Short Story Criticism

Guide to Gale Literary Criticism Series

For criticism on	Consult these Gale series
Authors now living or who died after December 31, 1999	*CONTEMPORARY LITERARY CRITICISM (CLC)*
Authors who died between 1900 and 1999	*TWENTIETH-CENTURY LITERARY CRITICISM (TCLC)*
Authors who died between 1800 and 1899	*NINETEENTH-CENTURY LITERATURE CRITICISM (NCLC)*
Authors who died between 1400 and 1799	*LITERATURE CRITICISM FROM 1400 TO 1800 (LC)* *SHAKESPEAREAN CRITICISM (SC)*
Authors who died before 1400	*CLASSICAL AND MEDIEVAL LITERATURE CRITICISM (CMLC)*
Authors of books for children and young adults	*CHILDREN'S LITERATURE REVIEW (CLR)*
Dramatists	*DRAMA CRITICISM (DC)*
Poets	*POETRY CRITICISM (PC)*
Short story writers	*SHORT STORY CRITICISM (SSC)*
Literary topics and movements	*HARLEM RENAISSANCE: A GALE CRITICAL COMPANION (HR)* *THE BEAT GENERATION: A GALE CRITICAL COMPANION (BG)* *FEMINISM IN LITERATURE: A GALE CRITICAL COMPANION (FL)* *GOTHIC LITERATURE: A GALE CRITICAL COMPANION (GL)*
Asian American writers of the last two hundred years	*ASIAN AMERICAN LITERATURE (AAL)*
Black writers of the past two hundred years	*BLACK LITERATURE CRITICISM (BLC-1)* *BLACK LITERATURE CRITICISM SUPPLEMENT (BLCS)* *BLACK LITERATURE CRITICISM: CLASSIC AND EMERGING AUTHORS SINCE 1950 (BLC-2)*
Hispanic writers of the late nineteenth and twentieth centuries	*HISPANIC LITERATURE CRITICISM (HLC)* *HISPANIC LITERATURE CRITICISM SUPPLEMENT (HLCS)*
Native North American writers and orators of the eighteenth, nineteenth, and twentieth centuries	*NATIVE NORTH AMERICAN LITERATURE (NNAL)*
Major authors from the Renaissance to the present	*WORLD LITERATURE CRITICISM, 1500 TO THE PRESENT (WLC)* *WORLD LITERATURE CRITICISM SUPPLEMENT (WLCS)*

ISSN 0895-9439

Volume 167

Short Story Criticism

Criticism of the
Works of Short Fiction Writers

Jelena Krstović
Project Editor

GALE
CENGAGE Learning®

Detroit • New York • San Francisco • New Haven, Conn • Waterville, Maine • London

GALE
CENGAGE Learning·

Short Story Criticism, Vol. 167

Project Editor: Jelena O. Krstović

Editorial: Dana Ramel Barnes, Sara Constantakis, Kathy D. Darrow, Matthew Derda, Kristen A. Dorsch, Dana Ferguson, Jeffrey W. Hunter, Michelle Kazensky, Michelle Lee, Marie Toft, Lawrence J. Trudeau

Content Conversion: Katrina D. Coach, Gwen Tucker

Indexing Services: Tonya Weikel

Rights and Acquisitions:Leitha Etheridge-Sims

Composition and Electronic Capture: Gary Leach

Manufacturing: Cynde Lentz

Product Manager: Mary Onorato

Gale
27500 Drake Rd.
Farmington Hills, MI, 48331-3535

LIBRARY OF CONGRESS CATALOG CARD NUMBER 88-641014

ISBN-13: 978-1-4144-8464-8
ISBN-10: 1-4144-8464-X

ISSN 0895-9439

Printed in Mexico
1 2 3 4 5 6 7 16 15 14 13 12

Contents

Preface vii

Acknowledgments xi

Literary Criticism Series Advisory Board xiii

Preface

Short Story Criticism (*SSC*) presents significant criticism of the world's greatest short-story writers and provides supplementary biographical and bibliographical materials to guide the interested reader to a greater understanding of the authors of short fiction. This series was developed in response to suggestions from librarians serving high school, college, and public library patrons, who had noted a considerable number of requests for critical material on short-story writers. Although major short-story writers are covered in such Gale series as *Contemporary Literary Criticism* (*CLC*), *Twentieth-Century Literary Criticism* (*TCLC*), *Nineteenth-Century Literature Criticism* (*NCLC*), and *Literature Criticism from 1400 to 1800* (*LC*), librarians perceived the need for a series devoted solely to writers of the short-story genre.

Scope of the Series

SSC is designed to serve as an introduction to major short-story writers of all eras and nationalities. Since these authors have inspired a great deal of relevant critical material, *SSC* is necessarily selective, and the editors have chosen the most important published criticism to aid readers and students in their research.

Approximately three to six authors, works, or topics are included in each volume, and each entry presents a historical survey of the critical response to the work. The length of an entry is intended to reflect the amount of critical attention the author has received from critics writing in English and from foreign critics in translation. Every attempt has been made to identify and include the most significant essays on each author's work. In order to provide these important critical pieces, the editors sometimes reprint essays that have appeared elsewhere in Gale's Literary Criticism Series. Such duplication, however, never exceeds twenty percent of an *SSC* volume.

Organization of the Book

An *SSC* entry consists of the following elements:

- The **Author Heading** cites the name under which the author most commonly wrote, followed by birth and death dates. Also located here are any name variations under which an author wrote, including transliterated forms for authors whose native languages use nonroman alphabets. If the author wrote consistently under a pseudonym, the pseudonym will be listed in the author heading and the author's actual name given in parentheses on the first line of the biographical and critical introduction. Uncertain birth or death dates are indicated by question marks. Single-work entries are preceded by the title of the work and its date of publication.

- The **Introduction** contains background information that introduces the reader to the author and the critical debates surrounding his or her work.

- The list of **Principal Works** is ordered chronologically by date of first publication and lists the most important works by the author. The first section comprises short-story collections, novellas, and novella collections. The second section gives information on other major works by the author. For foreign authors, the editors have provided original foreign-language publication information and have selected what are considered the best and most complete English-language editions of their works.

- Reprinted **Criticism** is arranged chronologically in each entry to provide a useful perspective on changes in critical evaluation over time. All short-story, novella, and collection titles by the author featured in the entry are printed in boldface type. The critic's name and the date of composition or publication of the critical work are given at the beginning of each piece of criticism. Unsigned criticism is preceded by the title of the source in which it appeared. Footnotes are reprinted at the end of each essay or excerpt. In the case of excerpted criticism, only those footnotes that pertain to the excerpted texts are included.

- Critical essays are prefaced by brief **Annotations** explicating each piece.

- A complete **Bibliographical Citation** of the original essay or book precedes each piece of criticism. Source citations in the Literary Criticism Series follow University of Chicago Press style, as outlined in *The Chicago Manual of Style,* 15th ed. (Chicago: The University of Chicago Press, 2006).

- An annotated bibliography of **Further Reading** appears at the end of each entry and suggests resources for additional study. In some cases, significant essays for which the editors could not obtain reprint rights are included here. Boxed material following the further reading list provides references to other biographical and critical sources on the author in series published by Gale.

Indexes

A **Cumulative Author Index** lists all of the authors that appear in a wide variety of reference sources published by Gale, including *SSC.* A complete list of these sources is found facing the first page of the Author Index. The index also includes birth and death dates and cross references between pseudonyms and actual names.

A **Cumulative Nationality Index** lists all authors featured in *SSC* by nationality, followed by the number of the *SSC* volume in which their entry appears.

An alphabetical **Title Index** lists all short-story, novella, and collection titles contained in the *SSC* series. Titles of short-story collections, separately published novellas, and novella collections are printed in italics, while titles of individual short stories are printed in roman type with quotation marks. Each title is followed by the author's last name and corresponding volume and page numbers where commentary on the work is located. English-language translations of original foreign-language titles are cross-referenced to the foreign titles so that all references to discussion of a work are combined in one listing.

In response to numerous suggestions from librarians, Gale also produces an annual paperbound edition of the SSC cumulative title index. This annual cumulation, which alphabetically lists all titles reviewed in the series, is available to all customers. Additional copies of this index are available upon request. Librarians and patrons will welcome this separate index; it saves shelf space, is easy to use, and is recyclable upon receipt of the next edition.

Citing *Short Story Criticism*

When citing criticism reprinted in the Literary Criticism Series, students should provide complete bibliographic information so that the cited essay can be located in the original print or electronic source. Students who quote directly from reprinted criticism may use any accepted bibliographic format, such as University of Chicago Press style or Modern Language Association (MLA) style. Both the MLA and the University of Chicago formats are acceptable and recognized as being the current standards for citations. It is important, however, to choose one format for all citations; do not mix the two formats within a list of citations.

The examples below follow recommendations for preparing a bibliography set forth in *The Chicago Manual of Style,* 15th ed. (Chicago: The University of Chicago Press, 2006); the first example pertains to material drawn from periodicals, the second to material reprinted from books:

Morrison, Jago. "Narration and Unease in Ian McEwan's Later Fiction." *Critique* 42, no. 3 (spring 2001): 253-68. Reprinted in *Short Story Criticism,* Vol. 57, edited by Jelena Krstovic, 212-20. Detroit: Gale, 2003.

Brossard, Nicole. "Poetic Politics." In *The Politics of Poetic Form: Poetry and Public Policy,* edited by Charles Bernstein, 73-82. New York: Roof Books, 1990. Reprinted in *Short Story Criticism,* Vol. 57, edited by Jelena Krstovic, 3-8. Detroit: Gale, 2003.

The examples below follow recommendations for preparing a works cited list set forth in the *MLA Handbook for Writers of Research Papers,* 7th ed. (New York: The Modern Language Association of America, 2009); the first example pertains to material drawn from periodicals, the second to material reprinted from books:

Morrison, Jago. "Narration and Unease in Ian McEwan's Later Fiction." *Critique* 42.3 (Spring 2001): 253-68. Rpt. in *Short Story Criticism.* Ed. Jelena Krstovic. Vol. 57. Detroit: Gale, 2003. 212-20. Print.

Brossard, Nicole. "Poetic Politics." *The Politics of Poetic Form: Poetry and Public Policy.* Ed. Charles Bernstein. New York: Roof Books, 1990. 73-82. Rpt. in *Short Story Criticism.* Ed. Jelena Krstovic. Vol. 57. Detroit: Gale, 2003. 3-8. Print.

Suggestions are Welcome

Readers who wish to suggest new features, topics, or authors to appear in future volumes, or who have other suggestions or comments are cordially invited to call, write, or fax the Product Manager:

Mary Onorato, Product Manager, Literary Criticism Series

Gale

27500 Drake Road

Farmington Hills, MI 48331-3535

1-800-347-4253 (GALE)

Fax: 248-699-8054

Acknowledgments

The editors wish to thank the copyright holders of the excerpted criticism included in this volume and the permissions managers of many book and magazine publishing companies for assisting us in securing reproduction rights. Following is a list of the copyright holders who have granted us permission to reproduce material in this volume of *SSC*. Every effort has been made to trace copyright, but if omissions have been made, please let us know.

COPYRIGHTED MATERIAL IN *SSC*, VOLUME 167, WAS REPRODUCED FROM THE FOLLOWING PERIODICALS:

American Imago, v. 39, spring, 1982. Copyright © 1982 by The Johns Hopkins University Press. Reproduced by permission of The Johns Hopkins University Press.—*British Journal for Eighteenth-Century Studies,* v. 10, autumn, 1987. Reproduced by permission.—*Clues,* v. 16, spring-summer, 1995. Copyright © Clues, 1995. Reproduced by permission of McFarland & Company, Inc., Box 611, Jefferson NC 28640. www.mcfarlandpub.com.—*Eighteenth-Century Fiction,* v. 23, fall, 2010. Reproduced by permission.—*Forum Italicum*, v.38, fall 2004. Copyright © 2004 by Forum Italicum. Reproduced by permission.—*Heliotropia,* v. 7, 2010 for "Boccaccio's Vernacular Classicism: Intertextuality and Interdiscoursivity in the *Decameron*" by Simone Marchesi. Reproduced by permission of the author.—*Heliotropia,* v. 1, 2010 for "New Lessons in Criticism and Blame from the *Decameron*" by Marilyn Migiel. Reproduced by permission of the author.—*Italica,* v. 87, summer, 2010. Reproduced by permission.—*MLN,* v. 125, January, 2010. Copyright © 2010 by The Johns Hopkins University Press. The Johns Hopkins University Press. Reproduced by permission of The Johns Hopkins University Press.—*Oxford German Studies,* v. 37, 2008. Reproduced by permission of Maney Publishing. www.maney.co.uk/journals/ogs and www.ingentaconnect.com/content/maney/ogs—*PMLA,* v. 43, June, 1928. Copyright © 1928 by the Modern Language Association of America. Reproduced by permission of the Modern Language Association of America.—*PMLA,* v. 124, May, 2009. Copyright © 2009 by The Modern Language Association of America. Reproduced by permission of the Modern Language Association of America.—*Romance Quarterly,* v. 54, summer, 2007 for "Work in Boccaccio's *Decameron*: Politics, Theology, and the Images of the Countryside" by Susanna Barsella. Copyright © 2007 Taylor & Francis. Reproduced by permission of Taylor & Francis Group, LLC, http://www.taylorandfrancis.com and the author.—*South Central Review,* v. 8, winter, 1991. Copyright © 1991 by The Johns Hopkins University Press. Reproduced by permission of The Johns Hopkins University Press.—*Women's Studies,* v. 31, Mar-April, 2002 for "The Critical Relevance of the Critique of Rationalism: Postmodernism, Ecofeminism, and Voltaire's *Candide*" by Helena Feder. Copyright © 2002 Taylor & Francis. Reproduced by permission of Taylor & Francis Group, LLC, http://www.taylorandfrancis.com and the author.—*Women's Writing,* v. 14, May, 2007 for "Experiments in Fiction: Charlotte Bronte's Last Angrian Tales" by Heather Glen. Copyright © 2007 Taylor & Francis Group, LLC. Reproduced by permission of Taylor & Francis, Ltd., http//:www.tandf.co.uk/journals and the author.

COPYRIGHTED MATERIAL IN *SSC*, VOLUME 167, WAS REPRODUCED FROM THE FOLLOWING BOOKS:

Baskins, Cristelle L. From "Scenes from a Marriage: Hospitality and Commerce in Boccaccio's Tale of Saladin and Torello," in *The Medieval Marriage Scene: Prudence, Passion, Policy.* Edited by Sherry Roush and Cristelle L. Baskins. Arizona Center for Medieval and Renaissance Studies, 2005. Copyright © 2005 Arizona Board of Regents for Arizona State University. Reproduced by permission.—Blom, Margaret Howard. From *English Authors Series:* Charlotte Bronte. Twayne Publishers, 1977. Copyright © 1997 Gale, a part of Cengage Learning, Inc. Reproduced by permission. www.cengage.com/permissions.—Braun, Theodore E.D. From "Chaos, Contingency, and Candide," in *1650-1850: Ideas, Aesthetics, and Inquiries in the Early Modern Era.* Edited by Kevin L. Cope. AMS Press, 2001. Copyright © 2001 by AMS Press, Inc. All rights reserved. Reproduced by permission.—Cooksey, Thomas L. From *Masterpieces of Philosophical Literature.* Greenwood, 2006. Copyright © 2006 by Thomas L. Cooksey. All rights reserved. Reproduced with permission of ABC-CLIO, LLC, Santa Barbara, CA.—Edmiston, William F. From "Sex as Satire in Voltaire's Fiction," in *An American Voltaire: Essays in Memory of J. Patrick Lee.* Edited by E. Joe Johnson and Byron R. Wells. Cambridge Scholars, 2009. Copyright © 2009 by E. Joe Johnson and Byron R. Wells and contributors. Reproduced by permission of the publisher and author.—Gold, Moshe. From "Those Evil Goslings, Those Evil Stories: Letting the Boys out of Their Cave," in *Levinas and Medieval Literature: The 'Difficult' Reading of English and Rabbinic Texts.* Edited by Ann W. Astell and J.A. Jack-

Gale Literature Product Advisory Board

The members of the Gale Literature Product Advisory Board—reference librarians from public and academic library systems—represent a cross-section of our customer base and offer a variety of informed perspectives on both the presentation and content of our literature products. Advisory board members assess and define such quality issues as the relevance, currency, and usefulness of the author coverage, critical content, and literary topics included in our series; evaluate the layout, presentation, and general quality of our printed volumes; provide feedback on the criteria used for selecting authors and topics covered in our series; provide suggestions for potential enhancements to our series; identify any gaps in our coverage of authors or literary topics, recommending authors or topics for inclusion; analyze the appropriateness of our content and presentation for various user audiences, such as high school students, undergraduates, graduate students, librarians, and educators; and offer feedback on any proposed changes/enhancements to our series. We wish to thank the following advisors for their advice throughout the year.

Decameron

Giovanni Boccaccio

The following entry presents criticism of Boccaccio's collection of tales, the *Decameron* (1348-53), through 2010. For additional information on Boccaccio's life and short fiction, see *SSC,* Vols. 10 and 87.

INTRODUCTION

A collection of one hundred *novelle,* or tales, the *Decameron* is recognized as Boccaccio's masterpiece and a classic of Italian and world literature. The stories are told by a *brigata* (or gathering) of city dwellers—seven women and three men—who escape from plague-ridden Florence, Italy, to nearby villas in the country-side where they pass time telling tales to each other over the course of a fortnight. Considered seminal to the development of the short story genre, the *Decameron* is praised for its sophisticated narrative framing devices which lend stylistic and thematic unity to a work that might otherwise appear disordered and fragmented. The formal innovations of the *Decameron* are matched by an ideological distinctiveness regarded as equally significant to the development of the Western literary canon. The *Decameron* puts forth a vision of human life that draws on medieval tradition while signaling the transition to the Renaissance in its refusal to offer a rigid set of moral values and an ostensible focus on secular rather than religious themes. Although most works of the Middle Ages were composed in Latin, the *Decameron* was written in the Italian vernacular. Famous for its risqué tales of love ranging from the tragic to the comic and the erotic, the *Decameron* proved highly popular among the literate merchant classes, whose language it valorized and whose values it appeared to elevate to classical status with its structural echoes of the one hundred cantos of Dante Alighieri's *Divine Comedy.* Yet it was not until the nineteenth century, when Francesco DeSanctis, in his *History of Literature* (1870), proclaimed the *Decameron* the "Earthly" equivalent to Dante's *Divine Comedy* that the collection received serious critical attention. Since that time, criticism on the *Decameron* has been voluminous, much of it confirming the cultural significance of the work as a reflection of its historical period, but also attesting to the impossibility of ever precisely determining the author's attitudes toward the world in which he lived because of his frequently ironic posture. In the centuries since the appearance of the *Decameron,* a number of famous writers including Geoffrey Chaucer, William Shakespeare, and Molière have imitated Boccaccio's style, paying tribute to his genius for storytelling.

PLOT AND MAJOR CHARACTERS

Boccaccio relied on a variety of classical and medieval sources in composing the stories of the *Decameron.* It is now believed that close to one-third of the tales were based on *fabliaux*—bawdy French tales popular throughout the Middle Ages. While there was nothing unique about Boccaccio's idea to cluster together a large set of tales, or *novelle,* critics agree that the *Decameron* is far superior in design to the episodic collections of stories typical of his day. Despite their diverse subject matter and styles, the stories of the *Decameron* read as a unified whole due to Boccaccio's masterly use of narrative framing devices. The primary framing structures in the *Decameron* include the "Proem," or preface, the introductions to the first and fourth days of storytelling, and the "Conclusion." Furthermore, the tales follow a logical, tightly structured progression of themes since the storytelling party has agreed that each member will tell one story every day and that each day a different member of the group will guide the speakers by choosing a particular subject to address. In addition, each day's storytelling session ends with a *canzone,* or song, as the young people play musical instruments, dance, and sing. The *brigata* does not return to Florence for two weeks, but since two days each week are set aside for chores and other activities, storytelling takes place over a total of ten days, thus accounting for the title of the work, which is derived from the Greek words for ten ("deka") and day ("hemera").

The *Decameron* opens with the "Proem," in which the author explains his purpose for writing. He states that he has recently suffered from the "pains of love" and that had it not been for the support of his friends and family, he never would have recovered. In order to return the favor, he maintains that he will attempt through his stories to offer comfort and entertainment to those who most need it: lovesick women who, due to the social restrictions of the time, are confined to their rooms without recourse to the pastimes available to lovesick men, such as hunting, fishing, and gambling. The intro-

1

duction to Day 1 realistically describes the horrendous effects of the Black Death, or plague, and introduces the ten young women and men who meet by chance in the church of Santa Maria Novella in Florence at the height of the epidemic in 1348. When the oldest woman in the group persuades the others to flee to their villas in the hills of Fiesole above the city, all agree to divide their stay among their respective estates, telling stories to occupy themselves and pass the time.

MAJOR THEMES

In addition to the daily themes connecting the stories, the *Decameron* is governed by some important controlling ideas. Although most of the stories deal with various degrees of moral and social corruption, the narrators typically let the guilty characters' actions speak for themselves instead of explicitly commenting on them. In this way, Boccaccio suggests the attitudes of the refined bourgeoisie of his time, who exhibited a certain degree of respect for convention but were inclined to be open-minded about personal behavior rather than being swayed by the dictates of religious dogma. Boccaccio documents as well the concerns of mercantile culture, which was at the time spreading across Europe. For this reason, some critics have referred to the *Decameron* as "the mercantile epic." But, since the stories of the *Decameron* are populated by over five hundred different characters, the social strata of fourteenth-century Italian life—including servant classes, artisans, clergy, and aristocracy—is also well represented.

The overwhelming majority of the stories in the *Decameron* depict love relationships in their many aspects: happy, unhappy, fraudulent, and erotic. The stories parade a cast of lucky and unlucky men and women immersed in the throes of affairs of the heart. There are virtuous women wronged and seductive temptresses; unfaithful, cuckolded, and inhumanely cruel husbands; and young boys and clerics caught in the middle of love triangles. Many of the stories turn on a *beffa,* a type of clever practical joke frequently involving masquerade, role reversal, or fast-tongued deception. For example, Day 1 is devoted to stories about human vice in which wit or ingenuity prevail over the forces of fate, and Day 6 features incidents in which quick thinking saves someone from danger or ridicule. Along with love and trickery, the notion of fate is a fundamental theme of the *Decameron.* The image of "Fortune's Wheel" presides over the collection, but many of the stories depart from the medieval belief in the randomness of fate by depicting characters who successfully overcome or even exploit Fortune with their cunning.

CRITICAL RECEPTION

DeSanctis's 1870 study reflected the nineteenth-century debate concerning the ethics of the *Decameron,* which since its first appearance had come under attack for its alleged profanity and anticlerical content. In labeling

the *Decameron* the "Earthly" Comedy (as opposed to Dante's *Divine Comedy*), DeSanctis argued that the work rejected the spiritualism of the Middle Ages and ushered in the humanism and rationalism of the Renaissance (see Further Reading).

Boccaccio's apparently ambivalent feelings toward the literary worth of the *Decameron* have complicated more recent critical interpretations, which have tended to emphasize the author's ambiguous commitment to the moral values expressed in the tales. Scholars have made much of a 1372 letter Boccaccio wrote to his patron, Mainardo Cavalcanti, in which he appears to repent the explicitly sexual content of the *Decameron.* In the letter, he refers to his "little books" as "domestic trifles" and warns of their "wicked" influence upon female readers. Boccaccio also expresses the hope that the immoral tales of his youth will not scar his lasting literary reputation: "For those who read my trifles will think me a filthy pimp, a dirty old man, a vile person, a foul-mouthed slanderer, and an eager teller of other people's wicked deeds. For there is not everywhere someone who can rise and say in my defence: 'He wrote when he was young and under compulsion from an older person.'" Yet a large number of critics have cautioned that this letter must be read with the same degree of attention to irony as would inform any insightful approach to the *Decameron* itself. It is more common for critics today to reject the "two Boccaccios" thesis in favor of a reading of the *Decameron* that takes account of the wide range of moral opinions offered by the various authorial intrusions, multiple narrators, and deliberate critiques of earlier literary models.

Fundamental to the debate concerning the *Decameron*'s reflection of medieval or Renaissance values is the question of whether it can truly be considered a work of moral instruction, especially since so many of the tales appear to be offered solely for the purpose of entertainment and diversion. The controversy over the ideological import of the *Decameron* has centered on Boccaccio's use of allegory and irony, his conflicting attitudes toward women, the significance of metaphor and symbol in individual stories, and Boccaccio's rejection or embrace of his literary predecessors. Many critics have celebrated Boccaccio's earth-bound subject matter as an early type of literary naturalism but, while some have denied the work any transcendent significance, others have argued that a moral message inheres in its dual presentation of love as both dangerous and enlightening. A number of scholars have proclaimed the *Decameron* a defense of storytelling in its own right and of its power to shape reality. In a 2010 essay Marilyn Migiel described the manner of the telling of the *Decameron* to be as thorny an issue as the matter of the stories: "Precisely *how* the *Decameron* complicates our moral views—how it goes about teaching us about moral reasoning, how it leads us to reflect on what we find praiseworthy or blameworthy, and above all how it demonstrates the value of literature to this enterprise—this is a matter unlikely to be resolved any time soon. It must continue to be discussed."

PRINCIPAL WORKS

Short Fiction

Decameron (novellas) 1348-53

Other Major Works

Caccia di Diana (poetry) 1334
Filostrato [*The Filostrato*] (poetry) 1335
Filocolo (prose) 1336-38
Teseida [*Book of Theseus*] (poetry) 1339-41
Ninfale fiesolano (poetry) 1341-45
L'amorosa visione [*Amorous Vision*] (poetry) 1342
Elegia di Madonna Fiammetta [*Amorous Fiammetta*] (poetry) 1343-44
Genealogie deorum gentilium [*Genealogy of the Gentile Gods*] (history) 1350-74
Corbaccio (satire) 1354-55
De casibus virorum illustrium (history) 1355-63
De montibus, silvis, fontibus et de nominibus maris liber (dictionary) 1355-64
De claris mulieribus (biographies) 1360-74
Trattatello in laude de Dante [*Life of Dante*] (biography) 1361
Buccolicum carmen (poetry) 1369-70
Esposizioni sopra la Commedia *di Dante* (lectures) 1373

CRITICISM

Julia M. Cozzarelli (essay date fall 2004)

SOURCE: Cozzarelli, Julia M. "Love and Destruction in the *Decameron*: Cimone and Calandrino." *Forum Italicum*, 38, no. 2 (fall 2004): 338-63.

[*In the following essay, Cozzarelli links the tales of Cimone (5.1) and Calandrino (9.1) because of their shared exploration of the human imagination. According to Cozzarelli, Cimone allows his transcendent vision of the beautiful Efigenia to devolve into a destructive passion, while Calandrino is made the dupe of his own distorted self-image.*]

Imagination, love, reason: these three elements come together in a delicate balance to form the workings of the human mind. This study explores these concepts and their intricate relationship as portrayed in the stories of two key characters in Giovanni Boccaccio's *Decameron.* On the face of it, the tales of Cimone (5.1) and Calandrino (9.5) told by, respectively, Panfilo and Fiammetta, have little to do with each other. Cimone expresses violence in the context of a story of education through love. Calandrino, on the other hand, is a character whose actions betray an extraordinary fusion of imagination and literal-mindedness. Although on the surface these two characters seem completely dissimilar, on closer inspection their stories bear striking resemblances at a thematic and conceptual level. If anything, Calandrino's tale presents itself as a comic counterpoint to that of Cimone; but a more vital and often dark thread binds these stories together. Both are dominated by the force of the imagination, with explosive results. The question I wish to explore is why Boccaccio artfully and subtly connects the tales from the viewpoint of imagination, love and rationality. I will show how he intertwines imagination and the passion of love, manipulating their fragile relationship with rational thought and forging a dangerous path to madness and destruction.

Behind Boccaccio there lies a well-known literary and philosophical tradition connecting the imagination, love, and the movement of reason towards knowledge. In the poetry of Dante, the passion of love both affects and is affected by the double-edged imagination, which is integral to the journey towards the divine.[1] In contrast, the *Decameron* moves in a predominantly horizontal direction, tying idealized love to the erotic love of human, earthly experience, and then bringing this passion to an extreme. Scholars examining Boccaccio's work have discussed the *Decameron*'s earth-bound subject matter and what has been called its "naturalism" at length.[2] Others have celebrated its realism, while also denying any morality in the text beyond that of its art; presenting it as a text without any transcendent values, and placing the work at odds with morally and spiritually guided literature.[3]

Yet, the passages of the *Decameron* that echo, linguistically or thematically, the works of Boccaccio's predecessors often demonstrate the author's deliberate critique of those earlier ideas. Of special interest to this study is the fact that throughout the *Decameron*, Boccaccio displays the concept of love with an emphasis not only on its failure to bring one to wisdom, but on its potential for danger. The *novella* of Cimone in particular embodies the rejection of the stilnovistic dream, through irony and even what has been described as flagrant parody (Mazzotta, *World* 200). This *novella* is the first story told on day five, a day on which Fiammetta[4] reigns as queen and has chosen the theme of "happy endings" for the day's tales. Panfilo, who has been seen as a spokesman for the rational faculty (Kirkham 87), narrates this story, whose introductory summary begins with the phrase: "Cimone amando divien savio e Efigenia sua donna rapisce in mare" 'Cimone acquires wisdom by falling in love with Efigenia, his lady, whom he abducts on the high seas' (593; 314).[5]

This theme of "amando divien savio" was a familiar one for Boccaccio, and it was also a motif seen in his own earlier works. In particular, the *Ameto* contains the theme of refinement of the rustic heart through love; and Boccaccio's earliest narrative, the *Caccia di Diana*, portrays Venus transforming animals into men. But the ***Decameron***'s version of the story has notable differences, along with some interesting and uncomfortable surprises for the reader.

The content of the tale and the character of Cimone begin to emerge when the narrator reveals that the name of Cimone's father is "Aristippo." This name is forged by the combination of two very different words. "Arist" forms the beginning of the name of the great philosopher Aristotle; and "ippo" derives from the horse. Thus, Cimone's father represents a hybrid between philosopher and beast. The image of the Aristotle-horse echoes D'Andeli's earlier *Lai d'Aristote*. There, the great philosopher humiliates himself by lusting after a girl and then allowing her to ride him like a horse. This story has been read to mean the triumph of Nature over Philosophy (Scaglione 67) or the ethical failure of the will to match the perfection of one's knowledge (Stone 25).[6]

The "nobilissimo" and "ricchissimo" Aristippo has everything he could want in life but has been bitterly disappointed with his son. Cimone (whose real name is Galeso) innately radiates exceptional physical beauty. However, despite his outward appearance, he is "quasi matto" and "di perduta speranza" (594), for no amount of persuasion or force succeed in educating him or teaching him manners. The translation of Galeso's description reads: "for all intents and purposes an imbecile whose case was hopeless" (314), but I would like to emphasize Boccaccio's choice of the term "matto," which carries implications of madness, lack of control, and obsession key to this tale.[7]

Galeso presents so hopeless a case that not only do all remedies fail to educate him, they cause him to go in the opposite direction, leaving him inarticulate and with "modi piú convenienti a bestia che a uomo" 'manners more suitable to a beast than a man' (594; 315). Everyone contemptuously calls him "Cimone," "il che nella lor lingua sonava quanto nella nostra 'bestione'" 'which in their language sounded something like 'numbskull' in ours' (594; 315). It is not by coincidence that the nickname Cimone sounds like "bestione" 'a great beast,' and Boccaccio clearly plays up this comparison. His

name also mimics "scimmione" or monkey.[8] In short, Cimone exemplifies a crude distortion of a human being. Significantly, the label "scimmione" can also be applied to victims of the tricks, or *beffe,* that we see elsewhere in the ***Decameron.***

This juxtaposition of beast and human in Cimone as well as his father calls to mind traditional views of animality and the pursuit of knowledge. In the Platonic system, the thinker needs to control his desires properly in order to reach knowledge—the bestial side of one's nature must be reined in. In the Aristotelian system, humans alone possess all three faculties of the soul (the vegetative/nutritive; the sensitive/imaginative; and the rational/intellective); animals possess only the first two. Humans are therefore able to reach unseen truths through their reason, whereas animals cannot.

An examination of Cimone's faculties reveals once again that he epitomizes an animal rather than a man. Communication, a certain sign of the human being and of reason itself, is a skill Cimone does not possess; and this also indicates the underlying madness of this character. Beast-like, inarticulate, and apparently incapable of learning, he is finally sent away to live in the country by his despondent father.[9] The move pleases Cimone greatly, for "i costumi e l'usanza degli uomini grossi gli eran piú a grado che le cittadine" 'the customs and the manners of unpolished countryfolk suited him better than those of city people' (595; 315). This relocation is significant—it has been understood to reflect his lack of civility and his naturalistic role, and it also embodies his rejection of rational thinking. But also, Cimone is entering a sort of utopia—a place that invites comparison with the setting of the narrators themselves who make up the *cornice* of the ***Decameron.*** The storytellers fleeing the chaos and destruction of the city for the tranquillity and pleasure of the country are attempting to create their own utopia, where they will dwell without trespassing "il segno della ragione" 'the bounds of reason' (35; 15).[10] Mazzotta explains that "ragione" in this context signifies "restraint" (*World* 42), a control we will see Cimone defy when he later returns to the city.

Up until this point, Boccaccio has successfully portrayed his protagonist as an uncultured, unimaginative and uncivilized brute. But Cimone's stubborn resistance to education and culture changes dramatically when, traveling through the countryside in springtime, he comes across Efigenia, a beautiful, nearly naked girl asleep with her servants. This turning point of the *novella* takes place in a beautiful meadow containing a fountain and surrounded by trees; the perfect setting for a romantic vision of beauty.[11] This idyllic scene, paired with the description in the chapter heading, leads us to expect that this will be the moment when through love Cimone will become wise. And, at least on the face of it, we are not disappointed.

The process of Cimone's metamorphosis is described in a paragraph that contains a microcosm of the ideas of Boccaccio's predecessors on the ennoblement of the soul through love. And here at last, the imagination stirs in Cimone, ignited by and also igniting the vision of beauty he sees before him: he is so taken with Efigenia that he becomes transfixed, and can only stare at her. The flow and style of the language evoke courtly and stilnovist poetry—he "sentí destarsi un pensiero il quale nella [. . .] mente gli ragionava" 'felt a thought awaken which within his [. . .] mind told him' that she was the most beautiful thing ever seen (596; 315). He then admires and praises the parts of her body, "lodando i capelli, li quali d'oro estimava, la fronte, il naso e la bocca, la gola e le braccia e sommamente il petto, poco ancora rilevato" 'praising her hair, which he thought made of gold, her face, her nose, her mouth, her neck, her arms, and especially her breasts, yet still undeveloped' (596; 315).

Cimone, beast-like, does not typify an imaginative creature; his eyes do not even note the beauty of nature surrounding him. But as he gazes on Efigenia, his imagination stirs. The imagination plays a very powerful role in traditional ideas of divine inspiration, as well as Platonic ideas of ascension through contemplation and love of beauty. The imagination works in tandem with the other senses to awaken the soul and guide it upwards. It is also crucial in the journey towards knowledge, even in its most basic sense as a strictly representational faculty rather than a creative one.[12] The vision of beauty and the philosopher's love of that beauty inspire the contemplation of the Ideal, and enable the philosopher, with the use of trained reason, to rise to that world. Love also guides the soul towards the knowledge of God in Dante.

On the surface, the process seems to be the same here. Cimone is stunned by Efigenia's beauty, which he perceives through his vision—in fact she is so perfect that "dubitava non fosse alcuna dea" 'he felt she might be some goddess' (596; 315). Cimone then moves very quickly through the internal changes that take him onto the path of ascension towards knowledge inspired by love. Then, after Efigenia wakes and fearing him, flees, Cimone returns to the city, where he re-creates himself. Here, in a brief description covering four years, he goes from "bestione" to the most accomplished and charming man in Cyprus. Refined in his speech, skilled at music and military arts, "valorosissimo tra' filosofanti divenne," he 'became most skillful among those who practiced philosophy' (598; 316). The tale explicitly relates the reason for the transition, "essendo di tutto ciò cagione l'amore il quale a Efigenia portava" 'the cause of it all being the love which he bore for Efigenia' (598, 316). Reason, which Cimone had initially seemed to lack, has come to life; beginning with the "ragionare" of Cimone's first thoughts on seeing Efigenia and reach-

ing its culmination in his philosophical excellence. This cooperative pairing of imagination and reason seem to cause Cimone to re-enter society and become the man his father had always hoped he would be.

However, this scene deserves closer scrutiny. Despite the traditional language of courtly and stilnovist love that litters this passage, and the connections with Platonic philosophy, Cimone's is an erotic love, more properly called lust. Critics frequently consider this type of love as dominating the *Decameron*.[13] In this tale, we note that Efigenia, the object of Cimone's desire, is asleep and her attire is transparent. Cimone feels particularly interested in closely examining every part of Efigenia's body.[14] Through the vision of her body, Cimone's powerful desire becomes a consuming wish to see Efigenia's open eyes. Traditionally, lovers' hearts are pierced by the arrows that leave the beloved's eyes, but the sleeping Efigenia's eyes are closed. When at last she wakes up and Cimone sees her eyes, "seco stesso parendogli che da quegli una soavità si movesse la quale il riempiesse di piacere mai da lui non provato" 'he seemed to sense such a sweetness coming from them that he was filled with a pleasure he had never before experienced' (597; 316).

No matter that Efigenia does not reciprocate Cimone's attraction, and that she in fact fears him; Cimone's desire burns so strongly that in his mind he creates this image of sweetness issuing from her eyes. This idea firmly binds him to her as in the great love of the poets. But Efigenia as a person has no role; Cimone has taken ownership over her in his mind and he will stop at nothing to possess her in the physical realm as well.[15]

The reader might well expect a man who becomes not only skilled in courtly manners, but also the greatest of philosophers, to follow a relatively positive, peaceful and wise course to win his lady love. We might also expect to see the workings of the new-found genius of our hero in the process. Instead, Cimone's actions snowball downwards into destruction and violence. When he cannot have Efigenia legitimately (she is already engaged), he will kidnap her and murder whoever stands in his way. Cimone rationalizes his violent actions by telling Efigenia "io sono il tuo Cimone, il quale per lungo amore t'ho molto meglio meritata d'avere che Pasimunda per promessa fede" 'I am your Cimone, whose long love for you makes me far more deserving to have you than does a promise made to Pasimunda' (601; 318). Cimone's learning and philosophizing do not enter into his forceful pursuit of Efigenia, who has become mere prey to his predatory behavior. Indeed, the "happy ending" of the tale is preceded by much bloodshed and death, culminating in the brutal massacre of Efigenia's fiancé and his brother at their marriage celebration.

When Cimone was initially described as an uncouth, ill-mannered boy, he still lived at peace with nature and also other human beings. Significantly, there were no indications at that point that Cimone was anything but a harmless creature, offensive though he may have been in manners and culture. But after his moment of inspiration, and despite, or rather assisted by, the cloak of "civilization," he becomes a raging beast unleashed on the innocents who happen, by ill-fate, to cross his path. There are other comparisons of him to beasts in the later paragraphs, especially concerning his immense strength and ferocity. Many read Cimone as a character that remains essentially unchanged—just as he desires to keep his bestial nickname rather than to return to his given name, he stays a beast throughout the *novella* (Scaglione 81; Stone 24). I would go further, however. Cimone not only retains his brutish connotations throughout the tale, but even becomes a far more destructive force as a result of the self re-creation that was sparked by his visual experience of beauty.[16]

The apparent schism between the two halves of the *novella* is so jarring that it has led some critics to dismiss the second half or to gloss over parts of the tale as inconsistent. This is especially apparent in writers who take the stilnovist "conversion" of Cimone at face value.[17] But the second half of the tale must not be dismissed, and its content does not permit a simplistic reading of the conversion. It demands instead the exploration of more complicated underlying messages. Ultimately, the tale can be seen as a demonstration of Cimone's failure to "truly" become ennobled by love, but this failure could be blamed on several things. The most simple might be the fact that he is, fundamentally, a beast; or that living in antiquity he lacks Christian guidance. But the character of the story suggests stronger and darker connotations.

The most striking aspects of this tale are its sweeping violence and Cimone's single-minded obsession. This obsessive "love" is more akin to madness, an implied feature of Cimone's personality even before his metamorphosis. This fixation, coupled with Cimone's excessive brutality, seems designed to inspire a strong reaction in the reader. Indeed, the impact of the violence is reinforced by the language tying the story to the *Decameron*'s frame.

The tale begins with an exhortation by Panfilo (also a lover) addressed specifically to the listening ladies. He claims he chose this story, one of his favorites, to demonstrate not only "il felice fine per lo quale a ragionare incominciamo" 'the happy ending which is to be the goal of our stories,' but also "quanto sian sante, quanto poderose e di quanto ben piene le forze d'Amore, le quali molti, senza saper che si dicano, dannano e vituperano a gran torto" 'how holy, how weighty, and how beneficent are Love's powers, which many people, who

do not know what they are saying, condemn and vituperate quite wrongly' (593-94; 314). This passage expresses a blatant irony, for the story, presented to women, in a text written ostensibly for the pleasure of women, has a "happy ending" only from the point of view of the male protagonist and his partner-in-crime—the ending is tragic from the female viewpoint. Efigenia, far from being a Beatrice-like guide to love, plays a role solely as helpless victim.[18] She is never described as desiring Cimone or in any way welcoming his advances. In fact, Boccaccio stresses her desperate resistance and horrified fear throughout the tale. Efigenia not only rejects, but curses, Cimone's love; blaming it even for the violent storm that forces the kidnappers' ship ashore. The final proof that the "happy ending" of the *novella* excludes the women lies in the language describing that ending—in a phrase that omits the women by its male gender markers.[19]

Through the story of Cimone, Boccaccio underscores not only the human frailty of having to cede to erotic love, but also its sheer destructive force, and especially its effects on those surrounding the lover. The tale serves as a strong warning to others (and especially women) about the dangerous fury of unrestrained love, a passion often seen as intimately connected with the imagination. The "happy ending" marriage is formulaic; a superficial gesture to calm the chaos of the tale and undercut the bestiality of its protagonist.[20] Marriage serves as the justification for Cimone's brutality—which includes the destruction of two other marriages—because he seeks a socially acceptable and civilized end. Simultaneously, by hiding beneath its veil of an orderly goal, an ironic Boccaccio can concentrate on the passionate and cruel forces that drive his characters.

This idea of Boccaccio condemning romantic love is not unique to the **Decameron.** The characters of the *Filocolo* also consider the subject when Fiammetta replies to the "questions of love." There, love is divided hierarchically into three types: "onesto" 'honest' (associated with God), "per diletto" 'for pleasure,' and that based on "utilità" 'utility.' The last is equated with hate, and the second is also a dangerous love that must be avoided by the wise (4.44).[21] Cimone could exemplify the danger in pursuing the wrong type of love. Indeed, his unrestrained sensual passion is also identified with an irreverent desire for glory. Cimone thinks to himself as if addressing Efigenia, "Io son per te divenuto uomo: e se io ti posso avere, io non dubito di non divenire piú glorioso che alcuno idio" 'Because of you, I became a man, and if I can succeed in winning you, I believe I can become more glorious than a god' (599; 317). This eagerness for greatness is in opposition to Dante's lover of knowledge and God, who must be humble. But the *Filocolo* discussion has also been used to support the idea that Cimone's tale condemns stilnovist love ("amore onesto") as contrary to human nature

(Toscano 28), and in fact, the tale is often read as a critique of the stilnovist philosopher.[22] Through each of these possibilities, the overarching characteristic shared by Cimone's tale and the *Filocolo* is earthly love's portrayal in a negative and destructive framework.

Filocolo also connects love with the language of the imagination through dream and vision.[23] Love and desire result from the pleasure experienced in contemplating the beloved in dreams and prolonged viewing.[24] Cimone's initial encounter with love is visual; his pleasure is awakened through his devouring eyes. But he feels unable to live without the object of his desire, which indicates that his imagination is also at work while they are apart, causing him to recall her image. Cimone seeks to possess Efigenia, and in that sense, the imagination is paradoxical. Imagination sustains Cimone's desire, but at the same time he wishes to turn away from imagination and fantasy and to cling tenaciously to the more concrete world of touch.

After Cimone sees his vision of Efigenia and decides to possess her, the imagination plays a surprisingly small part in this narrative. Panfilo emphasizes imagination's role in the context of stilnovistic love when, as narrator, he interjects at the moment seen as the dividing line between the two parts of the story. He states to the listeners that Amor is the "eccitatore degli adormentati ingegni" (598), translated as 'awakener of dormant talents' (317). Cimone's desire is portrayed as awakening his dormant reason, for it leads him to become, as we are told, the greatest of philosophers. The use of the term *ingegno* in Panfilo's words recalls love's connection not only to intelligence, but also to ingenuity and the creative imagination. In addition to being a philosopher, Cimone transforms himself into a musician and singer, roles intimately associated with the poetic art and creation. However, Cimone can only be posited as an example of imagination's stimulating effects if we consider this faculty at its most primitive level. Although his actions may have been initiated by the imagination's inspiration of erotic love, after he completes the period of transformation we see no more examples of original thinking. Cimone uses neither his vast reason nor his extensive creative skills to win Efigenia. Instead, he leaves imagination behind and relies on sheer force.

In fact, the new skills and creative ability Cimone is supposed to possess do not even assist him in his victory at the end of the *novella*. Only the fortuitous addition of another character provides the necessary ingenuity in the quest for Efigenia. It has been rightly pointed out that Cimone represents a dubious hero, considering it is Fortune who controls his life in the second part of the story (Ferreri 87).[25] Cimone sits silent in prison while the magistrate Lisimaco, presented as a naturally civilized person and also a lover, comes up with the plan to win the woman he himself desires, utilizing Cimone as a tool. Without Lisimaco, Cimone's effort would have been doomed to failure.

The imagination, we assume, inspired Lisimaco's passion as it did Cimone's; but unlike Cimone, Lisimaco employs his intelligence and knowledge (he is referred to as "savio") to win the day for both men. Lisimaco, evocative of Dante's Ulysses in *Inferno* XXVI, rouses Cimone with a speech, inciting him to be especially ferocious in a surprise attack. Lisimaco plans the event, but Cimone carries out the gruesome murders of the innocent fiancés. Although the killings are not by Lisimaco's hand, he is the one who initiates the bloodshed. Without his intervention, the joyful wedding celebrations for the women would have continued as originally planned.

The tale of Cimone is a cautionary one, one that shows that erotic passion, once inspired, can have devastating consequences. Traditional beliefs (posited also by physicians) considered the lover's passionate desire a sickness that resulted from the imagination stimulating the senses and overriding reason (Scaglione 61). Both Cimone and Lisimaco demonstrate the power of erotic desire. Lisimaco has been cited as an example of love's ability to destroy the powers of reason, and as Cimone's counterpart (Toscano 31-33).[26] However, in Cimone's case, the traditional system seems to be reversed: the love imagination inspires initiates Cimone's transformation into a philosopher, the epitome of rational control. But a greater irony is that although passion initiates Cimone's transformation, afterwards he neglects both reason and ingenuity, blindly ignoring all drives beyond that of his sexual desire. Cimone may in fact be read as an example of the stunted use of imagination's powers, for he is a man who begins and ends the tale as one with very little imaginative ability. While Lisimaco is able to utilize his ingenuity in order to succeed in his quest, Cimone demonstrates the true violence of this passion when borne in the heart of a person who is by nature unable to employ the full skills of his mind. Cimone's lack of imaginative development results in passion's free reign, for one idea alone consistently rules him: the obsession to fulfill his lust for Efigenia.

This single-mindedness leads Scaglione to read the story of Cimone as the manifestation of Boccaccio's "latent anarchism," for his values are so naturalistic "that all laws and policies are on the verge of crumbling under the sovereign tyranny of love, the only law" (80). But by setting the story against its framework through Panfilo's words and the narrative events themselves, Boccaccio gives structure to the tale's apparent chaos, and through its irony leads us to ponder the significance of the imagination not only in the text but also in its author. Boccaccio himself makes the connection between the literature produced by the creative imagination and danger from the very start of the *Decameron,* when he subtitles the work "Galeotto." This deliberate evocation of a text that, in *Inferno* V, leads Paolo and Francesca to eternal damnation warns the readers that they must "beware." Paolo and Francesca were unable to separate their reading from their reality—their imaginations instead inspired their inappropriate and disastrous lust. This warning by Boccaccio, situated so prominently in his *Decameron,* also serves as a warning to the ladies of the *brigata* not to take Panfilo's words, as a storyteller praising the merits of love, at face value. They must look beyond the surface of his words and use their own judgment.

Boccaccio's warning about the deceptive possibilities of the imagination bursts into vivid relief when we explore the workings of the imagination elsewhere in the *Decameron.* We have examined in Cimone the imagination's connections with love, and the destructive potential of that passion. An exploration of the later tales featuring the misadventures of Calandrino and his friends reveals a complementary theme. Here we witness more demonstrative examples of the workings and failures of the creative imagination. Calandrino is a painter—a person who works with images as the practical substance of his life.[27] The fact that he is also described as surrounded by other artists underscores the role played by the imagination in these stories. Imagination dominates these *novelle,* through both Calandrino and the perpetrators of the *beffe.* What varies, however, is the nature of the imagination expressed by each person, as well as its balance with the other faculties.

Readers know Calandrino best through the tale of his adventure with the heliotrope, which is also the first of the four *novelle* in which he appears. The four stories are often seen as forming the acts of a single play,[28] and they are distributed in a balanced manner. Each story also has a different narrator. The reader understands immediately that the treatment of the subject matter differs markedly from that in the tale of Cimone simply by the style of the narration. It is direct and straightforward, lacking the decorative language that overtly raised the image of the stilnovist tradition in Cimone's tale. But the last story in the Calandrino cycle presents a fascinating counterpart to that of Cimone. Both stories share a critical focus, one that is not typical of the *Decameron*'s tales as a whole. In them, Boccaccio highlights the concept of transformation through love in the mind of a male protagonist, while continuing to play with *stil nuovo* motifs. In this final tale, which receives much less attention from readers and critics than others in the cycle, Calandrino, like Cimone, is smitten by love.

The reader is well acquainted with the character of Calandrino by the time that Fiammetta narrates this tale on the Ninth Day. The peculiar characteristics of Calandrino and his "friends" are sharply delineated early in the cycle. Lauretta describes him on Day Eight as "uom semplice e di nuovi costumi" 'a simpleton of bizarre habits' (906; 483).[29] Bruno and Buffalmacco, fellow painters with whom he spends much of his time, are "uomini sollazzevoli molto ma per altro avveduti e sagaci" 'men who were pleasant enough but also very shrewd and sharp' (906-7; 483). These two, who are often blurred into a pair without individual identities, are always amused by Calandrino's simplemindedness. The reader realizes immediately who will be the object of the *beffe* to be narrated, and also glimpses the balance of power between the men. Calandrino, weaker in mind, will serve as the entertainment for his companions.

Calandrino exhibits many character flaws. He is greedy and egotistical (he believes himself clever)[30] and he is also gullible, a quality essential to the nature of his character. Most of all, Calandrino is ruled by his imagination. But the type of imagination that consumes Calandrino's life is an unquestioning fantasy, and he thrives in a world of deception that is almost impermeable. Paradoxically, as a creator of images, he scoffs at painting—and by inference the creative imagination—as a waste of time; but at the same moment he takes everything that others tell him at face value, immediately accepting words as truths.[31] Calandrino's literal-mindedness even allows his companions to convince him that he is invisible in the first tale. He trusts completely in the power of words, and especially when they come from the mouths of the two friends that he loves most.

On Day Nine, Fiammetta states that she has chosen to narrate the final Calandrino story because his tales are "tutti piacevoli" (1061), always pleasing the listeners.[32] At this point Fiammetta asserts the veracity of her tale, saying that she will not use fictitious names because "il partirsi dalla verità delle cose state nel novellare è gran diminuire di diletto negli'ntendenti" 'to depart from the truth of how things really happened in storytelling greatly diminishes the pleasure of the listeners' (1062; 574).

Fiammetta's assertion immediately draws the reader's attention to the very nature of the story as fiction, as well as stressing the connection of storytelling to pleasure. This recalls Boccaccio's reference to the text as "Galeotto." We know, after having already read three tales involving the same character, that we are about to hear another imaginative scene shaped to entertain and to distract its listeners from stark realties. Although Fiammetta indeed uses names of historical figures,[33] her request that we take what she says to be truth is, in effect, asking us to be Calandrino, and to take words at face value. Through her voice, Boccaccio again reminds us (if we will stop and consider it) not to allow the imaginative creation of the text to inspire images so strong in ourselves that we cannot distinguish them from reality. However, he is also reinforcing the truth that the shimmering illusions of art can lead to great pleasure. Such is imagination's paradox.

Warned, therefore, to be on our guard, we enter into the last story of Calandrino. The tale unfolds outside of Florence, a city whose inhabitants are supposed to be known for their wit, and against which Calandrino's apparent simplicity stands out.[34] Our protagonist is employed there with his friends (Bruno, Buffalmacco and another painter named Nello) painting frescoes on the walls of a beautiful mansion. The family is not in residence, but at times an unmarried son, Filippo, brings women to the home. This particular tale centers on Calandrino's romantic interest in one of them—never mind that he is a married man. Their initial meeting differs from that which took place between Cimone and Efigenia, but there are also some important similarities. Like Efigenia, the object of Calandrino's desire possesses a beautiful body dressed in white. Their encounter also takes place near a water source, although here it is not a fountain, but a well. Calandrino finds the woman beautiful yet "niuna cosa ardiva di dirle" 'he dared say nothing to her' (1063; 575), words that echo Cimone's reaction to Efigenia.

The contrasts between the two encounters are greater and also fascinating. The most obvious is in the style of the language, from the elegant courtly phrasing in Cimone's tale to the blunt and often crude language here. There are also significant differences in content. Here, the lady herself plays a very active role. In opposition to the passive, sleeping Efigenia, she initiates eye contact, staring at him "più perché Calandrino le pareva un nuovo uomo che per altra vaghezza" 'more because Calandrino seemed to her to be an odd individual rather than for any flirtatious reason' (1063; 575). Calandrino returns her stare, and when she notices this, "per uccellarlo" 'in order to make fun of him,' she would look at him now and then and "alcun sospiretto gittando" 'heave a sigh or two' (1063; 575). This interaction, connected by just a few coarse words to the doctrine of courtly love (the beautiful woman, the staring, the sighs) is all that Calandrino needs. "Per la qual cosa Calandrino subitamente di lei s'imbardò" 'Because of this, Calandrino immediately fell in love with her' (1063; 575). The lady he desires is named Niccolosa, and she is a prostitute, although Calandrino believes her to be Filippo's wife.

Cimone, the beast, re-creates himself in a solitary act inspired by his passion for Efigenia. His obsession then drives him to forcefully pursue the object of his desire. Calandrino, of course, has a very different reaction; he immediately asks his friend Bruno for help. His lack of ability to be autonomous is one of his greatest weaknesses, and the one that allows his friends to exploit

him for their amusement. Niccolosa initiates the *beffa* by actively triggering Calandrino's imagination, and now his other friends will join in the fun, shaping and sculpting it for him as the story progresses.

Calandrino's mind immediately begins to create fantasy. Naturally, his imagination makes Niccolosa stunningly beautiful. But Calandrino also declares, "è sí forte innamorata di me, che ti parrebbe un gran fatto" 'she is so passionately in love with me you'd be amazed' (1064; 575). Cimone, on the other hand, never paused to consider the feelings of the woman he desired—whether or not Efigenia loved him was meaningless. Interestingly, Boccaccio has a woman narrate the story of Calandrino, in which the female character plays an active role. However, Cimone's tale, in which the man aggressively initiates the action of the story, is narrated by a male.[35] Cimone's passion was inflamed by a contemplation of passivity; Calandrino's love springs from an imagination that takes flight as a reaction to external events, and yet his perception of those events is also distorted.

Discussing his belief that Niccolosa is married, Calandrino boasts to Bruno that he does not care, for "Io la fregherei a Cristo di cosí fatte cose, non che a Filippo" 'I'd steal her from Christ himself, let alone Filippo' (1064; 576). Similarly, an unsympathetic Cimone stole Efigenia from her fiancé and boasted that his power would exceed that of the gods (599; 317). In his earlier stories, Calandrino emulated what he believed to be intelligence and cunning; here, he masquerades as a lover in the style of Cimone. Calandrino also recalls the courtly lover, expressed in his words "ella m'ha morto!" 'she slays me!' (1064; 576).

An irony of Cimone was that, despite his transformation into a great philosopher and musician, he chose not to use these abilities to win Efigenia. Instead, Cimone relied upon force. Calandrino, also a parody of courtly love, does the reverse—although only in his mind. He does not linger long on the idea of taking Niccolosa by force. Rather, he soon proclaims, his great knowledge and musical skill will not fail to win her. Calandrino's self-image is so at odds with reality that he asserts "io so meglio che altro uomo far ciò che io voglio" 'I know better than any man how to get what I want' (1066; 577). This claim challenges the superiority of both Cimone's use of force and Lisimaco's use of intelligence in the earlier tale. Calandrino in a sense does undergo change as did Cimone, but with an important distinction. For Calandrino, it is a transformation in words only. Whereas Calandrino consistently acts upon the statements of his friends, which he accepts as truths, he does not do the same with his own words. Instead, Calandrino's transformation is hidden in his mind and his distorted self-image. This feature of Calandrino as unchanging allows him to be a repeat victim of the *beffe* in each tale. His companions carefully nurture his illusions and he never realizes that a joke has been played. Calandrino has been compared both to a child (Forno 136; Baratto 317), and to an animal, recalling the "scimmione" associations with Cimone.[36]

For the climax of this *beffa,* Bruno enlists the help of Buffalmacco and Nello in hatching a plot to prolong the fun at Calandrino's expense. They augment their pleasure by bringing Niccolosa as well as Filippo into the plan, telling them "chi era Calandrino" 'the kind of person Calandrino was' (1065; 576). Not only do these characters orchestrate Calandrino's life for the remainder of the *novella,* but they do so with his consent. Calandrino is more than cooperative when Bruno says "lascia far me" 'leave it all to me' (1065; 576).

Calandrino's friends enjoy the spectacle of his love affair for a good two months, until Calandrino begins to worry that he will not be able to fulfill his ultimate desire with Niccolosa. Rather than become more assertive towards the lady in his advances, Calandrino remains true to form and pressures Bruno to move things forward. Bruno complies by playing another trick on Calandrino's imagination, creating with him a magic formula (words on parchment) and instructing him to touch Niccolosa with the writing.[37] Calandrino believes the act will give him complete control over Niccolosa, but of course the magic with which he hopes to master his world has no true substance. Calandrino never tires of indulging his unquestioning imagination as he seeks out the strange ingredients for the formula, whose very form and purpose reminds us of his slavery to words.

At this point the story nears its end, and one that is commonly seen as the just retribution for the first story in the Calandrino cycle.[38] It acts as a counterpart to the violent episode that concludes Calandrino's first adventure, when he believed himself invisible due to a heliotrope's magic. That first shocking outburst was triggered when Calandrino's wife Tessa greeted him and he realized he was visible. Calandrino's dream of power came to an abrupt end and he blamed his wife, for women "fanno perder la vertú a ogni cosa" 'cause everything to lose its power' (918; 489). The ensuing disillusionment resulted in a rage so great that Calandrino savagely beat her nearly to death. In this final tale, Nello fetches Calandrino's wife on Bruno's orders, and tells her that this is her chance to be vindicated for the heliotrope incident. The stage is set, and Tessa arrives just at the moment when Calandrino believes he is to finally kiss Niccolosa. Tessa, burning with anger, beats her husband with a brutality reminiscent of the battering she had received from him in the first tale. And in both cases, Bruno and Buffalmacco serve as mediators, subduing the passions that have erupted, while laughing surreptitiously at the scene. Calandrino's clever companions have successfully and secretly manipulated every emotion and action of the characters in the tale.

Cimone and Calandrino appear to be very different characters but they are at base alike. Both exemplify the connections of the imagination with love, and how the balance between the two can lead to pleasure or to devastation and danger. Boccaccio uses these tales not only to demonstrate the destructive force of erotic love, but also to show the complicated ambiguity of the imagination. Cimone's passion is connected with a simplistic and limited form of imagination, leading him to become utterly controlled by his passion of desire. Calandrino's imagination is much more active and alive, but it is not under his own control. The movements of his imagination, and also the passions that they inspire, are orchestrated by those around him. Cimone ostensibly possessed the tools that could control his passions (wisdom and learning) but he did not use them, and in deciding to pursue his desire at any cost he caused devastation to those around him. In the end, it was only through the direction of Lisimaco that he succeeded in his quest. Calandrino, like Icarus and Phaethon, is overconfident in his own wisdom and abilities, and his arrogant delusions lead his quest for passion and knowledge—for ultimately all he wants is to be a clever man, like his friends—to fail. In both Cimone and Calandrino, the imagination is guided, but not by the one who possesses it.

The connection between Cimone's lustful passion and his violence was unquestionable as he slaughtered those around him. Although Calandrino is presented as a comic figure whose antics serve as entertainment for those around him, beneath the surface there always lurks the possibility of violence and danger. The passion that this character displays most intensely is anger, and he directs his rage against Tessa in these tales. She, as his wife, is the person with whom he is most intimately connected, yet also the one person who is not involved in the elaborate *beffe* played upon him. Tessa personifies the one element that threatens the stability of Calandrino's world built on fantasy. She is not afraid to show him the truth, and Calandrino, sensing this threat to his self-made utopia, resents her for it. The beating over the heliotrope is the most savage incident in the four tales, and the one that stands out in stark contrast to the "comic" purpose of the *novelle.* At that moment, in Calandrino's mind, Tessa actually does what he has always feared—she destroys the stone's magic, and by inference, also the illusions of his fantasy. It is when Calandrino's illusion is shattered that his character turns dangerous and his fury is unleashed.

The characters who seem to benefit the most from the Calandrino tales are the clever friends who manipulate him. Bruno and Buffalmacco are skilled in the use of the imagination, for they can combine it with their intelligence and with it create art (the theater of Calandrino). In Dante's works the term *ingegno* was used to signify, in effect, the creative imagination, especially in an artistic or poetic sense,[39] and the term is very fitting in this context as well. Cimone was not a shining example of such *ingegno,* despite his apparent miraculous conversion to wisdom, but the characters who plot the *beffe* in the Calandrino tales undoubtedly possess this faculty.

Boccaccio has been recognized as a writer who celebrates the *ingegno* of his characters, but Bruno and Buffalmacco (as well as the accomplices they draw into the various stories) are not uncomplicated examples of the merits of the creative imagination. Although they seem to benefit from the *beffe* and are themselves unscathed, they are toying with the passions of their victims. They are also well aware of Calandrino's dangerous anger. They do not hesitate—and in fact encourage, as in the case of Tessa—to rouse these violent passions, which even cause bodily harm. This provides further proof of their separation between *ingegno* and passion. Bruno and Buffalmacco understand that what Calandrino fears most is the unveiling of his illusions and having to face the truth of his own mental feebleness. They also sense that this is the basis for the rage he directs towards his wife. By perpetuating Calandrino's arrogant self-delusions and portraying themselves to him as the weaker-minded fools, Bruno and Buffalmacco are also protecting themselves from becoming targets of his violence.

The *ingegno* of the clever characters in the Calandrino cycle links them to the author of the *Decameron* himself. Boccaccio, too, is constructing a world of illusion and orchestrating the images we create in our own minds as we read. While Cimone and Calandrino as lovers experience violence, Bruno and Buffalmacco detach their own imaginations from that passion and so seem to remain unharmed. But they are rewarded for the exercise of their ingenuity with pleasure, a pleasure created by the humiliation of another that serves to prove the superiority of their own intellects. But even here love plays a role, for it is Calandrino's love for his friends that allows him to cede control over his imagination and his passions to them.

Ultimately, the two tales of Cimone and Calandrino are connected by Boccaccio's sovereign art, whereby he shows how vital, how unavoidable, and yet how dangerous the inspirations of the imagination can become. These two characters balance each other off. Cimone's actions reveal the inability to channel his passions to a constructive rationality. He yields to imagination's primitive phantasms all too readily. Calandrino, on the other hand, loses his sense of reality and quickly embraces the figments of his mind. Furthermore, both characters lack the more complex form of imagination as *ingegno. Ingegno* is essential to those who arrange the stories of Cimone and Calandrino—their unscathed companion characters and the author himself. Boccac-

cio, on his part, writes these two tales as if they were "exemplary novellas" (to use Cervantes' title): he shows that literature is forever flanked by two dangers. Readers can mistake, like Calandrino, fiction for reality; or they can, like Cimone, forget the order of rationality and yield to the impulses of destructive passions. These possibilities make the *Decameron* the privileged text of the contradictory, rich, and unpredictable experiences of life.

Notes

1. At the root of this tradition is the Platonic flight of the soul. For an analysis of Dante's ambivalence concerning the imagination, especially as linked to the visionary faculty and its ability to lead away from the physical world, see Mazzotta, *Dante's Vision* 116-34.

2. See Scaglione; see also Hastings for a reading of the relationship between nature and reason.

3. De Sanctis called the *Decameron* "earthly comedy," in contrast to the *Divina Commedia,* and described Boccaccio's work as "the cynical malicious world of the flesh, left in the low regions of sensuality" and "gross in its feelings, but polished and adorned by the imagination" (*History* 359); Auerbach echoes this concept saying Boccaccio uses an "intermediate style [. . .] which, combining the idyllic and the realistic, is designated for the representation of sensual love" (*Mimesis* 217). As is well known, Boccaccio himself expressed ambiguous views of his own text, between defending it and condemning it in his later years. Many authors have concentrated on the contradictions and polarities within the text itself (De Michelis; Sinicropi); or on the ambiguity of its content (Pagnamenta).

4. Note that "Fiammetta" is also the name of Boccaccio's professed Lady Love as well as the protagonist of the *Elegia di Madonna Fiammetta.* Paradoxically, the latter has been read alternately as a misogynistic and even a feminist text (see Calabrese). See Gómez Redondo for a discussion of the *Fiammetta* and the relationship between imagination and fiction.

5. Italian quotes from the *Decameron* are from the 1980 Branca edition; English quotes are from the translation by Musa and Bondanella, which is based on the authoritative edition by Branca done in 1975 for the Accademia della Crusca.

6. The last three lines of the *Lai* read: "Veritez est, et ge le di, / Qu'amors vänt tout et tout vaincra / Tant com cis siecles durera" (90).

7. *Matto* has many definitions, but those of greatest interest here include the following, all of which apply to Cimone at some point in the tale: "ha una

visione deformata [. . .] della realtà"; "si comporte come se avesse perduto la ragione"; "il contrario di *savio*"; "gravemente menomato nelle facoltà intellettuali; deficiente"; "posseduto, esaltato da [. . .] una passione particolarmente intensa, viva o violenta"; and "ossessionato." The term had been used in all of these contexts before Boccaccio's time ("Matto").

8. Marcus traces the etymology of Cimone to the Greek "chimaros," the male form of the she-goat "chimaira" ("Sweet" 10). Branca also connects the name with "montone" as one of its possible sources (*Decameron* 594). For discussion of man/beast metamorphoses and conflict in the *cornice* of this and other works of Boccaccio, see Surdich, *Cornice*.

9. While Boccaccio himself does not label Cimone a madman outright, his description of the events of the tale portrays him in many of the traditional trappings of madness. Valesio writes that, from the Middle Ages through the Renaissance, the iconic aspect of a character's madness is emphasized: "they discard all the refinements of culture and civilization, especially clothes, and revert to a state of nature, wandering in the wilderness; they rarely talk, and when they do, there are no specific linguistic elements in their speeches which indicate an abnormal state of mind" ("Language" 200).

10. See Kirkham for a discussion of this phrase in the *Decameron*.

11. See Cottino-Jones' *Order* for a reading on the meaning of the settings in this tale, and their role in her understanding of the *Decameron* as an aesthetic model of a chaotic society reorganized into a system based on individual and social values.

12. For a more in-depth discussion on the varied and multi-faceted definitions of the imagination and related terms, see Brann 18-26.

13. For example, Baratto 57 and Rossi, A xxvii.

14. Battaglia Ricci compares the contemplation of Efigenia with that of Masetto in the convent garden—the former inspiring a celebration of beauty and love, the latter a number of illicit sexual pairings (174-5). In a discussion of Griselda, Campbell connects the female body with the medieval concept of textuality, and its clothing (or lack thereof) with the masculine act of reading (192).

15. These types of depictions exemplify what some see as the overall victimization and anonymity of female characters in the *Decameron* (Fleming; Staples 66). For examples of the opposite view see Hastings 52.

16. For Toscano, the worsening of Cimone's character demonstrates the artificial and misleading nature of the love doctrine, and the conflict of nature and society (31). For Marcus, Cimone descends into monstrosity because he lacks the sense of humility required by *stil nuovo* lovers ("Sweet" 12).

17. Spera, for example, who also sees the division between the two halves as simply a device used to separate and then recombine "the lovers" (87), and the conflict of the story as one between the power of love and vicissitudes of fortune (86). See also Mulryan 392, Surdich's *Boccaccio* 150-51, and Branca's *Boccaccio medievale* 112-13.

18. In Ovid's *Metamorphoses* the character by this name has a small but significant role; she is a princess offered up as sacrifice by her own father in Book 12.

19. "Cimone con Efigenia lieto si tornò in Cipri e Lisimaco similmente con Cassandrea ritornò in Rodi; e ciascun lietamente con la sua visse lungamente contento nella sua terra" (608).

20. Mazzotta has pointed out that marriage in the *Decameron* serves to correct the imbalance between reason and the appetites in the context of the fall from Eden. Marriage is redemptive, reestablishing the dominant position of reason over the lower appetites (*World* 125-26).

21. "Onesto" is that which "il sommo e primo creatore tenne lui alle sue creature congiunto." Love "per diletto" is the one "al quale noi siamo suggetti [. . .] è il nostro iddio" (4.44). Toscano believes that the destructive description of "amore per diletto" is the immediate inspiration for the Cimone *novella* (29). That based on "utilità" is equated to hate by the speaker. She emphasizes the second type as dangerous and to be avoided if possible, for who, "se sarà savio," would not flee it for their own good? (4.44). *Filocolo* quotes in Italian are from *Tutte le opere,* and those in English are from the Cheney translation.

22. Marcus states that Boccaccio's critique of the *stil nuovo* also criticizes the point in his own literary career where he followed their poetics ("Sweet" 13). Another view is that the *Decameron* "rappresenta un mondo umano in preda a quella passione [amore] che il poeta ha superata e che perciò contempla ormai con distacco" (Givens 210). Bergin states that the tale "exemplifies the fundamental ambiguity of courtly or even romantic love" (*Boccaccio* 311). Stone believes that Boccaccio intended to "reinvent the very essence and purpose of philosophy" (24). He reads the tale as mocking the glorification, by Dante and others, of the philosopher whom they posit as "the only truly

nonanimalistic, [. . .] truly human, human being" (28). For Stone, Cimone embodies a new idea of philosophy based on the legislation of a desirable or pleasurable social order. Cimone is "the first Renaissance Man" (38), one who does not deny his animality and whose wisdom lies in renouncing the necessity of order to be "founded on rational knowledge of absolute truth" (37). This is a fascinating reading. However, the sheer destructiveness of the *novella* leads me to question its conclusion that Cimone serves simply as an example of the new philosopher who uses his mind to get what he desires. The context of violence invites further exploration.

23. We see this in a later question: is it better for a lover to see his beloved or to dream about her? (4.59). The queen answers that it is better to dream, for the "spiriti sensitivi tutti allora sentono mirabile festa," whereas in seeing the beloved, "solo il visuale spirito sente bene" (4.60), reminiscent of Cavalcanti. Graziosa (who posed the question) counters that the more one looks, the greater the pleasure.

24. Graziosa states: "nell'animo tale piacere si conferma, e generasene amore e quelli disii che da lui nascono" (4.61). A similar discussion takes place in *Filostrato* (Proemio 2-7). In this passage, the narrator confirms that dreaming of his beloved had given his imagination the freedom to envision her as reciprocating his affection, although he changed his opinion after feeling the pain of a separation from her.

25. Ferreri's interpretation then uses the conflict to illustrate a *rovesciamento* of the character of Cimone. Ferreri believes this reversal, together with its convergence of two narrative traditions, must be read in the context of the qualities of the mercantile Florentine society (90). See Branca for the concept of the *Decameron* as representative of that society. In any case, Cimone is not a character worthy of admiration or imitation despite the fact that he ultimately succeeds in his quest—but for a viewpoint in opposition to mine, see Cottino-Jones, *Order*. She sees Cimone in a much more positive light in her reading of the tale in terms of an individual vs. society conflict. She writes "our predisposition to admire Cimone, Lisimaco's presence as the true 'heavy' of the piece, Cimone's foreign origin, and his desire to win the woman who initiated his spiritual rebirth, all seem to mitigate his culpability in committing violence against an unfamiliar society which seeks to deny him love" (83).

26. Toscano believes the *novella* exemplifies "the irrational but quite natural form of love equated to madness" (26). Rather than becoming wise by falling in love, love can awaken natural human instincts that cannot be restrained through reason. For an interesting reading of the tale as Nature vs. *Ingegno* (Art), with Lisimaco's *ingegno* replacing that of Cimone, see Tronci.

27. This fact is emphasized when we meet Calandrino for the first time—he is in church, gazing at the paintings and bas-reliefs. See Mazzotta's *World* 194-95 for comments on the meaning of this scene.

28. Pierone 154; Russo refers to Calandrino's story as "la commedia di un mondo intellettuale e sensuale" (278).

29. The inclusion of "nuovo" in Calandrino's description can be seen as emphasizing his novelty and therefore his position as a target of pranks (Marcus, *Allegory* 82-83); as well as his "foreignness," and therefore his permanent exclusion from society.

30. Betti correctly calls Calandrino an "aspirante furbo," a person who "vuole agire sagacemente, intelligentemente, in un mondo che appare sovrappopolato da individui dotati di una mente molto più acuta della sua" (514-515). See Cottino-Jones for a very different conclusion, in which she states the heliotrope reflects Calandrino's "unconscious wish to make other people like himself, that is, incapable of seeing" ("Magic" 20). Passaro describes Calandrino as a "natural fool" for he lacks self-knowledge (151).

31. Mazzotta writes of this folly that "by mistaking what are only words for reality, Calandrino ultimately obliterates the value of words" (*World* 198).

32. Also see Forno for a reading on pleasure and the ambiguity of the *beffa* in the *Decameron*.

33. Calandrino, Bruno, Buffalmacco and Nello were indeed painters in the early 14th century. See Branca's notes in *Decameron* 906-07 and 1048 for more details about them.

34. See Cottino-Jones, *Order* 138-153; Baratto 309; Pierone 156. Mazzotta notes that Calandrino, as an outsider in the city, is also open to the possibility of anything happening in this unfamiliar world (*World* 194).

35. Migiel posits Fiammetta as presenting her companions with expanded and more complex views on the role of women in the *Decameron* ("How" 306-7).

36. Russo sees Calandrino as monkey in his antics (288); Salisbury reads ambiguous animal-human figures and their relationship with the passions ("animal") and reason ("human") in the Middle Ages.

37. See Cottino-Jones for a reading of magic in the *Decameron* as the stage on which Boccaccio celebrates human intelligence: it enables a clever person, who recognizes the power it has over the superstitious, to manipulate the shape of the world around them ("Magic" 30).

38. See Cottino-Jones, *Order* 165-66; Del Popolo reads this as Tessa's vindication not only of the previous tales, but as a reaction to the particular situation in the third tale, where she is blamed for getting her husband pregnant. In this tale, it is Niccolosa who is "di sopra." See Nissen for a reading of retribution as a link between the worlds of the "real" and "ideal." Calandrino merits punishment due simply to "who he is," because he violates the text's ethical norms (71). Nissen also views retribution as so prevalent that punishment must be viewed as a central theme in the *Decameron* (32). See also Surdich, *Boccaccio* 185. Migiel places the violent scenes of Calandrino within a larger context of domestic violence in the text. Increasing violence against women correlates with the potential for female empowerment while also demanding the examination of the reader's own perceptions within that context (*Rhetoric* 149).

39. *Ingegno* can be used interchangeably with *vis imaginativa* or *phantasia* in the tri-partite division of the internal senses (Wetherbee 46-47). Dante's use of *ingegno* is defined by Mario Trovato "as a poetical faculty [. . .] understood by Dante as the instinctive ability to evaluate and choose a suitable inventive material and transform it into artistic images" (261). Therefore, *ingegno* is a technical term equivalent to the formative process of the creative imagination, and for Dante, specifically to the poetic art. Hastings, placing the term under the heading of intelligence, defines *ingegno* in Boccaccio as "active, operative intelligence, resourcefulness, ingenuity" (74). Unfortunately, the creative aspect of *ingegno* often seems to be overlooked in scholarly writing, which focuses instead on it being one of the variants of "intelligence."

Works Cited

Auerbach, Erich. *Mimesis: The Representation of Reality in Western Literature.* Trans. Willard R. Trask. Princeton: Princeton UP, 1974.

Baratto, Mario. *Realtà e stile nel* Decameron. Vicenza: Pozza, 1970.

Battaglia Ricci, Lucia. *Boccaccio.* Roma: Salerno, 2000.

Bergin, Thomas G. *Boccaccio.* New York: Viking, 1981.

Betti, Franco. "Calandrino, eroe sfortunato: Aspetti del realismo boccacciano." *Italica* 54.4 (1977): 512-520.

Boccaccio, Giovanni. *Decameron.* Ed. Vittore Branca. Torino: Einaudi, 1992.

———. *The Decameron.* Trans. Mark Musa and Peter Bondanella. New York: Mentor-Penguin, 1982. xxi-xxx.

———. *Il Filocolo.* Trans. Donald Cheney and Thomas G. Bergin. New York: Garland, 1985.

———. *Tutte le Opere.* Ed. Vittore Branca. 12 vols. Verona: Mondadori, 1967.

Branca, Vittore. *Boccaccio medievale e nuovi studi sul* Decamerone. 5th ed. Firenze: Sansoni, 1981.

Brann, Eva T. H. *The World of the Imagination: Sum and Substance.* Lanham: Rowman and Littlefield, 1991.

Calabrese, Michael A. "Feminism and the Packaging of Boccaccio's *Fiammetta.*" *Italica* 74.1 (1997): 20-42.

Campbell, Emma. "Sexual Politics and the Politics of Translation in the Tale of Griselda." *Comparative Literature* 55.3 (2003): 191-216.

Cottino-Jones, Marga. *Order from Chaos: Social and Aesthetic Harmonies in Boccaccio's* Decameron. Washington: UP of America, 1982.

———. "Magic and Superstition in Boccaccio's *Decameron.*" *Italian Quarterly* 18.72 (1975): 5-32.

D'Andeli, Henri. *Le Lai d'Aristote.* Ed. Maurice Delbouille. Paris: Belles Lettres, 1951.

Del Popolo, Concetto. "Un'espressione di Calandrino: *Decameron IX* 3.21,24; 5.64." *Studi sul Boccaccio* 27 (1999): 107-112.

De Michelis, Cesare. *Contraddizioni nel* Decameron. Milano: Guanda, 1983.

De Sanctis, Francesco. *The History of Italian Literature.* Trans. Joan Redfern. 2 vols. New York: Harcourt, 1931.

Ferreri, Rosario. *Innovazione e tradizione nel Boccaccio.* Roma: Bulzoni, 1980.

Fleming, Ray. "Happy Endings? Resisting Women and the Economy of Love in Day Five of Boccaccio's *Decameron.*" *Italica* 70.1 (1993): 30-45.

Forno, Carla. "L'amaro riso della beffa." *Prospettive sul Decameron.* Ed. G. Barberi Squarotti. Torino: Tirrenia, 1989. 131-147.

Givens, Azzura B. *La dottrina d'amore nel Boccaccio.* Messina: D'Anna, 1968.

Gómez Redondo, Fernando. "De la imaginación a la ficción en el *Libro de Fiameta.*" *Romance Quarterly* 50.4 (2003): 243-258.

Hastings, R. *Nature and Reason in the* Decameron. Manchester: U of Manchester P, 1975.

Kirkham, Victoria. *The Sign of Reason in Boccaccio's Fiction.* Firenze: Olschki, 1993.

Marcus, Millicent Joy. *An Allegory of Form: Literary Self-Consciousness in the* Decameron. Saratoga: Anma Libri, 1979.

———. "The Sweet New Style Reconsidered: A Gloss on the Tale of Cimone (*Decameron* V,1)." *Italian Quarterly* 21.81 (1980): 5-16.

"Matto." *Grande dizionario della lingua italiana.* Ed. Salvatore Battaglia. Torino: UTET, 1975.

Mazzotta, Giuseppe. *Dante's Vision and the Circle of Knowledge.* Princeton: Princeton UP, 1993.

———. *The World at Play in Boccaccio's Decameron.* Princeton: Princeton UP, 1986.

Migiel, Marilyn. "How (thanks to a woman) Andreuccio da Perugia Became Such a Loser, and How (also thanks to a woman) Reading Could Have Become a More Complicated Affair." *RLA* [*Revista de linguistica*] 10.1 (1998): 302-307.

———. *A Rhetoric of the* Decameron. Toronto: U of Toronto P, 2003.

Mulryan, John. "The Three Images of Venus: Boccaccio's Theory of Love in the Geneology of the Gods and His Aesthetic Vision of Love in the *Decameron.*" *Romance Notes* 19.3 (1979): 388-394.

Nissen, Christopher. *Ethics of Retribution in the* Decameron *and the Late Medieval Italian Novella.* Lewiston: Mellen UP, 1993.

Pagnamenta, Roberta Bruno. *Il* Decameron: *L'ambiguità come strategia narrativa.* Ravenna: Longo, 1999.

Passaro, Maria Pastore. "Some examples of 'Wisdom' and 'Folly' in the *Decameron.*" *Forum Italicum* 31.1 (1997): 145-152.

Pierone, Claudia. "Per aver festa e buon tempo e non per altro . . ." *Prospettive sul* Decameron. Ed. G. Barberi Squarotti. Torino: Tirrenia, 1989. 149-163.

Rossi, Aldo, ed. *Il Decameron.* By Giovanni Boccaccio. Bologna: Cappelli, 1977.

Russo, Luigi. *Letture critiche del* Decameron. Bari: Laterza, 1956.

Salisbury, Joyce E. "Human Beasts and Bestial Humans in the Middle Ages." *Animal Acts: Configuring the Human in Western History.* Ed. Jennifer Ham and Matthew Senior. New York: Routledge, 1997. 9-21.

Scaglione, Aldo D. *Nature and Love in the Late Middle Ages.* Berkeley: U of California P, 1963.

Sinicropi, Giovanni. "Chastity and Love in the *Decameron.*" *The Olde Daunce: Love, Friendship, Sex and Marriage in the Medieval World.* Ed. Robert R. Edwards and Stephen Spector. Albany: State U of New York P, 1991. 104-120.

Spera, Francesco. "La buona sorte e la forza d'amore: V giornata." *Prospettive sul* Decameron. Ed. G. Barberi Squarotti. Torino: Tirrenia, 1989. 85-96.

Staples, Max Alexander. *The Ideology of the* Decameron. Lewiston: Mellen, 1994.

Stone, Gregory B. "The Philosophical Beast: On Boccaccio's Tale of Cimone." *Animal Acts: Configuring the Human in Western History.* Ed. Jennifer Ham and Matthew Senior. New York: Routledge, 1997. 23-41.

Surdich, Luigi. *Boccaccio.* Roma: Laterza, 2001.

———. *La cornice di amore: Studi sul Boccaccio.* Pisa: ETS, 1987.

Toscano, Antonio. "*Decameron*: Cimone's Metamorphosis." *Italian Quarterly* 29.114 (1998): 25-35.

Tronci, Francesco. *La novella tra letteratura, ideologia e metaletteratura: Studi sul* Decameron. Cagliari: CUEC, 2001.

Trovato, Mario. "The Semantic Value of *Ingegno* and Dante's *Ulysses* in the Light of the Metalogicon." *Modern Philology* 84.3 (1987): 258-266.

Valesio, Paolo. "The Language of Madness in the Renaissance." *Yearbook of Italian Studies* (1971): 199-234.

Wetherbee, Winthrop. "The Theme of Imagination in Medieval Poetry and the Allegorical Figure 'Genius'." *Medievalia et humanistica* 7 (1976): 45-64.

Cristelle L. Baskins (essay date 2005)

SOURCE: Baskins, Cristelle L. "Scenes from a Marriage: Hospitality and Commerce in Boccaccio's 'Tale of Saladin and Torello.'" In *The Medieval Marriage Scene: Prudence, Passion, Policy,* edited by Sherry Roush and Cristelle L. Baskins, pp. 81-95. Tempe: Arizona Center for Medieval and Renaissance Studies, 2005.

[*In the following essay, Baskins studies a set of fifteenth-century Florentine panels illustrating tale 10.9 of the* Decameron—*the story of Saladin, an Alexandrian sultan and merchant, and Torello, a Christian knight from northern Italy. Baskins argues that the panels and the tale reflect and reshape social practice and gender roles typical of the Middle Ages and are especially of interest for their commentary on diplomatic relations and trade customs between Europe and the East.*]

A pair of panels, painted in Florence in the 1420s, illustrates the tale of Saladin and Torello from Giovanni Boccaccio's **Decameron,** day 10, story 9 (figures 1 and 2).[1] Boccaccio's tale blends fact and fantasy, drawing on a host of earlier romances, poems, and anecdotes about Salah al Din (1138-1193 C.E.), the Muslim ruler of Egypt and Syria, who drove the Crusaders out of the Holy Land.[2] The panels have received scant attention and little analysis beyond clarifying the narrative source. Bruce Cole, for example, proposes a general, didactic reading; for him the pictures convey virtuous messages through action and suspense in an exotic location.[3] But Cole's reading does not take into account the material, cultural, or political factors shaping images of Saladin and Torello. In fact, fifteenth-century Florentines renewed their fascination with the Levant, "Saracens," and Saladin at a critical moment in the development of overseas trade and commercial privileges with the Mamlukes.[4] Representations of Saladin and Torello visualize relations between East and West as a domestic event, an encounter that results in fabulous gift exchange and courteous hospitality. The pictures translate immediate concerns, risks, and vulnerabilities into reassuring successes. Boccaccio's tale inspires images that merge the foreign and the familiar: ransom and marriage, crusade and commerce, trade and magic.[5]

Each of the panels features three polygonal fields framed by interlacing bands and gilt foliage in relief. The overall effect is reminiscent of decorative arts imported from Spain, North Africa, or the Levant. At the left of the first panel we see Torello, a Pavian knight, dressed in a pink mantle and helmet. He offers hospitality to Saladin and his companions, unaware that they are touring Europe disguised as Cypriot merchants in order to gain information about plans for a Christian crusade.[6] Saladin, wearing a yellow garment, tips his hat in greeting; Torello takes him firmly by the hand, leading him to his residence in the countryside. Boccaccio mentions that the Saracens happened to be fluent in Italian and that therefore language was no barrier to the exchange of compliments, chivalrous courtesy, and table talk at the banquet that Torello hastily arranges for his guests.

In the central scene, we see the events of the following day. Torello had sent word to his wife, Adalieta, to prepare their city residence for the arrival of his guests. The painter distinguishes the domestic architecture in the second scene from the fortified walls of the first. The assembled figures now stand before a Pavian townhouse while Torello's wife and their two children are shown accompanied by a maidservant. Adalieta begs the strangers, after they have bathed and eaten, not to refuse or to despise her "trifling" gifts:

> She then sent for two pairs of robes for each of the guests, one lined with silk and the other with fur, all of a quality more suited to a prince than to any merchant or private citizen. And these she presented to the gentlemen, along with three silken jackets and small-clothes, saying: 'Take these robes; they are like the ones in which I have arrayed my husband.'[7]

Saladin, shown wearing a turban and sporting a scimitar, reaches out to receive a dark, figured silk garment while the maidservant holds the remainder of the clothes to be given to his two companions. In the text, Boccaccio says that the Saracens could "scarcely believe their eyes . . . and for a moment they suspected, seeing that the robes were more sumptuous than those of any merchant, that [Torello] had seen through their disguise." The hospitality of the Pavian knight and his wife, including new garments for their servants, a tour of the city, fresh horses, and another magnificent feast, continues to impress the strangers. Saladin concludes that "there was never a more perfect gentleman than this, nor any more courteous or considerate." Saladin observes that if all Christian knights were like Torello they would be invincible. The Saracens depart for Alexandria with Saladin vowing someday to repay Torello's hospitality, or as he puts it, "to show him the quality of his merchandise."

The third scene from the first panel shows the departure of Torello for the long-anticipated crusade. We see Torello on horseback, accompanied by fellow soldiers, while his wife and maidservant bid them farewell on the threshold of their palace. Torello's cape matches the fabric of his wife's dress, as well as the magnificent garment she had given to Saladin; sumptuous figured silk thus links the three main protagonists. In the event of his death while on campaign, Torello makes Adalieta promise to wait a year, a month, and a day before remarrying. Despite her promise of fidelity, Torello knows that his wife's brothers and kinsfolk will be unable to avoid contracting a second marriage for a woman so young, beautiful, of good lineage, and exceptional gifts. The scene then illustrates Adalieta taking a ring from her own finger, presenting it to Torello, and kissing his other hand. If they never meet again, at least the ring will serve to remind Torello of his faithful wife.

The second panel opens at left with Torello in prison in Alexandria after having been captured during the crusade (figure 2). While in captivity he learns to train hawks and is eventually made the Sultan's falconer. The artist represents the moment when Saladin finally recognizes that his captive falconer is actually his old host, Torello. Saladin asks Torello if he recognizes the garments he is wearing, and Torello responds that they remind him of clothes he once wore himself and clothing that he had given to some travelling merchants. Overjoyed at the prospect of repaying Torello's generosity, Saladin dresses him in regal robes and declares him no longer a servant but co-ruler of the realm.

While Torello is enjoying his extraordinary reversal of fortune, his wife receives false reports of his death. The requisite waiting period has all but elapsed and she is about to be given in marriage. Torello hears of the impending wedding and begs Saladin to be allowed to return home. The middle scene of the second panel shows how Saladin's magicians transported Torello on an enchanted bed to the church of San Pietro in Ciel d'Oro at Pavia. The bed appears incongruously in the midst of the church where three monks gaze fearfully at the spectacle of Torello wearing a turban and Saracen clothing, reclining on velvet pillows, cloth of gold mattresses, and a quilt embroidered with gemstones. Further going-away gifts from the Sultan appear beside him: a crown, sword, brooch, golden bowl overflowing with coins, rings, belts, pearls, and a ruby ring of inestimable value. Saladin's ring parallels Adalieta's; it is another token of everlasting affection. The parallel rings remind us that the homosocial bond between the men—played out in identities ranging from host and guest, master and slave, or co-rulers—competes with the conjugal bond between spouses. A groom viewing the painted imagery of this wedding chest might well have recalled with nostalgia his carefree single days, hunting in the company of wealthy, powerful men, exempt from the cares of business or a household.

The third scene illustrates the happy conclusion in which Torello attends his wife's marriage feast still in disguise. Torello wants to test his wife's behavior and attitude before revealing his identity. Although Adalieta does not know who he is, Boccaccio says that she cannot stop looking at his extraordinary clothing. Satisfied as to her reluctance to marry again, Torello then drops the ring that she had previously given him into her chalice; after drinking from the cup she recognizes the ring and realizes that the stranger is none other than her husband, Torello. Adalieta is shown boldly leaning across the table to kiss her disguised husband. In Boccaccio's text she even overturns a table in her haste to embrace him and her actions are described as "berserk." The text explains that the unlucky bridegroom concedes Adalieta to Torello. Not only does she return the groom's marriage gifts, but Torello further compensates him for the cost of the banquet. Presumably the seated man to the right of the scene, shown conversing with a lady dressed in pink, represents the spurned bridegroom who knew better than to dispute Torello's claims.

In the story of Saladin and Torello, material goods, textiles, and gifts effortlessly criss-cross the Mediterranean as tokens of hospitality, affection, and worthiness. Whereas the tale appears to equate the courtesy of Christian and Saracen, demonstrating their essential similarity, Boccaccio characteristically undercuts such idealism in the conclusion. There the narrator Panfilo warns that those who are inept in carrying out courtesy may find that their deeds do *not* redound to their credit, and that the cost of courtesy may exceed its value. Panfilo's final word invites the reader and viewer to take another look at the systems of exchange dramatized in

the tale of Saladin and Torello and to speculate about the production of credit and value in late medieval Florentine domestic pictures.[8]

MARRIAGE GIFTS

The Saladin and Torello panels appear on domestic furniture, the wedding chests or *cassoni,* produced for wealthy merchants and patricians in late medieval Florence. The pictures not only illustrate gift exchange and magnificent changes of clothing, but the chests themselves were gifts commissioned by the bride's father or, as later became the norm, by the groom.[9] The chests were lavishly decorated with expensive pigments and gold leaf. The average cost for a *cassone* ensemble was sixty-five florins, or the equivalent of a working man's annual salary. The sumptuous enchanted bed that conveys Torello to Pavia might also have reminded contemporary viewers of the other key piece of furniture purchased for new couples. Artists decorated not only bedsteads and chests but also birth trays known as *deschi,* or wainscotting called *spalliere,* with scenes from ancient history, mythology, and vernacular literature. The works of Boccaccio and Petrarch remained popular as sources for domestic pictures well into the fifteenth century.

Wedding chests and their contents were subjected to intense scrutiny during the public procession in which they accompanied the bride to her new residence. *Cassoni* served as containers for the trousseau—the underclothes, linens, towels, gloves, belts, and ribbons—that the bride brought with her to her new home. The wedding procession itself could become a flash point for would-be suitors, who might threaten to kidnap the bride unless they were paid a ransom. In his tale, "The Precious Jewel," Agnolo Firenzuola describes how a clever bride convinces some gullible youths to accept a counterfeit ring in exchange for allowing her bridal procession to continue on its way.[10] Not only does she escape the encounter unmolested, but the youths suffer public humiliation for their stupidity and greed. Even if such mock kidnappings were highly choreographed street theater, they allowed participants to defuse aggression and to curb excessive competition over women and money.

As Christiane Klapisch-Zuber has suggested, the *cassoni* were a material reminder of the dowry received by the groom from the bride's father; whereas dowry payments could be delayed by investments, rents, or business proceeds, the decorated wedding chests carried visible and tangible goods. In return for the dowry, the groom provided a counter-dowry, the bride's outer clothing, and dresses often with elaborate, detachable sleeves displaying the arms or heraldry of the groom's family.[11] When Adalieta returns her marriage gifts to the suitor and Torello pays him for the marriage banquet, contemporaries would have recognized the complexity of gift exchanges and the amounts of money necessary for a wedding that would confer honor on both families involved.

The depiction of gifts of clothing on the Saladin and Torello panels recalls the exchange of dowry and counter-dowry between bride and groom, but it would be a mistake to think of the pictures as merely reflecting social custom. In Boccaccio's story and in the *cassoni* pictures, patrician Florentines encountered a pointed reversal of late medieval gender expectations. It is Adalieta, the wife, who gives silk and fur-lined clothing to her husband, as well as to Saladin and his companions (figure 1). Furthermore, whereas a contemporary bride might receive jewelry and rings from her relatives, it is Adalieta here who bestows a ring on Torello. It is not just the exotic Saracens who are strange in the story, but domestic conjugal identities are also estranged through the representation of atypical gift-giving. When wives take on the prerogatives of husbands, could they also be imagined as adulterous? After all, Adalieta comes very close to marrying another man while her first husband still lives. Perhaps even more titillating or threatening for contemporaries would have been the final scene in which Adalieta boldly kisses a man who appears to be an alien, a Muslim among Christians, a Saracen among the citizens of Pavia (figure 2). Even if viewers of the panel knew that Adalieta recognized her husband beneath the exotic costume, the image still visualizes miscegenation, and thus gives rise to the play of transgressive fantasy.

DOMESTIC ENEMIES

What would an average Florentine citizen of the 1420s know about Saladin, Muslims, or inhabitants of the Levant? Boccaccio's story portrays fictional Saracens travelling through northern Italy *incognito*. But in the early fifteenth century, Florence hosted actual travelers from the East, including Manuel Chrysoloras, emissary of the Byzantine emperor Manuel II. Chrysoloras occupied the first salaried chair of Greek at the University of Florence from 1397-1400 and he helped to train the next generation of Florentine classicists. The opening years of the fifteenth century also witnessed high hopes for an alliance of Mongols and Europeans to crusade against their common foe, the Turks; Timur, the Mongol leader, encouraged commercial ties as well as an alliance with the West. Even after his death in 1405, Timur was celebrated by humanists who placed him among exemplary "*uomini famosi*" like Alexander the Great, Augustus Caesar, or Charlemagne. Florentine authors such as Petrarch, Giovanni Villani, Andrea da Barberino, and Fazio degli Uberti included information about Islamic culture in their chronicles, poems, and romances. While such texts certainly relied on stereotypes and were fueled by Christian polemics and crusade fervor, Gloria

Allaire reminds us that they could occasionally impart accurate details about topography, landmarks, people, and customs in the region of the Levant.[12] Saracens might be characterized as having blue skin and worshipping improbable gods, but an author like Andrea da Barberino might also give a reliable description of a beverage made by steeping raisins in water or of the particular features of the buildings known as "*mosche*" or mosques.

Although the division between Christian and Muslim was theoretically fixed and absolute, identities could be more fluid in practice. Alterity was not so much a given, as an effect continually being produced and reinforced through social practices, including the making and viewing of precious objects like *cassoni*. Florentine patrician youths might encounter mock Saracen enemies while participating in military brigades or when looking at pictures. An anonymous mid-fifteenth-century *cassone* panel shows young men honing their skills by tilting at the "*Saraceno*" or quintain erected in the Piazza della Signoria (figure 3).[13] The quintain appears as a truncated male figure on a pole. Armed with a shield, helmet, and staff, the *Saraceno* is racially distinguished from its opponents by dark skin coloration. Curious women are shown leaning out of windows hung with carpets and rugs, domestic goods imported from the Levant, to watch the men compete in the piazza.

Another early fifteenth-century *cassone* panel attributed to Gherardo di Jacopo, known as Starnina, may represent an historical battle set in the Middle East or North Africa (figure 4).[14] Starnina went to Spain, working in Toledo and Valencia from 1393 to 1401, and he may have drawn details of costume and physiognomy from first-hand knowledge of Muslims. But Starnina's picture also recalls the mock battles between Moors and Christians that were staged during religious festivals throughout late medieval Europe.[15] Beneath their alien costumes, the supposed Saracen enemies represented in Starnina's picture or those participating in a Florentine pageant could turn out to be one's own neighbors or kin. Torello's exotic disguise, as represented on the Cini panel (figure 2), perhaps reminded contemporary viewers of the role-playing they enjoyed in mock battles, jousts, and civic pageantry.

Eastern "Tartar" slaves were also a common sight in late fourteenth- and early fifteenth-century Florence; Petrarch's term for these resident aliens brought to Italy from the Black Sea region was *domestici hostes,* or domestic enemies.[16] The vast majority of such imported slaves were female, women and girls intended for domestic service. The maidservant who appears with Adalieta twice in the Bargello *cassone* panel could perhaps be a reminder of such Tartar slaves (figure 1). Whereas Boccaccio's tale presents Torello dramatically taken into slavery during a Crusade, the actual traffic in slaves was mundane, commercial, and regulated. The Florentine Statutes of 1364 specify the conditions and terms of the trade with special provisions for the treatment of slaves, their potential wrongdoing or disobedience, and for those who might become fugitives.[17] The prices of Tartar slaves varied but they could equal the cost of a pair of decorated wedding chests, i.e. sixty-five florins. It was not unusual for a domestic slave to be included in a bride's dowry along with other objects of conspicuous consumption. But after the fall of Constantinople in 1453 and Turkish domination of the Levant, Tartar slaves were no longer readily available; those who could afford the increased expense of slaves looked to North African traders or to prisoners of war to supply their needs.

Unlike the royal, courteous, and chivalric Saladin featured in literature, actual Tartar slaves were considered uncivilized and prone to violence and lust. Boccaccio's Saladin, who already speaks Italian, lacks only a change of clothing to resemble his host Torello. Tartar slaves, on the other hand, were not so easily socialized. Their facial features, tattoos, or pox scars, as well as their strange clothing and unpronounceable names were obvious signs of difference. In order to absorb Tartar slaves into Florentine households, they were converted, baptized, and given new Christian names as well as a new set of clothes. Sumptuary legislation limited slave garments to a simple linen head scarf and a plain dress with low, flat shoes. The domestic slave pictured in the Bargello *cassone* panel can be differentiated from her mistress, Adalieta, by just such a plain white veil and red dress. Adalieta, in contrast, wears a figured silk garment trimmed with ermine while her hair is loose and crowned with a garland. The servant accompanying Adalieta represents the ideally acculturated, submissive and obedient slave that Florentines seldom enjoyed in practice. Instead, their letters complain about theft and threats of violence. Many Florentine mistresses expressed fear for their safety with Tartar slaves in the house.

Whereas in Boccaccio's story Saladin happily frees Torello after recognizing his former host, late medieval Florentines were ambivalent about emancipating female slaves and reluctant to recognize the children they might have fathered with them. The fictional Saladin helps Torello to return home to Pavia and to his legally sanctioned marriage, but Florentine men were only too interested in extramarital sex with their female slaves. In the Cini panel (figure 2), in contrast, it is the wife, Adalieta, who loses control and makes the first move on what appears to be a Saracen but turns out to be her own husband, Torello.

Bawdy carnival songs testify to the stereotypical lust and duplicity especially associated with Russian and Circassian slave women. A stanza from a typical sonnet by Antonio Pucci (d.1390) describes the potential for domestic conflict when the man of the house indulges in sexual relations with a slave:

> The slave is paid for and brought [home - *implicit*]
>   first;
> She doesn't wear a wedding ring on her finger,
> But she satisfies her appetite better
> Than her mistress, whom she checkmates.[18]

Pucci's *double-entendre* employs the images of food and gaming to describe how a slave might dominate her owner and intimidate her mistress. Of course, such an image of the pampered, spoiled slave derives its power from the anxiety, jealousy, and fear of wives who might be expected to tolerate concubines in the home and to raise their husband's "natural" children as their own.

The ubiquity of slaves in early fifteenth-century Florence makes it likely that the Saladin and Torello *cassone* panels resonated for contemporary viewers; but the pictures do not "reflect" social practice as much as they reshape it. In reality, Florentine slavery was based on class domination, racial prejudice, and gender subordination. In domestic painting, however, slavery could be pictured as a fantasy of decorum, of mutual friendship between men who exhibit the same degree of princely generosity, and chivalric spirit.

COUNCIL OF THE SEA

Boccaccio scholars have always noted the mercantile interests of the **Decameron,** but they have tended to assume that the text realistically illustrates aspects of contemporary business and commerce. The Saladin and Torello *cassoni* instead reveal a more complex relationship between cultural context and pictorial representation. Against the contingency and volatility of fifteenth-century international trade, the pictures present an appealing image of easy exchange, effortless travel, and fabulous profit. The *cassone* panels feature episodes that take place in Pavia, northern Italy, but the location shifts across the Mediterranean to Alexandria, Egypt, before it returns to Pavia again for the conclusion. The pictures reveal nothing of the physical effort and expense involved in making such a journey in the 1420s. The second panel shows Torello returning to his hometown not on a ship but rather on an enchanted bed; the trip is magical and instantaneous rather than requiring months at sea. And unlike those Florentine merchants who had to outsmart competitors and negotiate their way into foreign markets, Torello receives magnificent gifts and treasure out of friendship rather than as the result of business acumen.

Florentine viewers of the Torello and Saladin *cassoni* had reason to be especially attentive to the representation of Levantine travel and to the exchange of luxury textiles. While trading networks had operated between the Mediterranean and the Levant throughout the middle ages, landlocked Florence only gained control over the port of Pisa in 1406 and of Livorno in 1421. In order to compete with the maritime republics of Genoa and Venice the Florentines established a state galley system in 1422.[19] Representatives from the major guilds formed the *consoli del mare*; these Counselors of the Sea had to administer the building, financing, and outfitting of galleys, preside over a commercial court, as well as send trade embassies to foreign ports ranging from Southampton to Constantinople. Chroniclers describe the public rejoicing that took place in the streets on 17, 18, and 20 April 1422 with the introduction of the first galleys bound for Alexandria.[20] With hopes for divine approval of the enterprise, as well as financial success, the galleys were named after the patron saint of Florence, John the Baptist, and for Saint Anthony. For this portentous occasion all shops were closed while mass was celebrated and confraternity members and artisans marched in processions throughout the city.

The institution of a state galley system was aimed at two specific commodities, spice and silk, although many other items would find their way into the ships' holds.[21] In the fourteenth century, Florentines had depended on imported silk, *panni Tartarici,* from as far away as Mongol Asia; they also watched while their neighbors in Lucca developed a highly profitable silk industry. Although Florence already enjoyed the economic benefits of the wool trade, the ambitious oligarchs were determined to break into a new market.[22] The finest raw silk had to be obtained from the Levant but lower grades were also available from Spain, Greece, and from various Italian producers. In Florence the raw silk was processed, dyed, spun, and woven by increasingly specialized workers who learned to make brocade, velvet, and damask. By the 1420s silk manufacturing was sufficiently advanced to exceed domestic needs and to necessitate external outlets for Florentine products. In fact, in 1426 the Counselors of the Sea passed a regulation banning the importation of foreign silk cloth, thereby guaranteeing state protection of the silk industry against competition.

Recall that the central scene from the Bargello *cassone* (figure 1) features Saladin contemplating Adalieta's gift of silk garments. Here market strategy and state protection take the form of hospitable gift giving. Whereas Florentines once had been dependent on foreign silk, they now become the providers. In fact, they flooded Levantine markets not only with luxury goods but also with cheaper, coarse cloth that replaced local production.[23] Contemporaries in Alexandria might lament the introduction of cheap European goods, but the picture represents Saladin looking with rapt attention at Adalieta's gift, and Boccaccio confirms that the Saracens could not believe their eyes when they gazed at the sumptuous textiles. In the context of a growing trade imbal-

ance, Saladin's vow to show Torello the "quality of his merchandise" implies not only chivalric courtesy but also potential commercial competition over Levantine markets.

Merchants and artists also looked closely at silk, with particular visual acuity and calculation. Cennino Cennini's *Libro dell'Arte* or *Craftsman's Handbook,* dated circa 1400, with its attention to visual characteristics and reference to techniques, is a corollary to the skills of those merchants who traveled to market fairs and were able to assess quality merchandise, calculate freight, and realize a profit on resale. In the course of offering detailed instructions for the imitation of various kinds of fabric in panel painting or in fresco, Cennino singles out gold and silver brocade, velvet, wool, and silk.[24] The imitation of silk fabrics on the Saladin and Torello *cassone* panels corresponds to Cennino's instructions: the artist applies gold leaf, covers it with paint, then scrapes or scratches out fold lines, contours, and internal patterns. Afterwards the gold leaf can be stamped in order to vary the texture and to produce even more scintillation, more reflections of light. Cennino also carefully explains how to imitate the cut pile of velvet, a relatively novel textile. Viewing the Saladin and Torello *cassoni* was an education in how to appreciate and to value the silks or luxury textiles represented on their painted surfaces as well as those actual fabrics contained within. While viewers took in the painter's artifice, they were also affirming the value of domestic production over imported goods.

Visualizing the Saracen consumption of Italian silks in terms of gift giving rather than commerce leaves out a host of risks and dangers inherent in international trade. The lure of profits to be made in Levantine markets was countered by over-regulation and administrative inconsistency, by bribery, and by corruption. Constant threats of plague and pirates accompanied merchant galleys, while the ports they visited were not infrequently subject to civil unrest. Once they arrived in the Levant, Florentine merchants faced a bewildering number of port charges, duties, and taxes. Further complicating trading relations was the fact that units of measure varied from city to city and sometimes from product to product. And the preferred currency in the region remained the Venetian ducat rather than the Florentine florin. The smooth exchange of goods ran into very real and substantial snags at home and abroad. The state galley system, heralded with so much optimism in 1422, made slow progress and represented only a qualified success.

A preserved treaty of 1497, specifying commercial privileges granted to Florence by the Mamlukes of Cairo, describes the kinds of problems experienced by merchants throughout the fifteenth century.[25] The Sultan decrees that sales are to be recorded by notary so that neither party can break faith on an agreement. He promises to punish Turcoman thieves and others who might attempt to seize the property of Florentine merchants. He prohibits the taking of bribes and gratuities and condemns those who steal or interrupt foreign correspondence. But one of the most interesting provisions for an analysis of the Saladin and Torello *cassone* panels is the privilege granted to merchants to disguise themselves as Muslims:

> It has been mentioned that it is among the privileges of the Venetians that a number of their nation has business in the land of Syria, going from village to village for the purchase of cotton and Ba'albaki cloth, and that they fear for their persons and property from tribesman and robbers. And they have asked that they be permitted to wear the clothes of Muslims, Mamluk, and bedouin on their journeys, so that there be no temptation to rob them. So let his honorable Excellency promulgate his command permitting the aforesaid Florentine nation that, according to what is customary in conformity with the earlier privileges.[26]

In Boccaccio's tale and in the pictures that illustrate it, Saladin starts out in disguise as a Cypriot merchant only to be given a change of clothes by Adalieta. Torello, in Alexandria, exchanges his European dress for Saracen clothing when Saladin releases him from captivity and names him co-ruler. Throughout the story those disguises that appear to conceal identity in fact function to reveal a deeper, essential identity, one that transcends ethnic difference or national borders. But against the kinship displayed by Boccaccio's aptly disguised chivalric protagonists, Florentine merchants travelling in the Levant adopted alien clothing primarily to protect themselves and their goods. The performance of alterity that they may have enjoyed in battles with mock Saracens and when tilting at the *Saraceno,* or quintain, played to a different audience in Cairo or Damascus than it did at home. Merchants who took refuge in Muslim apparel while travelling on business may have had additional reason to appreciate Torello making strategic use of his Saracen costume to spy on his wife and test her fidelity since they, too, spent months or years away from home. If the adoption of Muslim disguise seems to expose the vulnerability of Florentine merchants, Torello's appearance as a Saracen allows him instead to exert control. From his assumed perspective as an "outsider," Torello interrupts his wife's unwelcome second wedding and restores his position "inside" the family. But despite being granted the privilege to dress as Muslims, Mamlukes, or bedouins, Florentine merchants remained outsiders with limited autonomy in the Levant.

CONCLUSION

A close reading of the Saladin and Torello *cassone* panels suggests two interrelated points. First, marriage was considered so important to late medieval Florentines that it warranted all kinds of gift exchanges, including wedding chests decorated with stories, like Boccaccio's tale, that relate to international trade and politics. Marriage in late medieval Florence does not function primarily as a bond between individuals nor even between families, but rather as a microcosm of the state. Second, the pictures reveal a desire to see foreign relationships in terms of the familiar, to domesticate the Saracen Other. In so doing, Florentine audiences could imagine exerting control and discipline in alien environments as they were accustomed to doing at home. The reunion of Torello and Adalieta in the final scene of the Cini panel (figure 2) presents a phantom marriage between Christian and Muslim, a fantasy of diplomatic ties between Europe and the Levant, and an ideal relationship between producer and consumer in a nascent capitalist economy.

Notes

1. The panels are Florence, Museo Nazionale del Bargello inventory number 160, and Venice, Collection Vittorio Cini, inventory number 994. There are several versions of the Bargello composition but only the Cini example illustrates the second half of the story. Tancred Borenius was the first scholar to read these panels as paired illustrations of *Decameron* 10.9; see "The Oldest Illustration of the Decameron Reconstructed," *Burlington Magazine* 35 (July 1919): 12. See also Ellen Callmann, "Subjects from Boccaccio in Italian Painting, 1375-1525," *Studi sul Boccaccio* 23 (1995): 19-78; and Paul Watson, "A Preliminary List of Subjects from Boccaccio in Italian Painting, 1400-1550," *Studi sul Boccaccio* 15 (1985-86): 149-66. For domestic painting in the first quarter of the fifteenth century, see Jerzy Miziolek, *Soggetti classici sui cassoni fiorentini alla vigilia del rinascimento* (Warsaw: Instytut Sztuki Polskiej Akademii Nauk, 1996). For discussion of the authorship of the panels and an attribution to Francesco di Michele, see Everett Fahy, "Florence and Naples: A Cassone Panel in the Metropolitan Museum of Art," in *Hommage à Michel Laclotte: Etudes sur la peinture du Moyen Age et de la Renaissance,* ed. J. Avril (Milan and Paris: Electa/Reunion des musées nationaux, 1994), 231-43.

2. For an overview see Americo Castro, "The Presence of the Sultan Saladin in the Romance Literatures," in *An Idea of History: Selected Essays of Americo Castro* (Columbus: Ohio State University Press, 1977), 241-69; and John V. Tolan, "Mirror of Chivalry: Salah Al-Din in the Medieval European Imagination," in *Images of the Other: Europe and the Muslim World before 1700,* ed. D. Blanks (Cairo: American University in Cairo Press, 1997), 7-38; idem, *Saracens: Islam in the Medieval European Imagination* (New York: Columbia University Press, 2002). See also Victoria

Kirkham and Maria R. Menocal, "Reflections on the Arabic World: Boccaccio's Ninth Stories," *Stanford Italian Review* 7 (1987): 95-110; and Janet Levarie Smarr, "Other Races and Other Places in the *Decameron*," *Studi sul Boccaccio* 27 (1999): 113-36.

3. Bruce Cole, *Italian Art 1250-1550* (New York: Harper & Row, 1987), 20-21. For a critique of conventional readings of domestic painting, see Cristelle L. Baskins, *Cassone Painting, Humanism and Gender in Early Modern Italy* (New York: Cambridge University Press, 1998).

4. For the Renaissance in global perspective, see *Circa 1492: Art in the Age of Exploration,* ed. Jay A. Levenson (New Haven and London: Yale University Press, 1991); Lisa Jardine, *Worldly Goods: A New History of the Renaissance* (London: W.W. Norton & Company, 1996); Lisa Jardine and Jerry Brotton, *Global Interests: Renaissance Art Between East and West* (Ithaca: Cornell University Press, 2000); and Rosamond E. Mack, *Bazaar to Piazza: Islamic Trade and Italian Art 1300-1600* (Berkeley: The University of California Press, 2001).

5. For a helpful discussion of approaches to Boccaccio, see Albert Ascoli, "Boccaccio's Auerbach: Holding the Mirror up to *Mimesis*," *Studi sul Boccaccio* 20 (1991-92): 377-97. See also the critique of realism in Frederic Jameson, *The Political Unconscious: Narrative as a Socially Symbolic Act* (Ithaca: Cornell University Press, 1981), 17-102.

6. Medieval popular tales feature Saracen spies dissuading Saladin from attacking Christian troops; see Roger S. Loomis, "The *Pas Saladin* in Art and Heraldry," in *Studies in Art and Literature for Belle da Costa Greene,* ed. D. Miner (Princeton: Princeton University Press, 1954), 83-91. In the Palazzo Galganetti (now Palazzo Arcivescovile), Colle di Val d'Elsa, a late fourteenth-century fresco shows Saladin and famous Crusaders from the *pas saladin*; see C. Jean Campbell, *The Game of Courting and the Art of the Commune of San Gimignano, 1290-1320* (Princeton: Princeton University Press, 1997), 253.

7. Boccaccio, *The Decameron,* trans. G. H. McWilliam (New York: Penguin, 1972), 800; all further references will be to this edition. The standard Italian edition is *Decamerone,* ed. Vittore Branca (Firenze: Sansoni, 1966). For an analysis of clothing in the *Decameron,* see Elissa Weaver, "Dietro il vestito: La semiotica del vestire nel *Decameron*," in *La novella italiana: Atti del convegno di Caprarola 19-24 settembre 1988* (Roma: Salerno, 1989), 701-10. For the clothing industry in Florence, see Carole Collier Frick, *Dressing Renais-*

sance Florence (Baltimore: Johns Hopkins University Press, 2002). See also *Encountering Medieval Textiles and Dress: Objects, Texts, Images,* ed. Desiree G. Koslin and Janet Snyder (New York: Palgrave, 2002); and Ann Rosalind Jones and Peter Stallybrass, *Renaissance Clothing and the Materials of Memory* (New York: Cambridge University Press, 2000).

8. For irony as a radical reading strategy, see Guido Almansi, *The Writer as Liar: Narrative Technique in the* Decameron (London and Boston: Routledge and Kegan Paul, 1975). For another destabilizing reading by a *Decameron* narrator, see Cristelle L. Baskins, "Griselda, or the Renaissance Bride Stripped Bare by her Bachelor in Tuscan *Cassone* Painting," *Stanford Italian Review* 10 (1991): 153-76.

9. On workshop practice, commissions, and costs, see Ellen Callmann, *Apollonio di Giovanni* (Oxford: Clarendon Press, 1974); and Kent J. Lydecker, "Il patriziato fiorentino e la committenza artistica per la casa," in *I ceti dirigenti nella Toscana del Quattrocento,* ed. Donatella Rugiadini (Firenze: Papafava, 1987), 209-21.

10. Brucia Witthoft, "Marriage Rituals and Marriage Chests in Quattrocento Florence," *Artibus et Historiae* 5 (1982): 43-59. See *Tales of Firenzuola,* ed. Eileen Gardner (New York: Italica Press, 1987), 73-81.

11. The public wedding cavalcade was no longer routine after the mid-1460s when the belongings of the bride were moved in simple baskets. See Christiane Klapisch-Zuber, *Women, Family and Ritual in Renaissance Italy* (Chicago: University of Chicago Press, 1985), 213-46, and eadem, "Le zane della sposa: La fiorentina e il suo corredo nel Rinascimento," *Memoria* 11-12 (1986): 12-23. See also Jane Fair Bestor, "Marriage Transactions in Renaissance Italy and Mauss's *Essay on the Gift*," *Past & Present* 164 (1999): 6-46; and Evelyn Welch, "New, Old, and Second-Hand Culture: The Case of the Renaissance Sleeve," in *Revaluing Renaissance Art,* ed. Gabrielle Neher and Rupert Shepherd (Aldershot: Ashgate, 2000), 101-20.

12. For the question of cross-cultural influence, see Maria Rosa Menocal, *The Arabic Role in Medieval Literary History: A Forgotten Heritage* (Philadelphia: University of Pennsylvania Press, 1987); see also Nancy Bisaha, "Petrarch's Vision of the Muslim and Byzantine East," *Speculum* 76 (2001): 284-314; Gloria Allaire, "Portrayal of Muslims in Andrea da Barberino's *Guerrino il Meschino*," in *Medieval Christian Perceptions of Islam,* ed. John V. Tolan (New York: Garland, 1996), 243-69; and eadem, "Noble Saracen or

Muslim Enemy? The Changing Image of the Saracen in Late Medieval Italian Literature," in *Western Views of Islam in Medieval and Early Modern Europe,* ed. David R. Blanks and Michael Frassetto (New York: St. Martin's Press, 1999), 173-84.

13. Richard C. Trexler, *Public Life in Renaissance Florence* (Ithaca: Cornell University Press, 1991), 233. See Richard Barber and Juliet Barker, *Tournaments: Jousts, Chivalry and Pageants in the Middle Ages* (New York: Weidenfeld and Nicolson, 1989), 86, 163. The *cassone* panel is untraceable; see *The Image of the Black in Western Art,* ed. Jean Devisse (New York: William Morrow and Co., Inc., 1979), vol. 2:2, 210.

14. Frederick Antal, *Florentine Painting and its Social Background* (reprint Cambridge, MA: Harvard University Press, 1986), 367.

15. Loomis, "The *Pas Saladin,*" 88; Joyce Kubiski, "Orientalizing Costume in Early Fifteenth-Century French Manuscript Painting (*Cité de Dames* Master, Limbourg Brothers, Boucicault Master, and Bedford Master)," *Gesta* 40 (2001): 176; and Max Harris, *Aztecs, Moors, and Christians: Festivals of Reconquest in Mexico and Spain* (Austin: University of Texas Press, 2000), 31-63.

16. See Iris Origo, "The Domestic Enemy: The Eastern Slaves in Tuscany in the Fourteenth and Fifteenth Centuries," *Speculum* 30 (1955): 321-66. See also Franco Angiolini, "Schiave," in *Il Lavoro delle Donne,* ed. A. Groppi (Rome and Bari: Laterza, 1996), 92-115; and Lauren Arnold, *Princely Gifts and Papal Treasures: The Franciscan Mission to China and its Influence on the Art of the West* (San Francisco: Desiderata Press, 1999). There is a new study by Steven A. Epstein, *Speaking of Slavery: Color, Ethnicity, and Human Bondage in Italy* (Ithaca: Cornell University Press, 2001). For female domestics in Florence, see Klapisch-Zuber, *Women,* 165-77.

17. For a translation of the document, see *The Society of Renaissance Florence: A Documentary Study,* ed. Gene Brucker (New York: Harper & Row, 1971), 222.

18. My translation. The poem is cited in Italian in Origo, "Domestic Enemy," 363-64; see also Ferruccio Ferri, *La poesia popolare in Antonio Pucci* (Bologna: L. Beltrami, 1909), 196. For the erotic significance of chess, see Maribel König, "Die profanen Fresken des Palazzo Davanzati in Florenz: Private Repräsentation zur Zeit der Internationalen Gotik," *Mitteilungen des Kunsthistorischen Instituts in Florenz* 34 (1994): 245-48; and Pat Simons, "(Check)Mating the Grand Masters: The Gendered, Sexualized Politics of Chess in Renaissance Italy," *Oxford Art Journal* 16 (1993): 59-74. On the excess pleasure of alien others, see Jeffrey J. Cohen, "On Saracen Enjoyment: Some Fantasies of Race in Late Medieval France and England," *Journal of Medieval and Early Modern Studies* 31 (2001): 113-46.

19. For the development of this new state enterprise, see Michael E. Mallett, *The Florentine Galleys in the Fifteenth Century* (Oxford: Clarendon Press, 1967). See also Gene Brucker, *The Civic World of Early Renaissance Florence* (Princeton: Princeton University Press, 1977).

20. Described by Armando Sapori, "I primi viaggi di Levante e di Ponente delle Galere Fiorentine," *Archivio storico italiano* 114 (1956): 69-91.

21. For an analysis of profits and balance of trade, see Eliyahu Ashtor, *Studies on the Levantine Trade in the Middle Ages* (London: Variorum, 1978), especially sections 9 and 10.

22. See the informative case study by Florence Edler de Roover, "Andrea Banchi, Florentine Silk Manufacturer and Merchant in the Fifteenth Century," *Studies in Medieval and Renaissance History* 3 (1966): 223-85; see also Fanny Podreider, *Storia dei Tessuti d'Arte in Italia* (Bergamo: Istituto Italiano d'Arti Grafiche, 1928), 93-164.

23. Eliyahu Ashtor, "L'exportation de textiles occidentaux dans le Proche-Orient musulman au bas Moyen-Age (1370-1517)," in *East-West Trade in the Medieval Mediterranean,* ed. B. Z. Kedar (London: Variorium, 1986), 305 and 369-75.

24. For the "period eye," see Michael Baxandall, *Painting and Experience in Fifteenth-Century Italy* (Oxford: Oxford University Press, 1972), 29-108. Cennino d'Andrea Cennini, *The Craftsman's Handbook: The Italian "Il Libro dell'Arte,"* trans. Daniel V. Thompson, Jr. (New York: Dover, 1960), 86-91. See also Brigitte Klesse, *Seidenstoffe in der italienischen Malerei des 14. Jahrhunderts* (Bern: Stämpfli, 1967). See the recent studies by Lisa Monnas, "The Artists and the Weavers: The Design of Woven Silks in Italy 1350-1550," *Apollo* 125 (June 1987): 416-24; eadem, "Silk Textiles in the Paintings of Bernardo Daddi, Andrea di Cione and their Followers," *Zeitschrift für Kunstgeschichte* 1 (1990): 39-58; and Rembrandt Duits, "Figured Riches: The Value of Gold Brocades in Fifteenth-Century Florentine Painting," *Journal of the Warburg and Courtauld Institutes* 62 (1999): 60-92.

25. See John Wansbrough, "Venice and Florence in the Mamluk Commercial Privileges," *Bulletin of the School of Oriental and African Studies* 28

(1965): 483-523; and M. Amari, *I diplomi arabi del R. Archivio di Stato Fiorentino* (Florence: Le Monnier, 1863). For another approach to the alterity of merchants in the Levant, see Kathryn L. Reyerson, "The Merchants of the Mediterranean," in *The Stranger in Medieval Society,* ed. F. R. P. Akehurst and Stephanie Cain Van D'Elden (Minneapolis: University of Minnesota Press, 1998), 1-13; and Kubiski, "Orientalizing Costume," 176.

26. Wansbrough, "Mamluk Commercial Privleges," 518.

Susanna Barsella (essay date summer 2007)

SOURCE: Barsella, Susanna. "Work in Boccaccio's *Decameron*: Politics, Theology, and the Images of the Countryside." *Romance Quarterly,* 54, no. 3 (summer 2007): 231-53.

[*In the following essay, Barsella investigates the practical and ethical dimensions of work as portrayed in the* Decameron, *emphasizing Boccaccio's focus on politics and the arts as civic professions reflecting the shift from a medieval Christian mentality to a humanistic perspective based on the classical virtues expounded by Aristotle.*]

The critical passage from a medieval to a humanistic vision of man during the fourteenth century led to a modified perception of the function and value of work, reflecting the changes in mentality and social structure that the urban culture had produced. The theme of work in Giovanni Boccaccio's *Decameron* is vast and relatively unexplored. An analysis of work in the *Decameron* suggests that rather than exalting the mercantile code of values, the *Decameron* illustrates its crisis and that of the ethical foundations of the communal world. In this article I will limit my investigation to its cornice ("framework") and to three *novelle* (*Dec.* 5.1, 3.1, 10.9), and I will focus on the political and theological implications of work in Boccaccio's idealized political community. The activities of the ten narrators during the period they spend in the countryside characterize their retreat as an exemplary, limited, period of *otium* ("leisure"). Boccaccio's critical view of the bucolic and religious themes traditionally associated to the image of the countryside casts light on the relevance that classical ethics assume in the ideal society he depicts in the *cornice.*

The ambivalent perception of work (as painful and creative) that is present in the Greco-Roman and Judeo-Christian traditions remained a distinctive trait in the perception and representation of work in the Middle Ages. During the centuries of expansion, maturity, and

crisis of the communal civilization, however, the importance of work in mercantile economy and thought steadily increased.[1] Literary, juridical, and religious sources attest to the progressive reevaluation of work that paralleled the development of urban civilization.[2] This trend accelerated with the stabilization of the growth of cities, and work started to be perceived as a positive force whose meaning went beyond the religious penitential dimension preached in churches.[3] Because the Christian, ultimate goal of salvation remained central to communal intellectual and religious life, the positive social effects related to the development of new working typologies rendered the relation between work and theology problematic.[4] These effects included economic growth, an almost general increase in welfare (within the ranges of a skewed wealth distribution), and augmented chances of social mobility.

These major shifts during the fourteenth century caused the insurgence of a new cultural sensibility that privileged ethical issues in realistic literary representations. Two belief systems—that nature could be read like a book of signs leading to knowledge of superior reality and that the eternal presence of divine laws could be found in the realm of contingent events—gave way to a focus on more practical than speculative philosophy. An increased attention on the human world led to an increased realism, and work became an object worth representing as an expression of human ingenuity and creativity. The philosophical inspiration and the natural realism of these literary representations revealed the central importance of work in a revalued human dimension.

Not all the activities animating the city expressed positive values, and their representation in the *Decameron* often symbolizes negative aspects of the mercantile mentality. The various occupations depicted in the *novelle,* from politics to husbandry, appear to be weighted against the ethical values that Boccaccio believed should be the milestone of a renovated Christian society. Since the early patristic commentaries on the six days of creation, work had been intimately connected to the very essence of human nature. The early Church Fathers saw humans creating as a means for them to achieve a resemblance to God.[5] In this theological tradition, work was significantly connected to the role man should play in the construction of the Christian community. The relevance of the theme of work in this particular meaning is visible in Boccaccio's title itself, *Decameron,* which shows his intention to recall hexaemeral literature and hints to the presence of an idea of a moral recreation of society after the crisis that the plague symbolically represented.[6]

The notion of work relevant to the analysis of the *Decameron* is that of productive activity as defined in Aristotle's *Ethics to Nichomacus,* a book Boccaccio not only read with the help of Aquinas's commentary but also carefully annotated.[7] This notion defines the human capacity of transforming existent resources into goods to satisfy individual or social needs. It requires both practical and theoretical training, the harmonious balance of experience and study. Technically, the end of productive activity is detached from the act of performance. Most of the work described in the **Decameron** requires craft and ingenuity, and as humble and socially debased as they might be, the activities of servants, peasants, traders, professionals, or rulers illustrate a productive form of labor. Even politics can be classified as productive work—as the conscious application of acquired notions and experience aimed at the production of the immaterial common good of governance. Some productive activities such as politics, writing, and oral narration involve self-building and moral education. Rather than insisting on the negative implications of work, Boccaccio seems more interested in its subjective and ethical dimension. In this perspective, both writing and narrating are *fatiche* that have an implicit moral dimension. An ethics of virtue related to work is at the core of all characters introduced as exemplary, even in a humble profession such as that of Cisti the baker, who is ennobled by his irreproachable virtue (**Dec.** 5.2).

THE FRAMEWORK (*CORNICE*)

In a previous study I have suggested that the proemial narrator of the **Decameron** is the figure of a civilizing, re-creative force in which the traits of Boccaccio's later reinterpretation of the myth of Prometheus emerge.[8] This myth of civilization, in which the classical and Christian ideals of ethical engagement of poetry combine, is central to the symbolic community of the ten narrators in the **Decameron**'s framework.[9] Although it is set in a realistic historical context, the company (*brigata*) presents the traits of an allegory of the beginning of a new era—that of the world after the plague.[10]

This allegorical dimension is further accentuated by the decision of the Florentines to return to a still plague-ridden city.[11] At the end of the two weeks in the countryside, Panfilo convinces his companions that social conventions and the necessity to defend their honesty from the risks of excessive familiarity oblige them to return to the city. He persuades them that it is time to end their re-creative *otium* and return, spiritually strengthened, to their roles in the city. In a similar way, Guido da Monteforte reminds King Charles d'Anjou of his duty to honor his high-position commands (**Dec.** 5.6). Thus, the adventure of the ten young people in pursuit of the purification of body and mind does not involve a refusal of the city.[12]

Much has been said about the places where the young people spend the two weeks dedicated to healing their moral and physical health. Many studies have described

the ideal space of the countryside as *locus amoenus* and the mythological settings of the company. Indeed, the *cornice* appears as an allegorical triumph of life, a distant fictional response to the triumph of death left behind in Florence.[13] In the framework, however—as some critics such as Luigi Surdich and Kurt Flasch have noticed—contrary to the typical scheme of a bucolic setting, there is no opposition between city and countryside. The relation of continuity is further stressed by Boccaccio's description of the effects of the plague in the *villa* outside of Florence. If natural reason recommends the ten young people to leave, the rules governing social *decorum* compel them to return and operate in the fictional society that the narrators reconstruct. The fortnight spent not more than two miles from Florence is a parenthesis in which the young people engage in a narrative labor whose aim fulfills the promise of the proemial narrator to meditate on what is to be pursued and what is to be avoided.[14] The author presents the elating narratives as the result of an intellectual effort, and his advice that this is a "work" cannot be underestimated.[15] The fact that the young people's temporary retreat is dedicated to narrative "labor" connotes it not as an escape from the city, but as a period of *otium,* intended in the classical sense of time spent far from the turmoil of the city to re-create the mind in between the commitments of civic life. Behind the minimal, symbolic, self-educating community of the narrators stands the author's ideal of the Promethean effort of civilization as the necessary premise on which to rebuild a new, Christian society founded on ethical values.

While the ancient models of the wise man of the classical and Christian traditions merge in the figure of the main narrator, the ideal of cenobitic community merges with the idea of "philosophical" school in the *cornice*. Enclosed in the circular movement of departure and return, the retreat ends with not a detachment but rather an acceptance of active life. A common trait to the images of wisdom texturing Boccaccio's prose is the functional interrelation between meditative life and social commitment, so that the abode, the monastery, or the *villa* are all positively connected to the city.[16]

Moreover, at that time in Florence the actual relation between countryside and city was not one of opposition. On the contrary, during the centuries of the mercantile economy's expansion, the city and the *villa* had evolved in synergy. Husbandry provided the rising city with the necessary resources while the city offered the peasants alternative working opportunities.[17] The difference between the two worlds was essentially cultural. The countryside represented a productive system regulated by natural time and reflected a mentality related to a feudal social structure. Conversely, the urban organization of work followed an artificial rhythm that the civic mentality of the communal republic echoed. In the

Decameron the image of the countryside is presented in a critical view as far as it symbolizes the values of feudal and monastic society. In the *cornice,* however, the *villa* where the young Florentines gather represents a symbolic spiritual pause spent in a countryside that was, as well as the city, ravaged by the plague.

The *brigata* does not engage in any work activity that may recall, even symbolically, the stigmatized manual, monastic labor. Nonetheless, the ten young Florentines are not a circle of idle courtiers trying to divert their thoughts from the hovering anguish of the Black Death.[18] Rather, they engage in a project of narration organized into themes and introduced and accompanied by a gloss, as would be appropriate to a collection of instructive texts. In addition, the narrators do not live without "modo" ("*decorum*") but, following Pampinea's suggestions, organize a well-structured court. As the queen of day 1, Pampinea organizes and distributes the various tasks among the servants, nominates a *seneschal,* and proposes to engage in their narrative activity (Intr. 1.98-101). *Novellare,* as well as writing for the author himself, is labor accomplished not without effort, and requiring organization by those who reign.

Besides establishing a miniature society, the ten young Florentines spend most of their time producing oral prose, engaging in healthy and seemly amusements, and ruling their fictional court. To give a complete picture of their duties, Boccaccio introduces a parodic deliberation on the comic *quaestio* by two servants, Licisca and Tindaro, at the beginning of day 6 (Intr. 6.4-16). The court represents an idealized society ruled by ancient aristocratic values and restrained by the inner force of the narrators' morality. These components are implicitly proposed as the essential traits of the generation that will rebuild a new society on the ruins left by the plague—a society founded on law and held together by ethical code.

The narrators' activities can be classified into two types: the political ruling of a temporary little kingdom—a formative exercise in political art—and other performances that, recalling the Aristotelian classification of the arts in the *Nicomachean Ethics,* may be defined as practical activities. The political fiction of a monarchy flanked by a counsel in which disagreement becomes embedded in the rule (Dioneo's privilege) is essential to understand the institutional aspect of civic life represented in the *cornice* and the model represented by the society of the ten young people. Boccaccio's elaboration of an ideal form of political organization parallels the ethical theme of an ideal community in which, ever since Plato's *Republic* and the early Fathers' social doctrine, work and division of labor played a crucial role. Politics and poetry are the main activities of the narrators and, respectively, the highest practical and poietic works. Boccaccio extols both activities, which in an-

cient practical philosophy were seen as complementary since there can be no virtuous city without virtuous citizens.[19]

Sometimes during the day, and always at the end of their story telling, the young people play musical instruments, dance, and sing on request of the king or the queen of the day. According to Aristotle's classifications, music, dance, and singing are not productive but practical (performative) arts, because their end is the performance itself. Narration and poetry, on the other hand, are productive arts because their end is the product of their creative process, the story itself. Texturing narratives engages the members of the court in an exercise that builds and reinforces the principles of communal life. As Pampinea observes, story telling is directed to an audience, whereas playing music only gives delight to the player (Intr. 1.111). The public value of story telling is thus in opposition to the self-contained value of the pastime symbolically related to the pre-communal courtly setting.

The ten narrators' activities, in addition to belonging to the sophisticated rituals of the courts, are also specific to the bucolic genre. Boccaccio experimented with this genre in the *Ninfale d'Ameto,* in which Ameto learns the arts of narration and poetry to become a civilized creature.[20]

Another type of work appearing in the *cornice* is that of the servants. Pampinea assigns the various organizational tasks to seven servants (Intr. 1.98-101). Her distribution of work reflects the different social status of the servants' respective lords and ladies. The most important task, that of the *seneschal*—a sort of courtly general manager—is assigned to Dioneo's servant, Parmeno. Panfilo's *famiglio,* Sirisco, is appointed treasurer (Intr. 1.98-101). Filostrato's man, Tindaro, takes care of the men's apartments while the attendants of the female characters are assigned to menial tasks. Pampinea's servant Misia and Filomena's Licisca rule the kitchen under Parmeno's supervision; Lauretta's Chimera and Fiammetta's Stratilia are the women's chambermaids. Emilia, Elissa, and Neifile have no servants, either because they are of inferior social status or because the plague had killed their maids. There are no other professional categories represented in the court, and these servants, although they use the comic language of some of the *novelle,* appropriately fit the model represented in the framework. They are loyal and efficient, without any apparent psychological scar of the plague. Like their masters and mistresses, they represent an exception to the Black Death's rule of destruction and, in demonstrating a stylized profile of theatrical characters, contribute to refining the framework's allegorical design.

THE *NOVELLE*

More than five hundred characters animate the *Decameron*'s fresco of communal life.[21] The array of different occupations in the text illustrates the economic and social stratification of communal society and the relevance that work, including political and religious occupations, had in the mercantile society.

Many of the main characters of the *novelle* have no name and are textually connoted only by their activities, as in the case of the story of the innkeeper in 9.6. Most characters are defined by their occupations, which in turn determine their social positions. Very few changes of status occur, and almost all of them involve the aristocracy. The aristocracy is a category that does not fully correspond to a standardized type of work, but it is associated with the political ruling function. Even in the *novelle,* aristocratic values appear as a possible alternative to mercantile logic when facing the issue of refunding a new, ideal, society. As the *novella* of Cimone (*Dec.* 5.1) suggests, these values, though, must be set in an ethical and Christian perspective.

That the ancient aristocratic code of value might provide a model for the ten narrators of the framework is testified to by its importance in the *Decameron.* The aristocrats are the most heavily represented class since its members account for 34% of the total number (502) of characters. In communal society the aristocracy had lost its power but not its blood privileges, and in Boccaccio's time it struggled to find a new political role in the city by compromising with commercial magnates.[22] As Daniel P. Waley observes, in the medieval city it was common to combine more than one activity—for example, banking and producing, diplomacy and trade—although in Boccaccio's time the professions had probably become quite specialized (11-31).[23] From this point of view, the most complex figures of the city were the great merchants (8% of the total characters), who often combined the activities of trading, banking, and manufacturing. If merchants, rich men, and professionals are pooled into one category, they make up the core of the urban secular middle-upper class, which would account for nearly 18% of the characters.

The importance of these figures is made clear by weighting the *novelle* by type of protagonist.[24] The stories with an aristocratic protagonist are 31 (30%), two of these concerning noblemen engaged in trade or banking activity (3.7 and 7.7).[25] Mercantile and religious protagonists in 20 and 13 stories, respectively, follow in order of importance. This classification shows a lessened discrepancy, in terms of relative significance, among the different categories. If "aristocratic" stories are compared with those dedicated to the entire class of urban activities (that is, all categories excluding the aristocracy, husbandmen, the religious, and the servants),

47% of *Decameron*'s *novelle* are dedicated to typical urban occupations. Thus, along with the aristocracy, merchants are the key protagonists in Boccaccio's world.

If the *Decameron*'s characters are considered by type of profession, all of the types of work that animate religious and exemplary texts—such as husbandry, commerce, trade, craftsmanship, and servitude—are present in large number. Artists are undoubtedly new protagonists with respect to tradition, and their presence reflects a progressive acquisition of identity and consciousness of this category.[26]

The central place that the aristocracy and merchants occupy is a sign that politics, the highest form of activity in the practical sphere, is at the center of Boccaccio's interest both in the *cornice* and in the *novelle.* These two upper classes, nobility and merchants, continually interact in the *Decameron,* and both are linked to the political sphere. Even if nobility found no place in the political organization of cities like Florence, it possessed a code of values and a culture of governance. The merchants, who actually ruled the city-states, had limited education and were devoted more to the laws of profit than to the ideal of common good.

The characters belonging to the aristocracy can be distinguished according to historical period and place. Most aristocrats are not Florentine and appear in *novelle* set in the feudal courtly world. Emperors, kings, *soldans,* and the highest ranks of aristocracy feature in *novelle* showing famous courts such as Naples (2.6, 3.6, 4.10, 10.6); Sicily (4.4, 4.10, 10.8); France (2.8, 3.9, 4.1, 4.9), the almost legendary realms of Egypt, Middle East, and Asia (1.3, 2.7, 2.9, 9.9, 10.3, 10.9); and of the Mediterranean islands of Cipri (1.9, 5.1), Ischia (5.6), Lipari (5.2), and Creti (4.3). Few *novelle* depict feudal courts in Northern Italy (Monferrato in 1.5, Verona in 1.7, Brescia in 4.6, Ravenna in 5.8, and Romagna in 10.5, 10.9, 10.10). Only two stories stage high nobility of ancient times: 3.2, set in Pavia during the Lombard kingdom, and 10.8, set in ancient Rome and Athens. Relatively few are the *novelle* showing Florentine aristocracy (only about the 17% of the total number of stories dedicated to the nobility), and almost all of them are set in contemporary times. Most of these are about exiles or decayed aristocrats connected in some way to the mercantile class. With respect to Florence, and regarding almost all the *novelle* set in contemporary times in which the aristocracy plays a relevant role, the focus is on the contradictions emerging from the necessity of nobility to compromise courtly values for the political code of the mercantile ruling class. In these stories, Boccaccio masterfully depicts the crisis of the aristocracy as a class relegated to a secondary role in the communal city. As in Petrarch's *Secretum*—in which Francesco recognizes the existence of a conflict between his Agostinian model and his real self, between what should be and what really is—so Boccaccio records the crisis of this political class facing a reality in which its power has faded and its prestige difficult to maintain.

The passage of power from the old nobility to the merchants created a political conundrum. The rich and powerful merchants wanted to be recognized and ennobled by the aristocracy while the disempowered aristocracy was inclined to make concessions to the nonnoble ruling class to maintain or regain its economic status. Merchants bartered their estates in exchange for blue blood at a high psychological price. As a consequence, social mobility became a complex issue whose different aspects conditioned the mercantile social climbing described in many Boccaccian *novelle*.

The *novelle* often provide examples of how aristocratic customs could be recovered, and adapted, to serve the formation of a new political class. An exemplary figure connected to the model of the *cornice* is Messer Torello da Stra (10.9). As Surdich remarks, Messer Torello represents the gentleman-citizen embodying the ideal suggested in the framework.[27] Torello, a man of noble spirit and plebian origins, represents the delicate moment of transition from early mercantile civilization to the culture of the *civitas* as expression of *humanitas*.[28] His story is emblematically the last "regular" tale of the **Decameron,** standing symmetrically in opposition to the negative exemplary figure of Ciappelletto. Messer Torello is a commoner, but Boccaccio deceives his reader by presenting him as acting, behaving, and thinking as a courtly aristocrat.[29] Only after the wise king Saladin makes Torello a prisoner does the agnition about his milieu occur:

> "Signor mio," disse messer Torello "io son lombardo, d'una città chiamata Pavia, povero uomo e di bassa condizione."
>
> "My lord," replied Messer Torello, "I am a Lombard, of a city called Pavia, a poor man, and of humble condition."
>
> (10.9, 54)

A first ambivalence characterizing Torello's description lies in the term *lombardo,* which Torello uses to define himself. The term has a double meaning. It refers to the foreign denomination and was used generally to indicate the "Italians" as the ancient inhabitants of the Lombard kingdom (whose capital was Pavia). More specifically, it designated Italian bankers and usurers. The term also occurs in the speech of the two brothers hosting Ciappelletto, who mention that the Burgundians call them "lombardi cani" because of their hatred for Italian usurers.[30] Another element that places Torello in an undistinguished middle (mercantile) class is provided by the Saladin's disguise of his military reconnaissance of Italian territory as an apparent pilgrimage by merchants:

> [S]embiante faccendo d'andare in pellegrinaggio, con due de' suoi maggiori e più savi uomini e con tre famigliari solamente, in forma di mercatante si mise in cammino.
>
> So, having ordered all things to his mind in Egypt, he made as if he were bound on a pilgrimage, and attended only by two of his chiefest and sagest lords, and three servants, took the road in the guise of a merchant.
>
> (10.9, 6)

The introduction of a disguised merchant-pilgrim (almost an oxymoron) seems to underline the relation of symmetry and inversion linking Torello and the Saladin. Although in the story the figure of the merchant is presented in a positive light, Torello's admission that he is not deceived by the Saladin's appearance as a merchant implicitly hints at the substantial difference between merchants and aristocrats. Torello's wife praises merchants' habits in the speech she makes to accompany her gifts to the Saladin in disguise:

> E fattesi venire per ciascuno due paia di robe, l'un foderato di drappo e l'altro di vaio, non miga cittadine né da mercatanti ma da signore, e tre giubbe di zendado e pannilini, disse: "Prendete queste: io ho delle robe il mio signore vestito con voi: l'altre cose, considerando che voi siate alle vostre donne lontani e la lunghezza del cammin fatto e quella di quel che è a fare e che *i mercatanti son netti e dilicati uomini,* ancor che elle vaglian poco, vi potranno esser care." (emphasis added)
>
> She then caused to bring forth for each of them two pair of robes, lined the one with silk, the other with vair, no such robes as citizens or merchants, but such as lords, used to wear, and three vests of taffeta, besides linen clothes, and: "Take them," quoth she. "The robes I give you are even such as I have arrayed my lord withal: the other things, considering that you are far from your wives, and have come a long way, and have yet a long way to go, and that merchants love to be neat and trim, may, albeit they are of no great value, be yet acceptable to you."
>
> (10.9, 30-31)

The adjectives *netto* and *dilicato* may seem excessive for the ambitious rich merchant, and not many are so described in the *Decameron*.[31] Another element that indirectly introduces the merchant figure to the structure of the *novella* is the Saladin's use of the word *mercatanzia* as a metaphor for his real condition and qualities in two occasions, both while speaking to Torello:

> "Messere, egli potrà ancora avvenire che noi vi farem vedere di nostra mercatantia, per la quale noi la vostra credenza raffermeremo: e andatevi con Dio."
>
> "Peradventure, Sir, we shall one day give you to see somewhat of our merchandise, and thereby confirm your belief: and so adieu!"
>
> (10.9, 38)

And again

"Voi siete messer Torel di Stra e io son l'uno de' tre mercatanti a' quali la donna vostra donò queste robe; e ora è venuto il tempo di far certa la vostra credenza qual sia la mia mercatantia, come nel partirmi da voi dissi che potrebbe avvenire."

"You," quoth he, "are Messer Torello d'Istria, and I am one of those three merchants to whom your lady gave these robes; and now is the time to warrant you of the quality of my merchandise, as, when I parted from you, I told you might come to pass."

(10.9, 57)

The use of technical financial language as "raffermeremo la vostra credenza" and "far certa la vostra credenza" is used allusively by the Saladin to mimic the mercantile jargon.

Torello is neither an aristocrat nor a saint; he stands in ethical opposition to the exemplary figure of the merchant found in religious moralizing literature and described in Ciappelletto's false confession.[32] He simply does not embody the religious ideal Ciappelletto mockingly presents in his confession. Abandoning a purely religious perspective, in the recovery of "civic" values, Torello merges the religious stereotypes of good merchants and aristocratic customs and sets them into a perspective influenced by Aristotelian ethics. In Torello, Boccaccio draws a model of a virtuous man whose customs are guided by practical reason toward his social realization. Being pious is a precondition that is necessary but not sufficient for becoming a "cittadino-signore." This was indeed the aim of the merchant class: to complete the passage from an old to a new social and political system. To complete this passage, however, it was necessary to place the basis of a new vision of the world and of the city on a religious model different from the one adopted by the feudal church. Boccaccio saw an alternative in the elaboration of a political system based on the ethical principles of classical virtue. Surdich's observations on the relation between the Saladin and Torello seems to confirm this hypothesis:

La distinzione di classe tra i due personaggi è annullata dalla pratica della cortesia che li accomuna e li rende uguali. Una uguaglianza che si realizza in alto, perché il modello cui conformarsi è quello aristocratico. [. . .] Tanto il Saladino quanto Torello sembrano allora essere esponenti virtuosi di una *upper class* nella quale trova ricomposizione, sul piano della morale e della comportamentistica, la frattura sociale prodotta dal declino della feudalità e dalla crescita della borghesia.

The distinction between the two characters is erased by the practice of courtesy, which renders them equal. It is an equality realized at a high level, since the model to conform with is that of the aristocracy. [. . .] Both Saladin and Torello seem to be the virtuous exponents of an upper class in which the social fracture produced by the decline of feudalism and the rise of bourgeoisie was reproduced at a moral and behavioral levels.

(Surdich, *Boccaccio* 269-70; my translation)

In proposing a model of an aristocracy of custom, Boccaccio had in mind the chivalric qualities of the pioneers of the "commercial revolution"—the great merchants who had explored the world and enriched their cities thanks to their spirit of initiative and adventure. At the very beginning of the commercial pre-capitalist era, these courageous people had worked not only for their own but also for the common good.[33] The image of the enterprising, virtuous merchant replaces the Church's traditional image of the pious merchant while maintaining an ethical perspective. Aristocratic customs would have been worthless without the value of work and moral principles.[34]

Two other *novelle* seem in dialogue with the *cornice*; both are set in the countryside: the *novella* of Cimone (5.1), dealing with the topos of uncontaminated natural life, and the *novella* of Masetto (3.1), dealing with the religious symbolism of peasantry. The medieval images of peasantry testify to the ambivalence between religious respect and social contempt.[35] In the High Middle Ages, peasants—whether landed or not, rich or poor—occupied a relevant place in the economic organization centered on the city. Although the country provided nearby urban centers with food and human capital, the town people looked down on its *laboratores* because of their menial occupations.[36] At the same time, husbandry maintained the religious connotation that had characterized it since antiquity. Almost nothing of the "sacrality" of the countryside remains in the *Decameron*; the *villa* of the frame is an ideal space of *otium*.[37] Moreover, the Hesiodian opposition between the vicious city and the virtuous country belonged to a precivic culture that the *Decameron* shows as fading away.

The stories in which peasants are protagonists or even in which they appear are very few, evidencing their diminished importance as exemplary figures of "natural" human beings. Peasants amount to only 3% of the total number of characters in the *novelle*, and only four stories have husbandry as a main or relevant object, including Griselda's parable in which her and her father, both shepherds, are in opposition to the lord of Saluzzo, who occupies the highest feudal rank (3.1, 3.8, 5.1, 10.10). The story of Cimone (5.1), with that of Masetto (3.1), can be seen in relation to the themes of "recreation" and education present in the *cornice*. Of these two *novelle*, only 3.1 is directly concerned with the allegorical value of agriculture in a perspective that interlaces peasantry and monastic work.

The story of Cimone (5.1) addresses the theme of passage from the state of "natural men" to that of "cultural men," which marks the progress of humankind toward civilization. The story touches on the Promethean myth of education and shows a critique of individual asceticism, affirming, although with specifications, the superiority of civic over natural life. In the *novella* "natural" has the negative meanings of "savage" and "uncivil"—the same meaning Boccaccio attributed to the Assyrian "natural men" in his allegorical interpretation of Prometheus' educative mission in *Genealogie* 4.44.

Born of a rich family, Cimone, a stranger to the customs of human consortium, chooses to abandon the city, thus relieving his renowned family of his embarrassing presence. The narrator presents Cimone's return to a state of nature as a regression with no ideological or religious appeal to the reader. In leading a primitive life, Cimone becomes more similar to a beast than to a human being; his happiness essentially derives from the oblivion of his human qualities and his loss of consciousness of what is good and what is bad.

One day, while Cimone is wandering in the woods, he is struck by the enlightening vision of Iphigenia's beauty. The vision upsets the young man so deeply that he decides to return to the city and undergo a long process of education in the arts to become a perfectly integrated and accomplished citizen.

The story is divided in two parts. The former follows the mythological pattern of man's emancipation from a natural to a civil state in a bucolic environment similar to that of Ameto's encounter with the Muses. Although in the *Ninfale* the educational process is perfected by Ameto's symbolic learning of the arts, in the **Decameron,** the same process takes place in the city. The countryside is a solitary space of vision where human beings may achieve an intuition of the truth that can be found in nature. So it is Cimone's vision of beauty. To pursue this image of perfection, however, Cimone must go back to the city and learn to become virtuous so as to deserve what he desires. Although the vision of beauty casts a Platonic light on the episode, the philosophical essence of Cimone's figure bears the influence of Aristotelian ethics. Man arrives at the truth by contemplating the natural world but perfects his nature only within the civic context. In this part of the *novella,* the countryside is not chosen as a place for meditation, a symbolic retreat in *otium*; rather, it represents the refusal of civilization and a consequent descent into a de-humanized world.

The second part of the *novella,* as Surdich remarks, has a completely different character, rhythm, and even language. Cimone moves to the city to undertake his education and makes incredible progress by becoming a polite gentleman in a short time:

> [U]sando co' giovani valorosi e udendo i modi, quali a' gentili uomini si convenieno e massimamente agl'innamorati, prima, con grandissima ammirazione d'ognuno, in assai brieve spazio di tempo non solamente le prime lettere apparò ma valorosissimo tra' filosofanti divenne. E appresso questo, essendo di tutto ciò cagione l'amore il quale a Efigenia portava, non so-

> lamente la rozza voce e rustica in convenevole e cittadina ridusse, ma di canto divenne maestro e di suono, e nel cavalcare e nelle cose belliche, cosí marine come di terra, espertissimo e feroce divenne.

> Mixing thus with the gallants, and becoming familiar with the manners proper to gentlemen, and especially to lovers, he very soon, to the exceeding great wonder of all, not only acquired the rudiments of letters, but waxed most eminent among the philosophic wits. After which (for no other cause than the love he bore to Iphigenia) he not only modulated his gruff and boorish voice to a degree of smoothness suitable to urbane life, but made himself accomplished in singing and music; in riding also and in all matters belonging to war, as well by sea as by land, he waxed most expert and hardy.

(5.1, 18-20)

Love pushes Cimone to seek excellence not only in courtly arts such as singing, playing, horse-riding, and soldierly bravery, but also in the fields of philosophy and literature. However, it also induces him to undergo a process of education that remains in some way incomplete as he is ready to transgress social conventions by becoming a corsair. If the *novella* is a celebration of the humanizing force of love, it also carries an implicit negative judgment on the kind of perfecting it may promote. It transforms Cimone into a refined gentleman, but it does not make him a good citizen. The traditional aristocratic values constitute only a part of the necessary virtues to become a civilized man; they must be complemented and guided by ethical values that lead to the respect of social conventions and thus assure the stability of communal life. Thus, if education in the traditional arts makes men apt to civil life, moral education makes human beings virtuous and capable to become righteous citizens of a just society.

If the story of Cimone critically revises the image of the countryside as an Edenic place in antithesis to the malicious city, the story of Masetto da Lamporecchio (3.1) evidences a criticism of another aspect of the religious value of the literary topos of the countryside. This story is a parody textured on the traditional image of the Christian laborer who tills and takes care of God's orchard. In this *novella* Boccaccio presents a situation that materializes the mythical metaphor of Genesis and expands its semantic field to include the monastic image of peasantry, which stressed the penitential function of work. This image was connected to the work of the monks or hermits who till their fields (worldliness) to transform them into a garden (the Eden recovered through grace and sanctified work). In this *novella* a peasant, instead of a monk, actually works the fields in a convent of nuns and makes it sexually fertile, showing a parodical literal materialization of God's orchard. In the *novella* of Masetto, however, instead of penitence, physical mortification, and heavenly reward, the protagonist obtains material wealth and pleasure by showing the inutility of physical restraints in avoiding the allures of concupiscence. In this way Boccaccio directly attacks one of the main tenets of the monastic conception of work, that work also helped in gaining dominion over passions, particularly over concupiscence. In Boccaccio not hard work but virtue tames the immoderate desires of the flesh. Only virtue can contain sexual desire without going against the natural law of human sexual appetites, thus negating rather than enhancing human nature. It is virtue that enables men to face and defeat the temptations of the secular world and to make exemplary figures of the narrators.

Boccaccio's parody in **Decameron** 3.1 is directed against the ascetical, penitential form of monasticism and against a false conception of virtue as a repression of natural impulses and escape from temptations. Filostrato introduces the literal theme:

> E similmente sono ancora di quegli assai che credono troppo bene che la zappa e la vanga e le grosse vivande e i disagi tolgano del tutto a' lavoratori della terra i concupiscibili appetiti e rendan loro d'intelletto e d'avedimento grossissimi. Ma quanto tutti coloro che cosí credono sieno ingannati, mi piace, poi che la reina comandato me l'ha, non uscendo della proposta fattaci da lei, di farvene più chiare con una piccola novelletta.

> And likewise not a few there are that blindly believe that, what with the hoe and the spade and coarse fare and hardship, the carnal propensities are utterly eradicated from the tillers of the soil, and therewith all nimbleness of wit and understanding. But how gross is the error of such as so suppose, I, on whom the queen has laid her commands, am minded, without deviating from the theme prescribed by her, to make manifest to you by a little story.

(3.1, 4)

Working the garden with no material compensation was the ordinary life of the anchorite. To make a sterile terrain fertile or to turn a piece of desert into a fruitful garden symbolized the work of Christ and recalled the image of a restored Eden. The anchorite's life, however, was no longer exemplary in the High Middle Ages because it was no longer compatible with the life of the city and the increased labor division of commercial development. Although the desert fathers lived in retreats close to urban centers and were spiritual guides for the Christian communities, the monks in Boccaccio's time simply lived separated from the city in a solitary form of asceticism. The hermit cut himself off from civic life leaving the function of spiritual leader to the secularized orders in town. Moreover, the ascetic autarkic model of the monks was no longer viable for the common citizen because life in the city implied a division of labor and economic interdependence that greatly reduced self-sufficiency. The ideal of ascetic life had therefore lost its practical appeal as a viable model of Christian life and had become exclusively associated with a radical choice of withdrawal from social life.

Masetto—"un giovane lavoratore forte e robusto e secondo uomo di villa con bella persona" ("a stout and hardy fellow, and handsome for a peasant," **Dec.** 3.1, 7)—is hired by the nuns whom the old peasant Nuto found so difficult to satisfy. His purpose is to plough the nuns' field, materially and metaphorically: "Se voi mi mettete costà entro, io vi lavorerò sí l'orto, che mai non vi fu cosí lavorato" ("Put me once within there, and you will see that I will do the work of the kitchen-garden as it never was done before," **Dec.** 3.1, 18). To obtain what he wants, Masetto pretends to be mute. The story deploys a three-level metaphorical development. Masetto literally works the nuns' fields and metaphorically plows their wombs. On a higher parodic level, he represents the material realization of the metaphorical image of the peasant as the Christian working God's orchard with the tools of love, with an equivocal exchange between physical eros and spiritual agape.

In the Bible, the kingdom of heaven is often referred to as a vineyard or an orchard. So it is in Jesus's parable of the master and the workers in Matthew 20.1-16:

> "Simile est regnum caelorum homini patrifamilias, qui exiit primo mane conducere operarios in vineam suam."

> "For the kingdom of heaven is like a landowner who went out early in the morning to hire laborers for his vineyard."[38]

and in John 15.1:

> "Ego sum vitis vera, et Pater meus agricola est."

> "I am the true vine, and my father is the vine grower."

For Paul, and subsequently in the Christian tradition, human beings are meant to cooperate with Christ; to became his *adiutores* ("coworkers") in taking care of God's earthly orchard. This image appears in Dante, who in *Paradise* 12 so speaks of Dominic:

> e io ne parlo
> sí come dell'agricola che Cristo
> elesse all'orto suo per aiutarlo.
>   I speak of him
> as of the laborer whom Christ
> chose to help Him in His orchard.

(*Par.* 12: 70-72)[39]

Dante used the image of the "orchard of God" to symbolize the Christian community as "orto cattolico." Significant for the analysis of Masetto's story is the passage of *Paradise* 26 in which Dante answers John's question about the intensity of his charity. The poet declares that God's love for humankind makes him love all the branches (human beings) adorning his orchard:

> "Le fronde onde s'infronda tutto l'orto
> dell'ortolano etterno, am'io cotanto
> quanto da lui a lor di bene è porto."

"The leaves with which all the orchard of the
eternal Gardener is embowered I love in the
measure of the good He has bestowed on them."

                                              (*Par.* 26: 64-66)

In these lines Dante refers to the passage from John 15
and uses the apostle's metaphor whereby *ortolano*
("peasant") is God and *orto* ("orchard") is the secular
world. Quite significantly, Dante translates *agricola* as
ortolano and not *vignaiolo,* as in modern translations.
The Latin word for *vignaiuolo* would be *vinitor* or *vi-
naecultor*; Dante, instead, intentionally uses a more
general term, referring to the biblical and Pauline metaphor of God as *agricola* and of the Christian as his *au-
diutor* ("coworker").[40] In the figure of Masetto we can,
then, recognize a Dantean presence and through Dante
the presence of the biblical tradition of the symbolic
value of the peasant.[41] In Boccaccio this metaphor is
made concrete, demoted (the whole story is played on a
"registro basso" key), and inverted according to the
scheme that characterizes Boccaccio's parodic technique.[42] Masetto, a sort of anti-monk, illustrates a parodic inversion of the ascetical principle that hard work
mortifies the body and restrains "concupiscible" appetites. The story, instead, shows the realization of the
very desire that hard work was supposed to avoid:

> Cosí adunque Masetto vecchio, padre e ricco, senza
> aver fatica di nutricare i figliuoli o spesa di quegli, per
> lo suo avvedimento avendo saputo la sua giovanezza
> bene adoperare, donde con una scure in collo partito
> s'era se ne tornò, affermando che cosí trattava Cristo
> chi gli poneva le corna sopra 'l cappello.

> Masetto, who had left Lamporecchio with a hatchet on
> his shoulder, returned thither in his old age rich and a
> father, having by the wisdom with which he employed
> his youth, spared himself the pains and expense of
> rearing children, and averring that such was the mea-
> sure that Christ meted out to the man that set horns on
> his cap.

                                              (3.1, 43)

A reflection on a fragment of what can be called a medieval theology of work thus surfaces in this *novella*
and reveals that the ethical dimension of the countryside in the *cornice* represents an alternative to the one
parodied here.

Conclusion

The relevance of work in the ***Decameron*** is a sign of
the progressive centrality that human productive activity was acquiring in humanistic thought. With this
changed perception of work, literature appears as the
product of the poet-philosopher, charged with an ethical, educative function that the community can recognize and value. Parallel to the work of the poet is that
of the symbolic community of the narrators in the
Decameron's framework. In the *villa* outside Florence,

Boccaccio establishes a model of political excellence
founded on aristocratic and ethical values. Analyses of
the *cornice* and of three *novelle* connected to the themes
of civilization and countryside—two major components
in Boccaccio's design of his idealized community—
reveal the influence of Aristotle's ethics.[43]

Two main types of work are represented in the *cornice*—politics and the arts (music, poetry, dance, and
narration)—that delineate a sort of mythical setting for
an ideal state. The *novella* of Torello suggests Boccaccio's ideal of the citizen of such a community. The *novelle* of Cimone and Masetto present a critical view of
different aspects of the traditional theological meanings
associated with the topos of the countryside. Cimone's
represents a case of failure in the self-educating process, whereas the *novella* of Masetto illustrates the superiority of active virtue over the ascetical withdrawal
in restraining passions within the limit of reason.

Notes

1. During the fourteenth century, Europe experienced
   political, financial, and natural distress as well as
   endemic waves of famine and plague. The 1330s
   were particularly grim years for Florence, which
   was submerged by a flood in 1333 and struck by
   the Bardi and Peruzzi economic crisis in 1336.
   The Black Death of 1348 was just the most catastrophic in a series of plagues that hit the country
   in the course of the century. On the economic crisis, its causes and consequences on subsequent
   developments in the fifteenth century, see Lopez;
   Malanima 201-03.

   Quotations and references are from Vittore Branca's edition of Giovanni Boccaccio's *Decameron*
   (Torino: Einaudi, 1992). Unless otherwise stated,
   English translations are from *The Decameron of
   Giovanni Boccaccio,* which is faithfully translated
   by J. M. Rigg (London, 1921). The text of this
   translation is from *The Decameron Web* <http://
   www.brown.edu/Departments/Italian_Studies/
   dweb>.

2. See, in particular, the twelfth-century juridical
   sources analyzed by Le Goff, *Time,* in the chapter
   "Labor, Techniques, and Craftsmen in the Value
   Systems of the Early Middle Ages (Fifth to Tenth
   Centuries)." A distinctive trait of the development
   of an urban working dimension was the attention
   dedicated to the working tools. It evidenced a progressive consciousness of the importance of work
   and its dependence on particular instruments. Parallel to the growth of urban centers was the inten-
   sification of both secular and ecclesiastical legislation regulating working time and modalities
   (*capitulares* and *corpus consuetudinum
   monasticarum*). See Le Goff, *Pour un autre* 122-
   23. The rise of a new labor-centered conscious-

ness was also present in contemporary medieval iconography. Starting from the twelfth century, for example, the iconography of the cycles of the months developed. Representations of urban work developed significantly in the fourteenth century, when the urban culture had become prevalent and reflected the increased economic relevance of the city. An element that characterized the specificity of urban work with respect to husbandry was the different perception of time. Le Goff emphasizes that artificial time, linked to the exigencies of manufacture and related productions typical of urban agglomerates, characterized the city, whereas the country (and the Church) still followed the natural time linked to seasonal cycles. This was made evident by the invention and adoption of the clock in the fourteenth century, which became a symbol of the city. See Le Goff, *Pour un autre* 46-65 and 66-79. The change in mentality regarding work was also witnessed in the (mainly Franciscan and Dominican) elaboration and diffusion of confessors' manuals after the twelfth century. These manuals were intended to provide confessors with a list of possible sins and misdemeanors peculiar to specific professions such as artisans, workers, and merchants, so that the confessor would be prepared to treat particular cases according to the general precepts of Christian doctrine. See Le Goff, *Pour un autre* 162-80.

3. Heretical sects' refusal to work also signaled the existence of a pervasive uneasiness toward the monastic theology of work. Their negative attitude toward work, on the one hand, shows a deep identification of monasticism with work, and on the other, a reaction against manual work as the only work compatible with religious life. The position of the heretics was opposite to that of Thomas Aquinas, who answered the exigency of freeing work from identification with manual monastic work by extending the Pauline concept of labor to typically urban professions. See Le Goff, *Pour un autre* 165, and Paolini's specific study on heretics and work (111-67).

4. See the data on production, income, and consumption in Italy during the fourteenth century as reported in Cipolla 183-208 and Malanima 480-571. Giovanni Villani described Florence's "magnificence" in the years immediately preceding the financial crisis of Bardi and Peruzzi (1336-39) in his *Nuova Cronica* 12.88, 91-94. For the relevance of the religious dimension in economic life and, in particular, the merchants' practice to leave bequests to the poor in their wills, see Le Goff, *La Bourse*. An example of this practice can be seen in Ciappelletto's *novella, Dec.* 1.1. For the idea of work in medieval juridical doctrine, see Bellomo 171-97.

5. See Basil of Caesarea's *Homélies sur l'*Hexaéméron, particularly homilies 10 and 12, attributed in the Middle Ages either to Basil or to Gregory of Nyssa. Ambrose based his *Hexaemeron* on Basil's.

6. An *Exameron beati Ambrosii* appeared in the inventory of Boccaccio's texts in Santo Spirito's "parva libraria," in a codex containing also the *De paradiso*. The codex is relevant because Ambrose's *Hexaemeron* was modeled on Basil's, and it attests to Boccaccio's indirect knowledge of the work. Both Ambrose and Basil shared a positive vision of work as one connected to man's capacity to imitate God's creating.

7. The manuscript Ambrosiano A f 204, Ambrosiana Library, Milan, contains Aristotle's *Ethics to Nichomacus* and, copied by Boccaccio, Thomas Aquinas's commentary.

8. On the myth of Prometheus in Boccaccio, see Marino, *The Decameron* and "Prometheus" 263-73; Gittes 125-57; and Barsella 120-41.

9. Giorgio Barberi Squarotti observed the mythological traits of the *Decameron*'s framework as illustrating an ideal re-creation of civil life. He paralleled the framework, metaphorically, to the industrial revolution myth of Robinson Crusoe: "in entrambi i casi è attiva l'intenzione di mostrare esemplarmente la vittoria sulle forze negative della natura, la possibilità di ricreare, per l'uomo, il suo mondo partendo dal vuoto provocato o dalla sciagura improvvisa" (135). The educational process from natural to civil, operating at a collective level, should be connected to Boccaccio's reinterpretation of the Promethean figure. In this framework, Boccaccio extended the model of the sage to a collective subject since his goal was not simply to illustrate the formation of a symbolic civil man but rather the re-creation of a civil community.

10. Millard Meiss argued that the plague of 1348 dramatically changed the modes of artistic expression and representation in Florence. According to this critic, the Orcagna's *pala* in Santa Maria Novella represents an iconographical symbol of the distinction between art before and after the plague. Boccaccio's *Decameron* preceded Orcagna's work and exemplified the same need for renovation in the poetic field. As Flasch suggests with the title of his book (*Poesia dopo la peste*), it represents "poetry after the plague." See, also, Meiss 157-65.

11. The vicinity to the city of the young people's retreat is another element suggesting the philosophical and religious subtexture of the *cornice*. Both the ancient sage and the anchorites' abodes were

situated in the proximity of cities. From there, the holy men could easily maintain a relationship with the community while subtracting themselves from secularized city life. See the introduction to day 1.89 for the location of the first retreat. Also, the other palace to which the narrators move in day 3 was not farther than two thousand paces from the first one. See the introduction to day 3.3.

12. See Panfilo's speech in *Conclusione,* day 10.2-7.

13. On the ideological role of the *cornice,* see Surdich, *La cornice* 227, 231-33; and Flasch 41-58. See, in particular, the analysis of the *cornice* as a metaphor of the world of art and of the moral value of its rituals in Marino, *The Decameron* 79-179.

14. In taking over her duties as queen of the second day, Filomena says, "[W]e will here resume our story telling, wherein, methinks, pleasure and profit unite in superabundant measure" ("[Q]ui al novellare torneremo, nel quale mi par grandissima parte di *piacere e d'utilità* similmente consistere," *Dec.* 1, concl. 9; emphasis added).

15. Alessandra Francesca Pennisi has already noted Boccaccio's insistence in presenting his labors as a writer and that of the young people as narrators as work. See Pennisi 70-78.

16. For the relation among desert fathers, hermits, and early cenobitic communities with the city, see Brown 112-32.

17. Both Surdich and Flasch observe that in the *Decameron* the city-country conflict underlined by Marga Cottino-Jones should be reconsidered.

"La campagna dunque, che è il contado immediatamente prossimo alle mura di Firenze, non ha un suo ruolo autonomo di opposizione alla città, non possiede uno statuto di valori peculiari. La contrapposizione tra un polo negativo rappresentato dalla città e un polo positivo costituito dalla campagna non si stabilisce secondo i parametri del codice bucolico (e dunque rende estraneo al contesto del *Decameron* il concetto di evasione)" (Surdich, *La cornice* 238). See, also, Cottino-Jones.

18. An essential element for the configuration of the activities of the *brigata* is that of "telling stories in a garden," which connotes an aristocratic form of social entertainment and connects the *cornice* with the image of the Court of Love. The narrators of the *Decameron,* however, do not simply entertain themselves but introduce and comment on the *novelle,* often overtly deliberating on their moral content. As Pier Massimo Forni remarks, the company is a special form of Court of Love,

closer perhaps to a court of justice: "It is clear that what happens in the *cornice* is, to a certain extent, related to the pattern of discussion of the juridical case, a pattern that combines narration and deliberation" (*Adventures* 2). For a comparison among Boccaccio's three different settings of the topos of the *brigata* in the garden, see Battaglia Ricci, *Boccaccio* 150-61, and Battaglia Ricci, *Ragionare* 168-79.

19. Thus Aristotle explained the relation between individual and political good at the beginning of the *Ethics to Nichomacus*: "For even though it be the case that the Good is the same for the individual and for the state, nevertheless, the good of the state is manifestly a greater and more perfect good, both to attain and to preserve. To secure the good of one person only is better than nothing; but to secure the good of a nation or a state is a nobler and more divine achievement" (*NE* 1094b 5-10). The English translation (ed. H. Racham) is from the classic archive at *The Perseus Digital Library,* <http://www.perseus.tufts.edu> (accessed Jan. 2007), which also includes the Greek text (ed. J. Bywater).

20. Surdich notices that the *Ameto* represents the successful emancipation from a natural (in the sense Boccaccio uses this term in the *Genealogie*) to a civil state after Ameto's uplifting encounter with the Muses in a pastoral setting. However, whereas in this work the protagonist's emancipation refers symbolically to the individual evolution in a mythical space, in the *Decameron* the primitive condition refers to the Florentine society of the fourteenth century. The company is therefore an ideological system that Boccaccio projects against the loss of the world's values. "Di fronte alle sollecitazioni drammatiche di una società storicamente determinata, il Boccaccio predispone una proposta ideologica che possa riguardare la collettività intera, non l'individuo singolo. [. . .] La brigata è un modello di vita comunitaria: un modello di comportamento, di rapporti, di valori" (Surdich, *La cornice* 233). According to Surdich, unlike Ameto, the company does not undergo an educational process. Although they have no personal transformation similar to that of Ameto, the young people's retirement in the *villa* has the same symbolic meaning of a temporary meditative detachment from the active life that seems to have an influence on their spiritual and moral refinement. At least they learn they have to go back and face reality. Moreover, the narrators consider the stories useful in the same sense used by the main narrator in the *Proemio.* See Boccaccio, *Comedia.*

21. Boccaccio criticism has widely analyzed the structure of the *Decameron* and the relations between

macro- and microtextuality. Since this theme only peripherally touches on the discussion of work, I will refer to the general bibliographies contained in Vittore Branca's edition of the *Decameron* (in *Boccaccio Medievale*) and in the studies by Forni, *Forme Complesse*; Battaglia Ricci, *Boccaccio*; and Surdich, *Boccaccio*.

22. An exemplary figure is that of the noble Federigo degli Alberighi in 5.9, who becomes a better manager (*miglior massaio*) by the end of the story.

23. On the degrees of specialization in the various professions see De Grassi; Pelner Cosman; and Robertson.

24. The total number of *novelle* includes the introduction to the narrator's tale of day 4.

25. Including these two, the number of mercantile stories rises up to twenty-two while that of the *novelle* having aristocratic protagonists diminishes to twenty-nine.

26. Marcello Ciccuto speaks of the "laicizzazione del sistema culturale intervenuta agli inizi del Trecento, in sintonia altresí con una trasformazione del ruolo dell'artista in seno alla società comunale e cortese che lo vede passare nel giro di due secoli dal livello di artigiano a quello di *divino artifex* in pieno Cinquecento" (116-17). According to Ciccuto, the artists appearing in the *Decameron* testify to the new aesthetic sensibility developed by communal culture that found expression in a new perception of the artist's role and in a new mode of representing reality both in figurative and literary arts. For a study on the relation between Giotto's naturalism and Boccaccio's realism as manifestations of a change in the medieval conception of knowledge, see Ciccuto 116-30 and 403-16.

27. "Torello, che mostra negli atti e nei fatti come si vive con gentilezza, è il prototipo umano ideale del Boccaccio, cui corrisponde come archetipo collecttivo e sociale la brigata. La celebrazione e la sublimazione di una borghesia che entra nell'area dominata dall'egemonia etica, morale e comportamentale del mondo aristocratico-nobiliare e che con l'aristocrazia fonda e gestisce una *upper class* a difesa di un'immagine di civiltà scossa e messa in pericolo dalla crisi abbattutasi sulla Firenze degli anni '40 del XIV secolo è l'operazione ideologica condotta dal Boccaccio scrivendo il *Decameron*: un'operazione i cui elementi di maggior spicco vanno individuati nella cornice-modello di civiltà e in un disegno dell'opera che, strutturato sulla simmetrica distanza di due archetipi negativi, viene a culminare con l'esempio massimamente positivo del 'cittadino' che è 'signore'" (Surdich, *La cornice* 282-83 and 266-71). See, also, Getto ch. 2.

28. Philip Jones distinguishes between "mercantile" and "civic" humanism in reference to the new vision of relations between wealth and common good that influenced political thought since the beginning of the fourteenth century: "Anche le nuove opinioni, favorevoli alla ricchezza, di un Albertano da Brescia o di un Remigio dei Girolami erano saldamente subordinate alla stessa generale filosofia del patriottismo civico e del "ben comun": in breve la filosofia dell'umanesimo—umanesimo civico (nonmercantile)—riscoperto e risuscitato (e molto tempo prima degli umanisti) della polis-comune italiana" (281).

29. "[T]hey chanced, between Milan and Pavia, to fall in with a gentleman, one Messer Torello d'Istria da Pavia, who with his servants and his dogs and falcons was betaking him to a fine estate that he had on the Ticino, there to tarry a while" ("[S]i scontrarono in un gentile uomo, il cui nome era messer Torello di Stra da Pavia: il quale con i suoi famigliari e con cani e con falconi se n'andava a dimorare a un suo bel luogo il quale sopra 'l Tesino aveva," *Dec.* 10.9, 7).

30. *Dec.* 1.1, 26. Branca observes, "Lombardi erano chiamati in Francia tutti gli italiani della parte settentrionale della penisola, Toscana inclusa (*Purg.* XVI.125-26): e 'lombardo' era sinonimo di prestatore e usuraio, cui si accompagnava spesso il dispregiatio di 'chien'. Ancora oggi esiste *rue des Lombards* e a Londra *Lombard Street*" (56n9).

31. Two characters are described as "azzimati": Ciappelletto and *messer* Zima in 3.5 (rich but not noble and with no direct clue in the story that he is a merchant).

32. But see, for example, Surdich, *La cornice* 271.

33. For the merchants' "heroic" saga, see Sapori, and Branca 134-64. See, also, Pirenne 29-32, who underlines the crucial support merchants provided to crusaders. For historians' differences of opinion about merchants' reputations in the Middle Ages, see Le Goff, *Pour un autre* 29.

34. We have so far analyzed the model of the merchant man. A further investigation should be done in parallel on the model of woman in the *Decameron*. *Novella* 10.9 is in a certain sense connected to 10.10, the closing exemplary story narrated by Dioneo, who—as only in 1.1—does not take advantage of his privilege. If we take into account the ideological components in the model represented by Torello (moral virtues, work, and Christian ideals), the two final stories are almost complementary. While Torello is the feasible positive model of "modern" man, Ghismonda is the ideal model of the new woman. Both have no noble origins, both work, and both ascend to higher social position because of their virtues.

35. "Whether servile or free, prosperous or indigent, the medieval peasants were above all defined as unprivileged and lowly, yet as productive. Elite regard of the peasantry displayed a fundamental ambivalence, conceiving of rustics on the one hand as inhabiting a completely different and lower world—if not literally 'other,' at least constructed as alien—and on the other hand as ur-human, exemplarily Christian, conforming most closely to what God had intended for humanity, people whose worthy labor supports all of humanity" (Freedman 12). In discussing the images of the wily and the pious peasant, Freedman finds that the connection between the popular prejudice of practical shrewdness associated with the peasant and its religious symbolism hinges on the idea of work: "[C]ertain ideas of peasant piety grew out of the functional identification of the peasant with work. To the extent that such work was regarded positively, as nourishing society, the peasant was at least worthy of esteem. To the extent that work was regarded as degrading or penitential, the peasant was credited with a spiritual benefit in God's eyes" (Freedman 234-35). The *sermones ad status,* sermons preachers addressed to different occupational groups, are a relevant source to judge the ambivalent image of the peasant in the Middle Ages. See the study by Van den Hoven (esp. 208-13) on the figures of peasants, merchants, and artisans in the *sermones ad status.*

36. Agriculture had lost the revered status of *techne* that it held in antiquity. For the dynamics of the relation between country and urban centers during the commercial revolution, see Cipolla 117-22; Lopez 148-67; and Cherubini 113-37.

37. Roman Stoics, particularly Seneca, exalted the country as the meditative space of the wise man and opposed it to the chaotic city life. Petrarch retrieved this classical ideal of the agricultural retreat as an element necessary to perfect the poet's intellectual life. The theme became dear to the humanists and Boccaccio. In the *Decameron,* however, the author does not associate the idea of intellectual retreat with monasticism.

38. Unless otherwise indicated, English quotations are from *The Jerusalem Bible* and Latin quotations from *Vulgata.* See also, for the same metaphor, Ps. 79.9-18 and Jr. 2.21.

39. The English translation is a revised version from the *Princeton Dante Project* (*The Divine Comedy,* <http://etcweb.princeton.edu/dante/index.html>). The word *garden* has been changed into *orchard* as closer to the original. By leaving the current translation of *orto* with *garden* and *ortolano* with *gardener,* much of the implicit biblical reference relevant to my analysis would have been lost.

40. The expression comes from Paul, 1 Cor. 3.9. The Greek text has, literally, "coworkers." The *Vulgata* translates the word as "adiutores."

41. This hypothesis is coherent with the *Decameron*'s continuous dialogue with Dante's *Commedia.* For the importance of Dante and the *Divine Comedy* in the *Decameron,* particularly in day 1, see Hollander, "Boccaccio's Dante: Imitative Distance (*Decameron* 1.1 and 6.10)" 1981-82 (169-98) rpt. in Hollander 21-52; Branca 3-30; and Bruni 289-302.

42. The inversion suggests that Boccaccio is constructing a parody of Dante's metaphorical orchard. The other two modes that characterize Boccaccio's pervasive parodic technique are also present here: concretization and demotion. See Forni, *Adventures* 110.

43. For both Plato and Aristotle, the end of politics was to realize the happiness of the city, which could be done only if it was previously understood what individual happiness was. For Aristotle, it was the result of the activity of the virtuous soul. Thus, individual and collective dimensions, ethics and politics, were strictly connected, for no individual happiness could be conceived outside the community, where men realized their nature. See Aristotle, *NE* [*Nicomachean Ethics*] 1094b 10 (*Perseus Digital Library*).

Works Cited

Alighieri, Dante. *La Divina Commedia.* Ed. G. Petrocchi. Milano: Mondadori, 1966-67.

Ambrose. *Hexaemeron, paradise, and Cain and Abel.* Trans. John J. Savage. Vol. 42. *The Fathers of the Church.* Ed. Thomas P. Halton. Washington, DC: Catholic U of America P, 1961.

Barberi Squarotti, Giorgio. "La 'Cornice' del 'Decameron' o Il Mito di Robinson." *Da Dante al Novecento. Saggi Critici Degli Scolari a Giovanni Getto Nel Suo Ventesimo Anno di Insegnamento Universitario.* AA.VV. Milano: Mursia, 1970. 111-58.

Barsella, Susanna. "The Myth of Prometheus in Giovanni Boccaccio's *Decameron.*" *Studia humanitatis: Essays in Honor of Salvatore Camporeale.* Spec. Supplement to *Modern Language Notes* 119.1 (2004): 120-41.

Basil of Caesarea. *Homélies sur l'*Hexaéméron. Trans. Stanilas Giet. Sources Chrétiennes 26. Paris: Éditions du Cerf, 1949.

Battaglia Ricci, Lucia. *Boccaccio.* Roma: Salerno, 2000.

———. *Ragionare nel giardino. Boccaccio e i cicli pittorici del "Trionfo della morte."* Roma: Salerno, 1987.

Bellomo, Manlio. "Il lavoro nel pensiero dei giuristi medievali. Proposte per una ricerca." Lavorare nel Medio Evo. Rappresentazioni ed esempi dall'Italia dei secc. X-XVI. Convegno del Centro Studi sulla Spiritualità Medievale. Università degli Studi di Perugia. XXI. 12-15 otto. 1980. Todi: Accademia Tudertina, 1983. 171-97.

Biblia Sacra Vulgatae Editionis. Sixti V Pontificis Maximi iussu recognita et Clementis VIII auctoritate edita. Milano: San Paolo, 1995.

Boccaccio, Giovanni. *Comedia delle ninfe fiorentine (Ameto).* Ed. Antonio Enzo. Firenze: Sansoni, 1963.

Branca, Vittore. *Boccaccio Medievale e Nuovi Studi Sul Decameron.* Firenze: Sansoni, 1992.

Brown, Peter. *The Rise of Western Christendom.* Oxford: Blackwell, 1996.

Bruni, Francesco. Boccaccio. *L'Invenzione Della Letteratura Mezzana.* Bologna: Il Mulino, 1990.

Cherubini, Giovanni. "The Peasant and Agriculture." *The Medieval World.* Ed. Jacques Le Goff. London: Collins and Brown, 1990. 113-37.

Ciccuto, Marcello. "Il Novelliere *en Artiste*: Strategie Della Dissimiglianza Fra Boccaccio e Bandello." *L'Immagine del Testo.* Marcello Ciccuto. Roma: Bonacci, 1990. 113-55.

Cipolla, Carlo Maria. *Before the Industrial Revolution: European Society and Economy 1000-1700.* New York: Norton, 1994.

Cottino-Jones, Marga. "The City/Country Conflict in the *Decameron.*" *Studi Sul Boccaccio* 8 (1974): 147-84.

De Grassi, Donata. *L'Economia Artigiana Nell'Italia Medievale.* Roma: Carocci, 1996.

Flasch, Kurt. *Poesia Dopo la Peste. Saggio su Boccaccio.* Bari: Laterza, 1995.

Forni, Pier Massimo. *Adventures in Speech.* Philadelphia: U of Pennsylvania P, 1996.

———. *Forme Complesse Nel Decameron.* Firenze: Olschki, 1992.

Freedman, Paul. *Images of the Medieval Peasant.* Stanford: Stanford UP, 1999.

Getto, Giovanni. *Vita di Forme e Forme di Vita Nel Decameron.* Torino: Petrini, 1958.

Gittes, Tobias Foster. "St. Boccaccio: The Poet as Pander and Martyr." *Studi Sul Boccaccio* 30 (2002): 125-57.

Hollander, Robert. *Boccaccio's Dante and the Shaping Force of Satire.* Ann Arbor: U of Michigan P, 1997.

Jones, Philip. "Economia e Società Nell'Italia Medievale: La Leggenda Della Borghesia." *Storia d'Italia.* Ed. Ruggero Romano and Corrado Vivanti. Torino: Einaudi, 1978.

Le Goff, Jacques. *La Bourse et la Vie.* Paris: Hachette, 1986.

———. *Pour un autre Moyen Âge.* Paris: Gallimard, 1977.

———. *Time, Work, and Culture in the Middle Ages.* Ed. Arthur Goldhammer. Chicago: U of Chicago P, 1980.

Lopez, Robert S. *The Commercial Revolution of the Middle Ages, 950-1350.* Cambridge: Cambridge UP, 1976.

Malanima, Paolo. *Economia Preindustriale: Mille Anni, Dal IX al XVII Secolo.* Milano: Bruno Mondadori, 1995.

Marino, Lucia. *The Decameron "Cornice": Allusion, Allegory, and Iconology.* Ravenna: Longo, 1979.

———. "Prometheus or the Mythos Grapher's Self-Image." *Studi sul Boccaccio* 7 (1980): 263-73.

Meiss, Millard. *Painting in Florence and Siena after the Black Death.* Princeton: Princeton UP, 1951.

The New Jerusalem Bible. [1966.] Ed. H. Wansbrough. New York: Doubleday, 1990.

Paolini, Lorenzo. "Gli Eretici e Il Lavoro: Fra Ideologia Ed Esistenzialità." *Lavorare Nel Medio Evo. Rappresentazioni Ed Esempi Dall'Italia Dei Secc. X-XVI.* Centro di studi sulla spiritualità medievale. Università degli studi di Perugia. Todi: Accademia Tudertina, 1983. 111-67.

Pelner Cosman, Madeline. *Women at Work in Medieval Europe.* New York: Checkmark, 2000.

Pennisi, Alessandra Francesca. *Endless Exchange: Money, Women, and the Writing of the* Decameron. Diss. Yale University. Ann Arbor: UMI, 1998.

Petrarch, Francesco. *Secretum.* Ed. Enrico Fenzi. Milano: Mursia, 1992.

Pirenne, Henri. *Economic and Social History of Medieval Europe.* New York: Harcourt Brace, 1936.

Robertson, Kellie, and Michael Uebel, eds. *The Middle Ages at Work.* New York: Palgrave Macmillan, 2004.

Sapori, Armando. *Le marchand italien au Moyen Âge.* Paris: Librairie Armand Colin, 1952.

Surdich, Luigi. *Boccaccio.* Bari: Laterza, 2001.

———. *La cornice di Amore. Studi sul Boccaccio.* Pisa: ETS, 1987.

Van Den Hoven, Birgit. *Work in Ancient and Medieval Thought.* Amsterdam: Gieben, 1996.

Villani, Giovanni. *Nuova Cronica.* Critical ed. Ed. G. Porta. 3 vols. Parma: Guanda, Fondazione Pietro Bembo, 1991.

Waley, Daniel P. *The Italian City-Republics.* London: Longman, 1988.

Stephen J. Milner (essay date 2008)

SOURCE: Milner, Stephen J. "Coming Together: Consolation and the Rhetoric of Insinuation in Boccaccio's *Decameron.*" In *The Erotics of Consolation: Desire and Distance in the Late Middle Ages,* edited by Catherine E. Léglu and Stephen J. Milner, pp. 95-113. New York: Palgrave Macmillan, 2008.

[*In the following essay, Milner argues that the "Proem" and "Conclusion" of the* Decameron *play with conventions of rhetoric as well as with the trope of consolation to eroticize female isolation, thereby placing the lovesick woman in a communal context, rather than in a courtly or spiritual one.*]

This [essay] examines how Boccaccio in the **"Proemio"** and **"Conclusione"** of the *Decameron* subverts the normative medieval discourses of consolation as found within the Italian vernacular traditions of the *Consolation of Philosophy* and the *ars dictaminis* to serve a wholly different and erotically charged function. By exploiting the mediating function of written texts, Boccaccio-narrator seeks to console by imagining a transition from being in touch literally to literally being in touch. In the process he parodies Boethius' and Dante's journeys of meditative ascent, offering in their place the fantasy of a pedestrian journey that climaxes in an erotic "rendezvous."

In the **"Proemio"** to the *Decameron,* Boccaccio famously explains how he had been saved from the pains (*noia*) of unrequited love and possible death by the "piacevole ragionamenti d'alcuno amico e le sue laudevoli consolazioni" ["agreeable conversation and the admirable expressions of sympathy offered by friends"].[1] In order to express his gratitude, he states his intention to offer his book as a gift to those friends to whom he felt indebted for his current well-being and healthy state of mind. Building upon the theme of recovery, he goes further in noting his desire to dedicate his book to all those still under the thrall of love, and especially women who had less access to the range of activities, such as hunting, riding, fishing, and gambling, which enabled men to more readily overcome their melancholy. From the outset, therefore, Boccaccio as narrator plays on the relation between love, suffering, and the gendered nature of behavioral norms to create the fantasy of a desiring female readership excluded from the consoling communities of affect available to men. It is into this space that he proposes to launch his text, drawing his imagined women readers into a fictive community that promised to perform a similar consolatory function. The gift of a book is particularly suited to this task, because of the ability of vernacular literature to overcome such cultural and spatial restrictions and reach a constituency characterized by the author as largely sedentary, listless, and confined within the domestic realm; factors, he adds, which merely serve to increase their suffering.[2]

Given this spatial constraint, Boccaccio-narrator's remedy for such lovesickness is predicated on the deployment of literature as a psychological rather than a physical form of *divertimento,* literature performing a metaphorical "diversion" rather than a literal "displacement" as a means of taking the mind off things. It was precisely the susceptibility of women to such metaphorical transport that interested Boccaccio. The avowed purpose of the text, therefore, was to supplant the melancholic thoughts (*ragionamenti*) of these suffering women with new, more enjoyable and consolatory ones. The author concludes the **"Proemio"** by declaring himself ready to undertake the task at hand and minister to these women's needs having himself been freed by Love "il quale liberandomi da' suoi legami m'a conceduto il potere attendere a' lor piaceri" ["which in freeing me from its bonds, has granted me the power of making provision for their pleasures"].[3]

To date, those who have sought to analyze the **"Proemio"** of the *Decameron* have tended to locate it within the literary register of the Ovidian *Remedia amoris* and the romance narratives of the chivalric epics, an association encouraged by the subtitling of the text as *prencipe Galeotto.*[4] In the process, however, the relation of the text to more mundane forms of communicative practice as experienced in late medieval communal Italy has been largely overlooked or simply taken for granted. For Boccaccio's text is typical of the dialogic nature of much literary and poetic writing produced in communal Italy with its emphasis on collective association, reunion and the overcoming of separation.[5] Indeed a prime concern of Boccaccio's vernacular literary output was the mediating function of literature and its relation to affairs of the heart.[6] It is somewhat incongruous, therefore, that the **"Proemio"** remains one of the least-studied parts of the *Decameron* when it actually testifies to the cultural obsession in communal Italy with the protocols of correct salutation and decorous address, as reflected in the manuals of the *ars dictaminis* and the various paraphrases and translations of Ciceronian classical rhetorical theory.[7]

It is within this communal context and the associated culture of textual production that I wish to locate my analysis of the *Decameron*'s rhetoric of consolation.[8] The dedication of the text to women suffering in love places it squarely within the late medieval genre of consolation literature, which is itself a by-product of communal life. Indeed, the narrator's description of women in love as suffering prisoners who "il più del tempo nel piccolo circuito delle loro camere racchiuse dimorano" ["spend most of their time cooped up within the narrow confines of their rooms"] (**"Proemio,"** 10) is far more redolent of one of the most translated and commented-upon texts of the late medieval period in Italy, namely Boethius' *Consolation of Philosophy,* than it is to courtly literature with its highly visible, if untouchable, women.

The perceived relevance of Boethius' text to the late medieval communal context is reflected in its reception history. Indeed, it was amongst the most widely available and commented upon Latin texts of the period.[9] Two popular Tuscan vernacular translations were already in circulation by mid-century, the 1332 version by the Florentine notary Alberto della Piagentina and the 1343 translation by the Sienese Grazia di Meo, which was completed in Avignon but produced for the Florentine patrician Niccolò di Gino Guicciardini.[10] The text was also used as a bridge between the minor and major authors in the teaching of grammar within the peninsula's schools.[11] Boccaccio's familiarity with the text is apparent from his earlier works including the *Amorosa visione* (VI, 83) and especially the *Filocolo,* in which Biancifiore is figured as an imprisoned lover in a clear adaptation of the Boethian trope.[12] Not only did he own a copy of the *Consolation,* but he also transcribed a copy in his own hand that is still extant (MS Vat. Lat. 3362), while his friend, Pietro da Muglio, gave public lectures on the *Consolation* that served as the basis for one of the two Latin Trecento commentaries on the text.[13]

The parallels between the **"Proemio"** of the *Decameron* and the *Consolation of Philosophy* are striking. The imprisoned women are described as involved in the kind of internal dialogue embarked upon by Boethius the prisoner, "volendo e non volendo in una medesima ora, seco rivolgendo diversi pensieri, li quali non è possibile che sempre siano allegri" ["wishing one thing and at the same time wishing its opposite, and reflecting on various matters, which cannot always be pleasant to contemplate"] (**"Proemio,"** 10). Where it is Philosophy that comes to the aid of the prisoner in the *Consolation,* in the *Decameron* it is the book itself that assumes the role, its "nuovi ragonimenti" seeking to displace any melancholic thoughts through a combination of *novelle* and *canzonette* (**"Proemio,"** 13), a form reminiscent of the Consolation's own *prosimetrum.* In addition, both texts seek to offer a palliative to the inconstancy of Fortune, the first by reconciling the prisoner to the contingency of all things she grants, the second by seeking to rectify the negligence of Fortune in her failure to grant them any favors on account of her preference for men, the text being written "acciò che in parte per me s'amendi il peccato dela fortuna" ["in order that I (Boccaccio-narrator) may to some extent repair the omissions of Fortune"] (**"Proemio"** 13). Similarly both

texts characterize the protagonists in need of consolation as inert, Boccaccio's suffering women being "sat in idleness" ("quasi oziose sedendosi") (**"Proemio"** 10) whilst Boethius prisoner is diagnosed by Philosophy as suffering "from lethargy, a sickness common to deluded minds" ("lethargum patitur communem inlusarum mentium morbum") (I.ii.10).

In a rare recognition of the parallels between the two texts, the Italianist Millicent Marcus has noted that the *Decameron* could equally be subtitled *The Consolation of Storytelling* such was its debt to the Boethian model, but the question remains concerning what kind of consolation the narrator is offering.[14] For Marcus, the *Decameron* is proof that Boccaccio the author "has welcomed the normative responsibilities of his art and composed a work of true consolation, dramatizing his faith in the human power to recreate the self and the world in the best tradition of Boethius."[15] However, this explanation is not altogether convincing, not least because Boethius' text can easily be read as a satire on the limits of philosophical consolation.[16] It is this satiric mode that I wish to stress through examining Boccaccio's ingenuity in adapting the trope of imprisonment, originally used to describe a state of male political marginalization to describe a state, or fantasy, of female social isolation.[17] The exploration of the erotic possibilities resultant from this adaptation lie at the heart of Boccaccio-narrator's consideration of what it means to console his female readers, for it simultaneously poses the question of what it means to be available to minister to women's pleasures, and alerts us to the text's subtitle that clearly aligns the author with another legendary fictive pander.[18] For by implicating the text within such processes of exchange between friends, Boccaccio-narrator conflates the libinal and social economies of *amicizia* and *clientelismo* and demands we question the nature of the bonds of mutual relation such gift giving seeks to establish. It is therefore instructive to set such textual strategies within the context of contemporary practices of address and correspondence, and examine their relation to spatial issues of distance and separation, for Boccaccio's **"Proemio"** clearly plays with the conventions of the Italian medieval form of the *ars dictaminis.*

Boccaccio was clearly versed in the compositional conventions of late medieval epistolography, the rudiments of which he would have learnt during his schooling in Florence and refined during his canon law training in Naples. In this context, Boccaccio's ability to write letters, be they personal or business related, were a constituent part of a skill set that also covered the accounting processes expected of an "arismetrica instructus."[19] The interpellation of such textual practices into his more overtly literary works comes as no great surprise given the verisimilitude of his realist fiction and it is in the modified Italian form of the *ars dictaminis* that we can trace the roots of what we may term Boccaccio's rhetoric of insinuation as manifest within the *Decameron,* specifically in relation to exordia and forms of address.

In many *ars dictamina,* the origins of epistolarity are traced to the need to overcome, or at least alleviate, some of the anguish caused by separation for letter writing provided a means of keeping in touch notwithstanding being apart. The communication of desire over distance was then the determining factor that led to the invention of the letter as a literary form. Written and sealed, they could also contain secrets that were not known to the bearer, who was more a carrier than a messenger. These characteristics of epistolary exchange were neatly summarized by the Bolognese *dictatore* Guido Faba in his influential *Summa dictaminis* (1228-29),

> Et ideo (the letter) non immerito fidelis nuntia dicitur secretorum, que crimen amici celat, verecundiam tegit, et absentes quantumcumque remotos inducit tamquam simul essent presentia corporali.[20]

> [And thus not without reason is it (the letter) called a faithful messenger of secrets, which conceals the trespass of a friend, covers shame, and unites those absent, no matter how distant from each other, as if they were bodily present together.]

In this respect the *ars dictaminis* was the secular counterpart to the *ars orandi* that furnished principles for effective communication with God.[21] In both cases the aim was to persuade through forms of mediation that sought to overcome separation and, ultimately, bring about union. As arts, or practices, both disciplines were rhetorical, not solely in the terms of constituting repertories of stylistic figures and tropes but also in the sense of being situated performances in which the situation was one of separation. The aim of both these mediating arts, therefore, was to foreclose the gap and bring the correspondents closer together through the medium of language. These are exactly the terms in which Boethius-prisoner prepares to address God in book 3 of the *Consolation of Philosophy:* "We must call upon (*Invocandum*) the Father of all things," I said, "for if this is omitted no beginning (*exordium*) can be rightly and properly based" (III, 103-105). Such an approach, therefore, had to be appropriately fashioned if it was to elicit a fitting response.

Understood in these terms, the way in which Italian late medieval writers of the *ars dictaminis* modified the early French tradition of letter writing is highly significant, not only in terms of understanding the relation between cultural practices and literary forms but also to provide the framework for a more nuanced reading of Boccaccio's **"Proemio"** in the *Decameron.* My contention is that Boccaccio adapts the conventions of rhetorical openings as presented within classical rhetorical theory to address a late medieval social constituency not imagined within the classical texts.[22]

The principal innovation of the Italian school was the increased prominence given to the discussion and exposition of the Ciceronian exordium as found in the two most famous texts of classical rhetorical theory known in the medieval period, the *De Inventione* and the pseudo-Ciceronian *Rhetorica Ad Herennium,* more commonly referred to as the *Rhetorica vetus* and the *Rhetorica nuova.*[23] Instead of focusing upon due recognition of social status through finely differentiated forms of the salutation, the return to the Ciceronian exordium marked a reorientation of practices of address that paid greater attention to the performative situation of the speech act and its intended audiences.[24] By stressing the importance of assessing the mood of the audience as a preliminary to the process of persuasion, greater emphasis was placed on rhetorical invention and argumentation within dictaminal and rhetorical writings of the late medieval communal period. In this respect it could meet the needs of communal speakers and writers who participated in deliberative assemblies, communal *parlamenti,* and intercommunal diplomacy, practices that required the debating of issues prior to voting or the establishing of consensus.[25] Bene da Firenze, writing in the 1220s, for instance, noted in his *Candelabrum* how Cicero had no use for salutations on account of the controversial nature of his rhetoric, the assumption being that each issue, or cause to be debated, had two sides.[26]

This more adversarial rhetorical paradigm is most clearly evidenced in the attention paid to the different forms of rhetorical exordium, or introduction, and specifically in relation to discussion of the closed, or indirect, exordium that was termed *insinuatio.* In the *Ad Herennium* the author differentiates between two forms of introduction, "the Direct Opening, in Greek called the *Prooimion,* and the Subtle Approach, called the *Ephodos*" ("principium, quod Graece prooemium appellatur, et insinuatio, quae ephodos nominatur").[27] The choice of type of exordium is conditioned by the nature of the issue (*causae*) being addressed, of which there were four types: "the honorable, discreditable, doubtful, and petty" ("honestum, turpe, dubium, humile").[28] The use of the subtle approach, *insinuatio,* was best suited to the pursuit of dishonorable causes. The author then treats insinuation at considerable length and in considerable detail before moving to discuss the next part of an oration, what translators have rendered as the "statement of facts," in Latin "narrationem"—narrative. Of the three forms of narrative he proposes, it is the first that is of most interest: "It is one type when we set forth the facts and turn every detail to our advantage (*ad utilitatem nostram*) so as to win the victory, and this kind appertains to the causes on which a decision is to be rendered."[29] The combination of assuming a subtle approach in constructing a narrative that seeks personal profit through persuading others to pursue discreditable courses of action is a suggestive combination when seeking to understand the Boccaccio-narrator's intentions in seeking to "console" his female readers. This is certainly apparent by the time we reach the **"Conclusione dell'autore."**

The suspicion is increased when we return to the *Ad Herennium*'s discussion of when to use this indirect or subtle approach. Here he gives us a detailed description of the forms of writing that can engender laughter and help raise the spirits of those who are tired of listening to other voices. The passage is worth quoting at length as the echoes we find in the *Decameron* **"Proemio"** are telling:

> If the hearers have been fatigued by listening, we shall open with something that may provoke laughter—a fable, a plausible fiction, a caricature, an ironical inversion of the meaning of a word, an ambiguity, innuendo, banter, a naïvety, an exaggeration, a recapitulation, a pun, an unexpected turn, a comparison, a novel tale, an historical anecdote, a verse, or a challenge or a smile of approbation directed at some one.[30]

> [Si defessi erunt audiendo, ab aliqua re quae risum movere posit, ab apologo, fabula veri simili, imitatione depravata, inversione, ambiguo, suspicione, inrisione, stultitia, exsuperatione, collectione, litterarum mutatione, praeter expectationem, similitudine, novitate, historia, versu, ab alicuius interpellatione aut adrisione.]

Boccaccio-narrator's positioning of his own narrative as a potential remedy for all those lovesick women cooped up in their rooms, exhausted by listening to their own voices, and in need of consolation seems to share distinct parallels with the Ciceronian rhetorical strategy of *insinuatio*. His intention to recount "cento novelle, o favole o parabole o istorie che dire le vogliamo" ["a hundred tales or fables, or parables or stories or what you will"] (**"Proemio,"** 13), which might proffer some "utile consiglio" (profitable advice) concerning what to pursue and what to avoid places his text within the deliberative rhetorical framework established in the *Ad Herennium*'s discussion of indirect narrative openings, their aims, and how those aims condition their mode of address.

What is significant concerning Boccaccio's application of this framework to a literary setting is that the vast majority of Italian writing on the Ciceronian exordium and insinuation had been applied to the political realm where resistance and hostility were understood in political terms. This was certainly the case with the rhetorical and political writings of Brunetto Latini nearly a century earlier in both his *Trésor* and *Rettorica* where the trope of insinuation receives extensive commentary and amplification, although Latini shows a rare literary interest in the third form of narration noted above in his

Trésor.[31] This domestication of a previously civic rhetorical device is highly original and focuses attention on the manner in which Boccaccio transposes feelings of hostility and resistance from the political to the personal sphere, at the same time giving the transposition a gendered twist in configuring women as the suffering exiles/prisoners rather than displaced men. Significantly, as will be demonstrated, it also adds a dimension to a previously established tradition of generic adaptation in relation to the *ars dictaminis* and the art of addressing women.

In this respect Boccaccio overcomes one of the key limits of Italian medieval Ciceronianism: its wholly political and male bias. Ciceronianism, as a republican- or communally orientated corpus of rhetorical doctrine, furnished no guidance on the composition of the kind of consolation literature that exile itself provoked.[32] The failure of Latini to complete his *Rettorica,* itself a commentary on the *De Inventione,* has been seen by some critics as a direct consequence of Latini's inability to reconcile the exclusively public and adversarial Ciceronian rhetorical model with the more broad ranging *Ars dictaminis* tradition that encompassed the private realm of personal correspondence and friendship, precisely the domain addressed by consolation literature.[33] The widespread dissemination of vernacular translations of Boethius' *Consolation of Philosophy* can therefore be read as meeting a demand that admitted to the possibility of removal from the political realm and to the social reality of exile. The evolution of the tradition of consolation literature in late medieval and Renaissance Italy actually runs parallel to the rhetorical republicanism of civic discourse, and in many ways constitutes its shadow side. This is most clearly illustrated by Albertano da Brescia's authoring of the *Liber de doctrina dicendi et tacendi* in 1245, a foundational text that examined the economy of the spoken and written word within a communal context, followed by his *Liber consolationis et consilii* the year after in 1246.[34] In keeping with Albertano's judicial background, the consolatory text is presented in the form of a deliberative dialogue that domesticates the genre of legal *consilia* in proffering advice on how best to overcome the grief suffered on the death of a relative in factional feuding, drawing extensively on Stoic and legal sources.[35] Boccaccio himself contributed to this genre of consolation literature in 1361 when he penned a *Consolatoria* to his friend Pino de' Rossi who had been exiled from Florence on account of his perceived involvement in a political plot. It was a text that enjoyed considerable popularity throughout the fifteenth century, as witnessed by the high number of copies included in Florentine miscellanies.[36]

Yet as a rule these texts were written by men and exchanged between men. The tradition of writing to women within the parameters of the *ars dictaminis* tradition is much less studied and less evident, but nonetheless is present amongst the rhetorically sophisticated teachers of the art in medieval Bologna, and specifically in the work of one of its most renowned practitioners, Boncompagno da Signa (c.1170-1240). Although Boncompagno claimed never to have read Cicero, there is no doubt he was familiar with both the *Rhetorica novus* and *Rhetorica vetus,* and certain characteristics of his adaptation of the *ars dictaminis* would seem to bear this out, especially in relation to his use of *insinuatio* and its relation to the possibility of "consoling" women readers. In his *Rhetorica novissima* of 1235, which contains a number of model letters, he illustrates the figure of *transumptio,* a figure primarily concerned with displacement and transport, by suggesting how a nun might seek to address her lover by appropriating the scriptural dictum "Virga tua et baculus tuus, ipsa me consolata sunt" ("Thy rod and thy staff they comfort (console) me").[37] Such usage is perfectly in keeping with the *Ad Herennium*'s advice that the indirect approach can be made through "an ironical inversion of the meaning of a word, an ambiguity, innuendo" as noted above. Indeed, in classical rhetorical theory metaphor in this sense was also used for the sake of avoiding obscenity, a theme glossed in several of the Trecento vernacular renditions of the *Ad Herennium.*[38]

Boncompagno took this play even further in his *Rota veneris,* a dictaminal tract that is exclusively concerned with the use of metaphors in persuading and dissuading within epistolary exchanges between lovers as suggested in the title *Tractatus amoris carnalis.*[39] A form of *summa dictaminis de arte amandi* the text has Venus appear to the protagonist "arrayed in richly broidered cloth-of-gold" and "like a queen she wore a crown and in her right hand held a regal scepter, in a manner most befitting a great lady."[40] The parody of Philosophy's appearance to the prisoner in the *Consolation of Philosophy* is suggestive; the dress is neither torn nor dusty, the crown is in place, and the scepter is held in the left rather than the right hand (I, I, 24-25). Significantly, there is not a book in sight. That lovers are all bound to wheels that turn in a circle would seem to collate the figure of Fortune with the figure of Venus in this instance. Yet for the purposes of establishing the significance of this text and this playful adaptation of epistolary exchange and verbal play to Boccaccio's **"Proemio"** in the **Decameron,** it is Venus' rebuke to the protagonist/fantasist that is most important. Upon greeting him "she emphatically declared that she was the goddess Venus, and at the same time demanded wherefore I had composed no greetings (*salutationes*) and delectable phrases (*delectabilia dictamina*) which seem so suitable for use by lovers."[41] Suitably chided, the protagonist takes up his pen and authors the tract.

My contention is that Boccaccio's **"Proemio"** stands within such a tradition of allusive amorous address, and that his use of metaphor and displaced meanings affords

the latitude required if the narrator's indirect approaches to women were to be successful, either in terms of reaching a female readership or indulging a male fantasy of reaching such a constituency. Nowhere is this clearer than in the punning found in the author's conclusion where Boccaccio returns to the issue of consolation and correct address: "Nobilissime giovani, a consolazion delle quali io a così lunga fatica messo mi sono . . ." ("Noble young ladies, for whose solace I undertook this protracted labor . . .").[42] In this epilogue, which forms the concluding part of the text, Boccaccio-narrator anticipates the criticism that he has taken inappropriate liberties ("troppa licenzia") in having his female protagonists say and hear words unbecoming to honest women. The term he uses is again a rhetorical one associated with unseemly address, namely "licenzia," license or speaking out of turn.[43] Yet, to be granted "licenzia" by the communal authorities also meant being given permission to move about unimpeded, and in legal terminology "licenziato" meant literally to be freed. The sense of the term, therefore, has both a spatial and linguistic performative dimension, and it is this duality that is played upon in Boccaccio-narrator's far from convincing denial of his use of linguistic insinuation within, and through, the text. His assertion that words literally mean what they say may offer a simple repost to any possible criticism, but the sheer weight of his metaphorical discourse suggests otherwise. It is metaphorical language, understood as a register in which signifiers are granted license and freed from signs, that permits the communication of nonliteral, and socially untoward, meanings.

The need to adopt insinuation as a linguistic and spatial tactic was in fact necessitated by the changed social conditions between the "then" of the narrated events and the "now" of their belated recording within the text. In the introduction to Day 1, the situating part of the cornice-narrative, Boccaccio-narrator presents us with a portrait of Florence during the plague in which the affective social bonds that were constitutive of society and community (illustrated in the Ciceronian foundation myths of the *De Inventione*) were systematically unpicked, and in which the conventions of decorous socialisation and address were abandoned: "E lasciamo stare che l'uno cittadino l'altro schifasse e quasi niuno vicino avesse dell'altro cura e i parenti insieme rade volte o non mai si visitassero e di lontano" ["It was not merely a question of one citizen avoiding another, and of people almost invariably neglecting their neighbours and rarely or never visiting their relatives, addressing them only from a distance"].[44] The matrix of family, friends, and neighbors is dissolved as brothers abandoned brothers, uncles their nephews, sisters their brothers, wives their husbands and, worst of all, parents their offspring. One consequence of this abandonment that is significant for the current argument is the narrator's observation that suffering women showed few scruples in revealing their bodies to male servants, a previously inconceivable practice. During the plague, therefore, the approach to women's bodies was direct and not oblique, whereas in the "now" of the narrative writing subsequent to the reinstatement of laws and cultural norms, a more subtle tactic is required by those seeking to serve suffering women, the very subject position that Boccaccio-narrator assumes in the **"Proemio."** That the parallel was in the forefront of the narrator's own mind is implicit in the observation that those women who participated in such revelatory practices and actually survived the plague were subsequently less chaste: "il che in quelle che ne guarirono fu forse di minore onestà, nel tempo che succedette, cagione" ["and this explains why those women who recovered were possibly less chaste in the period that followed"].[45] Indeed, the reassertion of cultural norms is read as coterminous with the reestablishment of the protocols of decorous address, which necessitates the renaming of the protagonists in order to preserve their reputations. Understood as a metaphor itself, what the plague serves to illustrate is the ambivalence of social aggregation as simultaneously a source of strength and a source of vulnerability as the benefits of contiguity are haunted by the specter of contamination. Coming together in such conditions, therefore, had not only potentially erotic but also potentially fatal consequences.

Once the license afforded by the plague was past, however, and culture was reestablished, those seeking union with their objects of desire had to resort to indirect forms of approach both linguistically and spatially, the very realm of insinuation. This was the time frame, the "now," within which the *Decameron* as text was authored. The text itself, therefore, can be read as an indirect approach to women readers, real or imaginary, a literary strategy in which linguistic insinuation seeks to contaminate the minds of its readership in the same way that the plague contaminated their bodies. Such thought processes were regularly addressed within contemporary handbooks on monastic meditation in which such ill-disciplined wandering thoughts were identified with the sin of curiosity and characterized as mental fornication.[46] The suggestion has already been made by Boccaccio-narrator that the plague had the effect of creating a female constituency more open to such suggestion and less risk-averse, more "curious" even. There is little doubt such a constituency appealed to our consoling author, yet culture dictated that the means of communicating such intentions had to be masked. The text, therefore, sought to elicit curiosity in the mind of the reader in the absence of the authorial body. Irrespective of the gender of the reader, metaphorical language was the ideal medium for such forms of communication, for the fantasy was one in which absence became presence and words became deeds, the text preparing the way for the coming together of reader and writer.

This dynamic is implicitly alluded to in the final section of the author's epilogue at the very end of the text where Boccaccio-narrator plays on the double sense of "lingua" in Italian as both language and tongue. Read literally there is nothing untoward about suggesting his text was a written version of his own speech. In a mid-Trecento Tuscan *volgarizzamento* of the most well-known Bolognese dictaminal tract from the early Trecento, Giovanni di Bonandrea's *Brieve introductione a dittare,* the definition of a letter is given as follow: "Epistola è orazione facunda \ cioè ornate \ vicaria della humana lingua" ["The letter is a fulsome oration, that is ornate, and acts in place of the human tongue"]. The term *"vicaria"* is then glossed in the margin as follows: "vicaria cioè che quello che l'uomo direbbe colla linghua se fosse presente, la epistola dicie per lui e così è vacaria della linghua però che fa il suo uficio" ["vicaria: since that which the man would say with his tongue if present the letter says for him and hence it is the messenger of the tongue since it fulfils its function"].[47] As deployed by Boccaccio-narrator in the epilogue to the *Decameron,* however, both senses of the word come together: the words of the text end and insinuation is imagined as a physical rather than a linguistic activity, a weaving of bodies rather than words:

> Confesso nondimeno le cose di questo mondo non avere stabilità alcuna ma sempre essere in mutamento, e così potrebbe della mia lingua essere intervenuto; la quale, non credendo io al mio giudicio, il quale a mio potere io fuggo nelle mie cose, non ha guari mi disse una mia vicina che io l'aveva la migliore e la più dolce del mondo.

> [I will grant you, however, that the things of this world have no stability, but are subject to constant change, and this may well have happened to my tongue. But not long ago, distrusting my own opinion (which in matters concerning myself I trust as little as possible), I was told by a lady, a neighbour of mine, that I had the finest and sweetest tongue in the world.][48]

The obscene allusion is clear, the fact that the lady in question was a neighbor adding to the sense of both spatial and linguistic insinuation, a fact reflected in the literal and figurative senses of the term itself. For literally a modern definition of "insinuation" means "to penetrate, insert gradually into a tight space . . . usually with caution and skill" ("far penetrare, intodurre a poco a poco in uno spazio angusto . . . per lo più cautamente e con abilità").[49] Figuratively it means "to inculcate in the spirit or in the mind of somebody a thought, an idea, a conviction" ("inculcare nell'animo e / o nella mente di qualcuno un pensiero, un idea, una convinzione"). This sense is further glossed as "to suggest, hint, refer to, make it understood, disclose, seek to persuade, advise (*consigliare*), bring to the attention of (in a more or less veiled or allusive manner)" ("suggerire, accennare, riferire, fare capire; palesare, cercare di persuadere, consigliare, mettere sull'avviso—

più o meno velatamente o allusivamente)." Coming together is here understood in both a literal and a metaphorical sense, addresser and addressee closing the physical space of separation and thereby overcoming the temporal belatedness of literary composition and reception. Hermeneutic closure is secured through the consensus of sexual communion in which acts replace words, both minds and bodies joining in a simultaneous and reciprocal dialogue.

In contrast to the Boethian and Dantean narrators, therefore, the Boccaccian narrator seeks, or claims to seek, bodily rather than spiritual union. The fantasy of physical access was privileged over that of metaphysical ascent, the joys of embodied pleasures consequent on coming together take precedence over the union with the divine and transcendental bliss. For reaching out to meet our maker, rather than a lover, is predicated and depends on the demise of the body, the mortification of the flesh. True happiness quenches all desires because it fulfils all lack. This is the perspective assumed by Boethius: "Now that is good which, once a man attains it leaves no room for further desires" ("Id autem est bonum quo quis adepto nihil ulterius desiderare queat") (II, 5). This state of bliss is only realized upon union with our maker, our Christian duty being to free the mind from its earthly prison, "terreno carcere," as it searches for its heavenly home (II, 85).[50] Boccaccio's homes were far more tangible, and as we have seen, even next door.

Using the same methods employed by preachers who largely relied upon their female congregations to insinuate the message of the gospels into the home and the minds of their menfolk, Boccaccio's insinuating text addressed the women in the house offering an alternative route to paradise.[51] The textual narrative of Boccaccio's *Decameron,* and especially its **"Proemio"** and **"Conclusione,"** is therefore rhetorical rather than grammatical as Todorov would have us believe.[52] For the subtlety of rhetoric permits us to circumvent the structures of grammar and the grammars of structuralism. The rhetoric of the authorial frame in the **Decameron** imagines its audience as being in a particular place and in a particular mental state. The book is sent on its way anticipating resistance, its closed exordium approaching obliquely, creeping under cover of metaphor as it works its way toward its intended audience. Hence the text is part of a larger socially situated communicative act that subverts the normative discourse of consolation as its seductive rhetoric seeks to reach places other stories cannot reach. As a communicative act the text is constitutive of its participants, both the writer and the reader, the seducer and the object being seduced.[53] Boccaccio in the very process of literary production creates a fantasy of literary consumption that privileges and empowers without compromising the male sender of the text as missive.[54]

The irony, however, lies in the temporal ordering of the imagined acts. Rather than speaking on behalf of the sender as if present, the traditional characterization of texts as surrogates, Boccaccio's book has already arrived and been consumed. The imagined coming together, therefore, postdates the production and consumption of the text in a sequencing that does not require that the sender speaks but rather that the consumer address the now present sender to establish the meeting of minds prior to the possibility of the meeting of bodies. The question that concerns the writer is whether his morally dubious counsel, his *utile consiglio,* has persuaded his deliberating audience; whether he has made himself clear; whether they have got his meaning. Only then will the reader as critic, knowing they are an object of desire, be able to decide whether to flee or follow: "in quanto potranno cognoscere quello che sia da fuggire e che sia similmente da seguitare" ["for they will learn to recognize what should be avoided and likewise what should be pursued"] (**"Proemio,"** 14). The *utile consiglio* empowers through teaching women how to subvert the paradigm of patriarchal *dominio* to facilitate coming together and seek relief from *noia,* a strategy that is as seductive to male fantasy as it is to any nominal female readership. In place of compounding melancholic lethargy, the text encourages activity in appealing to the senses as well as the intellect. While reading as an activity was one means of avoiding melancholy, most medieval medical writings advised it as part of a balanced regime of activities that also included the need for movement and the stimulation of the senses.[55] Such coming together of different parties, then, is active and consensual. The "weak women" ("delicate donne") imagined by the author of the **Decameron** are granted agency both spatially and linguistically in such opportunistic combining. As newly discerning readers, they dis-cern, in the literal sense of "prise apart," the gap between signs and signifiers, opening a space for the making of meaning. Boccaccio-narrator seeks out his idealized readership and through his oblique strategies aims to establish an affective bond with them and win them over through the medium of literature. In this respect he himself becomes a "familiar author" or even, if Fortune permits, an over familiar author whose consoling arm readily becomes a passionate embrace.[56] The verisimilitude of his realist fiction is predicated on the belief in the cognitive function of storytelling. Such playful fantasies of male and female empowerment and complicity and their location within the sensescape of late medieval Italian society is what renders Boccaccio's narrative "argumentum" so convincing.[57]

Notes

1. See Giovanni Boccaccio, *Decameron* in *Tutte le opere di Giovanni Boccaccio,* ed. Vittore Branca, 12 vols. (Milan: Mondadori, 1976), 4: proemio 4. All subsequent references are to this edition.

Translations are taken from Giovanni Boccaccio, *The Decameron,* trans. and ed. G. H. McWilliam (Harmondsworth: Penguin Books, 1972).

2. *Decameron,* Proemio, p. 10: "Esse dentro a' dilicati petti, temendo e vergognando, tengono l'amorose fiamme nascose, le quali quanto più di forza abbian che le palesi coloro il sanno che l'hanno provate." ["For the ladies, out of fear or shame, conceal the flames of passion within their fragile breasts, and a hidden love is far more potent than one which is worn on the sleeve, as everyone knows who has had experience of these matters."]

3. *Decameron,* Proemio, p. 15.

4. See Georges Güntert, *Tre premesse e una dichiarazione d'amore. Vademecum per il lettore del "Decameron"* (Modena: Mucchi editore, 1997), and Victoria Kirkham, *The Sign of Reason in Boccaccio's Fiction* (Florence: Olschki, 1993), pp. 117-119.

5. Claudio Giunta, *Versi a un destinatario: saggio sulla poesia del medioevo* (Bologna: Il Mulino, 2002).

6. See Francesco Bruni, *Boccaccio: L'invenzione della letteratura mezzana* (Bologna: Il Mulino, 1990).

7. A notable exception is Robert Hollander. See his 1993 essay "The *Proem* of the Decameron," in his collection of essays *Boccaccio's Dante and the Shaping Force of Satire* (Ann Arbor: University of Michigan Press, 1997), pp. 89-107. Even Hollander states (90), "in the group of those who do not understand it I unhesitatingly include myself." He makes a similar reading in his more recent study "The *Decameron* Proem" in *The "Decameron" First Day in Perspective,* ed. Elissa B. Weaver (Toronto: University of Toronto Press, 2004), pp. 12-28.

8. For an example of a historical materialist reading of Dante that sets his work in an identical sociopolitical milieu, see Justin Steinberg, *Accounting for Dante: Urban Readers and Writers in late Medieval Italy* (Notre Dame: University of Notre Dame Press, 2007), esp. pp. 171-179. Although a number of recent studies have sought to engage with the text's rhetorical strategies it is noticeable how rhetoric has been used as a synonym for discourse with little sense of its relation to the repertory of classical rhetorical forms found in late medieval Italian Ciceronianism and the *ars dictaminis.* This is a marked aspect of much Boccaccio criticism. See Marilyn Migiel, *A Rhetoric of the "Decameron"* (Toronto: University of Toronto Press, 2003), and Pier Massimo Forni, *Adventures in Speech: Rhetoric and Narration in Boccaccio's "Decameron"* (Philadelphia: University of Pennsylvania Press, 1996), neither of whom engage with medieval rhetorical doctrine.

9. See the Introduction to this volume for a survey of the text's medieval European diffusion.

10. On the vernacular tradition of Boethius, see Silvia Albesano, *"Consolatio Philosophiae" volgare: Volgarizzamenti e tradizione discursive nel Trecento italiano,* Studia Romanica 132 (Heidelberg: Winter, 2006). For an edition of Grazia di Meo's text, see Helmuth-Wilhelm Heinz, *Grazia di Meo. Il libro di Boeçio de chonsolazione (1343)* (Frankfurt, Bern, and New York: Peter Lang, 1984).

11. See Robert Black and Gabriella Pomaro, *La 'Consolazione della filosofia' nel Medioevo e nel Rinascimento italiano* (Florence: SISMEL, 2000).

12. See Stephen Grossvogel, *Ambiguity and Allusion in Boccaccio's "Filocolo"* (Florence: Olschki, 1992), pp. 33-55.

13. On Boccaccio's ownership of the *Consolation of Philosophy,* see Giovanni Boccaccio, *Amorosa visione,* ed. Vittore Branca (Milan: Mondadori, 1974), pp. 296-297. For the Latin commentaries, see Pierre Courcelle, *La Consolation de Philosophie dans la tradition littéraire: Antécédents et postérité de Boèce* (Paris: Études Augustiniennes, 1967), p. 326.

14. Millicent Joy Marcus, *An Allegory of Form: Literary Self-Consciousness in the "Decameron"* (Saratoga, CA: Anma Libri, 1979), pp. 110-125.

15. Marcus, *An Allegory of Form,* p. 125.

16. Joel C. Relihan, *The Prisoner's Philosophy: Life and Death in Boethius' "Consolation." With a Contribution on the Medieval Boethius by William E. Heise* (Notre Dame, IN: University of Notre Dame Press, 2007).

17. For Boccaccio as satirist and parodist, see Hollander, *Boccaccio's Dante,* and Luciano Rossi, "Ironia e parodia nel *Decameron*: da Ciappelletto a Griselda," in *La novella italiana: Atti del Convegno di Caprarola, 19-24 Settembre 1988,* ed. Enrico Malato, 2 vols. (Rome: Salerno Editrice, 1989), 1:365-405.

18. On Galeotto, see Robert Hollander, *Boccaccio's Two Venuses* (New York: Columbia University Press, 1977), pp. 102-106.

19. For Boccaccio's schooling and professional training, see Vittore Branca, *Boccaccio: The Man and His Works,* trans. Richard Monges (New York: Harvester Press, 1976), pp. 3-40.

20. Cited in Martin Camargo, "Where's the Brief? The *Ars dictaminis* and Reading/Writing Between the Lines," *Disputatio* 1 (1996): 2, 15 [1-17].

21. On prayer, see Marianne G. Briscoe and Barbara H. Jaye, *Artes praedicandi/Artes orandi*, Typologie des sources du Moyen Âge occidental, 61 (Turnhout, Belgium: Brepols, 1992), pp. 79-115.

22. In this respect I disagree fundamentally with the argument put forward by James A. Schultz, "Classical Rhetoric, Medieval Poetics, and the Medieval Vernacular Prologue," *Speculum* 59.1 (1984): 1-15, where he argues that the prologue tradition developed quite independently of the classical rhetorical tradition (15). The fact he considers only French and German cases, and overlooks Italy, where the classical and civic tradition was probably stronger, undoubtedly conditioned his conclusions.

23. See Martin Camargo, *Ars dictaminis/Ars dictandi*, Typologie des sources du Moyen Âge occidental, 60 (Turnhout, Belgium: Brepols, 1991).

24. James R. Banker, "Giovanni di Bonandrea and Civic Values in the Context of the Italian Rhetorical Tradition," *Manuscripta* 18 (1974): 3-20.

25. See Virginia Cox, "Ciceronian Rhetoric in Italy, 1260-1350," *Rhetorica* 17 (1999): 239-88. These themes are also dealt with in Virginia Cox "Ciceronian Rhetoric in Late Medieval Italy: The Latin and Vernacular Traditions," and Stephen J. Milner, "Communication, Consensus and Conflict: Rhetorical Principals, the *ars concionandi* and Social Ordering in Late Medieval Italy," both in *The Rhetoric of Cicero in Its Medieval and Renaissance Commentary Tradition*, ed. Virginia Cox and John O. Ward (Leiden: Brill, 2006), pp. 109-43, 365-408, respectively.

26. See *Bene Florentini Can delabrum*, ed. Gian Carlo Alessio (Padua: Antenore, 1983), p. 128 (book 3, chap. 55): "Moreover, Cicero only dealt with the complete parts of an oration, or, if you will, did it this way because the salutation has no place in controversies, to which Cicero reduced all rhetoric." ["Ipse (Tullius) autem de solis perfectis partibus orationis tractabat vel ideo fecit quia salutatio locum in controversiis non habet ad quas ipse totam rethoricam reducebat."]

27. [Cicero], *Ad C. Herennium. De Ratione Dicendi (Rhetorica Ad Herennium)*, trans. Harry Caplan (Cambridge, MA: Harvard University Press, 1964), I, iv, 6-7.

28. [Cicero], *Ad C. Herennium,* I, iii, 5.

29. [Cicero], *Ad C. Herennium,* I, viii, 12: "Unum est cum exponimus rem gestam et unum quidque trahimus ad utilitatem nostram vincendi causa, quod pertinet ad eas causas de quibus iudicium futurum est."

30. [Cicero], *Ad C. Herennium,* I, vii, 11.

31. See the excellent illustrative material on *insinuatio* in Virginia Cox and John O. Ward, "Appendix: The Commentaries in Action," in *The Rhetoric of Cicero,* pp. 430-45.

32. See Stephen J. Milner, "Exile, Rhetoric, and the Limits of Civic Republican Discourse," in *At the Margins: Minority Groups in Premodern Italy,* ed. Stephen J. Milner (Minneapolis: University of Minnesota Press, 2005), pp. 162-91.

33. See Ronald G. Witt, "Brunetto Latini and the Italian Tradition of *Ars Dictaminis*," *Stanford Italian Review* 2 (1983): 5-24.

34. See the edition *Albertano da Brescia, Liber de doctrina dicendi et tacendi. La parola del cittadino nell'Italia del Duecento,* ed. P. Navone (Florence: SISMEL, 1998). A resource site maintained by Angus Graham contains updated information on editions and secondary bibliography relating to Albertanus' work. See http://freespace.virgin.net/angus.graham/Albertano.htm

35. See Enrico Artifoni, "Prudenza del consigliare. L'educazione del cittadino nel *Liber consolationis et consilii* di Albertano da Brescia (1246)," in *"Consilium." Teorie e pratiche del consigliare nella cultura medievale,* ed. C. Casagrande, C. Cristiani, and S. Vecchio (Florence: SISMEL, 2004), pp. 195-216.

36. See Boccaccio, "Consolatoria a Pino de' Rossi," in *Tutte le opere di Giovanni Boccaccia,* ed. Giuseppe Chicchi, V, pp. 617-51.

37. See the edition Boncompagni da Signa, *Rhetorica Novissima,* ed. Augusto Gaudenzi, Bibliotheca Iuridica Medii Aevi, 3 vols. (Bologna: Piero Virano, 1892), 2:249-97, esp. 284 and the discussion in Josef Purkart, "Boncompagno of Signa and the Rhetoric of Love," in *Medieval Eloquence: Studies in the Theory and Practice of Medieval Rhetoric,* ed. James J. Murphy (Berkeley: University of California Press, 1978), pp. 319-31, esp. 329.

38. See [Cicero], *Ad C. Herennium,* IV, xxxiv, 45: "Obscenitatis vitandae causa, sic: 'Cuius mater cotidianis nuptiis delectetur.'" For a discussion of the relation between metaphor/*transumptio* in Boncompagno's *Rhetorica Novissima* and its use to underline extreme obscenity in the *Corbaccio,* see Guyda Armstrong, "Boccaccio and the Infernal Body: The Widow as Wilderness," in *Boccaccio and Feminist Criticism,* Studi e testi 8, ed. Thomas C. Stillinger and F. Regina Psaki (Chapel

Hill, NC: Annali d'Italianistica, 2006), pp. 87-93 [83-104]. I would like to thank Dr. Armstrong for bringing this piece to my attention and for her insightful observations on the final draft of this piece.

39. See Boncompagno da Signa, *Rota Veneris,* ed. and trans. Josef Purkart (Delmar, New York: Scholar's Facsimiles and Reprints, 1975).

40. Boncompagno, *Rota veneris,* fol. 2r, ll. 13-14 and 16-18; translation p. 73: "Ecce virgo in vestitu deaurato circumamicta varietatibus ex insperato comperaruit [. . .] Ad modum siquidem regine speciosam habebat coronam regine sceptrum in manu dextra dominabiliter deferendo venerat."

41. Boncompagno, *Rota veneris,* fol. 2, ll. 20-23; translation p. 73: "Illa vero interrogata firmiter asseruit se deam esse Venerem addendo pariter cur salutationes et delectabilia dictamina non fecissem que viderentur ad usum amantium pertinere."

42. *Decameron,* Conc. aut, p. 1.

43. See the discussion of "licenzia" in Bono Giamboni, *Fiore di rettorica,* ed. Giambattista Speroni (Pavia: Università degli studi di Pavia, 1994), pp. 31-33.

44. *Decameron,* I, Intr., p. 27.

45. *Decameron,* I, Intr., p. 229.

46. See Mary Carruthers, *The Craft of Thought: Meditation, Rhetoric, and the Making of Images, 400-1200* (Cambridge: Cambridge University Press, 1998), pp. 82-84.

47. Giovanni di Bonandrea, *Breve introductione a dittare,* Florence, Biblioteca Riccardiana, MS 2323, fol. 1r. For the Latin text, see the edition of Iohannis Bonandree, *Brevis introductio ad dictamen,* ed. Silvana Arcuti (Lecce: Congedo editore, 1993).

48. *Decameron,* Conc. aut, p. 27.

49. *Grande dizionario della lingua italiana,* ed. Salvatore Battaglia, 21 vols. (Turin: UTET, 1961-2002), 8:120-21.

50. Boethius, II, pp. 83-86: "If however a mind fully aware of its own nature, loosed from its earthly prison, is free to seek its heavenly home, will it not despise all earthly affairs, and in the joy of heaven rejoice to be freed from earthly things?" ["Sin vero bene sibi mens conscia terreno carcere resolute caelum libera petit, none omne terrenum negotium spernat quae se caelo fruens terrenis gaudet exemptam?"]

51. See Kate Cooper, "Insinuation of Womanly Influence: An Aspect of the Christianization of the Roman Aristocracy," *Journal of Roman Studies* 82 (1992): 150-64, and Sharon Farmer, "Persuasive Voices: Clerical Images of Medieval Wives," *Speculum* 61.3 (1986): 517-43.

52. Tzvetan Todorov, *Grammaire du Décaméron* (The Hague: Mouton, 1969).

53. See the suggestive observations in Ross Chambers, *Story and Situation: Narrative Seduction and the Power of Fiction* (Manchester: Manchester University Press, 1984), pp. 205-33.

54. For a contemporary literary critical examination of the multiple readers and audiences constructed through the text, see Migiel, *A Rhetoric of the Decameron.*

55. See G. Olson, *Literature as Recreation in the Later Middle Ages* (Ithaca and London: Cornell University Press, 1982), p. 175.

56. On the subject of "familiar authors" see A. J. Minnis, *Medieval Theory of Authorship: Scholastic Literary Attitudes in the Later Middle Ages,* 2nd edn. (Aldershot: Wildwood House, 1988), pp. 211-217.

57. On medieval theories of narrative, see Päivi Mehtonen, *Old Concepts and New Poetics: "Historia," "Argumentum," and "Fabula" in the Twelfth- and Early Thirteenth-Century Latin Poetics of Fiction* (Helsinki: Societas Scientiarum Fennica, 1996).

Select Bibliography

PRIMARY TEXTS

Boccaccio, Giovanni. *Tutte le opere di Giovanni Boccaccio.* Edited by Vittore Branca. 12 vols. Milan: Mondadori, 1976.

Boethius. *The Consolation of Philosophy.* Translated by Richard Green. London & New York: Macmillan, 1962.

Boncompagno da Signa. *Rhetorica Novissima.* Edited by Augusto Gaudenzi. Bologna: Piero Virano, 1892.

———. *Rota Veneris.* Edited and translated by Josef Purkart. Delmar, NY: Scholar's Facsimiles and Reprints, 1975.

SECONDARY MATERIALS

Albesano, Silvia. *"Consolatio philosophiae" volgare: volgarizzamenti e traduzioni discorsive nel Trecento italiano.* Heidelberg: Winter, 2006.

Black, Robert and Gabriella Pomaro. *La "Consolazione della filosofia" nel Medioevo e nel Rinascimento italiano.* Florence: SISMEL, 2000.

Bruni, Francesco. *Boccaccio: L'invenzione della letteratura mezzana.* Bologna: Il Mulino, 1990.

Camargo, Martin. *Ars dictaminis/Ars dictandi,* Typologie des sources du Moyen Âge occidental, 60. Turnhout, Belgium: Brepols, 1991.

Carruthers, Mary. *The Craft of Thought: Meditation, Rhetoric, and the Making of Images, 400-1200.* Cambridge: Cambridge University Press, 1998.

Courcelle, Pierre. *La Consolation de Philosophie dans la tradition littéraire: Antécédents et Postérité de Boèce.* Paris: Études Augustiniennes, 1967.

Cox, Virginia. "Ciceronian Rhetoric in Italy, 1260-1350." *Rhetorica* 17 (1999): 239-88.

Hollander, Robert. *Boccaccio's Dante and the Shaping Force of Satire.* Ann Arbor: University of Michigan Press, 1997.

Marcus, Millicent Joy. *An Allegory of Form: Literary Self-Consciousness in the "Decameron."* Saratoga, CA: Anma Libri, 1979.

Milner, Stephen J. "Communication, Consensus and Conflict: Rhetorical Principals, the *ars concionandi* and Social Ordering in Late Medieval Italy." In *The Rhetoric of Cicero in Its Medieval and Renaissance Commentary Tradition.* Edited by Virginia Cox and John O. Ward. Leiden: Brill, 2006. 365-408.

————. "Exile, Rhetoric, and the Limits of Civic Republican Discourse." In *At the Margins: Minority Groups in Premodern Italy.* Edited by Stephen J. Milner. Minneapolis: University of Minnesota Press, 2005. 162-91.

Minnis, Alastair. *Medieval Theory of Authorship: Scholastic Literary Attitudes in the later Middle Ages,* 2nd ed. Aldershot: Wildwood House, 1988.

Olson, Glending. *Literature as Recreation in the Later Middle Ages.* Ithaca and London: Cornell University Press, 1982.

Relihan, Joel C. *The Prisoner's Philosophy: Life and Death in Boethius' "Consolation." With a Contribution on the Medieval Boethius by William E. Heise.* Notre Dame, IN: University of Notre Dame Press, 2007.

William Rossiter (essay date 2008)

SOURCE: Rossiter, William. "Translation of Allegory or Allegory of Translation? Petrarch's Redressing of Boccaccio's Griselda." In *On Allegory: Some Medieval Aspects and Approaches,* edited by Mary Carr, K. P. Clarke, and Marco Nievergelt, pp. 156-82. Newcastle upon Tyne, U.K.: Cambridge Scholars Publishing, 2008.

[In the following essay, Rossiter suggests that Petrarch's Latin translation of the Decameron's *tale of Griselda (10.10) amplifies the allegorical potential of Boccac-* cio's spare version of the story. Rossiter proceeds on a theoretical framework using the tale's genre confusion to argue that neither fable nor history precludes allegory.]

Petrarch's Latin translation of the final tale in Boccaccio's vernacular work, the **Decameron**—in which patient Griselda is repeatedly subjected to cruelty and humiliation at the hands of her husband Gualtieri—is not the most immediately obvious example of the medieval allegorical mode. That is, the tale does not perhaps, for the modern reader, embody the aforementioned mode to the same stylistic degree that works such as the *Roman de la Rose* or Langland's *Piers Plowman* appear to, the landscapes of which are densely populated by personified abstractions. However, Jon Whitman has shown that while "personification is the most striking kind of compositional allegory, it is not the only kind. Allegorical composition need not employ abstract characters at all" (1987, 6). In order to illustrate this position one need only look to the *Commedia,* inhabited as it is by historical figures who serve as *exempla* no less effectively than their prosopopoeic counterparts; indeed, Whitman includes both the *Roman* and the *Commedia* under the same dispensation, namely "sustained psychic allegory" (1987, 47). From this perspective, Petrarch's allegorical translation may be considered post-*Commedia* both in terms of chronology and in terms of figurative strategy, despite his troubled relationship with Dante.[1]

And just as medieval allegory is frequently motivated by an exemplary ethical or pedagogical impulse, so Petrarch's translation is not only dependent upon an allegorical hermeneutics but also teleologically directed towards the spiritual and moral lesson which the literary technique aims to instil within its readership. Through being thus directed, the Latin redaction of Griselda's misfortunes may be seen to constitute a pivotal point in allegory's development from its mythopoeic origins to its humanized end, from personified abstraction to historical exemplar.[2] The crux of the matter is, as my chiasmic title suggests, distinction. To be more specific, the distinction, or lack of distinction, which Petrarch and his contemporaries perceived between the interrelated natures of translation and allegory, both of which fuse within the concept of "turning meaning" (Copeland 1987, 42); and how this, by extension, results in a conceptual distinction for the modern medievalist.[3] This discussion of the *Griseldis* then will examine just how allegory was and continues to be translated; how Petrarch's autoreflexive poetics redressed Boccaccio's tale, and how that *mutata veste* continues to generate debate as to the meaning beneath its "costume morale" (Martellotti 1951, 9).[4]

However, before these matters can be addressed directly, it remains necessary to establish the extent to which Petrarch's translation may be definitively classified as allegory. Might it not, in spite of Gualtieri's (Valterius's) extreme behaviour towards his wife, and Griselda's (Griseldis's) superhuman resolve, belong to the more explicitly didactic category of the *exemplum* book? Charlotte Morse, in her examination of Chaucer's *Clerk's Tale,* which draws both on Petrarch's Latin and an anonymous French translation, argues for the latter:

> The allegorizers justify Walter's tests of Griselda [. . .] by reading them as God's tests of the faithful Christian soul [. . .] Thus displacing the tale from itself and from themselves, readers make it safe, acceptable, and comfortable [. . .] the allegorizers, and outraged students—and, to varying degrees, the proponents of aesthetic failure—resist the example of Griselda's patience, her chief virtue.
>
> (1985, 52)[5]

Other critics, such as Martin McLaughlin, have indeed argued for the counterpoint, stating that "Petrarch saw his heroine as an allegory of the human soul" (1988, 56). I will return subsequently to the theological specifics of Petrarch's alleged allegoresis; for the moment I would like to focus briefly upon the perceived distinction between the two categories. The separation of allegory and *exemplum,* aside from constituting a false dichotomy—allegorical representations of the seven deadly sins, for instance, served specific exemplary ends—is central to the tale's problematic reception, and is related to the question as to whether it functions as *historia* or *fabula.* As Carolyn Dinshaw, amongst others, has argued, "the tale's attractiveness does indeed lie in its hermeneutic difficulty" (1989, 133).[6]

This difficulty has been central to the tale since its first recorded appearance in the **Decameron,** as Boccaccio's fictional company, the *brigata,* debate both its meaning and its merits:

> La novella di Dioneo era finita, e assai le donne, chi d'una parte e chi d'altra tirando, chi biasimando una cosa, un'altra intorno a essa lodandone, n'avean favellato.
>
> (Branca 1985, 905)

> Dioneo's tale had ended, and the ladies, some taking one side and some taking the other, some criticizing one thing about it and some praising another, had discussed the story at great length.
>
> (Musa and Bondanella 1982, 682)

The *novella*'s inherent potential for diverse interpretation is translated by Petrarch into his Latin rewriting, as he relates the contrasting responses of a Paduan and a Veronese reader, mutual friends of Petrarch and Boccaccio, in the letter following the *Griseldis* epistle (*Sen.,* 17. 4).[7] The Paduan interprets the tale as *historia,* and cannot finish reading it for crying; the Veronese reader on the other hand views it as *fabula,* and refuses to be-

lieve that any such figure as Griseldis could have existed due to her almost supernatural patience. However, this second response may hold the key to Petrarch's own understanding of the tale's verisimilitude, as he complains that "esse nonullus, qui quaecumque difficilia eis sint impossibilia omnibus arbitrent, sic mesura sua omnia metietes" ("there are some who consider whatever is difficult for them, impossible for everyone, and they so judge everything by their own measure") (Petri 1544, 606; Bernardo 1992, 670).[8] Petrarch had made a similar comment in relation to Boccaccio's critics in the preface to his translation: "esse hominum genus et insolens et ignavum, qui, quidquid ipsi vel nolunt vel nesciunt vel non possunt, in aliis reprehendunt" ("there is a breed of men who are insolent and lazy, who rebuke in others whatever they themselves do not want, do not know, or are unable to do") (Severs 1942, 290; Bernardo 1992, 655).[9] Furthermore, Petrarch proceeds to offer examples from history in order to qualify the verisimilitude of the tale, which confirms Martellotti's position that in

> accingendosi ad aggiungere questo di Griselda ai tanti esempi di virtù ch'egli ha descritti nelle sue opere storiche, sente il bisogno di considerare la vicenda almeno verosimile, se non vera; e su ciò egli insiste a lungo nelle due lettere che accompagnano la sua traduzione.
>
> preparing to link this tale of Griselda to the manifold examples of virtue that he has described in his historical works, [Petrarch] felt the need to consider the events as being at least possible, if not true; and it is on this point that he insists at length in the two letters which accompany his translation.
>
> (1951, 20)[10]

It may then be argued that Petrarch saw Boccaccio's tale of Griselda's misfortunes as being either a possible history, or a history which had passed into story as part of a gradual, ineluctable osmosis. At no point does he claim that the tale is pure fantasy. Yet this is not to deny its allegorical dimension; as was mentioned earlier in relation to Dante's figurative strategy, *historia* does not preclude *allegoria.* Moreover, as Robert Durling has argued in his discussion of the letter which recounts Petrarch's ascent of Mount Ventoux, "è possibile che lo stesso Petrarca abbia concepito il rapporto [. . .] fra senso letterale e senso allegorico come fra *integumentum* fittizio e contenuto vero" ("it is possible that Petrarch himself had conceived of a relationship [. . .] between the literal sense and the allegorical sense, as between fictional *integumentum* and true content"), although he renders them "volutamente inestricabili" ("deliberately inextricable"; 1977, 305).[11] In the same way that history may become story, so may it become allegory.

With the tale's allegorical potential *in situ* it is possible to return to the primary question of just how allegory is or was translated. In order to broach such a question as it relates to these two *trecento* texts, it becomes necessary to acknowledge and establish two preconditions: the first being Petrarch's own reception of a translative formula, the second being the concatenating principle of metaphor. In relation to the first precondition, we need look no further than the letter to Boccaccio in which Petrarch's redaction is embedded. In this epistle (*Sen.*, 17. 3), which effectively provides the exegetical framework for the translation, Petrarch informs Boccaccio that he adhered to Horace's precept that the careful translator "nec verbum verbo curabis reddere fidus / Interpres [. . .] imo alicubi aut paucis in ipsa narratione mutatis verbis aut additis" ("will not try to render word for word [. . .] [but will be found] changing or adding a few words at some points in the narrative"; Severs 1942, 291; Bernardo 1992, 656). This classical model, which is not only contiguous with Petrarch's humanist thought, but also indicative of the origins of medieval translation as a whole, in fact helps us to approach the second precondition, concerning metaphor—and by extension, allegory.

Rita Copeland has argued that the "commonplaces of translative theory descended to the Middle Ages (and in turn to us) from ancient rhetoric" (Copeland 1987, 44). Petrarch's translative methodology, at least as it stands in relation to his rewriting of Boccaccio's tale, although it appears to be humanistically based around classical *principia,* is in fact representative of an established medieval practice. Crucially, Copeland also posits the complex interrelation of interpretation and metaphor which characterized medieval *translatio,* and which is central to a clear understanding of Petrarch's allegoresis:

> As is well known, the standard rhetorical term for metaphor, *translatio,* also denoted translation in medieval usage. But in Latin, *translatio* as a term for translation long competed with the word *interpretatio,* a term from hermeneutics. [. . .] The word *interpretatio,* however, is also the Latin term equivalent to the Greek *hermēneia,* and it is this idea that informs both uses of *translatio,* as interlingual paraphrase and as metaphor. Both, as linguistic acts of turning meaning, are acts of interpretation.
>
> (1987, 42)

Medieval translation, therefore, is both an act of "interlingual paraphrase" and metaphorical "turning". Moreover, this concept of *translatio* as constituting the point at which periphrasis meets allegoresis is reinforced by the concretizing, disclosing nature of both, as the former "gives verbal expression to that which may be silent in [rather than absent from] the text but which the interpreter has discovered", whilst the latter "proposes itself as co-extensive with the [primary] text, as the realization, at the level of the text's 'proper' (as opposed to 'figurative') reference, of authorial intentionality" (Copeland 1991, 81-4). It is with this dual model of *translatio* in mind that Petrarch would have "vale omni-

bus ad tempus dicto, calamum arripiens, ystoriam ipsam tuam scribere" ("said goodbye to all of [my preoccupations] for a time, and, seizing my pen, set out to write that very story of yours"; Severs 1942, 291; Bernardo 1992, 656).[12]

At this point it perhaps ought to be made clear that I am working from a definition of allegory which is situated at an *intermezzo* between the modern and the medieval. The *OED*'s definition of allegory as signifying either symbolic representation or an extended metaphor places it well within the remit of medieval *translatio,* and also aligns it with the rather generalized use of the term as both Petrarch and Boccaccio would have understood it. Indeed, Petrarch, in a letter to his brother Gherardo, describes his conception of allegory in straightforward terms:

> theologie quidem minime adversa poetica est. Miraris? parum abest quin dicam theologiam poeticam esse de Deo [. . .] Quid vero aliud parabole Salvatoris in Evangelio sonant, nisi sermonem a sensibus alienum sive, ut uno verbo exprimam, alieniloquium, quam allegoriam usitatiori vocabulo nuncupamus? Atqui ex huiusce sermonis genere poetica omnis intexta est [. . .] sensibus intende, qui si veri salubresque sunt, quolibet stilo illos amplectere.
>
> (Rossi and Bosco 1933-1942, II: 301-3)

> In truth, poetry is not in the least contrary to theology. Does this astonish you? I might almost say that theology is the poetry of God. [. . .] Indeed, what else do the parables of the Savior in the Gospes echo if not a discourse different from ordinary meaning or, to express it briefly, figurative speech, which we call allegory in ordinary language? Yet poetry is woven from this kind of discourse [. . .] Concentrate on the meaning; if it is true and wholesome, embrace it regardless of the style.
>
> (Bernardo 1982, 69-70)

There is thus no need to refer to Lewis's famous distinction between allegorical and symbolical functions as he explains it in the *Allegory of Love,* as Petrarch and Boccaccio—like Dante before them—would have incorporated both within the single term.[13] And in any case, as Rosemund Tuve has pointed out, such a "Coleridgean definition of allegory (and symbol), [is] born of nineteenth-century German critical theory, not mediaeval usage" (Tuve 1966, 3).

However, even if the allegory-symbol dichotomy is disallowed by virtue of its anachronism, this is not to say that Petrarchan allegory is entirely amorphous, far from it. Petrarch and Boccaccio both understood a distinction which has become increasingly central to contemporary discussions of the allegorical mode. In order to highlight this distinction I refer to Paul Piehler's discussion of allegory proper in his work *The Visionary Landscape,* in which he states that: "allegory proper pleases by the appropriateness, ingenuity and wit displayed in the translation of the basic material into allegorical form" (1971, 10-11). This conception not only admits the translative element of allegory but also highlights a further bifurcation by default; that is, by avoiding it completely. Piehler's definition, whilst referring to the allegorization which takes place at the moment of the text's composition, may serve just as well as a definition of allegoresis: the exegetical hermeneutics whereby it is disclosed that the basic, ostensibly non-allegorical material possesses an extended metaphorical half-life. The dichotomy which Tuve denied Lewis has thus been succeeded by another:

> The older polarity "symbol-allegory", which valued symbol over allegory, appears to have been replaced with the polarity "allegory-allegoresis," in which allegory stands as the preferred mode. This is at least one implication of the term "imposed allegory" used by Rosemund Tuve to characterize a text like the *Ovide moralisé* as an example of allegoresis, against which the properties of "true" allegory can be defined.
>
> (Copeland and Melville 1991, 161-2)

My own interpretation of allegory is then predicated upon a correlation between the current definition (extended metaphor) and Petrarch's "figurative speech". And whilst this interpretation entails the acknowledgement of the division between allegory and allegoresis—as Petrarch and his peers would have made the distinction between Whitman's categories of allegorical composition and allegorical interpretation—it does not privilege one over the other, but does concede to the conjunction of translation and allegory within allegoresis.

Despite this conceptual or definitive correlation between the contemporary and the medieval, there remains an interpretative dilemma which the modern reader faces when reading Boccaccio's tale. The "basic material", that which Petrarch is not simply translating but transmuting "into allegorical form", is already amenable to charges of allegory proper; and yet if Petrarch's translation is not the most immediately obvious example of medieval allegory, then Boccaccio's original is even less so. However, this dilemma corresponds with Copeland's argument that "allegoresis proposes itself as co-extensive with the text", as it may be claimed that Boccaccio imbues his tale with the potential capacity for allegory, which he expected to be fulfilled by the commentator/reader; although it is unlikely that he would have anticipated Petrarch's translation. Indeed, it would be difficult to reconcile Gualtieri's actions, his "insane cruelty" or "matta bestialità" (Musa and Bondanella 1982, 672; Branca 1985, 892), as Boccaccio describes it, without recourse to such *interpretatio*.[14] It is only through allegory that the tale's action can be justified, otherwise when Boccaccio—or rather Dioneo, who relates the tale on the final day of the ***Decameron***—

declares that "ben ne gli seguisse alla fine" ("good did result from it in the end"; Branca 1985, 892; Musa and Bondanella 1982, 672), we would find it difficult to understand exactly *how*. Through a referral to the tale's mythological origins, however, and an examination of key elements within Boccaccio's original which are amplified by Petrarch's translation, we may reveal the allegorical basis necessary for semantic validation.[15] It may even be argued that the good which results is the fusion of the primary text's hermeneutic *potentia* with the secondary text's allegoresis.

Yet in order to enable evaluation of the Boccaccian text's exegetical afterlife, it is necessary to *redire ad fontem*. M. J. Marcus, drawing on previous studies by Griffith (1931), Cate (1932), and Severs (1942), asserts that the tale of Griselda's hardships and mistreatment constitutes a development of the Cupid and Psyche folktale, in which "an other-world creature marries a mortal and subjects the spouse to a series of tests", but

> the story had to adapt itself, through the process called rationalization, to the needs of more sophisticated, less credulous audiences. Accordingly, the other-world creature becomes a nobleman, and the mortal becomes a peasant [. . .] so that the original spiritual meaning is displaced from the literal to the allegorical level. Allegory thus becomes a way of maintaining the original supernatural purpose of this folk tale while allowing the narratives to rationalize according to the rules of medieval poetics.
>
> (Marcus 1979, 98-99)

Many of the allegorical commonplaces are indeed present in Boccaccio's tale, but implicitly or vestigially so, or rather in that state of orchestrated *potentia* expressed above. It is left to Petrarch's *translatio* to explicate the allegory which underpins its source. Furthermore, certain allegorical mainstays which are absent in Boccaccio's tale are reintroduced by Petrarch's translation. For example, Boccaccio (or Dioneo) begins his tale thus:

> Già è gran tempo, fu tra' marchesi di Sanluzzo il maggior della casa un giovane chiamato Gualtieri.
>
> (Branca 1985, 892)

> A long time ago, there succeeded to the Marquisate of Sanluzzo the firstborn son of the family, a young man named Gualtieri.
>
> (Musa and Bondanella 1982, 672)

Whereas the terseness of Boccaccio's style in the ***Decameron*** allows him to elaborate no further than the name of the place in which the tale is set, Petrarch begins with a lengthy description of the *locus amoenus,* that setting for the allegory which, as Piehler states, "is composed of images taken from the external world and transfigured by spiritual vision" (1971, 13). The actual region of Sanluzzo thus becomes Edenic, a *paradise* *terrestre,* and thereby sets the tone for "the generic confusion of history and fable introduced by Petrarch" (Edwards 2002, 131) discussed above:

> Est ad Ytalie latus occiduum Vesullus ex Apenini iugis mons unus altissimus, qui, vertice nubila superans, liquido sese ingerit etheri, mons suapte nobilis natura, Padi ortu nobilissimus, qui eius e latere fonte lapsus exiguo, orientem contra solem fertur, mirisque mox tumidus incrementis brevi spacio decurso, non tantum maximorum unus amnium sed fluviorum a Virgilio rex dictus, Liguriam gurgite violentus intersecat; dehinc Emiliam atque Flaminiam Veneciamque disterminans multis ad ultimum et ingentibus hostiis in Adriacum mare descendit. [. . .] et civitates et opida habet egregia. Inter cetera, ad radicem Vesulli, terra Saluciarum vicis et castellis satis frequens.

(Severs 1942, 254)

> On the western side of Italy there is a very high mountain of the Apennine chain called Monviso, whose summit, piercing the clouds, rises into the pure ether, a mountain famous for its size, but even more as the source of the Po which, flowing from a tiny spring from its side, moves toward the rising sun, and soon swollen by amazing tributaries over a short downward course, becomes not only one of the greatest streams, but is called "the king of rivers" by Virgil; with its strong current, it divides Liguria, then separates Emilia, Flaminia, and Venetia, and finally empties with many huge mouths into the Adriatic Sea [. . .] And [the area] has a number of outstanding cities and towns; among them, at the foot of Monviso, [is] the land of the Saluzzi teeming with hamlets and castles.

(Bernardo 1992, 656-7)

Petrarch has clearly chosen to translate Boccaccio's tale as allegory. The hyperbolic language he employs, "altissimus", "superans", "nobilissimus", imbues the landscape with a transcendent, aureate vision rhetorically removed from the historical reality of the place, which is nevertheless expressed through the proem's specificity and proper nouns. Petrarch is effectively filling in the gaps left by the Italian version in order to circumscribe his Latin redaction within the generic certainties offered by the allegorical form. Yet it is necessary to clarify exactly what is signified—apart from the tale's ascent from the vernacular of "nostro materno eloquio" ("our mother tongue"; Severs 1942, 290; Bernardo 1992, 655) to the language of the *patria*—by the "impertinent" use of this "heigh style", as Chaucer's Clerk terms it (IV [E] 54, 18 [Benson et al. 1987, 137]).[16]

The proem's allegorical function has been explored in detail by Emilie P. Kadish, who argues that "by tone and content it sets the mood for the story and directs attention to Griselda" (1976, 191). This is achieved through a form of *speculum* familiar to readers of the *Rime sparse.* In Petrarch's sonnet sequence the *Umwelt* of the natural world often reflects the *Innenwelt* of the poet-lover's mind, or rather the interior is projected upon the exterior.[17] However, it must be stressed that this is not what criticism terms the pathetic fallacy, which suggests a form of misreading; Petrarch is deliberately arranging a rhetorical and metaphorical balance. Also in the *Rime sparse* one finds the landscape following the template of Madonna Laura, as not only her body parts but also her name is scattered across it: she becomes the wind (*l'aura*); the dawn and its golden rays which blind the poet (*l'aurora* and *l'ora*); and of course the poeticized, eroticized laurel tree (*lauro*).[18] It is this same form of rhetorical equivalency, I would argue, which one encounters when reading the proem to Petrarch's *Griseldis,* and which Kadish exposits:

> Nature is here presented as sign or symbol of a reality that transcends both the physical world and its viewer [. . .] The physical beauty and perfection of the mountain and river—a vision of natural grandeur—are, as the story unfolds, to be equalled and exceeded by a vision of the spiritual beauty of a human being, a woman outwardly very frail both by nature and by reason of her humble social position. [. . .] The natural phenomena described in the poem represent not geography but poetry, in the sense that Petrarch understood poetry: a veil which tantalizingly conceals truth.

(1976, 193-6)

Interestingly, Kadish compares the unveiling of the proemical scene with the same letter that Durling (1977) refers to in his discussion of Petrarch's allegorical landscape, namely the ascent of Mount Ventoux. Arguing that in the proem Petrarch "introduced a mountain at once as physical and as abstract as Monte Ventoso" (1976, 201), Kadish also describes how the clouds pierced by Mount Monviso "now form a kind of veil to mask from mortal eyes the sacredness of a mysterious union" (1976, 193). In this sense, Petrarch's use of the mountain "qui, vertice nubile superans, liquido sese ingerit etheri" ("whose summit, piercing the clouds, rises into the pure ether") as an allegorical symbol, not only looks back to the account of Mount Ventoux but also to the shadow of the Augustinian mountain in which it was written, and with which it forms an intertextual union that clarifies the typological mystery. That is to say, the constancy of Griseldis, as it is prefigured by the proem's topography, reveals the Augustinian castigation of "the foolishness of men who willingly undertake a task as difficult and as pointless as the ascent of an earthly mountain but shrink before that much more crucial task of raising their souls to God" (Kadish 1976, 200).[19]

However, it is also possible that the Latin text's Edenic, rhetorically elevated and geographically enclosed *mise-en-scène* owes something to the *hortus conclusus* upon which the **Decameron** opens.[20] In the translation's framing epistle, Petrarch informs Boccaccio that he had received the work, but had been "occupatio me maior" ("too busy") to read it carefully, and so "excucurri eum

[. . .] festini viatoris in morem, hinc atque hinc circumspiciens, nec subsistens" ("leafed through it [. . .] like a hurried traveler who looks around from side to side without halting"; Severs 1942, 290; Bernardo 1992, 655). Yet Petrarch also reveals that "curiosius aliquanto quam cetera libri principium finemque perspexi" ("I looked into the beginning and the end somewhat more curiously then the rest"; Severs 1942, 290; Bernardo 1992, 655), as the *artes rhetoricae* dictate that these points are where the most potent matter ought to be located. His reading thus focussed upon the opening description of the plague which causes Boccaccio's company to flee from Florence to a country retreat, and upon the tale of Griselda. The idealized description of the estate to which the *brigata* repair appears on the first day (*giornata*), prior to the first *novella,* and does bear some resemblance to Petrarch's elevated 'Saluciarum':

> Era il detto luogo, sopra una piccola montagnetta, da ogni parte lontano alquanto alle nostre strade, di varii albuscelli e piante tutte di verdi fronde ripiene piacevoli a riguardare [. . .] con pratelli da torno e con giardini maravigliosi e con pozzi d'acque freschissime.
>
> (Branca 1985, 27)

> The place was somewhere on a little mountain, at some distance from the road, full of different kinds of shrubs and plants with rich, green foliage—most pleasant to look at [. . .] it was surrounded by meadows and marvelous gardens, with wells of cool water.
>
> (Musa and Bondanella 1982, 17)

Boccaccio's prospect "piacevoli a riguardare" almost serves as a miniature or *bonsai* version of Petrarch's Latin grandeur. The former's "una piccola montagnetta" is dwarfed in comparison with the latter's "mons unus altissimus", yet the comparison still exists, and Boccaccio's setting, although smaller, is no less abundant, and no less "maravigliosi".[21]

Yet Boccaccio does not omit the "seminal image" from the ***Decameron***'s closing tale—that is, the allegorical figure's "preliminary or invocatory state", whereby the "manifestation of the deity" (Piehler 1971, 15) or the personified virtue is summoned to the *locus amoenus*. Unsurprisingly, Petrarch amplifies the invocation in order to leave the reader in no doubt as to the tale's signification, or rather his individual *interpretatio* of its signification.[22] This becomes evident when we compare the two passages:

> più volte il pregaron che moglie prendesse, acciò che egli senza erede né essi senza signor rimanessero.
>
> (Branca 1985, 893)

> they [Gualtieri's vassals] begged him on many an occasion to take a wife so that he would not be without an heir and they without a master.
>
> (Musa and Bondanella 1982, 673)

unus cui vel auctoritas maior erat vel facundia maiorque cum suo duce familiaritas, "Tua," inquit, "humanitas, optime marchio [. . .] Libera tuos omnes molesta solicitudine, quesumus, ne si quid humanitus tibi forsan accideret, tu sine successore abeas, ipsi sine votivo rectore remaneant."

(Severs 1942, 256-8)

one of them, who was more influential or persuasive and on more familiar terms with his lord, said: "Most excellent Marquis [. . .] Free all your people from a disturbing anxiety, we beg you, lest perchance something, humanly speaking, happen to you: you depart without a successor, and we are left behind without a God-given lord."

(Bernardo 1992, 657-8)

Nevertheless, the invocation of the avatar, or the personification, poses a problem here, in that the roles have been reversed from the Cupid and Psyche model.[23] It is Griselda, and not Gualtieri, or Griseldis and Valterius to use Petrarch's Latinized names, who is summoned into being by the collective, whereas in the original myth it is the male figure (Cupid) who is the divinity, and the female figure (Psyche) who is mortal. Petrarch's emphasis upon the invocation, transfigured into the vassals' request that Valterius take a wife, underlines Griseldis's supernatural essence, yet the trials to which she is put maintain male authority. So what then is to be made of this reversal?

The solution to the conundrum, I would suggest, lies again in the epistolary framework to the tale, in which Petrarch posits the ostensible aetiology of his translation:

> Hanc historiam stilo nunc alio retexere visum fuit, non tam ideo, ut matronas nostri temporis ad imitandam huius uxoris pacienciam, que michi vix imitabilis videtur, quam ut legentes ad imitandam saltem femine constanciam excitarem, ut quod hec viro suo prestitit, hoc prestare Deo nostro audeant [. . .] Abunde ego constantibus viris ascripserim, quisquis is fuerit, qui pro Deo suo sine murmure paciatur quod pro suo mortali coniuge rusticana hec muliercula passa est.
>
> (Severs 1942, 288)

> I decided to retell this story in another language not so much to encourage the married women of our day to imitate this wife's patience, which to me seems hardly imitable, as to encourage the readers to imitate at least this woman's constancy, so that what she maintained toward her husband they may maintain toward our God. [. . .] I would number among the men overflowing with constancy whoever would suffer without murmur for his God what this little peasant woman suffered for her mortal husband.
>
> (Bernardo 1992, 668)

Valterius is allowed to retain a vestige of his divine origins; apparently he submits his wife to random acts of cruelty in a symbolic reflection of Providence as it unfurls as human fate. If this is the case, and, as Mazzotta argues, "Petrarch makes of the ordeals of Griselda and the cruel arbitrariness of Gualtieri the allegory of the soul tested by God" (1986, 123), then it may be argued that Petrarch is aware of the tale's mythological precedent, and has aligned it with a Christian gloss. The original folk-tale, after all, tells of a pagan god (Cupid) testing a representation of the soul (Psyche).

Yet despite Petrarch's Christian exegesis of his translation, the argument which refutes the tale's allegorical interpretation, by extension, denies its Christian tenor:

> However Christian Petrarch was, the subtext of his Griselda is not Christian. [. . .] Griselda's story occurred in Christian time, in the medieval not the ancient past, so that they [Philippe and Chaucer] simply ignored stylistic devices that linked Petrarch's prose to the ancient past and the restraint of Christian allusion that universalized his style. Petrarch thought of Griselda in terms of Pagan martyrs, Philippe, and implicitly Chaucer, thought of Christian martyrs.
>
> (Morse 1985, 80-1)

There is justification for reading Griseldis as a classical paradigm; indeed, Martellotti (1951, 7) had posited a stylistic link between Petrarch's translation and his earlier work, *De viris illustribus*. Morse points to Petrarch's naming of exemplary pagan martyrs in *Sen.,* 17. 4—"Portiam uel Hipsicrateam uel Alcestim & harum similes" ("Porcia, Hypsicratea, or Alcestis and others like them") (Petri 1544, 607; Bernardo 1992, 670)—as evidence of Griseldis's classical *virtù*.[24] Also, Boccaccio's description of Portia, whose "delixet integre atque caste ut, inter ceteras muliebres curas, is esset longe prima atque precipua" ("love for her husband was so complete and so pure that he was by far the first and most important of her wifely concerns") (Zaccaria 1970, 326; Brown 2001, 341), in *De mulieribus claris* certainly resembles Griseldis's declaration to Valterius that "nichil placere enim tibi potest quod michi displiceat. Nichil penitus vel habere cupio vel amittere metuo, nisi te" ("nothing can please you that would displease me; there is nothing whatever that I either hanker to have or fear to lose, except you") (Severs 1942, 270; Bernardo 1992, 661).[25]

Nevertheless, one cannot ignore the Christian elements within and without the tale. For example, before her daughter was taken Griseldis "benedixit ac signum sancta crucis impressit" ("blessed her and marked her with the sign of the holy cross"; Severs 1942, 270; Bernardo 1992, 662), and did the same for her son, whereas we are told that Boccaccio's Griselda only blessed (*benedettala*) her daughter, and no mention is made of how she bade farewell to her son. Petrarch also cites James 1: 13 in his exposition of the tale: "God cannot be tempted with evil, neither tempteth he any man" (Carroll and Prickett 1997, 281), which reinforces the

link between Griseldis's trials and *divina providentia.* Furthermore, in terms of a Christian subtext to apparently pagan matter one need look no further than Petrarch's detailed allegoresis of the first eclogue of his ostensibly Virgilian *Bucolicum Carmen,* which appears in that same letter to his brother in which is found his conception of allegory (*Fam.,* 10. 4). Yet there is no need here to set up a further dichotomy; as Petrarch reconciles *historia* and *fabula* so does he conjoin the classical with the Christian as part of what Charles Trinkaus has termed his "double consciousness" of both "an experienced and a revealed truth" (1979, 52). Petrarch's ability to perceive of antiquity as representing "*the possibility of a cultural alternative*" (Greene 1982, 90) did not prevent him from adhering to Augustine's method of reinforcing the Christian via the classical. Just as it is possible for the tale to be read as both *allegoria* and *exemplum,* so may Griseldis and even Valterius maintain classical virtues without diminishing their portrayal of Christian grace.[26]

However, the quasi-divinity which we are invited to read into Valterius's actions is undermined by Petrarch's conspicuous inclusion of "suo mortali coniuge ("her mortal husband"). I would suggest that Petrarch's Valterius may rather be read as an allegorical figuration of Man, who mistakenly aspires to Godhead in an attempt to justify his cruelty, his "matta bestialità". As Mazzotta posits, just as "God, who in his omniscience governs the design of history, [so] Gualtieri claims that he has manipulated the plot of the story" (1986, 124). This act of mimesis is borne out by the Marquis's asseveration that "ciò che io faceva a antiveduto fine operava" ("what I have done was directed toward a preestablished goal"; Branca 1985, 902; Musa and Bondanella 1982, 680). Alternatively, David Wallace has argued that "Walter is not to be compared to God, but he might be seen as an agent of God; he might as a tyrant, be compared to the Black Death" (1997, 281), yet this is dependent upon our reading Valterius as a tyrant, and upon the *exact* identification of him with Boccaccio's Gualtieri. As Martellotti and McLaughlin have shown, Petrarch's Valterius is an ameliorated Gualtieri; and would a tyrant be spoken to by his vassals as Valterius is by his? Their representative does not only demand that Valterius "collumque [. . .] legiptimo subicias iugo, idque quam primam facias" ("bend your neck to that lawful yoke [. . .] the sooner the better"), but also explains that "tua [. . .] humanitas [. . .] hanc nobis prestat audiciam [. . .] felices nos tali domino iudicemus" ("your kindness gives us the nerve to speak with you man to man [. . .] [and] we consider ourselves happy with such a lord"; Severs 1942, 256; Bernardo 1992, 657). Even if we were to interpret such statements as the platitudes of an oppressed, fearful people, Valterius's response ought to show that this is not the case, and also that he initially acknowledges the Providential source of his privileged position:

"Cogitis", inquit, "me, amici, ad id quod michi in animum nunquam venit; delectabar omnimoda libertate, que in coniugio rara est. Ceterum subiectorum michi voluntatibus me sponte subicio, et prudencie vestre fisus et fidei. [. . .] Quicquid in homine boni est, non ab alio quam a Deo est. Illi ego et status et matrimonij mei sortes, sperans de sua solita pietate, commiserim; ipse michi inveniet quod quieti mee sit expediens ac saluti. Itaque quando vobis ita placitum est, uxorem ducam: id vobis bona fide pollietor, vestrumque desiderium nec frustrabor equidem nec morabor [. . .]".

(Severs 1942, 258)

"Friends, you force me to do something that never entered my mind. I enjoyed total freedom, which is rare in marriage. However, I willingly submit to my subjects' wishes, relying on your forethought and loyalty. [. . .] Whatever good there is in man is from no-one else but God. Therefore, I will entrust to Him the destiny of my state and my marriage, hoping for His usual mercy. He will find for me what is expedient for my peace and well-being. And so, since it has pleased you, I shall take a wife; I promise you this in good faith, and I shall neither disappoint your desire nor delay it".

(Bernardo 1992, 658)

Valterius is then, as Wallace posits, an agent of God, but in accordance with medieval feudalism; his right to rule is God-given, but he must rule according to the wishes, needs and benefit of his subjects. Once he acts against the common good—which he does in his mistreatment of his wife, who "non virum modo sed totam patriam letam fecit" ("made not only her husband but the whole country happy"; Bernardo 1992, 661; Severs 1942, 268)—then he mistakes his divinely ordained position for a form of divinity in itself; a situation which creates the potential for tyranny. If we are to consider Valterius a tyrant at any point, therefore, it should not be at the beginning of the tale but at the point when he is seized by his "strange craving", Boccaccio's "matta bestialità".

Valterius's concern with self-aggrandizement following this point blinds him to the more valid allegorical manifestation of the deity represented by Griseldis's *figura Christi*. Indeed, Marga Cottino-Jones has argued for just such a reading of Boccaccio's original:

> Griselda stands out as a sacrificial character, a *pharmakos*, a *figura Christi* who is called on to offer herself as the innocent victim needed to restore her surrounding community to the harmony and happiness emblematic of a Golden Age condition of existence [. . .] Two central myths are also present and identifiable with the two main protagonists of the story, Gualtieri, the Marquis, signifying the Divine Father Archetype, and Griselda, typifying the Christ archetype.

(1973, 41)

One cannot help but suspect that such a reading of Boccaccio's tale has been tinted by an awareness of Petrarch's allegoresis, and again I doubt that Petrarch, at least, conceived of Valterius as "typifying the Divine Father archetype", but rather saw him as an emblem of human *vanitas,* an inflated sense of what would later be termed the Dignity of Man (*dignitate hominis*).[27] However, Marcus's interpretation of Griselda as representing Christ, and by extension Christian virtue, is reinforced not only by her public disrobing—a key scene in both Boccaccio and Petrarch which I will return to subsequently—but also by her occupation. Boccaccio describes his Griselda as a "guardiana di pecore" (Branca 1985, 896), whilst Petrarch's expanded *descriptio* informs us that "patris senium inextimabili refovens caritate, et pauculas eius oves pascebat, et colo interim digitos atterebat" ("[she] cheered her father's dotage with inestimable love, and would pasture his few sheep, all the while wearying her fingers on the distaff"; Severs 1942, 260; Bernardo 1992, 658). She is therefore a shepherdess, who undergoes physical pain tending her Father's flock; the analogy is waiting to be made, although it is but one allegorical interpretation of any number which Boccaccio's deliberately sparse tale instigates.

For example, aside from the *figura Christi* there is also the obvious allegorical reading of Griseldis as personifying the virtue of Patience, the medieval figure *Patientia,* whilst Valterius manifests Cruelty. This reading is qualified not only by the fact that the "external visible act most strikingly associated with patience is simply unswerving and silent endurance, passive bearing-up under all hardship" (Hanna 1978, 68) but also because in the late-medieval period

> the concept of the "good cause" becomes entwined with discussions of the "degrees" of patience, those levels of performance which separate the merely "good" from the perfect. In this context classical materials are regularly introduced to give a fuller paradigm [. . .] The patient man should recognize such unpleasant events, not as random ill fortune, but as a controlled Providential act. [. . . .] Patience is elevated to a fully heroic self-control, the constant recreation of an ordered inner-kingdom. And this inner citadel may be created only through continuous adjustment of the will to follow reason.

(Hanna 1978, 71-7)

All of these prescriptions resonate within Petrarch's translation. Griseldis's degree of patience rises in accordance with the elevation of her misfortune: first her daughter is taken away, followed by her son (which would have been considered a greater loss as he was the heir apparent), and finally she loses her husband, her love for whom outstrips that of her children, as Valterius is aware. The endurance of these hardships endows Griseldis with perfection, as opposed to mere goodness. Also, the passive acceptance of these "unpleasant events" in accordance with submission to Providence is congruent both with Valterius's misreading of himself as divinity, and his wife's more acute understanding that this misapprehension is itself Providential. Furthermore, her Stoical forbearance or *fortitudo in adversis,* not only allows Griseldis to be compared with "Porcia, Hypsicratea, or Alcestis and others like them", but also contributes to the "double consciousness" which underpins the translation, as "medieval Christianity inherited [concepts of *patientia*] from late classical ethical systems" (Hanna 1978, 69). Finally, the conception of the patient subject's "inner-kingdom" reinforces the allegorical import of the proem in relation to Griseldis's *habitus,* and Wallace's argument that she suffers in order that the body-politic might not, which in fact re-institutes her as a *figura Christi.*[28]

Alternatively, as Robin Kirkpatrick has argued, Griseldis, for Petrarch, may represent a personal ideal:

> It is not difficult to see that for the lover of Laura such a story would be especially valuable. Where Laura in the *Rime Sparse* had been as likely to signify doubt and lost days as much as peace, Griselda was an emblem of the constancy that human beings could achieve.
>
> (1983, 234)

Therefore Griseldis is potentially another Laura, the *donna angelicata* or heavenly lady of Petrarch's vernacular sonnet sequence, but an idealized (that is, submissive) version. Moreover, this *interpretatio* gains credence from Petrarch's transformation of his beloved, haughty *donna* into "la pastorella alpestra e cruda" ("the cruel mountain shepherdess") in *Rime* 52 (Durling 2001, 122-3).

The cumulative effect of these interpretations, however, is an indication of the "metaphorical turning" involved in *translatio.* The constant principle in Petrarch's allegoresis is the exemplification or deification of Griseldis and the dilution of Valterius's Godhead via a more ennobled rhetoric, what Copeland terms "vertical translation" (1987, 48); the process whereby a text passes from a lower to a higher linguistic existence.[29] Also, through Petrarch's *translatio* we are able to witness the multiformity of interpretation, the *polysemia* or variety of potential interpretations created by the artful bareness of Boccaccio's original text. In other words, Petrarch has translated an implicitly allegorical model which is formed around the potential entropy of the hermeneutic process—*id est,* the possibility of a variety of readings, some of which may directly oppose one another—and then reinforced the allegorical elements through *amplificatio,* in order to provide a univocal semantic and moral purpose, which is nevertheless itself on the verge of interpretative fragmentation. Furthermore, this entropic or fragmentary possibility is realized in the fourteenth century by the diverse translations of Petrarch's translation.

But the question of how Petrarch transmutes Boccaccio's tale into an allegory *of* translation is another matter, yet one that is—like the matter of the translated allegory—intertwined with the former's exegetical, epistolary framework. At the core of the transmutation is the disrobing and redressing of the textualized Griselda:

> Quam quidem an mutata veste deformaverim an fortassis ornaverim, tu iudica. Illic enim orta, illuc redit; notus iudex, nota domus, notum iter, ut unum et tu noris et quisquis hec leget: tibi non michi tuarum rationem rerum esse reddendam. Quisquis ex me queret an hec vera sint, hoc est an historiam scripserim an fabulam, respondebo illud Crispi: "Fides penes auctorem (meum scilicet Johannem) sit."
>
> (Severs 1942, 291-2)

> Whether I have deformed it or, perhaps, beautified it by changing its garment, you be the judge—for it all began there, and it goes back there; it knows the judge, the house, the way—so that you and whoever reads this may be clear on one point: that you, not I, must render an account of your works. Whoever asks me whether it is true, that is, whether I have written a history or just a tale, I shall reply with the words of Crispus, "Let the responsibility fall on the author", namely my Giovanni.
>
> (Bernardo 1992, 656)

Petrarch is here aligning the framing epistle with the redaction, focussing as he does upon one of the most crucial points in Boccaccio's tale, the translation of Griselda from peasant to princess:

> Allora Gualtieri, presala per mano, la menò fuori e in presenza di tutta la sua compagnia e d'ogn'altra persona la fece spogliare ignuda: e fattisi quegli vestimenti che fatti aveva fare [. . .] La giovane sposa parve che co' vestimenti insieme l'animo e' costumi mutasse.
>
> (Branca 1985, 895)

> Then Gualtieri took her by the hand, led her outside, and in the presence of his entire company and all others present, he had her stripped naked and the garments he had prepared for her brought forward [. . .] The young bride seemed to have changed her soul and manners along with her clothes.
>
> (Musa and Bondanella, 1982, 675)

That Petrarch understood the importance of this scene—and it may be thus called due to the crowd of onlookers attempting to interpret both Griselda and Gualtieri's choice—is attested to by his careful balance of *translatio* and *amplificatio*:

> nudari eam iussit, et a calce ad verticem novis vestibus indui [. . .] verecunde ac celeriter adimpletum est. Sic horridulam virginem, indutam, laceramque comam recollectam minibus comptamque pro tempore, insignitam gemmis et corona velut subito transformatam.
>
> (Severs 1942, 264)

> he ordered her to be undressed, and to be clothed from head to foot in new garments. This was carried out reverently and swiftly [. . .] Thus this girl was dressed;

her dishevelled hair was combed and braided by their hands, and she was adorned for the occasion with jewels and a crown, and, as it were, suddenly transformed.

(Bernardo 1992, 660)

The most interesting allegorical interpretation Petrarch applies to Boccaccio's text, it may be argued, is what Marcus terms an allegory of form, and Mazzotta "an allegory of order" (1986, 120). That is to say Boccaccio's tale may be read as an autoreflexive illustration of its own creative process and the reader's response to it—and it is vital to remember that day ten of the *Decameron* boasts a number of tales concerning artists of one kind or another. As Marcus argues:

If the people of Saluzzo constitute an internal reading public, offering a critical response to the tale as intimate witnesses of its action, then Gualtieri functions as the figure of the artist who manipulates the tale of Griselda as if from above. [. . .] Gualtieri's particular mimesis of the deity would thus take the form of the *deus artifex* in keeping with his aesthetic function as the author of Griselda's story.

(1979, 106)

This self-referential element of Boccaccio's tale is exactly what Petrarch is referring to in his accompanying epistle when he mentions "this change of dress" ("mutata veste"). Petrarch aligns himself with Valterius the Artist, the mortal author who mimics the actions of the *deus artifex*—which corresponds with his own emphasis upon the Marquis's aspirations to Godhead—and by extension parallels Boccaccio's authorial status via the translative process.[30] Petrarch inherits, or rather adopts, the autoreflexivity Boccaccio imbues his tale with, and so the Tale of Griselda, which allegorically tells the story of itself, becomes the Translation of the Tale of Griselda, which provides the concomitant allegoresis of itself. This interpretation or allegorical *translatio*, however, is dependent upon our reading of Griseldis as text, a reading which has been encapsulated by Carolyn Dinshaw's discussion of the "text as alien woman to be passed between men, stripped and reclothed for the bridal" and "the representation of allegorical reading as a trade, reclothing, marriage and domestication of a woman":

Griselda reads herself as an allegorical image, and thereby "authorizes" us to read her allegorically [. . .] She reads herself as religious symbol, moral allegorical image. We read her, in addition, as an allegorical image of a text, or as providing an homologous relation to a text. [. . .] We read Griselda then, both literally and figuratively.

(Dinshaw 1989, 133-47)

Petrarch strips away what he sees as the tale's ignoble vernacular clothing and redresses it, has it "collected and made smooth [. . .] as it were suddenly transformed" into the more respectable Latin, and after do-

ing so returns his Griseldis, the allegorical personification of her own text, "whence it came", just as Valterius returned her to Giannucolo, before finally reclaiming her. Boccaccio's tale of Griselda is translated into the text of Griselda by Petrarch's reading, and as part of that same metaphorical or allegorical *turning* whereby she is textualized, so does she become the translation of Griselda (into Griseldis), something both fixed—by Petrarch—and in flux—through the redactions of Philippe and Chaucer, amongst others.

In conclusion, Petrarch is practising a form of *translatio*, which through its very definition contains elements of both metaphor and interpretation, and, by extension, allegory and allegoresis; if we are to understand the latter elements as an extension of the former, as Petrarch would have. He reacts to an underlying allegorical tenor or possibility which Boccaccio insists that the reader must delineate for themselves if it is to serve any purpose, moral, spiritual or otherwise: "Ciascuna cosa in se medesima è buona a alcuna cosa, e male adoperata può essere nociva di molte; e così dico delle mie novelle" ("Everything is, in itself, good for some determined goal, but badly used it can cause a good deal of harm; and I say the same of my stories"; Branca 1985, 911; Musa and Bondanella 1982, 686). However, Petrarch, in addition to the Christian *exemplum* he expounds, reinforces the autoreflexive *interpretatio* of the tale as signifying its own process, and in doing so refutes any charges that his allegorical redressing results in its being displaced from itself, or renders it an "aesthetic failure" (Morse 1985, 52). His version of the tale is itself an allegory of the translation, and the translation an allegory of the tale—all in all a true Petrarchan paradox.[31]

Notes

1. For Petrarch's relation to Dante see *Fam.*, 21. 15 (Bernardo 1985, 202-7), and Brownlee (2005). Dante's conception of allegoresis, expounded at length in the famous *Epistle to Can Grande*, is concisely illustrated in *Inferno* 9. 62-3: "O voi ch'avete li 'ntelletti sani, | mirate la dottrina che s'asconde | sotto 'l velame de li versi strani." ("O you who have sound intellects, gaze on the teaching that is hidden beneath the veil of the strange verses.") (Durling 1996, 142-3).

2. See Lewis (1959): "If Dante is right—and he almost certainly is—we must begin the history of allegory with the personifications in classical poetry" (48). Whitman's comments on allegory's progress help to clarify its shift from such personification: "In the very process of challenging the old frameworks allegory necessarily generates new ones. It is simultaneously committed to radical acts of destruction and construction" (1987, 58).

3. I am using allegoresis as referring to the "allegorical *interpretation*" of a given text, which itself

may or may not be an "allegorical *composition*". See Whitman's discussion of the two categories (1987, 3-6).

4. Petrarch's "autoreflexive poetics" signifies his habit of illustrating the process by which his work develops; an illustration apparent within the work itself which advertises its textuality.

5. Philippe de Mézières, for example, who translated the tale into French ca. 1385-9 as part of his *Livre sur la vertu du sacrament du marriage,* evidently saw it as *exemplum,* as Morse rightly argues. Yet this is not to say that Petrarch did also, nor is it to deny the possibility that Philippe also understood an allegorical subtext to the tale—see Brownlee (1992, 867).

6. See also Middleton (1980).

7. See A. S. Cook (1918) and Vittore Branca (1976, 173) for discussion of the readers' possible identities. Martellotti (1951, 31) hints at the suggestion that they may even have been fictionalized: "La contrapposizione dei due episodi ha qualche cosa di stilizzato ed è lecito sospettare che la fantasia del poeta vi abbia qualche parte" ("The juxtaposition of the two [readings] has a stylized quality, and makes the reader suspect that the poet's imagination has played some part in it"). All translations from Martellotti are my own.

8. In the absence of a completed modern edition of the Latin *Seniles*—Elvira Nota's edition has so far covered books I-VII—I have followed the advice given by Bernardo in the introduction to his translation and referred to the early printed edition of Petrarch's *Opera* throughout when citing *Sen.,* 17. 4.

9. Petrarch suggests that all histories become stories eventually in any case: "nescio an res ueras an fictas, quae *iam non* historiae sed fabellae sunt" ("whether the contents are true or fictitious I know not, since they are *no longer* histories but just tales") (Petri 1544, 606; Bernardo 1992, 669 [my italics]). He thus excises the *historia* versus *fabula* debate by expositing the view that they are the same thing in different states of development. Petrarch's piqued response also appears to echo Augustine's *De civitate Dei.* XXI. 5-7 (see Dyson 1998, 1052-60).

10. See also McLaughlin (1988, 43-7).

11. Durling (1977) not only notes that the account of the ascent is a "testo capitale nel corpus petrarchesco" ("key text in the Petrarchan corpus") (304), but also that the problematic of *historia* and *fabula* which it details "non si risolve perfettamente" ("is not completely resolved") (305), indeed cannot be due to this inextricability. All translations from this article are my own.

12. It is interesting to note that Petrarch does not see his translation so much as a rewriting as a writing. Robinson and Rolfe's translation of *Sen.,* XVII. 3 was employed by various critics for a number of years; their translation of this section in particular, I believe, has shaped many readings of Petrarch's attitude towards *translatio*: "I suddenly sent everything flying, and, snatching my pen, attacked this story of yours" (2004, 193).

13. "The allegorist leaves the given—his own passions—to talk of that which is confessedly less real, which is a fiction. The symbolist leaves the given to find that which is more real. To put the difference in another way, for the symbolist it is we who are the allegory [. . .] However the personification [of Amor in *La Vita Nuova*] is to be defended, it is clear that Dante has no thought of pretending that it is more than a personification" (Lewis 1959, 45-7).

14. An echo of Virgil's words to the Pilgrim in *Inferno* 11. 79-83: "'Non ti rimembra di quelle parole | con le quai la tua Etica pertratta | le tre disposizion che 'l ciel non vole, | incontenenza, malizia e la matta | bestialitade?'" ("'Do you not remember the words with which your Ethics treats so fully the three dispositions that Heaven refuses, incontinence, malice, and mad bestiality?'"; Durling 1996, 174-5). This passage, however, as Anna Maria Chiavacci Leonardi argues, poses "a difficult question—and indeed it is one which is still discussed today—because it is linked to an apparent incongruity in [Dante's] text" (1991, 352 [my translation]). See also Durling (1996, 182) for a brief account of the critical debate as to the alleged Aristotelian referent, and Mazzotta (1986, 125-7) for a discussion of Dioneo's use of the phrase. Its import for Boccaccio's tale, I would argue, irrespective of any Aristotelian context, is that it intertextually condemns Gualtieri to hell and thereby introduces a theological dimension to the work, which Petrarch could expand upon. The Petrarchan equivalent to "matta bestialità" is "mirabilis [. . .] cupiditas", "a strange craving" (Severs 1942, 268; Bernardo 1992, 661), which has more of an Augustinian resonance.

15. Our knowledge of these origins, however, does not detract from Petrarch's belief in the tale's verisimilitude, from his belief in its historical possibility.

16. See Middleton (1980, 128-30) and Dinshaw (1989, 149-50) for a discussion of the shift from maternal to paternal language.

17. It is not surprising to find that Petrarch's poetical model was Virgil, whose technique, according to Whitman, "has deeper implications for the devel-

opment of allegory. By passing so smoothly between the outer and inner worlds [*Umwelt* and *Innenwelt*], he tends to blur the distinctions between them. The clear, hard outlines of the Homeric world, which limited the possibilities of allegory, are softening in focus" (1987, 52).

18. For a discussion of *Laura sparse* see Vickers (1982).

19. The Augustinian reference is *Confessions,* X. x (15). See Chadwick (1991, 187), and Durling (1977).

20. The *hortus conclusus* (enclosed garden) is a mainstay of allegorical composition, the most famous being that of the *Roman de la Rose*: "Si vi un vergier grant et lé | Tout clos de haut mur bataillié", "I saugh a gardyn right anoon | Ful long and brood, and everydell | Enclosed was, and walled well". (130-1 [Strubel 1992, 48]; A 136-8 [Benson et al. 1987, 688]).

21. It is also vital to remember that Petrarch, like the majority of his contemporaries, considered Latin superior to Italian. For a discussion of Boccaccio's *giardino* as constituting an allegorical, paradisiacal space see Mazzotta (1986, 107-17).

22. A central tenet of Petrarch's thought is his emphasis upon the centrality of individual experience, what may be termed his belief in a universal subjective. This tenet naturally applies to Petrarchan hermeneutics, as exemplified by his account of the divergent Paduan and Veronese responses.

23. I am using avatar to signify the earthly incarnation or representation of a divinity. Piehler explains how medieval allegory inherits the "seminal image" from pagan (classical) ritual: "In pagan religious rites, the preliminary to the manifestation of the deity was an elaborate process of nomination and evocation, translating him from a mere awareness of a desire for his presence to the full participation in the spiritual state he expresses and manifests. Surprisingly, the structure of such pagan ritual remains, with only slight modification, in the structure of allegory right up to the sixteenth century. Typically, a medieval allegory enacts the transformation of some bare personification or other static and unstructured image into a full visionary *potentia* in its appropriate *locus* [. . .] I have arbitrarily named the *imago* in its preliminary or invocatory state, a 'seminal image'" (1971, 15). Griselda, as *imago,* thus exists in her "preliminary or invocatory state" as the unspecific (or "unstructured") wife-to-be invoked by the vassals' "desire for [her] presence". She is translated into "full participation" when she is revealed in person, and in place (Giannucolo's hut), by Gualt-

ieri; when she involves herself in the management of the Marquis's estate; and extratextually when her exemplary patience provides a spiritual model through Petrarch's exposition of the tale.

24. It may be significant of Petrarch's fusion of *historia* and *fabula* that he names both historical (Porcia [Portia], Hypsicratea) and mythological (Alcestis) figures.

25. In the preface to *De mulieribus* Boccaccio links his work directly to Petrarch's *De viris*: "Scripsere iam dudum non nulli veterum sub comendio de viris illustribus libros; et nostro evo, latiotori tamen volumine et accuratiori stilo, vir insignis et poeta egregious Franciscus Petrarca, preceptor noster, scribit" ("long ago there were a few ancient authors who composed biographies of famous men in the form of compendia, and in our day that renowned man and great poet, my teacher Petrarch, is writing a similar work that will be even fuller and more carefully done"; Zaccaria 1970, 22; Brown 2001, 9).

26. For the possibility of Valterius as *vir illustris* see Martellotti (1951) and McLaughlin (1988, 49-50).

27. See Mazzotta: "By and large, the critical reaction has been such that one is led to infer that modern critics have hardly departed from Petrarch's reading of the story" (1986, 122-3). Yet Petrarch's comparison of Griseldis and Valterius as Human and Divinity is just that, comparative; it is not the definitive moral exegesis.

28. "Griselde's suffering begins when she becomes the object of the tyrannical gaze [. . .] Griselde contains the effects of Walter's gaze, and later of his acts, within herself" (Wallace 1997, 291). I would concur that Petrarch's Griseldis assumes such responsibility, but do not agree that Valterius is a tyrant, at least not initially. Mazzotta (1986, 123-4) and McLaughlin (1988, 56) recede beyond both the allegorical figure and the *figura Christi* by suggesting a possible interpretation of Griselda as Job, which reinforces Petrarch's own allegoresis of her as the soul's response to Providence. Compare "nuda e domo patris egressa, nuda itidem revertar" ("I left my father's home naked; I would return there naked"; Severs 1942, 280; Bernardo 1992, 665) with Job 1: 21: "Naked came I out of my mother's womb, and naked shall I return thither" (Carroll and Prickett 1997, 608).

29. In this case from Italian to Latin. As mentioned above, Petrarch, like the majority of his contemporaries, considered vernacular Italian as being inferior to the universal solidity of Latin. However, Foster (1984, 25-6) has argued that Petrarch did not conceive of vernacular Italian and Latin as be-

ing different languages, but rather inferior and superior modalities of the same language; his translation is not interlingual, therefore, but intralingual and contiguous.

30. See Dinshaw (1989, 133-7) and Wallace (1997, 282-6) for analogies between Petrarch and Valterius.

31. And as Durling admits: "Non m'illudo di poter risolvere i paradossi petrarcheschi, naturalmente: sono volutamente inestricabili" ("I do not delude myself that it is possible to resolve Petrarchan paradoxes, naturally: they are deliberately inextricable") (1977, 305).

References

Benson, Larry D., gen.ed. 1987. *The Riverside Chaucer.* 3rd ed. Oxford: Oxford University Press.

Bernardo, Aldo S., trans. 1982. *Francesco Petrarca: Letters on Familiar Matters: Rerum familiarium libri IX-XVI.* Baltimore: Johns Hopkins University Press.

————. trans. 1992. *Francesco Petrarca: Letters of Old Age: Rerum senilium libri I-XVIII.* Baltimore: Johns Hopkins University Press.

Branca, Vittore. 1976. *Boccaccio: The Man and His Works.* Trans. by Richard Monges. Ed. by Dennis J. McAuliffe. New York: New York University Press.

————. ed. 1985. *Giovanni Boccaccio: Decameron,* 2 vols. Vol. 4 of *Tutte le Opere di Giovanni Boccaccio.,* ed. by Vittore Branca. Milan: Mondadori. (1st publ. 1976)

Brown, Virgina, ed. and trans. 2001. *Giovanni Boccaccio: Famous Women.* The I Tatti Renaissance Library. Harvard: Harvard University Press.

Brownlee, Kevin. 1992. Commentary and Rhetoric of Exemplarity: Griseldis in Petrarch, Philippe de Mézières, and the Estoire. *South Atlantic Quarterly* 91: 865-890.

————. 2005. Power Plays: Petrarch's Genealogical Strategies. *Journal of Medieval and Early Modern Studies* 35: 467-88.

Carroll, Robert, and Stephen Prickett, eds. 1997. *The Bible: Authorized King James Version with Apocrypha.* Oxford: Oxford University Press.

Cate, Wirt Armistead. 1932. The Problem of the Origin of the Griselda Story. *Studies in Philology* 29: 389-405.

Chadwick, Henry, trans. 1991. *Saint Augustine: Confessions.* Oxford: Oxford University Press.

Chiavacci Leonardi, Anna Maria. 1991. *Dante Alighieri: Commedia. Volume 1: Inferno.* Milan: Mondadori.

Cook, Albert Stanburrough. 1918. The First Two Readers of Petrarch's Tale of Griselda. *Modern Philology* 15: 633-643.

Copeland, Rita. 1987. Rhetoric and Vernacular Translation in the Middle Ages. *Studies in the Age of Chaucer* 9: 41-75.

————. 1991. *Rhetoric, Hermeneutics, and Translation in the Middle Ages: Academic traditions and vernacular texts.* Cambridge: Cambridge University Press.

Copeland, Rita and Stephen Melville. 1991. Allegory and Allegoresis: Rhetoric and Hermeneutics. *Exemplaria* 3: 159-87.

Cottino-Jones, Marga. 1973. Fabula vs. Figura: Another Interpretation of the Griselda Story. *Italica* 50: 38-52.

Dinshaw, Carolyn. 1989. *Chaucer's Sexual Poetics.* Madison: University of Wisconsin Press.

Durling, Robert M. 1977. Il Petrarca, il Ventoso, e la possibilità dell'allegoria. *Revue des Études Augustiniennes* 23: 304-23.

————. trans. 1996. *The Divine Comedy of Dante Alighieri. Volume 1: Inferno.* Oxford: Oxford University Press.

————. trans. 2001. *Petrarch's Lyric Poems: The Rime sparse and Other Lyrics.* Cambridge, MA: Harvard University Press. (1st pub. 1976)

Dyson, R. W., ed. and trans. 1992. *Augustine: The City of God against the Pagans.* Cambridge: Cambridge University Press.

Edwards, Robert R. 2002. *Chaucer and Boccaccio: Antiquity and Modernity.* Hampshire: Palgrave.

Foster, Kenelm. 1984. *Petrarch: Poet and Humanist.* Edinburgh: Edinburgh University Press.

Ginsberg, Warren. 1998. Petrarch, Chaucer and the Making of the Clerk. In *The Performance of Middle English Culture: Essays on Chaucer and the Drama in Honor of Martin Stevens.* Ed. by James J. Paxson, Lawrence M. Clopper and Sylvia Tomasch. Woodbridge: Brewer.

Greene, Thomas M. 1980. *The Light in Troy: Imitation and Discovery in Renaissance Poetry.* New Haven: Yale University Press.

Griffith, Dudley David. 1931. *The Origin of the Griselda Story.* Seattle: University of Washington Press.

Hanna, Ralph. 1978. Some Commonplaces of Late Medieval Patience Discussions: An Introduction. In *The Triumph of Patience: Medieval and Renaissance Studies.* Ed. by Gerald J. Schiffhorst. Orlando: University Presses of Florida.

Kadish, Emilie P. 1976. The Proem of Petrarch's Griselda. *Mediaevalia* 2: 189-206.

Kirkpatrick, Robin. 1983. The Griselda Story in Boccaccio, Petrarch and Chaucer. In *Chaucer and the Italian Trecento*. Ed. Piero Boitani. Cambridge: Cambridge University Press.

Lewis, C. S. 1959. *The Allegory of Love*. Oxford: Oxford University Press. (1st pub. 1936)

Marcus, Millicent Joy. 1979. *An Allegory of Form: Literary Self-Consciousness in the Decameron*. Saratoga, CA: Anma Libri.

Martellotti, Guido. 1951. Momenti narrativi del Petrarca. *Studi Petrarcheschi* 4: 7-33.

Mazzotta, Giuseppe. 1986. *The World at Play in Boccaccio's Decameron*. Princeton, NJ: Princeton University Press.

McLaughlin, Martin. 1988. Petrarch's Rewriting of the Decameron X. 10. In *Renaissance and Other Studies: Essays Presented to Peter M. Brown*. Ed. Eileen A. Millar, 42-59. Glasgow: Dept. of Italian, University of Glasgow.

Middleton, Anne. 1980. The Clerk and His Tale: Some Literary Contexts. *Studies in the Age of Chaucer* 2: 121-150

Morse, Charlotte C. 1985. The Exemplary Griselda. *Studies in the Age of Chaucer* 7: 51-86.

Musa, Mark, and Peter Bondanella, trans. 1982. *Giovanni Boccaccio: Decameron*. New York: Norton.

Olson, Glending. 1976. Petrarch's View of the Decameron. *Modern Language Notes* 91: 69-79.

Piehler, Paul. 1971. *The Visionary Landscape: A Study in Medieval Allegory*. London: Arnold.

Robinson, J. H., and Henry Winchester Rolfe. 2004. *Petrarch: The First Modern Scholar and Man of Letters*. Honolulu: University Press of the Pacific. (1st pub. 1898).

Rossi, Vittorio, and Umberto Bosco, eds. 1933-1942. *Francesco Petrarca: Le Familiari*, 4 vols. Florence: Sansoni.

Severs, J. Burke. 1942. *The Literary Relationships of Chaucer's Clerkes Tale*. New Haven: Yale University Press.

Strubel, Armand, ed. 1992. *Guillaume de Lorris and Jean de Meun: Le Roman de la Rose*. Paris: Librairie Generale Francaise.

Vickers, Nancy J. 1982. The Body Re-membered: Petrarchan Lyric and the Strategies of Description. In *Mimesis: From Mirror to Method, Augustine to Descartes*. Eds. John D. Lyons and Stephen G. Nichols Jr. London: University Press of New England.

Tuve, Rosemund. 1966. *Allegorical Imagery: Some Medieval Books and Their Posterity*. Princeton, NJ: Princeton University Press.

Wallace, David. 1997. *Chaucerian Polity: Absolutist Lineages and Associational Forms in England and Italy*. Stanford, CA: Stanford University Press.

Whitman, Jon. 1987. *Allegory: The Dynamics of an Ancient and Medieval Technique*. Oxford: Clarendon Press.

Zaccaria, Vittorio, ed. 1970. *De mulieribus claris*. Vol. 10 of *Tutte le opere di Giovanni Boccaccio,* ed. by Vittore Branca. Milan: Mondadori.

Martin G. Eisner and Marc D. Schachter (essay date 2009)

SOURCE: Eisner, Martin G., and Marc D. Schachter. "*Libido sciendi*: Apuleius, Boccaccio, and the Study of the History of Sexuality." *PMLA*, 124, no. 3 (2009): 817-37.

[*In the following essay, Eisner and Schachter assert that scholars of the history of sexuality could learn much about the relationships among sex, desire, knowledge, and truth by studying Apuleius's novel* The Golden Ass *and Boccaccio's version of the same story in the* Decameron.]

Apuleius's story of a miller (*pistor*) who catches his wife at home with her young paramour and its reimagining by Boccaccio have figured prominently in an ongoing debate about how to study the history of sexuality. Whether the stories have been seen as demonstrating historical change in the relation between sex acts and social identities or used to disrupt the project of scripting a normative history of social types, they have been treated as discrete and essentially stable documents.[1] A woodcut from a 1519 edition of Matteo Maria Boiardo's Italian translation of *The Golden Ass,* however, shows that these tales had been combined long before their juxtaposition by modern scholars, since its conjunction of a hanged man and three figures in bed conflates the two versions. . . .[2] Apuleius's miller does facetiously propose a three-way, but it never takes place. Instead, he locks his wife in another room, rapes her would-be lover, and, after a series of magical machinations instigated by his estranged wife, hangs himself several days later. Boccaccio's version in the **Decameron,** on the other hand, fulfills the promise of the ménage à trois but omits the hanging. The woodcut thus combines these mutually exclusive resolutions to the love triangle and suggests how instead of predictably representing a distinct historical moment Boccaccio's retelling has at times interfered in the reception of its own source.[3]

Other, earlier readers found this image to be troubling, in one instance altering the woodblock from the 1519 edition to illustrate a later translation . . . and in another crossing out the uppermost figure in the bed.[4] While it is impossible to determine if these material witnesses from the past attest to objections about the sexual content of the picture or about the way it does not correspond to its textual source, they do record the practices of particularly active readers. The translation illustrated by the altered woodblock adds the further complication of omitting the rape scene altogether.[5]

Some modern scholars have similarly adapted these stories to fit their critical agendas in ways that foreclose the textual and sexual possibilities that this essay aims to explore. Whereas David Halperin acknowledges downplaying the literary sophistication of *The Golden Ass* and the **Decameron** because "the point [he] wish[es] to make is a historical one" (38), this article not only emphasizes how a literary work "increases the difficulty of identifying normative discourse" (Freccero 46) but also, taking up Michel Foucault's exhortation to explore the archives, addresses textual history. Going beyond the artificially stabilized modern critical edition, we draw on paratextual materials and manuscript variants to explore how attention to the variability of these documents could complicate the questions of historical identity and temporality that are central to studying the history of sexuality.

At the same time, this essay contributes to the discussion of Foucault's place in such a history, which Halperin inaugurated and the other participants in the debate extended, by drawing on Foucault's underappreciated reflections in the second and third volumes of his *History of Sexuality*. If according to the preface to volume 2 his original project had been an inquiry into "how individuals were led to practice, on themselves and on others, a hermeneutics of desire, a hermeneutics of which their sexual behavior was doubtless the occasion, but certainly not the exclusive domain" (*Use* 5), in the second and third volumes Foucault turned to antiquity and focused on a new question: before human beings became subjects of sexuality, "[w]hat were the games of truth by which [they] came to see themselves as desiring individuals?" (7). To respond in part to Foucault's question, the analyses of Apuleius and Boccaccio that follow investigate how both authors use sex to eroticize interpretation and generate epistemological uncertainty. In the light of Foucault's extension of his project to include a genealogy of the desiring subject reaching back to antiquity, we ask how Apuleius's and Boccaccio's literary and philosophical investigations into desire, interpretation, and epistemology (themselves, of course, historical) might contribute to a history of sexuality not tied to a history of social types, identities, or acts. The first section explores how *The Golden Ass* stages interpretive conundrums that seem to anticipate Foucault's concerns with games of truth and the production of knowledge, thereby rendering problematic attempts to access contemporary social norms through the novel.

The second turns to the **Decameron,** focusing on a textual crux to show how scholars have sought to fix the meaning of the text precisely where Boccaccio rendered it ambiguous and then raising larger questions about the roles of desire, sexuality, and interpretation in the novella collection.

HERMENEUTIC DESIRE IN *THE GOLDEN ASS*

The 1519 Italian image mentioned above appears to have influenced a woodcut illustrating the miller's tale made for a 1553 French translation of *The Golden Ass. . . .* On the left hangs the miller, now with an audience. On the right, where the earlier Italian illustration depicts a threesome, the French version offers a different scene *à trois* that actually does take place in the text: Lucius revealing to the miller the presence of a boy hidden under a tub. This woodcut puts into relief a significant detail that has been largely overlooked by participants in the history-of-sexuality debate—for most of the novel, its narrator is an ass.[6] While Mikhail Bakhtin invokes this scene in Apuleius's novel when he notes in "Forms of Time and Chronotope in the Novel" that "the position of an ass is a particularly convenient one for observing the secrets of everyday life" (122), the once-human Lucius is no mere observer, as the woodcut suggests. His insatiable curiosity (*curiositas*) as a biped is, if anything, even less restrained when he is a quadruped.[7] Indeed, Lucius's desire for knowledge is one of the chief motivating factors in the novel and one of its thematic preoccupations, and this desire is frequently linked to sex—for example, his transformation into an ass occurs after he seduces the servant Photis to gain access to the secrets of the witch Pamphile. In a now classic narratological interpretation of the novel, John Winkler argues that *The Golden Ass* shows how as an interpreter's "location shifts . . . conviction vanishes" (320). Winkler maintains that shifts in location invite the reader to engage in the "hermeneutic entertainment" to be found in unraveling the novel's interpretive enigmas (11). Drawing on Winkler's insight, we delineate in the following pages how *The Golden Ass* provokes, frustrates, and sometimes parodies *libido sciendi,* or the desire to know, both through its narration of hermeneutic desire in the novel's characters and through the implantation of the will to know in its readers. In other words, Apuleius conspicuously portrays—and repeatedly interpellates the reader within—ludic "games of truth," games that should give pause to the modern historian of sexuality eager to find the truth of sex in the novel.[8]

Epistemological uncertainty and hermeneutic desire are ostentatiously highlighted in a series of nested adultery tales Lucius recounts and refers to collectively as a "fabula" (2: 150-51; bk. 9, sec. 14).[9] In this fabula, the story of the miller and his amorous wife frames two other accounts of adulterous women and is itself framed by passages that impeach the reliability of its narrator. In a rare retrospective moment, just before introducing the miller and his wife, the extradiegetic, "authorial" Lucius proclaims his gratitude to the ass he was because "etsi minus prudentem, multiscium reddidit" 'he made me better informed, if less sensible' (2: 150-51; bk. 9, secs. 13-14 [trans. modified]).[10] At the conclusion to the fabula, the less *prudens* Lucius again explicitly calls attention to the question of his reliability. While recounting the miller's supernatural death, Lucius observes that the "lector scrupulosus" 'careful reader' may wonder how he could have known the details of the hanging (2: 152-53; bk. 9, sec. 30). By indicting his perspicacity just before the fabula and questioning his trustworthiness at its end, the embedded author incites the desire to know the truth about the details recounted in the fabula while provoking uncertainty about them. With its emphasis on the ass's subjectivity and questionable reliability as a narrator, the fabula's frame suggests that the tales are a difficult place to mine for evidence of social norms.

Lucius's *libido sciendi* also figures prominently near the outset of the miller's story when the ass overhears that the miller's wife has taken a young lover. Overcome with curiosity about this youth, he "cuius et faciem videre cupieba[t] ex summo studio" 'longed with the greatest zeal to see his face' (2: 152-53; bk. 9, sec. 15 [trans. modified]).[11] This longing evokes Psyche's "sacrilega curiositate" 'sacrilegious curiosity' to see her mysterious husband in the tale of Cupid and Psyche (1: 260-61; bk. 5, sec. 6), which Lucius has recently overheard. But whereas Psyche gets to see Cupid, if with near catastrophic consequences, Lucius does not manage to quench his ocular desire. Instead, he settles for another kind of satisfaction, one offered by his asinine body: "isto tamen vel unico solacio aerumnabilis deformitatis meae recreabar, quod auribus grandissimis praeditus cuncta longule etiam" 'I was at least uplifted by this one consolation in my painful deformity: namely, with my enormous ears I could hear everything very easily, even at considerable distance' (2: 152-55; bk. 9, sec. 15 [trans. modified]). This advantage of his new form recalls Lucius's earlier gratitude for his augmented genitalia (1: 170-71; bk. 3, sec. 24). The parallel between his enlarged phallus and enormous ears underscores the link between sex and listening to stories, or sexual desire and the desire for narrative, that Apuleius develops in the novel (Shumate 223; DeFilippo 490-91). The discussion of Lucius's ears at the beginning of his fabula also resonates with the invocation of the reading (or listening) audience's own ears in the novel's prologue (1: 2-3; bk. 1, sec. 1), suggesting retroactively how Lucius/Apuleius seeks to interpellate his audience into the novel's erotic economy from the outset.[12]

Because of his aural endowment, Lucius is able to overhear the conversation between the miller's wife and an old woman encouraging her to find a new lover. The old woman sings the praise of one Philesitherus, who, unlike the wife's current lover, is "adulescens et formosus et liberalis et strenuus" 'young, handsome, engaging, and vigorous' (2: 154-55; bk. 9, sec. 16), and then demonstrates his desirability by recounting a long tale about his clever cuckolding of a certain Barbarus. The wife's interest is piqued, and the old woman agrees to deliver Philesitherus to her. What appears, however, is not a bold lover but a mere youth, "adhuc lubrico genarum splendore conspicuus, adhuc adulteros ipse delectans" 'still conspicuous for the smooth brightness of his cheeks, still attracting male lovers himself' (2: 168-69; bk. 9, sec. 22). As Jonathan Walters and Halperin both note, this passage emphasizes the boy's youth and desirability to men. We would add that the discrepancy between what the old woman promises and the youth who appears invites the reader's scrutiny and reveals the wife's friend to be an unreliable narrator—or a sly one. Given that she chastises the wife for having taken a lover without her advice (2: 154-55; bk. 9, sec. 16), the old woman may misrepresent the boy in order to get revenge, or perhaps she is just doing a good job selling her ware. In either case, she skillfully incites the wife's desire both for gossip about Philesitherus's exploits during an affair with one of her classmates and for Philesitherus himself (2: 154-67; bk. 9, secs. 16-22). Lucius is not the only character ruled by an unmanageable desire for sex and knowledge. When the miller returns home unexpectedly from an interrupted dinner with his friend the fuller, the wife's desire for gossip is once again ignited, even displacing her fear that Philesitherus, hiding under a tub, might be discovered. "[N]oscendae rei cupiens" 'Desiring to know about the affair' (2: 170-71; bk. 9, sec. 23 [trans. modified]), she cajoles her husband into recounting the details of the *cena interrupta*, instead of trying to find a way to help the boy escape.

Lucius's own subjectivity once more comes to the fore when he expresses his desire to intervene in the scene he has been observing: "deliberabam si quo modo possem detectis ac revelatis fraudibus auxilium meo perhibere domino, illumque, qui ad instar testudinis alveum succubabat, depulso tegmine cunctis palam facere" 'I kept thinking . . . if there were any way I could help my master by uncovering and exposing her deceits, and dislodge the cover from that man who was lying under the vat like a tortoise, revealing him for all to see' (2: 174-75; bk. 9, sec. 26). The occasion of his nightly watering provides the willful and vindictive Lucius an opportunity to step on Philesitherus's fingers, as illustrated in the French woodcut. The boy then flings off the tub, and, as Lucius puts it, "conspectui profano redditus scaenam propudiosae mulieris patefecit" 'his appearance disclosed to the eyes of the uninstructed world the secret life of the shameless hussy' (2: 174-75; bk. 9, secs. 26-27). That Lucius should represent himself as a voice of prudence and moral comportment who reveals mysteries to the world, despite being a horny ass constantly ruled by his desires, points both to his hypocrisy and to the text's ludic relation to revelation. While Bakhtin emphasizes that Lucius is the forerunner of the servants and other "third man" figures in later novels who are "the most privileged witnesses to private life" (124-25), the ass turns out to be far from an ideal witness, not only partisan but participatory.

Lucius's partisan nature is curious. Why should Lucius have empathy for the miller rather than for the boy who also finds himself trapped in animal form, as a "tortoise"? Indeed, there are numerous parallels between the boy and the ass that suggest Philesitherus is a more natural object of identification. Before his transformation, Lucius was young and beautiful like Philesitherus.[13] In books 7 and 8, the text prefigures on Lucius's body the boy's implied anal rape, and the ass will later have sex with a married woman.[14] Nonetheless, instead of generating insight, self-knowledge, or compassion, Lucius's meddlesome *curiositas* leads him to take pleasure in the exercise of authority and in the execution of the law as long as he is not the one being punished. In this regard, he is like his own representation of the miller's wife, who eagerly imagines the punishment her adulterous neighbor merits despite the fact that she is guilty of the same crime. Rather than offer unmediated access to social norms, then, the details of Lucius's narration index the ass's subjectivity, through which these norms have been filtered. Determining the complex relation of Lucius's narration to the social and the normative would thus require careful adjudication.[15]

Lucius's representation of the miller and of the miller's self-presentation poses a similar challenge. After the ass has revealed Philesitherus, the miller says to the boy, "Nihil triste de me tibi, fili, metuas. Non sum barbarus, nec agresti morum squalore praeditus" 'You have nothing to fear from me, son. I am not barbarous, and I do not share the boorishness of rustic morality' (2: 176-77; bk. 9, sec. 27). The word "barbarus" evokes the previous story of Barbarus and can be read as an authorial wink at the reader or as another textual conundrum, since nothing in the fabula suggests that the miller knows of the event, if it ever took place. (We only have the old woman's word for it.) In any case, the miller does contrast his character with that of the fuller, another cuckold, whose story he recounts, to suggest that his own reaction will be urbane and moderate. The miller goes on to say that, rather than pursue the boy on capital charges for adultery,

> communi dividundo formula dimicabo, ut sine ulla controversia vel dissensione tribus nobis in uno conveniat lectulo. Nam et ipse semper cum mea coniuge tam con-

corditer vixi ut ex secta prudentium eadem nobis ambobus placerent.

> I will institute a suit to share common assets, contending that without controversy or dissension we three should enter into contract in the matter of one bed. You see, I have always lived in such harmony with my spouse that, in accordance with the teachings of the wise, we both have the same tastes.

(2: 176-77; bk. 9, sec. 27)

With his legalistic sophistry and invocation of "the teachings of the wise," the miller continues to imply that he will respond with equanimity and reason. Yet embedded in his speech lurks a series of obscene allusions that offer a different insight into his personality. In his best-selling and often-reprinted 1500 commentary on the novel, Philippus Beroaldus noted of *dividundo* ("to share or divide"), used by the miller to describe the sharing of the boy, that "potest videri subesse huic verbo obscenus intellectus. . . . ad pedicones refertur: & puerorum concubitores: quorum in libidine propostera & infanda nates quasi dividuntur" 'an obscene meaning can be seen under this word. . . . It refers to buggers and to men who sleep with boys, boys whose buttocks are, as it were, spread with preposterous and unspeakable desire' (209r [our trans.]).[16] Moreover, the miller himself perverts the implications of the law he invokes when he locks his wife in a separate room and leads "ad torum nolentem puerum" 'the unwilling boy to bed' (2: 178; bk. 9, sec. 28 [our trans.]) before enjoying "gratissima corruptarum nuptiarum vindicata" 'the most gratifying revenge for his ruined marriage' (2: 178-79; bk. 9, sec. 28).

According to Walters and Halperin, this entire incident tells us nothing unusual about the character of the miller. Unlike the comportment of Pietro, the miller's counterpart in the **Decameron,** the sweet revenge the miller will take on the boy is of no particular significance, something any "normal" Greco-Roman man might do. "Apuleius's text makes no incriminating association between the [miller's] sexual enjoyment of the adulterous youth and the [miller's] character, masculinity, or sexual disposition," remarks Halperin (41). The main lineaments of this argument conform to what has come to be the dominant view of ancient Roman masculinity and "sexuality" (Williams; Gleason). Attention to other elements in the representation of the miller, less determined by the horizon of modern sexuality, may, however, offer a more incriminating portrait. The miller's actions are hardly those of a man who was, in Lucius's words, "apprime modestus" 'extremely temperate' (2: 150-51; bk. 9, sec. 14). The editors of the Groningen Commentaries on Apuleius remind us that taking pleasure in revenge could be considered the comportment of "indocti" 'fools' (Hijmans et al. 244).[17] Moreover, when the miller implicitly criticizes the fuller by claiming not to be "barbarous" and not to have "rustic morality," he may show himself to be not so much an upstanding and cultured, if cruel, individual as a hypocrite whose self-importance is far from modest (another meaning of *modestus*).[18]

The complex characterization of the miller exemplifies what the fabula as a whole suggests about Lucius's untrustworthiness as a witness and relates to *The Golden Ass*'s overarching concern with epistemic uncertainty. Perhaps more provocative than this constant problematization of perspective is the novel's related meditation on the desire for knowledge. Instead of looking for representative subjects of sex and gender in *The Golden Ass,* an approach that contravenes the novel's ostentatious production of epistemic uncertainty, how might historians of sexuality use the novel's inquiry into *libido sciendi* to historicize the relations among sex, desire, knowledge, and truth—in a project similar to that proposed by Foucault at the outset of the second volume of his *History of Sexuality*—and perhaps reflect on their own desire to make meaning out of them? After all, the novel begins by announcing its narrator's desire to seduce the reader: "ego . . . auresque tuas benivolas lepido susurro permulceam" 'I would like . . . to caress your ears into approval with a pretty whisper' (1: 2-3; bk. 1, sec. 1).

Historians of sexuality could, for example, attend to the responses the novel has elicited from its readers. (Other possibilities will be suggested in the conclusion.) Take the Apuleian husband's evocative but unfulfilled proposal of "tribus nobis in uno . . . lectulo" 'the three of us in one . . . bed,' which has excited many readers' desires to know what might have happened in that bed. In his commentary on *The Golden Ass,* for example, Beroaldus, who knew Boccaccio's version of the story, lingers on the husband's bogus suggestion, writing of the expression "partario tractabo" 'I will split' (2: 176; bk. 9, sec. 27 [our trans.]): "ut scilicet dimidius sit uxoris ex membris anterioribus / dimidius sit ipsius ex membris posterioribus. & ita medius inter virum uxoremque discurrens hinc stupratus erit inde stuprator. Hinc paticus concubinus: inde masculus subactor" 'obviously so that the front parts would be for the wife and the rear parts for him. And in this way, rushing back and forth between the man and the wife, he would be both "screwee" and "screwer." Here a passive concubine, there a studly bugger' (209r [our trans.]). Later in the sixteenth century, Giovanni Morlini will rewrite the scene in yet more pornographic detail, in part by incorporating elements of Beroaldus's explication of it as well as phrases drawn from Lucius's sexual escapades with Photis in book 3.[19] Boccaccio, too, is fascinated by the configuration of desire in that bed, but he is less interested in the mechanics of the suggested or actual intercourse—which, as we shall see, also draw the atten-

tion of contemporary scholars—than in the epistemological questions they raise, which the next section of this essay explores.

AMBIGUOUS REVISION AND SUSPENDED
JUDGMENT IN THE *DECAMERON*, DAY 5,
NOVELLA 10

In comparing Apuleius's story of the miller and the ***Decameron,*** day 5, novella 10, Halperin suggests that "[i]n order to update Apuleius's plot it seems to have been necessary for Boccaccio to posit a sodomitical disposition or inclination on the husband's part; he seems to have had no other way of motivating the scandalously witty conclusion of the tale he had inherited from Apuleius" (41). We will suggest below that Boccaccio's representation of Pietro, the husband in his version of the tale, was not so much constrained by the medieval Florentine's limited options for making sense of or "modernizing" his Apuleian source as it was motivated by thematic and narratological concerns germane to the ***Decameron.*** Furthermore, as the woodcut . . . shows, Apuleius's ending, concluding as it does with a hanging, is anything but "scandalously witty." Halperin's conflation of the two endings demonstrates once again how the risqué conclusion of Boccaccio's version has influenced the reception and reading of its Apuleian source.[20]

While the idea that Boccaccio was simply updating Apuleius's story may be convenient for an analysis that aims to track historical change through literary adaptations, it overlooks Boccaccio's key role not only in the reception of this Apuleian story but also in the recovery and redeployment of Apuleius's works more generally; it overlooks, as well, the centrality of Apuleius to Boccaccio's own literary and philosophical projects.[21] In the *Genealogie deorum gentilium,* for example, Boccaccio uses the telling of the story of Cupid and Psyche in *The Golden Ass* to show that "[f]abulis laborantibus sub pondere adversantis fortune non nunquam solamen inpensum est" 'fiction has, in some cases, sufficed to lift the oppressive weight of adversity and furnish consolation' (2: 1416; bk. 14, ch. 9, sec. 13 [Boccaccio 50]) as part of his contention that "composuisse fabulas apparet utile potius quam damnosum" 'it is rather more useful than damnable to compose stories' (*Genealogie* 2: 1410; bk. 14, ch. 9 [our trans.]).[22] This mention of Apuleius not only shows his prominent place in Boccaccio's reflection on the functions of literature but also justifies in part the *Decameron* itself, which also has a consolatory purpose, announced in the first line of its proem (1: 5; our trans.): "Umana cosa è l'aver compassione degli afflitti" 'it is a human trait to have compassion for the afflicted' and reinforced in its **"Conclusione dell'Autore,"** where the "author" writes that the collection is intended "a consolazion" 'for the consolation' of ladies (2: 1254; our trans.).[23] *The Golden*

65

Ass is thus far more than a source of stories for Boccaccio to update in the *Decameron.*

An investigation of Boccaccio's own transcription of *The Golden Ass,* furthermore, reveals an intriguing variant that appears to show Boccaccio revising Apuleius from within. Where most early manuscripts, including the one that Boccaccio first read, describe the miller leading the boy to bed with the same words found in modern editions of the text, "deducebat ad torum nolentem puerum" 'he led the unwilling boy to bed,' Boccaccio's autograph copy . . . has "volentem" 'willing' in place of "nolentem" 'unwilling' (*Opera,* c. 1350, folio 51v). It is impossible to know whether Boccaccio is incorporating a reading from a now lost text, misreading his exemplar, or consciously (or unconsciously) rewriting it when he has the boy follow the miller willingly. In any case, the variant does insinuate into the original the much less vindictive spirit of Boccaccio's retelling of the story also found in illustrations of *The Golden Ass* that depict the Boccaccian ménage à trois that does not take place in Apuleius's text. Although this variant is unacknowledged in modern critical editions of the work, it invites a reconsideration of the ambiguous representation of the boy's experiences in Boccaccio's version of the story, a representation that has been central to the discussions of the tale by historians of sexuality.

In his essay, Halperin quotes the passage (in the translation by Charles Singleton) and interprets it in a manner similar to Beroaldus's imagining of the proposed threesome in Apuleius:

> [T]he husband in Boccaccio plays a sexually insertive role in intercourse with the wife's lover. That, after all, is the point of the story's punchline: "On the following morning the youth was escorted back to the public square not altogether certain which he had the more been that night, wife or husband"—meaning, obviously, *wife to Pietro or husband to Pietro's wife.*
>
> (40-41)

Jonathan Goldberg and Madhavi Menon question Halperin's interpretation and contest his claim to know exactly what the boy did in the bed. In their view, Halperin's argument that "the husband in Boccaccio plays a sexually insertive role in intercourse with his wife's lover" preserves what they call "normative distinctions" that they do not find in Boccaccio's Italian (1614). For Goldberg and Menon, G. H. McWilliam's translation, in which the boy is "not exactly certain with which of the pair he had spent the greater part of the night" (440), is preferable because it does not specify what any of the participants were doing and focuses instead on the indeterminate relations between the participants. This concern with relationality rather than roles or identities is consonant with Goldberg and Menon's resistance to arguments that depend on ossified and impoverished sexual categories such as inserter and insertee.[24]

While translations can certainly reflect ideological biases, the difference between Halperin's interpretation and Goldberg and Menon's reading, reflected in their choice of translation, also points to a particularly vexed moment in the original text.[25] Vittore Branca's standard critical edition, which Goldberg and Menon cite, is based on Boccaccio's autograph of the *Decameron,* now Hamilton 90 in Berlin's Staatsbibliothek. Boccaccio made this version late in his life (1370-72), when, according to Branca, copies of an earlier authorized version, written between 1349 and 1352, were already in circulation ("Variazioni" 5).[26] Branca identifies an authoritative witness of this earlier redaction in Italian 482, a manuscript housed at the Bibliothèque Nationale de France in Paris. Boccaccio scholars have not yet explored the hermeneutic potential of these variants, in part because the idea that they are in fact authorial variants is a quite recent one.[27] Most of the changes between the two versions are minor, but this passage shows an unusually elaborate revision.

In the first authorial version, the text reads "in su la piazza fu il giovane da Pietro accompagnato" 'the youth was accompanied into the piazza by Pietro' (Italian 482, folio 122ra; our trans.). Returning to the passage twenty years later, Boccaccio replaces Pietro's role as companion to the boy on his walk to the piazza with a phrase describing the boy's uncertainty, and in so doing has caused confusion among interpreters: "in su la piaça fu il giovane non assai certo qual piu stato si fosse la nocte o moglie o marito accompagniato" 'the youth was accompanied into the piazza, not very certain which he had been more that night, either wife or husband' (Hamilton 90, folio 72va; our trans.).[28] Our translation follows Branca's punctuation of the phrase in his critical edition, where "non assai certo qual più stato si fosse la notte o moglie o marito" appears between commas, which seems the most logical way to parse the sentence (2: 704; day 5, novella 10, sec. 63).[29] This reading suggests that Boccaccio intended the boy's uncertainty to involve whether he had been more husband or wife that night, but the sense of the passage remains confusing. The placement of "accompagnato," its distance from its complement "fu," the absence of punctuation in the authoritative holograph, and the potential association of "accompagnato" with what happens in the bed and thus with the boy's uncertainty all invite a reader's hesitation about the meaning of the passage and provoke the interpretation offered by McWilliam and shared by Goldberg and Menon.[30] It is a moment when, as Beroaldus writes in another connection in his commentary on Apuleius, "readers are not only readers but truly are made into commentators" (qtd. in Doody 206). While Goldberg and Menon's deconstructive emphasis on indeterminacy generally supports their critique of thinking that is dependent on stabilized categories and fixed binaries, in this case the critics fix the sense of the text to emphasize a meaning conducive to their argument. There may be a preferred interpretation that is more likely to convey authorial intent, but the complex syntax puts the reader in the boy's position, a perspective not unlike that of Apuleius's reader, eager to figure out what is going on even as the phrasing frustrates any certain satisfaction of that desire.

While the only critic to comment on Boccaccio's revision of this passage before this essay uses it as an index of Boccaccio's knowledge of Apuleius's text and contends that it shows "un'adesione maggiore alla versione apuleiana" 'a greater adherence to the Apuleian version' (Branca, "Variazioni" 204; our trans.), the later variant's focus on the boy's confusion about his nocturnal adventures actually emphasizes Boccaccio's distance from his source, where the boy is raped and beaten by the husband.[31] The epistemological uncertainty created by the variant reinforces the refusal to judge that is characteristic of both versions of Boccaccio's conclusion to the story, where the boy is introduced into a traditional place of public reckoning, the local piazza, but no judgment occurs.[32] Similarly, when Pietro's wife suggests that her husband wishes a heavenly fire would engulf all womankind, the image is "marked by the (deadly serious) play on the Biblical—but also literal—punishment for sodomy" (Freccero 46), but Boccaccio never makes Pietro its victim. Whereas Halperin contends that Pietro is "more than the juridical subject of a sodomitical act" (41), it is important to emphasize that Boccaccio never makes him a juridical subject at all.

This strategic suspension of judgment can already be found in the narrator Dioneo's advice to his female audience in the tale's introduction, where he provides an interpretive guide to the story as a whole:

> E voi, ascoltandola, quello ne fate che usate siete di fare quando ne' giardini entrate, che, distesa la dilicata mano, cogliete le rose e lasciate le spine stare: il che farete lasciando il cattivo uomo con la mala ventura stare con la sua disonestà, e liete riderete degli amorosi inganni della sua donna, compassione avendo all'altrui sciagure dove bisogna.
>
> (2: 693; day 5, novella 10, sec. 5)

> As you listen, do as you would when you enter a garden, and stretch forth your tender hands to pluck the roses, leaving the thorns where they are. This you will succeed in doing if you leave the knavish husband to his ill deserts and his iniquities, whilst you laugh gaily at the amorous intrigues of his wife, pausing where occasion warrants to commiserate with the woes of her lover.
>
> (McWilliam 432-33)

The narrator's remarks seem to encourage his female audience to pursue a binary reading strategy, but Dioneo acknowledges the limits of this strategy in the next sentence, where he instructs readers how to respond to the three characters of the story. They are to leave the

husband to an uncertain (but certainly not positive) fate, laugh at the woman's tricks, and have "compassione" for the boy's sufferings—an instruction that recalls the work's inaugural expression: "umana cosa è aver compassione degli afflitti" 'it is a human trait to have compassion for the afflicted.' Although the binary image of the rose does not quite fit the story it prefaces, it does integrate the erotic and the hermeneutic in a suggestive manner that is familiar from the *Roman de la rose* and central to the erotics of knowledge, or *libido sciendi*. As the rest of the story shows, Dioneo's point is to encourage his female audience's pursuit of sexual pleasure, a pursuit reinforced by the incitation to hermeneutic desire he includes in his introductory remarks.[33]

This concern with female desire may explain why Dioneo often tells stories about men who cannot or will not accommodate women's desires (1: 303-14; day 2, novella 10; 1: 570-83; day 4, novella 10): these men represent obstacles to the satisfaction of such desires and allow him to valorize those desires. Pietro is depicted as he is not because his specific sodomitical disposition was the only way for Boccaccio to update the character of the *pistor* from *The Golden Ass*—as Halperin contends in the passage cited at the outset of our discussion of Boccaccio—but rather because characters like Pietro are instruments in Dioneo's larger program of seduction.[34] "Unlike Freud," as Teodolinda Barolini quips, "Dioneo knows what women want"—to be satisfied sexually (288). For Dioneo, women's desires are of paramount interest, while the sexuality of boy and husband are not really problematic. Dioneo's use of the figure of the sodomite to advance a particular view about the "relations of symmetry and reciprocity between husband and wife" (Foucault, *Use* 253) might be located in the shift Foucault identifies from the problem of boys to the problem of women in his brief discussions of the medieval world at the end of the second and third volumes of *The History of Sexuality*.

Boccaccio's most significant structural change to the story reinforces this reorientation of the story toward a concern with women. Where Apuleius has the old lady tell a (potentially fictitious) story extolling Philesitherus's prowess, in Boccaccio she offers a long speech on sexual difference and female desires.[35] She describes this difference in biological and binary terms. As a younger woman, the old lady had to take every opportunity she could find to satisfy the fire of her desires because while men "nascono buoni a mille cose" 'are born good for a thousand things,' many of which they can continue to do as they grow older, "le femine a niuna altra cosa che a fare questo e figliuoli ci nascono" 'women are born for nothing other than doing this [i.e., having sex] and bearing children' (2: 697; day 5, novella 10 [our trans.]). For the old lady, the proof of this contention is that one woman exhausts many men but many men cannot exhaust one woman. Her speech "provides the theoretical foundation for a wife's infidelity" (Barolini 293-94) and reflects not only Dioneo's erotic interests but also the logic and rhetoric of sexual difference found in the work's proem.[36]

The old lady's advice to Pietro's wife that she give "pan per focaccia" (usually Englished as "tit for tat") anticipates the story's continued association of food and sex in a formulation that reflects Dioneo's concluding proverb, which seeks to reinforce the already enunciated binaries: "Per che così vi vo' dire, donne mie care, che chi te la fa; fagliele; e se tu non puoi, tienloti a mente fin che tu possa, acciò che quale asino dà in parete tal riceva" 'And so my advice to you, my dear ladies, is that whoever sticks it to you, stick 'em back, and if you can't, keep it in mind until you can; this way whatever the ass gives in butting a wall, he gets back in return' (2: 704; day 5, novella 10 [Bondanella and Musa 376]). The proverb's clever invocation of the figure of the ass indicates the tale's Apuleian origin in the style of *The Golden Ass,* whose ninth book, where the miller's tale appears, likewise ends with a puzzling proverb featuring an ass. Like Dioneo's earlier flawed interpretive frame of the rose and its thorns, however, the model of vengeance the proverb proposes does not correspond to the contours of the story itself. An analogical reading, whether of Boccaccio's two husbands arriving home early (the first threatens violence, while the second proposes sharing) or of Apuleius's version (rape, divorce, and death) compared to Boccaccio's (a satisfying threesome), shows a movement toward accommodation rather than retaliation.[37] Far from endorsing Dioneo's maxim "Whoso does it to you, you do it to him," to use Singleton's biblically inflected translation (441), the novella presents the possibility that reconciliation can take the place of punishment.

This tension between the narrative and its proposed meaning, visible in the novella's opening image of the rose and its final image of an ass, reflects the epistemological problems of interpretation and judgment that bookend the **Decameron** as a whole.[38] In the **Decameron**'s first novella, the possibility of definitive judgment about Ser Cepperello's damnation or salvation is left forever suspended, and in the final novella, the tale of Griselda, also recounted by Dioneo, the clamorous contrast between the story and Dioneo's interpretation has elicited numerous interpretations, from Petrarch's to those of modern critics.[39] The phrase Boccaccio adds to the conclusion of Dioneo's tale in the Hamilton autograph, "non assai certo qual più stato si fosse la notte o moglie o marito" 'not very certain which he had been more that night, either wife or husband,' generates a similar ambiguity and uses a playful sexual scenario to frame epistemological problems. This use of sex to thematize the difficulty of obtaining definite knowledge itself challenges the desire to locate definitive information in Boccaccio's text for any his-

tory, especially that of sexuality. The deployment of the correlative conjunctions "o . . . o" 'either . . . or' in the revision expresses a fundamental feature of Boccaccio's poetics in the **Decameron,** where characters invoke binaries whose status Boccaccio seeks to unsettle. Boccaccio is interested in performing dilemmas, not offering answers, in a manner consonant with his literary *ars combinatoria* ("combinatory art") and moral disposition toward accommodation rather than judgment. The revision exemplifies Boccaccio's desire to present polarities that he feels no obligation to resolve.[40]

The story of Pietro is also the story of Dioneo's rose, which concentrates the **Decameron**'s concerns with erotic and hermeneutic desires but fails to accommodate the full range of experiences the novella expresses, thus rehearsing an epistemological problem that is central to the study of the history of sexuality.[41] As the fiftieth tale in a collection of one hundred stories, the story is also central to the **Decameron**'s structure. While some features of its narrative have figured prominently in recent debates in the history of sexuality, the story's pivotal place in the **Decameron**'s "regime of imperfect symmetries" has not yet been adequately explored.[42] Although the next story in the collection, the novella of Madonna Oretta, has often been called "the center of the **Decameron**" (Fido, "Boccaccio's *Ars Narrandi*" 239) and has its own Apuleian pedigree (Usher), the fiftieth and fifty-first stories in a collection of one hundred tales can lay equal claim to being the work's center.[43] As **Decameron** critics continue to integrate issues of gender and sexuality with long-standing concerns for form and structure, the story's placement should prompt further explorations of the story's role in the **Decameron** as a whole.[44] As for historians of sexuality, they might give more consideration than they have to Boccaccio's decision to repeat with a difference a story that is itself constructed on differential repetition, a decision that anticipates the analogical reading practice to which his story and Apuleius's have been subjected in the recent debates.[45]

MULTIPLYING TEMPORALITIES AND DESIRES IN
THE ARCHIVE

Although the theoretical and methodological interventions offered by Halperin, Carla Freccero, and Goldberg and Menon exemplify quite different approaches to the study of the history of sexuality, they do share two common aims. They oppose the hegemony of normative understandings of sexual identity, and they seek to foster ways of being in the world that might evade what Foucault memorably referred to as "the austere monarchy of sex" (*Introduction* 159). Inspired by feminist and queer scholarship on the cultural politics of editing, this essay's aleatory encounters with the visual, textual, and commentary traditions of *The Golden Ass* and the **Decameron** have taken the study of the history of sexu-

68

ality beyond the straight and narrow of the critical edition and into the archives to explore how escaping the austere monarchy of the modern edited text might contribute to these goals. Instead of comparing and contrasting Apuleius and Boccaccio to generate evidence for exemplary social types, whether normal or abnormal, or for information about sex acts in the past and their social meaning, the current essay asks how these works' literary and textual histories, along with their literary—and philosophical—investigations into desire, narrative, interpretation, and epistemology (themselves historical) might contribute to a different kind of history of sexuality.

One way to pursue this project would be to place *The Golden Ass* within the shift in "moral reflection on sexual pleasures" from a focus on the problem of boys to a concern with women's chastity that Foucault outlines at the end of the second volume of *The History of Sexuality* (*Use* 253) and develops more fully at the conclusion to the third. Foucault locates the beginning of this transformation in the late antique novel, and the recent attention given to the pederastic dimension of the story of Philesitherus in *The Golden Ass* should not exclude consideration of the significant place of eroticized knowledge in several of the novel's key relationships between women and men—from Lucius's encounters with Photis and Pamphile at the novel's outset to Cupid's romance with Psyche in the middle and Lucius's salvation by Isis at the end. Another fruitful avenue of inquiry would consider how, despite Foucault's observation about the decreasing philosophical import of pederasty and the increasing scrutiny of relationships between men and women, men who desire boys and the figure of the sodomite are loci of intense epistemological uncertainty in texts such as the *Decameron* and Dante's *Commedia*.[46] These analyses might contribute to a larger historiographical inquiry framed by Valerie Traub's question "Why do certain figures and tropes of eroticism (and gender) become culturally salient at certain moments, becoming saturated with meaning, and then fade from view?" (130).

Such endeavors are most worthwhile if they do more than add to the accumulation of knowledge and actually change how knowledge is understood, following the kind of curiosity that Foucault defined in the second volume of *The History of Sexuality* as "the only kind of curiosity, in any case, that is worth acting upon with a degree of obstinacy: not the curiosity that seeks to assimilate what it is proper for one to know, but that which enables one to get free of oneself" (*Use* 8). Foucault's evocation of curiosity recalls the *curiositas* of Lucius, which leads to his metamorphosis into an ass. Whether this metamorphosis indicates actual change or instead denotes Lucius's nature—invariably bestial until his ambiguous redemption at the end of the novel—is a matter of scholarly debate.[47] One potential limitation of

this debate—and of the debate about Boccaccio, Apuleius, and the study of the history of sexuality in which the present essay participates—is that specimen texts provide examples to animate already articulated positions rather than occasions for transformation.

In the first volume of *The History of Sexuality,* Foucault contrasts a *scientia sexualis* interested in apprehending the truth of sex and desire with an *ars erotica* that seeks to cultivate erotic pleasure before he acknowledges that a *scientia sexualis* might have its own erotics (*Introduction* 57-58, 70-72). The preceding analyses of *The Golden Ass* and the *Decameron* offer novel paradigms for the understanding of these well-studied texts by focusing on their solicitation of *libido sciendi* instead of their representations of social history. These inquiries suggest that it would be possible to construct a genealogy of the links between sex, desire, and knowledge that would situate the contemporary apparatus of sexuality and the erotics of interpretation in the *longue durée*. They also suggest that the study of the history of sexuality should acknowledge and account for its place in this genealogy. "After all," Foucault continues, "what would be the value of the passion for knowledge if it resulted only in a certain amount of knowledgeableness and not, in one way or another and to the extent possible, in the knower's straying afield of himself?" (*Use* 8).

Notes

The authors would like to thank Albert Ascoli, Tobias Foster Gittes, Regina Psaki, Deanna Shemek, Michael Sherberg, and Valerie Traub for their valuable suggestions as well as Gary Ferguson for sharing forthcoming work. Our thanks go also to Erin C. Blake of the Folger Shakespeare Library, who provided expert assistance with the woodcuts; Carla Zecher of the Newberry Library, who kindly verified a crucial transcription from an early edition of Apuleius; and Davide Balbi, who helped obtain the image from Boccaccio's autograph of Apuleius.

1. Drawing on Walters's comparative study of masculinity in the episode from *The Golden Ass* and its reworking in the *Decameron,* Halperin inaugurated the debate with a critique of the historians of sexuality who, in his view, mistakenly find in the first volume of Foucault's *History of Sexuality* and then apply in their own work a rigid distinction between modern identities and premodern acts. Halperin calls for attention instead to the range of ways in which sex acts might be relevant to the consolidation of social identity at different historical junctures through the analysis of "partial identity, emergent identity, transient identity, semi-identity, incomplete identity, proto-identity, or subidentity" (43). Whereas Halperin acknowledges

that he simplifies the Boccaccian and Apuleian stories, Freccero emphasizes the implications of the complex literariness of the *Decameron* while arguing that investment in "produc[ing] truths about people of the past through sex" is antithetical to Foucault's project (46). In turn, Goldberg and Menon address the *Decameron* tale and, to a lesser extent, the Apuleian source in a manifesto about the methods and goals of queer historiography that draws on less frequented moments in the first volume of Foucault's *History of Sexuality* to emphasize how Boccaccio's text offers possibilities for desires and pleasures that cannot be plotted by identity-based models of sexuality. See also Traub, who offers a helpful disciplinary mapping of the debate and is skeptical of Freccero's and Goldberg and Menon's arguments, and Ferguson, whose disagreement is mostly with Halperin. Halperin's intervention was published first in *Representations* in 1998 and then again in revised form in his 2002 *How to Do the History of Homosexuality.* We quote throughout from the later version; when we make general remarks about Halperin's argument, they apply to both versions.

2. The 1518 editio princeps (*Apulegio volgare, tradotto . . .*) included half as many images as the 1519 edition (*Apulegio volgare: Diviso . . .*). For the history of their reprintings, see Acocella 146-47 and Mortimer 30-32. The images have been reprinted most recently by Rizzoli for a paperback Italian translation of *The Golden Ass* (*L'asino*). On the reception of *The Golden Ass,* see Gaisser and Carver, both of which appeared as this essay was being revised, and Moreschini, which focuses on the myth of Cupid and Psyche.

3. Fumagalli has discussed how the text of Boiardo's translation of *The Golden Ass* is influenced by Boccaccio's imitations of Apuleius in the *Decameron* (137-44).

4. The crossing out can be found in a copy of the 1544 edition of Boiardo's translation published in Venice by Bartolomeo detto l'Imperatore and Francesco Vinitiano, now in the Biblioteca Angelica in Rome (*L'Apuleio* 81r).

5. Despite these interventions, the altered woodblock's two figures in bed are the trace of the suppressed erotic encounter found in the original, just as the lingering nose and smile are the remnants of the three-way that Boccaccio realizes but Apuleius only suggests.

6. Walters does mention in passing that the narrator of the events he analyzes is "a donkey" (22). On the relation between shape and self-identity and on the continuity of consciousness in human-to-animal metamorphoses, see Bynum 1001-12.

Bynum focuses on werewolf stories around the year 1200, but, *mutatis mutandis*, her discussion remains illuminating for Lucius's case.

7. As has been frequently observed, the noun *curiositas,* which includes meanings not present in the English cognate, such as meddlesomeness, appears only once before Apuleius, in one of Cicero's letters to Atticus. The letter in question is not reproduced in the 1999 Loeb edition of Cicero's *Letters to Atticus,* edited and translated by D. R. Shackleton Bailey, but it can be found in the Teubner edition of the original Latin text (*Epistulae*), also edited by Shackleton Bailey (1: 68; bk. 2, letter 12, sec. 2). While there is a general consensus that *curiositas* is a crucial concept for the novel, whether it is celebrated as necessary for "salvation," condemned as enslaving man to desire, or treated ambivalently is contested. See Hijmans et al. 362-79; DeFilippo; Walsh; Schlam, "Curiosity."

8. On desire in *The Golden Ass,* see Konstan 125-38. On parody, especially the parody of literary texts, see Westerbrink; Finkelpearl 36-55. The use of *implantation* is meant to recall Foucault's discussion of "the perverse implantation" in the first volume of *The History of Sexuality* (*Introduction* 36-49).

9. Unless otherwise noted, the Latin text and English translations of *The Golden Ass* are drawn from Hanson's edition. For the Latin text with fuller apparatus, see Robertson's edition (*Les métamorphoses*). On the adultery tales, see Schlam, "Sex." There is another adultery tale earlier in book 9 that Boccaccio also takes up and reworks in the *Decameron* (798-804; day 7, novella 2), as discussed by Martinez.

10. There is considerable debate about this passage and about the significance of key terms in it. Disagreeing with Shumate's contention that *multiscientia* is a mature form of *prudentia* (247n36), Kenney argues that this passage demonstrates for the reader that the auctorial Lucius has not learned from his misadventures (168). Given our understanding of the Apuleius passage, *multiscientia* would here mean something like a not necessarily useful accumulation of information, while *prudentia* signifies prudence, practical judgment, or even wisdom. Kenney's essay offers a sustained discussion of the nuances in meaning and usage of these and semantically related terms. For a disagreement with Winkler's interpretation of prudence in this passage, see Hijmans et al. 377.

11. In "Curiosity," Schlam observes that "[p]rying, which finds particular delight in witnessing obscene activity, becomes a party to lust itself" (121).

12. On the prologue, see the essays in Kahane and Laird, especially Gowers's, which addresses ears at some length.

13. Lucius's youth and beauty receive more than passing comment. For example, his aunt Byrrhena warns him that he is "per aetatem et pulchritudinem" 'quite young and handsome enough' for the epheberastic witch Pamphile (1: 68-69; bk. 2, sec. 5). On epheberasty, see Turner, who also discusses in depth the eroticization of knowledge and addresses in passing Renaissance adaptations of the myth of Cupid and Psyche. On the significance of remarks concerning Lucius's human physiognomy, including Byrrhena's comments, see Keulen.

14. Lucius is anally penetrated by the old woman who recounts the story of Cupid and Psyche (2: 54-57; bk. 7, sec. 28), and an auctioneer tells a cinaedic priest looking to buy Lucius to thrust his face between the ass's thighs to see how great his "passivity" is ("quam grandem . . . patientiam" [2: 106-07; bk. 8, sec. 25]). On Lucius's gender, see Winkler 173-76. Foucault mentions the cinaedic priests in *The Golden Ass* during a discussion of continuities and ruptures in "sexual" morality across time (*Use* 19).

15. One element that would be particularly worthy of development is Lucius's misogyny, which manifests itself most spectacularly in a scene in book 8 when Lucius precipitously—and incorrectly—jumps to a conclusion about the depravity of Charity, announcing that "tunc . . . totarum mulierum secta moresque de asini pendebant iudicio" 'at that moment the character and principles of all womankind depended on an ass's verdict' (2: 22-23; bk. 7, sec. 10). Refusing to take responsibility for his metamorphosis, Lucius also routinely blames Photis for his transformation into an ass, although she only aided him reluctantly in his pursuit of magic. This recurrent element of Lucius's personality should be taken into account in discussions of the representation of the *pistor* and his wife.

16. When Beroaldus finds an obscene signification under *dividundo,* a word that evokes the medieval practice of parsing texts in order to interpret them, he luxuriates in the *libido sciendi* the novel represents and incites, as he does throughout his commentary. Compare Beroaldus's gloss with the marginal note to the same passage found in an early manuscript of *The Golden Ass,* transcribed in n21, below.

17. Hijmans and his fellow editors offer a sustained argument that the *pistor* is indeed a hypocrite (app. 6). Relating the regulation of sex to self-mastery

and the management of other forms of pleasure is one of the goals of the second and third volumes of Foucault's *History of Sexuality.*

18. In marshaling evidence that the *pistor*'s retribution against the youth was, "by the standards of Greco-Roman society, not an unreasonable one," Walters notes that after Valerius Maximus lists several extrajudicial punishments of adulterers, including castration and whipping, he concludes that "these men . . . were not held to have done anything wrong in giving vent to their anger" (24). But the examples Valerius gives concern adulterers found in flagrante delicto (1: 375; bk. 6, ch. 1, sec. 13). This is not the case in Apuleius, where the boy is discovered hiding after the husband's unanticipated return interrupts the would-be lovers' dinner. Moreover, the vengeful cuckolds Valerius lists all belong to the upper echelons of Roman society. Would their comportment have set the standard for that of a miller? Intriguingly, the *pistor* uses vocabulary that appears in Apuleius's defense of his own practice of writing love poetry about boys. In his "Apology" (*Pro se de magia*), Apuleius defends himself against the charge of poetic and sexual impropriety by describing one of his adversaries in the lawsuit as "agrestis quidem semper et barbarus" 'invariably rustic and uncivilized' (43; 34).

19. In addition to being imagined more graphically, the story was modified by censors. For example, the old woman's discourse is radically revised in a sixteenth-century edition (Chiecchi and Troisio 96).

20. Gaisser notes that the two stories "differ markedly in tone and characterization, and their endings are entirely different. . . . Boccaccio has written a comedy, Apuleius a tragedy—or at least a melodrama" (103-04).

21. Scholars have long appreciated Boccaccio's important role in the rediscovery of Apuleius. Sabbadini even attributed the discovery of the Montecassino manuscript of Apuleius's works, on which modern editions are based, to Boccaccio, but that discovery has since been disproved by Billanovich. Nevertheless, the oldest manuscripts of Apuleius do bear traces of Boccaccio's use of them in their margins (Fiorilla; Rafti, "Riflessioni"; Vio). One early manuscript of *The Golden Ass,* Biblioteca Medicea Laurenziana 29.2, includes a marginal comment, which may be in Boccaccio's hand, about the miller's misleading proposal: "Q[uasi] d[icat] nolo me totaliter ab uxore mea separare vel divortium cum ea facere propter adulterium per eam commissum, sed puellum adulescentem tamquam comunem inter nos dividere, vicissim eo utendo" 'As if to say, I do

not want to entirely separate myself from my wife or divorce her on account of her adultery, but to divide the adolescent boy as it were communally, using him in turn' (*Opera,* c. 1200, 60r). In their transcriptions of the Latin, previous scholars have omitted "vicissim" 'in turn' (Gaisser 107n131; Vio 155n23). On the legend of Boccaccio's visit to Montecassino, see also Coulter. For two more-recent assessments of Boccaccio's relationship with Apuleius, see Gaisser 93-99; Carver 127-41.

22. In the *Genealogie,* Boccaccio reads the story of Cupid and Psyche as an allegory of "superb[us] desideri[us]" 'overwhelming desire' (1: 568; bk. 5, ch. 22, sec. 16 [our trans.]), which suggests Apuleius also plays a significant role in Boccaccio's thinking about the problems of desire.

23. All quotations from the original text of the *Decameron* are from Branca's edition, unless otherwise noted. The issue of the *Decameron*'s place in Boccaccio's theoretical reflections in the *Genealogie* is a vexed one. Bruni, for example, argues that in the *Genealogie* Boccaccio rejects outright his amorous writings in the vernacular. In our view, such a reading simplifies the ambiguities of Boccaccio's own statements on the matter in the text, where he rejects the tales of old women as meaningless in one chapter and then in the next suggests that they do contain a hidden meaning. Whether he rejects his novellas or justifies them, his thinking on the matter is anything but unequivocal.

24. A similar divergence of interpretations can be found in other English versions: Bondanella and Musa share McWilliam's interpretation "with which," while Waldman's translation "not entirely sure whether last night he'd served more in the role of wife or husband" (380) agrees with Singleton's (*Decameron* [1982]). Note that Waldman's "in the role of" glosses the original, which Singleton renders more literally as "which he had the more been that night, wife or husband" (441).

25. For an exploration of the ideological investments of Boccaccio translations, see Migiel.

26. The most fully developed expression of this thesis can be found in Branca and Vitale.

27. The fashion for *variantistica,* the critical study of variants, remains strong in the wake of Gianfranco Contini's pathbreaking studies and it is surely only a matter of time before these materials are exhaustively mined.

28. The reading from Italian 482 can also be found in Branca, *Decameron* 1: cxxxiii, although not all the editions dated 1992 contain the list of variants. It can also be found in Branca, "Variazioni" 108.

The Hamilton 90 wording can also be found in Singleton's diplomatic edition (*Decameron* [1974]).

29. For a detailed analysis of Boccaccio's punctuation habits in Hamilton 90, see Rafti, "*Lumina.*" On the history of punctuation, see Parkes's magisterial study, as well as Carruthers's considerations of how, following Hugh of Saint Victor, "reading fundamentally proceeds by *divisio* ['division']" (174).

30. Ferguson suggests that the phrase may have been made intentionally ambiguous. Stone finds it "a celebration of the bisexual third party" (196).

31. After reading a draft of this essay during an exchange of work on Apuleius and Boccaccio, Ferguson added an interesting discussion of the variant in the autograph *Decameron* manuscripts to *Queer (Re)Readings* (60-61).

32. Bakhtin's comments on the role of the public square as a place for judgment in his discussion of *The Golden Ass* are illuminating on this point: "The everyday life that Lucius observes and studies is an *exclusively personal and private life.* . . . All its events are the personal affairs of isolated people. . . . These events are not liable to public reckoning on the open square. Events acquire a public significance as such only when they become crimes. The *criminal act* is a moment in private life that becomes, as it were, *involuntarily public*" (122). Boccaccio uses the public square as the place for judgment in the tale of Frate Alberto in *Decameron,* day 4, novella 2, a tale that Erich Auerbach memorably analyzed. For an incisive reading of Auerbach that explores issues of periodization that are important to the history of sexuality debate but beyond the scope of this essay, see Ascoli.

33. Noting that the rose is a conventional image of the female genitalia, Stone remarks that "[i]f Dioneo is not exactly telling his female audience to practice lesbianism, he is at least telling them to read homosexually" (198).

34. This is not to say that Pietro does not present a recognizable social type; rather, the specifics of his representation are determined by narrative requirements, not by Boccaccio's lack of options or by an idea of the medieval sodomite as a unified and stable being. Boccaccio's commentary on cantos 15 and 16 of Dante's *Inferno,* for example, provide an account of the sodomite very different from that found in *Decameron,* book 5, novella 10. See Cestaro, "Pederastic Insemination." On the range of manifestations of male same-sex desire in medieval Italy, see Rocke.

35. The importance of the change is noted by Radcliff-Umstead; Vio; Sanguineti White.

36. The affinities between the remarks in the proem and Dioneo's project require further investigation. The persona of the author of the proem should be carefully distinguished from the historical Boccaccio. For a useful categorization of the levels of narration in the *Decameron,* see Picone.

37. On the importance of accommodation in the *Decameron* more generally, see Greene; Marcus. Also note the importance of the theme in day 5 of the fulfillment of desire after extended tribulations (670-91; day 5, novellas 8-9). Here the happiness of all three is arranged immediately thanks to the "disonestà" 'iniquities' of Pietro rather than prolonged in the face of conflicting desires and obligations as in the earlier stories. (It is worth recalling, however, that Dioneo's privilege is not to have to follow any given day's topic.)

38. The ass and the rose are foundational—and related—plot elements in *The Golden Ass* since it is the consumption of roses that returns Lucius to human form.

39. For a careful consideration of the problem of truth and interpretation in day 1, novella 1, see Fido, "Tale." For Mazzotta, Dioneo's closing remark in his story of Griselda, that Griselda should have found another man to "scuotere il pilliccione" 'shake her skincoat' (2: 1248; day 10, novella 10 [McWilliam 795]), practically "unmakes the story he has just told" (128). Boccaccio's strategic suspension of judgments may be part of his ongoing, parodic engagement with Dante, which he announces in the appropriation of Dante's damned moniker *Galeotto* as the "cognome" 'surname' of his *Decameron.*

40. For similar observations about Boccaccio's treatment of gender, see Migiel, who argues that Boccaccio "polarizes sexual difference [while] mov[ing] away from clear polarizations of male and female" (162).

41. Boccaccio returns to the same floral image to figure the act of reading both implicitly, in the author's conclusion to the *Decameron,* when he commands, "[L]asci star quelle che pungono e quelle che dilettan legga" '[L]eave alone those that sting and read those that delight' (2: 1259; our trans.), and explicitly, in the dedication of *De mulieribus claris* (*Famous Women*) to Andrea Acciaiuoli: "You will find, at times, that an appropriate recital of the facts has compelled me to mix the impure with the pure. Do not skip over these parts and do not shy away from them, but persevere in your reading. As on entering a garden you extend your

ivory hands towards the flowers, leaving aside the thorns, so in this case relegate to one side offensive matters and gather what is praise-worthy" (Brown 5).

42. The quotation is a translation of the title of Fido's book on Boccaccio (*Il regime delle simmetrie imperfette*) and neatly captures the complex structures that Boccaccio builds into his work to encourage associations that seem to promise the discovery of some truth even as they thwart it.

43. If one counts the incomplete novella of the introduction to day 4, then day 5, novella 10, alone would occupy the central position. Gaylard follows Barolini's signaling of this centrality and offers a reading of the *Decameron* episodes that feature men who desire men.

44. It would be intriguing to read this novella in the light of some of the book's other erotic triangles, like the destructive one in day 4, novella 9, or the generously diffused one of day 10, novella 8. An equally important context is that constituted by the surrounding tales, like day 5, novella 8, and day 5, novella 9, as well as day 6, novella 1, whose connections with day 5, novella 10, have been mentioned.

45. Apuleius claims to have adapted his story from a Greek original, which would add another degree of differential repetition. Boccaccio includes this piece of information in his characterization of Apuleius in the second version of his *Amorosa visione* (canto 5, lines 37-39), and Castelvetro notes that Boccaccio stole his story from Apuleius just as Apuleius stole his tale of the golden ass (120). It is impossible to say whether Boccaccio knew, as modern readers do, that the miller's tale is not found in the Greek original, although it seems unlikely that he would have known enough about Lucian's work to be aware of that fact. One important dimension of the argument Goldberg and Menon put forth is their critique of approaches to history that presume a self-identical, knowable present anchored in its difference from a discrete, radically other past. This concern could be linked to the present essay's preoccupation with variants that demonstrate the instability of texts and with transmission histories that frustrate expectations of linearity.

46. Dante's treatment of sodomites has vexed scholars since Boccaccio. For some more-recent perspectives, see Pézard; Kay; Pequigney; Cestaro; Armour; Holsinger.

47. See the works listed in n46, above.

Works Cited

Acocella, Mariantonietta. *L'asino d'oro nel Rinascimento.* Ravenna: Longo, 2001. Print.

Apuleius. "Apology." Trans. Vincent Hunink. *Rhetorical Works*. By Apuleius. Ed. Stephen Harrison. Oxford: Oxford UP, 2002. 25-121. Print.

———. *Apulegio volgare: Diviso in undeci libri, novamente stampato & in molti lochi aggiontovi che nella prima impressione gli manchava, & de molte piu figure adornato, et diligentemente correcto: Con le sue fabule in margine poste*. Trans. Matteo Maria Boiardo. Venezia: Nicolo d'Aristotele da Ferrara; Vincenzo de Polo da Venetia, 1519. Print.

———. *Apulegio volgare, tradotto per il conto Mattheo Maria Boiardo*. Trans. Matteo Maria Boiardo. Venezia: Nicolo d'Aristotele da Ferrara; Vincenzo de Polo da Venetia, 1518. Print.

———. *L'Apuleio tradotto in volgare dal conte Matteo Maria Boiardo Historiato. Nuovamente, revisto, & ricorretto con ogni diligenza. Appresso aggiuntovi un breve discorso della vita dell'autore. Con una tavola da ritrovar tutte le novelle, sentenze, detti, fatti, & altre piu cose notabili, secondo che poste sono in margine; quello che per inanzi non era*. Venezia: Bartolomeo detto l'Imperatore; Francesco Vinitiano, 1544. Print.

———. *L'asino d'oro di Lucio Apuleio filosofo Platonico*. Trans. Pompeo Vizani. Venezia: Ghirardo Imberti, 1639. Print.

———. *L'asino, o Le metamorfosi: Con le 64 xilografie dell'edizione veneziana del 1519*. Trans. Claudio Annaratone. Milano: Biblioteca Universale Rizzoli, 2001. Print.

———. *Metamorphose, autrement, L'asne d'or*. Trans. George de la Bouthiere. Lyon: Jean de Tournes; Guillaume Gazeau, 1553. Print.

———. *Les métamorphoses*. Trans. Paul Vallette. Ed. D. S. Robertson. 3 vols. Paris: Les Belles Lettres, 1946-56. Print.

———. *The Metamorphoses*. Trans. J. Arthur Hanson. Ed. Hanson. 2 vols. Cambridge: Harvard UP, 1989. Print. Loeb Classical Lib. 44, 453.

———. *Opera*. C. 1200. MS. 29.2. Biblioteca Medicea Laurenziana, Firenze.

———. *Opera*. C. 1350. MS. 54.32. Biblioteca Medicea Laurenziana, Firenze.

———. *Pro se de magia*. Ed. Vincent Hunink. Vol. 1. Amsterdam: Gieben, 1997. Print.

Armour, Peter. "Dante's Brunetto: The Paternal Paterine?" *Italian Studies* 38 (1983): 1-38. Print.

Ascoli, Albert Russell. "Boccaccio's Auerbach: Holding the Mirror up to Mimesis." *Studi sul Boccaccio* 20 (1991-92): 377-97. Print.

Auerbach, Erich. "Frate Alberto." *Mimesis: The Representation of Reality in Western Literature*. 1953. By Auerbach. Trans. Willard R. Trask. Princeton: Princeton UP, 2003. 203-31. Print.

Bakhtin, M. M. "Forms of Time and Chronotope in the Novel." *The Dialogic Imagination: Four Essays*. By Bakhtin. Trans. Caryl Emerson and Michael Holquist. Ed. Holquist. Austin: U of Texas P, 1981. 84-258. Print.

Barolini, Teodolinda. "*Le parole son femmine e i fatti sono maschi*: Toward a Sexual Poetics of the *Decameron* (*Decameron* 2.9, 2.10, 5.10)." *Dante and the Origins of Italian Literary Culture*. By Barolini. New York: Fordham UP, 2006. 282-303. Rpt. of "*Le parole son femmine e i fatti sono maschi*: Toward a Sexual Poetics of the *Decameron* (*Decameron* II.10)." *Studi sul Boccaccio* 21 (1993): 175-97. Print.

Beroaldus, Philippus. *Commentarii a Philippo Beroaldo conditi in asinum aureum Lucii Apuleii*. Bologna: Benedictus Hectoris, 1500. Print.

Billanovich, Giuseppe. "I primi umanisti e le tradizioni dei classici latini." *Petrarca e il primo umanesimo*. 1953. Padova: Antenore, 1996. 117-41. Print.

Boccaccio, Giovanni. *Amorosa visione*. Ed. Vittore Branca. Milano: Mondadori, 1974. Print.

———. *Boccaccio on Poetry: Being the Preface and the Fourteenth and Fifteenth Books of Boccaccio's* Genealogia deorum gentilium. Trans. Charles G. Osgood. Princeton: Princeton UP, 1930. Print.

———. *Decameron*. Ed. Vittore Branca. 2 vols. Torino: Einaudi, 1992. Print.

———. *Decameron*. N.d. MS. Italian 482. BN, Paris.

———. *Decameron*. 1370-72, MS. Hamilton 90. Staatsbibliothek Preussischer Kulturbesitz, Berlin.

———. *Genealogie deorum gentilium*. Ed. Vittorio Zaccaria. 2 vols. Milano: Mondadori, 1998. Print.

Bondanella, Peter, and Mark Musa, trans. *The Decameron*. By Giovanni Boccaccio. New York: New Amer. Lib., 1982. Print.

Branca, Vittore, ed. *Decameron*. By Giovanni Boccaccio. 2 vols. Torino: Einaudi, 1992. Print.

———. "Variazioni stilistiche e narrative." Branca and Vitale vol. 2.

Branca, Vittore, and Maurizio Vitale. *Il capolavoro del Boccaccio e due diverse redazioni*. 2 vols. Venezia: Istituto Veneto di Scienze, Lettere ed Arti, 2002. Print.

Brown, Virginia, ed. and trans. *Famous Women*. By Giovanni Boccaccio. Cambridge: Harvard UP, 2001. Print.

Bruni, Francesco. *Boccaccio: L'invenzione della letteratura mezzana*. Bologna: Mulino, 1990. Print.

Bynum, Caroline Walker. "Metamorphosis; or, Gerald and the Werewolf." *Speculum* 73.4 (1998): 987-1013. Print.

Carruthers, Mary. *The Book of Memory: A Study of Memory in Medieval Culture.* Cambridge: Cambridge UP, 1990. Print.

Carver, H. F. Robert. *The Protean Ass: The* Metamorphoses *of Apuleius from Antiquity to the Renaissance.* Oxford: Oxford UP, 2007. Print. Oxford Classical Monographs.

Castelvetro, Lodovico. *Poetica d'Aristotele vulgarizzata, et sposta.* Wien: Gaspar Stainhofer, 1570. Print.

Cestaro, Gary. "Pederastic Insemination; or, Dante in the Grammar Classroom." *Poetics of Masculinity in Early Modern Italy and Spain.* Ed. Gerry Milligan and Jane Tylus. Toronto: U of Toronto P, forthcoming.

———. "Queering Nature, Queering Gender: Dante and Sodomy." *Dante for the New Millennium.* Ed. Teodolinda Barolini and H. Wayne Storey. New York: Fordham UP, 2003. 90-103. Print.

Chiecchi, Giuseppe, and Luciano Troisio. *Il* Decameron *sequestrato: Le tre edizioni censurate nel cinquecento.* Milano: Unicopli, 1984. Print.

Cicero. *Epistulae ad atticum.* Ed. D. R. Shackleton Bailey. 2 vols. Stuttgart: Teubner, 1987. Print. Bibliotheca Scriptorum Graecorum et Romanorum Teubneriana.

———. *Letters to Atticus.* Ed. D. R. Shackleton Bailey. 4 vols. Cambridge: Harvard UP, 1999. Print. Loeb Classical Lib.

Contini, Gianfranco. *Varianti e altra linguistica: Una raccolta di saggi, 1938-1968.* Torino: Einaudi, 1970. Print.

Coulter, Cornelia C. "Boccaccio and the Cassinese Manuscripts of the Laurentian Library." *Classical Philology* 43.4 (1948): 217-30. Print.

DeFilippo, Joseph G. "*Curiositas* and the Platonism of Apuleius' *Golden Ass.*" *American Journal of Philology* 111.4 (1990): 471-92. Print.

Doody, Margaret Anne. *The True Story of the Novel.* New Brunswick: Rutgers UP, 1996. Print.

Ferguson, Gary. *Queer (Re)Readings in the French Renaissance: Homosexuality, Gender, Culture.* Burlington: Ashgate, 2008. Print.

Fido, Franco. "Boccaccio's *Ars Narrandi* in the Sixth Day of the *Decameron.*" *Italian Literature: Roots and Branches, Essays in Honor of Thomas Goddard Bergin.* Ed. Glose Rimanelli and Kenneth John Atchity. New Haven: Yale UP, 1976. 225-42. Print.

———. *Il regime delle simmetrie imperfette: Studi sul* «Decameron». Milano: Angeli, 1988. Print.

———. "The Tale of Ser Ciappelletto (I.1)." *The* Decameron: *First Day in Perspective.* Ed. Elissa Weaver. Toronto: U of Toronto P, 2004. 59-76. Print.

Finkelpearl, Ellen D. *Metamorphosis of Language in Apuleius: A Study of Allusion in the Novel.* Ann Arbor: U of Michigan P, 1998. Print.

Florilla, Maurizio. "La lettura apuleiana del Boccaccio e le note ai manoscritti laurenziani 29,2 e 54,32." *Aevum* 73.3 (1999): 635-68. Print.

Foucault, Michel. *The Care of the Self.* Trans. Robert Hurley. New York: Vintage, 1986. Print. Vol. 3 of *The History of Sexuality.* 3 vols. 1976-86.

———. *An Introduction.* Trans. Robert Hurley. New York: Vintage, 1976. Print. Vol. 1 of *The History of Sexuality.* 3 vols. 1976-86.

———. *The Use of Pleasure.* Trans. Robert Hurley. New York: Vintage, 1985. Print. Vol. 2 of *The History of Sexuality.* 3 vols. 1976-86.

Freccero, Carla. *Queer/Early/Modern.* Durham: Duke UP, 2006. Print.

Fumagalli, Edoardo. *Matteo Maria Boiardo, volgarizzatore dell' «Asino d'oro»: Contributo allo studio della fortuna di Apuleio nell'umanesimo.* Padova: Antenore, 1988. Print.

Gaisser, Julia Haig. *The Fortunes of Apuleius and* The Golden Ass: *A Study in Transmission and Reception.* Princeton: Princeton UP, 2008. Print.

Gaylard, Susan. "The Crisis of Word and Deed in *Decameron* V, 10." *The Italian Novella: A Book of Essays.* Ed. Gloria Allaire. New York: Routledge, 2003. 33-48. Print.

Gleason, Maud. *Making Men: Sophists and Self-Presentation in Ancient Rome.* Princeton: Princeton UP, 1995. Print.

Goldberg, Jonathan, and Madhavi Menon. "Queering History." *PMLA* 120.5 (2005): 1608-17. Print.

Gowers, Emily. "Apuleius and Persius." Kahane and Laird 77-87.

Greene, Thomas M. "Forms of Accommodation in the *Decameron.*" *Italica* 45.3 (1968): 297-313. Print.

Halperin, David M. "Forgetting Foucault." *How to Do the History of Homosexuality.* Chicago: U of Chicago P, 2002. 24-47. Rpt. of "Forgetting Foucault: Acts, Identities, and the History of Sexuality." *Representations* 63 (1998): 93-120. Print.

Hijmans, B. L., Jr., et al. *Apuleius Madaurensis* Metamorphoses, *Book IX: Text, Introduction and Commentary.* Groningen: Forsten, 1995. Print. Groningen Commentaries on Apuleius.

Holsinger, Bruce W. "Sodomy and Resurrection: The Homoerotic Subject of the *Divine Comedy.*" *Premodern Sexualities.* Ed. Louise Fradenburg and Carla Freccero. New York: Routledge, 1996. 243-74. Print.

Kahane, Ahuvia, and Andrew Laird, eds. *A Companion to the Prologue of Apuleius'* Metamorphoses. Oxford: Oxford UP, 2001. Print.

Kay, Richard. *Dante's Swift and Strong: Essays on In*ferno *XV.* Lawrence: Regents P of Kansas, 1978. Print.

Kenney, E. J. "In the Mill with the Slaves." *Transactions of the American Philological Association* 133.1 (2003): 159-92. Print.

Keulen, Wytse. "*Ad Amussim Congruentia*: Measuring the Intellectual in Apuleius." Lectiones Scrupulosae: *Essays on the Text and Interpretation of Apuleius'* Metamorphoses *in Honor of Maaike Zimmerman.* Ed. Keulen, R. R. Nauta, and S. Panayotakis. Groningen: Barkhus; Groningen U Lib., 2006. 168-202. Print.

Konstan, David. *Sexual Symmetry: Love in the Ancient Novel and Related Genres.* Princeton: Princeton UP, 1994. Print.

Marcus, Millicent Joy. *An Allegory of Form: Literary Self-Consciousness in the* Decameron. Saratoga: Anma Libri, 1979. Print.

Martinez, Ronald L. "Apuleian Example and Misogynist Allegory in the Tale of Peronella (*Decameron* VII.2)." *Boccaccio and Feminist Criticism.* Ed. Thomas Stillinger and F. Regina Psaki. Chapel Hill: Annali d'Italianistica, 2006. 201-16. Print.

Mazzotta, Giuseppe. *The World at Play in Boccaccio's* Decameron. Princeton: Princeton UP, 1986. Print.

McWilliam, G. H., trans. *The Decameron.* By Giovanni Boccaccio. 2nd ed. New York: Penguin, 1995. Print.

Migiel, Marilyn. *A Rhetoric of the* Decameron. Toronto: U of Toronto P, 2003. Print. Toronto Italian Studies.

Moreschini, Claudio. "Towards a History of the Exegesis of Apuleius: The Case of the 'Tale of Cupid and Psyche.'" Trans. Coco Stevenson. *Latin Fiction: The Latin Novel in Context.* Ed. Heinz Hofmann. London: Routledge, 1999. 215-28. Print.

Mortimer, Ruth. *Italian Sixteenth-Century Books.* Vol. 1. Harvard Coll. Lib. of Printing and Graphic Arts Catalogue of Bks. and Manuscripts. Cambridge: Harvard UP, 1974. Print.

Parkes, M. B. *Pause and Effect: Punctuation in the West.* Berkeley: U of California P, 1992. Print.

Pequigney, Joseph. "Sodomy in Dante's *Inferno* and *Purgatorio.*" *Representations* 36 (1991): 22-42. Print.

Pézard, André. *Dante sous la pluie de feu (Enfer, chant XV).* Paris: Vrin, 1950. Print.

Picone, Michelangelo. "Autore/Narratori." *Lessico critico decameroniano.* Ed. Renzo Bragantini and Pier Massimo Forni. Torino: Bollati Boringhieri, 1995. 34-59. Print.

Radcliff-Umstead, Douglas. "Boccaccio's Adaptations of Some Latin Sources for the *Decameron.*" *Italica* 45.2 (1968): 171-94. Print.

Rafti, Patrizia. "*Lumina dictionum*: Interpunzione e prosa in Giovanni Boccaccio. IV." *Studi sul Boccaccio* 29 (2001): 3-66. Print.

———. "Riflessioni sull'*usus distinguendi* del Boccaccio negli zibaldoni." *Gli zibaldoni di Boccaccio: Memoria, scrittura, riscrittura.* Ed. Claude Cazalé Bérard and Michelangelo Picone. Firenze: Cesati, 1998. 283-306. Print.

Rocke, Michael. *Forbidden Friendships: Homosexuality and Male Culture in Renaissance Florence.* Oxford: Oxford UP, 1998. Print.

Sabbadini, Remigio. *Le scoperte dei codici latini e greci ne' secoli XIV e XV.* 2 vols. 1905. Firenze: Sansoni, 1967. Print.

Sanguineti White, Laura. *Boccaccio e Apuleio: Caratteri differenziali nella struttura narrativa del «Decameron».* Bologna: EDIM, 1977. Print.

Schlam, Carl C. "The Curiosity of the Golden Ass." *Classical Journal* 64 (1968): 120-25. Print.

———. "Sex and Sanctity: The Relationship of Male and Female in the *Metamorphoses.*" *Aspects of Apuleius'* Golden Ass. Ed. B. L. Hijmans and R. Th. van der Paardt. Groningen: Bouma's, 1978. 95-105. Print.

Shumate, Nancy. *Crisis and Conversion in Apuleius'* Metamorphoses. Ann Arbor: U of Michigan P, 1996. Print.

Singleton, Charles S., trans. *The Decameron.* By Giovanni Boccaccio. Berkeley: U of California P, 1982. Print.

———, ed. *Decameron: Edizione diplomatico-interpretativa dell'autografo Hamilton 90.* By Giovanni Boccaccio. Baltimore: Johns Hopkins UP, 1974. Print.

Stone, Gregory B. "The Prick of the Rose: Boccaccio's Bisexual Hermeneutics." *Boccaccio and Feminist Criticism.* Ed. Thomas C. Stillinger and F. Regina Psaki, Chapel Hill: Annali d'Italianistica, 2006. 189-99. Rpt. of "Two Ways Not to Read (and Going Both Ways)." *The Ethics of Nature in the Middle Ages: On Boccaccio's Poetaphysics.* By Stone. New York: St. Martin's, 1998. 173-203. Print.

Traub, Valerie. "The Present Future of Lesbian Historiography." *A Companion to Lesbian, Gay, Bisexual, Transgender, and Queer Studies.* Ed. George Haggerty and Molly McGarry. Malden: Blackwell, 2007. 124-45. Print.

Turner, James Grantham. *Schooling Sex: Libertine Literature and Erotic Education in Italy, France, and England, 1534-1685.* Oxford: Oxford UP, 2003. Print.

Usher, Jonathan. "*Desultorietà* nella novella portante di Madonna Oretta (*Decameron* VI, 1) e altre citazioni apuleiane nel Boccaccio." *Studi sul Boccaccio* 29 (2001): 67-103. Print.

Valerius Maximus. *Facta et dicta memorabilia.* Ed. John Briscoe. 2 vols. Stuttgart: Teubner, 1998. Print.

Vio, Gianluigi. "Chiose e riscritture apuleiane di Giovanni Boccaccio." *Studi sul Boccaccio* 20 (1991-92): 139-65. Print.

Waldman, Guido, trans. *The Decameron.* By Giovanni Boccaccio. Oxford: Oxford UP, 1993. Print.

Walsh, P. G. "The Rights and Wrongs of Curiosity (Plutarch to Augustine)." *Greece and Rome* 2nd ser., 35.1 (1988): 73-85. Print.

Walters, Jonathan. "'No More Than a Boy': The Shifting Construction of Masculinity from Ancient Greece to the Middle Ages." *Gender and History* 5.1 (1993): 20-33. Print.

Westerbrink, A. G. "Some Parodies in Apuleius' *Metamorphoses.*" *Aspects of Apuleius'* Golden Ass. Ed. B. L. Hijmans and R. Th. van der Paardt. Groningen: Bouma's, 1978. 63-73. Print.

Williams, Craig A. *Roman Homosexuality: Ideologies of Masculinity in Classical Antiquity.* New York: Oxford UP, 1999. Print.

Winkler, John. *Auctor and Actor: A Narratological Reading of Apuleius's* Golden Ass. Berkeley: U of California P, 1985. Print.

Moshe Gold (essay date 2009)

Gold, Moshe. "Those Evil Goslings, Those Evil Stories: Letting the Boys out of Their Cave." In *Levinas and Medieval Literature: The 'Difficult Reading' of English and Rabbinic Texts,* edited by Ann W. Astell and J. A. Jackson, pp. 281-303. Pittsburgh, Pa.: Duquesne University Press, 2009.

[In the following essay, Gold engages with Emmanuel Levinas's model of ethical criticism in analyzing two retellings of Plato's Allegory of the Cave, one from the Talmud and the other from the authorial introduction to Day 4 of the Decameron.*]*

A HYPERBOLIC LEVINASIAN ENCOUNTER
BETWEEN BOCCACCIO AND THE *TALMUD*

How can stories of allegorical caves help demonstrate the value of ethical criticism summoned and scrutinized by Levinas? Unlike narratives in which, according to Levinas, "image[s] neutralize [the] real relationship" between a concept and an object,[1] Boccaccio's introduc-

tion to the fourth day of **The Decameron** and the *Talmud*'s story of Rabbi Shimon bar Yochai in a cave, with their exposure of human bodies and fatherhood, with their complicated attitudes toward the women in their respective narratives, and with their frank attempt to expose the horror of being, reevaluate the Platonic good beyond being. In both stories, fathers must confront the other's finitude, frailty, and mortality. Both retellings of the allegory of the cave (from Plato's *Republic*) stress the Other's interruption of self-possession. In each narrative, the proximity between self and other ruptures the retreat from Being to a safe domicile, one, I should add, that conspicuously provides a domestic space without any women.

"TOWARD APPERCEIVING A NON-ALLERGIC
RELATION" WITH SHADOWS OF THE CAVE: ON
MY INABILITY TO WRITE A PROPER CRITICAL
PAPER ON LEVINAS AND LITERATURE

[2]However, before spelunking what I will call interruptive stories of caves—Platonic and otherwise—I feel a need to acknowledge my rhetorical situation. On the one hand, after creating the main essay title printed above, I know I should maintain my professional demeanor as a professor of literature engaged in a rhetorical act; hence, you, my readers, probably expect me to write clearly about ethics or about Levinas. If so, you might expect me to proceed by adducing textual and historical evidence that explicitly states Levinas's knowledge of, for example, Rabbi Shimon bar Yochai (henceforth sometimes called in shortened form, Rashbi). Here, I might have to quote from Levinas's essay "Judaism and Revolution": "Rabbi Simeon . . . is the famous Rabbi Simeon bar Yochai, who has a special place among the *Tanaim.* He and his son spend thirteen years in a cave hiding from the Romans. Jewish mystical tradition attributes the Zohar to him. These facts are important."[3] A large portion of my essay would then attempt to develop "the importance of these facts." In addition, I would need to support my selection of Rashbi as part of my essay's focus by finding evidence of his supreme vigilance, since I will claim that a critic's attitude toward an ethics of interruptive cave narratives should manifest extreme vigilance. For example, I might need to refer to the Talmud's claim that Rashbi's sole occupation was the study of Torah (Shabbas 11a), an occupation taken to an extreme. In addition, you would probably expect me to provide equal attention to both Boccaccio and the Talmud, possibly even supplying what I might call a reciprocal reading of all the texts discussed herein (same technique applied, same motivation expressed, same amount of significance interpreted, and so on). This kind of clear exposition, it would seem, is my responsibility to you.

However, on the other hand, I sense that Levinas's prophetic prose, at times reaching beyond my comprehension, actually lends ethical cadence to his reading of rabbinic texts and his critique of art; hence, to engage in ethical criticism, should I not speak hyperbolically, performatively, in excess of propositional clarity? Might not this be my responsibility to you? Would it then be too hyperbolic to say, right away, that my professed dilemma comes from not knowing what or how to write (or how to utter and undo my "said" in a Levinasian timbre)? After all, in the very last sentence of the preface to *Totality and Infinity,* does Levinas not declare that "the very essence of language . . . consists in continually undoing its phrase by the foreword or the exegesis, in unsaying the said" (*TI* [*Totality and Infinity*] 30)? Hyperbolic vigilance in unsaying, in fact, establishes the critical attitude at stake here. Rashbi's love of Torah was beyond vigilant. His was a Torah existence of constant hyperbolic obsession and elevation. In other words, instead of applying the same Levinasian terms yet again to different texts—only to have Levinas returned to us in the exact same state—I write this essay as an attempt to explore what a performance of hyperbolic ethical criticism might entail.[4]

Hyperbolic performativity, though, does not necessitate writing without clarity. Rather, it demands constant unsettling of one's knowledge of ethical responsibility. When Levinas himself speaks of his own method as hyperbolic, he even speaks of emphasis and exasperation as a philosophical method: "Emphasis signifies at the same time a figure of rhetoric, an excess of expression, a manner of overstating oneself, and a manner of showing oneself. The word is very good, like the word 'hyperbole': there are hyperboles whereby notions are transmuted. To describe this mutation is also to do phenomenology. Exasperation as a method of philosophy" ([*Of God Who Comes to Mind*] *GCM* 89)!

What kind of critical work does such exasperation, excess, and hyperbolic vigilance involve? For the purposes of this essay, I will provide what may seem like more analysis of the Talmud than of Boccaccio (thus I will not provide a reciprocal reading); however, there has still not been enough critical attention to the importance of talmudic narrative in Levinas's strong claims about art. Boccaccio, though, is not a secondary thinker or writer here; his own authorial interruptions to critics (as expressed in his introduction to the fourth day) will, in fact, alter the dynamics of the entire "excess of expression." Boccaccio's own criticism displays a different "manner of showing oneself" (*GCM* 89) by addressing his audience directly and by proclaiming his own attempt to please others. Boccaccio's interruptive cave tale enacts a rewriting of Plato's allegory of the cave in order to provide a defense of literature! The irony cuts deeply: when read with Plato's allegory of the cave from *The Republic*—the very work that (according to conventional interpretations) exiles most poetic mimesis—Boccaccio's cave story radically alters Plato's philosophical creation into a (narrative) defense of Boccaccio's literary writing.

The Talmud's use of narrative also provides a defense of stories in the midst of another (more technical and legal) discourse, which a cave story interrupts. If the work of hyperbolic ethical criticism demands extreme vigilance, then I must ask, what does the story of Rashbi—a critic of mediation and nonintensity—living in a (Platonic) cave mean for ethical criticism? In the Talmud, Rashbi is often depicted as a man of extremes. For example, he is quoted as saying "If a man plows in the plowing season, and sows in the sowing season, and reaps in the reaping season, and threshes in the threshing season, and winnows in the season of wind, what is to become of Torah? No; but when Israel performs the will of the Omnipotent, their work is performed by others" (Berakhot 35b). One must submit entirely to the will of the Infinite. In other versions, Rashbi expresses an even starker position: "Only to those who have manna to eat is it given to study the Torah. For behold, how can a man be sitting and studying when he does not know where his food and drink will come from, nor where he can get his clothes and coverings? Hence, only to those who have manna to eat is given to study the Torah" (Mekhilta de-Rabbi Yishmael, Va-Yassa 3). According to this sage, the location for rigorous study is the desert or a utopian messianic era when, under (ostensibly) supernatural conditions, there is no need for human beings themselves to deal with natural, earthly, agricultural work.[5] Sustenance will be provided by divine grace. One gets the impression that Rashbi wants nothing to do with grains or this earthly world. How can I suggest an "unsaying of the said" here? Can I really attend to much significance here beyond the said?

To make matters more problematic, my desire to grasp and enjoy my critical labor here tends to distance myself from you, my reading audience. I still want to hear and echo the solicitous sound of Levinas's ethical critique of stories, but the jarring voices of good storytellers fight against Levinas's own voice. Perhaps if I were to pose my problems as a theoretical question, I might ask: In a world of disease, plague, deception, and idolatry, how can we read an allegorical story of the Good without being contaminated by Being? Or, how can I direct my effort "toward apperceiving in discourse a non-allergic relation with alterity" (*TI* 47)? If many critics are correct, then for Levinas—especially in "Reality and Its Shadow"—stories behave without propriety by creating disorder and by causing us to evade our responsibilities; if so, then critical interpretations of stories might reset our responses back to their proper position. Art, it would seem, removes us from the real historical world of the other's needs and demands, but critique can make us acknowledge the other who utters a story.[6] In fact, Levinas himself supports such an understanding when he claims that criticism should move "the inhuman work of the artist into the human world" ([*Levinas Reader*] *LR* 142). In this essay, however, I suggest that we must, with utmost vigilance, continue to question this standard understanding of Levinas's position. The very last sentence of "Reality and Its Shadow" demands that we critics "have to introduce the perspective of the relation with the other without which being could not be told in its reality, that is, in its time" (143). So many of Levinas's own lectures on talmudic stories accentuate, in fact, the holiness of "the perspective of the relation with the other." Moreover, unlike one traditional acceptance of Plato's claims in *The Republic*—namely, if you want to tell stories make sure you tell nice stories that praise God—Levinas does not necessarily remove stories from what he names "religion," namely "the bond that is established between the same and the other without constituting a totality" (*TI* 40).

Moreover, Levinas's own voice, however compelling or dissonant, constantly interrupts my sense that I have heard his story. Perhaps Levinas suffers to create these interruptive moments because he wants his audience to rub abrasively against his language. At those moments when an author interrupts the narrative's sense of totality, when the author acknowledges the ruse, the rhetorical exploitation, the corruption involved in the story, then the proximity between art and criticism shifts.[7] Instead of applying a Levinasian method to stories—and I am not even sure what such a method would look like—I would rather personally heed the summons of Levinas's talmudic exegesis: "to rub in such a way that blood spurts out is perhaps the way one must 'rub' the text to arrive at the life it conceals . . . to make it spurt blood—I rise to the challenge! . . . One must, by rubbing, remove this layer which corrodes [the words of] the text" ([*Nine Talmudic Readings*] *NT* 47). By rubbing Levinas's texts, do I not cause the life of his words to spurt blood, and, by doing so, do I not respond to the obligation Levinas has summoned me to—the height of the good? This critical sensation, I should add, usually does not lead to pleasure. It, so to speak, rubs me the wrong way. It is discomforting. However hard I try to soothe or join Levinas's texts together, his blood keeps spurting out. Moreover, good ethical criticism demands something better than the onanistic enjoyment of more traditional critical strategies. A critical rub should not sacrifice stories as reductive examples of philosophy, the love of wisdom. Rather, by rubbing Levinas's reading of the good, I sacrifice my own understanding of Levinas to the higher wisdom of the love of the good. In other words, my inability to address you, my audience, properly and ethically, might just signify a trace of that which Plato's allegorical cave could never entirely reveal to us: the good. Indeed, the hyperbolic and holy vigilance of Rashbi's experience in and out of the

Platonic cave will reveal what Levinas might even consider calling "an extreme vigilance of the messianic consciousness" (*TI* 285).

UP TO THE NECK AND AGAINST THE GRAIN:
NATURAL LIVING AND A SPECIAL DIET

As it turns out, Plato's well-known allegorical story of life in and out of a cave is itself allegorized, I argue, in Boccaccio's **Decameron,** and can be read against its grain in the Talmud's famous story of Rashbi, who literally lives up to his neck in grains of sand when he lives in a cave. Unlike the latter tale, Boccaccio's interruptive tale (in his introduction to the fourth day) is much more familiar to Boccaccio scholars and Medievalists in general.[8] A perusal of the story reminds us that Boccaccio's narrative takes us to an author's incomplete story of Filipo Balducci, whose wife dies, and who withdraws to "a tiny little cave with his son, fasting and praying and living on alms."[9] With great resolve, the father takes "great care not to let [the son] see any worldly things, or even to mention their existence, lest they should distract him from his devotion" (*TD* 286). The boy never leaves the cave, nor does he see any living thing other than his father. Boccaccio then tells us that after many years, upon the son's first visit to Florence, Filippo's boy sees all sorts of objects that fill him with amazement. After receiving answers from his father that satiate the son's curiosity about these objects, Filippo and son "chance" upon "a party of elegantly dressed and beautiful young ladies," whom the father calls evil goslings ("papere") whose "bills are not where you think, and require a special sort of diet" (287). The father, though, realizes that "his wits were no match for Nature" (287); his son is now "captivated" (288) by these ladies. At this point, Boccaccio stops his narrative, claiming to "have no desire to carry this tale any further" (287), and proceeds to address his audience and his critics.[10]

The rabbinic narrative, I imagine, is not nearly as well known. Even though the text is relatively long, this talmudic digression, a critical interruption of sorts, might captivate you, my readers, enough to challenge traditional reading of Plato's cave and Levinas:

> R. Yehuda, R. Yose, and R. Shimon [bar Yochai] were sitting, and Yehuda ben Gerim was sitting next to them. R. Yehuda opened and said, "How pleasant are the deeds of this nation [Rome]. They established markets; they established bridges; they established bathhouses."

> R. Yose kept silent. R. Shimon bar Yochai answered and said, "All that they established, they established only for their own needs. *They established markets to house harlots there,* bathhouses to make their bodies beautiful, bridges to get tolls."

> Yehuda ben Gerim went and told over their words, and [the words] were heard by those in power. The governing authorities said, "Yehuda who elevated [Rome], he

shall be elevated. Yose, who kept silent, he shall be exiled to Tzipori. Shimon [bar Yochai] who disparaged [Rome], he shall be executed."

He [R. Shimon bar Yochai] and his son [R. Elazar] hid in the house of [Torah] study. Every day his wife would bring them bread and a pitcher of water, and they would eat. When the [Roman] proclamation became worse, he said to his son, *"Women are simple-minded [the minds of women are light on them ('nashim daitan kalah alahen')]; perhaps they [the Romans] will torture her ['metza-ari'/cause her to SUFFER] and she will reveal our [location]."*

They went and hid in a cave. A miracle happened; a carob tree and a spring of water were created for them. They removed their clothes, and would sit in sand up to their necks. All day they would study. When prayer-time arrived, they would put on their clothes, cover, and pray. Then they would go back and remove their clothes so they would not wear out.

They dwelled in the cave for twelve years. Elijah came and stood at the mouth of the cave. He said, "Who will inform the son of Yochai the ruler has died and the proclamation has been annulled?"

They came out [of the cave]. They saw men plowing and sowing. They said "[These men] forsake the life of the World-to-Come and busy themselves with the transitory life!" *Every place they turned their gaze would be burned immediately. A heavenly voice went out and declared to them, "Have you come out to destroY my world? Return to your cave!"*

So they returned and dwelled [in the cave] twelve months, a year. They said, "The sentence of the evil ones in Gehinnom [Hell] is twelve months." A heavenly voice went out and declared "Go out from your cave!"

They went out. Every place R. Elazar destroyed, R. Shimon would heal. He said, "My son, *the world* has enough with you and me."

As night began to arrive on Friday [twilight before the Sabbath], they saw a certain old man who was grasping two bunches of myrtles, running as twilight came. They said to him, "Why do you need these?" He answered them, "to honor the Sabbath." "But isn't one bundle enough for you?" "One is for 'zachor' [remember the Sabbath (Exodus 20:8)]; one is for 'shamor' [observe the Sabbath (Deuteronomy 5:12)]." He said to his son, "Look how dear the mitzvot [commandments] are to Israel." They were appeased.

R. Pinchas ben Yair, the son-in-law, heard and went out to greet him. He took him into the bathhouse, and was massaging his flesh; he saw that there were cracks in his [R. Shimon's] skin [body/flesh]. He started crying, and tears fell from his eyes and *caused him [R. Shimon] to cry out in SUFFERING ["metzavkha"].* He [R. Pinchas ben Yair] said to him, "Woe is me that I see you like this." He [R. Shimon] said to him, "Fortunate are you for seeing me like this, since if you had not seen me like this, you would not have found in me so [much knowledge of Torah]." For at the start, when R. Shimon ben Yochai would ask a question, R. Pinchas ben Yair would answer with twelve solutions.

However, in the end, when R. Pinchas ben Yair would ask a question, R. Shimon ben Yochai would answer with twenty four solutions.

He [R. Shimon bar Yochai] said, "Since a miracle transpired, I will go and improve [establish] something." Since it states, "And Jacob arrived whole ['shalem'/intact (Genesis 33:18)]." And Rav said, "whole in his body, whole in his money, whole in his Torah." "And he encamped ['vayikhan'—from 'khayn'/gracious] before the city [was gracious to the city]" (Genesis 33:18). Rav said, "He [Jacob] established a coin for [the city]." Shamuel said, "He established markets for them." And R. Yochanan said, "He established bathhouses for them."

He [R. Shimon bar Yochai] said, "Is there something to improve [fix]?" They said to him, *"There is a place that has unclear status of impurity, and it is difficult ['tza'arah'/causes SUFFERING] for Kohanim [priests] to go around."* He said, "Is there anyone who knows if there was a presumption of purity established here?" A certain old man responded to him, "Here, ben Zakkai would cut lupines of teruma [so a location of purity]." He also did the same. Everywhere [the ground] was hard, he proclaimed tahor [pure]; everywhere [the ground] was soft, he marked [as impure].

A certain old man [or the same certain old man] said, "Ben Yochai has made a cemetery pure." He [Rashbi] said to him, "If you had not been with us, or even if you had been with us, but had not been counted with us, then what you say would be fine. Now that you were with us, and you were counted with us, [others] will say *'Harlots braid each other's hair [paint/dye each other], should not Torah scholars certainly?!'"* R. Shimon turned his eyes on him and his soul left [he died].

He [R. Shimon] went out to the market; he saw Yehuda ben Gerim. He [R. Shimon] said, "Is this one still in the world?" He put his eyes on him and made him into a heap of bones.

(Shabbat 33b-34a, my translation and emphasis)[11]

The immediate similarities to Boccaccio's story are striking: Filippo's resolve "to withdraw from the world and devote his life to the service of God" (*TD* 286), and Filippo's time in the cave with his son—taking "great very great care not to let him see any worldly things . . . never permitting the boy to leave the cave or to see any living thing except his father" (286). Indeed, like Boccaccio's tale, the story of Rashbi presents us with another father and son who live in a cave glorifying "the life eternal" (286). Yet, there are important differences. For example, unlike the death of Filippo's wife, what motivates Rashbi's entry into the cave? The Talmud informs us of Rabbi Shimon bar Yochai's denouncement of Roman establishments. Someone tells over the Rabbi's derogatory remarks and the Romans overhear the remarks. A death sentence is immediately decreed on the Rabbi, who proceeds to leave his wife, since she might reveal his location under torture—a departure which intensifies the tale's challenges to human responses to suffering—and together with his son hides in a cave for many years.

When they first leave the cave, they scorch the earth when they see quotidian life seemingly not devoted to eternal pursuits. Commanded by a voice from heaven to return to their cave, they spend another year in exile. When they finally exit again, they see someone preparing for the holy time of the Sabbath, one of God's commandments, and the father rehabilitates his earlier sense of social justice, establishing and fixing social spaces for proper use. The wife, though, does not reappear in the narrative. However, women are not completely absent from the tale since the figure of harlots, for some reason, frames and interrupts the narrative structure. At the start, harlots—dare I say "evil goslings"?—are Rashbi's stated reason Rome established markets; at the end, harlots are better than the individual who critiques the Rabbi's purification of the earth, a decree that stops priests from their small suffering of unnecessary walking around impure ground. Moreover, as we move from the potential suffering of the wife to the actual suffering of the priests, we witness the Rabbi's own suffering body as his son-in-law rubs the wounds in his flesh, wounds caused by living naked in the sand of a cave. How might a Levinasian rubbing of these stories call out to these cave dwelling fathers and sons? What act of saying is a critic to attempt—either to vocalize, write, hear, or read—when faced with Balducci's goslings, or for that matter, with R. Shimon bar Yochai's wife? Can ethical criticism only address fathers and sons in the light of goodness? Are we left with boys who seek control of the dwelling space and even seek to expand their power beyond the confines of the cave?

Now, my responsibility to you, my readers, is once again, I feel, an impossible duty to fulfill; I cannot possibly provide an effective reading of all these texts in the allotted space of an academically published essay. With the hope that beyond the confines of the space here, you will critique these shadowy allegorical caves yourselves, I will just suggest a few ways these texts irritate and rub each other in order to convey the degree to which I feel something is amiss in the more calming readings of Levinas's ethics (including his own reading of art). These seemingly easy-to-read stories enact what is at stake: the interruptive dimension of the stories heightens the critical imperative to address the living time of the Other.

Is it not curious that both Boccaccio's story and the Talmud's story deal with a father and son who leave society to spend years in a cave before encountering human others? Plato's cave has been revamped. No longer is there a Platonic wise man who must leave the shadowy cave to experience the Sun, only to return with, pun intended, en*light*enment to others. The question is now what relation, if any, exists between these Platonic retellings and Levinas's seemingly Platonic denunciation of art and elevation of the good beyond being? After all, does not Levinas want to guard us against that deceitful idol of false forms and images, that thing known as art? And yet, if Levinas proclaims that meaning in the irreducible nakedness of the other's face "is to return to Platonism in a new way" ([*Collected Philosophical Papers*] CPP 101), might we not acknowledge "a new way" in Boccaccio and the Talmud, one that still realizes the risks of art's deceptions? Might "a new way" also entail what Levinas calls an experience? According to Levinas, genuine "experience must even lead us beyond the nature that surrounds us . . . Truth would thus designate the outcome of a movement that leaves a world that is intimate and familiar, even if we have not yet explored it completely, and goes toward the stranger, toward a *beyond,* as Plato puts it" (48). But how might interruptive cave stories (in Boccaccio and the Talmud) signify attempts to trace "a new way" toward a "beyond" as Plato might put it—yet a transcendent beyond embodied in specific human others, not abstract conceptions? Even an author, such as Boccaccio, must, after hundreds of pages, leave his comfort, his brigata, his by now intimate and familiar world to proclaim the fact that he is still here for his readers, giving himself to others. True, his art soon engulfs his interruption, but is he completely removed from any "new way"?

The possibility that Levinas is well aware that art can imitate imitation, thereby providing a critique of imitation in artistic form, needs to be faced if art is to be experienced as anything other than idolatrous mimesis. As Pierre Hayat suggests, "it can also be supposed that aesthetic experience, by its resemblance—even deceptive—to ethics, teaches the language of 'otherwise than being.'"[12] Levinas's critique of artistic shadowing does not simply repeat Plato's diatribe against mimetic ignorance. Epistemology is not Levinas's main issue. Rather, Levinas's writing attempts to confront the good emanating from the Platonic allegory of the cave itself. Does not Levinas himself say that it "matters little that Plato made of it [the good] an idea and a light source" ([*Otherwise Than Being or Beyond Essence*] OB 19)? If I were to use what critics might call Levinasian language, I would probably say that the allegory might passively be waiting to be read as ethical, not just mythic; critical, not just artistic; rupturing, not just totalizing; and most surprisingly, as holy, not just sacred.[13] Perhaps the cave in Plato, Boccaccio, and the Talmud takes us to a space wherein we can sense an ethical height, one Levinas calls a "curvature of intersubjective space [that] inflects distance into elevation" (*TI* 291). Perhaps this curvature and inflection might even help us deal with the fact that Boccaccio's cave does not appear in the midst of thematic conversation between members of the brigata, but surprises us when the author talks to us, in first person, interrupting his ordered design. Boccaccio's cave story, it turns out, is his unanticipated gift to his audience. His personal interruption at the start of the fourth day introduces ethical criticism in a form of narrative discourse.

"THE NAKEDNESS OF THE FACE" INTERRUPTING TALES—OR, HOW CAN NARRATIVE TRUTH BE FOUNDED ON THE CALL TO JUSTICE?

[14]There is something deeply unsettling about the way these stories abruptly break off from narrative closure. After all, to return to Rashbi, the last image we have of Rabbi Shimon bar Yochai in our talmudic narrative is the Rabbi's gaze upon another which kills the other person, turning him into "a heap of bones." This haunting image from the talmudic narrative, then, at least on an initial reading, appears to validate the violence of the self's vision.

Both the opening and the closing talmudic scenes reveal the intensity, the extreme, the excessive, the hyperbolic character of Rashbi. He must evaluate the Roman institutions as only abusive and horrid—period, without qualification. Either one embraces Roman idolatry or Jewish Torah; there is no possible passage from one to the other. Yet, Rashbi's wife interrupts this opposition. She silently passes sustenance from the outside world to her husband and son as they hide out in their house of study; Rashbi's response is to leave her since her future time contains the possibility of her "tza'ar"/her suffering, her torture and rape by Romans.[15] In other words, R. Shimon's response to an other's projected suffering is to flee. The woman, in between the Roman world and the masculine world of Torah study, leaves the narrative discourse as well. Yet, whose body suffers violently? The masculine body of Rashbi, out of which hyperbolic denunciation comes forth, scorching the earth and harming others! Even a cry from on high, from the highest good, orders R. Shimon to get back to his cave before he commits more violence!

Prior to cave existence and experience, Rashbi cannot attune his mood to the embodied goodness in women. After all, besides his comment that "the minds of women are light on them," he has also stated that the Romans established markets "to house harlots there." The figure of harlots obviously has nothing whatsoever to do with extreme Torah sages. Is this not what is said in the static narrative form? Yet, R. Shimon's adjusted attunement to embodied post-cave existence and suffering asserts a connection between scholars and harlots! Even though harlots were the reason for markets (in precave discourse), harlots become better than the man who critiques R. Shimon's purification of the earth, a decree that stops priests from their small suffering of unnecessary walking around impure ground: "Harlots braid each other's hair [paint/dye each other], should not Torah scholars certainly?!" This analogical saying acknowledges a possible passage from the market (which is the exact location R. Shimon "went out to" at the end of the story) to the hyperbolic existence of the male Torah scholar. Indeed, as Levinas says, to "explain the notion of [ethical] substitution, it is necessary that I say more, that I use hyperbole" (*GCM* 91).

If we look retrospectively at the moments of suffering in the text, we move from the priests' suffering, pass through R. Shimon's own bodily suffering (as his son-in-law rubs the flesh wounds caused by naked existence in the cave sands of the earth), and pass back to the futural, nonexistent suffering/rape of the unnamed wife. What transpires in this passage? Hyperbolic nature, supernatural transcendence in a cave: no baked bread, no society, no markets, no human others. The image captures the brute naked existence of bodies buried in the sand, only clothed to pray. Miraculously sustained, son and father study Torah. Would it be too much to say that Rashbi has found his messianic desert of miraculous manna (as the said would have seemed to indicate from our earlier sources)? No harlots; no wife. Torah itself with a male companion is taken here to the ultimate extreme. The story challenges us with hyperbolic existence and method par excellence. Indeed, the rebirth of father and son from the cave is, in a strong sense, autochthonous, without need for a woman's reproductive body. Yet Rashbi's wife turns out not to be a danger to humans; Rashbi is the danger! He leaves the cave to eliminate fecundity and life. The transcendence of height, the heavenly voice demands that father and son return to their exile.

After another year of cave existence, the men leave not really changed until they encounter a human other who engages in preparations for holy time. As Levinas would point out, the larger subject matter of this specific talmudic discourse is, in fact, the need to prepare for the holy time of the Sabbath. Indeed, our story is framed by (or better, interrupts legal discourses on) women's obligations to prepare for this holy time. The mishnah[16] before our cave claims that one reason women die in childbirth is that they were not careful regarding the kindling of Sabbath candles (Shabbas 31b). The mishnah after our cave claims that when a man comes home on Sabbath eve, he must ask his wife if she has properly prepared for the holy time—including kindling the Sabbath lights (Shabbas 34a). What is the significance of this frame and what is its relevance to the narrative of Rashbi?

This aside of mine, this move to the technical (halakhic) portions of the Talmud, turns out to be essential to any reading of Levinas. The Halakah, that is, the walking in life following Torah and rabbinic law, does not appear to provide justice here; for Levinas, justice should exceed any specific law. Why should a woman die for not properly kindling Sabbath candles? There is no biblical commandment that decrees any such law. Our cave narrative interrupts the more technically legal sections of the Talmud to respond with the ethical force of an interruptive cave that goes beyond previous Platonic versions. Preparation for holy time goes beyond the letter of the law. The human other who carries myrtles runs to bring pleasantness into his home.[17] This old man's very life is saved, and, one could argue, saves father and son from more exile, by the particular act that demonstrates a move, a running, beyond the letter of the law. Rashbi confronts an other's finitude, frailty, and mortality, but he also encounters human labor for the height of the good. The fecundity of the earth, the labors of plenitude, can create awareness of proximity between husband and wife, between self and other. At this point, Rashbi will not flee from corporeal suffering (real or futural) to a masculine-only space. He experiences the vulnerability to others that exists at the most extreme realm of the self.

However, the story interrupts any sense of security, safety, comfort, and ease of vigilance. We do not leave the story with a nice moral said. Rashbi kills. We are left with a haunting image, a grotesque image of flesh leaving a human corpse's bones. The violence of Rashbi's totalizing vision radically transforms a human being into "a heap of bones." Perhaps the Talmud's overall representation of Rashbi presents us with an ultimate example of Levinas's contention (in *Totality and Infinity*) that a separated self has the potential to be a tyrant and has the potential to welcome the other.

What, we must wonder, can sanction such violent murder? Unlike many children's stories of goodness, in which readers end with a feel-good sense of "be good and kind and nice to others"—a morality we can too easily think we understand—this story demands adult acknowledgement of ongoing power over others. In a completely unexpected manner, does the story not suggest the holiness of infinite goodness? Rashbi's burning of the very earth in which we labor and enjoy, echoes, in fact, the violence of Levinas's goodness (albeit the trace of the good in *Otherwise Than Being*). The good that is other than being, says Levinas, "destroys without leaving souvenirs, without transporting into museums the altars raised to idols of the past for blood sacrifices, it burns the sacred groves in which the echoes of the past reverberate" (*OB* 18). The irreducible signification of the good violently burns sacred accounts of being, especially a being (Yehuda ben Gerim) whose account heard by oppressive political authorities casts more than aspersions on someone's ethos.[18] Rabbi Shimon's violent irruption reacts to more than a breach in courtesy. Rubbed critically, until we suffer to understand, the violence tears us away from easy and clear notions of religion and ethics; it demands that we counter slander, that we oppose those who would easily dismiss the life of those in this world and the life of this world itself. As the heavenly voice of the infinite Other proclaims to father and son when they first scorch the earth, "Have you emerged from your isolated existence with Torah study in your miracle-filled cave in order to destroy My world? Return to your cave!" We must learn from the miracle of nature, from the sensuousness of our naked bodies and our burial in the earth, from the power of

the shadowy cave to help those in the sun who suffer to cultivate their gardens. Only by "taking up a position in being such that the Other counts more than myself" can we confront those who oppose others (*TI* 247).

My own writing cannot take up such a position consistently or constantly. So I ask a basic question: why am I horrified at the end of this story? In part, I feel either my inability to comprehend death, or feel my desire to provide a clear resolution to murder (perhaps by saying, "well, the individual must have been an evil person or intended evil"). The Talmud demands nearly unbearable vigilance. There is no real total solace for others. This narrative keeps interrupting my complacency. But more than any interruption, this "new way" out of Plato's cave traces, or marks, or signifies something and some time that can never be represented fully, namely a messianic time and perspective in this world—"an extreme vigilance of the messianic consciousness" (*TI* 285). It addresses the obligation for unending, hyperbolic vigilance to others. Indeed, it challenges notions of utterly mutually exclusive realms between Torah and non-Torah realms. Where is Rasbhi at the end? In the market, the exact location that Rashbi first said was despicable and inhabited by harlots! Before encountering the old man with myrtles who prepares for holy time, the hyperbolic lover of ideal existence (an ancient version of Platonism) can still contrast his self with all inferior forms. Once encountering the pleasantness beyond the letter of the law, once in the bathhouse suffering from rubbed wounds, once purifying ground that caused suffering for priests, the figure of Rashbi, beyond the said, signifies a trace of true transcendence in this world, a trace of goodness and ultimate responsibility.

The story—that which risks being totalizing, idolatrous, corrosive, and corruptive—makes literal and particular what one experiences as complex and difficult to comprehend. The Rabbi needs the holy connection to divine transcendence in the cave to gain Torah wisdom (indeed, as the bathhouse discourse clarifies, Rashbi's analytic skills have multiplied dramatically; he is now a master Teacher). This Sophia, this wisdom, this techne, is absolutely valuable, crucial, and necessary, but insufficient for ethics. A philosophy, a love of wisdom that evades (and even does violence to) proper responsibility to others, a philosophical attunement to wisdom without acknowledgment of the good in the gift of the physical, material, labored-over world and embodied in human production and reproduction (including storytelling)—such wisdom will not suffice to help the suffering of others, nor will it heed the demands and commands of the infinite goodness of the ultimate height of supreme elevation (as the voice from heaven enunciates). As Levinas declares elsewhere, "in rabbinical thought, to obtain grace it is absolutely necessary that there be a first gesture coming from man. Even in Maimonides" (*GCM* 94). The revised Platonism demands a messianic vigilance of acknowledging this-worldly suffering, do-ing deeds for others (no matter how small and insignifi-cant their suffering might seem), not speaking slander to others, preparing for the time of holiness, creating pleasantness for others, and giving even bread and wa-ter for mouths without food or drink, all to counter im-purity and suffering, all to acknowledge a passing from Torah brilliance to marketplaces and harlots.[19] To braid an other's hair, to paint an other's countenance, to pret-tify an other's body, to acknowledge eros without con-cupiscence (as Levinas might put it)—should critics not engage in such activities? Is it too much beneath our own self assumed height?

And what soul-serarching resounds from Boccaccio's frame-tale and critical reply to his critics, which Boc-caccio narrates in the form of an interruptive cave tale? Let us remember that before any of his 100 stories, Boccaccio describes mass death, which describes, as Levinas might say, an "anxiety over Being—horror of Being—[that is] just as primal as anxiety over death" ([*Existence and Existents*] *EE* 5). Part of the horror here is my inability to comprehend death, but, as impor-tantly, might we sense this affect in art as well as in a corpse? Levinas himself writes, "A corpse is horrible; it already bears in itself its own phantom . . . [In fact] this impossibility of escaping from an anonymous and uncorruptible existence constitutes the final depths of Shakespearean tragedy" (56-57). During the plague of the Black Death (as depicted in the start of *The Decameron*) there are humans who desire to escape from existence while acknowledging that they cannot take possession of their own being. They have not yet come to be ethical subjects for others, taking on the ob-ligations of the others' suffering.[20] They must leave; they cannot dare breathe the air around them; there is simply too much brute existence and too much brute death. The question becomes: will they leave to ac-knowledge the stranger who knocks on their door or the servants who interrupt their storytelling, or will they build a stronger, safer, home? Will their stories mobi-lize or immobilize; or, is the real issue here one of radi-cal passivity?

In a sense, prior to portraying ten humans who say sto-ries, ten awake states of consciousness, Boccaccio nar-rates an inescapable persistence of bodies that are acted upon. By removing themselves from this horror of ex-istence, the brigata attempts to become a group of indi-vidual existents. All of their storytelling away from the horror attempts to create a private, safe home where they can pretend that the horror of brute existence does not, in fact, stand at their front door. The entire *Decameron* contains this trace of mass death, of injus-tice, so that when interruptions happen, Boccaccio makes us aware that stories do not offer real total so-lace, but stories can both point to a past that can never be represented, and address the need for unending com-

passion. Whereas a direct representation of the Levina-sian *il y a* is impossible, narrative allegory that per-forms interruptive ethical criticism, can inflect a curvature of space in which a trace of that which can-not be represented echoes in the shadows.

Stated otherwise, Boccaccio rubs against the human de-sire to be removed from horror. Each story in *The Decameron* tries to help the escape from existence, but those moments that interrupt the comprehension of a full story, mark Boccaccio's awareness that stories in-evitably draw consciousness out of its retreat. When Boccaccio interrupts his *Decameron* with his allegori-cal cave, he seems to be saying, "I know as a storyteller I cannot portray true transcendence," but by doing so, he leaves us with a trace of responsibility. How? A story cannot exist as an anonymous moment; it is fated to stay in its state continuously. However, by interrupt-ing this state at unexpected instances, Boccaccio cri-tiques his own narrative's fate. In other words, an inter-ruptive narrative shows us an author responding to those critics of art who complain that the "eternal duration of the interval in which a statue is immobilized differs radically from the eternity of a concept; it is the mean-while, never finished, still enduring—something inhu-man and monstrous" (*LR* 141). Boccaccio dramatizes for us how often humans try to use monstrous stories to escape the horror of being. Without the interruptive nar-rative in the fourth day, we might be right to distrust stories; do not stories cover over the murder of the Oth-er's immediacy with an idolatrous layer? However, when we remember Boccaccio's earlier depiction of the plague, we indirectly recall our own coming forth from "the irremissibility of pure existing," from the *il y a*. Boccaccio himself, in other words, tries to rub that idolatrous narrative layer away by interrupting our con-templation of and participation in the 100 stories.

The brigata might wish, and the bulky volume of *The Decameron* might seem (to some readers) to indicate that storytelling in this safe environment away from the plague-ridden others, might somehow be salubrious. But if this is so, why does Boccaccio not attempt to portray what happens upon the brigata's return to the openness of mass death? Can it be that Boccaccio en-acts a Levinasian obsession? According to Levinas, "the openness of space as an openness of self without a world, without a place, utopia, the not being walled in, inspiration to the end, even to expiration, is proximity of the other which is possible only as responsibility for the other . . . what took place humanly has never been able to remain closed up in its site" (*OB* 182-84). This new sense of utopian justice, acknowledged in my re-sponsibility for the other, cannot remain closed up or walled in. The other breaks open my illusory invulner-ability and sense of neat completeness.

In addition to our mini cave story, one that upsets the ordered 100—titular—stories, the mini story of the servants' own Decameron (which erupts at the start of day six), and the literary criticism Boccaccio performs in his own frame tale (his preface and epilogue), all upset the neat ordering of criticism and literature. These disorderly events expose the impossibility of fully telling what Levinas calls the *said,* not just the *saying* (as, again, a more standard reading of Levinas would have us believe).[21] The said of Boccaccio's interruptive stories of critique actually shows and tells us about those stories' untellability. Like the boy in the introduction to the fourth day, we need to do what Boccaccio calls "natural": we need to exit the (Platonic) cave of isolation and encounter the disorderly interruptions of our own self-narratives, what Boccaccio calls "not a complete story," "a part of one," a "digression" (all words used to tell us the critique-story of the fourth day's introduction). Nature, here, must include the ins and outs (from the cave), the elevations and degradations, the breaks in language (for example, the misnaming that names ladies "goslings," not women) the distress at the loss of the thing one loves.[22] It is even in the nature of ethical criticism to ask how to suffer need. After all, once the incomplete cave story is said, Boccaccio says, "All that remains to be said, then, is that [my critics] are perfectly free to turn me away if I should ever come asking them for anything. Thank God, I am not yet starving in any case; and even if I were, I know, in the words of the Apostle [Paul], both how to abound and to suffer need" (*TD* [*The Decameron*] 289). Is it really so surprising that this particular journey out of the cave turns into an experience with sexual difference? The boy only expresses desire for women after the father hides the literal word for women and names them "goslings." The boy desires what his father says "evil looks like"; the boy desires "goslings"; we desire narrative closure. Boccaccio's sense of nature and criticism connects the "tiny little cave" to language used by those who lie. In a word, the alterations of language and erotic desire might be no match for the father's wits, but such movement is exposed by the author in his interruptive saying.[23] The very first sentence after the unfinished tale is said resounds with Boccaccio's own natural wit: "But I have no desire to carry this tale any further." Boccaccio's own desire is for his own immediate audience.

Through interruptive stories of critique, we can move beyond the image of the cave as a caricature. By doing so, we go beyond Levinas's own call to his audience: "to introduce the perspective of the relation with the other" to criticism. I read the cave stories with a sense of the good here in this world, in this earth, in sexed bodies, yet somehow charging us beyond being. Those who stand in the way of even the smallest acts of kindness to others threaten to remove the good from society, the embodied good rooted in bodies and nature. Who truly interrupts Rashbi's constant estrangement from and endangerment of human others? Not the supreme deity in whose light Rashbi learns wisdom from when

in the cave. The interruptive other is the human other who prepares for holy time and the human who suffers, the human who, despite horrid conditions, circumstances, and setting, provides basic human pleasantness to others.

Like Rashbi's wife, we must act responsibly for others and acknowledge the proximity between the cultural institutions of knowledge, knowledge without cultural institutions, and the marketplace. If we are not vigilant in preparing for an other, for shortening distances others must walk, if we do not silence ourselves from words—even unintentional ones—said that can harm, might not we (critics and readers, myself and you, my audience) hear someone say of us, as we walk out in the market one fine day, "Is this one still in the world?" Torah is the supreme value for Rashbi (who endeavors as Levinas says, "To Love the Torah more than God"), but Torah learning must not be disembodied from this worldly existence with others. Empirically and ethically, Rashbi uses his imagination to enact messianic time in the here and now. A hyperbolic methodology and attitude are maintained, but brought down to this earth so that an elevated height can be attained here and now. Even agricultural work (collecting myrtle branches or farming) for the sake of ethical living for others and the commandments of the Infinite can be preparations for the time of holiness. Rashbi is still obsessively hyperbolic, but, in a sense, it is exactly excessiveness—in going beyond the letter of the law, in myrtles, in food and water, in braiding an other's hair, in the death that can happen if a self does not prepare candles—that breaks Rashbi out of his own being.

And from Boccaccio's perspective, those fathers who try to negate sexual difference in their sons soon learn that the metaphysical desire for the other can, in reality, become manifest in a plot to desire real women. When speaking of his ability "to suffer need," Boccaccio rubs harshly against Saint Paul's words: "I know both how to be abased, and I know how to abound: every where and in all things I am instructed both to be full and to be hungry, both to abound and *to suffer need*" (Phil. 4:12). The other who interrupts Boccaccio's father and son is not Christ, but women; the other who interrupts Rabbi Shimon bar Yochai is not the supreme deity in whose light the Rabbi learns wisdom when in the cave; the interruptive other is the suffering other. Rashbi's wife is given no words to utter, but her face speaks, perhaps in a way not that much unlike the speaking described by Levinas: "The face speaks. The manifestation of the face is already discourse" (*TI* 66). Harlots, better than uncivil men, introduce the perspective of the relation with the other. The silent wife, the unseen harlots, the evil goslings, each, in her own way beyond the self's previous capacity to understand, forces the male self to question what it means to be an ethical subject. To suffer interruptive cave narratives ethically, signifies a metaphysical desire, in hyperbolic vigilance, that exceeds self-enjoyment and even totalizing critiques of art. The self is never finished with the possibility of violence; vigilance means being for others beyond all frames of self-conception or reference.

Notes

1. Emmanuel Levinas, "Reality and Its Shadow," *LR* 132.

2. The "shadows" here are not simply allusions to Socrates' allegorical story told over in Plato's *Republic*. I refer as well to skepticism, which would question my very attempt to perform in this essay what I will refer to as hyperbolic ethical criticism: "Philosophy is not separable from skepticism, which follows it like a shadow it drives off by refuting it again at once on its footsteps . . . Skepticism is refutable, but it returns" (*OB* 168). I have borrowed the line, "toward apperceiving a non-allergic relation," from Emmanuel Levinas, *TI* 47.

3. *NT* 108. The Aramaic term "tanaim" (plural form of "tanna") indicates the teachers or sages whose sayings can be found in the Mishnah. Note also, a kabbalistic tradition attributes R. Shimon bar Yochai with the creation of the Zohar, a work that reveals, according to this tradition, usually hidden transcendent mysteries of the Torah. Quite a few stories portray R. Shimon bar Yochai as an extremely holy individual. During his life, one of the stories declares, there was no need for a rainbow (a "sign" from heaven), since R. Shimon bar Yochai was so suffused with holy radiance that he was a sufficient sign for his generation.

4. For a similar charge to Levinas scholars (one that concerns the problem of writing about ethics at the expense of enacting ethical criticism), see Adam Zachary Newton, "Versions of Ethics; Or, the SARL of Criticism: Sonority, Arrogation, Letting-Be," *American Literary History* 13, no. 3 (2001): 603-37.

5. See David Hartman's *A Living Covenant: The innovative spirit in traditional Judaism* (New York: The Free Press, 1985), 281-85. By not addressing the full story in the Babylonian Talmud, Hartman, I would argue, reduces the complexity of Rabbi Shimon bar Yochai's positions. Compare "In All Your Ways, Know Him: Two Modes of Serving God," the second chapter of *By His Light: Character and Values in the Service of God,* Based on addresses by Rabbi Aharon Lichtenstein, adapted by Rabbi Reuven Ziegler (Jersey City, N.J.: Ktav Publishing House, 2003), 27-48.

6. I am indebted to those who have written on Levinas and art before me, in particular, Jill Robbins, *Altered Reading: Levinas and Literature* (Chicago: University of Chicago Press, 1999); Colin Davis, "After Ethics: Levinas without stories," *After Poststructuralism: Reading, stories, and theory* (London: Routledge, 2004), and his "Hermeneutics and Ethical Encounters," *Ethical Issues in Twentieth Century Fiction: Killing the Other* (Basingstoke: Macmillan, 2000); Adam Zachary Newton, *Narrative Ethics* (Cambridge, Mass.: Harvard University Press, 1995), and his "Versions of Ethics"; Edith Wyschogrod, "The Art in Ethics: Aesthetics, Objectivity, and Alterity in the Philosophy of Emmanuel Levinas," *Ethics as First Philosophy: The Significance of Emmanuel Levinas for Philosophy, Literature and Religion,* ed. Adriaan T. Peperzak (New York: Routledge, 1995), 137-48; Robert Eaglestone, *Ethical Criticism: Reading After Levinas* (Edinburgh: Edinburgh University Press, 1997); Gerald L. Bruns, "The concepts of art and poetry in Emmanuel Levinas's writings," *The Cambridge Companion to Emmanuel Levinas,* ed. Simon Critchley and Robert Bernasconi (Cambridge: Cambridge University Press, 2002), 206-33; and Richard Cohen, *Ethics, Exegesis and Philosophy: Interpretation after Levinas* (Cambridge: Cambridge University Press, 2001). More than any of the other writers, Cohen serves as a constant reminder to me that performative interruptions risk turning, all too easily, into the kind of aestheticism/idolatrous rhetoric that Levinas takes to task severely and effectively. In addition, I greatly admire both Cohen's clarity and his vigilant awareness of the Jewish traditions raveling Levinas's discourses. While several of my concerns overlap with those addressed by all of these writers, my readings of Boccaccio, Levinas, and Rabbi Shimon bar Yochai present significant challenges that, I hope to show, have not yet been addressed adequately by Levinasian criticism.

7. *TI* 47. For a nuanced reading of rhetoric in Levinas, see Susan E. Shapiro's "Rhetoric, Ideology, and Idolatry in the Writings of Emmanuel Levinas," *Rhetorical Inventions and Religious Inquiry: New Perspectives,* ed. Walter Jost and Wendy Olmsted (New Haven: Yale University Press, 2000), 254-78.

8. Scholars often recall this tale, perhaps because of the author's personal reappearance in the midst of all *The Decameron*'s tales, perhaps because of the author's direct responses to critics. At the very least, the first person singular form of "I" throughout the introduction to the fourth day (and the frame tale) refers to Boccaccio's implied author/personae.

9. Boccaccio, *The Decameron* [*TD*], trans. G. H. McWilliam, 2nd ed. (New York: Penguin Classics, 2003), 286. Hereafter cited parenthetically by page.

10. For a wonderful philosophical reading of this specific narrative (in particular, his chapter "The Nature of Desire"), see Gregory B. Stone, *The Ethics of Nature in the Middle Ages: On Boccaccio's Poetaphysics* (New York: St. Martin's Press, 1998). I have learned much about "nature" in the Middle Ages from Stone's work. However, whereas Stone connects his analysis of Boccaccio to Heidegger and Lacan, I read Boccaccio from within a response to interruptive sayings in the Talmud and Levinas. Whereas Stone's aim is to show reality imitating language and to argue "the birth of desire as the effect of language, lawgiving, and the name of the father" (76), my explorations attend to what Levinas would call "metaphysical desire." In other words, it is important that the son feels satisfied about objects in Florence, but his encounter with human others (and sexually different others), not "objects," begins to break apart the father's (and the son's) restrictive conceptions of existence and existents. More importantly, the entire cave narrative is the only story told by Boccaccio himself, and the interruptive story is addressed directly to his audience, in an attempt to create a sense of immediacy.

11. The most comprehensive close textual exegesis in English of this talmudic narrative remains Jeffrey L. Rubenstein's "Torah and the Mundane Life" in his *Talmudic Stories: Narrative Art, Composition, and Culture* (Baltimore: John Hopkins University Press, 1999). However much I gained by his "explication of the text"—as literary critics have often said—I feel that Rubenstein's focus on comparative versions of the story and particular historical contexts actually reduces the ethical significance and rigor of the overall text. A Levinasian approach to the suffering in story, and to those moments that require a critical rub, addresses significance in the story beyond the attention to historical exigencies of textual production. In addition, I am not sure that Levinas would agree with several of the generalizations Rubenstein posits, such as "the union of husband and wife is the most elementary human relationship" (112). As I will argue, Rashbi's wife actually enacts a primary ethical force in the narrative. Overall, whereas Rubenstein tends to desire mediations, I attempt to acknowledge ethical interruptions that go beyond reconciliation or mutual recognition. Nonetheless, despite significant differences, I remain indebted to his attentive reading of nuances in the Talmud's phrasing.

12. Pierre Hayat, "Introduction to the French Edition: Challenging History, Demanding Reflection," *Unforeseen History,* trans. Nidra Poller (Urbana: University of Illinois Press, 2004), 10.

13. Here I rub against the recent tendency to use pairs of opposed terms to explain Levinas. For example, the entire "Part One" of Michael B. Smith's *Toward the Outside: Concepts and Themes in Emmanuel Levinas* (Pittsburgh: Duquesne University Press, 2005), which Smith calls "Concepts," addresses seven splits, such as "Sacred/Holy" and "Totality/Infinity." However accurate any of these "concepts" might be (after all, Levinas himself uses these terms), the constant reinforcement of these oppositions often begs the critical question of how passage is possible from the Sacred to the Holy or from Totality to Infinity.

14. I have borrowed the line, "the nakedness of the face," from *TI* 74.

15. When "tza'ar" (her suffering) is coupled with "megalyah" (revealing), the text suggests the forced sexual revealing of a woman (for critics interested in sufficient textual evidence, see Ketuvos 39a-b, Bava Kama 59a, and Nedarim 91b). For those critics interested in the textual evidence and variants, see Rubenstein.

16. The Mishnah is, among other things, a compilation of Oral Laws (edited probably in the end of the 2nd century CE).

17. Rubenstein nicely draws out the implications of the semantic constellation involving linguistic forms of "pleasantness" throughout the entire narrative.

18. For an intriguing perspective on what she calls "a tragic aspect at the heart of Levinas' Good" (80) see the last section of Bettina Bergo's third chapter of her *Levinas Between Ethics and Politics: For the Beauty that Adorns the Earth* (Dordrecht: Kluwer Publishers, 1999). According to Bergo, "If the violence of the Good is to be sought in its disruption of the order of being, it remains for all that, a violence—one which transforms immanence into the for-the-other of the prophet, and of any self or subject" (81). In general, Bergo's work is noteworthy for attending to the challenges of the biblical, prophetic, and talmudic inflections and—perhaps most significantly—the messianic consciousness of Levinas's writing in addition to what has become the more standard passages and emphases in Levinas criticism.

19. In the very last sentence of the first paragraph of the very last section of *Otherwise Than Being,* Levinas brings us back to Plato: "It is as though the Platonic Ideas themselves owed their eternity

and their purity as universals only to the perishing of the perishable, before requiring a republic so as to come out of their bad idealism and be efficacious" (176). Might a revision of Plato's *Republic*, perhaps even the cave, keep haunting Levinas? Perhaps Levinas is even obsessed with bringing, so to speak, the Platonism (and utopianism) of Rashbi's cave out into the quotidian world of work and specific embodied existents?

20. For the existent's movement out of existence, see Levinas's *On Escape,* trans. Bettina Bergo (Stanford: Stanford University Press, 2003) as well as his *Existence and Existents.* See Bergo (especially at the beginning of her *Levinas Between Ethics and Politics*) for a particularly insightful exploration of this process.

21. See the work of Colin Davis for a more expansive treatment of these issues.

22. My reading of Boccaccio remains indebted to the thoughtful and critical discussion of "nature" in Gregory B. Stone's *The Ethics of Nature in the Middle Ages.* Stone effectively dismantles any reading of Boccaccio that would keep what is "natural" removed entirely from what is linguistically constructed. However, again, Stone's focus is on what is often called "natural desire," not what Levinas calls "metaphysical desire." If Stone is correct—if Boccaccio's interruptive story is a culturalist, not naturalist, manifesto, and if the boy does not start desiring until after he hears improper linguistic constructions ("goslings")—then Levinas's ethical claims would be even more important for reading Boccaccio: "metaphysical desire" can exist on a more basic level in the self than erotic desire or social constructions of desire do! A more significant dilemma arises once Irigaray's critique of Levinas enters any hyperbolic ethical criticism, but her question of an ethics of sexual difference deserves much more space than this essay will permit.

23. There is not enough space here to pursue the ethical implications, but perhaps I can suggest that Boccaccio here becomes, for a moment, more open to Irigaray's sense of otherness than Levinas's. That is, it might be possible to read Boccaccio's interruptive cave story as a critique of Levinas's position in *Totality and Infinity* that the son challenges the father's experience of time. In Boccaccio, the "young ladies" influence the son, who in turn, challenges the father's sense of time and obligation. The son, in other words, does not start the breaking open of the self's sense of time. Particular, embodied (sexually different) others first break open the son's sense of self.

Abbreviations

LR: *The Levinas Reader.* Ed. Sean Hand. Oxford: Basil Blackwell, 1987.

NT: *Nine Talmudic Readings.* Trans. Annette Aronowicz. Bloomington: Indiana University Press, 1998.

OB: *Otherwise than Being or Beyond Essence.* Trans. Alphonso Lingis. Pittsburgh: Duquesne University Press, 1996.

TI: *Totality and Infinity.* Trans. Alphonso Lingis. Pittsburgh: Duquesne University Press, 1969.

Irene Albers (essay date January 2010)

SOURCE: Albers, Irene. "The Passions of the Body in Boccaccio's *Decameron*." *MLN*, 125, no. 1 (January 2010): 26-53.

[*In the following essay, Albers takes a historical approach to the Romance novella, exploring how the* Decameron *contributes to research into the "language of the body"—the involuntary expressions that are natural and physiological signs of emotion, and the voluntary gestures that are rhetorical and stylized, such as the swooning feigned by the courtly lover.*]

I. PATHOGNOMY IN THE NOVELLA

The[1] sixth day of Boccaccio's **Decameron** begins with a very short and apparently insignificant story. A knight wants to shorten a woman's long journey with a narrative, a "novella," but he is a bad storyteller, who mixes up names, muddles, and hopelessly botches the story. The reaction of his female listener is described in the following terms: "Di che a madonna Oretta, udendolo, spesse volte veniva un sudore e uno sfinimento di cuore, come se informa fosse stata per terminare [. . .]."[2] Thus, Madonna Oretta reacts bodily to the aesthetic and linguistic failure of the novella: the blockage of the narration causes the sweat to flow from her pores and her heart to miss a beat. Sentences like this one are often skimmed over, as if they referred only to formulaic bodily reactions and gestures, long become cliché, that do not contribute to the meaning of the text. In contrast, the purpose of this article is to explore such notations of the physical by regarding their ambiguous reference to language and body, poetics and somatics, literature and anthropology. The novella about Madonna Oretta shows both the close relation between bodily and linguistic gestures and the poetological dimension of the theme, since it refers to the bodily and emotional impact of storytelling, which was already a subject of ancient rhetoric. As a "metanovella" that thematizes novella telling, the story which Boccaccio places at the exact center of his **Decameron** hints at a poetics of the bodily emotions that will remain specific to the genre of the novella until the seventeenth century.[3] Whether in Marguerite de Navarre's *Heptaméron,* Bandello's *Novelle,* Boaistuau's and Rosset's "histoires tragiques," Cervantes's *Novelas ejemplares* or María de Zayas's *Novelas amorosas y ejemplares,* just to name the major works, one always encounters numerous references to both expressive body movements and gestures related to emotions. Because the subject of the novella, from Boccaccio onwards, is the tragic or comic encounter between physiological needs and moral or social norms, between "nuritura" and "natura," this form of affective and pathetic body language is of fundamental relevance to the overall meaning of the text.[4] The novellas refer, in particular, to what today are often called the somatic automatisms or vegetative epiphenomena of emotions.[5] These include such involuntary physiological symptoms as blushing, turning pale, being paralyzed by fear, crying, fainting, horripilation (i.e. goose bumps), sweating, trembling, fever, etc. The conspicuous frequency of such somatic automatisms is also found in Kleist's stories (in part drawing on the Romance novella). While the phenomenon has often been commented on in Kleist scholarship, it has hardly attracted attention in research on the Romance novella.[6]

The superordinate area of "gestures," that which Lavater calls, in the context of his research on physiognomy, "pathognomy,"[7] and Darwin, "expression of emotion,"[8] and Wilhelm Wundt, the "expressive movements" (the German word is "Ausdrucksbewegungen")[9] of the body, has always received exceptional status, because it can neither be fully assigned to the psyche, nor to the body. Thus, the actor Johann Jakob Engel (1741-1802), in his important treatise *Ideen zu einer Mimik* (1785-86), endeavors to differentiate between bodily reactions which do have purely somatic causes (when exhaustion causes one's eyes to close or quick running leaves one out of breath) and those, which can be ascribed to "effects of the soul." Engel refers to the latter as "physiological gestures":

> Among the physiological gestures, there are many which simply do not obey the free will of the soul, which can neither be kept back when real sentiment draws them forth, nor be generated when real sentiment is lacking. Thus are the tears of sorrow, the paleness of fear, the blushing of shame: phenomena which I should not properly call gestures, but which may be so called according to my somewhat broader explanation.[10]

The main distinction in this passage is that between voluntary and involuntary, intended and unintended (and impossible to intend) acts of expression. The nineteenth century does not come to terms with this problem. Thus, Wilhelm Wundt's psychophysics of expression treats the unity of an involuntary process that encompasses both the emotions and the body: "Every

change of psychic condition is connected to simultaneous changes of correlative physical processes."[11]

Even if the psychology of expression and its terminology is now considered obsolete, many traces of it remain in the cultural and literary theory of the first half of the twentieth century, especially in German scholarship.[12] It is not fortuitous to note that the majority of scholarly works on gestures ("Gebärden" in the German literature of the time) in literary texts—especially from antiquity and the Middle Ages—stem from this field.[13] Representative of work in this direction is the dissertation by the second editor of the *Altfranzösische Wörterbuch,* Erhard Lommatzsch (1886-1975). In his *System der Gebärden-Dargestellt aufgrund der mittelalterlichen Literatur Frankreichs* (Berlin, 1910), he investigates medieval texts, on the one hand, using Wundt's terminology and the differentiation between voluntary and involuntary gestures, and on the other, inquires, like Darwin, into the original purposefulness of the bodily automatisms as vestiges of evolution.[14] Literature is regarded here as a document for the theories of Wundt and Darwin. In spite of the great historical distance and difference, medieval texts confirm anthropological constants. In this regard, involuntary gestures are often distinguished from "conventional gestures," as if the former, even in literary texts, do not refer to cultural conventions but directly to bodily processes and emotions.[15] However, the references to "physiological" or "involuntary" gestures in literary texts concern, at the most, what one must call a secondary level of automatism, for they are ultimately employed consciously by the author of the text. Thus, if the following treats a "language of the body," this language is not a "body language" that can be reduced to a language; rather, it treats narrated and written bodies as they are presented to the reader in the language of the novella.[16] The body does not speak; it is due to cultural, social and aesthetic systems of meaning that we interpret body movements as a "language" and consider specific movements to be expressions of specific emotions. Literature partakes in these systems of meaning without merely reproducing them. The anthropologically and psychologically oriented study of expression passes over this phenomenon of literarily mediated and staged body language. Conversely, the same applies to the studies in the tradition of research on "non-verbal communication" from the beginning of the 1970s onwards, which newer literary studies employ to approach the body language found in literature. In contrast to the earlier works on literary body language, with their lack of awareness of the textuality and literariness of the phenomenon, in these studies anthropological and other context relevant questions are often set aside completely in favor of an occasionally overly systematic classification of the literary representation of "nonverbal communication."[17] This is motivated by the effort to keep semiotics and communication theory free from anthropological questions (such as the relationship between body and culture, body and aesthetic representation). Consequently, this line of research has little to say concerning pathognomy. The prevalence of a semiotic approach passes by the fact that the somatic automatisms are indeed always encoded according to literarily and culturally predetermined formulae, but, in the fictional communication situation, also stand for a non-cultural entity and are ascribed to physiological processes. Since the representation of pathetic emotion, even since antiquity, has been encoded, a repertoire of set phrases has been developed, especially in the area of the rhetoric of lamentation and the representation of love.[18] This has led to a tension between a physiologization, which refers to universalized assumptions on the human body, and a rhetorization of these "physiological gestures," which refers to the code. Therefore, the article on "Gebärde" (gesture) in a dictionary of rhetoric states:

> Thereby gesture is considered partly as an involuntary, unforced expression of nature by the soul, employed and understood by all persons, but beyond this, as the speaker's or actor's willfully-created, conventionalized, and learnable means of representation, which later makes its appearance as the courtly art of affectation.[19]

Whether involuntary bodily expressions are the effects of universal physiological automatisms or particular cultural, historical, or even gender specific condifications, is to this day treated as controversial. Just as perspectives from the sciences and humanities are in opposition concerning the status of these bodily expressions, novellas express ambiguity between physiological determinism and rhetorical *topos,* authenticity and simulation, reference to nature or to culture.[20] Instead of understanding from the outset every reference to the physiology of basic emotions as a historical construct, and turning to Boccaccio's *Decameron* as an example, the proposal will be developed that the conflict between physiology and rhetoric, between body and language, must itself be historicized.[21] In this way one may observe in the comic or tragic encounter between bodily desire and social norms in the Romance novella and its history, the difference between sign and body, rhetorical and physiological reading, literature and anthropology, and how these are configured text-internally and how they make an essential contribution to the constitution of the genre.

II. BOCCACCIO: BODIES BETWEEN *DIGNITAS* AND *MISERIA*

Boccaccio's *Decameron* is a work full of bodies of ideal beauty. Seldom does a novella lack a reference to a character's impeccable "bellezza," a term which represents moral values at the same time.[22] This neat correspondence between visible appearance and invisible characteristics, however, is fundamentally challenged even before the beginning of the storytelling: The frame narrative of the *Decameron* begins, as is well known, with the portrayal of the devastating epidemic of the Plague in 1348, which ruins both the individual body and the body of society; humans are reduced to animal savagery. Also left in ruins is the unproblematic analogy between the outside and the inside of the body, for even the medical experts of antiquity are said to have failed when faced with the Plague, because they were simply not able to recognize the signs of infection: "Quanti valorosi uomini, quante belle donne, quanti leggiadri giovani, li quali non che altri, ma Galieno, Ipocrate o Esculapio avrieno giudicati sanissimi, la mattina desinarono co' lor parenti, compagni e amici, che poi la sera vegnente appresso nell'altro mondo cenaron con li lor passati" (19). Medicine loses its authority.[23] It not only fails to heal the Plague, but even to diagnose it correctly. This failure comes as no surprise, since the symptoms of the deadly disease vary: if in the East nosebleeds are the "manifesto segno di inevitabile morte" (10), in Florence the "certissimo indizio di futura morte" (11) are the "black or blue bruises" ("macchie nere o livide"; 10) that extend across the body. The *o* is significant: Boccaccio's hypotactic syntax, rife with "o che" structures, figures the falling apart of knowledge, the now only hypothetical character of statements concerning the meaning of the "signs." The uncanny epidemic renders the body opaque and the creatureliness of man contingent, for not only has medical knowledge (along with the authorities of antiquity) succumbed to a crisis; the signs, "segni," of the body have become just as unreadable as the Plague as a whole.[24] This question, too, is met by Boccaccio with a laconic either/or sentence: the Plague, he writes, is either the effect of an astrological configuration ("per operazion de' corpi superiori") or a just, divine punishment ("o per le nostre inique opere da giusta ira di Dio"; 10). The theological explanation of the Plague thus becomes a single hypothesis among others; it is referred to as if it were only a cited interpretation of the occurrence. In contrast to Dante's earthly world, this world's lack of transparency conceals the immaterial beyond.[25] In light of this finding, Kurt Flasch has coined a phrase (referring to the famous dictum of Adorno) to describe the *Decameron*: "poetry after the Plague."[26] This suggests, and it has often been so understood, that the worlds of the narratives contrast the Plague; the former are a mere form of "divertimenti,"[27] and create a maximal distance from the heteronomy that the group of seven women and three men leave behind.

The majority of the hundred novellas, however, treat another, hardly less dangerous illness, lovesickness,[28] which is associated with the Plague through a multitude of linguistic and thematic isotopies, and also causes the body to share in the mental suffering it causes.[29] When, for example, in the eighth novella of the fourth day, the "forze d'amore," is deemed a "maravigliosa cosa," Boccaccio resorts to the exact same formulation of the "Introduzione": "Maravigliosa cosa è a udire quello che io debbo dire," which refers to the "qualità della pestilenzia" (11).[30] The analogy between Plague and lovesickness is also based on the fact that the emotions in Boccaccio's work, according to premodern theories of emotion, are external instances and entities which "overcome" and "seize" the subject. They are not the result of "elezione," but of the "appetito," which does not obey the will.[31] This is reflected by the use of common metaphors from the realm of nature, like the fire metaphors that often appear in passive constructions: "essendo acceso stato d'altissimo e nobile amore" (3); "in fiero furore accesa" (189); "dello amor di lui mi s'accese un fuoco nell'anima" (893); "di subita ira acceso."[32] In other cases, the passivity of the subjects is shown by verbs like "venire" and "cadere": "ed andando gli venne un pensier molto pauroso nell'animo"; "cadde in un crudel pensiero" (165).

The analogy between lovesickness and plague corresponds to the doubling of the frame: if the narrator in the "Proemio" offers his book to the women as a medicine for lovesickness and "malinconia,"[33] the "therapeutic fiction"[34] of the frame means that the storytelling can offer protection from the Plague. Accordingly, one cannot understand the novellas as mere diversion from the catastrophe of the disease. The research of Hans-Jörg Neuschäfer already includes the argument that the novellas also stage the bipolarity of humankind between "miseria" and "dignitas," between limits and possibilities, as is so prevalent in the frame.[35] With this thought, he founds the still controversial classification of the *Decameron* as a text of typical Renaissance characteristics. But if here the "dignity" of the human is derived above all else from his capacity for linguistic and aesthetic production, and the "misery" of the human is derived from the limits set by his bodily nature, in the following it will be argued that this bipolarity not only applies to the body itself, but also to language: just as in Boccaccio's work, on the one hand, the language of the body is freed from its determination through bodily processes, the language of the novella, on the other, is tied back to the body and is thought to affect it. The body becomes semiotic and language becomes bodily.

III. THE LANGUAGE OF THE BODY IN THE *DECAMERON*: PHYSIOLOGY AND SIMULATION

In the **Decameron,** Boccaccio employs the whole repertoire of pathognomic gestures: He lets his characters blush, turn pale, faint, cry, laugh, sigh, tremble, break into a sweat and scream in agony. Their hair is raised, their pulses or their hearts race.[36] These (psychogenic) pathognomic bodily expressions are to be differentiated from the unambiguously somatogenic phenomena, such as the sneezing in the presence of sulfur in the tenth novella of the fifth day (521). It is clear that this emphasis does not simply reflect a static repertoire of formulae,

not only because of the great frequency and diversity of these expressive movements: the eighth novella of the first day thematizes, in the form of a joke, a "beffa," the impossibility of pictorial representation of involuntary body movements: when a courtier wants to know how he can adorn a room with something which has never been seen and never been painted, the humorous retort is that he should have a "sneeze or something like one" painted, "starnuti o cose a quegli simiglianti" (79). That which eludes the medium of pictorial representation is, in terms of its linguistic representation, representable, outside of the existing repertoire of formulae, as something "never read."

Surprisingly, no studies seem to exist on this complex of gestures and body-bound expressiveness in the **Decameron.** If the body is treated in Boccaccio research, then only in the context of the discussion of "naturalistic" interpretations: here, Boccaccio is deemed the discoverer of sensuality, and the *Decameron* is read as a carnival of fantasy and insurgence of the flesh against clerical asceticism[37] in the name of a morality of "nature" stemming from the tradition of the fabliau.[38] Pasolini's well known film adaptation of the *Decameron* (*Il Decameron*, 1970) is founded on this interpretation (although politicized and updated in his version). The body's adverse counter-thesis, in a manner of speaking, claims that the **Decameron** is a quasi-religious textbook on overcoming this sensual love.[39] Recently, the attempt has been made, inspired by discourse analysis, to separate moral from medical discourse on the body, leading to the view that the so called poetic naturalism of the **Decameron** is indebted to a traditional, amoral form of medical naturalism.[40] If Boccaccio is seen as taking on the role of a doctor intending to dispel melancholy among women, then one can only argue on the level of the contents (as in the sexual morality reconstructed by Schnell with the help of medical discourse) and must lose sight of the difference between two forms of providing therapy against melancholy and lovesickness: on the one hand, medical treatises, and on the other, literary texts. However helpful the reconstructed medical-historical context may be, problems in poetics cannot, apparently, be solved through discourse analysis alone. Precisely the bodily expressions are involved in a form of play of perspectives, between the character-level and the narrator-discourse, between the fictional communication in the novella and that between the narrator-reader.

The question as to the aesthetics and poetics of the body in the **Decameron** cannot be answered in this way; for in the novellas, the medical-naturalistic reading of body language is only one option, and applicable at the character level. It is not the narrator but the characters who assume that the movements of the soul correspond to bodily changes and, inversely, that from the observation of bodily changes valid conclusions on the

status of the soul can be drawn. In the scholastic terminology of the Middle Ages, which draws on the medicine of classical antiquity, one already observes *motus
animi* and *motus corporis* in an analogy or continuity:
the "movements" affect the body through the heart.
Scholarship has been able to document that Boccaccio
was not only familiar with the Latin commentary on
Guido Cavalcanti's song, "Donna me prega," but also
copied it down himself.[41] In this commentary there is
also a passage explaining the psychophysical mechanism which connects the emotions to bodily processes
by triggering "alterations" to, and "movements" of, the
body:

> Deinde cum dicit, Move cagiando colore, loquitur auc-
> tor de motibus ipsius amoris, id est, de diversis alter-
> ationibus quas haec passio inducit in corpus, et vult
> dicere quod in hac passione corpus alteratur diversis et
> contrariis alterationibus, quod quia non accidit in aliis
> passionibus animae ut in ira, in tristitia, in timore, et in
> similibus. Nam in amore corpus alteratur nunc ad istum
> colorem, nunc ad illum qui est oppositus; similiter
> etiam alterat nunc ad risum, nunc ad planctum; et hoc
> est quod vult dicere, post cum dicit, Muove cangiando
> colore, riso in pianto [. . .] Causa autem istarum diver-
> sarum alterationum quas amor inducit in corpus est
> propter diversitatem ymaginationum quae representatur
> sibi de re quam amat. Nunc autem representatur sibi al-
> iquid propter quod timet, tristatur et desperat, et secun-
> dum hoc accidit quod in ipso diversimode movetur
> calor naturalis et spiritus, quia nunc movetur ad intra,
> nunc ad extra, nunc partim ad intra, nunc partim ad ex-
> tra, secundum quod diversimode movetur in diversis
> passionibus animae, ex cuius motu diverso accidit di-
> versificatio coloris corporis ita ut nunc sit unius coloris,
> nunc alterius, et nunc assimiletur figura eius figurae ti-
> mentis, nunc gaudentis, nunc ridentis, nunc plorantis.[42]

Emotions cause not only changes to the physiological
system, but they are understood to be identical with
these changes.[43] The soul has body parts. The modern
(Cartesian) problem of the interaction between the body
and the soul, between the material and the immaterial,
between *commercium mentis et corporis* is not yet
posed, because speculative physiology in the Aristotelian tradition claims that the pneuma (*spiritus*), formed
from blood in the heart, is that which connects them.
The *spiritus* conveys impulses of desire or rejection
from an imagination or perception to the heart, where
emotions are located, and causes the heart to move.
Joyful and pleasant excitement coincides with the expansion of the heart, so that the *spiritus* spreads
throughout the whole body, while fear and grief coin-
cide with the *spiritus* flowing back into the heart, which
constricts.[44] The idea, then, concerns forms of alternate
movements: expansion and contraction, movement out-
wards from the heart or inwards towards it, warmth or
coolness, broadening or narrowing, the flowing out of
bodily fluids or their holding back. Compared to the
other emotions (such as anger, sorrow, fear), each of
which corresponds to a typical change to the body, the

changes to a person in love, according to Dino del
Garbo, are inconsistent: laughing followed by crying,
blushing followed by sudden pallor. Based on the dominant state of emotions and the imaginings of the
lovesick patient, the heart expands or contracts. Dino
del Garbo's commentary reflects the prevailing conception of medicine of the time: the emotions include the
above described somatic processes, which were the subjects of elaborate works, especially concerning so called
"lovesickness."[45] It is to be assumed that Boccaccio
made use of this medical knowledge.[46] This does not
mean, however, that his novellas reproduce it or integrate it into appropriate passages as the narrator's explanatory comments; rather, knowledge of the physiology of emotions in the ***Decameron*** appears on the level
of the characters, who employ it, for example, to understand the behavior of others. It is narratively staged
knowledge that is contradicted by the voice of the narrator on more than one occasion. For this reason, the
phenomena of body language must be observed, with
great exactitude, in the constellation of narrative perspectives and acts of communication of a concrete text.
For example, King Agilulf, who, in the second novella
of the third day, wants to find out which stableboy has
had an affair with his wife, checks the pulse of every
sleeping servant and thus discovers the culprit:

> Preso adunque un picciolissimo lume in una lanter-
> netta, se n'andò in una lunghissima casa che nel suo
> palagio era sopra le stalle de' cavalli, nella quale quasi
> tutta la sua famiglia in diversi letti dormiva; e esti-
> mando che, qualunque fosse colui che ciò fatto avesse
> che la donna diceva, non gli fosse potuto ancora il
> polso e 'l battimento del cuore, per lo durato affanno,
> potuto riposare, tacitamente, cominciato dall'un de'
> capi della casa, a tutti cominciò a andar toccando il
> petto per sapere se gli battesse. Come che ciascuno al-
> tro dormisse forte, colui che con la reina stato era non
> dormiva ancora; per la qual cosa, vedendo venire il re
> e avvisandosi ciò che esso cercando andava, forte com-
> inciò a temere, tanto che sopra il battimento della fatica
> avuta la paura n'agiunse un maggiore; e avvisossi fer-
> mamente che, se il re di ciò s'avvedesse, senza indugio
> il facesse morire. E come che varie cose gli andasser
> per lo pensiero di doversi fare, pur vedendo il re senza
> alcuna arme diliberò di far vista di dormire et d'attender
> quello che il far dovesse. Avendone adunque il re molti
> cerchi né alcun trovandone il quale giudicasse essere
> stato desso, pervenne a costui e trovandogli batter forte
> il cuore seco disse: "Questi è desso."

(251)

This involuntary confession of the body, as analyzed by
sociologist Alois Hahn,[47] is, however, of little use to the
king, since he cannot identify the man in the dark. In
order to mark him with a "segnale" (252), he cuts his
hair off on one side. By replacing a physiological symptom, which cannot be feigned for long and cannot be
portrayed, with an arbitrary sign, he renders it vulner-

able to manipulation: the clever stableboy cuts off one side of each of the other servants' hair, so that on the following morning identification is no longer possible.

That even physiological signals can be manipulated is shown in the eighth novella of the second day: the same woman, in possession of all the clear symptoms of being deeply in love, attempts to seduce the Conte d'Anguersa and pretends, when he rejects her, that he has raped her. Although she was heteronomous, even somatically, against the "stimoli della carne" and the "forza d'amor" (188),[48] shortly afterwards she regains control of her body and uses it as evidence of her version of the story. She is successful, for the audience of her theatrical pretense employ the model of unity between *motus animi* and *motus corporis* and are thus deceived:

> E così detto, a una ora messesi le mani ne' capelli e rabuffatigli e stracciatigli tutti e appresso nel petto squarciandosi i vestimenti, cominciò a gridar forte: "Aiuto aiuto! ché 'l conte d'Anguersa mi vuol far forza" [. . .] Al romor della donna corsero molti, li quali, vedutala e udita la cagione del suo gridare, [. . .] dieder fede alle sue parole [. . .].
>
> (189)

The reader can observe how the characters fall for the woman's cunning play with body language. He finally asks himself whether the symptoms of her passionate excitement for the Conte were not also feigned. After all, relevant treatises, such as Andreas Capellanus's *De amore,* taught that even bodily symptoms, from which others determine one's psychic disposition, can be voluntarily produced.[49] As agents, Boccaccio's characters have access to this courtly discourse, which presents love as an art to be learned; as interpreters of the behavior of others, they tend to commit a "naturalistic" fallacy.

Whereas from the perspective of the characters the analogical reading of the language of the body dominates, in the juxtaposition of character perspectives and narrator discourse arises an awareness of the fundamental ambiguity of bodily expression, between reflection of nature and simulation of a code. As "movimento subito e inconsiderato" (378), the bodily phenomena triggered by passion (in this case anger) are beyond control, but can, nevertheless, be simulated. The language of the body is for Boccaccio both the expression of the natural "concupiscibile appetito" (105, cf. 239), or other passions, and a medium which, like language, enables the production of distance, freedom from the heteronomy of creatureliness and carnality.[50]

The very first novella of the first day teaches that the analogy between emotional gestures and interior conditions is definitely unreliable. Just as the doctors in the frame narrative fail to diagnose the Plague, so the cler-

gyman who hears Ser Cepparello's general confession, and the cause of his failure is that he believes he can see the sinner's supposed remorse.[51] The "pessimo uomo in vita" (32) takes advantage of the assumption that the movements of the body, over which humans have no control, must automatically show the honest truth rather than deceive: "E in brieve de' così fatti ne gli disse molti; e ultimamente cominciò a sospirare e appresso a piagner forte, come colui che il sapeva troppo ben fare quando volea" (42).[52] The confessor infers especially intense contrition from the tears ("sempre piagnendo forte") and sighing ("gittò un gran sospiro": 43) that accompany the confession: he takes them as visible proof of the truth of the speech and believes he can actually see the contrition.[53] Cepparello, however, who can be considered an author figure, or a master of lies,[54] deceives not only with language but also with his body, creating a fictive character, San Ciappelletto, the saint.[55] He can willfully control his tears ("quando volea"). As the doctors no longer are able to read the body and cannot detect those who are infected with the Plague, the theologian errs concerning the inner life, in that he believes he can arrive at the internal through the external (the tears and sighs).[56] The internal and the external, body and emotion, can be dissociated. This destruction of the "correspondence between truth and appearance, between ethos and gesture, between soul and body, signifies new "spaces of fictionality," writes Walter Haug.[57] Such spaces of fictionality also arise in the realm of bodily expression. The implicit reader is thus offered a form of casuistics on body reading, which encourages skepticism and case-by-case decision making, since bodily expressions do not simply make visible the inner movements of the soul. The crisis of language and nominalistic inspiration in the ***Decameron*** (which has been shown by others in addition to Kurt Flasch), also includes the language of the body. Moreover, a pure "phenomenalism" is also faced with the problem that even appropriately encoded bodily expressions can have more than one meaning. This is often reflected by Boccaccio in passages on the reactions of the *brigata* to the novellas. For example, after the story of Alatiel (second day, seventh novella), the sultan's daughter, who manages to get married as a virgin although she has "slept with eight men perhaps ten thousand times" ("con otto uomini forse diecemilia volte giaciuta era"; 184), the *brigata* sigh, and the narrator speculates on the meaning of their sighing: "Sospirato fu molto dalle donne per li varii casi della bella donna: ma chi sa che cagione moveva que' sospiri? Forse v'eran di quelle che non meno per vaghezza di così spesse nozze che per pietà di colei sospiravano" (185). These unclear relations also serve a poetological purpose: when Boccaccio, in his **"Conclusione dell'autore,"** claims that one could read, from the summaries of the novellas, what happens in them, just as one can see in the "fronte," a person's forehead, what is occurring in their "seno," in their mind, the relationship between the body and the inner self becomes a metapoetical metaphor.[58] To the extent that the signs of the body become opaque, so do the stories in terms of the "morals" associated with them, according to the model of the exemplum. This corresponds to the problematization of the role of the exemplum in the **Decameron,** associated with Boccaccio's breaking with the Middle Ages.[59]

IV. IMAGES OF THE BODY AND "PATHOS FORMULAE" IN THE *DECAMERON*

Even though pathetic gestures themselves form a code that can be simulated, there are several novellas that are not affected by this ambiguity and in which the suspicion of simulation is not brought up at all. These novellas tend to create images of bodies rather than body signs: concise images of bodies, suffering, mourning, or otherwise excessively impassioned. Such passages do not concern the fictional communication among the characters, but rather, the communication between narrator and audience. The heightening of the body's susceptibility to manipulation, apparently, leads to an increase rather than a reduction of its inaccessibility. This observation applies especially to the tragic novellas. The few interpreters who mention this aspect include Erich Auerbach, who, however, aesthetically stigmatizes the tragic novella by calling it "melodramatic."[60] A different interpretation comes to light when considering the eighth novella of the fourth day, which is dedicated to tragic love stories. According to the narrator, Neifile, her novella is to be understood as criticism of persons who oppose the "natura delle cose" (411). She means both Girolamo's mother, who brings about her son's death when she wants to end his love for a tailor's daughter, Salvestra, because of the couple's class difference, and she means Salvestra herself, who believes she can "extract love from a heart in love" ("dello innamorata cuor trarre amore" [411]), without also removing the "anima" from the body, or ending a life.[61] Before nature offers the "consiglio," she "consumes herself": the reflexive verb "consumarsi" describes what is represented in the novella as a strange form of passive suicide. When Girolamo, after a two year stay in Paris, returns to Florence, Salvestra is married. The mother's hope that the son will forget the tailor's daughter when distanced from her is not fulfilled. Salvestra, who in the meantime has married a tradesman, seems to have forgotten Girolamo and does not react to his absence in front of her house. He thus hides in her house one evening, waits until her husband has fallen asleep, "places his hand on her breast," and addresses her: "O anima mia, dormi tu ancora?" (414). These are his only words in the whole novella. Salvestra holds back a scream and sends the man, who she has now recognized, away. Girolamo desires his own death and asks her if he can lie next to her to warm up, because he has gotten cold in his hiding place. She accepts through

compassion: "Coricossi adunque il giovane allato a lei senza toccarla: e raccolti in un pensiero il lungo amor portatole e la presente durezza di lei e la perduta speranza, diliberò di più non vivere; e ristretti in sé gli spiriti, senza alcun motto fare, chiuse le pugna allato a lei si morì" (415). In his desire to die, Girolamo compels his own body to stop living. The formulation "ristretti in sé gli spiriti" requires explanation.[62] It means not only (as the English translation implies) that "he held his breath,"[63] but the "spiriti" refer to the Galenic theory of pneuma, and the theory of the vitally important function of the flowing out of the air-enriched blood, the "pneuma zotikon" or "spiritus vitalis," out of the "fountain" or heart.[64] By holding back inside himself these fully material "life spirits," Girolamo removes the life from his body.[65] Since every form of external violence is lacking, the action can hardly be called suicide; anthropologists, such as Claude Lévi-Strauss, refer to such an occurrence as a "voodoo death."[66] Since the doctors who later examine Girolamo's body find no organic causes, they diagnose pain as the cause of death.[67] The image of this pain is his clenched fists. Fist clenching is encoded as a sign of anger and strained will, but also figures, in this novella, the physiological effects of held back "life spirits," which include a brief struggle for life and a body cramped in pain.[68] Decision and result, voluntary and involuntary behavior of the body, are thus integrated into the one gesture. The third part of the sentence, after the second semicolon, with four syntagmas connected only by the repeated "and," ending in "si morì" transforms the gestures into a concise linguistic figure. This is an example of Boccaccio's "poetic prose." The syntactical caesuras between the syntagmas also figure the breathing pauses taken by the narrator, who is moved himself by the pathetic death.

Is Girolamo's death an effect of the self-consuming "nature of things" or his active desire to die? A sudden death by pain or a voluntary act? The novella does not end with the diagnosis of the doctors, although it is already entirely sufficient, as an exemplum, to show what Neifile announced at the beginning: as is so often the case, the novella simply does not end as an exemplum, either semantically or narratively. Salvestra goes to the church to attend the lamentation, where Girolamo's body is laid out, and the women, says Neifile, according to the custom of "usanza nostra" (416), lament. Neifile's motivation for attending, on the level of the plot, is not her own passion but the suggestion of her husband. Only now does she become "pietosa" and desire to see the dead man whom she rejected when he was alive. The narrator comments on this change with an exclamation that the "forze d'amore" are a "maravigliosa cosa" (416), and it is not mere chance that this recalls the phrase in the "Introduzione" concerning the Plague. The closing scene now shows how Salvestra, while engaged in the ritual of lamentation, falls over dead on Girolamo's corpse:

Quel cuore, il quale la lieta fortuna di Girolamo non aveva potuto aprire, la misera l'aperse, e l'antiche fiamme risuscitatevi tutte subitamente mutò in tanta pietà, come ella il viso morto vide, che sotto il mantel chiusa, tra donna e donna mettendosi, non ristette prima che al corpo fu pervenuta; e quivi, mandato fuori uno altissimo strido, sopra il morto giovane si gittò col suo viso, il quale non bagnò di molte lagrime, per ciò che prima nol toccò che, come al giovane il dolore la vita aveva tolta, così a costei tolse. Ma poi che, riconfortandola le donne e dicendole che sù si levasse alquanto, non conoscendola ancora, e poi che ella non si levava, levar volendola e immobile trovandola, pur sollevandola, a una ora lei essere la Salvestra e morta conobbero; di che tutte le donne che quivi erano, vinte da doppia pietà, rincominciarono il pianto assai maggiore.

(416-17)

The gestural plotting of the scene follows the lamentation and its "pathos formula," showing the ritual and symbolic completion of a "basic experience." Further, the ritual behavior is laden with meanings in the opposite direction. Salvestra's pain is so overburdening that she dies of it. The scream is her last utterance, and marks the moment of her death. In this scene, one finds a reversal typical to Boccaccio: while in other novellas (especially in those one would call pornographic today) he parodies language games, generally to a humorous end,[69] here, the now topical formulae of ritualized bodily behavior, Girolamo's fist clenching and Salvestra's scream, are given other emotional content and thus tied back into other physiological processes.[70] Aby Warburg's term "pathos formula," which he applies to the visual arts of the Renaissance, seems to appropriately describe the specific poetics of such expressive gestures in Boccaccio. Pathos formulae, according to Warburg, are a repertoire of "expressions of maximum inner pathetic movement" (in German: "Ausdrucksformen des maximalen inneren Ergriffenseins"), which arise in antiquity and, in the following ages—always with increasing specificity—are assimilated by art.[71] Especially in the Renaissance, these static formulae from the Middle Ages are charged with new energy. They are to be seen as "memoranda of archaic excitements and fears [. . .] so called 'engrams of passionate experience' whose emotions, only allegedly overcome through a history of civilization, along with the objects thereof, can be brought back to life in differing historic situations."[72] Warburg turned to Wundt's and Darwin's theories of facial expression, among others: for Darwin, gestures are an unconscious bodily memory-trace of evolutionarily older and biologically necessary behavior; for Warburg they are signs of an afterlife for the "primitive," and mark the exchange between the biological and the symbolic of which culture is composed.[73] Pathos formulae, thus, are situated between the somatic and the aesthetic, and articulate the tension between these two poles, the body-bound pathetic and the formulaic conventional: "Pathos formula" ("Pathosformel"), writes Salvatore Settis in an important interpretation, "is therefore a

word with inner "explosive force," it includes both the fixedness of the formula and the impetus of the pathos: in this internal tension lies its richness and fruitfulness."[74]

Attempts have been made to render this "explosive force" available to literary scholarship, but Ernst Robert Curtius's research on the *topos,* pertinent here, turns away from the anthropological question and ends in a mere categorization of gestures of sorrow in medieval literature.[75] The same applies to the many above cited investigations of gestures, which appeared around the turn of the century, particularly in studies of medieval literature. The medievalists limit themselves to the positivistic collection of concrete kind of gestures. Such programs relinquish two forms of insight: first, they miss the irreducible internal tension in Warburg's term, between the historical invariance of the physiological symptoms of emotions and the historic transformation of their symbolization; second, they disregard the fact that Warburg's is a theory of art based on anthropology. As a "magically effective image of excitement" ("magisch wirksames Erregungsbild"), the pathos formula serves simultaneously as the articulation and the warding off or distancing of passionate emotions.[76]

This cause and effect relationship of expressive linguistic body images can also be discerned in Boccaccio. Situations of reception internal to the fiction are components of many of his novellas. Nastagio degli Onesti's famous novella (the eighth novella of the fifth day), recalling Dante's visions of hell, describes the dreadful sight of a naked woman hunted in a pine forest by a horseman and two dogs.[77]

E essendo già passata presso che la quinta ora del giorno e esso bene un mezzo miglio per la pigneta entrato, non ricordandosi di mangiare né d'altra cosa, subitamente gli parve udire un grandissimo pianto e guai altissimi messi da una donna; per che, rotto il suo dolce pensiero, alzò il capo per veder che fosse e maravigliossi nella pigneta veggendosi. E oltre a ciò, davanti guardandosi, vide venire per un boschetto assai folto d'albuscelli e di pruni, correndo verso il luogo dove egli era, una bellissima giovane ignuda, scapigliata e tutta graffiata dalle frasche e da' pruni, piagnendo e gridando forte mercé; e oltre a questo le vide a' fianchi due grandi e fieri mastini, li quali duramente appresso correndole spesse volte crudelmente dove la giugnevano la mordevano; e dietro a lei vide venire sopra un corsier nero un cavalier bruno, forte nel viso crucciato, con uno stocco in mano, lei di morte con parole spaventevoli e villane minacciando. Questa cosa a un'ora maraviglia e spavento gli mise nell'animo e ultimamente compassione della sventurata donna, dalla qual nacque disidero di liberarla da sì fatta angoscia e morte, se el potesse.

(504)

Before the horseman kills her and throws her "cold heart" to the dogs to be eaten, he explains to the appalled witness, Nastagio, that what he has seen is not reality, but the enactment of a punishment in hell, to which both are sentenced. He is punished because he killed himself over the woman who turned him down; she because she is pleased by the suicide. The woman is repeatedly revived and the hellish hunt begins anew. Every Friday, he overcomes her at the same place where she was cruel to him. The chase lasts one year for each month during which she previously turned him down. Nastagio's hair is raised when he hears the story: "udendo queste parole [. . .] quasi non avendo pelo addosso che arricciato non fosse" (506). This is a bodily symptom of his terror, his "spavento."[78] He wavers between "compassion" and "terror" ("compassione" and "spavento"), or in other words, "tra pietoso e pauroso" (506). The pathos formula of the image of the screaming naked woman is made bodily in the text-internal pragmatics, transformed into a bodily reaction, one that, as has been shown by Hellmut Flashar, was already connected to "phobos" in Aristotle's thought.[79] Boccaccio's Nastagio now has an entirely pragmatical idea: he can use the play acting that takes place in the forest every week—virtually a "theater of cruelty," as Artaud puts it—to frighten the "cruel woman" ("crudel giovane" 508), whom he has been pursuing for years in vain, so that she relents.[80] The plan is successful. The viewers of the event, which resembles a play staged by Nastagio, react with fear and "maraviglia." The women cry, as if they themselves were subjected to what Guido degli Anastagi, the horseman, does to the woman: "tutte così miseramente piagnevano come se a se medesime quello avesser veduto fare" (507). The greatest "spavento" is experienced by the woman Nastagio targets (cf. 508). In the end, she marries Nastagio out of fear rather than for love. He uses the vision of hell as an instrument for the profane interests of his individual desire.[81] The pathetic body images in this episode act forcefully on the recipients; the transfer of emotions (modeled after the Plague) almost amounts to contagion. However, the irony of the ending—which states that all women in the city then became more accessible (508)—suggests criticism of this form of the exemplum's employment of emotional effects.[82] The author-reader communication breaks with the communication between the fictional characters.

V. The Effects of Language on the Body: The Therapeutic Fiction of the Frame

It is not in the novellas alone that characters react bodily and emotionally to what they see and hear. Such situations are also formed in the frame narrative, in the commentary following the individual novellas, in which the reactions of the *brigata* are conspicuously portrayed as bodily. This first occurs among the narrators: in the introduction to the tenth novella of the first day, Pampinea says that when a person wants to use storytelling to cause others to blush, he often ends up blushing himself.[83] The same applies when one tells of others' tears,

"raccontar l'altrui lagrime" (354), the words with which Fiammetta announces the Ghismonda novella. The narrator of a novella also becomes moved himself—in rhetoric, this is a well-known requisite for the successful transfer of emotion to the audience.[84] The occurrence of such a transfer is demonstrated by the many references to the audience's blushing (63, 247, 560), sighing (392, 185), crying (159, 366, 763), "compassione" (159, 392, 418, 738), and above all, their at times uncontrollable and boisterous laughter (48, 71, 100, 142, 185, 479, 556, 575, 593, 644, 674, 681, 702, 710, 763, 802, 817, 842, 843). Often, multiple reactions occur simultaneously. After the Masetto novella (III.1) some of the women blush while the others laugh: "Essendo la fine venuta della novella di Filostrato, della quale erano alcuna volta un poco le donne arrossate e alcuna altra se n'avean riso, piacque alla reina che Pampinea novellando seguisse" (247). Or the women blush first, only to break into laughter: "La novella da Dioneo raccontata prima con un poco di vergogna punse i cuori delle donne ascoltanti e con onesto rossore nel loro viso apparito ne diede segno; e poi quella, l'una l'altra guardando, appena del rider potendosi abstenere, soghignando ascoltarono" (63, cf. 560). The narrator of the *Decameron* apparently finds it important that speaking about passion and hearing novellas have direct bodily effects, causing, according to the medical assumptions of the epoch, either the expansion (in laughter) or the contraction (in weeping or sighing) of the heart. The humors are set into a motion that "cleans" the subject, or frees him from harmful emotions and humors.[85]

Winfried Wehle has contributed most to the development of the thesis that the narration of novellas in the Renaissance is based on an "emotion-triggering poetics" ("affektive Wirkungspoetik"), which aims to serve as a therapy for melancholic illnesses.[86] One could also speak of a "somatic poetics," since—in the tradition of rhetoric and the medical theory of catharsis—physiological effects, beyond those moral or psychological, are ascribed to poetic language. In his defense of poetry in the fourteenth book of his *Genealogie deorum gentilium libri*, Boccaccio explicitly mentions this effect.[87] It corresponds to the therapeutic fiction of the *Decameron*'s **"Proemio,"** in which Boccaccio offers his work to the lovesick women for the restoration or re-creation of the humors' and emotions' balance.[88]

But can one reduce the Renaissance novella to a form of therapy for melancholy and the psyche? One cannot, for the text-internal acts of communication are undermined by fiction. The reader of the *Decameron* is not identical with the audience in the frame narrative. When Boccaccio claims of the *Decameron* in the **"Conclusione dell'autore"** that his stories, like wine, might improve or ruin ones health depending on how they are used (cf. 961), his earlier promise to the women becomes ironic: the reader, not the author, becomes responsible for the effects of his work. What is exhibited by his novellas also applies to his poetics: bodily effects are unpredictable and susceptible to manipulation. What helps one person might hurt another. It therefore remains unresolved, whether the *brigata,* on their return to Florence, will survive the Plague. In this passage, Boccaccio no longer addresses his reader in the second person, as he did at the beginning; rather, the use of the third person suggests a critically reflective reader, who, like the characters in the novellas, can free himself from the somatic automatisms. Through aesthetics and language, this reader might continuously participate in play involving both the manipulable and inaccessible nature of the body. Any "Principe Galeotto" who becomes infected, in the sense of the Dante-citing subtitle of the *Decameron,* will, at the very least, not end up in hell. In contrast to Nastagio, Boccaccio does not want to coerce his readers, regardless of whether such coercion would benefit or harm either of the parties; he does not want to subject them to a new heteronomy of the body, but to protect their freedom. The poetics of the body play a decisive role to this end, since rhetorical and physiological readings constantly undermine one another, and there is no position of equilibrium between the manipulable and inaccessible nature of the body.

The texts of the novellas treat not only the effects of culture on the body, but also the return of the body to culture and society, and give central importance to what, today, is explored by neurophysiological theories of emotion (in opposition to more cognitivist approaches). Novellas thus engage in a form of literary anthropology. As an alternative to other anthropological discourses, which seek normativeness and systematic coherence, the novella negotiates the open spaces between the cultural and natural determination of the body. This corresponds to the significance of affective poetics in the novella, in which narration has the ability to affect the body and experiments with this ability. In this sense, the implicit poetics of the novellas and their communities of narrators is already an "anthropology of literature," which investigates the ability of literature and narration to influence the passions and imbalances in the metabolism of the body. Even beyond Boccaccio, the language of the novella is a language of the body.[89]

Notes

1. Special thanks to Aaron Whittington for his support as a native speaker.

2. Giovanni Boccaccio, *Tutte le opere,* ed. Vittore Branca (Milan: Mondadori, 1976) 4: 537. Unless otherwise noted, page numbers refer to this edition of the *Decameron.*

3. This is emphasized in Guido Almansi's, "Lettura della novella di Madonna Oretta," *Paragone* 270 (1972): 139-42: "[. . .] è una novella su come raccontare o come non raccontare una novella. Si tratta quindi di una metanovella, cioè di una novella sull'arte di novellare": 142. By contrast, in Regina Psaki's analysis failed story-telling stands for failed sexuality and Madonna Oretta for the female audience who are "ill-treated by raconteurs (lovers) less expert and amiable than the narrator": "Women in the *Decameron,*" ed. James H. McGregor, *Approaches to Teaching Boccaccio's* Decameron (New York: Modern Language Association, 2000) 83.

4. Hans-Jörg Neuschäfer, *Boccaccio und der Beginn der Novelle: Strukturen der Kurzerzählung auf der Schwelle zwischen Mittelalter und Neuzeit* (Munich: Fink, 1969) 62ff.

5. Klaus Scherer's influential component-process model of emotion lists, among the five components, the "neurophysiological component (bodily symptoms)" and the "motor expression component (facial and vocal expression)," without discussing the difficulties of differentiating between, for example, an instance of blushing, which is a "physiological symptom," and tears, which are a "motor expression" with the function of "communication." I want to show that the difference between "symptom" and "expression" has a long and debated history and that, at least in literary texts, the meaning of unintended and involuntary "symptoms" (or "expressions") should be analyzed in the context of a concrete narrative setting. See Klaus Scherer, "Emotion as a Process: Function, Origin, and Regulation," *Social Science Information* 21 (1982): 555-70 and his more recent "What are emotions? And how can they be measured?" *Social Science Information* 4.4 (2005): 695-729.

6. With the exception of Gisèle Mathieu-Castellani's discussion of the "physiologie de la passion" in her book on Marguerite de Navarre, *La Conversation conteuse: Les nouvelles de Marguerite de Navarre* (Paris: Presses universitaires de France, 1992) 211ff.

7. On the difference between physiognomy and pathognomy, see Johann Caspar Lavater, *Physiognomische Fragmente zur Beförderung der Menschenkenntnis und Menschenliebe,* ed. Christoph Siegrist (Stuttgart: 1984) 275 (my translation): "*Pathognomy, the interpretation of passion* or the *science of the signs of the passions.* One [physiognomy] shows the *fixed,* the other the *moved* character [. . .] *Physiognomy* is the mirror of the natural scientist; pathognomy, the mirror of the courtiers and worldly persons. Everyone reads *pathognomically*—very few read *physiognomically.* Pathognomy has to struggle with pretense. Not so with *physiognomy.*" The differentiation between pathognomy and physiognomy lies at the

center of Lichtenberg's polemic against Lavater and his axiom of the body's readability. Pathognomy is, for Lichtenberg, the "comprehensive semiotics of the emotions or knowledge of the natural signs of the expression of mood": Georg Christoph Lichtenberg, "Über Physiognomik," *Schriften und Briefe,* ed. Wolfgang Promies (Munich: Wissenschaftliche Buchgesellschaft 1972) 3: 264.

8. Charles Darwin, *The Expression of Emotions in Man and Animals,* ed. Paul Ekman (1872; London: Fontana, 1999). According to Darwin, in the course of evolution the purposefulness of bodily movements, necessary among the animals, is reduced among humankind. While the furrowing of one's brow, for example, serves the purpose of protecting an animal's eyes in a fight, as an expressive movement among humans it only retains the symbolic vestiges of this purpose. Since, in Darwin's formulation, such movements are to be called "associated habitual movements" and have become engrained through repetition, the expressive movements of humans are still related to the instinctive forms of reaction among animals.

9. Wilhelm Wundt, *Völkerpsychologie: Eine Untersuchung der Entwicklungsgesetze von Sprache, Mythus und Sitte,* 10 vols. (Leipzig: Engelmann, 1900). A synthesis of the psychology of expression, including its roots in physiognomy, can be found in Karl Bühler, *Ausdruckstheorie: Das System an der Geschichte aufgezeigt* (Jena: Fischer, 1933).

10. Johann Jakob Engel, *Ideen zu einer Mimik, Johann Jakob Engels Schriften* (1801-06; Frankfurt: Athenäum, 1971) 7: 59. All translations by the author unless otherwise indicated.

11. "Mit jeder Veränderung psychischer Zustände sind zugleich Veränderungen physischer Korrelatvorgänge verbunden." Quoted in Bühler, *Ausdruckstheorie,* 131.

12. One might recall André Jolles's theory of "simple forms" ("Einfachen Formen") as "language gestures" ("Sprachgebärden"): *Einfache Formen: Legende, Sage, Mythe, Rätsel, Spruch, Kasus, Memorabile, Märchen, Witz* (1928, Tübingen: Niemeyer, 1982), but also the Warburg school and its term "pathos formula," to which I will return (see below).

13. To provide only a few examples: Franz Bernhard Zons, *Von der Auffassung der Gebärde in der mittelhochdeutschen Epik. Studie über drei Hauptarten mittelalterlicher Gebärdendarstellung,* diss. (Munich: Fahle/Münster, 1933); Otto Schulz, *Die Darstellung psychologischer Vorgänge in den*

Romanen des Kristian von Troyes (Halle: Niemeyer, 1903); Carl Sittl, *Die Gebärden der Griechen und Römer* (1890; New York: Olms, 1970); Werner Habicht's *Die Gebärde in englischen Dichtungen des Mittelalters* (Munich: Bayerische Akademie der Wissenschaften, 1959).

14. Erhard Lommatzsch, *System der Gebärden: Dargestellt aufgrund der mittelalterlichen Literatur Frankreichs,* diss. (Berlin: 1910) 9. Also see, from the same author, "Darstellung von Trauer und Schmerz in der altfranzösischen Literatur," *Zeitschrift für Romanische Philologie* 43 (1922): 20-67.

15. Thus, Lommatzsch writes as follows on the difference between involuntary and voluntary gestures: "These are posed as the plastic manifestations of feelings and emotions, independent of will and reflection and whose course can only be blocked through forcible effort. The others alone form the proper vocabulary of the language of gestures: this "language without words" is spoken entirely consciously and with the intention of sharing a thought or disposition": *System der Gebärden* 9.

16. This is analogous to Roland Barthes's differentiation between the worn article of clothing and the "vêtement écrit." Barthes uses this distinction as a basis for his semiotic analysis of the "language of fashion," the title given in the English translation of *Système de la mode* (Paris: Seuil, 1967).

17. See, for example, Hartwig Kalverkämper, "Literature und Körpersprache," *Poetica* 23 (1991): 328-73.

18. One might recall the description of anger and its bodily expression in Seneca's "On Anger," *Moral and Political Essays,* eds. John M. Cooper and J. F. Procopé (Cambridge: Cambridge UP, 1995) 1-116.

19. Alexander Košenina, "Gebärde," *Historisches Wörterbuch der Rhetorik,* ed. Gert Ueding (Tübingen: Niemeyer, 1996) 2: 564.

20. The principal question is whether the forms of involuntary expression of certain simple emotions—such as anger, sorrow, fear, sadness, happiness, and disgust—are innate universals of human behavior or determined by historical and cultural differences. The main proponent of universality has been Paul Ekman. See, for example, "Universal and cultural differences in facial expression of emotion," *Nebraska Symposium on Motivation,* ed. J. R. Cole (Lincoln: Nebraska UP, 1971); and Paul Ekman, Wallace V. Friesen and Phoebe Ellsworth, *Emotion in the Human Face: Guidelines for Research and Integration of Findings* (New York: Pergamon, 1972) 207-83. The cultural

thesis has been represented by Weston LaBarre, "The Cultural Basis of Emotions and Gestures," *Journal of Personality,* 16 (1947): 49-68. As I intend to give this never-ending debate a historical turn, my main reference for this article is the approach of sociologist Alois Hahn. For Hahn, the concept of a "language of the body" is constructed socially and historically, for it is not the body which speaks. Rather, society interprets its seemingly "natural" and involuntary manifestations as text, as something like the trace of a truth which the subject wants to hide. See Alois Hahn, "Kann der Körper ehrlich sein?" *Konstruktionen des Selbst, der Welt und der Geschichte. Aufsätze zur Kultursoziologie* (Frankfurt a.M.: Suhrkamp, 2000) 358.

21. Constructivism in the history of the body has now also been criticized by the historians themselves. The criticism is started by Caroline Walker Bynum: "Why All the Fuss About the Body? A Medievalist's Perspective," *Critical Inquiry* 22 (1995): 1-33.

22. Just one example for now: "la donna tra tutte l'altre donne del mondo era bellissima e valorosa" (64).

23. The following develops an interpretation of the criticism of medicine and the portrayal of the Plague in the frame from Kurt Flasch, *Giovanni Boccaccio: Poesie nach der Pest: Der Anfang des* Decameron *Italienisch-Deutsch,* trans. and ed. Kurt Flasch (Mainz: Dieterich, 1992) 87: While the experts believe in their knowledge, Boccaccio's portrayal of the Plague is limited to the description of contradictory phenomena, which renders the medical knowledge invalid and legitimizes the knowledge found in literature.

24. Galen is mentioned again (in the sixth novella of the first day) and again made the subject of irony.

25. The implications for Dante's portrayal of the body and its expressions—principally the body of the sinner—are shown in Anna Cerbo, *Poesia e scienza del corpo nella* Divina Commedia: *Dicer del sangue e de le piaghe* (Naples: Dante & Descartes, 2001). According to her thesis, all of Dante's descriptions have a double reading, since they refer both to medical and theological knowledge; physiology and allegory are connected.

26. Flasch, *Giovanni Boccaccio: Poesie nach der Pest.* Also see, from the same author, *Vernunft und Vergnügen: Liebesgeschichten aus dem* Decameron (Munich: Beck, 2002).

27. Neuschäfer, *Boccaccio und der Beginn der Novelle,* 130.

28. For Joachim Küpper, the references to the concept of lovesickness in the *Decameron* are legion. See his article on the medical references to lovesickness in Petrarca: "(H)er(E)os. Petrarcas *Canzoniere* und der medizinische Diskurs seiner Zeit," *Romanische Forschungen* 111 (1999): 178-224. An example can be found in the eighth novella of the second day, in which there is a medical diagnosis of a diffuse case of melancholy. The employed pulse test recalls Valerius Maximus's exemplum on Antiochus and Stratonike (the beloved woman comes into the room and the pulse beats more quickly, when she leaves it slows down, as in *Decameron* [193]). Lovesickness and its somatic symptoms have been studied with relative intensity. See especially Mary Francis Wack, *Lovesickness in the Middle Ages: The Viaticum and Its Commentaries,* (Philadelphia: Pennsylvania UP, 1990). On Boccaccio, see Massimo Ciavolella, *La "Malattia d'amore" dall'Antichità al Medioevo* (Rome: Bulzoni, 1976); and from the same author, "La tradizione dell' 'aegritudo amoris' nel *Decameron*," *Giornale storico della letteratura italiana* 147 (1970): 498-517.

29. The affinity between the Plague and lovesickness is underlined by Giuseppe Mazzotta in, *The World at Play in Boccaccio's* Decameron (Princeton: Princeton UP, 1986): lovesickness "stands in a metonymic contiguity to the plague" 30. The argument is developed by Jessica Levenstein in, "Out of Bounds: Passions and the Plague in Boccaccio's *Decameron,*" *Italica* 73.3 (1996): 313-35. In Boccaccio's mythological handbook, *Genealogia deorum gentilium,* "amor concupiscibile" is associated with "peste": Boccaccio, *Tutte le opere,* ed. Vittore Branca, vol. 7: 142, 8.1: 1086. In the *Genealogia* one often encounters references to the theory of humors when mythological figures also represent characters defined by humoral pathology (e.g. "Morbo" [158]).

30. "Maravigliosa cosa è a pensare quanto sieno difficili a investigare le forze d'amore" (416). See also, Mazzotta, *The World at Play* 30.

31. Boccaccio has Lisa use these terms in the seventh novella of the tenth day: "niuno secondo debita elezione ci s'innamora ma secondo l'appetito e il piacere" (898).

32. Examples following Bernard Chandler, "Man, Emotion and Intellect in the *Decameron,*" *Philological Quarterly* 39.4 (1960): 405.

33. In the "Conclusione dell'autore," too, the book is offered "per cacciar la malinconia delle femine" 963.

34. This term employed by Riva, "Hereos/Eleos: l'ambivalente terapia del mal d'amore nel libro chiamato *Decameron,* cognominato prencipe Gakleotto," *Italian Quarterly,* 36 (2000): 69-106. Fol-

lowing Riva, the "therapy" is ambiguous, because the novella does constitute a distraction from the emotional fixation considered responsible for lovesickness, but also gives wings to the fantasies which should be quelled by it, so that readers might either be healed or infected.

35. Neuschäfer writes: "In the frame of the *Decameron, miseria* and *dignitas* are weighed against one another, without, as in the exemplum, either of the two possibilities settling absolutely. And exactly this seems to be the function of the Plague in the frame: it allows such *miseria* and *dignitas* to be placed on the scale in such a fashion. Death, ruin, chaos, mass graves, decomposition, and moral decay—these are the aspects of *miseria* arising through direct contact with the Plague. Beauty, civilization, social virtues, fantasy, and intelligence—these are, distanced from the Plague, the aspects of *dignitas* or the opportunities for human nature" (131). "Thus, it becomes suddenly clear that there is a thematic relationship between the frame narrative and the individual novellas, for ambiguous human nature and the dialectic of its possibilities and limits is also, basically, the continually recurrent theme of the novellas themselves" (134).

36. Additionally, one might mention the erection, metaphorically present at least (as "la resurrezion della carne" [334]), in the novella of Alibech and the monk Rustico (III.10), and that of Gianni and Gemmata (IX.10). Also see Boccaccio 841.

37. Francesco de Sanctis, "Il 'Decamerone,'" *Storia della letteratura italiana,* 4th ed. (Bari: Laterza, 1949) 281-345. Flasch seeks to provide a reading of Boccaccio's collection of novellas and "Boccaccio legends" alternative to the two traditions, which classify it as either frivolous, or an educational, primarily philosophical, work (177-96).

38. See the authoritative elaboration of this interpretation: Aldo Scaglione, *Nature and Love in the Late Middle Ages. An Essay on the Cultural Context of the* Decameron (Berkeley: California UP, 1963).

39. This position is mainly represented by Vittore Branca, *Boccaccio medievale,* 6th ed. (Florence: Sansoni, 1997).

40. "Female sexuality is viewed in total sobriety, amorally as a physical state, which can be kept in balance or deeply unsettled by physiological processes and events." And also: "Since Galen, the doctors considered the suppression of sex drive a serious or, in certain circumstances, deadly danger. The retained humors, determined by nature to be expelled, can transform into deadly poison in the body": Rüdiger Schnell, "Mittelalter oder Neu-

zeit? Medizingeschichte und Literaturhistorie. Apologie weiblicher Sexualität in Boccaccios *Decameron,*" *Gotes und der werlde hulde. Literatur in Mittelalter und Neuzeit. Festschrift für Heinz Rupp zum 70. Geburtstag,* ed. Rüdiger Schnell (Bern: Francke, 1989) 275-76.

41. On Boccaccio's familiarity with the manuscript (before 1366), see Rüdiger Schnell 267 and Robert Hollander, *Boccaccio's Two Venuses* (New York: Columbia UP, 1977) 60. See also: Marie-Madeleine Fontaine, "La lignée des commentaires à la chanson de Guido Cavalcanti *Donna me prega*: Évolution des relations entre philosophie, médecine et littérature dans le débat sur la nature d'Amour," *La Folie et le corps,* eds. Jean Céard, Jean Naudin, and Michel Simonin (Paris: École Normale Supérieure, 1985) 159-78.

42. Otto Bird, "The *Canzone d'Amore* of Cavalcanti According to the Commentary of Dino del Garbo. Text and Commentary," *Medieval Studies* 2 (1940): 170.

43. This difference from the modern understanding of a quasi-bodiless, interior space of the mind, for which psychology alone is responsible, has been emphasized often enough. Küpper ("(H)er(E)os" 185) writes pointedly on the "somatism" of the early modern theory of the soul, which is developed into a form of "materialism" in medical discourses.

44. Compare Otto Bird's commentary with the corresponding citations from Aristotle, Avicenna, and Albertus Magnus, to which Galen could be added (131).

45. See literature listed in note 27.

46. Boccaccio's medical knowledge is dealt with in greater depth in Marga Cottino-Jones, "Boccaccio e la scienza," *Letteratura e scienza nella storia della cultura italiana,* eds. Vittore Branca et al. (Palermo: Manfredi, 1978) 356-70; and Rüdiger Schnell, "Mittelalter oder Neuzeit?"

47. See Hahn's essay, "Kann der Körper ehrlich sein?" in which he speaks of the social institutionalization of the body as an "organ of truth," and "honesty" of the observation of the body as a "lie detector," as a process during which the social attention paid to the involuntary bodily expressions is enhanced, for everyone is afraid of being betrayed by liars (357).

48. "A queste parole sopravvennero in tanta abbondanza le lagrime, che essa, che ancora più prieghi intendeva di porgere, più avanti non ebbe poter di parlare, ma bassato il viso e quasi vinta piagnendo sopra il seno del conte si lasciò con la testa cadere" (188).

49. See Küpper, "(H)er(E)os," 196.

50. In his commentary, Branca points out that this is a recurring construction in Boccaccio: 1055.

51. This parallel following Flasch, *Poesie nach der Pest,* 152.

52. Even Frate Alberto (IV.2) can willfully bring forth tears ("piagneva la passione del Salvatore, sì come colui al quale poco costavan le lagrime quando le volea" [368]).

53. Flasch, *Poesie nach der Pest,* 142.

54. See Georges Güntert, *Tre premesse e una dichiarazione d'amore. Vademecum per il lettore del* Decameron (Modena: Mucchi, 1997) 57.

55. In some sense, this applies to Griselda as well, only the other way around: Griselda can keep her body perfectly under control; it arises repeatedly that, despite great inner excitement, she keeps her face perfectly motionless ("senza mutar viso" [947], "col viso non solamente asciutto ma lieto" [954], "con fermo viso" [949], "con lieto viso" [951], "ritenne le lagrime" [949-50], etc.). The difference between interior and exterior is continuously mentioned. Her famous "pazienza" thus comprises a generally successful form of body control. According to Flasch, Boccaccio wanted to show here that women, too, are capable of stoic "detachment of their emotions from themselves," that the "wisdom" and self-determination of stoic ethics is not available to men alone (*Vernunft und Vergnügen* 254).

56. See also Flasch, *Poesie nach der Pest* 152.

57. Walter Haug, "Literaturgeschichte und Triebkontrolle. Bemerkungen eines Mediävisten zum sog. 'Prozeß der Zivilisation,'" *Jahrbuch der Heidelberger Akademie der Wissenschaften für 1993* (Heidelberg: Akademie der Wissenschaften, 1994) 56.

58. "Tuttavia chi va tra queste leggendo, lasci star quelle che pungono e quelle che dilettano legga: elle, per non ingannare alcuna persona, tutte nella fronte portan segnato quello que esse dentro dal loro seno nascose tengono": 962.

59. See Karlheinz Stierle, "Three Moments in the Crisis of Exemplarity: Boccaccio-Petrarch, Montaigne, Cervantes," *Journal of the History of Ideas* 59.4 (1998): 581-95.

60. See Erich Auerbach, *Zur Technik der Frührenaissancenovelle in Italien* (Heidelberg: Winter, 1921) 36.

61. This novella is not among those frequently commented. See Raffaello Ramat, "Girolamo e la Salvestra, *Decameron* IV, VIII," *Studi di varia umanità in onore di Francesco Flora* (Mailand: Mondadori, 1963) 340-52; Valter Puccetti, "Girolamo, Salvestra e l'inferno degli amori nel *Decameron,*" *Studi sul Boccaccio* 20 (1991-92): 85-129.

62. Vittore Branca comments: "ritirati in loro stessi gli spiriti vitali" (1248). And Cesare Segre states, "chiamate a raccolta le sue facoltà sensitive": Boccaccio, *Decameron,* ed. Cesare Segre (Milan: Mursia, 1966) 304.

63. Giovanni Boccaccio, *The Decameron,* trans. G. H. McWilliam, 2nd ed. (London: Penguin Classics, 1995) 346.

64. The basics on Galen: Rudolph E. Siegel, *Galen's System of Physiology and Medicine. An Analysis of his Doctrines and Observations on Bloodflow, Respiration, Humors and Internal Diseases* (New York: Karger, 1968). And on the theory of pneuma: Marielene Putscher, *Pneuma, Spiritus, Geist. Vorstellungen vom Lebensantrieb in ihren geschichtlichen Wandlungen* (Wiesbaden: Steiner, 1973).

65. Bandello uses the same formulation to describe the death of Giulietta: "Ristretti adunque in sé gli spirti, con il suo Romeo in grembo, senza dir nulla se ne morí": Matteo Bandello, *Novelle,* ed. Ettore Mazzali (Milan: Rizzoli, 1990) 315. The commentary of this edition points out the reference to Boccaccio (622).

66. See Claude Lévi-Strauss, "Le sorcier et sa magie," *Anthropologie structurale* (Paris: Plon, 1958) 183-203. He draws upon the research of Walter B. Cannon, "'Voodoo' Death," *American Anthropologist* 44 (1942): 169-81.

67. "Di dolore esser morto," (416). The novellas of the fourth day comprise a series of deaths, which, in contrast to that of Girolamo, are not caused by flawed human behavior, but through contingency or fortuna, as in the case of the sage bush poisoned by a toad (IV.7) and the sudden death of Gabriotto by organic causes (IV.6); the doctors find a sort of tumor on the heart of his body: "alcuna posta vicina al cuore gli s'era rotta, che affogato l'avea" (403).

68. A reference to angry fist balling is found, for example, in Wolfram von Eschenbach. See Dietmar Peil, *Die Gebärde bei Chrétien, Hartmann und Wolfram: Erec—Iwein—Parzival* (Munich: Fink, 1975) 225.

69. See, above all, the Alibech novella (third day, tenth novella).

70. The thesis that in Giotto's paintings the conventionalized gestures are restored to "natural" (physiological) gestures, is developed by Moshe Barash, *Giotto and the Language of Gesture* (Cambridge: Cambridge UP, 1987). Also see Barash, *Gestures of Despair in Medieval and Renaissance Art* (New York: New York UP, 1976).

71. Aby Warburg, "Mnemosyne. Einleitung," *Der Bilderatlas. Mnemosyne,* eds. Martin Warnke and Claudia Brink (1929; Berlin: Akademie Verlag, 2000) 3.

72. This is Ulrich Port's reformulation in his article "'Katharsis des Leidens': Aby Warburg's 'Pathosformeln' und ihre konzeptionellen Hintergründe in Rhetorik, Poetik und Tragödientheorie," *Wege deutsch-jüdischen Denkens im 20. Jahrhundert,* ed. Gerhart v. Graevenitz, *Deutsche Vierteljahrsschrift für Literaturwissenschaft und Geistesgeschichte,* special issue 73 (1999): 6-7. In his reconstruction of the term's "linguistic-literary background tradition" (along with the Aristotelian theory of catharsis), Port advocates for the possibility of a re-importation of the problematic term "pathos formula" into literary studies (8). On this, see also pages 40-42. The suggested analysis of literarily staged pathognomy in Romance novellas aims to profit from the introduction of such a term, insofar as it allows both the body-bound poetic and the aesthetic, literarily-topical to be combined into a literary anthropology of body language.

73. Warburg's reception of Darwin's, *The Expressions of Emotion in Man and Animals* is presented in detail in Bernd Villhauer, *Aby Warburgs Theorie der Kultur. Detail und Sinnhorizont* (Berlin: Akademie Verlag, 2002) 44-48. The critical discussion of the psychology of expression in the Warburg circle is also documented in Fritz Saxl, "Die Ausdrucksgebärden in der Bildenden Kunst," Aby Warburg, *Ausgewählte Sachriften und Würdigungen,* ed. Dieter Wuttke (1931; Baden-Baden: Koerner, 1980) 419-32.

74. Salvatore Settis, "Pathos und Ethos: Morphologie und Funktion," *Vorträge aus dem Warburg-Haus,* eds. Wolfgang Kemp et al. (Berlin: Akademie Verlag, 1997) 1: 41.

75. Ernst Robert Curtius, "Antike Pathosformeln in der Literatur des Mittelalters," *Gesammelte Aufsätze zur romanischen Philologie* (Bern: Francke, 1960) 23-27.

76. Werner Kaegi, 1932, quoted in Martin Warnke, "Pathosformel," *Die Menschenrechte des Auges: Über Aby Warburg,* eds. Werner Hofmann, Georg Syamken, Martin Warnke (Frankfurt: Europäische Verlagsanstalt, 1980) 66.

77. This novella has been commented on several times, above all before the background of the possible sources of the "hell hunt" and in the context of the question concerning the reference to Dante's *Commedia*: See Nino Scivoletto, "Fonti latine e trovatoriche di una novella del Boccaccio," *Romania: Scritti offerti a Francesco Piccolo nel suo 70 compleanno* (Naples: Armania, 1962) 499-513.

78. In Pampinea's description of her fear of the Plague, Boccaccio uses a formulation that sounds similar: "impaurisco e quasi tutti i capelli adosso mi sento arricciare" (21).

79. Hellmut Flashar, "Die medizinischen Grundlagen der Lehre von der Wirkung der Dichtung in der griechischen Poetik," *Hermes: Zeitschrift für Klassische Philologie* 84 (1956): 12-48. On the knowledge of the Aristotelian terms before the rediscovery of the *Poetics* in the sixteenth century, see Güntert, *Tre premesse,* 142. Here one might mention in passing that Botticelli transformed the Nastagio novella into a series of pictures in 1482 and that Warburg included this depiction in his Mnemosyne atlas, which was planned as an "atlas of gesture-language"—under the rubric of "mixed style in reference to antiquity [. . .] punished coldness [. . .]": Warburg, *Der Bilderatlas. Mnemosyne,* plate 38, 66f. See, on the Botticelli pictures, Georges Didi-Huberman, *Ouvrir Vénus. Nudité, rêve, cruauté. L'image ouvrante* (Paris: Gallimard, 1999) 1. Also: Vittore Branca, ed., *Boccaccio visualizzato. Narrare per parole e per immagine fra Medioevo e Rinascimento,* 3 vols. (Turin: Einaudi, 1999) 64ff.

80. Artaud, in "Le Théâtre et la peste," uses Boccaccio's description of the Plague to compare contagion with the effects of the theater (where he inverts Augustine's motifs of theological theater-criticism): Antonin Artaud, "Le théâtre et la peste," *Œuvres complètes* (Paris: Gallimard, 1964) 2: 19-39; reference to Boccaccio on p. 28; to Augustine on p. 32.

81. See Kurt Flasch's convincing interpretation, in *Vernunft und Vergnügen* (136), which sees in this novella a parody of Dante's hell, a "persiflage" made to serve earthly purposes.

82. Gregory B. Stone also reads the novella as criticism of the exemplum: it shows, according to Stone, that the transmission of the hellish spectacle to Nastagio and his "crudel giovane" functions as a deception, based on an identification between characters (Nastagio with Guido degli Anastagi and the two women) which in truth are not similar (Nastagio did not kill himself because of lovesickness). Boccaccio's novellas thus show that the exemplum must reduce difference to be effective and function as an instrument of power: *The Ethics of Nature in the Middle Ages: On Boccaccio's Poetaphysics* (London: St. Martin's, 1998) 187ff.

83. [. . .] credendo alcuna donna o uomo con alcuna paroletta leggiadra fare altrui arrossare, non avendo ben le sue forze con quelle di quel cotal misurate, quello rossore che in altrui ha creduto gittare sopra sé l'ha sentito tornare" (84).

84. On the principal of "ut moveamur ipsi" as a commonplace of rhetoric, see Klaus Dockhorn, *Macht und Wirkung der Rhetorik. Vier Aufsätze zur Ideengeschichte der Vormoderne* (Zürich: Gehlen, 1968) 53.

85. Boccaccio himself employs the medical term "purgatio" when he has Dioneo say, for example, in the introduction to the tenth novella of the fifth day: "[Il] diletto può porgere" (517). The tradition of the theory of literature as "medicina animi" and medium of "purgatio" (i.e. the physiological removal of damaging humors from the body) has been studied in detail in Heinz-Günther Schmitz, *Physiologie des Scherzes. Bedeutung und Rechtfertigung der Ars Iocandi im 16. Jahrhundert* (New York: Olms, 1972) 50.

86. Winfried Wehle, *Novellenerzählen: Französische (und italienische) Renaissancenovellistik als Diskurs* (Munich: Fink, 1984).

87. *Genealogie deorum gentilium* XIV.9: "Veramente leggiamo che dalle favole, che costoro così disprezzano, a causa del vocabolo, furono talvolta acquetati gli animi accesi di pazzo furore e ridotti alla mansuetudine di prima [. . .] Con le favole talora è stato dato conforto a coloro che sono travagliati sotto il peso dell'avversa fortuna [. . .]." Boccaccio, *Tutte le opere*, 7: 1416-17.

88. For a detailed discussion of literature as "recreation," see Glending Olson, *Literature as Recreation in the Later Middle Ages* (Ithaca: Cornell UP, 1986). Laughing is supposed to increase one's resistance to infection from the Plague. The medical justification of laughing as "ars iocandi" is also presented by Schmitz, in *Physiologie des Scherzes*.

89. I am preparing a book on the passions of the body in the Romance novella from Boccaccio to Madame de Lafayette in the context of a larger interdisciplinary project on "Languages of Emotion"at the Free University Berlin. Also see my article on fainting ("desmayos") in Cervantes's *Novelas ejemplares*: "La razón de los desmayos en 'El celoso extremeño' de Cervantes," *Escenas de transgresión. María de Zayas en su contexto literario-cultural*, ed. Irene Albers and Uta Felten (Madrid: Vervuert, 2009) 189-224.

Francesco Ciabattoni (essay date summer 2010)

SOURCE: Ciabattoni, Francesco. "Boccaccio's Miraculous Art of Storytelling: *Dec.* I.1, II.1 and VI.10." *Italica*, 87, no. 2 (summer 2010): 167-78.

[*In the following essay, Ciabattoni identifies narrative and thematic strategies linking four tales (1.1, 2.1, 4.2, and 6.1) about faked miracles in the* Decameron.]

The aim of this paper is to highlight unifying patterns in some of the *Decameron*'s tales that deal with the topic of miracles: I.1, Ser Cepperello; II.1, Martellino; and VI.10, Fra Cipolla. These three *novelle* are interconnected by elements that suggest we read them as a triptych about the delicate matter of belief in miracles.

As Pier Massimo Forni showed, consciously organized complex forms link the single texts in the *Decameron* system to one another.[1] Sometimes these links provide the occasion for a mutual validation between members of the brigade, and sometimes for ironic rewriting or even parodical reversal.[2] My research moves along these lines, identifying characteristics of responsiveness among I.1, II.1, and VI.10.

Both I.1 and VI.10 are built upon multiple narrative levels. In I.1 we can identify a *meta-novella*: the main narrator tells a story about the brigade, and one member of the brigade, Panfilo, narrates the story of Cepperello, who, in turn, tells the story of himself as the perfect Christian. Here, as in Fra Cipolla's account, the protagonist is the same as the narrator but modified by the clever lies that transform an almost demonic creature into an example of chastity and virtue. But Cepperello's fictional self-portrait is in itself a figure of irony—a rewriting and point-by-point reversal of the description given by Panfilo at the beginning of the tale: there Cepperello was a professional liar, one who "testimonianze false con sommo diletto diceva, richiesto e non richiesto;"[3] in his confession, Cepperello claims that the only false witness he ever bore was to save a woman from a violent husband. The real Cepperello—a man "delle femine [. . .] cosí vago come sono i cani de' bastoni; del contrario piú che alcuno altro tristo uomo si dilettava"[4]—in his confession reluctantly admits, lest he commit vainglory, to being "cosí vergine come [. . .] usci' del corpo della mamma mia."[5] His avowal of gluttony during confession is a masterwork of ironic hyperbole: "con quello diletto e con quello appetito l'acqua bevuta aveva, e spezialmente quando avesse alcuna fatica durata o adorando o andando in pellegrinaggio, che fanno i gran bevitori il vino; e molte volte aveva disiderato d'avere cotali insalatuzze d'erbucce."[6] The ridiculous zeal of denouncing a craving for herbs and water as gluttony clashes marvelously with the figure of the real Cepperello as "Gulosissimo e bevitor grande, tanto che alcuna volta sconciamente gli facea noia"[7] preparing for the graver sins to come. In Panfilo's description, Cepperello is a murderer and the most irascible of men; in his confession he only unleashes his wrath against the sacrilegious, blasphemous, and tavern-goers—a righteous reaction, like the one by which Dante wins Virgil's commendation for pushing away Filippo Argenti, except that we know that Cepperello "a chiesa non usava giammai, e i sacramenti di quella tutti come vil cosa con abominevoli parole scherniva; e cosí in contrario le taverne e gli altri disonesti luoghi visitava volentieri e usavagli.'"[8] The same care and devotion that the real Cepperello puts forth with regard to stealing, the confessional, re-born Cepperello puts into donating four farthings he found in excess in his merchant's box to the poor.

With this painstaking, contrapuntal revision, Cepperello writes his new self as the perfect Christian, the ultimate saint—the reverse of the novel Judas figure he was at the beginning. Cepperello goes from "piggior uomo che mai nascesse" to the epitome of a saint.

The presence of the aware audience—the two Florentines who know the truth—is essential for the successful result of his sacrilegious joke. Cepperello's awareness that the merchants know that his confession is false and that he is deceiving the friar, the whole monastery, the worshippers, and lastly the entire Christendom, who raised a repellent sinner to the honor of sainthood, makes his satisfaction much greater than it would have been if no one knew the truth about his final deception. The biggest of all ironies is that Cepperello's lie must be unveiled to show its author's ability: had there been no one to collect and diffuse the real version of the story, Cepperello's confession would have been worth nothing, and Panfilo, or we, would never have learned it.

Cepperello's fictional speech, like that of his worthy colleague, orator Fra Cipolla, is made necessary by a situation that implies danger for someone. The Florentine merchants hosting Cepperello are in danger of not only losing their reputation and their business in the town, but also being killed by a rioting mob:

> . . . il popolo di questa terra, il quale sí per lo mestier nostro, il quale loro pare iniquissimo e tutto il giorno ne dicon male, e sí per la volontà che hanno di rubarci, veggendo ciò si leverà a romore e griderà: 'Questi lombardi cani, li quali a chiesa non sono voluti ricevere, non ci si voglion piú sostenere'; e correrannoci alle case e per avventura non solamente l'avere ci ruberanno ma *forse ci torranno oltre a ciò le persone*: di che noi in ogni guisa stiam male se costui muore.
>
> (*Dec.* I.1.26)[9]

Both fictional speeches (Cepperello's and Cipolla's) go beyond mere goal accomplishment in their artistic quality: Cepperello could have told an ordinary man's confession in order to save the merchants from danger and shame, but he takes his confession to an extreme for the fun of the hoax. Fra Cipolla, the other master of oratory—a new Cicero or Quintilian indeed—faces a crowd full of expectations about the relic of the archangel Gabriel he has promised to show. When, instead of the promised feather, he finds charcoals, the clever friar crafts a fantastic story on the spot to bewilder his audience, which results in a double wonder: not only is the charcoal a miraculous relic, too, but it was God's direct intervention that led his hand to it instead of to the feather.

Cipolla's oratorical technique is quite simple: he makes up names of places, perhaps after well-known streets of Florence, in a quick succession rich with details and novelty so as to baffle the slow minds of his audience. But before he can serve up the grand finale to his listeners, he has to validate the authenticity of the relics he is about to present so that those relics can later guarantee the veracity of the miracle he will invoke. How does he do so? By relating his abbot's initial caution regarding showing them and then claiming previous miracles for the relics themselves:

> È il vero che il mio maggiore non ha mai sofferto che io l'abbia mostrate infino a tanto che certificato non s'è se desse sono o no; ma ora che per certi miracoli fatti da esse e per lettere ricevute dal Patriarca fatto n'è certo m'ha conceduta licenzia che io le mostri; ma io, temendo di fidarle altrui, sempre le porto meco.
>
> (*Dec.*VI.10.48)

Note Cipolla's *bravura,* here: not only does he claim that the relics are authentic because they have performed miracles, so these miracles are also real, but he even inserts a hidden rebuke for his negligent servant, Guccio Imbratta, by stating that he would never entrust them to anyone. This ironic wink, addressed to Guccio as well as the two yet unknown pranksters, contrasts with the thought of Guccio's negligence which ran through Cipolla's mind when he found the charcoal in the box.

After the fireworks of his travel account, he foists not one, but two miracles on his audience: God's leading his hand to take the wrong box and the "extraordinary" effect of St. Lawrence's coals, since "chiunque da questi carboni in segno di croce è tocco, tutto quello anno può viver sicuro che fuoco nol cocerà che non si senta."[10] Cipolla's artful speech is all balanced on amphibology: from the outset of his speech/journey to the land of Menzogna, the friar's words "play on a double-level effect, duping the faithful Certaldesi with the apparent meaning, and winking, with the real meaning, to the intelligence of the two pranksters (Giovanni del Bragoniera and Biagio Pizzini) and the readers."[11] This is what Dilwyn Knox calls *mendacium ironicum*[12]—a statement that is only apparently wondrous or extraordinary. In fact, whoever is touched by the coals may live secure that he will indeed feel any fire that touches him! (This is the same rhetorical ploy Panfilo uses for Cepperello who "avea grandissima vergogna quando uno de' suoi strumenti, come che pochi ne facesse, fosse altro che falso trovato."[13] Ironically, strictly speaking, Cipolla does not even lie about the miracle because the unsophisticated Certaldesi are, at this point, so bedazzled by the sparkling galore of exoticism that they do not realize the obviousness of his sentence. The audience hears what they expect to hear: whoever is touched by the charcoals will feel no fire, in antiphrasis with the real meaning. The dull tautology, the pure obviousness, and the musicality of the final hendecasyllable are cast like a magic formula onto the simpleminded crowd.

This sudden switch from anticipated extraordinariness to what is obvious and flippant appears to be the signature of Fra Cipolla's oration: always playing on the edge of risk, he actually leaves a chance for his audience to see the trick because, by listening carefully to the real meaning of the words, the swindle would be evident. But the slow-minded Certaldesi are incapable of such subtlety and are thus ravished in the swirls of invention. The beginning of the oration already points to this style: "Signori e donne, voi dovete sapere che, essendo io ancora molto giovane, io fui mandato in quelle parti dove apparisce il sole, e fummi commesso con espresso comandamento che io cercassi tanto che io trovassi i privilegi del Porcellana, i quali, ancora che a bollar niente costassero, molto più utili sono a altrui che a noi."

Manlio Pastore Stocchi notes that Fra Cipolla's account bears a debt to a very popular literary scheme of the time:[14] the *itinerarium ultramarinum,* which were travellers' voyage accounts, especially those of merchants journeying to the East, such as Marco Polo's *Milione.* Thus, when we read "io fui mandato in quelle parti dove apparisce il sole," we are tempted to understand "where the sun rises," that is "to the East," but Cipolla says instead "where the sun is visible,"[15] so "to no particular place." The "Privilegi del Porcellana" are something mysterious just made up by the clever friar from the name of a Florentine street, so in spite of the evocative name, they mean nothing, are worth nothing ("a bollar niente costassero"), and serve no purpose ("molto piu' utili a altrui che a noi"). And a few lines below, ". . . molti de' nostri frati e d'altre religioni trovai assai, li quali tutti il disagio andavano per l'amor di Dio schifando, poco dell'altrui fatiche curandosi dove la loro utilità vedessero seguitare,"[16] where the expectable traditional depiction of the helping missionary is subtly reversed into the image of the lazy friars who, pretending to care about other people's trouble, would rather seek their own advantage.

The *novelle* of Cepperello and Fra Cipolla share a number of structural similarities in scene arrangement. In both we find the following:

- a third-level narrator who makes an invented self the protagonist of the story (the good Christian Cepperello; Cipolla the wayfarer);

- a deceived audience unaware of the truth and appearing quite ready to believe in miracles (the confessor, who reverberates Cepperello's story onto the Burgundians; the Certaldesi);

- and a second audience which knows the truth (the two merchants eavesdropping on Cepperello's confession from behind a wall; Giovanni del Bragoniera and Biagio Pizzini hiding among the crowd and enjoying Ci-

polla's tale more than anyone else because they know it is a big yarn.) In fact, the smothered laughter of the merchants hiding behind the wooden plank is echoed in Giovanni and Biagio's outward gales of laughter.[17]

- a faked miracle (Cepperello's irreprehensible conduct and God leading Cipolla's hand to the box with saint Lawrence's coals).

When the two protagonists speak, they have an audience of many. Even Cepperello knows that if he is good enough to convince the friar of his sanctity, his speech will be turned into the subject-matter of sermons and his lie will be disseminated by the clergy (the organ that is, ironically, supposed to check the veracity of miracles), which will make his deception even more complete. And these audiences will easily believe what they are told, not only because their orators are extremely refined ones, but also because believing something is, after all, what they are there for. The Certaldesi, as much as the friar, listen to the speech uncritically (the confessor does too, not because he is simple-minded, but because his faith keeps him from conceiving that anyone could attach more importance to a joke than to the salvation of his own soul); they are willing to trust the orator as long as his speech fulfils the characteristics of genre (the *ars praedicandi* for Fra Cipolla and the intimate confession for Cepperello).

Fra Cipolla's account of his fictional journey also represents a *meta-novella*: we read a story told by Boccaccio about Dioneo who tells a story about a friar named Cipolla who tells a story about himself. Thus the protagonist of the inside story is still Cipolla, although an invented one, who appears to be younger, adventurous, and an experienced traveler as opposed to the lazy and modest figure presented at the story's beginning. The false Cipolla ventures in the East and gains the friendship of the Patriarch of Jerusalem, the venerable Nonmiblasmete Sevoipiace, who offers him several relics from his collection.

The polemic against the church's granting easy approvals for sanctifications and miracles patently underlies both Cepperello's and Cipolla's tales and is heavily stressed in the absurd canonization of "il piggior uomo che mai nascesse" and in Cipolla's long listing of the sacred items in Nonmiblasmete's collection. This topic is also at the core of II.1, the story of Martellino in Treviso. A Florentine jester, Martellino earns his living with his friends Stecchi and Marchese by entertaining the nobles in the courts with his traveling show. When the three get to Treviso, they find the city in a state of unrest because of a humble porter who has just died in the odor of sanctity. What is more, at the moment of his death the bells of the Treviso cathedral began to toll of their own accord. The three jesters become so captivated with this story that they want to see the body of the saint. But how are they going to wade their way through the thick crowd? Martellino knows: he will pretend to be a paralytic while Stecchi and Marchese will hold him up, and the people will have to make way for them. But the hoax slips out of their hands when Martellino simulates a sudden healing and the crowd invokes the miracle: the Florentines' initial goal was simply to see the saint, but their improvisatory nature takes over and they impress a multitude of believers with a miracle. Things precipitate when another Florentine, who is coincidentally in Treviso, recognizes Martellino and blows his cover: "Domine fallo tristo! [. . .] Egli è stato sempre diritto come qualunque è l'un di noi, ma sa meglio che altro uomo, come voi avete potuto vedere, far queste ciance di contraffarsi in qualunque forma vuole."[18] At this point the crowd grows into a mob and starts beating and kicking Martellino for impersonating a paralytic and mocking the saints:

> Sia preso questo traditore e beffatore di Dio e de' santi, il quale, non essendo attratto, per ischernire il nostro santo e noi, qui a guisa d'attratto è venuto!" E cosí dicendo il pigliarono e giú del luogo dove era il tirarono, e presolo per li capelli e stracciatili tutti i panni indosso gl'incominciarono a dare delle pugna e de' calci; né parea a colui essere uomo che a questo far non correa. Martellin gridava "Mercé per Dio!" e quanto poteva s'aiutava, ma ciò era niente: la calca gli multiplicava ognora addosso maggiore. La qual cosa veggendo Stecchi e Marchese cominciarono fra sé a dire che la cosa stava male, e di sé medesimi dubitando non ardivano a aiutarlo anzi con gli altri insieme gridando ch'el fosse morto, avendo nondimeno pensiero tuttavia come trarre il potessero delle mani del popolo; il quale fermamente l'avrebbe ucciso, se uno argomento non fosse stato il qual Marchese subitamente prese.[19]

Marchese's *argomento* is to report Martellino to the police for theft, causing him to be arrested and, thus, saving him from the beating which would have certainly killed him.[20] Eventually Martellino is indeed arrested for theft and spared fair punishment thanks to the intervention of yet one more Florentine, Sandro Agolanti, who, *Deus ex machina*, beseeches the lord of Treviso to set the jester free.

This story bears several points in common with those of Cepperello and Cipolla, so that it can be considered, in the system of *forme complesse* that Forni identifies, a response to Cepperello's story and an anticipation of Cipolla's. First of all, we can identify a structure in the layout of the scene which is similar to that in I.1 and VI.10, for II.1 contains the following:

- a deceived audience unaware of the truth (the Trevigiani, like the Burgundians and the Certaldesi, are quite ready to believe in miracles but also potentially dangerous should they become a mob);

- a second audience aware of the truth (Stecchi and Marchese as well as the Florentine who recognizes Martellino);

- and a faked miracle (the healing) plus another miracle (the cathedral's bells tolling on their own) on which Neifile (and therefore the author) does not take a stance.

Given these precedents, when the reader gets to VI.10 he knows how dangerous it is to simulate a miracle: Martellino's nearly deadly beating prepares the reader to anticipate serious trouble for Fra Cipolla as he opens his box before a crowd full of expectations. Boccaccio further prepares this ground with one more *novella* on the way to VI.10. In IV.2, the tale of the *agnolo Gabriello*, another unlikely friar, Alberto, is forced to abandon his archangel Gabriel accoutrements in his mistress's chamber when her family discovers the affair:

> I cognati della donna entrati *nella camera* trovarono che *l'agnolo Gabriello, quivi avendo lasciate l'ali,* se n'era volato.[21]

Alberto, too, simulates a miracle: in order to seduce Lisetta he lets her believe that no less than the archangel Gabriel has fallen in love with her and subsequently beds her by impersonating Gabriel. Now, Lisetta is as ingenuous as she is vain, and Alberto has an easy way with her, at least until her brothers-in-law enter the picture. This scene and the danger it brings immediately come to mind when Cipolla publicly announces that he will be displaying his relic—the feather which Gabriel left in Mary's chamber after the annunciation:

> "questa è *una delle penne dell'agnol Gabriello,* la quale *nella camera* della Vergine Maria rimase quando egli la venne ad annunziare in Nazarette."[22]

Frate Alberto, like Martellino, will end up severely battered, publicly ridiculed, and imprisoned, indeed even dead in prison. Pampinea will close her tale by stating that Frate Alberto ended up vituperated and imprisoned because he "ardì di farsi l'agnolo Gabriello."[23] His sin, in other words, was not so much his deception of Lisetta, who after all was all too ready to accept whatever fabrication would appease her vanity, as his impersonation of the angel Gabriel and his simulation of a miracle.

The procession of worshipping Certaldesi, submitting to the grotesque rite of being marked with charcoal, mirrors the Burgundians thronging around Cepperello's body to touch it and tear off a bit of his clothes. In I.1 and VI.10, the relics are consumed by the faithful as they approach to receive their benefits: Cipolla's charcoals are consumed as he daubs crosses on the people's vests, and the nearly-savage assault of the Burgundians, eager to touch the saint, almost destroys Cepperello's body.

> con la maggior calca del mondo da tutti fu andato a baciargli i piedi e le mani, e *tutti i panni gli furono indosso stracciati,* tenendosi beato chi pure un poco di quegli potesse avere.[24]

The textual link between *novella* I.1 and *novella* II.1 appears clear when we read the real quasi-dismemberment of the body of Martinello (who had started his simulation precisely to get near the saint's body and touch it):

> il pigliarono e giú del luogo dove era il tirarono, e presolo per li capelli e *stracciatili tutti i panni indosso* gl'incominciarono a dare delle pugna e de' calci.[25]

The reverence of the Burgudians touching Saint Cepperello's body is ironically reversed, with the same wording, in the hateful attack on Martellino by the Trevigiani. This *novella,* with its scene of an enraged mob, realizes the danger foreshadowed in the story of Cepperello and nourishes the expectation of danger in the story of Cipolla. The responsiveness of these three *novelle* pivots on Martellino's violent beating, which makes him so battered he almost becomes the paralytic he had impersonated or even the dead body he wanted to touch. The triptych of these *novelle* points at a negative exemplum of what can happen to those who make fun of their neighbors "e massimamente di quelle cose che sono da reverire"[26]—i.e., miracles.

In this context, the consumption of the relics (Cepperello's corpse, St. Lawrence's charcoals, and wretched Martellino's body) becomes a symbol of the inflation of false miracles: real miracles might lose their significance and be misbelieved if the clergy continue to take advantage of the humbles' gullibility. Hence the double polemic against the ignorants who do not deserve real saints or real miracles and against the superficiality of some clergy in dealing with the delicate matter of miracles. The *Decameron*'s author does not solve the doubt about Cepperello's metaphysical destiny; Bocaccio does not venture in defense of the church as the warden of faith, but rather lets the evident corruption of the institution paradoxically prove the truth of the Christian faith, as in I.2, the *novella* of Abraham the Jew who travels to Rome, eager to see by his own eyes the heart of the Christian Faith, and is so shocked by the scandalous corruption of the Papal See that he ends up converting to Christianity because, he reasons, if this religion has so many followers despite the terrible example of the clergy, it certainly is the right one.

Boccaccio bows at Cepperello's and Fra Cipolla's rhetorical ability, pitting their successes against Martellino's failure. What, then, makes the art of Cepperello and Cipolla different from Martellino's? Neifile's insistence on the word "contraffare"[27] with respect to Martellino's masquerade reveals a valuable hint regarding Boccaccio's rhetorical strategy: pointing to the jester's nature as a counterfeiter. Martellino's act fails because it is a pantomime, a merely physical performance. Its nearly deadly outcome restates the power of words over deeds. On the contrary, it is the miraculous art of story-telling that can bring salvation and safety both within the tales and without. Storytelling, indeed, is a healthy practice: the ten youngsters use words in the form of stories as entertainment and psychological therapy against the terrible perils of plague-ridden Florence.[28] Storytelling, with its *diletto* and *utile consiglio,* is the help Boccaccio offers the women of his intended audience.[29] The *Decameron* is meant as a therapeutic intervention not only for these lovesick women but also for the critical situation in Florence after the devastation of the plague.

The power of words to shape reality has been stressed before, to different extents: Giovanni Getto highlights Cepperello's rhetoric as that of an "artist of pure word" and Giorgio Barberi Squarotti depicts Cepperello as a competitor with God himself.[30] Pier Massimo Forni points out that, in III.5, Zima's speech proposes and realizes an alternative reality: the reality that would have existed if the husband had not prohibited his wife from speaking.[31] This effect also follows after Cepperello's words: by depicting himself as a saint, he actually becomes a saint (at least to human eyes), the real man being dead and replaced by the new, legendary character created by his fiction and made famous by the friar. On the contrary, and ironically, Martellino's pathetic pantomime gets him "tutto pesto e tutto rotto"[32] and nearly killed, and it almost causes him to become the paralytic he had pretended to be.

The real miracle in Cepperello's and Cipolla's stories is, then, that words, if used skillfully, can shape reality, changing one's destiny in this life and perhaps the next (if Cepperello did indeed go to Heaven). We can then steal a page from Guido Almansi's book[33] and make out the figure of the author behind these excellent liars. If this is so, Boccaccio is to the *Decameron* what the storytellers are to their lies. Boccaccio's words, then, like the storytellers', are imbued with the miraculous power to change reality.

Notes

1. "Forme complesse, coscientemente architettate." P. M. Forni, *Forme complesse nel Decameron,* Firenze: Olschki, 1992, 17.

2. "E' chiaro che V.4 viene configurandosi come riscrittura ironica, come liquidazione comica di IV.1." P. M. Forni, *Forme complesse nel Decameron,* 106; "The brigade engages in an edifying mutual ritual validation of principle and experience." P. M. Forni, *Adventures in Speech,* Philadelphia: U of Pennsylvania P, 1996, 7.

3. "False witness he bore, solicited or unsolicited, with boundless delight;" *Dec.* I.1.11. Translated by J. M. Rigg, London, 1921 (first printed 1903).

4. "as fond of women as a dog is of the stick: in the use against nature he had not his match among the most abandoned." *Dec.* I.1.14.

5. "I am virgin even as when I issued from my mother's womb." *Dec.* I.1.39.

6. "he had quaffed the water with as good a gusto and as much enjoyment, more particularly when fatigued by devotion or pilgrimage, as great drinkers quaff their wine; and oftentimes he had felt a craving for such dainty dishes of herbs." *Dec.* I.1.41.

7. "most gluttonous . . . and inordinately fond of his cups, whereby he sometimes brought upon himself both shame and suffering." *Dec.*1.14.

8. "was never seen at church, held all the sacraments vile things, and derided them in language of horrible ribaldry. On the other hand he resorted readily to the tavern." *Dec.* I.1.14.

9. "the folk of these parts, who reprobate our trade as iniquitous and revile it all day long, and would fain rob us, will seize their opportunity, and raise a tumult, and make a raid upon our houses, crying: 'A way with these Lombard dogs, whom the Church excludes from her pale;' and will certainly strip us of our goods, and *perhaps take our lives also*; so that in any case we stand to lose if this man die." *Dec.*I.1.26, my emphasis.

10. "who has the sign of the cross made upon him with these coals, may live secure for the whole of the ensuing year, that fire shall not touch him, that he feel it not." *Dec.* VI.10.51.

11. C. Del Corno, "Ironia/parodia" in *Lessico critico decameroniano,* P. M. Forni and R. Bragantini eds. Torino: Bollati Boringhieri, 1995, 171.

12. D. Knox, *Ironia. Medieval and Renaissance Ideas on Irony,* Brill: Leiden, 1989, 51. Quoted from C. Del Corno, "Ironia/parodia." *Lessico critico,* 169.

13. "Great was his shame when they [Cepperello's documents] were found anything but false." *Dec* I.1.10.

14. M. Pastore-Stocchi, "Dioneo e l'orazione di Frate Cipolla." *Studi sul Boccaccio* 10 (1977-1978) 207.

15. It is Branca that attributes the meaning of "si vede," "è visibile" to "apparisce." V. Branca ed, *Decameron,* Einaudi, 1980, 768, in footnote.

16. "I met with many of our own brethren, and of other religious not a few, intent one and all on eschewing hardship for the love of God, making little account of others' toil, so they might ensue their own advantage," *Dec.* VI.10.39.

17. "Avevan tanto riso ch'eran creduti smascellare" ("They . . . laughed till they thought their jaws would break;") *Dec.* VI.10.55.

18. "God's curse upon him [. . .] He has always been as straight as any of us; he has merely shown you

that he knows better than any man alive how to play this trick of putting on any counterfeit semblance that he chooses." *Dec.* II.1.14-16.

19. "Seize this traitor who mocks at God and His saints; who, being no paralytic, has come hither in the guise of a paralytic to deride our patron saint and us." So saying, they laid hands on him, dragged him down from where he stood, seized him by the hair, tore the clothes from his back, and fell to beating and kicking him, so that it seemed to him as if all the world were upon him. He cried out: "Pity, for God's sake," and defended himself as best he could: all in vain, however; the press became thicker and thicker moment by moment. Which Stecchi and Marchese observing began to say one to the other that 'twas a bad business; yet, being apprehensive on their own account, they did not venture to come to his assistance, but cried out with the rest that he ought to die, at the same time, however, casting about how they might find the means to rescue him from the hands of the people, who would certainly have killed him, but for a diversion which Marchese hastily effected." *Dec.* II.1.17-21.

20. "avendo nondimeno pensiero tuttavia come trarre il potessero delle mani del popolo; il quale fermamente l'avrebbe ucciso," *Dec.* II.1.20.

21. ". . . the lady's brothers-in-law entered *the room,* and found that the *Angel Gabriel had taken flight, leaving his wings behind him.*" *Dec.* IV.2.47, my emphasis.

22. "One of *the feathers of the Angel Gabriel, which he left behind him in the room* of the Virgin Mary, when he came to make her the annunciation in Nazareth." *Dec.*VI.11, my emphasis.

23. "presumed to counterfeit the Angel Gabriel." *Dec.* IV.2.58.

24. "they *tore off the cerements,* each thinking himself blessed to have but a scrap thereof in his possession;" *Dec.* I.1.86, my emphasis.

25. "they laid hands on him, dragged him down from where he stood, seized him by the hair, *tore the clothes from his back,* and fell to beating and kicking him, so that it seemed to him as if all the world were upon him." *Dec.* II.1.18, my emphasis.

26. "Especially of things worthy to be had in reverence." *Dec.* I.1.2.

27. "l'uno era chiamato Stecchi, l'altro Martellino e il terzo Marchese, uomini li quali, le corti de' signor visitando, di contraffarsi e con nuovi atti contraffaccendo qualunque altro uomo li veditori sollazzavano." *Dec.* II.1.6; "Io mi contraffarò a guisa

d'uno attratto." *Dec.* II.1.10; "Egli è stato sempre diritto come qualunque è l'un di noi, ma sa meglio che altro uomo, come voi avete potuto vedere, far queste ciance di contraffarsi in qualunque forma vuole." *Dec.* II.1.16.

28. P. M. Forni, "Therapy and Prophylaxis in Boccaccio's *Decameron.*" *Romance Quarterly* 52 (No.2 Spring 2005) 159-62.

29. "Who shall read them, may derive both pleasure from the entertaining matters set forth therein, and also good counsel, in that they may learn what to shun, and likewise what to pursue." *Dec.* Proem, 14.

30. G. Getto, *Vita di forme e forme di vita nel* Decameron, Torino: Petrini, 1966, 68; G. Barberi Squarotti, *Il potere della parola,* Napoli: Federico & Ardia, 1983, 103-09. See also S. Grossvogel, "What Do We really Know of Ser Ciappelletto?" *Il veltro* 40 (1995) 133-37 and M. Codebò, "True Biography versus False Biography in Boccaccio's Short Story of Ser Ciappelletto" *West Virginia U. Philological Papers* 46 (2000) 10-15. For a bibliographical orientation on this broadly studied tale, see F. Fido, "The Tale of Ser Ciappelletto (I.1)." *The "Decameron" First Day in Perspective,* Volume One of the Lectura Boccaccii. Ed. E. B. Weaver. Toronto: U of Toronto P, 2004, 59-76.

31. P. M. Forni, *Adventures in Speech,* 94-94.

32. "All bruised and battered" *Dec.* II.1.22.

33. G. Almansi, *The Writer as a Liar,* London and Boston: Routledge & Kegan Paul, 1975.

Works Consulted:

Almansi, Guido. *The Writer as a Liar.* London and Boston: Routledge & Kegan Paul, 1975.

Barberi Squarotti, Giorgio. *Il potere della parola.* Napoli: Federico & Ardia, 1983.

Branca, Vittore, *Decameron.* Torino: Einaudi, 1980.

Codebò, Marco. "True Biography versus False Biography in Boccaccio's Short Story of Ser Ciappelletto." *West Virginia U. Philological Papers* 46 (2000) 10-15.

Fido, Franco. *Il regime delle simmetrie imperfette.* Milano: Franco Angeli, 1988.

———. "The Tale of Ser Ciappelletto (I.1)." *The "Decameron" First Day in Perspective,* Volume One of the Lectura Boccaccii. Ed. Elissa B. Weaver. Toronto: U of Toronto P, 2004. 59-76.

Forni, Pier Massimo. *Forme complesse nel Decameron.* Firenze: Olschki, 1992.

———. *Adventures in Speech.* Philadelphia: U of Pennsylvania P, 1996.

———. "Therapy and Prophylaxis in Boccaccio's *Decameron.*" *Romance Quarterly* 52 (No.2 Spring 2005) 159-62.

Getto, Giovanni. *Vita di forme e forme di vita nel Decameron.* Torino: Petrini, 1958.

Grossvogel, Steven. "What Do We really Know of Ser Ciappelletto?" *Il veltro* 40 (1995) 133-37.

Pastore-Stocchi, Manlio. "Dioneo e l'orazione di Frate Cipolla." *Studi sul Boccaccio* 10 (1977-1978) 47-61.

Usher, Johnathan. "Frate Cipolla Ars praedicandi or a 'recit du discours' in Boccaccio." *The Modern Language Review* 88 (no.2: Apr 1993) 321-36.

Van Der Voort, Cook. "Convergenze e divaricazioni tra la prima e la sesta giornata del Decameron." *Studi sul Boccaccio* 11 (1979) 207-41.

Marilyn Migiel (essay date 2010)

SOURCE: Migiel, Marilyn. "New Lessons in Criticism and Blame from the *Decameron.*" *Heliotropia,* 7, nos. 1-2 (2010): 5-30.

[In the following essay, Migiel invites readers to reflect on how they form opinions regarding the tales by directing them to ambiguous narratives in the Decameron. *Migiel approaches the question from the standpoint of Boccaccio's good women wronged, illustrating how readers' perceptions can be influenced by the manner in which the women's stories are reported and by the language the women use to respond to the reprehensible behavior of their husbands.]*

One of the great innovations of the *Decameron,* with respect to the tradition, is that it aims to complicate our moral views and our ethical responses.[1] If one believes, as I suspect many of us do, that the *Decameron* is neither immoral nor amoral in its stance, and if one believes, as I suspect many of us do, that the *Decameron*'s purpose is not solely to entertain, this claim won't strike us as earth-shaking. Precisely *how* the *Decameron* complicates our moral views—how it goes about teaching us about moral reasoning, how it leads us to reflect on what we find praiseworthy or blameworthy, and above all how it demonstrates the value of literature to this enterprise—this is a matter unlikely to be resolved any time soon. It must continue to be discussed.

Over the years, we have discovered that there are multiple ways in which the *Decameron* teaches us to view things differently and anew: by its search for harmony and joy out of confusion and chaos, by its irreverent stance toward unfounded authorities, by its spirited dialogue with sources and analogues, by its multiple languages, voices, and stylistic registers, by its use of pointed juxtapositions and pointed ironies. All these features are important to the *Decameron*'s success, and in many cases, they constitute significant innovations in the Italian and the European literary tradition.

We have also recognized, over the years, that the *Decameron* teaches us to reflect on what it means to speak and listen (or write and read) and that it does so by offering us a panoply of authorial and audiential role models—some seemingly reliable, some far less so, some puzzlingly uncertain.[2] Reading the *Decameron,* it turns out, is much like finding oneself in an academic setting. It's tempting to think that all the teachers are going to be fabulous and that learning from them is going to be a quite straightforward enterprise. The real educational process happens in a much less straightforward way, however, as students seek to determine the soundness of those teacherly voices, seek to identify other contributors who could be just as insightful (if not more so), and seek to figure out which books are actually worth reading, what facts stand out, and what theories have any validity.

Consistent with my own pedagogy and consistent with what I think Boccaccio was trying to achieve in the *Decameron,* I believe that the burden is on those of us who are readers and students. When we hear an opinion touted as gospel truth or rejected as utterly loathsome, when we get a report of something done well or something done badly, how careful are we to take measured account of the manner in which the information has been delivered to us? Are we confident that we have enough information to pronounce praise or to blame?

In fact, the *Decameron* offers us a spectacular opportunity to witness how information can be expertly controlled. The narrators and the Author function as "filtering mechanisms." To the extent that any fictional construct can be said to choose, they make choices about what to report in direct discourse or indirect discourse. They represent thoughts that could belong to a given character, could belong to alternate publics, or could be some combination thereof. Such reporting happens with the greatest frequency when frametale narrators re-present a scene that has been imagined, heard about, read about, or actually witnessed. It also happens as the Author conveys the frametale narrators' reactions or tells us what the stories are about (as for example, in the Author's rubrics). There are plenty of other medieval literary texts that expertly control information—the French fabliaux provide some outstanding examples of this—but on account of its length and complexity, the *Decameron* provides an especially sustained reflection on the ethics of reporting.

I would like to draw our attention to a specific kind of reported event in the *Decameron,* namely, moments where a wife—most especially a wronged, virtuous wife—criticizes her husband for behavior that a reader could objectively find blameworthy. Since the *Decameron*'s Author offers that women in love will be able to take useful advice and pleasure from his book, we are led to pause, almost inevitably, over instances where the woman reader could reasonably expect to find "advice about how to speak," most especially when a woman addresses a man whom she knows intimately and to whom she is joined by legal and perhaps emotional bonds. As I intend to show here, multiple voices from the *Decameron* come together in order to tell a story about how "good women" (which is to say women who are both virtuous and of elevated social standing) should speak when they have been aggrieved. The situation I describe has broader implications. It raises questions such as: Can the less powerful ever really speak truth to power? Can they ever really name blameworthy behavior as such?[3] I suspect that those were fascinating questions for Boccaccio, whose socio-economic, intellectual, and psychological condition may have predisposed him to identify, at least in part, with people outside the accepted circles of power. Finally, I shall ask us to reconsider how we, as critical readers of the *Decameron,* assign praise and blame and I shall propose some strategies for "new lessons in criticism."

* * *

Among the wronged wives of the *Decameron,* perhaps none is more striking than Madonna Zinevra (II, 9), whose denunciation of the injustices done to her emerges as the model against which all subsequent criticisms of husbands will be judged. Looking to Madonna Zinevra, we will gain a more accurate understanding of how a narrator can handle a situation in which a woman reprimands her husband, shaping our perceptions of how admirable or blameworthy she may be.

In the moment that interests us, Madonna Zinevra, disguised as Sicurano da Finale, stands in the presence of three other men: 1) the Sultan; 2) Ambrogiuolo, who has falsely claimed to have taken his pleasure with Zinevra, winning a bet against Zinevra's husband Bernabò; and 3) Bernabò himself, who had ordered Zinevra killed and believes she is dead. Sicurano has already managed to have Ambrogiuolo tell his entertaining version of story to the Sultan, and then to arrange a situation in which the Sultan forces Ambrogiuolo to tell the truth of the matter in the presence of Bernabò. Exactly what that truth is, we are not fully certain at first, since we learn only that Ambrogiuolo told all ("narrò ogni cosa" [II, 9, 60]).[4] When Sicurano asks Bernabò, "E tu che facesti per questa bugia alla tua donna?" ("And what did you do to your wife on account of this lie?" [II, 9, 61]), we learn what the summary statement had stopped short of saying: namely, that Ambrogiuolo lied.

In exposing the lies about her, Zinevra demonstrates superb rhetorical control. It no doubt serves her well that she had begun speaking as Sicurano (i.e., as a man), in a public setting, and to a figure of authority. In a single, skillfully crafted sentence, she labels each of the personages in the dramatic situation she has constructed: first she acknowledges the Sultan as her lord, then she identifies herself, then she identifies the perpetrator of the wrong done to her and the nature of the injury, and finally, she indicates the man who must be her husband Bernabò and the wrong he had committed against her:

> Signor mio, io sono la misera sventurata Zinevra, sei anni andata tapinando in forma d'uom per lo mondo, da questo traditor d'Ambrogiuol falsamente e reamente vituperata, e da questo crudele e iniquo uomo data a uccidere ad un suo fante e a mangiare a' lupi.
>
> (II, 9, 69)

> My lord, I am the poor unfortunate Zinevra, who spent six years wandering the world as a man, who was by this traitor Ambrogiuolo wrongly and maliciously dishonored, and who was by this cruel and unjust man given over to one of his servants to be killed and then eaten by wolves.

Throughout her eloquent condemnation of lies,[5] Madonna Zinevra refrains from identifying her husband by name or calling him a "murderer," though she does call him "cruel and unjust" ("crudele e iniquo"). This may indicate an unwillingness to assign to Bernabò the kind of blame that has been placed squarely on Ambrogiuolo, whose name appears prominently along with the designation of "traitor." This moment asks us to reflect on how we assign gradations of culpability. Is attempted murder a lesser offense than fraud and treachery? How does ordering someone's murder compare to providing false testimony that could lead to the ordering of someone's murder?

Thus far, Madonna Zinevra's speech is directed at the Sultan, so we have not yet seen anything like a direct reprimand of a guilty party. This changes when, with dramatic flair, Madonna Zinevra, seals her statement with visual proof of her identity. Having proved that she is indeed a woman, she can now prove that Ambrogiuolo is the traitor she has claimed him to be:

> E stracciando i panni dinanzi e mostrando il petto, sé esser femina e al soldano e a ciascuno altro fece palese, rivolgendosi poi ad Ambrogiuolo, ingiuriosamente domandandolo quando mai, secondo che egli avanti si vantava, con lei giaciuto fosse; il quale, già riconoscendola e per vergogna quasi mutolo divenuto, niente dicea.
>
> (II, 9, 69)

> And ripping her clothes and baring her breast, she made it manifestly clear both to the sultan and to everyone else that she was a woman; turning then to Ambrogiuolo, with great indignation she asked him when, as he claimed previously, he had ever lain with her. Recognizing her and falling just about mute with shame, Ambrogiuolo said nothing.

Let us pause over the information that the narrator, Filomena, offers in indirect discourse: "ingiuriosamente domandandolo quando mai, secondo che egli avanti si vantava, con lei giaciuto fosse" ("with great indignation she asked him when, as he claimed previously, he had ever lain with her"). How might Madonna Zinevra have formulated her question to Ambrogiuolo? One possibility slips out of the indirect discourse. It is a shimmeringly elegant question, consisting of two septenaries cloaking a hendecasyllable: "Ambrogiuolo, quando mai, secondo che tu avanti ti vantavi, sei tu giaciuto con me?" (As for the shamed Ambrogiuolo's silence, we might reproduce it, as would Elsa Morante, with "! . . .") This, of course, assumes that we translate "ingiuriosamente" as "with great indignation" (as I have) or "scathingly" (as Guido Waldman translates it).[6] What if we render the word, as G. H. McWilliam does, as "haughtily"?[7] I could imagine Zinevra being haughty here—after all, she certainly has the right to be haughty, seeing how her virtuous behavior gives her the upper hand. But what if we translate "ingiuriosamente," along with Mark Musa and Peter Bondanella, as "abusively"?[8] What if we understand "ingiuriosamente" to mean, as Fanfani does, "mescolando alla domanda parole d'ingiuria" ("mixing in with her question words of insult and injury")?[9] I admit that I would not like to think of Madonna Zinevra as "abusive." And I am not sure how much insult and injury can we imagine in her speech before she stops being Zinevra and becomes instead Bartolomea (II, 10), or Catella (III, 6), or Tessa, the wife of Calandrino (IX, 5).

The indirect discourse asks us not to think about Madonna Zinevra's language. Or rather, it asks us to believe what we may already be too willing to believe, namely, that whatever we imagine her to say is what she might actually have said. Indirect discourse can serve as a protective mechanism. It can allow for the possibility of insult and injury without ever tarnishing Madonna Zinevra's reputation with any undignified words.

In a later passage, Filomena again uses indirect discourse to describe a moment that some readers will have long awaited: the reconciliation of Madonna Zinevra and her husband. The Sultan orders that dresses and women's companions—both markers of femininity that must be present for the situation to right itself—be brought for Madonna Zinevra. Furthermore, Bernabò gets pardoned. Exactly what that pardon looks like should be of great interest to us:

> E, fattile venire onorevolissimi vestimenti femminili e donne che compagnia le tenessero, secondo la dimanda fatta da lei a Bernabò perdonò la meritata morte; il quale, riconosciutala, a' piedi di lei si gittò piagnendo e

domandando perdonanza, la quale ella, quantunque egli mal degno ne fosse, benignamente gli diede, e in piede il fece levare, teneramente sì come suo marito abbracciandolo.

(II, 9, 71)

Having ordered fine dresses and women that could keep her company, in response to her request he pardoned Bernabò the death that he deserved. Bernabò, having recognized her, threw himself at her feet, weeping and asking forgiveness, which she kindly granted him, though he was not deserving of it; and she had him rise to his feet, where she tenderly embraced him as her husband.[10]

What precisely does Madonna Zinevra say when she advances her request? Could it be "Vi prego di perdonare mio marito" ("I beseech you to pardon my husband")? In that case, the comment about a death well deserved would be attributed to the narrator. Or might Madonna Zinevra herself recognize the gravity of Bernabò's crime, with a request such as "Vi prego di perdonare a mio marito la meritata morte?" ("I beseech you to pardon my husband the death that he deserves")?

Even more pressing would be the questions that arise when Zinevra forgives Bernabò "even though he didn't deserve it" ("quantunque egli maldegno ne fosse"). Is it conceivable that Zinevra would say to him "I forgive you even though you do not deserve it?" To whom should we attribute this comment? To Madonna Zinevra? To Bernabò? To the Sultan? To the narrator Filomena? Here, editorial interventions are telling. Although the original autograph text reveals no punctuation that would allow us to decide about where to assign responsibility for this comment, editors in the sixteenth century intervene with punctuation in order to set the comment off as a parenthetical interpolation, thus encouraging us to read the comment as belonging to the narrator rather than to Zinevra. Representative is the following from a 1522 edition of the *Decameron* published in Venice by Aldo Romano and Andrea Asolano:

secondo la domanda fatta dallei a Bernabo perdono la meritata morte. Il quale riconosciutala a piedi di lei si gitto piagnendo; & domando perdonanza: la quale ella (quantunque egli mal degno ne fusse) benignamente gli diede.[11]

in response to her request he pardoned Bernabò the death that he deserved. Bernabò, having recognized her, threw himself at her feet, weeping and asking forgiveness, which (though he was not deserving of it) she tenderly granted him.

Only by reflecting on the use of indirect discourse can we realize that we never have to come to terms with what a Zinevra openly critical of her husband would sound like. Would we agree with her particular combination of disapproval and forgiveness? Would we find

that she strikes the right balance? The indirect discourse draws a veil over this, simply reassuring us with its elegant formulations that a resolution has been achieved.

* * *

Now let us look at another approach to criticism and blame, one from which we are invited to distance ourselves. I am thinking of Catella (III, 6), who, believing that she has successfully substituted herself for her husband's presumed lover, has sex in the dark with the man she believes to be her husband and then proceeds to reveal her true identity and to rail against him. (Unfortunately for Catella, the man she is railing against is Ricciardo, who has tricked her into this sexual encounter.) Here is what Catella says:

Ahi quanto è misera la fortuna delle donne e come è male impiegato l'amor di molte ne' mariti! Io, misera me, già sono otto anni, t'ho più che la mia vita amato, e tu, come io sentito ho, tutto ardi e consumiti nello amore d'una donna strana, reo e malvagio uom che tu se'. Or con cui ti credi tu essere stato? Tu se' stato con colei la qual con false lusinghe tu hai, già è assai, ingannata mostrandole amore ed essendo altrove innamorato. Io son Catella, non son la moglie di Ricciardo, traditor disleale che tu se': ascolta se tu riconosci la voce mia, io son ben dessa; e parmi mille anni che noi siamo al lume, ché io ti possa svergognare come tu se' degno, sozzo cane vituperato che tu se'. Oimè, misera me! a cui ho io cotanti anni portato cotanto amore? A questo can disleale che, credendosi in braccio avere una donna strana, m'ha più di carezze e d'amorevolezze fatte in questo poco di tempo che qui stata son con lui, che in tutto l'altro rimanente che stata son sua. Tu se' bene oggi, can rinnegato, stato gagliardo, che a casa ti suogli mostrare così debole e vinto e senza possa! Ma, lodato sia Idio, che il tuo campo, non l'altrui, hai lavorato, come tu ti credevi. Non maraviglia che stanotte tu non mi ti appressasti: tu aspettavi di scaricar le some altrove e volevi giugnere molto fresco cavaliere alla battaglia: ma lodato sia Idio e il mio avvedimento, l'acqua è pur corsa all'ingiù come ella doveva. Ché non rispondi, reo uomo? ché non di' qualche cosa? Se' tu divenuto mutolo udendomi? In fè di Dio io non so a che io mi tengo che io non ti ficco le mani negli occhi e traggoglti! Credesti molto celatamente saper fare questo tradimento? Par Dio! tanto sa altri quanto altri; non t'è venuto fatto, io t'ho avuti miglior bracchi alla coda che tu non credevi.

(III, 6, 33-38)

Oh, how wretched is women's lot! how thankless is the love that many of them have for their husbands! Me—wretched me!—for eight years now I have loved you more than my life itself, and you, as I've heard, are completely consumed with passion for another woman, evil and wicked man that you are! Now who do you think you've been with? You've been with the woman you have been deceiving with bogus flattery for quite some time, exhibiting love for her when all the time you were enamored elsewhere. I am Catella, I am not Ricciardo's wife, you dishonest traitor that you are. Listen—do you recognize my voice? It really is me. I can't wait until we're out of here so that I can shame you the way you deserve, dirty shameful dog that you are. Oh, wretched me! Who have I loved for all these years? This dishonest dog who, thinking he had another woman in his arms, offered me more caresses and affection in this little bit of time that I've been here with him than in all the rest of the time that I was his. Today, you two-timing dog, you were daring and bold, while at home you prove feeble and defeated and lifeless. But praise be to God that it was your own field, not someone's else's that you were plowing, contrary to what you thought! It's no surprise that you didn't come near me last night! You were waiting to unload yourself elsewhere, and you wanted to be a fully rested knight entering the battlefield. But praise be to God and to my keen foresight, the water ended up running down the way it was supposed to! How come you don't answer, you wicked man? How come you aren't saying anything? Have you become mute as you've been listening to me? By God, I don't know what's keeping me back from sticking my fingers into your eyes and tearing them out! You thought you would know how to keep this affair secret? By God, other people know how things work too. It didn't turn out as you expected—I had better hounds on your tail than you thought.

While the first words out of Catella's mouth could have been spoken by Madonna Zinevra, the resemblance between these "virtuous wives" soon starts to look shaky. That double repetition of "misera" ("quanto è misera la fortuna delle donne . . . ! . . . Io, misera me! . . .") forecasts the excess that will soon be evident. The attack turns exceedingly vicious and vulgar. Catella's relies on pounding repetitions and frequent jabbing monosyllables (with a particular emphasis on the pronoun "tu" with which she addresses him). Harsh dental consonants T and D reinforce the sense of attack. She moves from calling him "evil and wicked man that you are" to "dishonest traitor that you are" to "dirty shameful dog that you are" to "dishonest dog," "two-timing dog" and "wicked man" ("reo e malvagio uom che tu se'," "traditor disleale che tu se'," "sozzo cane vituperato che tu se'," "questo can disleale," "can rinnegato," "reo uomo"). This moment is presumably about self-revelation and intended to shame a wayward husband by making him see that he has had sex with his own wife while believing he was having sex with another woman. But Catella goes beyond naming him a wrongdoer (as does Zinevra with her husband in II, 9, and as the wife of Guglielmo Rossiglione will do with her husband in IV, 9); she descends into name-calling. This attempt to define Filippello soon proves to be her greatest blunder. As Catella attacks Filippello for his sexual shortcomings over the eight years she has been with him—shortcomings redressed in the encounter she has just had—she reveals her own sexual frustration and gives Ricciardo hope that he can indeed win her over.

Nor does Catella's self-revelation stop here. After a brief interlude in which Fiammetta represents Ricciar-

do's pleasure at hearing this ("in se medesimo godeva di queste parole" [III, 6, 39]) and in which she calls attention to Ricciardo's pleasuring of Catella ("e senza rispondere alcuna cosa l'abbracciava e basciava, e più che mai le facea le carezze grandi" [III, 6, 39]), Catella is given yet another long speech, in which she continues the name-calling, in which she repeats that Filippello has performed sexually beyond what is usually the case for him, in which she threatens Filipello with public shaming, and in which she concludes by saying that perhaps it would not be so bad after all if she were to take up with Ricciardo, who has always loved her. This speech reinforces our perception that 1) Catella has a few notes that she sounds insistently, and 2) the more she rants, the more she will reveal information that will undermine her authority.

This is the first time in the story that we hear Catella speak at any length, so we might assume that this is the only register available to her. Yet in her final speech, delivered after she is stunned to discover the identity of the man she has been with, she strikes a different tone:

> Ricciardo, io non so come Domenedio mi si concederà che io possa comportare la 'ngiuria e lo 'nganno che fatto m'hai. Non voglio gridar qui, dove la mia simplicità e soperchia gelosia mi condusse, ma di questo vivi sicuro, che io non sarò mai lieta se in un modo o in un altro io non mi veggio vendica di ciò che fatto m'hai; e per ciò lasciami, non mi tener più: tu hai avuto ciò che disiderato hai e ha'mi straziata quanto t'è piaciuto. Tempo hai di lasciarmi; lasciami, io te ne priego.
>
> (III, 6, 47-48)
>
> Ricciardo, I do not know how the lord God will grant me the ability to withstand the injury and the deception you have perpetrated on me. I do not wish to scream here, where my foolishness and excessive jealousy have brought me, but be certain of this: that I shall never be content if, in one way or another, I do not see myself avenged of what you have done to me. And so leave me, let me go. You have gotten what you longed for and you have tormented me as much as you liked. It is time for you to leave me; leave me, I beg of you.

Now we have evidence that Catella is capable of delivering a composed and deliberate speech. The string of septenaries and hendecasyllables at the conclusion of this speech render it elegant and memorable. Even more stunning is the mournful lamenting sound "ai" that sounds repeatedly, particularly at the end of sentences. Catella is saying "hai" (that is, "you have" done this or that) but the effect on the listener is also to register "ahi!", an exclamation that in Italian would be pronounced the same way. What if Catella had begun her earlier speech with a phrase like, "Filippello, io non so come Domenedio mi si concederà che io possa comportare la 'ngiuria che fatto m'hai" ("Filippello, I do not know how the lord God will grant me the ability to withstand the injury and the deception you have perpetrated on me")? Would she have descended as easily into name-calling? I suspect not. Rather, I would think that an exordium like this would have more likely led into an elegant hendecasyllable like "ha'mi straziata quanto t'è piaciuto" ("you have tormented me as much as you liked") and, in closing, to polished double septenaries, marked by a poignant chiasmus: "Tempo hai di lasciarmi: lasciami io te ne priego" ("It is time for you to leave me; leave me, I beg of you" [III, 6, 48]).

And what do we make of the fact that, when Catella actually has her chance to call Ricciardo a fraudulent rapist, she does not do so? It is as if Catella has used up all her rhetorical weaponry and is no longer able to apply to Ricciardo all the epithets she hurled at him when she thought he was Filippello. This affects the reader's perception of him. If Catella doesn't find it within herself to call him a dirty dog, can we?

But Catella may not be the only person protecting Ricciardo from criticism. The narrator of the story, Fiammetta, also, by means of her selective use of direct and indirect discourse, can also shape our reaction.

When Ricciardo reveals himself to Catella, Fiammetta gives us the entire text of his speech. Already from the opening lines, we see his rhetorical power: "Anima mia dolce, non vi turbate: quello che io semplicemente amando aver non potei, Amor con inganno m'ha insegnato avere, e sono il vostro Ricciardo" ("Sweet darling, don't be upset. What I could not have simply by loving, Love taught me to have by deception, and I am your Ricciardo" [III, 6, 42]). From the opening phrased as a hendecasyllable ("Anima mia dolce, non vi turbate") to the closing septenary ("sono il vostro Ricciardo"), this is a statement remarkable for its mellifluous sophistication. As Ricciardo proceeds to demonstrate that what has happened cannot be otherwise, and as he asserts that Catella has no recourse to justice, he reveals a full arsenal of literary, historical, and judicial weaponry. Multiple footnotes alert us to the sources for his argumentation: Livy, Valerius Maximus, and a range of passages in Boccaccio's earlier works.[12] The direct discourse asks us to consider the basis for his authority.

When Ricciardo responds to Catella's threat of retaliation, however, Fiammetta opts for indirect discourse:

> Ricciardo, che conoscea l'animo suo ancora troppo turbato, s'avea posto in cuore di non lasciarla mai se la sua pace non riavesse: per che, cominciando con dolcissime parole a raumiliarla, tanto disse e tanto pregò e tanto scongiurò, che ella, vinta, con lui si pacificò . . .
>
> (III, 6, 49)

> Ricciardo, who saw that she was still very agitated, had made up his mind not ever to leave her until he reconciled with her. So, beginning by placating her with sweet words, he spoke at length and pleaded at length and appealed at length, with the result that she, defeated, made peace with him.

Ricciardo has already exerted control over Catella by putting his hand over her mouth, and he has already stated that she has no recourse other than to accept him as a lover. What could he possibly say to pacify her? Why is his speech not rendered with direct discourse? I think it is because, no matter what Ricciardo says—and it clearly was quite a bit—we would not look kindly upon his arguments. If in reading "tanto disse e tanto pregò e tanto scongiurò" "he spoke at length and pleaded at length and appealed at length" [III, 6, 49]) we imagine the progression that could be required if Catella were to mount resistance, it would have to look something like "tanto disse e tanto pregò e tanto scongiurò e tanto implorò e tanto esortò e e tanto invocò e e tanto impetrò e tanto sollecitò e tanto supplicò" ("he spoke at length and pleaded at length and appealed at length and implored at length and exhorted at length and invoked at length and importuned at length and solicited at length and beseeched at length"). In the final accounting it is better—better for Ricciardo, that is—to leave his exact words cloaked in mystery.

The story of Catella and Ricciardo, along with the story of Madonna Zinevra, shows that, if we wish to position ourselves to make informed judgments, we must be aware of how the information we receive (and the form in which we receive it) will affect our judgment. Direct and indirect discourse can be used selectively to solicit approval (even if tacit) or blame. We would do well to remember these lessons from literature every time that we ourselves report events to others and every time that we listen to the accounts that others offer us.

* * *

I have long maintained that we must attend not only to single exemplary moments that invite praise or blame but also to the dialogue among the narrators that emerges as they are drawn to certain narrative moments, pause over them, draw out the narrative possibilities, contest the conclusions that others draw, and use the stories as ways of exploring ways of being in the world.[13] Many are the questions that the stories of Zinevra and Catella pose, so I cannot in good faith claim that the story I am about to tell you is the lone one. I urge readers to consider what other stories there may be. As for myself, when I begin with the story of a virtuous wife who responds to the husband who has wronged her, and when I begin to examine other wives who respond to husbands who are blameworthy, this is what I hear:

Against the bet of a man like Ambrogiuolo and in a certain sense against all odds, Madonna Zinevra upholds ideals of loyalty, resourcefulness, prudence, foresight, and commitment to the truth. When she defends herself and exposes the wrongdoing of others, she does so in a language that is presented as above reproach. With Zinevra, the narrators will begin in earnest a series of reflections about marital fidelity, about women's abilities, about their right to self-assertion, about their use of deception, and about the strategies that a wife might use to criticize blameworthy behavior in her husband. How legitimate is the kind of deception that Zinevra uses to unearth Ambrogiuolo's deceptions? How realistic is it to expect women to respond to adversity as she does? (Just for starters, how many women can go about for six years dressed as men? What if you don't happen to have collegial relations with a wealthy ruler outside the Western legal system? And how deep do the wells of forgiveness run if your husband has ordered you killed and left as repast for the wolves?)

Upon hearing Zinevra's story, Dioneo attacks Bernabò for his foolishness and showcases Bartolomea of Pisa, who advocates rights to sexual fulfillment that her husband Ricciardo Cinzica has denied her. Extraordinarily important, as Mario Baratto has shown is the moment when Bartolomea, quite unexpectedly, becomes the arbiter of the situation. She vituperates her husband for his pitiful sexual performance. Dioneo's story turns on the question of male sexuality: if you're a real man, unlike Ricciardo, you'll remember that women need to be satisfied and you won't try to advertise your abilities beyond what they are. The narrators—all of them—laugh. They approve of Dioneo's story and agree that Bernabo was a fool. As for what they think of Zinevra, we are not told. The question arises, however: Was Zinevra also a fool? Should she have acted and spoken like Bartolomea?

Catella (III, 6) is the next woman to assert herself as a wronged wife by bringing to light her husband's failings. In fact, we have every reason to believe that Catella will triumph, since she has the scales of the literary tradition tipped in her favor. In the sources and analogues for *Decameron* III, 6, when a woman sets about to expose her husband's infidelities, and seeks to do so by trapping him with a bed trick, she is generally guaranteed success.[14] In some stories, even when she is an equally guilty partner, she substitutes herself for the woman with whom her husband believes he is having sex and, when she angrily confronts him, the shamed husband learns his lesson. In "Le Meunier d'Arleux" ("The Miller of Arleux"), the fabliau often considered to be Boccaccio's direct source, the wife not only manages to successfully substitute herself for the other woman, but her husband ends up acting as his own pimp when he allows another man to have sex with her too. Boccaccio has Fiammetta, the narrator of Catella's story, turn all this on its head. The literary tradition might say one thing, but *Decameron* III, 6 shows us that things don't always work out for the wife who wishes to expose her husband's infidelities, no more than things work out for a man like Ambrogiuolo who wishes at all cost to broadcast that women are unfaithful. When Catella finds herself in the darkened room,

all the literary and historical narratives that put the wife in control get lost. What is foregrounded is Catella's excess in her attack on her husband. In addition, superimposed on the narratives of faithful wives who seek to teach their wayward husbands a lesson is a narrative of a faithful wife who maintains her own (and her husband's) honor: Lucretia. Lucretia takes the sword to herself. Now Catella is in a bind. The literary tradition predicts success; the narrative about Lucretia tells us that a suicide could be in the making. As it turns out, in the *Decameron,* the result is neither self-assertion nor suicide, but making do. For Catella, that means accepting failure and humiliation, accepting her own excesses, and accepting that hers is a society that will not recognize the wrong done to her.

In the wake of *Decameron* III, 6, the narrators work off two possibilities: the wronged wife as played by Madonna Zinevra (who is a difficult exemplar to criticize, even though her kindness toward a husband who tried to kill her does strike some of us as inexplicable) and the wronged wife as played by Catella (who displays a kind of excess that we are invited to condemn, even if we know that she has been duped by Ricciardo). These are not the only two possibilities that the world offers us, of course, but the fact is that the narrators of the *Decameron*—like people in general—tend to work off binaries like this.

Neifile, the Queen of Day III, is the first to take up the challenge presented by Zinevra and Catella. In *Decameron* III, 9, her female protagonist Giletta di Narbona appears as a redeemed blend of those earlier wives. Not to be deterred by a husband (Beltramo) who sets her aside, Giletta successfully conceals her identity, substitutes herself for a woman with whom Beltramo intends to have sex, and succeeds in fulfilling the ostensibly impossible conditions he himself has established: she acquires Beltramo's ring and bears his offspring.

At pains to render Giletta a wronged virtuous wife, Neifile describes the sexual encounter between Giletta and Beltramo in a most summary fashion. Once another woman arranges for Giletta to lie with the count, this is what we are told:

> Ne' quali primi congiugnimenti affettuosissimamente dal conte cercati, come fu piacer di Dio, la donna ingravidò in due figliuoli maschi, come il parto al suo tempo venuto fece manifesto. Né solamente d'una volta contentò la gentil donna la contessa degli abbracciamenti del marito ma molte, sì segretamente operando che mai parola non se ne seppe, credendosi sempre il conte non con la moglie ma con colei la quale egli amava essere stato; a cui, quando a partire si venia la mattina, avea parecchi belle e care gioie donate, le quali tutte diligentemente la contessa guardava.
>
> (III, 9, 49)

In these first embraces most affectionately sought out by the count, as it pleased God, the woman conceived two sons, as their birth later made evident. The noblewoman arranged for the countess to enjoy the embraces of her husband not only once, but many times. The whole matter was managed so secretly that no word was ever known about it, and the count believed unwaveringly that he was not with his wife but with the woman he loved. When he had to leave her in the morning, he presented her with a number of beautiful and precious jewels, all of which the countess preserved most carefully.

We might not find this exercise of discretion strange, but for the fact that, up until now in the novella, Giletta has been doing quite a bit of talking in direct discourse, mainly to other women who will provide her with necessary support for her plan to win back her husband. By drawing a veil over Giletta and Beltramo's sexual encounters, Neifile neatly circumvents the problem of what they might be saying to each other. There is no risk that Giletta could sound like a woman of whom an audience could disapprove.[15]

Our lasting memory of Giletta, then, comes near the very end of the story when dressed as a pilgrim and carrying her two children, she reenacts a version of a plea to authority that readers will recognize as Zinevra's:

> E sentendo le donne e' cavalieri nel palagio del conte adunati per dovere andare a tavola, senza mutare abito, con questi suoi figlioletti in braccio salita in su la sala, tra uomo e uomo là se n'andò dove il conte vide, e gittataglisi a' piedi disse piagnendo: "Signor mio, io sono la tua sventurata sposa, la quale, per lasciar te tornare e stare in casa tua, lungamente andata son tapinando. Io ti richeggio per Dio che le condizioni postemi per li due cavalieri che io ti mandai, tu le mi osservi: e ecco nelle mie braccia non un sol figliuol di te, ma due, ed ecco qui il tuo anello. Tempo è adunque che io debba da te sì come moglie esser ricevuta secondo la tua promessa."

(III, 9, 57-58)

Hearing that the ladies and knights had gathered in the count's palace and were ready to dine, she went forward—in the clothes she was wearing and with these children of hers in her arms—to the head of the room when she saw the count. Then, crying, she threw herself at his feet and said, "My lord, I am your unfortunate bride, who has long gone wandering through the world in order to allow you to return and remain in your home. I ask, by God, that you respect the conditions placed on me by the two knights I sent to you. Behold here in my arms not one but two children by you, and behold here your ring. The time has come therefore that I should be received as your wife, as you promised."

In passages preceding and following this one, Neifile refers insistently to Giletta as the "countess" ("contessa" [III, 9, 60]), reminding us that Giletta is Beltramo's legitimate spouse. Giletta reaffirms her own parity with Beltramo when she addresses him with the informal second-person singular even as she calls him her "lord." Like Zinevra, whose words she echoes, Giletta remains

humble supplicant and, like Zinevra, she receives new clothes and a sumptuous celebratory feast. Giletta also, like Zinevra, mutes her criticism of a husband who has not acted very admirably. As for the aspects of Zinevra's behavior that could raise eyebrows, Neifile deftly transforms them. There is no cross-dressing, and no ripping open a bodice to reveal breasts. Rather, "proof" of Giletta's femininity is displaced onto the twins that she holds in her arms even as she throws herself dramatically at Beltramo's feet.

Up until this point, as I have provided textual examples of women who criticize men in indirect or direct discourse, and in oblique or abusive language as the case may be. I have not yet broached the issue of the women's class or social standing. And that is because I believe that for the first third of the *Decameron,* while we are encouraged to believe that women who are truly classy will speak only in the most oblique of terms— witness, for example, the message sent by marchioness of Monferrato with her all-chicken banquet in *Decameron* I, 5—we are not yet encouraged to believe that abusive language is a marker of the lower class woman. Beginning with Day IV of the *Decameron,* however, women of confirmed social standing do not criticize their husbands (or anybody else who is trying to act like a husband or even a prospective husband) in abusive language. If these women of the upper class criticize at all, as do Ghismonda in IV, 1 (told by Fiammetta) and the wife of Guglielmo Rossiglione in IV, 9 (told by Filostrato), they exit this life soon afterwards. Or they can, like Madonna Sismonda of VII, 8 (told by Neifile), benefit from the presence of a surrogate who can deliver a vituperative speech against the husband.[16] Or, like Monna Giovanna of V, 9 (told by Fiammetta), they pull their punches by blaming first (though not in direct discourse that we could examine) and then offering extensive praise (granted, again in indirect discourse).

In fact, the case of Federigo degli Alberighi and Monna Giovanna is worth a second look, despite the fact that they are not yet married at the time when they exchange some crucial words. In the following passage, narrated by Fiammetta, Federigo degli Alberighi proves to Giovanna that she has indeed eaten his beloved falcon, which he has killed and served to her because he had nothing else to offer, and she responds to him:

> E questo detto, le penne e' piedi e 'l becco le fé in testimonianza di ciò gittare avanti. La qual cosa la donna vedendo e udendo, prima il biasimò d'aver per dar mangiare a una femina ucciso un tal falcone, e poi la grandezza dell'animo suo, la quale la povertà non avea potuto né potea rintuzzare, molto seco medesima commendò.

(V, 9, 37)

Having said this, he had the feathers and the feet and the beak thrown before her as proof. The woman, upon seeing and hearing this, blamed him at first for having killed such a falcon in order to give it to a mere female to eat, and then, to herself, she praised greatly the nobility of his soul, which poverty had not blunted and which it would never be able to blunt.

This passage is doing a good deal to bolster the courtesy and good manners of both Federigo degli Alberighi and Monna Giovanna. The first challenge is presented by Federigo's gesture, which follows a most elegantly-phrased justification for his being without a falcon that Giovanna now requests as a gift. Having the leftover body parts of his falcon thrown before her "as proof" seems openly aggressive, but for the fact that the body parts stand as testimony to his just-concluded courteous statement. And how do the feathers and feet and beak "get thrown down"? Does Federigo do it himself, and much more nicely, as Musa and Bondanella assert when they translate "And after he had said this, he laid the feathers, the feet, and beak of the bird before her as proof?"[17] Was it that he "caused the feathers, talons, and beak to be cast on the table before her," as McWilliam tells us?[18] If Federigo directs a servant to bring out the bird's remains, it seems improbable that a servant would, without specific orders from Federigo, choose to "throw" them before Monna Giovanna. But then, given what we know about Federigo, it also is hard for us to accept that Federigo would tell a servant "Have the feathers and the feet and beak thrown before her as proof of this" ("le penne e' piedi e 'l becco le farai in testimonianza di ciò gittare avanti"). Given contradictory bits of evidence, many readers will eliminate details that do not conform to their assumptions. The second challenge to courtesy and good manners is posed by Monna Giovanna, whose first response is blame. Multiple rhetorical features of this passage lead us to see her as justified in her attack on Federigo, or as not really attacking him at all. First, if she is being excessive, it might only be in response to Federigo's barely hidden aggression. Second, she denigrates herself as a "mere female" at the same time that she blames Federigo. Third, as several other readers of this passage have pointed out to me, if we imagine Giovanna to have said something like "Really, you shouldn't have!," her reproach to Federigo could have the rhetorical force of a move to console him.[19] Finally, her blame is counterbalanced by what seems (particularly given the syntax and metrical rhythms of the Italian) a lengthy moment of praise.

What is most curious about this passage is that it encourages us to see the praise cancelling out any possible blame. This is true for Federigo, whose courteous speech, delivered in direct discourse just before he has pieces of his bird thrown before Monna Giovanna, seems to guarantee that readers will not look unkindly on him. For Federigo, it appears that words speak louder than actions, perhaps because the words were rendered at length in direct discourse. And we find that Monna

Giovanna receives similar protection. She delivers a reproach, but manages, thanks to a round of praise that she does not even deliver out loud, to emerge untainted by ungraciousness that can easily earn a woman harsh criticism, at least in the *Decameron.* For Monna Giovanna, it appears that mentally articulated words speak louder than words that are verbalized, perhaps because the mentally articulated words appear in a climactic moment of a lengthy sentence.

Once the *Decameron*'s narrators make sure that upper-class women have renounced any claim on the abusive language of Bartolomea and Catella, that abusive language becomes the inheritance of women from whom the frametale narrators can distance themselves. It is a language that belongs to a comic register such as we find in the stories of Calandrino. When Tessa, Calandrino's wife, finds him with another woman (Niccolosa) in IX, 5, she gets her nails into his face and screams:

> Sozzo can vituperato, dunque mi fai tu questo? Vecchio impazzato, che maladetto sia il ben che io t'ho voluto: dunque non ti pare aver tanto a fare a casa tua, che ti vai innamorando per l'altrui? Ecco bello innamorato! Or non ti conosci tu, tristo? Non ti conosci tu, dolente? che premendoti tutto, non uscirebbe tanto sugo che bastasse a una salsa. Alla fé di Dio, egli non era ora la Tessa quella che ti 'mpregnava, che Dio la faccia trista chiunque ella è, ché ella dee ben sicuramente esser cattiva cosa a aver vaghezza di cosí bella gioia come tu se'!

> (IX, 5, 63-64)

> You dirty rotten dog, this is what you do to me? You crazy old fool—damn the love that I've felt for you! So you didn't think you had enough to do at home so you went around falling in love elsewhere! There's a fine lover boy! Now don't you see what you're doing, you twerp? You don't, you miserable creep? If you got squeezed dry, there wouldn't be enough juice to make a sauce. By God, it wasn't Tessa who got you pregnant, and goddam whoever she is, because she really must be a piece of trash to take a fancy to a fine jewel like you!

Tessa seizes upon a vituperative language used by Bartolomea and Catella in private conversation with their husbands and showers it on Calandrino in a more public setting, where four other people (Niccolosa, Bruno, Buffalmacco, Filippo) serve as witnesses. As the four spectators laugh, open criticism of a husband is reinforced as a marker of lower-class behavior.

* * *

At the end of Day X, there appears a twofold "solution" to the problems raised by the prospect of wives criticizing their husbands. The first solution is Panfilo's, and it appears in X, 9, the story of Messer Torello and his wife Adalieta (X, 9), which can be seen as the first of two conclusions to the storytelling.[20] Panfilo renders

Adalieta an exemplary wife to a husband who is above reproach.[21] At least when people behave in ways we recognize as exemplary, we can avoid instances where husbands act badly or wives speak badly about them.[22]

Then, in very final story of the series, Dioneo offers a most striking solution to the problem of critical wives. In a crucial moment in this novella, Griselda—the lower class woman who has been cruelly tested by her upper-class husband Gualtieri—is invited by him to comment on his new bride. Griselda offers a criticism that masks its status as criticism. Recognizing the superiority of her muted response, Gualtieri then reinstates her as a wife worthy of him. The passage reads as follows:

> . . . in presenza d'ogni uomo sorridendo le disse: "Che ti par della nostra sposa?"

> "Signor mio," rispose Griselda "a me ne par molto bene; e se così è savia come ella è bella, che 'l credo, io non dubito punto che voi non dobbiate con lei vivere il più consolato signor del mondo; ma quanto posso vi priego che quelle punture, le quale all'altra, che vostra fu, già deste, non diate a questa, ché appena che io creda che ella le potesse sostenere, sì perché più giovane è e sì ancora perché in dilicatezze è allevata, ove colei in continue fatiche da piccolina era stata."

> Gualtieri, veggendo che ella fermamente credeva costei dovere esser sua moglie, né per ciò in alcuna cosa men che ben parlava, la si fece sedere allato e disse: "Griselda, tempo è omai che tu senta frutto della tua lunga pazienzia, e che coloro li quali me hanno reputato crudele e iniquo e bestiale conoscano che ciò che io faceva a antiveduto fine operava, volendoti insegnare d'esser moglie e a loro di saperla tenere, e a me partorire perpetua quiete mentre teco a vivere avessi . . .

> (X, 10, 58-60)

> . . . in the presence of all, he smiled and said, "What opinion do you have of our bride?"

> "My lord," replied Griselda, "my opinion is very positive, and if she is as wise as she is beautiful, which I believe she is, I do not doubt at all that you will live with her as the happiest man in the world. But I beg you, as much as I can, that you not inflict on her the wounds you inflicted on that other woman, who was once yours, for I hardly believe that she would be able to bear them, because she is younger and also because she was brought up in great comfort, whereas the other woman had been in continuous hardship from the time she was a small child."

> When Gualtieri saw that she firmly believed that the girl was to be his wife, and this notwithstanding, she said nothing but good, he had her sit beside him and said, "Griselda, it is now time that you should reap the fruit of your long patience, and it is time for those who have considered me cruel, unjust, and brutish to realize that what I did was directed toward a foreseen goal, given that I wanted to teach you how to be a wife, to show those other people how to handle a wife, and to create for myself perpetual serenity for as long as I should live with you . . .

Griselda abstracts herself from her own material experience by speaking about herself in the third person. Thus, if there is any discontent to be registered, it is displaced onto that "other woman" and the offense to Griselda is unrecognizable. She is the lower class woman *who shows the upper class woman how to speak.*[23]

Or does she? Is Griselda (like Zinevra before her) put forward as a model of how women should respond to objectively blameworthy behavior in their husbands or is she (like Zinevra before her) meant to show us what women (and like them, anyone who wields less power) end up having to tolerate?

Praise or blame? That is the question before us. It is a question that Boccaccio posed repeatedly throughout the *Decameron* and indeed, throughout his career. It is a question that we find ourselves grappling with repeatedly as we read the *Decameron* and other of Boccaccio's works. It is—as I have argued elsewhere—a question that threatens us with critical impasse, since we can find ourselves getting nowhere as we take sides about who to praise and who to blame.[24] So Petrarch and others in his wake found nothing but praise for Griselda's patience. Women today are likely to offer nothing but resistance to Griselda's example. Perhaps we are simply condemned to a cycle where, based on our own shifting values over time, we are destined to praise or blame the so-called "virtuous wives" of the *Decameron*?

To attempt to answer this question, I would like to modulate our methodologically aware and critical voices toward a voice that overlaps more with the pronouncements of the *Decameron*'s non-analytic (and critical) wives.

In examining the story of Griselda, I have been struck by how much people seem to relish retelling it, and in particular how much they seem to relish retelling the scene I have just cited. I am referring not only to Petrarch, Chaucer, and other such writers whose retelling can be found in the Rare Book rooms of our research libraries. I am referring also to people whose retellings can be found on personal websites and in other such arenas. Readers appear fascinated by a moment of "criticism and blame" that is barely recognizable as such. They assume the voices of Gualtieri and Griselda. They reenact the scene. They editorialize. They explore motivation and intention. They appear to take considerable pleasure in doing so.

Here is one of the most engaging renditions I have found:

> She's lost her children, remember: she thinks he murdered them. In fact, he merely took them away and had them raised secretely [sic] in Bologna, and now the boy is six and the daughter twelve, and he arranges it so the daughter, his daughter by Griselda, is brought ceremoniously into town as the young bride-to-be.

So Grisdelda's [sic] standing quietly by in her crummy rags and Gualtieri asks her what she thinks of his beautiful young thing, the next Mrs. Gualtieri.

. . . "Oh, my lord," she says. "She seems very beautiful to me. And if she is as wise as beautiful, I have no doubt that you will live with her as the happiest lord in the world."

And here she does get in a word. (Trumpets! stuffed with rags for mutes) She doesn't quite chide him, but she reflects so as to protect the young bride. Please don't treat this one as you did your last wife, she says. That woman (herself, in third person) was tough, raised tough from the start—a peasant after all. This lovely one is so young, and has obviously been brought up ". . . in a more delicate fashion."

The Marquis is so pleased now that he begins to fess up: Now's the time for you to reap the fruit of your long patience, he tells her. And for everyone to realize that he had always had a plan—he wasn't really cruel as some might think. "For I wanted to teach you how to be a wife, and to show these people how to know such a wife and how to choose and keep one, and to acquire for myself lasting tranquility for as long as I was to live with you." He's not a big risk-taker. At the very outset, he says, he was afraid she'd screw up his tranquility, so he tested her. And now she's passed with flying colors.

And then he has her reinstated, introduces her to her 12 year old daughter and 6 year old son, sets them straight on who she is, sets up her poor old dad in a manner he'd never dreamed of, and everyone is really, really happy.[25]

This passage is doing some very curious work. Adopting a complicit tone with us, the narrator sets out the details we need to remember as we witness the dialogue between Gualtieri and Griselda. Then the narrator pauses over three sections of the story: Griselda's statement, in which open acceptance and oblique criticism co-exist; Gualtieri's response, in which open self-justification and oblique awareness co-exist, and a speedy rush to the happiest of endings (lest such an ending escape us). It seems manifest that the narrator is on Griselda's side. S/he evokes sympathy for what we would imagine to be Griselda's emotions and her physical condition. S/he celebrates (if in muted fashion) any attempt on Griselda's part to stand up to Gualtieri. Gualtieri's assertions to the contrary, the narrator leads us to see him as both cruel and capricious.

A reader might object that it would now be relatively easy to create a space for an ironic reading of a character like Griselda. After all, haven't many readers in the last thirty years been insisting on precisely such ironic readings, ones that display the enormous lengths we have to go to in order to insist on the happy ending?[26]

This leads me to think about what might happen if we were to give the floor to a character like Madonna Zinevra, who continues to inspire admiration, even if

some readers may perceive her as an unserviceable exemplar. So here below, I reproduce the full text of a letter, under the signature of Madonna Zinevra, that was written in response to an assignment that I gave to my spring 2006 First-Year Writing Seminar ("The Craft of Storytelling: The *Decameron*") at Cornell University.[27] Zinevra's letter, authored by Nathan Peter Sell, Cornell '09, reads[28]:

> My dear Abbot,
>
> Firstly, I must congratulate you and Alessandro for finding each other and starting a beautiful marriage together. I also must commend you in your efforts of restoring the relatives of Alessandro to their previous wealth, the act being definite testimony to your undoubtedly firm devotion to your husband. From personal experience, I can tell you that loyalty and dedication to your loved one are the primary foundations of any marriage. My husband even tried to have me *killed,* but, I forgave him anyway, since he was impoverished and I couldn't just leave him like that.
>
> But enough of me, I wanted to talk about a few things that you did while you were on your little pilgrimage. I did enjoy how you kept your true identity and purpose a secret even from the men following you on your journey. I know firsthand that this is no trivial task, as I was forced to parade around as a man for a number of years, all because my husband *tried to have me killed,* but that's neither here nor there. I think that you conducted yourself perfectly during your trip, and if I were in your shoes, I would have done just as you did. The way you directly but courteously addressed the Pope especially caught my attention, as you combined both your ambitious nature with your respect for proper authority. All of these facets of your character are truly laudable.
>
> However, I do happen to disagree with the way that you went about introducing yourself to Alessandro. Now, my husband may be a bit hasty, jumps to conclusions, and isn't exactly perfect, but I know that at least he of all people would understand a decent approach from a woman, as opposed to an immoral proposal. I think you scared poor Alessandro half to death when you invited him to your bed and started to caress him while he was still under the impression that you were a man, thinking you were stuck "in the grip of some impure passion" (88). Then right there, on the spot, you ask him to take your hand in marriage. Now, I'm not the biggest fan of brash decisions, seeing as how one almost killed me (but of course all is forgiven!), but I cringed when you asked him to marry you just moments after revealing the fact that you are actually a woman. Imagine what the bewildered Alessandro must have been thinking! I understand that you were under a certain time constraint, but I still do believe that you could have exercised a bit more modesty.
>
> In any case, I wish you all the best with Alessandro and the future that you two have before you. And if anyone ever asks you to hold a large trunk in your room, you say no to that person. I hope to hear from you soon!
>
> Sincerely,
>
> Zinevra

In this creative and nuanced response, Nate Sell does not limit himself to what a good many other readers can see, namely, the similarities between Zinevra and the abbot/princess (loyalty, respect for authority, intelligence, ambition) and the manifest divergence between them (the abbot/princess's forward sexual advances). Rather, his Madonna Zinevra struggles to suppress a terrible truth, only to have it peek through repeatedly: "My husband even tried to have me *killed* . . . But enough of me . . . I was forced to parade around as a man for a number of years, all because my husband *tried to have me killed,* but that's neither here nor there . . . Now, I'm not the biggest fan of brash decisions, seeing as how one almost killed me (but of course all is forgiven!)." Remarkable for their sophistication are Sell's timing and his ability to vary the ways in which Zinevra keeps returning to the site of emotional trauma only to keep tamping down anything that would sound like open criticism of her husband. At less than 500 words, this letter from Madonna Zinevra provides insights into *Decameron* II, 9 that go far beyond what first-year university students are able to express in an analytic essay—indeed, it goes far beyond what most of us can express in the language and argumentation of academic discourse. It dramatizes the issue of control that is, I believe, at the heart of all of the instances of wifely criticism in the *Decameron.* It reminds us that a story like II, 9 poses questions like: What are women allowed to say? What might they want to say? What can they get away with saying? It tells us that happy endings often require discarding unhappy and disturbing details. Above all, I believe, this letter reminds us what *literature* can do. Although this letter was written by a very young person—or perhaps precisely because of that—it shows us how creative and literary responses can expertly capture the delicate balance of enthusiasm and unease, of praise and blame, that hovers in the final reconciliation scene of a novella like II, 9.

And, I might as well just say it: That delicate balance of enthusiasm and unease is quite distinctively Boccaccian. In the *Decameron,* we hear praise that is not quite praise and blame that is not quite blame. That is why we have such difficulty agreeing, as we read Boccaccio's masterpiece, whether certain behaviors are the object of approbation or not. The *Decameron,* which steadfastly refuses to tell an uncompromised story about what to praise and what to blame, invites us to reflect on how we form our opinions. It describes for us situations that will elicit a range of responses (often contradictory ones), and then, as a great and innovative literary text, it invites us to examine how we might be encouraged by its own (often contradictory) rhetorical formulations to accept certain judgments and to discard others. From this we can derive a crucial lesson about our responsibility to think critically about the assumptions we make, the evidence we cite, the judgments we proffer.

Notes

1. The argumentation in this essay has benefited from careful critical readings offered by Kathleen Perry Long, Anna Paparcone, Daniel Tonozzi, and Hannah Chapelle Wojciehowski.

2. Interested in the "various ways in which Boccaccio teaches us to read the text," Millicent J. Marcus draws our attention to the internalized artist figures and internalized publics of the *Decameron.* See her *An Allegory of Form: Literary Self-Consciousness in the "Decameron"* (Saratoga, Cal.: Anma Libri, 1979), p. 9. She emphasizes the *Decameron*'s resistance to univocal interpretation - particularly evident from the final story of the collection where, as she notes, "Boccaccio subjects his readers to the severest of tests" (9).

3. Let me be more straightforward, at least in the parenthesis offered by this footnote. It is quite astonishing to see the increasing pressure, especially in the United States today, against anything that would look like assigning responsibility for bad behavior. Speaking out against bad behavior is considered "bad form," an indication of less than collegial activity. Little concern is shown, however, for the ways in which *not* speaking out is a form of complicity.

4. All citations from the *Decameron* are drawn from Giovanni Boccaccio, *Decameron,* ed. Vittore Branca, 2 vols. (Torino: Einaudi, 1992). All English translations are mine, unless otherwise noted.

5. Zinevra's rhetorical skill is evident not only in the succinctness and the moral pointedness of this denunciation, but also in the material vocalizing of her pain. Her self-identification is broadened by two adjectives preceding her name ("io sono la *misera sventurata* Zinevra") and by the series of wailing "ah" sounds that characterize both this revelation of her name and the adjectival modifying phrase that follows it ("sei *anni* and*ata* tapin*a*ndo in forma d'uom per lo mondo"). The open wail is rendered even more stunning by the alternately accented morpheme AN, which suggests that Zinevra is swept away by repeated waves that overpower her. We could visualize this as follows. The first accented "AN" is followed by a non-accented (and therefore muted) "an," making us think that the pain might have receded, only to return, after a warning "DA ta ta," in a third accented AN: *sei AN*ni an*DA*ta tapi*NAN*do.

6. Giovanni Boccaccio, *The Decameron,* trans. Guido Waldman (Oxford: Oxford University Press, 1993), p. 156.

7. Giovanni Boccaccio, *The Decameron,* trans. G. H. McWilliam, 2nd ed. (1995; rpt. New York: Penguin Books, 2003), p. 177.

8. Giovanni Boccaccio, *Decameron,* trans. Mark Musa and Peter Bondanella (New York: New American Library, 2002), p. 177.

9. See the footnote to this passage, in Boccaccio, *Decameron,* ed. Branca, vol. 1, p. 300.

10. One other edition adds a comma that could alter our reading: "E, fattili venire onorevolissimi vestimenti femminili e donne che compagnia le tenessero, secondo la dimanda fatta da lei, a Bernabò perdonò la meritata morte" (See the text of II, 9 in Giovanni Boccaccio, *Decameron,* in *Antologia (frammentaria) della Letteratura Italiana,* available on the World Wide Web at <http://www.crs4.it/Letteratura/Decamerone/Seconda/2_09.htm>, date of access 23 August 2006). The comma makes it less certain that Madonna Zinevra's request regards Bernabò's fate. Her request may refer just as easily to the clothes and the attendant women, which the Sultan has just provided.

11. *Il Decamerone di Giovanni Boccaccio novamente corretto con tre novelle aggiunte* (Venice: Case d'Aldo Romano e Andrea Asolano, 1522), p. 71. The passage can also be found in *Il Decamerone di M. Giovanni Boccaccio Di nuovo emendato secondo gli Antichi essemplari, per giudicio Et diligenza di piu autori con la Diversità di molti testi posta per ordine in margine, & nel fine con gli Epiteti dell'Autore, con la espositione de' proverbi Et luoghi difficili, che nell'opera si contengono, con tavole e altre cose notabili & molto Utili alli studiosi della lingua volgare* (Venice: Gabriel Giolito de Ferrari, 1550), p. 116. In the Deputati edition, the relevant portion of the passage reads "domandando perdonanza, la quale ella (quantunque egli mal degno ne fosse) benignamente gli diede" (*Il Decameron di Messer Giovanni Boccaccio Cittadino Fiorentino, Ricorretto in Roma, et Emendato secondo l'ordine del Sacro Conc. Di Trento, Et riscontrato in Firenze don Testi Antichi & alla sua vera lezione ridotto da' Deputati di loro Alt. Ser.* [Florence: Giunti, 1573], p. 129).

12. See Boccaccio, *Decameron,* ed. Branca, vol. 1, p. 387.

13. Marilyn Migiel, *A Rhetoric of the "Decameron"* (Toronto: University of Toronto Press, 2003), especially the Introduction and Conclusion, and also Marilyn Migiel, "The Untidy Business of Gender Studies: Or, Why It's Almost Useless to Ask if the *Decameron* is Feminist," in *Boccaccio and Feminist Criticism,* eds. Thomas C. Stillinger and F. Regina Psaki (Chapel Hill, N.C.: Annali d'Italianistica, 2006), pp. 217-33.

14. On the identified sources and analogues for III, 6, see A. C. Lee, *The "Decameron": Its Sources and Analogues* (1909 rpt; New York: Haskell House Publishers, Ltd., 1972), pp. 79-91.

15. Yet, listening to the text, I wonder if it is not alerting us to the incomplete resolution that this silence offers. In the Italian, I register an insistent turn toward nouns that end in *-menti* (*congiugnimenti, abbracciamenti*) and adverbs that end in *-mente*: (*affettuosissimamente, solamente, segretamente, diligentemente*). This persistent refrain announces "you lie!" (*menti*), "she lies!" (*mente*).

16. Playing the part of the virtuous wife, Madonna Sismonda does not criticize her husband who claims to have beaten her and cut her hair. Since the acerbic criticism comes instead from her mother, Madonna Sismonda remains above reproach. For this observation, I am indebted to Kathleen Perry Long (conversation on August 31, 2005).

17. Boccaccio, *Decameron,* trans. Musa and Bondanella, pp. 430-31.

18. Boccaccio, *Decameron,* trans. McWilliam, p. 431.

19. This is reading advanced by John Najemy and seconded by Kathleen Perry Long at a department colloquium where I presented my current work on the *Decameron* (October 19, 2006).

20. Although Franco Fido does not explicitly make this claim, his reading of X, 9 leads us to recognize this story as a privileged endpoint of the frametale narrators' interests. See his "Il sorriso di messer Torello," in *Il regime delle simmetrie imperfette: Studi sul "Decameron"* (Milano: Franco Angeli, 1988), pp. 11-35.

21. Adalieta, as Irene Eibenstein-Alvisi has argued, is a "perfect wife" who functions as viable model for the genteel women narrators of the *Decameron.* See her essay "The *Decameron*'s Perfect Wives," chapter 5 of Irene Eibenstein-Alvisi, "The Dialogic Construction of Woman in the Italian Renaissance," unpublished Ph.D. diss. (Cornell University, 2003).

22. Panfilo may be preparing for this solution, I believe, as he tells IX, 6, a story in which he revises the fabliau sources so that the husband is not a thief and so that the wife never has occasion to confront the husband for blameworthy behavior. For a summary of the possible sources and analogues for IX, 6, see A. C. Lee, *The "Decameron": Its Sources and Analogues,* pp. 281-87.

23. This passage would merit further analysis, particularly for the way it forces us to reevaluate our view of a husband, Bernabò, whom we might have been content to define as foolish rather than bestial. When Gualtieri states that others have marked him as "crudele e iniquo e bestiale" ("cruel, un-

just, and brutish"), we must remember that these are the very words applied earlier to Bernabò. Zinevra had referred to her husband as "crudele e iniquo" ("cruel and unjust" [II, 9, 69]). Dioneo had highlighted Bernabò's "bestialità" ["asinine stupidity" [II, 10, 3]). The women of the group had all agreed with Dioneo that Bernabò had been a "bestia" ("fool" or "ass" [II, Conclusione, 1]). Thanks to an overlay from Dante's "mad bestiality" ("matta bestialitade"), which Dioneo recalls at the very beginning of the novella of Griselda, Bernabò's foolishness begins to look more like Gualteri's bestiality and brutishness. (For this particular observation about how moral and emotional charge of *bestialità* can change over the course of the *Decameron,* I am indebted to Michael Papio, who drew our attention to this during the discussion following my presentation of an earlier version of this essay at the University of Wisconsin-Madison.)

24. In both my book *A Rhetoric of the "Decameron"* and in my essay "The Untidy Business of Gender Studies: Or, Why It's Almost Useless to Ask if the *Decameron* is Feminist," I have argued that the debate about whether the *Decameron* is misogynist or philogynist has produced an impasse in our thinking.

25. Unfortunately, I no longer know who authored this. My notes show that I had found this passage at a website entitled "Patient Griselda" (date of access 21 January 2006), but the website is no longer available and the professor I believed to be the author has told me that she is not.

26. Shirley S. Allen is representative of the readers who believe that Boccaccio must want us to read X, 10 ironically. See her "The Griselda Tale and the Portrayal of Women in the *Decameron,*" *Philological Quarterly* 56 (1977): 1-13.

27. For Assignment 1d (part of an assignment sequence focused on II, 9), I had instructed students to assume Zinevra's voice and to write a letter to either the abbot/princess (II, 3) or Bartolomea of Pisa (II, 10).

28. I have reproduced the assignment exactly as it was submitted to me, including with the one textual citation from p. 88 of McWilliam's translation of the *Decameron.*

Simone Marchesi (essay date 2010)

SOURCE: Marchesi, Simone. "Boccaccio's Vernacular Classicism: Intertextuality and Interdiscoursivity in the *Decameron.*" *Heliotropia,* 7, nos. 1-2 (2010): 31-50.

[*In the following essay, Marchesi uses the* Decameron *to illustrate the validity and necessity of the intertextual gloss as a technique of literary interpretation. Referencing the Latin rhetorical tradition and the medieval French poem* Roman de la Rose, *Marchesi provides an intertextual gloss on two sections of the* Decameron: *Boccaccio's definition of the* novelle *in the "Proem" and the description of the bucolic storytelling garden that opens Day 3.*]

In the following pages, I would like to explore two related questions that should be considered every time we are tempted to gloss a literary work such as the *Decameron* intertextually. The first question is one of method: when is a gloss necessary? What are the conditions in a work that require—rather than suggest, invite, or simply permit—that we bring a different text to its interpretation? The second question relates to the merit of the gloss: when is the intertext pertinent? How can we establish that a precise intertext is relevant to the understanding of the work we are studying? According to what parameters can we, in particular, advance the claim that an individual text rather than a permeating discourse, a book rather than common parlance, are to be taken into account? To put it another way, and in more essentially practical terms, when do we start looking for meaning outside the text? And most importantly, when do we stop looking for it?

Let me anticipate my theoretical conclusions, so that we may concentrate on the textual examples. An intertextual gloss is necessary when there is something odd about the text we study, when its terminology, syntax, theme or motifs are so peculiar that any reading, no matter how attentive, still leaves an inexplicable residue.[1] That is, an intertext is called for when a text diverges from a discourse: when it does not merely rehearse common wisdom, when it is not fully endorsing the party line of its culture. Correspondingly, an intertextual gloss is pertinent when the target text has literal connections with the one we are glossing; there is a cluster of elements (themes, syntax, and lexicon) that resonates in the text; and the evocation of the target text is able to reduce all elements of disturbance. In other words, an intertext is pertinent when it fully brings the text back into the discourse: when it makes its peculiar statements dialogue rather than clash with common wisdom, when it makes it a distinct yet harmonious interlocutor in a cultural debate.[2]

The hermeneutic process thus sketched out is, of course, circular. It moves from text to context and back. In order to suggest that it may be also virtuously circular, I will explore two cases of intertextual interference, moving back and forth between the spheres of classical and romance antecedents with which the *Decameron* most closely dialogues. I will proceed mainly through examples, a series of flashcards, in order to stay as close to the *Decameron* as possible. Doing so will also allow me to provide examples of what kind of meaning intertexts may produce. By studying the parameters determining the intertextual dynamics of the *Decameron* we should be able to learn something about what the evoked intertexts tell us.

1. When is an intertextual gloss necessary?

A good example of what I deem a necessary intertextual gloss is the self-definition that the *Decameron* gives in its proem:

> Adunque, acciò che in parte per me s'amendi il peccato della fortuna, la quale dove meno era di forza, sì come noi nelle dilicate donne veggiamo, quivi più avara fu di sostegno, in soccorso e rifugio di quelle che amano, per ciò che all'altre è assai l'ago e 'l fuso e l'arcolaio, intendo di raccontare *cento novelle, o favole o parabole o istorie che dire le vogliamo,* raccontate in diece giorni da una onesta brigata di sette donne e di tre giovani nel pistelenzioso tempo della passata mortalità fatta, e alcune canzonette dalle predette donne cantate al lor diletto.

(*Decameron* "Proemio" 13)[3]

Boccaccio's definition consists of two parts. The generic term that should be defined ("novelle") and its threefold, hierarchically subsumed, specification: "favole, parabole, istorie." The triad's rhetorical pedigree has long since been recognized, and there is a wide range of texts that may be (and have been) offered as gloss. All fundamental Latin manuals of rhetorical instruction from antiquity agree in their content and terminology on this point: Cicero, the *Rhetorica ad Herennium,* Quintilian, and Isidore converge in their assessment that there may be, in theory, three kinds of narrative: fables (which tell of events that have never taken place and couldn't have), histories (dealing with events which could take place, and indeed they did), and "arguments" (today we might call them "plots"): a third intermediate category of narratives recounting events that did not take place, but could have. The terminological compactness of the tradition is astounding. One would expect a higher degree of inconsistency from a series of texts spanning five centuries and belonging to a tradition which was notoriously belligerent when it came to issues of nomenclature:

> Ea, quae in negotiorum expositione posita est, tres habet partes: fabulam, historiam, argumentum. Fabula est, in qua nec verae nec veri similes res continentur, cuiusmodi est: "Angues ingentes alites, iuncti iugo . . .". Historia est gesta res, ab aetatis nostrae memoria remota; quod genus: "Appius indixit Carthaginiensibus bellum". Argumentum est ficta res, quae tamen fieri potuit. Huiusmodi apud Terentium: "Nam is postquam excessit ex ephebis, [Sosia] . . .

(Cicero, *De inventione* I.19.27)

> Id, quod in negotiorum expositione positum est, tres habet partes: fabulam, historiam, argumentum. Fabula est, quae neque ueras neque ueri similes continet res, ut eae sunt, quae tragoediis traditae sunt. Historia est gesta

res, sed ab aetatis nostrae memoria remota. Argumentum est ficta res, quae tamen fieri potuit, uelut argumenta comoediarum.

(*Rhetorica ad Herennium* I.8.13)

> Et quia narrationum, excepta qua in causis utimur, tris accepimus species, fabulam, quae uersatur in tragoediis atque carminibus non a ueritate modo sed etiam a forma ueritatis remota, argumentum, quod falsum, sed uero simile comoediae fingunt, historiam, in qua est gestae rei expositio.

(Quintilian, *Inst. or.* II.4.2)

> Item inter historiam et argumentum et fabulam interesse. Nam historiae sunt res verae quae factae sunt; argumenta sunt quae etsi facta non sunt, fieri tamen possunt; fabulae vero sunt quae nec factae sunt nec fieri possunt, quia contra naturam sunt.

(Isidore of Seville, *Etymologiae* I.44.5).[4]

When offered as a background for Boccaccio's introductory remarks, this host of authoritative sources seems to provide readers of the *Decameron* with an ideal situation. They are presented with a meta-poetic statement that reflects their readerly expectations. In proposing a new genre, the *novella,* the work certainly challenges its immediate audience in their understanding of the literary canon. In doing so, however, the *Decameron* also appeals to its audience's most traditional habits of categorization. For modern readers, Boccaccio's definition of his new genre seems to constitute a typical case of learned interdiscoursivity: it reduces what is "new" in the text to what is "known" in its context. A compact body of writing, the capillary cultural diffusion of which is unquestionable, concurs in content and language with what we read in the text.[5]

Boccaccio's strategy is apparently so clear-cut that, in theory, a gloss might not even be needed. Were it not for the purpose of establishing a classical pedigree for the **"Proem"**'s words (as opposed to a Romance or neo-Latin one), the gloss is redundant. In practice, things are a little less neat than they appear. The problem is, of course, the second term of the triad, which sources coherently render with the Latin *argumentum,* but that Boccaccio, surprisingly, chooses to render with *parabola.* In the tradition just explored, there is really nothing (or very little) that could justify his choice. The terminological difficulty is the second essential stumbling block in the text. As a corrugation that attracts attention to itself, it also works as an invitation, almost a provocation, for readers to account for its presence. The inconsistency in the passage, in other words, invites a supplement of interpretation.

There are more ways in which such a stumbling block may be removed; none, however, may prove more satisfactory than further intertextual research, especially when the text itself has already opened an intertextual possibility. If the Latin rhetorical tradition unanimously agrees on listing *fabulae, historiae,* and *argumenta* as the only three kinds of possible narratives, one may wonder if the voice of this tradition was the *only* voice that was available to writer and readers of the **Decameron.** As a matter of fact, it was not. The text that is at the origin of the Latin rhetorical tradition, Aristotle's Greek treatise on the art of rhetoric, has something to offer as an intertext. Proposing to look into the Aristotelian corpus in order to gloss a text by Boccaccio requires a small stretch of the limits of philological probability: Aristotle's Greek was most likely out of Boccaccio's reach. However, what was fully within his reach was one of its translations, and a relatively new one at that: Aristotle's *Rhetorica* enjoyed a renewed interest at the end of the thirteenth century and was circulating in a new translation through the Latin West. A crucial passage from that text, in the *nova translation,* drafted in 1270 by William of Moerbecke at the bequest of Thomas Aquinas, offers the most precise equivalent of the terminological triad we have found in Boccaccio's passage. Aristotle's definition of rhetorical example reads:

> Primo quidem igitur *de exemplo* dicamus. Simile enim inductioni exemplum; inductio autem principium. Exemplorum autem due specie sunt. Una quidem enim species exempli est cum dicet *res prius gestas*; una autem cum quod ipse facit. Huius autem unum quidem *parabula,* unum autem *fabule*—velud Esopice et Lybice.

> (Aristotle, *Rhetorica* II.xx.1-6)[6]

The closer literal cogency of this new intertext changes the quality of the gloss we may decide to append to Boccaccio's passage. Far from being interdiscursive, the required gloss is definitely intertextual. And it bears some hermeneutic implications, the first of which should probably be that the *novella* is not Boccaccio's vernacular equivalent of the Latin generic *narratio,* but rather his allusive equivalent that of the more specific Latin *exemplum* or, if you will, of the strictly Aristotelian, Greek *enthymeme.* Glossing Boccaccio with Aristotle, in sum, may change our understanding of *novella* as a literary genre.[7]

Beyond the eventual adjustments that this self-definition may impose on our perception of the generic nature of the *Centonovelle,* we must pay attention to a further facet of Boccaccio's authoritative (because authorial) definition of the work.[8] The definitional precision exercised in the coherent application of Aristotelian terminology is immediately balanced and perhaps neutralized in a lighthearted aside: *cento novelle, o favole o parabole o istorie, che dire le vogliamo.* While it may be phrased as to betray some impatience with the strictures of the potentially argumentative grammarians who may object to the **Decameron**'s distinctive mixture of actual, potential, and implausible stories, the sentence

that follows the definition potentially makes the carefully posited distinction completely obsolete. After we have been told with such allusive care that what we are about to read falls within the limits of a very specific rhetorical and literary category, we learn that we may call the novellas that make up the body of the work in whatever way we please. The gesture is, of course, ironic—if it means, as it should, that the new generic identity of the *novella* sums up and supersedes the three-fold typology in which narratives and *exempla* are traditionally articulated.[9] The new model pushes the old ones out of the inventory. And yet, one may ask, is irony all that there is to it? In positing a distinction only to immediately undo it, the author makes a gesture that, again, may invite interpretation.

Interpretive obstinacy is, of course, not a virtue, and my insistence on searching for additional meaning in the sentence might border on "aggressive hermeneutical treatment." Yet there is an additional notable element to Boccaccio's phrasing, which draws attention to its presence and calls for interpretation. The sentence is not only peculiar for its semantic import; it is also actually unprecedented in its syntax. The expression "che dir le vogliamo" is by now part and parcel of the zero-degree of Italian language. We use the phrase "che dir si voglia" so often in Italian that even a restricted Google search for the four-word idiom yields about 259,000 hits.[10] However, in spite of its current overwhelming popularity, I have not been able to find any use of this expression to mean what Boccaccio meant with it before Boccaccio himself. Reading for exclusionary purposes is, of course, no exact science, and it may certainly be the case that I (or the OVI search engine) have missed some instance of this concessive relative clause in texts dating before Boccaccio's death.[11] Even if its absence from any earlier text may never be proved conclusively, its statistical density in the late Boccaccio (**Decameron** and *Esposizioni*) is certainly telling. Boccaccio is fond of the expression, enough at least to re-use it three more times, always with definitional import. See, for instance, the following cases:

> Oltre a questo, niuno scudiere, o famigliare *che dir vogliamo,* diceva trovarsi il quale meglio né più accortamente servisse a una tavola d'un signore, che serviva ella, sì come colei che era costumatissima, savia e discreta molto.

> (**Decameron** II.9.9)

> L'aere, ancora per non esser dal fuoco risoluto, gli fugge inanzi e, quando tiene la via che fa l'umido, volendo tutto insieme essalare, e trovando i pori stretti, uscendo per la strettezza di quegli, fa col suo impeto quello stridore, o cigolare *che dir vogliamo*; e, convertito dall'impeto in vento, va via.

> (*Esposizioni* XIII (i) 40-42)

> Dice adunque l'autore nello essemplo il quale induce, o comparazione *che dir la vogliamo*. . . .

> (*Esposizioni* XVI (i) 94.99)[12]

Boccaccio might not have been the one who invented it (if anyone may be said to invent anything in language), but it is perhaps safe to say that he is most likely the first to make it graduate to a literary use in the charged locus of the **"Proem."** The end result of Boccaccio's syntax is a double order of frames: the initial quasi-neologism "novella" is reinforced by the syntactic neologism "che dire le vogliamo" at its end; wedged between the two novelties we find what is most traditional, the series ranging from "favole" to "istorie"; wedged between the two well-known, perfectly traditional terms, we surprisingly find the novel "parabole." The structure of the sentence and its heightened rhetorical tone suggest that we might not have yet exhausted its potential for meaning. Boccaccio's alternation of confirmations and surprises may indicate that the **Decameron** resonates again with the voice of another intertext. It might be coincidental, but a text that comes close to Boccaccio's definitional musing does indeed exist, and it is located in a context no less self-conscious than the **"Proem"** to the **Decameron.** In the present context, I will refrain from discussing the specific coordinates and the philological probability of the classical fragment that I propose should be used to gloss once more Boccaccio's phrasing.[13] Instead, I would like to concentrate on its syntax and, however subtle and impalpable it may be, on its tone. Here is a snippet of text from the *Epistles* of Pliny the Younger, which may illuminate Boccaccio's wording:

> Proinde, sive epigrammata sive idyllia sive eclogas sive, ut multi, poematia seu quod aliud vocare malueris, licebit voces; ego tantum hendecasyllabos praesto.
>
> (Pliny, *Ep.* 4.14.9)[14]

Any evaluation of the fragment cannot do away with the differences it exhibits when paired with Boccaccio's: the object of the present classificatory meditation is poetry rather than prose; the Latin author fully embraces responsibility for the classification of his work, the vernacular apparently avoids it; finally, the movement from the term which is being defined to the dismissed alternatives is the opposite from the one we find in Boccaccio—in Boccaccio, "X equals either A or B or C, whatever one may call it": the Latin theorist postulates "either A or B or C, or D, or whatever, amounts to X." All these differences notwithstanding, however, there might be something to say in favor of the pertinence of a classical discussion of a book's title for a book that, like the **Decameron,** programmatically if defensively claims it is "senza titolo," and with that alludes to the most classical *sine titulo* status of Ovid's *Amores.*

Again, a measure of skepticism might be healthy. Even if we accept the pertinence of this accessory gloss, it remains to be seen whether it may also be in any way useful. I believe that it is. The first aspect that the new intertext illuminates is the idiosyncratic quality of Boccaccio's expression "che dire le vogliamo": one may invoke the Latin passage as an antecedent, in accounting for the syntactic neologism that concludes Boccaccio's typology. As a still tentative and perhaps merely erudite note, a classicizing gloss may be appended to indicate that what appears to be Boccaccio's new coinage has indeed clear Latin antecedents: *quod aliud vocare malueris* explains *che dire le vogliamo.* When I say that the Latin antecedent "explains" the vernacular turn of phrase, I do not mean that it determines its semantic value, but only that it helps to recover some sense of its surprising appearance. In theory, there is no compelling reason to intervene in the intertextual apparatus of the passage beyond its contextual relevance. It might be intriguing to speculate about the possible connection between Boccaccio and the Latin author who penned that definition of his poetry, but nothing imposes a strict intertextual reading. Unlike Aristotle's discussion of enthymeme, the intertextual gloss we may agree should be appended to the passage is merely accessory: it is not susceptible, as far as I can see, to further interpretation.

There are, however, further aspects of Boccaccio's syntax that the Latin passage may help illuminating: first, the value of the threefold "o" which articulates the typology of exemplary narratives in the **Decameron.** The Latin background, against which we may decide to project Boccaccio's classification, clarifies that the ambiguous Italian disjunctive conjunction is inclusive rather than exclusive: Boccaccio presents the alternatives of *favole, parabole* and *istorie* in a system of *sive-sive,* not as *aut-aut's.* But there is more. The initial inclusiveness is designed to produce a deeper exclusion—perhaps in both texts. The Latin author's strong claim of independence may in some way resonate with Boccaccio's terminological supersessionism. Pliny's insistence on classifying his poetry as technically "hendecasyllables" against all other alternatives may anticipate Boccaccio's use of *novelle* not only as a generic term that embraces fables, parables and histories in a wider scope, but also as the term to be used in their stead. The authorial irony, so typical of the **Decameron,** hides beneath a very thin veil the seriousness of his metapoetic statement. To be sure, it is a small interpretive step, one we may have taken anyway; but having a precise classical antecedent in mind may help us take it. The search for one extra-antecedent may have proved not to be otiose after all.

2. When is an intertextual gloss pertinent?

If the hermeneutic necessity of an intertextual gloss is the result of a tear in the semiotic fabric of the text, a void that readers are asked to fill, a consensus on what to use in order to fill this gap is often difficult to reach. The question is now one of choice: when can we say that an intertext is so precisely fitting, so convincing, that none other is needed? What are the conditions that allow us to argue, with some degree of confidence, that we have spotted the book that Boccaccio's text invited his readers to keep open alongside his **Decameron**? More importantly, is it an individual text or a diffuse discourse?

In order to explore this next set of questions, we move from the dense meta-poetic locus, which was treated in the first section, to a more pleasantly descriptive locus—technically, we move into one of the *loci amoeni* in the **Decameron**. The context of the following extended quotation is famous. We are at the beginning of Day III, and the *brigata* has just moved from its first meeting-place into a second palace on the hills surrounding Florence.[15] A summary description of the new villa has just concluded with the highest praises being lavished on the "signore" of the palace ("sommamente il commendarono e magnifico reputarono il signor di quello," notes the narrator at III.*intro*.4), and the *brigata* is ready to move into the garden. It is here, in the most perfect setting one may imagine, that the three following rounds of story-telling will be staged. As the segments I have strategically bolded show, the passage—with all its literary beauty—is a patchwork of recycled literature. The *Roman de la Rose* takes, as we know, the lion's share in providing material for the topical description:

> Appresso la qual cosa, FATTOSI APRIRE UN GIARDINO che di costa era al palagio, in quello, CHE TUTTO ERA DA TORNO MURATO, se n'entrarono [*RdR 129-35*]; e parendo loro nella prima entrata di maravigliosa bellezza tutto insieme, più attentamente le parti di quello cominciarono a riguardare. Esso avea dintorno da sé e PER LO MEZZO IN ASSAI PARTI VIE AMPISSIME, TUTTE DIRITTE COME STRALE [*RdR* 1320-22] e coperte di pergolati di viti, le quali facevano gran vista di dovere quello anno assai uve fare, e tutte allora fiorite sì grande odore per lo giardin rendevano, che, MESCOLATO INSIEME CON QUELLO DI MOLTE ALTRE COSE CHE PER LO GIARDINO OLIVANO, PAREVA LORO ESSERE TRA TUTTA LA SPEZIERIA CHE MAI NACQUE IN ORIENTE. [*RdR* 1337-44] Le latora delle quali vie tutte di rosa' bianchi e vermigli e di gelsomini erano quasi chiuse: PER LE QUALI COSE, NON CHE LA MATTINA, MA QUALORA IL SOLE ERA PIÙ ALTO, SOTTO ODORIFERA E DILETTEVOLE OMBRA, SENZA ESSER TOCCO DA QUELLO, VI SI POTEVA PER TUTTO ANDARE. [*RdR* 1362-71] QUANTE E QUALI E COME ORDINATE POSTE FOSSERO LE PIANTE CHE ERANO IN QUEL LUOGO, LUNGO SAREBBE A RACCONTARE [*RdR* 1358-61]; ma NIUNA N'È LAUDEVOLE LA QUALE IL NOSTRO AERE PATISCA, DI CHE QUIVI NON SIA ABONDEVOLEMENTE. [*RdR* 1323-26] Nel mezzo del quale, quello che è non meno commendabile che altra cosa che vi fosse ma molto più, era un prato di minutissima erba e verde tanto, che quasi nera parea, dipinto tutto forse di mille varietà di fiori, chiuso dintorno di verdissimi e vivi aranci e di cedri, li quali, avendo i vecchi frutti e' nuovi e i fiori ancora, non solamente piacevole ombra agli occhi ma ancora all'odorato facevan piacere. Nel mezzo del qual prato era UNA FONTE DI MARMO BIANCHISSIMO E CON MARAVIGLIOSI INTAGLI: iv'entro, non so

se da NATURAL VENA O DA ARTIFICIOSA, [*RdR* 1429-35?] per una figura, la quale sopra una colonna che nel mezzo di quella diritta era, gittava tanta acqua e sì alta verso il cielo, che poi NON SENZA DILETTEVOL SUONO nella fonte chiarissima ricadea, che di meno avria macinato un mulino. LA QUAL POI, QUELLA DICO CHE SOPRABONDAVA AL PIENO DELLA FONTE, PER OCCULTA VIA DEL PRATELLO USCIVA E, PER CANALETTI ASSAI BELLI E ARTIFICIOSAMENTE FATTI FUOR DI QUELLO DIVENUTA PALESE, TUTTO LO 'NTORNIAVA; E QUINDI PER CANALETTI SIMILI QUASI PER OGNI PARTE DEL GIARDIN DISCORREA, [*RdR* 1432-42] raccogliendosi ultimamente in una parte dalla quale del bel giardino avea l'uscita, e quindi verso il pian discendendo chiarissima, avanti che a quel divenisse, con grandissima forza e con non piccola utilità del signore due mulina volgea. Il veder questo giardino, il suo bello ordine, le piante e la fontana co' ruscelletti procedenti da quella TANTO PIACQUE A CIASCUNA DONNA E A' TRE GIOVANI, CHE TUTTI COMINCIARONO A AFFERMARE CHE, SE PARADISO SI POTESSE IN TERRA FARE, NON SAPEVANO CONOSCERE CHE ALTRA FORMA CHE QUELLA DI QUEL GIARDINO GLI SI POTESSE DARE, né pensare, oltre a questo, qual bellezza gli si potesse agiugnere. [*RdR* 635-44] Andando adunque contentissimi dintorno per quello, faccendosi di varii rami d'albori ghirlande bellissime, tuttavia udendo FORSE VENTI MANIERE di canti d'uccelli quasi a pruova l'un dell'altro cantare, s'accorsero d'una dilettevol bellezza, della quale, dall'altre soprappresi, non s'erano ancora accorti: ché essi videro IL GIARDIN PIENO FORSE DI CENTO VARIETÀ DI BELLI ANIMALI, E L'UNO ALL'ALTRO MOSTRANDOLO, D'UNA PARTE USCIR CONIGLI, D'ALTRA PARTE CORRER LEPRI, E DOVE GIACER CAVRIUOLI E IN ALCUNA CERBIATTI GIOVANI ANDAR PASCENDO E, OLTRE A QUESTI, ALTRE PIÚ MANIERE DI NON NOCIVI ANIMALI, CIASCUNO A SUO DILETTO, QUASI DIMESTICHI, ANDARSI A SOLLAZZO: le quali cose, oltre agli altri piaceri, un vie maggior piacere aggiunsero.

> [*RdR* 1372-79]

We are in a clear situation of intertextuality. In the table that follows, I have included some passages from the *Roman de la Rose* that appear most pertinent to appreciate Boccaccio's combinatory art.[16] This time, I have bolded what may be considered the connective segments in the primary intertext: the lexical and syntactic "hooks" that hold the two extended passages together.

> 1) Quant j'oi ung pou avant alé,
> Si vi un vergier grant et lé,
> TOUT CLOS DE HAUT MUR BATAILLIÉ,
> Portrait et dehors entaillié
> A maintes riches escritures,
> Les ymages et les pointures
> Du mur volentiers remiré
>
> *RdR* 129-35
>
> 2) Et sachiés que JE CUIDAI ESTRE
> POUR VOIR EN PARADIS TERRESTRE,
> Tant estoit li leus delitables,
> Qui sembloit estre esperitables:
> Car si com il m'estoit avis,
> NE FÉIST EN NUL PAREVIS
> SI BON ESTRE, COM IL FEISOIT
> OU VERGIER qui tant me plaisoit.
>
> *RdR* 635-44

3) Li vergiers par compasseüre
Fu faiz par droite quarreüre,
S'ot autant de lonc con de large;

                    RdR 1320-22

4) Nus arbres n'i a qui fruit ne charge,
Se n'est aucuns aubres hideus,
Dom il n'i ait ou ung ou deus
Où vergier, ou plus, se devient.

                    RdR 1323-26

5) Si trovast qu'en eüst mestier,
Où vergier, mainte bone espice,
Clos de girofle et requalice,
Graine de paradis novele,
Citouaut, anis, et canele
Et mainte espice delitable,
Que bon mangier fait apres table.

                    RdR 1337-44

6) Que iroie-je ci notant?
De divers arbres i ot tant,
Que moult en seroie encombrez,
Ainz que jes eüse nombrez;

                    RdR 1358-61

7) Me lis arbres, ce sachiez, furent
Si loing a loing con estre durent.
Li uns fu loins de l'autre asis
Plus de cinq toises, ou de sis:
Mès li rain furent gent et haut,
Et por le lieu garder dou chaut,
Furent si espes par deseure,
Que li solauz en nes une eure
Ne pooit a terre descendre,
Ne faire mal a l'erbe tendre.

                    RdR 1362-71

8) Où vergier ot dains et chevriaus,
Si ot grant plente d'escuriaus,
Qui par ces arbres gravissoient;
Conins i avoit qui issoient
Toute jor fors par lor tanieres,
Et en plus de trente [.XXX.] menieres
Aloient entr'aus donoiant
Seur l'erbe fresche verdoiant.

                    RdR 1372-79

9) Il ot par leus cleres fontaines,
Sans barbelotez et sans raines,
Cui l'aubre fesoient ombre;
Je n'en sai pas dire le nombre.
Par petiz roissiaus et conduiz
Q'ot fet faire danz Deduiz,
S'en aloit l'eve aval, fesant
Une douce noise et plesant.
Antor les ruissiaus et les rives
Des fontaines cleres et vives,
Poingnoit l'erbe menue et dru.

                    RdR 1380-90

10) Dedeanz une pierre de marbre
Ot Nature par grant mestrisse
Souz le pin la fontaine assise:
Si ot dedanz la pierre escrites
Ou bort amont lettre petite
Qui devisoient qu'anqui desus
Se mori li biaus Narcisus.

                    RdR 1429-35

In two texts that certainly pay remarkable attention to the irrigation systems they depict, the "hydraulic" metaphor with which we are now used to describing the "influx" a text exerts on its "tributaries" is not completely out of place. The Garden of Deduit is for all intents and purposes the "source" of Boccaccio's new Garden: the presence of singing birds, an almost impregnable canopy of leaves and trees, fresh running water, odorous spice-plants, and caroling animals—in sum, the explicit Eden-like quality of Boccaccio's garden finds its main antecedent in Guillaume's garden of Deduit. And yet, is the *Rose* so compellingly unique?

As a matter of fact, there are other texts that could make a legitimate claim to the role of generic antecedents for the passage. The second table contains a small sampling of texts, one of which is again from Pliny the Younger, the Latin author whose definition of poetry we have used to gloss the authorial definition of the **Decameron**. All these examples may be used to contrast our first response to the text. They may help us second-guess the assurance with which we consider the *Rose* as the sole and exhaustive antecedent for Boccaccio. They show that we may be facing a collection of fragments of a common discourse, bridging vernacular and Latin descriptions of villas:

Several details converge in these parallel places: the context of Boccaccio's own *Filocolo* represents the closest thematic antecedent, linking the bucolic setting of **Decameron** III with the *questioni d'amore* and the structured proceedings of an embryonic *brigata* of storytellers. Folgòre's sonnet is a stringent antecedent in its detailing of privileged essences and fragrances for the garden, the activities of the *brigata,* and the *giochi d'acqua.* The Latin fragments insist on the secluded quality of the garden, its shadowed paths, the hydraulic complexity of its irrigation system, its overall artistry. Though for different reasons, and admittedly with different degrees of pertinence, all these intertexts contribute something, probably worth a footnote.

These similarities having been noted, however, Latin and vernacular contextual sources do not exclude the *Rose*. Rather (and at the most), they suggest that in reading the **Decameron** we are presented with a complex interplay between a wider array of common places (*topoi*) and a specific text. Guillaume's *Rose* is certainly part of a topical discourse into which Boccaccio's taps: together with these and other parallel sources they form one of the most classical common places, that of the *locus amoenus,* in its specific garden-variety. However, the density of lexical connections, the clusters of thematic and verbal resonances, the presence of differential thematic elements such as the choice of spices, the perhaps merely accidentally divergent numberings in the catalogue of peaceful animals (thirty in the *Rose,* twenty in the **Decameron**), and the rhetorical

BOCCACCIO, *Filocolo* IV.18.

Andò adunque Filocolo, lodando il consiglio della donna, dietro a' passi di lei, e con lui i suoi compagni, e Caleon e due altri giovani con loro: *e vennero nel mostrato prato, bellissimo molto d'erbe e di fiori, e pieno di dolce soavità d'odori, dintorno al quale belli e giovani albuscelli erano assai, le cui frondi verdi e folte, dalle quali il luogo era difeso da' raggi del gran pianeto. E nel mezzo d'esso pratello una picciola fontana chiara e bella era, dintorno alla quale tutti si posero a sedere*; e quivi di diverse cose, chi mirando l' acqua chi cogliendo fiori, incominciarono a parlare. Ma però che tal volta disavvedutamente l' uno le novelle dell' altro trarompeva, la bella donna disse così:—Acciò che i nostri ragionamenti possano con più ordine procedere e infino alle più fresche ore continuarsi, le quali noi per festeggiare aspettiamo, ordiniamo uno di noi qui in luogo di nostro re, al quale ciascuno una quistione d'amore proponga, e da esso a quella debita risposta prenda. E certo, secondo il mio avviso, noi non avremo le nostre quistioni poste, che il caldo sarà, sanza che noi il sentiamo, passato, e il tempo utilmente con diletto sarà adoperato—Piacque a tutti, e fra loro dissero: - Facciasi re -.[17]

1) *omnia maceria muniuntur*: hanc gradata buxus operit et subtrahit.

3) *Ambit hunc ambulatio* pressis varieque tonsis viridibus inclusa; ab his *gestatio* in modum circi, quae buxum multiformem humilesque et retentas manu *arbusculas* circumit.

7) Medius patescit [hippodromus] statimque intrantium oculis totus offertur, *platanis circumitur; illae hedera vestiuntur utque summae suis ita imae alienis frondibus virent. Hedera truncum et ramos pererrat vicinasque platanos transitu suo copulat.* Has buxus interiacet; exteriores buxos circumvenit laurus, *umbraeque platanorum suam confert.*

Rectus hic hippodromi limes in extrema parte hemicyclio frangitur mutatque faciem: *cupressis ambitur et tegitur, densiore umbra opacior nigriorque*; interioribus circulis—*sunt enim plures*—purissimum diem recipit.

9-10) pratum inde non minus *natura* quam superiora illa *arte* visendum; campi deinde porro multaque alia *prata* et arbusta. . . .

FOLGÒRE, *Sonetti de' mesi* 7.

Di giugno dovvi *una montagnetta*
coverta di bellissimi *arbuscelli,*
con trenta ville e dodici castelli
che sieno intorno ad una cittadetta,

ch'abbia nel mezzo una sua fontanetta;
e faccia mille rami e fiumicelli,
ferendo per giardini e praticelli
e rifrescando la minuta erbetta.

Aranci e cedri, dattili e lumíe
e tutte l' altre frutte savorose
impergolate sieno per le vie;

e le genti vi sien tutte amorose,
e faccianvisi tante cortesie,
ch' a tutto 'l mondo sieno grazïose.

. . . contra mediam fere porticum diaeta paulum recedit, *cingit areolam,* quae quattuor platanis inumbratur. inter has *marmoreo labro aqua exundat . . .*

. . . nec cedit gratiae marmoris *ramos insidentesque*
ramis aves imitata pictura. fonticulus in hoc, in fonte
crater; circa *sipunculi plures* miscent *iucundissimum murmur . . .*

. . . sed ante piscinam, quae fenestris servit ac subiacet, *strepitu visuque iucundam*: nam *ex edito desiliens aqua* suscepta marmore albescit.

Hic quoque *fons nascitur simulque subducitur.*

Per totum hippodromum inducti strepunt rivi et, *qua manus duxit, sequuntur. His nunc illa viridia,* nunch haec, interdum simul omnia lavantur.

Contra fons egerit aquam et recipit; nam expulsa in altum in se cadit iunctisque hiatibus et absorbetur et tollitur.

(Pliny, *Ep.* 5.6)

insistence on a summative *praeteritio* in enumeration, all have a cumulative effect in singling out the Old-French garden as the target of a specific allusion for the **Decameron.** In sum, if the parallels traditionally proposed are found convincing, the intertextual connections thus established should not be seen as questioning in absolute terms the pre-eminence of the *Rose*: the issue is not one of absolute relevance, but of stratification and differential interplay. Paradoxically, bringing contextual parallels to the understanding of Boccaccio's redeployment of the *topos* actually reinforces the pertinence of the choice intertext as specific and unique. While Boccaccio's readers are invited to keep in mind a plurality of traditional texts—a discourse—when they are reading the **Decameron,** they are asked to keep the *Roman de la Rose* open on their desk.

If this is the case, and Boccaccio's intertextuality is actually a direct and straightforward allusion, a supplementary question arises: is the *Rose* able to account for *all* of Boccaccio's text as an antecedent? The answer is obviously negative. Not everything in Boccaccio's description finds a convincing antecedent in the *Rose*. Allusion and 'imitation' are, of course, creative activities. But in the present case, there is perhaps more: there is at least one crucial detail of innovation. Boccaccio's text twice insists on the final destination of the water that the fountain at the center of the garden so forcefully pours forth. In what may appear at first reading as a mere quantitative simile, the authorial voice suggests that the water "might have been enough to propel a millstone"; at the end of the passage, the millstone comes back as a literal presence outside the garden but intimately connected to it: the water, "verso il pian discendendo chiarissima, avanti che a quel divenisse, con grandissima forza e con non piccola utilità del signore due mulina volgea." Of course, a simple argument could always be made that the detail of the millstone is motivated merely by extra-literary circumstances: Boccaccio adds a millstone to his villa description because the villa he imagines as the backdrop for the next two days of story-telling actually had one. Barring unforeseen archeological discoveries, the claim cannot be proved—and the argument perhaps is to be discarded.[18] To an argument *a rebus* one may add a converging, and perhaps more compelling, argument *a verbis*: what at first makes its appearance in the text as a simile is then materialized. The fountain's water which started out "as if it could move a millstone" is in the end described as actually "moving a millstone—or two." Both arguments, however, risk missing the central cultural point the text is probably making. When set alongside the *Rose*, the **Decameron** appears to be insisting on the practical function of the fountain. In addition to the aesthetic pleasure that the garden-dwellers may derive from the admirable, gushing fountain and the murmuring streams and

rivulets, something that unites them with the *compaignie* of the *Rose*, the *signore* of *this* garden has designed it so that it may offer at once pleasure and profit, *diletto* and *utilità*.[19]

Pleasure and profit, were already explicitly (albeit incidentally) at the core of the *Filocolo* passage. In the context of that work, time well spent was at once pleasurable and useful: the irrigation system of the present garden replicates that ideal verbal setting in its architecture. In their *longue durée,* the notions thus joined represent Boccaccio's distinctive and contrasting signature. The garden of Deduit, with its cortège of idleness and levity, was all about pleasure and in no way about profit. Once we put this feature of Boccaccio's garden in focus, its presence acquires the value of a precise antithetical statement, one specifically targeting the *Roman de la Rose*. The pursuit of utility-with-pleasure is the specific difference that separates the members of Boccaccio's *brigata* from the court of love they intertextually mimic.

It may not be a random coincidence that the dialectics between pleasure and profit, beauty and usefulness, can be found in a different, and for Boccaccio radically alternative tradition. *Amoenitas* and *utilitas* are at the core of Classical treatments of villa gardens. In Roman literature, discussions of how the country estates owned by the cultivated ruling class should look like and what purposes they should serve was entrusted to the contrastive terminological couple we find joined in Boccaccio. The theme, first expounded in Varro's *De re rustica,* reaches as far as Pliny the Younger. In the summer of 2005, while collaborating on a study of Boccaccio's use of Livy in the **Decameron,** an Italian colleague, Professor Gaetano Braccini, directed my attention to two epistles by Pliny, which are devoted to a detailed, painstakingly precise and yet fully literary, description of two of his country estates.[20] *Ep.* II.17 presents the Laurentine villa (a property Pliny owned on the coast of Latium); *Ep.* V.6 repeats the ekphrastic exercise for a second villa, one he owned in Tuscany.[21] While the coupling of *amoenitas* and *utilitas* is spelled out in the first letter, it is the second one that may be more interesting to readers of Boccaccio. Below, I quote the text of this second epistle almost in its entirety. In addition to the group I have listed above, I have now bolded other *loci* in the epistle that may be suggested as antecedents for descriptive and thematic details in the **Decameron.** In what may appear a perverse chronological order, I am now glossing Pliny with Boccaccio:

C. PLINIUS DOMITIO APOLLINARI SUOS.

1 Amavi curam et sollicitudinem tuam, quod cum audisses me aestate Tuscos meos petiturum, ne facerem suasisti, dum putas insalubres. 2 Est sane gravis et pestilens ora Tuscorum, quae per litus extenditur; sed hi procul a mari recesserunt, quin etiam Appennino salu-

berrimo montium subiacent. 3 Atque adeo ut omnem pro me metum ponas, accipe temperiem caeli regionis situm villae amoenitatem, quae et tibi auditu et mihi relatu iucunda erunt.

7 Regionis forma pulcherrima. IMAGINARE AMPHITHEATRUM ALIQUOD IMMENSUM, ET QUALE SOLA RERUM NATURA POSSIT EFFINGERE. LATA ET DIFFUSA PLANITIES MONTIBUS EINGITUR, MONTES SUMMA SUI PARTE PROCERA NEMORA ET ANTIQUA HABENT. 8 Frequens ibi et varia venatio. Inde caeduae silvae cum ipso monte descendunt.

11 PRATA FLORIDA ET GEMMEA TRIFOLIUM ALIASQUE HERBAS TENERAS SEMPER ET MOLLES ET QUASI NOVAS ALUNT. Cuncta enim perennibus rivis nutriuntur; sed ubi aquae plurimum, palus nulla, QUIA DEVEXA TERRA, QUIDQUID LIQUORIS ACCEPIT NEC ABSORBUIT, EFFUNDIT IN TIBERIM. [*Dec.* VI. concl.20-24]*

14 VILLA IN COLLE IMO SITA PROSPICIT QUASI EX SUMMO: ITA LEVITER ET SENSIM CLIVO FALLENTE CONSURGIT, ut cum ascendere te non putes, sentias ascendisse. [*Dec.* III.intro.3] A tergo Appenninum, sed longius habet; accipit ab hoc auras quamlibet sereno et placido die, non tamen acres et immodicas, sed spatio ipso lassas et infractas.

17 AMBIT HUNC AMBULATIO PRESSIS VARIEQUE TONSIS VIRIDIBUS INCLUSA; AB HIS GESTATIO IN MODUM CIRCI, QUAE BUXUM MULTIFORMEM HUMILESQUE ET RETENTAS MANU ARBUSCULAS CIRCUMIT. [*Dec.* III.intro.6] OMNIA MACERIA MUNIUNTUR [*Dec.* III.intro.5]: hanc gradata buxus operit et subtrahit. 18 PRATUM INDE NON MINUS NATURA QUAM SUPERIORA ILLA ARTE VISENDUM [*Dec.* III.intro.8-9]; campi deinde porro multaque alia prata et arbusta.

20 Contra mediam fere porticum diaeta paulum recedit, cingit areolam, quae quattuor platanis inumbratur. INTER HAS MARMOREO LABRO AQUA EXUNDAT [*Dec.* III.intro.10] circumiectasque platanos et subiecta platanis leni aspergine fovet.

23 Fonticulus in hoc, in fonte crater; CIRCA SIPUNCULI PLURES MISCENT IUCUNDISSIMUM MURMUR. In cornu porticus amplissimum cubiculum triclinio occurrit; aliis fenestris xystum, aliis despicit pratum, sed ante piscinam, quae fenestris servit ac subiacet, strepitu visuque iucunda; 24 nam EX EDITO DESILIENS AQUA SUSCEPTA MARMORE ALBESCIT. [*Dec.* III.intro.9-10]

32 Hanc dispositionem amoenitatemque tectorum longe longeque praecedit hippodromus. Medius patescit statimque intrantium oculis totus offertur, PLATANIS CIRCUMITUR; ILLAE HEDERA VESTIUNTUR UTQUE SUMMAE SUIS ITA IMAE ALIENIS FRONDIBUS VIRENT. HEDERA TRUNCUM ET RAMOS PERERRAT VICINASQUE PLATANOS TRANSITU SUO COPULAT. Has buxus interiacet; exteriores buxos circumvenit laurus, UMBRAEQUE PLATANORUM SUAM CONFERT. 33 Rectus hic hippodromi limes in extrema parte hemicyclio frangitur mutatque faciem: cupressis ambitur et tegitur, DENSIORE UMBRA OPACIOR NIGRIORQUE. [*Dec.* III.intro.6]

36 [. . .] In capite stibadium candido marmore vite protegitur; vitem quattuor columellae Carystiae subeunt. Ex stibadio aqua velut expressa cubantium pondere sipunculis effluit, cavato lapide suscipitur, gracili marmore continetur atque ita occulte temperatur, ut impleat nec redundet. 37 [. . .] CONTRA FONS EGERIT AQUAM ET RECIPIT; NAM EXPULSA IN ALTUM IN SE CADIT IUNCTISQUE HIATIBUS ET ABSORBETUR ET TOLLITUR.

40 HIC QUOQUE FONS NASCITUR SIMULQUE SUBDUCITUR. [. . .] PER TOTUM HIPPODROMUM INDUCTI STREPUNT RIVI, ET QUA MANUS DUXIT SEQUUNTUR: HIS NUNC ILLA VIRIDIA, NUNC HAEC, INTERDUM SIMUL OMNIA LAVANTUR. [*Dec.* III.intro.9-11]

45 Habes causas cur ego Tuscos meos Tusculanis Tiburtinis Praenestinisque praeponam. Nam super illa quae rettuli, altius ibi otium et pinguius eoque securius: nulla necessitas togae, nemo accersitor ex proximo, placida omnia et quiescentia, quod ipsum salubritati regionis ut purius caelum, ut aer liquidior accedit. 46 IBI ANIMO, IBI CORPORE MAXIME VALEO. NAM STUDIIS ANIMUM, VENATU CORPUS EXERCEO. MEI QUOQUE NUSQUAM SALUBRIUS DEGUNT; USQUE ADHUC CERTE NEMINEM EX IIS QUOS EDUXERAM MECUM,—VENIA SIT DICTO—IBI AMISI. Di modo in posterum hoc mihi gaudium, hanc gloriam loco servent! Vale.

*) For the pertinence of this fragment, cf. the description of the *valle delle donne*: Secondo che alcuna di loro poi mi ridisse, IL PIANO, CHE NELLA VALLE ERA, COSÍ ERA RITONDO COME SE A SESTA FOSSE STATO FATTO, QUANTUNQUE ARTIFICIO DELLA NATURA E NON MANUAL PARESSE. [. . .] Le piagge delle quali montagnette cosí digradando giuso verso il pian discendevano, COME NE' TEATRI VEGGIAMO dalla lor sommità i gradi infino all'infimo venire successivamente ordinati, sempre ristrignendo il cerchio loro. [. . .] Il piano appresso, senza aver piú entrate che quella donde le donne venute v'erano, ERA PIENO D'ABETI, DI CIPRESSI, D'ALLORI E D'ALCUN PINI SÍ BEN COMPOSTI E SÍ BENE ORDINATI, COME SE QUALUNQUE È DI CIÒ IL MIGLIORE ARTEFICE GLI AVESSE PIANTATI: e fra ESSI POCO SOLE O NIENTE, allora che egli era alto, entrava infino al suolo, il quale era tutto un prato d'erba minutissima e piena di fiori porporini e d'altri. (*Dec.* VI.*concl.*20-24)

When we consider it in its entirety, Pliny's letter appears to be more than simply casually related to Boccaccio's text. First, a geographical consideration: Pliny's villa is in Tuscany. Its larger topographical coordinates (with the peculiar metaphor of the amphitheater common to the two texts) anticipate those of the *Valle delle Donne* on which Day VI comes to a close. Architectural and landscaping details also correspond across the texts: the garden is fully enclosed (che *tutto era da torno murato: omnia maceria muniuntur*); the tender trees (*albuscelli: arbusculas*); the meadows (*pratelli: prata*), the central court in the palace (*un cortile nel mezzo: diaeta cingit areolam*); the fountain pouring forth water (una *fonte di marmo* da cui *usciva* l'acqua *che soprabondava al pieno: marmoreo labro aqua exundat*); the little channels irrigating the garden (*canaletti: spicunculi plures, inducti rivi*); the murmuring waters (*dilettevole suono: iucundissimum murmur*); the central water-show (l'acqua *alta verso il cielo, che . . . nella fonte chiarissima ricadea: ex edito desiliens aqua*). We have seen all of this, listed as part of the 'common discourse' on villa gardens.

Beyond the frequency of parallel details, however, it is the opening and ending of the letter that seem particularly resonant of the larger themes of the ***Decameron***. The care with which Pliny tells his correspondent not to worry about the salubrious nature of his estates in Tuscany brings to the surface a term that might have caught Boccaccio's eye. Pliny admits that the rest of Tuscany is infested (most likely with malaria), especially along the coast, but his villa is in a more remote area, away from the "gravis et pestilens ora." Fleeing the plague-ridden city, and searching for a similarly safer place (even if only relatively so), the *brigata* seems to be driven by similar considerations (see ***Dec.*** I.*intro.* 65-66). Coming from the perspective of the ***Decameron,*** the evocative power of the word *pestilens* can hardly be overestimated. Both Pliny and Boccaccio's *brigata,* moreover, seem to have been right in their choice: in the envoy of his epistle, Pliny comes back to the practical concern of health and notes, with a touch of *scaramanzia,* that no one of his family (that is, of his slaves) has ever died there. The villa is apparently able to fend off death; the plague cannot walk through the threshold of its garden. Boccaccio's Edenic setting offers a similarly comforting, if just as temporary, shelter.

One final general interpretive remark may bring this exploration of some of Boccaccio's antecedents full circle. For Pliny's letter to be a good intertext, a viable hermeneutic supplement (if not a real alternative) to the overwhelmingly present *Roman de la Rose,* his texts should also be interpretable. The classical intertext should, in other words, be able to bear an alternative meaning—a semantic, cultural advantage over the garden of Deduit. Indeed, in its closing, the epistle may contain a hint at precisely that element of distinction, which will bring us back to the dichotomy of pleasure and profit with which we started. When Pliny writes that his health is never better than when he is in his villa, he also posits an important distinction. The health he refers to is both physical and intellectual: *Ibi animo, ibi corpore maxime valeo. Nam studiis animum, venatu corpus exerceo.* While a regimen of hunting exercises takes care of the body; *studia,* a generic term that embraces all intellectual activities, is what guarantees the mind's health. Being active rather than leisurely, Pliny's retreat into the countryside works as the counter-model for the one set by Guillaume's poem: the winning formula for the ***Decameron*** is not the one offered by Deduit in the vernacular romance, but a classical *otium cum studiis.* If Eden is to be recovered in full, the first pre-lapsarian mandate needs to be enforced as well: unlike the leisurely company of Deduit, Boccaccio's *brigata* has been given a literary and moral garden to tend. In their story-telling, this is precisely what its members will do.

Notes

1. See M. Riffaterre, *La production du texte* (Paris: Seuil, 1979), 86.

2. Background to these arguments and terminology may be found in C. Segre, *Teatro e Romanzo* (Torino: Einaudi, 1984), 103-18; for the debate in classical studies, see S. Hinds, *Allusion and Intertext: Dynamics of Appropriation in Roman Poetry* (Cambridge: Cambridge University Press, 1998), and for its modern counterpart G. Machacek, "Allusion," *PMLA* [*Proceedings of the Modern Language Association*] 122.2 (March, 2007), 522-36. M. Orr, *Intertextuality: Debates and Contexts* (Cambridge: Polity Press, 2003) can still prove useful.

3. All citations from the *Decameron* are from Giovanni Boccaccio, *Decameron,* ed. V. Branca (Torino: Einaudi, 1992^3).

4. I quote the texts from: Cicéron, *De l'invention,* ed. G. Achard (Paris: Les Belles Lettres, 1994); Cicerone, *La retorica a Gaio Erennio,* ed. F. Cancelli (Milano: Mondadori, 1992); Quintiliano, *L'Istituzione oratoria,* ed. R. Faranda (Torino: UTET, 1968); Isidori Hispaliensis *Etymologiarum sive originum libri xx,* ed. W. M. Lindsay (Oxford: Clarendon Press, 1911).

5. Still essential is the treatment of this issue in P. Stewart, *Retorica e mimica nel "Decameron" e nella commedia del Cinquecento* (Firenze: Olschki, 1986); but see also P. M. Forni, "Realtà/Verità," *Studi sul Boccaccio* 22 (1992), 235-56.

6. The text is cited from the manuscript Laurenziano 13.sin.6, f. 214v, sec. XIV^i, a codex to which Boccaccio might have had access.

7. For a more extended treatment of this argument, see S. Marchesi, *Stratigrafie decameroniane* (Firenze: Olschki, 2004), 1-16; analogous conclusions about the peculiar kind of 'exemplarity' embodied in the *Decameron* have been reached independently (and based on a different set of considerations) by T. Kircher, *The Poet's Wisdom: The Humanists, the Church, and the Formation of Philosophy in the Early Renaissance* (Leiden: Brill, 2006), esp. Chapter 3, and T. Foster Gittes, *Boccaccio's Naked Muse: Eros, Culture, and the Mythopoeic Imagination* (Toronto: University of Toronto Press), esp. Chapter 4.

8. The nature of the *novella* has become the recurrent subject of discussion: see the three main volumes of conference proceedings, *La Nouvelle: Actes du Colloque International de Montréal* (McGill University, 14-16 octobre 1982), eds. M. Picone, G. Di Stefano, and P. Stewart (Montréal: Plato Academic Press, 1983); *La novella italiana: Atti del Convegno di Caprarola,* 19-24 settembre 1988 (Roma: Salerno Editrice, 1989); and *Favole Parabole Istorie: Le forme della scrittura novellistica dal medioevo al rinascimento* (Atti del Convegno di Pisa, 26-28 ottobre 1998), G. Albanese, L. Battaglia Ricci, and R. Bessi, eds. (Roma: Salerno, 2000).

9. *Sed contra,* see M. Picone, "L'invenzione della Novella italiana: tradizione e innovazione," in *La novella italiana,* 119-54.

10. Results from a Google search for "che dir si voglia"; the same parameters entered into Yahoo's search engine yield 229,000 hits (October 29, 2007).

11. The search engine for the *Opera del Vocabolario Italiano* is part of the ItalNet consortium. It can be accessed via the University of Notre Dame or University of Chicago servers at: http://www.lib.uchicago.edu/efts/ARTFL/projects/OVI/.

12. I cite the text of the *Esposizioni* from Giovanni Boccaccio, *Esposizioni sopra la Commedia,* ed. G. Padoan (Milano: Mondadori, 1965).

13. The so-called "one-hundred letter form" (1.1-5.6) of Pliny's *Epistles* is the philological bridge between his collection and Boccaccio's *Decameron.* I have discussed Boccaccio's knowledge of that branch of the tradition, in particular of ms. F., the Mediceo Laurenziano S. Marco 284, in "The two halves of a dialogue: Petrarch, Boccaccio, and the invention of the epistle," in *Inventing History: Italian Literature between Philology and History,* F. Finotti and W. Storey, eds. (forthcoming).

14. All citations from Pliny come from C. Plini Caecili Secundi *Epistularum libri decem,* ed. R. A. B. Mynors (Oxford: Clarendon Press, 1963).

15. On the axiological charge investing gardens in the *Decameron,* see L. Battaglia Ricci, *Ragionare nel giardino: Boccaccio e i cicli pittorici del "Trionfo dela Morte"* (Roma: Salerno, 1987), 125-32 and 166-80. For the literary tradition behind Boccaccio's treatment of the *topos,* see E. G. Kern, "The Gardens in the *Decameron* Cornice," *PMLA* 66.4. (June, 1951), 505-23. See also G. Mazzotta, *The World at Play in Boccaccio's "Decameron"* (Princeton, NJ: Princeton University Press, 1986), 107-11, similarly insisting on the *Roman de la Rose* as central intertext.

16. I cite the text of the *Rose* from Guillaume de Lorris et Jean de Meun, *Le Roman de la Rose. Édition d'après les manuscrits BN 12786 et BN 378,* ed. A. Strubel (Paris: Librarie Générale Française, 1992).

17. I cite the text from Giovanni Boccaccio, *Filocolo,* ed. A. E. Quaglio (Milano: Mondadori 1967).

18. Having no investment in promoting a specific site, I will refrain from putting Boccaccio's villa on any map. Traditionally, however, Villa Palmieri has been considered the strongest candidate. See, for instance, C. Bichi and M. Zoppi, *Giardini di Toscana* (Firenze: Edifir, 2001).

19. For an analysis of the two terms in the *Decameron,* see R. Hollander "*Utilità,*" in *Boccaccio's Dante and the Shaping Force of Satire* (Ann Arbor: The University of Michigan Press, 1997), 69-88.

20. See G. Braccini and S. Marchesi, "Livio XXV, 26 e l'*Introduzione alla prima giornata:* di una possibile tessera classica per il *cominciamento* del *Decameron,*" *Italica* 80.2 (2003), 139-46. The notes that follow about the resonance of Pliny's description of his gardens are deeply indebted to my conversations with Professor Braccini.

21. For Pliny's treatment of villas in an archeological and cultural vein, see G. Mansuelli, "La villa nelle *Epistulae* di C. Plinio Cecilio Secondo," *Studi Romagnoli* 29 (1978), 59-76; J. Bodel, "Monumental villas and villa monuments," *Journal of Roman Archaeology* 10 (1997), 5-35; and A. Riggsby, "Pliny in Space (and Time)," Arethusa 36 (2003), 167-86. J. S. Ackerman's vast study *The Villa: Form and Ideology of Country Houses* (Princeton, NJ: Princeton University Press, 1989) clearly outlines the cultural debates surrounding the Roman estates (for Pliny's case, see Chapter 2). For literary meditations on villas, see most recently J. Henderson, *Morals and Villas in Seneca's "Letters": Places to Dwell* (Cambridge: Cambridge University Press, 2004).

Jason M. Houston (essay date 2010)

SOURCE: Houston, Jason M. "Boccaccio *Dantista* and the *Decameron.*" In *Building a Monument to Dante: Boccaccio as "Dantista,"* pp. 163-69. Toronto: University of Toronto Press, 2010.

[*In the following essay, drawn from Houston's full-length study of Boccaccio's debt to Dante Alighieri, Houston analyzes tale 5.8 from the* Decameron *for its Dantean elements.*]

Aside from Boccaccio's work as *dantista,* the **Decameron** itself has left a monumental imprint on European literary culture. In the Introduction to this book I admitted that trying to discover Boccaccio's attitude through a reading of his **Decameron** and his fictional works in general was a slippery proposition at best. However, the presence of Dante, both explicitly and implicitly, in Boccaccio's own works of creative fiction make the text impossible to ignore in any study of Boccaccio's relationship to Dante. Therefore, I will conclude this book about Boccaccio's construction of his monumental Dante with a brief consideration of Boccaccio's fiction and the presence of Dante. Specifically, I will examine one story from the **Decameron** that is both overtly Dantean in nature and implicitly linked to

Dante's biography: the story of Nastagio degli Onesti (Day V, 8). In reading this most Dantean of all of the stories in light of Boccaccio's project as *dantista,* I hope to more fully explain Boccaccio's *dantismo* in terms of his entire intellectual career.

The *Decameron* represents the fullest expression of Boccaccio's artistic genius, but it is not his earliest attempt to incorporate Dante into his fiction. The earliest phase of his work as a *dantista,* somewhat previous and peripheral to his monumentalizing project, involved his attempts to imitate Dante's poetic style. In the wake of Dante's impact on the literary scene in trecento Italy, especially Tuscany, it would be surprising if Boccaccio did not imitate Dante. Boccaccio's efforts as an imitator of Dante begin with his earliest recognized work. *La caccia di Diana,* which overtly recalls Dante through the utilization of the *terza rima* rhyme scheme, attests that Dante was Boccaccio's first reference for poetic style, and he continues to rely on Dante's forms throughout his early career as a vernacular poet. Despite the clear borrowings from Dante, however, Boccaccio never seems to approach Dante in spirit; the early works copy his style while glossing over the philosophical implications of Dante's *dolce stil novo.* Boccaccio as imitator is less concerned with shaping Dante than with adopting the literary mode of his great Tuscan literary ancestor in an exercise of style.[1]

However, one of Boccaccio's early works does attempt to follow Dante in both style and substance. The *Amorosa Visione,* written shortly after Boccaccio's return to Florence from his long sojourn in Angevin Naples, once again takes up Dante's *terza rima* and adopts the conventions of the dream-vision narrative from the *Commedia.* While not philosophical in nature this rather poetic compendium of tropes of Venus nevertheless closely imitates Dante's poetics. I doubt that many readers will argue with my characterization that it represents Boccaccio's greatest artistic failure. In addition to holding to Dante's allegorical vision and complicated metrical structures, Boccaccio burdens the poem with an acrostic that provides a cumbersome superstructure over the poem. What previous critics have found ambiguous, whether it is seen a moralistic poem or a proto-humanist celebration of classical learning, turns out to be Boccaccio's struggle between his two masters: Dante and Petrarca.[2] It is ironic but not surprising that the *Amorosa Visione* mediated Petrarca's most Dantean text, the *Trionfi.*[3] As is the case with many attempts to imitate two masters in a single work, the *Amorosa Visione* is an aesthetic and intellectual hybrid of a text that only points up the limits of Boccaccio's poetic craft.

It may well be that Boccaccio realized the failings of his imitation of Dante in the *Amorosa Visione* as he never again attempted such close reproduction of Dante's poetics. Indeed, the many instances of Dantean borrowings that pervade the *Decameron* pointedly avoid direct imitation or citation. Just as with the *Corbaccio,* as I argue in chapter 3, Boccaccio uses Dante's matrix of language and imagery to populate the *Decameron* with echoes that would resonate with his reading public.[4] These intertextualities simultaneously recall and re-cast Dante's text in a metalepsis. In the case of the *Corbaccio,* Boccaccio wanted to protect Dante from the critiques of the Dominican preachers and others who had rejected Dante's *Commedia* for its vernacularity. I will now turn to one story from the *Decameron* to evaluate how Boccaccio as *dantista* reads and shapes Dante's *Commedia* in his own fiction.

There are a number of stories that carry more or less specific references to Dante's literary world. Readers of the *Decameron* have not been reticent to call out the myriad resonances in many of the *novelle.* Panfilo's opening lines in the first story of the *Decameron* about the wicked Ser Cepparello and his eventual *translatio* to sainthood in Burgundy as San Ciappelletto challenge Dante's entire poetic claim to truth in the *Commedia.*[5] In the last story about patient Griselda, Dioneo opens with an obvious quotation from Dante's *Inferno* in his description of the wicked Gualtieri's actions as 'matta bestialità.' As I discussed in chapter 4 Dioneo's citation of Dante is both evident and problematic, as is much of Boccaccio's citation of Dante in the *Decameron.* Indeed, even Boccaccio's one explicit reference to Dante in the Introduction to Day IV provides few clues about his attitude to his predecessor. In the frame(s) and stories of the *Decameron,* Dante exists specifically as a literary *auctoritas,* but Boccaccio never accepts or rejects this model.

In considering the eighth story from the Day V (V, 8) I apply Boccaccio *dantista's* architectural hermeneutic to both this story and to the entire *Decameron.* Boccaccio privileges the public and present value of literature, its monumental value, over the private and philosophical. He prefers that his Dante reach a wide, public audience rather than remain within the confines of the elite, literate culture of Latin humanism. In this story, Boccaccio constructs an overtly Dantean episode at the crossroads of the public, private, political, and religious: courtship and marriage. Although written a few years before beginning his project of monumentalizing Dante, the *Decameron,* and this story in particular, prefigures Boccaccio as *dantista.*

Before the story begins, Filomena's opening introduces a central theme of this book. 'Amabili donne, come in noi è la pietà commendata, cosí ancora in noi è dalla divina giustizia rigidamente la crudeltà vendicata: [Adorable ladies, just as our pity is commended, so is our cruelty severely punished by divine justice] (*Dec.* V., 8, par. 3). The juxtaposition of divine justice with cruelty and vengeance is, of course, an oft-cited disagreement between Boccaccio and Dante; in this *novella* Boccaccio, as in the *Corbaccio,* refits a Dantean literary structure with his own ethical, rather than speculative, façade.

The story takes place in Ravenna, where a young and wealthy man, Nastagio degli Onesti, nurses an unrequited love for the daughter of a nobleman Paolo Traversari. Spurned despite the lavish nature of his courtship ('spendere smisuratamente'), Nastagio leaves Ravenna only to end up in Classe, a coastal town only three miles from Ravenna. He brings enough baggage on this excursion to set up a pavilion and entertain friends in a lordly fashion. One day Nastagio wanders into a pine forest; he witnesses a naked woman running through the woods chased by a black knight on horseback with a pack of hounds. Attempting to intervene and lacking weapons, Nastagio presents himself to the knight armed with a tree branch. The knight explains that Nastagio need not protect the lady as they are both actually in Hell and this is their mutual punishment. He is punishing her for being too well pleased at his suffering by her cruelty, and in playing his role in this scene he is punished for his act of suicide out of despair for this lady's refusal. Nastagio watches as the knight stabs the lady with his sword, and also witnesses the knight carving open her back, removing her heart, and feeding it to the mastiffs. The lady then rises and runs off again chased by the knight to replay the chase to the same end on the following Friday.

This point is not the end of the story, but it marks the end of the particularly Dantean elements. As one reader has remarked, the entire story is generically Dantean.[6] Indeed, the forest setting recalls the woods of *Inferno* I as well as the idyllic landscape of the Garden of Eden in *Purgatorio*; the chase through the underbrush is reminiscent of the suicides in Canto XIII, while the punishment of the woman (a suicide in the story) recalls the punishment of those who brought scandal and discord in Canto XXVIII. The nature of the punishment suggests Dante's *contrapasso*. Nastagio's position as spectator of this event and interlocutor with one of the two members of the coupled sinners evokes the entire structure of Dante's *Inferno,* especially the Paolo and Francesca episode in Canto V. Moreover, Nastagio's own profligacy in his pursuit of his lady reminds the reader that the suicides in *Inferno* XIII share their environment and punishment with the profligate chased by hounds: thus, Nastagio is a spectator but also a participant in this drama. These allusions and others mark this story with the undeniable sign of Dante's *Inferno.* Just as I have shown for the *Corbaccio,* Boccaccio employs a metaleptical narrative strategy in the simultaneous restaging and reshaping of Dante's *Inferno.* Other critics have noted that for this text Boccaccio draws upon other dream-vision narratives, both classical and medieval, including *De amore libri tres* (*The Art of Courtly Love*) by Andreas Capellanus.[7] However, the story, 'generic' as it might be, most pointedly echoes Dante's afterworld.

Boccaccio's clues in the description of the story suggest more than a 'generic' reference to Dante by bringing out specifically biographical details about Dante. By setting the story in Ravenna, Boccaccio places the reader in the place of Dante's own death and burial. Only a few years later Boccaccio will call for the return of Dante's remains to Florence. By specifically naming the lady as one of the Traversari family, Boccaccio links the characters with characters in Dante's *Commedia.*[8] The woods at Classe not only recall a generic wood in Dante's *Inferno,* but more specifically allude to the Garden of Eden in *Purgatorio* XXVIII. As in the *Corbaccio,* this story has the unmistakable Dantean stamp, but Boccaccio conflates different scenes from the *Commedia* into one hybrid scene. Once again, he wants to recall Dante's text in its structure without resurrecting the entire philosophical or moral edifice.

The second half of the story offers an example of Boccaccio's architectural instinct. He uses the existing structure of Dantean imagery to construct a uniquely Boccaccian literary scene. The *novella* converts a distinctly Dantean narrative of personal sin and punishment into a public drama. Having beheld this scene, Nastagio is at first horrified by the event, but then he decides to make use of this occurrence of ritualistic punishment to his benefit. He gathers his friends and family and asks them to help him stage a show.

> 'Voi m'avete lungo tempo stimolato che io d'amare questa mia nemica mi rimanga e ponga fine al mio spendere, e io son presto di farlo dove voi una grazia m'impetriate, la quale è questa: che venerdí che viene voi facciate sí che messer Paolo Traversari e la moglie e la figliuola e tutte le donne lor parenti, e altre chi vi piacerà, qui sieno a disinar meco. Quello per che io questo voglio, voi il vedrete allora.'
>
> (*Decameron* V, 8, par. 33-4)

> [For some little time you have been urging me to desist from wooing this hostile mistress of mine and place a curb on my extravagance, and I am willing to do so on condition that you obtain for me a single favour, which is this: that on Friday next you arrange for Messer Paolo Traversari and his wife and daughter and all their womenfolk, together with any other lady you care to invite, to join me in this place for breakfast. My reason for wanting this will become apparent to you on the day itself.]

Thus Nastaglio convinces the Traversari family to witness this Dantean spectacle of punishment. The tale ends with a fantastic banquet that becomes dinner theatre as the Traversari family and the other young ladies behold the terrible punishment of this young woman. Of course, the young lady understand Nastagio's intended message in staging the scene and agrees to do anything Nastagio pleases; as Filomena the storyteller concludes, the women of Ravenna were much more tractable to men's desires after that day. Nastagio saves the *novella* from out and out ethical parody by proposing marriage to the terrified lady, but the ambiguity of Boccaccio's reframing remains. The Dantean elements that seed this story grow into a new narrative of indefinite sin—Is it cruel to refuse illicit love?—and mock punishment that performs its function, admonition, and persuasion, in a public, civic space.

In a sense, Boccaccio's conclusion to this story prefigures his public reading of the *Inferno* before the citizens of Florence in 1372. Just he delivered his readings on the steps of the church of Santo Stefano Badia, Boccaccio translates Dante's ethics to the public sphere. In his work as *dantista* he sought to bring Dante's poetic story of sin, redemption, and grace to a larger audience by tempering some of the more radical claims. For Nastagio in the **Decameron,** the hellish scene serves as a path to his redemption through his marriage into the noble Traversari family and his return from self-imposed exile. This scene also leads to the civil tranquillity of Ravenna by teaching young women how to treat, or rather how not to mistreat, the young men of the city. Boccaccio's sharp irony, of course, makes this second conclusion somewhat problematic for the reader. As in the *Corbaccio,* Boccaccio irrigates this Dantean moment with a critique of Dante's system of divine justice that takes root in human vengeance and violence. Although both the characters in the story and the members of Boccaccio's *brigata* find the conclusion a happy one, the reader—this reader at least—finds Nastagio's moral play disturbing.[9]

Written between Boccaccio's failed attempts to imitate Dante's poetics and his decades-long project to monumentalize the poet, the **Decameron** offers clues about how Boccaccio developed as a *dantista*. This story contains the same elements that I have identified in Boccaccio's work as *dantista*. First, Boccaccio places Dante's work within a larger group of source texts; Boccaccio's Dante is first among equals, not revolutionary. Moreover, as in many of his texts, Boccaccio craftily reworks his source material into playful texts that simultaneously recall and subvert the tradition. The second element of Boccaccio's work as *dantista* prioritizes the ethical importance of poetry; for Boccaccio, poetry serves a goal of civic virtue. In this story Boccaccio transports the dream-vision narrative from the world of personal consolation and salvation to the public sphere. Nastagio makes this vision in the forest a theatre of ethics for his unwilling beloved and for the city of Ravenna. When Boccaccio penned this story, redolent with Dante's presence in the city of Dante's death, he foreshadows his own performance of Dante's *Inferno* in Florence twenty years later. Just as Boccac-

cio had risked censure for exposing the Muses in his public readings of Dante, so too in this *novella* Boccaccio unveils his subject—literally the naked lady who receives punishment, but figuratively the eschatological valence of Dante's *Commedia*—for the edification of his audience.[10]

Despite Petrarca's dismissal of the **Decameron,** this text has secured Boccaccio a place as a monumental author in Italy and in the Western canon. Through his work as a *dantista,* he has had a quiet but similarly profound impact on the Italian literary landscape. In both fields of work, Boccaccio understood that his own reputation depended on his relationship to his two contemporary authors: Dante and Petrarca. Indeed, Boccaccio understood the practical workings of transmission of texts and influences. In laying bare the mechanics of his work as a *dantista,* I hope to have made evident Boccaccio's important role not only in fashioning the figure of Dante (and for that matter, the category of the *tre corone* as well) that has persisted to this day but also in translating the emerging culture of humanism to vernacular culture.

Notes

1. One might regard Boccaccio's early poetic texts as exercises similar to his earliest known epistolary writings. His first three letters are written to a fictitious personage, to Petrarca (but never delivered), and to an unknown and probably fictional correspondent.

2. For the critical view of the *Amorosa Visione* as an ambiguous text, see S. Huot, 'Poetic Ambiguity and Reader Response in Boccaccio's *Amorosa Visione,*' *Modern Philology* 83 (1985): 109-122. For the discussion of Boccaccio's position between Dante's *Commedia* and Petrarca's *Trionfi,* see V. Branca, 'Implicazioni espressive, temi e stilemi fra Petrarca e Boccaccio,' in *Boccaccio medievale e nuovi studi sul 'Decameron'* (Florence: Sansoni, 1996), pp. 300-32.

3. Branca proposes the Dantean influence of the *Amorosa Visione* in V. Branca, *Boccaccio medievale* (Florence: Sansoni, 1996), 315. See also M. Eisner, 'Petrarch Reading Boccaccio,' in *Petrarch and the Textual Origins of Interpretation,* ed. T. Barolini and H. W. Storey (Leiden: Brill, 2007), 130-46.

4. I refer the reader to the Introduction to this book for details on the critical perspectives on Dante's presence in the *Decameron*. The two most important articles about the actual textual presence of Dante in the *Decameron* are both by Attilio Bettinzoli: 'Per una definizione delle presenze dantesche nel *Decameron*': I—I registri ideologici, lirici, drammatici,' and II—'Ironizzazione ed

espressivismo antifrastico-deformatorio,' *Studi sul Boccaccio* 13 (1981-2): 257-326, and 14 (1983-4): 209-40. Indeed, almost every book or article on Boccaccio must, in some way, discuss for Dante's presence in Boccaccio's writing.

5. On the relationship of this story to Dante see, Hollander, 'Imitative Distance,' 21-52. See also G. Mazzotta, *World at Play in Boccaccio's 'Decameron,'* 47-74.

6. For this characterization of Day V, 8, see R. Hollander, *Boccaccio's Dante and the Shaping Force of Satire,* 4.

7. For one such view, see G. Mazzotta, *World at Play in Boccaccio's 'Decameron,'* 86-9. For more a more systematic discussion of sources for this story see, G. Kamber, 'Antitesi e sintesi in "Nastagio Degli Onesti,"' *Italica* 44 (1967): 61-8; C. Segre 'La novella di Nasagio delgi Onesti (*Dec.* V, 8): i due tempi della visione.' *In ricordo di Cesare Angelini* (Pavia: Saggiatore, 1980), 65-74.

8. Dante mentions the Traversari family as model of virtue in *Purgatorio,* Canto XIV, 107.

9. Of course, I am not alone in questioning the conclusion of this story; see M. Migiel, *A Rhetoric of the Decameron* (Toronto: University of Toronto Press, 2003), 156-7.

10. Gittes has shown how Boccaccio's 'naked muse' is a necessary result of his project to translate literary culture to his contemporaries. He speaks specifically of Boccaccio's bitter sonnets written after the delivery of his public lectures on the *Commedia*; see Gittes, *Boccaccio's Naked Muse,* 166-8.

Works Cited

PRIMARY SOURCES

Frequently cited editions of works by Boccaccio, Dante, and Petrarca are indicated by a dagger (†). Unless otherwise indicated, the translations are my own, prepared with reference to published translations marked with a double dagger (‡).

†Boccaccio, Giovanni. *Amorosa Visione.* Ed. Vittore Branca. Vol. 3 of *Tutte le opere di Giovanni Boccaccio.* Milan: Mondadori, 1964-92.

———. †*Corbaccio.* Ed. Giorgio Padoan. Vol. 5, tome 2, of *Tutte le opere di Giovanni Boccaccio.* Milan: Mondadori, 1994.

———. †*Decameron.* Ed. Vittore Branca, vol. 4 of *Tutte le opere di Giovanni Boccaccio.* Milan: Mondadori, 1964-92.

———. *Tutte le opere di Giovanni Boccaccio.* Series ed. V. Branca. Milan: Mondadori, 1964-92.

Dante Alighieri. ‡*The Divine Comedy of Dante Alighieri,* Trans. A. Mandelbaum. 3 vols. New York: Bantam, 1980.

SECONDARY SOURCES

Bettinzoli, Attilio. 'Per una definizione delle presenze dantesche nel *Decameron.*' I, 'I registri ideologici, lirici, drammatici,' Part II, 'Ironizzazione e espressivismo antifrastico-deformatorio.' *Studi sul Boccaccio* 13 (1981-2): 257-326 and 14 (1983-4), 209-40.

Branca, Vittore. *Boccaccio medievale e nuovi studi sul 'Decameron'.* Florence: Sansoni, 1996.

Eisner, M. 'Petrarch Reading Boccaccio.' In *Petrarch and the Textual Origins of Interpretation.* Ed. T. Barolini and H. W. Storey. Leiden: Brill, 2007, 130-46.

Gittes, Tobias Foster. *Boccaccio's Naked Muse: Eros, Culture, and the Mythopoeic Imagination.* Toronto: University of Toronto Press, 2008.

Hollander, Robert. *Boccaccio's Dante and the Shaping Force of Satire.* Ann Arbor: University of Michigan Press, 1997.

Huot, S. 'Poetic Ambiguity and Reader Response in Boccaccio's *Amorosa Visione.*' *Modern Philology* 83 (1985): 109-22.

Kamber, G. 'Antitesi e sintesi in "Nastagio Degli Onesti."' *Italica* 44 (1967): 61-8.

Mazzotta, Giuseppe. *The World at Play in Boccaccio's 'Decameron.'* Princeton: Princeton University Press, 1986.

Migiel, M. *A Rhetoric of the Decameron.* Toronto: University of Toronto Press, 2003.

Segre, C. 'La novella di Nasagio delgi Onesti (*Dec.* V, 8): i due tempi della visione.' In *In ricordo di Cesare Angelini: Studi di letteratura e filologia.* Ed. Franco Alessio and Angelo Stella. Pavia: Saggiatore, 1980, 65-74.

FURTHER READING

Criticism

Brown, Katherine A. "Boccaccio Reading Old French: *Decameron* IX.2 and *La Nonete.*" *MLN,* 125, no 1. (January 2010): 54-71.

Argues that tale 9.2 of the *Decameron* takes a single French *fabiau*—Jean de Condé's *La Nonete*—as its primary source and points out thematic, lexical, and syntactical similarities between the two stories.

Civitarese, Giuseppe. "Abstraction and Aesthetic Conflict in Boccaccio's '(L)Isabetta.'" *Journal of Romance Studies,* 10, no. 3 (winter 2010): 11-25.

Attempts to account for the disturbing appeal of tale 4.5 of the *Decameron,* the story of a woman who digs up her husband's corpse and cuts off his head.

De Sanctis, Francesco. *The History of Italian Literature.* Trans. Joan Redfern. New York: Harcourt, 1931.

Seminal criticism on the *Decameron,* originally published in 1870.

Daniels, Rhiannon. "Rethinking the Critical History of the *Decameron*: Boccaccio's Epistle XXII to Mainardo Cavalcanti." *Modern Language Review,* 106 (2011): 423-47.

Questions standard critical assumptions surrounding Boccaccio's 1372 letter to his patron, Mainardo Cavalcanti.

Kuhns, Richard. *Decameron and the Philosophy of Storytelling: Author as Midwife and Pimp.* New York: Columbia University Press, 2005, 208 p.

Develops a philosophy of the story and storytelling based on a close reading of sexual themes in the *Decameron* and on a study of the work's incorporation of paintings from the Florentine art world.

Additional information on Boccaccio's life and works is contained in the following sources published by Gale: *Classical and Medieval Literature Criticism,* **Vols. 13, 57;** *European Writers,* **Vol. 2;** *Gale Contextual Encyclopedia of World Literature;* *Literature Resource Center;* *Reference Guide to Short Fiction,* **Ed. 2;** *Reference Guide to World Literature,* **Eds. 2, 3;** *Short Stories for Students,* **Vol. 28;** *Short Story Criticism,* **Vols. 10, 87;** *Twayne's World Authors***; and** *World Literature and Its Times,* **Vol. 7.**

Charlotte Brontë
1816-1855

(Also wrote under the pseudonym Currer Bell) English novelist, short story writer, poet, and essayist.

The following entry presents criticism on Brontë's short fiction.

INTRODUCTION

Best known as the author of *Jane Eyre* (1847), Brontë came to success as a novelist after a long period of literary apprenticeship during which she composed a vast quantity of short fiction that remained unpublished for many years after her death. Almost all of Brontë's attention in these shorter works was devoted to the creation of an imaginary saga about a mythic West African kingdom that she and her siblings named Angria. Although the existence of these manuscripts had been discovered as early as 1857 by Brontë biographer Elizabeth Gaskell, scholars tended to regard them as negligible. The reasons for this are manifold, having much to do with the circumstances surrounding the production and dissemination of the stories.

Growing up in the seclusion and poverty of Haworth parsonage with their widowed father, Brontë and her siblings Anne, Emily, and Patrick Branwell developed an elaborate scenario of British colonization in Angria drawn on their wide reading of the classics and contemporary politics and history. As the stories evolved over the course of more than ten years, their execution was largely taken over by Charlotte, with considerable input from Branwell. These tales, now known as the Angrian cycle, in total run to hundreds of thousands of words, were originally contained in over one hundred booklets that the Brontë children enclosed in covers of blue and brown wrapping paper. Owing to their shortage of paper, the children printed the stories in miniscule letters on tiny pieces of paper, some as small as one-and-a-half by one-and-a-quarter inches, that were stitched into miniatures.

In 1859 Brontë's widower, Arthur Bell Nicholls, entrusted the collection to Brontë biographer Clement Shorter, who then turned the manuscripts over to bibliophile Thomas J. Wise. Wise privately printed some of the stories and then sold the bulk of them to collectors. The task of locating all the various manuscript collections proved exceedingly difficult for twentieth-century scholars, compounded by the existence of limited editions that were abridged or transcribed incorrectly. Since some of the pieces were

signed UT (Us Two) or WT (We Two), the precise contributions of Charlotte and Branwell, respectively, have in certain instances remained elusive. Perhaps because of the deterioration of some of the manuscripts and their disordered state, literary scholars appeared more than willing to dismiss the juvenilia as inconsequential. Before the publication of Christine Alexander's three-volume *An Edition of the Early Writings of Charlotte Brontë* (1987-91), fewer than half of the stories had been made available to the public. With the rise in feminist studies in the 1970s, literary critics began to reassess Brontë's youthful work, finding in it important evidence of her technical development as a writer and of the themes that were to occupy her throughout her adult career.

BIOGRAPHICAL INFORMATION

The third child of Patrick Brontë, an Anglican priest, and Maria Branwell, Brontë was born in 1816 in the village of Thornton, England. Patrick Branwell was born a year later, and sisters Anne and Emily, both of whom would also become famous authors, were born in 1818 and 1820, respectively. Around the time of Anne's birth, the family moved to Haworth, where Patrick Brontë had been appointed village pastor. From an early age, Brontë's life was one of hardship and tragedy. Her mother died of cancer in 1821 and her older sisters, Maria and Elizabeth, succumbed to typhoid in the spring of 1825. Educated by their father at home, the remaining Brontë children devoted much of their time to reading and writing plays and to other imaginative games. One such game, involving twelve wooden toy soldiers that Branwell had received as a gift from his father in 1826, marked the inception of the Angrian cycle. The children named the soldiers after their favorite military heroes. These play heroes gradually evolved into the explorer-colonists who would seize control of Angria from the native Ashanti and found a confederacy of twelve free states. The Angrian tales occupied Charlotte for the next thirteen years.

In 1831 Brontë was sent to Roe Head, a private school in the nearby town of Mirfield, with money given her by her godparents. She returned home after little over a year to help with the tutoring of her younger sisters, but was invited back to Roe in 1835 as an instructor. Her diary entries describe her time teaching there as "wretched bondage," relieved only by her secret fantasies of Angria. An entry dated 1836 records a vision of Angria in a state of rebellion that came upon her in a "trance . . . whirl[ing] me away like heath in the wilderness for five seconds of ecstasy." Brontë's long hours of duty at Roe left her little time to write, but she and Branwell corresponded often about new ideas for the storyline. Brontë left Roe Head in December, 1838. Her family's increasing financial difficulties forced her to seek new work, and in the spring of 1839, she took a governess position with a wealthy family in Stonegappe. She clashed with the children, however, and left after just three months. Another governess position two years later also proved intolerable.

In 1842 Brontë and her sisters decided to found their own school in Haworth. To that end, Charlotte and Emily, with the financial assistance of their Aunt Branwell, traveled to Brussels, Belgium, to study foreign languages at the Pensionnat Heger. However, the Brontës' school never materialized for lack of students. Branwell, meanwhile, had developed a severe alcohol addiction, and his deteriorating physical and psychological health began to exert an enormous strain on his three sisters. In the midst of the turmoil, Charlotte, Emily, and Anne collaborated on publishing their first book, *Poems by Currer, Ellis and Acton Bell* (1846). Brontë subsequently used Currer Bell as a pseudonym for all of her published works. The year 1847 saw the publication of Charlotte's *Jane Eyre* as well as her sisters' first novels: Emily's *Wuthering Heights* and Anne's *Agnes Grey*. This wave of literary success was followed by great tragedy. In September, 1848, Branwell died suddenly of acute bronchitis and tuberculosis. Emily succumbed to tuberculosis in December of that year, and Anne's death followed in May 1849 after a long battle with influenza. Grief-stricken, Charlotte tried to lose herself in her writing. On visits to her London publishers, she also became acquainted with such famous authors as William Makepeace Thackeray, Mathew Arnold, and her future biographer, Elizabeth Gaskell. Brontë had little tolerance for the trappings of literary fame, however, preferring to spend her time with her ailing father at Haworth. A year after publishing her third novel, *Villette* (1853), Brontë married Arthur Bell Nicholls, a young Irish pastor in her father's parish. She died in 1855 of complications experienced in pregnancy.

MAJOR WORKS OF SHORT FICTION

It was not until 1829 that Charlotte and Branwell began to record their tales about the wooden soldiers. By this time, Anne and Emily had taken their favorite soldiers, named after the Arctic explorers William Edward Parry and John Ross, and founded a second kingdom. Charlotte christened her favorite soldier the Duke of Wellington, after the military leader who had defeated Na-

poleon at Waterloo in 1815. Branwell named one his soldiers Napoleon. From these two competing figures derived the idea of a rivalry between two powerful men that would drive the plot of the Angrian tales for the next ten years. Early on, the "Young Men," the Brontë children's collective name for the soldiers, left their military careers in England and traveled in 1793 to the Ivory Coast, where they overpowered the native inhabitants and established the Glass Town Confederacy consisting of four provinces. In this effort they were aided by the four genii who ruled the land. As the stories progressed, the reliance on magic and the supernatural would remain a constant, as would Gothic elements such as ghosts, secret passageways, and graveyards. The children designed a publication named after their favorite journal, *Blackwood's Edinburgh Magazine,* which they filled with poems, stories, songs, and other writings supposedly written by Glass Town's inhabitants. Charlotte soon took over the editorship of *Blackwood's Young Men's Magazine* and began to expand on the Duke of Wellington's story. The centrality of Glass Town to the stories was replaced by Angria, a rival adjacent kingdom. The four volumes of "Tales of the Islanders" set the stage for a future scenario of revolution, political chaos, family feuds, incest, adultery, and murderous revenge.

These tales outline the Duke's political opponents and the hatred between his two sons, Arthur and Charles. Arthur would become the principal figure in the tales as the Duke of Zamorna and, later, King of Angria. Scholars consider Arthur the first of Brontë's Byronic heroes. A genius in battle strategy, he is ruthless in the conquest of his enemies and irresistible to women, though he treats them with great cruelty. He is reviled by his brother, Charles, who is portrayed as small and homely, but equally vindictive. Branwell's Napoleon figure gradually transformed into Zamorna's arch-antagonist, Alexander Percy, who attains the status of a lord through his second marriage to Lady Zenobia Ellrington. Zamorna leaves his wife, Marian Hume, for Percy's daughter by his first wife, Maria. When Marian dies of a broken heart over Zamorna's infidelity, Zamorna hands their infant son over to the care of his mistress, Mina Laury, but marries Maria. Zamorna is repeatedly frustrated in his quest for omnipotence by Percy, who enlists the aid of the native Ashanti in his attempt to overthrow Zamorna. Zamorna is motivated by both political and private revenge, and he threatens to get back at Percy by killing his own wife, Maria, who is Percy's daughter. The disintegration of colonial conquest gives way to more chaos when Quashia, the leader of the Ashanti, invades Maria's private rooms in the palace Zamorna has abandoned. These rooms have figured prominently in the story as the place where Maria has imprisoned herself, waiting for her faithless lover, Zamorna, to return.

The last of the Angrian tales, written in 1838 and 1839, turn the focus over to Mina Laury and another of Zamorna's lovers, the young Caroline Vernon, daughter of Percy and his mistress, Louisa Danci. Caroline's hero worship of Zamorna, who is at first her guardian, turns into the same obsessive and destructive love to which Zamorna's other female conquests had fallen prey. The romantic, political, and familial connections with Alexander Percy and Zamorna are returned to again and again in the plots of the stories; very often incidents already narrated are revisited and retold from different angles, and characters are killed off and then resuscitated. Late in 1839 Charlotte wrote what critics refer to as her "Farewell to Angria." In this piece, she relates her intent to "quit for awhile that burning clime where we have sojourned too long . . . [T]he mind would cease from excitement and turn now to a cooler region where the dawn breaks grey and sober. . . . [It] is not easy to dismiss from my imagination the images which have filled it so long; they were my friends and intimate acquaints . . . who peopled my thoughts by day, and not seldom stole strangely even into my dreams by night."

CRITICAL RECEPTION

Reassessments of Brontë's Angrian fiction have stressed its importance to the study of her output as a whole and scholars have been impressed by the sophistication of the stories on a variety of levels. Brontë has been praised for her literary borrowings from William Shakespeare, Lord Byron, John Milton, and the *Tales of the Arabian Nights*; for her demonstrated understanding of the politics and class struggles of colonization; for her increasingly realistic approach; and for her focus on the psychological motivations of her characters. Many critics have looked to the stories as sources for the themes and characters of Brontë's later and longer fiction. The principal themes of the Angrian tales—seduction, adultery, betrayal, the linking of male potency with violence, and the urge to self-destruction—have given rise to a number of Freudian readings. Critics have interpreted the stories as manifestations of Brontë's grief over the deaths of her mother and sisters, or as evidence of her repressed sexuality. Some have argued that her depiction of the Ashanti rebellion attests to Brontë's growing recognition of her marginalized position in society as a lower-middle-class woman. According to Susan Meyer, "[If] Brontë's imaginative images are speaking the culture, they are speaking the culture's nightmares—successful black and working class revolt—and using them to express her own subversive fantasies—the rebellion of the working woman, the invasion of the structures of privilege, unloosed sexuality, and the routing and disempowerment of the ruling class." Following similar lines of analysis, commentators have examined how Brontë transformed the sensational material of the Angrian stories into the more conventional narratives of her novels. Margaret Howard Blom has observed that, "Angria is, in a sense, the province of the id; Charlotte's superego dictated her conception of reality. The resulting tension between what she was naturally drawn to and the values she thought she should uphold is apparent in all of her adult novels. . . . Indeed, Charlotte's struggles to subdue the subconscious self which produced Angria are echoed in the works of her maturity as again and again—and most powerfully in *Villette*—she describes the agony of the individual who discovers within himself powerful impulses, desires, and fears which are not subject to the control of the rational mind." In a 2007 essay Heather Glen lamented that far too many studies of the Angrian cycle had proceeded on the premise, drawn from Brontë's diary entries, that the tales were written in a "trance-like" state suggestive of Brontë's subconscious desires. Emphasizing Brontë's experimentation with a variety of short fictional forms, such as vignettes, sketches, and miscellanies, as well as her efforts to emulate the popular episodic fiction of Charles Dickens, Washington Irving, and Sir Walter Scott, Glen argued for greater recognition of the Angrian cycle as serious literature.

PRINCIPAL WORKS

Short Fiction

The Life and Works of Charlotte Brontë and Her Sisters. 7 vols. [with Anne Brontë and Emily Brontë] (novels, short stories, and poetry) 1899-1900
The Twelve Adventurers and Other Stories (short stories) 1925
The Shakespeare Head Brontë. 19 vols. [with Patrick Branwell Brontë, Anne Brontë, and Emily Brontë] (short stories, novels, poetry, and letters) 1931-38
Legends of Angria: Compiled from the Early Writings of Charlotte Brontë (short stories) 1933
The Miscellaneous and Unpublished Writings of Charlotte and Patrick Branwell Brontë. 2 vols. [with Patrick Branwell Brontë] (short stories and poetry) 1936
Five Novelettes (short stories) 1971
An Edition of the Early Writings of Charlotte Brontë. 3 vols. (short stories) 1987-91
Tales of Angria (short stories) 2006

Other Major Works

Poems by Currer, Ellis, and Acton Bell [as Currer Bell; with Emily Brontë and Anne Brontë] (poetry) 1846
Jane Eyre: An Autobiography. 3 vols. [as Currer Bell] (novel) 1847
Shirley: A Tale. 3 vols. [as Currer Bell] (novel) 1849

Villette. 3 vols. [as Currer Bell] (novel) 1853
The Professor. A Tale. 2 vols. [as Currer Bell] (novel)
   1857
*The Poems of Charlotte Brontë: A New, Annotated, and
   Enlarged Edition of the Shakespeare Head Brontë*
   (poetry) 1984
The Belgian Essays (essays) 1996

CRITICISM

Fannie E. Ratchford (essay date June 1928)

SOURCE: Ratchford, Fannie E. "Charlotte Brontë's
Angrian Cycle of Stories." *PMLA* 43, no. 2 (June 1928):
494-501.

[*In the following essay, Ratchford reassesses theories of
Brontë's literary development in light of her Angrian
cycle of stories.*]

The existence of voluminous Brontë juvenilia has long
been known. Anyone who has read Mrs. Gaskell's *Life
of Charlotte Brontë* must remember the astonishing list
of twenty-two 'books' therein enumerated as having
been completed by August 3, 1830, near the end of
Charlotte's fourteenth year. Mr. Clement K. Shorter
continues the list through 1839, bringing the number of
titles up to forty. To these may be added from sources
not included in his list an almost equal number of
sketches and fragments, making a total which in volume approximates the author's published works.

The appearance of these curious little 'books' has become fairly familiar through the descriptions and reproductions of bibliographers. Books they are indeed,
though hand-made, with elaborate title-pages, prefaces,
and colophons containing signature and date. They vary
in size from miniatures 1½ × 1¼ inches to large octa-
vos. The leaves are usually carefully sewed together inside a cover of blue or brown wrapping paper. Their
texts are executed in a minute hand-printing impossible
to read except under a strong glass. A few of the stories
have been printed and more or less widely distributed,
but it is doubtful if as many as a dozen persons, including even the author, have known the juvenilia as a
whole; and it is only as a whole that they assume biographical and critical importance.

Except for the Introduction to **"Tales of the Islanders"**
and a portion of the **"History of the Year,"** quoted to
illustrate Charlotte's unusual precocity and the strange
home life of the Brontë children, Mrs. Gaskell made no
use of the manuscripts which she lists. Unused and ap-

parently unread, they were returned to Mr. Nicholls. After lying forty years in his desk with their mailing wrap-
per unbroken, they were purchased from him by Mr.
Shorter for Mr. Thomas J. Wise. A few of the manuscripts Mr. Wise kept for himself and friends, the rest
he allowed to become scattered among private collectors of England and America, who have valued them
only as literary curiosities. A large number of them
have, fortunately, found their way into the hands of a
collector in Philadelphia, whose kindness in lending me
transcripts of them has made my study possible.

Mr. Shorter, like Mrs. Gaskell, made no use of the
manuscripts as they passed through his hands except to
list them. After a brief general description, he dismisses
them with one sentence: "Perhaps the only juvenile
fragment which is worth anything is also the only one
in which she escapes from the Wellington enthusiasm."

The story exempted from Mr. Shorter's general condemnation is **"An Adventure in Ireland,"** dated April,
1829, a childish fairy tale written under the influence of
Arabian Nights. In stating that this is the only story in
which Charlotte escapes from the "Wellington enthusiasm," Mr. Shorter is mistaken, but he errs more seriously, I think, in pronouncing all the others worthless.

When Charlotte was but thirteen years old she wrote a
story which she called **"The Twelve Adventurers,"** in
which twelve of her favorite heroes, including the Duke
of Wellington, are shipwrecked on the coast of Africa,
near the mouth of the Niger River. By the help of the
genii who rule the land they overcome the hostile blacks
and found a city. At the end of twenty years, when the
population of the settlement had grown to 15,000, the
Duke of Wellington was unanimously chosen as "a fit
and proper person to sit on the throne of these realms."

Other stories followed, extending and developing the
situation created in the first. The city, called at first
Glass Town, later Verdopolis, grows with the rapidity of
magic. It is soon the commercial metropolis of the
world, "the Queen City of Neptune," beautiful above all
others for situation, with magnificent public buildings
and residences. The element of magic disappears, for
Charlotte soon outgrew the influence of *Arabian Nights,*
but Verdopolis continues to expand. In the course of
time it spreads northward up the Valley of the Niger
and sends out colonies into the fertile lands to the east,
until there is evolved a far-flung empire of unrivalled
wealth and power.

The government is at first a simple confederacy of
twelve free states, ruled by the twelve original heroes
or their descendants, under the leadership of the Duke
of Wellington. In the course of the second generation
the Verdopolitan Confederacy is subverted by Arthur
Wellesley, Marquis of Douro, elder son of the Duke.

This young man, after saving his country in a military crisis, demands the cession of three of the richest provinces to himself in full sovereignty and control, to be known as the Kingdom of Angria. His successive titles, Duke of Zamorna, King of Angria, and Emperor Adrian, tell the story of his continued aggressions and usurpations.

Through all the Verdopolitan and Angrian stories, except the very early ones in which his father holds the center of the stage, this tyrant moves as the arch-hero with a supremacy of interest which Mr. Shorter terms Charlotte's "Wellington enthusiasm." The term loses its aptness when applied to the second half of the cycle and becomes even misleading, for by this time the Duke of Wellington has disappeared from the scene, and in his son there remains only the reminiscence of the Wellesley name. He has become the typical Byronic hero, supreme and unrestrained. One might now more properly speak of Charlotte's Byron enthusiasm.

The composition of the Angrian Cycle, if the term be used to include the earlier stories of Verdopolis, covered a period of ten years or more, and the group includes every form of literature known to its young authors—essays, poems, dramas, short sketches, and novels—more than a hundred in number. To its astonishing volume Charlotte and Branwell Brontë seem to have contributed about equally, for from the very founding of Verdopolis, Branwell had added his effusions to his sister's, introducing some very interesting, if incongruous, elements. It was he who brought revolution and war into Verdopolitan politics and created the Kingdom of Angria. His contributions, usually wildly imaginative, confused, contradictory, and verbose, Charlotte accepted without question and transmuted by her genius into an integral, natural, and permanent part of the whole. Indeed, no character or situation, whether of Charlotte's or Branwell's creation, was ever lost. So easily and naturally did each catch up and use the conceptions of the other that it is impossible to separate their contributions with certainty.

In this imaginary world of her own creation Charlotte lived and moved from her thirteenth to her twenty-third year. It was her playground in childhood and her land of refuge in the troubled years of young womanhood. To it she transferred all she knew of life, whether from her wide reading or her own narrow experiences, and to its creation she devoted the whole force of her genius. Written with the intimacy and frankness of a diary and with far less self-consciousness, the Angrian stories picture clearly the development of Charlotte's mind, emotions, and views of life during her formative years.

How vividly Charlotte's mind realized Angria, both the land and its people, is betrayed by innumerable passages such as follow, written in the course of her unhappy months of teaching in Miss Wooler's school.

I now after a day of weary wandering return to the ark which for me floats alone on the flood of this world's desolate and boundless deluge. It is strange that I cannot get used to the ongoings that surround me. . . . It is the still small voice alone that comes to me at eventide that—like a breeze with a voice in it—over the deeply blue hills and out of the now leafless forests and from the cities on distant river banks of a far and bright continent, it is that which takes my spirit and engrosses all my living feelings, all my energies which are not merely mechanical. . . . Last night I did indeed lean upon the thunder-waking wings of such a stormy blast as I have seldom heard blow, and it whirled me away like heath in the wilderness for five seconds of ecstacy. As I sat by myself in the dining room, while all the rest were at tea, the trance seemed to descend on a sudden. Verily this foot trod the war-shaken shores of the Calebar and these eyes saw the defiled and violated Adrianopolis shedding its lights on the river from lattices whence the invader looked out.

. . . . The other day I appeared to realize a delicious hot day in the burning height of summer, a gorgeous afternoon . . . descending upon the hills of Africa, . . . a day when fruits visibly ripen, when orchards appear suddenly to change from green to gold over the distant Sydenham Hills in Hawkscliffe Forest. . . . It seemed to me that the war was over, that the trumpet had ceased but a short time since, and that its last tones had been pitched on a triumphant key. . . . After months of bloody toil a time of festal rest was now bestowed on Angria. The noblemen, the generals, and the gentlemen were at their country seats and the Duke, young but war-worn, was at Hawkscliffe, stupendous still in influence.

All this day I have been in a dream. . . . I sat sinking from irritation and weariness into a kind of lethargy. . . . I flung up the sash. An uncertain sound of inexpressible sweetness came on a dying gale from the south. . . . I shut the window and went back to my seat. Then came on me, rushing impetuously, all the mighty phantasm that this had conjured from nothing to a system as strong as some religious creed. I felt as if I could have written gloriously. The spirit of all Verdopolis, of all the mountainous North, of all the woodland West, of all the river-watered East, came crowding into my mind. If I had had time to indulge it, I felt that the vague suggestion of that moment would have settled down into some narrative better than anything I ever produced before. But just then a dolt came up with a lesson. . . .

Charlotte had apparently passed her twenty-third birthday when she bade farewell to Angria and her Angrians in a paragraph which constitutes a landmark in her literary career.

I have now written a great many books and for a long time have dwelt on the same characters and scenes and subjects. I have shown my landscape in every variety of shade and light that morning, noon, and evening—the rising, the meridian, and the setting sun can bestow on them. . . . So it is with persons. . . . But we must change, for the eye is tired of the picture so often recurring and now so familiar.

Yet do not hurry me too fast, reader. It is no easy task to dismiss from my imagination the images which have filled it so long; they were my friends and intimate acquaintances, and I could with little labour describe to you the faces, the voices, the actions of those who peopled my thoughts by day and not seldom stole strangely even into my dreams at night. . . . Still, I long to quit for a time that burning clime where we have sojourned too long. Its skies flame, the glow of sunset is always upon it. The mind would cease from excitement and turn now to a cooler region, where the dawn breaks gray and sober and the coming day for a time at least is subdued by clouds.

Had either of the two biographers who have had access to the Angrian cycle made more adequate use of it, little of the familiar speculative and controversial Bronteana would have been written, for to most of the disputed questions these stories afford conclusive answers.

In the first place the stories furnish an accurate record of Charlotte's reading through her most impressionable years and reflect the successive influences under which her own style evolved. Into her imaginary world, along with characters drawn from her reading and imagination, she projected herself, her brother and sisters, and other familiar figures. Accordingly, the Angrian literature becomes an important piece of family and neighborhood biography. Her teasing satires of Branwell, woven throughout the Cycle, are particularly illuminating, and, together with his own stories, enable the reader accurately to estimate the nature and extent of her literary debt to her brother.

It has been the universal custom to take *The Professor* as the earliest of Charlotte's novels and the starting point for critical study. The contrast between its commonplace dullness and the fire and passion of *Jane Eyre* has led to interesting attempts at explanation, chief of which is the well known theory that Charlotte, while in school at Brussels, conceived a passion for her teacher, M. Heger, which fired her latent genius into activity. Miss May Sinclair, on the other hand, suggests that it was Emily's *Wuthering Heights* which roused Charlotte's latent talent for emotional and dramatic writing.

The Angrian stories, however, disprove both theories by showing that Charlotte's genius had no sudden awakening, but developed normally and gradually. The record of its development from month to month, from year to year, through her childhood and early womanhood, is not to be disputed. By the time that Charlotte took leave of Angria in the paragraph quoted above she had developed all the best characteristics of her literary style. The simplicity and realism, the passion, the flights of imagination, and the lyrical quality of her prose at its best in *Jane Eyre* and *Villette* had all been displayed re-

peatedly before *The Professor* was written. In truth, *The Professor*, in its attempt to establish a "set of principles," shows the conscious imposition of a self-discipline against the long indulgence of her imagination and emotions, which characterizes her subsequent work. *Jane Eyre* is a partial return to her natural style of expression.

The conclusion to which one is forced upon re-reading Charlotte Brontë's published novels in the light of the Angrian Cycle is that after she quitted Angria, that is after her twenty-third year, she created nothing. She modified, re-shaped, and adapted in conformity with her two adult experiences—teaching and study in Brussels—but she *created* practically nothing. The characters, plot incidents, and general situations which make up *The Professor, Jane Eyre, Shirley,* and *Villette* were all drawn from her Angrian storehouse.

When she bade goodbye to Africa for England she brought with her the dear and familiar characters. Fortunately there are extant fragments showing the successive steps by which her Angrian lords and ladies were transformed into ordinary English men and women. A few examples will support these statements. The opening chapters of *The Professor* are a subdued and condensed version of a chapter of a story, "Wool is Rising," written by Branwell Brontë and dated June 26, 1834. The remainder of the book is drawn from other stories concerning the same characters, as Charlotte herself adapted and continued them throughout the Angrian cycle. Names, situations, phrases, and even whole paragraphs are identical. The only new element in the story is the Belgian setting. Even the name of the Belgian school-mistress, Zoraïde, at which Charlotte pokes fun—"the continental nations do allow themselves vagaries in the choice of names such as we sober English never run into"—is borrowed from one of her own Angrian heroines. Two distinct versions of *The Professor* are found among the transition fragments mentioned above, but curiously enough the published version is nearer than either of the others to the original.

Shirley furnishes an even better example than *The Professor*, both because it is further removed from Angria in time of composition and because it has a much greater number of characters. Shirley herself is the continuation of an Angrian beauty, named Jane Moore, who represented Emily Bronte. She is the only character in Charlotte's published novels who retains her Angrian halo of happiness and good fortune. Robert and Louis Moore are counterparts of the originals of Edward and William Crimsworth in *The Professor*; Sir Philip Nunnely is a lineal descendant of "young Soult, the Rhymer," a character under which Charlotte early began satirizing her brother's propensity for writing verse. The curates, though apparently drawn from living models, had their Angrian prototype in one Henry

Warner. The mill-strike and the shooting of Robert Moore from ambush have their earlier sketch in a Verdopolitan story without a title, dated August 20, 1832, of a strike and the shooting of Colonel Greenville. The use which Charlotte here makes of the Methodists as literary material is a subdued and restrained reworking of earlier and less merciful satires on this denomination, which are among the best things she ever did.

Both Rochester, in *Jane Eyre,* and John Bretton, in *Villette,* are derived from her arch-hero, Arthur Wellesley, with different sides of his varied nature emphasized and modified under different influenzas. The much discussed Paul Emanuel is preëminently an Angrian. One would hardly expect to find among the gay and brilliant women of Angria the prototype of Jane Eyre and Lucy Snowe, yet near the end of the cycle she appears once in the person of Miss Hastings, the companion and foil of Jane Moore, "the Rose of Zamorna," and again as Miss West, governess to the daughters of Mr. Lonsdale.

Many of the incidents which direct the plots of both *Jane Eyre* and *Villette* have either evident originals or very suggestive parallels in the juvenilia. Rochester's mad wife; Jane's betrayal of her love to Rochester in the garden; and the mysterious exchange of call and answer between the two had been used before in connection with Arthur Wellesley. Similarly in *Villette* many incidents usually considered autobiographical are echoes from Angrian stories written long before the supposed incident in Charlotte's own life could have occurred. Among these are the voice bidding Lucy to try her fortune in a foreign land; her feverish dream while left alone in Madam Beck's school during the long vacation; the effect of the opiate administered to her by Madam Beck; the visitations of the ghostly nun; the gay concert scene; and many others. Even the description in *Villette* of Rachel's acting of Vashti before the royalty and fashionable world of Brussels bears more than an accidental likeness to a purely imaginary description of Mrs. Siddons' acting of a native tragedy before the royalty and nobility of Verdopolis.

These assertions, I am well aware, in order to carry conviction, must be supported by more extensive quotations from the text of the Angrian stories than is possible in the present paper. This proof I hope later to submit in a longer work now in preparation.

Margaret Howard Blom (essay date 1977)

SOURCE: Blom, Margaret Howard. "Early Unpublished Writings." In *Charlotte Brontë,* pp. 37-60. Boston: Twayne, 1977.

[*In the following essay, Blom describes the plot, setting, and characters of Brontë's Angrian stories, at the same time noting her increasingly realistic approach to writ-*ing. *Blom describes in detail Brontë's attention in the later stories to the psychological motivations of her characters, arguing that the themes of the Angrian cycle—the violence of sexual desire, the impulse to self-destruction, and the loss of identity—are those that also figure most prominently in Brontë's novels.*]

When Charlotte Brontë wrote in the preface to *The Professor* that this first novel was the product of a "pen . . . worn a good deal in a practice of some years," she was referring to a long literary apprenticeship spent compulsively chronicling the events which occurred in her imaginary "infernal world." This early material—written between 1829 and 1839, and comprising hundreds of thousands of words—richly deserves attention, since it not only illuminates Charlotte's adult novels but also offers a unique opportunity to examine a great novelist's technical development and the means by which she remodels private fantasies to suit the demands of her conscience and her public.

A study of the juvenilia is no easy task, for the individual manuscripts are the component parts of a complex saga which describes in particular detail the political and social history of the imaginary West African kingdom of Angria and the Glasstown Confederacy of which Angria is a part. During her ten-year apprenticeship, Charlotte obsessively returned again and again to this subject; instead of abandoning old characters, settings, and situations for new ones, she chose to revise, refine, and retell her story. The intensity of her fascination is made clear in her descriptions of the creative process which produced Glasstown and Angria: the world she wrote about seemed to her to have an independent existence; it possessed her so completely that she frequently closed her eyes and allowed her pen to move automatically over the page. Thus she speaks not of *inventing* these realms, but of being lifted by vision to see and hear what is happening in another world:

> Never shall I, Charlotte Brontë, forget what a voice of wild and wailing music now came thrillingly to my mind's—almost to my body's—ear; nor how distinctly I, sitting in the schoolroom at Roe-head, saw the Duke of Zamorna leaning against that obelisk, with the mute marble Victory above him, the fern waving at his feet, his black horse turned loose grazing among the heather, the moonlight so mild and so exquisitely tranquil, sleeping upon that vast and vacant road, and the African sky quivering and shaking with stars expanded above all. I was quite gone. I had really utterly forgot where I was and all the gloom and cheerlessness of my situation.[1]

Unable and, in part, unwilling to free herself from her visionary world, Charlotte tried as she grew older to remodel its details in conformity with insights afforded by her increasing aesthetic and psychological maturity. As she sought to explain the motives which underlay actions she had so vividly imagined in the past, she continually reexamined key incidents in the plot and elaborated upon their cause and consequence. The resulting Byzantine complexities of the juvenilia make it necessary to summarize the major stages in the development of the plot and the relationships of the major characters before attempting a critical commentary.

I Actors, Setting, and Plot

For several years before the Brontë children began to record their fantasies in writing, they created tales about the activities of Branwell's wooden soldiers, to whom they had assigned names and personalities. Each child became the protector of one special soldier: Emily and Anne chose for their particular attention Parry and Ross, named for the Arctic explorers William Edward Parry and John Ross; Branwell, whose original choice had been Bonaparte, renamed his hero Sneaky; Charlotte chose as her special favorite the Duke of Wellington. The story which gradually evolved took the "Young Men," as the soldiers were collectively known, to the West Coast of Africa. Here, with the help of despotic Genii (the children themselves), the Young Men defeated the aboriginal inhabitants in a fierce war and established the Glasstown Confederacy made up of four provinces—Parrysland, Rossesland, Sneakysland, and Wellingtonsland. In 1829, inspired by his love of *Blackwood's,* a popular magazine, Branwell began writing tiny booklets containing articles and poems chronicling the activities of the soldiers. Charlotte was his eager collaborator, and from 1829 until 1831, when she was sent away to Roe Head School, she also wrote accounts of the establishment and development of the Glasstown Confederacy under the rule of her particular hero, the Duke of Wellington, and his two sons, Arthur (also known as Lord Douro) and Charles Wellesley. A main source of the drama in the early materials derives from these three essentially virtuous characters' conflict with Branwell's new hero, Rogue, a proto-Byronic villain. While at school, Charlotte had little time to write, but during vacation periods, she contributed to the story, which during her absence, Branwell both expanded and particularized with new details of past and present political and military history. Meanwhile, Emily and Anne abandoned Glasstown and established Gondal, their own fantasy kingdom.

Her education at Roe Head completed, Charlotte returned home in 1832 and began anew to collaborate with Branwell on the Glasstown saga, which underwent a major transformation as the result of new events in both the political and domestic spheres. Arthur Wellesley, Lord Douro, gradually usurped his father's dominant position in Charlotte's writing; and as he gained importance, Charlotte altered his character, adding more and more Byronic qualities, chief among which were a magnetic power over and a cavalier attitude toward women. In earlier sketches, Charlotte described Douro's romantic love for a sweet, passive young girl, Marian Hume, whom he eventually married and who bore him a son; but in 1833, both Charlotte and Branwell moved their focus to Douro's relationship with a new heroine, Mary Percy—daughter of Rogue, now known as Alexander Percy.

Douro and Mary love passionately at first sight; and Marian, knowing she is powerless to command her husband's fidelity, dies of a broken heart. Douro, having given his infant son into the keeping of his mistress Mina Laury, marries Mary, whom he soon begins to torture with hints of his marital infidelity. As Douro's private life undergoes these dramatic changes, his public role is also transformed; after blocking Napoleon's invasion of the land east of the Glasstown Confederacy, Douro demands through Percy, now his ally, that parliament grant him sovereignty over the area he defended. When his demand is met, a new kingdom called Angria—comprised of the provinces of Etrei, Calabar, Douro, Arundel, Northangerland, Zamorna, and Angria—is formed under the control of Douro, who receives the titles of Duke of Zamorna and Emperor Adrian of Angria.

Douro, now commonly referred to as Zamorna, and his wife Mary soon fall prey to the machinations of her father, Percy. Although Zamorna has rewarded his father-in-law with the title of Earl of Northangerland and with the position of prime minister, Percy is dissatisfied; and motivated by ambition and jealousy, he creates trouble for Zamorna in the Angrian parliament and among the citizenry. The manuscripts of 1834 and 1836 describe the outbreak and progress of a long war in which Zamorna struggles to maintain control of a kingdom that is threatened by internal rebellion and by invasion.

Although Charlotte began her three-year career as a teacher at Miss Wooler's School in the summer of 1835, during school holidays she eagerly returned to the Angrian saga and contributed a series of writings which concentrated on the psychological effect of the rebellion on Zamorna, Mary, Percy, and Mina Laury. In accounts written in 1837, the final phase of Angria's history begins when Zamorna triumphs over his foes and reinstates Mary as his queen after having earlier abandoned her as a means of revenging himself upon his father-in-law. Charlotte's last Angrian manuscripts deal with Zamorna's increasingly complex affairs of the heart and focus primarily on his relationships with two of his mistresses, Mina Laury and Caroline Vernon, and with his bitterly jealous wife, Mary.

II Guilt and Growing Mastery

At the age of twenty-three, Charlotte consciously severed relations with this fictional world, because she had come to feel that the mental activity which produced it was dangerously seductive; but ironically, in rejecting Angrian characters and history, she cast out only that material which had come to limit rather than to facilitate her exploration of the themes of passion thwarted and unleashed, violence, and threatened identity which are the essential core of her imaginative vision. During the ten years she wrote about her "world below," her emotions, insights, and understanding matured; but the heroes and heroines of her adult novels, like those she wrote about in childhood, are always the victims of their own violent emotions and of others' unpredictable malevolence.

The childish ingenuity—even crudity—of the literary devices to which Charlotte resorted as a young author may have served to focus her attention on and to sustain her interest in violence and passion. For example, recourse to the simple explanation "magic was at work" enabled her to dismiss the laws of causality and to explore with unrestrained relish incidents which, without supernatural intervention, would result in an early termination of the saga. Since the Genii who ruled the destinies of all could resurrect a hero or a villain, Charlotte could safely revel in the treacherous murder of her hero, in the murderer's cynical refusal to repent, and in his horrible punishment of death by torture.[2] Magic also permitted a tentative, safe exploration of subjects too advanced, complex, or even distasteful for realistic treatment by a young, ambitious author. Attracted to the theme of sexual passion, jealousy, and betrayal in even her earliest writing, Charlotte employs supernatural intervention to avoid difficult material, as in **"The Fairy Gift"** (1830), in which a sprite rescues the hero from his insane wife's sexual jealousy, or as in **"The Bridal"** (1832), in which the Byronic hero's marital infidelity is excused on the grounds that his mistress used magic to lure the passionate man away from his wife.

But it must be stressed that Charlotte avoided such material only because it was for the moment beyond her literary powers, not because of her inhibitions: early and late, the most striking quality of her fictional world is its violence. In the adult novels, characters smolder with rage and desire which only occasionally breaks out into physical action but which consistently drives them to brutalize others psychologically. In Glasstown and Angria, physical restraint is unknown; and the basic plot line focuses on war, rebellion, political chaos, and family disintegration. The central incident in the earliest narration is the destruction of the aboriginal Ashantee tribe after "many bloody and obstinate battles" which reduce the land to "the wildest and most appalling desolation which the mind of man can conceive of."[3]

Once in control of the disputed territory, the English colonists—men who consider cruelty and pride to be the requisites of power and the hallmarks of nobility—establish a strife-torn society. The very descriptions of

the Angrian leaders suggest their proud, tempestuous natures. Charlotte's first hero, the great Duke of Wellington, whose "appearance came up to [the] highest notions of what a great General ought to be," has a "stern forehead, noble Roman nose, compressed disdainful lip" and "a certain expression of sarcasm about his mouth which showed that he considered many of those with whom he associated much beneath him" (*MUW* [*The Miscellaneous and Unpublished Writings of Charlotte and Patrick Branwell Brontë in Two Volumes*], I, 37). Percy has a "polished" manner, but "his mind is deceitful, bloody, and cruel" (*MUW,* I, 42). Lord Douro, originally "mild and humane but very courageous, grateful for any favour that is done, and ready to forgive injuries" (*MUW,* I, 38), becomes the Byronic Zamorna, a "keen, glorious being," whose "glancing" eyes "bode no good": "Man nor woman could ever gather more than a troubled, fitful happiness from their kindest light. Satan gave them their glory to deepen the midnight gloom that always follows where their lustre has fallen most lovingly" (*MUW,* I, 361).

These vicious, proud men control not so much a society as a mob of ruthless individualists who, bound together only by proximity, feel no need to inhibit their fierce passions. In such a world, the common forms of courtesy are disregarded; in fact, as a matter of course, the winner of a debate is "challenged . . . to single combat" (*MUW,* I, 58); a man who marries above his station is openly "despised" by his guests and "insulted . . . with impunity" by his servants (*MUW,* I, 55). The common folk of the city witness impassively as two of "some 20 or 30 naked, lean, miserable-looking children" are cast into a "fiery brazier" where they "fling themselves into all imaginable attitudes, till their extremities [are] entirely consumed" (*MUW,* I, 229-30).

The family unit is torn by the same violence which rends the fabric of city and state; for brother turns against brother; and parents, children, husbands, and wives battle murderously. The Wellesley brothers are filled with such hatred for one another that Charles tells a vicious story about his brother's faithlessness "out of malignity for the injuries that have lately been done me";[4] and in another tale, his brother, Douro, savagely beats Charles and then threatens to "hardly leave a strip of skin on his carcass" if he offends again (*LA* [*Legends of Angria*], 7). In **"The Fairy Gift,"** a witch-wife rushes upon her husband, who has discovered her magic rites, and attempts to strangle him (*MUW,* I, 56). Maddened by jealousy, Percy turns on his wife, saying, "You shall not die the easy death of having your brains blown out. No! I'll thrust this sharp blade slowly through you, that you may feel and enjoy the torture" (*MUW,* I, 260).

As Charlotte passed from childhood and adolescence to maturity, her increased experience, perception, and technical ability modify the Angrian world. Verisimilitude takes precedence over the fantastic. Perhaps the most obvious indication of the increasing realism of her work appears in late stories such as **"Mina Laury"** (1838) and **"Caroline Vernon"** (1839), in which the nominally African landscape comes to resemble that of northern England and Yorkshire: "The air is dimmed with snow careering through it in wild whirls—the sky is one mass of congealed tempest—heavy, wan, & icy—the trees rustle their frozen branches against each other in a blast bitter enough to flay alive the flesh that should be exposed to its sweep."[5] Yorkshire dialect, attitudes, and concerns also intrude. A bluff, blunt military man dismisses his wife's terrifying dreams in accents which recall Joseph's speech in *Wuthering Heights* (*MUW,* II, 384), and another character pokes cynical fun at the assumed piety of his landlord and the activities of Methodist Ranters in a scene set not in the never-never land of Angria but in mid-nineteenth-century Yorkshire (*MUW,* II, 281-82).

Deriving great satisfaction from realistic portrayal, Charlotte worked consciously to remodel her fictional world. In 1836 she invokes her muse to "paint to the life," "detail with graphic skill," "scribe so well that each separate voice shall speak out of the page in changeful tone," and "shew us even those details that give truest life to the picture," for all these characteristics have the power to "astonish us" (*MUW,* II, 125). Charlotte's invocation is highly significant, for it reveals her changed attitude toward her materials, a change dictated by growing awareness of a new sort of involvement in the writer's craft. Later in the same year, Charlotte describes the pleasure given her by one of Branwell's Angrian accounts, and her delight derives not from entering vicariously into represented dramatic action but from feeding her imagination on scenes carefully and realistically delineated in minute detail:

> About a week since I got a letter from Branwell containing a most exquisitely characteristic [Angrian] epistle. . . . I lived on its contents for days; in every pause of employment it came chiming in like some sweet bar of music—bringing with it agreeable thoughts such as I had for many weeks been a stranger to— some representing scenes such as might arise in consequence of that unexpected letter, some unconnected with it, referring to other events, another set of feelings. These were not striking and stirring scenes of incident—no—they were tranquil and retired in their character, such as might every day be witnessed in the inmost circles of highest society. A curtain seemed to rise and discover to me the Duchess as she might appear when newly risen and lightly dressed for the morning—discovering her father's letter in the contents of the mail which lies on her breakfast-table. There seems nothing in such an idea as that, but the localities of the picture were so graphic, the room so distinct, the clear fire of morning, the window looking upon no object but a cold October sky, except when you draw very near and look down on a terrace far beneath, and, at a still dizzier distance, on a green court with a fountain

and rows of stately limes—beyond, a wide road and wider river, and a vast metropolis.

(MUW, II, 256-57)

The pleasure Charlotte received from the imaginative contemplation and creation of scenes realistically portrayed marks the last accounts of her fantasy world. In **"Caroline Vernon,"** Wellesley House, the home of the ruler of Angria, retains its grand title but shrinks to a suburban villa. The Duke and Duchess of Zamorna shed the garments of romance to become a blustering, guilty husband and a foolish, protective wife. Mary, whose tortured love for her erring Zamorna was once the most interesting and pathetic of subjects to Charlotte, becomes an unperceptive, jealous, doting housewife waiting up to interrogate a husband guilty of keeping late hours; Zamorna, her husband, once described as a figure of "faultless elegance" with "features . . . regularly beautiful" (*MUW,* I, 241), is shown "stepp[ing] on his toes like a magnified dancing-master." He who once drew all women to him with a glance, now creeps into his darkened house like "a large Tom-Cat" (*FN* [*Five Novelettes*], 331).

Charlotte's handling of the romantic dreams of Caroline Vernon, her last Angrian heroine, indicates clearly that the maturing artist has not only viewed her past imaginative ventures with detached amusement but has also realized the literary potential of objective—even ironic—introspection and description; for what she here presents as being ridiculous fantasy actually parodies many passages in her earlier writings:

> . . . something there was of a Hero—yet a nameless, a formless, a mystic being—a dread shadow—that crowded upon Miss Vernon's soul—haunted her day & night when she had nothing useful to occupy her head or her hands—I almost think she gave him the name of Ferdinand Alonzo Fitz-Adolphus, but I don't know— the fact was he frequently changed his designation— being sometimes no more than simple Charles Seymour or Edward Clifford, & at other times soaring to the titles of Harold, Aurelius Rinaldo, Duke of Montmorency di Valdacella—a very fine man no doubt— though whether he was to have golden or raven hair or straight or acquiline proboscis she had not quite decided—however, he was to drive all before him in the way of fighting—to conquer the world & build himself a city like Babylon—only it was to be in the moorish style—& there was to be a palace called the Alhambra—where Mr Harold Aurelius was to live, taking upon himself the title of Caliph, & she, Miss C. Vernon, the professor of Republican principles, was to be his chief Lady & to be called the Sultana Zara-Esmerelda—with at least a hundred slaves to do her bidding—as for the gardens of roses & the Halls of Marble & the diamonds & fine pearls & the rubies—it would be vanity to attempt a description of such heavenly sights—the reader must task his imagination & try if he can conceive them.

(FN, 312-13)

Charlotte's growing interest in realism and her increasing perception and technical skill lead her to probe the complexity of character. The idea that appearances belie reality, hinted at in the earliest pieces by figures who are witches and magicians in disguise, becomes a dominant concern in later works and leads to her analysis of the complex emotional states that play a role in an involved response to life. After Zamorna's defeat by the Angrian rebels and his subsequent exile, Charlotte turns her attention in **"The Return of Zamorna"** (1836-1837) to the reaction of his deserted wife, Mary Henrietta. Although Charlotte follows the convention of the day by describing her grief-stricken heroine's fall into a physical decline, the ambitious young author does not rest content with convention; rather, she probes deeply into Mary's emotional state, matching psychological insight with impressive literary technique. When Mary rises "wan and pallid from the bed that a month since it seemed she would never leave again," she enters a terrible existence: her body lives, but her soul has died. Unable to bear the memory of the past she has lost, she is unable to accept the present to which it has led; thus, her identity is stripped from her, for to call herself either mother or wife is to remind herself of happiness that is forever gone. The stirring of memories she is desperate to repress is suggested both by her question "was I ever married?" and by the fact that although she "continued to wear round her neck, a little miniature of the Duke . . . she never opened the case that contained it."

Fearing to unlock the past, she walks in a trance through the maze of corridors in her winter-besieged palace. Her spiritual deadness is objectified in falling leaves and autumnal groves, symbols of sterility and death, and the aimless wandering of her body through endless, echoing passages suggests the confused straying of her mind through the labyrinth of past experience: "The last days of Autumn were now dimly closing. . . . the leaf-strewn walks and embrowned groves of Alnwick prophesied how nigh were the snows of Winter. . . . Too feeble to bear the chill . . . , she never walked but in the lengthened and sounding corridors . . . and there all day long the light rustle of her dress might be heard as she traversed the measured walk with noiseless and languid tread, more like a flitting shade than a living woman" (*MUW,* II, 285-87).

There is yet another level of significance in Charlotte's description. As Angria's queen drifts through a decaying world, her war-torn nation sinks toward death. The impression of destruction which permeates the entire passage culminates in the image of the pearl-like tear which falls from Mary's eye. Consistently described as ornamented with "chains" and rings of pearl, Mary is herself "a priceless pearl which a strong man had found and which he kept and guarded jealously" (*MUW,* II, 27); now the strong man is gone; the rich setting of

Zamorna Palace, with its "warm lights" and "rich deep sombre hangings" (*MUW,* II, 26), has been ravaged. And the tear on Mary's eyelid, which falls "like a single pearl on the pavement" (*MUW,* II, 286), is symbolic of Mary herself, the most treasured, the most guarded jewel of the kingdom. The destruction is complete: physically and mentally, Mary dies; and her land and her world die with her.

III PERCY AND ZAMORNA

The impulse toward self-destruction which is implicit in this description of Mary's responses continued to intrigue Charlotte and ultimately became the focus of her juvenile writings. As her growing insights and technical ability enabled her to provide more complex character sketches of the individuals engaged in the never-ending series of battles upon which Branwell insisted, she began to use the framework of war to probe into the problem of psychic conflict; for she saw political strife as emblematic of and stemming from ambivalent and mutually destructive internal impulses. The very fact that the two men who most actively attempt to overthrow Emperor Zamorna are bound to him by familial and quasi-familial ties intensified her perception that actual and potential warfare is symbolic of the tearing apart of what is by nature a single unit: Quashia, who threatens to invade Angria and to drive out the English colonists, was raised as Zamorna's foster brother; Percy, who foments internal rebellion, is Zamorna's surrogate father, father-in-law, prime minister, and spiritual twin.

The relationship between Percy and Zamorna—which was from the beginning the crucial source of conflict in the overall plot of the saga—increasingly tantalized Charlotte as she strove to provide psychological motivation for the actions she and Branwell in their earliest writings had attributed to these two central figures. Again and again she returns to the intriguing riddle of the bond that unites the two in mutual ruin; and her awareness of her fascination with this topic is apparent when, at one point, after having once again recapitulated the history of the Zamorna-Percy relationship, she remarks: "All this I have written before, but the subject is a strange one and will bear recurring to, and the fact is, when I once get upon the topic . . . I cannot help running on in the old track at a most unconscionable rate" (*MUW,* II, 361).

Gradually, Charlotte perceives and clarifies a meaningful pattern in the interaction between these two men, Percy and Zamorna. Drawing upon Grecian and Christian tradition, using ideas gleaned from Shakespeare, Milton, and Byron, Charlotte finally interprets the political battle between Zamorna and Percy as the epic struggle of beings bound together by a mutual love and hate for each other and for themselves. In one of her last Angrian pieces, **"The Duke of Zamorna"** (1838), she attempts to bring together the pieces of the psychological puzzle. Four years earlier, in **"The Wool Is Rising,"** Branwell had explained that Percy, fearing his young sons had inherited his own evil nature, condemned them to death.[6] Making use of this information to illuminate the background of the confederacy between Percy and Zamorna, Charlotte now describes how Percy, "spent almost with sin" after the infanticide, chose young Douro as his "confidant" and revealed to him "the tenderest, the holiest feeling his heart had ever known."

Although, we are told, if Percy "had discerned anything like attachment to his person in any other man or boy," he would have responded with "intense and eternal hate," he accepted Douro's "glances of feeling—clashing, ardent, enthusiastic" (*MUW,* II, 360). Too proud to serve another, Percy finds his love for Douro doubly intolerable, for it forces awareness of his emotional dependency upon him while winning him the subordinate position of prime minister in Zamorna's Angrian government. Thus Charlotte is able to support and clarify her previous assertion in **"The History of Angria III"** (1836) that Percy's rebellious acts, inexplicable in pragmatic terms, are indeed "not a disease in themselves, but merely the symptoms of some grand latent malady" (*MUW,* II, 139) in Percy's heart and soul.

Her analysis of Zamorna's motivation is much more complete. Always the central figure in Charlotte's Angrian writings, Zamorna is transformed from a Prince Charming, a child of good fortune, into a tortured and doomed man. Possessing a personal magnetism that gives him virtually total political and sexual power, Zamorna is driven by inner defects to destroy those he loves, his empire, and ultimately himself. Much of Charlotte's later Angrian material is devoted to an analysis of his complex character. In **"The History of Angria III,"** Charlotte remarks that "notwithstanding [Zamorna's] outside shew of rich vigorous health, . . . in the timber of this stately tree there was a flaw which would eat ere the lapse of many years to its heart" (*MUW,* II, 155). The flaw is his dependency upon Percy, who has betrayed him, but whom he continues against his will to love and to whom he believes his fate is linked by destiny. Conceiving of himself and Percy as two halves of a whole which seeks a dissolution that will bring ruin on itself and all about it, Zamorna says of his antagonist, "You are a fiend . . . I'm no better, and we two united / Each other's happiness have fiend-like blighted" (*MUW,* II, 240).

In Charlotte's writings, the civil war Percy instigates against Zamorna thus emblematizes and expresses the love-hate struggle of two men whose self-destructive rage encompasses the nation which they created together and which, therefore, represents to each a mutually hated interdependence. In **"The History of Angria III,"** Zamorna's supporters rightfully accuse him of seeking not so much military victory as private revenge; and Zamorna, although he remains adamant in his purpose, acknowledges the truth of this interpretation. Turning to his Home Secretary, General Warner, Zamorna announces,

> two living creatures in the world know the nature of the relations that have existed between Alexander Percy and myself. From the very beginning in my inmost soul, . . . I swore that if he broke those bonds and so turned to vanity and scattered in the air sacrifices that I had made and words that I had spoken; if he made as dust and nothingness causes for which I have endured jealousies and burning strife and emulations amongst those I loved; if he froze feelings that in me are like living fire, I would have revenge.
>
> (*MUW,* II, 156)

The relationship Zamorna here discusses is explained further in **"The Duke of Zamorna,"** written two years later. Charlotte recounts how Zamorna had once

> sought [Percy's] society—followed his footsteps—hung spellbound on his persuasive lips—insinuated his way to his confidence—. . . and Douro was not repulsed: he was retained—almost clung to.
>
> True [Percy] broke upon his young comrade sometimes with fury, and at other times he seemed to freeze and turn away with hollow coldness from his enthusiasm. This [Douro] felt at his heart's core.
>
> (*MUW,* II, 360)

Zamorna, therefore, sees Percy's overt political rebellion primarily as the last and most drastic of a series of emotional withdrawals and rejections. And his thwarted love for Percy drives him to seek military triumph over him as a means of gaining personal revenge and of proving his psychological dominance; but he foreknows that victory over Percy will be final defeat for himself, as he admits when he cries out in anguish and rage, "He has no heart and I'll rend mine from my bosom before its quick hot pulsations shall interfere with what I see, with what I feel, with what I anticipate by day and night. Why else were we born in one century? His sun should have set before mine rose, if their blended shining was not destined to set Earth on fire" (*MUW,* II, 30). Thus for Zamorna the political and military struggle against Percy is, in fact, the acting out of a death-wish, a suicide, the "tearing up [of] something whose roots had taken deep hold in [his] very heart of hearts" (*FN,* 137). He acknowledges that his battle with Percy produces a "mental anguish" which "shortens . . . my very brief allotment of life on earth. . . . I loved Percy, and what it is costing me to send him to the D—1!!" (*MUW,* II, 158).

So uncontrollable is Zamorna's desire for omnipotence that he would rather destroy the thing he loves than be thwarted in his desire to possess it totally: Angria, the nation he lovingly created; Mary, his adored wife; Percy, his beloved surrogate father—all become the targets of his hate and are destroyed by him in a series of actions which only increase his agony. By thus using the civil war that he wages with monomaniac fury as the expression of Zamorna's sadomasochistic tendencies, Charlotte establishes the link between sexual desire and the willingness to inflict and suffer pain which informs all her work. That she equates Zamorna's emperorship with aggressive sexual potency is apparent in his address to the kingdom he has willfully "ruined," for he remembers his days of political power as the time when

> I was king in thee,
> And when thy wildest mountains, heather palled,
> With all their iron vassalage knew me,
> And my land's daughters, now with bondage galled,
> Were as the Gordon red deer, chainless, free,
> And thousands of their ruby lips have known
> The touch of [Zamorna's] when he claims his own.
>
> (*MUW,* II, 246)

Angria had once been "gilded by [his] hand from the crown of [her] head to the sole of [her] foot," but she has been betrayed by her lover-king, who "should have been [her] mantle and . . . shield," her "warder, [her] counsellor." The effect of his "rashness . . . cruelty, [and] selfishness" (*MUW,* II, 162-63) is, significantly enough, presented as the symbolic rape of his queen, Mary, who is both an emblem of his nation and his deserted wife. Left free to invade the capital Zamorna has abandoned, Quashia, the savage aboriginal heir to the land, marches through the "defiled and violated" city, and at last enters into the undefended private rooms of the palace, where he lolls "intoxicated to ferocious insensibility" upon the couch of the Queen he has long desired:

> Aye, where she had lain imperially robed and decked with pearls, every waft of her garments as she moved diffusing perfume, her beauty slumbering and still glowing as dreams of [Zamorna] for whom she kept herself in such hallowed and shrine-like separation wandered over her soul, on her own silken couch [stretched] a swart and sinewy Moor. . . . I knew it to be Quashia himself, and well could I guess why he had chosen the Queen of Angria's sanctuary for the scene of his solitary revelling. . . . he was full before my eyes, lying in his black dress on the disordered couch, his sable hair dishevelled on his forehead, his tusk-like teeth gleaming vindictively through his parted lips, his brown complexion flushed with wine, and his broad chest heaving wildly as the breath issued in snorts from his distended nostrils.[7]

From 1836 to 1838 most of Charlotte's writings concern Zamorna's decision to make Mary suffer, even die, to achieve what he knows will be a Pyrrhic victory over Percy; and this concern leads Charlotte to probe ever more deeply into psychological complexities and to examine more fully her controlling theme of the destruc-

tive power of sexual desire. At one point, Mary says that Zamorna sees her as "the bodiless link between himself and my terrible father" (*MUW,* II, 147) whom Zamorna had "loved intensely" (*MUW,* II, 330) but who had defied his will and betrayed his love. Mary is the perfect victim not only because of the effect her agony and death will have upon her father but also because she is the incarnation of Percy in feminine form and thus, unlike her father, is susceptible to Zamorna's sexual charm:

> [Mary's] sweet eyes
> Showed in their varied lustre—changing, fleeing—
> Such warm and intense passion—that which lies
> In [Percy's] own breast and, save to the All-seeing,
> Not fully known to any, could not rise
> To stronger inspiration than their ray
> Revealed when I had waked her nature's wildest play.
>
> (*MUW,* II, 241)

These lines provide the key to the situation. Percy remains forever the enigma; the passions which govern him are fully divined only by the "All-seeing"; but Zamorna, by virtue of his sexual power, controls Mary totally: it is he who "waked her nature's wildest play." Unlike her father, she does not reject Zamorna's passion; instead, she delights in it, pleads for it, and will die without it:

> "Why have you chained me to you, [Zamorna], by
> Such days of bliss, such hours of sweet caressing,
> Such looks of glory, words of melody,
> Glimpses of all on earth that's worth possessing
> And now, when I must live with you or die
> Out of your sight distracted, every blessing
> Your hand withdraws, and, all my anguish scorning,
> You go and bid me hope for no returning?
>
> "[Zamorna], don't leave me—" then the gushing tears
> Smothered her utterance.
>
> (*MUW,* II, 328)

The equation of male potency and violence which runs throughout the Angrian writings is explicit in Zamorna's plan for victory: "In all but one quarter [Percy] is fortified and garrisoned. He can bid me [Zamorna] defiance, but one quarter [Mary] lies open to my javelin, and dipped in venom I will launch it quivering into his very spirit—so help me Hell!" (*MUW,* II, 156).

Because killing and loving are thus inextricably connected in this world, some of Charlotte's characters attempt to repress all emotion in order to avoid becoming either victims or victimizers. This response, only slightly touched upon in the Angrian writings, is fully developed in the adult novels: emotional withdrawal is chosen as a way of life by Yorke Hunsden, St. John Rivers, Mrs. Pryor, and the Reverend Helstone; it is seriously considered by Jane Eyre, Robert and Louis Moore, Lucy Snowe, Paul Emanuel, and William Crimsworth. The original of this last character is William Percy of the Angrian saga, who prides himself on having "denied [his] feelings . . . absolutely" (*MUW,* II, 390). Yet even as he thus congratulates himself, he realizes that he has imprisoned himself in a vast and empty wasteland. To him the people who crowd the thoroughfares of the capital are of no more significance than phantoms in a dream: he sees before him only a prospect of "wide Squares . . . long Streets"; and when he commands himself to "think again—surely some one breathes who will wish thee well," he admits, "I thought and thought—and all seemed vacant" (*MUW,* II, 392).

William's ability to choose an alienation so total that it is itself a kind of psychological suicide is unusual in the Angrian writings. Most of the characters in these manuscripts succumb totally and with little struggle to the passions which rage within them. Believing that human beings are by nature highly sexed, self-seeking, violent, and capable of brutality, Charlotte depicts sexual desire as an overwhelming force which robs both men and women of both the capacity and the will to defend the self against the innate aggressiveness of a lover. In the Angrian writings, all-engrossing passion blots out even the instinct for self-preservation; and the besotted individual, perceiving the sadomasochistic nature of the relationship into which he is ineluctably drawn, frequently sees death as the inevitable result, or even the equivalent of, sexual consummation. On the simplest level, the lover, therefore, offers himself willingly to the blood lust of his sexual rivals; and Lord Hartford's actions when he is spurned by Zamorna's mistress Mina Laury epitomizes this response. Knowing he can never possess her, he madly challenges Zamorna to a duel; and when a mediator attempts to intervene, saying "all is in vain, the lady in question can never be yours," Hartford answers, "I know that, Sir, & that is what makes me frantic—I have no motive left for living, & if Zamorna wants my blood, let him have it" (*FN,* 154).

In the 1836-1839 manuscripts, the focus of interest is on Zamorna's dealings with three women—Mary, Mina Laury, and Caroline Vernon; and Charlotte's treatment of these relationships suggests that men are capable of sexual response only when they subjugate and inflict pain on women and that women choose to submit themselves to sexual brutalization which leads to the loss of psychological and moral identity. Indeed, the story of Zamorna's sadistic victimization of his wife Mary, whose masochism makes her his willing accomplice, is the paradigm of sexual relationships in the early writings. In the poem **"And When You Left Me"** (1836), Zamorna, thinking about Mary's response to his brutality, suggests that on her own initiative she is pursuing a suicidal course: "She said she'd die for me—and now she's keeping / Her word far off at Alnwick o'er the sea" (*MUW,* II, 243).

Zamorna is quite right in his inference; for Mary, rejected by Zamorna and fearing he is dead, passively courts death by living "almost without food" and sitting "from morning to night in one place, almost in one position" (*MUW,* II, 287). Eventually, she consciously chooses death over a life of continued separation: "I adored him . . .—and Oh God, is that radiant, resistless being truly dead? Am I to feel rest for my aching agony no more? If this were my certain doom I would live not an instant longer" (*MUW,* II, 290). Returning to this theme in **"Well, the Day's Toil Is Over"** (1837), Charlotte examines the full extent of Mary's perverse nature, suggesting that she is most fully aroused sexually when she is most threatened. Thus at the moment when Mary understands the truth and says to Zamorna, "You love me, yet you'll kill me," she feels "an electric thrill and passion [wake] / In all her veins" (*MUW,* II, 327).

IV MINA LAURY AND CAROLINE VERNON

In Charlotte's final Angrian stories—written between 1838 and 1839—she continued to define the sexual myth which she had been slowly evolving and which is also central to the novels of her maturity. Her last two heroines, Mina Laury and Caroline Vernon, differ greatly from each other and from Mary Percy in social position, character, and psychological maturity; but all are willing victims of the brutal male lover—Zamorna. Overwhelmed by sexual desire, they renounce social standing and brush aside moral considerations to become his slaves; and though they recognize that their relationship with him entails suffering, they find perverse pleasure in such danger and in the fear that Zamorna's aggressive sexuality awakens in them. The heroines of the adult novels are sisters of these women, all of whom are tempted to act in accordance with Shirley Keeldar's statement that in choosing a mate she "prefer[s] a *master*. . . . A man I shall find it impossible not to love, and very possible to fear."[8]

The story of Mina's relationship with Zamorna is both complex and tragic. Possessing both capacity and drive for independence, and a sensibility which makes her aware of fine moral distinctions, Mina freely chooses to sacrifice herself in order to fulfill emotional needs which she herself defines as evil because they place her in a position which she finds shameful and which robs her of worth in her own eyes. Capable of supervising the financing of Zamorna's military campaigns and the upbringing of Zamorna's son, she wins the admiration of his military supporters who, seeing her as "sagacious, clever, and earnest," "did not hesitate to communicate with her often on matters of first-rate importance" (*MUW,* II, 133).

Mina takes pleasure in her superior powers, finding a sense of herself in her ability to meet every test, as she acknowledges: "when I was at Fort Adrian and had all the yoke of governing the garrison and military house-hold, I used to rejoice in my responsibility and feel firmer the heavier weight was assigned me to support" (*MUW,* II, 134). But her love for Zamorna vitiates these capacities: "Miss Laury belonged to the Duke of Zamorna—She was indisputably his property as much as the Lodge of Rivaux or the stately woods of Hawk-scliffe, & in that light she considered herself" (*FN,* 143). Seeing herself thus, she considers herself dis-graced and unworthy of contact with society. Suspi-cious that all must scorn her as she scorns herself ("Every body knows me . . . 'Mistress' I suppose, is branded on my brow" [*FN,* 160]), she still becomes so dependent on the man she idolizes that she says of the relationship which has corrupted her: "I've nothing else to exist for; I've no other interest in life" (*MUW,* II, 134).

Thus she is trapped in an increasingly self-destructive pattern. In **"The History of Angria III,"** Charlotte de-scribes how "an unconscious wish of wild intensity filled [Mina] that she were dead and buried, and insen-sible to the shame that overwhelmed her" (*MUW,* II, 137). And in the sketch written two years later that con-cludes Mina's story, her passion has led to the fatal consequence she unconsciously pursued, for she now insists, "[my] feelings [for Zamorna] . . . were so fer-vid . . . they effaced everything else—I lost the power of properly appreciating the value of the world's opin-ion, of discerning the difference between right & wrong." She is herself aware that loss of her moral sense and concomitant sacrifice of her identity add up to psychic death: "Unconnected with him my mind would be a blank—cold, dead, and susceptible only of a sense of despair" (*FN,* 147).

Charlotte Brontë's belief in the fatal power of sexual desire is nowhere more succinctly stated than in the story of this heroine. Although Mina is "strong-minded beyond her sex—active, energetic, & accomplished," her love for Zamorna makes her "weak as a child." Ul-timately, "her very way of life . . . swallowed up in that of another," she comes to function merely as the extension of her vicious lover's will. That she finds pleasure in his brutalization of herself and others is made clear when Zamorna—who can respond sexually only when he has proved his total power over her by taunting her until she faints and lies "stretched at his feet"—proceeds to offer her as proof of his love, not an embrace, but the announcement that he has been will-ing to kill the man who threatened to take her from him. For Mina accepts his statement not only as appro-priate evidence of his passion, but as the consummation of their perverse sexual relationship: "Miss Laury shud-dered, but so dark & profound are the mysteries of hu-man nature, ever allying vice with virtue, that I fear this bloody proof of her master's love brought to her heart more rapture than horror" (*FN,* 165).

"Caroline Vernon," the last of Charlotte's Angrian writings, is a study of a young girl's awakening to sexual desire, which inevitably leads her to surrender her entire identity to her lover. While the basic theme is the familiar one traced in the histories of Mary and Mina, in this sketch Charlotte examines the psychology of her heroine even more fully; by making use of inte-rior monologue and reflective passages, she reveals the tension between fear of and desire for sexual experi-ence. Caroline is introduced as a hoydenish fifteen-year-old girl who gives promise of great beauty and who, as the daughter of Percy and his emotionally un-stable mistress Louisa Danci, has inherited a highly passionate nature and a rebellious spirit. Charlotte im-plies that Caroline's childish hero worship of Zamorna, who is her guardian, holds within it the seeds of sexual desire which Caroline can neither understand nor ac-knowledge. Her conversation with Zamorna on the eve of her departure for Paris to finish her education makes the situation plain. Zamorna, responding to her plea that he show his affection for her as openly as he had when she was a little girl, commands her to come to him; but she draws back, saying, "I don't know [why]—I didn't mean to draw back." Zamorna replies, "But you always do, Caroline, now—when I come near you—& you turn away your face from me if I kiss you, which I seldom do—because you are too old to be kissed & fondled like a child" (*FN,* 365).

In Paris, Caroline, for the first time treated as a woman, makes "discoveries concerning men & things which sometimes astounded her"; specifically, she learns that "she [is] a very attractive being & [has the power of in-spiring love] in a very high degree" and that Zamorna is "a man vicious like other men—perhaps . . . more than other men—with passions that sometimes con-trolled him—with propensities that were often stronger than his reason—with feelings that could be reached by beauty" (*FN,* 319-23). She revaluates her love for him; but knowing he is married, she disavows any sexual in-terest on the grounds that such feeling would be "wicked" and insists instead that she merely wants al-ways "to be doing something that would please him" (*FN,* 337). Yet when she is alone in the privacy of her darkened room, her passion overwhelms her moral prin-ciples: "I can't go to sleep, I'm so hot & so restless—I could bear now to see a spirit come to my bed-side and ask me what I wanted—wicked or not wicked, I would tell all—& beg it to give me the power to make the Duke of Zamorna like me better than ever he liked any-body in the world before" (*FN,* 337).

On her return from Paris, she takes "secret enjoyment . . . from the idea of shewing herself to [Zamorna]—improved as she knew she was" (*FN,* 327). And an-gered by her father's efforts to protect her by keeping her from Zamorna's sight, she runs off to join him, al-though she attempts to hide the consequences of her rash act from herself with childish fantasies: "He did not know the restless, devouring feeling she had when she thought of him . . . she would crush the feeling & never tell that it had existed—She did not want him to love her in return—no—no—that would be wicked—She only wanted him to be kind—to think well of her, to like to have her with him—nothing more—unless indeed the Duchess of Zamorna was to happen to die, & then—" (*FN*, 349).

But when Zamorna and Caroline meet, he refuses to allow her the luxury of such equivocation; despite the fact that she has tried to present her elopement as the act of a wayward and affectionate child, she knows "he looked upon her with different eyes to what he had done, & considered her attachment to him as liable to another interpretation than the mere fondness of a Ward for her Guardian" (*FN*, 351).

Caroline is thus doomed by the mere fact that she has become sexually mature. "All the ladies in the world . . . hold the Duke of Zamorna to be matchless, irresistible" (*FN*, 315); and having become a woman, Caroline must acknowledge and act upon her all too natural desire for this man whose hypnotic sexual power both titilates and terrifies her:

> Miss Vernon sat speechless—She darkly saw or rather felt the end to which all this tended, but all was fever & delirium round her—The Duke spoke again—in a single blunt & almost coarse sentence compressing what yet remained to be said. "If I were a bearded Turk, Caroline, I would take you to my Harem"—His deep voice, as he uttered this—his high-featured face, & dark large eyes, beaming bright with a spark from the depths of Gehenna, struck Caroline Vernon with a thrill of nameless dread—. . . all at once she knew him—her Guardian was gone—Something terrible sat in his place. . . . She attempted to rise—this movement produced the effect she had feared, the arm closed round her—Miss Vernon could not resist its strength, a piteous upward look was her only appeal.
>
> (*FN*, 352-53)

Thus the inevitable pattern is completed; and Caroline, like Mary and Mina, becomes the possession of Zamorna, who gloats over his sexual triumph, saying to Percy, "You cannot take her from me, & if you could—how would you prevent her return?—She would either die or come back to me now" (*FN*, 358).

"Caroline Vernon," Charlotte's last extant Angrian tale, focuses upon the moment when, having left the protective innocence of childhood behind, the heroine becomes "one of the Gleaners of Grapes in that Vineyard—where all man & woman-kind—have been plucking fruit since the world began, the Vineyard of Experience" (*FN*, 363). The quotation effectively summarizes Charlotte's view of the consequences of female sexuality. The skillful portrayal of Caroline's fluctuation between passionate ecstasy and fear foreshadows the similarly ambivalent responses of Jane Eyre, Shirley Keeldar, and Lucy Snowe to their aggressive lovers.

V THE EARLY WRITINGS AND THE ADULT NOVELS

In writing the annals of Glasstown and Angria, Charlotte codified her conception of psychological truth; and despite her avowal in 1839 that she "long[ed] to quit for awhile that burning clime," the Angrian mode of perception, synonymous as it was with her creative imagination, could not be wholly suppressed or denied. The adult novels complete the process begun years earlier of reshaping fantasy to a surface accord with reality. Not only do some of the characters from the earlier writings appear in the four novels, but Angria itself, fragmented by war and dominated by vicious and self-seeking leaders, is the paradigm of the strife-ridden Yorkshire of *Shirley*, the morally corrupt cities of *The Professor* and *Villette*, and the desolate and inimical social environment of *Jane Eyre*. Ruled by an omnipotent emperor whose acts are expressions of his destructive impulses and idiosyncratic needs, the Angrians are placed in a situation which prefigures that of the protagonists of the later works.

All of Charlotte's novels concentrate upon the individual and his own needs, rather than upon social context. The Angrian manuscripts are filled with characters who seek their private fulfillment at the expense of all others and even of society, if need be. This egoism is sometimes tempered, sometimes disguised, in the mature novels; but Charlotte's militant Protestantism in these works functions, oddly enough, to allow her heroes and heroines something of the same freedom. For by extending the basic Protestant doctrine that the individual needs no mediator between himself and God, these characters are able not only to deny the teachings of the ministers of the Church but to reject or to reinterpret Scripture in accordance with their own desires and to insist that the only true commands of God are those which conform to the individual's own deeply felt needs. This total reliance of the individual upon himself accounts for the fact that the crisis of each of Charlotte's novels comes when the protagonist reaches a crucial decision which introspection rather than the advice or teaching of others reveals to him as right.

In fact, Charlotte's assumptions about the nature of the human condition expressed in her depiction of Angria remain essentially the same in her adult novels and are in conformity with the Christian view that man is a fallen being in a fallen world. The protagonists of both her juvenile and adult fiction exist amid violence and danger. They are the prey not only of vicious enemies but also of their own passionate natures which urge them toward social and psychological destruction. And the linking of sex with self-destruction and violence which appears throughout her work echoes the fear of sexuality which is basic to Pauline doctrine.

Charlotte's own sense of her Angrian writings as dangerous and revelatory of her sinful state stems from the fact that her juvenile works imply that there is no force sufficient to control man's evil, sensual nature—and, indeed, that there is no good reason for controlling it. Glasstown and Angria are Zamorna's world: there is no power superior to his; and he, like the Byronic hero he is modeled upon, is a demonic figure. Convinced of his damnation, he ruthlessly makes others suffer, not in the hope of achieving happiness himself, but because his insatiable ego finds momentary satisfaction only in his ability to prove his power by inflicting pain. Ineluctably fascinating and, as Emperor, the holder of the reins of all social and political power, he is an omnipotent force against whom there is no defense. Those who hate him, hopeless of any remedy in law, can respond only with a viciousness similar to his own; those who love him, since they are inhabitants of a world bereft of meaningful religious, ethical, or moral standards, suffer his cruelty in an agony of self-destructive passion which they can appeal to no superior values to control.

Angria is, in a sense, the province of the id; Charlotte's superego dictated her conception of reality. The resulting tension between what she was naturally drawn to and the values she thought she should uphold is apparent in all of her adult novels. In all of these works, the unresolvable conflict between romantic fantasy and reality, passion and control, imagination and reason, is observable not only in tone but also in atmosphere and in conception of human psychology. At times the burning light of Angria flashes out, illuminating her prosaic settings and transforming them into a landscape of dream or nightmare as a ghostly nun walks the shadowy attics of a school and as a goblin laugh rings out in the third story of an English country house.

Indeed, Charlotte's struggles to subdue the subconscious self which produced Angria are echoed in the works of her maturity as again and again—and most powerfully in *Villette*—she describes the agony of the individual who discovers within himself powerful impulses, desires, and fears which are not subject to the control of the rational mind. The sexual relationships which form the center of her plots force the protagonists to recognize the claims of these latent and potentially dangerous impulses of their deeply divided natures. Priggish, smug, self-complacent, they pay lip service to the conventional values of Protestant, puritan, nineteenth-century society; but at the same time, they are highly unconventional, deeply passionate, and self-centered. Because her heroes and heroines are thus driven by antithetical desires, frustration suffuses all of Charlotte's work.

On the one hand, her central characters seek what reason tells them is desirable and attainable: position, respect, economic success, and above all, independence. But these men and women search with equal fervor for that which their romantic imaginations envision: not just for conventional love or fulfillment of burning physical passion, but for a soul mate—the one individual who meets the needs of their inner natures and who will allow them to complete themselves. For Charlotte's protagonists, no measure of social or economic success, no sense of conforming to abiding moral principles, is ever sufficient in itself—the soul mate must be sought and won. Yet because the search for and commitment to this unique human being militates against the achievement of other, more reasonable aims, no ultimate, satisfactory solution is possible. The images of abysses, sterility, fragmentation, and death which fill Charlotte Brontë's works bespeak a deep conflict within herself; and her novels reflect this tension, since they chronicle the rending internal conflict suffered by individuals who desperately desire both to be supremely independent and to be merged, twinned, with another.

Notes

1. *The Poems of Charlotte Brontë and Patrick Branwell Brontë,* ed. T. J. Wise and J. A. Symington (Oxford, 1934), p. 186.

2. *The Miscellaneous and Unpublished Writings of Charlotte and Patrick Branwell Brontë in Two Volumes,* ed. T. J. Wise and J. A. Symington (Oxford, 1938), I, 278-79; hereafter cited as *MUW*.

3. *Legends of Angria,* ed. Fannie Ratchford and William Clyde DeVane (New Haven, 1933), p. 65; hereafter cited as *LA*.

4. Ratchford, Fannie Elizabeth. *The Brontë's Web of Childhood.* New York: Columbia University Press, 1941; reissued, New York: Russell and Russell, 1964, p. 45.

5. *Five Novelettes,* ed. Winifred Gérin (London, 1971), p. 127; hereafter cited as *FN*.

6. Ratchford, pp. 142-43.

7. Ratchford, pp. 113-14.

8. *Shirley,* 2 vols. (Oxford, 1931), II, 256.

Robert Keefe (essay date 1979)

SOURCE: Keefe, Robert. "Death and Art: Juvenilia." In *Charlotte Brontë's World of Death,* pp. 45-76. Austin: University of Texas Press, 1979.

[*In the following essay, Keefe provides a Freudian interpretation of the Angrian story cycle focusing on the centrality of death, killing, and corpses, contending that the frequent killing and resuscitation of characters in the stories is a form of wish fulfillment indicative of Brontë's unconscious mind working to dispel her own demons—bereavement and self-hatred.*]

It would be a mistake to see the fictional world which the Brontë children built up out of the shards of their existence as an escape from their death-filled surroundings. Nobody escapes. Charlotte Brontë's early fiction does not run from death; it concentrates obsessively on the act of dying. From her earliest scribblings to the final chapter of *Villette,* Brontë's imagination is fascinated with death, approaches it with affection and fear, examines it tentatively but persistently, backs away from it only to creep up again, to grapple with it and overcome it temporarily without gaining any real respite from the compulsion to struggle with it again and again, in work after work after work. But it is in her juvenilia, where no one was listening but her sisters and brother, that her struggle and her strategies for temporary victory are clearest.

The Brontë children began to create their imaginative world in June, 1826, when Patrick Brontë returned from a trip to Leeds with a new set of twelve painted wooden soldiers for Branwell. The date is crucial, though its full significance has escaped Brontë scholars: exactly a year had elapsed since the death of Elizabeth, following closely on that of Maria, had rocked the Brontë household. Thus the shiny toys which Branwell received after the period of formal mourning must have represented his father's attempt to lead his children back along the first tentative steps to the land of the living. The effect of the gift was to be astounding, although Patrick Brontë would learn nothing of it until after the last of his children had died.

Branwell's toys were not the only new playthings which the children discovered as they awoke on the morning of June 6; their father had left a present beside the bed of each sleeping child. He had bought a set of ninepins, a toy village, and a dancing doll for the girls. But it was the soldiers which captured the children's fancy. They did not begin to play house with the toy village, as their father had hoped. Rather, they took the toy soldiers and played at life and death. They gave the individual riflemen names. Charlotte christened the largest and handsomest figure after the Duke of Wellington, who had beaten Napoleon at Waterloo a year before her birth. Branwell, characteristically, named one of the soldiers Napoleon. Emily and Anne named their favorites in honor of Edward Parry and William Ross, the Arctic explorers. The children began a game which would soon channel and control their imaginations. The twelve wooden soldiers gave up their military careers to become explorer-adventurers, leaving England for a life of excitement and eventual wealth on the Ivory Coast. The children followed the escapades of their toys avidly

and soon began to write them down. The resultant literary game went through many permutations during the next twenty years or so. At first all of the children played it together. Later, after Charlotte had left home to become a pupil at Roe Head, Emily and Anne rebelled against Branwell's rule and founded their own game and their own kingdom, Gondal, which they kept up till their deaths. Charlotte and Branwell went on chronicling their mythical realm for at least another decade. As late as her second year in Belgium, Charlotte, then in her late twenties, could be caught in the mental web of her childhood game.

Charlotte and her brother composed over one hundred booklets, printing their stories laboriously in a tiny hand in order to fit hundreds of words onto pages as small as one by two inches. Their secret books and magazines chronicled the events of the world they had created. At first the children founded Glass Town, located somewhere on the Ivory Coast. Later, as Branwell's knowledge of Greek and Latin increased, it seemed more dignified to them to translate Glass Town into Verreopolis. That name quickly blurred into Verdopolis, as the children shifted their attention from the city's miraculous buildings to its lush setting. At a still later date Charlotte and Branwell created Angria, an adjacent and rival kingdom. For the sake of simplicity, the entire body of magazines, novellas, poems, political pamphlets, and miscellanies can be called the Angrian cycle.

Almost from the beginning, two characters dominated the game. On the one hand there was Northangerland, the successor to Napoleon in Branwell's affections. Early in the cycle he had been a pirate with the functional name of Rogue, but on land Branwell's personal toy soldier aspired to greatness again and took the name of Alexander Percy. He attained through marriage the title Lord Ellrington, and ended the cycle as the Earl of Northangerland. For the reader's sake I shall refer to him anachronistically as Northangerland throughout this chapter.

Northangerland's antagonist, the hero of the cycle, is Zamorna, the son of the Duke of Wellington. Whether Charlotte calls him Arthur Wellesley, Marquis of Douro, or gives him his later, more ornate identity, Arthur Augustus Adrian, Duke of Zamorna and King of Angria, her favorite character remains an unconscious parody of the Byronic hero.[1] And there is ample evidence that Charlotte worshipped him.[2] Her brother exorcised his anguish by pushing his malicious toy into battle against the fathers of Glass Town; Charlotte assuaged her loneliness by adoring a wooden soldier who could never leave her because he did not exist.

Zamorna is surrounded by admiring women and married in turn to two young girls whose only functions are to love, to pine, and to die. Marian Hume and, later,

Maria Henrietta Percy, whose first names bear a suspicious resemblance to Charlotte's sister and mother, are innocent young girls who have the misfortune to be the first and second wives of a rake. They suffer continually, and their suffering only increases the cruelty of Zamorna. We will watch them die repeatedly in this chapter.

Much of their pain comes from the machinations of an evil older woman who cannot stand to see them happy. Lady Zenobia Ellrington is old enough to be their mother—she is in fact the step-mother of Maria Percy—and carries out her role of Oedipal rival with malignant flair. She is the second wife of Northangerland, Maria Percy's father, and takes an occasional turn as Zamorna's mistress. A precursor of *Jane Eyre*'s Bertha Mason, Zenobia is highly intelligent, but brutalized by years of vaguely suggested debaucheries into a nervous if brilliant wreck. She is large, stout, and powerful enough to throw Zamorna's younger brother down the stairs from time to time. She would kill Marian Hume or, later, Maria Percy if she could.

These main figures and the dozens of other characters of the cycle populated a world which did more for the still mourning children than merely supplement an existence grown suddenly and irrevocably thin. For well over a decade their obsessive dream—"the infernal world," or "the world below," as Charlotte termed it—was the focal point of their lives. Fannie Ratchford claims that it was a world "where sin was shorn of its consequences."[3] Certainly sin's outcome was softened, and that was important to the children. For in their unconscious patterning of the world, the most crucial of sin's consequences was death. And the game of the toy soldiers, which Mr. Brontë hoped would set a period to the year of mourning, became for Charlotte and the others a mediatory device, a stage on which they could examine and tinker with death, over and over, as they obsessively set into motion the event they most feared.

In *Beyond the Pleasure Principle*, Freud describes a game played by a one-and-a-half-year-old child. The boy (Freud's grandchild) would take small objects and throw them as far as he could, making a sound which his parents decided represented the German word *fort* ("gone"), followed by gurgles of pleasure and interest. One day Freud observed a more complicated game. Sitting on the floor, the little boy held a reel by its string and tossed it up over the edge of his crib so that it disappeared from his sight. He then pulled the string so that the reel fell back out of his crib. As he did so he squealed *da* ("there"). "This, then, was the complete game—disappearance and return," Freud comments.[4] By throwing the reel away and then pulling it back, the child was training himself to undergo with fortitude the temporary loss of a beloved object by demonstrating to himself that a thing which has gone can return when one needs it.

But what of the simpler game, the disappearance without return of a toy? Why would the child play this game, and play it with obvious pleasure? Freud's answer is both simple and profound. The child never cried when his mother left him for a few hours, although he was greatly attached to her. The complete game, the rejection and retrieval of the toy, lessened his fears by assuring him that beloved objects do return. The starker, more frightening game of disappearance strengthened his resolve to do without that which had gone away, whether it came back or not. In the first place, it was an act of defiance, a demonstration that he could do without the presence of a favorite toy or even a mother. And, more profoundly, the child could derive a bitter pleasure from his ability to initiate and thus in a sense control a painful occurrence: "At the outset he was in a *passive* situation—he was overpowered by the experience; but, by repeating it, unpleasurable though it was, as a game, he took on an *active* part. These efforts might be put down to an instinct for mastery."[5]

The Angrian cycle provided Charlotte with both the game of disappearance and the game of disappearance and return. We will look at both games. Working thematically rather than chronologically, we will examine a small group of representative tales from the period 1829-1834, written by Charlotte between the ages of thirteen and eighteen. These will be followed by a later group. Charlotte's artistic strategies for dealing with death changed considerably during this period. But her basic feelings toward death seem to have remained relatively static and fixed, since the spring of 1825 when her sisters sickened and died. Charlotte's image of her sister Maria's death seems never to have softened, never to have changed; it remained a timeless abrasive which tortured her for the rest of her life. And that is understandable, for the death was traumatic in and of itself, and seems to have served as an emblem for the other deaths—for Elizabeth's, and years later for Branwell's, and Emily's, and Anne's; above all, it must have functioned as a screen for the first loss, the death of Charlotte's mother. But what follows will for the time being concentrate on Charlotte's sister Maria herself as the figure of the lost beloved.

"Albion and Marina" (1830), like so many of Charlotte's contributions to the game, centers on the death of a young girl. As in *Jane Eyre*, the plot depends on a mysterious communication between widely separated lovers. But the message here is from the dead to the living.

Albion, the nineteen-year-old son of a nobleman from the south of England, falls in love with Marina, the daughter of his family physician. His father reluctantly accepts the idea of eventual marriage to a commoner, but insists on first taking his son to Glass Town for a visit which lasts four years. Albion wiles away his African years by writing great epics, the most famous of which, fittingly enough for an Angrian poem, is a Byronic extravaganza entitled "Necropolis, or the City of the Dead," which features a heroine patterned after Marina. At a dance in Glass Town the young poet meets Lady Zelzia Ellrington, who fascinates him momentarily. Walking home later that night, he is confronted by a vision of Marina, who tells him: "Do not forget me; I shall be happy when you return."[6] Albion rushes back to his English estates to find total desolation. On his arrival at Marina's house he sees his beloved playing the harp and singing of her loneliness, but the apparition vanishes leaving him staring at her ruined home. A small boy comes out of the bushes and leads him to Marina's grave; she had died, the victim of Albion's neglect, at precisely the moment her spirit appeared to him in Glass Town. The forlorn lover leaves the south of England and is never heard from again.

The story could be taken simply as one piece of evidence that Charlotte quite naturally hates to see girls with names like Maria die. But more lies under the surface. The narrative purports to be written by Charles Wellesley. It is prefaced by a confused and guilt-ridden statement in which Charles tries to explain to the reader and to himself why he wrote the story: "I have written this tale out of malignity for the injuries that have lately been offered to me. Many parts, especially the former, were composed under a mysterious influence that I cannot account for" (I, 24). Charles explains that Albion represents his older brother, Zamorna, that Marina is Zamorna's wife, Marian Hume, and that Lady Zelzia is modelled on Lady Zenobia Ellrington, Zamorna's mistress. In effect, then, Charles, as the author of the piece, has killed off his sister-in-law and driven his older brother from the country. Seen in this light the tale is an act of outright aggression. But Charles negates the results of his aggression with this denial: "The conclusion [of the story] is wholly destitute of any foundation in truth, and I did it out of revenge. Albion and Marina are both alive and well for aught I know" (1, 25). The narrator of the tale seems both fascinated and horrified by the possibility of creating a fictional homicide. As creator he can kill, but he regrets his godlike power.

Charles is a complex man, and one of Charlotte's intimates; she uses him constantly as the narrator of her stories in the early years of the Angrian cycle. In "**The Foundling**" an innkeeper describes him to a foreign visitor as a rather nasty man:

> "Has the [Duke of Zamorna] any sisters?"
>
> "No, but he has a small imp of a brother."
>
> "Any likeness in their dispositions and persons?"
>
> "Not the least. Lord Charles is a little vile, ugly, lying, meddling, messing, despicable dirty ape, who delights in slandering all good and great men and in consorting with all wicked and mean ones."
>
> (1: 241)

Charles is a favorite of both Branwell and Charlotte, but they handle him in crucially different ways. Branwell tolerates him as an impertinent clown, a tiny imp who intrudes farce into tragic scenes. Charlotte, too, likes the clever little man. But frequently her humorous affection turns to screaming rage or bitter sarcasm; she will turn from her proper narrative pursuits to growl out a gratuitous insult at her hapless friend. Poor Charles has no role to play in "**The Foundling**"; he never even appears in the story. Thus the innkeeper's slander leads the plot nowhere.

A casual digressive reference like this need imply nothing more than the author's imperfect control over the material. But digressions piled high enough take on a central meaning of their own. Charlotte seems to treat Charles as a masculine projection of herself. The similarity of her name to that of her creature is obvious but in itself proves nothing. The frequency with which her stories are filtered through Charles is a further step toward identification. However, the most important indication of the face behind the mask is the similarity between his features and Charlotte's image of herself. She felt she looked horrid. "I notice," she told Mrs. Gaskell, "that after a stranger has once looked at my face, he is careful not to let his eyes wander to that part of the room again!" (Gaskell, *Life,* p. 380). In her early writing she could slough off her ugliness onto Charles and poke fun at it. Charles does not mind; he is a man and feels no need of beauty.

But that "little vile, ugly . . . despicable dirty ape" is not always able to laugh off his lack of beauty; for his homeliness is in Charlotte's hands often the mirror of his vile soul. Charles' occasional anguish over his looks arises at least in part from his fear that ugliness might not be merely skin-deep.

The impulse behind "**Albion and Marina**" goes beyond Charles' usual malice; his misery has turned homicidal. Why does he kill Marina? "Out of malignity, . . . out of revenge," he claims in the Preface. But his revenge is sadly displaced. Charles refers in the Preface to Marina's "incomparable superiority" over her rival, Lady Zelzia. He bears no animus toward Marian Hume, the Angrian counterpart of Marina; his hatred is reserved for his older brother, who treats him like dirt throughout the cycle. In fact one of Charles' main characteristics is his impotent hatred for this older sibling who is the adored favorite of the Verdopolitan aristocracy. If one is not permitted to kill one's sibling in reality, one may at least punish him in a short story. But even there, released aggression causes extreme anxiety: "Many parts . . . were composed under a mysterious influence that I cannot account for." And aggression's consequences are unpredictable: Charles discovers that his malice has produced, not the death of the hated sibling, but the destruction of a girl whom he loves as a sister.

Marina is Marian Hume; is she also Maria Brontë? If so, then Charlotte has produced a tale which must indeed have troubled her, as well as her persona. But Charles' malediction can be cancelled: "The conclusion is wholly destitute of any foundation in truth . . . Albion and Marina are both alive and well." Thus one can kill and not kill. In fiction one can release the most aggressive tendencies of one's nature and yet know beforehand that they will have no "real" effect. Charles tells the reader at the outset that Marina isn't dead, that the report of her death is a strange little lie, a make-believe. Death may obsess the imagination, but in "real" life, the life of Glass Town which provides the setting in which Charles Wellesley writes his aggressive tale, it shall have no dominion. Both Charles and the young girl writing furiously behind the mask of Charles can breathe freely again, having committed no crime. In this limited sense the Angrian writings constitute a literature of escape. But neither literature nor any other form of activity provides a true escape from the dilemmas of existence. Fiction can bring a temporary release of mental pressure, but there is no real exit from the prison of the mind.

Thus throughout the Angrian cycle Charlotte Brontë finds herself repeatedly confronted with variations of the same situation, a dilemma which she has herself constructed out of her unconscious need to track her agony back to its traumatic source, to confront and conquer the causal event: the beloved has died—how can one explain it, who is to blame for it, how can death's echo be muted once and for all? The Angrian cycle, like Albion's poem, is a Necropolis, lingering with tenderness and horror and remorse over the figure of a corpse.

In the early years of the cycle the children developed a filter through which they could continually gaze without pain on death. Their solution to their problem resembles an unwitting parody of the novelistic practice of their era. The young artists took on the attributes of gods. They appear in their early stories as genii: Chief Genius [sic] Brannii [Branwell], Chief Genius Talii [Charlotte], Chief Genius Emii [Emily], and Chief Genius Annii [Anne]. Their playthings, the fictional characters, retain their autonomy only so long as the genii are willing to hide from them. But the authors step into their fictive world at moments of crisis to make certain that the story goes well. Their physical appearance and the exotic names they give themselves are reflections of *The Arabian Nights,* but their function is at bottom a childish variation of the role of the nineteenth-century narrator: out of the chaos of the essential vision they create the artificial order of novelistic form and authorial intervention. Their most frequent intrusion into the "natural" order of events is the resuscitation of the dead.[7] Blatant resurrection would of course be objected to by an adult reading public. But the children themselves were their only audience, and the return to life of the dead was without doubt a fulfillment of one of their deepest wishes. Out of grief and resentment they kill off character after character in their writings, but they need carry no heavy burden of guilt for their actions, since they can cancel the death of their victims. The subplot of **"The Foundling"** (1833) provides a good example of the pattern.

The main plot of the tale concerns the adventures of Edward Sydney, one of the dozens of orphans who appear in Charlotte Brontë's fiction. Abandoned as an infant on the doorstep of a Derbyshire peasant, he travels in his adulthood to Glass Town, where he finds out that he is the grandson of England's George III. Jane Eyre's discovery that she has inherited a few thousand pounds is dwarfed by comparison with Edward's good fortune. Orphans do not simply find their relatives in Charlotte's juvenilia; they find them in hilariously high positions. Edward Sydney is only momentarily discomposed by the revelation that his father is the Duke of York, for he knows through experience that Glass Town is a land where loss is offset by miraculous gain. He has already seen Zamorna reborn.

Zamorna had been poisoned. Northangerland and a friend, Montmorency, while sipping a casual one hundred and thirty glasses of rum, had plotted his death. Northangerland had heard of the perfect weapon, a potion compounded by Manfred, the sage of Philosopher's Island. A bit later the reader meets this sage, and hears Manfred explain to his disciples what happened when he discovered an elixir of life: "I at last succeeded in compounding a fluid, so pure, so refined, so ethereal that one drop of it distilled on our mortal clay penetrated to the soul, freed it from all grosser particles, raised it far above world troubles, rendered it capable of enjoying the calm of heaven amid the turmoil of earth, and, as with a shield of adamant, forever warded off the darts of death" (1: 276). But the Genii, enraged at Manfred's presumption, have transformed his discovery into an elixir of death. (They had presumably not noticed that the state of euphoria produced by the original fluid was itself suspiciously deathlike.) The conclusion to be drawn from their action is obvious, though neither they nor Manfred draw it: the Genii have made themselves accomplices to any murder committed with the new weapon.

The sage announces that someone has poisoned Zamorna. And then a scene occurs which will be staged in slightly varying form repeatedly throughout the Angrian cycle: "He paused again and made a mystic sign with his sceptre. An iron door immediately unfolded, and six dark figures, bearing a bier covered with a white sheet, entered" (1: 277). Zamorna's corpse is followed by two men in chains, Northangerland and Montmorency. They confess to the murder and must themselves drink the elixir.

By the time Edward Sydney and the Duke of Wellesley arrive at Philosopher's Island, the Duke's son and his murderers have been buried, and Manfred is crooning a dirge:

> Damp lies his corpse in the folds of the shroud;
> Low to the dust his bright forehead is bowed.
>   . . . . .
> And why was that fair form, all fettered and shrouded,
> So early laid down in its long dreamless sleep?
> What hand can dispel that dense, shadowy gloom
> Which hides from our vision the volume of doom?

> (1: 286)

In Haworth, Manfred's question would be rhetorical and futile. But Glass Town is a kingdom where death has lost its finality: "On looking up they perceived the four chief Genii, who rule the destinies of our world, appearing through an opening in the sky. 'Mortals,' they cried, in a voice louder than . . . thunder, 'We, in our abundant mercy, have been moved to compassion by your oft-repeated and grievous lamentations. The cold corpse in the grave shall breathe again the breath of life, provided you here pledge a solemn oath that neither he nor his relatives shall ever take revenge on those who slew him'" (1: 288). And they resurrect both the victim and his murderers.

In the context of the story, the men whom the Genii are shielding from revenge are Northangerland and Montmorency. But on a deeper level Charlotte, the author as Genie, is protecting herself. For she is an accomplice to the crime in two crucial senses. In the first place she is one of the demi-gods who changed the nature of the potion from benevolent to malign; her jealousy of her creatures' potential immortality fashioned the weapon which killed Zamorna. Secondly, she is the author of the tale: her imagination plotted the murder, guided the poison to the victim's lips, and destroyed him. Yet the narrative insists that death is not the immutable end of life, that destructive impulses can be blunted in the mind's arena, that victims of those impulses can even be called back to life in an act of generosity—under the condition that the risen victims bear no animosity toward their killers. The reign of death is provisional, even whimsical.

Not all Glass Town corpses rise from the grave, however. In one strange fragment included in **"My Angria and the Angrians"** (1834), Charlotte imagines Northangerland dead. His widow, Lady Zenobia Ellrington, is troubled, but cannot fathom the cause: "Detached fragments of the past, the long-past, the never to return, have since morning been gliding through my memory like that cloud. And still as they vanished one haunting fancy remained behind and what is it? A foolish one but I cannot think it unfounded—that I had something to do before midnight, some important and

solemn duty to perform. I know not its nature. I only feel the impression, and that at times is so strong that I have started from my seat in urgent horror" (2: 36). Her anxiety is soon focused; a courtier arrives to remind her of a promise they had made to her husband. The three of them years before had argued about the nature of death. Northangerland had ended the discussion by making his wife and his friend swear that they would open his coffin and examine his corpse on the twentieth anniversary of his death. Lady Zenobia thus seems to resemble her creator, Charlotte Brontë: they are both compelled to stare at death. Moreover, both have repressed that need, banished it from consciousness. Neither the character nor the author analyzes the nature of the compulsion; but each of them apparently feels and is disturbed by an amorphous "haunting fancy," which Zenobia will act out while Charlotte stares down on her surrogate and pulls its strings.

Now throughout the Angrian cycle Zenobia normally despises her husband. In one typical conjugal chat she calls him a "base villain" and a "wretch," and scorns his "blood-stained . . . crime-blackened hand" as he threatens to kill her (1: 260). But in this fragment, thinking of a vision she had while gazing on his portrait, she can talk of her love for him:

> [The face] vivified, as it often does when I am alone and thoughtful, into Life, flesh and existence. Though dead he yet lived. The eye looked at me so strangely. A melancholy, a warning, a commanding light, filled it and inspired it, till I trembled with the marvellous reality of the likeness. Then a recollection rushed on, of what I had said, what I had promised. . . . I tried to keep and unfold it. I gasped with eagerness. I gazed again and again on the picture that it might enlighten me, but vainly, all died off. Alexander's form was no longer the one I had known and loved."

> (2: 36-37)

Death changes hatred into desperate love. As we saw in Chapter 1, Charlotte too had looked on the faces of the dead in her dreams; they, like Northangerland, had gazed at her in solemn and mournful admonition, perhaps commanded services which she could not understand. Perhaps they commanded her to resurrect them. Zenobia Ellrington does not notice it, but in gazing on the picture of her dead husband she had attempted to resuscitate him. The portrait "vivified . . . into Life . . . Though dead he yet lived." The miracle could not be sustained; "All died off." Now she must visit his crypt, lift the coffin's lid despite her repulsion, and gaze on his face. Perhaps her unconscious mind hopes to resurrect him. Or, just as plausibly, perhaps it is the need to prove that her husband is still in the coffin, still dead, which impels her toward his tomb. Securely locked in their coffins, the dead cannot carry out schemes of revenge on the living. The Genii had been forced to proscribe vengeance before they called Zamorna back to life. The desire for revenge would be natural for one who had lain motionless in a grave for years while the luckier ones romped in the free air over one's body. Surely then the corpse, its mind slowly decomposing into sheer malice, would wish to elicit obscure promises from the living, to circumscribe and gradually compress their freedom till they too were locked as in a coffin.

Northangerland has forced the living to come and do homage to the dead. Probably Zenobia, like her creator, wonders with a mixture of hope and fear whether she will find the corpse inside the coffin. The courtier urges Zenobia:

> Bride of his living breast draw near,
> Bend Lady o'er thy husband's bier;
> For ere the night lamps farther wane
> We'll look on Percy's face again!
>
> (2: 41)

And then the fragment breaks off, ending with an anti-climactic stage direction: *"Lifts the coffin lid, curtain drops"* (2: 41). Charlotte has not been able to carry out her resolve to see the corpse.

But for a few moments she has identified herself with a character she usually hates. Zenobia's normal role in the cycle is that of Oedipal rival to a series of young girls. When Charlotte sends the older woman into a tomb, however, Zenobia seems to become Charlotte's surrogate; she takes on a new personality in order to act out her creator's own compulsion.

The fragment is one of the few tales in the Angrian cycle in which the reader does not get even a glimpse of a corpse. More normally the body lies like a gruesome centerpiece, profoundly disturbing but inescapable, in the middle of the tale. This is the case, for example, in **"The Fairy Gift"** (1830). Captain Bud, who tells Charles Wellesley the story, is an Angrian politician who comes from humble origins. In the days when he was still a farmhand, he was approached by a fairy who offered him three wishes. The first was the crucial one: the ugly young man wished for beauty. He immediately became handsome: "There I stood, tall, slender, and graceful as a young poplar tree, all my limbs moulded in the most perfect and elegant symmetry, my complexion of the purest red and white, my eyes blue and brilliant, swimming in liquid radiance under the narrow dark arches of two exquisitely-formed eyebrows, my mouth of winning sweetness, and lastly, my hair clustering in rich black curls over a forehead smooth as ivory" (1: 53). The description of the rough laborer's transformation is feminine to the point of being unintentionally comic. Surely the rugged Captain Bud would never want to look like that. But Charlotte Brontë might.

Armed with new beauty, Bud meets and marries a rich hag, Lady Beatrice Ducie. He tires of the marriage almost immediately; the neighbors snub him, the servants insult him, his wife is insanely jealous. His misery comes to a climax when, having met young Lady Cecilia Standon, he is foolish enough to praise her beauty in front of his wife, who he soon discovers is a witch. That night Bud secretly follows Beatrice to the dungeon, where his wife's magic calls forth this scene: "At length the dead silence that had hitherto reigned unbroken was dissipated by a tremendous cry which shook the house to its centre, and I saw six black, indefinable figures gliding through the darkness bearing a funeral bier on which lay arrayed . . . in robes of white satin and tall snowy ostrich plumes, the form of Cecilia Standon. Her black eyes were closed, and their lashes lay motionless on a cheek pale as marble. She was quite stiff and dead" (1: 56).

The understandable desire of the young man to overcome his physical ugliness by supernatural means has resulted in the death of a young girl he was beginning to love. He had wished for beauty, for the power to be loved, and his hatred of his inadequacy caused the death of an innocent girl; he repudiates the gift of beauty when he sees its victim's corpse. In other words, **"The Fairy Gift"** represents yet another variation of the pattern of self-assertion, death, and remorse which we have seen in **"Albion and Marina"** and **"The Foundling."**

But there is more to the problem than that. Throughout the Angrian cycle the corpse is a constant obsession. The point is not simply that Charlotte is fascinated with death, though that fact should be obvious by now. More particularly, she seems obsessed with visions of the grave, the crypt, the corpse itself. In their most developed state, her compulsive visions take the form of a coldly beautiful corpse in white surrounded by six pallbearers dressed in black.

The corpse which would seem to be the immediate object of Charlotte's obsession is that of her oldest sister, Maria. Not that Charlotte didn't love her sister; she clearly adored her. She thought of Maria as a saint. But this very adoration, which the other Brontës shared, must have helped to reinforce and disguise an unacknowledged resentment of the model held up before her. The underlying pattern of destruction, observation, and regret which controls much of the Angrian cycle can best be understood as the mirror of the little girl's quite understandable ambivalence toward her sister, an ambivalence which was accompanied by the wish to replace her rival in her elders' affections. That wish received a horrifying fulfillment: Maria died, Elizabeth followed her to the grave, and Charlotte became the oldest child.

In reality there was no way of repudiating the abhorrent fairy gift of preferment. In Charlotte's adult writings, aimed at a public audience, death is an absolute. Charlotte was to portray Maria as Helen Burns, who dies in *Jane Eyre*. Jane describes her burial site: "Her grave is in Brockleridge churchyard: for fifteen years after her death it was only covered by a grassy mound; but now a grey marble tablet marks the spot, inscribed with her name, and the word 'Resurgam.'"[8] In adult fiction only the pious hope of resurrection remains: "I shall arise." In the imaginative world of the adolescent, however, unrestrained by the thought that adults are watching, the wish can be given more concrete form. The dead really do awake—not in an insubstantial afterlife, but now, in the body, in Glass Town.

The provisional hypothesis of sibling rivalry is useful but ultimately inadequate as an explanation of the myth of disappearance and return which structures the Angrian cycle. Most significantly, the victim in many of the tales is totally innocent of any offense against the murderer. If we were dealing only with sibling rivalry, it would seem that the victim would normally have somehow insulted the sensibilities of the murderer. But in many cases there had been no prior tension between them. Instead, the aggressor rushes blindly at the thing he hates only to discover that he has killed the thing he loves.

A sequence of tales later than the one we have so far examined sheds light on this drama of displaced revenge which seems to have haunted Charlotte's psyche. In 1834, Charlotte and Branwell decided to reward Zamorna by giving him a kingdom, Angria, just east of Glass Town. Perversely, they chose Northangerland as his prime minister. It was a strange alliance, and quickly broke down. In January, 1836, Branwell decided to let Northangerland begin a full-scale civil war, gathering together the Ashantee army, the dissident democrats of Angria, and the conservative aristocracy of Glass Town to form a coalition which quickly overwhelmed Zamorna.

The Zamorna-Northangerland alliance and feud were further complicated by the fact that they had for several years been related by marriage. In **"Politics in Verdopolis"** (1833), Branwell had introduced a new character to the cycle, Maria Henrietta Percy (known also as Mary Percy), Northangerland's daughter by his first wife. Maria had been reared in absolute retirement in the countryside and only now, on the verge of adulthood, entered the aristocratic world of Glass Town. She quickly became engaged to an aristocratic nonentity, but then met Zamorna. They fell in love, Zamorna told his wife Marian of the affair, and Marian obligingly dropped dead.

It must have been painful for Charlotte to let Branwell kill Marian Hume. Fanny Ratchford indicates one of the mechanisms which made it psychologically possible for Charlotte to get rid of the original heroine of the

Angrian cycle: "Charlotte did not give her up any more than she had given up the wooden soldiers who fell in battle; she merely resorted to a new form of resuscitation, and continued to write about her in retrospect, adding new traits of character from time to time and new incidents to her life, until Marian Hume dead grows into a vastly different person from Marian Hume living, gradually merging into Mary Percy, and through her into Paulina Mary Home of *Villette*."[9]

In her late adolescence Charlotte was devising more sophisticated mechanisms for overcoming death. The blatant intervention of the author into the processes of life and death had disappeared; instead there was now the manipulation of the past tense and the merging of the characters of one work into their literary descendants in the next. In replacing the discarded Marian with her double, Maria, Charlotte had rediscovered a mature novelistic defense against death; she had taken a step closer to becoming an adult artist, resolving her psychological dilemmas with the standard tools of her trade.

By the time the Angrian Civil War began, Charlotte was teaching at Roe Head, separated from Branwell by twenty long miles. She was unable, except during vacations, to read her brother's manuscripts. Thus when Branwell wrote to her that he was going to kill Maria Henrietta Percy, Charlotte was thrown into an agony of suspense. For nearly a year Charlotte tried desperately to come to terms with this new tragedy, the death of yet another girl named Maria. And this time she was able to stave off the hated event.

Maria Percy was to be a victim of the feud between her husband and her father. Charlotte's long poem, **"And, When You Left Me,"** dated July 19, 1836, describes the family situation. The poem, patterned after Byron's "Childe Harold's Pilgrimage," is a monologue spoken by Zamorna. He has been captured by his father-in-law and sent off to exile on a ship wandering around the Mediterranean. The poem is an imagined confession to the absent Northangerland. Zamorna describes the mutually sadistic relationship between Northangerland and himself, in which each partner was able to inflict exquisite psychological wounds on the other. Moreover, both were masochists; each willingly offered the other the opportunity to return the wound:

> if one
> Had in his treasures some all priceless thing,
> Some jewel that he deeply doated on
> Dearer to him than life, the fool would fling
> That rich gem to his friend.

> (2: 241)

And the friend would immediately destroy it.

Zamorna's analysis of the relationship is followed by the charged statement: "Percy, your daughter was a lovely being" (2: 241). In Charlotte's eyes the Angrian Civil War was simply the mechanism which triggered the compulsion of two people to kill the thing they loved.

In a manuscript dated April 29, 1836 (its modern title is **"History of Angria III"**), Charlotte had discussed the relationship between Northangerland, Zamorna, and Maria in more political terms than in Zamorna's poetic monologue, but even that work had stressed the taut emotional quality of the situation. Zamorna had told his aide-de-camp: "I swore that if he broke those bonds and so turned to vanity and scattered in the air sacrifices that I had made and words that I had spoken; if he made as dust and nothingness causes for which I have endured jealousies and burning strife and emulations amongst those I loved; if he froze feelings that in me are like living fire, I would have revenge" (2: 156). The language here is vivid but vague. It is possible to read the passage in entirely political terms. But the vocabulary bears a striking resemblance to that of love, described, as in *Jane Eyre,* in terms of fire and ice.

If there is any doubt that Zamorna views his father-in-law with outraged love, Zamorna makes the point perfectly clear a bit later on: "You know what accursed way I tend after my Mother, and you know how I loved Percy, and what it is costing me to send him to the D . . . l!" (2: 158). The older man had taken the younger as his son-in-law. But the relationship is closer to that of parent and child. In substituting Maria Henrietta Percy for Marian Hume, Charlotte and Branwell had made explicit a relationship which had become more and more strongly implied in the earlier years of the cycle. The compact of mutual torture understood so fully by both the older man and his son-in-law thus becomes intelligible: it is a romantic reflection of the paradigmatic stance of parent and child. They are allies, they present for a time a common front to the world, they love and admire one another, but they are also the victims of a compulsive need to inflict pain on each other. Maria Henrietta Percy is a pawn in this libidinal game, beloved and used by both men in their struggle with one another.

In the poem we have been examining, **"And, When You Left Me,"** Maria is still alive, but Zamorna already speaks of her as if she were dead. He envisions a way in which a woman might die. His companion, a courtier named Robert King, who, quite appropriately for Charlotte's juvenilia, is known by the nickname "Sdeath," had suggested that they should have taken Maria along on the voyage and drowned her while she was asleep. Zamorna contemplates the thought:

> It would look well, says Sdeath, to see her sinking,
> All in white raiment, through the placid deep,
> From the pure limpid water never shrinking,

> Calmly subsiding to eternal sleep,
> Dreaming of him that's drowning her, not thinking
> She's soon to be where sharks and sword-fish leap;
> And, if she rose again a few days hence
> Looking like death, it would but stand to sense.

> To common sense, a corpse laid in the water
> Must putrefy whosever corpse it be,
> And neither [Zamorna's] wife nor
>   [Northangerland's] daughter
> Can be left out in Nature's great decree.

(2: 244-245)

Charlotte is now twenty years old and her vision of death has apparently lost its connection with the childish hope for immediate resurrection in the flesh. The compulsive pattern is still there: a murder occurs, the aggressor stares at the corpse, and the dead girl rises. But she bobs to the surface in bitter parody of the earlier myth. The blotted resurrection takes Charlotte a long step in her adolescent journey to an acceptance of reality. The genii have been left behind with the other toys of childhood. Still, Charlotte insists on holding a buffer between herself and death. Maria's drowning was merely a suggestion, and Zamorna can luxuriate in the vision while refusing to take his counsellor's advice.

Meanwhile Branwell was forging implacably ahead in his neurotic need to kill once again the saintly ghost who tormented him. Maria must die no matter how much Charlotte complained. By the end of the summer Charlotte was undergoing the remorseful agonies of an accomplice:

> I wonder if Branwell has really killed [Maria]. Is she dead? Is she buried is she alone in the cold earth on this dreary night with the ponderous coffin plate on her breast under the black pavement of a church in a vault closed up, with lime and mortar. No body near where she lies—she who was watched through months of suffering—as she lay on her bed of state. Now quite forsaken because her eyes are closed, her lips sealed and her limbs cold and rigid. . . . A set of wretched thoughts are rising in my mind, I hope she's alive still partly because I can't abide to think how hopelessly and cheerlessly she must have died, and partly because her removal if it has taken place, must have been to Northangerland like the quenching of the last spark that avoided utter darkness.[10]

Charlotte was apparently able to dissuade her brother from killing the duchess. For although in a manuscript dated September 19, 1836, Branwell had written that she could last "not more than an hour or two" (2: 216), Maria still lingers on in Charlotte's **"The Return of Zamorna,"** written in the winter of 1836-1837. The language of that story mirrors its author's need to compromise her dream of resurrection with reality. Maria is still sick, but is now at least ambulatory. Charlotte writes: "Wasted and blanched as she looked, her attendants wondered often how she could bear to walk so long, but her uncomplaining melancholy awed them too much for expostulation. They never dared advise her to seek more repose, and there all day long the light rustle of her dress might be heard as she traversed the measured walk with noiseless and languid tread, *more like a flitting shade* than a living woman."[11]

Though in Branwell's imagination Maria had been scheduled to die on the night of September 19, for Charlotte her death had become metaphorical. The device of the simile, which allows her to state a proposition and cancel it at the moment of its expression, will continue to function throughout Charlotte's career as a mediator between dream and reality. In the long progression from the wild romances of her childhood game to the somber close of *Villette,* the simile becomes one of Charlotte's most successful tools for balancing her private vision with the need for a myth which is acceptable both to her own sense of reality and to a public audience. In the description of Maria Percy she continues her metaphoric play with death. She writes: "The remembrance of the thousand characters who had moved and shone around her was grown dim and vague. . . . Their appearance in her presence would have startled her as though one had returned from the dead" (2: 286). Other devices used in the story also approximate and cancel death. For example, a servant tells the narrator: "I have thought it would not be long before we should have to dress her corpse in its shroud and to lay her out, young as she was and divinely beautiful, stiff and icy in her coffin" (2: 287-288). The subjunctive here has much the same function as the similes above. And Maria herself asks: "How is it that I am kept here in such solitude, such deadliness of Life?" (2: 288). Again, an approximation of death is followed by life.

The attempted murder of Maria Henrietta Percy contains the necessary material for moving a step beyond the provisional hypothesis of sibling rivalry developed in the first part of this chapter. Maria was to die because her father had deserted Zamorna. If we schematize the triangular relationship between the three characters, the implications of this statement become clearer. Zamorna loves Maria. But he is willing to let her die because her father has turned against him. Zamorna's indignation is not simply the result of rational political considerations. Rather, he sees himself as a man whose offer of love has been rejected. How will he take revenge on this father-figure whom he loved (and hated) and who repudiated him? He will wound Northangerland in his only vulnerable spot, his love for his daughter Maria.

The stance of rejected love is common to Charlotte Brontë's works from **"Albion and Marina"** to *Villette.* But the poem **"And, When You Left Me"** seems to me the clearest statement of the paradigm which the later

fiction echoes and distorts. The speaker has been cast off by an older man; therefore he will destroy that man's daughter, the only creature the older man really loves. The pattern bears a striking resemblance to the emotional constellation of the Brontë household, in which Patrick Brontë's loved ones were taken from him one by one until he was left face to face with his only remaining child.

Charlotte's unconscious identification with the mighty Zamorna which this pattern of rejection and revenge implies may at first sight seem strange. But although her worship of Zamorna had made her identify with his forlorn mistresses, she had at the same time almost certainly viewed him as a projection of the self-assurance and aggressiveness she longed for and lacked. Like all idols, Zamorna had always served his worshipper in part as compensation for her own inferiority complex. Zamorna had been repeatedly attracted to the daughters of rough or evil men: Marian Hume, Maria Percy, Maria Sneaky and Caroline Vernon are all daughters of less than admirable fathers, and all are loved and mistreated by Zamorna.

A parent-figure is punished and a young girl mistreated in **"The Green Dwarf"** (1833). And the perpetrator of the crimes bears a strong resemblance to Charlotte Brontë. The tale, an imitation of *Ivanhoe,* centers on a triangle consisting of the Count of St. Clair, Northangerland, and the woman they both love, Lady Emily Charlesworth. The fourth major figure of the story is Northangerland's spy in the service of St. Clair, Andrew, known as the Green Dwarf because of his costume and his height. After Andrew has nearly managed to get his master executed as a traitor, St. Clair complains: "I know not what demon has possessed my vassal's breast, what hell-born eloquence has persuaded the orphan, who, since his birth, has existed only on my bounty, to aid in the destruction of his lord and benefactor."[12] The demons which possess Andrew are those which possessed Charlotte Brontë: bereavement and self-hatred. He has lost his parents, and he is painfully aware of his ugliness. At one point he is said to have "withered, unnatural features" (p. 94), and elsewhere Charlotte refers to his "keen eyes and shrivelled, ill-favoured" looks (p. 82). In punishment for betraying his master Andrew is sentenced to a term as a galley slave. On his release he takes up an occupation which will exploit his alienation and channel his aggression away from crime: "He . . . took to the trade of author, published drivelling rhymes which he called Poetry, and snivelling tales, which went under the denomination of novels" (p. 102). Andrew, then, seems to serve as a projection of Charlotte's self-hatred and repressed aggression. But though he gives the story its title, he is not the main character nor does Charlotte seem particularly fascinated with him. Her interest seems focused more on the heroine, Lady Emily Charlesworth. Lady Emily can be seen as a composite character: to the qualities associated in the Angrian cycle with the Maria-figure, she adds the names of Emily and Charlotte. She does not die, but she faces the danger of starvation, and her peril is a crucial point in the psychological pattern of Angria.

Andrew helps Northangerland abduct her. (The dwarf has learned that the most effective way to punish his fatherly benefactor is to take the older man's most prized possession away from him.) Northangerland imprisons Lady Emily in a tower which is guarded by a woman named Bertha, whom Charlotte describes as a malevolent shrew: "The portal [of the tower] slowly unfolded and revealed . . . an old woman bent double with the weight of years. Her countenance, all wrinkled and shrivelled, wore a settled expression of discontent, while her small red eyes gleamed with fiend-like malignity" (p. 59). But Bertha's supposed malice breaks forth in nothing worse than brusque speech. Most of the time she merely ignores her captive: "During a period of four weeks Lady Emily had pined in her lonely prison under the surveillance of the wretched Bertha, who regularly visited her three times a day to supply her with food, but at all other times remained in a distant part of the castle" (p. 99). And then Bertha drops dead, leaving Emily to starve. The young poacher who saves the heroine tells her that "in his perambulations through the desolate halls he had, to his horror, stumbled upon the corpse of an old hideous woman, who, to his mind, looked for all the world like a witch" (p. 100). He had buried the corpse under a heap of stones.

Thus in **"The Green Dwarf"** Charlotte as author does not gaze for a long time at a beautiful corpse, but takes only a timid peek at a dead old crone and passes on. Moreover, the body is removed from direct view by a series of narrators. The story is told by Charles Wellesley. It has been recounted to him by Captain Bud, whom Emily had presumably told of her adventures in the tower. She in turn had been informed by the poacher of his discovery of Bertha's corpse. The compulsive view of the body, in other words, is separated from Charlotte's eyes by four protective layers of narrative. This filtering device seems to me to indicate that something about Bertha's death disturbs Charlotte profoundly.

Normally the author succeeds in satisfying her need to stare at dead Angrians. The dead are not coy: Zamorna's corpse in **"The Foundling"** and Lady Cecilia's in **"The Fairy Gift"** had thrust themselves into the viewer's gaze with festive shamelessness; at the first hint of incantation they had been carried in sad triumph onto the stage to take up their role in the gloomy ritual. But when the corpse is of someone older, a parent-figure, then the voyeuristic desire of the author remains unsated. Thus the curtain closes when Zenobia lifts the lid of her husband's coffin in the fragment from **"My An-**

gria and the Angrians." And here, in **"The Green Dwarf,"** the poacher hauls the hag's carcass into the yard with unceremonious haste and piles stones on it before Charlotte can get her fill of staring. Charlotte seems to have exercised unconscious censorship and placed a barrier before the eyes of the curious.

The cause of this taboo can be seen if, ignoring the surface plot, we concentrate on the abstract pattern of Lady Emily's agony. The young heroine is abducted from her friends and taken to a lonely building where she is neglected; the man who has kidnapped her never reappears, and the woman who feeds and cares for her spends most of her time in another part of the tower. The wrinkled, grumpy, red-eyed woman, bent double with age and pain, caps her malign neglect by dying, leaving the heroine totally alone with no one to care what happens to her. The story seems like a distortion of Charlotte Brontë's childhood. In all probability Bertha's corpse cannot be seen because she represents Charlotte's mother, and the sight of her remains would send the whole traumatic year flooding back into her daughter's consciousness, overwhelming it with pain and remorse. It must remain walled up, blocked from Charlotte's view by the long line of younger, more beautiful corpses on which the Angrian narratives dwell.

Fanny Ratchford finds Bertha the most interesting character in the story. She writes: "Bertha is a direct adaptation of the Saxon Ulrica of Front de Bœuf's castle in *Ivanhoe*. Commonplace and childish as the plagiarism seems in itself, it fixed in Charlotte's mind an image which under the heat of her imagination fused in the course of years with Lady Zenobia Ellrington to become Bertha Mason, the mad wife of *Jane Eyre*."[13] True. But we must try to go beyond the mere recognition of similarity to ask what it was that heated Charlotte's imagination to the point where it could fuse a slattern like Bertha with the voluptuous, brilliant Zenobia, wife of Northangerland and mistress of Zamorna. I would suggest that the catalyst lies in the fact that both women are projections of Charlotte's complex infantile image of her mother. And one more character should be added to the mix: Lady Beatrice Ducie, the witch in **"The Fairy Gift."**

Lady Beatrice is as rich and powerful as Lady Zenobia. Unfortunately she is as hideous as Bertha. But ugly mothers are better than none at all, and Bertha's considerable drawbacks do not stop Bud from hoping that his new-found beauty will attract her attention and love: "Though her ladyship had passed the meridian of life, was besides fat and ugly, and into the bargain had the reputation of being a witch, I cherished hopes that she might take a liking for me, seeing I was so very handsome" (1: 54). Lady Beatrice does love Bud in her insanely possessive way, to the point of murdering Cecilia Standon out of jealousy. And then she turns on Bud:

At this appalling sight I could restrain myself no longer, but uttering a loud shriek I sprang from behind the pillar. My wife saw me. She started from her kneeling position, and rushed furiously towards where I stood, exclaiming in tones rendered tremulous by excessive fury: "Wretch, wretch, what demon has lured thee hither to thy fate?" With these words she seized me by the throat and attempted to strangle me.

I screamed and struggled in vain. Life was ebbing apace when suddenly she loosened her grasp, tottered, and fell dead.

When I was sufficiently recovered from the effects of her infernal grip to look around I saw by the light of the candle a little man in a green coat striding over her and flourishing a bloody dagger in the air.

(1: 56)

It is the fairy whose gift to Bud was beauty. Like the Green Dwarf this little man in green has struck down a parent-figure.

The maternal figures of Angria hate young girls. Lady Zenobia is prettier than her two ugly doubles, but no nicer: "Who would think that that grand form of feminine majesty could launch out into the unbridled excesses of passion in which her ladyship not infrequently indulges? . . . it would seem as if neither fire nor pride nor imperiousness could awaken the towering fits of ungoverned and frantic rage that often deform her beauty. . . . is it natural that such hands should inflict the blows that sometimes tingle from them?"[14]

In the early stages of the Angrian cycle, the object of Zenobia's fits is often Marian Hume. **"The Rivals"** (1830) dramatizes the contest between the woman and the girl for Zamorna's love. Marian (who, like the Green Dwarf and Lady Beatrice's murderer, is dressed in green) cannot understand Zenobia's accusation that she loves the Duke: "'Tis to me a problem, / An unsolved riddle, an enigma dark" (1: 48). She has no conscious need of Zamorna's love, since she receives enough affection at home: "I've a father" (1: 47). The statement enrages Zenobia. Screaming "Wretch, I could kill thee!" (1: 48), she seizes Marian and tries to decide whether or not to throttle this presumptuous girl who brags of her father's love. When Zamorna calls from the woods and Marian tries to run to him, Zenobia restrains her, saying: "Nay! I will hold thee firmly as grim death!" (1: 49). In Angria the deathlike grasp of the older woman who restrains the young girl from the enjoyment of love is often quite powerful. Zamorna comes out of the woods with a rose for Marian. When he gives in to Zenobia's cajolery and presents her the rose instead, Marian falls down as if dead. Zenobia has won the round.

"The Rivals" presents in relatively straightforward fashion the Oedipal triangle of an older woman, a young girl, and the man they both love. Often the constellation is more complex, but in one form or another it runs throughout the cycle. One of the constants in Charlotte's juvenilia is Zenobia's hatred for whatever young girl happens to fall in love with Zamorna. When Marian Hume dies and Zamorna marries Maria Henrietta Percy, the daughter of Northangerland's first wife, the picture comes into even sharper focus. For Northangerland's second wife is Zenobia. Thus Zenobia is both Maria's stepmother and her rival.

Maria Percy was named after her mother, a gentle, quiet woman who died when Maria was an infant. It is apparent that Charlotte has split off the two aspects of motherhood which fascinate and torment her: separation and jealousy. The good mother, who if she were only alive would love and understand her daughter, is dead. The one who is there is an evil stepmother who stands between the young girl and sexual love.

Despite the maternal barrier, however, girls do fall in love in Angria—usually with Zamorna—but they quickly find themselves caught in a trap as restrictive as the lonely existence they sought to escape. Two emotions, anguish and love, dominate Angria, and each of them is a psychological prison. Anguish turns to aggression: the sufferers hurl themselves like weapons at an imagined persecutor, unmindful of the consequences to themselves. Love too results, not in the expansion of the lover's sense of self, but in dehumanization: the lover becomes an object. Charlotte describes one of her lovesick young girls: "Miss Laury belonged to the Duke of Zamorna. She was indisputably his property, as much as the Lodge of Rivaulx or the stately wood of Hawkscliffe, and in that light she considered herself."[15]

Mina Laury is the most interesting character in the late years of the Angrian cycle. In a sense she is a transitional figure between Charlotte's juvenilia and her adult novels. She does not suffer the anguish of bereavement. Her problem is not how to scramble back to a hiding place in the mind where she can stare at a beautiful corpse, her gaze forming the last tenuous bond between the living and the dead. Rather, like the characters of Charlotte's novels she is concerned with the dilemma of psychological survival in an empty, alien world. She has found a simplistic and excruciating solution— love—and she grips it with the ardor of a woman dangling from a cliff: "You know Sir, my mind is of that limited and tenacious order, it can but contain one idea, and that idea whilst it lasts affords a motive for life, and when it is rent away leaves a vacancy which makes death desirable as a relief" (**"The Return of Zamorna,"** 2: 298). Mina and the other young girls who took up more and more of Charlotte's attention in the fiction of her late adolescence are creatures who desperately need a tangible motive for their existence. Charlotte's novels will concern themselves with the quest for such a motive; the protagonists of her maturity will change and develop as they wander in search of meaning. Mina and the other Angrian heroines cannot develop, for they are chained to their premature and faulty solution of the dilemma of their loneliness.[16] Love has given them a reason for living, the love-object filling the conscious mind to the extent that it disguises existence's void. Take away the idol, and a blank would be left which the worshipper would not be strong enough to face.

In **"Mina Laury"** (1838), one of the last of the Angrian tales, Charlotte examines this emotional trap. Mina is kept in a location which will reappear in *Jane Eyre*. There it will be called Ferndean Manor, the gloomy haven where Jane and Rochester will spend their married life. Here it is a hunting lodge with the significant French name of *Rivaulx* ("rivals"), an out-of-the-way mansion where Zamorna hides his young mistress from the jealous wrath of his wife. Charlotte's ambivalence toward both her older sister and her mother is mirrored in the complex nature of her Oedipal fictions: Maria Percy, usually the victim of Zenobia's jealousy, is herself an older rival of Mina Laury. Maria is a tortured woman. In fact, of all the characters of the novella only Zamorna is relatively happy. But the most tormented of all is Lord Hartford, a middle-aged man who has the audacity to try to seduce Mina away from her master. The attempt fails. In his anguish the rejected suitor can only think to fight a duel with Zamorna. Not that he believes it would gain him anything; it is simply that anguish must find its outlet in aggression. Zamorna wounds Hartford mortally, and then tells Mina what he has done: "She said not a word, for now Zamorna's arms were again folded round her, and again he was soothing her to tranquillity by endearments and caresses that far away removed all thought of the world, all past pangs of shame, all cold doubts, all weariness, all heart-sickness resulting from hope long deferred. . . . She lost her identity; her very life was swallowed up in that of another."[17] Angrian love is psychic suicide. Like the sage Manfred's elixir of life in **"The Foundling,"** it solves life's puzzle too effectively; its victims, cuddled in the possessive embrace of the man who owns them, will never search further for meaning. A piece of property defines itself through reference to its owner. With so many dying around them the young women of Angria cling to an idol who will help them forget their mortality. The protagonists of Charlotte's adult novels, however, will not be so easily trapped by the paralyzing solution to the problem of emptiness which Angria poses. Unattached, all of them orphaned, they will have to ask who they are, not simply whose they are.

By the time she wrote **"Mina Laury,"** Charlotte was becoming more and more aware of the psychological fetters which the shape of the Angrian world placed on her mind. Angria had served its purpose; for well over a decade it had provided her with the means of working through her grief and her loneliness. But its solutions were immature and its boundaries, established by years of description, could not be stretched to cover the adult woman's soberer sense of reality. In a fragment probably written in 1839, Charlotte expressed her resolve to break out of her imaginative confinement:

> I have now written a great many books and for a long time have dwelt on the same characters and scenes and subjects. I have shown my landscapes in every variety of shade and light which the morning, noon, and evening—the rising, the meridian and the setting sun can bestow upon them. . . . So it is with persons. My readers have been habituated to one set of features. . . . but we must change, for the eye is tired of the picture so often recurring and now so familiar.

> Yet do not urge me too fast, reader: it is no easy theme to dismiss from my imagination the images which have filled it so long; they were my friends and my intimate acquaintances, and I could with little labour describe to you the faces, the voices, the actions, of those who peopled my thoughts by day, and not seldom stole strangely even into my dreams by night. When I depart from these I feel almost as if I stood on the threshhold of a home and were bidding farewell to its inmates. When I strive to conjure up new inmates I feel as if I had got into a distant country where every face was unknown and the character of all the population an enigma which it would take much study to comprehend and much talent to expound. Still, I long to quit for awhile that burning clime where we have sojourned too long— its skies flame—the glow of sunset is always upon it— the mind would cease from excitement and turn now to a cooler region where the dawn breaks grey and sober, and the coming day for a time at least is subdued by clouds.

> (2: 403-404)

It was to take Charlotte several more years before she could leave the cruelly familiar homeland of her imagination. Before she could break away imaginatively, she had to go to Belgium and act out her sense of exile. And that would not happen until 1842. Four years later, after two years in a foreign country and two more years of separation from the object of her own worship, Heger, she finally left her fictional home to become a professional novelist. For the rest of her life she looked back on Angria with an expatriot's fondness, drawing constantly on the experiences of her childhood game for the characters and incidents of her novels.[18] She would never feel comfortable in the realistic middle-class world of the Victorian novelist, but her very discomfort would be her greatest advantage. For in her impatience with the attenuated minutiae of the novel of manners, she would turn to the only subject she knew thoroughly, the soul's hunger.[19] And her work would attain a psychological depth which the English novel had not known since Richardson.

Notes

1. The importance of the Byronic hero for the development of Charlotte Brontë's vision of life, and

her need to wean herself away from that conception of masculinity, are discussed in Moglen, *The Self Conceived.*

2. Peters, in *Unquiet Soul,* discusses Charlotte's attraction for Zamorna: "Gradually her old idol, the white-haired, fatherly Duke of Wellington, faded from her imagination to be replaced by his magnificent son, Arthur Augustus Wellesley. . . . [He] in turn gradually lost his filial aspect, evolving into the Duke of Zamorna, dark, cruel, sexually magnetic, and sinning. Unconsciously she turned from her father to his son to a stranger. The new branches shot from the old tree, however: her male idol continued to be masterful, domineering: she could not separate sexuality from domination since she could not free herself from the powerful authority of her father" (p. 34). Peters continues a few pages later: "The figure of Zamorna loomed gigantic over her life. . . . He was all she longed to be—rich, despotic, adored, sinning, and masculine. From this deep well of imagination she thus slaked her sexual and creative thirst" (p. 43).

3. Fannie Ratchford, *The Brontës' Web of Childhood,* p. 102.

4. Sigmund Freud, *Beyond the Pleasure Principle,* trans. James Strachey, p. 33.

5. Ibid, p. 35.

6. *The Miscellaneous and Unpublished Writings of Charlotte and Patrick Branwell Brontë,* ed. T. J. Wise and J. A. Symington, 1: 32. Unless otherwise indicated, all quotations from Charlotte Brontë's juvenilia will be taken from this edition. The reader should be warned that since T. J. Wise, who controlled the juvenilia for decades, has been proven a forger, we cannot be certain that Charlotte, and not Branwell, wrote all of the stories attributed to her. Thus I have rested my argument on a general pattern discernible throughout the juvenilia, rather than on any one story. For more information on this difficulty, see Winnifrith, *The Brontës and Their Background,* p. 16 and p. 225, notes 43 and 44, where he calls into question the authorship of "The Foundling" on the basis of a larger than normal signature and some rather coarse stanzas in the story. Although his evidence is unconvincing on this point, I do not mean to rule out the possibility that he may just be correct.

7. Gérin, *The Evolution of Genius,* p. 17, notes: "The effect of the successive deaths of their mother and sisters was to drive them far from all thought of mortality—as far as the wings of invention could bear them—towards the creation of an existence of which they held the key and of whose permanence they themselves could be the guarantors. It was not for mere love of magic that, for years after, in their games and dramatized stories, they claimed to 'make alive again' the casualties of the day."

8. Brontë, *Jane Eyre,* p. 72.

9. Ratchford, *Web of Childhood,* p. 75.

10. Quoted from the Roe Head Journal by Gérin, *The Evolution of Genius,* p. 107.

11. 2: 286. My italics.

12. "The Green Dwarf," *Legends of Angria,* ed. Fannie E. Ratchford and William C. DeVane, p. 90. All quotations from "The Green Dwarf" will be taken from this edition.

13. Ratchford, *Web of Childhood,* p. 62.

14. "A Peep into a Picture Book," *The Twelve Adventurers and Other Stories,* ed. Clement Shorter and C. W. Hatfield, pp. 168-169.

15. "Mina Laury," *Legends of Angria,* ed. Ratchford and DeVane, p. 173.

16. Moglen, *The Self Conceived,* pp. 49ff., discusses Charlotte's treatment of the later heroines of the Angrian cycle insightfully and intelligently. Readers may also wish to consult Margaret Blom's discussion of Brontë's juvenilia in *Charlotte Brontë* (Boston: Twayne, 1977). Unfortunately I was not able to obtain a copy of this book before my own study was completed.

17. "Mina Laury," *Legends of Angria,* ed. Ratchford and DeVane, p. 206.

18. Ratchford, *Web of Childhood,* Chapter 26, discusses the correspondences between the characters of Charlotte Brontë's novels and those of her juvenilia.

19. On April 12, 1850, Brontë told Williams: "[Jane Austen's] business is not half so much with the human heart as with the human eyes, mouth, hands and feet; what sees keenly, speaks aptly, moves flexibly, it suits her to study, but what throbs fast and full, though hidden, what the blood rushes through, what is the unseen seat of Life and the sentient target of death—*this* Miss Austen ignores" (Wise and Symington, *Correspondence,* 3: 99).

Bibliography

Works by Charlotte Brontë

The Brontës: Their Lives, Friendships, and Correspondence. Edited by T. J. Wise and J. A. Symington. 4 volumes. Oxford: Shakespeare Head Press, 1932.

Jane Eyre. Edited by Richard J. Dunn, New York: Norton, 1971.

Legends of Angria. Edited by Fannie Elizabeth Ratchford and William C. DeVane. New Haven: Yale University Press, 1933.

The Miscellaneous and Unpublished Writings of Charlotte and Patrick Branwell Brontë. Edited by T. J. Wise and J. A. Symington. 2 volumes. Oxford: Shakespeare Head Press, 1936-1938.

The Twelve Adventurers and Other Stories. Edited by Clement Shorter and C. W. Hatfield. London: Hodder and Stoughton, 1925.

Villette. Edited by Geoffrey Tillotson and Donald Hawes. Boston: Houghton Mifflin, 1971.

OTHER WORKS

Blom, Margaret. *Charlotte Brontë.* Boston: Twayne, 1977.

Freud, Sigmund. *Beyond the Pleasure Principle.* Translated by James Strachey. New York: Bantam Classic, 1959.

Gaskell, Elizabeth Cleghorn. *The Life of Charlotte Brontë.* London: J. M. Dent, 1960.

Gérin, Winfred. *Charlotte Brontë: The Evolution of Genius.* London: Oxford University Press, 1967.

Moglen, Helene. *Charlotte Brontë: The Self Conceived.* New York: Norton, 1976.

Peters, Margot. *Unquiet Soul: A Biography of Charlotte Brontë.* Garden City, N. Y.: Doubleday, 1975.

Ratchford, Fannie Elizabeth. *The Brontës' Web of Childhood.* New York: Columbia University Press, 1941.

Winnifrith, Tom. *The Brontës and Their Background: Romance and Reality.* London: Macmillan, 1973.

Branwen Bailey Pratt (essay date spring 1982)

SOURCE: Pratt, Branwen Bailey. "Charlotte Brontë's 'There Was Once a Little Girl': The Creative Process." *American Imago* 39, no. 1 (spring 1982): 31-9.

[*In the following essay, Pratt offers a Freudian reading of Brontë's earliest surviving piece of writing, a story she wrote at the age of eight for her sister Anne. Pratt maintains that the story expresses Brontë's grief over the death of her mother as well as her nurturing instinct, a character trait that figures prominently in the heroines of her later juvenilia and novels.*]

Studies of creativity must begin, paradoxically, not at the beginning, with the initial creative impulse, but at the end, with the completed work of art. The psychoanalytic critic, in search of a full understanding of the literary text and the creative act that produced it, sel-dom has access to the artist's psychic history or to the first efforts of the child who becomes that artist. Although a few writers—the Rossettis, Jane Austen and A. E. Housman among them—have left fugitive childhood poems and stories, a body of juvenile work substantial enough to illuminate the early workings of the creative process is rare.

Unique among major novelists, Charlotte Brontë preserved thousands of pages of fiction written between her eighth and twenty-third years, stories that record the elaborate fantasy life that dominated her childhood and her prolonged adolescence. Most scholars ignore these tales as mere child's play; some consult them as sources of characters for the mature writing; many consider them near-incomprehensible chaos, "the dark hinterland of the novels."[1] In a letter of her middle age, the author herself both acknowledges and disclaims the unconscious content of the poems that were her first publication: "[They] are chiefly juvenile productions; the restless effervescence of a mind that would not be still. In those days, the sea too often 'wrought and was tempestuous,' and weed, sand, shingle—all turned up in the tumult."[2]

It is precisely the "weed, sand, shingle"—evidence of intense activity beneath the surface of the writer's mind—that makes Brontë's early work useful in the psychoanalytic study of the artist. The author of *Jane Eyre* and *Villette,* major *Bildungsroman* of woman's inner life, began to chronicle her responses to experience early on. The juvenile narratives are as emotionally complex as they are artistically naive; their very lack of sophistication reveals with unusual clarity the interplay between primitive fantasy and the ordering imagination. As they expose the author's mind in the process of creating a child's version of art, these conscious fictions—and the unconscious fantasies that underlie them—afford new insights into the functions that creativity performs in the psychic evolution of the artist.

The image of the lonely woman isolated on the Yorkshire moors has led scholars to regard Brontë's work from an at least implicitly Freudian perspective, as an attempt to sublimate in fiction desires impossible to gratify in reality. Circumstances justify this approach: Left motherless at five, bereft of her two older sisters at nine, Charlotte Brontë was almost symbiotically attached to her only brother throughout adolescence. She then conceived a passionate admiration for an older man she called her "Master," but did not consciously acknowledge as a sexual being. Her devotion to her father in adulthood so impressed her first biographer, Elizabeth Gaskell, that Gaskell's *Life of Charlotte Brontë* presents its subject as a tragic Antigone figure, the spinster caretaker of an old man with failing eyesight. Filial duty, not love, finally decided the novelist's marriage at thirty-nine; only her minister father's need for a competent curate outweighed her doubts about her future husband's sensibilities. Her death from complications of pregnancy nine months later fulfilled her father's longstanding prophecy that she would never survive childbirth. It is small wonder that ever since Lucille Dooley's 1920 study, psychoanalytic critics have ascribed oedipal causes to Brontë's artistic effects.[3]

Since all human beings have in some way come to terms with oedipal conflicts, such interpretations have been readily accepted. But they limit understanding of the texts as much as they deepen it: Artist and reader are more than their drives, and powerfully influential psychic events occur both before and after the passing of the oedipus complex. Brontë's work presents the reader not with a single consistent subtext, but with many, each overlapping, partly obscuring, contradicting and reinforcing the others.

Charlotte Brontë began to write fiction almost as soon as she could read. Her earliest surviving work, a small, hand-bound "book," is a matter-of-fact narrative written when she was about eight years old for her younger sister, Anne. An exact transcription of the manuscript (conjectural wording indicated by [?]) reads:

> There was once a little girl and her name was Ane she was born at a little vilage name Thorn[?ton and by and by she grew] a good [?girl] her father and mother was very rich M[r] and M[rs] Wood were there names and she was there only child but she was not too muc indulged once little Ane and her mother went too see a fine castle near at London about ten miles from it Ann was very much pleased with it. once Ane and her papa and her Mama went to sea in a ship and they had very fine weather all the way but Anns Mama was very sick and Ann attended her with so much care. she gave her her meddcine.[4]

This tale, like many manifest dreams, is so innocuous on the surface that interpretation seems almost superfluous. Yet, the author chose these events and characters as her subject, rather than any of the others she could have selected—the Yorkshire folk legends she heard from the family housekeeper, the fairy tales she read, the adventures she and her brother and sisters enjoyed during their walks on the moors. Like the construction of a dream or a joke, the creation of fiction has psychic determinants and emotional consequences: The little girl who travelled with her parents surely had particular significance for the little girl who wrote about her, and the writing of this simple story particular functions in its author's emotional life.

Most obviously, the tale acts as compensation for her deprivations: At this time, Brontë was one of six motherless children living in a remote village with their Calvinist aunt and their minister father, whose stipend was no more than adequate for their needs. Little Ane's po-

sition as only child of wealthy Mr. and Mrs. Wood bolsters the writer's self-esteem through the fantasy of possessing parents more desirable and more devoted than her own—the phenomenon and common literary theme of the family romance. No excursions for pleasure are recorded in accounts of Brontë's childhood: She was not much indulged. Ane's expeditions vicariously fulfill the wish for a larger, more varied life that impels Jane Eyre, the same "urgent thirst to see, to know, to learn" the author repeatedly expresses in her adult letters. The mother's serious illness—she was "very sick"—hints at the daughter's desire to replace her in the father's affections; Ane's care of her mother is both negation of this oedipal wish and the positive return to the mother as love object, frequently observed in girls approaching adolescence. The story does involve the issues psychoanalytic interpretation would emphasize; its author's major interests, however, are the child's perception of herself, enjoyment of broadened experience, and relationships with her parents, especially her mother.

When Charlotte Brontë was five and a half years old, her mother died, ending a painful decline that had begun after Anne was born not quite two years before. The birth of the writer's youngest sister was therefore closely related to the death of the mother. When Charlotte wrote this story for her, Anne was five—a correspondence in age that, in a variant of the anniversary reaction, may have recalled to the older child her own reactions at the time of her mother's death. These would normally include grief at the loss of the loved object, fear at the absence of the protector, anger at abandonment and guilt at the fulfillment of unconscious hostile wishes—feelings whose traces might be expected in a story about a child with a sick mother written by a child whose mother had died three years earlier. In the same way that a positive image is discernible in a photographic negative, or a patient's conflicts are evident in seemingly innocent associations, these traces are there—not as painful emotions, but as defenses against them. By employing an omniscient narrator and third-person narrative, Brontë distances the events she describes; by naming her heroine not for herself, but for her sister, she can express her own feelings at a safe remove.[5]

Ane's care of her Mama is one of three assertions in a total of ten lines that identifies her as good (she "grew a good girl," "she was not too much indulged"). Repeated affirmation—protesting too much—suggests an unconscious attempt to negate its opposite, a sense of badness that guilt over the death of a significant object commonly arouses. In a kind of reverse accusation, the author exonerates her heroine from some implied, but unacknowledged action; Ane's attempt to rescue her mother from illness translates into a giving of life, an undoing of the unconscious crime of matricide.

The child's giving medicine to her mother is especially suggestive in light of the fantasies object relations theory attributes to the infant at the time he realizes that the mother is a separate being. The mother's death revives these disturbing hostile fantasies, particularly when the daughter, at around age five, is subject to intense oedipal conflicts. The odd circumstance that it is the child rather than the adult father who cares for the mother points to an unconscious purpose: By making the central action of her story an act of reparation by oral means, the author substitutes a conscious fantasy of reparation for an unconscious fantasy of destruction; the external situation is unchanged, but, within the mind, an emotional equilibrium is achieved.

However, this ending is not the "happily-ever-after" that would naturally follow the "once-upon-a-time" beginning. The story breaks off abruptly with the statement that Ane gave her mother medicine; what happened after that is uncertain. The reader's inference will depend upon his own emotional history—his conscious and unconscious relationships with objects, responses to loss, sense of identity. For the writer and original reader, whose mother had died, the implication is presumably not that Ane has recovered, but that loving feelings have triumphed over hostile ones, that the child was not responsible for the mother's death. Little Ane is a "good girl," caring and capable—a negation of the helpless (and possibly bad) girl who could not (or did not choose to) save her mother's life. In circumstances that her creator could only suffer passively, Ane reverses the parent-child relationship and becomes the active nurturer of the mother-as-child.

Like many other works of art, "There was once a little girl" is a continuation of the uncompleted work of mourning. By realigning the relationship between the self and the lost object, it changes the writer's image of herself in a way that ameliorates unconscious fear, grief, anger and guilt. Axiomatically, art can serve as a catharsis for painful feelings. Ane's story suggests that the creative work also contributes significantly to the formation of identity in two ways: Within the narrative, the artist asserts her heroine's (and therefore her own) strength and goodness, altering her inner reality; as the author of the story, she transforms herself from the passive sufferer to the active interpreter of experience in the external world. The writing of fiction is a kind of play which allows Brontë to imagine alternative reactions to actual events, to conceive a way of being that is different from the one external reality has imposed on her. In this instance, at least, the creative process adds something new to the artist's unconscious perceptions, as well as to the reality she consciously recognizes.

This "playwork," like the dreamwork or the jokework, can accomplish its ends entirely within the mind; fantasies can be effective without validation in the external world. It is when the individual communicates his inner experience to someone else that fantasy begins to move in the direction of art—of communication intended, consciously or unconsciously, to produce an effect on an audience. In Ane's story, Charlotte Brontë presents her sister with a fantasy that assures the real child of the fictional child's goodness, and by implication reassures her of her own. In so doing, the writer is unconsciously taking responsibility for her younger sister's well-being, and thus identifying with the mother in her protective aspect.

Both psychoanalytic observation of bereavement and the course of Brontë's later life lead to this hypothesis. Freud points out that the bereaved person takes a representation of the lost object into the inner self, and that this internalized object profoundly influences the formation of the ego as the character develops; Charlotte Brontë, whose earliest extant story describes a child's mothering her mother, became, as she grew up, the maternal caretaker of her father and siblings. Her sense of herself as the nurturer rather than the nurtured, the powerful rather than the powerless, emerged as a major element in her "identity theme" (Heinz Lichtenstein's term).[6] Throughout her writing, she created protagonists who define themselves through their relationships with others. The heroines of her juvenilia devote themselves totally to the men who are their sexual objects; Jane Eyre changes from a motherless waif to Rochester's powerful protector and supporter; Shirley Keeldar (in *Shirley*), stronger and more vital than her fiancé, turns over her fortune to him; Lucy Snowe (in *Villette*) begins her school with the help of the man she loves, but survives and makes a success of it after he dies. All are variations on the theme of object relationships as primary motivation; the traditionally weaker partner emerges as the stronger—the same reversal that little Ane accomplishes. As a daughter and sister, Brontë appropriated the position of the protector; as a novelist, she continued her early role of interpreter of experience and creator of meaning—the story teller, not the listener, the active agent, not the passive recipient.

Winnicott sees creativity as growing out of the child's attempt to repair the damage done to the mother in fantasy. Achieving the "capacity for concern"—the realization that the mother is a being like himself, with her own needs and vulnerabilities—the child moves toward "actively loving behaviour in his limited world, reviving the object, making the loved object better, rebuilding the damaged thing . . . the solution to the problem of the destruction of what is loved turns into the urge to work and to acquire skills."[7] Charlotte Brontë invents a fictional child who tries to make the loved object better, but she does not simply tell her story to her sister. Instead, she produces a manuscript which is a demonstration of skills: It is carefully printed in a minuscule imitation of type, illustrated with painstaking watercolor drawings, and sewn together between figured paper covers. In writing and "publishing" Ane's story, Brontë not only gave her reparative fantasies the authenticity of material existence, she also created an actual physical object, a child's version of a book.

"There was once a little girl," the child's play of a little girl who became a novelist, had for her—and has for the reader—all the seriousness that play involves. From her childhood onward, writing was for Brontë a way of working through emotional disturbance, of comprehending and integrating psychic and physical experience within the safety of fiction—in what Winnicott calls the "play space." But it was more than that. Just as dreams and jokes are not simply reactions to experience, this "playwork" is not merely a description of events. It is in itself a significant psychic event, an actual creating of new feelings.[8] In writing this story, the author took an important step in the formation of her identity as an artist, a maker of new objects. In the transitional space between the inner self and the outer world, where artist and audience meet, she created for herself new relationships with inner and external objects, and new ways of feeling about them.

Neither reading nor writing fiction is only a defense against an emotionally threatening reality. The creative act which produces the work of art and the creative act which is the reader's response to it effect psychic transformations which integrate the inner and outer worlds, and influence the growth and the shape of the self. Charlotte Brontë's earliest surviving story is, like all art, an intrinsic part of actual life which changes the reality in which child and adult, writer and reader, live.

Notes

The author is grateful to the American Council of Learned Societies for a year's fellowship which supported the research for this essay and the longer study of which it is a part, and to Dr. Albert D. Hutter of the Southern California Psychoanalytic Institute, who read and commented on an early draft.

1. Kathleen Tillotson: *Novels of the Eighteen-Forties* (Oxford: Oxford Univ. Press, 1954), p. 270-1.

2. Elizabeth Gaskell: *The Life of Charlotte Brontë* (New York: Dutton, 1974 [repr. of 1857 edition]), p. 314.

3. Gaskell, cited above, and Winifred Gerin, *Charlotte Brontë: the Evolution of Genius* (Oxford: Oxford Univ. Press, 1967) are the sources for biographical information in this essay. Psychoanalytic studies of Brontë include Lucille Dooley, "Psychoanalysis of Charlotte Brontë as a Type of the Woman of Genius," *American Journal of Psychology* 31, No. 3 (1920); Rosamund Langbridge,

Charlotte Brontë: a Psychological Study (New York: Doubleday, 1929); Charles Burkhart, *Charlotte Brontë: a Psychosexual Study of Her Novels* (London: Gollancz, 1973); Helene Moglen, *Charlotte Brontë: the Self-Conceived* (New York: Norton, 1976).

4. Unpublished, undated manuscript from the Bonnell Collection, Brontë Parsonage Museum, Haworth; published by permission of the Curator. Transcription by the author, who gratefully acknowledges the assistance of Professor Christine Alexander, University of New South Wales. Fannie Ratchford, *The Brontës' Web of Childhood* (New York: Russell and Russell, 1964) dates this story 1829. On the basis of language, style and subject matter, the date of 1824 assigned by C. W. Hatfield, *The Early Manuscripts of Charlotte Brontë: a Bibliography* (Haworth: Transactions of the Bronte Society, 1924) is clearly more probable.

5. Norman N. Holland: *The Dynamics of Literary Response* (New York: Norton, 1975) discusses at length the concept of literary form as a defense.

6. Heinz Lichtenstein: *The Dilemma of Human Identity* (New York: Jason Aronson, 1977).

7. D. W. Winnicott: *The Maturational Processes and the Facilitating Environment* (New York: Int. Univ. Press, 1977), p. 103.

8. Stephen A. Black, *Whitman's Journeys Into Chaos* (Princeton: Princeton Univ. Press, 1975) elaborates the idea that works of art do not *describe* psychic events, but *are* those events, a concept I first encountered in conversation with Professor Black and borrow from him here. Susanne Langer, *Problems of Art* (New York: Scribner's, 1957), asserts that the artist conceives the feeling in a work of art as he is creating the symbolic form that represents it; the work is not a cathartic, involuntary venting of feeling.

Susan Meyer (essay date winter 1991)

SOURCE: Meyer, Susan. "'Black' Rage and White Women: Ideological Self-Formation in Charlotte Brontë's African Tales." *South Central Review* 8, no. 4 (winter 1991): 28-40.

[*In the following essay, Meyer argues that Brontë's vision of British imperialism evolved from an unquestioning acceptance of white racial superiority to a halting identification with Quashia, the Ashanti tribal leader who is the nemesis of the white aristocracy in the Angrian tales. Meyer attributes the change to Brontë's growing recognition of her own financial and social marginality as a lower-middle-class woman.*]

Critics of Charlotte Brontë's juvenilia have noticed the passionate interest in contemporary politics reflected in her early writings: her fascination with the Duke of Wellington, the characters named after other contemporary figures, the allusions to current affairs, such as Catholic Emancipation, and the important formative influence of *Blackwood's Edinburgh Magazine.* Yet the way in which the Brontë children's early tales are most fundamentally involved with British politics has received virtually no sustained attention. From their very beginnings, as the prominence of the Duke of Wellington might suggest, the Brontë children's juvenile tales are centrally about imagining the British empire.

The story of the founding of the children's imaginary world is well known. As it is usually told, the game grew up around the twelve toy soldiers the Reverend Brontë brought home for Branwell one June night in 1826. The next morning Branwell brought his soldiers into the girls' bedroom to show them to his sisters, and Charlotte leapt out of bed, seized a soldier, and named him after her military hero, the Duke of Wellington, who had been posted in India and had defeated Napoleon in the Napoleonic Wars. Following her lead, each of the children chose and named a soldier to use as a personal hero. The twelve individually carved and individually named soldiers became the first characters in a childhood game which was to develop into the creation of a complicated imaginary world: a city called first Glass Town and then Verdopolis, expanding into the larger region of Angria, about which Charlotte and Branwell were to write hundreds of pages over the next thirteen years.[1]

But two crucial aspects of the story are given little attention by Brontë biographers and critics. The retellings of this story tend not to emphasize the historical specificity of this imaginary world: Glass Town is an imaginary British colony established by British soldiers on the west coast of Africa. The Brontë children, avid readers of the Tory journal *Blackwood's,* founded their fictitious colony on the Niger river delta, near Fernando Po, following one *Blackwood's* writer's advice on how to strengthen the British position in Africa.[2]

A second crucial element of the story, which can be found in Branwell's version of the origin of the games, is also rarely mentioned by the biographers. The gift Reverend Brontë brought home for Charlotte that night in June was also used in the game in the early stages in which the children were still physically enacting their stories. The children used her toy, a set of small ninepins, to represent the black Africans, the Ashantis (or, as the Brontë children spelled it, the Ashantees) whom the white soldiers encountered as they arrived in Africa.[3] The children's choice to array the ninepins, as the Ashantees, against the toy soldiers—the representation of the Africans with objects which were all alike, not in

human shape, and designed to be knocked over—suggests the relative degree of humanity accorded the two groups in the initial conception of Glass Town.

By recalling the existence of those black ninepins, and by attending to the African setting of the Brontë tales, we can see to what degree the Brontë children's tales were about their imagination of empire. The juvenile texts provide important early evidence of the significance British imperialism and racial conflict have for Charlotte Brontë, of the way in which, in fact, the British empire is associated with the very beginnings of her fictional inspiration and her creation of herself as a writer. But if being a writer for Brontë arose out of the "drama" and tensions of empire, out of the desire to imagine and tell its stories, becoming a woman writer required negotiating a more complex relation to British imperialism. In her earliest juvenile texts, Brontë's sense of herself as a writer is as a transcendent, god-like, genderless creator: she figures in the tales as the "Genius Tallii," who, along with the Genii Brannii, Emmii, and Annii, moves the characters around like pawns. But in her later juvenile texts, as Brontë becomes more aware of herself not as transcendent but as socially situated, the nature of her representation of empire and racial hierarchy begins to evolve.

Charlotte Brontë's early juvenile tales, like Branwell's, unabashedly thematize knocking over the black ninepins. Branwell describes the violence of the colonial process with matter-of-fact bluntness: in his history of the founding of the Glass Town colony he recounts that the heroic British soldiers "speedily . . . began the business of founding towns in various eligible situations, exploring lands and shooting negroes."[4] Charlotte Brontë's history of the founding of the colony is only slightly less ruthless. Her early stories, dated in the late 1820s and early 1830s, describe, without emphasis or comment, the soldiers' possession of the Ashantees' cultivated land, and the capture of black slaves.[5] Charlotte Brontë's early tales, like Branwell's, seem to voice without ambivalence the dominant imperialist ideology of the period—attitudes of triumphant conquest and of white racial superiority which pervaded British writing on the colonies. But as Brontë's own biography follows a course of greater alienation and social disempowerment, the nature of the representation of empire in her juvenile writing changes. The representations of empire and race relations in Brontë's later juvenilia no longer calmly affirm white racial domination; they reveal an ideology in flux.

The shift in Brontë's representation of empire, I will argue, her motivation to question imperialist ideology, arises from an increasing awareness of her social position as a lower-middle-class woman. It was a common rhetorical move in nineteenth-century writing, used in the service of affirmations of middle-class white male superiority, to compare both white women and the white working class to blacks. Nineteenth-century scientists described an intellectual inferiority common to both white women and the "lower races," noting that, among other evidences of this mutual inferiority, the brain size of both white women and of blacks was smaller than that of white men.[6] Insensitivity to physical pain also revealed the similarities among "the lower human races, the lower classes of society, women and children."[7] Such analogies were invoked particularly in times of perceived threat to the social order. In response to the working-class agitation of the 1820s, which was to develop into the Chartist movement of the 1830s, for example, *Blackwood's* published a poem mocking white working men by associating them with blacks: they debate in taverns, according to the writer, about "How to relieve the wide world of its chains, / Pluck Despots down, / And thereby crown / Whitee- as well as Blackeeman-cipation."[8] Such analogies circulated widely in early nineteenth-century British culture as a whole as well as in the Tory intellectual and political environment within which Charlotte Brontë grew up. As Brontë became aware, as her childhood progressed, that she was not personally in the position of social privilege enjoyed, for instance, by the middle-class male writers of *Blackwood's,* her attitude toward the associated complex of social hierarchies underwent significant changes. Brontë's increasing awareness of the constraints of her position as a woman of the lower-middle class, who faced a lifetime of labor at subsistence-level wages, gradually led her into a more oppositional representation of empire than is evident in her earliest Glass Town writings.

This transformation is apparent in two texts from different moments in Brontë's adolescence in which she creates imaginary images of empire. The first passage was written in 1831 or 1832, when she was about fifteen years old and was away at school for the second time in her life. It was a time when Brontë had reason to feel relatively socially fortunate. Unlike the disastrous experience of charity-school education which she had undergone five years previously at Cowan Bridge, and which she was later to recreate as the Lowood School in *Jane Eyre,* Brontë's brief three terms at Roe Head boarding school were an experience not of deprivation but of privilege. Even with assistance from her godparents, the family could only afford to keep Charlotte at Roe Head, which was attended by much wealthier girls, for a year and a half, but in that time, by all accounts, she was the most eager and diligent student at the school, so conscious of this period of formal education as a privilege that she studied even during play time and set herself double lessons.[9]

The one passage in which we have evidence of Brontë's imaginative vision of empire during this period reveals her attempt to fit into and affirm the structures of Brit-

ish society. It is from an account of Brontë in her school days by Ellen Nussey, one of her school friends:

> When her companions formed the idea of having a coronation performance on a half-holiday, it was Charlotte Brontë who drew up the programme, arranged the titles to be adopted by her companions for the occasion, wrote the invitations to those who were to grace the ceremony, and selected for each a title, either for sound that pleased the ear or for historical association. The preparations for these extra half-holidays (which were very rare occurrences) sometimes occupied spare moments for weeks before the event. On this occasion Charlotte prepared a very elegant little speech for the one who was selected to present the crown. Miss W[ooler]'s younger sister consented after much entreaty to be crowned as our queen (a very noble, stately queen she made), and did her pupils all the honor she could by adapting herself to the role of the moment. The following exquisite little speech shows Charlotte's aptitude, even then, at giving fitting expression to her thoughts:
>
> 'Powerful Queen! accept this Crown, the symbol of dominion, from the hands of your faithful and affectionate subjects! And if their earnest and united wishes have any efficacy, you will long be permitted to reign over this peaceful, though circumscribed empire.'
>
> [Signed, etc., etc.],
>
> Your loyal subjects.
>
> The little fete finished off with what was called a ball; but for lackofnumbers we had to content ourselves with one quadrille and two Scotch reels. Last of all there was a supper, which was considered very *recherché,* most of it having been coaxed out of yielding mammas and elder sisters, in addition to some wise expenditure of pocket-money. The grand feature, however, of the supper was the attendance of a mulatto servant. We descended for a moment from our assumed dignities to improvise this distinguishing appanage. The liveliest of our party, 'Jessie Yorke,' volunteered this office, and surpassed our expectations. Charlotte evidently enjoyed the fun, in her own quiet way, as much as any one, and ever after with great zest helped, when with old schoolfellows, to recall the performances of the exceptional half-holidays.[10]

The speech written by Charlotte Brontë, along with the elaborate pageant subsequently invented by the students, uses the imagery of empire to represent the hierarchy of Roe Head School. All, in this empire, is decorous, orderly, and peaceful. The head schoolmistress, Miss Wooler, represented in the actual pageant by her more cooperative younger sister, also a teacher at the school, is a "Powerful Queen" who is willingly given power by her "faithful and affectionate subjects," the students, and who does her subjects honor by accepting their tribute. The hierarchy of this empire, we might say, is both justified and earned: the teacher gains her queenly position by a superior knowledge and experience. In the nonconflictual vision of empire Brontë presents in this speech, monarchs and subjects mutually honor each other with pleasure and respect.

The ceremonies after the pageant were not of Brontë's individual invention; instead they seem to have been a group conception arising spontaneously from the imagery of her speech. For these British schoolgirls, the idea of the attendance at the supper of the undignified and comic mulatto, the "grand feature" of the evening, grew out of and was evidently seen as continuous with the vision of empire Brontë had created for the pageant. The status of the mulatto, in 1832, six years before the full emancipation of the slaves in the British colonies in 1838, is disguised by Nussey's polite term, "servant."[11] The subordination of this "happy darky" enhances the glory of the imagined empire: he (or she?) is a "distinguishing appanage" who, by enacting subjection, makes the British subjects of the "Powerful Queen" more exalted. Nussey's diction equates the unnamed and ungendered mulatto with the "recherché" supper: the word "appanage" is of French derivation from the Latin "ad" ("to") and "pan-is" ("bread"). This "provision made for the maintenance of the younger children of kings," or, as the word is used more loosely, this "specially appropriated possession" is, in more than one sense, "feeding" the British subjects (OED, sb. 1, 2). Nussey's word choice reveals the way in which the mulatto servant is distinguishing by the very subordination which servitude and comic characterization provide. Like fine food, or lands, or property, the mulatto boosts the status of those of middling rank, the white British, rather than the dark colonial subjects of the queen. This is the vision of empire—orderly, ceremonial, with each cheerfully filling an appointed place—evoked by the imperial pageant Brontë created during her relatively privileged year and a half as a student at Roe Head School.

One might add, though, that the passage also reveals a slight sense of strain—that this celebration of idealized hierarchy does not come with complete ease to Brontë even at this relatively privileged moment in her life. The white British subjects here, despite their cheerful acceptance of hierarchy, seem actually to be in control of the pageant: they hand the imperial crown to the queen and "permit" her to reign over them. Brontë's word choice suggests that the subjects have it in their power no longer to accept the queen's rule. Even in this grand celebration of hierarchy, the slight indication of a tension which will emerge later in Brontë's juvenile writing is evident.

In 1835, a few years later, Brontë returned to Roe Head, this time to work as a teacher. Teaching at Roe Head she had virtually no time to herself, for the writing and imagining already so important in her life. It was a situation she had no reason to expect would change: at the age of nineteen she faced a lifetime of such work. Now at Roe Head as a teacher, she felt her class difference from the majority of the students with a new sharpness. In her journal and letters, she expresses her discontent and anger about becoming a servant and a nursemaid to the students: she worked for twelve hour days, she records, did the students' mending and packing, in addition to teaching them, and at times was even called on to babysit the children of Miss Wooler's sister.[12] Brontë refers to her students, in these private writings, with great hostility: she terms them "the ladies," and "asses" and "Dolts," and she describes her teaching, and her sister Emily's, as "bondage" and "slavery."[13] "[A]m I to spend all the best part of my life in this wretched bondage," she writes in a typical passage, "forcibly suppressing my rage at the idleness, the apathy, and the hyperbolical and most asinine stupidity of those fat-headed oafs, and on compulsion assuming an air of kindness, patience, and assiduity?"[14]

One of Brontë's journal entries from these years, known by its first sentence as "Well, here I am at Roe Head," dated 1836, opens with Brontë's worries, after an arduous week of teaching, about her dislike for her work and her difficulty in adjusting to it. In this journal entry, written at a time in which Brontë is beginning to experience her financial and social marginality, a quite different vision of her place in society and of empire begins to emerge:

> Well, here I am at Roe Head. It is seven o'clock at night; the young ladies are all at their lessons. . . . I now assume my own thoughts. My mind relaxes from the stretch on which it has been for the last twelve hours and falls back onto the rest which nobody in this house knows of but myself. . . . It is strange. I cannot get used to the ongoings that surround me. I fulfil my duties strictly and well. I must, so to speak. If the illustration be not profane—as God was not in the wind nor the fire nor the earthquake so neither is my heart in the task, the theme or the exercise.

Brontë then goes on to describe a vision of the private world she had been writing about since the age of twelve, that secret "rest" which no one else at Roe Head knew to be sustaining her. The imaginary African colony is in the throes of a revolution. Zamorna, the white king of Angria, husband to Queen Mary Percy, is contending against an uprising by his white, aristocratic arch-rival, Alexander Percy, in league with the French, the Angrian working class, and the native black "Ashantees," under their leader, Quashia. The rebels have now occupied the palace of Adrianopolis, capital city of Angria. Brontë notes that the Angrian vision had come upon her in a "trance" the previous night, during a wild storm: "it whirled me away like heath in the wilderness for five seconds of ecstasy." She first describes herself, in the vision, walking along the "latticed arches" of a palace: "passing along quick as thought, I glanced at what the internal glare revealed through the crystal." No longer a participant in imperial dignities, Brontë is now an outsider to the aristocratic palace. Brontë, as narrator, goes on to recall what she has earlier seen through these windows: Queen Mary Percy, in melancholy despondency and devotion, waiting for the return of the husband who has abandoned her to revenge himself on her father. The white queen, in the scenes the narrator recalls, was sadly but passively accepting the ill treatment of men. But what the narrator now sees in the queen's rooms is quite different. The scene she describes is, like the school pageant she designed, a vision of empire, but this private and secret vision is very different from the one she had enacted publicly a few years before:

> The red ray of the fire flashed upon a table covered with wine flasks, some drained and some brimming with the crimson juice. The cushions of a voluptuous ottoman, which had often supported her [Queen Mary Percy's] slight fine form, were crushed by a dark bulk flung upon them in drunken prostration. Aye, where she had lain imperially robed and decked with pearls, every waft of her garments as she moved diffusing perfume, her beauty slumbering and still glowing as dreams of him for whom she kept herself in such hallowed and shrine-like separation wandered over her soul on her own silken couch, a swarth and sinewy moor intoxicated to ferocious insensibility had stretched his athletic limbs weary with wassail and stupified [sic] with drunken sleep. I knew it to be Quashia himself, and well could I guess why he had chosen the Queen of Angria's sanctuary for the scene of his solitary revelling. While he was full before my eyes, lying in his black dress on the disordered couch, his sable hair dishevelled on his forehead, his tusk-like teeth glancing vindictively through his parted lips, his brown complexion flushed with wine, and his broad chest heaving wildly as the breath issued in snorts from his distended nostrils, while I watched the fluttering of his white shirt ruffles, starting through the more than half-unbuttoned waistcoat, and beheld the expression of his Arabian countenance savagely exulting even in sleep—Quamina, triumphant lord in the halls of Zamorna! in the bower of Zamorna's lady!—while this apparition was before me, the dining-room door opened, and Miss W[ooler] came in with a plate of butter in her hand. "A very stormy night, my dear!" said she.

> "It is, ma'am," said I.[15]

What is perhaps most immediately striking about Brontë's vision is its racism. Quashia is a stereotypically drunken and hyperbolically sexual black male, rolling on the queen's couch with heaving chest and disordered clothes. The reference to "tusk-like teeth" simultaneously suggests his sexuality and his resemblance to beasts. The association of Quashia with African elephants also suggests an imperialist perspective in which he is both expendable and capable of being turned into a product for British imperialist consumption.[16] Quashia's very name derives from the racist epithet "Quashee," a British racial slur equivalent to the word "nigger."

Yet despite the blatant racism of the passage, the way in which the empire is represented is dramatically different from that in the school pageant passage. Unlike

that peaceful, orderly hierarchy, with its cheerfully subordinate blacks, this empire is in a state of chaotic upheaval and revolution. The black character has moved to the center of the imagined scene, and is no longer a "distinguishing appanage" but a triumphant revolutionary. Quashia's surname, Quamina, is a more ambiguous designation than his first name, and could even be seen as heroic: he seems to have been named after Quamina Gladstone, one of the black slave leaders in British Guyana who led the Demerera uprising of 1823.[17] In her stolen "five seconds of ecstasy," Brontë envisions overturned hierarchies and successful revolution. The delight with which she describes her vision suggests both the pleasure with which, in this moment of wildness, she contemplates the overturning of the white aristocracy, and the identification she feels with her triumphant black male character. The narrator's positioning outside the crystal windows of the palace also links her with Quashia, the outsider. The crystal windows recall the name of the first imperial city—Glass Town—with its suggestion of visible but inaccessible grandeur and privilege. The image of a watcher outside windows recurs later in her work when Quashia complains of being positioned outside the palaces of privilege, looking in at those who "walk in silks & velvets & live in a diamond House with golden windows."[18] Like Quashia, Brontë is outside those windows. And when the narrator remembers seeing Mary Percy in those rooms, she recalls her sense of marginality and of the queen's remote inaccessibility: "I always felt as if I dared not have spoken to her, for my life." But with Quashia in the palace, the impenetrable crystal barrier dissolves: he is "full before [her] eyes," so close that she can watch his breathing and read his expression. The sense of dissolving barriers between narrator and characters, as well as the narrator's initial positioning outside the windows of privilege suggests Brontë's identification with Quashia.

The ironic ending of the journal entry also reveals a dramatic shift in Brontë's attitudes since the days of the school pageant empire. Brontë mockingly juxtaposes the "apparition" of Quashia, who aptly embodies the wildness and disorder of the storm, with the literal apparition of Miss Wooler who, with her butter plate and polite commentary on the weather, becomes, in contrast, the epitome of banality. The juxtaposition is entirely in Quashia's favor—Miss Wooler's entrance is an interruption of Brontë's storm-inspired vision, a vision which she obviously prefers, as her note of irritated irony indicates, to her abrupt, enforced return to the dining room of Roe Head school. Oddly, despite her racist representation of Quashia, Brontë identifies with this character, rather than with the once-idolized headmistress, making him a representative of the wild storm which gives her such pleasure, of her own transgressive imaginative trance, and of her social marginality, and contemplating with "ecstasy" a vision of his triumph over the white aristocracy.

In fact, Brontë's meditations, at the beginning of this journal fragment, about her discontent at Roe Head as an overworked and poorly paid teacher, are closely connected with the Angrian vision which she then describes. The few critics who cite this journal entry overlook this connection and tend to cite the "autobiographical" part separately from the Angrian vision.[19] The whole manuscript is driven by Brontë's discontent in her social position: Brontë's discontent at her "bondage," at her "governessing *slavery*" to the "young ladies" of Roe Head school, finds release in this manuscript in "five seconds of ecstasy" in a vision of the successful revolution of the oppressed Angrian blacks against the white Angrian aristocracy. Quashia—and the Ashantees whom he represents and the working class with whom he is allied—break from their bonds just as Brontë is inwardly rebelling against her "slavery." This momentary release comes abruptly to an end when her employer, Miss Wooler, enters the room with a plate of butter. In doing so, she disrupts Brontë's brief moment of privacy, and acts in this instance to represent, despite all of Brontë's affection for her, the oppressive conditions of her working life. When she enters, Brontë is restored to her own subordinate place in the social hierarchy, agreeing, in deferential tones, to the banalities of her superior: "'It is, ma'am,' said I."

It is interesting, however, that Brontë does not describe this moment of visionary release as disrupted by a detestable student; instead it is the head teacher, for whom Brontë felt some affection, who forcibly returns her to drab reality. The queen is absent from Brontë's Angrian vision, but she returns here in the form of Miss Wooler, once seen as "Powerful Queen," but now, carrying a plate of butter, demoted to the rank of servant. Miss Wooler appears at the end of the vision as Brontë's employer, but also as a figure for the servitude of the lives of women teachers. The passage demystifies the idealization of hard-working middle class women as queens of the hearth, by demoting the former queen into a domestic servant.[20] And the passage indirectly suggests a female rebellion against that role by transforming the docile, slumbering white queen, in a subtle bed trick, into an enraged, revolutionary black man.

"Well, here I am at Roe Head" reveals that by this point in the development of her imaginary world Charlotte Brontë is using the rebellious Angrian blacks as a figure for her rage against gender and class constraints. In her "five seconds of ecstasy," represented in this journal entry, Brontë vicariously takes pleasure in the overturning of the social system which Quashia's act symbolizes. Yet at the same time that the passage reveals an identification with the oppressed and now revolutionary African blacks, it is unquestionably racist. The passage is, at its core, ambivalent. Quashia, who stands for a part of Brontë's personality about which she is extremely uneasy, is represented in terms simultaneously celebratory and reflective of all the language of nineteenth-century British racist judgment. In fact, interestingly the racism is more blatant in this passage than in the school pageantry. The racist characterization of blacks seems to intensify when they are imagined as more real, more central, and more powerful—as well as more linked to disturbing impulses in the white self. In the world the children appropriately named "Angria," Brontë explored the disturbing impulses of anger in herself, her social discontent and ambivalence, an ambivalence which is then enacted in the racist characterization of blacks. The echo of the word "Africa" in the name "Angria" emphasizes the way in which Brontë is using the Africans to express her own "black" rage.

To read Brontë's stories in this way is not in any way to deny their racism. Indeed, such a use of black characters—to represent a white woman's rage at her gender and class limitations—obviously reveals only a very incomplete identification with the oppressed Africans. Brontë's figurative strategy is appropriative: her juvenile writings are not exploring the reality of race relations under British colonialism, but are rather exploring gender and class relations in Brontë's Britain through the setting of an African colony and the figure of the revolutionary black leader. Her use of African blacks to represent rage reduces them to this one dimension of character, making them less fully human than other characters in the imaginary colony.

Yet it is interesting to find that Brontë's resistance to gender and class hierarchies sustains, rather than impedes, an impulse to imagine the overturning of racial hierarchies. The Roe Head journal entry is a manifestation of the struggle for ideological self-definition, in a moment in which the author's relation to social hierarchies is in flux. The young Charlotte Brontë is no longer simply "speaking the culture"—affirming, with her imaginative images, the rightness and inevitability of imperialist racial hierarchy. Instead here, if Brontë's imaginative images are speaking the culture, they are speaking the culture's nightmares—successful black and working class revolt—and using them to express her own subversive fantasies—the rebellion of the working woman, the invasion of the structure of privilege, unloosed sexuality, and the routing and disempowerment of the ruling class.

The apparent trajectory in Brontë's ideological self-formation, the apparent movement toward the rejection of racial along with gender and class hierarchy, is not borne out, as I argue elsewhere, in the fiction of Brontë's maturity.[21] Brontë's anger about class and gender constraints, while expressed through metaphors which draw their energies from the conflicts of imperialism, does not finally lead her to a rejection or an imaginative overturning of racial hierarchy. Yet that such an ideological trajectory was possible can be seen in the disruption of complacency about empire to which Brontë's other forms of discontent could lead her. Gayatri Chakravorty Spivak has asserted that nineteenth-century British feminism was complicitous with imperialist ideology, while Elin Diamond, in a reading of the drama of Aphra Behn and Caryl Churchill, finds similarly that while one might expect feminist playwrights to be conscious of imperialist oppression, in fact they are not: "the foregrounding of gender inequalities in texts by women dramatists does not perforce include, and may not even imply an awareness of racism's violence."[22] While I would not assert that such a linking by feminist writers is either necessary or automatic, Brontë's juvenile writings demonstrate that a linking of class as well as gender oppression with racial oppression is both possible in her historical moment and a logical and consistent response to the ideological structures to which she was exposed.

The ideological struggle which we can see at work in Brontë's Roe Head journal provides an instance of one of the ways in which a writer can come to work out an oppositional position in relation to the dominant ideology. Comparisons between one hierarchy and another in nineteenth-century texts—comparisons of white women and the white working class to blacks—were intended to reinforce the ideology of white male supremacy. Yet when viewed from an oppositional perspective, these comparisons not only manifest some strain, some sense of conflict with resistant thought, and a need for ideological reinforcement, but could be turned into strategies for resistance which the dominant ideology had unintentionally authorized. Stephen Greenblatt has described colonialist power as all-encompassing and preemptive, contending that "subversiveness . . . was produced by the colonial power in its own interest."[23] Laura Brown has argued in response that "we can read the literature of those in power not only for the massive and elaborate means by which power is exercised, but also as a source of leverage for those in opposition, that while sites of resistance may be produced within a dominant ideology . . . they do not serve it. They are produced despite it."[24] I would add that not only are strategies of resistance unintentionally produced within a dominant ideology, but that possibilities for resistance are produced precisely at those cultural moments when the dominant ideology is experienced as under attack or in need of reinforcement. The moves of ideological reinforcement themselves create the opening for resistance, the possibility for distancing oneself from a dominant ideology and imagining another mode of thought. Charlotte Brontë's juvenile writings about Africa provide an example of a young writer in such a moment of ideological struggle.

Notes

1. Christine Alexander is in the process of editing a standard critical edition of Charlotte Brontë's juvenilia for the Shakespeare Head Press, of which one volume out of three has been published: Christine Alexander, ed., *An Edition of the Early Writings of Charlotte Brontë, Volume I: The Glass Town Saga 1826-1832* (New York: Basil Blackwell, 1987). My quotations of the later juvenilia come from the following editions: Thomas James Wise and John Alexander Symington, ed., *The Miscellaneous and Unpublished Writings of Charlotte and Patrick Branwell Brontë*, 2 vols. (Oxford: The Shakespeare Head Press, 1936); Charlotte Brontë, *Five Novelettes,* ed. Winifred Gerin (London: The Folio Press, 1971); and the juvenile texts edited by Christine Alexander included in Richard J. Dunn, ed., *Jane Eyre: A Norton Critical Edition,* 2nd ed. (New York: Norton, 1987). I also use excerpts from texts published only in the following studies of the juvenile writings: Fannie Elizabeth Ratchford, *The Brontës' Web of Childhood* (1941; New York: Russell & Russell, 1964) and Christine Alexander, *The Early Writings of Charlotte Brontë* (Oxford: Basil Blackwell, 1983). An indispensable tool in studying Charlotte Brontë's juvenile writings is Christine Alexander, *A Bibliography of the Manuscripts of Charlotte Brontë* (Keighley, West Yorkshire: The Brontë Society-Meckler Publishing, 1982).

2. See Alexander, *Early Writings* 30.

3. Branwell Brontë, "The History of the Young Men," Wise and Symington, *Unpublished Writings* 1: 78. I will use the spelling "Ashantees" when I am referring to the Brontë children's representations of the Ashantis.

4. Branwell Brontë, "History of the Young Men," transcript from C. W. Hatfield, quoted in Ratchford 116.

5. Charlotte Brontë, "A Romantic Tale," Wise and Symington, *Unpublished Writings* 1: 5, 10.

6. See Cynthia Eagle Russett, *Sexual Science: The Victorian Construction of Womanhood* (Cambridge, Mass.: Harvard UP, 1989) 55.

7. William I. Thomas, "On a Difference in the Metabolism of the Sexes," *American Journal of Sociology* 3 (1897): 50, quoted in Russett 56.

8. T. H., "The Monkey-Martyr: A Fable," *Blackwood's Edinburgh Magazine* 21 (1827): 706-08.

9. See Winifred Gerin, *Charlotte Brontë: The Evolution of Genius* (Oxford: Clarendon Press, 1967) 54-76.

10. "Ellen Nussey's Narrative," Thomas James Wise and John Alexander Symington, ed., *The Brontës:*

Their Lives, Friendships, and Correspondence, 4 vols. (Oxford: The Shakespeare Head Press, 1932) 1: 95-6.

11. England abolished slavery in its colonies in 1834; full emancipation, however, did not occur until 1838. See Michael Craton, *Sinews of Empire: A Short History of British Slavery* (Garden City, New York: Anchor Books, 1974) 239-84.

12. See Gerin, *Evolution* 107, 112.

13. Gerin, *Evolution* 103, 113.

14. Charlotte Brontë, "All this day I have been in a dream," ed. Christine Alexander, in Dunn 413.

15. Charlotte Brontë, "Well, here I am at Roe Head," ed. Christine Alexander, in Dunn 410-12.

16. The British trade in ivory was well under way by this period. See J. D. Fage, *A History of Africa* (New York: Knopf, 1978) 326-27. I am grateful to Ophelia Dahl for pointing out this comparison of Quashia to African elephants harvested for their ivory in class discussion at Wellesley College.

17. For an account of the uprising, see Robin Blackburn, *The Overthrow of Colonial Slavery 1776-1848* (New York: Verso, 1988) 428-31.

18. Charlotte Brontë, *Caroline Vernon,* Gerin, *Five Novelettes* 284.

19. See for example Ratchford 109, 114; Alexander, *Early Writings* 217.

20. Joan Burstyn notes that the nineteenth-century English middle class held that the most ideal, saintly woman's life was one blissfully occupied with care of the home and children. This ideal, Burstyn argues, was in ironic conflict with a reality in which the wealthy women of the middle class handed over the duties of the household and child-rearing to women of lower economic status. Joan N. Burstyn, *Victorian Education and the Ideal of Womanhood* (Totowa, New Jersey: Barnes & Noble, 1980) 132-34. The middle-class ideology of selfless female service thus fell upon "every woman who has the sacred duty of training up the young committed to her trust" as Mrs. Sarah Ellis, author of conduct books for middle-class women, put it in a carefully ambiguous phrase. Sarah Ellis, *The Women of England, Their Social Duties, and Domestic Habits* (Philadelphia: Carey & Hart, 1839) 2: 209. For the most part, women bearing the burden of this "sacred duty" toward upper-middle-class and upper-class children, were hired governesses working both in schools for girls and in private families, who were, like Brontë, from the lower middle class. These women had virtually no other employment options which their class

considered respectable, yet the cold economic compulsion under which they performed the "sacred duty" was obfuscated by this middle-class ideology of the joys of domesticity, care for others, and womanly self-abnegation.

21. See my "Colonialism and the Figurative Strategy of *Jane Eyre*," *Victorian Studies* 33 (1990): 247-68; reprinted in *Macropolitics of Nineteenth-Century Literature: Nationalism, Exoticism, Imerialism,* ed. Jonathan Arac and Harriet Ritvo (Philadelphia: U of Pennsylvania P, 1991) 159-83.

22. Gayatri Chakravorty Spivak, "Three Women's Texts and a Critique of Imperialism," *Critical Inquiry* 12 (1985): 243-61; Elin Diamond, "Closing No Gaps: Aphra Behn, Caryl Churchill, and Empire," *Caryl Churchill: A Casebook,* ed. Phyllis Randall (New York: Garland, 1988) 172.

23. Stephen Greenblatt, "Invisible Bullets: Renaissance Authority and its Subversion in *Henry IV* and *Henry V,*" *Political Shakespeare: New Essays in Cultural Materialism,* ed. Jonathan Dollimore and Alan Sinfield (Ithaca: Cornell UP, 1985) 24.

24. Laura Brown, "The Romance of Empire: *Oroonnoko* and the Trade in Slaves," *The New Eighteenth Century: Theory, Politics, English Literature,* ed. Felicity Nussbaum and Laura Brown (New York: Methuen, 1987) 61.

Heather Glen (essay date May 2007)

SOURCE: Glen, Heather. "Experiments in Fiction: Charlotte Brontë's Last Angrian Tales." *Women's Writing* 14, no. 1 (May 2007): 4-22.

[*In the following essay, Glen presents the last five Angrian fictions as evidence that Brontë was self-consciously experimenting with the wide variety of short fictional forms—vignettes, tales, sketches, papers, and miscellanies—then featured in the fashionable magazines. According to Glen, Brontë purposely avoided constructing the Angrian cycle on a cohesive master narrative, desiring instead to emulate the aesthetics of "disjunction and inconclusiveness" characteristic of the popular episodic fiction of the day.*]

The last five of Charlotte Brontë's surviving Angrian fictions—**"Mina Laury," "Stancliffe's Hotel," "The Duke of Zamorna," "Henry Hastings"** and **"Caroline Vernon"**—were written between 1838 and 1839.[1] These "tales", as I shall call them, for want of a better term, have long been known to Brontë critics and scholars. But they have scarcely been considered as serious works of art. Because their scenes and characters are those of the imaginary world of Angria, it has often been assumed that they are more private and more solipsistic than in fact they are. Indeed, they have been pathologized as obsessive, unstructured "trance-writing", unselfconsciously and fervidly reproducing the sexist and racist ideology of their time.[2] At best, they have been seen as giving evidence of Charlotte Brontë's developing skill in presenting psychologically realistic character or of her growing capacity to subject her fantasies to moral scrutiny.[3]

It is certainly true that sexist and racist stereotypes are prominent in these tales. They are set in a fashionable world of dissolute sexual mores—of amoral Byronic heroes and their passionately devoted mistresses; of romantic intrigue, and seduction, betrayal and adultery. Their protagonists are aggressive colonizers in an Africa whose natives are depicted as drunken, marauding savages. Conversely, it is true that there is a growing psychological complexity in their representation of character. They explore the love-hate relationship between their Byronic heroes; the insecurities of dandyish masculinity; a young girl's dawning awareness of her sexuality. The "independent woman" of Brontë's later novels here makes her first appearance. Female characters developed in the earlier juvenilia—the courtesan Louisa Vernon, cynically transferring her affections from one "protector" to another; Mina Laury and Mary Percy, each differently losing self in all-consuming romantic love—are counterbalanced here by more ambiguous figures, women not defined by their relationship to men: Jane Moore, who baffles her would-be adorers with her cheerful self-composure; Elizabeth Hastings, the governess, independent and alone. Indeed, this latter figure—small, plain and insignificant, but with a steely determination and a capacity for passionate love—has been seized upon by critics as a forerunner of Jane Eyre.

Yet these apparently similar characters are represented very differently; and the difference might prompt us to consider these tales of Angria not as early attempts at the psychological realism that contemporaries were to hail in Charlotte Brontë's first published novel[4], but as fictions of a rather different kind. For Elizabeth Hastings' ambitious self-cultivation is far more cynically observed than Jane Eyre's struggle to survive. That identification with the protagonist that readers of *Jane Eyre* were to cherish is checked in these tales of Angria by a deflating narrative voice. Where Jane speaks with intimate directness of her longings for "incident, life, fire, feeling" (ch. 12), **"Caroline Vernon"** offers a more sardonic view of its daydreaming young heroine—one whose brain is "filled with the rawest hash of ideas imaginable", and who is first seen strumming a song that was all the rage in 1838 (373, 363). The narrator throughout is the cynical Charles Townshend, who in his dandyism, his self-irony and his voyeuristic curiosity is far closer to the eponymous narrator of Bulwer-

Lytton's best-selling silver-fork novel *Pelham* (1828) than to the passionate, serious Jane Eyre. These ironic little fictions are not, it appears, private, obsessive "trance-writings", but sharply and wittily responsive to the literary fashions of their time—silver-fork fiction throughout, the Newgate novel in **"Henry Hastings,"** and (especially in **"Caroline Vernon"**) the Gothic and romantic tales that their author had first encountered in old copies of "the Lady's Magazine".[5] They were evidently written in the confidence that the "reader" or "readers" frequently addressed within them would pick up topical allusions and respond to generic cues. And, as I shall be suggesting, they play with, exploit and reflect upon the potentialities of fiction in surprisingly sophisticated ways.

Yet the reader who comes to these tales with expectations shaped by the high Victorian novel will find them disconcerting. They are quite conspicuously lacking in many of the qualities that we have come to associate with the form—extended, psychologically realistic development of character, moral seriousness, structural coherence, symbolic or thematic patterning, and complex unifying plot. Characters appear abruptly, with no introduction;[6] they are not continuously developed, but "seen now in profile, now in full-face, now in outline, and again in finished painting, varied but by the change of feeling or temper or age"—as Charlotte Brontë put it, in the fragment that has become known as her **"Farewell to Angria"**.[7] Instead of moral reflection, there is witty social comedy—the Duchess of Zamorna and her husband's mistress each dissembling to the other; Elizabeth Hastings leaving Sir William Percy high and dry in the moonlight; "Messrs Clarke and Gardiner" disconcerted by Jane Moore (50-52, 305, 98-101). None of these tales tell a single story leading to denouement and resolution. Each consists instead of a series of "scenes", much of the narrative implied in the spaces between. Loose ends are not tied together; things are not followed through. The sense at the end of each is less of tensions resolved and a stable future assured than of a peculiarly fragile stasis and continuing unease.

There is nothing here like the unifying symbolism that shapes those later novels: *Villette*'s sunshine and shadow; *Jane Eyre*'s "war of earthly elements".[8] The details and images in these tales have a peculiarly disruptive, inconsequential quiddity: a troop of half-savage little girls in a room whose walls are hung with "wild Salvator scenes"; an old man showing too much "spindle" in tights; a sudden mental vision of "legs jammed into the body like a telescope" (179, 69, 259). There seems to be, indeed, a quite deliberate emphasis on the accidental, the random, the arbitrary, what simply happens by chance—a carriage overturned; a dog catching a bat; the bump that appears when the heroine bangs her head (49, 149, 399). And as if in reflection on this heterogeneity, there are recurrent images throughout of miscellaneous, disconnected things—a meal of "rice-currie, devilled turkey and guava"; a list of disparate entries from a "fashionable intelligence" column; a bundle of pilfered letters, "all unconnected"; the contents of a dandy's carpet bag (68, 75, 139, 77). "Will you take some salmagundi, Mr Clarke?" asks Jane Moore in **"Stancliffe's Hotel"** (99). Grose's *Dictionary of the Vulgar Tongue* (1811) tells us that "salmagundi" was "a dish composed of chopped meat, anchovies, eggs, apples and onions, with oil and condiments", and that it was used often in a figurative sense to mean a potpourri or a miscellany. The term had been adopted by Washington Irving as the title of the popular series of "papers" on "an infinite variety of characters and circumstances"[9] which had launched his career as a writer of sketches more than 30 years before—and which was still in 1841 to be found in the library of the Keighley Mechanics' Institute, from which, in the late 1830s, the Brontë family borrowed books.[10] The joking little allusion is characteristic of these tales. It signals to the reader that these first of Charlotte Brontë's adult fictions are not attempts at or fragments of novels, but distinctive, self-conscious experiments in a different, and—to her and her readers—quite familiar, literary form.

Perhaps the most potent influence on the Brontë children's first "plays" had been a collection of short stories. For them, as for thousands of early nineteenth-century children, *The Arabian Nights' Entertainments* were a rich and long-remembered imaginative resource. The *Arabian Nights* seems to have been important to Charlotte Brontë not merely as a source of ideas and images (such as the all-powerful genii) but for the example it provided of a collection of short prose fictions, discontinuous but connected, each embedded within a larger narrative frame. By 1838, when the first of these tales were written, Charlotte Brontë may also have encountered another such collection, likewise enjoying a resurgence of popularity in early nineteenth-century England. Margaret Wooler, headmistress at Roe Head school, was a noted Italian scholar; if, as Charlotte's journal fragments suggest, she introduced her prize pupil to Italian literature, it is very likely that she included at least some of that other great collection of separate yet related stories, Boccaccio's *The Decameron*.[11]

It is the end of the nineteenth century that is usually seen as the period of the flowering of the short story. But as the Corvey project's listings show, there was a huge amount of interest in and experiment with the possibilities of short fiction in the years in which Charlotte Brontë was serving her literary "apprenticeship".[12] If the *Arabian Nights,* loved since childhood, was to continue to haunt her imagination, a whole variety of early nineteenth-century short fictions was available to her. Such fictions appeared both in the popular annuals and keepsakes from which the young Brontës copied prints,

and in the periodicals which were their main point of access to the contemporary literary world. Since the late eighteenth century, the *Lady's Magazine* (old copies of which were to be found in Haworth Parsonage, and with which, in her early twenties, Charlotte Brontë connected her literary experiments) had been printing short Gothic and romantic tales.[13] *Blackwood's Magazine,* which the Brontës "read and re-read" in childhood[14], specialized in "tales" of sensation and in first-person "anecdotes" (defined much later by Henry James as "something that has oddly happened to someone");[15] Charlotte Brontë knew both of these, and imitated both in her early contributions to the Glass Town *Blackwood's Young Men's Magazine.*[16] Regional tales were also popular: in the 1820s and 30s the young Brontës' childhood favourites Walter Scott and James Hogg were famous as authors of these. Perhaps the finest of all early nineteenth-century short fictions, Scott's "The Highland Widow" (one of his *Chronicles of the Canongate*), was much praised and very extensively quoted in an enormous review in *Blackwood's* in November 1827 by the Brontës' admired "Christopher North".[17] Hogg's tales appeared first in *Blackwood's* and later in *Fraser's,* which was launched in 1832 and taken in Haworth Parsonage.[18]

Indeed, as that reference to "salmagundi" suggests, short fiction in these years comprised not merely tales and stories, but a variety of other kinds. Both through periodicals and through the holdings of Keighley Mechanics' Institute Library, the young Brontës would have been familiar with the early nineteenth-century literary "sketch". Washington Irving, whose enormously popular *Sketch-Book of Geoffrey Crayon* had appeared in 1820, was probably the most famous contemporary writer of short fictions of this kind. His example seems to have led to numerous other series of "sketches" and "papers" in the period; and it was as authors of these that Dickens and Thackeray, who were to be the most famous novelists of the next decade, were, in the late 1830s, still principally known. Dickens had shot to fame with *Sketches by Boz* in 1836-37; *The Pickwick Papers,* at least one catchphrase from which is echoed in these tales, began publication as a series of similarly disconnected comic "sketches" in April 1836.[19] Thackeray's *Yellowplush Correspondence* appeared in *Fraser's* from November 1837 to August 1838.

Like many other short fictions in these years, these latter were not free-standing. An episodically evolving narrative and the fact that each part contained the same familiar characters, no less than the presence of their facetiously presented fictional "editor", linked them together as parts of a larger whole. In *Blackwood's,* in *Fraser's,* and in the earlier *Lady's Magazine* (all familiar to the young Brontës), and in *Bentley's Miscellany* (which they very possibly knew), more or less fictional "sketches" of place or character, "scenes", "papers", "tales" and short stories, in a variety of styles and tones, loosely connected by setting, theme or narrator, were often published as series over a number of months.[20] In the 1820s and 30s many series like these were collected into volumes. The tales and essays Hogg published in *Blackwood's* between 1819 and 1828 under the running title *The Shepherd's Calendar* appeared, along with some other stories, as a two-volume collection in 1829. Samuel Warren's wildly popular series of fictional medical case histories, *Passages from the Diary of a Late Physician* (first published in *Blackwood's,* and pirated in America under the title *Affecting Scenes*), with its stories of familial affection and dissipated young "men about town", seems to have been of some interest to the Brontë sisters; it was to be echoed in Anne Brontë's much later novel, *The Tenant of Wildfell Hall.*[21] Branwell would probably have been more interested in first-person tales of military and naval adventure, such as those collected in William Hamilton Maxwell's *Stories of Waterloo* (1829), William Nugent Glascock's *Naval Sketch Book* (1834), Matthew Barker's *Tough Yarns, A Series of Naval Tales and Sketches* (1835), and Michael Scott's much admired *Tom Cringle's Log* (1829).[22] All these collections, along with Washington Irving's *Salmagundi, The Sketch-Book of Geoffrey Crayon* and *Tales of a Traveller,* appear in the 1841 catalogue of Keighley Mechanics' Institute Library.[23] None of the narratives which linked such volumes together were as elaborate or as developed as that of Angria. But they may well have suggested to the young Charlotte Brontë, for whom that "mighty phantasm"[24] had for years provided a framework for writings of various kinds, ways in which a series of separate but related short fictions might be developed to distinctive aesthetic effect.

For the form was one within which, by the time of these Angrian tales, she had been working for a number of years. Whereas her brother Branwell's contributions to Angria were extensive "histories" of its battles and politics, and "lives" of its famous men, hers were briefer, more varied and disconnected from one another, rather than parts of a single "sage" elaborated over time. Partly, this must have been because she could write only in snatches, when her other commitments allowed. Yet it seems also to have been a matter of conscious choice. Her earlier Angrian writings are not abortive fragments of a single continuous narrative, but modelled, it appears, on quite other contemporary fictional forms: the "sketch", the "character", the vignette. *A Peep into a Picture Book* (1834), *Corner Dishes: A Small Collection of Mixed and Unsubstantial Trifles in Prose and Verse* (1835), *Arthurian or Odds & Ends Being A Miscellaneous Collection of Pieces in Prose & Verse* (1835), *The Scrap Book. A Mingling of Many Things* (1835): what such titles indicate is an awareness of an aesthetic of brevity, disjunction and juxtaposition that others besides Charlotte Brontë were developing in these years.

"I consider the story merely as a frame on which to stretch my materials", wrote Washington Irving in 1824, explaining why he had chosen to write "sketches & short tales rather than long work".

> It is the play of thought, and sentiment and language; the weaving in of characters, lightly yet expressively delineated; the familiar and faithful exhibition of scenes in common life; and the half concealed vein of humour that is often playing through the whole—these are among what I aim at, and upon which I felicitate myself in proportion as I think I succeed.[25]

Short fictions in the early nineteenth century were sophisticated and self-reflexive, and designedly different from the novel in their effects. "Sketches sometimes possess an interest that is often not found in more finished performances", announces the epigraph to Lady Blessington's *Sketches and Fragments* (1825).[26] In 1824, the author of a volume of stories about the west of Scotland writes:

> It has often occurred to the Author, that these legends, presenting alternately features of horror, of pathos, or of comic humour, were peculiarly adapted to furnish materials for [. . .] the short TALE; where, without any elaborate attempt to delineate character, or to excite a sustained and prolonged interest by a succession of incidents, the attention is directed to a few striking events, and characters exhibited only under some brief and momentary aspects.[27]

The popularity of such collections of variegated short fictions meant that by the 1830s the sequence of "sketches" and "tales", "linked together by a chain of interest strong enough to prevent their appearing unconnected", yet each "to a certain extent, complete in itself" (as one of its most accomplished practitioners described it) could be seen as a distinctive literary form.[28]

Such collections as these were usually written in the first person, with a more or less elaborately characterized narrator. Washington Irving's *The Sketch-Book of Geoffrey Crayon, Gent.* (1820) is a vehicle for the sensibility of the dilettantish "Geoffrey Crayon", a genial, sentimental flâneur. The framing narrative of Scott's *Chronicles of the Canongate* (1827), in which Chrystal Croftangry describes his situation and introduces other, subsidiary narrators, is almost as long as the stories themselves. "I have been eccentric from my cradle. At Eton I was called an odd boy, and at Oxford was considered a character", begins William Hamilton Maxwell's *Stories of Waterloo.*[29] Sometimes (as in *Tom Cringle's Log*) the teller is a central protagonist; sometimes, like Charlotte Brontë's Charles Townshend, at an ironizing remove from the world of the narrative. But a foregrounding of the narrator is characteristic of the genre, as in the great prototypes for such collections, *The Arabian Nights' Entertainments* and *The Decameron.* This gives considerable opportunity for self-reflexive focus upon the processes of storytelling, and also for experimentation with different fictional styles. Hogg's and Scott's fictive worlds are places within which different kinds of stories circulate and multiply, and reverberate against one another to distinctive aesthetic effect. The tragic Ossianic poetry of Scott's "The Highland Widow" stands out with stark authority from its frame within Chrystal Croftangry's more garrulously circumstantial narrative; rollicking humour and bawdiness are counterpointed in *The Shepherd's Calendar* by lyric beauty and supernatural suggestiveness.[30] Washington Irving (who, like Charlotte Brontë, considered Hogg a writer of "extraordinary genius")[31] was to exploit such contrasts of tone in his development of the "sketch". His *Sketch-Book of Geoffrey Crayon* was calculatedly "miscellaneous, and written for different humours"; the whole point of the collection lay in its play of lights and shadows, its diversity of moods.[32]

As the titles of many collections suggest, the distinction between "tale" and "sketch" was often blurred in the period. But some broad distinctions can be drawn. If tales such as Hogg's might be seen as having roots in rural oral storytelling, the "sketch", with its connotations of polite accomplishment, was rather more urbane.[33] Its focus was less on "story" than on the depiction of "scene" or character; its emphasis was on the moment, the situation, rather than development over time. The titles of collections of short fictions of this kind—"sketches", "papers", "scenes", "pictures"—emphasized their difference from more plot-driven narratives, and also their affinities with the visual arts. Thus Geoffrey Crayon, in the "Author's Account of Himself" that forms the opening of his *Sketch-Book,* tells of observing "the shifting scenes of life [. . .] with the sauntering gaze with which humble lovers of the picturesque stroll from the window of one print shop to another, caught sometimes by the delineations of beauty, sometimes by the distortions of caricature, and sometimes by the loveliness of landscape", and likens himself to those tourists who "bring home portfolios filled with sketches [. . .] for the entertainment of [. . .] friends".[34] Collections both of "sketches" and "tales" were characterized by shifts of tone, from melodrama to comedy, from sentiment to knowingness. Yet both worked not simply by contrast, but also as coherent wholes. The tales of Hogg's *Shepherd's Calendar* offer a cumulative picture of the manners, customs and superstitions of a whole vanishing society; each of the stories included in Scott's *Chronicles of the Canongate* in its different way reflects on "progress" from the perspective of those left in its wake. Irving, says his modern editor, worked over his *Sketch-Book,* revising it "into a volume with increasing internal consistency and literary purposiveness".[35] A series of short fictions could develop themes and motifs from a number of different angles, and invite the making of connections and the picking up of echoes—sometimes sardonic, sometimes

confirmatory—between the discrete pieces of which it was composed.

The shared, familiar world of Angria provided Charlotte Brontë with a framework within which she could experiment with the potentialities of this form. Just as Hogg's *Tales of the Wars of Montrose* (1835) and Scott's *Chronicles of the Canongate* draw upon a background of a well-known Scottish history, so these tales are premised on the reader's knowledge of the characters and events of Angria; they allude to a larger "story" that they themselves do not tell. In some, story is more important than in others. **"Mina Laury," "Henry Hastings"** and **"Caroline Vernon"** all contain climactic events—a duel, a proposal, a meeting between wife and mistress; a dramatic pursuit and arrest, the seduction of a young girl. These are closer, perhaps, to "tales" than are the more disconnected "scenes" of **"The Duke of Zamorna"** and **"Stancliffe's Hotel."** But unlike the Gothic tales that Brontë would have read in *Blackwood's,* none of these Angrian fictions present a single story leading to climax and resolution, or even to the quieter "point" of the contemporary "anecdote". Threading through each are suggestions of a number of different narratives, some more developed than others. Moments of apparent closure are pregnant with suggestions of new, disquieting stories. Their climaxes resolve nothing; each ends abruptly, inconsequentially.

These tales are suggestively different from the "histories" of battle and politics, the "lives" of famous men in which Branwell Brontë was chronicling the story of Angria in these years. His are the master narratives of the hero and "historian" of Angria, the Byronic Alexander Percy, the gallant Henry Hastings—flawed but commanding figures of narrative authority. Here, instead, the narrator is the mocking, marginalized Charles Townshend, in whose debunking narration heroics are diminished and great events sardonically reported or distanced into lyric memory. Instead of linear development there is disconnection and contrast. The breaks and gaps both within each tale and between them are emphasized rather than harmonized away. One is reminded of Ian Duncan's suggestion that Hogg's refusal, in his collections, of "an extensive, complex, unifying plot" might be seen as "expressing a thoroughgoing ideological refusal" of contemporary narratives of nationhood.[36] Just so, in these tales of Angria, the master narrative of achievement is ironically undermined. The sense throughout is of elusiveness rather than possession, vulnerability rather than mastery.

Yet this aesthetic of disjunction is also an enabling one. In a passage that would have been well known to Charlotte Brontë, Thomas Moore had written of Byron's "idea of writing a poem in fragments" as

> [. . .] enabling him to overleap those mechanical difficulties, which, in a regular narrative, embarrass, if not

chill, the poet,—leaving it to the imagination of his readers to fill up the intervals between those abrupt bursts of passion in which his chief power lay.[37]

Just so, these tales exploit the expressive possibilities of disjunction and inconclusiveness, leaving spaces for the "reader" so frequently addressed within them (most immediately, Branwell) to respond, to imagine, to reflect. Blank spaces are left between "scenes" in the manuscripts that survive; this seems to be not simply because the writing was often interrupted, but a matter of deliberate choice. The movement from scene to scene allows a play with contrasts between past and present situations, between comedy and seriousness. Thus, in **"The Duke of Zamorna,"** the melodrama of Augusta di Segovia's death is counterpointed by the flippant comments of the voyeuristic Charles Townshend, reading the pilfered letters of the "western aristocracy" (133); thus, in **"Caroline Vernon,"** the poignant depiction of Mary Percy's anxious, fading beauty is offset against the image of her husband creeping up the stairs on tiptoe "like a magnified dancing-master" so that she will not hear (405). Sharp satiric observation is here and there punctuated by moments of lyric beauty—a girl standing in a doorway; a voice singing in the distance; a portrait smiling all by itself in an empty room.

Each individual tale consists of a succession of scenes, in which familiar characters appear in different lights and groupings, familiar landscapes at different seasons and from different points of view. In **"Stancliffe's Hotel,"** Jane Moore, "the beautiful Angrian", is recalled as "a very imposing figure, in her white satin dress and stately plume of snowy ostrich feathers" at "the music festival which was held last September in the minster at Zamorna"; then she suddenly appears "like an apparition" in a domestic drawing room, "just a girl in white, plump and very tall" (95, 97-98). Charles Townshend, in **"Henry Hastings,"** gazing at a group of figures in a room "closed, curtained, and lighted up", is reminded of "another picture—like this, but yet how different!"—a past moment in which the broken-down figure at its centre was "a bold, handsome, hardy soldier", "surrounded by a circle of lovely women, young and unfaded with vice" (218-19). What the reader is offered is (as Charlotte Brontë put it in her **"Farewell to Angria"**) a series of reconfigurations of "the same characters and scenes and subjects" in "every variety of shade & light"[38]; different yet related patternings of the same familiar materials, like the patterns produced amongst the same group of coloured pieces by the recently invented kaleidoscope.

For the structure of these tales is not quite as inconsequential as it might at first appear. **"Stancliffe's Hotel"** begins with Louisa Dance affectedly quoting Byron, and concludes with Zamorna and his wife reading Byron together. **"Caroline Vernon"** opens with a "mad"

letter from the African king, Quashia, demanding Caroline's hand, and ends with the revelation of her actual seduction by her guardian—as if to emphasize that she is mere "clay in the hands of the potter" (384), she herself is significantly absent from both scenes. And if each tale articulates its own distinctive configuration of feeling, each also echoes and chimes against the others to distinctive and cumulative effect. The sense, as in music, is that themes and preoccupations are being revisited, developed and elaborated in different keys and tones; complicating, deepening, gathering new resonances. In **"Mina Laury,"** with its bleak wintry landscapes and aristocratic interiors, a half-elegiac romanticism, evocative of Scott (men galloping, quarrelling, duelling, gripped by furious passions; women no less passionate, waiting in enforced passivity), is poised on the edge of cynicism: the story pivots on the half-farcical near discovery of Zamorna's adultery. **"Stancliffe's Hotel,"** set mainly in a busy, industrializing town, is explicitly anti-romantic, sometimes descending to farce (as in its portrayal of "two chits" attempting to court the unflappable Jane Moore); yet it ends with a scene of Byronic melancholy. In **"The Duke of Zamorna"** those "two chits" reappear, one of them at least a lonelier, more complex figure: the melodramatic darkness of a remembered aristocratic past is set against the flippancies of a differently unhappy present day. In **"Henry Hastings,"** the decadence of a fading aristocracy (the courtesan Louisa Vernon, Sir William Percy's rakishness, Zamorna's deception of his wife) is counterpointed by the narrative of Elizabeth Hastings' construction and maintenance of a "character"—the hard work and respectability of a rising middle class. And in **"Caroline Vernon"** a young girl's ridiculous but "really romantic" (383) dreams are abruptly, catastrophically fulfilled. It seems that a heroic or lyrical romanticism is being interrogated, in each rather differently, from the cooler, more ironic distance of a disenchanted modernity. It is a sense that grows in resonance and in complexity as each tale succeeds the last.

For like the series of short fictions that appeared in contemporary periodicals, these tales would have been read in succession by that eager audience in Haworth; they would also have been remembered, returned to, and re-read.[39] The effect of each, their author could assume, would thus have been modified, ironized and enriched in the light of subsequent tales.[40] If their readership was tiny (only the author's siblings), it was extraordinarily sophisticated—made up of practising writers, who were used to criticizing and imitating all kinds of contemporary writings; two of its small number were to become major novelists. These tales were offered to the "reader" frequently addressed within them (most immediately, it seems, Branwell) not merely as contributions to an unfolding "Angrian saga", but as experiments in writing, to be admired and/or judged for their literary effects. They showcase an extraordinary variety of different styles of writing, from romantic landscape description to Quashia's Ossianic bombast; from fragments of lyric poetry to letters in a number of different "hands". The heroics of Branwell's histories are mocked in Charles Townshend's sardonic style of parliamentary reporting and in Sir William Percy's parodic "quotations" of news reports from the front (208-11, 86). Throughout, the writing is punctuated by reflections upon itself. "I began this work with the intention of writing something high and pathetic", says Charles Townshend in **"The Duke of Zamorna."** "Let it suffice to say that I found this pitch far too high for me. I could not keep it up. I was forced to descend a peg" (161, 163). An eloquent description of a midnight debate in the Verdopolitan parliament is succeeded by the debunking comment: "The above concerning the agony of flayed eels, the attention of breathless lookers-on, the ferocity of infernal operators, I wrote merely as a specimen of a certain style" (210).

Tzvetan Todorov has argued that short fiction is of its nature more self-referential, more self-consciously literary than the novel "because there is no time, in reading a short work, to forget it is only 'literature' and not 'life'".[41] "When, in the narrators' tales, I was shewn, as through a glass darkly, some scene of love either in splendid saloon or shaded grounds of a hall, what would I have given to cast away the medium and behold the figures face to face!" says Charles Townshend, recalling the anecdotes he was told in servants' halls in childhood (132). Throughout these tales, stories are seen as filtered always through a "medium"; tellers, letters and newspapers are prominent in them, as are references to the act of writing and to themselves as "books". Their subversive relation to the pretensions of grand narrative is figured not merely in their marginal, mocking narrator, but also in their constantly foregrounded sense that any single story is only one amongst many, and their allusions to and fragments of other possible stories throughout. The developing presentation of psychologically realistic character is repeatedly punctuated by a witty interrogation of different ideas of "character"—as essential nature, as performance, as moral standing in the world. And most strikingly, in a series of moments of formal self-reflexiveness, these tales image and reflect upon the tension between narrative and "scene" that is the mainspring of their fictional form.

For the scenes of which they are composed have often a charged suggestiveness which, like that of the epiphanic moments of later modernist fiction, crystallizes and suspends the linear progression of narrative. And they are self-reflexively punctuated by comic and lyric images of such suspension: Zamorna and his prime minister, like two figures in a Dutch painting, caught in a moment of perpetual, pointless "play"; Caroline Vernon, left "for a period of about four months" in the act of stepping into a carriage, in the interval between the

two parts of **"Caroline Vernon,"** like an actress holding her pose in a contemporary tableau vivant; the portrait of a girl in **"Henry Hastings"** like the Sleeping Beauty, frozen in time (305-06, 388, 255-56). Such images work against the different "suspense" of narrative development and offer a distinctive reflection on the virtual timelessness of art. Thus, the fleeing Henry Hastings, watching from the outside darkness, sees his sister through the window of a lonely country house:

> A figure came towards the window, and then paced back again, and was almost lost in the shadow of the opposite end. Again it appeared, drawing near slowly; as slowly, it withdrew to the dusk of distance. To and fro it paced with the same measured step down the whole length of the large old parlour, and there was nothing else visible. A single person walking about there in that remote mansion embosomed amid boundless fields.
>
> (231)

The frame of the lighted window (quite different from those "boundless" fields) contains an arresting image of rhythmic movement without progression: an anxious, ambitious young woman appears less as purposeful character than as a vulnerable, abstract "figure" of formal patterning. The sense, finely caught in the present participle that replaces the verb in the final sentence, is of a moment suspended in time. One is reminded of Mrs Gaskell's description of the "household custom" amongst the Brontë sisters of discussing their writing in the evening when their duties were done:

> They put away their work, and began to pace the room backwards and forwards, up and down,—as often with the candles extinguished, for economy's sake, as not,— their figures glancing into the fire-light, and out into the shadow, perpetually.[42]

All too few years later, as Mrs Gaskell tells, the last surviving sister was to pace that parlour alone.[43] But in these tales of her early twenties, written in a happier time, that pacing becomes an image of how the fragility of the moment, the relentlessness of time passing, might be countered and rendered meaningful by the formal shapings of art. Thus, these tales' recurring image (reflective of the moment, all too well known to their author, when the writing had to stop) of light fading and candles burning down—Zamorna's lamp expiring in the darkness of his chamber; William Percy glimpsing "the pallid gleam of sculpture" in a garden in the gathering dusk; Caroline Vernon's candle falling from its socket and leaving her in the dark (22, 185, 399)—is poignantly and suggestively developed at the end of **"Henry Hastings,"** as Mary Percy and her husband withdraw in an uneasy truce:

> The candle remained burning on the toilet, the two chairs stood vacant before it, the splendid little room reflected around its fairy beauty, but the living figures

of the scene were gone. Solitude and silence lingered behind them. The candle burnt soon to its socket. The flame flickered, waned, streamed up in a long tongue of light, sank again, trembled a moment, and finally vanished in total darkness. Then a piano was heard playing in the drawing-room below, and, when the first note had stilled the clamour of children, a voice sung:

[. . .] Merrily, rapidly,
Our sunny hours flit by,
Then gratefully, cheerily,
Enjoy them as they fly.

(321-22)

The room is emptied; the candles burn down; the "living figures" disappear. But counterpointing this, as activity becomes stillness, before the implied observer the room becomes a "scene": the past tense of narrative gives way to the timeless present of "song", as the dwindling, vanishing moment takes on aesthetic form.

Shortly after she finished the last of these tales, Charlotte Brontë seems to have bidden farewell to Angria; and also, apparently, to her experiments with shorter fictional forms. In that letter to Hartley Coleridge, written in 1840, she gives voice to her awareness that a wider audience might expect a different kind of fiction, in which character was more coherently introduced and developed, and the desire for "story" more obviously satisfied.[44] Certainly, by 1840, the novel was both prestigious and profitable. "Readers in this country have a decided and strong preference for works (especially fiction) in which a single and connected story occupies the whole volume, or number of volumes, as the case may be", wrote Poe's American publishers, refusing his short fiction sequence, *Tales of the Folio Club,* in 1836.[45] Publishers and circulating libraries wanted three-volume novels. It is unsurprising that the Brontë sisters' first attempts at fiction for publication should have been of this kind.

But the tales in which Charlotte Brontë used the framework of Angria to experiment with fictional form are very far from clumsy apprentice work. They raise questions about her later novels that have scarcely yet been asked. Were the "three distinct and unconnected tales" with which the Brontë sisters tried to enter the fictional marketplace[46] meant to reverberate against each other in ways now lost to us? The refusal, in these Angrian fictions, of authoritative grand narrative might lead us to look beyond the narrative suspense of *Jane Eyre* to its disconcerting lack of closure, the questions left suspended by the invocations of scripture at its end. They cast a different light on the ironies and disjunctions of *Shirley*—that "portfolio of random sketches", as G. H. Lewes called it, criticizing its lack of "unity"[47]—and on its elegiac romanticism. Their play with echo and difference, with the poignancies and ironies of recurrence, points toward the way in which the past is reworked in

a different key in *Villette.* These final tales of Angria— less the last of Charlotte Brontë's juvenilia than the first of her adult fictions—bear eloquent, suggestive testimony to the artfulness of the writer who was to produce the deceptive "artlessness" of *Jane Eyre.*

Notes

1. These last five tales of Angria were published together for the first time in Heather Glen, ed., *Tales of Angria* (London: Penguin, 2006); page references given in the text are to this edition. This essay is an expanded and revised version of material that appears in the introduction to that volume.

2. Winifred Gérin's suggestion, apparently derived from the Roe Head journal fragments, that the Angrian manuscripts were written in a "trance-like" state (Winifred Gérin, ed., *Five Novelettes* [London: Folio, 1976] 16) has been repeated by successive critics. See, for example, Sandra M. Gilbert and Susan Gubar, *The Madwoman in the Attic: The Woman Writer and the Nineteenth-Century Literary Imagination* (New Haven: Yale UP, 1979): 311; Christine Alexander, *The Early Writings of Charlotte Brontë* (Oxford: Blackwell, 1983): 243 and Dianne F. Sadoff, *Monsters of Affection: Dickens, Eliot and Brontë on Fatherhood* (Baltimore: Johns Hopkins UP, 1982) 120. On sexist and racist stereotyping in these tales, see Firdous Azim, *The Colonial Rise of the Novel* (London: Routledge, 1994) and Carl Plasa, *Charlotte Brontë* (Basingstoke: Palgrave, 2004) 14-28.

3. See, for example, Alexander 244-46 and Sally Shuttleworth, *Charlotte Brontë and Victorian Psychology* (Cambridge: Cambridge UP, 1996) ch. 6.

4. See, for example, the review by G. H. Lewes in *Fraser's* 36 (December 1847), which praises the novel for its "perception of character, and power of delineating it" and its "deep, significant reality". Qtd in Miriam Allott, ed., *The Brontës: The Critical Heritage* (London: Routledge and Kegan, 1974) 84.

5. Charlotte Brontë, *The Letters of Charlotte Brontë, Volume I: 1829-1847,* ed. Margaret Smith (Oxford: Clarendon, 1995) 237. Further references to this edition are given as *CBL.*

6. "It is very edifying and profitable to create a world out of one's own brain and people it with inhabitants who are like so many Melchisedecs—'Without father, without mother, without descent, having neither beginning of days, nor end of life'", Charlotte Brontë was to write ironically to Hartley Coleridge of her fictions in December 1840 (*CBL* 240).

7. "Farewell to Angria" (*c.* 1839), repr. Charlotte Brontë, *Jane Eyre,* 3rd ed., ed. Richard Dunn (New York: Norton, 2001) 424-25.

8. David Lodge, "Fire and Eyre: Charlotte Brontë's War of Earthly Elements," *The Language of Fiction: Essays in Criticism and Verbal Analysis of the English Novel* (London: Routledge and Kegan, 1996) 114-43.

9. Richard H. Dana, Snr., North American Review 9 (1819): 345.

10. *Salmagundi: or The Whim-Whams and Opinions of Launcelot Langstaff, Esq., and Others,* a series of satirical essays and poems by Washington Irving, his brother William, and James Kirke Paulding, appeared in 20 periodical pamphlets and then in two volumes between 1807 and 1808. On Keighley Mechanics' Institute Library, see Clifford Whone, "Where the Brontës Borrowed Books: The Keighley Mechanics' Institute," *Brontë Society Transactions* 11 (1950): 344-58.

11. New English translations of *The Decameron* were published in 1802 and 1825. There were many early nineteenth-century retellings of various of its tales, and its 10-day frame was employed in a number of early nineteenth-century works. See Herbert G. Wright, *Boccaccio in England from Chaucer to Tennyson* (Fair Lawn, NJ: Essential Books, 1957).

12. Peter Garside and his co-researchers at the Centre for Editorial and Intertextual Research at Cardiff University note the "large increase in the output of works of fiction consisting of a variety of individual tales and sketches" and the "relatively high proportion of works of fiction incorporating a variety of separate tales", as well as "compilations of shorter fiction, usually presented as edited by one person" in the years between 1830 and 1836. See *The English Novel, 1830-1836: A Bibliographical Survey of Fiction Published in the British Isles,* compiled by Peter Garside, Anthony Mandal, Verena Ebbes, Angela Koch and Rainer Schöwerling, 12 May 2006 <http://www.cf.ac.uk/encap/corvey/1830s/>. See also the checklist of 150 such titles from the 1820s in P. T. Killick, "The Rise of the Tale: A Preliminary Checklist of Collections of Short Fiction Published 1820-29 in the Corvey Collection," *Cardiff Corvey: Reading the Romantic Text* 7 (Dec. 2001), 8 May 2006 <http://www.cf.ac.uk/encap/corvey/articles/cc07_n04.html>.

13. The immensely popular *Lady's Magazine* merged with *La Belle Assemblée* in 1832. In a letter sent to Hartley Coleridge with a sample of her fiction in December 1840, Charlotte Brontë speaks of reading old copies in "antiquated print [. . .] before I knew how to criticize or object [. . .] I shall never see anything which will interest me so much again [. . .] With all my heart I wish I had

been born in time to contribute to the Lady's Magazine" (*CBL* 240).

14. Branwell Brontë to John Wilson ("Christopher North"), 8 Dec. 1835. Qtd in T. J. Wise and J. A. Symington, eds., *The Brontës: Their Lives, Friendships and Correspondence,* vol. 1 (Oxford: Shakespeare Head, 1932) 133-34.

15. See Robert Morrison and Chris Baldick, eds., *Tales of Terror from Blackwood's Magazine* (Oxford: Oxford UP, 1995) and Henry James, *The Art of the Novel: Critical Prefaces* (New York: Scribner's, 1962) 181.

16. See Heather Glen, *Charlotte Brontë: The Imagination in History* (Oxford: Oxford UP, 2002) 12-16. In *Jane Eyre,* ch. 34, there is a reference to William Mudford's "The Iron Shroud", published in *Blackwood's* 28 (Aug. 1830): 364-71.

17. "Christopher North", "A Preface to a Review of Chronicles of the Canongate" and "Review of Chronicles of the Canongate," *Blackwood's* 22 (Nov. 1827): 531-56, 556-70.

18. Hogg's *Winter Evening Tales,* a miscellaneous collection of tales and sketches, many of which had appeared in *Blackwood's,* was first published as a collection in 1820, and was an immediate success. Short fictions by Hogg appeared in *Blackwood's* and in *Fraser's* through the 1820s and into the 1830s. Scott's first short story, "Wandering Willie's Tale", appeared in his novel *Redgauntlet* (1824); his first series of *Chronicles of the Canongate,* comprising three short stories—"The Two Drovers", "The Highland Widow" and "The Surgeon's Daughter"—with an extensive framing narrative, was published in 1827. Three more short stories originally intended for *Chronicles of the Canongate*—"My Aunt Margaret's Mirror", "The Tapestried Chamber" and "Death of the Laird's Jock"—appeared in *The Keepsake* for 1828. On Hogg, Scott, Washington Irving and the development of the short fiction form in this period, see R. J. Lyall, "Intimations of Orality: Scotland, America and the Early Development of the Short Story in English," *Studies in Short Fiction* 36 (1999): 311-25.

19. Early critics praised Dickens as a "brilliant sketcher of detached scenes" and suggested that he was imitating Washington Irving. "Unfinished as this tale still is," writes one reviewer of *Oliver Twist,* "it is the best example which Mr Dickens has yet afforded of his power to produce a good novel; but it cannot be considered a conclusive one", for it cannot yet "be viewed as a connected whole". See T. H. Lister, "Dickens's Tales," *Edinburgh Review* 68 (Oct. 1838): 75-79, repr. John

Charles Olmsted, *A Victorian Art of Fiction: Essays on the Novel in British Periodicals 1830-1850* (New York: Garland, 1979) 270, 274. Most of Thackeray's writings of the 1830s appeared pseudonymously in *Fraser's*: they included *The Yellowplush Correspondence* (1837-38), later collected as *The Yellowplush Papers* in Thackeray's *Comic Tales and Sketches* (1841).

20. In *Blackwood's,* the Brontës could have found, for example, John Wilson, *Lights and Shadows from Scottish Life* (1820-21); Mrs A. Gillespie-Smith, *Tales of the Wedding* (May-July 1826); John Galt, *My Landlady and Her Lodgers* (August-November 1829); Michael Scott, *Tom Cringle's Log* (1829-33) and Samuel Warren, *Passages from the Diary of a Late Physician* (18 instalments from August 1830 to August 1837). *Fraser's* published stories by "the Ettrick Shepherd", James Hogg, from 1830 until 1836 (after his death). Among the numerous other short fiction series to be found in *Fraser's* in the 1830s were John Galt's sketches and stories of Canada and the West Indies, and Andrew Picken's Scottish tales. Thackeray's *Yellowplush Correspondence* appeared there from 1837 to 1838. The *Ingoldsby Legends,* a series of tales in verse and prose by Revd R. H. Barham, began to appear in *Bentley's Miscellany* in 1837, and were to be published in book form in 1840. The Brontës may have known these; they would certainly have known Barham's Gothic short story, "Singular Passage in the Life of the Late Henry Harris", which introduced the Ingoldsby framework, and was published in *Blackwood's* in 1826.

21. See Tom Winnifrith, *The Brontës and Their Background* (London: Macmillan, 1973) 92-93.

22. On the military stories of the French wars which appeared in great quantities in the periodicals of the 1830s, see Kathryn Chittick, *Dickens and the 1830s* (Cambridge: Cambridge UP, 1990) 107-09.

23. See Whone. The collections of short fictions in Keighley Mechanics' Institute Library included four volumes of Edgeworth's *Tales* (1804-12); Washington Irving, *Salmagundi* (1808), *Knickerbocker's History of New York* (1809), *The Sketch-Book of Geoffrey Crayon* (1820) and *Tales of a Traveller* (1824); Walter Scott, "The Highland Widow" (1827), apparently in a separate edition; James Hogg, *The Shepherd's Calendar* (1829); Michael Scott, *Tom Cringle's Log* (1829); William Hamilton Maxwell, *Stories of Waterloo* (1829) and *Wild Sports of the West* (1832), a collection of Irish sketches and tales; Samuel Warren, *Passages from the Diary of a Late Physician* (1832); William Nugent Glascock, *Naval Sketch Book* (1834); [Matthew Henry Barker], *Tough Yarns, A Series of Naval Tales and Sketches to Please All Hands. By

an Old Sailor* (1835) and Thomas Miller, *A Day in the Woods* (1836).

24. Charlotte Brontë, Roe Head Journal, 11 August 1836, in Glen. ed., *Tales of Angria* (1836): 453.

25. Washington Irving to Henry Brevoort, 11 Dec. 1824. Qtd in Washington Irving, *The Sketch-Book of Geoffrey Crayon, Gent.,* ed. Susan Manning (Oxford: Oxford UP, 1996) xxviii. Future references are to this edition.

26. Her source for this quotation is given as *Critique on the Art of Painting.* I have been unable to trace this perhaps fictional work.

27. Thus Archibald Crawford in his preface to *Tales of My Grandmother,* 2 vols. (Edinburgh and London, 1825). Qtd in Tim Killick, "Hogg and the Collection of Short Fiction in the 1830s," *Studies in Hogg and his World* 15 (2004): 21-31 (25).

28. The phrases in quotation marks are taken from Dickens's preface to the first complete edition of *The Pickwick Papers* (1837). Edgar Allan Poe, who reviewed *Sketches by Boz* in 1836, and was very familiar with the tales and sketches appearing in *Blackwood's* and other English periodicals, planned an analogous collection of short fictions designed around a group of characters belonging to "the Folio Club". Although the proposed volume never appeared, individual tales were published separately in the *Philadelphia Saturday Courier* and the *Southern Literary Messenger* between 1832 and 1836. See James M. Hutchinson, *Poe* (Jackson: UP of Mississippi, 2005) ch. 3.

29. William Hamilton Maxwell, *Stories of Waterloo, and other tales,* vol. 1 (London: Colburn and Bentley, 1829) 1.

30. Ian Duncan suggests that the Shakespearean echo in the title of his *Winter Evening Tales* "situates Hogg's enterprise in a genealogy of sophisticated literary meditations on the 'primitive' conditions and effects of storytelling". See Ian Duncan, introduction, *Winter Evening Tales Collected Among the Cottagers in the South of Scotland,* by James Hogg (Edinburgh: Edinburgh UP, 2002) xxvii. Vol. 11 of *The Stirling/South Carolina Research Edition of The Collected Works of James Hogg* (16 Volumes, 1995-2005). Fiona Robertson has pointed to the importance of "storytelling" as a theme in Scott. See Fiona Robertson, *Legitimate Histories: Scott, Gothic, and the Authorities of Fiction* (Oxford: Oxford UP, 1994) 130.

31. "He is an extraordinary genius of Natures own production", writes Irving of Hogg to his publisher early in 1818. See Washington Irving, *Letters. Volume I: 1802-1823,* ed. Ralph M. Aderman

et al. (Boston: Twayne, 1978) 537. "James Hogg a man of most extraordinary genius a Scottish Sheppard", the 12-year-old Charlotte Brontë calls him in "The History of the Year" (1829). See Charlotte Brontë, *Juvenilia 1829-1835,* ed. Juliet Barker (London: Penguin, 1996) 2.

32. "L'Envoy", in Irving, *Sketch-Book* 322.

33. Indeed, silver-fork fiction itself may have originated in "sketches" of fashionable life. See, for example, Lord John Russell, *Essays and Sketches of Life and Character—by a Gentleman who has left his Lodgings* (1820) and Miss E. H. McLeod, *Tales of Ton* (1821-22, three series). Alison Adburgham speculates that Lady Blessington's *The Magic Lantern, or Sketches of Scenes in the Metropolis* (1822), a series of vignettes of fashionable life, may have inspired the publisher Henry Colburn's promotion of the genre. See Alison Adburgham, *Silver Fork Society: Fashionable Life and Literature from 1814 to 1840* (London: Constable, 1983) 33.

34. Irving, *Sketch-Book* 13.

35. Manning, "Note on the Text", in Irving, *Sketch-Book* xxxi.

36. Duncan xxv, xxx.

37. Thomas Moore, *Letters and Journals of Lord Byron: With Notices of his Life,* vol. 1 (London: Murray, 1830) 481. He is discussing "The Giaour: A Fragment of a Turkish Tale".

38. Christine Alexander, *The Early Writings of Charlotte Brontë,* (Oxford: Basil Blackwell, 1983) 199.

39. "Perhaps my readers may recollect a description of this young lady which appeared some time since, in a sort of comparison between eastern and western women", says Charles Townshend in "Stancliffe's Hotel" (95).

40. Cf. Forrest Ingram's description of the short-story cycle as "a book of short stories so linked to each other by their author that the reader's successive experience on various levels of the pattern of the whole significantly modifies his experience of each of its component parts". See Forrest Ingram, *Representative Short Story Cycles of the Twentieth Century* (The Hague: Mouton, 1971) 19.

41. Tzvetan Todorov, *The Poetics of Prose,* trans. Richard Howard (Oxford: Blackwell, 1977) 107.

42. Elizabeth Gaskell, *The Life of Charlotte Brontë,* ed. Elisabeth Jay (Harmondsworth: Penguin, 1997) 111.

43. Gaskell 412.

44. *CBL* 239-41.

45. Harper and Brothers to Poe, 1836. Qtd in Kevin J. Hayes, *Poe and the Printed Word* (Cambridge: Cambridge UP, 2000) 58.

46. Charlotte Brontë to Messrs Aylott and Jones, 6 Apr. 1846 (*CBL* 461).

47. G. H. Lewes, *Edinburgh Review* 91 (1850): 84.

Additional information on Brontë's life and works is contained in the following sources published by Gale: *Authors and Artists for Young Adults,* **Vol. 17;** *Beacham's Guide to Literature for Young Adults,* **Vol. 2;** *British Writers,* **Vol. 5;** *British Writers: The Classics,* **Vol. 2;** *British Writers Retrospective Supplement,* **Vol. 1;** *Concise Dictionary of British Literary Biography,* **Vol. 1832-1890;** *Dictionary of Literary Biography,* **Vols. 21, 159, 199, 340;** *DISCovering Authors; DISCovering Authors 3.0; DISCovering Authors: British; DISCovering Authors: Canadian Edition; DISCovering Authors Modules: Most Studied Authors* **and** *Novelists; Exploring Novels; Feminism in Literature: A Gale Critical Companion,* **Ed. 1:2;** *Gale Contextual Encyclopedia of World Literature; Gothic Literature: A Gale Critical Companion,* **Ed. 2** *Literature and Its Times,* **Vol. 2;** *Literature Resource Center; Nineteenth-Century Literature Criticism,* **Vols. 3, 8, 33, 58, 105, 155, 217, 229;** *Novels for Students,* **Vols. 4, 36;** *Twayne's English Authors; World Literature and Its Times,* **Vol. 4; and** *World Literature Criticism,* **Ed. 1.**

Voltaire
1694-1778

(Born François-Marie Arouet) French novelist, short fiction writer, essayist, playwright, poet, historian, critic, and autobiographer.

The following entry focuses on Voltaire's short fiction. For additional information on his short fiction, see *SSC,* Vol. 12; for information on his novella *Candide,* see *SSC,* Vol. 112.

INTRODUCTION

Considered a key figure of the French Enlightenment, a seventeenth- and eighteenth-century movement that spurred new developments in the fields of philosophy and science, Voltaire is most remembered for his *contes philosophiques* (philosophical tales), especially *Candide; ou, l'optimisme* (1759; *Candide*), *Micromégas* (1752; *Micromégas,*), and *Zadig* (1747; *Zadig, or the Book of Fate: An Oriental History*). Using irony, satire, and playful black humor in these works, Voltaire proceeds from the belief that humanity can perfect itself through reason, but then goes on to show how human nature, corrupt politics, hypocritical religiosity, and the thirst for power undermine the possibility of an ideal world. As Voltaire scholar Haydn Mason has observed (see Further Reading), all of Voltaire's *contes* "aim to shake the reader's conventional assumptions, to make him think for himself. Enlightenment is all. Satire, irony, dream-like imaginings, solid historical fact, parody: these are some of the tools which Voltaire uses in his pursuit of that end."

BIOGRAPHICAL INFORMATION

Voltaire was born François-Marie Arouet on 21 November, 1694, in or around Paris. His parents were Marguerite Daumard and François Arouet, a notary in Paris. Voltaire was so weak at birth that he was not expected to live, and he remained in poor health for much of his life. Biographers have suggested that the young François-Marie made up for a feeble body by developing an extraordinary mind; even as a student he was known for his brilliance, wit, and impulsive nature. His sister and mother, with whom he was quite close, both died when he was young, and he and his brother parted ways over the issue of religious tolerance. He was educated by the Jesuits at the Collège Louis-le-Grand in Paris. His godfather, the abbé Châteauneuf, also over-saw parts of his education. The abbé introduced him to abbé Chaulieu, who in turn introduced him to the philosophy of Deism and the art of writing poetry. Abbé Châteauneuf also acquainted his godchild with his lover, the courtesan Ninon de Lenclos, who further encouraged the young man's studies in philosophy and literature. After completing school, François-Marie planned to pursue a career as a poet, but his father intervened, instead sending him to Holland to work for the French ambassador. Holland was the home of exiled Huguenots, victims of religious intolerance in France; François-Marie fell in love with a young Huguenot girl known as "Pimpette" and was swiftly recalled home. He entered law school to please his father but also began his literary career in earnest, using his connections to move in the highest Parisian social circles. After writing a poem lampooning the regent Phillipe d'Orleans, François-Marie was exiled from Paris, but later pleaded successfully for his return. However, after again mocking the regent in verse in 1717, he was sent to the Bastille prison for a year. While there, he wrote one of his greatest works, *La ligue; ou Henry le Grand,* an epic poem on the subject of Henry IV and his advancement of religious freedom in England. The poem was not published until 1723, and was printed secretly.

After his release from prison in April, 1718, Voltaire began his long association with the theater. The stage production of his *Oedipe* in November of that year and its publication the following year were a tremendous critical and financial success. In February, 1719, François-Marie changed his name, first to Arouet de Voltaire and then simply to Voltaire. In 1720 he visited Lord Bolingbroke, an influential English writer, beginning an ongoing connection with English intellectuals that served him well throughout his lifetime. As his reputation grew, Voltaire became a favorite with royalty, accepting substantial gifts from the kings of England and France, but even this did not protect him from attack. When events related to a love triangle between Voltaire, the actress Adrienne Lecouvreur, and the chevalier de Rohan-Chabotchevalier lead to a threat of arrest, Voltaire arranged to be exiled in England instead. He lived there from May, 1726, to March, 1729, learning English and meeting with leading intellectual figures who would, in turn, influence his own thought. During this period Voltaire wrote several works in English and released a revision of his poem on Henry IV as *The Henriade*—a tremendous popular success which he dedicated to the English Queen.

He returned to France secretly, remaining in hiding until he could obtain permission to stay in Paris. Voltaire also returned to the theater, with several successful productions mounted in the 1730s, but his *Letters Concerning the English Nation* (1733), which celebrated the openness of the English monarchy and English society, was burned and its publisher jailed. Voltaire soon opted to leave Paris again, moving in with his friend and lover, Mme. Emilie Du Châtelet, at her estate at Cirey. Du Châtelet was a scientist with a strong understanding of Isaac Newton—whose writings were of great interest to Voltaire—and of Gottfried Leibniz, whose philosophy of optimism Voltaire would eventually assail in *Candide*. They lived, studied, and wrote together for nearly fifteen years, but their relationship as lovers waned as Voltaire began a new affair, a scandalous relationship with his young niece, Mme. Denis. Nevertheless, Voltaire and Du Châtelet remained close friends until her death in 1749.

Seeking a new home, Voltaire traveled to the court of Frederick II of Prussia, but he soon ran into trouble again for satirizing one of the King's favorites. After a brief period of detention, Frederick allowed him to leave and Voltaire moved on to Switzerland with his niece, from where he carried on extensive correspondence with such figures as Russia's Catherine the Great. He also took on several legal battles involving religious prejudice—often securing reversals of imposed sentences—and he began writing more forcefully against institutional religion and superstition. After a thirty-year absence, he returned to Paris in April, 1778, having been invited to a gala performance of his play *Irene* (1778). Queen Marie Antoinette asked to meet him, crowds came to greet his carriage, and he was crowned with a laurel wreath. Perhaps, as biographers speculate, overwhelmed by this personal and professional triumph, Voltaire fell ill and died less than two months later. Before his death, he had agreed to sign a statement saying that he accepted Catholicism, likely to avoid the ignominious burial of the unsaved. However, when he refused, in his dying days, to recognize the divinity of Jesus, church authorities decided not to accept his earlier statement of faith and attempted to deny him a Christian burial. His nephew secretly moved Voltaire's body to a monastery in Champagne for burial by setting the body upright in a carriage. In 1791 his remains were exhumed and reburied in the Pantheon at Paris.

MAJOR WORKS OF SHORT FICTION

Voltaire began writing short fiction late in his career, during a stay with the Duchesse du Maine at Seaux, where he recited parts of his philosophical tales each evening. Most of his twenty-five tales are written in the oriental style popularized by the exotic stories of Antoine Galland's translation of *The Arabian Nights* (published between 1704 and 1717) and by Montes-

quieu's *Lettres persanes* (1721). Short fiction provided Voltaire with a convenient and safe format for expressing his criticism of political, social, and religious institutions because he set his tales in foreign locales that offer the protagonists opportunities to learn about and react to various philosophies and cultures. Typically, the protagonist of each *conte* undergoes a journey (actual or metaphorical) to a strange place where he or she is made to learn certain life lessons—often by accident—and where the familiar world and inherited beliefs are called into doubt. As Mason has noted, "Behind the central character stands the author, ever present, guiding the reader towards a conclusion that, in a host of different ways, mocks at set patterns of faith. All around us complexity and contradiction reign. Once we begin to appreciate that, we may possibly start to show greater tolerance for others, avoiding dogmatic attitudes which bring only oppression and cruelty in their wake."

Always didactic, Voltaire's tales impart lessons through entertaining, witty, and satirical narratives. His reliance upon reason and his belief that injustice could be examined dispassionately and eliminated define the themes of his short fiction. For example, *Zadig* concerns the role of divine Providence in human affairs. The protagonist, an ideal figure who is confident in his value system, encounters several persons who represent the potential for evil in human nature, and he is tempted to despair. But his experiences also teach him that there is a plan for mankind despite the fact that human nature cannot be changed, and he eventually accepts his place in that cosmic plan. *Micromégas* is tale of two extraterrestrial beings—one a giant, one a dwarf—who discuss the gap between human ability and achievement, resulting in a satire on anthropocentrism. In *La monde comme il va* (1748; *Babouc, or the World as It Goes*), Voltaire poses the mock question of whether the city of Paris deserves to be saved from destruction, presenting a list of arguments for and against that notion. The conclusion asserts that people are naturally weak and so it is folly to expect them to behave perfectly. *L'Ingénu* (1767; *The Pupil of Nature*) focuses on the subject of religious persecution, condemning religious intolerance through its portrayal of suffering and its appeal to common sense. Critics have noted that the inexperience and innocence of Voltaire's protagonists allow them to offer a fresh perspective on various social issues, while at the same time embodying the theme of personal happiness at odds with the desire to lead a moral life. In *Candide*, Voltaire's best known *conte*, published anonymously, he uses the trials and tribulations of the title character to satirically undercut various philosophies, including Optimism and Manicheanism, while also rejecting the Nihilism that remains when all conventional beliefs are proven bankrupt. Though the hero starts with the notion, imparted to him by the scholar Pangloss, that the world we live in is in fact the best of all possible worlds, Voltaire satirizes this optimistic view by creating a series of misfortunes for Candide and the other characters that serve to emphasize the cruelty of human beings and the widespread indifference to suffering in the world. Along the way, Voltaire also criticizes the hypocrisy of organized religion and the clergy, the aristocracy, and the effects of greed.

CRITICAL RECEPTION

Over the course of his life Voltaire was both celebrated and despised for his satires of the political and philosophical trends of the day, paying for his outspokenness with imprisonment and exile. Nevertheless, *Candide,* widely considered his masterpiece and a signature work of the French Enlightenment, was an immediate bestseller, as numerous pirated editions that proliferated in the first year of its publication attest. Upon its publication, a spokesman for the Parlement of Paris, the highest court in France proclaimed the work indecent and detrimental to religion and public morality, ordering it removed from bookstores. Voltaire did not acknowledge his authorship of the work until 1768. Readers, however, embraced *Candide,* as well as Voltaire's other *contes,* and their popularity as well as critical reputation have been unflagging from the eighteenth century onward. Over the years scholars have taken numerous and diverse approaches to the tales. Johnson Kent Wright has recently reexamined the biographical, historical, and intellectual context of *Candide* and Thomas L. Cooksey has written about Voltaire's handling of generic conventions in the *contes. Amabed* has received renewed critical attention as well, with Robin Howells discussing it as a critique of Roman Catholicism and William F. Edmiston focusing on the tale's treatment of sexuality as an attack on the Roman Catholic Church. Critics have also taken a fresh look at *Zadig,* with Norman J. Tanguay proposing the tale as a precursor of modern detective fiction. *Candide* has been revisited by such scholars as Theodore E. D. Braun, who brings chaos theory to bear on his discussion of the structure of the novella, and Helena Feder, who links Voltaire's acceptance of the material world in *Candide* with contemporary ecofeminist theory. Evaluating the relevance of *Candide* for contemporary readers, Ricardo J. Quinones has noted that the work still remains vital because it offers a glimpse of Voltaire's own inner conflict between a jaded and an optimistic view of the world—a conflict that is eternal, and universally and essentially human.

PRINCIPAL WORKS

Short Fiction

Memnon: Histoire orientale [*Zadig, or the Book of Fate: An Oriental History*] 1747; also published as *Zadig, ou la destineé*

La monde comme il va [*Babouc, or the World as It Goes*] 1748
Le Micromégas de Mr. Voltaire, avec une histoire des croisades & un nouveau plan de l'histoire de l'esprit humain [*Micromegas: A Comic Romance*] 1752
Le deux consolés 1756
Candide; ou, l'ptimisme, traduit de l'Allemand, de Mr. le Docteur Ralph [*Candide; or, All for the Best*; also translated as *Candide; or, Optimism*] 1759
Histoire d'un bon brahmin 1759
Le blanc et le noir 1764
Les aveugles juges des couleurs 1766
L'Ingénu: Histoire véritable tirée des manuscrits de Père Quesnel [*The Pupil of Nature*; also published as *The Sincere Huron*] 1767
L'homme aux quarante écus [*The Man of Forty Crowns*] 1768
La princesse de Babylon [*The Princess of Babylon*] 1768
Les lettres d'Amabed 1769
Le toureau blanc [*The White Bull: An Oriental History*] 1774
Histoire de Jenni, ou l'athée et le sage 1775

Other Major Works

Oedipe (play) 1719
La ligue, ou Henry le Grand [*Henriade; an Epick Poem*] (poetry) 1723; also published as *La Henriade,* 1728
Lettres philosophiques [*Letters Concerning the English Nation*] (essays) 1733
Oeuvres de M. de Voltaire. 12 vols. [*The Works of Voltaire*] (essays, plays, philosophy, prose, history, and criticism) 1738-60
Poèmes sur la dèsastre de Lisbonne, et sur la loi naturelle (poetry) 1756
Dictionnaire pholosophique portaif [*Philosophical Dictionary for the Pocket*] (nonfiction) 1764; also published as *La raison par alphabet*
Irene (play) 1778

CRITICISM

Robin Howells (essay date autumn 1987)

SOURCE: "Processing Voltaire's *Amabed.*" *British Journal for Eighteenth-Century Studies* 10, no. 2 (autumn 1987): 153-62.

[*In the following essay, Howells discusses Voltaire's* Amabed *as an extended critique of Roman Catholicism, also pointing out that the "text seems to work against itself" on the narrative and thematic levels.*]

Little critical attention has been given to the less popular of Voltaire's 'contes'. *Les lettres d'Amabed* is among these.[1] The story centres on a young Hindu couple, Amabed and Adaté. Living in a part of India occupied by the Portuguese, they are the victims of a Catholic missionary who falsely accuses them of apostasy. They are sent for trial in Rome, where they are seduced by the pleasures of a corrupt Papal court. The medium of narration is their letters to a Bramin. Their naive account serves to expose to us, contrastively, the cruelty and cynicism of Roman Catholicism. Among the 'contes', *Amabed* has two distinctions. It is the only one in the epistolary form. And it is almost the only one widely regarded, then and now, as an aesthetic failure.[2] I do not propose to deny that adverse judgement directly. But I want to point to another kind of 'failure' which brings out a much more satisfying dimension to this tale. On the narrative and thematic levels, but especially on the figural, this text seems to work against itself. Most interestingly, rational and moral norms are dissolved in a figure of organic violence. Recognizing the powerful expression of this vision enables us to derive more pleasure from *Amabed*. Opening up this marginal 'conte' may also encourage us to re-read more central ones.

In positing certain normative values in the text, I am in effect assuming an authorial intention to establish them. The intention to denounce the Roman Inquisition seems, from internal and external evidence, a safe assumption. In their own country the young Indian couple are imprisoned. The woman is terrified by a monkish tribunal, and she is sexually assaulted by Father Fa tutto. Yet her account of these shocking events reveals a degree of ambivalence. In Rome the man finds the practices of the Papal city increasingly attractive. The simple certainties with which the protagonists began are replaced by a sense of complexity and paradox. Of course such a journey, literal and philosophical, is commonplace in the 'contes'. An initial position of naive optimism is broken down by the multiplicity of experiences to which the protagonist—and the reader—are subjected. Here however, on the one hand clerical usurpation and violence are not just one subject among many, but the main focus throughout. On the other, the protagonists and apparently Voltaire compound with it. In fact, 'l'infâme' is presented as the life-force.

The key notion here is that of conversion. *'Io la converteró'* says Fa tutto of Adaté, a proposition that she duly misunderstands as 'Je la retournerai' (p. 487).[3] Conversion operates on the two protagonists not in the obvious religious sense (Hindu belief changed to Catholic belief), but in several others. Cultural conversion: from Indian to European mores. Linguistic conversion: in the first letter we are told that the Hindu couple are learning Italian from Father Fa tutto; they continue to encounter new meanings. Sexual conversion: from the

heterosexual monogamy which is their initial ideal to the five-sided affair with two young cardinals at the end.[4] The linguistic and the sexual conversions—synechdoches of the cultural—are the more interesting. They are worked as conceits right through the text. The former, linguistic conversion, links with all the problems of language. It is particularly appropriate where writing itself, and the difficulty of comprehension, are principal elements in the story. Misspellings are the ultimate literalization of such uncertainties. The sexual domain is equally a literalization, the organic *reductio* of all human relations. European sexual aggression is linked with European killing and eating, carnivorous activity contrasted with the gentle vegetarian practices of the Hindus. The Indian couple themselves undergo this process, signified in terms of penetration and swallowing up. The insistent presence of these elements in the text clearly suggests an authorial intention here too. Being more figural, they are probably however less consciously controlled. In any case they work against the rationalist and moralistic norms which are evident on the discursive level. They offer a carnivalesque vision of the world in which ambiguity and paradox are celebrated, violence liberates and conversion is the material principle. Unable to resolve these tensions, the text ends by re-representing them as ritual.[5]

The authority of certain holy texts is placed in question in Amabed's first letter. Hindu, Chinese, Egyptian, and Zoroastrian revelation are juxtaposed by the pious Amabed, exposing to us their curious coincidences and contradictions. Then we are told that he is learning 'un jargon [. . .] qu'on nomme l'*italien*', in order to read 'les livres européens'. His teacher is the missionary Father Fa tutto, his fellow-pupil his fiancée Adaté. 'Nous avons conjugué ensemble le verbe *j'aime* dès le premier jour' (p. 478). Thus language-learning is straightaway linked to European cultural discourse, and to sexual love. The traditional romance conceit of 'studying love' (Paolo and Francesca, Abelard and Héloïse, or Saint-Preux and Julie) is given new twists. The Indian pupils are learning from a European teacher, who intends to do violence to them. 'Conjuguer ensemble' offers a sexual sense which will later be more explicit in other verbal ambiguities.

What 'European' means, in all its multivalency, is sketched out in the next two letters. The Portuguese conqueror of Goa is 'un des plus illustres brigands qui aient désolé la terre. [. . .] Il a noyé dans leur sang des hommes justes et paisibles'. Owing to their different climate, Europeans lack the agricultural resources of India, 'ils ne connaissent qu'une liqueur, qui leur fait perdre la raison' (Réponse d[u Brama] Shastasid, p. 480). Amabed's second letter repeats this picture of European violence and inconsistency. The latter appears in their authoritative texts. Their *Histoire universelle* actually ignores much of the world. Their Bible, which contradicts itself, tells odd tales like that of 'un Noé qui planta des vignes après que l'océan eut submergé tout le globe'. As to violence, the 'cruautés épouvantables' that they have committed in Calicut '[font] frémir la nature indienne'. They appear to differ entirely from Indians, because 'leurs estomacs sont carnassiers. Ils s'enivrent avec le jus fermenté de la vigne, plantée, disent-ils, par leur Noé. Le père Fa tutto lui-même, tout poli qu'il est, a égorgé deux petits poulets; il les a fait cuire dans une chaudière, et il les a mangés impitoyablement' (pp. 481-82). Here is something of an Indian 'cru' opposed to a European 'cuit'. But more particularly, a gentle and vegetarian order is opposed to one which deals in transformation and appropriation by violence. The presentation of the violent order poses problems. We are clearly urged to abhor the brutality of the Catholic conquerors, and presumably to deplore inebriation. Yet the violence to chickens, and to grapes, with which it is identified does not seem to call for such reactions. We are invited to mock the Bible, yet it is presented too as the fount of wine-making. A principal motif first appearing here in both accounts of the European is that of a universal immersion. The conqueror of the world drowns Indians in their own blood. The Deluge drowns the earth. Yet from the latter comes fruitfulness and change. Will the same then be true of the Indian couple forcibly submitted to the European process? Baptism, the text will point out, signifies immersion. Fa tutto's sexual assault on Adaté will also be presented as an immersion. Finally we may note that the universal and the sexual are already linked in European linguistic activity. Amabed naively notes that Fa tutto is giving more attention to Adaté. 'Il a même fait pour elle deux vers italiens qui finissent en *o*' (p. 482). We can imagine the subject, verb, and predicate of his short text. The agent is European, the object Indian, the verb active. The sexual reading—ours, not Adaté's—is surely invited too by the end of the sentence (Fa tutto's, and Voltaire's). Carnal knowledge, for the male, finishes in 'o'. So indeed does the European violence to other creatures, which pass through his cooking-pot, then his mouth, to enter his carnivorous stomach. These are figures of interpenetration, and of comprehension. 'O' represents wholeness. Fa tutto, as his name implies, is the universally active missionary.

These linked motifs are kept before us in the next few letters between the Bramin and Amabed. The Bramin warns against 'ton Fa tutto, qui tue des poulets, et qui fait des vers pour ta chère Adaté' (p. 482). Killing, eating, Italian, and loving are placed together (indeed superimposed if we see a pun in 'poulets'). Amabed in reply joyfully reports his marriage with Adaté. Fa tutto, we are not surprised to learn, has been happy to take part. Amabed naively contrasts the blameless life of the Bramin 'sans passions' with his own present state. 'Je ne touche plus à la terre, je suis dans le ciel', '[je suis] absorb[é] dans une mer de voluptés' (pp. 483-84). Then we learn that Fa tutto has persuaded them to go on a

journey, to Goa where Italian is widely spoken. Adaté 'brûle d'envie de faire usage d'une langue qu'elle vient d'apprendre. Je partage tous ses goûts' (p. 484). The established *double-entendre* of 'using Italian' points to that of 'sharing all tastes'. To the elements of air and water, in which love has immersed Amabed, Adaté adds that of fire. But the Europeans will bring him literally back to earth. Adaté's dramatic letter spells it out. 'Birmah, entends mes cris [. . .]. Mon cher Amabed [. . .] est dans une fosse que les barbares appellent *prison*'. Here is the third case where European appellation is called to our attention. The second was sexual love, the first 'l'italien' itself (the naming of the naming). The enclosure of the Indians by the Europeans is emphasized, and its senses multiplied. 'Ces monstres [. . .] saisirent mon mari et moi, et nous mirent chacun dans une fosse'. 'Il fallait du moins nous ensevelir ensemble'. 'J'ai dit à mes anthropophages: "Où est Amabed [. . .]?"' (p. 485). The Europeans seize them and bury them in the earth, perhaps in a bodily cavity or a sexual cleft. The Europeans may literally ingest them. Adaté's second letter,—with 'gouffre', 'se nourrir de sang humain', etc.—offers the same configuration.

Adaté's second letter is presented as being from the enclosure, 'écrite de la prison de l'Inquisition'. She is brought for trial. The key words for the Inquisitors are those for our figure of the world-process: baptism and conversion. Their religious sense is degraded and profoundly enriched. The president of this tribunal asks just one question: 'Est-il vrai que vous avez été baptisée?' Father Fa tutto promises just one thing: '*Io la converteró*'. Adaté misinterprets both utterances. Having received Hindu baptism in the Ganges, she answers the Catholic question in the affirmative, and is therefore accused of apostasy. Of Fa tutto's undertaking she notes, 'cela signifie en italien, autant que j'en puisse juger: *Je la retournerai*'. 'Veut-il dire qu'il me rendra à ma patrie? Ah! père Fa tutto, lui ai-je dit, retournez donc le jeune Amabed'. We must reserve judgement on the status of Hindu baptism. What is clearer is that Adaté's conscious understanding looks back to her own culture, whereas the story will take her forward to the 'baptism' and 'conversion' practised by the Europeans. The sense of sexual conversion, and entry from the rear, are signalled to us in her mistranslation. Her request that Fa tutto give this treatment to Amabed implies homosexuality. This is promptly underlined by her reference to the monks bowing to a picture of crucified Jesus. 'Tous ont fait une profonde révérence au tableau qui représente un homme tout nu'. Fa tutto's heterosexual desires however are not excluded. As the final frolic in Rome will indicate, front and rear, heterosexual and homosexual, are not contradictory but complementary. On wider senses of 'baptism' the text is equally insistent. 'Amabed [. . .] est dans une fosse! Pourquoi y ai-je été plongée? qui sont ces spectres qui m'ont demandé si j'avais été baignée?' (pp. 485-87). Both of the Indians are imprisoned, buried, immersed, bathed. They will emerge to the new life that is parodic of spiritual rebirth and far fuller.

Adaté undergoes Fa tutto's conversion and baptism, a single event. He rapes her. A sexual meaning for conversion is already well established. The figure of baptism is offered in her account of the climax of the event. 'Le détestable Fa tutto a fait pleuvoir dans mon sein la brûlante rosée de son crime'. She is flooded by his power, which is elemental and paradoxical ('pleuvoir', 'brûlante'). It is clear that despite her conscious detestation she is attracted by this conquering violence. She describes Fa tutto as 'enflammé, invincible, inexorable, [. . .] indomptable'. As if to prove it, he promptly repeats his act upon Déra, her serving-maid. Déra is the subaltern ingénue, with the usual reductive role of repetition and contrast. Treated like Adaté, her reaction is likewise ambiguous. '"Ah! ma chère maîtresse, quel homme! Tous les gens de son espèce sont-ils aussi cruels que lui?"'. Fa tutto's manly violence is assimilated to that of the Europeans. The contrast with the Indian order is made explicit in the complementary episode presented in this letter to complete the figure. 'On ne nous a point apporté à manger à l'heure accoutumée.' Vulgar Déra has complained about this, whereas to Adaté 'il me paraissait bien honteux de manger après ce qui nous était arrivé. Cependant nous avions un appétit dévorant [. . .]'. There is much more here than the traditional burlesque juxtaposition of high thought and low hunger. They are served with roasted fowl and wine. After what we have suffered, writes Adaté, 'c'est le tour le plus sanglant qu'on puisse jouer'. To them as vegetarians, 'c'est un péché horrible de manger du poulet: mais on nous y force'. They plead to the Hindu deity that 'l'âme n'est point souillée de ce qui entre dans le corps', and urge that all these crimes be attributed to Father Fa tutto. Indeed Adaté prays that in the next incarnation she and the Dominican might change places, so that she can be 'plus impitoyable encore pour lui qu'il ne l'a été pour moi'. Then 'nous nous sommes mises à table' (pp.494-95). Thus the two appetites, for sex and for food, are not only juxtaposed. They are identified: through their missionary origin, through the theme of violence ('on nous y force'), through the metaphor and synechdoche of 'sang', through the conceit of penetration and enclosure ('ce qui entre dans le corps'), through the degrading 'souillure', and through the implication that the women really desire both. Religious, sexual and alimentary communion are superimposed, in a figure of violence, reversal, and flow.

Adaté is maximally enclosed—by the earth, the prison and Fa tutto—at the time she is penetrated. She is immersed from the inside. The paradoxical figure is repeated in the next stage of the narrative. The Indians are brought out of prison, and despatched on a journey half-way round the world (for judgement in Rome). In the account of the voyage enclosure is emphasized. It is stressed for itself: 'nous aurons une petite chambre [. . .]'. Stressed for paradox within enclosure: 'nous avons pour compagnons de voyage des marchands d'Europe, des chanteuses, deux vieux officiers, [. . .]'. And for the particular juxtaposition: 'moi et ma chère Déra, être enfermées dans le même vaisseau avec le père Fa tutto!'. But emphasized too is openness to the universe, identified with European language and violence: 'nous ne voyons plus que les airs, nommé *ciel* par ces brigands si peu dignes du ciel, et cette grande mer que l'avarice et la cruauté leur ont fait traverser' (pp. 497-99). On board too is a Franciscan almoner, Father Fa molto, who contributes to a more dynamic figure. Landing at the Cape, 'Fa molto a conduit notre jeune Déra tout doucement dans une petite maison [. . .]'. But then 'Fa tutto [. . .] est entré dans le cabaret en furieux. Il y avait deux matelots qui ont été jaloux aussi'. '[Ils] avaient beaucoup bu [. . .].' 'Les deux hommes de mer et les deux bonzes d'Europe se sont gourmés violemment; [. . .] tous quatre changeant de main à tout moment, deux contre deux, trois contre un, tous contre tous, chacun jurant, chacun tirant à soi notre infortunée [. . .]'. The paradox is marked at every level: men of the sea; European bonzes; all engaged with an Indian, and with each other. Religion and sex; 'tout doucement' and 'violemment'. The Indian is enclosed and then almost taken to pieces, an opening up no doubt repeated more gently by her rescuer the captain '[qui] l'a menée dans son quartier, où elle est enfermée avec lui depuis deux heures' (pp. 504-505).

On the voyage the Indians study the European Bible in which they find further variants of the world-process. St Paul, notes Amabed, '[a] été comme moi au cachot; il ajoute qu'il a eu cinq fois trente-neuf coups de fouet [. . .] sur les fesses; plus, trois fois des coups de bâton, sans spécifier le nombre; plus, il dit qu'il a été lapidé une fois: cela est violent'. Quite. He too is enclosed then literally opened up. 'Plus, il jure qu'il a été un jour et une nuit au fond de la mer [. . .]; mais en récompense, il a été ravi au troisième ciel.' This is literal and elemental enclosure and release, contradictory ('en récompense') yet complementary. Thus we come to the archetype of Jonah—swallowed by the world-whale—flanked by linguistic and elemental paradoxes. In the Old Testament, 'tantôt c'est un âne qui parle, tantôt c'est un de leurs saints qui passe trois jours et trois nuits dans le ventre d'une baleine, et qui en sort de fort mauvaise humeur. Ici c'est un prédicateur que s'en va prêcher dans le ciel [. . .]'. Fa molto leaves them to read for themselves 'son livre sacré'. They promptly find incest, and the attempted homosexual rape of angels (pp. 500-502). The exemplary value of such images is by now clear. Their paradoxical force is doubled by their sacred context.

The juxtaposition of sacred and sexual continues in the rest of *Amabed.* The denomination of the Pope is abbreviated in advance from 'ce vice-Dieu' to 'ce vice' (p. 496). At the Cape we encounter the naked Hottentots, whose women have a kind of natural apron of skin to cover their private parts. 'Ce tablier couvre leur joyau, dont les Hottentots sont idolâtres.' However, in Amabed's opinion, 'un Hottentot [. . .] n'a plus rien à désirer quand il a vu sa Hottentote par devant et par derrière' (pp. 503-504). The antithesis will be repeated in Rome—itself the antithesis of the African Cape—reworking both the 'cabaret' and 'Hottentot' images. Déra enters a church, where 'un brame du pays, vêtu magnifiquement, se courbait sur une table; il tournait le derrière au peuple. On dit qu'il faisait Dieu. Dès qu'il eut fait Dieu, il se montra par devant. Déra fait un cri, et dit "Voilà le coquin qui m'a violée!"' (p. 523). The suggestion of a Divine fecundity appears in other religious/sexual juxtapositions too. We are told that 'les Portugais regardent les femmes grosses comme des personnes sacrées' (p. 506). On the same page the organic power of life is stressed in Fa molto's rejection of priestly celibacy. 'Il est vrai que j'ai fait ce vœu; mais si j'avais promis que mon sang ne coulerait jamais dans mes veines, et que mes ongles et mes cheveux ne croîtraient pas, vous m'avouerez que je ne pourrais accomplir cette promesse'. Once in Rome, the converts are taken through the crowds in triumph. 'Le peuple y suivit en criant *Cazzo, Cazzo,* en nous donnant des bénédictions' (p. 511). When they meet the Pope, he asks them about Hindu techniques of love-making, and whether Brama has a seraglio (p. 523). The final sexual encounter is organized by two cardinals.

In this final five-sided encounter—for 'Déra était du voyage'—the Indians seem to participate with some willingness. Its avatar was the violent five-sider at the Cape. It is clear that the European missionary process has changed them. 'Ce monsignor me paraît bien dessalé; je me forme beaucoup avec lui, et je me sens déjà tout autre', noted Amabed between times (p. 511). We may say that, like Adaté, he has been 'retourné(e)'. The fullest configuration is probably that offered by another prelate—his denomination underlined—who cheerfully urges them to absorb European victuals. 'Le *préféré* nous a dit que, puisque nous étions baptisés, il fallait manger des perdrix et boire du vin de Montepulciano; que tous les vice-Dieu en usaient ainsi; que c'était la marque essentielle d'un véritable chrétien'. Adaté explains that her baptism was not Christian but 'dans le Gange. "Eh, mon Dieu! madame, dit le *préféré*, dans le Gange ou dans le Tibre, ou dans un bain, qu'importe! Vous êtes des nôtres. Vous avez été convertie par le père Fa tutto; c'est pour nous un honneur que nous ne voulons pas perdre. Voyez quelle supériorité notre religion a sur la vôtre!"' (p. 513). Adaté was baptised and converted by the missionary's sexual violence. The couple are now urged to ingest (immerse/convert/

comprehend) flesh which has already been subject to violence and wine which may produce it. This multiple communion is true Christianity, the best religion. As with the final five-sider, the Indians no longer need to be forced. Partly because they are converted. Partly because Rome represents a civilized resolution of the opposition in India between Hindu gentleness and European colonialist violence.

But if we are indeed dealing with a world-process, it cannot neatly stop. The text seems to recognize this. 'Il faudra donc qu'il y ait des révolutions dans la religion de l'Europe' (p. 522). Catholicism too, we may say, will be 'retourné', broken down, changed. Nor can the world-process have neatly started. The text goes partway to breaking down its own structure of opposition. Adaté has already been immersed in the Ganges. The prelate seems to say that any kind of immersion will do. Adaté earlier also links Ganges baptism with a sexual baptism given to her—after Fa tutto—by Amabed. 'Mon tendre époux [. . .] a effacé la tache du crime dont cet abominable Fa tutto m'avait souillée; semblable à l'eau sainte du Gange, qui lave toutes les macules des âmes, il m'a rendu une nouvelle vie' (p. 497). Fa tutto's baptism was violent, soiling, and enriching, whereas that of the Indian and his river are sterile. But along with the dualist opposition is variety and succession. Adaté looked forward to the next incarnation, in which she would do violence to Fa tutto. The final stage in the story is the five-sider, whose permutations are unfinished. To 'return'—both to restore and to reverse—implies here an unending cycle of replacement and change.

I noted initially that this celebration of the world-process goes against the moralistic and didactic bias of the text. Positive festivity emerges from negative satire. There is however another contradiction here. The process is sometimes presented not just with nominal disapproval but with disgust. Here the visceral does not form a single figure with the sacred, but remains irreconcilable. In the Old Testament rape and incest can be assimilated, but what of consuming faeces, 'manger de la matière louable sur son pain' (p. 501)? At Rome the Papal states are described as 'le cloaque de la nature' (p. 510). Theologians are compared, curiously, to 'les derniers valets dans une maison; ils font la grosse besogne, portent les ordures, [. . .]' (p. 515). Most striking is a set-piece comparison between Rome and a banquet, which is not joyous, nor even satirical so much as appalled. 'Je le compare [le gouvernement de Rome] au repas que nous a donné la princesse Piombino. La salle était propre, commode, et parée; l'or et l'argent brillaient sur les buffets; la gaieté, l'esprit et les grâces animaient les convives; mais, dans les cuisines, le sang et la graisse coulaient; les peaux des quadrupèdes, les plumes des oiseaux et leurs entrailles, pêlemêle amoncelées, soulevaient le cœur, et répandaient l'infection'

(p. 514). Here one has no sense of a view beyond Amabed's view. The underlying violence and flow are presented with puzzlement and with horror. The Indians have learned to enjoy high European civilization. But behind it they can still see what Adaté called earlier 'ce galimatias infernal, ce mélange incompréhensible d'absurdités et d'horreurs' (p. 491).

'Comprehension' in the linguistic sense has been linked since the beginning of the story with its ontological sense. The Indians 'learn European' in the fullest way. As they are converted they attempt to convert it, world-process and word-process. The first letter presented them studying 'un jargon qui a cours dans l'Europe, et qu'on nomme l'*italien*'. Subsequently various European or Catholic terms (Italian is their common synechdoche) are foregrounded in their letters. The effect is to recall repeatedly the gap between their understanding and European reality. Sometimes the Indians are simply baffled by these lexical items. '*Apostata*! Je ne sais ce que ce mot veut dire' (p. 486). But positive misinterpretation offers far more satisfactory possibilities. Sometimes they give a naive explanation. 'Un *obispo* est [. . .] un intendant de leur religion; il est vêtu de violet, et il porte aux mains des souliers violets' (p. 496). 'J'ai su que c'est un des seigneurs, c'est-à-dire un des valets du vice-Dieu, qu'on appelle *préférés, prelati*' (p. 513). The first adduces apparently trivial particularities as if they had equal value with the essential; the second uses etymology to imply a more down-to-earth significance. Both suggest a reductive truth which may be valid. In some sense then the Indians do indeed comprehend. The nub of the matter, Fa tutto's 'Io la converterò', was correctly mistranslated by Adaté. Though she did not realize it, already she was beginning to recognize the world-process. And she was stripping away from words both their cultural prestige and their equivalence with what they appear to mean.

On the minimum level the linguistic problem is signalled through misspelling. Rome first appears in the text as 'une ville magnifique qu'on nomme *Roume*' (p. 498); 'son nom est Pual' is our introduction to St Paul (p. 500). These forms are then maintained throughout. On the maximum level, the gap between meaning and reality can lead to a statement about universal incomprehension. On board is 'un personnage considérable qu'on nomme *l'aumônier*. Ce n'est pas qu'il fasse l'aumône; au contraire on lui donne de l'argent pour dire des prières dans une langue [. . .] que personne de l'équipage n'entend; peut-être ne l'entend-il pas lui-même' (p. 500). But language is not just verbal. '[Fa tutto] ne m'a répondu qu'en levant les yeux et les mains au ciel, mais avec une attitude si douloureuse et si tendre que ne savais plus que penser' (p. 486). More emphatically: 'Il est sorti de ma chambre en prenant ma main, et en la mettant sur son cœur. C'est le signe visible, comme tu le sais, de la sincérité, qui est invisible.

Puisqu'il a mis ma main sur son cœur, il ne me trompera pas [. . .]' (p. 488). She is wrong. In Rome the Church deals publicly in the same manner. 'Nous avons fait du mariage le signe visible d'une chose invisible': all the court cases and profits therefore come to us, 'parce que nous seuls pouvons voir des choses invisibles' (p. 516). In making the claim to know the reality behind the sign they too are wrong. But they know it.

Rome knows its own ignorance, though cynically pretending to know reality. It knows the world-process, though it puts a gloss on it. Its response is laughter and ceremony. This is presented through Roman high society, and through the Pope. It is the itinerary of the Indians. Adaté had trusted that the truth would be established by the Pope, 'cet être extraordinaire qui ne se trompe jamais' (p. 498). The event is different. 'L'infaillible [. . .] nous a fait baiser son pied droit en tenant les côtés de rire.' 'Il a donné deux baisers à ma femme et à moi aussi'. 'Il nous a congédiés en nous recommandant le christianisme, en nous embrassant, et en nous donnant de petites claques sur les fesses' (pp. 522-23). Back and front, top and toe, kiss and smack, male and female, he offers only a comic ritual reprise of the world-figure. Amabed has understood this already. 'Je crois que le plus sage est de rire comme les autres, et d'être poli comme eux' (p. 515). The Indians attend a performance of Machiavelli's *Mandragora*, in which a monk seduces a woman and Catholicism is mocked throughout, 'mais la comédie est si jolie que le plaisir l'a emporté sur le scandale' (p. 520). This *mise en abyme* is also Voltaire's solution, and that offered to us. The 'conte' as a figure of the world circles round to meet itself, without denying the contradictions within it.

Notes

1. No study of this tale is listed in 'Voltaire's "contes": an "état présent"', by H. T. Mason, *Modern Language Review*, 65 (1970), 19-35, or in the bibliography of the Pléiade *Romans et contes,* ed. F. Deloffre and J. Van den Heuvel (Paris, 1979). The latter contains a substantial 'Notice' (pp. 1087-118), but this deals mainly with the stages of Voltaire's composition of the tale and the historical sources. The briefer literary assessment also cites remarks from Dora Bienaimé Rigo, *Gli Ultimi Racconti di Voltaire* (Pisa, 1974), which contains a chapter on *Amabed*. The Preface to the separate edition of *Amabed* by A. Josipovich (Paris, 1961) has little to say on its quality as a fiction. Some observations on literary technique in D. A. Bonneville, *Voltaire and the Form of the Novel,* 'Studies on Voltaire and the Eighteenth Century', 158 (1976).

2. See the Pléiade 'Notice', pp. 1111-16. In a word, the anti-Catholic satire is perceived as predictable and repetitive, the style throughout heavy-handed.

3. References are to the Pléiade edition (see note 1). The text occupies about fifty pages.

4. The Pléiade editors note '*converteró*' as 'l'élémént central du conte', though pointing only to its sexual realisation at the end (pp. 1126-27). On the linguistic side, the importance of a 'démontage étymologique' of religious vocabulary is noted but not developed (p. 1116). The chapter in Rigo points to the oniric quality of Adaté's account, and studies Amabed's changing response to Rome, but tends to be drawn back into 'ideas' and the problem of Good and Evil.

5. This analysis has its origins in the model of reading offered by M. Bakhtin in his classic *Rabelais and his world,* English translation (Cambridge, Mass., 1968), though going beyond the model in finding unresolved tensions. Bakhtin's notion of the 'grotesque body' I have already used to 'open up' a major tale in my '"Cette boucherie héroïque": *Candide* as carnival', *Modern Language Review,* 80 (1985), 293-303. I have argued for a materialist dimension in the 'contes', which may go beyond authorial intention, in 'The burlesque as a philosophical principle in Voltaire's "contes"', in the Festschrift for W. H. Barber, *Voltaire and his World* (Oxford, 1985), pp. 67-84. The present study of *Amabed* points further in showing the positive strength of the figure of violence, its links with ambiguous language, and the contradiction between the discursive and the figural levels of the text. The figural for me is any literary or poetic element—from metaphor to narrative segment—which is at once concrete and expressive.

Norman J. Tanguay (essay date spring/summer 1995)

SOURCE: Tanguay, Norman J. "Voltaire's *Zadig*: Precursor of the Modern Gumshoe?" *Clues: A Journal of Detection* 16, no.1 (spring/summer 1995): 141-51.

[*In this essay, Tanguay examines the evidence for the claim that Voltaire's* Zadig *is "the grandfather of detective stories."*]

Is Voltaire's *Zadig,* as Ellery Queen (Frederic Dannay and Manfred B. Lee) claims, the great grandfather of the detective story? It is certainly one of his most entertaining stories and predates *Candide* by 12 years. Zadig, like Candide, experiences a series of outrageous, even harrowing, adventures. Although ostensibly set in ancient Babylon, Clarence Darrow points out that,

> The story of *Zadig,* while outwardly a romance, was recognized by every one who read it at the time as picturing plainly the people at the French Court, the ab-

surd manners and customs and the stupidity of it all. There was scarcely a custom or habit prevalent at court that was not satirized by the keen wit and facile pen of Voltaire in this romance.

(xiv)

To qualify as a detective story, however, *Zadig* must have an individual who is capable of deductive reasoning, someone who is a keen observer. All other elements, be they red herrings or locked rooms, merely indicate the mystery story. Does Zadig measure up? Benvenuti and Rizzoni write, "The character of Zadig . . . is often seen as the modern detectives prototype, with his ability to see the significance in signs and to discover the unknown through clues" (2). He may be less than brilliant; there is some debate about his mental acuity. Roy S. Wolper states:

> Zadig's brain cannot be depended upon. His perceptiveness admittedly enables Azora to be less censorious: Ogul, less gluttonous; Setoc, less narrowly religious. At its best his wisdom has a solomon-like ingenuity: he is able to make a stone bear witness to convict a corrupt moneylender. And without seeing the lost horse he can identify it microscopically. . . . Although Zadig is a picaresque hero on the surface, he nevertheless is constantly presented as a fool. (But since he is often perceptive, he is not a Panglossian dunce.) He is at different times, then, hero and fool.

(237-48)

In other words, he is a normal human being.

The episode of the lost horse is by far the most famous example in *Zadig* of what Poe would have called ratiocination, practiced by *his* detective, C. Auguste Dupin. However, as John Butt points out, there are a number of other instances in which Zadig can be recognized as an early example of the modern gumshoe:

> Zadig owes his first success (in Chapter 3) to skill in interpreting evidence such as Sherlock Holmes would have admired, but he maintains it (through the next four chapters) by his wisdom, his discretion, and his gentle behaviour . . . good sense, patience in persuasion, ingenuity, and courage ensure his eventual triumph.

(xv)

The episode in question is a wonderful example of deductive reasoning, equal to anything expounded by Sherlock Holmes, Ellery Queen, or Nero Wolfe:

> One day, when he was walking near a little wood, he saw one of the queen's eunuchs running to meet him, followed by several officers, who appeared to be in the greatest uneasiness, and who were running hither and thither like men bewildered and searching for some most precious object which they had lost.
>
> "Young man," said the chief eunuch to Zadig, "have you seen the queen's dog?"
>
> Zadig modestly replied: "It is a bitch, not a dog."

"You are right," said the eunuch.

"It is a very small spaniel," added Zadig; "it is not long since she has had a litter of puppies; she is lame in the forefoot, and her ears are very long."

"You have seen her, then?" said the chief eunuch, quite out of breath.

"No," answered Zadig, "I have never seen her, and never knew that the queen had a bitch."

Just at this very time, by one of those curious coincidences which are not uncommon, the finest horse in the king's stables had broken away from the hand of a groom in the plains of Babylon. The grand huntsman and all the other officers ran after him with as much anxiety as the chief of the eunuchs had displayed in his search after the queen's bitch. The grand huntsman accosted Zadig, and asked him if he had seen the king's horse pass that way.

"It is the horse," said Zadig, "which gallops best; he is five feet high, and has small hoofs; his tail is three and a half feet long; the bosses on his bit are of gold twenty-three carats fine; his shoes are silver of eleven pennyweights."

"Which road did he take? Where is he?" asked the grand huntsman.

"I have not seen him," answered Zadig, "and I have never even heard anyone speak of him."

For his trouble, Zadig is disbelieved and fined. He finally explains himself, though rather unctuously:

> Stars of justice, fathomless gulfs of wisdom, mirrors of truth, ye who have the gravity of lead, the strength of iron, the brilliance of the diamond, and a close affinity with gold, inasmuch as it is permitted me to speak before this august assembly, I swear to you by Ormuzd that I have never seen the queen's respected bitch, nor the sacred horse of the king of kings. Hear all that happened: I was walking toward the little wood where later on I met the venerable eunuch and the most illustrious grand huntsman. I saw on the sand the footprints of an animal, and easily decided that they were those of a little dog. Long and faintly marked furrows, imprinted where the sand was slightly raised between the footprints, told me that it was a bitch whose dugs were drooping and that consequently she must have given birth to young ones only a few days before. Other marks of a different character, showing that the surface of the sand had been constantly grazed on either side of the front paws, informed me that she had very long ears; and, as I observed that the sand was always less deeply indented by one paw than by the other three, I gathered that the bitch belonging to our august queen was a little lame, if I may venture to say so.

> With respect to the horse of the king of kings, you must know that as I was walking along the roads in that same wood, I perceived the marks of a horse's shoes, all at equal distances. 'There,' I said to myself, 'went a horse with a faultless gallop.' The dust upon the trees where the width of the road was not more than seven feet, was here and there rubbed off on both sides, three feet and a half away from the middle of the road. 'This horse,' said I, 'has a tail three feet and a half long, which, by its movements to right and left, has whisked away the dust,' I saw, where the trees formed a canopy five feet above the ground, leaves lately fallen from the boughs; and I concluded that the horse had touched them, and was therefore five feet high. As to his bit, it must be of gold twenty-three carats fine, for he had rubbed its bosses against a touchstone, the properties of which I had ascertained. Lastly, I inferred from the marks that his shoes left upon stones of another kind, that he was shod with silver of eleven pennyweights in quality.

This passage may be favorably compared with any number from the Holmesian canon. Here is a typical example, from "The Red-Headed League":

> Sherlock Holmes's quick eye took in my occupation, and he shook his head with a smile as he noticed my questioning glances. "Beyond the obvious facts that he has at some time done manual labour, that he takes snuff, that he is a Freemason, that he has been in China, and that he has done a considerable amount of writing lately, I can deduce nothing else."

> Mr. Jabel Wilson started up in his chair, with his forefinger upon the paper, but his eyes upon my companion.

> "How, in the name of good-fortune, did you know all that, Mr. Holmes?" he asked. "How did you know, for example, that I did manual labour? It's true as gospel, for I began as a ship's carpenter."

> "Your hands, my dear sir. Your right hand is quite a size larger than your left. You have worked with it, and the muscles are more developed."

> "Well, the snuff, then, and the Freemasonry.?"

> "I won't insult your intelligence by telling you how I read that, especially as, rather against the strict rules of your order, you use an arc-and-compass breastpin."

> "Ah, of course, I forgot that. But the writing?"

> "What else can be indicated by that right cuff so very shiny for five inches, and the left one with the smooth patch near the elbow where you rest it upon the desk?"

> "Well, but China?"

> "The fish that you have tattooed immediately above your right wrist could only have been done in China. I have made a small study of tattoo marks and have even contributed to the literature of the subject. That trick of staining the fishes' scales of a delicate pink is quite peculiar to China. When, in addition, I see a Chinese coin hanging from your watch-chain, the matter becomes even more simple.

(177)

There is much more to *Zadig* than the episode of the dog and the horse. There are several episodes which employ devices still used by detective, mystery, and suspense writers today. One of these perennial favorites is the cryptic message, usually incomplete because it has been torn, which defies interpretation or is misinterpreted. It is normally the detective's job to make sense out of the situation. Zadig writes verses which he does not want to read, so he tears them in half and throws them away. The Envious man, his enemy, searches diligently and finds . . . one fragment of the leaf, which had been torn in such a way that the halves of each line made sense, and even rhymed verse, in shorter meter than the original. But by an accident still more strange, these short lines were found to contain the most opprobrious libel against the king. They read thus:

> By heinous crimes
> Set on the throne
> In peaceful times
> One foe alone.

The Envious man shows the verse to the king, and Zadig is imprisoned. However, on the way to his execution,

> . . . the king's parrot escaped from its perch, and alighted in Zadig's garden, on a thicket of roses. A peach had been carried thither by the wind from a tree hard by, and it had fallen on a piece of writing paper, to which it had stuck. The bird took up both the peach and the paper, and laid them on the monarch's knees. The king, whose curiosity was excited, read some words which made no sense, and which appeared to be the ends of four lines of verse. He loved poetry, and princes who love the muses never find time hangs heavy on their hands. His parrot's adventure set him thinking. The queen, who remembered what had been written on the fragment of the leaf from Zadig's notebook, had it brought to her.

> Both pieces were put side by side, and were found to fit together exactly. The verses then read as Zadig had made them:

> By heinous crimes I saw the earth alarm'd
> Set on the throne one king all evil curbs:
> In peaceful times now only Love is arm'd,
> One foe alone the timid heart disturbs.

Zadig is set free and the Envious man is punished. Devices such as cryptic messages or misplaced letters may seem farfetched, but they are still used in detective fiction today. They have also been used extensively in mainstream fiction (Thomas Hardy leaps to mind). Here is a typical example from Mary Roberts Rinehart's *The Circular Staircase*:

> The second scrap, folded and refolded into a compass so tiny that the writing had been partly obliterated, was part of a letter—the lower half of a sheet, not typed, but written in a cramped hand.

> "—by altering the plan for—rooms, may be possible. The best way, in my opinion, would be to—the plan for—in one of the—rooms—chimney."

That was all.

"Well?" I said, looking up. "There is nothing in that, is there? A man ought to be able to change the plan of his house without becoming an object of suspicion."

"There is little in the paper itself," he admitted; "but why should Arnold Armstrong carry that around, unless it meant something? He never built a house, you may be sure of that. If it is this house, it may mean anything from a secret room—"

"To an extra bath-room," I said scornfully. "Haven't you a thumb-print, too?"

(55)

Ms. Rinehart is acknowledged as the founder of the Had I But Known school of detective fiction, and this sort of device is widely used to create suspense.

Not all detectives are great analytical thinkers; some catch criminals through their knowledge of psychology and humanity. Christie's Hercule Poirot, Simenon's Jules Maigret, and Chesterton's Father Brown are all excellent examples of this type of detective. They can often trick criminals into giving themselves away. Zadig displays this quality also:

> "Pillar of the throne of equity, I come here to claim from this man, in my master's name, repayment of five hundred ounces of silver which he will not restore."

> "Have you witnesses?" asked the judge.

> "No, they are dead; but there still remains a large stone upon which the money was counted out; and, if it please your lordship to order someone to go and fetch the stone, I hope that it will bear witness to the truth. We will remain here, the Jew and I, until the stone arrives; I will send for it at my master Setoc's expense."

> "I am quite willing that that should be done," answered the judge; and then he proceeded to dispatch other business.

> At the end of the sitting he said to Zadig:

> "Well, your stone is not arrived yet, is it?"

> The Jew laughed, and answered:

> "Your lordship will have to remain here till tomorrow before the stone could be brought; it is more than six miles away, and it would take fifteen men to move it."

> "Now then," exclaimed Zadig, "did I not say well that the stone itself would bear witness? Since this man knows where it is, he acknowledges that upon it the money was counted." The Jew was abashed, and was soon obliged to confess the whole truth. The judge ordered him to be bound to the stone, without eating or drinking, until the five hundred ounces should be restored, and it was not long before they were paid.

The above passage compares favorably with this passage from Ellery Queen's "The Mad Tea Party":

> Their eyes went with horror to the tall mirror set in the wall, winking back at them in the glitter of the bulbs. And when I discovered the secret, I looked *through the looking glass* and what do you suppose I—a clumsy Alice, indeed!—found there?"

No one replied.

Ellery went swiftly to the mirror, stood on tiptoe, touched something, and something happened to the whole glass. It moved forward as if on hinges. He hooked his fingers in the crack and pulled. The mirror, like a door, swung out and away, revealing a shallow closet-like cavity.

The women with one breath screamed and covered their eyes.

The stiff figure of the Mad Hatter, with Richard Owen's unmistakable features, glared out at them—a dead, horrible, baleful glare.

Paul Gardner stumbled to his feet, choking and jerking at his collar. His eyes bugged out of his head. "O-O-Owen," he gasped. "Owen. He *can't* be here. I b-b-buried him myself under the big rock behind the house in the woods. Oh, my God." And he smiled a dreadful smile and his eyes turned over and he collapsed in a faint on the floor.

(262-63)

Zadig could lay claim to being the great grandfather of detective stories from these incidents alone, but there are several other episodes in the relatively short romance. You set a trap to catch a thief. Sometimes it works only too well, as the following illustrates:

The same day he issued a public notice that all who aspired to the post of receiver-in-chief of the revenues of His Gracious Majesty Nabussan, son of Nussanab, were to present themselves in garments of light silk, on the first day of the month of the Crocodile, in the king's antechamber. They duly put in an appearance to the number of sixty-four. Fiddlers were posted in an adjoining hall; all was ready for dancing; but the door of the hall was fastened, and it was necessary, in order to enter it, to pass along a little gallery which was pretty dark. An usher was sent to conduct each candidate, one after another, along this passage, in which he was left alone for a few minutes. The king, prompted by Zadig, had spread out all his treasures in this gallery. When all the competitors had reached the hall, his majesty gave orders that they should begin to dance. Never did men dance more heavily and with less grace; they all kept their heads down, their backs bent, and their hands glued to their sides.

"What rogues!" said Zadig, under his breath.

There was only one among them who stepped out freely, with head erect, a steady eye, and outstretched arms, body straight, and legs firm.

"Ah! The honest fellow! The worthy man!" said Zadig.

The king embraced this good dancer, and declared him treasurer; whereas all the others were punished with a fine, and that most justly, for each one of them, during the time that he was in the gallery, had filled his pockets so that he could hardly walk. The king was grieved for the honor of human nature that out of those sixty-four dancers there should have been sixty-three thieves.

The above style of entrapment was much used by Erle Stanley Gardner's Perry Mason and Earl Derr Biggers' Charlie Chan.

Zadig also shows himself adept at answering riddles, as many detectives must do to arrive at the correct solution:

The grand magian first proposed this question:

"What, of all things in the world, is alike the longest and the shortest, the quickest and the slowest, the most minutely divided and the most widely extended, the most neglected and the most regretted, without which nothing can be done, which devours everything that is little, and confers life on everything that is great?"

Itobad was to speak first; he answered that such a man as he understood nothing about riddles, that it was enough for him to have conquered by the might of his arm. Some said that the answer to the riddle was fortune; according to others it was the earth, and according to others again light. Zadig said that it was time:

"Nothing is longer," added he, "since it is the measure of eternity; nothing is shorter, since it fails to accomplish our projects. There is nothing slower to one who waits, nothing quicker to one who enjoys. It extends to infinity in greatness, it is infinitely divisible in minuteness. All men neglect it, all regret its loss. Nothing is done without it. It buries in oblivion all that is unworthy of being handed to posterity; and it confers immortality upon all things that are great."

Finally, Zadig's mental powers are transferable. Toward the end of the tale, when he is reunited with his beloved Astarte, she shows talents similar to his:

At these words Zadig threw himself at her knees, and bathed them with tears. Astarte raised him tenderly, and continued thus:

"I saw myself in the power of a barbarian, and a rival of the crazy woman who was my fellow-prisoner. She told me what had befallen her in Egypt. I conjectured from the description she gave of your person, from the time of the occurrence, from the dromedary on which you were mounted, and from all the circumstances of the case, that it was Zadig who had fought in her behalf. I had no doubt that you were at Memphis, and resolved to betake myself thither."

What a pity that Dr. Watson and Captain Hastings (Hercule Poirot's sometime companion) had not paid closer attention. They never seem to acquire the knack of detection.

Works Cited

Benvenuti, Stefano, and Gianni Rizzoni. *The Whodunit: An Informal History of Detective Fiction.* New York: Collier Macmillan, 1981.

Butt, John. *Voltaire's Zadig—L'Ingenue.* Introduction. Middlesex, England: Penguin, 1964.

Darrow, Clarence. *The Best of All Possible Worlds: Tales and Romance by Voltaire.* New York: Vanguard, 1929.

Doyle, Arthur Conan. *The Complete Sherlock Holmes.* Garden City, NY: Doubleday, 1930.

Queen, Ellery. *The Adventures of Ellery Queen.* New York: Pocket, 1954.

Rinehart, Mary Roberts. *The Circular Staircase.* New York: Grosset, n.d.

Wolper, Roy S. "Zadig, a Grim Tragedy?" *Romantic Review* 65.4 (1974): 237-48.

Theodore E. D. Braun (essay date 2001)

SOURCE: Braun, Theodore E. D. "Chaos, Contingency, and *Candide*." *1650-1850: Ideas, Aesthetics, and Inquiries in the Early Modern Era*, 6 (2001): 199-209.

[*In the following essay, Braun applies chaos theory in an interpretation of* Candide, *noting that its "shimmering surface perfection and regularity" is undermined by the plot's nonlinearity and by Candide's rejection of a Providential worldview.*]

Voltaire has proven to be a formidable obstacle to many modern critical approaches; not impervious, but a kind of unmovable object successfully resisting an irresistible force. Few indeed have been the scholars who have applied to his works the methods of recent approaches such as structuralism, deconstruction, or chaos theory (of course, with the latter being scarcely a decade old, this is perhaps to be expected). Whatever the cause, the effect is clear, and in terms of chaos theory, Voltaire appears to be virginal: I have not found in the MLA bibliography any critic examining any work of his from this point of view, nor have I found it in recent books by Haydn Mason, Roger Pearson, or Thomas Kavanagh.[1]

One of the problems to be faced in approaching Voltaire and *Candide* from the point of view of chaos theory is that with most authors—and in particular, most postmodern authors—chaos theory helps us to see the order in apparent disorder, to make sense out of texts that seem to lead nowhere. With Voltaire and with *Candide* in particular the problem is more complex: we must first look under the crystalline surface of the narration to find the murkiness that represents life in this tale, that is, we must find the disorder hidden beneath an apparent order, and then look for a different order, a kind of order that may surprise us, perhaps taking us away from traditional views but certainly towards greater depth and complexity than we have been accustomed to in Voltaire.

Chaos, as it is understood by modern scientists and mathematicians, is not used only in "the older sense of chance, randomness, disorder" that most literary and historical scholars are likely to associate with the word;

chaotic systems all contain an order in the midst of disorder, they are "both deterministic and unpredictable," they raise questions (when applied to human beings) of free will and determinism; "chaos leads to order, and order back to chaos."[2] As Crutchfield, Farmer, Packard, and Shaw express it in their seminal article, "Chaos,"

> simple deterministic systems with only a few elements can generate random behavior. The randomness is fundamental; gathering more information does not make it go away. Randomness generated in this way has come to be called chaos.[3]

Among the features of chaotic systems that we will examine here are *nonlinearity* (which can be seen, from one point of view, as a refutation of some Newtonian principles, such as the proportionality of cause and effect [a small deviation may sometimes have large consequences], and from another point of view as complexity rather than simplicity in design, which leads to "a new awareness of the importance of scale"); *recursive symmetries between scale levels* (recalling on the one hand, fractal geometry which finds recursive patterns in many natural phenomena in going from the large-event scale to the component-unit scale, as in studies of waves and flows, and exploring, on the other hand, minute fluctuations or differences in the events studied which might bring about unpredictable results); and *sensitivity to initial conditions,* which either are not identical or cannot be specified with infinite precision, in either case causing chaotic systems to become quickly and increasingly unpredictable. It should be noted, for the analysis that follows, that contingency (and therefore unpredictability) is implied by chaos, and that teleology (which, viewed in this manner, is a mechanistic, linear system) requires predestination. ***Candide*** argues consistently against teleological interpretations of human life and for a sense of the contingent, unpredictable nature of Nature.

The shimmering surface perfection and regularity, the limpid style that appears to so many critics to be the trademarks of Voltaire's style, the easy-to-grasp philosophical message that to many critics is not only the heart of a Voltairean *conte* but also its raison d'être, all make it easy to miss what Voltaire surely understood, that things are never as simple as they seem; that systems of thought never work according to their design because they are flawed and their flaws, once exposed, never cease expanding; that the turbulence that is often hidden by surface calm is nevertheless governed by rules or laws, that is by an order the exact nature of which we are not at present able to comprehend.[4]

Let us begin our examination of chaos in Voltaire by a brief examination of *nonlinearity* and *recursive symmetries between scale levels* in the story, which because they overlap in this tale can be conveniently explored together. The narrative seems to proceed in a linear fashion, picking up Candide's life at the time he is about 18 or 20 and following him for an undeterminable span of years, probably in the order of 5 to 10 years, through many adventures in Europe, in South America, and back in Europe. His adventures tend to begin in a rosy manner only to end in disaster—thus his life at Thunder-ten-Tronckh, his life as a soldier, the war he describes, his career with Jacques the Anabaptist, his rescue by Cunégonde, his trip to Argentina, the Eldorado episode, the 100-day trek to Surinam, the Parisian and Venetian interludes, and the Constantinople episode until the end of the last chapter.[5] This recurring pattern, like waves breaking on a shore, gives the story not only depth but also a gradual darkening of spirit: the early chapters seem far more suffused with the light of hope than the later ones, and the experience of Candide certainly gives the reader, if not the central character, a tragic sense of life. The story seems to move forward, but in fact keeps starting over again, only in a different spot, like a huge spiral pulling its characters down and around as well as forward. Far from being simple, it is revealed as complex, unpredictable, nonlinear.

Candide's American adventures, covering about one-third of the book, can serve as a model of the workings of non-linearity and recursive patters. They begin when, by chance, he finds a ship ready to sail from Cadix in need of an officer to train the troops who will fight the Jesuits in Paraguay. Captain Candide sets off for Argentina a hunted man, it is true, the killer of the Grand Inquisitor and of dom Issachar, moneylender to the throne of Portugal. But he cheerfully travels with Cunégonde, the Old Lady, and (we learn later) a part-Indian, part-Spanish valet, Cacambo. He is looking for a new life in a new world: "Tout ira bien," he says in chapter IX; "la mer de ce nouveau monde vaut déjà mieux que les mers de notre Europe; elle est plus calme, les vents plus constants. C'est certainement le nouveau monde qui est le meilleur des univers possibles."[6]

At this point, the Old Lady tells her story. Daughter of a Pope, Princess of Palestrina, about to begin her adult life by entering into a fairy-tale marriage, her ordered, calm, predictable world falls apart, the contingent nature of life erupts and reveals the chaos beneath the surface. Her fiancé is poisoned; she is captured by pirates, repeatedly raped, sold into servitude, partly cannibalized; she works her way into old age across Europe, her life progressively more miserable, until she becomes a maid to Cunégonde. An accessory to two murders, she is now sought along with her mistress and Candide. She has often contemplated killing herself, and finds that every single passenger aboard ship has also at least once in life thought of suicide.

The same downward spiral is evident when the stories of Candide's friends are examined: Pangloss, Cunégonde, Jacques, the young Baron, Martin, Cacambo, Paquette, Frère Giroflée—all their adventures follow the same pattern, extend the geographic bounds of the story to North Africa and Asia Minor and Eastern Europe, include religious, political, ethnic, and moral backgrounds of the greatest variety, and come together at the same place. They are like smaller eddies that become absorbed for a time in a large whirlpool while somehow keeping their identities and at times breaking off from the main vortex in one or more cases never to return.

In the case of Candide, this pattern, like a fractal, continues on even as we see shorter pieces of his life. He is in Buenos Aires for a few scant hours at most. The high hopes he had had on board prove to be groundless: for when don Fernando d'Ibarra, y Figueora, y Mascarenes, y Lampadouros, y Souza sets eye on Cunégonde and learns that she is not Candide's wife, the downward spiral takes hold of the young man again and is made more dangerous by the unexpected and unpredictable arrival of the Spanish authorities, who wish to seize him. He is forced to flee with Cacambo, and finds himself in a Jesuit compound in Paraguay where the Indians are virtually enslaved. Unpredictably, he finds that the baron had not after all been killed; but he does the job himself when in a heated argument the old friends draw swords, and then flees with Cacambo towards the north and west. The fugitives are captured and—in a scene that recalls the barbarity of the Turks against the Old Lady and her companions, another recursive incident in the story—are themselves almost cannibalized. When they finally reach Eldorado, seemingly by miracle, their lives seem to start anew, their fortunes mount, their dreams of peace and happiness are about to be fulfilled. But soon they long for the life they have left behind, and their misadventures begin again. Thus, all but two of their llamas die during their 100-day trek to Surinam; they see the horrors of slavery; the friends part; Candide finds people even more miserable than he; he is robbed by the Judge and the Courts as well as by an evil slave-owning Dutch sea captain.[7]

The apparently linear, forward-moving pattern of the story is interrupted by countless flashbacks to other times and other places, where different but uniformly tragic adventures enrich the readers' understanding of the complexities of life, and where ever-renewed patterns, like waves endlessly crashing onto the shore, display in the differences in detail the chaotic nature of human experience and where simplistic notions of the nature of Nature or of evil or of God are shown to be deficient.

Which is to say that *Candide* is a story that is nonlinear and characterized by recursions that can be seen at every narrative scale. The novel itself, the overall adventures of any of the numerous characters, the individual adventures they have, all display a pattern that recalls what fractal geometry shows in nature. Furthermore, the disproportionality in *Candide* between cause and effect (another marker of nonlinearity) is apparent from the very first chapter, when Candide is driven from the château for having kissed Cunégonde, and when his absurd deficiency in quarterings makes it impossible for him to pretend to her hand. The harshness of the punishment meted out to Pangloss and the Baron for their heterosexual and homosexual drives (Pangloss spends too much time, we remember, in retrieving a bouquet from an apparently willing woman's cleavage, and the Baron is arrested for skinny-dipping with a young Muslim), Admiral Byng's execution, and the huge fine imposed on Candide in Surinam for making too much noise knocking on the judge's door—further examples of the disproportionality of cause and effect—are among scores that appear in the book.

The recursive symmetries that can be found in *Candide* are of similar but not identical life stories. One of the reasons the stories vary in detail is, in chaoticist terms, the *sensitivity to initial conditions* that the narrator and the author present. Hayles notes that "unless the starting conditions can be specified with *infinite precision,* chaotic systems quickly become unpredictable" (p. 14). Now since the initial conditions of the characters are of necessity different and since it is not possible to specify the starting conditions with infinite precision, the life story of one character will be unpredictable even to a reader already familiar with the life of another character. For example, Candide and the young baron, apparently of the same age, brought up together in the same castle and educated by the same tutor, will have radically different life stories. The initial conditions set up by the narrator make it possible for them to lead similar lives but not to have identical futures.

Even if the baron had fallen in love with a clone of Cunégonde and kissed her, trembling, behind a screen, he would surely not have been driven out into a harsh winter without ceremony and without support: he is, after all, the heir of the Thunder-ten-tronckh family name and fortune, and the overweening pride that goes along with the title and the stereotypical characteristics of German nobility prevalent in the book. A second initial condition is eventually revealed, the differing sexual orientations of the two young men, which of course help determine the course of events in their lives. Yet who could predict that the baron would become a Jesuit? By chance a Jesuit priest finds him alive, is attracted to him, takes care of him, and arranges to have him enter the order; eventually he finds himself in Paraguay and meets Candide there.

Meanwhile, Candide's experiences have been quite different. Trained as a soldier but flogged for exercising his free will (as the narrator humorously puts it), saved

from a sure death by the chance passing of the King who pardons him, experiencing in the midst of a terrible battle the evil that men visit upon one another and the hollowness of the Catholic religion, he escapes only to find that the Protestant religion is no less hollow; he works for an Anabaptist, is one of only three persons saved in a shipwreck, finds himself condemned to a second flogging for having apparently agreed with Pangloss's deterministic philosophy (and need I remind the reader that he had met Pangloss in an unpredictable state and under unpredictable circumstances?), is saved once more from a certain death, this time by Cunégonde who by chance is the mistress of the very same Grand Inquisitor who condemned Pangloss to death and Candide to a flogging . . . ; eventually, he meets up with the baron in Paraguay, and their stories, converging unexpectedly for a few hours, take separate but once again unpredictable paths when Candide "kills" his friend and future brother-in-law.

In short, the similar but not identical initial conditions of their lives lead to startlingly different results. As Crutchfield and his colleagues explain it, "In principle, the future is completely determined by the past, but in practice small uncertainties are amplified, so that even though the behavior is predictable in the short term, it is unpredictable in the long term" (p. 46).

Initial conditions, recursive symmetries between scale levels, and nonlinearity are all part of the structure of this story, and all contribute to what might be sensed as an implicit moral lesson. To date, only Roy S. Wolper and critics who agree with him seem to have had an intuition of this internally-generated moral (see n. 5. *supra*). Evil in *Candide* is regularly associated with stupidity (or Dullness, in Wolper's Swiftian vocabulary) and violence, and often also with greed. Part of the humor of the description of life at the chateau of Thunder-ten-Tronckh comes from the incredibly stupid philosophy of Pangloss, which masks the truth about the Baron's domain: he is in fact an impoverished minor nobleman living in an unpleasant world. And Candide's life in the chateau ends with a violent act on the part of the Baron, whose intellectual prowess we can infer by the fact that Pangloss is his children's tutor. The mindless violence that Candide encounters upon his desertion is magnified by that which he sees during battle. The Protestant preacher who, despite his hour-long sermon on tolerance, berates Candide and refuses to give him alms because he does not believe that the Pope is the Antichrist, and his wife who dumps a chamber pot on the young man's head, add a note of greed to the stupidity and violence of their actions. This association of stupidity and violence and often of greed with evil continues throughout the story and is indeed inextricably intertwined with it right to the end. It is difficult not to see this association and its implied opposite: wisdom and kindness and generosity are attributes of good. This moral (which has nothing directly to do with Optimism or with an interpretation of "il faut cultiver notre jardin") is embedded in the very structure of the story, in the life history of every character, in every episode we read. It is revealed clearly by chaos theory.

But are we free to choose good or evil? Do we have, in other words, free will? The repeated patterns we noted earlier, the interactions of the characters and their experiences, the constantly changing tempo of the narrative, bring to the tale a sense of unpredictability, of anti-Providential design, of *contingency*. How different this is from Pangloss's summary, on the very last page of the novel, of Candide's life and adventures:

> Tous les événements sont enchaînés dans le meilleur des mondes possibles: car enfin si vous n'aviez pas été chassé d'un beau château à grands coups de pied dans le derrière pour l'amour de mademoiselle Cunégonde, si vous n'aviez pas été mis à l'Inquisition, si vous n'aviez pas couru l'Amérique à pied, si vous n'aviez pas donné un bon coup d'épée au baron, si vous n'aviez pas perdu tous vos moutons du bon pays d'Eldorado, vous ne mangeriez pas ici des cédrats confits et des pistaches.

Pangloss, ever true to his philosophical beliefs, adopts the perspective of God, and gives to the chain of events that link the characters and bring them to their little tenant farm near Constantinople a teleological slant. He simply cannot accept a universe that is not planned in every detail by an all-powerful deity. His entire thought is essentially Providential, non-contingent, non-chaotic: in the great scheme of things, earthquakes, wars, rape, murder, crimes of all sorts exist in order to support a greater good, the stability of the universe. In this context, Candide's response to Pangloss's interpretation of the events that have led the small group to their little farm can be seen as a denial of teleology and an acceptance of contingency: "Cela est bien dit," the words are fine, the logic impeccable if one accepts the premises, "mais" [sous entendu: "je n'en crois plus une syllabe"], if we are to escape boredom, vice, and poverty, "il faut cultiver notre jardin." Only in this way can we be sure to remove some of the contingencies in this world, to reduce the disproportionality between cause and effect, and more importantly, to take on responsibility for our lives in this non-Providential world, that is, to exercise our free will. Candide might not yet be able to accept a chaotic world view, but he can reject a Providential one that seems to leave little room for free will.[8]

Had Voltaire lived another two centuries, he would have found scientific evidence through chaos theory that it is possible to conceive of free will existing even in a deterministic world; this, as we know, is one of the central problems that Optimism posed for Voltaire, the apparent irreconcilability of free will and determinism, of contingency and Providence, or more broadly speaking,

of man in a God-created universe. Indeed, wedded as he was both to Newtonian mechanics and to the existence of God, while at the same time keenly aware of the existence of moral and physical evil in the world, Voltaire suffered throughout much of his career from the intellectual and moral disquietude that is so evident in such stories as *Zadig* and *Candide*. His knowledge of probability theory, described by Kavanagh in the first chapter of his book, would have brought him little comfort, for if anything it served to shore up the premises upon which Optimism was based.

On the other hand, what Crutchfield, Farmer, Packard, and Shaw conclude in their article on chaos would at least have given Voltaire some hope in resolving this central dilemma of his life:

> Even the process of intellectual progress relies on the injection of new ways of connecting old ideas. Innate creativity may have an underlying chaotic process that selectively amplifies small fluctuations and molds them into macroscopic coherent mental states that are experienced as thoughts. In some cases the thoughts may be decisions, or what are perceived to be the exercise of will. In this light, chaos provides a mechanism that allows for free will within a world governed by deterministic laws.
>
> (p. 57)

Optimism, as taught by Pangloss, is dead at the end of *Candide.* But even if the world seems deterministic, chaos theory lets us know both that we cannot predict events in the long term, and that the decisions we make are real. It lets us know, as a result, that free will and therefore individual responsibility may be alive and well in this best of all possible worlds.

Chaos theory, as we have suggested earlier, also leads us to an unexpected interpretation of the apparent utopia at the novel's end: the recursive patterns in the story—rosy beginnings in each adventure, rapid deteriorations, disastrous conclusions—should alert us to the fact that *Candide* ends but has no more a real conclusion than *Zadig.*[9] We can predict (to the extent that prediction is possible, at least) that this utopian community will soon entropy and deteriorate, and that Candide and his friends will encounter unimaginable disasters. We are back, so to speak, at the beginning, the pattern is about to recur. Chaos will reign.

Notes

1. Haydn T. Mason, *Candide: Optimism Demolished* (New York: Twayne, 1992), and Roger Pearson, *The Fables of Reason: A Study of Voltaire's* Contes philosophiques (Oxford: Clarendon Press, 1993) present fresh views based on traditional methods. Thomas M. Kavanagh, *Enlightenment and the Shadows of Chance: The Novel and the Culture of Gambling in Eighteenth-Century France*

(Baltimore and London: Johns Hopkins University Press, 1993) approaches the analysis of *Candide* from the point of view of probability theory, a field invented by Pascal in the previous century and developed throughout the eighteenth. Chapters 1 (The Triumph of Prability Theory) and 7 (The Ironies of Chance: Voltaire's *Candide* and *Zadig*) are most relevant to this study, but do not broach the question of chaos theory.

2. N. Katherine Hayles: *Chaos Bound: Orderly Disorder in Contemporary Literature and Science* (Ithaca and London: Cornell University Press, 1990), 115, 14, 82, 128. See also the work of critics like Patrick Brady, who gives essentially identical categories for chaotic systems, as in his articles "Chaos Theory, Control Theory, Literary Theory: Or, A Story of Three Butterflies," *Modern Language Studies,* 20 (1990): 65-79, and "Théorie du chaos et structure narrative," *Eighteenth-Century Fiction,* 4 (1991), 43-51, among others.

3. James P. Crutchfield, J. Doyne Farmer, Norman H. Packard, and Robert S. Shaw, "Chaos," *Scientific American,* 225 (December 1986): 46.

4. Theodore E. D. Braun makes some of these points in his chapter, "Interpreting *Candide*: The Anvil of Controversy," in *Approaches to Teaching Voltaire's Candide,* ed. Renée Waldinger (New York: The Modern Language Association of America, 1987), 75, which is based on Roy S. Wolper's hermeneutic study of Voltaire's tale, "*Candide*: Gull in the Garden?" *Eighteenth-Century Studies* 3 (1969): 265-77. Since the bibliography on *Candide* is immense, and the interpretations of the ending of *Candide* are not only diverse but also the starting point of most critical studies of the book, I will refer the reader to Arthur Scherr's recent article, "Candide's Garden Revisited: Gender Equality in a Commoner's Paradise," *Eighteenth-Century Life* 17 (1993): 40-59.

5. Indeed, in the light of this recurring pattern critics should have been on the alert, they should have been—and we should be—unwilling to accept the end of the story as the conclusion of the little group's odyssey but only the opening act of a new tragedy; but that is another problem with this book and the history of its critical reception.

6. Voltaire, *Candide,* in *Romans et contes,* ed. René Pomeau (Paris: Garnier-Flammarion, 1966), 169-259; the present quotation is found on p. 198.

7. In studies such as Manuel Moreno Alonso's "América española en el pensamiento de Voltaire," *Anuario de estudios americanos,* 38 (1981): 57-100, the critical point of departure is a polemical interpretation of Voltaire's thought as it is per- ceived to be presented in the work(s) under consideration; in this case, Voltaire is seen as presenting a negative view of Spain and Spanish customs. Arguments are often—one might be tempted to say usually—supported by biographical data. In this Moreno Alonso follows the practice of most Voltairean scholars, whether they wish to support Voltaire or attack him. The villains in *Candide,* however, even those in South America, are not necessarily Spanish or Portuguese: they are also Dutch, German, French, English, Turkish, Arab, Russian, Oreillon, etc.

8. Rob Roy McGregor, Jr. presents a different point of view, finding in Pangloss's summary an irony missed by both Pangloss and Candide, but intended by the narrator (and possibly by the author). Unfortunately, McGregor himself falls into one of Voltaire's traps, brought about by the apparent simplicity of the story masking its underlying complexity. McGregor finds that a "great and preferable good *has* resulted from a series of physical and moral evils; namely, Candide has escaped the world of illusions . . ." (p. 364). Could he not have learned his lesson without countless deaths and other tribulations? This disproportion between cause and effect is one of the markers of nonlinearity, as we have seen.

9. Few contemporary critics have come as close to incorporating an intuition of this continuing pattern into an overall interpretation as has Roy S. Wolper in the work cited and others. Indeed, in his note, "Professor Wolper's Interpretation of *Candide*," *Eighteenth-Century Studies* 5 (1971): 145-51, Lester Crocker reiterates without fresh examination generations of interpretations that see in Candide's garden at the end of the book a conclusion and a message; even Arthur Scherr's sensitive study fails to take into account the recursive character of the narration and the open-endedness of the tale.

Susan Klute (essay date 2002)

SOURCE: Klute, Susan. "The Admirable Cunégonde." *Eighteenth-Century Women: Studies in Their Lives, Work, and Culture* 2 (2002): 95-107.

[*In this essay, Klute focuses on the character of Cunégonde and her relationship to the theme of optimism in* Candide, *asserting that of all the characters in the novella, she is the most down-to-earth and the most capable of overcoming the obstacles life presents.*]

Most critics agree that Voltaire's goal in his philosophical tale **Candide** was to ridicule the optimist philosophy of Gottfried Wilhelm von Leibniz. These same critics have also tended to concentrate their efforts on Candide and Pangloss with little regard for the principle female character, Cunégonde. Apart from the fact that she is the object of Candide's affection, what can one say about the personality, mind, and spirit of one of the most famous fictional women of the eighteenth century? To date, little or no critical analysis exists of Cunégonde's character nor of her function in the novel. In the late 1970s, Nellie Severin covered the hagiographic meaning of the name "Cunégonde" in articles for *French Review* and *Romance Notes* but did not extend her study to a general consideration of the character, which is the task I have set myself here. I intend to show that, far from being a member of the cast of philosophical adherents of optimism, Cunégonde is a positive force in the work and, in the end, fares far better than either Candide or Pangloss, despite her misfortunes and a less-than-flattering first impression.

From the outset, by virtue of the narrator's description, Cunégonde is defined by her body, or at least the "physical charms" that Candide sees in her. The narrator states that she is "haute en couleur, fraîche, grasse, appétissante" (147) [high in color, fresh, plump, appetizing]. If one believes the narrator, and assumes he shares Candide's point of view, she is an attractive young woman. If, however, one reads the passage with a more discerning eye and does *not* assume that the narrator is of the same opinion as Candide, Cunégonde is a rather stout young woman who resembles a roast more than a girl at the peak of her youthful beauty. For Candide, a young man who is familiar neither with the world, nor with women other than Cunégonde and the comtesse her mother (who herself weighs 350 pounds), a prettier or more "tasty" woman is unimaginable. The link between Cunégonde and food, suggested here in a rather negative sense, will be taken up later in the story in a different, positive light that will underscore the fundamental incompatibility of Candide and Cunégonde.

Even at this point, early in the story, Cunégonde's inherent sensuality stands in stark contrast to the total innocence and naïveté of Candide. When she sees Pangloss giving "une leçon de physique expérimentale" (148) [an experimental physics lesson] to one of the maids, instead of being shocked, as every well-born and well-bred girl should be, she is curious and watches the entire private moment. Immediately after, "toute remplie du désir d'être savante" (149) [full of desire to be knowledgeable], her thoughts turn to Candide and she wonders if she could be "la raison suffisante" (149) [sufficient reason] for him as he could for her. This short scene is, in fact, full of allusions to the sensual aspect of Cunégonde's nature.

Most importantly, there is the play on the word "physique," which according to the *Robert,* includes both the "science qui étudie les propriétés générales de la matière et établit des lois qui rendent compte des phénomènes matériels" [the science which studies the general properties of matter and established laws that explain material phenomena] and that which "concerne le corps humain" [concerns the human body]. Pangloss's *leçon* thus has two meanings: as the tutor of the household, he could have taught "la physique" as a science, but it is clear that the second definition applies to what Cunégonde witnessed and is no doubt the "physique" which interests her vis-à-vis Candide. Later on, Cunégonde will be the one to initiate physical contact with Candide by first "se trouv[ant]" [finding herself] behind a screen (as though by accident), by letting her handkerchief fall to the ground for Candide to retrieve, and finally by putting into practice what she saw demonstrated by Pangloss (149).

While on one hand, this exploration of her sexuality results in Candide's dismissal from the château, it also shows remarkable initiative on Cunégonde's part. Rather than wait for Candide to make a move, which he might never have done, she sets the scene for their encounter and makes it possible, even though she knows that her parents would disapprove (hence her falling into a faint when they are discovered). In a sense, female initiative and sexuality are punished, first comically by Cunégonde's fainting and then being slapped when she comes to, and then more seriously by the events which follow: the arrival of the soldiers, her rape, and finally with her being passed or sold from man to man. With Candide's dismissal from the château, Cunégonde is largely forgotten by the narrator, and the reader is thus left with an unflattering portrait of her as a large, loose young woman capable of leading young men astray.

As has been shown, Cunégonde is defined by her physical nature; the narrator even goes so far as to say that she had "beaucoup de disposition pour les sciences" (148) [great inclination for the sciences], the "sciences" in question being of the sort she saw Pangloss "teach" the maid. In contrast to this, Candide is defined by his studies and by the optimist philosophy that he learned from Pangloss. The following dichotomy pervades the story: Cunégonde belongs to the physical world while Candide belongs to a "philosophical" world of ideas and ideologies; she perceives the world in concrete terms, he in abstract terms; she acts, he reasons.

Candide remains, quite improbably and in spite of everything that befalls him, Pangloss' attentive pupil and a faithful adherent of optimist philosophy. Thus, he is often referred to as a "philosophe" [philosopher], forever trying to reconcile the cruelty and the violence he sees in the world with this philosophy. Cunégonde, on the other hand, faces the same cruelty and violence in a completely different manner.

Whatever happens to Cunégonde, she recounts the episode in concrete terms and, above all, remains *practical*. One can see this trait most clearly when she tells Candide what happened to her after he left the château. To express the pain and fear she must have felt, she simply says that a Bulgarian soldier "se mit à me violer" (163) [began to rape me]. She details her vain efforts to free herself, but the result is not a narrative full of embellishments designed to provoke the sympathy of Candide. He misses the point of her stoicism and, showing little concern for her well being, asks to see the scar on her thigh. Her sensual side comes to the fore once again in this scene for she replies, "Vols le varies" (164) [You will see it], as though the sight of the scar (and no doubt other parts of her body) were no more than a matter of time. It becomes clear that her sensuality and her practical view of the world are inextricably intertwined. If she were not so "in tune" with her body, she would be more like Candide, who so distances himself from the physical world that he is no longer able to function effectively and remains a bewildered victim of the events and the people that surround him.

The connection between Cunégonde's sensuality and practicality also governs her living situation with Don Issachar and l'In quisiteur. To begin with, she says, "quand il plut au ciel d'envoyer les Bulgares dans notre beau château" (163) [when it pleased the heavens to send the Bulgars to our beautiful château], thus accepting the arrival of the soldiers as a matter of fate and of fact. The fact that they *came* is enough, and she concerned herself more with *how* to survive the war than *why* these things happened. After the war, reduced to the position of servant and maid to the captain who captured her, she was then sold to Don Issachar. She states without embellishment that Don Issachar "s'attacha beaucoup à [sa] personne, mais il ne pouvait en triompher" (178) [was greatly attached to her body, but could not triumph over it].

She apparently doesn't mind the idea that he wants her solely for her body, but she is not "easy" (even though the Old Woman says later that he had enjoyed "ses bonnes graces" [her good favor]). The most important result of the war and her travels, and the one that Candide misses entirely, is the fact that she began to question the ideas that Pangloss had taught her. She saw that the château of Thunder-ten-tronckh was perhaps not the most beautiful of all châteaux and later says openly, "Pangloss m'a donc bien cruellement trompée quand il me disait que tout va le mieux du monde" (165) [Pangloss tricked me cruelly when he said that everything was the best in the world].

Freed from the optimism that she was taught, she manages to live with Don Issachar and l'Inquisiteur in relative peace. She has some worth in their eyes, even if only because they desire her physically, but she does

have a house of her own and a servant. In many respects, she has regained some of the stability and material well being that she enjoyed at her parents' home in Germany. That is, until Candide arrives and manages to destroy it all by playing the jealous lover, murdering both Don Issachar and l'Inquisiteur and forcing them all to flee Portugal.

Cunégonde's reaction to the murder is revealing: "qu'allons-nous devenir? Un homme tué chez moi! Si la justice vient, nous sommes perdus" (167) [what is going to become of us? A man killed in my house! If the law comes, we are lost.] She sees the inherent danger in their situation whereas Candide, instead of reacting, only thinks of Pangloss and the advice he could have given them, if only he weren't dead: "Si Pangloss n'avait pas été pendu, il nous donnerait un bon conseil dans cette extrémité, car c'était un grand philosophe" (167) [If Pangloss had not been hanged, he would have given us some good advice in this situation because he was a great philosopher.] The only excuse he can give for putting them all in such a precarious position is that "quand on est amoureux, jaloux et fouetté par l'Inquisition, on ne se connaît plus" (167) [When you are in love, jealous, and have been whipped by the Inquisition, you no longer know yourself.]

What's more, Candide shows himself to be incapable of taking action without consulting another person. In this case, he consults the Old Woman. It is curious, though, that it never occurs to him to ask advice of Cunégonde, who has obviously learned to survive with some success. By not asking her opinion, Candide reveals his own narrow thinking concerning women: he does not entertain the possibility that she could have grown wiser in their time apart because *he* has not and thus it does not occur to him that she could offer good advice. Rather than lament the loss of Pangloss when their own lives are at stake, Cunégonde concerns herself with the situation at hand and would like to know how Candide is going to handle it. He, unfortunately, is unable to put aside his *philosophy* long enough to save them from certain death and must rely on the Old Woman's counsel to see that acquiring some horses and leaving Portugal posthaste is a good idea. The subsequent voyage to the New World and the events that befall the party also posit Cunégonde as a positive figure in the novel by reason of her practicality, and by her ability to change her behavior and to adapt to her surroundings.

When first reunited with Candide, she was convinced that no one could be "plus malheureuse" [more unlucky] than she. Once the Old Woman tells the story of her life, Cunégonde realizes that, while her story is sad and she has had to bear much unhappiness, she is relatively lucky compared to the Old Woman. At this moment, Cunégonde opens her eyes to the people who surround her and becomes less egocentric than her upbringing had taught her to be. Listening to the Old Woman's story and asking each of the people on the boat to tell their stories shows a genuine interest in others that Candide does not seem to possess, except insofar as their stories either prove or disprove his optimist philosophy.

In the New World, Cunégonde is again presented with a practical dilemma: accept the offer of the governor and all the wealth and stability that come with him, as well as knowing herself to be desired by a powerful man in spite of her past, or stay with her young, impractical, and now outlawed lover. In a remarkable display of womanly solidarity, Cunégonde's old servant puts her situation into perspective and advises her to stay with the governor, portraying her attachment to Candide as so much romantic nonsense: "est-ce à vols de vols piquer d'une fidélité à toute épreuve" (178) [Can you really flatter yourself with fidelity against all odds?] The Old Woman shows a true concern for Cunégonde's well being and knows from experience that a liaison with the governor is her best chance for a "normal" life. Cunégonde sees the validity of this argument and accepts the proposal of the governor, sending Candide off as best she can and helping him avoid the long arm of Portuguese justice. This decision speaks volumes, not only about the position of women in the eighteenth century, but also about Cunégonde's practicality and her ability to see *reason*.

While it seems extremely improbable that *all* the misfortune that befalls Cunégonde could actually happen to one person in one lifetime, in many ways her life serves as an unembellished version of the life of many women in France before, during, and after the French Revolution. As Cissie Fairchild makes clear in her article "Women and Family," "seventeenth- and early eighteenth-century noblewomen found little emotional fulfillment in marriage" while "Noblewomen of the late eighteenth century were clearly fascinated by the idea of marrying for love" (90-99). One can see this evolution in Cunégonde: she loves (or is at least attracted to) Candide and reveals her feelings in a way suitable for a romantic heroine. Her father's anger no doubt stems from what he sees as a "ruining" of his daughter's chance to make a better (more lucrative) marriage. For "In the traditional patriarchal family, wives and children were clearly subordinate to their husbands and fathers, who exercised both legal and actual power over their property and their persons" (Fairchild 97). Her father, then, had every right to expel Candide and to punish his daughter, but he could not dictate her feelings for the young man and she gives up material comfort with l'Inquisiteur and with the governor to follow Candide.

In a more negative sense, Cunégonde could also represent the feelings of some French noblewomen concerning their own marriages. If a young woman is made to marry an older man because her father wills it and is then expected to bear the children of her husband and in every sense be subordinate to him, it seems that the only difference between this state of affairs and Cunégonde's life is a matter of vocabulary. While in real life, a father might have used the terms "suitable match" or "advantageous marriage," in Cunégonde's case, Voltaire actually uses the words "rape" and "slave"; the meaning is much the same. The events of Cunégonde's life, while no doubt embellished for the sake of the story, taken as a whole might well have struck a cord with some female readers. In light of this resonance and of Voltaire's conclusion of the satire, it seems unfair to label Cunégonde a "one dimensional character [who] sets out on the road of bodily pleasure at the age of seventeen and follows it vigorously to the story's final line" (Russo 289).

Even though she was born "baronne," she had absolutely no resources: no money of her own, no family, no network to support her in time of need. Lacking all this, she had to find a way to support herself, which, for a woman of her birth in the eighteenth century, meant marrying a man wealthy enough to support her. In the New World, her title meant little and she had no skills by which to earn a living. Her support had to come from a man, and her servant made it clear that her romantic notions about love would not bring stability or any sort of material comfort. Given her situation, it is not surprising that Cunégonde chose to stay with the governor rather than follow Candide into an uncertain future. It is unfortunate, too, that she eventually went against her own judgment and allowed herself to be persuaded to leave the governor to be with him.

Here again, the conflict between the reality of a woman's situation and the idea of love is made apparent. Twice, Cunégonde had to choose between material comfort and love, much as other women must have had to put aside their feelings for one person once their marriages were arranged. It seems that in this story, as well as in real life, love and marriage are, more often that not, incompatible. While marriage (including Cunégonde's relationship with the governor) meant material well-being, love engendered loss, privation, crime, and outlawry as witnessed by the murder of l'Inquisiteur, the flight to the New World, Cunégonde's enslavement, etc. In a curious twist, once Cunégonde and Candide are married, it is revealed that he is no longer in love with he—once again, love and marriage are mutually exclusive.

To return to the narrative itself, when Candide finally catches up with her in Constantinople, it becomes clear that, however he might protest his love for her, he is still a man of his time, concerned more with the beauty of his lover and her feelings for him than with her well being. He says to Cacambo, "Est-elle toujours un prodige de beauté? M'aime-t-elle toujours? Comment se porte-t-elle?" (231) [Is she still a marvel of beauty? Does she still love me? How is she?]. It is not insignificant that the question about her health and well being came last, for although Candide sees himself as a model lover, he is, in fact, terribly selfish when it comes to looking out for Cunégonde.

In order to be reunited with Candide, Cunégonde is bought from the governor by Cacambo and then robbed at sea by pirates, leaving her once again without resources and forcing her to become a slave. When Candide sees her and buys her freedom, he does so out of a sense of duty: not because he feels himself responsible for her situation, but because it befits the image that he has of himself as a faithful lover. The idea of a romantic reunion is further dampened by the fact that "Le tendre amant Candide, en voyant sa belle Cunégonde rembrunie, les yeux éraillés, la gorge sèche, les joues ridées, les bras rouges et écaillés, recula trois pas, saisi d'horreur, et avança ensuite par bon procédé" (237-38) [The tender lover Candide, upon seeing his beautiful Cunégonde sunburnt, her eyes dried, her chest dry, her cheeks wrinkled, her arms red and scaly, recoiled three steps, seized by horror, and then advanced by dint of will]. There is no mention of love or longing in this description, and one cannot help but feel some sympathy for Cunégonde, who left security to follow her lover only to find herself bought and sold, forced into slavery, and then perceived as horrific by the very lover for whom she gave up so much.

As an ironic twist, it is noteworthy that Candide's sense of honor, which first got them into trouble with the murders in Portugal, is now her only hope of survival as a free woman for, having lost her beauty, she now does not even possess the one thing that had pulled her from misery twice before. In Constantinople, she is now entirely dependent on Candide's generosity and can expect help from no other quarter; no other man will have her.

What is even more unfortunate is that Candide, seeing her thus reduced to slavery and a pathetic caricature of her former beauty, no longer desires her and finds the idea of marriage to her distasteful. The narrator states that, "Candide, dans le fond de son coeur, n'avait aucune envie d'épouser Cunégonde. Mais l'impértinence extrême du baron le déterminait à conclure le mariage, et Cunégonde le pressait si vivement qu'il ne pouvait s'en dédire" (238) [Candide, in the bottom of his heart, had no desire to marry Cunégonde. But the extreme impertinence of the baron pushed him to go through with the marriage and Cunégonde hurried him so insistently that he could not say no.] So much for the romantic ideals that Candide espoused in the beginning of the novel and which, it appears, Cunégonde came to accept. Candide, the "tender lover" who once thought only of his Cunégonde, now is prompted to marry her out of spite and revenge. The baron's refusal to give his permission, Cunégonde's insistence, and the collective advice of Pangloss, Martin and Cacambo, all manage to convince Candide to do something which obviously does not interest him. From this weakness of character, it becomes evident that Candide has not fundamentally changed since the beginning of the novel: he is still impressionable and unable to make a decision without consulting those around him.

The marriage, in any event, is not exactly the happy union that one would imagine: they marry "de la main gauche" (239) [by the left hand] which, according to editor René Pomeau's note, is a far less binding sort of marriage than the traditional one, and Cunégonde gradually becomes more and more ugly and bitter. In spite of this physical degradation, Cunégonde emerges, at the end of the novel, as a positive image of survival. Following the advice that "Il faut cultiver notre jardin" (243) [We must tend our garden], she becomes an "excellente pâtissière" (243) [an excellent baker].

The fact that she becomes a "pâtissière" is quite symbolic, as well. She obviously has some talent for it, or she would not be "excellente" and the act of cooking is a link to her principle traits of physicality and practicality. By becoming a baker, she is producing something useful and necessary that will nourish others. But she is more than a baker—she is a baker of pastries and so the products of her labor are not just the necessary, but the rich foods that people eat when they want to indulge. Initially referred to as "grasse" [plump] and "appétissante" [appetizing], one could no doubt apply the same adjectives to her baked goods. By cultivating her garden, and exploiting her natural talent, Cunégonde nourishes herself by earning a living and nourishes others by the goods she sells. Candide cannot claim anything so noble.

In light of this embodiment of survival and practicality that finds self-worth in things other than physical beauty, Candide's reasons for not wanting to marry her and then *for* marrying her are insulting. He, apparently, is unable to see these qualities, blinded as he is by the physical changes that life worked upon her. While "cultiver notre jardin" becomes a positive notion for Cunégonde, for Candide it seems a bitter resignation. Cunégonde, abused by men, disillusioned by the world, and a *survivor,* is truly an odd partner for Candide, who, in comparison, seems petty and shallow rather than philosophical.

While it is clear that the narrator finds Candide's and Pangloss's blind adherence to the optimist philosophy of Leibniz laughable, the narrator does not take the same stance with Cunégonde. She is portrayed, in the beginning, as a somewhat loose young woman responsible for leading Candide astray, but that image does not last. Through her misfortunes, Cunégonde becomes more of a realist than Candide could ever be; she realizes that Pangloss was wrong: that misfortune is misfortune and to survive in the world, one cannot hold to such a ridiculous philosophy and hope to find comfort. She was a sensual young woman whose very sensuality and awareness of her body, though punished in her youth, allowed her to escape from poverty. Her fatal mistake, it seems, was in believing that it would be better to run away with Candide than to stay with the governor in the New World. When she put faith in herself and acted on her own, she was more successful than when she trusted Candide to be able to save them both.

Given the differences in their personalities and their different ways of dealing with the world, one must ask the questions "What attracts her to Candide? Are they truly in love with each other?"

On one hand, her attachment to Candide could be seen as an emotional compensation: she had lost her family in the war and perhaps she was looking for a link to happier time. On the other hand, she must have known that she would no longer be admitted to polite society after having been the slave and/or mistress of several different men; Candide would then have been a way to recover some of her former stature by accepting the traditional role of a wife. A third possibility is that she felt genuine gratitude toward Candide for having freed her from slavery and thus her attachment could stem from a sense of obligation. And, lastly, Candide is perhaps the only person in the story, save Pangloss, who can remember a time when she was young and pretty, when her worst crime was sharing a kiss with a young man. He would then be a constant reminder of a happier time, before the war and before her misadventures.

While it may be intriguing to analyze her in this way, it would be anachronistic to enter too deeply into the psychoanalysis of Cunégonde; the novel does not really allow for it. After all, the philosophy of Leibniz is in question and not the individual psychology of the characters. That said, one can still see that Cunégonde is a strange partner for Candide.

If one follows the pattern of good fortune that suddenly changes to misfortune that impregnates the novel, it becomes increasingly difficult to believe that the true ending of the story is the final image of the (happy) couple cultivating their garden. Their fortunes have been reversed several times before—why would it be different for their life together? Because of the apparent conflict between Cunégonde and Candide, one must consider Voltaire's reason for creating such a woman to "play" opposite the protagonist.

As Nellie Severin makes clear in the articles mentioned earlier, the name "Cunégonde" is in fact the name of a Saint Cunégonde, who was not only "a model of virgin-

ity, but also had founded several cloisters" ("Note on the Name" 215). There exists, then, a good deal of irony in the choice of this saint's name for Voltaire's Cunégonde, who first explores her own sexuality with Candide and then suffers numerous rapes. The name "Cunégonde" also reinforces Voltaire's mockery of the German nobility because in the convent established by Saint Cunégonde "the applicants had to prove at least 'seize quartiers de noblesse' before being accepted" (Severin, "Hagiographic" 884). Even though there exist hagiographic references to several Saint Candides, the contrast in this case between the saints and the fictional character is not so clear; Voltaire was in all likelihood mocking the improbability of the events recounted in the tradition of saints' lives ("Hagiographic" 843).

The association with Saint Cunégonde and her monastery for ladies of a certain birth allowed Voltaire to poke fun at what he saw as the ridiculous German obsession with "quartiers de noblesse." But, given the odd nature of this couple based on their widely disparate world views, it seems as though Voltaire must have had something else in mind when he created Cunégonde. The most likely raison d'être for this choice of partner for Candide, and the one which supports the general goal of the novel, is that Cunégonde gave Voltaire yet another means to ridicule Leibniz's philosophy.

Compared to the two representatives of optimism, Cunégonde (and to a lesser extent the Old Woman) shows a greater ability to reason and to surmount obstacles in a firm, sensible manner. Pangloss, great philosopher that he is, consistently finds himself a victim of his own bad judgment. Candide, rather than judging poorly, does not judge at all; he almost never questions the truth of optimism even though every event that occurs contradicts what he was taught. He also allows himself to be carried away by his emotions. Cunégonde, on the other hand, concerns herself with the here-and-now, the world "ici-bas" [down here] which, as works such as "Le Mondain" and "Poème sur le désastre de Lisbonne" reveal, was of the greatest importance to Voltaire and which makes her, in spite of the loss of her beauty, an admirable figure and one that Candide would have done well to imitate.

Works Cited

Braun, Theodore E. D. "Voltaire, *Zadig, Candide,* and Chaos." *Studies on Voltaire & the Eighteenth Century* 358 (1998): 1-20.

Fairchild, Cissie. "Women and Family." In *French Women and the Age of Enlightenment.* Ed. Samia Spencer. Bloomington: Indiana UP, 1984. 97-110.

Russo, Gloria. "Voltaire and Women." In *French Women and the Age of Enlightenment.* Ed. Samia Spencer. Bloomington: Indiana UP, 1984. 285-95.

Severin, Nellie H. "Hagiographic Parody in *Candide*." *French Review: Journal of the American Association of Teachers of French* 50 (1977): 842-49.

———. "A Note on the Name of Cunégonde." *Romance Notes* 19 (1979): 212-16.

Voltaire [François-Marie Arouet]. *Micromégas, Zadig, Candide.* Ed. René Pomeau. Paris: Garnier Flammarion, 1994.

Helena Feder (essay date 2002)

SOURCE: Feder, Helena. "The Critical Relevance of the Critique of Rationalism: Postmodernism, Ecofeminism, and Voltaire's *Candide*." *Women's Studies* 31 (2002): 199-219.

[*In this essay, Feder identifies a link between Voltaire's criticism of rationalism in* Candide *and contemporary ecofeminists' critique of rationalism, building a case for her assertion that Voltaire's embracing of materialism in the novella is an example of protoecological thought.*]

> I write in order to act.
>
> —Voltaire, Letter to Vernes, 15 April 1767

> *Voltaire makes the very act of living lucidly a form of active revolt.*
>
> —Patrick Henry

Scholars of the eighteenth century are challenging aspects of the prevailing characterization of the Enlightenment and, conversely, certain postmodern critics are rethinking their understanding of eighteenth-century thought and literature. Similarly, ecocritics must reexamine the idea of the Enlightenment as the monolithic embrace of "reason" (systematic rationalism) and its attack on nature, women, non-European peoples, and the poor. As Voltaire's most influential critique of rationalism, **Candide** exemplifies the relevance of eighteenth-century thought to contemporary discourses of engagement. It is my hope that an ecocritical approach to **Candide** will demonstrate a clear link between Voltaire's critique of rationalism and the ecofeminist critique of rationalism and, in turn, that an examination of the ecofeminist vision informed by this critique will vibrantly develop the protoecology of **Candide**'s materialism.

ENLIGHTENMENT RECONSIDERED

Daniel Gordon's "On the Supposed Obsolescence of the French Enlightenment" and the collection in which it appears, *Postmodernism and the Enlightenment*, seeks to initiate a broad movement among scholars of various backgrounds to bring eighteenth-century texts and ideas into productive conversation with contemporary theory. Such a conversation first requires that certain misconceptions about the Enlightenment be refuted. For instance, Gordon cites Jean-François Lyotard's definition of postmodernism as "incredulity toward metanarratives," the mistaken belief that skepticism of cultural narratives, as a critical practice, is unique to postmodern thought (201-2). **Candide,** as Gordon points out, is *not* only not a metanarrative, but is also its opposite, what Jean Starobinski calls "'the simulacrum of a narrative'—a parody 'whose moral is to beware of all morals'" (qtd. in Gordon 202). Voltaire's *conte* flatly rejects the metanarrative most commonly attributed to the Enlightenment, that of the progress and unification of human knowledge and the resulting mastery of nature (Gordon 202). With reference to Max Horkheimer and Theodor Adorno's well-known theory of the dialectic of the Enlightenment, Gordon suggests that we instead "see this dialectic as a process internal to the Enlightenment—a process in which a certain degree of historical optimism immediately produced doubts about the completeness of the society desired" (204).

In many respects Karlis Racevskis's *Postmodernism and the Search for Enlightenment,* published prior to Gordon's essay, anticipates the direction Gordon advocates. Racevskis's interest in the Enlightenment comes from a Foucauldian concern with power:

> while the Enlightenment handed down the belief that reason legitimates power—indeed, that reason is power—we are now able to appreciate the extent to which it is power that gives reason its prerogatives, that power, in short, produces the reason—or reasons—it needs.
>
> (3)

Power producing reason producing power: this is the machine of our age, the machine which many blame the Enlightenment for putting into motion. And yet, as we have seen, this critique of what we call the Enlightenment was, in many respects, already embodied by Voltaire's philosophical skepticism.

So it is not surprising that Racevskis chooses **Candide** to create a dialogue between Foucauldian logic and Enlightenment ideals. He presents a strong case for **Candide**'s continued relevance, drawing a number of important parallels between the mature Candide and the postmodern critic. Both eschew abstractions in favor of practical reason; both realize that solutions to social problems must be grassroots and communal, not dictated by intellectuals or "experts"; and both share the knowledge that work isn't protected by transcendental reason, destiny, or "a nature that will ensure humanity's survival in the face of the greed, cruelty, and stupidity of humans" (85-6). Racevskis concludes that:

> we are rediscovering something that Voltaire believed in profoundly: that the recourse to abstract systems and metaphysical explanations is the way to delusion and

catastrophe; and that constant vigilance, critical attention, and skepticism are still the best weapons for confronting the reality of the human condition.

(87)

It is in this context—that of power and oppression—that Voltaire's attack on systematic rationalism clearly links him to ecological thought, most specifically to the ecofeminist critique of reason. Australian philosopher Val Plumwood remains ecofeminism's most perceptive critic of rationalism; in *Feminism and the Mastery of Nature,* she links rationalism to the human mastery of nonhuman nature. The kind of reason that embodies the "master identity," Plumwood asserts, is that which produces "a dualised conception of self and other, reason and emotion, universal and particular," thus underpinning "the instrumental treatment of nature and its exclusion from ethical significance in western (now global) culture" (6). And yet,

> critiquing the dominant forms of reason which embody the master identity and oppose themselves to the sphere of nature does not imply abandoning all forms of reason, science and individuality. Rather, it involves their redefinition or reconstruction in less oppositional and hierarchial ways.
>
> (Plumwood 4)

Just as Plumwood's critique of "reason" also affirms its importance, she acknowledges that an

> analysis of the philosophical past [ancient Greek] throws into the foreground the many conflicts and tensions in [. . .] accounts of the origins of the domination of nature and of women, especially those which locate the entire problem in the Enlightenment and the rise of atomistic science.
>
> (5)

Like Voltaire, then, Plumwood distinguishes between reason and systematic rationalism, between the cognitive faculty and its institutionalization, even if the terminology ("reason") remains the same.

CANDIDE

Throughout his lifetime, François-Marie Arouet de Voltaire struggled with many of the questions that ecological thinkers continue to ask in the twenty-first century: What are the limits of reason and knowledge? What is the "good" life and how do we achieve it in an uncertain world? Voltaire's *contes philosophique* demonstrate the absurdity of attempting to answer such questions through systematic rationalism and other forms of abstraction. With *Candide,* first published in 1759, Voltaire attacks Leibnizian optimism, and seventeenth-century systematic rationalism generally, thus dramatizing the primary concern of the Enlightenment. As Ira O. Wade proposes in *The Intellectual Origins of the French Enlightenment,*

> The central problem of the Enlightenment would be to grasp the way in which rationalism, having set out to become aware of its possibilities, has encountered hidden forces within itself which have made it conscious of its impossibilities. Simply stated, it is the story [of] how the human mind came to know and to turn into realities its inner powers, but how, in doing so it discovered not only their ultimate unreality, but their uselessness in achieving human satisfactions.
>
> (16)

Candide repeatedly demonstrates that we as human beings are neither the masters of the earth nor of our fate—and yet Voltaire ultimately, I argue, casts his assertion of the limits of reason, knowledge, and human power in positive terms. Candide's education concludes with the first exercise of his newly gained wisdom: he famously insists, *"mais il faut cultiver notre jardin"* (we must cultivate our garden). His injunction responds not only to Pangloss's blind optimism and Martin's visionless pessimism, and to systematic theorizing altogether, but also to the natural and social crises witnessed on his voyage.

Of course, a long history of inquiry into the meaning of the text's conclusion has produced strikingly varied interpretations. While many view the injunction to "cultivate our garden" as a positive call for productive community action in the face of uncertainty or evil (cf., Jerry L. Curtis, D. Langdon, William F. Bottiglia, and Patrick Henry), others, such as John Pappas and Giovanni Gullace, argue that Candide's final statement reflects resignation or even pessimism (Waldinger 19). And still other critics, notably Ira Wade and Geoffrey Murray, claim the ending to be ambivalent or ambiguous (Henry 178; Murray 188).

Invariably, however, both eighteenth-century scholars and postmodern critics read Candide's injunction to "cultivate our garden" as mere metaphor (Racevskis, for instance, construes the famous line as a metaphoric call to cultivate practical reason in terms of critical praxis [86-7]). Yet in the context of a tale that insists on the inescapability of material reality, it makes no sense at all to read Candide's dictum as a metaphor or transcendental ideal. Whatever else it may signify, the garden, I contend, must also signify a real, material garden—and, as we shall later see, Voltaire's actual experience with gardens reinforces this idea.

THE MATERIALITY OF THE GARDEN

Many eighteenth-century scholars claim Voltaire invented the genre of the *conte philosophique,* the pantomime-like tale that uses flat characters (the mere shadows of characters) to symbolize and enact various philosophical concepts. Voltaire's *contes* (which also include *Zadig* and *Micromégas*) satirize philosophical ideas and social institutions. Most famously, of course,

Candide attacks the Leibnizian concept of optimism, which can be summed up by Alexander Pope's dictum from *Essay on Man,* "Whatever is, is right," or as Pangloss has it, that we live in the "best of all possible worlds." It also attacks the Catholic clergy (especially the Jesuit sect), provincial nobility, and the pandemic institutions of slavery, prostitution, and war.

The most fascinating—and paradoxical—aspect of *Candide* is its successful refutation of metaphysical thought through an insistence on the inescapability of material reality, using the equivalent of cardboard cut-outs for characters and settings. As the pedagogical fulcrum of the tale, Candide is the only character who may be said to develop; his actions anchor every scene and chapter, and he is the primary audience for every character's narration of physical suffering and catastrophe. These narratives, combined with the suffering and catastrophe Candide himself witnesses on his journey—storm, shipwreck, earthquake, war, and disease—layer to achieve the tale's philosophical theme: the inescapability of materiality and, therefore, the benefit of cultivating one's garden.

Many characters relate harrowing tales of woe, but the most significant of all is told by an old woman. After Cunégonde recounts her misfortunes to Candide, her servant boasts, "Alas! You have never seen misfortunes like mine" (*Candide* 60). In the course of chapters 11 and 12, this old woman recounts her kidnapping, bondage, repeated rape, mutilation, and bout with the plague. Her narrative stands out as particularly awful, which seems significant because she is the only character in the tale, aside from Candide, who achieves a modicum of wisdom. The narrator repeatedly describes her as prudent and, tellingly, it is she that Candide consults for advice in Pangloss's absence (*Candide* 57-8, 67). In other words, this old woman who speaks "from age and experience" serves as a foil to Pangloss's and Martin's abstractions (*Candide* 67).

On the surface it would seem troubling, from any feminist perspective, that Voltaire chooses male characters (and only male characters) to represent philosophical concepts and an old woman to represent experience (as a lifetime of suffering). It certainly wouldn't be the first time a woman has been made to bear the weight of the world's, particularly men's, materiality.[1] However, nearly everyone in the tale, male and female, suffers physically—both Cunégonde and her brother are stabbed and raped, and Pangloss is whipped and hanged. In the final chapter, the old woman recounts their collective suffering in one stroke: "I'd like to know which is worse—to be raped a hundred times by Negro pirates, to have a buttock cut off, to run the gauntlet among the Bulgars, to be shipped and hanged in an auto-de-fé, to be dissected, to row on the galleys, in short, to experience every misfortune we have known—or to stay here without anything to do?" (*Candide* 117).

One need not claim Voltaire as a feminist[2] to acknowledge the significance of the old woman's position; as the voice of experience, she is shown to be wiser than both Pangloss (who represents optimism) and Martin (who declares himself a Manichean, but may be said to represent pessimism generally). Because the tale ultimately recommends experience over theory, both as the vehicle for and the conclusion of Candide's enlightenment, Voltaire's symbolic use of the old woman seems less like misogyny and more like shrewd observation. In the eighteenth century and still today, most of the world's women suffer some form of gender-related oppression, social and economic. In many countries women and female children are still regularly bought and sold, and rape remains a preferred strategy for non-combatant subjugation in conflicts across the globe.[3] Nowhere in *Candide* does it indicate that Voltaire condones this oppression; rather, Candide is highly sympathetic to the plight of the prostitute Paquette and to the sufferings of Cunégonde and the old woman (all of whom become valued members of Candide's little commune). Yet ultimately, the crucial gesture lies in the text's privileging of the experience of material life as more philosophically valid and meaningful than any abstract idea conjured through metaphysics (which, as we know, was almost entirely a male pursuit in the eighteenth century). And, of course, it was not Pangloss or Martin but the old woman "who suggested to Candide that they settle into it [a little farm in the area] until the destiny of the group improved" (*Candide* 115).

We must recall, for a moment, the old woman's question (what is worse—horrific physical suffering or philosophical arguments, debates and boredom?) to understand the answers put forward by the text. Naturally, the question leads Martin and Pangloss to philosophize, and after the arrival of the miserable Paquette and Giroflée (further confirmation of Pangloss's philosophical error), Pangloss, Candide, and Martin seek the advice of "a very famous dervish who was reputed to be the best philosopher in Turkey" (*Candide* 117). Not only does the dervish have no answer to the question of human life and its relation to the world, he is utterly indifferent to the question, and hostile to the curious. "'Why meddle in that?' said the dervish. 'Is it any business of yours?'" (*Candide* 118). He also has nothing to say on the nature of evil or how to live in a world of suffering, save "'Keep silent'" (*Candide* 118). On the way back to their farm, the three encounter a kindly old farmer resting in his orange grove. They had just heard rumors of the murders of several Constantinople court officials, and, hoping for more information, they ask the old Turk the name of the strangled mufti. The old Turk replies:

> I have no idea. [. . .] I assume that in general those who meddle in public affairs perish, sometimes miser-

ably, and that they deserve it. But I never think about what people are doing in Constantinople. I am content to sell them the fruits of the garden that I cultivate.

(*Candide* 188)

Having been presented with these two inadequate approaches to life (the dervish's attempt to transcend life and the Turk's insular materialism, both utterly antisocial), Candide achieves his own answer to the old woman's question from the fruits of his own experience (we will come back to this in a moment). Neither physical suffering nor the frustrated pursuit of philosophical ideals is more painful than the other; in fact, *Candide* demonstrates that they exacerbate each other. Candide's former estrangement from the world he wandered proceeded not from his human faculty of reason but from Pangloss's metaphysics, as it came into conflict with the calamitous reality Candide experienced. For example, in chapter 23, Candide asks the reason for the Admiral's execution.

"It's because," came the answer, "he didn't kill enough people. He was engaged in a battle with a French Admiral and was later judged to have kept too great a distance from the enemy."

"But," said Candide, "the French Admiral was as far from the English Admiral as the latter was from the former."

"That's incontestable," was the response. "But in this country they think it's good to kill an Admiral from time to time, to encourage the others."

Candide was so stunned and shocked by what he saw and heard that he would not even set foot on land.

(*Candide* 99)

At the end of the tale, Candide's full cognizance of the futility of Pangloss's systematic rationalism (the insanity of attempting to control or even construe the complexities of the world through reason) leads him to create his communal garden, which he does with his rational faculties clearly intact. His answer to the old woman is clear: "we must cultivate our garden" (*Candide* 119).

Or, at least, it is certainly clear why Candide chooses the practical materiality of the garden over empty abstractions, after all the unhappiness they have caused him and the rest of the world (in the form of patriotism and religion). However, why doesn't Candide set up a garden exactly like the Turk's? Upon returning from the Turk's home, Candide proclaims, "That kindly old man seems to have made a better life than the six kings we had the honor of eating supper with" (*Candide* 119). The answer, I believe, is in the comparison. The Turk's garden is not unlike the courts of noble households we see in *Candide*—insular, selfish, uncaring, and uncompromising; it is, ultimately, antisocial.[4] Yet, Candide clearly sees the benefit of practical, material activity—

keeping away the "three great evils: boredom, vice, and indigence" (*Candide* 119). If we consider the practice of metaphysics to be a vice, or at least a cause of vice, then Candide's "little society" becomes a social antidote to transcendental ideas and the very real problems they cause. Everyone participates in the collective freedom from the three evils:

Each began to exercise his talents. The little bit of earth became productive. Cunégonde was undeniably very ugly, but she baked excellent pastries. Paquette embroidered. The old woman took care of the linen. No one failed to contribute, not even Brother Giroflée. He was a good carpenter and even became a sociable fellow.

(*Candide* 119)

Unlike a king's court or the Turk's garden, Candide's "little society" functions like a commune—each contributes according to ability for the welfare of the group. *Candide*'s portrait of the good life is one in which individuals function together organically, without an idealistic plan, for their mutual benefit.

LES DÉLICES, FERNEY, AND TOURNAY

The question still remains, why did Voltaire choose gardening or small-scale agriculture to represent the good life? Aside from the fact that every community depends on agriculture, Voltaire may have been suggesting that a return to the earth, to a life lived within its cycles, to the practice of material awareness, remains the best course for social happiness. Certainly, he believed this idea enough to practice it in his own life. Although for many years Voltaire's life was, like Candide's, one of movement—from one part of Europe to another, as courtier and exile—Voltaire eventually made his way to Switzerland, and then to nearby France, where he purchased several country properties over a number of years. The first was *Les Délices* (House of Delights), just outside Geneva, where he resided during the fall of 1758, when *Candide* was probably composed.[5]

An examination of excerpts from Voltaire's letters from *Les Délices* and *Ferney,* Voltaire's second and favorite farm (he eventually sold *Les Délices* but he kept *Ferney,* where he lived until just shortly before he died in 1778), reveals his material commitment to gardening and to rural community life. Douglas Chambers' *The Planters of the English Landscape Garden* provides an excellent context for Voltaire's interest in gardening:

[T]hroughout the first half of the eighteenth century, much garden design and writing began with a reaction against the artificialities of both Dutch and French garden design. In doing so its celebration was of a landscape that aspired toward the condition of an ideal farm as Pliny [and Horace describe . . . ,] and Virgil in lines 458-540 of *Georgics* II. Another much-cited tag from the *Georgics*, "laudato ingentia rura, exiguum *colito*" (praise a large farm but cultivate a small one), became the hallmark of the *ferme ornée*. That most Augustan invention represented the unity of beauty with profit and use with pleasure that was within the means of a man of modest income: the smallholding of a man of philosophical mind.

(6)

Voltaire's gardens could easily be described as *ferme ornée* (which loosely translates as florid or charming farm), as they were productive instead of merely ornamental. From *Les Délices* on 28 March 1775 (a few months after taking possession of the property), Voltaire writes to his close friend Jean Robert Tronchin,

> My thanks for the lavender. I have promised you to have some planted round the edges of your kitchen garden. I have already planted 250 trees for you [. . .] I am now sowing Egyptian onions. The Israelites did not love them more than I. Whereupon I abuse your kindness. I beg you to send me all that you can in the way of flowers and vegetables [seeds]. The garden is absolutely lacking them.

(*Select* 147)

Voltaire's reference to "your kitchen" is a little joke; Tronchin had to register as the legal owner of the property because in Calvinist Geneva, a Catholic (even a lapsed one) could not own property. That aside, this letter, and dozens more like it, demonstrate Voltaire's hands-on work in his gardens.

While the roots of Voltaire's gardening begins at *Les Délices,* the scope and depth of his enthusiastic commitment reach fruition at Ferney, in nearby France. From the *Chateau de Ferney* on 1 August 1772, Voltaire writes to Sir William Chambers (Chambers had recently sent him a copy of his monograph, "Dissertation on Oriental Gardening"):

> It is not enough to love gardens, and to have them: one also needs eyes with which to look at them and legs with which to walk in them. [. . .] I have something of everything in my gardens: flower beds, little pieces of water, formal walks, very irregular woods, valleys, meadows, vineyards, kitchen gardens with walls covered by fruit trees, the groomed and the wild, the whole in little [. . .].

(*Select* 169)

In *The Life of Voltaire,* S. G. Tallentyre records that although the grounds at *Ferney* were rather elaborate, containing acres for wheat and hay, poultry yards, sheepfolds, an orchard, beehives, vegetable gardens, and more, Voltaire not only oversaw every detail of this garden, he also cultivated a good bit of it with his own hands, which were no longer so young (86). Tallentyre describes *Ferney* thus: "In the garden were sunny walls for peaches; vines, lawns, flowers. It was laid out with a charming imprévu and irregularity most unfashionable

in that formal day. Voltaire [. . .] made his gardens as English as he could" (86). From Voltaire's letters and this description, we see that Voltaire had indeed abandoned the Dutch and French fashion for formal, purely decorative gardens in favor of a somewhat wilder, productive *ferme ornée.*[6] Voltaire once said: "I have only done one sensible thing in my life—to cultivate the ground. He who clears a field renders a better service to humankind than all the scribblers in Europe" (Tallentyre 87).

Perhaps even more importantly, *Ferney* was not an estate, such as *Les Délices,* but a community. In his autobiography, written in the third person, Voltaire observes

> [T]he village of Ferney, which at the time of his purchase, was only a wretched hamlet tenanted by forty-nine miserable peasants, devoured by poverty, scrofula and tax-gatherers, very soon became a delightful place, inhabited by twelve hundred people, comfortably situated, and successfully employed for themselves and the nation.

(qtd. in Besterman 662)

Indeed, one of the chief reasons why Voltaire purchased the land was to alleviate the tremendous suffering of the people of the region; in a letter to a French correspondent he writes, "One's heart is torn when one witnesses so much misery. I am buying the estate of Ferney only to do a little good" (qtd. in Besterman 407). Numerous biographers, including Besterman and Tallentyre catalogue Voltaire's activism on behalf of this little society (including financial support; the removal of the local *curé,* who ruthlessly beat his parishioners; the drastic reduction of taxes; and the construction of roads and communal buildings).

In contrast, Geoffrey Murray's *Voltaire's Candide: the Protean Gardener, 1775-1762,* repeatedly suggests that Voltaire used his "garden" as a detached vantage point from which to observe the horrors of the Seven Years War (153-221).[7] In so many words, Murray claims that Voltaire was an escapist who justified his intellectual pursuits with humanitarian rhetoric from the security of an ivory tower-like garden. But might we, instead, see Voltaire as engaged in quite the opposite activity? We might consider that *Les Délices* and, even more so, *Ferney* were part of an experiment to engage fully with the materiality of human life through the meaningful practice of the daily activities of existence. For Voltaire as for Candide, the good life meant the moral, purposeful life or, as Henry David Thoreau later called it, living deliberately. And like Thoreau's little garden at Walden Pond, Candide's "little bit of earth" and Voltaire's garden "became productive" (**Candide** 119).

VOLTAIRE AND THE ECOFEMINIST CRITIQUE OF RATIONALISM

As Patrick Henry writes in *Voltaire and Camus: the Limits of Reason and the Awareness of Absurdity,*

"When not linked with experience, for example, we have seen that Voltaire not only considers reason an ineffectual instrument [. . .] but also a potentially dangerous one. [. . . Voltaire] also insisted upon the inability of reason to systematize reality" (50). In many ways, Voltaire's critique of rationalism greatly resembles Plumwood's; as we have already seen, Plumwood rejects disembodied forms of reason and the resulting abstraction of ethics. However, in light of **Candide** and Voltaire's actual experience of nonhuman nature, an even more fundamental level of connection becomes apparent; both critiques are not only materialist but *explicitly* earth-centered. Compare, for instance, their critiques of Cartesian thought, the pinnacle of rationalism and keystone of western dichotomy. Voltaire strongly rejects two of Descartes' most basic concepts, that of animals as *animaux-machines* and humans as *res cogitans*. Henry writes, "Voltaire not only considered this option to be empirically untenable, but also perceived that it created a cleavage in the zoological chain of being and was essentially an offshoot of the old anthropocentric vision of the world (35).[8] While Voltaire recognizes and critiques anthropocentric solípsism, Plumwood laments its mirror image, the debasement of nature:

> Cartesian thought has stripped nature of the intentional and mindlike qualities which made an ethical response possible. Once nature is reconceived as capable of agency and intentionality, and human identity is reconceived in less polarized and disembodied ways, the great gulf which Cartesian thought established between the conscious, mindful human sphere and the mindless, clockwork natural one disappears.
>
> (5)

While these connections do not position Voltaire as an ecological thinker of the contemporary variety, we might easily consider his materialism to be protoecological. In any case, the ecofeminist critique of rationalism and dualism, consciously or not, operates within a tradition of skepticism that owes much to Voltaire's thought.

Voltaire's staunch rejection of metaphysical epistemological channels and his preference for "pragmatic moral eclecticism" over lifeless abstractions demonstrates, as Henry argues, that "Voltaire wanted to establish a way of life, not a body of thought. His main concerns were practical, not speculative" (89-91). **Candide** does not construct an abstract philosophy; rather, it satirizes the rationalist philosophies of the previous century and suggests that the communal practice of a materialist, practical realism is the best road to social harmony. The fact that Voltaire chose gardening, both in his *conte* and in his life, as the embodiment and practice of this materialist realism seems much more than mere coincidence, especially when one examines where the critique of rationalism has led ecofeminist philosophy.

In her book, *Feminism and Ecology,* ecofeminist philosopher Mary Mellor argues that historical materiality, the embodied and ecological embeddedness of human existence, may serve as the basis for an ecofeminist immanent realism, an epistemology for a politics of nature. For Mellor, as for ecofeminist Mary O'Brien, the real work isn't "the struggle for liberation, or some abstract humanism, but [. . .] the regeneration of and reintegration of historical and natural worlds" (qtd. in Mellor 91).[9] This is, fundamentally, an argument against western, dualistic epistemologies that cast knowledge as transcendent, over and against the reality of nature; it is an argument for an immanent realism "revealed through patterns of subjugation and the perspectives they generate within the human community, and through an awareness of the interrelatedness of humanity and nature in ecological processes" (Mellor 111).

For Mellor (and, as she acknowledges, for many other ecological thinkers) "the immanence of human existence is always framed in radical uncertainty about material conditions in their widest and deepest sense" (148). This radical skepticism forms the epistemological and ontological core of Mellor's materialist ecofeminism. A material subjective ontology is not, in this framework, a metanarrative, but rather a "grounding awareness" (Mellor 185). And such an awareness isn't deterministic but processual. Mellor writes, "Neither humanity nor 'nature' are determinant; what is inescapable are the consequences of the dynamics between them." (13).

Of course, Voltaire's concept of the use of reason can differ sharply from ecofeminist theory, as it does with the concept of rights. Both Mellor and Plumwood find the discourse of rights inescapably problematic for theoretical and historical reasons that are quite clear to most feminists. In "Nature, Self, and Gender: Feminism, Environmental Philosophy, and the Critique of Rationalism," Plumwood critiques ethical universalization and its discourse of rights that still dominate the field of environmental ethics:

> Universalization [. . .] is the moral complement to the account of the self as "disembodied and disembedded," as the autonomous self of liberal theory, the rational egoist of market theory [. . .] A more promising approach for an ethics of nature [. . .] would be to remove rights from the center of the moral stage and pay more attention to some other, less dualistic, moral concepts such as respect, sympathy, care, concern, compassion, gratitude, friendship, and responsibility. [. . .] They are moral "feelings" but they involve reason, behavior, and emotion in ways that do not seem separable.
>
> (6, 8-9)

Plumwood argues that an "ethic of care and responsibility" extends far more easily to nonhuman nature than the discourse of rights, and provides a better basis for noninstrumental relations with nature (9). Nevertheless, Voltaire's and Plumwood's critiques of rationalism are, ultimately, more similar than dissimilar. Plumwood concludes,

> What is involved here is a reconceptualization of the human side of the human/nature dualism, to free it from the legacy of rationalism. Also in need of reconceptualization is the underside of this dualism, the concept of nature, which is construed in polarized terms as bereft of qualities appropriated to the human side, as passive and lacking in agency and teleology, as pure materiality, pure body, or pure mechanism. So what is called for here is the development of *alternatives to mechanistic ways of viewing the world,* which are also part of the legacy of rationalism.
>
>   (18, emphasis mine)

What Plumwood really advocates here is more complex than a revision of ideas, of our concept of nature or, as I would suggest, our concept of materiality. We also require practical means by which to physically and daily enact a more expansive vision of the world. As Voltaire was fond of saying, "I write in order to act."

TECHNOCRACY VS. THE BIOREGIONAL LAND
ETHIC

As ecologists and a variety of activists have noted for decades, technological "advancements" and global "development" usually mean the maldevelopment, and even the destruction, of entire bioregions, countless species of flora and fauna and human cultures.[10] In this context, "globalization" is synonymous with technocracy, the contemporary incarnation of the mechanistic worldview. As part of his call for a new kind of reason, Racevskis comments on the systematic rationalism of "the contemporary technological arrangement":

> This perspective [the tendency, inherited from Kant, to believe that social progress must accompany the growth of knowledge, and that knowledge is logically independent of the social conditions of its acquisition and communication] also shows that the possibility of placing knowledge outside the conditions that produced it [. . .] constituted a mechanism that is fundamental to the contemporary technocratic arrangement. Thus, it is evident that attempts to rationalize society in order to make it transparent to the scientific, technical mind are still driven by a desire to fulfill the telos of an Enlightenment-oriented ideology. The technical expert has given rise, for example, to the "heroic expert," the incarnation of the dominant instrumental ethic, which is also a dominant masculine ethic, as a number of feminists have argued.
>
>   (83)

Although the drive to master nature, to force a feminized nature to divulge her "secrets," characterizes Cartesian logic and Baconian science rather than an Enlightenment ethic, this drive nevertheless exists as part of an intricately woven technological power structure. As Maria Mies argues in *Ecofeminism,* since the time of Bacon and Descartes, scientists "have consistently concealed the impure relationship between knowledge and violence or force (in the form of military power, for example) by defining science as the sphere of a pure search for truth. Thus they lifted it out of the sphere of politics. [. . .] [T]he separation of politics (power) and science [. . .] is based on a lie" (46). The real political power of this lie even problematizes aspects of the science of ecology, with its host of technical experts and its seemingly endless co-optability.[11] Donna Haraway expresses the frustration of this position in her call for a "successor science," which would take "account of radical historical contingency for all knowledge claims . . . [while making] a no-nonsense commitment to faithful accounts of the 'real world'" (qtd. in Mellor 123).

The bioregional land ethic, or the gardening model, stands in opposition to the universalizing, instrumental rationalism of technocracy through its commitment to the lived stewardship of particular bioregions or parcels of land.[12] Voltaire often made the seemingly contradictory claims that he was a citizen of all nations and a citizen of no nation, a citizen of the world and a resident of the *pays de Gex* and Geneva (Murray 72). These claims have been variously interpreted, but I suggest that Voltaire's cultivation of *Les Délices* was a rejection of national systems in favor of a kind of regionalism, a commitment to a particular place, just as Candide's garden functions as a kind of land stewardship, as a form of community action and care. In a sense, the bioregional land ethic comes close to the successor science Haraway imagines; it is an embedded, embodied, contextual basis for knowledge claims and a commitment to the real world. Specifically, the garden model means the utilization of local knowledge and experience to care for our regions and ourselves simultaneously; in this way, communal gardening also embodies the ethic of care and responsibility that Plumwood advocates. Unlike the rational models of ecological science, bioregional stewardship (or "gardening") is democratic, requiring the lived interconnectedness of human and nonhuman nature.

"'I know,' said Candide, 'that we must cultivate our garden.' 'Your are right,' said Pangloss, 'for when man was placed in the Garden of Eden, he was placed there *ut operaretur eum,* in order to work on it, which proves that humankind was not made for rest'" (*Candide* 119). As *Candide* indicates, the garden model is not without its dangers: when this way of life leaves no room for wilderness, then "gardening" becomes another form of systematic management that privileges the human over the nonhuman. In other words, when certain species require separate niches—places free from human habitation—the bioregional land ethic or garden model must not become yet another justification for human omnipresence at the expense of nonhuman nature, like Pangloss's invocation of the Judeo-Christian tradition that commands human dominion over nonhuman nature.[13] However, by embracing philosophy as a lived, materially critical praxis, Candide's dictum to "cultivate our garden" avoids the cold transcendentalism of the dervish, the logical extension of Pangloss's systematic rationalism, and the unthinking individualism of the Turk—the logical extension of Martin's creed, "let us work without theorizing" (**Candide** 119).

A Politics of Nature

A recent article on "extreme gardening" in *The New York Times Magazine* relates the experience of two professors who created a garden tended by smart-machines that could be manipulated "virtually" through the Internet (Nussbaum 24). The professors explain that the idea was intended as a short-term "dystopian vision"; however,

> over the last three years, 30,000 people have planted seeds via modem. "It gets pretty ugly in there," sighs Goldberg. "On the Website, there's a quote from Voltaire, which basically says, tend your own garden. A lot of people seem to miss that."
>
> (24)

This story exemplifies the ecocritical belief that between living deliberately in nature and the mastery of nature is all the difference in the world. Candide's injunction to cultivate our garden only makes sense in the context of a lived skepticism toward systematic rationalism in all its guises, particularly in the form of technocracy.

For this reason, the Enlightenment critique of rationalism has never been more relevant. The spirit of **Candide** remains alive in the work of philosophers and activists who connect forms of rationalism to the domination of human and nonhuman nature. But this is not enough. The critique of rationalism, as Mellor argues, must become part of a politics of nature, a politics that requires not only resistance but positive action. It is not enough to garden like the Turk, with no thought or care for the rest of the world, and it is not sufficient to philosophize like the dervish, in abstraction from the meaning of material life. We can neither ignore nor transcend pain and suffering; we must cultivate our garden deliberately and with care for all.

Notes

1. From Eve's fall in the Garden of Eden to the eighteenth-century salon remark that women are but large children (often attributed to Rousseau), western culture has associated women with materiality as opposed to intellect (another version of emotion vs. reason), particularly fleshiness (both the sins and suffering of the flesh).

2. Although I do not make claims for Voltaire as a feminist in any contemporary sense of the word, others have. In "Women's Equality in *Candide*," Arthur Scherr claims that one of *Candide*'s primary themes is the equality and interdependence of the sexes. Also Gloria M. Russo's "Voltaire and Women," from *French Women and the Age of Enlightenment*, makes a similar and compelling claim for *La Pucelle* and the *contes philosophique* based on textual and biographical evidence.

3. There are a variety of statistics on these subjects. MADRE (an international women's rights organization), Feminist Majority, International Association for Feminist Economics, United for a Fair Economy, and the Recent UN Report on Women's Progress provide a wealth of information.

4. Voltaire's chief argument against Liebnizian optimism is that it is fundamentally quietist. In a letter to Elie Bertrand on 18 February 1756, he writes, "Optimism is despairing. It is a cruel philosophy under a consoling name. [. . .] We will go from misfortune to misfortune to become better off. And if *all is well,* how do Leibnizians allow for something better?" (*The Selected* 183).

5. There are varying opinions on this. In *Voltaire's* Candide: *the Protean Garden, 1775-1762,* Geoffrey Murray advances this claim, while Theodore Besterman believes that he may have been staying at Schwetzingen when *Candide* was composed (24-7; 408).

6. The intentional and unusual informality (or unstructured quality) of Voltaire's gardens, both in *Candide* and at *Les Délices* and *Ferney,* seems particularly important in light of Pope's *Essay on Man,* which, of course, *Candide* was written against every bit as much as Leibniz's treatises. Chambers summarizes Pope's metaphoric use of landscape in terms which make the comparison clear: "In the words of Pope's *Essays on Man,* the universe is a landscape garden: a mighty maze, but not without a plan" (5).

7. Murray also connects *Candide* with Voltaire's life; his book catalogues Voltaire's progressive interest in agriculture and animals with the purchase of *Les Délices* in 1755. Despite his conclusions, I agree with Renee Waldinger's assessment of the book: "Murray demonstrates convincingly that the language of this [Voltaire's] correspondence is the very language of *Candide* and that the final garden is not an abstraction but a real spot on earth where productive life is possible" (17).

8. Henry culls this summary from a great many sources, including *Micromégas, Letters philosophiques,* and several volumes of correspondence.

9. I use the phrase "real work" with reference to Gary Snyder's concept of "what needs to be done" (cf. *The Real Work: Interviews and Talks 1964-1979, The Practice of the Wild,* and *A Place in Space*).

10. There are a number of accounts of this process. See Carolyn Merchant's *The Death of Nature for a historical account,* and Maria Mies and Vandana Shiva's *Ecofeminism* for a theoretical overview.

11. This has been the subject of much debate in ecological circles. Many deep ecologists, social ecologists, and ecofeminists feel that the entire program of "land management," including conservation reserves, is complicit in imperialist land-grabs, corporate "greenwashing" campaigns, the commodification of ecological activism, and the perpetuation of dualistic thought which defines nature as Other, as "out there." Other ecological thinkers maintain that land management has never been more necessary.

12. While some ecological thinkers may claim superficial differences between the bioregional movement, Aldo Leopold's land ethic, and gardening as an ecological model, I believe that they advocate the same thing: embedded and embodied stewardship of particular places as ethical practice and ecopolitical activism. And so I have collapsed bioregionalism and the land ethic into bioregional land ethic, which I use interchangeably with the concept of the "gardening model."

13. Frederick Turner's garden model is a particularly telling example of this danger; see "Cultivating the American Garden" in *Rebirth of Value: Meditations on Beauty, Ecology, Religion, and Education.*

Works Cited

Besterman, Theodore, *Voltaire.* Banbury: Cheney and Sons, 1969.

Chambers, Douglas. *The Planters of the English Landscape Garden: Botany, Trees and the* Georgics. New Haven, Yale UP, 1993.

Gordon, Daniel. "On the Supposed Obsolescence of the French Enlightenment." *Postmodernism and the Enlightenment.* Ed. Daniel Gordon. New York: Routledge, 2001, 201-221.

Henry, Patrick. *Voltaire and Camus: The Limits of Reason and the Awareness of Absurdity.* Banbury, Cheney and Sons, 1975.

Mellor, Mary. *Feminism and Ecology.* New York: New York UP, 1997.

Merchant, Carolyn. *The Death of Nature: Women, Ecology, and the Scientific Revolution.* San Francisco: Harper & Row, 1980.

Mies, Maria, and Vandana Shiva. *Ecofeminism.* London: Zed Books, 1993.

Murray, Geoffrey. *Voltaire's* Candide: *The Protean Gardiner, 1775-1762.* Geneva: Institut et Musée Voltaire, 1970.

Nussbaum, Emily. "The Green Reaper." *The New York Times Magazine,* 1 July 2001, 24.

Plumwood, Val. *Feminism and the Mastery of Nature.* London: Routledge, 1993.

———. "Nature, Self, Gender: Feminism, Environmental Philosophy, and the Critique of Rationalism." *Hypatia,* 6(1) (1991), 3-27.

Racevskis, Karlis. *Postmodernism and the Search for Enlightenment.* Charlottesville and London: U of Virginia P, 1993.

Russo, Gloria M. "Voltaire and Women." *French Women and the Age of Enlightenment.* Bloomington: Indiana UP, 1984. 285-295.

Scherr, Arthur. "Women's Equality in Candide." *Readings in Candide.* San Diego: Greenhaven, 2001. 129-140.

Snyder, Gary. *A Place in Space: Ethics, Aesthetics, and Watersheds.* Washington. D. C.: Counterpoint, 1995.

———. *The Practice of the Wild.* San Francisco: North Point, 1990.

———. *The Real Work: Interviews and Talks 1964-1979.* New York: New Directions, 1980.

Tallentyre, S. G. *The Life of Voltaire.* Vol. 2. London: Smith, Elder, & Co., 1903. 2 vols.

Turner, Frederick. *Rebirth of Value: Meditations on Beauty, Ecology, Religion, and Education.* Albany: State University of New York P, 1991.

Wade, Ira O. *The Intellectual Origins of the French Enlightenment.* Princeton: Princeton UP, 1971.

Waldinger, Renee, ed. Part one: Materials. *Approaches to Teaching Voltaire's* Candide. New York: MLA, 1987.

Voltaire, François-Marie. *Candide.* Trans., Ed. Daniel Gordon, Boston: Bedford/St. Martin, 1999.

———. *Select Letters of Voltaire.* Trans., Ed. Theodore Besterman. London: Thomas Nelson and Sons, 1963.

———. *The Selected Letters of Voltaire.* Trans., Ed. Richard A. Brooks, New York: New York UP, 1973.

Diane Johnson (essay date 2005)

SOURCE: Johnson, Diane. Introduction to *Voltaire: Candide, or Optimism,* translated by Peter Constantine, pp. xi-xvii. New York: Modern Library, 2005.

[In the following essay, Johnson presents an overview of Voltaire's life and of the themes of Candide, *stressing*

the ambivalence inherent in the author's notion of optimism as well as the need for each reader to judge for him/herself whether it is actually borne out by the novella.]

Candide is, for the English reader, Voltaire's most familiar work, a production of his maturity—written when he was sixty-five—and seems to present in most concise and apposite form the considered opinions of his life. In this odd work, a credulous young hero, Candide, is driven, like Adam from Eden, out of the happy precincts of his childhood in Westphalia, which in Voltaire's day was in reality one of the poorest and most embattled parts of Germany. *Candide* is set in this distant German province at least in part to protect the author from any supposition that it was intended to comment on the political situation or moral condition of France. Voltaire had had a number of run-ins with kings and cardinals because of his volatile political writings, and was pointedly careful to avoid direct references to recognizable autocrats. Indeed, like many of his colleagues and friends, he had been imprisoned a number of times in the Bastille, imprisonments, to be sure, made comfortable enough by the rules of the day—but prison all the same. Though wishing to avoid its consequences, he throve on political controversy and courted it constantly. *Candide* was only one of his Swiftean attacks on political abuses, but it is somehow the one that has remained current.

Without reference to the real events of Voltaire's time, and to the ideas he contributed with his satire to the evolving social and political discourse, *Candide* can seem a picaresque tale of limited fascination. One soon understands the design: a naïve young man, trustfully adhering to the lessons of his fatuous teacher, Professor Pangloss, that all is created for the best in this best of all possible worlds, is launched into a series of adventures that reasonably would lead most people to despair. His intended wife, Cunégonde, is kidnapped, raped, and eviscerated. He himself is kidnapped, beaten, imprisoned, loses his home, and loses his loved one.

Though the characters miraculously survive most of the horrors they suffer—for basically Voltaire is an optimist—the contrast between what they suffer and their optimism serves only to point up the folly of belief in general and optimism in particular. Everyone Candide encounters exemplifies the greed and brutality that seem to characterize mankind, though he himself, Cunégonde, Pangloss, and their other companions are finally the very models of people who survive by patiently focusing on their work. This was Voltaire's own recipe for survival, and there may be more than a bit of himself as he thought of himself in the naïve, good, and good-looking Candide.

The hundreds of books that have been written about Voltaire, the most admired and famous writer of the eighteenth century and perhaps for us the most famous of all French writers, together give the vivid impression of an amazing human being—merry, difficult, brilliant, indefatigable, productive, witty, and wise. It may be helpful to an American reader to place him in his epoch, complete with powdered wig and ruffled neck-cloth, by remembering that Voltaire and Benjamin Franklin knew each other and shared the paradoxically hopeful cynicism that seems to characterize the late eighteenth century.

They were introduced in Paris by admirers who believed that these two great thinkers should meet. Whether either had ever heard of the other is unclear, but at the urging of a crowd at a meeting of the scientific society, they politely embraced and perhaps exchanged a few words—in which language is not recorded, but it was likely English, for Voltaire knew English well, read it, and had even written in English; he had spent a few years in exile in England during one of his many periods of being in disfavor with two of the three kings Louis who reigned during his long lifetime. This disfavor was earned by his lifelong, vigilant criticism of a variety of the political and humanitarian issues pungently expressed in *Candide.*

Above all was Voltaire's belief in freedom. At the time of his meeting with Franklin in 1778, the American Revolution was in full force, and Voltaire was predicting a French one that he would not live to see. He died the same year, at the age of eighty-four, in the reign of Louis XVI, praising the revolution that must inevitably come.

> I won't have the pleasure of beholding it. The French catch on to everything late, but they understand at last. Young people are lucky—they will see great things. I shall not cease to preach tolerance upon the housetops until persecution is no more. The progress of right is slow. The roots of prejudice are deep. I shall never see the fruits of my efforts, but their seeds must one day germinate.

Later thinkers would agree that his ideas on individuality, industry, religion, and human rights may have indeed fostered the French Revolution, which followed the American one by thirteen years, and must also have influenced the earlier one, given that Jefferson, Franklin, and indeed Washington, all valued his works. (Though Jefferson never met Voltaire, he kept a copy of Houdon's bust of him at Monticello.)

"Voltaire" was a nom de plume he invented after the success of his first literary works; he was born François-Marie Arouet in November (or February) 1694, in the reign of Louis XIV. The particle he gave himself (in "Arouet de Voltaire") suggests a certain conflict about his own place in society. Though his father was a member of the bourgeoisie, a prosperous *notaire* (a kind of legal functionary), the boy had the common (according to Freud) fantasy of being of noble birth, and thought of himself as the illegitimate son of an aristocratic neighbor. Whatever his parentage, he was exceptional, and excelled at his studies, though the ideas of the Jesuits who taught him only incited his mockery and anticlericalism. Like Jefferson and Franklin, he counted himself a Deist and was a lifelong resolute critic of the Catholic church and of religion in general. Religious skepticism among freethinking French intellectuals (again like the American founders) had generally replaced unquestioning, conventional piety, and neither Deism nor atheism was actively persecuted. Yet *Candide,* when it was published in 1759, would be condemned in both Catholic France and Protestant Geneva.

The temperament that initially led young Arouet to study law accounts for his interest in politics and even his role as a French spy, when adviser to his friend Frederick the Great of Prussia, and for his bitter portrayal of rulers in *Candide.* Though he became very rich, like other artists and intellectuals of the period, he had a lively sense of the prevailing idea of noblesse oblige, and he had a number of patrons, of whom Frederick was the most highly placed. He never married, but lived for twenty years with the great love of his life, the almost equally remarkable Madame du Châtelet, a young, rich, and intellectually ambitious aristocrat, in a chateau tactfully distant from the court, where they did scientific experiments and entertained a variety of courtiers, intellectuals, and the simply amusing among their friends. When Madame du Châtelet died (after giving birth to a child by another lover), Voltaire lived with King Frederick, still later with his niece (said also to be his mistress) and, until his last year, at his own estate on the Swiss border at Ferney, where he could escape France when, as often happened, his outspoken criticisms of the crown endangered his freedom. He had just moved to Ferney while he was writing *Candide,* and was greatly under the charm of rural domestic life, as we see from the tale's denouement.

The almost casual brutalities—torture, mutilation, rape, and murder—that the hapless Candide and his beloved Cunégonde behold or endure in their flight from Westphalia are perhaps shocking to the modern reader, yet they are only slight exaggerations of actual practices in Voltaire's world. To be sure, France in the seventeenth century, which produced Voltaire himself at the end of it, had slightly improved over its northern neighbors. The bitter wars of religion that had raged during the sixteenth and seventeenth centuries and had divided all of Europe, and within France pitted Catholics against Huguenots, had somewhat subsided but were still very much in Voltaire's mind.

In the middle of their travels and misfortunes, Candide and his party at one period find themselves in El Dorado, a marvelous, peaceable land, more or less Peru,

full of gold and jewels that people are not driven to acquire, wonderful food, religious tolerance, an enlightened king, and general happiness. This astonishing place makes Candide and his company almost uncomfortable, and too excited by the prospect of going back home laden with jewels and gold to remain. They resume their journeys, having to spend all their fortune on bribing and hiring their way back to Europe to rescue Cunégonde.

When eventually Candide and his companions are able to find and save her, she has become hideously ugly. He marries her anyway, still trusting that everything is for the best in this best of all possible worlds, the credo, intended as a satire on Leibnitz, that Dr. Pangloss has not wavered from. They settle down on a small farm, where each exercises his talents, far from "boredom, vice, and want," and endorses the principle that each of us must "cultivate his garden."

Despite its specific targets, in *Candide,* it is the entire human race—greedy, cruel, inconstant—that is called into question:

> "Do you believe that men always butchered one another the way they do today?" Candide asked. "Do you believe they have always been liars, rogues, traitors, ingrates, brigands, weaklings, inconstant, cowards, enviers, gluttons, drunkards, misers, self-seekers, bloodthirsty, slanderers, debauchees, fanatics, hypocrites, and fools?"
>
> "Do you believe that hawks have always eaten pigeons wherever they have found them?" Martin asked.

By the time he wrote this, Voltaire had seen enough of humanity and its institutions to confirm his harsh opinion of them. Perhaps current events have given contemporary Americans more of a sense of the effects of religious fanaticism than we could have had even a few decades ago. Roland Barthes remarked in 1964, of the pertinence of Voltaire's philosophy, that while today we have no Inquisition, ours is still a world rife with persecutions and horrors committed in religion's name. He believed that only the theater, the spectacle of persecution, had vanished, and the bonfire and axe supplanted by more insidious methods of torture and killing. But at the beginning of the third millennium we are in a position to say that the theater has been rediscovered, too, with video-taped beheadings—and Voltaire's dim view of human nature is confirmed.

Yet, is his an entirely dim view? The complex mixture of cynicism and optimism in *Candide,* which is subtitled *ou, l'optimisme,* has generated numerous arguments. Is it finally Voltaire's view that man is redeemed, and his life made worth living, by the exercise of hope, good nature, and industry ("*cultiver son jardin*") in the face of cruelty and wickedness? Or is this simply the warring of his own good nature with the plain facts apparent to his intelligence, of the fundamental cruel and wicked character of mankind? The reader can make this judgment for himself.

Michael Wood (essay date 2005)

SOURCE: Wood, Michael. Introduction to *Voltaire: Candide, or Optimism*, translated by Theo Cuffe, pp. xi-xxviii. New York: Penguin Books, 2005.

[*In the following essay, Wood explores the meaning and philosophical underpinnings of Voltaire's notion of optimism in* Candide, *pointing out that the novella teaches the reader to view its narrative with skepticism and suspicion.*]

THE BEST OF ALL POSSIBLE WORLDS

The word optimism, first used in print in 1737, represents a philosophical position, a claim that in spite of errors and appearances God's creation is as good as it could be, and Voltaire's subtitle glances at just this doctrine. But the young hero of this book is also an optimist in the modern sense. Candide looks on the bright side when he can, and not one of his many moments of discouragement can prevent his innate cheerfulness from returning. Voltaire has not made it easy for him. Candide inhabits a world which may seem freakishly full of disasters, of war and earthquake, repeated rape and the persistent exploitation of the frail and the innocent by the rabid and strong. He suffers a good deal himself and carefully and kindly notes the catastrophes of others. He despairs at the sight of a slave in Surinam, who has lost an arm in a sugar-mill accident, and a leg as punishment for an attempt to escape. The slave is very forthright—'It is the price we pay for the sugar you eat in Europe' (chapter 19)—and provides one of the book's coolest and wittiest condemnations of inhuman practices. Dutch missionaries have taught the converted African slaves that we are all, black and white, children of Adam, and therefore members of the same family. 'You must admit,' the slave says, 'that no one could treat his relatives much more horribly than this.' It is at this point—the only place in the book, apart from the subtitle—that the word optimism is used. The abomination of slavery, Candide cries, would make even his teacher Pangloss renounce the doctrine of optimism. Candide's servant Cacambo does not know the word. 'What is Optimism?' he asks. Candide replies that 'it is the mania for insisting that all is well when all is by no means well'. Candide looks at the black man and weeps.

Voltaire, famously ridiculing the doctrine that all is for the best in the best of all possible worlds, is more subtly attacking (at least) three other, more insidious as-sumptions: that we can totally transcend our selfishness or provincialism; that a final accounting of the balance of good and evil in the world is achievable; that human philosophies bear some sort of direct relevance to human behaviour. Optimism is involved in all of these enterprises, and although our modern sense is anachronistic, and Candide's bitter definition is a mirror of his despair, these different meanings are not unrelated, as the mutilated slave might say; and it is their relation to each other and to the word's older, official meaning that matters to us. Indeed we scarcely see optimism in *Candide* except in the form of broad and damning travesties of it, and it takes an effort of the imagination to see that the doctrine isn't, or doesn't have to be, sheer parochial folly.

Theodore Besterman defines optimism as the theory 'that all that is and happens is for the best'.[1] 'For the best' already tilts the argument slightly. One meaning of 'All is well' is simply that all is as it has to be, that things could not be otherwise, and in this sense Voltaire had no significant quarrel with optimism. He merely regarded it as tautological and redundant. Thinking of English optimists like Henry St John Bolingbroke, the Earl of Shaftesbury, and Alexander Pope, he wrote in his *Philosophical Dictionary* (1764), 'their *All is well* means nothing more than that all is controlled by immutable laws. Who does not know that?'[2] The best of all possible worlds turns out to be the only possible world, there were never any other options. Free will is not subordinate to destiny, but certainly colludes with it in the long run.

But this is not optimism's most interesting claim. The idea that all is well implies a perspective—well for whom?—and may supply a useful corrective to limitations of vision. The world doesn't have to be a bad place because things are going badly for me. Voltaire himself was drawn to this view earlier in his career. 'What is bad in relation to you is good in the general arrangement,'[3] he wrote in his *Elements of the Philosophy of Newton* (1738). And of course the Christian notions of a benevolent God and a fortunate fall are optimistic in this sense: all is ultimately for the best even if there is nothing but a vale of toil and tears to be going on with. We may think of Alexander Pope's lines in *The Essay on Man* (1734):

> All Nature is but art, unknown to thee
> All chance, direction, which thou canst not see;
> All discord, harmony not understood;
> All partial evil, universal good[4]

When Candide quotes Pangloss as saying that the ills of the world are shadows in a beautiful painting, he is also quoting the German philosopher Gottfried Wilhelm Leibniz, a leading proponent of eighteenth-century optimism, who claimed that 'the shadows bring out the colours'.⁵ This is not a negligible argument, even if we may feel closer to the position of Candide's dour companion Martin, who thinks such shadows are 'dreadful stains' (chapter 22). What turned Voltaire away from this more complex form of optimism was not a refusal of its logic or a conviction of its untruth but a perception of its potential heartlessness and a belief that the claim, even if true, couldn't be tested, and worse, couldn't be articulated without incurring some sort of complicity with the unacceptable, too eager an embrace of the idea that certain horrors are not only unavoidable but necessary. 'I respect my God,' Voltaire wrote in his *Poem on the Lisbon Disaster,* 'but I love the universe.' And elsewhere, thinking of Pope: 'A strange general good! composed of the stone, gout, all crimes, all suffering, death and damnation.'⁶ Peter Gay, in *Voltaire's Politics,* goes so far as to say that 'Voltaire's objection to "whatever is, is right" was not to its complacent optimism but to its half-complacent, half-despairing pessimism . . . Voltaire's attack on "optimism" was an attack on pessimism in the name of a philosophy of activity'.⁷ In other words, Voltaire saw pessimism as just too easy. The word pessimism, I should add, was not used until 1794, and appears to have been coined by Coleridge, although the frame of mind clearly existed long before, and Voltaire knew he didn't like it.

The book's first onslaught on optimism finds the doctrine in its crassest and most comfortable form: a combination of ignorance and complacency, which asserts that all is well everywhere because I'm doing pretty well in the tiny corner of the world I happen to know. Much of the fun here depends on Voltaire's parodies of sloppy argument, his deliberately loose connections between clauses, and an extravagantly restrictive sense of what a world is. The Baron von Thunder-ten-tronckh is 'one of the most powerful lords of Westphalia, for his castle had a gate and windows' (chapter 1). The relative sophistication of the baron's home—Westphalia is Voltaire's model of perfect backwardness—is the result rather than the cause of his greatness, but Voltaire's language mischievously pretends the reverse. And of course, as long as Westphalia is the world, this must be the best castle in the world. Candide too follows this lamentable style of inference when he thinks that Pangloss is the greatest philosopher in the province, 'and therefore in the whole world'. Voltaire has taken a grand phrase from Pope and toppled it into triviality. 'Whatever is, is right' becomes in *Candide* 'I like things the way they are because they suit me and because I don't know any better'.

This position is not only selfish but dependent on conditions beyond one's control, and it is rapidly rendered untenable by Candide's expulsion from the castle, by Pangloss's moral and physical ruin, and by the invasion of the castle by the Bulgars. Pangloss, undeterred, develops more complicated, if deeply muddled arguments

as he and Candide start their travels: if Columbus had not brought syphilis from the New World we would not have chocolate in the Old; if private ills make up the general good, then the more private ills there are, the more all is well. In Pangloss's absurd assertions, we have our first inkling of what becomes fully clear only at the end of the book: Pangloss insists on his system not because he believes in it but because it is his system. It would not do for him to recant, he says, and in this statement Voltaire is offering us a sly definition of philosophy: never having to say you are wrong. 'I hold firmly to my original views,' Pangloss says in the last pages (chapter 28). 'After all I am a philosopher.' And Voltaire, in an uncharacteristically informative moment, tell us that Pangloss maintains his position 'while believing nothing of the kind' (chapter 30).

Candide is a philosopher too, in the sense that he loves to talk about philosophical ideas, but above all he is young, and his youth permits him attitudes which are not all that far removed from the initial provincialism of his native Westphalia. Candide is not complacent, and can't remain ignorant, but he does find it hard to believe the world is a bad place if his own affairs are going well. Voltaire remorselessly returns to this point, as strict with his likeable hero as he is with everyone else, but also interested in the *energy* of self-concern, as long as it is combined with curiosity and compassion. Candide's advantage over Martin, we learn, is that he has hope, 'for he still hoped to see Mademoiselle Cunégonde again, whereas Martin had nothing to hope for' (chapter 20). As well as hope, however, Candide has gold and diamonds, and he also has a good appetite. In the following stealthy sentence Mademoiselle Cunégonde is squeezed between money and food as only a part of what makes for the best of all possible worlds: 'when he thought of what remained in his pockets, and when he spoke of Cunégonde, especially at the end of a good meal, he still inclined towards the system of Pangloss'. And when Candide says 'once again I see that Pangloss was right: all is well' (chapter 27), he means nothing more than that he believes the desired end of his journey is near. Voltaire makes a slightly different point when he has Candide claim, while putting away a hearty meal, that he is too unhappy to eat, but the jokes all have the same theme: happiness and misery are contingent, local and material; philosophical optimism and conventional melancholy are postures. There is certainly a selfishness in Candide's repeated resorting to Pangloss's system; but there is also an ultimate moral health in his inability to be unhappy for long, even if his own intelligence says he should be.

THE WORST OF ALL POSSIBLE WORLDS

To speak of the best of all possible worlds, as Pangloss and Candide repeatedly do, is not only to espouse optimism as I have described it, it is explicitly to compare worlds and implicitly to say what a world is. 'If this is the best of all possible worlds,' Candide says after the Lisbon *auto-da-fé* in which he has been flogged and Pangloss has been hanged, 'what must the others be like?' (chapter 6). He is probably thinking of the whole earth, but one can also think smaller, as we have seen. If Westphalia is a world, then so are other regions and countries. If Europe is a world, then so are the Americas, and Candide himself says so. 'We are going to another world,' he remarks. 'No doubt it must be there that all is well' (chapter 10). He is both right and wrong about this, as we shall see.

But persons are also worlds in **Candide,** each enclosed in a circle of need and individual experience, and each convinced of precisely the opposite of Pangloss's proposition, namely that there is no world worse than his or hers. This is one of Voltaire's favourite themes, and he elaborates it with the greatest relish. Candide learns of Cunégonde's terrible fate from Pangloss: she has been raped and disembowelled by Bulgar soldiers. The disembowelling, it turns out, was something of an exaggeration, since she did survive, and Voltaire later devotes a whole chapter to her story, which she recounts to Candide. She became the mistress of her rapist's superior officer, and was then sold to a Jewish merchant, who shares her favours, or almost-favours, with a Portuguese grand inquisitor. She and Candide and the old woman who accompanies her have just finished supper when the Jewish merchant arrives to exercise his proprietorial rights. Furious at the sight of Candide, the merchant draws a dagger, only to find that Candide is even swifter with his sword, and 'his gentle disposition notwithstanding . . . lays the Israelite out, stone dead at the feet of the lovely Cunégonde' (chapter 9). Within minutes the Portuguese inquisitor arrives, and Candide, thinking fast about the spot he finds himself in, decides he had better kill him too. The situation gives rise to one of Voltaire's most spectacular set-pieces, a stunning piece of absurdist repartee. 'What on earth has got into you,' Cunégonde asks, 'you who were born so gentle, to do away with a Jew and a prelate in the space of two minutes?' (chapter 9). It's hard to think there could be a good reply to this question, but Candide finds one. 'My dear young lady . . . when you are in love, and jealous, and have been flogged by the Inquisition, there's no knowing what you may do.' The joke about Candide's gentle nature is not a sarcasm, it is a suggestion that no one is gentle all the time, and also glances more generally at the possibility that anyone's nature can be radically altered by circumstance. Voltaire returns to this thought, and to this tone, when Candide, in another fit of self-defence, kills (or thinks he has killed) Cunégonde's brother. This time it is Candide himself who naively proclaims his surprise: 'I am the mildest man alive, yet I have now killed three men, two of them priests' (chapter 15). Is he still a mild man? How many killings will it take to change this ascription?

Cunégonde's personal world seems pretty bad, but she has some competition, and for some time now her companion the old woman has been hinting that she too has a story to tell. When Cunégonde insists she has been 'so horribly unhappy' (chapter 10) in her world, the old woman says she herself has suffered far worse misfortunes. Cunégonde almost has to laugh, and lapses comically into that boasting about suffering which so marks the book, and she multiplies everything by two, partly for the sake of argument and partly no doubt because she feels as if she has suffered everything twice.

> Alas, my good woman . . . unless you have been raped by two Bulgars, been stabbed twice in the stomach, had two castles demolished, had the throats of two mothers and two fathers slit before your very eyes, and watched two lovers being flogged in an *auto-da-fé*, I really cannot see that you have the advantage over me.
>
> (Chapter 10)

The number of the Bulgars appears to be correct, the rest is competitive accounting.

The old woman, of course, now tells her story and her considerable travails put Cunégonde's into the shade. She is Italian, the daughter of a pope and a princess and the mere scenes of her sorrows cover much of the then known world: Tunis, Tripoli, Alexandria, Smyrna, Constantinople; Moscow, Riga, Rostock, Wismar, Leipzig, Kassel, Utrecht, Leiden, the Hague, Rotterdam. The old woman also likes to boast, both of her former beauty and fortune and of her later torments, and she too indulges in absurd comparisons, insisting that the plague is worse than the earthquake, as if there were anything to be said in favour of either. But she has her own form of wisdom—'I have lived, and I know the world,' she says (chapter 12)—and makes a wager she knows she can't lose. She suggests that Cunégonde ask each of their fellow travellers to tell his story, 'and if you find a single one of them who has not repeatedly cursed his existence, who has not repeatedly told himself that he is the unhappiest man alive, then you may throw me into the sea head first'. She is suggesting that everyone, in a phrase Voltaire uses in his story **Zadig,** regards himself or herself as 'the model of misfortune'. Later, Candide remembers the old woman's proposition and organizes a competition. He will take with him on his trip back to Europe the person who is 'the most unfortunate and most thoroughly disgusted with his condition in the whole province'. In the end he can't tell which of the candidates is the most wretched, and chooses one who is certainly miserable but probably more amusing than most, the Manichean Martin. The very idea of supremacy in sorrow or distress is self-defeating for all but the strictest misanthropes, and it is the old woman who has the most compelling view of what we may call the theory of the worst of all possible personal worlds. She says that there have been a hundred times when she has wanted to kill herself, but she is still 'in love with life'. She goes on to call this love a 'ridiculous weakness' (chapter 12) but plainly it is a form of radical heroism, a love that not only needs no reasons, but persists in spite of hosts of counter-reasons. There is an echo here of Candide's inability to sustain despair, however plausible the grounds. The old woman has seen, she says, 'a prodigious number of individuals who held their lives in contempt; but only a dozen who voluntarily put an end to their misery: three negroes, four Englishmen, four Genevans and a German professor named Robeck'. The list is carefully designed. The negroes are presumably slaves, the English as melancholic as French myth would have them, the Genevans doubtless too dour and Calvinistic to live, and Robeck was a historical person who argued that loving life was ridiculous and sought to prove his point by deliberately drowning himself in 1739.

As for the New World, Candide is clearly wrong about this being the place where all is well, because cruelty, conflict and greed are not restricted to the Old World, and Cacambo points out to him that 'this hemisphere is no better than the other one' (chapter 17). But Candide is right in another sense, because in the Americas he does find Eldorado, a world where all really is well, a version of the utopia sketched out in Michel de Montaigne's essay on cannibals,⁸ and echoed (and mocked) in Shakespeare's *Tempest*. Here in Eldorado there are no courts, prisons or lawyers, and no one is interested in gold and silver. The natives believe in God but they don't pray, in the sense of asking for help or grace or cure, because they already have all they need. Their form of prayer is simple worship and giving of thanks.

Yet the happiness and innocence of the citizens of Eldorado rests on total isolation, assured by an edict, to which they have all consented, that no one will ever leave this realm. And of course no stranger can enter it either, except by the kind of accident that brought Candide and Cacambo there. Voltaire seems to be saying that the best of all worlds can be found and enjoyed, but only at the cost of total separation from the turbulent and changing world humans have the habit of living and dying in, and in this context the remark made by Candide and Cacambo, both equally bemused and bewildered by Eldorado even before they have seen much of it, is exceptionally revealing. They say this is 'probably the land where all is well, for clearly such a place has to exist' (chapter 17). Has to exist? The place doesn't have to exist in material reality, and as far as we know it never has. But it does, it seems, have to exist as an expression of need and longing, because we cannot do without the dream of perfection it embodies. Voltaire includes it in his book for just this reason. 'All may be well,' he wrote in the *Poem on the Lisbon Di-*

saster . . . , 'that hope can man sustain, / All now is well; 'tis an illusion vain'. Eldorado is the fictional illusion that represents the historical hope.

Well, not quite. Eldorado is perfect, but perfection itself is a problem in Voltaire's view, as his recurring allusions to the Garden of Eden also suggest. We can certainly wish that people might be less unhappy than so many of them are, less tormented by disease and poverty and the rabid violence of their neighbours, but should we hope for an ideal happiness for anyone? This goal may be not only unattainable but undesirable, because its achievement would leave no room for human restlessness and the intensity of our interest in the opinions of others. 'Nothing is so disagreeable,' Voltaire drily writes in an essay called 'Historical Praise of Reason', 'as to be hanged in obscurity'⁹—that is, without any public attention to one's martyrdom. And on the subject of happiness he offers one of the tersest and most complex statements in *Candide.* After a month in Eldorado, Candide decides the place is not for him because Cunégonde is not there, and also because he doesn't want to be like everyone else. If he takes a few sheeploads of gold and jewels with him back to Europe, he will be richer than all the kings there put together. Cacambo agrees: it's good to be on the move, we all like to go home and tell stories about our travels. Voltaire's comment is 'our two happy wanderers resolved to be happy no longer'. Why would anyone resolve to abandon happiness? Because it wasn't happiness? Or because it was? The paradox certainly contains an element of criticism, a measurement of folly: these two (genuinely) happy people don't know how to live with their happiness. But another and perhaps stronger reading will insist on the backhanded praise: the two are right to leave, happiness isn't everything, and a full life must include risk and adventure, and even a bit of pettiness.

And if Cacambo is ready to join his master in leaving Eldorado and happiness, he is also himself a model of goodness and loyalty, and a significant figure in the text for this reason. Reading *Candide,* we become experts in suspicion, attuned to the obliquity of the book's language. An 'honest' person is someone who is about to do something crooked; 'good' or 'worthy' means naive or foolish. And so when Candide gives half his fortune to Cacambo and asks him to look for Cunégonde, with Voltaire telling us, for good measure, that 'he was a worthy fellow, this Cacambo' (chapter 19), we know what to expect. And when Candide says he trusts Cacambo as he trusts himself, that 'All is well, all goes well, all goes as well as it possibly can' (chapter 23), we merely wonder what form his terrible disappointment will take when it comes. Martin reinforces this idea by calling Candide 'a simpleton' for expecting 'a half-caste valet' to remain faithful when he has such an opportunity to defect. Ten pages later we are told there is still no sign of Cacambo. But then he turns up. He has been working for Candide all this time, he has found Cunégonde. 'The faithful Cacambo' turns out to be just what the epithet says he is: faithful. The interpretative rule in this deeply ironic text seems to be that the suspicious reading of words, persons and events is always correct—except when it is not. We certainly cannot count on human kindness, Voltaire is saying; but we cannot absolutely count on human betrayal either.

THE SATIRIST'S GARDEN

Italo Calvino remarks on the 'rhythm' and 'speed' of Voltaire's writing in *Candide*,[10] and Jean Sareil, in what is still the most subtle and far-reaching critical study of the book, asks a cluster of key questions.[11] If Voltaire is offering us such a disenchanted vision of the world, why is there so much gaiety in the writing? Why does the account of so many catastrophes have a happy ending? Why does this philosophical tale contain no real philosophical discussion? Why is Cunégonde the only person to age and become ugly?

Sareil himself offers an array of interesting responses. *Candide* is a satire, not a confession. Voltaire is not giving us his opinion about the universe; he is looking at persistent problems whose solutions, including the ones he has himself proposed, do not satisfy him. He wishes to represent a world that is not absurd and useless, but mysterious, forever inexplicable; a world that is 'simultaneously livable and bad'.[12] And most explicitly, Voltaire's 'lesson' is both that life is not worth much, and that this 'not much' is of the highest value. These are excellent answers. Voltaire's gaiety is a matter of style rather than philosophy, the happy ending is at once ironic and an invitation not to overdo our sense of misery. Voltaire's philosophy doesn't require philosophical discussion, indeed requires its absence. There is plenty of confirmation of these claims in Voltaire's other works. The hero of *Zadig* turns to philosophy when he has a problem, but receives 'only knowledge', and no relief. In his *Philosophical Dictionary,* Voltaire pretends to wonder why we are arguing about the supreme or sovereign good. 'You might as well ask what is the sovereign blue, or the sovereign stew, or the sovereign way of walking, or the sovereign way of reading . . . There are no extreme pleasures or extreme sufferings which will last a whole lifetime: the sovereign good and the sovereign evil are chimeras.'[13] And again (on the subject of destiny): 'Man can have only a certain quantity of teeth, hair, and ideas. A time comes when he necessarily loses his teeth, his hair and his ideas'.[14] But there is more to be said, and not only about the loss of Cunégonde's looks.

It may help if we slow Voltaire down a little, look at the details of his speed. Many critics have remarked on his strategic use of the little word 'but'. In *Zadig* it rep-

resents an incomplete discussion. An angel explains to the hero that things are what they are, and if they were different, this would be a different world. Zadig, wanting to argue and philosophize, says, 'But . . .' The angel is not listening, he is already on his way to another sphere. In *Candide,* however, the use of 'but' usually indicates not a wish to continue talking but the existence of a material fact needing immediate attention, something that supersedes talk. Does Candide believe, as certain Protestant zealots do, that the Pope is the Anti-Christ? Candide replies that he has not heard it said before, 'but whether he is or is not, I am in need of food' (chapter 3). Meeting up with the syphilitic Pangloss, Candide listens patiently to a long argument about the best of worlds and sufficient reasons, then says, 'This is all very interesting . . . but now we must get you treated' (chapter 4). Caught up in the Lisbon earthquake, Pangloss seeks a scientific connection between this tremor and an earlier one in Peru. 'There must certainly be a seam of sulphur running underground from Lima to Lisbon' (chapter 5). Candide, trapped under fallen masonry and believing himself close to death, says, 'Nothing is more likely . . . but, for the love of God, some oil and wine!'. Pangloss says, 'What do you mean, "likely"?', and Candide passes out. On a milder note, but preserving the same corrective pattern, Voltaire has Candide say there is nothing certain in the world (the French literally says nothing solid in the world) but virtue and the happiness of seeing Mademoiselle Cunégonde again. Cacambo says, 'I agree . . . but we still have two sheep laden with more treasure than the King of Spain will ever own' (chapter 19). There are other uses of the word 'but' in *Candide,* moments of conventional argument or discussion, but the general tilt is obvious, and prepares us for the most famous 'but' of all. Pangloss, correctly but trivially, summarizes all their adventures as a chain of cause and effect. Candide answers, in the last words of the book, 'That is well said . . . but we must cultivate our garden' (chapter 30). The garden is what there is, beneath and beyond our words; and even philosophy is welcome in the garden, as long as it doesn't insist on having any consequences, or getting in the way of work, the active cultivation of that earth.

To cultivate the garden, then, is not simply to mind one's own business, a wiser, more sophisticated version of the selfishness the book attacked at its outset. It is to decide not to seek answers to questions that can have none; to remember the concrete 'buts' that lie in wait for every grand abstraction. Still, it is hard not to feel there is a certain blandness in this philosophy that refuses philosophy, a betrayal of Voltaire's own best, angriest moments, and Roland Barthes, not intending a compliment, called Voltaire 'the last of the happy writers', or perhaps, given a certain fluidity in the meaning of the French word, 'the last of the lucky writers'. Voltaire was lucky, Barthes wrote, to have history on his side, a world of atrocities and visible, idiotic villains, making way for the great wave of improvement that ended in the French and American revolutions. And lucky to have been able to ignore another kind of history, since he couldn't know anything about Hegel or Marx or evolution. 'For Voltaire, there is no history in the modern sense of the word, nothing but chronologies. Voltaire writes historical works expressly to say that he didn't believe in history.'[15] History, for Barthes, is not simply what happens to human beings in time but a particular, post-Enlightenment project of making sense of progress and its discontents. Voltaire's third piece of luck or happiness, Barthes says, was the welcome his contemporaries gave to his refusal of all systems. And not only Voltaire's contemporaries, but those of Barthes too. Voltaire 'ceaselessly dissociated intelligence and intellectuality, asserting that the world is an order if we do not try too much to order it, that it is a system only if we renounce systematizing it: this conduct of mind has had a great career subsequently: today we call it anti-intellectualism'.[16]

'Today' for Barthes was 1964, and we may feel the idea of history as change and evolution has taken a few hits since then. But the charge of intellectual complacency retains its force, it seems to me, only as long as we try to capture Voltaire's thought, or more precisely, as long as we try to separate his thought from the movement of his prose. Seeking to understand Voltaire, we forget what it is like to read him. At the level of the words, what Barthes calls luck turns into what Calvino calls speed, and the gaiety of the writing, far from diminishing the described horrors or providing an argument for ignoring them, actually enhances them. They are beyond mere sentimental condemnation, and beyond philosophy too, in another sense: philosophy is not only helpless but tasteless, a form of unkindness. Here, for example, is Candide, who is said to have 'trembled like a philosopher', escaping from Voltaire's version of the Seven Years' War:

> Climbing over heaps of the dead and dying, he came first to a neighbouring village; it was in ashes . . . Here old men riddled with wounds or lead shot looked on as their wives lay dying, their throats cut, clutching their children to their blood-stained breasts; over there lay young girls in their last agonies, disembowelled after having satisfied the natural urges of various heroes; others still, half burned to death, cried out for someone to come and finish them off. Brains were scattered over the ground, amidst severed arms and legs.
>
> (Chapter 3)

A little later, in a village belonging to the other side in the war, Candide is said to be 'still stepping over twitching torsos'. 'Dead and dying', which sounds like a cliché, turns out to be an exact announcement of an enormity: this is what it means not to be dead yet, only shot, slashed, burned and dismembered. The anger is

directed at those who lead people into war (we hear it especially in the sarcasm about heroes, which is merely another word for rapists), but we are also to remember that Candide, endlessly described throughout the book as a good person, is not stopping to help anyone, or even register his shock.

Late in the book, Candide, once again called 'the worthy Candide', meets up with Paquette, the chambermaid from the Westphalian castle, the one who gave Pangloss his syphilis. She is still pretty, and now a prostitute in Venice, having passed through the hands of a monk, a doctor and a judge, and is apparently some sort of expert on the professions:

> Oh, Monsieur, if you could imagine what it is like to have to caress, with the same enthusiasm, an elderly merchant, a lawyer, a monk, a gondolier and an abbé; to be exposed to every insult and affront; to be reduced often to borrowing a petticoat so as to go and have it lifted by some disgusting man or other; to be robbed by one of what you have earned with another, or have it extorted from you by officers of the law; to have nothing to look forward to but a hideous old age, the poor house and the refuse-heap; then you would agree that I am one of the unhappiest creatures alive.
>
> (Chapter 24)

This is another worst-of-all-possible-worlds story, of course, but it is hard to argue with it, and Voltaire adds a cruel and subtle twist. Candide expresses his surprise that Paquette should seem so happy, and she points out that seeming happy is precisely part of her job, and not the least of its horrors: 'Ah! Monsieur . . . that is another of the miseries of our profession. Yesterday I was beaten and robbed by an officer; today I must seem in good humour to please a monk.'

In a short story called **'Adventure of Memory'**, Voltaire says the Muses don't compose satires because 'satires don't correct anyone, irritate the foolish, and make them even more mean'.[17] Does he believe this? He probably does, at least in part. He himself composes satires not because they work but because he is a writer, lucky or not. Pointless war, ubiquitous rape, endless prostitution, miserable dying, miserable living, the selfishness of even the best of men, good humour as the professional mask of pain—these are just a few features of the world Voltaire evokes for us, and I am not even mentioning natural disasters and ordinary human greed and crookedness. In such a universe cultivating one's garden is neither complacency nor wisdom, but a therapy of forgetting, a way of conjugating one's own good fortune and the distress of others. But if your garden happens to be the world of writing, then cultivating it is not even a work of forgetting. It is a work of unrelenting memory, a recurring assemblage of words that remind us what the world is like and invite us to think about which pieces of it we can change. Satires don't correct anyone, but some readers may find their mingled horror and laughter suggest work for them to do. That would be their garden.

There remains the question of Cunégonde's aging and becoming ugly. It is not strictly true that she is the only person this happens to—the old woman was once a beautiful princess—but she is the only person it happens to in the time of the immediate narrative, and the contrast with Paquette is important. Paquette needs to retain her looks so that the gap between the appearance of happiness and the hard grind of sexual labour can finally become clear, and in the economy of Voltaire's writing the situation alludes to the gap between many other bright appearances and dark realities. And Cunégonde needs to lose her looks so that . . . There are really too many possibilities.

Perhaps Cunégonde's aging happens simply so that Voltaire can get a laugh out of this sour turn in what Candide, if no one else, keeps seeing as a fairy tale: the hero marries not the princess he dreamed of, but the old toad the princess has become. Voltaire does go to town on this subject. When Candide first hears that Cunégonde has become 'fearfully ugly' (chapter 27), he quickly strikes the correct posture: 'I am a man of honour, and my duty is to love her always.' At the end of the same paragraph, though, the change is still on his mind: 'What a shame she has become so ugly'. And, as Voltaire adds with mock gratuitousness, Candide sets out to catch up with her, 'however ugly she might be'. When he finally sees Cunégonde again, he is 'seized with horror', and recoils, before pulling himself together and stepping forward 'out of sheer good manners' (chapter 29). His surprise is not too surprising, since Voltaire has just described Cunégonde as 'all weather-beaten, her eyes bloodshot, her breasts sunken, her cheeks lined, her arms red and chapped'. She is clearly the victim of more than ordinary aging; the victim of her author, we might say. Not only has she not aged well, she has become an anti-beauty.

The fairy tale has turned sour, but the sourness has its reasons. The tale was deluded to begin with, a distracting dream or retarded fantasy. Cunégonde is the withered goal of Candide's longing, indeed she is what happens to all longing that pursues only an idea of a person or a passion. She has to change not in order to disappoint Candide or to allow him to do the right thing after all, but in order to remind us that the objects of our desire have histories of their own, and histories we may not like. She is the incarnation of the book's most cruel 'but'. Candide finds his great love again, but she is ugliness personified, and has become nasty into the bargain. The unfortunate Cunégonde loses her looks, it turns out, for precisely the same reasons as the unfortunate Paquette retains hers: appearances alter or don't alter, but they are never more than appearances, a place to start but not to end.

Notes

1. Theodore Besterman, *Voltaire* (London, 1969), p. 301.

2. Voltaire, *Philosophical Dictionary*, trans. Theodore Besterman (London, 1972), p. 72.

3. Voltaire, *Candide et autres contes* (Paris, 1979), p. 414.

4. Alexander Pope, *Poems*, ed. John Butt (New Haven, 1963), p. 515.

5. From Leibniz's *Theodicy*, quoted in notes to *Candide et autres contes*, p. 420.

6. *Philosophical Dictionary*, p. 72 (see Appendix 3: 'Bien (Tout Est): All Is Good').

7. Peter Gay, *Voltaire's Politics* (Princeton, 1959), p. 21.

8. Michel de Montaigne, 'Des Cannibales', *Essais*, book 1, chapter 30.

9. Voltaire, 'Eloge historique de la raison' (1775), in *Candide et autres contes*, p. 279.

10. Italo Calvino, 'Candide: An Essay in Velocity', in *The Literature Machine*, trans. Patrich Creagh (London, 1987).

11. Jean Sareil, *Essai sur 'Candide'* (Geneva, 1967).

12. Sareil, *Essai sur Candide*, p. 31.

13. *Philosophical Dictionary*, p. 67, entry 'Bien (Souverain Bien): Good (Sovereign Good)'.

14. *Philosophical Dictionary*, p. 173 (see Appendix 3: 'Destin: Fate').

15. Roland Barthes, *Barthes: Selected Writings*, ed. Susan Sontag, trans. Richard Howard (London, 1983), p. 154.

16. Barthes, *Selected Writings*, p. 156.

17. Voltaire, *Aventure de la mémoire* (1775), in *Candide et autres contes*, p. 275.

Johnson Kent Wright (essay date 2005)

SOURCE: Wright, Johnson Kent. "Introduction: *Candide*, Voltaire, and the Enlightenment." In *Candide, or Optimism*, by Voltaire, translated by Burton Raffel, pp. xiii-xxv. New Haven, Conn.: Yale University Press, 2005.

[*In this essay, Wright discusses* Candide *in its biographical, historical, and intellectual context, suggesting that, perhaps more than any other factor, its "sheer exhuberance" is responsible for its continuing popularity with readers.*]

As Burton Raffel remarks in the prefatory note to his sparkling new translation, **Candide** has been "compulsory reading" for nearly two hundred and fifty years now. At first glance, the explanation for this staying power seems obvious. It clearly reflects **Candide**'s undiminished capacity to move, delight, and instruct its readers, according to the classical maxim. Yet it remains to explain exactly *how* Voltaire's novella still manages this feat, so long after the world in and for which it was written has passed away. For **Candide** is a satire—one of the most celebrated examples of the genre in modern literature—and satire, no matter how captivating at the time, has a notoriously short shelf-life, once its object and moment have passed. What has kept Voltaire's lampoon of eighteenth-century philosophic "optimism" so fresh and so engaging, after all these years? Raffel rightly suggests that the answer lies in the *universality* of Voltaire's themes—the sense that we still recognize ourselves in the mirror of his characters and their concerns, as if we would not be surprised to encounter Candide or Cunégonde on the streets of Manhattan today. Paradoxically, however, any attempt to explain this sense of familiarity and currency must return us to the very particular context in which **Candide** was produced—above all, to the intersection between an unprecedented intellectual movement and an extraordinary individual life.

The movement was the Enlightenment, the great revolt against inherited intellectual authority—classical and Christian alike—that swept across Europe in the eighteenth century. Its seeds can be traced to a set of intrepid thinkers from the middle of the preceding century: the major figures of what was later called the Scientific Revolution—Galileo Galilei, William Harvey, and Isaac Newton; philosophers such as René Descartes, Benedict de Spinoza, and Gottfried Leibniz; and theorists of "natural rights"—Hugo Grotius, Thomas Hobbes, and John Locke. It is no accident that most of these came from or lived in either England or the Dutch Republic, countries that had succeeded in overthrowing the rule of divine-right or absolute monarchy in the course of the seventeenth century. Nor is it surprising that their ideas began to make their way into France early in the eighteenth, when that nation was in recovery from the long and exhausting reign of the greatest of all absolute monarchs, Louis XIV. For this was what the Enlightenment amounted to, in the first instance: the process by which French thinkers translated and popularized the ideas of their more advanced Dutch and English predecessors, for presentation to a far wider audience than they had ever reached before. These ideas never formed a single coherent doctrine. But by the time the Enlightenment reached its maturity, in the middle years of the century, there was a rough consensus among its leading thinkers in regard to certain key themes: rejection of orthodox, scriptural Christianity, in favor of deism or natural religion; conviction of the su-

periority of modern over ancient thought, above all owing to recent achievements in the natural sciences; extension of this natural-scientific model to a host of new social sciences, including economics, psychology, and sociology; and a protoliberal political program, aimed at protecting what were now seen as the equal natural rights of individuals. The most famous vehicle for the propagation of these ideas was, of course, the great collective enterprise of the *Encyclopedia* edited by Jean le Rond d'Alembert and Denis Diderot between 1751 and 1772. But it is also striking how easily the themes of the Enlightenment lent themselves to expression in imaginative literature. The French Enlightenment was in fact launched with an epistolary novel, the Baron de Montesquieu's dazzling *Persian Letters* (1722), which held up a critical mirror to European society by recounting the visit of two Muslims to France. A little over a half-century later, the Enlightenment closed, in a sense, with the supreme expression of its cosmopolitan and egalitarian values, Wolfgang Amadeus Mozart's opera *The Marriage of Figaro* (1786)—the joint product of a French Protestant, an Italian Jew, and an Austrian Catholic.

But of all the literature and art associated with the Enlightenment, none has had quite the success of **Candide.** It literally flew off the presses at the moment of its publication in early 1759, appearing almost immediately in multiple editions in every European language, eventually selling more copies than any other eighteenth-century book. Today, two and a half centuries later, it has a wider readership than ever, one that is almost certainly still increasing—not least because of the historical shorthand that has turned it into a veritable icon of the Enlightenment. How did it happen that this one novella managed to capture the essence of this large and complicated intellectual movement?

The achievement has everything to do with the remarkable career of its author, who, more than a mere "writer," was in many ways the first *intellectual* of the modern world, a social role he virtually invented. He was born François-Marie Arouet in Paris on November 21, 1694, the son of a lawyer and banker prosperous enough to furnish him with an education at the finest Jesuit school of the time—where, Voltaire later claimed, he was also sexually abused by his warders. By his mid-twenties, he had abandoned the legal career chosen by his family for a life of letters, rapidly establishing a reputation as a leading dramatist and poet. By this point, he had also discarded his patronymic, adopting as a pen name an anagram of Arouet (with *le jeune,* "the younger") that echoed the French verb *volter,* "to turn abruptly." Nimbleness was a useful trait, given Voltaire's chafing against the social constraints that a bourgeois poet naturally encountered in the aristocratic world of regency France. His satirical verse already landed him in the famous Bastille prison in 1717-18. A more serious run-in with a petty noble in 1726 led to a severe beating on the streets of Paris, another stint in the Bastille, and then prudent exile in England.

The two years Voltaire spent there were a first turning point in his life. For in England, he encountered a society that was not only very different from that of France, but one that seemed more *advanced,* in every respect— freer and more tolerant, richer and more rational. The result was an enthusiastic traveler's report, *Letters Concerning the English Nation* (1733), which in one stroke placed Voltaire at the forefront of the early Enlightenment. The book was in fact more subversive than Montesquieu's *Persian Letters* had been, since it sang the praises of a very real neighbor, where the fruits of England's religious toleration and political liberty were to be seen both in scientific accomplishments of the English and in the commercial prosperity they enjoyed. The Parlement of Paris, France's highest court of appeals, reacted accordingly and banned the *Letters Concerning the English Nation* in 1734. Voltaire was forced to resume his wanderings, which now went on for a quarter-century. He spent most of the years 1734-43 in happy and productive cohabitation with Madame du Châtelet, a formidable Enlightenment thinker in her own right, with a cooperatively absent husband, at her estate at Cirey, in Lorraine. In addition to an unabated flow of dramas and verse, Voltaire now became the most innovative historian of the early Enlightenment. His great study of Louis XIV in fact restored him briefly to favor at Versailles, where he became historiographer to the king in 1745. Relations with Madame du Châtelet had in the meantime soured, though she and Voltaire reunited in 1749 at her deathbed, during childbirth, together with her husband and current lover. Voltaire was now banished from the capital again, and later in the same year, he finally accepted the long-standing invitation of Frederick, Prussia's energetic young king, to join the royal court at Berlin. A shorter, more intense replay of his life at Cirey ensued: an initial period of blissful productivity—Voltaire, who was probably bisexual, and Frederick, certainly homosexual, may even have been lovers for a time—was followed by a fractious blowup between the two powerful personalities. House arrest and flight back to France followed in 1753. Having failed to establish himself at two absolutist courts, Voltaire was now virtually a man without a country. He was, however, wealthy, thanks in part to his literary success but still more to his skills as financier and investor. In 1755, he leased a modest estate in the Swiss city-state of Geneva. As Voltaire remarked at the time, Les Délices (the Delights), as he called it, which he shared with his niece, Madame Denis, the other great female love of his life, was the first household that he actually headed rather than lived in as a guest.

It was at Les Délices, in 1758, that Voltaire wrote **Candide,** which was preceded by a number of earlier exer-

cises in the genre of the "philosophical tale." He was sixty-four at the time. Surprisingly, given a lifetime of complaints about ill health, **Candide** proved not to be a swan song but instead ushered in an entirely new phase of Voltaire's life, one of even greater hyperactivity. In 1759, he purchased the more ample estates of Ferney and Tournay, just across the border from Geneva, in France. Scandalized by the dismal state of peasant life in the villages he now superintended, Voltaire threw himself into improving the local agricultural economy, with notable success. More important, it was from Ferney that he launched the great public campaigns against judicial abuse that were the hallmark of the political activity of his later years. Voltaire had in fact tried unsuccessfully some years earlier to intervene on behalf of Admiral Byng, the British naval commander shot for cowardice—the inspiration for chapter 23 of **Candide.** In 1762, Voltaire's attention was captured by the brutal public execution in Toulouse of Jean Calas, a Protestant businessman falsely accused of having murdered his son, a suicide. Voltaire devoted three years of incessant labor to clearing Calas's name, during which time he sheltered his widow and children. The Calas campaign was the first of a string of militant interventions on behalf of victims of religious persecution and social abuse, inspired by the sentiment expressed in the motto Voltaire now used to sign letters: "Ecrasez l'infâme!"— "Crush the infamy!" Voltaire's correspondence was in fact gargantuan: the evidence suggests that he may have written more than forty thousand personal letters in his lifetime, of which some fifteen thousand survive. Meanwhile, his formal literary output flagged not a bit in this period. His *Philosophical Dictionary* (1764) is a masterpiece of the mature Enlightenment. Accompanying it were any number of tales, essays, dramas, and poems, which continued to pour forth from Voltaire's pen until his last days. These were in fact spent in Paris in the first half of 1778, where Voltaire finally returned, after an absence of nearly thirty years, to attend the première of one last tragedy. There his health finally failed him, but before his death on May 30, the eighty-four-year-old writer was treated to rapturous public celebrations.

Voltaire's conquest of Paris was more than a personal victory, of course. It was the moment of greatest triumph for the Enlightenment itself, with which he had by now become so closely identified. The intimate association between writer and movement, however, poses a question about **Candide,** the greatest literary success of Voltaire's lifetime. A reader coming to the story anew might be forgiven for finding the relation between text and context puzzling—or even discrepant. For there is, of course, no idea more commonly associated with the Enlightenment, in its maturity, than a belief in "progress"—a fundamental optimism about the capacity of modern Europeans to reshape the social and political world for the better. Yet **Candide** is, of all things, a *satire* on "optimism," whose object is precisely one of those intellectual pioneers that the Enlightenment, and Voltaire in particular, tended otherwise to honor—the German philosopher Leibniz, author of the doctrine ventriloquized by Pangloss in the story. Indeed, the ordeals to which its protagonist is subject—expulsion from an Edenic home; a succession of misadventures whose hallmark is hyperbolic physical violence; and final capture of the object of his affections, only to find that he no longer desires her—seem designed to make the case for the opposite doctrine, the *pessimism* (a word Voltaire may have invented), urged by Pangloss's opposite number, Martin. In the meantime, as if to agree that this is the worst of possible worlds, the Old Woman who arrives so memorably in chapters 11 and 12 has already insisted that *every* human life is fundamentally a tale of misfortune and suffering. If we compare the outlook of **Candide** to, say, *The Marriage of Figaro,* with its triumphantly happy end, then Voltaire's story might look less like an advertisement for the Enlightenment than the announcement of his defection from it.

There were, in fact, contemporary commentators who read **Candide** that way and suggested an obvious biographical explanation for Voltaire's disenchantment. After all, the relative happiness of his life at Cirey, when he and Madame du Châtelet were indeed enthusiasts for Leibniz, ended with a series of heavy personal blows—the breakup with Châtelet and her premature death, permanent loss of favor at Versailles, the imbroglio with Frederick and expulsion from Prussia. These private tragedies were then followed, in the mid-1750s, by two major public catastrophes, which deeply engaged Voltaire's imagination—the great earthquake that destroyed Lisbon in 1755, claiming thousands of lives, and the outbreak of the Seven Years' War, strewing destruction around the globe, the following year. The earthquake was, in fact, the occasion for a famous poem, in which Voltaire explicitly attacked Leibniz. **Candide,** the argument goes, simply clinched the case against "optimism" by distilling these experiences into a thinly veiled autobiography: the sufferings of its main characters mirror those of its author all too exactly, for which the Seven Years' War (that is, the war between Bulgars and Avars in chapters 2 through 4) and the Lisbon earthquake (experienced at firsthand by Candide and Pangloss in chapter 5) furnish the appropriate historical backdrop. On this view, which has had many adherents, **Candide** was indeed out of step with the Enlightenment, a grumpy exception to its optimism and faith in progress.

However, this is not the only way to understand the relation of **Candide** to its biographical and intellectual context. The historian David Wootton has recently proposed an alternative account, arguing that the book played an even more pivotal role in Voltaire's life than has hitherto been recognized. Laying special stress on Voltaire's well-attested and frequently repeated complaints about being sexually abused by his Jesuit teach-

ers as a child, Wootton contends that this defining experience—together with the ordeals of physical violence, imprisonment, exile, exaltation and degradation, love and loss that followed over the next forty years—did indeed supply the raw material for **Candide.** By the time he wrote it, however, Voltaire had reached the safe shore of Les Délices and was now genuinely *happy,* for perhaps the first time in his life. **Candide** is testimony to that achievement. Far from announcing an embrace of pessimism, what the story reveals is the *means* by which Voltaire freed himself from an unhappy past: he unburdened himself by finally telling his story, in precisely the manner that his main characters do. That the purge was successful, Wootton concludes, is shown by what followed in the last phase of Voltaire's life, with his turn to energetic and effective political activism.

There are limits to any biographical explanation of a work of imaginative literature, of course. But Wootton's interpretation has the advantage of explaining salient features of **Candide,** difficult to account for otherwise. First, if there is any single characteristic of **Candide** on which all readers agree, it is surely its sheer *exuberance* as a piece of writing—a bubbling gaiety of form, belying its apparently grim contents, that accords perfectly with Voltaire's frequent descriptions of his newfound happiness in his correspondence of the time. As for those contents, the basic component part of the story is, of course, the slip on the banana peel—the sudden dashing of hopes, reversal of fortune, puncturing of illusions. The constant repetition of this joke, in myriad forms, is, in fact, what supplies the basic evidence for the "pessimistic" reading of **Candide.** However, once larger narrative patterns come into sight—above all with the numerous "stories-within-the-story," as new characters appear or old ones reappear—a more complicated picture emerges. For these narratives all focus obsessively on precisely the topic indicated by Wootton's interpretation—sexuality, and sexual violence in particular. Violation at the hands of men is the fate of every female character in **Candide,** suffering as a result of their own sexual sins the lot of all the men. This is true for the protagonist no less than for the rest: Candide is exiled from a happy home for a sexual slip, and his dogged pursuit of his lost love object across three continents ends in what might be thought of as the bitterest ironic reversal of all.

That the ending of **Candide** is not at all bitter, however, is owing to its *other* narrative thread, which more than compensates for this bleak depiction of sexuality and erotic love. **Candide** opens with a depiction of a community that is an elfin model of Old Regime European society as a whole—hierarchical, authoritarian, laughably unaware of its own poverty, convinced that it is the best of possible worlds. In fact, the smallest sexual indiscretion is enough to unravel Thunder-ten-Tronckh, flinging its inhabitants out into a world of violence and misfortune. Halfway through his journey toward a new home, however, Candide stumbles on a second community, Eldorado, which is the exact opposite of the first—"enlightened," egalitarian, blissfully unaware of its own wealth, oblivious to the fact that it *is* the best of possible worlds. But Candide learns its lessons and departs a wealthy man. By the end of the story, he has forged a new community out of the debris of the first one, replacing the Baron (old and young) at the head of a society that is egalitarian, wealthy enough to be well fed, and undeluded about its place in the cosmos. For if the ridiculous "optimism" of Pangloss is indeed formally abandoned, immediately on leaving Eldorado, Candide does not thereby embrace the equally absurd "pessimism" advocated by Martin. Philosophically, the last word belongs to the dervish of chapter 30, who literally slams the door on dogmatic speculative philosophy of every kind. Far more convincing than any speculative system is the concluding example of the old farmer, who, more contented than any king in Europe, demonstrates that happiness is well within reach, to be secured by pulling together and *working* at it.

From Thunder-ten-Tronckh via Eldorado to the farm outside Constantinople—an itinerary perhaps not all that far from *The Marriage of Figaro* after all. What this suggests, at the least, is that posterity has made no mistake in regarding *Candide* as the best of all possible renderings of Enlightenment ideas in literary form. Trying to explain the unique place of Shakespeare in English literature, the poet Ted Hughes once suggested that "it is only those poets whose make-up somehow coincides with the vital impulse of their times who are able to come to real stature." Voltaire is a lesser writer, of course, but there was clearly a happy coincidence between the biographical material that found expression in *Candide* and the "vital impulse" of his time. The result was a winning allegory of the process of enlightenment itself, as Candide's journey through the European world gradually causes the dogmatic scales to fall from his eyes. Along the way, the reader is treated to the entire catalogue of great Enlightenment themes—condensed into the charming mini-utopia of Eldorado but, above all, leaping out from Voltaire's scathing description of the injustice, irrationality, and violence of European society, metropolitan and colonial, in the rest of the text. For all of Voltaire's circumspection in dealing with the various kings who cross his pages—objects of pathos as much as ridicule—the silhouette of a revolutionary politics is not hard to glimpse in *Candide*. Shortly after its initial publication, the American and French Revolutions in fact started start the process of dismantling the social world of aristocrats and kings that we now call the Old Regime. What is striking, two and a half centuries later, is not merely how violent that undertaking turned out to be but also how slowly it has proceeded. This is true for the world of thought as well—which, of course, is precisely why *Candide*'s sat-

ire has remained so actual, and so entertaining, over the years. Despite the efforts of Voltaire, his fellow Enlightenment thinkers, and their successors, our own intellectual scene teems with Panglosses and Martins, peddling prefabricated systems of thought of every kind. The consolations of facile "optimism" and "pessimism" alike are as attractive as ever. But so long as this is the case, *Candide* is not likely to lack for readers.

Thomas L. Cooksey (essay date 2006)

SOURCE: Cooksey, Thomas L. "Voltaire, *Candide*." In *Masterpieces of Philosophical Literature*, pp. 93-114. Westport, Conn.: Greenwood Press, 2006.

[*In the following essay, Cooksey examines the intellectual and literary background of* Candide, *Voltaire's handling of generic conventions, and the influence of the novella on later works.*]

> [S]he came to a prim little villa with a very amateurish garden which was being cultivated by a wizened old gentleman whose eyes were so striking that his face seemed all eyes, his nose so remarkable that his face seemed all nose, and his mouth so expressive of a comically malicious relish that his face seemed all mouth until the black girl combined these three incompatibles by deciding that his face was all intelligence.
>
> —George Bernard Shaw

Voltaire thought of himself first and foremost as a poet, and believed that his fame rested upon his verse tragedies, such as *Oedipe, Mahomet,* or *Mérope,* his epic *La Henriade,* or the mock-heroic *La Pucelle.* The tale (*conte*) was a literary genre that he dismissed as false, frequently using the word in disparagement, especially when applied to philosophical systems, theological doctrine, or political and economic theories. Ironically, Voltaire's most enduring achievement are his philosophical tales (*contes philosophiques*). From about 1715 to 1775, he produced some 26, many of which, including *Micromégas, Zadig, L'Ingénu,* and most notably *Candide,* remain popular. *Candide, or Optimism* is the greatest of Voltaire's *contes,* exemplifying the complex spirit of the Enlightenment. On one hand it gleefully punctures authority, whether social, political, religious, or philosophical, inviting its heroes (and readers) to think for themselves. On the other, it recognizes the limits of human reason and enterprise, undercutting human arrogance and pretension to grandeur. As a Turkish dervish asks Candide, "[w]hen his highness sends a ship to Egypt, does he worry whether the mice on board are comfortable or not?" (*Candide* 73). In place of various false tales and ideologies that too often are the source of our misery, Voltaire offers a tolerant and skeptical realism.

Voltaire stands among Denis Diderot and Jean-Jacques Rousseau as one of the towering French *philosophes* of the eighteenth century. R. G. Saisselin aptly describes the *philosophes* as the "fighting wing of the Enlightenment elite" (qtd. in Yolton 395). They were public intellectuals, their fields of battle the salons of Paris and the general reading public. While centered in France, and including among their number such notables as Montesquieu, Condillac, Helvétius, d'Holbach, La Mettrie, D'Alembert, and Mme. d'Épinay, their spirit was international, embracing the Scotsman David Hume, the Neapolitan Abbé Galiani, the Milanese Cesare Beccaria, the Americans Benjamin Franklin and Thomas Jefferson, and the Germans Friderich Melchior Grimm, Gotthold Ephraim Lessing, and Moses Mendelssohn (the prototype for Lessing's Nathan the Wise). Among their political supporters (at least in spirit, if not always in practice or pocketbook), Frederick the Great of Prussia, Catherine the Great of Russia, and Mme. de Pompadour, long-time mistress of Louis XV of France.

VOLTAIRE AND THE ENLIGHTENMENT

Writing in 1784, within 5 years of the French Revolution and in many regards at the end of the Enlightenment, the German philosopher Immanuel Kant offers a definition in his "Was is Aufklärung? [What is Enlightenment?]": "Enlightenment is man's leaving his self-caused immaturity," he declares. Explaining, he adds, "Immaturity is the incapacity to use one's intelligence without the guidance of another. Such immaturity is self-caused if it is not caused by lack of intelligence, but by lack of determination and courage to use one's intelligence without being guided by another. *Sapere Aude!* [Dare to be wise!]" (Kant 132). Two themes emerge, a rejection of authority and, in its place, a challenge to think for one's self. This included not only challenging political and religious authority as it related to the power of the state and the Church, the unquestioned privilege of tradition and social hierarchy, but more broadly a questioning of systems in general, whether they be related to science, philosophy, law, medicine, or theology. Instead of authority, whether in the form of royal or papal pronouncements, revelation, the Bible, or even rational systems, they proposed an appeal to reason supported by empirical observations. "The Enlightenment," says historian Peter Gay, "was not an Age of Reason but a Revolt against Rationalism" (Gay 27). Indeed, for many *philosophes* the most dangerous and persistent enemy was what Voltaire termed the "spirit of system [*l'esprit du système*]." He considered Plato more a poet than a philosopher, "an eloquent moralist and bad metaphysician" (Gay 29). Leibniz, Voltaire told Condorcet, was a great man, especially with regard to mathematics, but also "a bit of a charlatan." Descartes' system was "an ingenious novel [*un roman ingénieux*], at best seeming probable to the ignorant" (*Philosophical Letters* 64), and Malebranche's development of Cartesian doctrine, "sublime hallucinations" (*Philosophical Letters* 53). Each case illustrated the dangers of a mind detached from the grounding of

empirical data. It was not Montaigne, Locke, Bayle, Spinoza or the other great skeptics who caused discord and social upheaval, Voltaire notes, but the dogmatic theologians, "who having first had the ambition of being leaders of their sect, have soon afterward desired to be heads of parties" (*Philosophical Letters* 58, 59).

By the time Voltaire entered the public arena around 1718, the dominant themes of the Enlightenment were already well established. Growing out of the rise of science in the wake of Galileo, Bacon, and Descartes, as well as a general exhaustion from the bloody sectarian strife caused by the Reformation and Counter-Reformation, the spirit of Enlightenment called into question the traditional authority of philosophy, theology, and science, and by extension law and medicine. Descartes' repudiation of the scholastic curriculum, his rejection of Aristotelian science (and by extension the science of Thomas Aquinas), and his the call to start again from the foundations in order to make progress in the sciences set the tone and terms for debate. We must think for ourselves and reject anything that is not "clear and distinct." Voltaire himself acknowledged the importance of Descartes. His response was, however, nuanced. Comparing Descartes to Locke in his *Philosophical Letters,* Voltaire writes, "Our Descartes, born to bring to light the errors of antiquity and to put his own in their place, being led astray by that spirit of system which blinds the greatest of men, imagined he had demonstrated that soul is the same thing as thought, just as matter, according to him, is the same as extension" (53).

Historian Jonathan Israel distinguishes two wings to the Enlightenment. The moderate wing, including Newton and Locke in England, Montesquieu in France, and Wolff in Germany, sought to synthesize reason with faith. Appealing to verifiable empirical evidence, they tried to ground religion in science, thereby conquering ignorance and superstition. Ethically, they advocated a spirit of toleration and the importance of education. The radical wing, including many of the later *philosophes,* tended to be atheistic or deistic, denying miracles and the notion of a divinely ordained hierarchy. They often evoked the work of the Dutch Jewish philosopher Baruch de Spinoza (1632-1677), especially his *Tractatus Theologico-Polititus* (1670) and the posthumously published *Ethics* (1677). Anticipating modern biblical criticism, Spinoza had advocated religious toleration and freedom of thought, based on a historical reading of the Bible. The *Ethics,* developed out of a rigorous geometrical method of proof, equates God and existent nature ("*deus sive natura*"). This led many in the Enlightenment to consider him a radical materialist. (Later the Romantics would reverse this identity and read him as a pantheist.) Though increasingly anti-clerical, Voltaire was largely of the moderate wing, famously writing in his poem "Trois imposseurs," "If God did not exist, it would be necessary to invent him [*Si Dieu n'existait pas, il faudrait l'inventer*]" (Voltaire, *Oeuvres* 10.405). Once, upon witnessing a glorious sunrise, he is reported to have raised his hat and declared, "Oh mighty God, I believe!" To this, however, he quickly added, "As to Monsieur the Son and Madame his mother, that is another matter!" (qtd. Durant 750).

To understand Voltaire's relation to the Enlightenment, two thinkers are worth briefly considering, Pierre Bayle (1647-1706), and Gottfried Wilhelm von Leibniz (1646-1716). Bayle was born to a Protestant family in France, converted to Catholicism and then reverted to Protestantism. He saw himself in the skeptical tradition of Montaigne, rejecting fanaticism. He remained Christian throughout his life, but advocated religious toleration for Protestants, Catholics, Jews, Muslims, and even atheists. His most influential work, *Dictionnaire historique et critique* (1697, 1702), an inspiration for Voltaire's own *Philosophical Dictionary,* offers historical examinations of religious and philosophical figures, including Arminius, David, Eve, Mahomet, Rosarius, and Spinoza. Among his central themes are an attack on Calvinist orthodoxy, a call for the separation of religion and morality, a discussion of the limits of human reason, and a critical examination of the systems of Descartes, Spinoza, and Leibniz. While these great rationalists supposed that the acquisition of knowledge advanced in a causal, linear fashion, one step inevitably leading to another, Bayle held that knowledge was provisional, acquired through a process of incremental revision. The *Dictionnaire* thus became an important source book for later skeptics, influencing many, including Hume and Gibbon. In his poem, "Poème sur le désastre de Lisbonne," Voltaire finds consolation only in Bayle.

> What do I learn from Bayle, to doubt alone?
> Bayle, great and wise, all systems overthrows,
> Then his own tenets labors to oppose.
>
> (*Portable Voltaire* 567)

For both Bayle and Voltaire, the point is not doubt for its own sake, but a rejection of incomprehensible dogmas. Skepticism is not nihilism, but a withholding of assent when there is a lack of evidence, an honest confession of "I don't know," in the face of uncertainty.

Philosopher, mathematician, scientist, lawyer, librarian, and diplomat Leibniz was one of the towering thinkers of the seventeenth century. Along with Newton, he was the co-discoverer of differential calculus. Leibniz developed his mature philosophy in a series of books and papers, especially *The Discourse on Metaphysics* (1685), *The New System* (1695), the *Theodicy* (1710), the *Monadology* (1713), and the *Nouveaux Essais* (1701-1709), a running commentary on Locke's *Essay Concerning Human Understanding* His philosophy grew out of his de-

sire to reconcile science and religion. To explain the physical concept of force, the capacity to cause change, which is the basis of time, space, and mass, Leibniz argued that infinitesimal units of force comprised the basic substance (or being) of the universe. He concluded that reality is composed of an infinite number of independent substances, or monads, each potentially an alternative universe, a sort of spherical mirrors reflecting the other monads from its own perspective, each monad acting to realize its own potential. The world as we know it is the resulting unity, the pattern emerging from the competing forces (like vector addition in algebra and calculus). Thus, from the myriad activities of infinite possible universes emerges a single optimum pattern. The interaction of forces that produces the optimum pattern is what Leibniz terms "sufficient reason," and given this particular sufficient reason, no other reality is possible. This is the "best of all possible worlds" that Voltaire satirizes in **Candide.**

BIOGRAPHICAL CONTEXT

Voltaire's life was marked by turbulence, controversy, and brilliance. He was born François-Marie Arouet in Paris, November 21, 1694, in the twilight of the Sun King, Louis XIV. Voltaire's father was a lawyer and official in the Chambre-des Comptes (Office of the Auditor). From 1703 to 1711, Voltaire studied at the Jesuit college of Louis-le-Grand, awakening and nurturing his literary gifts. After a brief stint as a secretary to the French ambassador to Holland, he began legal studies in 1714, but soon found himself in trouble with his father and the authorities for his inflammatory writing. He was exiled from Paris in 1716, and imprisoned in the Bastille from March 17, 1717, to April 11, 1718. In June, he began calling himself Voltaire, completing his play *Oedipe,* first performed November 1718. His version of the story of Oedipus draws on both Sophocles and Corneille and centers on the theme of religious superstition. The play was Voltaire's first literary triumph, making him an overnight success, and establishing his reputation. For the rest of his life, he produced a continuous stream of plays, poems, histories, tales, polemical writings, and letters. Only a few can be mentioned given the scope of this book. In 1723 he published his verse epic, *La Ligue,* later retitled *La Henriade.* The ten-book poem, written in spirit of Virgil's *Aeneid,* focuses on Henry of Navarre, who converted to Catholicism, becoming Henry IV of France (Henri le Grand) with the famous quip that Paris was worth a mass. Much of Voltaire's epic is a polemic against religious fanaticism, though his account of the Saint Bartholomew's Day Massacre remains powerful.

1723 saw three of Voltaire's plays performed as part of the wedding celebration for Louis XV. In 1726 he quarreled with the Chevalier de Rohan, culminating in his being beaten by the Chevalier's servants. Despite his fame, Voltaire found no legal redress, and was himself imprisoned again in the Bastille when he threatened to challenge Rohan to a duel. Soon released, he went into exile in England from 1726 to 1728. During his stay in England he met the great British satirists, poet Alexander Pope, the playwright John Gay, and the essayist Jonathan Swift. He also met the philosopher and statesman Henry St. John, Viscount Bolingbroke. A deist, Bolingbroke developed a philosophy of optimism that impressed Voltaire. Later Pope summarized Bolingbroke's position in his poem, *An Essay on Man.* Arguing a sort of natural theology that "Whatever is, is RIGHT" (1.291), Pope declared, "Know then thyself, presume not God to scan; / The proper study of mankind is Man" (2.1, 2). The most important work to emerge from the visit to England was Voltaire's *Letters on England* (1733), also known as the *Lettres philosophiques.* Here he described English institutions and religious toleration, with special admiration for the Quakers. He also wrote extensively on English letters and philosophy.

Probably the most enduring influence of the English sojourn was Voltaire's introduction to the philosophies of John Locke and Sir Isaac Newton. Locke's *Essay Concerning Human Understanding* (1690) offered an explanation of human knowledge that, unlike that of Descartes, did not fall back on the notion of innate ideas. An empiricist, Locke argued that the mind is like a blank piece of paper (the *tabula rasa* or blank slate in Aristotelian terms) written on by sense experience. In the early philosophical tale **Micromégas,** composed around 1738 and published in 1751, Voltaire's hero receives a book of philosophy written by a giant from the star Sirius, which turns out to be nothing but blank pages. Newton's *Philosophiae Naturalis Principias Mathematica* (1687), one of the monuments in the history of science, offered a comprehensive description of the universe, based on observation and without appeal to metaphysical first causes. As Voltaire later wrote in his *Elements of the Philosophy of Newton* (1739),

> Only quacks boast of universal medicines; and he would be a quack in philosophy, who should refer everything without proof to the same cause: the same force of mind, which enabled Newton to discover the power of attraction [gravity], made him confess that that power was far from being the sole agent of nature.
>
> (117)

In other words, Newton exemplified the Enlightenment spirit of Pierre Bayle.

Voltaire was finally allowed to return to Paris in 1729, thereafter making a fortune by stock speculation. He continued producing plays and began work on his *Histoire de Charles XII,* published in 1732, and *Le Siècle de Louis XIV,* eventually appearing in 1751. During this

period he also entered into two profound relationships. The first was with Emilie, Marquiese du Châtelet, whom he met around 1733, the second with Frederick II of Prussia, who began a correspondence in 1736, initiating a long, if at times difficult, friendship. From 1733 until her death from childbirth on September 10, 1749, Mme. du Châtelet and Voltaire enjoyed a deeply personal and intellectual partnership. Much of their shared passion centered on the sciences, carrying out studies at the Château de Cirey, Mme. du Châtelet the better mathematician. When the 24-year-old Frederick began his correspondence with Voltaire, he was still crown prince of Prussia (he assumed the throne in 1740). A passionate Francophile, he preferred French to German, and saw himself an enlightened monarch. In 1740, Voltaire helped to publish Frederick's *Anti-Machiavel,* a political treatise arguing that the ruler is the first servant of the people. At loose ends after the death of Mme. du Châtelet, Voltaire accepted Frederick's invitation to move to Berlin in 1750. The relationship quickly soured, and Voltaire was caught up in financial schemes and court intrigues, pillorying another of Frederick's *philosophes,* Pierre Maupertuis, president of the Berlin Academy of Sciences, in his *Diatribe du docteur Akakia* (1752). Fleeing Berlin in 1753, Voltaire and his niece, Mme. Denis, were detained in Frankfurt for a month by Frederick's agents. Subsequently, Voltaire would allude to Frederick's homosexuality, joking about "Potsdamites" (a conflation of Potsdam, Frederick's capital, and sodomite).

By 1755, unwelcome in both Berlin and Paris, Voltaire purchased Les Délices, an estate on the outskirts of Geneva, his first home of his own (and today the Institut et Musée Voltaire). In that year he published *La Pucelle,* a ribald mock-heroic treatment of Joan of Arc, noted, says George Bernard Shaw, for its "extravagant indecorum." On November 1, 1755 (All Saints Day), a deadly earthquake devastated Lisbon, Portugal. This terrible natural disaster set into sharp relief for Voltaire the relationship between natural evils and moral evil, challenging the optimistic view that "whatever is, is RIGHT." In response he composed "Poème sur le désastre de Lisbonne." The following year witnessed the start of the Seven Years War, pitting Prussia against France. Finally in 1757, Voltaire became entangled in controversy over the *Encyclopédie* of Diderot and D'Alembert, to which he had contributed a number of articles. The article "Geneva" composed by the editor D'Alembert, but influenced by Voltaire, declared that there was religious tolerance in Geneva because most of the Calvinist pastors were essentially deists, a statement putting Voltaire and his friends among the clergy in an awkward position. It was amid these conditions of controversy that Voltaire began work on *Candide* around 1757, publishing it in 1759 to immediate and continued success.

In 1759, Voltaire bought a château and park near the village of Ferney. Now the "patriarch of Ferney," he became a magnet for the leading men and women of letters, hosting visits from James Boswell, Adam Smith, and Edward Gibbon. Here too, Voltaire wrote his *Dictionnaire philosophique,* appearing in 1764, and carried out various campaigns, most notably that to restore the good name of Jean Calas, wrongly executed in 1762. In the last two months of his life, Voltaire returned to Paris in triumph, where he was feted and crowned with laurels at the Comédie Française during a performance of his last play, *Irène.* He died in Paris May 30, 1778, though arranged that his body be smuggled out of town for fear that the clergy would prevent its burial. During the French Revolution, Voltaire's body was returned to Paris where it was interred with great honor and ceremony in the Panthéon of Paris, where it still rests, near that of Rousseau.

CANDIDE: PLOT DEVELOPMENT

The text of *Candide* begins with the narrative fiction that it is translated from a German manuscript ostensibly found in the pocket of a certain Doctor Ralph upon his death at the Battle of Minden, August 1, 1759, a Prussian victory over the French during the Seven Years War. (The significance of the narrator Dr. Ralph is a point of debate, though it may allude to the character Ralpho, from Samuel Butler's *Hudibras* [1663, 1664, 1678], a long satirical poem patterned on *Don Quixote,* and much admired by Voltaire.) The narrative itself unfolds along a sort of three part dialectic, tracing the growth of Candide's mind, as he moves first from a position of naive optimism to an equally naive cynicism, finally emerging in a mature skeptical realism. Opening on a note reminiscent of a fairy tale, *Candide* begins with the narrator telling us that in Westphalia, in the castle of the Baron of Thunder-Ten-Tronckh, there lived a young man, who "combined an honest mind with a great simplicity of heart," for which reason, the narrator speculates, he is named Candide. He is under the care of the baron, and may be the illegitimate son of the baron's sister. The young Candide is in love with the baron's nubile daughter, Mademoiselle Cunégonde. Affirming the spirit of the fairy tale (ironically) Doctor Pangloss, the tutor of the baron's son has taught Candide that this is the "best of all possible worlds [*ce melleur des monde possibles*]," and correspondingly that the baron's castle is the most beautiful, and that the 350-pound baroness is the best of all possible baronesses. Pangloss, Voltaire's satire on the philosophical system-building of the philosophers Leibniz and Wolff, is a professor of "La métaphysico-théologo-cosmolonigologie." The name Thunder-Ten-Tronckh suggests a Frenchman's perception of what German sounds like. Westphalia is a real place, at the time a province of lower Rhineland near Holland. For Voltaire it was vast and empty, a fact that underlines the foolishness of the

snobbery and pretensions of the baron and his family, who claim a pedigree stretching back over "seventy-one quarterings," several thousand years. With a straight face, the narrator relates that "[t]he Baron was one of the most mighty lords of Westphalia, for his castle had a door and a window. His great hall was even hung with a tapestry" (*Candide* 1).

One day Mademoiselle Cunégonde observes Pangloss in the underbrush, "giving a lesson in experimental physics" to the lady's maid Paquette. Playing on this euphemism and parodying the language of Leibnizian metaphysics, the narrator adds, "as Mademoiselle Cunégonde had a natural bent for the sciences, she watched breathlessly the repeated experiments which were going on; she saw clearly the doctor's sufficient reason, observed both cause and effect, and returned to the house in a distracted and pensive frame of mind, yearning for knowledge" (2). When she attempts a similar experiment with the pliant and innocent Candide, they are discovered and Candide is ejected from "the earthly paradise." Thus expelled from his Eden, Candide begins years of wanderings and misadventures in search of happiness.

The cause of Candide's many misfortunes, and the targets of Voltaire's satire include the brutality of war, religious hypocrisy, intolerance, sectarianism, and colonialism, each in turn informed by greed, lust, violence, and foolishness. Almost immediately he is dragooned into the army of the Bulgars (the Prussians in Voltaire's political allegory) who are at war with the Abares (the French). Trained in the manual of arms, repeatedly flogged, and witness to a horrific battle, Candide eventually deserts, "climbing over ruins and stumbling over twitching torsos" (5). Candide next makes his way to Holland, where he is first spurned by a Christian who had been preaching the virtues of charity, next has a chamber pot emptied over his head, and is then finally befriended by Jacques, a good Anabaptist who owns a Dutch Persian-rugs factory.

One day Candide encounters a wretched beggar who turns out to be none other than Doctor Pangloss! The doctor explains that the castle of Thunder-Ten-Tronckh had been destroyed by the Bulgars and the baron and his family killed. Pangloss himself had received from Paquette a syphilitic inflection with a pedigree almost as venerable as that of the baron's family. Pangloss is cured through the good offices of Jacques with "only the loss of an eye and an ear" (8). (A lifelong hypochondriac, Voltaire never missed an opportunity to satirize physicians.) Despite his hardships Pangloss continues to maintain that this is the best of worlds. Jacques, being a good Anabaptist, rejects his optimism, but takes Pangloss on as a bookkeeper, and together all three sail to Lisbon on a business trip. As it turns out, it is none other than November 1, 1755, and they approach the harbor in time to experience the terrible tempest and the fatal earthquake of Lisbon. Jacques drowns, and Pangloss prevents Candide from trying to rescue his benefactor by logically demonstrating to him that the bay of Lisbon had been formed to drown the poor Anabaptist, an ironic death given his sectarian beliefs.

Amid the devastation of Lisbon, Pangloss and Candide are arrested and condemned to be sacrificed at an auto-da-fé as a preventative against future earthquakes. Pangloss is hanged, and Candide flogged yet again, this time to musical accompaniment. "If this is the best of all possible words," he muses to himself, "what are the others like?" (12). Anticipating a central theme, however, he adds that his own misfortune was not as bad as that which had befallen the dear Pangloss, the good Jacques, and the beloved Mademoiselle Cunégonde. At this point Candide is approached by an old woman (*la vieille*) who leads him to none other than Mademoiselle Cunégonde. After much ecstatic fainting at this unexpected reunion, she unfolds her story, explaining that although the rest of her family had been butchered by the Bulgars, she herself had became the mistress of a "handsome" Bulgar captain, initiating a series of exchanges that brought her in Lisbon, where she was currently the joint mistress of Don Issachar, a Jewish money lender, and the Grand Inquisitor. It is evident from her tone that Mademoiselle Cunégonde remains enthusiastic about "experimental physics." This sentimental interlude is suddenly interrupted with the unexpected appearance of Don Issachar, who attacks the couple with a dagger. Acting on reflex, Candide runs him through with his sword. At this point they are interrupted by the unexpected appearance of the Grand Inquisitor, who is similarly dispatched. "How is it that you, who were born so gentle," asks Mademoiselle Cunégonde, "could kill a Jew and a prelate in two minutes?" Candide replies, "when a man is in love, jealous, and just whipped by the Inquisition, he is no longer himself" (17). Recognizing the peril of their situation, Candide, Mademoiselle Cunégonde, and the old woman flee Lisbon for Cadiz where they take ship for Buenos Aires, a move from the Old World to the New. This interlude gives Voltaire an opportunity to cast light on the themes of utopia and European colonialism.

On the voyage, the old woman unfolds her story. She explains that she is none other than the daughter of Pope Urban X (historically there have only been eight Pope Urbans), that her beauty rivaled the Venus de Medici, and that she was engaged to a handsome prince. "[A]ll Italy composed sonnets in my honor of which not one was passable" (19). Here her troubles began. Her fiancé was poisoned by his mistress; she and her mother were captured and raped by Moroccan pirates. After plagues, earthquakes and further misfortune, she is sold into slavery, finding herself in the possession of a Turkish officer during the Russian siege of Azov. To

fend off starvation, the besieged Turkish defenders first ate the eunuchs, then the buttocks of the women. After the city falls, the old woman survives as a chambermaid, eventually working herself across Europe to Lisbon. "I grew old in misery and shame, having only half a *derrière* and remembering always that I was the daughter of a Pope." To this she adds, "A hundred times I wanted to kill myself, but always I loved life more" (23). The old woman's words, like Candide's earlier, underline a central theme in Voltaire's ethics. Experience teaches that humans seem to have a natural instinct to live, allowing us to endure misery and persevere, even when there is no apparent point to life. Paradoxically, everyone thinks his own suffering is worse than everyone else's, yet few consider their suffering so bad that they would willingly end their lives.

The New World proves no utopian escape from the Old. First the viceroy takes a fancy to Mademoiselle Cunégonde, then the authorities from Portugal arrive, seeking Candide for the murder of the Grand Inquisitor. Accompanied by a multilingual multi-racial servant named Cacambo, also a happy mixture of good nature and common sense, Candide flees to Paraguay. In the eighteenth century, Paraguay was a colony governed by the Jesuit missions (the Reductions). In his *Essai sur les moeurs,* Voltaire described this religious Arcadia as repressive, and Candide's experiences concur. (The 1986 Roland Joffé movie, *The Mission,* offers a different take on the Reductions as bastions of Enlightenment and tolerance until suppressed by the Portugese.) Here Voltaire again satirizes the conventions of the *conte* when it turns out that the reverend father commander of the Jesuits is none other than the young Baron Thunder-Ten-Tronckh, brother of Mademoiselle Cunégonde. He also had somehow survived the slaughter of the Bulgars, and through a series of (implied) homosexual relationships, become a priest and risen in the Jesuit order. Their tearful reconciliation is shattered when Candide tells the baron of his desire to marry Mademoiselle Cunégonde. The baron berates Candide's presumption and slaps him. Candide responds by running the baron through with his sword. Voltaire's portrait of the baron as a homosexual Jesuit is a satirical amalgam, alluding both to the Prussian arrogance of Frederick the Great and to the ingratitude of Jesuit Abbé Desfontaines, who had betrayed him in his *La Voltairomanie,* even though Voltaire had come to Desfontaines' aid in 1725 when the latter had been incarcerated for sodomy. Sizing up the danger, Cacambo and Candide disguise themselves as Jesuits and ride off into the wilderness towards Peru.

The next episodes develop the theme of utopia most explicitly. After various adventures in the "state of nature," they are caught by cannibals who are delighted at the prospect of roasting Jesuits. Trying to translate through Cacambo, Candide argues that Christian ethics forbade cannibalism. Instead Cacambo tells the cannibals that "the law of nature teaches us to kill our neighbor, and that's how men behave the whole world over. Though we Europeans don't exercise our right to eat our neighbors, the reason is simply that we find it easy to get a good meal elsewhere" (32). They are finally released when Cacambo convinces them that he and Candide are not really Jesuits. Here Voltaire plays with the philosophical concept of the state of nature, central to seventeenth and eighteenth century political thought, imagining the human condition outside the restraints of civil society. Do laws and human rights derive from nature, or are they constructed by society? British philosopher Thomas Hobbes likened it to a state of war, famously describing the natural human condition as "solitary, poor, nasty, brutish and short." Society, for Hobbes, is a means of protection from each other. Jean-Jacques Rousseau, on the other hand, saw humanity as fundamentally good, corrupted by the distortions produced by artificial systems that impede our natural instincts. Voltaire takes a more skeptical approach, echoing the views of Michel de Montaigne's essays, "On the Cannibals," and "On Coaches." Human nature remains universal, adapting itself to its circumstances. There is little fundamental difference between cannibals and Europeans, Montaigne concludes, aside from the fact that Europeans wear breeches.

Their journey next brings them to the Eldorado, the legendary land of gold sought by the conquistadores. They discover that the land is indeed covered with gold and precious gems, but also discover that the citizens of Eldorado are indifferent to or even contemptuous of the "yellow mud." Borrowing from Thomas More's *Utopia,* Voltaire imagines that gold and jewels are dismissed as merely suitable for children's toys. The citizens are well fed and educated, pursuing with enthusiasm the study of science and mathematics, much like Voltaire at Mme. du Châtelet's château de Cirey. There are no law courts or prisons, and no priests, except in the sense that everyone is a priest giving thanks to the goodness of God. When Candide asks an old man about religion in Eldorado, he replies, "Can there be two religions? . . . I suppose our religion is the same as everyone's, we worship God from morning to evening" (36). The old man's ingenuousness, underlines Voltaire's sad irony about the rest of the world.

Despite having actually found the real earthly paradise, the polar opposite of the estate of Baron Thunder-Ten-Tronckh, Candide still longs for Mademoiselle Cunégonde. This time he willingly chooses to leave Eden for the sake of his Eve. With a train of one hundred giant sheep (probably Voltaire's notion of the llama) packed with gold and jewels, Candide and Cacambo continue their journey to Surinam in order to find a ship for Europe. On the way they encounter a negro slave who had been mutilated and pinioned to the ground by his master, a Dutch sugar planter. "This" the

wretched slave explains, "is the price of the sugar you eat in Europe" (40). His words paraphrase those of Helvétius, who wrote in 1758 that "not a barrel of sugar arrives in Europe which is not stained with human blood" (qtd. in Mason 42). This is the final straw for Candide, who finally renounces his Panglossian optimism. Once in Surinam, Cacambo is sent off to Buenos Aires to find Mademoiselle Cunégonde and then to rendezvous with Candide in Venice. The latter then sets sail for the Old World with a new companion and mentor, Martin, a Manichean Dutchman. An absolute and dogmatic pessimist, Martin is the polar opposite of Pangloss, seeing an active force of evil in the world. While ultimately Candide (and Voltaire) reject the extreme cynicism of Martin's position for something more realistic, he offers an important corrective that allows Voltaire to sermonize on a number of political and social ills.

Candide's stay in Paris is the longest chapter and somewhat breaks the brisk pace of the narrative. Voltaire uses it as an occasion to satirize various aspects of Parisian society. Because he is now rich, he finds himself surrounded by "intimate friends" he did not know he had, and doctors he did not call. "[A]s a result of medicines and bleeding, Candide's illness became serious" (*Candide* 47). He also finds himself invited to various elegant salons, where he is seduced by beautiful ladies, and cheated at cards. The optimistic Candide is always surprised, the cynical Martin, never. For Voltaire (the playwright), however, the main target is the theater and the state of literature. Attending a play, Candide is moved to tears, only to be informed by a wit that the acting was bad and the play worse. He is impressed that some five or six thousand plays were written each year. Martin is impressed that as many as fifteen or sixteen were any good. Voltaire's position on art is most fully advocated by a dinner guest described as "a man of learning and taste [*un homme savant et de goût*]," who argues that too many tragedies fail because they try to be like novels. A good tragedy must aspire to naturalness in language and action, coming from a real understanding of the human heart. "[O]ne must know the language perfectly, speak it purely, and maintain a continual harmony without sacrificing sense to mere sound" (50). The man of learning and taste could well be Voltaire himself.

Finally fed up with Paris, Candide and Martin set sail for Venice, on the way encountering the execution of the English admiral, John Byng. The case of Admiral Byng had been one of Voltaire's many causes, and he had tried unsuccessfully to prevent the execution. When the incredulous Candide observes that the French admiral seemed as guilty of the same technicalities as the English, he is informed that "it is useful from time to time to kill one admiral in order to encourage the others" (55). In Venice, Candide is distressed not to find

Cacambo. The cynical Martin is not surprised at all. They do encounter Paquette, the baroness's former lady's maid, who is now working as a prostitute. She also has a lover, Brother Giroflée, a young Theatine monk. Both are in love, but both miserable. During the Venetian interlude, Candide and Martin visit the Venetian nobleman, Lord Pococurante; like the encounter with the man of learning and taste, this provides an opportunity for Voltaire to expound his views more explicitly.

The sixty-year-old Pococurante lives in fabulous luxury. His palazzo is surrounded by large gardens, adorned with beautiful statues, and hosts a fine art gallery and well-stocked library. Despite this he is bored with everything, except an occasional tryst with his two pretty serving girls, but admits that they are also starting to bore him. The encounter with Pococurante points out two themes, elaborating on the visit to Eldorado and the exchange with the Parisian man of learning and taste. On one hand Pococurante has created a sort of earthly paradise. He has no wants and can enjoy any material or cultural amenity that money can buy, yet he also is unhappy. By contrast, the citizens of Eldorado, who also enjoy great prosperity, are portrayed as truly happy. The difference is that they focus their attention on the pursuit of scientific knowledge while Pococurante seeks amusement.

Underlying this contrast, Voltaire reiterates the Aristotelean doctrine of happiness. In the *Nichomachean Ethics* Aristotle argues that happiness (*eudaimonia*) is the "highest realizable good" (1095a). Do we pursue happiness for some goal or purpose other than itself, or for its own sake? Aristotle deduces that if it is the highest good, then it represents an end in itself, and so has no other purpose than itself. He argues that two activities satisfy his criteria, amusement and contemplation, concluding that it is absurd to suppose people would willingly endure the pains and hardships of life simply in order to enjoy some amusement. He concludes that happiness is related to contemplation, the most godlike of activities, by which we struggle to go beyond ourselves by trying to understand the world. In pursuing material comfort and amusement, Pococurante has merely cultivated the animal side of human nature, and while he has found a surfeit of pleasure, he has not achieved happiness. By contrast, the citizens of Eldorado are active in the contemplation of nature. As such, they are continually discovering and creating, while Pococurante is merely the connoisseur of other people's creativity, simply repeating the same things over and over. The position is aptly summarized when Cacambo remarks to Candide, on their entry into Eldorado, "If we don't find anything pleasant, at least we may find something new" (33).

Pococurante's views on art and high culture also echo those of Voltaire. Like the man of learning and taste, Pococurante is dismissive of art that substitutes virtuos-

ity or effect for nature. Speaking of painting, he declares, "I like a picture only when I can see in it a touch of nature itself." Speaking of music, he notes, "[m]usic today is only the art of performing difficult pieces, and what is merely difficult cannot please for long" (60). For similar reasons, he is equally dismissive of most classical and modern literature. For Pococurante, the authority enjoyed by any of these cultural icons is based more on the opinion of other authorities than any self-evident merit. We admire them because we are told that we ought to admire them, supposedly a mark of our sophistication or cultural accomplishment. Too often, our culture is a display of vanity and pretension. "Fools admire everything in a well-known author," he says. "I read only for my own pleasure; I like only what is in my style" (61). For Candide, who had been trained never to think or judge for himself, this revelation is a moment of profound enlightenment.

The precariousness of political power is illustrated several days later, when Candide is dining in a hotel. Also dining are six strangers who had come to Venice for the carnival. They turn out to be Achmet III, former Sultan of Turkey; Ivan VI, dethroned Czar of Russia; Charles Edward of England (the so-called Young Pretender, Bonnie Prince Charlie); Augustus III, a King of Poland, deposed by Frederick the Great; Stanislas Leczinski, abdicated King of Poland (an actual friend and correspondent of Voltaire's); and finally Theodore, former King of Corsica. Such a convergence is historically impossible, but history is not Voltaire's point here. Each ruler had once enjoyed the authority of political power, and each had been overthrown. Candide, as a private citizen, has more freedom and means of action. Also present in this dining room is Sultan Achmet's slave, who turns out to be none other than Cacambo! His apearance is an important counter force on Martin's cynicism, for we learn that Cacambo had tried to keep faith with Candide. Telling his story, Cacambo explains how he had bought Mademoiselle Cunégonde from the viceroy in Buenos Aires, and then how they had been attacked by pirates and sold into slavery. Mademoiselle Cunégonde and the old woman are now slaves, washing dishes in the household of a Transylvanian prince living in Constantinople.

Liberated by Candide, the faithful Cacambo arranges passage for themselves, Martin, Paquette, and Giroflée on a galley headed for Constantinople. The final goal of the novel, however, is Candide's own liberation. Among the galley slaves they discover none other than Doctor Pangloss and the young Baron Thunder-Ten-Tronckh. Each had managed to survive his supposed demise, each had suffered further hardships, and each had been sentenced to the galleys for sexual indiscretions, Pangloss with a Turkish girl, and the baron with a Turkish boy. Candide buys their liberty and they join the growing band. Arriving finally in Constantinople Candide liberates Mademoiselle Cunégonde and the old woman. After so many years and hardships, however, reality does not live up to the long-cherished idea. Satirizing the romantic convention, Voltaire writes, "[t]he tender lover Candide, seeing his lovely Mademoiselle Cunégonde with her skin weathered, her eyes bloodshot, her breasts fallen, her cheeks seamed, her arms red and scaly, recoiled three steps in horror, and then advanced only out of politeness" (71). When the baron still persists in objecting to someone of Candide's class marrying his sister, the absurdity of the situation is more than Candide can stand. "You absolute idiot" he explodes, "I rescued you from the galleys, I paid your ransom, I paid your sister's; she was washing dishes, she is ugly, I am good enough to make her my wife, and you still presume to oppose it! If I followed my impulses, I would kill you all over again" (71). At long last Candide liberates himself from the vestiges of the old order, and dares to be wise.

In the end, Candide decides to marry Cunégonde more to spite the baron than from any desire. The baron is returned to the galleys and then Rome, providing the "double pleasure of snaring a Jesuit and punishing the pride of a German baron" (72). The rest of the band set up a household together on the outskirts of Constantinople. One day they visit a Turkish farmer who seems prosperous and happy. Supposing that he must own enormous lands, they are surprised when the Turk replies, "I have only twenty acres. . . . I cultivate them with my children, and the work keeps us from three great evils, boredom, vice, and want [*l'ennui, le vice, et le besoin*]" (74). So inspired, the group sets up its own little farm. The men work the fields, Paquette embroiders, the old woman does laundry, and Cunégonde, though "remarkably ugly," is an excellent pastry cook. And whenever there are any doubts, Candide reminds them, "we must cultivate our garden [*il faut cultiver notre jardin*]" (75). Having begun with expulsion from a symbolic garden of Edean, the *conte* closes with the creation of a new garden, the creation of a real (if provisional) earthly paradise.

CANDIDE AND THE CONVENTIONS OF THE TALE

Voltaire was widely read, and his work plays with and against assorted conventions of the tale, subverting the genre to foreground his thematic targets. The *conte* or tale was a popular literary genre in the eighteenth century, written in prose rather than verse, and manifest in a variety of types, including the allegory, the Italian *novella,* the picaresque novel, the apologue (moral fables such as those of Aesop), the exemplary tale, the oriental tale, the extraordinary voyage, the chivalric romance, the novel of education. Often the types overlapped. Extraordinary voyages are also occasions for didacticism and exotic perspectives. The basic plot of **Candide** follows that of the extraordinary voyage. This type of tale

looks back to ancient works such as Lucian's satirical *True Histories,* which inspired works such as Thomas More's *Utopia,* Cyrano de Bergerac's *Voyage dans la lune* (1657), and Swift's *Gulliver's Travels* (1726). Voltaire admired and drew on all four. The oriental tale, with prototypes in the *Arabian Nights,* and contemporary works as Montesquieu's *Persian Letters,* play on the perceived exoticism of the Middle East. The clash between cultural perspectives allows the author to look at European culture from a foreign perspective, bringing out irony by making the everyday appear strange. Elements of this directly occur when Candide and company find themselves in Turkey. In a deeper sense, however, Candide's complete innocence makes him an exotic stranger in his own world.

Since much of **Candide** is about its hero's education, the novel of education (the *bildungsroman*) is particularly important. François Fénelon's *Télémaque* (1699) was one of the most popular novels in eighteenth century France, setting the pattern. This book purports to fill in the gaps in Homer's *Odyssey,* relating the adventures of Odysseus's son Telemachus as he searches for his father. Integral to the conventions of this literary type, he is guided by the sage Mentor (Athena in disguise), who teaches him about morality, politics, and religion. Another novel of education of special importance is the philosophical novel *El Criticón* (1651, 1653) by the Spanish Jesuit Baltasar Gracián, much admired by Voltaire (and later Nietzsche and Borges). Its lengthy dialogues between the wise realist Critilo and his naive charge Andrenio, strongly resemble the exchanges between Martin and Candide.

The Italian *novella* featured stories ranging from the mixture of chivalry and scandalous love found in Boccaccio's *Decameron* to the frankly erotic *Dialogos de cortesanas* of Pietro Aretino. Madame de La Fayette's *Princesse de Clèves* (1678), which many consider the first psychological realistic novel, is one of the finest French novels derived from this type. Closely related to the *novella* is the Spanish picaresque novel, featuring the adventures of lowlife scoundrels and tricksters, the *picaro.* Among the most famous of these is *La Vida de Lazarillo de Tormes* (1554), itself an important source for Cervantes' *Don Quixote.* All of these look back to the Roman *Satyricon* of Petronius, about the sexual misadventures of the sponging Encoplius, Ascyltus, and Giton in their quest for a free dinner. The misadventures of Mademoiselle Cunégonde and the old woman owe much to the *novella,* and Cacambo to the *picero.*

Candide's name, like that of most of the characters, carries both comical and allegorical significance. Candide plays on the English "candid" in its eighteenth century usage, implying honesty, and the Latin "candidus," meaning "white" or "pure." The name of Mademoiselle Cunégonde, suggests either the medieval Germanic saint

Cunegunde, or an off-color amalgam of *cune* or *conne* ("bitch") and *gonde* ("cunt"), indicative of her active sexuality. Doctor Pangloss's name is constructed from Greek, signifying "all tongue," underlining the fact that his systems are empty words. The name Cacambo plays on the Spanish *caca,* a child's expression for excrement, or *caco,* signifying a "pickpocket" or "coward." The name of Paquette, the lady's maid who infects Pangloss, may pun variously on *pâquerette* ("daisy") and the English "pox," slang for syphilis. The name of her lover, Brother Giroflée derives from *giroflée* ("gillyflower"). The name of the Venetian nobleman Pococurante means "small care" in Italian. Finally, the passing reference to the King of the Bulgars (*le roi des Bulgares*) puns on the French *bougre* (a derogatory term for homosexual, related to the British expression *bugger,* which derives ironically from the adjective Bulgarian through a process of semantic narrowing). The Bulgars represent the Prussians, thus "King of the Buggers," another sly reference to Frederick the Great, one of Voltaire's many inside jokes.

Philosophical Themes

Amid the myriad philosophical references, inside jokes, and allusions, three prominent philosophical themes emerge. The first relates to utopia and the realistic limits of human happiness, the second relates to questioning authority and learning to judge for oneself, and the third to the provisional nature of life. *Candide* deploys a succession of communities, real and imaginary, from the Edenic Westphalia, the states of Holland, the New World, the Jesuit Reductions, Eldorado, the Republic of Venice, to the Turkish farm. Each is posited as a ideal community, a utopian "happy place," but an ideal inevitably subverted by a reality delivered with deadpan matter-of-factness. Each is really just a false tale, a philosophical fantasy. All of this underlines the fact that utopia, or the happy place, is not a location, but a state of mind. The dreary backwater of Baron Thunder-Ten-Tronckh's castle was the best of all possible worlds for Candide because he knew no better and because he was content with his life. The Turkish farmer is content with his lot because the satisfaction of his needs prevents him from being bored. Pococurante lives in real luxury, but is nevertheless bored because he prefers to amuse himself rather than stretch his mind; the Eldoradians have their needs satisfied, but then use their surplus of time to contemplate nature and are therefore happy. Underlying all of this is the persistence of human nature, paradoxically the one fundamental constant, our restlessness. For Voltaire, once our needs for survival are addressed, the best way to satisfy the mind is to keep busy, and best of all to pursue something new. The old woman summarizes the situation,

> I should like to know which is worse, being raped a hundred times by negro pirates, having a buttock cut off, running the gauntlet in the Bulgar army, being

flogged and hanged in an auto-da-fé, being dissected and rowing in the galleys—experiencing, in a word, all the miseries through which we have passed—or else just sitting here and doing nothing?

(72, 73)

Anticipating the Romanticism of a Goethe and the modern worldview, Voltaire sees life as open-ended, humans driven by a curiosity, or at least a restless impulse to assuage boredom. In his *Pensées,* philosopher and mathematician Blaise Pascal remarked "I have often said that the sole cause of man's unhappiness is that he does not know how to stay quietly in his room," Voltaire would have agreed with this diagnosis, if not Pascal's implication. What makes us human is the willingness and the courage to leave the room, a theme and metaphor that existentialist Jean-Paul Sartre picks up later in his 1944 play *No Exit.*

Closely related to the drive of curiosity is the willingness to question authority, to assume the Enlightenment spirit of skepticism, to judge for ourselves. The trajectory of Candide's education involves learning how to question his authorities, and ultimately learning how to trust his own judgement. The succession of his mentors traces a sort of dialectical pattern in which his wisdom comes from a process that both cancels and preserves: he first experiences the absolute optimism of Dr. Pangloss. This is then corrected by the absolute pessimism of Martin. Both dispositions are necessary states of mind, for without optimism we would find it hard to go forward, to face the risks of something new. Yet without pessimism, we would find ourselves the constant victims of experience. In the end Candide is left with a realistic view, neither the absolute certainty of Pangloss's optimism nor the absolute certainty of Martin's pessimism, but the skeptical position of "I don't know."

Several readers complain that the conclusion of *Candide* leaves us hanging. We do not know whether the farm will thrive or fail. We do not know if there will be yet another remarkable reunion or unexpected disaster. Perhaps members of the little band will become bored and strike out on yet another adventure. Such a conclusion is consistent with life and Voltaire's concept of realism. He rejects the artificial closure of the traditional tale or romance in which we are told that the heroes live happily ever after. Life and reality offer no such assurances. Whether in Paris or Potsdam, Cirey or Les Délices, Voltaire learned that life in the happy place is always provisional and precarious, always subject to the unexpected earthquake. Voltaire might well have appreciated the title to the closing chapter to Samuel Johnson's novel *The History of Rasselas, Price of Abyssinia,* published the same year as *Candide* and dealing with many of the same themes: "The Conclusion, in Which Nothing Is Concluded." Such an ending is closer to reality, to life as we actually experience it.

SUBSEQUENT INFLUENCE

By the end of its first year in publication (1759) *Candide* had gone through 17 editions, some 20,000 copies in print, in eighteenth century terms, a major achievement, and this despite the immediate condemnation of its "depravation" (Mason, *Candide* 14). It has remained widely in print ever since, drawing readers attracted to its crackling wit and gleeful subversiveness. The Marquis de Sade's novel *Justine* and George Bernard Shaw's play *Candida* and novella *The Adventures of the Black Girl in her Search for God* are direct parodies of *Candide,* and Leonard Bernstein turned it into a successful musical. Goethe considered Voltaire the greatest writer of all times, and Flaubert claimed to have read *Candide* 100 times. Later satirists as diverse as Mark Twain and Lytton Strachey took inspiration from it, as did the early economist Adam Smith, who alludes to Pococurante it in *The Wealth of Nations.* Finally, perhaps the enduring power of *Candide* rests in Voltaire's power to capture and articulate the human condition in a way that we still recognize. Writing in 1922 in the wake of the First World War, the novelist Aldous Huxley, himself skeptical of the utopian spirit of the modern world, observes, "the world in which we live is recognizably the world of Candide, Cunégonde, of Martin and the Old Woman. . . . The only difference is that the horrors crowd rather more thickly on the world of 1922 than they did on Candide's world" (Huxley 20, 21). In our age of competing ideologies, each a narrative tale claiming absolute authority, Huxley's assessment remains valid.

Suggested Readings

Aristotle. *The Basic Works of Aristotle.* Ed. Richard McKeon. New York: Random House, 1941.

Durant, Will and Ariel. *The Age of Voltaire,* Vol. 9 of *The Story of Civilization.* New York: Simon and Schuster, 1965.

Gay, Peter. *Voltaire's Politics: The Poet as Realist.* New Haven: Yale University Press, 1988.

Huxley, Aldous. *On the Margin: Notes and Essays.* New York: George H. Doran Co., 1923.

Kant, Immanuel. *The Philosophy of Kant: Immanuel Kant's Moral and Political Writings.* Ed. Carl J. Frederich. New York: Modern Library—Random House, 1977.

Mason, Haydn. *Candide: Optimism Demolished.* New York: Twayne Publishers, 1992.

————. *Voltaire: A Biography.* Baltimore: The Johns Hopkins University Press, 1981.

Pope, Alexander. *The Poems of Alexander Pope.* Ed. John Butt. New Haven: Yale University Press, 1963.

Voltaire. *Candide, or Optimism.* Trans. Robert M. Adams. 2nd. ed. New York: W. W. Norton, 1991.

————. *The Elements of Sir Isaac Newton's Philosophy.* Trans. John Hanna. London: Cass, 1967.

————. *Lettres philosophiques.* Ed. Frédéric Deloffre. Paris: Gallimard, 1986.

————. *The Philosophical Dictionary.* Trans. Peter Gay. New York: Harcourt, Brace & World, 1962.

————. *Philosophical Letters.* Trans. Ernest Dilworth. Indianapolis: Bobbs-Merrill, 1961.

————. *The Portable Voltaire.* Ed. Ben Ray Redman. New York: Viking Press, 1958.

Yolton, John W., ed. *The Blackwell Companion to the Enlightenment.* Oxford: Blackwell Publishers, 1991.

Melora G. Vandersluis (essay date 2007)

SOURCE: Vandersluis, Melora G. "Fate, Faith, and Freewill: Voltaire's *Candide* and Pascal's *Pensées.* In *Sublimer Aspects: Interfaces between Literature, Aesthetics, and Theology,* edited by Natasha Duquette, pp. 40-50. Newcastle upon Tyne, U.K.: Cambridge Scholars Publishing, 2007.

[*In the following essay, Vandersluis compares notions of fate, free will, and optimism in* Candide *with those in Blaise Pascal's* Pensées, *concluding that Voltaire depicts a random, hostile universe, while Pascal stresses the role of humankind's free will through self-knowledge and a relationship with God.*]

In "Lines Written in Early Spring" (1798), William Wordsworth asks, "Have I not reason to lament / What man has made of man?" (23-24). This powerful question is voiced in a myriad of ways by various artists, philosophers, writers, and social critics who follow Wordsworth, and by many who precede him. Of those predating Wordsworth, two with similar questions include Voltaire and Pascal; and both philosophers ask such questions with some degree of urgency, angst, and longing.[1] In Pascal's *Pensées* we find interwoven threads that ultimately form the patterns of an intricate tapestry. Reverberating issues include Pascal's thoughts on fate, freewill, and faith. Likewise, Voltaire writes *Candide* as a culmination of his thoughts on the nature of humanity, government, and religion. Though separated from Pascal by some fifty years, Voltaire, too, grapples with the same issues of fate, faith, and freewill.

Short and punchy, *Candide* will become Voltaire's most famous work. The under-girding question in *Candide* has to do with the nature of humankind—fraught, as he sees it, with evil tendencies and desires. Voltaire expounds on the "why" of the question through characters such as the Dervish and Martin. In Chapter Thirty of *Candide* the Dervish says,

What does it matter whether there is good or evil? When his highness sends a ship to Egypt, does he worry whether the mice on board are comfortable or not?[2]

This is the culmination of the bizarre and fantastical events of *Candide*: a sort of mild despair mitigated only slightly by the notion of cultivating one's garden to stave off boredom and depression. The message of the text—that God is not necessarily present or active on earth—is highlighted by the many atrocities that happen to humankind throughout *Candide.*

One of the goals of *Candide,* explored by many critics, is to dismantle the absurd notions of Pangloss (a.k.a. Leibniz or his followers) who maintains that all shall be well "in this best of all possible worlds."[3] Toward the end of the book, Candide sardonically asks Pangloss,

> [N]ow that you have been hanged, dissected, beaten to a pulp, and sentenced to the galleys, do you still think everything is for the best in this world?

With the gloss of Leibnizian philosophy, Pangloss replies,

> I am still of my first opinion . . . for after all I am a philosopher, and it would not be right for me to recant since Leibniz could not possibly be wrong.[4]

While no one, perhaps, is safe from the bitingly satirical pen of Voltaire in *Candide*—the Church, the Government, the French nobles, the naïvely trusting—his greatest remonstrance seems to go to representatives of Christianity, Protestant and Catholic alike. He finds in Christianity a palpable mixture of greed, narcissism, neglect of the poor, lechery, and absurdity.[5]

Paquette, the "pretty maidservant" to the Baroness, who gives Pangloss syphilis,[6] says that she "was perfectly innocent" until a Franciscan, her confessor, easily seduced her.[7] This is only one of the many misdeeds of the Franciscans, Jesuits, and most notably those who make up the Inquisitors. The Hebrew Don Issachar and the Grand Inquisitor both share Cunégonde for sexual favors; as Cunégonde explains,

> [H]e [the Grand Inquisitor] took notice of me at mass; he ogled me a good deal, and made known that he must talk to me on a matter of secret business. I was taken to his palace; I told him of my rank; he pointed out that it was beneath my dignity to belong to an Israelite [Don Issachar].[8]

Ultimately, a bargain is struck so that Don Issachar will spend time with Cunégonde on "Mondays, Wednesdays, and the Sabbath, the inquisitor would get the other days of the week."[9] In ironical fashion, Cunégonde says she is granted "an excellent seat" at the hangings and burnings ordered by the Grand Inquisitor for those heretical to the faith.[10]

In addition to being lecherous, the Franciscans and Jesuits are also painted as greedy, unscrupulous and hypocritical. The old woman, also known as the "daughter of Pope Urban the Tenth and the Princess of Palestrina,"[11] suspects the friar of pilfering their things, and she is right.[12] While they are in Paraguay, Cacambo, Candide's valet, says,

> I myself know nothing so divine as Los Padres, who in this hemisphere make war on the kings of Spain and Portugal, but in Europe hear their confessions; who kill Spaniards here, and in Madrid send them to heaven; that really tickles me.[13]

And it is the Jesuit brother of Cunégonde who is found living in luxury in Paraguay, dismissing "the negro slaves and the Paraguayans who [serve] his drink in crystal goblets"[14] while the natives are oppressed. He "thank[s] God and Saint Ignatius" a thousand times, but seems to have little gratitude for his servants and slaves.[15] He is further proved to be absurd when he initially embraces Candide as a brother and friend, and within minutes threatens to kill him because Candide wants to marry his sister.[16]

The absurdity associated with those who claim to be Christians is also highlighted in conjunction with Protestants. The orator from Chapter Three says to Candide, "[D]o you think the Pope is the Antichrist?" When Candide replies:

> I haven't considered the matter . . . but whether he is or not, I'm in need of bread," the orator sputters, "You don't deserve any . . . away with you, you rascal, you rogue, never come near me as long as you live.[17]

This is followed by "religious zeal" that prompts the orator's wife to empty a pot of something "scandalous" on their heads.[18]

In his *Voltaire,* Hadyn Mason argues that the Lisbon earthquake of 1755 has a profound effect on Voltaire and was "'a terrible argument against Optimism'" for him.[19] Yet, on 16 December 1755 Voltaire writes,

> [M]en do still more harm to each other on their little molehill than nature does to them. Our wars massacre more men than are swallowed up by earthquakes. If we had to fear only the Lisbon adventure in this world, we should still be tolerably well off.[20]

Mason argues that Voltaire's views increasingly lean towards Manichaeism, a belief system in which good and evil exist in the same time and space and where "evil has a life of its own quite independent of the forces of good in the universe."[21] In a letter to Mme du Deffand in May 1756, Voltaire wonders if "the evil cask [out of Jupiter's two casks of good and evil] could have constructed itself'; he senses that evil is a gargantuan and unruly force not necessarily controlled by human will.[22]

The world is not inherently good, Voltaire argues; natural catastrophes claim thousands of lives through pestilence, disease, calamity, and hunger. This is not the best of all possible worlds, and all is not well. Yet, the greater issue for Voltaire is the nature of humankind itself, imbued as it is with self-destructive tendencies, violence, and avarice. In extreme and even surrealistic terms, Voltaire paints a world in which everyone has philosophical opinions and no one makes sense. It is a world of physical and spiritual hunger in which the carrot is ubiquitously dangled and never able to be tasted.

Certainly there are personal connections between Voltaire's life and the characters in **Candide.** These autobiographical resonances range from Vanderdunder, "a name intended to suggest VanDuren, a Dutch bookseller with whom Voltaire had quarreled,"[23] to Voltaire's "unhappy experiences with Jewish financiers" leading to his unsavory depiction of Jews.[24] Voltaire's own personal experiences with the Parisienne government form much of the basis for **Candide.** As John Butt argues,

> The tortures, humiliations, and reversals of fortune which Candide and his friends undergo can all be traced in Voltaire's experience and reading.[25]

These experiences include being imprisoned in the Bastille twice and exiled from Paris for his writings. Voltaire also had his political reasons for setting Protestant against Catholic, and highlighting the hypocrisy of those proclaiming to be Christians. He had hopes of toppling what he saw as a stranglehold that the Church had over those in powerful positions.

Yet, beyond the personal vendettas, and political backdrop, Voltaire contemplates the problem of evil. He goes from asking why God would create a world of natural calamities and disasters to why he would create beings so riddled with pride and selfishness that they would destroy each other. Ultimately, Voltaire questions how much control and responsibility human beings have over themselves and their actions, and how much responsibility God has for creating them.

It is Candide who asks Martin,

> Do you believe . . . that men have always massacred one another as they do today? That they have always been liars, traitors, ingrates, thieves, weaklings, sneaks, cowards, backbiters, gluttons, drunkards, misers, climbers, killers, calumniators, sensualists, fanatics, hypocrites, and fools?

To which Martin replies,

> Do you believe . . . that hawks have always eaten pigeons when they could get them? . . . if hawks have always had the same character, why do you suppose that men have changed?[26]

Voltaire does not let the interchange continue after this; Candide merely trails off with a word about "freedom of the will" and they go on to the next event elucidating human folly.[27] Martin, the Manichean, says:

> [A]s I survey this globe . . . I think that God has abandoned it to some evil spirit . . . I have scarcely seen one town that did not wish to destroy its neighboring town, no family that did not wish to exterminate some other family.[28]

Even Candide concedes that there is "something devilish in this business."[29] Events are portrayed as out of the control of human choice or will.

In Chapter Twenty Two, while Martin and Candide are in France, they briefly discuss Pangloss, and Candide says, "The blemishes [on Pangloss] are made by men . . . who cannot do otherwise," to which Martin responds, "Then it is not their fault."[30] According to Haydn Mason, Voltaire's own letters reveal an intriguing coalescence between himself and "the self-styled Manichean Martin."[31] John Butt concurs with this view, contending that it is Martin "who comes as near as any character to speaking with Voltaire's voice."[32] Voltaire supports the idea of life as a cosmic game where humans are mere pawns and where the devil holds the unfair advantage.

It is interesting to note the congruence of Voltaire's work with the ethos of the Enlightenment. As a reaction to the religious wars of the sixteenth century, many *philosophes* and thinkers—among them Montaigne, Descartes, Hobbes, and Locke—found comfort in the idea of Rationalism: reliance on reason "rather than sense-perceptions, revelation, tradition, or authority."[33] Remarkably, it is Pascal, a mathematician and scientist, who argues that factual analysis is not incongruent with faith, and that humans do have freewill and are responsible for their choices.

Pascal, similar to Voltaire, grew up in precarious times, in what Ernest Mortimer describes as a period of "spiritual exhaustion."[34] With the onset of the Thirty Years' War, according to Mortimer, France became a "country given over to banditry, looting, sporadic forays and political anarchy."[35] Raised by his father after his mother's early death, Pascal was forced to flee with his father "for a time to Auvergne" because of the displeasure of Richelieu.[36] In 1647, Pascal fell ill "perhaps through overwork"[37] and the last "twelve months of Pascal's life were dark with sickness and grief." Yet he "died in physical distress but spiritual serenity."[38]

Although Voltaire wants to "defend humanity against this 'sublime misanthrope'" (Pascal),[39] perhaps Pascal and Voltaire are actually preoccupied with the same thing: "the relation between faith and reason, which is in effect the question of original sin."[40] Original sin in *Candide* is manifest in a number of chilling ways. Robert Adams contends,

> If man's reason, no less than his will, is fatally corrupted from birth, his only hope of understanding himself or the world lies in supernatural faith. In opposition to this crucial point, all the Enlightenment philosophers united.[41]

This includes Voltaire.

Yet, Pascal argues for such a faith—imbued with God's grace—and contends not that humans are powerless before a greater evil, but that humankind is riddled with inconsistencies, humanity being at once "sublime and abject, great and wretched, strong and powerless, all in one."[42] Humankind is

> chaotic, contradictory, prodigious, judging everything, mindless worm of the earth, storehouse of truth, cesspool of uncertainty and error, glory and reject of the universe.[43]

The answer, though, is not despair or ennui. In a beseeching passage, Pascal says,

> Be aware, then, proud men, what a paradox you are to yourselves! Humble yourself . . . Learn that humanity infinitely transcends humanity and hear from your Master your true condition of which you are unaware. Listen to God.[44]

It is through concerted listening that one comes to know something of God's grace—mysterious, bountiful, and transforming—and something of one's own heart. Ultimately, Pascal argues for anagnorisis, or seeing one's face in the mirror.

The notion of self-knowledge in the *Pensées* is complex, however, because it is likened to infinity. Ann T. Delehanty argues that Pascal must use approximations and representations—and that he ultimately finds human knowledge can only take one so far. "The concept of infinity," she contends, "has opened up hemorrhages in time, and in knowledge" for Pascal.[45] Knowledge—including self-knowledge—is ever expanding and sometimes elusive. Further, according to Alban Krailsheimer in *Pascal,* "there are three ways to knowledge [for Pascal] . . . authority, reason, [and the] senses," rather than Descartes's "pure reason."[46] "The purely human dualism of mind and matter must be transcended," states Krailsheimer, "which can only be done by grace, a third order not within our control, but which comes as a free, unearned gift from God."[47]

For Pascal, knowledge of the self must come from God, and God does not reveal everything to us. Pascal says,

> If we are made up of mind and matter, we can never totally understand simple things since the instrument which helps this understanding is partly spiritual.[48]

He adds, "not knowing by ourselves who we are, we can only learn it from God."[49] Pascal includes excerpts in the *Pensées* where God speaks in the first person, and it is He who says: "I am the only one who can teach you what your true good is and what your true state is. . . . [b]ut I do not want this knowledge to be so plain."[50]

In essence, Pascal insists that individuals must see themselves *as they are*—riddled with contradictions and inconsistencies, and in need of faith and God's grace. The emphasis is on self-knowledge—seeing one's face in the mirror—and being humbled and duly sobered by the reflection one receives. It is not "through the proud workings of our reason but the simple submission of reason that we can truly know ourselves,"[51] contends Pascal.

Pascal supports the notion of freewill—in the form of penitence, reflection, good decisions—and, simultaneously, he explores the mystery of faith and self-knowledge—ever expanding, defying categorical definition, and ephemeral. According to Pascal, we must seek to know ourselves, so that we may see our own limitations, but not so much that we become proud or self-sufficient.

The idea of self-knowledge is also interesting to ponder in *Candide,* for while all the characters are continually scandalized, saddened, and ultimately educated by the evil people and happenings around them, not much is said about the self-examination of the characters themselves. It is not for a lack of time that could be devoted to self-reflection, for on several occasions characters will "debate for fifteen days in a row,"[52] tell long and elaborate stories,[53] or argue at length "over metaphysics and morals."[54] But everything is about what is external to them: the injustice, depravity, and absurdity of others and of various philosophies. Little is said about a character's own epiphany. Cunégonde does not know she is ugly;[55] the Baron does not know he is absurd;[56] Pangloss does not know he is ridiculous—yet, each of these, along with Martin, Candide, and others, are quick to point out what is wrong with others (including God).

In the Greek world, both fatalism and the mandate of the oracle at Delphi, "know thyself," are interwoven; Voltaire hearkens back to the former, and Pascal, to the latter. "Know thyself" in the Greek system, however, meant knowing the prodigious capacity of humanity to explore facets of heaven and earth—congruent with Protagoras's claim that man is the measure of all things. Humankind comes to deceit, ruin, and infamy because of the capricious Gods and Goddesses—external forces outside of oneself. Pascal argues that the enemy is within; Voltaire's work—though complex—points to the idea that there are forces at work outside of humankind that cause destructiveness.

Candide ends with the concept of boredom—also explored in Pascal's *Pensées.* In Chapter Eight, "Contradictions," Pascal argues:

> [People] do not themselves know themselves. . . . They sincerely think they are seeking peace and quiet, whereas they are really seeking agitation. . . . The whole of life goes on like this. We seek repose by battling against difficulties, and once they are overcome, repose becomes unbearable because of the boredom it engenders.[57]

Voltaire faces this same conundrum in *Candide.* At the end of the book, "the boredom [is] so intolerable" that the old woman remarks:

> I should like to know what is the worst, to be ravished a hundred times by negro Pirates, to have one buttock cut off, to run the gauntlet of a Bulgar regiment, to be whipped and hanged at an auto-da-fé, to be dissected, to row in the galleys—in fact, to experience all the miseries through which we have passed—or just stay here with nothing to do?[58]

Martin's conclusion is that "man [is] born to suffer from the restlessness of anxiety or from the lethargy of boredom."[59] Even though Candide does not comment and Pangloss prattles on about things turning out for the best, the narrator says that an incident "confirms Martin" in his views.[60] The incident also involves the Dervish who seems to have the last word. It is he who argues that humankind is like the mice on a ship: not to be worried about by the powers that rule. When asked what can be done about this, the Dervish exclaims, "Keep your mouth shut!"[61]

Candide closes with the idea that the cosmic game goes on and humankind cannot change certain things. Perhaps the garden can be tended to, but for how long before a skirmish threatens the peace due to dissention or sheer boredom? Even God seems to be entertained by such sport; it is all part of the show.

For Pascal, humankind is intensely paradoxical, but freewill imbues us with both accountability and the prospect of change. He insists that humans must choose both grace and works in order for true transformation to take place. "If you are united with God," he asserts, "it is through grace, not nature. If you are humbled, it is through penitence, not nature."[62] Penitence is made possible only through acknowledgement and ownership of one's own failings. Rather than mice on a ship, humans are endowed with will, reason, and responsibility. This means both suffering and joy.

Pascal also places great emphasis on thinking. "All our dignity consists therefore of thought," he says, ". . . [s]o let us work on thinking well."[63] Yet, the mystery of faith is also found ubiquitously throughout the *Pensées.* It is a free gift that nevertheless costs everything. It is

no work at all and it is simultaneously the most demanding of all work. One must choose each day whether or not to accept it.

Voltaire courageously and colorfully addresses questions relevant to all: what is the nature of humankind? To what extent do we have freewill? What is the nature of evil? Ultimately, he seems to question whether there is anything to be optimistic about in a world imbued with inexplicable puzzles. Yet, while it is "foolish self-deception to close our eyes to the evils which everywhere confront us,"[64] Pascal offers hope in the admonishment to truly see oneself—and one's great need.

Notes

1. Interestingly, Wordsworth shares another similarity with Pascal. It was William Wordsworth who struggled ardently to write *The Recluse,* which he believed would be his magnum opus. However, it is Wordsworth's *The Prelude,* meant to be his simple introductory comments, that today is his most remembered, revelatory, and celebrated text. Similarly, Pascal, some three hundred years earlier, strove to write "his projected work on religion" with "'proofs,' 'persuasion,' 'marks of certainty and evidence'" (xix) and ended up with the *Pensées*—an unfinished collection of thoughts "never meant to be read." Levi, xx, xix, & vii. The *Pensées* remains his most accessible and successful work, though it was never intended to be so.

2. Voltaire, *Candide,* 73.

3. Ibid., 2. Albert Schweitzer in *The Philosophy of Civilization* contends that Gottfried Wilhelm Leibniz (1646-1716) holds to the "religion of reason," which Schweitzer describes as the "optimistic-ethical world-view reproduced in a Christian phraseology . . . preserving within it the Christian theism, and the belief in immortality. An all-wise and wholly benevolent Creator has produced the world, and upholds it in corresponding fashion. Man is endowed with freewill, and discovers in his reason and his heart the moral law which is meant to lead individuals and mankind to perfection." Schweitzer, 170.

4. Voltaire, *Candide,* 70.

5. Interestingly, there is one notable exception here: a very brief reference to "a good Anabaptist named Jacques," who helps Candide when he is in need. Jacques is referred to specifically as a "man who had never been baptized," and who seems separated from organized religion. Apparently, Voltaire "had a high opinion of contemporary Anabaptists" perhaps because of their "radical views on property and religious discipline" which ultimately

"made them unpopular during the sixteenth century" (6). It is significant, however, that Voltaire satirically has Jacques die by drowning two chapters later, which Pangloss says is for the best (9).

6. Voltaire, *Candide,* 8.

7. Ibid., 57.

8. Ibid., 15.

9. Ibid.

10. Ibid.

11. Ibid., 19. Voltaire argues that he has used "extreme discretion" in "avoiding attributing a bastard to a known pope," as "hitherto there has never been a pope named Urban X." Ibid.

12. Ibid., 17.

13. Ibid., 26.

14. Ibid., 28.

15. Ibid.

16. Ibid., 29.

17. Ibid., 6.

18. Ibid.

19. Hadyn Mason, *Voltaire,* 79.

20. Quoted in Mason, 80.

21. Mason, 81.

22. Ibid.

23. Ibid., 40.

24. Ibid., 72.

25. Butt, Introduction to *Candide,* 10.

26. Voltaire, 46.

27. Ibid.

28. Ibid., 44.

29. Ibid.

30. Ibid., 104.

31. Mason, 81.

32. Butt, 11.

33. Harmon and Holman, *A Handbook to Literature,* 427.

34. Mortimer, *Blaise Pascal: The Life and Work of a Realist,* 28.

35. Ibid.

36. Krailsheimer, *Pascal,* 5.

37. Ibid., 8.

38. Ibid., 11.

39. Quoted in Cassirer, "Religion," 145.

40. Adams, 167.

41. Ibid.

42. Cassirer, 143.

43. Pascal, 41.

44. Ibid., 42.

45. Delehanty, "Morality and Method in Pascal's *Pensées,*" 80.

46. Pascal, 23.

47. Krailsheimer, 53.

48. Pascal, 71.

49. Ibid., 56.

50. Ibid., 54.

51. Ibid., 43.

52. Voltaire, 45.

53. Ibid., 14-16; 19-21, etc.

54. Ibid., 72.

55. Ibid., 71.

56. Ibid.

57. Ibid., 46.

58. Ibid., 140.

59. Ibid., my italics.

60. Ibid.

61. Ibid., 142.

62. Pascal, 55.

63. Ibid., 73.

64. Cassirer, 147.

Bibliography

Butt, John, trans. Introduction to *Candide,* by Voltaire, 7-15. London: Penguin, 1947.

Cassirer, Ernst. "Religion." In *The Philosophy of the Enlightenment,* edited and translated by Fritz Koelln and James P. Pettegrove, 134-96. Princeton: Princeton UP, 1951.

Delehanty, Ann T. "Morality and Method in Pascal's *Pensées.*" *Philosophy and Literature* 28 (2004): 74-88.

Harmon, William and C. Hugh Holman. *A Handbook to Literature.* 7th ed. Upper Saddle River: Prentice Hall, 1996.

Krailsheimer, Alban. *Pascal.* New York: Hill and Wang, 1980.

Levi, Anthony. Introduction to *Pensées and Other Writings,* by Blaise Pascal, vii-xxxvii. Oxford: Oxford UP, 1995.

Mason, Haydn. *Voltaire: A Biography.* Baltimore: The Johns Hopkins UP, 1981.

Mortimer, Ernest. *Blaise Pascal: The Life and Work of a Realist.* New York: Harper and Brothers, 1959.

Pascal, Blaise. *Pensées and Other Writings.* 1660. Edited by Anthony Levi and translated by Honor Levi. Oxford: Oxford UP, 1995.

Schweitzer, Albert. *The Philosophy of Civilization.* Translated by C. T. Campion. Tallahassee: University Presses of Florida, 1981.

Voltaire, François Marie Arouet. *Candide.* 1759. Translated and edited by Robert Adams. 2nd ed. New York: Norton, 1991.

Wordsworth, William. *William Wordsworth: Selected Poems and Prefaces.* Edited by Stillinger. Boston: Houghton Mifflin, 1965.

Robert Vilain (essay date 2008)

SOURCE: Vilain, Robert. "Images of Optimism? German Illustrated Editions of Voltaire's *Candide* in the Context of the First World War." *Oxford German Studies* 37, no. 2 (2008): 223-52.

[*In this essay, Vilain surveys the implications of the artwork in various German illustrated editions of* Candide *in the period of 1913-1922 (when France was an enemy nation to Germany), discussing the personal and political context of each edition as well as its implications for interpreting the idea of optimism.*]

I

'Es ist ein bitteres Buch, dieser **Kandide** [**Candide**], der die ganze Verlorenheit unserer Existenz mit schneidender, grausamer Erbarmungslosigkeit aufdeckt', writes the editor of a 1920 German edition of Voltaire's classic *conte* in his afterword, repeating himself for good measure a page later: 'Es ist ein bitteres Buch, dieser **Kandide,** eines der bittersten, pessimistischsten, die je geschrieben wurden, erbarmungslos und schneidend im verzweifelten Hohn seiner Satire.'[1] One of the leading contemporary Anglo-Saxon Voltaire scholars takes a rather different view of this most famous of

tales: 'It is, of course, a satire on Optimism [. . .]. It is also a satire on systems; a discussion of the problem of evil; a comparison of Utopia and reality; a pursuit of the secret of happiness; an education; and, above all, a comedy.'[2] At first sight there is a fairly simple explanation for this radical difference of approach, since the German editor, the poet and essayist Peter Hamecher, was writing shortly after the end of the First World War, in the wake of turmoil likely to mute anyone's sense of humour. The catalogue of violence that is **Candide**—which includes rape, decapitation, murder at the sword, torture, disfigurement, burning, hanging, drowning and shooting, to mention only those inflicted by one human being on another—may have been drawn up some 150 years previously, but in 1920 memories of the violence of a world war were very recent. Hamecher reads **Candide** exclusively as a response to the Lisbon earthquake, Voltaire's 'vernichtende Satire', an articulation of his fury at the inadequacies of Leibnitzian Optimism in the face of physical and moral ills: 'Ein grausamer Enthüller reißt die Binden von den Wunden und Gebresten der Menschheit.'[3] He does not make explicit the comparison with his own time, but his own anger and frustration with humanity's inhumanity is evident in every line.

Candide has often been the vehicle for reflections like this on the problems of an age far removed from the Enlightenment. In the programme notes to the spectacular recent production of Leonard Bernstein's **Candide** at the English National Opera, Nicholas Cronk deftly indicates just how richly resonant Voltaire's work has been for succeeding generations of writers:

> When W. H. Auden contemplated Fascism in Europe in 1939, he wrote a poem 'Voltaire at Ferney'. When Bernstein was a witness to McCarthyism in the USA in the early 1950s, he composed **Candide.** When the Italian novelist Sciascia observed the conflict between Marxism and Christianity in post-war Italian society, he wrote his novel *Candido* (1977). For as long as there are fanatics promoting their '-isms', we will go on reading and re-reading **Candide.**[4]

One might almost expect the generation that produced a cluster of editions of **Candide** on either side of the First World War in the second and third decades of the 20th century to make such links, and indeed some did so. However, the political context was certainly not the only factor influencing their choice to illustrate this work and the picture that emerges from comparing a series of five sets of images produced between 1913 and 1922 for German readers of the French classic is a more complex one than Hamecher's indignation has room to accommodate.

From the outset there has been a strong tension with German and the German lands inscribed both within **Candide** and in its contexts.[5] Not only is the opening set in a fictional Westphalian castle owned by Baron Thunder-ten-tronckh, the story was originally published in 1759 as if it had been translated from the German of a certain 'M. le docteur Ralph'. From the 1761 edition onwards we learn that the text also includes additions supposedly retrieved from Dr Ralph's pocket when he died in Minden in 1759.[6] Both names are in fact more English than German—most German translators have even felt that Thunder-ten-tronckh needs to be translated as Donnerstrunkshausen or Donnerstrunckh—probably because, whilst Voltaire had learned some English during his exile in London between 1726 and 1729, he always hated German and never troubled to master even the basics of the language. He also especially loathed '[la] détestable Westphalie' and its 'chien de territoire', writing to Frederick II during a journey through Germany in 1740, 'O champs westphaliens, faut il vous traverser? / Destin où m'allez vous réduire!'[7] It was the Seven Years War (including the Battle of Minden) that provided the backdrop for the warfare in *Candide*, too—and Frederick II appears in the form of the King of the Bulgares to save and pardon Candide—so Voltaire's choice of a German province as the location for Candide's supposed 'paradis terrestre' (p. 147) is suffused with irony. In a further twist, German commentators in 1759 originally took Dr Ralph's nationality seriously and claimed to have identified Gottsched as the true author of *Candide*—which provoked a fierce rebuttal by Gottsched and some counter-teasing by Moses Mendelssohn and Lessing.[8]

The first German version of *Candide* appeared two years after its first publication in French, in 1761, under a pseudonym, without place of publication, dated wrongly (1751) and entitled simply *Die beste Welt*.[9] The translator was Johann Albrecht Philippi, who was in 1771 to become Berlin's 'Stadtpräsident' and its Chief Constable and was the architect of a policing system based on French models. Philippi also appended a continuation of *Candide* attributed to Thorel de Champigneulles. In a move that multiplies the false trails most entertainingly, he pretended to be 'Dr Ralph'—now equipped with Johann and Albrecht as his first names—translating the work of a Spanish priest and member of the Inquisition, Don Ranudo Maria Elisabeth Francisco Carlos Immanuel de Collibradoz. This is, in fact, an embellishment of the name of an impoverished scion of the old nobility in a comedy by the Danish dramatist Ludvig Holberg, *Don Ranudo de Colibrados* (written in 1723 and adapted by Kotzebue in Switzerland in 1745). Ranudo is of course 'O du Nar[r]' spelt backwards, which would no doubt have amused Voltaire had he been aware of it.

None of these editions is illustrated and Voltaire himself was opposed to the inclusion of any illustrations in editions of his works, writing to the publisher Panckoucke in 1778, 'Je crois que des Estampes seraient fort in-

utiles. Ces colifichets n'ont jamais été admis dans les éditions de Cicéron, de Virgile et d'Horace. Il faut imiter ces grands hommes dans cette simplicité si on ne peut pas imiter leurs perfections.'[10] Nevertheless, Charles Monnet made six engravings for a 1778 edition of the *Romans et contes de M. de Voltaire*,[11] and two small sets (of four and seven engravings) were produced in France in 1787 and 1803 by Jean-Michel Moreau Le Jeune.[12] An early German edition, a 1778 translation by Wilhelm Christhelf Sigismund Mylius entitled *Kandide oder die beste Welt,* has six engravings by the prolific Polish-German painter and printmaker Daniel Nikolaus Chodowiecki,[13] who was thus, with Monnet, the first of *Candide's* illustrators. Mylius's translation was generally well received (and re-issued four times). A contemporary reviewer fully appreciates the humour of the original:

> Bey Produkten von der Art des hochberühmten Kandide ist die Uebersetzung nur alsdann wichtig, wenn unsere Sprache dabey durch Uebertragung launichter Gedanken Zuwachs gewinnt, neue glückliche Wendungen erhält; kurz reicher und geschmeidiger wird. Ohne diese Vortheile mag Kandide immer unübersetzt, und von ehrlichen deutschen Lesern ungelesen bleiben. Die andern, Glückliche und Große, die zur Beförderung der Verdauung ekelhafter Gemälde des menschlichen Elendes nöthig haben, mögen ihn im Originale lesen, und sich an der verstellten Wahrheit satt lachen, gegen die man hier mit Witz, wies oft geschieht, zu Felde zieht.[14]

The Mylius version soon displaced Philippi's as the standard German text and served as the basis for some of the 20th-century editions of *Candide* that are the subject of this article.

II

On the centenary of Voltaire's death Friedrich Nietzsche dedicated *Menschliches, Allzumenschliches* to his memory: 'Dem Andenken Voltaire's geweiht zur Gedächtnis-Feier seines Todestages, des 30. Mai 1778', adding on the back cover: 'Dieses monologische Buch [. . .] würde jetzt der Öffentlichkeit nicht übergeben werden, wenn nicht die Nähe des 30. Mai 1878 den Wunsch allzu lebhaft erregt hätte, einem der größten Befreier des Geistes zur rechten Stunde eine persönliche Huldigung darzubringen.'[15] Another individualist, just as implacably opposed to the injustices that societies inflict upon those who fail to conform, Nietzsche nonetheless admired 'Voltaires maßvolle, dem Ordnen, Reinigen und Umbauen zugeneigte Natur', and praised him as the last of the great dramatists, 'welcher seine vielgestaltige, auch den grössten tragischen Gewitterstürmen gewachsene Seele durch griechisches Maß bändigte', possessing 'griechische Schlichtheit und Anmut' and a unique combination of intellectual freedom with an 'unrevolutionary' temperament.[16] To be sure, Nietzsche's admiration for Voltaire is by no means unqualified, and it is sometimes deployed more strategically than unselfishly, Voltaire serving 'merely as the stick with which to chastise Wagner',[17] but it represents a turning-point in the reception of Voltaire in Germany after a century of under-appreciation in the wake of Goethe's rather tepid response. In the notes to *Le Neveu de Rameau* (1805), for example, Goethe had described Voltaire guardedly as 'der höchste unter den Franzosen denkbare, der Nation gemäßeste Schriftsteller'.[18] The standards of the French with respect to their 'great men', he says, are 'wo nicht größer, doch mannigfaltiger als die andrer Nationen'. If in later life he was more respectful of Voltaire's integrity, he never manifested true enthusiasm.[19]

By the turn of the 20th century, however, Voltaire had become representative amongst Germans worried about their country's increasing nationalism for tolerance, rationality, and the defence of civil liberties, individual rights, social reform and freedom of confession.[20] In 1916 Gustav Landauer published a short introduction entitled 'Zu Ehren Voltaires' in the periodical he edited, *Der Sozialist,* where it precedes extracts from Josef Popper's 1878 volume on social reform, *Das Recht zu leben und die Pflicht zu sterben,* whose subtitle refers specifically to the importance of Voltaire for the modern age.[21] The section quoted by Landauer begins: 'Die europäische Menschheit atmete im schweren Dunkel, sie ging eingebeugt einher; die Menschen hatten nicht den Mut, sich aufrecht zu erhalten', which in its original context is a reference to the *ancien régime,* but which, published in Germany in 1914, targets the militaristic Wilhelmine regime. Many other Socialist writers, including René Schickele, Hugo Ball, Iwan Goll, Ludwig Rubiner and Kurt Tucholsky, drew upon the symbolic force of Voltaire and on his individual works to construct a mirror in which their own society might contemplate its increasingly erratic and disastrous development. Victor Hugo's address to the Académie Française on the hundredth anniversary of Voltaire's death was translated and published in 1917—during the war itself, therefore—as the first volume in the series 'Der rote Hahn' published by the Verlag die Aktion. The brothers Mann articulated aspects of their protracted and paradigmatic differences during and after the war by propounding the virtues of two contrasting emblematic figures, Goethe (Thomas) and Voltaire (Heinrich).

Such interest rested partly on the publication of German editions of Voltaire during the late 19th and early 20th centuries, and on a spate of academic interest in him. A volume of *Erzählungen* in versions by Ernst Hardt appeared in 1908, reprinted in 1924; *Die Romane und Erzählungen* under Ludwig Rubiner's editorship and illustrated with the drawings by Moreau le Jeune, were published by Kiepenheuer in 1920.[22] There is no shortage of scholarly investigation of Voltaire and his works during this period. The journal *Die Hilfe* published a

two-part essay on Rousseau and Voltaire in 1912;[23] Hermann August Korff's huge study *Voltaire im literarischen Deutschland des XVIII. Jahrhunderts* appeared during the war, in 1917. A few years later, in 1923, a translation of Georg Brandes's two-volume study entitled simply *Voltaire* appeared with Erich Reiss in Berlin. The opening paragraphs of Brandes's work reflect something of the passion of the epoch:

> Es war einmal ein Nervenbündel, mit Elektrizität geladen, das Europa einnahm und erleuchtete. [. . .]
>
> Es war einmal ein Dämon, dessen Geist Feuer und dessen Einfälle blitzartig waren, dessen Herz warm in Hingebung und Freundschaft schlug, während sein Verstand in leuchtender Klarheit kalt war.[24]

This work made a great impression, as a note in Thea Sternheim's diary confirms.[25] Sternheim at one stage planned her own edition of Voltaire in conjunction with the Institut Jean Jacques Rousseau, but it never came to fruition.[26]

III

Candide attracted more attention during this period than any of Voltaire's other works.[27] In 1912 the Georg Müller Verlag in Munich brought out a reprint of the 1782 Berlin edition in Mylius's translation with the illustrations by Chodowiecki.[28] Müller was a bibliophile 'Kulturverleger' who concentrated on making *belles lettres* from Europe, Britain and the United States accessible in German to as broad a public as possible in series such as 'Klassiker des Altertums', 'Perlen älterer romanischer Prosa', 'Welttheater' and 'Denkwürdigkeiten aus Altösterreich' that sometimes had as many as thirty titles. Many of these reprinted original illustrations, since for all his vision and zeal, the redoubtable Müller was with a few exceptions (such as Alfred Kubin) not especially interested in contemporary or avant-garde book illustration *per se.*[29]

Another edition of *Candide* appeared in 1913, in Ernst Hardt's translation and with twelve full-page woodcuts and thirty capitals by Max Unold.[30] This was one of the Insel Verlag's limited editions (albeit hardly a typical one, quite unlike its more famous editions of Oscar Wilde or Hugo von Hofmannsthal by Heinrich Vogeler). It was a single edition of only 800 copies, the first 30 on China paper, and unlike the Müller publication was intended for art-lovers rather than a diverse readership. 1920 saw two editions, the first another (edited) version of the Mylius translation brought out by Morawe & Scheffelt in Berlin with illustrations by Josef von Divéky[31]—which combined a popular edition with a luxury subscription version of 250 copies, including separate full-page illustrations—and, by far the more famous, Kurt Wolff's edition with Paul Klee's drawings.[32] Wolff had made a name for himself as a publisher of Expressionist literature—his influential series 'Der jüngste Tag' announced itself in 1913 as 'eine Reihe von Schöpfungen der jüngsten Dichter, hervorgebracht durch das gemeinsame Erlebnis unserer Zeit'[33]—and Klee's drawings are sometimes described as variants of Expressionism. Alfred Kubin's illustrations for *Candide* appeared two years after Klee's with Steegemann in Hanover,[34] a mass edition with some fifty additional copies printed on luxury paper, and in the same year Ottomar Starke produced a set of fourteen lithographs with a foreword by Franz Blei—an edition of 100, 85 copies of which were sold by subscription.[35]

Of the six illustrated editions of *Candide* issued in German between 1912 and 1922, therefore, the first maintained the illustrations that had been current in German-language versions of Voltaire since 1778 and the last actually dispenses with Voltaire's text altogether. The artists are of varying origins: two are German (Unold and Starke), one Swiss-born (Klee), one Polish-born (Chodowiecki), one born in Bohemia (Kubin) and the last Hungarian (Divécky). Only one set of illustrations—Klee's—is nowadays widely regarded as of special artistic or aesthetic importance, although as we shall see it is somewhat anomalous within Klee's own *oeuvre*. Four of the six were aimed at a broad public, two exclusively at wealthier book or arts collectors. Despite these variations and inconsistencies, however, this group of works is unified by having been inspired by a work from what was between 1914 and 1918 an 'enemy' culture and from a bygone age.

The illustrations by Daniel Nikolaus Chodowiecki (1726-1801) are of course genuine products of that bygone age and offer a useful benchmark against which to assess the others. They are highly detailed, naturalistic renderings of five moments in Candide's history, densely drawn, all with patches of heavy shadow, and—from the perspective of a 21st-century reader—at first sight a little ponderous.[36] When Pangloss explains the 'raison suffisante' (p. 147) for the existence of the human nose (which exists to rest spectacles on), for example, Chodowiecki depicts the whole baronial family arrayed before him in a dark corner of a decorated chamber, their lower bodies and most of the background in heavy shadow. In fact, however, there is much humour here. The text of Voltaire's tale makes no mention of 'group tuition'; the implication is that only the younger members of the household are instructed; so by including the portly Baron (head bowed, mouth turned down in what looks like a groan) and his even portlier and rather sulky 350-pound wife as part of a captive audience, Chodowiecki's Pangloss is made to look even more martinet-like. In contrast to the Baron and his wife, Candide is especially slim; he and Cunégonde's brother are listening, Candide with his hands in his pockets, but Cunégonde is staring out of the image at the reader.[37] The light from the window falls in a pool

on the five faces of the audience and full-length on Pangloss himself, capturing the absurdity of the scene almost in a snapshot.

Composition is one of Chodowiecki's strengths. Another illustration shows Candide at the point where he is being booted out of the château of Thunder-ten-Tronckh because of his hanky-panky with Cunégonde behind a screen. Only Cunégonde's face is visible—the two men are seen from the back only, the Baron's more elaborate frock coat and curlier wig brightly lit in the foreground, Candide's simpler vestments in the middle distance, their shadows falling across each other on the tiled floor. Cunégonde is entirely in shadow. The Baron's right arm and leg are lifted and Candide is leaning forward, propelled away from the swooning Cunégonde to his left. As one commentator has put it, the two men seem to be moving *into* the picture,[38] and indeed Chodowiecki has created a marvellous impression of depth, in part by reducing the space in which the action occurs to its simplest components—a corner of a rectangular room and the five-panelled screen—placing the whole emphasis of the scene on the protagonists. There are no props, except the handkerchief that triggered the lovers' moment of passion still clutched in Cunégonde's hand, and there is only the merest sliver of decoration on part of one of the screen panels to the left of the picture. And yet the image is full of emotion, shock, anger and fear on the part of the three figures.

Chodowiecki became the best known German book-illustrator of his age. He was hugely prolific and widely respected, ending his career as director of the Kunstakademie in Berlin. Many of his most famous works—including another Voltaire-inspired subject, *Jean Calas Bidding Farewell to his Family* (1767), and the self-portrait with his own family, *A Painter's Cabinet* (1771)—have elements of sentimentality about them, but the *Candide* illustrations are entirely free of this. Their tone is set by the vignette of Voltaire himself on the title page, hunched over a desk, the peak of his cap echoing the jut of a determined chin and the protrusion of a large, sharp nose; Chodowiecki's characteristic light-effects illuminate the intimate scene from over the writer's shoulder, shedding light on his face and his quill. Voltaire is smiling, a little grimly perhaps, and without much of a glint in his eye, but with a wry determination that was shared by many in the generation we are considering, the young satirists, rebels and reformers of the late Wilhelmine Empire and the Weimar Republic.

Chodowiecki's illustrations of *Candide* were the last for several generations; there were no German illustrated editions in the whole of the 19th century.[39] Unsurprisingly, none of the illustrators of *Candide* in the 20th century is nearly as naturalistic as their 18th-century predecessor, although one at least, Max Unold, made his name from his powerful adaptations of traditional styles from previous periods. Unold (1885-1964) was south German, born in Memmingen and spending most of his career in Munich.[40] Between 1908 and 1913 he spent part of each summer in the south of France and, inspired by Van Gogh and Cézanne in particular, he joined the vanguard of the German anti-traditionalists, winning the Gold Medal at the Spring 1913 exhibition of the Munich Secession with *Dame in Blau* and forming part of the avant-garde breakaway group, the 'Neue Secession', in the same year. However, he was simultaneously a gifted woodcut artist, originally favouring strong lines and decorative space in the Jugendstil mode, but from 1912 onwards—with illustrations for Nicolas de Troyes *Der große Prüfstein der neuen Novellen* and Christian Reuter's *Schelmuffsky* in particular[41]—he made an intensive study of woodcuts from the 15th and 16th centuries and cultivated a historicizing approach: 'Auf diese Weise bewegt sich Unolds Holzschnittkunst von einer malerisch naturalistischen zu einer flächig abstrakten Auffassung hin, die in der illusionsfreien Holzschnittkunst der Vordürerzeit wurzelt.'[42] This is the context of his illustrations for *Candide.*

Unold's illustrations are in black and white with no shades of grey, in this respect often reminiscent of the work of Frans Masereel. Standing alone on a right-hand page facing the text, their heavy-edged frames seal in situations often of destruction and terror. This is certainly the case with the image he created to depict the Lisbon earthquake for chapter 5 of *Candide.* . . .[43] All is instability: the buildings on the left are leaning in and crumbling; the masts of the boats on the right are crossed in the turbulent harbour; the corner building in the centre ground is shedding its roof and threatens to split in two. Even the hill behind the city seems to be collapsing inwards, and the sky above is creased and furrowed, much like the sea below, which is encroaching onto the land. People on the decks of the boats are prostrate or tumbling down steps; small clusters on the harbour front have their hands raised as if to fend off falling masonry; their legs are suggestive of panicked running. The stark contrast of the solid patches of black and the open patches of white lend these images an element of simplicity that is preserved even when the relative complexity of the action depicted is recognized.

The other Lisbon picture, of the 'bel auto-da-fé' . . . , is just as terrible, but much more sinister. It shows two huge pyres with a gallows between them; in each a body hangs down in the middle of the flames—white streaks in the midst of jet black clouds of smoke; the flames reach high above the piles of logs and the topmost plumes of smoke bump against the layers of cloud that form the top of the picture as if the world has a lid on it, denying the possibility of an ascent to the heavens of any kind, physical or spiritual. All the figures in

the image are solid black silhouettes with rudimentary details of limbs and clothing; one has his hand on his hips in a gesture of awful nonchalance, another is leaning on a walking-stick. Many of them are hooded or cowled; a curving procession of monks holding crosses moves away from the fires, turning their backs on the victims, but the scene is also encircled by an 'audience' in canopied enclosures as if for a medieval joust or a modern sporting competition—the faces of the spectators are invisible, indicated only by small white dots for eyes. Even the lines of houses on the edge of the square in the background seem to be observing, their hundreds of 'eyes' black dots in white backgrounds. The white ground of the square underlines the isolation of the men being killed and their separation from the rest of society. The whole is so threatening, partly because of the starkness of the black/white contrast, and partly because of the monstrous nature of the 'spectacle'. The central scene is in effect a counter-facture of Calvary, with two pyres and a gibbet instead of three crosses, but one that offers no possibility of redemption, only abandonment. There is little or nothing of the irony that Voltaire effortlessly draws out of the same situation—with his parodic use of the terminology of cuisine ('quelques personnes brûlées à petit feu', p. 157), his unceasing mockery of the language of Optimism, exposing the grotesquely theatrical nature of the events as Candide is 'fessé en cadence, pendant qu'on chantait' (p. 158)— and nothing to suggest a way out, which Voltaire always provides. In the fervid period leading up to world war, Unold was impervious to all the elements of the Enlightenment that he found in Voltaire.

The core of Unold's striving for a modern style was his need to free himself '[vom] konstruierten, perspektivistisch realen Raum' (Margot Lehner describes it as his 'Kampf gegen die konstruierte dritte Dimension'), and the influence of Expressionist and Cubist artists such as Klee, Jawlensky, Beckmann, Pechstein and Kanolt was crucial.[44] The personal artistic context for the *Candide* illustrations comprised—in broad terms—a turn away from realism, and from the artificial constructions of space and perspective that realist art paradoxically requires, towards a more dynamic, rough-edged and brittle perception of reality, its twists, shears, fractures and incompleteness not defects but essential components. The works that Unold chose to illustrate in order to achieve this between 1912 and 1914—Nicolas de Troyes' *Le Grand Parangon de nouvelles Nouvelles* (1535), Vicente Espinel's *Marcos de Obregón* (1618), Christian Reuter's *Schelmuffsky* (1696) and Ludwig Aurbacher's version of the 16th-century folk-tales of the 'Sieben Schwaben' (1827-29)—have many things in common with *Candide,* and these shared features complement the stylistic and aesthetic struggle that was in progress. Most of these books are adventure tales in the picaresque style, with pace, verve, danger and violence; they share a simplicity of narrative (and often a degree of simplicity in their protagonists); they hold a mirror up for society to contemplate its own defects and failures, but one that exaggerates, magnifies and distorts the world for comic, satiric and usually educative effect. Their heroes, or anti-heroes, are somehow larger than life and are treated with a mixture of censure and sympathy that matches Voltaire's critical indulgence of Candide. Unold had an obvious fondness for the romping 'Schelmenroman' or the proto-'Bildungsroman'—this sequence is immediately preceded by pictures for Rabelais's *Gargantua* in 1911[45]—but the comic aspects of the texts he illustrated are muted in the images themselves.

The opposite is true of Josef von Divéky's illustrations, which are light, decorative, often comic and decidedly optimistic. Where Unold focused on scenes where individuals were unrecognizable except as gestural encapsulations of fear, panic or turmoil, in his fifty-one illustrations Divéky only depicts people—the novel's principle players, of course, but also soldiers, doctors, clerics, natives and all the 'bit parts' that Voltaire passes before us, all in historically appropriate garb. Most of the illustrations are in the manner of small vignettes, of single individuals or pairs (often too small to be appreciated fully), but every dozen or so pages there are more elaborate groups; all, however, are integrated into the pages with the text flowing smoothly past them.[46] Divéky's images are plain to the point of naivety; they have sufficient background detail to anchor them in their context; the characters express their emotions straightforwardly, their postures are simple and eloquent. There is some stylization, but it tends towards the children's comic or cartoon—Candide's pose in the illustration for Chapter III, his escape from the Bulgares . . . is exaggerated and melodramatic in this vein, for example. The pile of dead soldiers on which he stands allows him to strike a mock-heroic pose, but despite the smoking garrison in the background, the broken wheels in the pile and the clenched fist of the dead soldier on the right, the scene is not cruel or gruesome. Voltaire refers to 'des cervelles [. . .] répandues sur la terre à côté de bras et de james coupés' (p. 150), but Divéky shows no broken limbs, no blood and no slashed throats; his carnage is sanitized to a high degree. This has the effect of making the scene comic, but not in the way that Voltaire's satirical clash between the mock-sobriety of his language and the awfulness of the injuries is comic.

Divéky offers some variation in technique. The illustration to Chapter XVI, in which Candide shoots the ape-lovers of the girls *in puris naturalibus* . . . , is rather more stylized than the image just discussed. The two native girls are to some extent caricatured, running in parallel, their arms outstretched, hair flowing, one looking across to the other in excitement rather than fear—making it clear that where Candide is uncertain as to whether 'ces cris étaient de douleur ou de joie' (p. 180), the reader should not be. The ape, too, is comic: on all fours, stalking the girls with long digits outstretched, the ruff like a lion's mane and the positively lecherous look in its eye beneath the rather louche raised eyebrows suggest no trace of bloodthirstiness. Divéky has chosen to depict a romp rather than a hunt, and by completely desexualizing what is in Voltaire's story an episode with something of a shock-factor, he again sanitizes the tale. His earlier illustration of Candide's treatment by a doctor after running the gauntlet amongst the Bulgares is similar because of the almost neutral stance it takes towards the violence. Candide's face is flushed, more surprised than agonized, and we don't see his wounds—he has been beaten with rods until the nerves and muscles on his back are laid bare. The doctor is leaning over him about to wind a bandage around him. With a handlebar moustache, thick spectacles and large clumsy hands, the surgeon does not promise great finesse; he almost seems to be wondering how to go about the task.[47] Pictures such as this are graphic enactments of the very optimism and escapism that Voltaire both conjures up and undermines.

Divécky (1887-1951) was born in Hungary but studied and lived in Vienna from 1892, becoming a member of the 'Wiener Werkstätte' before moving briefly to Brussels which he left in 1918 for Switzerland, where he remained until 1941. He was best known as an illustrator and book designer, but also produced greetings cards, *ex libris,* business cards and menus! All his work shows virtuosity and fluency, much of it (like the illustrations for an edition of Münchhausen's adventures in 1913[48]) is comic; but it also has the kind of plainness, even workmanlike quality that these illustrations show. His approach to **Candide** was to keep the atmosphere light-hearted; he suppressed intimations of threat, instead playing up the charm that is also a genuine component of Voltaire's story. The extreme violence that also characterizes **Candide** is absent, which, given that Divéky served at the front during the war, was wounded, and became a war artist when unfit for active service, must be seen as a deliberate response. Whether it is a gesture of optimism or one of displacement is not possible to judge.

The **Candide** illustrations that have the highest art-historical profile are undoubtedly Paul Klee's. This was one of only two books that Klee ever illustrated, despite plans for others, including Goethe's *Reinecke Fuchs* and Boccacio's *Decamerone.*[49] He seems to have had reservations about the business of illustrating a pre-existing work that complement Voltaire's doubts about the need for pictures to accompany a written text: 'Nie habe ich ein litterarisches Motiv illustriert sondern ich habe bildnerisch geformt und mich erst dann gefreut, wenn ein dichterischer und ein bildnerischer Gedanke "zufällig" sich deckten.'[50] He read **Candide** enthusiastically in January 1906—'Drei Ausrufzeichen'—noting in his diary in 1909, 'Es ist an Candide ein Höheres was mich anzieht, der kostbar-sparsam-treffende Ausdruck der Sprache des Franzosen.'[51] He began to produce his drawings in 1911 and by the end of 1912 had completed twenty-six, without any form of contract or even encouragement from a publisher. One critic describes Voltaire as Klee's 'kindred spirit',[52] but even if this was so, a letter to Paul Eluard describes the process of producing the images less comfortably as a 'battle'.[53] He saw these illustrations explicitly as the basis for his own 'Ausarbeitung des Persönlichen'.[54] There is documentary evidence of the extreme care that he took with these illustrations and of the complexity of his work-processes—his text has underlinings and annotations in four different pens or pencils to show how he tried to vary the number of figures and the 'props' to indicate settings and there are drafts that show his care with compositional relationships.[55] His correspondence with the eventual publisher, Kurt Wolff, shows how keen he is to get right even the details of type face and fount size,[56] and all twenty-six are reproduced at exactly the same size to fit the page layout perfectly, all heading their respective chapters, placed above the chapter-titles and numbers.

In a sense there is no need to look for a reason why any artist takes such care with his work, but in this case a very plausible explanation for Klee's particular interest in *Candide* has been suggested, one that combines an aesthetic or stylistic struggle with a view of the content or substance of the text that is not unlike that suggested for Max Unold above. One of Voltaire's major targets is Leibnitzian Optimism and Providentialism; Leibnitz's *Essais de théodicée* are famously both attacked and travestied throughout the *conte* in a savagely parodic manner. Klee had been interested in the work of the Nobel Prize-winning chemist Wilhelm Ostwald (1853-1932) for some years before his work on *Candide,* and Ostwald was another implacable opponent of Leibnitz. He had developed a theory of 'energetics', seeing matter not as an independent reality but as a complex of energy factors. His theories radically question the Leibnizian ideas of 'pre-established harmony' and 'sufficient reason': 'According to Ostwald, every cause and its corresponding effect constitute a temporal sequence generated not by sufficient reason, but by nervous energy that is unleashed in response to external stimuli and in turn is transformed into other forms of energy. Ostwald's concept of nervous energy seems to have been the catalyst that triggered Klee's unique graphic response to Voltaire's *Candide.*'[57] Aichele notes that Klee's initial reading of *Candide* coincided with his attempts to find graphic equivalents of energy and that he specifically chose those scenes in the text that most clearly debunk Candide's naivety and optimism to create 'visual metaphors of what Ostwald would have characterized as nervous energy, thus anticipating [Klee's]

own often quoted aphorism that the purpose of art is to make visible, not to reproduce the visible'.[58] Ironically, then, the illustrations to *Candide* are themselves a perfect illustration of why Klee usually chose not to illustrate literary works.

The images themselves are complex although several commentators make the point that at first sight they are deceptively innocent—'like doodles which are virtually pointless', 'nervous scrawls', 'recht eigenwillig'.[59] Klee himself whimsically called them his 'Candideln'.[60] Their complexity does not derive from abstraction—far from being abstract art, they are clearly representational, although they are in some respects highly schematic and highly reductive of the detail of the outside world. Klee used the phrase 'psychische Improvisationen' to characterize the field of art most profoundly his own and these illustrations certainly fit that description.[61] There is something ascetic, even primitive about them, too, making them reminiscent of cave paintings. The scenes are mostly empty of scenery and have few 'props' except for a piece of clothing or furniture or a screen to anchor them in the text.[62] The pictures depict movement; they are always dynamic rather than static (even when their subject-matter is dead); gesture is crucial to each of them. The figures themselves are provocatively strange, grotesque even, ghostly, skeletal, dematerialized, 'dünngliedrige Schattenwesen',[63] a little like Giacometti's spindly bronzes from the 1940s and 1950s.[64]

Whilst they may be highly stylized, the figures are far from being undifferentiated: in the illustration of Candide's double-murder of Don Issacar and the Grand Inquisitor . . . , 'La Vieille' is clearly recognizable from her bent neck, Cunégonde is wringing her hands ineffectually and Candide has a fashionable pigtail; the murdered Jew has a caricatured hooked nose. There is no intimation of a room surrounding the characters—the scene might as well be taking place in the open air. The whole is a study in the tension between action and inaction. Cunégonde is upright, turned away from what is happening, almost with her back to the events that are taking place on her behalf. The Old Woman, however, is leaning forwards, stretching out perhaps in order to stay Candide's hand, with none of the massive energy of the young man in her ancient and mutilated frame, but at least gesturing. There are two bodies on the floor, one totally lifeless, crumpled and flat (almost *flattened,* the forearms pressed hard down on the ground, for example), the other depicted in a gesture of self-defence, his right arm trying to parry the sword, his left arm behind and beneath him as if to break his fall. Candide himself is leaning extravagantly across the dead body of Don Issacar to thrust his sword into the Grand Inquisitor; he is overwhelming and agile, his legs and torso and the weapon forming an energy-laden arc, 'with contours that are as malleable and elongated as stretched rubber bands'.[65]

The use of the line is a vital key to Klee's decisive move away from naturalistic art: 'Die naturalistische Malerei [. . .] hat vor allem den Nachteil, dass kein Absatz hier für meine lineare Produktionsfähigkeit vorhanden ist. [. . .] Über den Naturalismus geht ein Kunstwerk schon hinaus, wo die Linie [. . .] als selbständiges bildnerisches Element auftritt'.[66] The illustration to Chapter XIII . . ., however, shows clearly how this can be achieved without at the same time losing the representational dimension of the drawings. The commanding figure in the centre with the long twirly moustache is Don Fernando d'Ibaraa, y Figueora, y Mascarenes, y Lampourdos, y Souza, the Governor of Buenos Aires, who is sending Candide away to review his company so that he can make advances to Cunégonde. His imperious gesture with his left hand virtually cuts Candide apart from Cunégonde, forcing them to lean backwards away from each other. He incarnates Voltaire's character perfectly: 'un homme qui [. . .] parlait aux hommes avec le dédain le plus noble, portant le nez si haut, élevant si impitoyablement la voix, prenant un ton si imposant [. . .] que tous ceux qui le saluaient étaient tentés de le battre' (p. 173). Candide on the left is arching his back almost painfully; Cunégonde (whose charms for the Governor are manifested in her naked breasts) is also leaning towards Don Fernando, a gesture that is once more perfectly in keeping with her somewhat fickle character. The Old Woman on the right is again recognizable by her hunched back and she seems to have her hands clasped, perhaps in satisfaction rather than in anguish—it is she, after all, who reminds Cunégonde of the benefits of marriage to a man with such a fine moustache, asking 'est-ce à vous de vous piquer d'une fidelité à toute épreuve?' (p. 174). Klee shows how stylization need never be at the expense of the narrative value of the pictures.

Klee's ***Candide*** figures have often been likened to marionettes,[67] a comparison that has also been made of Voltaire's characters.[68] It is true that in some of the images Klee's figures seem almost to have hinged joints like puppets, and in none of them does he endow his figures with any overt emotion (as distinct from energy), which may be why such a comparison is made. When Candide and Cacambo meet the mutilated slave in Surinam in Chapter XIX, Klee shows the slave half-naked on the ground, his right arm and left leg both cut short, an earring dangling from his right ear and Candide leaning over him. Nothing suggests what the feelings of each character are, there are no gestures of overt sympathy or repugnance; only Cacambo, in the middle of the picture, seems to be looking out to the reader, almost drawing us into the scene, inviting us to allow our own emotions to fill it. The figures are not devoid of feeling, they are merely receptive. Seen within the context of Klee's concern with 'energetics', too, the suggestions of passivity implied by the comparisons with marionettes seem out of place. The lines of Klee's drawings may

dissolve the corporeality of the bodies they represent but they are both outlines and energy lines: in concentration they show skies, ground, the edges of a scene, a prop, but 'the principle function of Klee's "swarming scribbles" is to animate the figures and fill the space they occupy. [. . .] often they appear to swarm around the figures like a visible atmospheric force.'[69] Nothing comparable could be said about Voltaire's figures, whose speech and actions are 'flattened' rather than filled out, where eloquence and richness paradoxically derive from simplicity, or from irony.

Klee initially had problems finding a publisher for his illustrations. His diary for the summer of 1912 records how Franz Marc took them to his friend Reinhardt Piper, doubtless thinking that Piper & Co.'s emphasis on art books would make it a suitable home for Klee's work, but he was turned down. Alfred Richard Meyer was hugely enthusiastic about them—'Für meine Candides entflammte er sich so sehr, das er sich mit mir auf den Georg Müller Verlag begibt, um auf Grund dieser Leistung einen Vertrag abzuschliessen'—but Müller was unable to commit, having already published a version of ***Candide*** recently. Meyer was himself a publisher, who between 1910 and 1914 brought out works by Zech, Benn, Leonhard, Lasker-Schüler, Lichtenstein and Goll, but he focused on contemporary and avantgarde authors and did not, it seems, consider finding a place for Klee's Voltaire. In 1913, Hans Arp took the illustrations under his wing and tried to persuade Otto Flake to publish them in the Verlag der Weissen Blätter. Flake was by all accounts 'für mich gewonnen' and planning an edition, but it came to nothing: two years later, in 1915, Klee noted 'Meine Candide-Illustrationen möchte ich gerne zurückhaben. Sie liegen auf dem Verlag der Weissen Blätter, der schon vor dem Krieg merkwürdig zögerte'.[70] After a delay of four more years the illustrations were taken over by Kurt Wolff, who offered a kind of apology for the delay by referring to the absene of appropriate 'Herstellungsmöglichkeiten für ein gutes Buch' during the war years.[71] He produced an elegant but affordable volume with photo-mechanical reproductions.[72]

It is telling that the war significantly dulled Klee's excitement about these works. 'Was Candide betrifft', he wrote to Kubin in April 1915, 'habe ich jetzt kein Bedürfnis nach seinem Erscheinen, nach dem Krieg muß es dann sein. Überhaupt ruhig Blut!' and in April 1918, 'An Candide denke ich gar nicht mehr, das ist schon gar nicht mehr wahr.'[73] They had served their purpose for him artistically, fulfilled their function in the development of his ideas on line and energy. Despite the tale's obvious potential relevance to the situation in which these artists found themselves in 1918, Klee had not read it as a commentary on his own age or as a warning of any kind, as Unold seems to have done, but the intervention of the war between the completion of his illustrations and their publication seems to have alienated him from the comic aspects of their original context. The effects of the war were, of course, much more far-reaching than that. He wrote to Kubin on 10 April 1916 from the garrison town of Landshut in terms that suggest a profound personal crisis:

> Lieber Kubin, nun schreibt Ihnen der Soldat. Ist es möglich, daß ich das bin, der da in der Kolonne schwergestiefelt abgebräunt und bestaubzuckert mittrottet. Nein man kann es sich nicht vorstellen, nur die Chirurgie der Tatsachen macht es möglich. Und hier beginnt meine Traumwelt. Die Dinge zweiten Gesichts hab ich stets verdammt real aufgefaßt und nur Eingriffe dahinein waren schmerzlich. Zwar sah ich schon diese Sachen um mich herum aber was hinderten sie? War eins krank mußte ich pflegen, manchmal wochenlang einmal monatelang, ich sah hindurch. Momente des an der Wirklichkeit strauchelnden Auges waren kurz. Im Dienst nun sind sie etwas länger. Hier heißt es manchmal rasch sich diesseits orientieren und je diesseitiger, aufdringlicher diesseitig, desto phantastischer. Daß ich der bin, sein soll—wie grotesk, welch ein Traum! Wie unmöglich, greifbar unmöglich . . .[74]

Ironically, whilst the grotesque reality that the world of *Candide* once represented for him artistically might now be thought to be *reinforced* by current events, it is in fact *supplanted* by an enforced reorientation towards the here-and-now that Klee paradoxically compares to the onset of a dream.

Kubin's illustrations for *Candide* appeared in the same year as Klee's and the tale had been a major catalyst for their relationship. Kubin had had some experience as an illustrator of literature (for his own novel *Die andere Seite* [1909] and works by Poe and Nerval, for example[75]), and seems to have encouraged Klee, who travelled to see Kubin in his Upper Austrian home, Schloß Zwickledt, in June 1912 possibly in order to show his colleague the recently completed series. Kubin was certainly impressed by them sufficiently to attempt to incorporate their stimulus into his own works,[76] but his 28 illustrations for *Candide* are usually seen both as wholly uninfluenced by Klee and as untypical of his own tortured view of the world.

Kubin was usually little short of obsessive in his artistic practice. He began by immersing himself in the works he was illustrating to an almost pathological degree: 'Erst dann kam die Tat, mit der er sich von den Gespenstern, die ihm keine Ruhe ließen, befreite: dem Geist und die Figuren des Werkes bildlich Ausdruck zu verleihen.'[77] The relationship between text and image was always an intimate one and in no sense were his illustrations to be considered 'incidental' or 'additions'. Of the figures he drew Kubin wrote,

> meine Gestalten sind weder auf irgendeinen ästhetischen Kanon festgelegt, noch sind sie Karikaturen; sie entgleiten jeder Formulierung, ich aber weiß um den

Schaffenszwang, der hier unerbittlich am Werk ist. Ich sehe die Welt nicht etwa 'so', sondern in seltsamen, wie halbwachen Augenblicken erspähe ich erstaunt diese Verwandlungen, die oft kaum spürbar sind, so daß sie im Stadium des ersten Gewahrens selten klar geschaut werden, sondern erst allmählich tastend erwittert werden müssen. Meine Räume, Beleuchtungen, Proportionen und Perspektiven sind weder in der Natur noch im Kopf vorhanden, und SIND DOCH, eben im Zwischenreich der Dämmerung. Die Figuren und Gespenster, die zeichnerisch festgehalten werden, tragen alle das Signum, den unverwechselbaren Duft als gemeinsames Erkennungszeichen für jeden, der verwandte Erlebnisse hat.[78]

Restless and driven, he was fascinated by the fantastic, the mysterious and the demonic, as eight volumes of Poe between 1909 and 1920, Balzac's *Mystische Geschichten* (1920) and Barbey d'Aurevilly's *Teufelskinder* (1921) make manifest. All these were published by Georg Müller in Munich, but after the war he began to receive commissions from a much wider field of publishers. One such was from the forward-looking (but ultimately short-lived) firm of Steegemann, also in Munich, to illustrate *Candide*. Horodisch's judgement of the results is typical of many: 'die Illustrationen zu Candide vermögen uns nicht zu überzeugen. Die beißende Ironie, die schonungslose Satire Voltaires sind nicht Kubins Sache. Diese Blätter gehören zu den wenigst transzendentalen in Kubins Schaffen, und keineswegs mangelt es ihnen an Humor. Aber der Humor Kubins entspringt ganz anderen Quellen als Voltaires kaustischer Witz.'[79]

It is true that there is little in his *Candide* drawings that is obviously reminiscent of the dark and demonic, nothing to connect them with the crisis states of *Die andere Seite*. They are deftly executed, detailed without being naturalistically over-stuffed, often decorative in the rococo manner, but always with a fundamental simplicity. His own description of his pen drawings emphasises this aspect: 'Ich verzichte auf alle Abtönungen und Farben und pflege ausschließlich die Federzeichnung. Das einfachste Mittel—Striche, Flecken und Punkte—soll den ganzen imaginären Bau der Zeichnung tragen.'[80] Many are elegantly reminiscent of the 18th-century world that they depict, but sometimes they are more mysterious, too—especially in the sections of the tale set in Eldorado. Kubin also had an eye for the gruesome detail: in his picture of the naked girls with the apes, for example, the girls' distress is perfectly evident and one is holding up her dead lover by the tail. The description just quoted continues: 'Nach langen Irrfahrten glaube ich endlich gefunden zu haben, was mir zukommt, und ich habe die Hoffnung, meine Art noch weiter zu vervollkommnen, um diese verdrehte Welt zu spiegeln', and the twisted nature of his world is not wholly hidden.

Most of the illustrations are full-page images, although a few of the smaller ones are topped or tailed by text as necessary. The first, immediately preceding Chapter I . . . , shows Pangloss instructing Candide and Cunégonde in the arcana of 'métaphysico-théologo-cosmolo-nigologie' (p. 146)—in the last component of which is hidden one of the French words for 'fool' ('nigaud'). Both are depicted fittingly as naïve innocents; Cunégonde looks up admiringly at Pangloss, straight-backed and with her hands laid gently on her knees, and Candide looks across adoringly at Cunégonde, leaning forward a little eagerly, sitting on his hands to contain his ardour. Pangloss is the most interesting figure, however. He seems to be talking principally to Cunégonde, their gazes constructing an axis that links them without excluding Candide himself. Here 'l'oracle de la maison' (p. 147) is leaning on the table, his face is wrinkled, his back a little hunched—he is an old man, somewhat infirm, and by no means the commanding figure that his pupils seem to see in him.[81] Looking more carefully at Kubin's version of Pangloss, while keeping in mind all that Voltaire tells us about his sexually voracious character, it may be that Kubin has deliberately shown in his face the ravages of the pox that we know he has contracted by a long and circuitous route—which rather undercuts the rococo elegance of the image.

A similar tension is visible in another image of Pangloss, from Chapter XXVII, Candide's journey to Constantinople. . . . He and Cunégonde's brother have been sold into slavery and, as luck would have it, are the very two slaves set to row Candide, Cacambo and Martin across the Propontis. Kubin depicts a very cheerful slave-master cracking a whip vaguely in their direction, his top-knot flying in the breeze, but the two rowers are shown genuinely suffering. Both are chained to the boat, semi-naked and emaciated, pulling hard on the oars and showing the strain in their faces. Cunégonde's brother has his eyes shut and his mouth slightly open. Pangloss looks considerably older than in the first illustration, his cheeks are hollowed, his eyes gaze unseeing ahead of him, his neck is scrawny and his head nearly bald. It is certainly possible to see this illustration as humorous—the stereotyped whip-cracking slave-driver is whimsical in a manner reminiscent of Edward Ardizzone's mock-oriental drawings, perhaps—but the presence of pain makes it more complex than that. Wackermann is right to observe that '[Kubin] konnte hier hintergründige Unnatur des Menschen, Dämonisches, Brüchigkeit der Welt und mehr aufzeigen.'[82] In the uneasy tension between the slave-driver and his rowers Kubin has recognized and captured the crucial Voltairean truth that blithe optimism cannot hide the very real presence of oppression and misery in the world. Horodisch may have found these illustrations 'unconvincing', but in reality they are penetrating commentaries on Voltaire's satire, and as such not perhaps quite such poor relations of Klee's as is usually thought.

The final set of *Candide* illustrations to be considered here was published in a limited edition without a reprint of the text itself. Ludwig Emil Georg Ottomar Starke (1886-1962) was a writer and actor as well as a stage designer and graphic artist; he studied at the Kunstgewerbeschule in Munich from 1906 to 1907 and worked as a set designer in Frankfurt and Mannheim and the Landestheater in Darmstadt between 1911 and 1922. His plays include *Journaille, Die Welt* and an adaptation of Molière's *L'Avare* called *Die Nachbarn*; he wrote novels, too (such as *Der Glatzkopf,* and *Das Loch in der Schöpfung*) and a volume of verse. He was also a journalist and commentator, and in the early 1920s co-edited *Der Querschnitt* with Alfred Flechtheim (the *Candide* illustrations were published by Flechtheim's gallery) and contributed to Bruno Cassirer's *Der Bildermann* from its foundation in 1916. Starke illustrated a large number of books by his contemporaries and others—Carl Sternheim in particular, and Gustav Freytag,[83] but also René Schickele, Max Brod and Alfred Wolfenstein, as well as Flaubert, Grillparzer and Shakespeare. Sternheim contributed the foreword to his book of fifty caricature lithographs entitled *Schippeliana,* after Bürger Schippel.[84]

Starke's *Candide* illustrations are more elaborate than any so far discussed—perhaps partly because they stand alone, without the text, in a publication designed exclusively for art-lovers—and are full of wit and irony as well as a heavy dose of social and cultural critique. His version of the auto-da-fé . . . maximizes the use of grotesque to underline Voltaire's anti-clerical satire, although it is based on a mis-reading of the tale: it is entitled 'Pangloß wird verbrannt', but in Chapter VI of *Candide* Pangloss is hanged; the Biscayan and two Jews are the ones burned to death. Be that as it may, Starke uses Pangloss as the centre-piece of a vigorous indictment of hypocrisy. He has Pangloss chained to a stake, semi-naked and wearing only a loincloth. Smoke rises from the fire beneath him as his mouth opens in what is clearly a groan rather than a scream, his eyes bulging, a conical hat on his head. This last detail is an authentic prop for the Inquisition's burnings: Voltaire's source for this was Gabriel Dellon's *Relation de l'Inquisition de Goa* (originally published in 1688 but often reprinted), which notes: 'Ensuite je vis paraître des bonnets de carton, élevés en pointe à la façon d'un pain de sucre, tout couverts de diables et de flammes de feu.'[85] The other condemned man on the right, perhaps the Biscayan, has a similar 'mitre de papier' (p. 158), and on the left there is a true mitre worn by a furious Bishop, eyes narrowed with hatred, hand raised not in benediction but in accusation, his huge cross towering above poor Pangloss. There are three crucifixes in the picture, ironically underlining the godlessness of the actions being carried out. No less ironic is the presence of a diminutive tonsured thurifer on the far left, censing the scene with burning incense to try to mask the smell of burning flesh (he and a number of others in the crowd are holding their noses) rather than for any more orthodox purificatory purpose. The whole scenario is set against a dark backdrop, unspecific but highly suggestive of storm clouds or encroaching darkness—a symbolic rendition of the blackness of a world that can inflict such cruelty for such implausible reasons.

Even greater devastation is visible in another of Starke's bleak images, one in fact that records a happier moment, when Candide is reunited with Pangloss after the war between the Bulgares and the Abares. . . . Again the letter of the text has been ignored—this reunification does not take place on a battlefield as is suggested here, but during a walk after Candide has been helped by the Anabaptist Jacques, specifically 'hors du théâtre de la guerre' (p. 150). Starke's purpose is clear: he lays a potentially optimistic image (as two old friends embrace after a period of separation, each imagining the other had been killed) over the smoking battlefield only so as to debunk that optimism more effectively. There are two buildings in the scene, one burnt out with smoke rising from the ruins; the other with black windows and a crumbling roof; a human figure on the left is hanging by a rope from a charred tree, observed pathetically but poignantly by a small dog; to the left of the main figures there is another human figure lying on its back with a sword sticking out of its chest; more gruesome still is the severed head bottom right. In the midst of this carnage Candide embraces his old tutor: Pangloss is in rags—not quite 'tout couvert de pustules' (p. 151) as Voltaire records, but certainly ravaged, 'les yeux morts'—and whilst Candide still has his peruke, he also has a wooden leg (a detail from the inauthentic 'Second Part' of *Candide* rather than from Voltaire). The battlefield is generic, as it were: it need not be read only as a snapshot from the Seven Years War; the most recent conflict will have left similar images in the minds of many readers. The smile on Candide's face is certainly one of genuine happiness at the recovery of his friend and mentor and Pangloss is happy to be rescued from his misery, but, just as in Voltaire's original story, any such evidence of the rightness of the Optimistic philosophy must be tempered by a simultaneous awareness of the horrors on which the moment of anagnorisis is predicated.

IV

An English contemporary of these illustrators spelt out the powerful relationship that potentially existed between *Candide* and their age:

> In the good old days, before the Flood, the history of Candide's adventures seemed to us quiet, sheltered, middle-class people only a delightful fantasy, or at best a high-spirited exaggeration of conditions which we knew, vaguely and theoretically, to exist, to have existed, a long way off in space and time. But read the

book today; you feel yourself entirely at home in its pages. It is like reading a record of the facts and opinions of 1922; nothing was ever more applicable, more completely to the point. The world in which we live is recognizably the world of Candide and Cunégonde, of Martin and the Old Woman who was a Pope's daughter and the betrothed of the sovereign Prince of Massa-Carrara. The only difference is that the horrors crowd rather more thickly on the world of 1922 than they did on Candide's world. The manoeuvrings of Bulgare and Abare, the internecine strife in Morocco, the earthquake and *auto-da-fé* are but pale poor things compared with the Great War, the Russian Famine, the Black and Tans, the Fascisti, and all the other horrors of which we can proudly boast.[86]

The illustrators of the German editions of *Candide* of this period were not for the most part 'quiet, sheltered, middle-class people', but that does not mean they could not share Huxley's sense of the relevance of its world to theirs.

None of the sets of illustrations considered here was produced during the war itself. Unold's and Klee's precede the war, even though the latter were not published until afterwards. Ottomar Starke's images are most obviously the product of the political upheaval of their age and these are the illustrations that make most overt reference to the conflict of 1914-18, albeit not in any narrowly allegorical way. Yet he also preserves Voltaire's satirical stance and the edgy humour of the work, which means that there is a dimension to his reading of Voltaire that moves beyond Hamecher's repeated 'Es ist ein bitteres Buch, dieser *Kandide.*' Whilst also clearly reflecting the threatening nature of the physical and the social world, in his illustrations Max Unold chose not to try to accommodate the satire. He was to be wounded in the war and spent a long period in a military hospital in 1916-1917. Even before this, however, his images are bleakly impersonal; no faces are shown; individuals are often victims of crowds; where Starke proliferates detail in the way that Voltaire does—pragmatically rather than decoratively—Unold eschews elaboration altogether. Likewise, Paul Klee has no room for embellishment. His 'battle' with the illustrations was, however, a purely personal one, concerned above all with the identification of a means of finding a 'graphic language' that communicated the unease and nervous energy that he found in *Candide,* that articulated a relationship between science and art that was important to him and that drew him away from naturalistic art by giving priority to the use of the line.

Unold had also used Voltaire as a stage in his own personal development away from perspective and representationalism, but he maintained a clear association with the events of the world outside and reflects the imminence of catastrophe. Klee is in some respects a more 'faithful' illustrator of Voltaire than Unold: he captures the outline of the narrative and on occasion its ironic dimensions, too. However, none of his illustrations depicts absurdity, and whilst his figures are in an obvious way caricatures they possess a poignancy and an inner seriousness that ensure they are not mocked. Alfred Kubin might be said to be bluffing with some of his illustrations. Inspired to some extent by Klee's engagement with **Candide,** but wisely avoiding the faintest hint of imitation in his own versions, Kubin reaches back into the 18th century and to elements of Chodowiecki's images for the costume and style missing entirely from Unold and Klee. However, he layers them thinly over his own acutely painful existential anxieties.

It is an irony that the plainest and most truly optimistic illustrations for Voltaire's tale are those that adorn the edition with Peter Hamecher's doom-laden afterword. Josef von Divéky's studies of small groups and individuals give precisely the opposite message from the accompanying commentary. Hamecher's brief translator's introduction makes much of his efforts to make a French classic accessible to a German readership—exchanging references to French culture for 'Anspielungen auf *deutsche* Autoren, *deutsche* Schriften' in a tale that was after all 'auf *deutschem* Grund und Boden [gewachsen]'.[87] His stress on the contemporary German dimensions of the story sits ill with Divéky's continual recourse to the stylistic world of Voltaire's France. If Voltaire inspired all five of the early 20th-century artists, he inspired them very differently. The group shows no consistency in interpretation and no shared core of values inherited from Voltaire. They all demonstrate the flexibility of the new contexts for the work, personal and political. Eckermann contrasted Goethe with Voltaire, to the latter's disadvantage: 'Von Voltaire läßt sich nicht sagen, daß er auf junge Poeten des Auslandes einen Einfluß der Art gehabt, daß sie sich in seinem Geist versammelten und ihn als ihren Herrn und Meister erkannten.'[88] The illustrated editions of **Candide** between 1913 and 1922 certainly confirm the truth of this statement, although not necessarily in the way that Eckermann apparently intended. Voltaire would surely have been pleased to inspire, but, as a free spirit, he would have been just as content to be nobody's master.

Notes

1. Peter Hamecher, 'Nachwort', in Voltaire, *Kandide, oder: Es ist doch die beste Welt!,* trans. by Wilhelm Christhelf Mylius, revised by Peter Hamecher, illus. by Josef von Divéky (Berlin: Morawe & Scheffelt, 1920), pp. 150-53, here pp. 151 and 152.

2. Roger Pearson, *The Fables of Reason: A Study of Voltaire's 'Contes Philosophiques'* (Oxford: Clarendon Press, 1993), p. 110.

3. Hamecher, 'Nachwort', in Voltaire, *Kandide,* p. 152.

4. Nicholas Cronk, 'Candide, comedy and chaos', in the programme for Leonard Bernstein, *Candide,* English National Opera 2008, directed by Robert Carsen [n.p.].

5. There is relatively little secondary literature on the topic of Voltaire and Germany, but key works include: Hermann August Korff, *Voltaire im literarischen Deutschland des XVIII. Jahrunderts: Ein Beitrag zur Geschichte des deutschen Geistes von Gottsched bis Goethe,* 2 vols (Heidelberg: Winter, 1917); *Voltaire und Deutschland: Quellen und Untersuchungen zur Rezeption der Französischen Aufklärung. Internationales Kolloquium der Universität Mannheim zum 200. Todestag Voltaires,* ed. by Peter Brockmeier and others (Stuttgart: Metzler, 1979)—which has no paper on *Candide;* Ernst Hinrichs and others, '*Pardon, mon cher Voltaire . . .': Drei Essays zu Voltaire in Deutschland* (Göttingen: Wallstein, 1996), where there is an essay by Roland Krebs devoted to the reception of *Candide* from its publication until the early 19th century: '"Schmähschrift wider die weiseste Vorsehung" oder "Lieblingsbuch aller Leute von Verstand"? Zur Rezeption des "Candide" in Deutschland', pp. 87-124.

6. The French text of *Candide* is quoted from Voltaire, *Romans et contes,* ed. by Frédéric Deloffre and Jacques van den Heuvel, Bibliothèque de la Pléiade, 3 (Paris: Gallimard, 1979), here p. 145. Henceforth page numbers for this edition will be given in parentheses in the text.

7. Voltaire to Francesco Algarotti and Frederick II, 28 November and 6 December 1740: *Voltaire's Correspondence,* ed. by Theodore Besterman, 107 vols (Geneva: Institut et Musée Voltaire, 1953-65), XCI, 374 and 363 (letters D2382 and D2369). Quoted in Voltaire, *Romans et contes,* p. 855.

8. See the 91st of the 'Literaturbriefe' (20 March 1760): Gotthold Ephraim Lessing, *Werke,* ed. by Herbert G. Göpfert and others, 8 vols (Munich: Hanser, 1970-79), v, 266-68. For more detail, see Krebs, '"Schmähschrift"', pp. 90-92.

9. *Die beste Welt. Eine Theologische, Philosophische, Praktische Abhandlung aus dem Spanischen Grund-Text des Don Ranudo Maria Elisabeth Francisco Carlos Immanuel de Collibradoz, Beysitzer der heiligen Inquisition, übersetzt; und mit einer Vorrede, auch Zuschrift und Register begleitet von Johann Albrecht Ralph* (Riga and Leipzig, 1751 [sic]). See also Paul Wallich and Hans von Müller, *Die deutsche Voltaireliteratur des achtzehnten Jahrhunderts* (Berlin: [Liebheit & Thiesen], 1921), pp. 30-31.

10. Voltaire to Charles Joseph Panckoucke, 12 January 1778: *Voltaire's Correspondence,* XCVIII, 18 (letter 19825). Despite Voltaire's views, Robert

Tucker, *The Illustrated Editions of Candide: An Examination & Checklist,* with an introduction by Giles Barber (Church Hanborough: The Previous Parrot Press, 1993), has a checklist of 104 illustrated editions of this work, and Hans-Ulrich Seifert's online 'Verzeichnis der illustrierten Ausgaben' (http://ub-dok.uni-trier.de/candide.htm) has many more.

11. *Romans et contes de M. de Voltaire* (Bouillon: Société Typographique, 1778).

12. See Emile Dacier, 'Moreau Le Jeune: Illustrateur de Voltaire,' in Voltaire, *Romans et Contes,* 2 vols (Paris: Aux Horizons de France, 1934), I, i-vi; for a fascinating analysis of the 'shift in the French cultural imaginary' that these represented, see also Mary L. Bellhouse, 'Candide shoots the monkey lovers: Representing black men in eighteenth-century French visual culture', *Political Theory,* 34.6 (2006), 741-84 (p. 741).

13. Voltaire, *Kandide oder die beste Welt aufs neue verdeutscht,* mit sechs Chodowieckischen Kupfern (Berlin: Himburg, 1778). A French edition with the same illustrations (but without the title vignette) was published simultaneously.

14. J. E. Biester, [review of the Mylius translation], *Allgemeine deutsche Bibliothek,* 50.1 (1782), 209-10.

15. Friedrich Nietzsche, *Werke,* ed. by Karl Schlechta, 3 vols (Munich: Hanser, 1954-56), III, 1385. The dedication was removed from the second edition. For a brief sketch of Nietzsche's intellectual relationship with Voltaire, see Hermann Hofer, 'L'image de Voltaire dans les lettres allemandes de Strauss et Nietzsche à Heinrich Mann', in *Voltaire und Deutschland,* pp. 491-99.

16. Nietzsche, *Werke,* I, 677 and 578-79.

17. Erich Heller, 'Nietzsche, the teacher of "free spirits"', in *The Importance of Nietzsche: Ten Essays* (Chicago: University of Chicago Press, 1988), pp. 58-60 (p. 60).

18. Johann Wolfgang von Goethe, *Werke,* ed. by Erich Trunz, 14 vols (Munich: Beck, 1981), XII, 269.

19. Even begrudging remarks such as 'Eigentlich [. . .] ist alles gut, was ein so großes Talent wie Voltaire schreibt, wiewohl ich nicht alle seine Frechheiten gelten lassen möchte' (16 December 1828) are relativized by others that denigrate '[das] Voltairesche leichte oberflächliche Wesen' (5 April 1829). Johann Peter Eckermann, *Gespräche mit Goethe in den letzten Jahrzehnten seines Lebens,* ed. by Fritz Bergemann (Frankfurt a.M.: Insel, 1987), pp. 284-85 and 314.

20. This paragraph is a summary of points developed more fully in my essay '"Maske des Lächelns": Voltaire und der deutsche Expressionismus', in *Frankreich und der deutsche Expressionismus/ France and German Expressionism,* ed. by Frank Krause (Göttingen: V&R unipress, 2007), pp. 115-40.

21. *Das Recht zu leben und die Pflicht zu sterben: Sozialphilosophische Betrachtungen, anknüpfend an die Bedeutung Voltaires für die neuere Zeit* (Leipzig: Koschny, 1878). Nietzsche owned the second edition of this work (1879) and a further two editions appeared in 1903 and 1924.

22. Voltaire, *Erzählungen,* trans. by Ernst Hardt (Berlin: Wiegand & Grieben, 1908); Voltaire, *Die Romane und Erzählungen,* ed. by Ludwig Rubiner, trans. by Frida Ichak and Elsa von Holländer, 2 vols (Potsdam: Kiepenheuer, 1920).

23. Otto Bollnow, 'Rousseau und Voltaire', *Die Hilfe,* 18.26 (1912), 411-13 and 18.27 (1912), 429-32.

24. Brandes, *Voltaire,* I, 5.

25. Thea Sternheim, *Tagebücher 1903-1971,* ed. by Thomas Ehrsam and Regula Wyss (Göttingen: Wallstein, 2002), I, 704 (entry 1418, 13 December 1924).

26. Other studies that had appeared since the hundredth anniversary of Voltaire's death include those by Richard Mahrenholtz, *Voltaires Leben und Werke,* 2 vols (Oppeln: Franck, 1885) and *Voltaire im Urteile der Zeitgenossen* (Berlin: Gronau, 1883); Käthe Schirrmacher, *Voltaire: Eine Biographie* (Leipzig: Reisland, 1898); Joseph Popper, *Voltaire: Eine Charakteranalyse in Verbindung mit Studien zur Ästhetik, Moral und Politik* (Dresden: Reissner, 1905); Paul Sakmann, *Voltaires Geistesart und Gedankenwelt* (Stuttgart: Frommann, 1910).

27. The other works by Voltaire that appeared in illustrated German editions at the time are *La Princesse de Babylone* (by Rolf Schott, 1920, Friedrich Heubner, 1922, and Walther Klemm, 1924) and *Cosi Sancta* (by Otto Linnekogel, 1921). See Adolf Sennewald, *Deutsche Buchillustratoren im ersten Drittel des 20. Jahrhunderts. Materialien für Bibliophile* (Wiesbaden: Harrassowitz, 1999) and Erwin Wackermann, 'Die beste der Welten. Deutsche Illustrationen zu Candide. Zur 200. Wiederkehr des Todes von Voltaire', *Illustration 63,* 15.1 (1978), 16-22 [pre-WW2] and 15.2 (1978), 59-66 [post-WW2].

28. Müller produced another edition of 300 copies in 1924 with 20 engravings by Carl Sturzkopf, which is not illustrated in Tucker, *Illustrated Editions,* and is described by Wackermann as 'fast unauffindbar', but focusing on 'die Urfehde zwischen Adel und Nichtadel' ('Die beste der Welten',

p. 22). Other elusive editions from the period not considered in this essay are: *Candide,* illus. by Erhard Amadeus-Dier (Vienna: Wolf, [*c.* 1922]) and *Candide,* illus. by Paul Scheurich (Berlin: Gurlitt, [*c.* 1925]).

29. See *Literatur und Zeiterlebnis im Spiegel der Buchillustration 1900-1945,* ed. by Ulrich von Kritter (Bad Homburg: von Kritter, 1989), pp. 139-40.

30. *Candid [sic] oder der Optimismus: Eine Erzählung von Voltaire,* with 12 woodcuts and initials by Max Unold (Leipzig: Insel Verlag, 1913).

31. See note 1; this is described rather patronizingly as a 'modest little German edition' by Tucker, *Illustrated Editions,* p. 59.

32. *Kandide oder die beste Welt: Eine Erzählung von Voltaire,* with 26 drawings by Paul Klee (Munich: Wolff, 1920).

33. Quoted in *Literatur und Zeiterlebnis,* p. 163.

34. Voltaire, *Candide: eine Erzählung,* trans. by Johann Freking, with 28 drawings by Alfred Kubin (Hanover: Steegemann, 1922).

35. Ottomar Starke, *14 Lithographien zu Voltaires 'Candide',* with a foreword by Franz Blei (Berlin: Galerie Flechtheim, 1922).

36. For brief descriptions of each illustration, see Elisabeth Wormsbächer, *Daniel Nikolaus Chodowiecki: Erklärungen und Erläuterungen zu sienen Radierungen* (Hanover: Bauer, 1988), pp. 44-45. Peter Tucker describes 'Chodowiecki's scenes and his preference for interiors' as 'rather dull' (*The Illustrated Editions of Candide,* p. 22).

37. Wackermann, 'Die beste der Welten', p. 19, writes of Chodowiecki's 'sprechende Physiognomien' as one of his strongest features: 'diese sprechen auch aus, was in ihren Gehirnen und Seelen vor sich geht'.

38. *Candide: Illustrierte Ausgaben eines Klassikers. Katalog einer Ausstellung der Universitätsbibliothek Trier 2000* (Trier: Universitätsbibliothek, 2000), p. 76.

39. See Wackermann, 'Die beste der Welten', p. 19. The only illustrated edition that appeared between the end of the 18th century and those considered here is a 1901 two-volume set published by Schupp in Munich and illustrated by Christian Wild in the Jugendstil manner (described by Wackermann as "eigenwillig und gegen die gezielten Absichten von Voltaire').

40. For biographical details and an essay on Unold's artistic development in the context of Modernism, see *Max Unold (1885-1964): Ausstellung in Memmingen 18. September bis 13. Oktober 1985,* ed. by Germaid Ruck (Memmingen: Stadt Memmingen, 1985), pp. 9-28. See also Max Unold, 'Selbstbiographie', in Wilhelm Hausenstein, *Max Unold* (Leipzig: Klinkhardt & Bierman, 1921).

41. Nicolas de Troyes, *Der grosse Prüfstein der neuen Novellen,* trans. by Paul Hansmann, Perlen älterer romanischer Prosa, 21 (Munich: Müller, 1913); Christian Reuter, *Schelmuffskys wahrhaftige, kuriöse und sehr gefährliche Reisebeschreibung,* ed. by Gottlieb Fritz, Hausbücherei der Deutschen Dichter-Gedächtnis-Stiftung, 41 (Hamburg: [Verlag der Stiftung], 1912).

42. Germaid Ruck, 'Bemühungen um einen Anschluß an die Moderne', in *Max Unold (1885-1964),* pp. 13-28 (p. 19), who refers to Wilhelm Höck, 'Max Unold als Illustrator', *Illustration 63: Zeitschrift für die Buchillustration unserer Zeit,* 3 (1965).

43. Every effort has been made to trace copyright ownership for all images reproduced in this article; the author would be grateful for further information concerning any artist for whom we have been unable to trace a copyright holder.

44. Margot Lehner, 'Von der Schönheit der Buchillustration', in *Max Unold (1885-1964),* pp. 29-34 (p. 31).

45. Rabelais and Voltaire are coupled more than once in this period. The 1912 edition of *Candide* that Chodowiecki illustrated was part of the 'Bücherei der Abtei Thelem' founded by Otto Julius Bierbaum and named after the Abbey of Thelema in *Gargantua.* There were more than thirty volumes published in this series between 1910 and 1923, beginning (and almost ending) with the Rabelais-inspired Laurence Sterne (*Tristram Shandy* and *A Sentimental Journey*), but including other English satirists such as Fielding and Smollett. Controversial French literature alongside Voltaire included Diderot's *Jacques le fataliste* and Mme de La Fayette's *La Princesse de Clèves*; German authors in the series (such as Christoph Martin Wieland and the rather lesser-known August Moritz von Thümmel or Johann Gottfried Schnabel) were also no strangers to the techniques of comedy and satire, or to the invention of utopian worlds for the purposes of reflecting a contemporary critique.

46. Wackermann notes that 250 copies were produced in a luxury edition with additional full-page illustrations, but that no example of these can now be traced ('Die beste der Welten', p. 20).

47. See also Sandra Schwarz's commentary in *Candide: Illustrierte Ausgaben eines Klassikers,* p. 122.

48. *Des Freiherrn von Münchhausen wunderbare Reisen und Abenteuer: Mit vielen Bildern v. J. v. Divéky, Brüssel* (Berlin: Morawe & Scheffelt, 1913).

49. See *Paul Klee: Handzeichnungen, 1: Kindheit bis 1920,* ed. by Jürgen Glaesner (Bern: Kunstmuseum Bern, 1973), pp. 178-83 (p. 178). The other work he illustrated was Curt Corrinth's *Potsdamer Platz,* with 10 lithographs.

50. Klee, *Togebücher 1898-1918: Textkritische Neuedition,* ed. by the Paul-Klee-Stiftung Kunstmuseum Bern and Wolfgang Kersten (Stuttgart: Teufen, 1988), p. 495 (1905).

51. Klee, *Tagebücher 1898-1918,* pp. 232 and 296-97. Interestingly, considering links already noted between the two authors, Klee was reading Rabelais at about the same time, too (p. 496).

52. Kathryn Porter Aichele, *Paul Klee's Pictorial Writing* (Cambridge: Cambridge University Press, 2002), p. 24.

53. Letter of 21 April 1928, quoted in *Paul Klee: Handzeichnungen,* I, 179.

54. 'Von Paris habe ich allerdings allerlei starke Eindrücke mitgebracht. So sehr ich die neuesten Bestrebungen auch gerade da schätzen lernte, sehe ich doch ein, daß *ich* weniger forschen und noch mehr als bisher an die Ausarbeitung des Persönlichen gehen soll. Meine Candide Illustrationen erscheinen mir z. Zt. als Basis zu solchen Bestrebungen geeignet': letter to Alfred Kubin of 19 May 1912 published in Jürgen Glaesemer, 'Paul Klees persönliche und künstlerische Begegnung mit Alfred Kubin', *Pantheon,* 32 (1974), 152-62 (p. 154).

55. See Aichele, *Paul Klee's Pictorial Writing,* pp. 26-27. Klee had a copy of the 1897 Hachette edition.

56. Kurt Wolff, *Briefwechsel eines Verlegers 1911-1963* (Frankfurt a.M.: Scheffler, 1966), p. 358. See also Tucker, *Illustrated Editions,* p. 28: 'the original is [. . .] cleanly printed in Unger-Fraktur type which harmonizes with the feathery pencil lightness of the drawings.'

57. Aichele, *Paul Klee's Pictorial Writing,* pp. 28-29. See also the same author's 'Paul Klee and the energetics-atomistics controversy', *Leonardo,* 26.4 (1993), 309-15.

58. Aichele, *Paul Klee's Pictorial Writing,* p. 29. See Paul Klee, 'Creative credo', in *The Inward Vision: Watercolours, Drawings and Writings by Paul Klee,* trans. by Norbert Guterman (New York: Abrams, 1959), p. 1.

59. Tucker, *Illustrated Editions,* p. 28; Aichele, *Paul Klee's Pictorial Writing,* p. 22; Lothar Lang, *Expressionistische Buchillustration in Deutschland 1907-1927* (Lucerne: Bucher, 1975), p. 51.

60. Klee, *Tagebücher 1898-1918,* p. 330 (summer 1912).

61. Klee, *Tagebücher 1898-1918,* p. 282 (November 1908).

62. See for example the illustrations on pp. 5, 8, 19, 21, etc.. A draft for one of the Lisbon illustrations experiments with a much more detailed spatial setting, but was eventually rejected; it is reproduced in Glaesemer, 'Paul Klees [. . .] Begegnung mit Alfred Kubin', p. 154.

63. *Paul Klee: Handzeichnungen,* I, 180.

64. See Angela Graas's commentary in *Candide: Illustrierte Ausgaben eines Klassikers,* p. 148.

65. Aichele, 'Paul Klee and the energetics-atomistics controversy', p. 310.

66. See Klee, *Tagebücher 1898-1918,* p. 282 (November 1908).

67. See *Paul Klee: Handzeichnungen,* I, 180: 'Das Spiel ihrer Bewegungen steht unter dem Gesetz einer höheren Macht, und sie gehorchen ihm wie die Marionetten dem Zwang der unsichtbaren Fäden' (see also I, 182); Lang, *Expressionistische Buchillustration,* p. 51; Tucker, *Illustrated Editions,* p. 31; Aichele, 'Paul Klee and the energetics-atomistics controversy', p. 310.

68. 'Der philosophisch unbelastete Candide, sein optimistischer, sein pessimistischer Freund, seine Geliebte, ihr adelsstolzer Bruder: alle sind Puppen, sie können das gräßlichste Unheil erleiden, die scheußlichsten Verstümmelungen, sie können zu Tode kommen, und doch stehen sie immer wieder auf': Viktor Klemperer, 'Voltaire und seine kleinen Romane', in Voltaire, *Sämtliche Romane und Erzählungen,* 2 vols (Leipzig: Dieterich, 1964), I, 35-36.

69. Aichele, *Paul Klee's Pictorial Writing,* p. 27. See the illustration to Chapter XII, the Old Woman's history, p. 31.

70. See Klee, *Tagebücher 1898-1918,* pp. 502, 329, 516, 330 and 369.

71. Wolff, *Briefwechsel eines Verlegers,* p. 357 (24 September 1919).

72. Much later it was reissued as Insel-Taschenbuch, Nr. 11 (Frankfurt a.M.: Insel Verlag, 1972); there are several other (Dutch, French and American) editions with Klee's drawings.

73. Quoted from Glaesemer, 'Paul Klees [. . .] Begegnung mit Alfred Kubin', p. 156.

74. Quoted from Glaesemer, 'Paul Klees [. . .] Be-gegnung mit Alfred Kubin', p. 160.

75. Kubin's catalogue of illustrated books has more than a hundred entries from writers such as E. T. A. Hoffmann, Achim von Arnim, Hauff, Jean Paul, Dostoyevsky, Barbey d'Aurevilly, Haupt-mann, Hardy and Balzac to Expressionist contem-poraries such as Mynona, Panizza, Werfel and Scheerbart. See Abraham Horodisch, *Alfred Kubin als Buchillustrator* (New York: Aldus-Buch-Compagnie, 1949), pp. 46-48.

76. See Glaesemer, 'Paul Klees [. . .] Begegnung mit Alfred Kubin', pp. 154 and 156.

77. Horodisch, *Kubin*, p. 12.

78. Cited by Horodisch, *Kubin*, pp. 13-14.

79. Horodisch, *Kubin*, p. 16.

80. Quoted by Wackermann, 'Die beste der Welten', p. 22.

81. Britta Roeske surely misidentifies Candide's prin-cipal object of interest ('er [nimmt] das "Ge-schwätz" des Lehrmeisters begierig in sich auf') and fails to spot Voltaire's irony concerning. Pan-gloss himself: 'Pangloss [. . .], der in der Erzählung als das Orakel des Hauses, als der größte Philosoph der Welt beschrieben wird, wirkt in der Zeichnung lächerlich, alt und schwach' (*Candide: Illustrierte Ausgaben eines Klassikers*, p. 74). Voltaire never seriously suggests that Pan-gloss is anything but a self-deluding systematizer.

82. Wackermann, 'Die beste der Welten', p. 22.

83. See Detlef Haberland, '"Der Zeichner liest mit einem besonderem Verstand"'. Ottomar Starke als Illustrator Gustav Freytags', *Oberschlesisches Jahrbuch*, 10 (1994), 163-85.

84. Ottomar Starke, *Schippeliana, Ein bürgerliches Bilderbuch* (Leipzig: Wolff, 1917).

85. Quoted in Voltaire, *Romans et contes*, p. 863.

86. Aldous Huxley, 'On re-reading *Candide*' (1923), in *Complete Essays*, ed. by Robert S. Baker and James Sexton, 6 vols (Chicago: Dee, 2000-02), I: *1920-1925* (2000), pp. 63-65 (p. 64).

87. Peter Hamecher, [Translator's note], in Voltaire, *Kandide*, [p. 5].

88. Eckermann, *Gespräche mit Goethe*, p. 375 (7 March 1830).

William F. Edmiston (essay date 2009)

SOURCE: Edmiston, William F. "Sex as Satire in Vol-taire's Fiction."[1] In *An American Voltaire: Essays in Memory of J. Patrick Lee,* edited by E. Joe Johnson and Byron R. Wells, pp. 80-96. Newcastle upon Tyne, U.K.: Cambridge Scholars Publishing, 2009.

[*In this essay, Edmiston examines Voltaire's handling of sexuality in his short fiction, finding that although ex-cessive female sensuality and male homosexuality are often the targets of the author's satire, its ultimate aim is to attack "not sex but that which tries to rise above sex and deny it"—especially the Roman Catholic Church.*]

In Voltaire's fictional prose narratives, sex is one of the privileged vehicles for satire.[2] Sex is often depicted in a negative way, as something brutal and venal, and used to denounce the abuse of power. Masculine desire is of-ten accompanied by coercion and violence—of which women are usually the victims. Sexual violence is so much a common and regular occurrence in *Candide* that Roger Pearson claims that "human sexual organs are the single most important cause of evil" in that text.[3] Haydn Mason has noted that human sexual rela-tions in *Candide* are shown to be completely subverted and devoid of positive content.[4] Sex is viewed nega-tively when it is a motivation for corruption, injustice, or violence, and this is also true in other tales. In the *Lettres d'Amabed,* Adaté describes her own rape at the hands of Père Fa Tutto. Cosi-Sancta is a victim of sexual extortion by a magistrate and by a physician, while Mlle de Saint-Yves undergoes the same fate at the hands of a government minister. Quite often in these narra-tives, however, sexual references are comic, intended to provoke laughter, and these often involve female sensu-ality and sometimes male homosexuality. Since the comic is a weapon in the Voltairean arsenal, the refer-ences are usually intended to be satiric, to attack a tar-get. Lynn Hunt tells us that in early modern Europe, writing about sex in an obscene way was linked to free-thinking and heresy, ideology, satire, and social criti-cism. Obscenity, she continues, was most often a ve-hicle for using the shock of sex to attack absolutist political authority, religious institutions, and moral con-ventions.[5] In this essay I will examine Voltaire's use of sex as a vehicle of satire. Specifically, I propose to demonstrate that female sensuality and male homosexu-ality, ancient sources of humor in literature, are de-ployed by the author to satirize and criticize his pre-ferred targets, especially the Roman Catholic Church. Sexuality is an effective weapon for unmasking and de-nouncing religious bigotry and especially the hypocrisy of the theological system that denies and condemns hu-man sexuality in most of its multiple aspects.

As a point of departure, let us begin by examining a well-known passage from *Candide*:

> Un jour, Cunégonde, en se promenant auprès du châ-teau, dans le petit bois qu'on appelait *parc*, vit entre des broussailles le docteur Pangloss qui donnait une

leçon de physique expérimentale à la femme de chambre de sa mère, petite brune très jolie et très docile. Comme Mlle Cunégonde avait beaucoup de dispositions pour les sciences, elle observa, sans souffler, les expériences réitérées dont elle fut témoin; elle vit clairement la raison suffisante du docteur, les effets et les causes, et s'en retourna toute agitée, toute pensive, toute remplie du désir d'être savante, songeant qu'elle pourrait bien être la raison suffisante du jeune Candide, qui pouvait aussi être la sienne.

(Voltaire, 146-47)

The lesson that Pangloss teaches to the chambermaid Paquette (and inadvertently to the young Cunégonde) in the first chapter of **Candide** is undoubtedly the most famous sexual reference in Voltaire's fictional prose narratives. It is paradigmatic of many sexual references in the *contes philosophiques* on three counts. . . . First, sexual desire and acts are expressed by means of preterition. Preterition involves designating something unmentionable in classical and more acceptable language—which can range from metaphors to phrases in Italian—in order to attenuate the breach of decency. As Philip Stewart points out with regard to *La Pucelle*—and the same can be said of the *contes*—Voltaire never uses illicit language, instead he tests the limits of how explicit one can be without stylistic indelicacy.[6] Second, the reference is intended to provoke laughter, and the comic element is actually enhanced by the preterition. Third, the goal of Voltaire's obscene reference is not the titillation of pornography but the sting of satire. What is the satiric target of our exemplary episode? Pangloss is the perpetrator of the act, and Cunégonde is the witness. One target is clearly the "métaphysico-théologo-cosmolonigologie" taught incessantly by Pangloss, which is denigrated here by its close proximity to a sexual act. Can we see a second satiric target in female sensuality? The heroine's nascent lust for the young hero is expressed in a scientific and metaphysical vocabulary that will come to be associated with Pangloss. I would argue that the satiric thrust is aimed more at the intellectual pretentiousness of Pangloss than at the sensual desire of Cunégonde.

Many sexual references in Voltaire's fiction are periphrastic descriptions, referring to a sexual act with vocabulary from a non-sexual domain. Since the sexual domain is frequently linked with and opposed to higher, "intellectual" domains, preterition often involves using the vocabulary of the latter to describe familiar, recognizable acts of the former. The scientific-philosophical terminology of **Candide** has already been noted. Zadig's orgasms with Astarté's chambermaid are said to occur "dans les instants où plusieurs personnes ne disent mot, et où d'autres ne prononcent que des paroles sacrées" (Voltaire, 75). Sexual activity can be expressed in religious terms, as in the **Histoire de Jenni** ("je donnai secrètement plus de la dîme des offrandes," Voltaire, 600), or in medical terms, by the doctor in **Cosi-Sancta**

("guérissez-moi seulement du mal que vous me faites, et je rendrai la santé à votre fils. . . . Cosi-Sancta . . . acheta le remède au prix qu'on voulut . . . ," Voltaire, 14). These clever circumlocutions enhance the comic by associating two unlikely domains, one more physical and the other more intellectual, such as sex and religon, or sex and philosophy. Preterition diminishes the shock of indecency by avoiding the language of sex and by substituting the more intellectual language. As Sigmund Freud wrote, the offensive element is replaced by one that is neutral, appearing innocuous to the censorship.[7] The obscenity is thus "smuggled in," as it were, past the internal censor whose standards of decency have not been breached, while the reader is allowed to indulge in all of it. The satiric effect is a carnivalesque debunking of intellectual pretension and an unmasking of hypocrisy.

Sexuality has always been used as a comic device in Western literature. Doubtless this is true in part because sex is a forbidden subject, one of the most hidden and private parts of life, so that the very mention of it in public discourse—even when veiled and oblique, or perhaps especially when the reference is veiled and oblique—will often provoke a smile or a laugh. Sexual organs, acts, and desires provide a rich repository of comic devices because they attract attention to the physical, to the animal nature of humankind and away from the intellectual dignity and the lofty morality to which members of the species aspire. The opposition between the physical and the intellectual constitutes a crucial component in the theoretical relationship between sex and comic discourse. Arthur Schopenhauer is the principal proponent of what is known as the incongruity theory of the comic, according to which humor involves tracing connections where none seems to exist. Laughter arises from a sudden perception of an incongruity, which might stem from a juxtaposition of emotional attitudes that are normally kept separate, from an unexpected disproportion, from a mismatch between sensory knowledge of things and an abstract knowledge of those same things. Schopenhauer called attention to what is considered by some to be the most essential element of humor, the "tricking of the mind," an intellectual component rather than an affective one.[8] In Schopenhauer's terms, the perceived (the forbidden subject) is subsumed into the conceived (a respectable and innocuous one), so that we are "tricked" into reading about the former. To return to our opening example, we thought for a moment that the narrator was talking about Cunégonde's initation into experimental science, but it turned out to be her first knowledge of sex. The indecent reference by itself, without the tricking of the mind, would not be funny. But as D. H. Monro has noted, the intrusion of sex reinforces the joke in a way that no other subject could, and we must therefore take into account "the whole complex of ideas, beliefs, inhibitions and fears which surround the subject of sex."[9] In other words, sex is a privileged category, one that makes incongruity easier to achieve and funnier in its effect. The incongruity between the intellectual and the sexual is almost always funny but not always wholly in fun, and Monro explains how it can be exploited as satire:

> It is important to notice that the satire may be of two kinds. It may be directed at the more exalted of the two ideas, which is degraded by being connected with the other one. Or it may be a debunking of the whole system of values which keeps the two ideas rigidly apart.
>
> (157)

In the case of Voltaire, as we shall see, sexual reference often accomplishes both satiric aims at once.

The elements of incongruity, sexuality and satire have been synthesized by Mikhail Bakhtin from an historical perspective.[10] In his monumental study of Rabelais, Bakhtin distinguishes between medieval folk humor and modern satire by postulating a bipolar and ambivalent image of the human body. According to his formulation, the medieval culture of folk humor accepted both the negative and positive poles; this culture denied and degraded, but at the same time it renewed and regenerated. Medieval folk humor degraded by materializing, by transferring all that is spiritual to the "material bodily lower stratum," to the genital organs and buttocks and to their biological functions. But it also emphasized the regenerating element of the body, that of birth and renewal. Medieval folk humor viewed the body as both positive and negative, as something universal, and made no pretense to renunciation of the flesh. For Bakhtin, the laughter of modern satire is only negative: the mirth places itself above the object of its mockery. Its function is still to liberate from established truth, to purify from dogmatism, intolerance and fanaticism, but its force is deprived of the regenerating element, that is, the positive pole of the bodily image. The sexual humor of Voltaire differs from that of Rabelais because, according to Bakhtin, it has been deprived of that positive pole.[11]

Women hold a special place in the negative pole of the bodily image. Women, especially their sensuality and their libidinous desire, had long been a target of comic satire in Western literature, dating back to Aristophanes. As Thomas Laqueur writes, "the commonplace of much contemporary psychology—that men want sex while women want relationships—is the precise inversion of pre-Enlightenment notions that, extending back to antiquity, equated friendship with men and fleshliness with women."[12] Michel Foucault discusses the virile character of moderation in the ethics of the ancient Greeks.[13] Being a man meant being able to control the manly activity that one directed toward others in sexual practice. To rule one's pleasures, wrote Aristotle, is to bring them under the authority of the logos, the rational principle. Aristotle gave moderation an essentially masculine structure. As a consequence, writes Foucault, "immoderation derives from a passivity that relates it to femininity. To be immoderate was to be in a state of nonresistance with regard to the force of pleasures, and in a position of weakness and submission . . ." (2: 84). The unbridled lust of women was considered to be more difficult to control than that of men because of women's supposed feeble-mindedness. In the older scheme of things, women's desires knew no bounds, and their reason offered little resistance to passion. Their minds were completely subjected to the hunger of their sexual bodies. This notion of the fundamental subjection of women's minds to their reproductive anatomy had not disappeared by the eighteenth century. Comparing the Hippocratic corpus of medical texts to articles in the *Encyclopédie,* Paul Allen Miller demonstrates that

> the same basic conceptions underlying the Hippocratic understanding of the relations between women's mental capacities and their reproductive anatomy, common from classical Greece through the Middle Ages, find themselves fully re-expressed in the scientific idiom of the Age of Reason.
>
> (48)[14]

These conceptions had been readily incorporated into the Church's negative view of female sensuality and the role of woman in the Fall.

There were, in fact, two traditions surrounding female sexuality throughout the Middle Ages. Bakhtin explains that the *tradition gauloise,* or Gallic tradition, represented not one but two lines of thought. The first was a popular comic tradition that was in no way hostile to women. It incarnated the material bodily lower stratum that degraded and regenerated simultaneously. The second was the ascetic tradition of medieval Christianity, which saw in woman the incarnation of sin, the temptation of the flesh. In a number of medieval writings hostile to women, the two tendencies are combined, but Bakhtin asserts that the popular comic tradition was profoundly alien to the ascetic tradition. The ascetic tendency, he maintains, gained predominance in the early modern period, so that the Gallic image of the female body lost its positive pole and became purely negative (240-41). It is my contention that Voltaire uses this ascetic view of women, this ancient and negative image of female lust, not to mock the sensuality of women but to call into question the very theological system that affirmed and perpetuated the ascetic view.

Voltaire's texts frequently emphasize the sensuality of women. His female characters bear such names as Las Nalgas (Spanish for "buttocks") and Signora Fatelo (Italian for "do it"). Cunégonde notices that her Bulgar captain is handsome and she does not find sexual relations with him to be repugnant. Seeing Candide about to die at the hands of the Inquisition, she is phlegmatic enough to make a comparison between his body and that of the captain. Cunégonde is not the only female character to show an interest in male nudity. The eponymous heroes of *L'Ingénu* and the *Histoire de Jenni* strip off their clothes for a bath or a baptism, exposing their naked bodies for the admiration of women. When L'Ingénu is given the baptismal name of a saint who deflowered fifty virgins in a single night, "Toutes les dames baissèrent les yeux, et jugèrent à la physionomie de l'Ingénu qu'il était digne du saint dont il portait le nom" (Voltaire, 299). Saints are not supposed to deflower virgins, of course, and women are not supposed to be interested in the male body. The revelation that saints act on their sexual desires and that women lust for men makes us laugh, while revealing the hypocrisy of the respective value systems. The narrator of *La Princesse de Babylone* makes repeated reference to the beauty of Amazan and to the sensual desire of the women who encounter him. While Formosante is compared favorably to "la *Vénus aux belles fesses*" (Voltaire, 350), Amazan is described as having "le visage d'Adonis sur le corps d'Hercule" (Voltaire, 352). According to the oracle, the Princess of Babylon would be given in marriage to the man who could bend the bow of Nembrod, which the handsome Amazan proceeds to do. In Voltaire's text, "tendre l'arc de Nembrod" soon gives way to "bander l'arc," and the repeated substitution of the transitive form of this verb evokes the obscene meaning of its intransitive form ("bander" = to have an erection): "toutes les dames . . . s'émerveillèrent qu'un homme qui bandait si bien un arc eût tant d'esprit" (Voltaire, 354). Such references are comical because they mix the sexual with the nonsexual and because they call attention to the material side of would-be spiritual beings. By portraying fictional women who were interested in sex and in the male body, Voltaire seems to be paying tribute to the ancient Gallic tradition by satirizing the fickle nature of women and female sensuality. At the same time, however, he is mocking a social ethic underpinned by a theological system that viewed all sexual desire as shameful and sinful.

In Voltaire's fiction sexual desire is often linked with and opposed to religious devotion. Simple juxtaposition of sensual pleasure and piety may be seen in the opening pages of *L'Ingénu*. The abbé de Kerkabon, he writes,

> était un très bon ecclésiastique, aimé de ses voisins, après l'avoir été autrefois de ses voisines. . . . Il savait assez honnêtement de théologie; et quand il était las de lire saint Augustin, il s'amusait avec Rabelais. . . . Mlle de Kerkabon . . . aimait le plaisir et était dévote.
>
> (Voltaire, 285-86)

As Freud and others have pointed out, there is a wide gulf between the sexual and the non-sexual. The linkage between the two is even funnier if it involves not merely the non-sexual but the pious, which explains why clergymen figure so prominently in smutty jokes. It is this gulf between the sexual and the pious that is exploited by Voltaire. The bridging of this gulf is accomplished very effectively in the figure of the pious woman, the *dévote*. To the themes of the sexual and the pious, the *dévote* adds a certain concept of the feminine, the weak-willed and lustful female. Before and after Voltaire, the *dévote* was the character used to embody the feminine in the Church and also to mock it. The *dévote* was considered a sensual creature but also one who was concerned for her reputation, and therefore a hypocrite.

In Voltaire's tales, the coupling of the sexual and the religious is often directed at women in a way that aims to debunk their outward piety by revealing their sensual nature. The narrator of *Micromégas* exploits this notion of feminine hypocrisy—viewed as decency masking sensuality—when he refers to a part of the hero's anatomy as "un endroit que le docteur Swift nommerait, mais que je me garderai bien d'appeler par son nom à cause de mon grand respect pour les dames" (Voltaire, 32). The implication is that ladies are interested in the male body, but their concern for their reputation as moral and religious individuals forces them to deny any such interest. Mlle de Kerkabon worries that L'Ingénu will circumcise himself in a clumsy fashion: women, we are told, are always interested in such matters, "par bonté d'âme" (295). Mlle de Saint-Yves, gazing at the young man's naked body, "poussait de profonds soupirs qui semblaient témoigner son goût pour les sacrements" (Voltaire, 296-97). Las Nalgas and Boca Vermeja are astounded not only by the beauty of Jenni—he too is described as having "le visage d'Adonis sur le corps d'un jeune Hercule"—but also by the contrast with what they expected to see, the monstrosity of an English Protestant: "Saint Jacques, me dit-elle, et Sainte Vierge! est-ce ainsi que sont faits les hérétiques? Eh, qu'on nous a trompées!" (Voltaire, 599). Voltaire uses women to join two disparate domains—feminine sensuality and religious piety—and thereby to degrade the latter. Put differently, he uses a conception of the feminine, already degraded, to attack the Church. It must be noted here that the *contes philosophiques* contain examples of male sensuality as well, and I will return to this point further on.

In emphasizing the lust of the clergy, Voltaire drew upon another literary tradition stretching back to the Middle Ages, one that mocked monks and priests by revealing their sensual desires behind a pious and abstemious countenance. The material bodily lower stratum proves to be more insistent than the lofty ideals of religion. Voltaire also drew upon a medieval tradition of ascribing homosexual desire to clerics, which represents presumably a step further down into degradation, thus providing another comical way to discredit the Church. Comical insinuation of sodomy was a recurring feature in anticlerical humor since the Middle Ages, and it crops up often in Voltaire's satires against his enemies, especially the Jesuits. Almost all of the homosexual references in the philosophical tales occur in *Candide,* and they have been noted by others.[15] I reiterate some of them here because I wish to make a point about their satiric function. A close look at the homosexual references in the text of *Candide* reveals an objectivity that is curiously in keeping with contemporary queer theory. What is remarkable is that the homosexual references, though at times just as comic as the heterosexual ones, are not positioned hierarchically with regard to the latter. The homosexual references contribute to the general satiric attack on the army and on the clergy, but homosexual acts are not more vilified than heterosexual acts. There is no moral hierarchy of sexual desire, and the text makes no judgmental distinctions between heterosexual and homosexual conduct. It is especially interesting to note here that Foucault, in the first volume of his enormously influential *History of Sexuality,* posited that before the nineteenth century in Europe, homosexual acts were treated no differently than pre-marital and extra-marital heterosexual acts by the confessional manuals of the Church. Canonical law, Christian pastoral codes, and civil law, Foucault avers, "did not make a clear distinction between violations of the rules of marriage and deviations with respect to genitality. Breaking the rules of marriage or seeking strange pleasures brought an equal measure of condemnation" (1: 37-38).

Many of the homosexual references in *Candide* involve soldiers and sailors (the army of the Bulgars and the shipmates of Christopher Columbus) and Jesuits, especially the young baron Thunder-ten-tronck, who is coincidentally both a soldier and a Jesuit priest in Paraguay. According to Patrick Henry, by portraying the young baron as homosexual, Voltaire was taking aim at two professions he detested (46).[16] In chapter two Candide is drafted into the Bulgar army, and when he attempts to flee the horrors of war, he is forced to undergo a severe beating by the entire regiment, "à passer trente-six fois par les baguettes." The text implies, for most twenty-first-century readers, nothing sexual: "Le régiment était composé de deux mille hommes; cela lui composa quatre mille coups de baguette, qui, depuis la nuque du cou jusqu'au cul, lui découvrirent les muscles et les nerfs" (Voltaire, 149). However, for more than fifty years scholars have claimed that "le roi des Bulgares" in chapters two and three designates the Prussian king Frederick II, and that this reference would have put the eighteenth-century reader in mind of the word "bougre" ("bugger"), since both words derive from the same origin and since Frederick had the reputation of being a sodomite. Peter Gay, for example, has commented on the sardonic implication of Voltaire's use of the term "bulgare," which signified to an eighteenth-century French reader both "hérétique" and "sodomite" (1: 198).[17] Claude Courouve corroborates that the term "bougre" was used as early as the twelfth century to designate the Bulgars and their heretical beliefs, and by the fourteenth century it also designated homosexual practices (70).[18] Courouve quotes the eighteenth-century jurist L'Averdy who wrote in 1750 that the term "bougrerie" is applied to heretics such as the "Albigeois" and the "Bulgares," and it also signfies the "crime contre nature" (Courouve, 77).

Knowledge of this association for the eighteenth-century reader thus conveyed a much different meaning to Candide's punishment by the Bulgars. The *double entendre* allows for the possibility of sodomy, of punishment by rape, further emphasizing the brutality of the soldiers. That the Bulgars use rape as punishment is confirmed when Pangloss explains what happened to Cunégonde and her brother at the time of the attack: "[Cunégonde] a été éventrée par des soldats bulgares, après avoir été violée autant qu'on peut l'être; . . . mon pauvre pupille, traité précisément comme sa soeur . . ." (Voltaire, 152). The rape is treated in a matter-of-fact way, like much of the brutality in *Candide.* Pangloss's serene, nearly detached manner of narration is almost comic. It suggests that such acts of violence are part and parcel of the best of all possible worlds and must be accepted as such. The homosexual innuendo about the Bulgars crops up again when the hero is in Spain, as Candide profits from his military/sexual experience: "Candide, ayant servi chez les Bulgares, fit l'exercice bulgarien devant le générale de la petite armée avec tant de grâce, de célérité, d'adresse, de fierté, d'agilité, qu'on lui donna une compagnie d'infanterie à commander. Le voilà capitaine . . ." (Voltaire, 166). The innuendo turns comic when the context turns from the military to the ecclesiastical. Later in the tale Candide and Cacambo arrive in Paraguay, which is under control of the Jesuits. Cacambo assures his master that the young hero's treatment by the Bulgars will ingratiate him with the Jesuits, who will value his initiation into a practice they hold dear: "Quel plaisir auront Los Padres quand ils sauront qu'il leur vient un capitaine qui sait l'exercice bulgare!" (Voltaire, 176).[19] Rape is thus juxtaposed with homosexual pleasures, with no hint of moral condemnation of either. This morally neutral view of homosexuality is characteristic of *Candide.*

The same neutral tone is used by Pangloss in his narration of the syphilitic genealogy, ending with his encounter with Paquette at the château in Westphalia. He recounts that his venereal disease has been traced back to one of Christopher Columbus's shipmates, through a number of heterosexual and homosexual relationships:

> Paquette tenait ce présent d'un cordelier très savant, qui avait remonté à la source; car il l'avait eue d'une vieille comtesse, qui l'avait reçue d'un capitaine de

cavalerie, qui la devait à une marquise, qui la tenait d'un page, qui l'avait reçue d'un jésuite, qui, étant novice, l'avait eue en droite ligne d'un des compagnons de Christophe Colomb."

(153)

No distinction is made between these encounters. As Jean Sareil remarks, "Pangloss ne se permet pas le moindre jugement sur les déviations curieuses par lesquelles passe la maladie; le rôle de l'historien est d'instruire, non de nous faire connaître son opinion" (7).[20] None of the sexual acts responsible for the transmission of the disease is given a morally hierarchized position in Pangloss's deadpan narration, a neutrality of view which contributes to the comic. Homosexuality is presented as part of the spectrum of human sexuality, without moral privilege or opprobrium. Venereal disease, no matter how it is contracted, seems to be just another evil in the best of all possible worlds.

The most important character in **Candide** who is overtly homosexual is the young baron Thunder-ten-tronck, who is given no other name than "le jeune baron."[21] The young baron is the subject of only one sentence in the opening chapter, a statement that says he resembled his father in every way, meaning vain and arrogant, qualities he will display later in the story. First-time readers of the text tend to forget this character who is mentioned so briefly and who is given no name. The young baron is more fully developed as a character in chapters 14 and 15, in which Candide finds him in Paraguay as a Jesuit commandant. There we learn that his youthful beauty had curried him favor with the Jesuits and led to his promotion in their ranks. The young baron relates that, after his rape by the Bulgars, he was taken to a nearby Jesuit chapel. He explains his subsequent success quite laconically: "Vous savez, mon cher Candide, que j'étais fort joli, je le devins encore davantage; aussi le révérend père Croust, supérieur de la maison, prit pour moi la plus tendre amitié; il me donna l'habit de novice; quelque temps après je fus envoyé à Rome" (Voltaire, 178).[22] The young baron explains how his good looks served him well with men, as any heroine might do, and indeed as Cunégonde speaks of her success with the Bulgar captain, the Jew, the Grand Inquisitor, and so on. The textual language is expressionless and completely non-judgmental.

In a sudden dispute over Candide's wish to marry Cunégonde, the hero kills the young baron and is forced to flee Paraguay. In chapter 27 the young baron again arises from the dead, as it were, when Candide, during a sea voyage to Constantinople, discovers him to be one of the galley slaves on the ship. The young baron explains how he came to Constantinople and how he ended up as a slave:

> Il n'y avait pas huit jours que j'étais entré en fonction, quand je trouvai sur le soir un jeune icoglan très bien fait. Il faisait fort chaud: le jeune homme voulut se

baigner; je pris cette occasion de me baigner aussi. Je ne savais pas que ce fût un crime capital pour un chrétien d'être trouvé tout nu avec un jeune musulman. Un cadi me fit donner cent coups de bâton sous la plante des pieds, et me condamna aux galères.

(Voltaire, 226)

It is clearly the young baron's sexual interest in the young Turk that led him into the Turkish bath, a traditional venue for homosexual eroticism in fiction. Yet he is arrested for a religious infraction, not for a sexual one: as a Christian he could not be found naked with a Muslim. Voltaire's text is totally silent on the homosexual infraction.[23] This refusal of sexual hierarchy is underscored by the fate of Pangloss. In the same chapter, Pangloss proceeds to explain why he too has become a galley slave in Constantinople:

> Un jour il me prit fantaisie d'entrer dans une mosquée; il n'y avait qu'un vieil iman et une jeune dévote très jolie qui disait ses patenotres; sa gorge était toute découverte: elle avait entre ses deux tétons un beau bouquet de tulipes . . . ; elle laissa tomber son bouquet; je le ramassai, et je le lui remis avec un empressement très respectueux. Je fus si lontemps à le lui remettre que l'iman se mit en colère, et, voyant que j'étais chrétien, il cria à l'aide. On me mena chez le cadi, qui me fit donner cent coups de latte sur la plante des pieds, et m'envoya aux galères.

(Voltaire, 227)

No hierarchical distinction is made, either by the Turkish judge or by Voltaire's text, between the homosexual desire of the young baron and the heterosexual desire of Pangloss. The judge metes out the same punishment to both characters, who are sentenced to the galleys because of religious infractions, not sexual ones.

It has long been noted that Voltaire's narrator relates numerous acts of violence—heterosexual and homosexual rape, public executions, amputation of the limbs of slaves, etc.—with a tone of calm detachment, as if such horrors were an ordinary and acceptable part of life. The intended reader is expected to smile and perhaps laugh at the deadpan narration while realizing that these atrocities ought not to exist in the best of all possible worlds. What has not been sufficiently noted is that the narrator treats sexual desire and behavior in the same way, making no moral distinction between heterosexual and homosexual desire and behavior. I do not mean to suggest that Voltaire held no negative attitudes toward homosexuality.[24] What I do mean to suggest is that Voltaire's deadpan narration presents—oddly enough—a queer approach to sexuality, a morally neutral and non-judgmental presentation of sexual acts and desires. Homosexual desire is no more a satiric target than is heterosexual desire. Clearly, however, the association of Jesuits with homosexual behavior is a weapon against the Church and its ascetic ideology. I would like to comment on Robert Adams's claim that "the theme of homosexuality that attaches to Cunégonde's brother seems to have no general satiric point . . ." (7).[25] What I believe Adams means to say—and I would agree—is that homosexuality itself is not the target of satire, except to the extent that sexual activity of any description is forbidden to the clergy. The young baron is a priest who, according to Christian doctrine, has supposedly renounced the flesh.

We have seen that Voltaire deployed ancient comic traditions concerning female sensuality and male homosexuality to unmask religious hypocrisy and to discredit the Church and its clergy. But there are plenty of examples of male heterosexuality and male fickleness in the tales, even among the protagonists. Even men like Zadig and Candide, who have vowed fidelity and shown extraordinary single-mindedness in their devotion to one woman, yield to the weakness of the flesh when seduced by a prostitute or a chambermaid (and possibly a valet and an abbé). Candide's sexual interest in Cunégonde is never far beneath the surface of his yearning for happiness and is the sole motivation for his departure from Eldorado. Sexual desire is often a natural phenomenon in Voltaire's narratives, one that is used to characterize the human condition. Pleasure, as the hermit explains to Zadig, is "un présent de la Divinité" (Voltaire, 54).

There are a few instances in Voltaire's fiction in which sexuality is viewed outside a European context, when it is glimpsed in its so-called "primitive" form. When Candide happens upon two naked South American girls cavorting in a sexual manner with monkeys, he reacts with horror and shoots the monkeys, but his European misunderstanding of this incredible form of eroticism nearly costs him his life. L'Ingénu, a young North American man, is endowed with "une vertu mâle et intrépide, digne de son patron Hercule, dont on lui avait donné le nom à son baptême; il allait l'exercer dans toute son étendue" with his beloved Saint-Yves, in the name of natural law, but Saint-Yves resists this attempted act because she is "une personne qui a de l'éducation" (Voltaire, 302-03). In the *Histoire de Jenni,* another North American man, upon learning that Freind is the venerable grandson of William Penn, enthusiastically cries out: "Un fils de Penn! Que je baise ses pieds et ses mains, et ses parties sacrées de la génération" (Voltaire, 625-26). The man is quickly told that such is not the custom in England.

These examples of "natural" sexuality are comic, but are they satiric? They have no real target except European ethnocentrism, which turns out to be, once again, produced and controlled by the Church. In such cases, human sexuality collides with Christian notions of sexual propriety. Such passages evoke a sense of cultural relativity (similar to Montesquieu's Persians), and

they constitute an amusing wink at cultures that do not complicate sexuality (such as Diderot's Tahitians). These passages call into question the value system that sets religion and sex at odds in the first place. While Voltaire knew how to use sex to debase and criticize his enemies, one can find sexual references in his works that are characteristic of Bakhtin's positive pole of the material body, naturalness and regeneration. If the positive pole is to be found in Voltaire, it is surely in the first part of *L'Ingénu,* in which sexual desire appears to be an integral characteristic of essentially sympathetic characters. The good-natured interest in sex manifested in the Bas-Bretons and especially in the Bas-Bretonnes, as well as in the handsome young Huron from Canada, contrasts sharply and favorably with the sexual intrigue and extortion evident in the royal, ministerial, and ecclesiastic world of Versailles.

Lustful women and homosexuals are not Voltaire's targets. Nor is sex in general, which although it brings pains along with joys, is shown to be a natural part of the human condition. The portrayal of women in his texts—and also of homosexuals—is predicated on a preconceived notion of the feminine as something feeble-minded, weak-willed, and lustful, an Aristotelian notion that Voltaire uses to attack his principal enemy, the Church. This is accomplished in two ways. On one hand, pious women and priests are portrayed as dominated by their passions. The exalted, spiritual idea (Christianity) is degraded, contaminated by its association with sex, by the revelation that its devotees are lustful, bodily, material, and therefore hypocritical. On the other hand, the whole intellectual system of Christianity is called into question because it makes a pretense of renunciation of the flesh and denies the attraction of sex. What is attacked is not sex but that which tries to rise above sex and deny it, notably metaphysics and religion. As a universal phenomenon, sex is a leveling element. It degrades the presumptious intellectual ideas attached to philosophy and religion by encumbering them with the material demands of the body.

Notes

1. Initial research for this essay was done in 1994 for a paper I presented at a conference celebrating the tercentenary of Voltaire's birth. J. Patrick Lee was in the audience and later told me that he found my treatment of the subject very interesting. It is for this reason that I have chosen to expand upon it for this volume. The original conference paper was published as "Making Connections: Sexuality as Satire in Voltaire's Philosophical Tales," *Voltaire et ses combats,* ed. Ulla Kölving and Christiane Mervaud, (Oxford: Voltaire Foundation, 1997), 189-97.

2. By "fictional prose narratives" I designate the 26 philosophical tales often grouped under the title *Romans et contes.* All subsequent quotations from

Voltaire's *contes* will refer to the following edition: François Marie Arouet de Voltaire, *Romans et contes,* ed. Frédéric Deloffre and Jacques Van den Heuvel (Paris: Gallimard, 1979) and be indicated as "Voltaire."

3. Roger Pearson, *The Fables of Reason: A Study of Voltaire's "Contes philosophiques"* (Oxford: Oxford University Press, 1993), 125.

4. Haydn Mason, *Candide: Optimism Demolished* (Boston and New York: Twayne, 1992), 59-62.

5. Lynn Hunt, ed., *The Invention of Pornography: Obscenity and the Origins of Modernity, 1500-1800* (New York: Zone Books, 1993), 10-11.

6. Philip Stewart, *Engraven Desire: Eros, Image and Text in the French Eighteenth Century.* (Durham and London: Duke University Press, 1992), 320.

7. Sigmund Freud, *The Joke and Its Relation to the Unconscious,* trans. Joyce Crick (New York and London: Penguin, 2003), 166.

8. Arthur Schopenhauer, *The World as Will and Representation,* trans. E. F. J. Payne, 2 vols. (New York: Dover Publications, 1958), 2: 91-101.

9. D. H. Monro, *Argument of Laughter* (Melbourne: Melbourne University Press, 1951), 156.

10. Mikhail Bahktin, *Rabelais and His World,* trans. Hélène Iswolsky (Bloomington: Indiana UP, 1984), 116-19.

11. Bakhtin's remarks on Voltaire are somewhat attenuated by the following comment: "It must be added, however, that Voltaire in his *Contes philosophiques* and in his 'Maid of Orleans' . . . [was] not far removed from Rabelaisian imagery, though in a somewhat limited and rationalized aspect" (118).

12. Thomas Laqueur, *Making Sex: Body and Gender from the Greeks to Freud.* (Cambridge and London: Harvard University Press, 1990), 3-4.

13. See Michel Foucault, *The History of Sexuality,* Vol. 1, *An Introduction,* trans. Robert Hurley (New York: Vintage Books, 1990) and his *The History of Sexuality,* Vol. 2, *The Use of Pleasure,* trans. Robert Hurley (New York: Vintage Books, 1990).

14. See Paul Allen Miller, "Floating Uteruses and Phallic Gazes: Hippocratic Medicine in the *Encyclopédie*" *Intertexts* 2.1 (1998): 46-61.

15. See Patrick Henry, "On the Theme of Homosexuality in *Candide,*" *Romance Notes* 19 (1978): 44-48, and, for the most recent and detailed work on the subject, E. M. Langille, "Allusions to Homosexuality in Voltaire's *Candide*: A Reassessment," *Studies on Voltaire and the Eighteenth Century* 2000 (05): 53-63, and "Cacambo and Candide: A New Look at Voltaire's 'Valet-Master' Duo," in *Voltaire; Raynal; Rousseau; Allégorie,* Studies on Voltaire and the Eighteenth Century 2003:07 (Oxford: Voltaire Foundation, 2003), 3-17; and, co-written with G. P. Brooks, "How English Translators Have Dealt with *Candide*'s Homosexual Allusions," *Literary Research/Recherche littéraire* 18.36 (2001): 367-87.

16. This might seem to be the case at first glance, but more recent commentators have uncovered homosexual allusions that are not restricted to these groups but instead involve Candide himself. Daniel Gordon, in his translation of *Candide,* makes a case for an allusion to Candide's having a sexual encounter with the *abbé périgordien* in Paris (32); see Daniel Gordon, trans. *Candide,* by Voltaire (Boston: Bedford/St. Martin's, 1999). E. M. Langille, in several recent articles, argues convincingly that references to homosexuality in *Candide* suggest a wider pattern of satirical allusion than has been previously recognized. Langille goes farther than Henry and others, extending the homosexual sub-theme to the tale's hero and suggesting an erotic relationship between Candide and his valet Cacambo, "an eroticism curiously at odds with the homosexual satire detected elsewhere in the novel" ("Cacambo," 4). Since I am dealing with satire here, I shall restrict my comments to the homosexual references whose satiric target is more obvious.

17. See Peter Gay, *The Enlightenment: An Interpretation,* 2 vols. (New York: Knopf, 1969). Gay limits the connotation to a parodic reference to Frederick, but Henry points out—correctly in my view—that it must apply to the whole group of Bulgar soldiers (45).

18. See Claude Courouve, *Le Vocabulaire de l'homosexualité masculine* (Paris: Payot, 1985).

19. Recent English translations include: "a captain who knows the Bulgar drill" (Pearson, *Candide* 35) and "a captain who knows how to move like a Bulgar" (Gordon, 69). For a comparison of the English translations of these allusions, see the aforementioned essay by Langille and Brooks. See Roger Pearson, trans. *Candide and Other Stories,* by Voltaire (Oxford: Oxford University Press, 1990).

20. Jean Sareil, "Sur la Généalogie de la vérole," *Teaching Language Through Literature* 26/1 (1986): 3-8.

21. Interestingly, in Leonard Bernstein's musical dramatization of *Candide,* the young baron is given a name, Maximilian, and promises at the outset to

be an important character. He is characterized in one of the first musical numbers as a narcissist, totally infatuated with his own beauty. For those who do not know Voltaire's text, this narcissism, this obsession with one's own beauty, are nonetheless comic. For those who do know the text, it appears to be portending of things to come. Yet Maximilian plays almost no part in subsequent scenes (he reappears briefly as he does in Voltaire's text), and his homosexual nature is entirely effaced.

22. Pearson's translation is even more equivocal, perhaps unintentionally so: "You know how good-looking I was, my dear Candide. I became even more so, with the result that the reverend father Croust, who was Father Superior, developed the most tender affection for me. He *initiated* me as a novice" (*Candide* 38, emphasis added).

23. I disagree totally with René Pomeau when he states that "le sodomite baron jésuite, frère de Cunégonde" is the only totally unsympathetic figure among the tale's recurring characters and that he is the only one excluded from the garden because of his sexuality (247). It is quite clear that the young baron is banished from the garden only because of his arrogant opposition to the marriage of his sister to the illegitimate Candide. See René Pomeau, "Voltaire, du côté de Sodome?" *Revue d'histoire littéraire de la France* 86 (1986): 235-47.

24. One need read only the article "Amour nommé socratique" in his *Dictionnaire philosophique* to be convinced of the contrary: "Non, il n'est pas dans la nature humaine de faire une loi qui contredit et qui outrage la nature, une loi qui anéantirais le genre humain si elle était observée à la lettre" (20) See François Marie Arouet de Voltaire, *Dictionnaire philosophique*, ed. Raymond Naves (Paris: Garnier, 1967).

25. See Robert M. Adams, trans. *Candide*, by Voltaire, 2nd ed. (New York and London: Norton, 1991).

Julia V. Douthwaite (essay date fall 2010)

SOURCE: Douthwaite, Julia V. "On *Candide*, Catholics, and Freemasonry: How Fiction Disavowed the Loyalty Oaths of 1789-90." *Eighteenth-Century Fiction* 23, no. 1 (fall 2010): 81-117.

[*In the following essay, Douthwaite discusses accounts of the 14 July 1790 Festival of Federation in France and the loyalty oaths required of citizens in support of it, focusing on the bawdy parody* Julie philosophe, ou le bon patriote *(1791) as a satire of Voltaire's* Candide.]

The literary historian who ventures into the French Revolution faces mighty challenges: most of the writers who penned the 800-some fictions published 1789-99 are largely unknown, and their works are anchored in a cultural field marked by radical, rapidly changing political alliances, linguistic innovation, and social upheaval. Historians of the political, social, and religious past have long dominated this epoch, and for good reason: their work lends itself to sifting through heterogeneous documentary evidence in service of larger historiographical claims. As Daniel Gordon famously noted: "History is a distinct form of art . . . The material that the historian writes about always appears to be a concrete particular—a monument, a document, an action—but that is because the rays of history can be detected only through such specifics. The search is ultimately for something that lends other objects their hue but is itself invisible."[1] For literary historians, the task is somewhat different: we analyze the cultural significance of sophisticated works of art in, not through, the works themselves. Our focus is acute as we decipher texts written to entertain, instruct, or provoke a public that died years ago, and whose preoccupations were very different from our own. Through historically contextualized close readings, and careful study of the work's reception, we sometimes have the good fortune to stumble upon traces of phenomena that underline the strangeness of revolutionary France. What appears to be an unexpected alignment of ***Candide,*** Catholics, and Freemasons offers an excellent case in point.

While it cannot be denied that sex and political critique run through almost all works from this period, in three novels published 1790-91—*Julie philosophe* (1791), *La Boussole nationale* (1790), and *L'Isle des philosophes* (1790)—one finds a representative set of themes and aesthetics that transcends the inconsequential coupling of most revolutionary satire and suggests a deliberate critique of oath-taking and national unity. Moreover, based on a study of 60 politically inflected fictions published from 1789-91, I contend that the trio selected here represents a rare combination of relatively elevated literary craftsmanship and in-depth sociopolitical reflection.[2] Two of the three had some measurable impact in their day. Unlike much of the ephemera produced in these early years of the Revolution, all three are hefty little tomes (in octodecimo and octavo); the shortest counts 331 pages; the longest weighs in at over 950 pages. Two are illustrated and were reprinted shortly after the original publication; the most famous, *Julie philosophe,* still enjoys a certain renown today thanks to reprints in 1910 and 1968 and links to the libertine genre. Such texts written during the age of federation-building complement the better-known records of newspaper and correspondence with wicked wit, humour, and some poignancy, suggesting the pain felt by believers during the months that saw the first major attempts on the primacy of the Catholic Church.

In the history of the French Revolution, the 14 July 1790 Festival of the Federation has the distinction of being the only event upon which everyone seems to agree: it is the apex of the patriots, the one moment when people across the country unanimously supported the new French nation. In this article, I analyze three of the most popular fictions of oath-taking written around the festivities, ancestor of modern Bastille Day,[3] in order to demonstrate how literary analysis does more than generate a glow for history; it allows us to "get it"—to get the jokes, the innuendoes, and the sarcasm deployed by contemporaries on socio-political issues of their day. Historians have detailed the elaborate physical land works and propaganda campaign that prepared the site and spectators of the July 1790 ceremonies around the country, and have unearthed fascinating traces of the emotional residue left in the thousands of letters, speeches, and diaries of Parisian and provincial deputies.[4] The novels in question shine an intriguing light on some of the political jockeying that may have unfolded behind the scenes, as refracted through the prism of satire and sentiment. Whether through subversion, co-optation, or resistance, they mark a distance from nationalist rhetoric while ostensibly supporting the revolutionary impulse towards solidarity. Moreover, they announce bedfellows that are rarely conjoined in modern-day accounts o patriotic oath-taking: Voltairean wit, Roman Catholicism, and Freemasonry.

The corpus identified here dialogues with the political history of the first year of the Revolution in three ways: (1) it underlines modern-day historians' work on the Assembly's attempt to seek unity in the midst of a contentious political environment; (2) it complements the literature on eighteenth-century sociability by reminding us of the fraught relationship between fraternity and Freemasonry; and (3) it casts a jaded eye on the ability of political innovations to break with deep-anchored networks of kinship and Catholic belief. These fictions focus specifically on oath-taking to reshape and reinterpret the act: by inscribing oath-taking into the long duration of the novel, they make what was a theatrical expression of national bonhomie into a seriously vulnerable subject of inquiry and debate.

Politics cannot tell the whole story, however. To fully appreciate *Julie philosophe, La Boussole nationale,* and *L'Isle des philosophes,* we must dig deeper into long-term trends in literary history. Like many novels of the years 1789-99, all three recycled and combined existing genres into hybrid forms. Rewriting Voltaire's philosophical tale **Candide** as a female picaresque, *Julie* features an ingénue prostitute who makes a fortune by declaring her patriotism at the most intimate of moments, and in the most didactic of styles. Her clients sign up to serve the nation in a farcical sort of oath-taking that proves as ephemeral as their libidos. *La Boussole* recalls Scarron's *Roman comique* (1651) by relating the

burlesque adventures of a peasant in foreign lands, but it combines comic portraits of national types with edifying comments on agriculture, engineering, and industrial practices that reveal a debt to the economically minded Physiocrats. Aligned overtly with the Jacobins, this text displays the most convincing patriotism of the three. But *La Boussole* nevertheless co-opts the constitutional *pacte fédératif* with another pact, sworn by brother Masons to the transnational society of their Lodge. *L'Isle des philosophes* seems at first glance to be an ironic, Swiftian voyage narrative to ideologically charged islands. However, the arrival of enthusiastic dispatches sent by a young patriot from revolutionary Paris ends up discombobulating the chronology and cultural relativism expected of this genre. In the clash between the various worlds encountered here, faith trumps all.

By underlining the impact of recent political developments on otherwise old-fashioned characters and their *péripéties,* these novels bend inherited conventions and exemplars. All three articulate a sceptical attitude towards patriotism and popular enthusiasms that presages the wry attitude of early nineteenth-century writers towards their public, thereby dispelling—if any further dispelling were needed—François Furet and Denis Richet's claims about the "happy year" of 1790.[5] Upturning national loyalties through recourse to the body, the intellect, and the conscience, they affirm a kind of liberty that transcends efforts at nation-building, and suggest that, despite claims to the contrary, France remained divided indeed during this great year of unity.

OATH-TAKING AND ITS TRACE

> Nous jurons d'être à jamais fidèles à la Nation, à la Loi et au Roi; de maintenir de tout notre pouvoir la Constitution décrétée par l'Assemblée nationale et acceptée par le Roi; de protéger, conformément aux lois, la sûreté des personnes et des propriétés, la libre circulation des grains et subsistances dans l'intérieur du royaume, la perception des contributions publiques, sous quelque forme qu'elles existent; de demeurer unis à tous les Français par les liens indissolubles de la fraternité.
>
> —Oath of the Federation[6]

While organizers were surely dismayed by the terrible weather, that so many thousands of people participated in the Festival of the Federation underscores its particular ethos: a determination to celebrate.[7] Commemorative prints . . . capture the key features: the spectacularly rain-soaked setting in the Champ de Mars outside Paris, where King Louis XVI, Queen Marie-Antoinette, General Lafayette, and Bishop Talleyrand, along with some 50,000 armed national guardsmen and soldiers and a crowd of 300,000 citizens, endured a long and surely tedious parade in the mud. According to the now classic historiography of Mona Ozouf, Samuel F. Scott, and

Henri Leclercq, this festival was basically a military gathering with the purpose of reining in the national guards by having them pledge an oath alongside the king's regular line troops.[8]

Also significant were the festival's repercussions outside the capital. The Paris festivities mirrored events being held all around the nation, from tiny Provençal villages to major Atlantic seaports, where huge numbers of Frenchmen joined together and, when the clocks hit noon, pledged a solemn oath of mutual support and defence. The proceedings followed a careful script to symbolize union, but left out a significant portion of the population and blurred over the exact meaning of the union in question. After Bishop Talleyrand celebrated high mass, General Lafayette read the oath and the thousands of guardsmen and soldiers raised their right hands and repeated: "je le jure." Next, the king swore his oath to maintain constitutional law as decreed by the Assembly, and the queen showed her young son to the crowd and promised, to much applause, that he would do likewise. Apart from the small contingent accompanying the royal family, the celebrants were primarily middle-class military men and deputies. Most flagrant in their absence were the upper classes. As for the poor (*le menu peuple*), they were neither excluded nor involved, rather they served as witnesses to the national regeneration. Despite this exclusion, Ozouf's history represents the nation as uniting under the oath; as she notes: "It was met nearly everywhere with enthusiasm, even by those not normally enthusiastic about the Revolution."[9] From an untruth emerged a legend, made truth by the retelling. How did this come about?

The Parisian event did not simply promote patriotism and religion; it announced de facto that both were already reconciled in the new constitution. Historians Leclercq and Suzanne Desan claim that for many *fédérés* oath-taking was an explicitly sacred event.[10] Feudal oaths had a long history dating back to *La Chanson de Roland* (c. 1100); more recently, deputies had sworn oaths at the 1614 Estates-General to restore unity following the assassination of Henri IV. Vowing to uphold a constitution, however, was a new idea; and yet the unfinished status of the constitution gave pause. Making a constitution for France was a primary preoccupation for the deputies assembled at Versailles in May 1789; they believed that they had been elected for this purpose, and by 7 July 1789 they adopted the name "National Constituent Assembly." By August 1789, they approved the Declaration of the Rights of Man and of the Citizen that laid down the principles—of equality under law, free speech, and national sovereignty—to secure the break with feudalism, and named a committee to begin drafting a constitution. But the first constitution was not officially installed until 14 months after the Federation, and the binding power of the oath remained unclear. Most perplexing was the hazy relation between

the constitution, the Gallican Catholic Church, and the French state, the loyalty implied to each, and the question of how oath-taking might impact the delicate balance between the two bastions of French identity.[11]

Readings based on the iconography of euphoric *pactes fédératifs* spreading across the nation must be tempered by awareness of the social, military, and religious tensions that divided France in fall 1789 through summer 1790. Georges Lefebvre noted in his classic work of rural history that by summer 1789, many long-term antipathies proved impervious to fraternal good will, and old animosities flared anew.[12] As word spread of legislation that restricted feudal rights and formalized tolerance of Protestantism,[13] towns witnessed latent hostilities turning into skirmishes between the newly formed local militias or National Guards, the king's line troops, and the disgruntled civilians who appealed to both for protection. In a juxtaposition of official harmony and bloody conflict, cities large and small, from Lille to Marseilles, saw violent confrontations and civic oath-taking that spring and summer. The year 1790 not only found French society caught in "the widespread, if not general, breakdown of law and order," writes Scott, but it was also the "year of disintegration" for members of the regular army, whose allegiance to the king and obedience to officialdom were repeatedly tested by the increasing popularity of the National Guards.[14] Faced with an unstable signifier, it is not surprising that the oath would assume radically different meanings when voiced by a Catholic or a Freemason, for example, as opposed to a free-thinking libertine. The meaning of the festival lay less in the performance than in the legitimacy attributed to its performers.

The loyalty oath taken by festival participants in the French capital and countryside on 14 July 1790 was only one in a long sequence of performances that marked that year. Oath-taking had already swept through the nation beginning in summer 1789, first at the Tennis Court Oath of June 20, then following the news of the Night of August 4 and Declaration of the Rights of Man and the Citizen. The vogue became especially pronounced after Louis XVI's dramatic appearance in the Constituent Assembly on 4 February 1790; during spring and summer 1790, *pactes fédératifs* spread across the provinces. The gesture brought to mind virtuous Spartans and other heroes of Antiquity such as the Horatii of Jacques-Louis David's tableau, but it also infringed on individual honour.[15] Some claimed that oath-taking itself was an affront, since any worthy citizen would not need a public audience to confirm his virtue.[16] Partisan politics were not uninvolved: the now-famous Tennis Court Oath was itself a result of partisan positioning. As Claude Langlois points out, the deputies' euphoric gesture was considered just one event among others until the fateful day when the king swore his allegiance at the Assembly. From that moment on, the oath "to the nation, the law, and the king" was on everyone's lips, and this first oath acquired its status in the patriot press. Reacting to the upsurge in popularity of Louis, journalists suddenly inscribed the June event as a founding moment of the Revolution, an interpretation that would be consecrated by David's drawing presented to the Salon in 1791.[17] The delay between signifier and signified here reveals the artist's debt to left-wing activism, and testifies to the potent symbolism of oath-taking in the public eye.

The year 1790 saw the large-scale promotion of a performative sort of public political culture as had never before been experienced in France. Marie-Hélène Huet and Susan Maslan have focused on the distinction between the performed and the performative enacted in these rituals, and have shown how contemporaries demanded a classically inspired "virtuous spectacle" that would eschew the theatricality and artifice of the *ancien régime* court.[18] Focusing on the words spoken and the actors speaking in fictionalized rituals of oath-taking can reveal much about the oath's shaky content and the weakening prestige of the monarchy in the months surrounding the writing of the constitution. No matter how earnest its performers, ritual could not amount to much as long as its key player—the constitution—remained off-stage. When performance is seen to be enacted by illegitimate actors, the results elicit even greater scepticism. The three works studied here tackle the issue of legitimacy: the first undermines oath-taking with sly innuendo, the second co-opts it to extra-national purposes, and the third refuses it outright, but in moral not political terms. Literary performances thus parallel the paradoxes of real-life drama, and through their strategies of indirection and allusion, they illuminate the political repressed.

JULIE PHILOSOPHE, OR CANDIDE TURNS A TRICK

A Voltairean irony imparts much of the humour to the anonymous *Julie philosophe, ou le bon patriote* (1791), a fictional autobiography that enjoyed some contemporary success, judging from its second edition in 1792, and which continues to intrigue readers today. Its eroticism may account for its popularity; that *Julie* was considered pornography comes out clearly in a police report of An IX (1801) that includes the novel alongside *Thérèse philosophe* and *Le portefeuille du fouteur* in a list of books seized for immoral content.[19] The 1910 edition by Guillaume Apollinaire and more recent scholarship emphasize the salacious nature of *Julie's périples*.[20] Courtesan, spy, and adventuress, Julie is regarded by critics as one in a series of independent whores celebrated in libertine fictions of the Enlightenment, such as *Fanny Hill* (1748-49), *Moll Flanders* (1722), or *Margot la ravaudeuse* (1750), who masterfully practice their trade in order to gain wealth and prestige. But when one looks behind the plot line to the

logic underpinning *Julie,* one espies a politicized satire of Voltaire's best-known tale, **Candide, ou l'optimisme** (1759).

Although Julie's early education conforms to conventions of period erotica, the narrative also explicitly refers to a penchant for explanatory life-writing that recalls the ridiculously doctrinaire stances embraced by Voltaire's optimist Candide and Diderot's fatalist Jacques. "J'ai toujours aimé à raisonner mes actions," Julie notes on one occasion; and "j'ai déjà dit que toutes mes actions étaient raisonnées, et j'étais ingénieuse à les justifier vis-à-vis de moi-même après coup, quand la faiblesse, la passion, ou les circonstances m'avaient entraînée" (1:30; 1:67). Like Candide, her desire for "learning" gets her expelled from home and sets off the journey plot. The philosophical tic takes on a more topical air when Julie wanders into war-torn regions of the Brabant and émigré circles in London, before returning to revolutionary France at the end of the novel.

Just as the Legislative Assembly would do in 1791 and the Convention government in 1792, Julie undertakes her own liberating mission to neighbours abroad, and with such success![21] Thanks to one of her first lovers, a rebellious Amsterdammer whose grandiose ambition compensates for his tiny penis, the heroine claims to become a "proselyte of the cause" and her ardour—metaphorical and literal—never flags (1:91).[22] The diverse origins of her clients drive home the essentially transnational libertinism of their practices: the Dutch ship captain who initiates her into the useful practice of prostitution deploys an appealingly "republican" energy in their tryst; and an English lover is praised for pumping her with "spirits of liberty" (1:71; 1:204). As Harvey Chisick has noted, this notion of "patriotism" was intended to connote a value that was not exclusive but universalist; its opposite was not cosmopolitanism but selfishness.[23] So thoroughly enthused do these experiences make her, that one suspects a certain tongue-in-cheek intent. Although Julie's mercantile affirmation of individual freedom turns Candide's deterministic casuistry upside down, the function of patriotism in *Julie philosophe* feels strangely familiar. Perhaps patriotism is to this heroine what optimism was to Candide.

In episode after episode, Julie's principles are tested, and always she reiterates the same blind devotion to the cause. Her most harrowing adventure occurs back in France, where she narrowly escapes a hanging by a mob of irate citizens. Here too the heroine proves surprisingly tolerant of violence against her person, and comments: "Quoique victime innocente . . . la cruelle épreuve par laquelle j'ai passé n'a point changé mes sentiments; je suis toujours patriote" (2:62). In ironic understatement, she admits that "il est toujours fort désagréable d'avoir été pendu, fut-ce pour la bonne cause"; nevertheless her support for the people remains steadfast (2:66). This absurd metaphor of reduction—calling a hanging a "disagreeable" experience—casts a broad wink at another Voltairean hero, Babouc who, after enjoying weeks of high living in the operas, theatres, and homes of elegant Persepolisans, realizes that his "trials" are minor compared to Jonah's imprisonment three days in a whale's belly.[24] Babouc's reliability is debunked by his exaggerated self-importance and the ease with which he changes his mind; Julie's reliability proves just as dicey but for the opposite reason. Like Candide, she never allows events to impact her beliefs. Her simple-minded patriotism robs the narrator of the credibility she might otherwise have claimed with the tell-all strategy of the autobiography. How can one be so blind to the dangers of ideology?

As narrated by this diarist, patriotism justifies any number of moral transgressions, and the loyalty oath absolves all kinds of sins. Prostitution comes across as a not only lucrative but also virtuous enterprise: even the most formidable noblemen become *sans-culottes* under the influence of Julie's persuasive harangues. A sort of revolutionary casuistry runs through these sordid details, as when the heroine explains her decision to accept the lewd advances of Louis XVI's former finance minister Calonne as a gesture comparable to the sacrifices committed by the heroes of Antiquity, such as the Horatii celebrated in David's painting: "'Je parviendrai peut-être à le changer, me dis-je, à en faire un honnête homme, un bon citoyen' . . . je me comparais à ces anciens Romains qui se dévouaient généreusement pour leur Patrie" (2:34). After bedding several times with this ugly yet energetic client, Julie's plot succeeds: he realizes the errors of aristocratic prejudice and he writes to the Assembly asking for permission to return to France from exile in England and to take a civic oath (2:43-44).

Before accepting a liaison with an aristocratic émigré in Austria, Julie demands a conversion as well: "Je suis d'un parti opposé au vôtre; la cause de la liberté n'a pas un plus zélé partisan que moi. Ah! s'il en est ainsi, dès ce moment, je déteste, j'abjure une cause qui n'est point la vôtre, et je suis prêt à vous immoler mes intérêts les plus chers pour vous prouver mon amour . . . il n'est rien que je ne fasse pour vous plaire, et je suis prêt à m'engager par serment à tout ce que vous voudrez m'ordonner" (2:201-2). Days later, after embracing new principles—but nothing else—from the coy taskmistress, he seals the deal with a "most sacred oath," and finally receives his reward (2:205). When an accident leaves him on his deathbed shortly thereafter, the one-time conspirator regrets only that he did not have time to "expiate his errors" and prove that he had become "as uncompromising a patriot as he had once been a flagrant aristocrat" (2:217).

Based on this recurrent plot device, I disagree with Margaret Jacob's dismissal of the novel as a "preachy"

kind of failed pornography, and propose rather that *Julie* be read for the Voltairean spirit it incarnates.[25] Along with its rocambolesque erotica, *Julie philosophe* presents a sustained, ironic conversion tale that satirizes the mania for oath-taking which swept the French nation in 1789-90. Even modestly knowledgeable readers of 1791 would remember Calonne's despicable role in the Diamond Necklace Affair.[26] With rumours running thick of his activism among the émigrés in London in 1789, the notion that this roué might swear a loyalty oath to the nascent French nation was surely a burlesque gesture. The oaths in *Julie philosophe,* like the patriotism they profess to symbolize, function in the same way that the tenets of Leibnizian optimism functioned in **Candide.** They are vain gestures involving a vacant signifier: they cannot explain the world or even predict a character's intent.

Julie philosophe ends as did **Candide** by exposing her principles as a sham. Thanks to the lucrative traffic in sex, Julie becomes a wealthy landowner. Despite her oft-cited love of equality, she admits no desire to share the fortune except with a strapping peasant husband. In an explicit wink to **Candide** that ends with the famous adage "Il faut cultiver notre jardin," *Julie philosophe* concludes: "Adieu mon cher lecteur; il m'en coûte de ne plus pouvoir bavarder avec toi, mais je te quitte pour aller trouver mon cher Jérôme, qui laboure une pièce de terre derrière notre maison, car, quoique nous soyons riches, nous n'en travaillons pas moins . . . et je finirai en disant comme Candide: 'Tout cela est bien, mais il faut labourer notre jardin'" (2:229).[27] Note the titillating slip of vocabulary; from the elegant verb of agricultural and intellectual work *cultiver* to the double-entendre implicit in *labourer* (to work and to dig or plow, as in the poetic expression *labourer les sillons de Vénus,* to plow the furrows of love). Just as Voltaire's naive hero ultimately found himself slaving as a subsistence farmer, this fiery patriot concludes her life as the kind of genteel aristocrat that she all along professed to despise, though she too dabbles in gardening.

Julie was not the only text to satirize the vogue for civic oath-taking. Consider the caricature *Ma Constitution* (ca. 1791 . . .) that depicts General Lafayette placing his right hand in a gesture of oath-taking onto the genitals—*res publica*—of a scandalously exposed lady. This insulting caricature marks an affront to all three subjects of the real oath—*La Nation, la loi et le Roi*—by showing a *putto,* symbol of love and lust, knocking the royal crown off the globe on the right, while a penis ejaculates below. It implies that the world is now governed neither by the Assembly nor by the monarchy, but by the leader of the nation's military who is himself led by his prick.[28] Also relevant are the bawdy jokes that appeared in newspapers, such as the September 1791 *Journal des sans-culottes,* which depicts a patriot swearing fidelity to the constitution as if she were a slutty girlfriend: "Madame, si j'avais l'honneur d'être votre mari, je ne vous caresserais jamais le cul que la main droite posée sur la Déclaration des droits de l'homme."[29] In *Julie philosophe,* as in period caricature and journalism, the ritual of oath-taking is transformed from a solemn event into a trivial or burlesque gesture heralding sexual favours to come.[30] Oath-taking becomes a sly joke to share among friends, a cynical reminder that patriotism—or indeed any ideology—can hardly rival the libido.

LA BOUSSOLE NATIONALE, OR THE FEDERATION OF MASONS

Where these last examples explicitly skewer revolutionary idioms with irreverent humour, the irony that seems to cloak oath-taking in Pochet's *Boussole nationale* (1790) derives from a political innuendo of an entirely different nature.[31] This novel, whose beautifully illustrated title page . . . announces its attribution to a "true Patriot," includes a dedication to a most distinguished ally: Jean-Sylvain Bailly, academician, astronomer, and Mayor of Paris from 1789, who presided over the Assembly during the famous Tennis Court Oath. Although largely unknown today, *La Boussole* was well received by the press and went into a second edition in 1791 with the title *Voyages et aventures d'un laboureur descendant du frère de lait d'Henri IV* (Travels and Adventures of a Labourer, Descendant of the Foster-Brother of Henri IV). The editors' instructions for its dissemination are tantalizing yet enigmatic. The preface describes Bailly's support for the novel—deemed "l'ouvrage d'un bon Citoyen"—and exhorts compatriots to stage public readings or *veillées* as soon as possible. Moreover, it offers grandiose instructions aiming for wide distribution: "Nous bornons nos vœux pour qu'à l'imitation de nos Concitoyens qui forment des Sociétés des Amis de la Constitution, établies dans les villes municipales de Besançon et Strasbourg, MM. les chefs de districts villageois, les curés de campagne, les chefs de régiment et de manufactures, établissent des Sociétés de lecture, qu'on y lise les aventures survenues aux inconséquens parens du descendant du frère de lait de notre bon roi Henri, [et] que cette histoire soit pour eux l'œil du maître, avec lequel ils acquerront les lumières nécessaires à tout bon citoyen."[32] Even if this lengthy little book (more than 950 pages in three volumes in octavo) was not read aloud as the editors requested, it was apparently promoted among the Jacobins.[33] Four book reviews appeared in June-October 1791 in the leading newspapers, *Le Journal de Paris, Le Moniteur Universel, La Chronique de Paris,* and the more specialized *Feuille de correspondence du libraire,* and *La Boussole* is praised as a "very useful" book, which offers not only a "faithful and lively tableau of the happy life in France," but also warns of the "evils found in foreign lands by those unwise enough to betray their country in guilty emigrations."[34] The agricultural lessons of *La*

Boussole may be banal borrowings from didactic publications such as the *Feuille villageoise;* more intriguing are the *lumières* that every good citizen needs.[35]

Most of the novel relates the travails of the peasant-hero Jaco as he travels through Holland, Russia, Poland, Germany, and England; wherever he goes, he is duped by unscrupulous swindlers, is welcomed by fellow Masons, learns about new agricultural technologies and tips on topics such as sheep breeding and crop rotation, and seeks to locate his lost relatives who had fallen prey to "guilty emigrations" in search of work—and religious freedom—abroad.[36] His main goal throughout is to convince his cousins to return home and join the family farm in rural France, where they are now welcome thanks to the king's lifting of restraints against non-Catholics.[37] At the end, all the relatives and many more peasants, who have followed their lead, settle on the farm and adopt a lifestyle that is as heavily legislated as the other schemes for social engineering found in period fiction.[38] Despite its strenuous support for the constitutional monarchy, King Louis XVI and the legislative reforms afoot in France in 1789-90 are not mentioned as much as the localized reforms being enacted on Jaco's territory. When Louis XVI is held up for praise, his name is invariably coupled with the hero's great-great-grandfather's foster-brother Henri IV, and Louis' policies are compared favourably with the religious tolerance and agrarian reforms of that illustrious forebear, or it is suggested that he look to his ancestor or to his loyal labourers for advice.[39] This genre of kingly dialogue reveals the connection between *La Boussole nationale* and the dozen or so brochures known as the *Entretiens des Bourbons* that were published the same year.[40] However what is relevant here is not the king's presence but rather his relative absence from the tale.

Especially significant is the blurred constitutionalism behind the ritualized oath-taking that marks the grandiose finale of *La Boussole nationale*: a spectacular 30-page tableau of rustic festivals on Jaco's farm, where he convokes a meeting of what he calls his "petite monarchie." Counting more than 1,200 inhabitants, this compound includes 32 farms, workshops housing weavers, tanners, and a stocking factory, all set up according to the most modern criteria. But the final oath taken by the men in Pochet's version of the Federation is not a constitutional oath at all, rather it is a pledge to Freemasonry.

Although the novel's last page is illustrated with emblems indicating support for the constitutional king (. . . note the lilies winding around a sword and a bugle, while a banner-bedecked beehive sits atop a book of laws), and it bears the familiar slogan of *Le Roi, La Nation, réunis et soumis à la loi,* the text conflates constitutionalism with an initiation into the Freemasons. The villagers do join together at one moment to read the Declaration of the Rights of Man and the Citizen, and take an oath to the National Assembly and the king (3:313-18). But the emotional high point of the event emerges at the end. After three days of Rousseauian open-air merrymaking in which Jaco, the village noble-man, and the parish priest choreograph the distribution of prizes to the best citizens and celebrate marriages be-tween young couples, they bring together the hundreds of men who head the community households and offer them three objects. Each man receives a symbolic in-strument that corresponds to his Masonic rank, a copy of the "Duties and rights of men and citizens," and a copy of *La Boussole nationale* itself, which they are in-cited to learn by heart so they can repeat it to their families, each one incarnating the virtuous transparency of life under the "eye of the master."[41] Before closing, the men also learn the secret rites and password of the Freemasons, they raise a glass of wine in a toast, and they make a pledge. This pledge invokes unity and brotherhood, which resembles the rhetoric of the Fed-eration, except that the pledge exactly reproduces the language of the well-known Masonic *Apprentices' Song* (*La Chanson des apprentis*). The *Boussole* pledge goes: "Joignons-nous de mains en mains / Tenon-nous fermes ensemble / Rendons grâce aux destins / Du nœud qui nous rassemble"; the *Chanson des apprentis* reads: "Joignons-nous, mains en mains / Tenons-nous fermes ensemble, / Rendons grâce au destin / Du nœud qui nous assemble."[42] There are only a few letters, and a very slight emphasis, differentiating the first from the second: *le destin* becomes *les destins,* and *assemble* be-comes *rassemble.* This striking similarity between the novel's language and imagery of the all-seeing eye and the discourse of Freemasonry may be chalked up in part to the borrowings that were known to operate between revolutionary and Masonic symbolism.[43] One thing is sure, however: this vow does not conform to the *pacte fédératif* seen above. By introducing the transnational dimension of Masonic brotherhood, this vow departs radically from the original national pledge—"demeurer unis à tous les Français par les liens indissolubles de la fraternité"—which bolstered support for the French in and only among the French.

It is also significant that the constitution, the National Guard, and the Assembly, which was entrusted with drafting the document, are all missing from this climax. Those agents who are present—the Masonic leader, the village nobleman, and the local curate—represent an amalgam of old-fashioned and newfangled authority figures. All three orders being equal, it is nevertheless Jaco the peasant who heads the "little monarchy." This juxtaposition of old regime sociability, egalitarianism, and fraternity seems to be a deliberate move on the part of author Pochet that reveals much about the unsettled state of constitutional politics in 1790. It also brings an important nuance to our idea of the French *mentalité.*

The positive image of helpful, intelligent, and organized Freemasons in this book and in Robert Lesuire's novel *Charmansage* (1792; reprint 1795) should ring a bell of caution to those modern critics who may hastily con-flate Freemasonry with conspiracy theory, or misunder-stand its resonance in 1790-91. Although the work by Roger Chartier, among others, has seen Masonic socia-bility as an early model for revolutionary ideals of re-generation and equality, opinion also ran strong against it, and on all sides of the political spectrum. The mas-terful Ronald Paulson and Margaret Jacob both cite 1793 as the turning point—Jacob notes that "by 1793 freemasonry was suspect to both the French left and the French right"—but neither explains how this shift oc-curred.[44] Evidence of confusion and ambivalence over the secretive group emerges strikingly in François Dop-pet's novel, *Zélamire, ou les liaisons bizarres* (1788, re-print 1791), where the narrator describes his father as a goodly Freemason who was nevertheless seduced by an unscrupulous *illuminé* with dastardly powers of mind control over his initiates.[45] That rumours conflated Free-masonry with other shady sects is attested by the dis-tinction in *Zélamire* between the Freemasons and the *il-luminés,* but their shared predilection for magic ends up costing his father his life. Moreover, this learned au-thor—a medical doctor who during the Revolution would serve as general in the republican army—inserts a note that declares: "Quoi! Les illuminés vont aussi en Savoie? Il faut avouer que cette secte ridicule se multi-plie singulièrement. Ce qu'il y a de plus étonnant, c'est la protection dont jouissent ces imposteurs [par].. des gens en place."[46] The political power of the Freemasons was part of their allure, and explains some of the alarm.

Regardless of the doubtful innuendoes that cloaked the Freemasons among some camps, the fact remains that the positive representation of the group in *La Boussole* was a significant support. That the novel was well-received in the press, and that both the author and the purported ally of the book in the revolutionary govern-ment supported them, lend credence to our appeal for caution. Moreover, the instructions included in the pref-ace suggest a fascinating reciprocity between literature and the civic activism of the Freemasons. The cities where *La Boussole* is to be sent—in imitation of the good work being done in Besançon and Strasbourg—will by association join with what Daniel Ligou labels the "rationalist" Lodges of the Freemasons, where mem-bers were attempting to distinguish themselves from their more mystical confederates by setting up literary and scientific academies to respond to local needs.[47] Clearly, the Freemasons in 1790-91 appeared to some, if not all Frenchmen, as wielding the potential to pro-vide important assistance and structure ("the eye of the master") to the rural citizenry—and perhaps more effec-tively than the nation could do for itself.

L'ISLE DES PHILOSOPHES: AN OBJECT LESSON
ON SILENCING THE OATH

Refusing outright to take the constitutional oath presents an even more provocative challenge to revolutionary reform, and yet it appears the most sensible choice in Abbé Balthazard's epistolary novel, *L'Isle des philosophes* (1790). Through dialogues between an enthusiastic patriot and his long-suffering yet loyal friend, Abbé Balthazard portrays the ambiance of uncertainty affecting a broad cross-section of French society in the months leading up to the festival. Sympathy for the Church is unsurprising given that Balthazard's only other publication is *L'Année chrétienne* (1789), a book of Christian exercises.[48] Both books project an image of the author as citizen-priest: less a sacred intercessor or miracle worker than a spiritual educator and willing servant of society.[49] Immediately upon opening this tome, however, the reader encounters the dilemma confronting the would-be patriot; as the "Preliminary reflections" declare: "Et moi aussi, je crie vive la Nation! Je désire son bonheur, & je crains sa ruine plus que personne au monde. Qu'elle vive donc, la Nation françoise, qu'elle prospère à jamais, & qu'elle ne perde rien de son antique splendeur! Tel est mon vœu, tel est le vœu de tous les bons patriotes."[50] From these prophetic words, the campaign of resistance begins, as the partisans of "good patriotism" and "ancient splendour" defend tradition against the innovators.

Reworking a satirical leitmotif inherited from what is now commonly known as the counter-Enlightenment, *L'Isle des philosophes* proves deeply enmeshed in the anti-philosophical debates of the early Revolution.[51] Composed of eight long letters and commentaries dated from May 1789 to March 1790 and sent by a nobleman (*le chevalier*) to his nephew in Paris, the fiction relates a voyage among strange and quixotic peoples residing on a number of islands off the coast of America. In a genre made popular by early modern novelists such as Gabriel de Foigny, Jonathan Swift, and Restif de la Bretonne, and reworked in numerous revolutionary allegories, the voyage format allows the author to comment upon different social systems and expound upon the philosophies that they represent.[52] Each landfall encountered in *L'Isle des philosophes* prompts the two Frenchmen to engage in a heated exchange on issues regarding the origins of man and the Earth, the moral superiority of man over beast, and other debates inherited from the 1750s to the 1770s. Critics have proven Balthazard's debt to the reactionary polemics spawned by Abbé Barruel, whose best-selling *Mémoires pour servir à l'histoire du jacobinisme* would deliver a major jolt to left-wing literati in 1797.[53] But its dialogue with the vogue for oath-taking and the spirit of Federation remains unexplored.

The temporal disjunction running through *L'Isle des philosophes* may be one of its most valuable legacies to modern readers. Thanks to the multivocal epistolary genre, the numerous inset tales, and the paratextual materials appended to the voyage story, Balthazard's novel allows its readers to experience vividly the anxiety felt by his contemporaries in the summer of 1790. That is when it appears to have been written, judging from the author's criticism of the press for condemning people who "still think the way they did 15 months ago": presumably a reference to the pre-Bastille days of spring 1789 (*L'Isle,* vii). Reading this book is befuddling, because each letter relating the voyagers' adventures includes a P.S. where the hero comments on the news from Paris as relayed by his nephew and relates the often heated conversations they elicit with his friend (*le vicomte*), but these appendices frequently focus on events that happened months after the dates of the letters. Such chronological incongruities point to a crisis of temporality that doubtless mirrored the lived experiences of many French in this turbulent moment.

After a shipwreck strands them in the midst of the ocean, the travellers discover a number of islands inhabited by deformed humans and gifted animals. Most disconcerting are the Swiftian Island of the Bears (where intelligent bears dominate dull-witted human beasts of burden) and the Island of Chance (where humanoid horses rule over hooved homo sapiens).[54] Here they witness the surprising results of chance, as when a cup holding the letters of a word game is accidentally knocked over during an earthquake and spells out the king's speech to the National Assembly on 4 February 1790. Insisting on the veracity of this anecdote, the narrator claims that he would never have imagined the king of France bowing before the people, and a footnote echoes the irony by exclaiming: "En effet, qui auroit prévu que Louis XVI seroit dans le cas de parler de la sorte en 1790?" (*L'Isle,* 88).

The metaphorical distance between new worlds and the old gradually shrinks until the travellers disembark on the Island of Philosophers. There they meet a "learned man" who expounds on principles that clearly parallel legislative battles in France, as when he describes the methods that he and his faction employed to annihilate religious feeling among the populace. Initially, they made religion the butt of ridicule, clever sarcasm, and jokes, he explains, before adopting print media, distributing and reading anticlerical brochures in the streets, and finally insinuating their views into philosophical writings, catechisms, and academic tirades. The result is splendid, as he announces with satisfaction: "Ainsi grâce à nos efforts, la religion est aujourd'hui reléguée parmi le petit peuple, & ne sert plus d'aliment qu'aux esprits faibles" (*L'Isle,* 120-22).

Although set in a faraway land, this campaign would ring familiar to many Frenchmen who feared that the Assembly, under the cloak of budgetary reform, was launching a veritable campaign of de-Christianization. The future of the Catholic Church in France had inspired much anxious debate since the fateful night when feudal privileges were abolished (4 August 1789), and it suffered its first major setback with the 2 November 1789 law that placed church property at the disposal of the nation for possible future sale. In the next six months, the National Assembly adopted ever more aggressive measures against the Church, going beyond fiscal appropriation of property to launch a frontal attack on the status of the Catholic organization in France. This trend culminated in the 13 April 1790 Assembly rejection of Catholicism as the state religion, the Civil Constitution of the Clergy on July 12, and the more punitive measures against non-juror priests that followed in 1791.[55]

The postscript following this visit makes the connection between *philosophie* and de-Christianization explicit, and furthermore anchors such sacrilege in French history. The chevalier naively enthuses: "Quand j'entendais le recteur nous conter la manière dont les philosophes de l'isle . . . avaient dépouillé le clergé, je ne m'imaginais pas que les philosophes français imiteraient sitôt un si bel exemple" (*L'Isle*, 200-1, 209). But his friend retorts morosely that the deputies would never live down this infamous act, and compares them to heretics who had tried to sully the Church in earlier times. In its contrast between present enthusiasm and anxiety for the future, this exchange reveals the different use of time in revolutionary and monarchist discourse. Where the former celebrates the nation's break with the past, the latter emphasizes continuity and perceives the disconnection from repeatable exempla as a kind of cultural melancholy.[56] This tendency also runs through royalist caricature, which insisted that the Revolution was not a rupture and was not irreversible or instantaneous; instead, it was a specific time, a present stretched out beyond measure and not easily understandable, which constantly required the evocation of the immediate past and the anticipation of the near future.[57] In this invocation of historical sweep lay the counter-revolutionaries' greatest arm, for it replaced the patriots' reassuring fictions of newness with reminders of their shameful hubris and spectres of a guilty future looming ahead.

Most relevant for my purposes is the seventh letter dated 25 February 1790, where the chevalier describes hearing from his nephew about the patriotic oaths being celebrated in France: "Cette lecture m'a comme électrisé, j'ai partagé l'enthousiasme de l'assemblée nationale, & j'ai prononcé sur le champ à la compagnie, presque toute composée de Français, de faire le serment civique et de jurer de *maintenir de tout notre pouvoir la nouvelle constitution de la France*" (*L'Isle*, 252). Much to his surprise, he finds that the others disagree. Here Balthazard offers his most precious insights into the conflicted feelings of Frenchmen in early 1790, as he

represents a number of different social types explaining why they all refuse to swear. A nobleman refutes the oath on legal grounds, arguing that it enacts a kind of emotional and political violence against individual free will: "vous tyrannisez ma conscience, vous forcez mon opinion, & vous violez l'article XVIII de cette même constitution qui laisse à l'homme la liberté de penser sur-tout, même en matière de religion" (*L'Isle*, 253). A Quaker refuses on doctrinal grounds, arguing that his religion forbids oath-taking and moreover, the declaration of rights protects religious freedoms. A Catholic refuses because of his great respect for such a "religious act," deferring judgment until the constitution is finished (*L'Isle*, 254). A writer refuses because he feels the oath binds his critical judgment ("je ne veux pas enchaîner mon opinion," *L'Isle*, 254). A parish priest refuses because he would have to convince his parishioners that the constitution is fair, even if he does not believe so. Finally, and most compelling, an ordinary man (*un bonhomme*) takes the floor and explains:

> Je suis comme des millions de Français, un être nul, par rapport au gouvernement & aux affaires de l'Etat. Si vous exigez seulement de moi de me soumettre au nouvel ordre de chose, qui sera adopté par toute la nation, & en attendant de ne point fomenter de trouble, de ne point soulever les peuples contre la constitution, à la bonne heure; ma religion elle-même me défend d'exciter des révoltes. Cette religion qui m'inspire des sentiments pacifiques, est plus utile qu'on ne pense à la tranquillité publique, & on a grand tort de ne pas la déclarer la religion de l'Etat.
>
> (*L'Isle*, 256)

With this, the episode abruptly ends. Unlike other scenes, it is followed by no dialogue with the vicomte, no spirited repartee, no attempt to defend the Revolution. Conscience and faith trump partisan politics.

Whereas historical accounts of early 1790 polarize between the images of spontaneous intra-village goodwill that dominate Ozouf's account, on the one hand, and the visions of religious persecution and infighting penned by Catholic historians and historians of rural France,[58] on the other hand, here is a portrait of ordinary Frenchmen as conscientious citizens who support Catholicism, remain wary of change, and justify their views with intelligent reasons. The novel concludes with a scene where the *vicomte* relates the despair of a monk forced to leave his monastery, lists all the reasons why Catholicism should be the state religion, and then challenges his interlocutor to practice the virtue of tolerance. In a deft move, the author turns the doctrine of free speech against the enemies of the Church, and demonstrates that refusing to take an oath makes more sense than swearing to obey. As in *Julie philosophe* (but what a difference of tone, style, and humour!), the meaning of oath-taking lies less in the performative aspect of the act than in the legitimacy attributed to the words and the performers. Where the 1791 novel showed a promiscuous seductress using patriotic rhetoric to make an ironic statement on political expediency, Balthazard's work provides a roll call of upstanding individuals whose close scrutiny of the oath, in word and in deed, rejects the integrity of a supposedly democratic ritual. By the end of *L'Isle*, the legitimacy of the revolutionary state lies in tatters. Unlike Swift's example, it is not the interlocutors encountered on the fantastic voyage who bring about this sea change, but rather the French themselves who are faithful to a higher power.

MAKING SENSE OF HISTORY WITH FICTION

If we fast-forward to later years of the Revolution, the issues of constitution-drafting and oath-taking continue to concern French writers, yet the stakes have changed considerably since the Federation. Fervour for oath-taking spread around the country in the days following the king's attempted escape in June 1791, and a vow to "live free or die" helped instil a common purpose among a worried populace.[59] In pledging to defend a National Assembly that was now perceived as the sole site of governmental power, people shifted allegiance from the monarch to the state: some claim this was a signal moment in the emergence of French nationalism. But counter-revolutionary caricature tackled the uncertainty with oaths of its own. Consider the 1792 image entitled *Le Serment de la noblesse françoises* [*sic*] (*Oath of the French Nobility*) which shows Louis XVI and Henri IV as two heads sitting on a pedestal and watching a procession of woeful aristocrats and clergymen pay their respects and take a vow of loyalty to the monarchical cause. . . . Although buttressed by the beloved Henri IV on his right, it is the king's brothers on his left—the émigré princes—who emerge as the true heroes of the day, as they rally the group to pledge a counter-offensive against the republic.[60]

The line between burlesque and grotesque, comedy and horror, depends on the observer: while the caricature above may strike some as a playful yet acerbic satire of the battle between monarchical and constitutional politics, a number of contemporaries took the imagery as a real warning of imminent attack. Caricatures insulting the monarchy and threatening vengeance against the nobility who remained in France were routinely produced in the press during 1790-92, and were apparently sent to members of court and rural noblemen to urge them to join émigré forces abroad. According to influential witnesses, cartoons actually did succeed in this attempt. In their frontal attacks on the monarch and constitutional state, political imagery contributed to the rising fears of reprisal among one-time partisans, and thus hastened the increase of emigration from the French countryside in 1790-91.[61]

Such guerrilla tactics were operational at other moments in revolutionary history as well, according to the literary record, and they served various political pur-poses. Oath-taking runs through many of the Thermidorian fictions that emerged after the fall of Robespierre (July 1794): in prison tales and other accounts of suffering under the Montagnards, victims whisper oaths to each other in order to nourish the flame of freedom while awaiting better days to come.[62] The subject of their oath is no longer the king or the constitution, but rather the basic ideals of '89—*liberté, égalité, fraternité*—that were obfuscated by the Terrorist state and its judiciary during the terrible years 1793-94. An oppositional kind of oath-taking punctuates dramatic moments in royalist fiction as well, where family ties re-emerge with special poignancy. In novels such as *Adolphe ou la famille malheureuse* (1797) or Elisabeth Guénard's best-selling *Irma, ou les malheurs d'une jeune orpheline* (An VII [1799]), oath-taking abounds: a kindly stranger vows to adopt a lonely orphan in the first, and a sorrowful daughter (Irma being a partial anagram for Marie, sole survivor of the Bourbons) takes a vow over her father's grave in the second.[63] That these gestures were of key significance can be verified by the concrete evidence of the books' production: frontispieces to both celebrate the vow-taking scene, and the political stance of *Irma* is further underlined by the hidden profile of a furious-looking Robespierre jutting out of the folds of her gown. . . . Emulating the vogue for hidden profiles of the royal family found on porcelain and medallions of weeping willows and "mysterious urns,"[64] these images are clearly not ordinary families but stand-ins for the Bourbon monarchy, and their vows of filial sentiment form a resistance to republican nationalism. Ceremonies of allegiance to Masonic and other secret societies pepper many fictions of the late 1790s as well, where secrecy and religious liberalism, often interpreted as libertine sexuality, made Freemasonry a magnet for counter-revolutionary myth-making.[65] Oath-taking thus transfers from a public and patriotic spectacle of civic unity into a private issue of individual honour and duty, or a clandestine gesture of allegiance to an oppressed or illicit minority.

The mixed messages and paradoxes that underlie the historiography of the year of the Federation now make more sense. As this brief incursion into literary history has shown, the period from August 1789 to July 1790 saw a major conflict between patriots and monarchists over the meaning of democratic political processes and the allegiance required of citizens in a constitutional state. Although the language of *L'Isle des philosophes* may seem tame in comparison to the harsh invective of journalism, the ordinary Frenchmen depicted by Abbé Balthazard do important cultural work.[66] By voicing opinions freely exchanged between believers and non-believers, revolutionaries and royalists, Balthazard proffered what might be the most significant service to the nation: he inscribed into the long duration of a novel the most important achievement of his day—freedom of conscience and thought—and depicted ordinary Frenchmen as politically informed, active citizens of the *patrie*. Their refusal of the oath highlights a genuine dilemma experienced by many in 1789-90, and to a greater extent in 1791-94: how to understand the role of religion separate from politics. Although David Bell celebrates the advent of state *laïcité* and nationalism as breakthroughs realized by the Revolution, this novel casts a tragic aura around the people's sense of being forced to abandon their belief in an apostolic church and a divinely ordained king for a new deity of uncertain origin and future.[67] The moral ambivalence depicted in literature such as *L'Isle des philosophes,* like the heart-breaking dilemma in Victor Hugo's *Quatre-vingt-treize* (1874) where the characters must choose between kinship, love, or honour, injects a much-needed human dimension into the discourse of nationalism.

The ceremonies of oath-taking that marked 1789-90 were based on a myth: that words might conquer an invisible enemy. But the organizers of the many festivals in Paris and the provinces did not reckon with the vulnerabilities of the rite, including its essential illegitimacy. By interpreting the fictions of oath-taking on their own historically specific terms, we are able to "get it": we get the anxieties felt by ordinary parishioners faced by the attacks on their clergymen, their lack of confidence in the unknown constitution, and their curiosity about the shadowy, powerful Freemasons. Moreover, we share in some of the humour, the gossip, and political jockeying that apparently surrounded the famous ceremony. Using strategies still operative among political satirists today—undermining through ridicule, co-optation, and resistance—the literature of the early Revolution presented a parallel competing field of performance where the politically repressed found full expression.

Notes

1. Daniel Gordon, "The Glow of History," *EMF: Studies in Early Modern France* 6 (2000): 61-65. For research support, I would like to thank the John Simon Guggenheim Memorial Foundation and the Institute for Scholarship in the Liberal Arts at the University of Notre Dame. For their intellectual acumen and expert readings, thanks go to Tom Kselman, Lesley Walker, Ted Cachey, and the Nanovic Institute "War and Revolution" discussion group.

2. According to the most reliable bibliography of the period, 210 novels (including translations) were published in French between 1789 and 1791; of that total, only about 80 are new titles by French authors and are explicitly tied to French politics. Research to date can thus be considered relatively exhaustive. See Angus Martin, Vivienne G. Mylne, and Richard Frautschi, *Bibliographie du genre romanesque français, 1751-1800* (London: Mansell, 1977).

3. For more on the history of how this festival became the French national holiday, see Christian Amalvi, "Le 14-juillet, du *Dies irae* à *jour de fête,*" in *Les Lieux de mémoire,* ed. Pierre Nora, 3 vols. (Paris: Gallimard, 1984), 1:421-72.

4. See, for example, Timothy Tackett, "Conspiracy Obsession in the Time of Revolution: French Elites and the Origins of the Terror, 1789-1792," *American Historical Review* 105 (June 2000): 698-713.

5. François Furet and Denis Richet baptized 1790 as the "happy year" in chap. 4, "L'Année heureuse," in *La Révolution française* (Paris: Fayard, 1973), 99-124. Although their account is not devoid of tensions, it evinces an essential optimism, as in its conclusion: "Juillet 1790. Le péril est passé, le ressort se détend. Satisfaction du travail accompli, goût naturel de l'ordre, l'alimentation populaire devenue normale, tout laisse espérer un climat de stabilité et de paix. À elle de bâtir, sur les décombres de l'ancien régime, la belle maison de demain dont rêve le troisième état" (125). Many others have nuanced this claim, however; for example, David Bell points out the country's fractured linguistic identities in *The Cult of the Nation in France* (Cambridge: Harvard University Press, 2001), 169-71.

6. Cited in Dom Henri Leclercq, *La Fédération (janvier-juillet 1790)* (Paris: Librairie Letouzey et Ané, 1929), 351-52. Unless otherwise noted, all translations are my own.

7. Tackett's account of the months surrounding the Federation nuances this impression of complete unity, noting that "not all of the deputies were equally enthralled by the idea" of mounting this extravaganza. Tackett, *Becoming a Revolutionary: The Deputies of the French National Assembly and the Emergence of a Revolutionary Culture (1789-1790)* (Princeton: Princeton University Press, 1996), 296-301, esp. 297.

8. Mona Ozouf, *Festivals and the French Revolution,* trans. Alan Sheridan (Cambridge: Harvard University Press, 1988); Samuel F. Scott, "Problems of Law and Order During 1790, the 'Peaceful' Year of the French Revolution," *American Historical Review* 80, no. 4 (1975): 859-88; and Leclercq, *La Fédération.* The military purpose of the gathering is underlined in Talleyrand's report: "C'est la France armée qui va se réunir, ce n'est pas la France délibérante," cited in Ozouf, *La Fête révolutionnaire, 1789-1799* (Paris: Gallimard, 1976), 56. On military anxieties behind the festival, see William Doyle, *The Oxford History of the French Revolution* (Oxford: Oxford University Press, 1989), 127-29. See also Bronislaw Baczko,

"Serments et perjures," in *Starobinski en mouvement,* ed. Murielle Gagnebin and Christine Savinel (Seyssel: Éditions Champ Vallon, 2001), 331-45.

9. Ozouf, *Festivals,* 34. Ozouf underlines this sentiment, noting that "the truth of these untruthful accounts derives, therefore, precisely from this consensus. The harmony between the language used in the festival and that used by the ordinary people in the towns was no doubt temporary, but for the moment complete" (*Festivals,* 60). Furet and Richet echo Ozouf's sentiment: "Fête de l'utopie? Ce fut surtout l'image d'une unité volontaire, confiante et pacifique qui aurait voulu être l'aube d'une époque nouvelle" (114).

10. Leclercq highlights the January 1790 ceremony in Pontivy, where some 200 guardsmen, volunteer soldiers, and ecclesiastics from Brittany and Anjou joined to "d'unir l'amour de la patrie à celui de la religion, pour fixer le caractère de la sainte confédération" (*La Fédération,* 251-53). Framed by celebration of two masses, their oath was spoken in the front of the village church and invoked the protection of God. Suzanne Desan comments that "ceremonies throughout France fused patriotic and Christian symbolism as priests baptized babies with the sign of the cross and the cockade and sang the Te Deum to honor the unity of the nation." Desan, *Reclaiming the Sacred: Lay Religion and Popular Politics in Revolutionary France* (Ithaca: Cornell University Press, 1990), 7.

11. Accounts of Assembly deliberations from September 1789 to May 1790 show that most deputies assumed devotion to the nation could co-exist with Catholicism, but a vocal minority disagreed. M. Picot, *Mémoires pour servir à l'histoire ecclésiastique pendant le dix-huitième siècle,* 3rd ed., 7 vols. (Paris: Librairie d'Adrien Le Clere, 1856), 6:2.

12. One must also recall the great surge of peasant uprisings continuing sporadically from December 1789, the early appearance of counterrevolutionary sentiments among the nobility, notably with the suppression of noble titles in June 1790, and the violent antirevolutionary rhetoric of conservative newspapers. The scholarship on these symptoms of dissent and unrest is voluminous; classic titles include John McManners, *The French Revolution and the Church* (London: S.P.C.K. for the Church Historical Society, 1969); Georges Lefebvre, *The Great Fear of 1789: Rural Panic in Revolutionary France,* trans. Joan White (New York: Schocken Books, 1989); and Jeremy Popkin, *Revolutionary News: The Press in France, 1789-1799* (Durham: Duke University Press, 1990).

13. For more on the application of the "Edit de Tolérance," see Dom Henri Leclercq, *Vers la*

Fédération (janvier-juillet 1790) (Paris: Librairie Letouzey et Ané, 1929), 369-89.

14. Within a month of the May 1790 ceremonies in Lyon, for example, peasants and guardsmen engaged in battles against the upper-class municipal officers and regular army units stationed in town. A similarly dramatic crisis followed the April 1790 pact between the soldiers of Languedoc and the National Guard of Montauban and Toulouse. The August mutiny of the Swiss troops and National Guards in Nancy and Châteauvieux ended with 300 dead: although restitution was attempted through a symbolic ceremony on the Champ de Mars, memories of this bloody feud remained bitter. For more on these conflicts, see Scott; on the mutinies and insurrections of 1790, see Leclercq, *La Fédération,* 460-534.

15. Tackett, *Religion, Revolutions and Regional Culture in Eighteenth-Century France: The Ecclesiastical Oath of 1791* (Princeton: Princeton University Press, 1986); Harold T. Parker, *The Cult of Antiquity and the French Revolutionaries: A Study in the Development of the Revolutionary Spirit* (Chicago: University of Chicago Press, 1937), 24.

16. This reaction was elicited by Jacques-Louis David's painting *Le Serment des Horace* (1787); as a review in *Le Journal de Paris* exclaimed: "je vous avoue que l'action de prêter serment, pour faire son devoir, a selon moi, quelque chose d'avilissant et de bas, et fort au-dessous du caractère Romain." Review of *Le Serment des Horace* by Jacques-Louis David, in *Journal de Paris* (12 May 1787), cited in Thomas Crow, *Emulation: Making Artists for Revolutionary France* (New Haven: Yale University Press, 1995), 310n47.

17. Claude Langlois, "Counter-Revolutionary Iconography," in *French Caricature and the French Revolution, 1789-1799* (Los Angeles: Grunwald Center for the Graphic Arts, UCLA, 1988), 42. See also Jean Starobinski, "Le Serment: David," in *1789: Les Emblèmes de la raison* (Paris: Flammarion, 1973), 81-93.

18. The focus on the "virtuous spectacle" is in Susan Maslan, *Revolutionary Acts: Theater, Democracy, and the French Revolution* (Baltimore: Johns Hopkins University Press, 2005). See also Marie-Hélène Huet who, in a pioneering study of the conjunction between revolutionary justice and drama, reveals not only the political relevance of discursive content but also its transmissibility to audiences in *Rehearsing the Revolution: The Staging of Marat's Death, 1793-1797,* trans. Robert Hurley (Berkeley: University of California Press, 1982), 27-45. On performative speech acts as a site of individual theatrical performance, see J. L.

Austin, *How to Do Things with Words* (Oxford: Clarendon Press, 1962); on the performative as a cultural iteration of individual identity, see Judith Butler, *Gender Trouble: Feminism and the Subversion of Identity* (New York and London: Routledge, 1990); Butler, *Bodies That Matter: On the Discursive Limits of "Sex"* (New York: Routledge, 1993); and Butler, *Excitable Speech: A Politics of the Performative* (New York: Routledge, 1997). Cecilia Feilla presented an interesting take on this question in "The Oath in Revolutionary Literature and Culture: A Performative Paradigm of Action" (lecture, New Paradigms for Revolutionary Studies: French-American Colloquium, South Bend, IN, 6 October 2008).

19. Archives de la Préfecture de la Police, Paris. AA/132, no. 178 (Vendémiaire, An IX).

20. Guillaume Apollinaire attributed *Julie* to the well-known author of libertine fiction, Chevalier Andrea de Nerciat. Malcolm Cook has noted, however, that textual clues are unreliable and that no biographical evidence supports this attribution. Cook, *Politics in the Fiction of the French Revolution, 1789-1794*, in *Studies in Voltaire and the Eighteenth Century* 201 (1982): 270-72. On *Julie*'s place in the libertine tradition of Margot and Moll, see Kathryn Norberg, "The Libertine Whore: Prostitution in French Pornography from Margot to Juliette," in *The Invention of Pornography: Obscenity and the Origins of Modernity, 1500-1800*, ed. Lynn Hunt (New York: Zone Books, 1993), 225-52; Pamela Cheek, "Prostitutes of 'Political Institution,'" *Eighteenth-Century Studies* 28, no. 2 (1995): 193-219; and Stéphanie Genand, *Le Libertinage et l'histoire: politique de la séduction à la fin de l'ancien régime, SVEC [Studies in Voltaire and the Eighteenth Century]* 2005:11 (Oxford: Voltaire Foundation, 2005). *Julie philosophe* was originally published as 2 vols. in octodecimo, with no place or publisher. *Julie philosophe ou le bon patriote: Histoire à peu près véritable d'une* CITOYENNE ACTIVE *qui a été tour à tour agent et victime des dernières révolutions de la Hollande, du Brabant et de la France*, ed. Guillaume Apollinaire, 2 vols. (1910; Paris: Tchou, Briffaut, 1968). References are to this edition.

21. Alan Forrest, "La Révolution et l'Europe," in *Dictionnaire critique de la Révolution française*, ed. François Furet and Mona Ozouf (Paris: Flammarion, 1988), 146-55.

22. The prostitute's ridicule of her clients for their "flabby" organs and impotence corresponds to the conventions of libertine literature outlined in Norberg, 237-38.

23. Harvey Chisick, *The Limits of Reform: Attitudes Towards the Education of the Lower Classes in Eighteenth-Century France* (Princeton: Princeton University Press, 1981), 215-25.

24. Babouc is the hero of *Le Monde comme il va, ou Vision de Babouc* (1748). The comparison between the voyage of Babouc (luxurious foods and pleasures in a wealthy foreign city) and the trial of Jonah (imprisonment in a whale's belly with nothing but fish to eat) emerges at the end of the tale. As the narrator notes: "Babouc fut bien loin de se plaindre, comme Jonas qui se fâcha de ce qu'on ne détruisait pas Ninive. Mais quand on a été trois jours dans le corps d'une baleine, on n'est pas de si bonne humeur que quand on a été à l'opéra, à la comédie, et qu'on a soupé en bonne compagnie." Voltaire, *Le Monde comme il va, ou Vision de Babouc*, in *Les Œuvres complètes de Voltaire*, ed. Theodore Besterman, 65 vols. (Oxford: Voltaire Foundation, 2004), 30B:63. On the unreliability of language in *Babouc*, see Roy Wolper, "The Final Foolishness of Babouc: The Dark Center of 'Le Monde comme il va,'" *Modern Language Review* 75, no. 4 (1980): 766-73, esp. 772-73.

25. Interpreting *Julie philosophe* as a poor remake of *Thérèse philosophe* (1748[?]), Margaret Jacob argues that Julie is "hardly as naughty or philosophically astute as her mid-century predecessor," and judged the novel unfavorably because of its disconnect from the "complexities of the materialist world that pornography sought to narrate and describe." Jacob, "The Materialist World of Pornography," in *The Invention of Pornography*, 200.

26. For more on Calonne's involvement in this scandal, see Robert Lacour-Gayet, *Calonne: financier, réformateur, contre-révolutionnaire 1734-1802* (Paris: Hachette, 1963); and Sarah Maza, "The Diamond Necklace Affair Revisited: The Case of the Missing Queen," in *Eroticism and the Body Politic*, ed. Lynn Hunt (Baltimore: Johns Hopkins University Press, 1991), 63-89. Calonne would move to Turin and then to Koblenz in 1790, where he became "prime minister" of the Count d'Artois.

27. On the ambivalence implicit in the dénouement of *Candide* and its philosophy of optimism, see Lionel Gossman, "Voltaire's Heavenly City," *Eighteenth Century Studies* 3, no. 1 (1969): 67-82; and David Langdon, "On the Meanings of the Conclusion of *Candide*," *SVEC [Studies in Voltaire and the Eighteenth Century]* 238 (Oxford: Voltaire Foundation, 1985), 397-432. A similar Candidean plot, where a cynical narrator travels the world, sees much injustice, and finally gets a nice job as a librarian and gardener, marks Abbé Jean-Jacques Gaudier, *Jean le noir, ou le misanthrope* (Paris: Hôtel de Bouthillier, 1789).

28. There is debate about the identity of the woman in this image. Vivian Cameron and Michel Vovelle claim it depicts Queen Marie-Antoinette, whereas Langlois, citing an advertisement in *Le Journal de la Cour et de la ville* (1792), argues it is Sophie de Condorcet. See Vivian Cameron, "Political Exposures: Sexuality and Caricature in the French Revolution," in *Eroticism and the Body Politic*, 97; Michel Vovelle, *La Révolution française: Images et récit*, 5 vols. (Paris: Editions Messidor, 1986), 2:66; and Langlois, *La Caricature contre-révolutionnaire* (Paris: Presses du CNRS, 1988), 242. Whether or not this particular caricature meant to insult the queen is irrelevant, since it resembles many other texts and images targeting Lafayette and Marie-Antoinette. See, for example, *Soirées amoureuses du Général Mottier et de la belle Antoinette* (Persepolis, 1790) and the image reproduced in Langlois, *La Caricature*, 151.

29. Cited in Antoine de Baecque, *Le Corps de l'histoire: métaphores et politique (1700-1800)* (Paris: Calmann-Lévy, 1993), 75.

30. That the oath would re-emerge as an important plot device in the Gothic and royalist fiction of the late 1790s is evident in the analysis below. Vow-taking plays an equally dramatic function in the dénouement of Stendhal's *Le Rouge et le noir* (Paris: Levasseur, 1830), although the gesture is veiled in irony for its overly melodramatic sentimentality.

31. Little biographical information on Pochet is extant. Apart from his literary work, he was once director of l'Ecole Gymnastique of the Military School in St Petersburg and author of *L'Héroïsme uni à l'espérance par la félicité publique à l'autel de la liberté. Fête Gymnastique et Athénienne, Allégorique, composée pour être exécutée par des jeunes Patriotes, dédiée à Louis XVI, Roi des Français, inventée par le Sieur Pochet, pensionnaire du Duc des Deux-Ponts, à l'occasion de la nouvelle Constitution, acceptée par le Roi, le 4 septembre, l'an troisième de la Liberté* (n.p.: De l'Imprimerie de Pain, c. 1792). Alexandre Cioranescu, *Bibliographie de la littérature française du dix-huitième siècle* (Paris: Editions du CNRS, 1962), 2:1407.

32. [A. Pochet], *La Boussole nationale ou Aventures historico-rustiques de Jaco surnommé Henri quatrième laboureur, descendant du frère de lait de notre bon roi Henri IV. Recueillies par un vrai patriot*, 3 vols. (Paris: De l'imprimerie de la liberté sur la Place de la Bastille, 1790), 1:n.p. References are to this edition.

33. On the network of Jacobin clubs and their role in educating rural populations, see Michael Kennedy, "Les Clubs des Jacobins et la presse sous l'Assemblée nationale, 1789-1791," *Revue historique* 264, no. 1 (1980): 49-63; Ozouf, *Varennes: La mort de la royauté* (Paris: Gallimard, 2005), 354; and Françoise Parent, "De nouvelles pratiques de lecture," in *Histoire de l'édition française: Vol. 2, Le Livre triomphant*, eds. Henri-Jean Martin et Roger Chartier, 4 vols. (Paris: Promodis, 1984), 2:606-21.

34. "Les lecteurs trouveront dans ces anecdotes le tableau fidèle et animé du bonheur que l'on goûte en France, et des maux que rencontrent dans les pays étrangers les imprudents qui trahissent leur pays par de coupables émigrations," Review of *Voyages et aventures d'un laboureur descendant du frère de lait d'Henri IV, Le Moniteur universel* 283 (10 octobre 1791), in *Réimpression de l'Ancien Moniteur*, 32 vols. (Paris: Henri Plon, 1862), 10:74. See also the reviews in *Le Journal de Paris* (June 1791) and *Chronique de Paris* (September 1791) reprinted in *Feuille de correspondance du libraire* (3:61; 10:237-38). Unlike the emigrations of nobles which would shortly rob the nation of its financial and military might, when news of the royal family's failed escape attempt launched a massive exodus of the wealthy, the characters in *La Boussole* emigrated for religious reasons. As members of a Huguenot clan, they fled the French hostility against Protestants by taking their trades abroad. But the author's warning against emigration may well have explained its appeal to readers in the post-Varennes days of Fall 1791. Massimo Boffa, "Emigrés," in *Dictionnaire critique de la Révolution française*, 348.

35. For more on the kinds of teachings included in the popular *Feuille villageoise*, see Michel Vernus, "Lectures et pratiques de lecture en Franche-Comté (1780-1800)," in *Livre et révolution*, ed. Frédéric Barbier, Claude Jolly, and Sabine Juratic (Paris: Aux Amateurs des Livres, 1988), 172; and James Livesey, *Making Democracy in the French Revolution* (Cambridge: Harvard University Press, 2001), 96-99.

36. On the links between the character of Jaco and the ideal of the reforming farmer, a republican prototype that was embraced and promoted with particular fervour during the Directory period, see Livesey, 88-166.

37. On the "Edit de Tolérance," see Leclercq, *Vers la Fédération*, 369-89.

38. The detailed recommendations on space usage, work timetables, and gender-specific leisure pursuits recall the elaborate scheme of Gaspard Guillard de Beaurieu, *L'Élève de la nature* (Lille: Le-

houcq, 1762; reprint 1778). For more on these topoi, see Julia V. Douthwaite, *The Wild Girl, Natural Man, and the Monster: Dangerous Experiments in the Age of Enlightenment* (Chicago: University of Chicago Press, 2002), 124-25.

39. The voyage narrative relays a number of comments on fiscal and commercial policies, as when the narrator offers advice on the import-export business: "Si le gouvernement n'est pas plus attentif, désormais à retenir par de bonnes primes, récompenses, privilèges, les bons ouvriers manufacturiers, fabriquants, et ceux des bons ouvriers, qui nous donnent encore l'avantage sur nos concurrents, d'ici à la fin du siècle, les fabriques des autres nations auront plus de bras que nous, et par conséquent feront baisser leur prix" (*La Boussole,* 2:316). For more on the history of Freemasons in France, see Margaret C. Jacob, *The Origins of Freemasonry: Facts and Fictions* (Philadelphia: University of Pennsylvania Press, 2005); and Pierre Chevalier, *Histoire de la francmaçonnerie française,* 3 vols. (Paris: Fayard, 1984).

40. As Annie Duprat has noted, these hostile pamphlets exemplify a hard-line monarchism that violently condemns Louis XVI. Duprat, "Louis XVI morigéné par ses ancêtres en 1790: *Les Entretiens des Bourbons,*" *Dix-huitième siècle* 26 (1994): 317-32; and Duprat, *Les Rois de papier: La caricature de Henri III à Louis XVI* (Paris: Belin, 2002).

41. "L'œil du maître peut tout, c'est lui qui rend la vie / Au mérite expirant sous la dent de l'envie, / C'est lui dont les rayons ont cent fois éclairé / Le modeste talent dans la foule ignoré / Un roi qui sait régner nous fait ce que nous sommes, / Les regards d'un héros produit de grands hommes" (*La Boussole,* 3:325).

42. *La Boussole,* 3:326. The *Chanson des apprentis* is reproduced in *Le Parfait maçon: Les débuts de la maçonnerie française (1736-1748),* ed. Johel Coutura (St Étienne: Publications de l'Université de St Étienne, 1994), 284.

43. The combination of a Mason with a representative of the First and Second Estates would not have been as shocking to period readers as it may seem to us. As Roger Chartier has noted, the rituals and principles of Freemasonry were not democratic; rather they replicated many features of old regime sociability, including honorary distinctions and an exclusivism based on social standing. Chartier, *Les Origines culturelles de la Révolution française* (1990; Paris: Seuil, 2000), 290-91. Richard Cobb and Colin Jones have usefully pointed out the prevalence of Masons in the Estates General (at least 200 were elected) and the borrowing of sym-

bols (the eye representing vigilance, the level symbolizing equality) and mottoes (*liberté, égalité, fraternité*) from Freemasonry into patriotic rhetoric of the early Revolution, and they too stress that Masonic political views were seldom radical. Cobb and Jones, *The French Revolution: Voices from a Momentous Epoch, 1789-1795* (London: Simon & Schuster, 1988), 109. On the links between Bailly, the Physiocrats and Freemasonry, see Edwin Burrows Smith, "Jean-Sylvain Bailly: Astronomer, Mystic, Revolutionary, 1736-1793," *Transactions of the American Philosophical Society* 44 (1954): 427-538.

44. Jacob, *Living the Enlightenment: Freemasonry and Politics in Eighteenth-Century Europe* (Oxford: Oxford University Press, 1991), 203; Ronald Paulson, *Representations of Revolution (1789-1820)* (New Haven: Yale University Press, 1983), 223. In *Charmansage,* the Masons are more cautiously referred to as a *société mystérieuse* or *le sabbat des philosophes,* but the gestures of solidarity and promotion of intelligence sound Masonic, as does the Fête de la Rosière that the hero hosts to celebrate the villagers' virtue. See Robert Martin Lesuire, *Charmansage, ou mémoires d'un jeune citoyen faisant l'éducation d'un ci-devant noble,* 3 vols. (Paris: Defer de Maisonneuve, 1792), 2:118-36. Another Masonic link lies in the work of François-Félix Nogaret, who published prolifically throughout the revolutionary decade. See Janet Burke, "Leaving the Enlightenment: Women Freemasons After the Revolution," *Eighteenth-Century Studies* 33, no. 2 (2000): 255-65, esp. 259.

45. Describing his father, the narrator writes: "Mon père étoit d'une secte connue sous le nom de *Franche-Maçonnerie*; j'ignore ce qui se pratique dans ces assemblées, mais j'ose assurer que, puisque mon père étoit un Francmaçon la plupart sont certainement des honnêtes gens." François Amédée Doppet, *Zélamire, ou les liaisons bizarres, Histoire récente, mise au jour d'après les Mémoires de l'Héroïne, & publiée par l'Editeur de 'Célestina'* (1788; Paris: Marchands de Nouveautés, 1791), 17-18.

46. Doppet, *Zélamire,* 18. François-Amédée Doppet (Chambéry, 1753-1800) was also author of several works of medicine, poetry, history, most notably *Mémoires politiques et militaires du général Doppet* (1797). An ardent Jacobin, he founded a newspaper after the coup d'état of 18 Fructidor An v (4 September 1797), entitled *L'Écho des Alpes, journal démocratique,* but it only lasted a few months. *Index biographique français,* 3rd ed., ed. Tommaso Napo (Munich: K. G. Saur, 2004), fiche I, 325, 20-40.

47. Daniel Ligou, "Franc-maçonnerie," in *Dictionnaire historique de la Révolution française*, ed. Albert Soboul (Paris: Presses Universitaires de France, 1989), 475-81.

48. Little is known of Abbé Balthazard (or Baltazard), save his ecclesiastical functions as priest in the diocese of Metz and his death in Chartres in 1801.

49. The concept of "citizen priest" is drawn from Desan, 77.

50. [Abbé Balthazard], *L'Isle des philosophes et plusieurs autres, Nouvellement découvertes, & remarquables par leurs rapports avec la France actuelle* (n.p., 1790), iv. According to Barbier, *L'Isle* was published in Chartres by Deshayes. Antoine-Alexandre Barbier, Gustave Brunet, and J. M. Quérard, *Dictionnaire des ouvrages anonymes,* 2 vols. (Paris: F.-J. Féchoz, 1889), 2:888.

51. My research and the data in the Martin, Mylne, and Frautschi *Bibliographie* indicate that *L'Isle des philosophes* may have gone into two editions in 1790, but it was not reviewed in the contemporary press. For more on Balthazard's debt to the counter-Enlightenment, see Darrin M. McMahon, *Enemies of Enlightenment: The French Counter-Enlightenment and the Making of Modernity* (Oxford: Oxford University Press, 2001), chap. 2.

52. For more on these traditions as reworked in the 1790s, see Anne-Rozenn Morel, "Modes d'engagement de l'utopie: Le ludique et le juridique," in *Littérature et engagement pendant la Révolution française,* ed. Isabelle Brouard-Arends and Laurent Loty (Rennes: Presses de l'Université de Rennes 2, 2007), 79-89; Gillian Beer, "Discourses of the Island," in *Literature and Science as Modes of Expression,* ed. Frederick Amrine (Dordrecht: Kluwer, 1989), 1-27; Philip Babcock Gove, *The Imaginary Voyage in Prose Fiction* (London: Holland, 1941).

53. See Darrin M. McMahon, "Narratives of Dystopia in the French Revolution: Enlightenment, Counter-Enlightenment, and the *Isle des philosophes* of the Abbé Balthazard," *Yale French Studies* 101 (2002): 103-18; Joël Castonguay-Bélanger, *Les Écarts de l'imagination: pratiques et représentations de la science dans le roman au tournant des Lumières* (Montréal: Presses de l'Université de Montréal, 2008); Anne-Rozenn Morel-Daryani, "Lettre et utopie dans l'œuvre contre-révolutionnaire de l'Abbé Balthazard," *Revue de l'Aire* 30 (2004): 40-47; and Cook, 253-55.

54. Both these islands are clearly indebted to Jonathan Swift's *Gulliver's Travels* (1726) and especially part 4, "A Voyage to the Country of the Houyhnhnms."

55. For more on this complex history, see Tackett, *Religion, Revolution, and Regional Culture*; and Dale Van Kley, *The Religious Origins of the French Revolution: From Calvin to the Civil Constitution, 1560-1791* (New Haven: Yale University Press, 1996).

56. Lynn Hunt, *Measuring Time, Making History* (Budapest: Central European University Press, 2008), 74.

57. Langlois, "Counter-Revolutionary Iconography," 50.

58. For a Catholic interpretation of the 4 February 1790 oath of loyalty, see Picot, 5:403-21; and on the July 1790 Civil Constitution of the clergy, see Picot, 6:1-54. For more on disturbances in rural France, see Lefebvre.

59. Tackett, *When the King Took Flight* (Cambridge: Harvard University Press, 2003), 158.

60. Langlois, *La Caricature contre-révolutionnaire,* 123. For an alternative interpretation of this caricature that situates it within the tradition of the "talking heads" automaton evoked by the two kingly busts, see Julia V. Douthwaite and Daniel Richter, "The Frankenstein of the French Revolution: Nogaret's Automaton Tale of 1790," *European Romantic Review* 20, no. 3 (2009): 381-411, esp. 390-92.

61. On persecution through caricature, see Mme de la Tour du Pin, *Mémoires de la marquise de la Tour du Pin; Journal d'une femme de cinquante ans (1778-1815),* ed. Christian de Liedekerke Beaufort (1979; reprint, Paris: Mercure de France, 1989), 161.

62. This scenario is replayed several times in Joseph de Rosny, *Les Infortunes de La Galetierre pendant le régime décemviral* (1797, 1st ed.; Paris: Leprieur, An VII [1799]), vi; 60; 70-71.

63. "Je te jure d'être bon père," declares the kindly father-figure in *Adolphe*; standing in front of Louis XVI's tomb in *Irma*, the hero (Duke d'Angoulême) vows: "Je te jure par l'ombre sacrée de ton père, que je n'existerai jamais que pour toi," and his intended (Marie-Thérèse) repeats the same vow. In the second, however, a horrific spectre of Robespierre appears shortly after these solemn oaths, and threatens to devour all the cadavers buried in royal tombs (2:203-4). Mme Grandmaison Van Esbecq, *Adolphe, ou la famille malheureuse,* 2 vols. (Paris: Lepetit, An V), 1:26; Elisabeth Guénard [Mme Brossin de Méré], *Irma ou les malheurs d'une jeune orpheline; histoire indienne,* 2 vols. (Paris: Chez l'auteur, An VIII), 2:202. There are many other examples of oath-taking in revolu-

tionary literature; see Olympe de Gouges, *Les Voeux forcés* (1790), and Stéphanie Félicité Genlis, *Les Voeux téméraires ou l'enthousiasme* (1798).

64. A German medallion bearing the image of a girl vowing filial loyalty to the tomb of Louis XVI, with the slogan "Seule consolation d'Irma" is found in Vovelle, *La Révolution française: Images et récit,* 2:351. For more on the fad for hidden profile imagery in this epoch, see Langlois, *Les Sept morts du roi* (Paris: Anthropos, 1993), 13-15; and Richard Taws, "Trompe l'Œil and Trauma: Money and Memory after the Terror," *Oxford Art Journal* 30, no. 3 (2007): 355-76.

65. Abbé Barruel was the principal theoretician of this movement in the religious-political realm, but the revelation of Masonic secrets forms a veritable subgenre in literature of 1797-1820 as well. For one of the most lurid descriptions of Masonic initiation rituals and mysterious beliefs, see J.-J. Regnault-Warin, *Spinalba, ou les révélations de la Rose-Croix,* 4 vols. (André: An Onze, 1803).

66. For more on revolutionary newspapers, see Popkin; Robert Darnton and Daniel Roche, eds., *Revolution in Print: The Press in France, 1775-1800* (Berkeley: University of California Press, 1989); Béatrice Didier, *Écrire la Révolution, 1789-1799* (Paris: Presses Universitaires de France, 1989), 89-120; Jean Sgard, ed., *L'Écrivain devant la Révolution, 1780-1800* (Grenoble: Université Stendhal de Grenoble & Société Française d'Etude du XVIIIᵉ siècle, 1987).

67. Bell, 7-8.

Ricardo J. Quinones (essay date 2010)

SOURCE: Quinones, Ricardo J. "The Survivors: *Praise of Folly* and *Candide*." In *Erasmus and Voltaire: Why They Still Matter,* pp. 123-42. Toronto: University of Toronto Press, 2010.

[*In the following essay, Quinones evaluates the relevance of Desiderius Erasmus's* Praise of Folly *and Voltaire's* Candide *to modern readers. Candide, he asserts, continues to resonate because it offers insight into Voltaire's conflict within himself, with the two main characters in the novella, Martin and Candide, representing a jaded (but accurate) view of the world versus an optimistic one.*]

Satire is a lesser genre. It is to the great credit of both *The Praise of Folly* and *Candide* that they triumph over satire. Satire depends upon the debasement of an object, a practice, or a person. It objectifies and separates the

author from his target. Erasmus's satire derives from situation, where the derelictions are very obvious and dependent upon our awareness of an implied or distinctly stated code of values. The code of values for *Praise of Folly* had been provided by the Christian doctrine of the *Enchiridion.* Quite different in method Voltaire's satire proceeds by caricature. He decontextualizes, or isolates, a practice or other particularities, and removing from them all sense, reduces them to their absurd external manifestations. The larger relevancy of symbols as tripwires is ignored. The enemy is well recognized by a simple name (legitimate or mocked), while the author roams relatively freely, present only by his moving hand. While such moments have their modest appeal, *The Praise of Folly* and *Candide* would not be classics on the basis of their satire alone. Their greatness emerges when their authors enter into the works and themselves become players and victims among the rest. They themselves acquire an identity, are objectified, and their work acquires a dialectic. But that is a very drab phrase to describe what happens when an author submits the limits and liabilities of his own cherished commitments to critical scrutiny, when in the operations of solitude he becomes two-in-one, that is, he becomes a thinking person. Then he ceases to be the satiric manipulator but rather he becomes a player himself. He breaks out of the conventional mode of giving the enemy a face and a name and discovers that he too harbours the face of an enemy.

There are other related reasons why *The Praise of Folly* and *Candide* have survived in the historical memory. Such preservation represents something of an anomaly, because in their basic principles—the reasons for their preeminence—they contain much that runs counter to Erasmian or *Voltairien* values. They do not prioritize, they present no scale of proportionate values; they are not accommodating. Rather they present contests of values, agons, clashes of principles and values. And by such dialectic they have endured and found their constant appeal. This is not a question of complexity versus simplicity (for as Shakespeare reminds us, there is such a thing as simple truth that might be miscalled simplicity; see Sonnet 66), but rather of what emerges when an author engages in debate with himself, presenting the most stringent of auto-critiques. His most cherished opinions and activities are called into question, challenged at their core. In such moments of self-impressment, he has taken himself prisoner. In such a magnificent and rare encounter the writer (or artist) manages to bring out the neglected or invisible self, one that had been recognized but never acknowledged in the public face of the author. The whoreson must be acknowledged. This is a true 'overcoming,' or '*dépassement*' and revels in the presentation of a more superior confrontation, not with the other, the common enemy with names, the 'sophists,' the Jesuits, the Jansenists, and others, but with that unnamed part of the self that had been so elusive but now is brought forward, unmasked in stupendous recognition and admission.

The Praise of Folly is a genuine masterpiece. Yet Erasmus, with his customary deprecatory (and self-defensive) tic, dismisses it as being tossed off in a matter of weeks when he was ill in Thomas More's house.[1] The ease of its coming should not belie its profundity, nor Erasmus's receptivity. In discounting it, he had adopted something of a labour theory of value, neglecting the years of keen observation, the convictions born of personal experience, and the diligent study that went into its making. Ease of composition does not indicate slackness in conception or flabbiness of information. Like all good satire, *The Praise of Folly* has a firm moral grounding that extends back to his much earlier *Enchiridion,* where Erasmus first postulates his *philosophia Christi* and his spiritual hermeneutics. But *The Praise of Folly* achieves its measure of greatness by the wider extent of its pitch, by the rapid-fire mobility of its thought, by the fullness of detail and thought. The Erasmian profile is very present in the work, despite the persona of Folly. Acts of denunciation do not hide the maker's hand. Erasmus knew what he was talking about, and covered familiar terrain when he attacked the number of superstitions that attend any popular adherence to a materialized religion. And this is further witnessed in his satiric roll-call of the professions, with its detailed description—with one thought following rapidly upon another—of the derelictions of those who should be better leaders of the people. But in two areas Erasmus outdoes himself. The first is a self-portrait of the weaknesses and fallibilities of the wise, who fall victim to what could be called the tragedy of Nature. The second occurs near the end, where Erasmus, for the moment loosening his normal sense of preferring the spiritual over the corporeal, admits to an 'irreconcilable warfare,' a profound difference of parts that can no longer be subordinated but rather exist in inveterate unending lateral opposition.

Superstition is always present in the popular imagination. In the early sixteenth century Erasmus subjected it to particularly strenuous review. Not that he had to, as others were only too willing to pronounce against its deviations. Many of the issues that Luther would later denounce, such as indulgences, masses for the dead, and the human ordinances that have no basis in scripture, Erasmus had already demeaned. But he shows a special hostility to those practices that inspire a false confidence and that interfere with a direct worship of Christ. Icons and images, stained-glass windows and murals might well be the 'Bible of the people,' or, as later, 'silent poetry.' But that is one thing; it is totally another, and quite misleading, to allow them to be the objects of religious veneration on the part of the people. Against this latter transposition Erasmus wars decisively with all the tools of his rational theology. Such unbecoming substitution results in the veneration of saints, even of Mary herself, the adoration of icons and pilgrimages to faraway places to bow before and kiss dubious relics (CWE [*Collected Works of Erasmus*] 27:122). These are the same critical qualities that show themselves in the *Colloquies* such as 'Shipwreck' and 'A Pilgrimage for Religion's Sake,' among the most prominent. More than intermediaries such poetical and legendary saints as George, Christopher, and Barbara stand in lieu of a faith in Christ, surrogates to whom one turns for grants of their specialized favours (114). The inclusion of Mary is somewhat surprising, when one considers her restitution as the Mother of Christ so beautifully invoked in 'A Pilgrimage for Religion's Sake.' But just as to the pseudosaints who have their particular wares, so people turn to her for many things, her, the Virgin Mother, 'to whom the common people do in a manner attribute more than to the Son' (115). But Erasmus is quick to indicate the proper meaning of Mary in Christian thought: 'How many are there that burn candles to the Virgin Mother, and that too at noonday when there's no need of them! But how few are there that study to imitate her in pureness of life, humility, and love of heavenly things, which is the true worship and most acceptable to heaven!' (120).

The ways of the common people differ in their simplicity from those of the learned. If the first follow docilely and unthinkingly, the second are guilty of overly subtle disputations turns to debate and definition. Yet, they are joined together, as each is ignorant of or ignores the teachings of Christ, the Gospels and apostles, and the early church fathers, all those that form the basis of Erasmus's Christian formation and practice. A large portion of *The Praise of Folly* is made up of portraits of the so-called leaders of the Christian society; these depictions comprise a veritable rogue's gallery, a mustering of the professions, and in their massive detail and keen insights they are examples of Erasmus at his satiric best.

While there are nine such portrayals, three of the longest and the most discerning are those, understandably enough, devoted to the grammarians, the theologians, and the monks. In his objections to Erasmus's treatment of the theologians, Maarten van Dorp obviously could not have had in mind Erasmus's dire portraits of the grammarians—which may have been added later. The latter are pedants in their work and tyrants in their classrooms. Merged with school teachers they are kings of the kids (and of their doting parents as well). Their scholarship is devoted to petty trifles, over which they crow if they discover any new phrase. Their comings and goings are devoted to punctuation and to parts of speech, and woe to any person who manages to make a small mistake. 'What uproars, what bickering, what taunts, what invectives!' One specific culprit, who spent twenty years sorting out the parts of speech, makes it a matter for the sword if someone makes a conjunction out of a preposition. Then there are the pluckier ones who simply steal others' works, and in the tangled publication industry of the time, pass off the pirated work as their own (the same outcry heard from Voltaire in his letter to Rousseau). They have the effrontery to adopt classical names (and here Erasmus is cutting close to home), and as a form of defensiveness against bad reviews resort to an inbred, incestuous chumminess with their fellow grammarians, each engaging in mutual back-scratching (CWE 27:123-5). The portrait is far from limited to Erasmus's own time.

The theologians (CWE 27:126ff) have a heavy weapon at hand to persuade their opponents, the charge of heresy. Otherwise their lives are spent in the pursuit of 'subtle trifles,' of pretending to answer questions that no sensible person would ever think of asking, such as 'whether it was possible that Christ could have taken upon Him the likeness of a woman, or of the devil, or of an ass, or of a stone, or of a gourd.' And then, throughout these novel transformations, whether he could have performed the miracles and died on the cross (127)? Obviously this is a generation and a profession, which through specialized training, run-away speculative imaginations, and a forward tendency to dispute and debate, along with professional pressures to make a mark, has lost its bearings, its compass of centred direction. What they have lost is direct contact with Christ, the Gospels, the apostles and the church fathers. Paul knew what faith and charity were but his understanding was far from the definitions of the scholastics, with all the subclassifications and distinctions (127). The urge to define has violated two codes essential to Erasmus: respect for the mysteries and obscurities of the world and the need for direct experience. There are questions beyond our knowing and there are experiences within our telling. The apostles were able devoutly to consecrate the Eucharist, but they had no need of the terminologies and specific processes of transubstantiation (127). They knew the mother of Jesus, but had no need to prove her preserved from original sin (128). They baptized but did not need the support of further argumentation. They do not search out the various compartments of hell (130). In all of this not only do the current theologians fall short of the apostles, but they even refrain from reading the Gospels or Paul's epistles. They pay even less heed to the early church fathers, including Jerome. And yet—here we must understand the immensity of Folly's indictments—these are the people with their abstruse intellectual convolutions who control the thought of the church. They believe that their certainly more subtle and rarified questionings and procedures have raised theology to the level of a higher physics, to which not everyone is entitled to ascend. But Erasmus and his numerous cohorts, including Luther, regarded their obfuscations as nothing more than gibberish. Erasmus is particularly attuned to their errors in speech and their inelegant, if not barbarous, Latin. A tonic for its time, a chronicle of generational warfare, Erasmian satire at its most potent steps out of its time and continues, even in its specifics, to resonate down to the cultural wars of our own day.

Just as Erasmus discovered early his distaste for the 'modern' theology, so too he discovered quickly and decisively his aversion to the monastic life. But in the latter case it came after he had already entered the monastery at Steyn, and thus much of the efforts of his later life were devoted to fruitful attempts to free himself from that first misstep. Very early he announced in the *Enchiridion* that the monastic life has no monopoly on piety, that one can as a layperson lead a fully Christian life. In fact, Erasmus's intellectual efforts might be summarized by that belief and by his efforts to reach out and persuade eminent laity of that possibility. Yet monks and their cohort friars exercise a strong hold on the susceptible popular imagination. Like the theologians they wield threatening powers: the charge of heresy, excommunication, and worse. And the friars, who hear confessions, have access to people's innermost secrets (thus he urges that confession, when necessary, be heard by the parish priest). The two are further bound together by a heavy regimen of rules and by intra- and extramural rivalries. The rules extend to petty trifles, which are however treated with the exactitude of mathematics, and the rivalries accumulate both within and without the various orders, with all their pullulating new crop of subdivisions and breakaway reorganizations (CWE 27:131). But what most galls Erasmus is that along with literal-mindedness there is often joined illiteracy, a fumbling intonation of Latin phrases meant to impress and entrance the populace. Folly is amused that these people 'with their petty ceremonies, ridiculous trifles and noise exercise a kind of tyranny among mankind' (ibid.).

If this is what we were to be left with from *The Praise of Folly*—a theology derived from the *Enchiridion,* the satiric roll-call of the professions—then we would have a remarkable record of the times, even in several cases extending beyond the times to recurrent issues in Western culture, but we would not have a world classic. Nor would we have an Erasmus whose insights suggest comparison with Montaigne or one whose arguments and figures are recognizable in some of Shakespeare's greatest plays. This Erasmus we get when in the very same *Praise of Folly* he reaches both beyond himself and within himself, exposing the tragic imbalance of the intellect and Nature, the obscurities of existence, and the paradoxes and conflicts inherent in the human condition. This is not only an Erasmus of some relevancy but an Erasmus who is profoundly perennial.

At length realizing that she has produced more of a satire than an 'oratio,' the chagrined Folly (Erasmus) abandons this task. These pages, constituting almost one third of the volume, are concerned with the perversions and violations of true knowledge. The earlier portion, to my mind the most important section, amounting to a bit more than one fifth of the volume is devoted to the liabilities of learning. In the one instance Erasmus calls for the restitution of good learning and true piety, based upon the imitation of Christ and familiarity with the Gospels, the works of the apostles, and those early church fathers. In the other instance it is learning itself that is out of step with Nature, with the regular workings of society, and with the general condition of humankind. In the first he rebukes deviations from essential guides to life; in the second he records the painful lesson that learning may be ill-suited to the requirements of existence. The first deviation suffers from the mania of definition and debate as well as intellectual hubris; the second disjunction from modesty and fear.

The earlier section could be called a defence of ignorance and opens a clear path to Montaigne and eventually to Rousseau's first *Discours*. It is based upon three under-emphasized components of Erasmian thought. The first is his deeply held sense of the obscurity of things. In his letter to Marcus Laurinus of 1523 he addresses his apparent lack of spiritual conviction: he knows so little of himself, he writes, how can he bring any certain judgment to the motivations of others and their springs of action? Then there is the famous Silenus head of Alcibiades (102-3) suggesting the great difference between appearance and reality. But more important and finally all things are ruled by the principle of dissimilarity (Silenus's two faces are 'dissimiles'), thus generating difference and conflict, which becomes an operating rule in human life. Intellect and Nature are dissimilar: where mind is complex, Nature is simple; where intelligence is sharp, Nature is blunt, which makes it so that intelligence or learning is a great inconvenience in all normal human dealings.

Thus the 'fool' has an advantage. At this point, Erasmus, whom we can designate as one of the founders of the modern *studia humanitatis* (not forgetting his Italian predecessors), exposes the hazards of such learning itself. The wise man has recourse to the books of the ancients, and from them picks nothing but verbal subtleties (CWE 27:102). The liabilities of modesty and fear fill the wise man with unwarranted anticipations, the hesitations that hinder any call to action. But the foolish person (now become audacious) suffers none of these inhibitions, from which folly sufficiently frees us. 'Few mortals realize how many other advantages follow from being free from scruples and ready to venture anything' (102), which the older Wilson translation renders more succinctly, 'Few there are that rightly understand of what great advantage it is to blush at nothing and attempt everything' (42-3). These are searing insights of self-recognition where Erasmus sees in himself the de-

ficiencies of the overly-compunctious learning that he laboured so sedulously to establish. The century that witnessed the tragic transformations of humanism was marked at its early beginning by *Praise of Folly* and at its later ending by *Hamlet*.

Delusion, like folly, is of immense value, for it conceals or overlooks the ugliness of existence, the processes of aging and finally dances in the face of death itself. If one were to look at life squarely, at the thing itself, who would not be justified in committing suicide (CWE 27:105)? But from these terrible truths delusion spares us. The old man marries a young wench; the old woman still uses cosmetics to preserve appearances (105-6). But these are more than appearances; they represent attempts to keep hold of identity and to fight off the inevitable nothingness that awaits in the wings. Shakespeare's Richard II, captive in the crushing reality of the thick prison walls, still sends up flashes of imaginary beings: 'Nor I, nor any man that but man is, / With nothing shall be pleased, till he be eased / With being nothing' (V.v.39-41). Life is a play and we are merely players: we change into many costumes along the way, until the 'property manager' calls upon us to return our dress. 'Thus are all things ruled by counterfeit, and yet without this there were no living' (Wilson 44).

The scholar, who had demystified so many saints, now has recourse to fable and to myth. It is not the precepts of Plato or Aristotle that hold cities together, but rather the fetching tales and symbols of myth and mythology (Wilson 40). All the silly parades and the added paddings of names of honour for the victors may be mocked, 'and yet from this source sprang deeds of valiant heroes which the pens of so many eloquent men have extolled to the skies' (CWE 27:102, Wilson 41).

As in Shakespeare, the allowed fools are able to utter truths without censure (Wilson 56-60). Like the lilies of the field, they neither spin nor weave, harbour no fearful anticipations nor wish for future good. They exist totally in the innocent nonchalance of the present, and for this their company is sought out and embraced by all. Contrast this with the lucubrations of the wise man, one 'who has frittered away all his boyhood and youth in acquiring learning, has lost the happiest part of his life in endless wakeful nights, toil, and care, and never tastes a single drop of pleasure even in what's left to him. He's always thrifty, impoverished, miserable, grumpy, and harsh to himself, disagreeable and unpopular with his fellows, pale and thin, sickly and bleary-eyed, prematurely white-haired and senile, worn out and dying before his time. Though what difference does it make when a man like that dies? He's never been alive. There you have a splendid picture of a wise man' (CWE 27:110, Wilson 60)—and a self-portrait of Erasmus himself.

One can well imagine Erasmus's pained grimace as he draws that curriculum vitae. The 'great wise man' has his true complement in the most perfect of men, the Stoic. Each is a born party-killer. The first poisons either by morose silence or screeching argumentation, the other with a deadly eye scrutinizes all human festivities. Which city would choose him as a governor, what wife as a husband? Better to stay with 'boon companions,' as one who thinks nothing human to be alien (CWE 27:103-5).

Two recurrent points of reference underlie the value scheme of this remarkable part of *The Praise of Folly*. They are the bounds and limits of Nature herself, and the regularity of ordinary life. While all other creatures are content to exist within those boundaries that Nature has set for them, only humankind has the effrontery to try to exceed them (CWE 27:108). It is Nature that establishes 'the common lot of all mankind. There's no misery about remaining true to type' (106). Such commonality extends to the social order as well, with which the wise man is similarly out of sync. The wise man's learning has rendered him incapable of carrying on the normal businesses of life, 'and all because he is wholly ignorant of ordinary matters and far removed from any common way of thinking and current practice. And so inevitably he is disliked, doubtless because of the great dissimilarity in mentality and way of life' (propterea quod communium rerum sit imperitus, et a populari opinione, vulgaribusque institutis longe lateque discrepit; 101. Wilson 54). But the main reason he attracts such odium is that there is such a great 'dissimilitudinem' existing between them in both their 'lives and souls.' The word *dissimilitudo* recalls the 'dissimilar' parts of the Silenus head. Such difference means opposition; such 'unlikes,' as Coleridge tells us, cannot but end in dislikes.

The sublime conclusion of *The Praise of Folly* invokes the numerous connections between folly and the religious life, particularly the affinities between folly and Christianity: 'the foolishness of the cross,' 'let us be fools for Christ's sake.' As a scholiast, a concordance compiler, Erasmus evidenced a pedantic passion in this multiplication of citations. But the true function of the finale is to bring together in confrontation the two codes of values that have thus far been exemplary. In the earlier section it is natural wisdom, what Huizinga calls 'spontaneous energy' (71), the teachings of nature, and the ways of the ordinary world that prevail. In the longer more satiric survey of the professions, it is imitation of Christ, immersion in the Gospels, and the authority of the apostles and the early church fathers that matters. The quarrel is between Nature and holiness. How can these two be reconciled? In fact, Erasmus tells us, they cannot. There exists an 'irreconcilable enmity' (irreconciliabile bellum; Wilson 145, CWE 27:204) between them. The one is attached to the corporeal, the other to the spiritual, the invisible. Each takes on the colour of his mental attachments, and so where the one is competent the other a blockhead, and where the one finds his habitat the other lives in the shadows. Hence it follows that there is 'so great [contrarity] of opinion between them, and that too in everything' (Wilson 147, 206). Erasmus's phrase is actually 'dissension,' rendered in the CWE translation as 'disagreement.' But John Wilson in his translation from 1668, to which I have been attached, is intuitively right in that throughout this episode Erasmus proceeds by contrast, starting many a sentence with the word 'contra,' or, 'contrariwise,' as if he were setting up a table of oppositions, emphasizing rhetorically the non-alignment, the inherent disagreement or 'dissensio' between the two dominant ways of viewing the world as if they must always exist in a state of mutually uncomprehending difference, if not warfare.

But what is most remarkable here is how at odds this description of eternal warfare, or lateral opposition, is to Erasmus's normal rhetorical procedures and his ways of viewing the world and resolving conflicts. Rhetorically Erasmus has been given to defusing differences, to finding ways of incorporation and of amelioration. Normally he does this by prioritizing, as Chomarat has indicated. The one kind of assertion or procedure might be of lesser importance but still it figures as having some merit in any proportionate scale of values. This is just one of the rhetorical devices employed by Erasmus in order to bridge difference. Yet here for page after page Erasmus, as he did in the earlier sections, emphasizes 'dissensio,' 'dissimilitudo,' irreconcilable enmities. Obviously he cannot leave it at that, and even Folly serving as arbiter must finally come down on the side of the spiritual, but as being at one with the madness of Christian selflessness. Despite this attempted restoration, the real greatness of *The Praise of Folly* emerges in those pages where Erasmus presents conflict, clashes of visions, and the recognition of the liabilities of the life he has made his own, and eventually of the division within his own life between the practical man he was and the holiness toward which he aspired, but from which he knew he fell short.

In her classic work, *The Fool: His Social and Literary History* Enid Welsford draws upon the two discrepant elements for her understanding of *Praise of Folly* (236-42). On the one hand, by means of Folly Erasmus 'defends the creative vital instincts of humanity against the encroachments of the analytical reason . . . Folly is really the sane normal world according to Nature.' She fosters the pleasing illusions, the counterfeits that make life possible, 'Without Counterfeit there were no living.' Under the watchful eye of the stern Stoic, who could accept without anxieties the pleasing measures offered by Nature? While noting that Folly expends a good deal of time on satiric portraits of the professions, Welsford turns to Folly's higher purpose, which is the appropriateness of another kind of folly for the true Christian. This higher folly disregards 'with a wild recklessness' the goods of this world, but in regard to the next world experiences an ecstasy which renders the soul 'beside herself,' swallowed up in the love of the divine (241) It should be noted that it is these two features—and not the satiric—that Huizinga invokes to account for the work's great appeal. The satire may dominate the middle parts of *The Praise of Folly,* 'but in the other parts it is something far deeper' (74). Here again he sides with posterity's judgment: '[*The Praise of Folly*'s] lasting value is in those passages where we grant that folly is wisdom and the reverse' (75).

By virtue of these divergent characteristics Folly finds her fullest literary incarnations in two of Shakespeare's greatest comedies, *As You Like It* and *Twelfth Night,* and even more imaginatively so, in *King Lear* (thus providing support for Craig Thompson's later notion of the influential roles of the Oxford Reformers in the flowering of Elizabethan literature). Walter Kaiser admirably supplements Welsford's repertoire by including as praisers of Folly, Erasmus's foremost French disciple, Rabelais, and Shakespeare's preeminent Lord of Misrule, Falstaff. Falstaff is dislocated: a figure from the happy world of comedy, he is misplaced in the iron world of history, from whence he must suffer his own tragic discharge. All the ironies of Erasmus's *Praise of Folly* and tensions of Shakespeare's *Henriad* are well observed by Kaiser.[2]

In *As You Like It,* the first contention indicated above occurs between Touchstone and melancholy Jaques, the wearied world traveller, who 'has sold his own lands to see other men's.' The clown is the real touchstone of the play, and Jaques is revealed to be a mere 'poseur.' The fool finds his natural home in the comic freedom of the world of Arden, from which 'the over-clever victim of ennui excludes himself' (Welsford 249-50). One could well picture Erasmus's own delight at this portrayal so consonant with some of the more piercing arguments of *Praise of Folly*. He would perhaps have had some moral scruples at the undoing of Malvolio in *Twelfth Night,* where Touchstone finds his true brother in comic arms in Feste the clown. A mutual dislike and more separates the worlds of Feste and Malvolio. The clown finds his congenial pace in the festival spirit of Saturnalian comedy. Malvolio, however, cannot even be denounced as a Puritan, but rather as a self-serving careerist, who in his eagerness to please his superiors abuses his powers by squelching the riotous behaviour of the free-spirited. He is rebutted by Sir Toby's immortal response to the up-tight: 'Dost thou think because thou art virtuous there shall be no more cakes and ale?' While this is supposedly a temporary seasonal licence (which most certainly Toby is guilty of abusing) it nevertheless serves its purpose in expressing a more

exuberant attachment to living and in exposing the authoritarianism of the censorious. In Shakespeare's festive comedy clowns and fools speak for a spirited vitality while the worldly wise are cast out. Such comparisons are never perfect fits, and trite summaries are hardly helpful, but Jaques and Malvolio can certainly be enrolled in Erasmus's gallery of life-deniers who are undermined and exposed in their foolish wisdom by wise fools.

It is in *King Lear* that Shakespeare addresses the same dialectic as does Erasmus in the final, fitting climax to *The Praise of Folly.* In some brief sixteen pages that are among the best ever written on Shakespeare's greatest tragedy Welsford demonstrates how Erasmus's twofold argument is completed and enhanced, as kings and clowns are brought together, change roles, and achieve in their downfalls a universal wisdom. In the face of a classical decorum that would prohibit such cohabitation, Shakespeare insists on the dramatic effectiveness of bringing together these grandly representative types, in building on and altering the historical structures and traditions of their roles. The fool rises to the level of moral sanctity while the king in his madness expresses philosophical and human truths that represent the highest consciousness of the play.

King Lear is a morality play without that genre's predictable outcomes. The good characters are obviously good and the evil characters identifiable as evil. But in their differences they are mutually uncomprehending, just as Erasmus indicated they should be. There are no hands across the barriers. In many of their coolly rational arguments Goneril, Regan, and Edmund are obviously correct; only in their consequences are their reasonings catastrophic. The equally obvious good characters are innocently trusting and easily duped. That is, the one type, the malevolently rational, considers the other to be imbecilic, and the other cannot comprehend their deviousness or hardness of heart. Indeed, two worlds, with two different mental and emotional instruments, are in conflict. But in Shakespeare's tragedy, as in *The Praise of Folly,* such equivalency and irreconcilable warfare does not produce a stalemate. Each of the viewpoints 'is not equally valid, not equally true.' When pushed to the play's apocalyptic extremes, they all reveal their genuine natures. One great turnabout occurs in the nature of the fool. In the end, fidelity and loyalty are his true provinces:

> But I will tarry, the fool will stay
> And let the wise man fly;
> The knave turns fool that runs away:
> The fool no knave perdee.

Welsford makes a direct connection between this practice of foolish loyalty—a trait that finally distinguishes the 'good' characters—and the conclusion of *Praise of*

Folly. 'That Shakespeare's ethics were the ethics of the New Testament, that in this play the mightiest poetry is dedicated to a reiteration of the wildest paradoxes of the Gospels and of St. Paul that seems to me quite certain' (268). But the presence of that doctrine as reassurance is not so clear, as the good suffer from what the evil have wrought and the evil devour themselves.

Voltaire had no need of a Shakespeare to bring his thoughts dramatically alive: he had a Voltaire. Yet, this was a Voltaire whose sense of artful decorum could not tolerate kings and clowns pitched together, or a prince and a grave-digger bandying wits. In Shakespeare's great imagination, however, they do represent universal types and conditions of humankind. Still, despite his unwillingness to step out of the decorum of his age into a more creatural universality, Voltaire did achieve greatness by virtue of the freedoms he allowed himself in the once demoted genre of **Candide.**

It is strangely wanting to seek in Voltaire that which he has in 'common' with us, as does Roland Barthes (94), when we should be seeking the exceptional, that which carries us beyond our normal worlds of perception. There are three main clasps that open up the books of *Voltairien* appeal. The first is found in **Zadig,** where Voltaire shows his rare faith in the possibility that good faith and rectitude will eventually be vindicated. Intellectual justice will pierce through the dense fog of slander, resentment, and ill-will. One can think back to the time when he turned the disaster after the Rohan affair into the opportunity of England, or the humiliation at Frankfurt into the rehabilitation at Ferney, but perhaps, looking ahead, his greatest vindication occurred when he returned to Paris, the site of his earliest triumphs, the native city he had known so well but which he had not seen in twenty-eight years, come back to be crowned with laurels and carried by the crowd to the old Comédie Française, the house that Voltaire built, with the splendid statue by Houdon fronting it all.[3]

The second clasp is of a different order. It reveals in **L'Ingenu** Voltaire's refusal to be comforted, to accept consolation. Not all the grave injustices that have been committed can be washed away. The complacent sexual banter and bartering of **Cosi-Sancta** falls short when compared with the death of Mlle Saint-Yves. The culture of mundanity does not suffice when there are some losses that are beyond repair, that do not lead to reconciliation, and like raw wounds have only to be touched to be reopened. Voltaire insists upon his God-given right to hold to such outraged conviction, not to absolve the sins of the world by the consolations of theodicy, which is only a type of fatalism that does away with the reality of things. Oddly enough, Voltaire needs a God as a warrant of his right to accuse the world as it is presented to him.[4]

The third clasp opens the world of **Candide** at those places where Voltaire argues with himself. It is present in the last of his *contes,* **Histoire de Jenni ou le Sage et l'Athée** (1775) in the debate between Freind and Birton. It may well be that Voltaire is showing the fatal consequences of the materialistic theories of Diderot and d'Holbach, but the greatness of the debate between Freind and Birton derives from the fact that Voltaire is arguing with himself (Deloffre's *'notice'* and notations are excellent, **RC** [**Romans et Contes**] 1215-27, 1233-65). This clasp opens up the dramatic world where Voltaire is not arguing a settled case of Spirit, or Intelligence, against Stupidity and Fanaticism, engaging in too easy combat, where there is really no contest. There is another Voltaire, who arrives at his true stature when he is able in some ways to outface himself, to set in contention his own firmly held beliefs. While the outcome might still be a foregone conclusion, the presentations of Birton (who advances the arguments of the atheist, although he is not one) are too powerful to be simply trod upon or stepped over. Birton is ready to acknowledge that there is a Supreme Intelligence, but how or when this being enters into human affairs is open to question. As in the stupendous lengthy series of notes to the *Poème sur le désastre de Lisbonne,* Birton demolishes the assumptions of the great Chain of Being. He asks what possible relation there can be between the Infinite Being and us other 'worms of the earth.' This Being did not create the world as evidence of his glory, because that would be an act of vanity. And if this Being created the earth so that human beings could live happily, 'Je vous laisse a penser s'il est venu à bout de ce dessein . . .' (I leave it to your judgment as to whether he ever completed his design) (RC 647). He than affirms the question that Voltaire in other writings found unacceptable. We may call God that intelligent and powerful principal that animates all of nature, but did he deign to make himself known to us?

Freind in his more *Voltairien* counterarguments has recourse to the evidence of our senses, an appreciation of the magnificent order of nature, and the gift of life itself. Voltaire has him echo Rousseau's arguments so fully expounded in *Émile* about the ever-present power of conscience and even finally the mendacious wager of Pascal, hardly suitable for a true religious experience. At length, despite the pragmatic victory of Freind, there remains the comment of Voltaire's editor, Frédéric Deloffre, who concludes that Birton does not represent the adversary of Voltaire but rather 'that part of himself that rebels against his very fideism' (**RC** 1262). These are parts of himself exposed in a true dialectic, each taking animation from Voltaire's own firmest convictions, convictions that he cannot totally eliminate or crown in triumph (van den Heuvel 327).

Criticism can no longer treat **Candide** in superior isolation. While this means its primacy of place is open to some challenge (particularly from *L'Ingenu,* which Voltaire himself considered superior because of its greater *vraisemblance,* or truth to being), it also means we can gain a better understanding of this masterpiece. Burlesque in style, and lacking in affective power, *Candide* has a different field of interest. Yet, we are strangely moved by this young man's need to search out the truths of existence, *une raison d'exister,* to test the philosophies that encircle him. The candour of his name represents his openness to what experience brings his way. This is why Rousseau was intuitively correct in asserting that Voltaire did indeed respond to his *Letter on Providence* of 1756, Rousseau's impassioned answer to the pessimism of the *Poème sur le désastre de Lisbonne.* In it, Rousseau implicitly asks, if what you (Voltaire) say is true, that evil stalks the earth, then how are we to lead our lives? *Candide* is Voltaire's delayed answer.

While finally with *Candide* we open the third clasp, where Voltaire argues against himself, the first half of this *récit* teeters perilously on the brink of failure. Voltaire has little interest in arguing against Pangloss's philosophy, the Leibnizian quality of which he long before discarded, or embraced in only lukewarm fashion, riddled by the famous aborted questioning 'Mais . . .' Pangloss is merely a figure of straw and the *roman* does not turn until the Eldorado episode, chapters XVII and XVIII. Eldorado is not Utopian, but rather *Voltairien,* where the author's most valued goals for human society are introduced. By its very inaccessibility, Eldorado might as well be 'nowhere'; nevertheless its practical ways are for Voltaire quite feasible. Borrowing from the comfort-seeking Voltaire of the *Mondain* poems, all the carriages are good and the cuisine is superb. For the exponent of natural religion and rational theology, there is only one God (it is beyond comprehension that anyone would think to worship more). There are no monks, and showing Voltaire's further leanings toward Protestantism, everyone is a priest and the only prayers are those of universal thanks-giving. For the progressive Voltaire, who learned well the lessons of his stay in England, Eldorado is a centre of technology, with its own palace of science and industry. The elements of Eldorado might be out of sight, but they are not out of reach.

After Eldorado the orbit of *Candide* changes. The murder and mayhem that existed in the first half—so reminiscent of the comic violence typical of Bugs Bunny or the Roadrunner cartoons, where the victims manage to escape uninjured or recover sufficiently—is notably lacking. So is the need to controvert the theological questions of Pangloss; his own words undo him. At the end, while averring that he had suffered terribly, he continues to sustain his thesis that 'tout allait à merveille,' to which Voltaire, in one of his typical ironic locutions, adds, 'et ne croyait rien' (and didn't believe a word of it; *RC* 230). Later, trying to resurrect his customary prying into the final causes of things, Pangloss gets the door slammed in their faces.

Now questions of Providence rarely intrude as Candide has acquired a new interlocutor in the person of Martin, and their discourse takes place on the plain turf of purely earthly understanding. As in *Jenni,* Martin represents Voltaire's worst fears, stated as matters of fact, meeting his best wishes. Rather than a satire of the emptiness of Pangloss's vapid thinking, there emerges a real encounter, an unbridgeable one (as in Erasmus's *Praise of Folly*) between benevolent hopes and the brute facts of evil. In this new ethos of significant exchange and encounter, it is quite striking that no statement in the second half of the *roman* is allowed to pass unqualified or uncontradicted.

The second half of *Candide* is an amazing venture in self-presentation, of the self in conflict. Voltaire's encounter with his own values is reproduced in two portraits, that of the savant and that of Pococuranté, where Voltaire is indeed showing portions of himself while not exempting these proto-Voltaires from serious criticism. The savant gives a splendid synopsis of Voltaire's own poetics of tragedy: to be new without being bizarre, to be sublime yet always natural, to be a great poet while none of the characters appear as such, to know the human heart and to let it speak simply and in a pure and harmonious language, and never to let the rhyme control the meaning (*RC* 204-5). Like Shakespeare's having Hamlet give advice to the players, Voltaire stands behind the voice of his character. But not for long, as the hostess marquise (whose gaming house is quite crooked) soon lets Candide know that the savant's own literary success is quite meagre: his one play was hooted off the stage and his book was left unsold. Candide replies that this savant is another Pangloss. Pursuing this advantage, and showing how diminished his former mentor has become, he then asks the savant if everything is 'au mieux' (for the better) in this world. But unlike Pangloss the savant embraces the philosophy of the new interlocutor, Martin. Not at all, is his answer; in fact 'chez nous' everything goes crosswise (tout va de travers). Eternal warfare is the rule and enmity of opposing forces the composition of the times.

Pococuranté, that languid Venetian nobleman, also displays much of the *Voltairien* critical manner (as Voltaire himself admits, *RC* 882n1, 214). Like Montaigne, he reads for his own pleasure and the exercise of critical judgment. Fools admire everything from an esteemed writer (they are exegetes), whereas he only reads for himself and for what he can take from a work ('Je ne lis que pour mois; je n'aime que ce qui est à mon usage'). All things must be brought before the bar of critical judgment, and in Voltaire's time, the canons of good taste. Accordingly, the seemingly unending battle scenes of the *Iliad* are deplored; the *Aeneid* can only be accepted in Books 2, 4, and 6, and Milton is beyond repair (216-18). But more than critical judgment, one senses in Pococuranté the fatiguing weight of books. He has read all the books and his flesh is weakened thereby. Candide is taken in by this example of independent critical thinking. But where Candide reads full self-possession (a man who exists above all that he possesses), Martin detects in Pococuranté a more disfiguring disgust at all that he possesses. And when Candide questions whether there is not great pleasure in this ability to criticize everything, Martin answers, 'C'est-à-dire, qu'il y du plaisir à n'avoir pas de plaisir' (219)? As if there can be pleasure in not taking pleasure. And the delight that Voltaire always took in genuine works of art, even where he was alert to their shortcomings, finds its voice to repeal the part of himself that was abused in Pococuranté.

The real opposition in *Candide* exists between the jaded yet usually accurate views of Martin and the character of Candide. To this dichotomy there appears to be no resolution. But there is a reason for this: each represents permanent parts of the 'complex vocation' of Voltaire himself. On the one side, his is an 'esprit sans illusions' but on the other, this same esprit without illusions is capable of great enthusiasms, expressing a 'volonté prête à toutes les aventures' (Naves, 19). Thus Voltaire presents in his two main characters the opposing aspects of his own personality.

Yet like a cropped photo the conclusion of *Candide* is much diminished, as this gathering of war-torn refugees is confined to working a sparse farm under a limited motto—and perhaps this reduced picture of desolation is the true basis of its modern appeal. However, the problem with isolating *Candide* is that one tends to view Voltaire through the critical lens of these narrow passages. Able writers have felt the pressure to enlarge the dimensions of each, to gather up a philosophy more in keeping with Voltaire's larger aspirations and accomplishments. For some, the conclusion of *Candide* is already 'dépassée' (Pomeau, *De la Cour au jardin* 355). Van den Heuvel and Pomeau (along with others) are most instructive here, using extraliterary and literary methods to arrive at a fuller assessment of *Candide*. Each cites appropriately the great difference between the cold comforts offered by the *metairie* and the magnificent work of rehabilitation Voltaire brought both to the adjoining village of Ferney and its people (Pomeau, 353-6, van den Heuvel, 276-81). From a few barren and poorly cultivated farms (the region was badly hurt by the loss of the Protestant workers after the revocation of the Edict of Nantes), Voltaire at great expense and with much concern and diligence managed to restore it to a level of some 1200 households.

Both Pomeau and van den Heuvel also use the same kind of language when placing *Candide* in Voltaire's development. The oft-repeated phrase 'mais il faut cul-

tiver notre jardin,' becomes both a conquest and a point of departure. It represents a conquest over the need to cut a figure with the great and also a contentedness with one's own more restricted possibilities. *Candide* thus contains 'the stirrings of a new humanism.' In itself, 'not very exalting,' the ending of *Candide* represents a new beginning, a certain 'ouverture' (RC 830). In van den Heuvel's more benign reading, the new, remodelled humanism, while more limited, also represents the possibilities of bringing into realization 'le rêve de l'Eldorado.' Pomeau for his part, as does van den Heuvel, situates *Candide* in the larger enterprises of Voltaire at this time. But he also calls it a masterpiece; *Candide* was 'une lecture roborbative pour les temps d'épreuve' (*De la Cour au jardin* 374). But the germination of *Candide* does not end there; it has its role as a point of departure: '*Candide* donne le coup d'envoi à la campagne contre l'Infâme' (Candide is the starting shot for the campaign against the *infâme*; 347-75, 374).

Quite clearly the critical tradition encasing *Candide* needs to be supplemented. The book needs to be seen in its relation with Voltaire's other works; it needs to be judged in balance with the larger aspirations and successes of Voltaire in reclaiming the farmlands near the chateau of Ferney, and it needs to be regarded as a new manifesto, an 'opening,' from which, with a more solid base, his public campaigning starts out on a solid footing. *Candide* is remarkable because within it Voltaire finds the insight and the courage to give full expression to his antiself, or to the portraiture of himself through others, to bring crashing down the outmoded philosophy ('of which he did not believe a word'), and to set in motion the challenges represented by the clash and conflict of new ways of looking at the world. *Candide* may not stand alone, but it does stand tall; witness its astonishing immediate success when an estimated 20,000 volumes were sold in 1759. Although Voltaire persistently denied authorship, he took great pains to have it printed in various outposts so as to elude the watchful authorities. The genre of the *conte philosophique,* to which he took reluctantly, became the capstone of his continuing fame, overshadowing other works which, by some criteria, should be better known. In this of course it is like *The Praise of Folly*. But in being so overbearing such classics have also the reverse effect of attracting some vagrant attention to the lives of their authors, and thus serendipitously to their other works as well.

Notes

1. See the introduction to Clarence Miller's translation of *The Praise of Folly* ix. For the Latin original I have been obliged to resort to the *Erasmus*

von Rotterdam, Ausgewälhlte Schriften (AS), vol. 2. Where the Latin original is given in the text, the page number after the slash refers to this edition.

2. See Kaiser, *Praisers of Folly* [Cambridge, Mass.: Harvard University Press, 1964].

3. Jacques Gengoux has written an admirable suite of essays, '"*Zadig*" et les trois puissances de Voltaire,' *Les Lettres Romanes* 16 (1962), wherein he introduces the three powers that, brought together, form the *Voltairien* ideal. They are body (*corps,* including bravery and physical appeal); mind (*esprit,* including wit, intelligence, and philosophical bent); and heart (*coeur,* or the capacity for affection that underlies the others). Taken individually each of these powers is insufficient, but brought together into a developing whole, as in *Zadig* or *L'Ingenu* (note the absence of *Candide*), they represent the fullness of *Voltairien* virtue (in marked contrast to the same triadic elements employed by Pascal.) The three clasps I invoke are not individual forces or qualities but rather subjects of concern—one could call them personal myths or themes. Two of them refuse to enter into any ideal development or notions of reconciliation. They balk at any attempt to show the unity of Voltaire's thought and instead reveal its dire complexity.

4. Paul Hazard, in the aforementioned essay, 'Le Problème du mal dans la conscience européene du dix-huitième siècle,' traces the widespread appeal of the Leibnizian adage that this is the best of all possible worlds. He attributes its dissolution to the developing confidence in the powers of observation and common sense. In Voltaire, this may be confirmed by his long-standing allegiance to Locke, but it would appear that Hazard's thesis would have the consequence of locating Voltaire in that genius of mediocrity by overlooking his insistence on the just expression of an outraged sense of humane sentiment.

Works Cited

Barthes, Roland. 'Le dernier écrivan heureux.' *Essais Critiques.* Paris: Gallimard, 1962.

Erasmus, Desiderius. *The Praise of Folly.* Trans. Clarence H. Miller. New Haven: Yale UP, 1979.

Naves, Raymond. *Voltaire.* 8th ed. Paris: Hatier, 1972.

Pomeau, René. *De la Cour au jardin* (with Christine Mervaud). Oxford: Voltaire Foundation, 1991.

Welford, Enid. *The Fool: His Social and Literary History.* New York: Farrar and Reinhart, 1935.

Wilson, Derek. *England in the Age of Thomas More.* London and New York: Hart-Davis McGibbon, 1978.

Abbreviations

AS: Erasmus, Desiderius. *Encomium Moriae Erasmus von Rotterdam.* Ausgewählte Schriften. Darmstadt: Wissenschaftliche Buchgesellschaft, 1976.

CWE: Erasmus, Desiderius. *Collected Works of Erasmus.* Toronto: University of Toronto Press, 1974-.

OC: Voltaire. *Oeuvres Complète.* Paris: Garnier, 1877-85.

RC: Voltaire. *Romans et Contes.* Paris: Gallimard, 1979.

E. M. Langile (essay date 2010)

SOURCE: Langile, E. M. "*Candide* and *Tom Jones*: Voltaire, Perched on Fielding's Shoulders."[1] In *Mentoring in Eighteenth-Century British Literature and Culture,* edited by Anthony W. Lee, pp. 85-107. Farnham, U.K.: Ashgate Publishing Limited, 2010.

[*In this essay, Langile analyzes similarities between* Candide *and Henry Fielding's* Tom Jones, *tracing the influence of Fielding's novel on Voltaire and arguing that in* Candide *"Voltaire takes issue with the moral certainties [of] Fielding."*]

In the late summer of 1722 the then 26-year-old Voltaire encountered an Englishman of high intellectual and social attainment.[2] To the budding poet and man about town, the exiled Tory statesman and free-thinker, Henry St. John, Viscount Bolingbroke (1678-1751), embodied a type of cultural pre-eminence that appealed to the ambitious and snobbish young man.[3] Voltaire's portrait of Bolingbroke expresses not only his enthusiasm for the British aristocrat's cosmopolitan refinement, vast learning, and worldly experience; it also implicitly pays homage to England and her social and cultural institutions.[4] Five years after this decisive encounter, Voltaire gained first-hand experience of England and English life (1726-8), and his later writings bear witness to a deeply held admiration for English social models as well as for English scientific, philosophical, and political thought.[5] Until the end of his life Voltaire was a committed, though not always an uncritical anglophile.

In the field of English literature too, the young Voltaire was eager to make a name for himself as a pioneering critic. His writings in the 1730s, for example, did much to advance English literature in France. Several creative works from that period also pay tribute to his newly acquired knowledge of English literature both established and contemporary. According to the author's preface, *La Mort de César*—written at Wandsworth in 1726 and published ten years later—started out as a translation of Shakespeare's *Julius Cesar.* Likewise, the *Discours en vers sur l'homme* (1740) can only be fully appreciated as an imitation of Pope's *Essay on Man* (1734). By the 1750s, however, Voltaire's youthful zeal gave way to a more critical and often subversive reading of English literature. His reaction to contemporary English fiction, for example, betrays impatience and irritation. This is certainly true of Voltaire's reading of Richardson, but also of his response to Fielding, whose works had the unenviable distinction, at least in Voltaire's eyes, of having been translated into French—and worse—made popular, by his bitter rivals Desfontaines and Pierre-Antoine de La Place.[6] And yet even as he gives the appearance of rejecting the English novel as a trivial and unworthy art form, Voltaire unquestionably felt its attraction. Perhaps the author doth protest too much. And so do the critics who have long acknowledged the inspiration Voltaire drew from contemporary English fiction, the best-known case being Chapter 20 of *L'Ingénu*, where the account of mademoiselle Saint Yves' agony is derived from *Clarissa*.[7] In the same vein I have recently brought to light the remarkable similarities that exist between *Candide* and Fielding's *Tom Jones* in its 1750 French translation.[8] My findings suggest very strongly that Voltaire's most enduring masterpiece makes explicit reference to La Place's *Histoire de Tom Jones, ou l'enfant trouvé* (*ET*) both in terms of characters and the situational conflict that sets the tale in motion.

It can be demonstrated, for instance, that Candide, Cunégonde, and Pangloss derive from La Place's treatment of Fielding's Tom Jones, Sophia Western, and the philosopher Square. Consistent with my view that Voltaire's aim was to reverse what he perceived as Fielding's original intent, the creation of the overtly sexual Cunégonde from two different characters—the virginal Sophia and the bawdy Jenny Jones—ironically and subversively undermines Candide's symbolic pursuit of love in the person of "la perle des filles," his beloved Cunégonde. What is also clear is that *Candide*'s episodic structure in Chapters 1-3, can be seen to parody La Place's version of Fielding's novel. Tom's life in a country idyll, his picaresque adventures on the road (and most notably, his encounter with a company of soldiers massing to fight the Jacobites in Scotland) prefigure Candide's early life in Thunder-ten-tronckh, his sudden expulsion from the *meilleur des châteaux*; and then, in quick succession, his adventures as a recruit in the Bulgar army, and subsequent travels to Holland. By the same token, Jones's enthusiasm for the Hanoverian cause against the Scotch rebels—"Tom s'entretenait paisiblement avec celui qui paraissait commander et de qui il apprit que la troupe qu'il conduisait était une compagnie de recrue pour l'armée du duc de Cumberland destinée à combattre les *rebelles d'Écosse*" (*ET* I 299)—finds its counterpart in Candide's eagerness to serve the kings of Spain and Portugal in their fight

against Jesuits, accused of endorsing a native rebellion in Paraguay. *Candide* transforms the details of the rebellion accordingly:

> On y équipait une flotte, et on y assemblait des troupes pour mettre à la raison pères jésuites du Paraguai, qu'on accusait d'avoir fait *révolter une de leurs hordes* contre les rois d'Espagne et de Portugal, auprès de la ville du Saint-Sacrement
>
> (*C* [*Candide*] 151).

A further indication that Fielding was an inspiration for Voltaire comes not from *Tom Jones,* but rather from his earlier *Joseph Andrews* (1742), a novel translated into French 1743 (and reprinted in 1750) by the aforementioned Abbé Desfontaines.[9] Written in the style of *Don Quixote* to ridicule Richardson's *Pamela, Joseph Andrews* makes use of a curious motif inherited from Socrates' wife Xanthippe, who, according to one tradition, emptied a chamber pot on the philosopher's head. That motif occurs twice in *Joseph Andrews,* though the first time the pot contains pig's blood rather than excrement. In both instances, Parson Adams, who is arguably another curious forerunner of Pangloss, has the filthy contents of the pot dumped on his head, first by the choleric innkeeper's wife, Mrs Tow-wouse, and second, inadvertently by Joseph Andrews himself.[10] Precisely the same motif appears in Chapter 3 of *Candide* where the Calvinist orator's fanatical wife takes the place of Mrs Tow-wouse and empties a chamber pot on the innocent and unsuspecting Candide. Ever conscious of the *bienséances*, Voltaire scrupulously avoids naming that infamous receptacle, or describing its contents, though he must have known that this unflattering allusion would remind contemporary readers of Fielding's novel and more pointedly, perhaps, of one his most irritating adversaries and long standing target of ridicule, Desfontaines[11]:

> La femme de l'orateur ayant mis la tête à la fenêtre, et avisant un homme qui doutait que le pape fût antéchrist, lui répandit sur le chef un plein.. O Ciel! à quel excès se porte le zèle de la religion dans les dames!
>
> (*C* 128)

Finally, with regard to *Joseph Andrews,* Parson Adams, is credited with so much learning that he would scarcely meet his equal "in the most famous" German University. This is how Desfontaines renders that passage:

> Monsieur Adams était très savant. La plus grande partie de sa vie s'était passée dans ces études et sa profonde érudition faisait bien voir qu'il n'avait pas perdu son temps, puisqu'on aurait à peine trouvé son pareil dans la plus célèbre université d'Allemagne.
>
> (*JA* 1:11)

In *Candide*'s final chapter, Pangloss, in spite of his many misfortunes and dwindling academic prospects, still hopes for recognition, as Voltaire puts it . . . "in any" German University.[12] This too strikes me as an ironic reference to *Joseph Andrews* and one that squares neatly with *Candide*'s original German setting.

And yet, notwithstanding these two specific examples, Fielding's influence on *Candide* was almost certainly precipitated by *Tom Jones* in La Place's 1750 translation. Consider first the novels' shared narrative formula. *Candide* parallels Fielding's story of a well-meaning, but poor and naïve orphan boy brought up in a nobleman's house. In both stories, the cause of the protagonist's brutal expulsion from a childhood paradise relates to his sexual awakening. Both story lines recount their protagonists' wanderings in search of their inamoratas. Voltaire clearly appropriated the moral dimension of Tom Jones's odyssey—his exposure to evil, and suffering; his gradual acquaintance with the world, its cruelty, and hypocrisy; his interactions with a rogue's gallery of social types; and his intermittent involvement with the darker side of human nature. It is no coincidence, therefore, that both Tom and Candide attain a degree of philosophical detachment and maturity before they are reunited with the women they love. Tom wins the hand of the lovely Sophia whose very name means wisdom, while Candide accepts his fate and marries Cunégonde, in spite of his obvious misgivings—for at the tale's conclusion he discovers to his dismay that she has grown hopelessly ugly. What I hope now to demonstrate is the extent to which *L'Enfant trouvé* contributed to *Candide*'s episodic structure and overall arrangement far beyond the first three chapters previously examined, thus clearly establishing Fielding, through the conduit of La Place's translation, as a key intertextual mentor to Voltaire.

Both *Tom Jones* and *Candide* are based on an Aristotelian tripartite narrative design. Tom Jones is divided into 18 books, where each six-book unit corresponds to a specific geographical and psychological space: six books for the country, six for the road, and six for the city.[13] *Candide,* likewise, is composed in 30 chapters and can be neatly divided into three philosophical segments, each roughly ten chapters long. Ervin Beck has written that Candide's symbolic journey is contingent on three allegorical guides: the optimistic Pangloss (Ch., 1-10), the sceptical Cacambo (Ch., 11-20) and the pessimistic Martin (Ch., 21-30). Each of these guides represents a particular philosophical disposition and each, moreover, is associated with a specific, yet symbolic, geographical region.[14] Voltaire's borrowings in the early chapters of *Candide* are not difficult to identify in spite of the tale's being set, at least initially, in the very real region of Westphalia.[15] *Candide*'s spatial-temporal dimension—and notwithstanding Voltaire's satire on Frederick the Great and Prussian militarism, and his send-up of the Inquisition—is an abstract construct with virtually no basis in reality.[16] The tale could have taken place anywhere (or everywhere) and in a certain sense

it does. For example, *Candide*'s opening lines replicate, in almost identical phrasing, the conceptual sequence clearly detectable in the first paragraph of *L'Enfant trouvé*.[17] The important thing is not the actual geographical setting, but rather, the psychological and moral one, which, initially, both Tom Jones and *Candide* share:

> Il y avait en Westphalie, dans le château de monsieur le baron de Thunder-ten-Tronckh, un jeune garçon à qui la nature avait donné les mœurs les plus douces. Sa physionomie annonçait son âme. Il avait le jugement assez droit avec l'esprit le plus simple; c'est je crois, pour cette raison qu'on le nommait Candide.
>
> (*C* 118)

One wonders if Voltaire's choice of Westphalia might have been suggested by Fielding's "the *western* division of this kingdom" (cette Partie *Occidentale* de l'Angleterre)? Or perhaps by the family name of Fielding's heroine, Sophia Western, a character we know to have been modelled on Fielding's wife, Charlotte Craddock. Coincidentally, the names Charlotte/Sophia (Sophie in French)—and keeping in mind my contention that Cunégonde is in part built on the Sophia character—tie in neatly with Deloffre's view that *Candide*'s "illustre Westphalienne" was inspired by Voltaire's long time friend and paramour, a woman he refers to famously as "cette franche Westphalienne": *Charlotte-Sophie* von Altenburg, Countess Bentinck.[18] Voltaire was certainly in a position to know the name of Fielding's wife and a great deal too about his domestic life and career. From the 1720s he was on intimate terms with Fielding's cousin, Lady Mary Wortley Montagu (1689-1762), who he celebrates in his *Lettres Philosophiques*.[19] Voltaire also had more than a passing acquaintance with one of Fielding's most intimate friends and admirers, George Lyttleton (1709-73), *Tom Jones*'s dedicatee. That dedication was translated at the beginning of *L'Enfant trouvé,* and again in Book 13:1 where Lyttleton is mentioned by name along with Fielding's benefactor Ralph Allen (1693-1764), the model for Squire Allworthy.[20] In the absence of a better explanation (and there is none), one could plausibly trace the name of "Dr. Ralph," *Candide*'s supposed author, to Fielding's Ralph Allen. Voltaire obviously knew that Ralph is not a German name, even though the tale's final version (1761) maintains and extends the fiction that the work was translated "from the German" of Dr. Ralph. Such half revelations are entirely consistent with Voltaire's arch style, though, admittedly, they are not easy to confirm. They also tell us very little about how Voltaire's familiarity with Fielding's *Tom Jones* (through *L'Enfant trouvé*) influenced *Candide*. Here again, we must rely on La Place's translation to uncover further textual evidence that Voltaire followed Fielding's archtectonic plot in almost parallel sequence, and that several important narrative segments in *Candide,* including, the Old Woman's story; Candide and

Cacambo's adventures in the land of the Oreillons, and in Eldorado; Candide's entrance into Paris, his evening at the theatre; and finally, his sojourn in Venice can be seen to derive from prominent passages in Fielding's *Tom Jones.*

An uncharacteristic *lapse* at the beginning of Chapter 2 of **Candide** shows the eponymous hero sleeping rough in a snow storm, perished with cold in the depth of a Northern winter.[21] Just a page earlier, however, Pangloss was observed by Cunégonde giving his outdoor lesson in "experimental physics" to a docile chamber maid. This scene, which I believe derives from two different chapters in Book 5 of *L'Enfant trouvé*: (the philosopher Square's trousers down exposure in Molly's room 5:3; and Tom's summer time tryst with the same Molly in a *petit bois* 5:7), must surely have taken place in warm weather, just like the analogous scene in *L'Enfant trouvé,* where La Place specifically mentions that the evening was balmy:

> *La soirée était belle*; & il [Tom] se promenait seul dans un petit bois, en rêvant aux charmes de sa chère Sophie, lorsque ses réflexions amoureuses furent interrompues par l'apparition d'une femme, qui l'ayant regardé fixement, se sauva dans le plus épais du bois.

> (*ET* I 206)

The sudden change in climate from Chapter 1 to Chapter 2 has puzzled more than one critic. René Pomeau, for example, has written that the falling snow in Chapter 2 provides evidence that Voltaire began writing the first chapters of **Candide** in January 1758: "s'il écrivait ces lignes en janvier 1758, un coup d'œil par sa fenêtre lui a procuré ce parfait raccourci du malheur de Candide, nouvel Adam chassé du Paradis terrestre."[22] Another, more plausible, explanation for the narrative incoherence noted, one consistent with my reading of *L'Enfant trouvé,* can be found in Book 7 where we learn that Tom's expulsion from the Allworthy estate takes place in the dead of winter—symbolic, in both *Tom Jones* and **Candide,** of the cold and heartless world into which the protagonists have been expelled. The sudden change of season from Chapter 1 to Chapter 2 can accordingly be seen as a result of the way Voltaire, working from a pre-existing narrative, compressed the first seven books of *L'Enfant trouvé,* to forge **Candide**'s first two chapters. Having left a country inn accompanied by Partridge, Tom—who has not yet conceived of regaining Sophia—hopes to join a group of soldiers and head north to Scotland (Book 7.7). At this point, still warmed by thoughts of his true love, he is resigned to a cold, dark, and desolate journey on foot. Partridge, however, complains bitterly of the cold:

> De tels amants, ajouta Jones en poussant un soupir avaient sans doutes des cœurs bien capables de sentir tout ce que l'amour a de plus sublime et de plus délicat! . . . Cela est assez probable, répondit Partridge en

murmurant, mais j'envie encore plus leur bonheur, si leurs corps étaient insensibles au froid. Quant à moi, je suis *transi* et si nous ne trouvons bientôt un gîte convenable, je crains bien de perdre mon nez en route.

> (*ET* II 46-7)

In spite of the frosty weather, Tom is consumed by romantic longings and wishes to continue his night journey. He proposes that he and Partridge climb a steep hill from where: "la vue [. . .] doit être charmante par ce beau clair de lune et surtout pour quelqu'un qui aime à s'entretenir dans ses idées mélancoliques" (*ET* II 52). Here again Partridge pleads with him to seek shelter from the cold: "Il fait déjà assez froid ici sans risquer d'aller nous morfondre là-haut. Cherchons plutôt quelque trou où nous puissions nous réfugier et reprendre des forces . . ." (*ET* II 53). As chance would have it, Partridge spies a far-off light, and then an ancient cottage. The two travellers make their way to the cottage, where, *"demi-morts de froid"* (*"mourant de faim et de lassitude"* in **Candide,** *C* 122) they eventually encounter the Man of the Hill. Tom finally asks for shelter and a place by the fire (*ET* II 55).

Thus Fielding introduces a "tale within a tale," a narrative device inherited from Cervantes and exploited to great effect in both *Joseph Andrews* and *Tom Jones,* and which, incidentally, Voltaire also uses in **Candide.** Following Cunégonde's example (Ch. 8: *Histoire de Cunégonde),* the Old Woman tells a story that differs in detail, but is strikingly similar in both structure and theme to the Man of the Hill's tale in *Tom Jones.* Fielding's Man of the Hill segment both adumbrates and encapsulates Voltaire's dual purpose in **Candide**: the pursuit of love and the defeasance of Optimism. The thematic concordance between the tales is indicated by the titles of the chapters in which they are told. La Place's *Histoire de l'homme de la montagne, Suite de l'histoire de l'homme de la montagne,* and his *Conclusion de l'histoire de l'homme de la montagne* (8.10, 11, 12, 13) have their parallel in Voltaire's much shorter *L'Histoire de la vieille,* and the *Suite des malheurs de la vieille* (Ch. 11 and 12). This similarity in titles is hardly surprising. Both tales recount the same archetypal story of an individual blessed by good looks and fortune, and raised in a secure and loving home who comes, through suffering and abandonment, to know extreme disillusionment. The Man of the Hill is led astray at college; he wastes his life gambling and drinking, is disowned by his family, and abandoned by the woman he loves. Eventually his best friend betrays him as well.

The Old Woman's ribald saga relates how a once a beautiful princess engaged to marry a handsome prince only to find herself the victim of rape, war, disease, and, finally, decrepitude. Hobbling from one scene to the next, minus half her bottom, the Old Woman is an obvious alter ego for the toothless and emaciated Voltaire himself. Proffering wise counsel to the young lovers, she reiterates almost word for word the Man of the Hill's corrosive pessimism.[23] An unusual theme common to the Man of the Hill's tale and the Old Woman's story is that of suicide.[24] Reduced to misery, the Man of the Hill tells of a time when he began to abhor life and contemplated suicide:

> [. . .] l'état horrible où je me trouvai alors est au-dessus de toute expression [. . .]. Le projet d'attenter sur moi-même devint le plus sérieux de mes réflexions.
>
> (*ET* II 50-51)

> [. . .] l'horreur que je me sentis pour moi-même, me saisit au point de regarder la vie comme un supplice."
>
> (*ET* II 54)

The Old Woman expresses precisely the same idea. Her plaint, which is also clearly Voltaire's, magnifies the Old Man's lamentation and projects his suffering to the whole of humankind:

> [. . .] y a-t-il rien de plus sot que de vouloir porter continuellement un fardeau qu'on peut toujours jeter par terre? D'avoir son être en horreur, et de tenir à son être?
>
> (*C* 162)

Thus Candide makes explicit a point that is hinted at in *L'Enfant trouvé*. The Old Woman clings to life, in spite of misery, suffering, and disappointment for the simple reason that she wants to live: "j'ai vieilli dans la misère et dans l'opprobre, n'ayant que la moitié d'un derrière, me souvenant toujours que j'étais fille d'un pape; je voulus cent fois me tuer, mais j'aimais encore la vie" (*C* 162). She then adds ludicrously that she has only known 12 people to have taken their own life: "trois nègres, quatre Anglais, quatre Genevois, et un professeur allemand nommé Robeck" (*C* 162). Within the thematic context of our respective tales, the Man of the Hill and the Old Woman are narrative substitutes strategically positioned to resist the younger protagonists' optimism. The warm-hearted Jones cannot help challenging the Man of the Hill's misanthropy. He protests that he still believes in Sophia's love. The Man of the Hill replies that at Tom's age he too held fast to such illusions. The same thing happens in *Candide* at the beginning of Chapter 13, where, notwithstanding the Old Woman's dire warnings, the two lovers cling to their youthful optimism. It is only after they have taken up her challenge to hear the stories of all the other passengers that they, reluctantly, see the point of her despair: "Candide et elle avouèrent que la vieille avait raison" (*C*: 164). Significantly, Voltaire is careful to point out that the Old Woman's gloominess undermines Pangloss' mindless cheer. Having listened to the Old Woman, Candide decides that, were Pangloss still alive: "je me

sentirais assez de force pour oser lui faire respectueusement quelques objections" (*C* 164). Pangloss, of course, comes back to life in Chapter 27.

Further confirmation that the Old Woman's story derives from that of the Man of the Hill's tale is revealed by the comparable wording at the each tale's conclusion. The Old Man sums up his story by saying: "J'ai beaucoup voyagé, [. . .] il est même peu de parties de l'Europe qui me soient inconnues" (*ET* II 120). The Old Woman, who admittedly has travelled a great deal—(je m'enfuis; je traversai toute la Russie; je fus longtemps servante de cabaret à Riga, puis à Rostock, à Vismar, à Leipsick, à Cassel, à Utrecht, à Leyde, à la Haye, à Rotterdam (*C* 162)—says almost exactly the same thing. She speaks of the "pays que le sort m'a fait parcourir," and concludes by saying: "j'ai de l'expérience, je connais le monde . . ." (*C* 162). The two stories are in fact so similar that reading them out of sequence, one might conclude that the Man of the Hill's tale was inspired by Old Woman's wager at the end of Chapter 12 to encourage the passengers on board the South American bound ship to tell each his tale of woe.[25]

The Old Woman's tale leads us to Buenos Aires, where "Cunégonde, le capitaine Candide, et la vieille, allèrent chez le gouverneur [. . .]" (*C* 164). Here too another curious verbal clue links Cunégonde to the character of Jenny Jones, (now Mme Waters). In *L'Enfant trouvé* (9:2), Jones rescues a naked Mme Waters from the evil clutches of the ensign Northerton. He then proceeds with her to the inn at Upton where Mrs Waters is at first taken for a prostitute. She is soon identified by a sergeant in the Army billeted in the inn as the "wife" of "Captain" Waters, counterpart here to the recently promoted "capitaine Candide." Then we note that just like the Governor of Buenos Aires, the sergeant has curled mustachios, which he twirls repeatedly. The sergeant's offer of service to Mrs Waters, who at this point has only a pillow case to hide her nakedness, brims with double entendre (Je connais la générosité du capitaine). In other words, in much the same way that the Governor of Buenos Aires plans to cuckold Candide, the sergeant hints that the Captain will not mind if he, the sergeant, has his way with his comely (and naked) wife:

> Quoique ce gentilhomme ait fait pour vous, s'écria le sergent, en retroussant sa moustache, il peu compter sur la reconnaissance du capitaine et j'en suis le garant. En attendant, Madame, si je puis vous rendre quelque service, ordonnez, disposer de moi sans façons. Je connais la générosité du capitaine, ce sera m'obliger.
>
> (*ET* II 132-3)

The phrasing *retroussant sa moustache* (*relevant sa moustache* in *Candide*) and the attendant erotic gesture (twirling the mustachios) are almost identical in *Can-*

dide where the Governor's mustachio suggests Spanish pride and aristocratic bearing as well as lasciviousness: "Don Fernando [. . .] relevant sa moustache, sourit amèrement, et ordonna au capitaine Candide d'aller faire la revue de sa compagnie (*C* 166). The Governor's sexual prowess, synonym of his authority, is underscored by the prudent Old Woman. She reminds the penniless, but still vacillating Cunégonde that she should have no scruples about abandoning Candide in favor of the Governor, the most impressive nobleman in Latin in America, who, after all, has a "splendid moustache":

> La vieille dit à Cunégonde: "Mademoiselle, vous avez soixante et douze quartiers et pas une obole; il ne tient qu'à vous d'être la femme du plus grand seigneur de l'Amérique méridionale, qui a une très belle moustache; est-ce à vous de vous piquer d'une fidélité à toute épreuve."
>
> (*C* 166)

Another verbal clue in the same chapter, linking Cunégonde to Sophia is the Old Woman's observation that Cunégonde "[*n'a*] *pas une obole*." La Place uses the phrase at the conclusion of Book 6, where Jones prepares to quit the Allworthy estate. In a fit of compassion, Sophia instructs her maid to give Jones all her ready money: "prends donc tout mon argent [. . .] n'en réserve *pas une obole*" (*ET* I 266). Voltaire's use of the same phrase in connection with Cunégonde strengthens my view that *Candide*'s baronette is a composite character, combining elements from both Jenny Jones and Sophia. The subtle but consistent verbal signals I have identified are significant and suggest that Voltaire was acting deliberately.

At this point Candide, accompanied by Cacambo, flees the Argentine. The two make their way, first, to the Jesuit kingdom of Paraguay (Chapter 15) and then, via the land of the Oreillons, they enter the mysterious nation of Eldorado. Having escaped the wrath of the Jesuits, Candide and Cacambo find themselves wandering in a strange country where their adventures echo the encounter Tom and Partridge have with an itinerant puppet show in Book 12. As elsewhere, a number of verbal coincidences link the two scenes. Voltaire refers, for example, to the central characters as "nos deux voyageurs" (*C* 176), a term used twice in this segment of *Candide,* once when Candide and Cacambo enter the land of the Oreillons (Ch. 16), and again when they leave Eldorado (Ch. 19). La Place uses the similar phrase "nos voyageurs" seven times in Book 12 and it seems plausible that its repetition had an impact, perhaps an unconscious one, on Voltaire, whose rewriting of this segment includes other analogies as well. Thus we note that Fielding's travellers find themselves lost in "une *vaste plaine coupée* par différents chemins" (*ET* II 295). Candide and Cacambo, who are, after all, in the wilderness without roads, halt in a "*belle prairie entrecoupée* de ruisseaux" (*C* 176). Then as night begins to fall, both pairs of travellers hear an unexpected noise. In *L'Enfant trouvé* that noise is a drum heralding the puppet show that Partridge takes for a rebel army: "Ils s'arrêtaient pour déterminer lequel de ces chemins il était à propos de prendre lorsque le bruit d'un tambour vint frapper leur oreille" (*ET* II 295-6). In *Candide,* the protagonists hear the cries of the two maidens pursued by the amorous monkeys: "Le soleil se couchait. Les deux égarés entendirent quelques petits cris qui paraissaient poussés par des femmes. Ils ne savaient si ces cris étaient de douleur ou de joie" (*C* 176). At first glance *Tom Jones'* puppets are very different from the "sauvages nommés Oreillons" whose creation was dictated by the plot, now situated in Amazonia. It is nonetheless not hard to see how the Oreillon sequence in Chapter 16 resembles a puppet show, or, perhaps more accurately, a pantomime or magic-lantern performance. *Candide*'s puppet-like dimension has long been noted, and certainly the tale's slap-stick humour is borne out here by the spectacle of the naked Oreillons preparing a cauldron to cook the tale's hero.[26] In reality the Oreillons are only slightly more present in *Candide* than the marionettes in *L'Enfant trouvé* which are not described at all. We learn that there is a puppet show attended by Partridge and Tom, but we do not witness it. The Oreillons are similarly elusive: they tie up Candide and Cacambo in their sleep without their knowledge.[27] At this point the novels converge in terms of storyline rather than content. Both Tom and Candide go to sleep, and both wake up facing a crisis. Tom has to settle a noisy and violent dispute between the puppeteers: "Jones, qui s'était couché sans souper au sortir des marionnettes, avait déjà dormi neuf bonnes heures et en eut peut-être dormi davantage, si un bruit des plus violents qui se faisait à la porte de la chambre ne l'eût pas réveillé en sursaut" (*ET* II 301). Candide and Cacambo waken and are horrified to discover that they are about to be boiled alive: "Nous allons certainement être rôtis ou bouillis" (*C* 179). In both stories the crisis is quickly resolved and the travelers soon resume their journey. There is, however, one instance in the Oreillon sequence where Voltaire uses almost identical phrasing to that of La Place. Convinced that the puppeteers are a force of invading French troops, Partridge exclaims: "Les voilà, Monsieur! . . . *Je l'avais bien dit,* [. . .] voilà leurs drapeaux! Voilà la couronne et le cercueil!.. Ah ciel! vit-on jamais rien de plus terrible? . . ." (*ET* II 297). In *Candide,* Cacambo claims he predicted that killing the amorous monkeys would bring him and Candide bad luck, and his rebuke echoes Partridge's chiding in *L'Enfant trouvé*: "*Je vous l'avais bien dit,* mon cher maître, s'écria tristement Cacambo, que ces deux filles nous joueraient d'un mauvais tour" (*C* 178).

The next important narrative anecdote from *L'Enfant trouvé* that evidently worked its way into *Candide* is derived from Book 12:6, (*Voyage nocturne. Étrange aventure*)—Jones's entry into the city of Coventry and his encounter with a band of gypsies. This sequence corresponds to Candide's arrival in Paris in Chapter 22, then, backtracking, to his sojourn in Eldorado in Chapters 17 and 18. There are two versions of **Candide**'s Paris chapter; the one that Voltaire published, and a curious 60-line fragment included in the La Vallière manuscript, the earliest known arrangement of the tale. That manuscript, the only preparatory work to have survived, was copied under Voltaire's dictation in the autumn of 1758, and corrected in his own hand. It belonged to Voltaire's friend and protector, the duc de la Vallière, who reputedly helped Voltaire publish **Candide** in Paris in February 1759. The manuscript was sold in the eighteenth century and eventually found its way into the Bibliothèque de l'Arsenal where it was catalogued in the nineteenth century under the heading: "*Invertaire succinct des manuscripts de m. le duc de La Vallière: Candide ou loptimisme. MS. In-$^0_4$ sous la dictée de M. de Voltaire*". None of the nineteenth century's great Voltaire scholars, (Beuchot, Moland, Lanson, Desnoireterres, Morize) knew of the manuscript; its discovery in 1957 by Ira O. Wade constituted a major breakthrough in Voltaire studies.[28] Of interest to my purpose is the unpublished version of Chapter 22, which presents striking evidence that La Place's report of Tom's entry into Coventry directly inspired the passage where Candide enters Paris. A comparative reading of the two passages offers a unique glimpse of how **Candide** incorporates identifiable fragments of *L'Enfant trouvé*.[29]

The relevant scene in *L'Enfant trouvé* is set on a dark winter's night, evocative of a witches' sabbath and it presents key elements also found in the unpublished fragment from Chapter 22, where Candide and Martin witness the hysterical antics of Jansenist convulsionaries in a Parisian cemetery. The witches in *Tom Jones* turn out to be a band of celebrating gypsies, about whom more will be said presently. Thus Tom, Partridge, and their guide (*postillon*) enter the outer reaches (*faubourgs*) of Coventry on a narrow and dirty road. That phrase in the La Place translation "ils se trouvèrent dans un chemin très sale et très étroit" (*ET* II 315) is very similar and expresses the same thought as **Candide**'s reflections on his arrival in Paris when he thinks the faubourg's shabbiness no better than the most dilapidated village in his native Westphalia[30]:

> Il entra par le faux bourg S^t. Marceau, et crût être dans la plus vilain vilage de la Westphalie. [. . .] Ah bon Dieu! dit Candide à Martin; est-ce ainsi que la capitale d'un grand roïaume est faite! quelle différence de ce cloaque à la ville d'Eldorado.
>
> (*C* 261-2)

In La Place's text the roads are foul. Both Partridge and the guide fall off their horses into a quagmire and are soaked to the skin in mud and horse manure: "Partridge

"tomb[e] avec son cheval dans un bourbier [. . .]" (*ET* II 316). The metonymy "*cloaque*" meaning cesspool in **Candide** to describe Paris expresses the same idea as La Place's "bourbier," the two words being synonyms. A further link between our two texts is the presence in both of the guide or *postillon*. Voltaire uses precisely that term to designate the guide in connection with Paris and its stinking streets:

> Le postillon qui conduisait les deux voyageurs eut beaucoup de peine à passer, à peine fut-il arrivé à un carrefour voisin plus puant mille fois que tous les morts du quartier, qu'ils virent tout en tumulte.
>
> (*C* 263)

The published version of **Candide** leaves out the guide altogether. It does, however, make elliptical reference to the scene of public hysteria referred to above. As Candide prepares to enter Paris in Chapter 21, Martin comments: "Je connus la canaille écrivante, la canaille cabalante, et la canaille convulsionnaire" (*C* 205). This reference to the antics of the convulsionaries in St-Médard cemetery is greatly expanded in the manuscript fragment where Voltaire actually describes the macabre scene witnessed by Candide. He hears terrifying cries in a cemetery:

> Il entra par le fauxbourg S^t. Marceau, et crût être dans le plus vilain vilage de la Westphalie. Un moment après il passa prés d'un cimetière; *c'étaient des cris, des hurlements horribles,* on eut dit que tous les morts étaient ressuscités pour faire cet épouvantable sabat.
>
> (*C* 261)

The novel then reflects on what is actually taking place. The convulsionaries bark, gnash their teeth, and roll on the ground:

> il [Candide] vit des petites filles, des abbés, des colporteurs, des sacristains, de vieilles qui aboïaient, qui grinceaient les dents, qui se roulaient par terre, qui sautaient, qui chantaient des psaumes, et tremblaient et qui b[a]vaient en criant miracle, miracle.
>
> (*C* 262)

It is my belief that this entire sequence was prompted by a parallel scene in *Enfant trouvé* where Partridge's over-active imagination leads him to take a group of revelling gypsies for ghosts and hobgoblins. Read in sequence, the unpublished fragment's thematic and verbal affiliation with the La Place translation is unmistakable:

> Ils avançaient, en tâtonnant, lorsqu'une lumière éloignée frappa les yeux de Jones et jeta la terreur dans l'âme du pédagogue. C'est un feu follet, Monsieur, s'écriat-il . . . prenez garde! Ne vous y fiez pas! Ah la maudite sorcière! Sa lanterne, si nous la suivons va nous précipiter dans quelque abîme. Mais quel redoublement de frayeur pour le pauvre Partridge lorsque nos voyageurs approchant un peu plus près de cette, ou plutôt maintenant de ces lumières, entendirent un bruit

confus de voix humaines! *Des cris, des chants, des éclats de rire,* qui, mêlés au son de quelques instruments formaient un concert si difficile à définir que Partridge devint à peu près pardonnable en affirmant d'une voix presque éteinte que c'était un *sabbat.*

(ET II 318-19)

Apart from the overall tone and similar phrasing, the use of the unusual word "*sabbat*" provides compelling evidence that the La Vallière fragment presents an intermediary text stylistically and thematically closer to *L'Enfant trouvé* than to the published novel. The interesting point, however, is not that Voltaire copied the anecdote. Rather, what we must consider is how he transforms it to fit **Candide.** Partridge's witches' sabbath has been completely interiorized; Voltaire has infused a verbal image with his own longstanding enmity toward superstition and religious fanaticism. It is also instructive to grasp the extent to which **Candide** encapsulates a lifetime of observation and experience. At issue are the convulsionaries who, 30 years before **Candide** was written, would congregate at the grave of the ascetic churchman François Paré. Paré died in 1727 from self-imposed privations shortly after completing his Jansenist profession of faith. The cemetery where he was buried became the focal point of loud, chaotic and emotional worship: the so-called convulsionaries marched, sang songs, danced, twitched, and shouted. They were fervent believers in miracles, especially in faith healing, and, before long, their emotional outpourings were deemed to constitute civil disorder. The cemetery was closed by the Lieutenant of Police in 1734.

Finally, the La Vallière fragment reveals an association between Paris and Eldorado—"*quelle différence de ce cloaque à la ville d'Eldorado*". Pomeau has gone so far as to surmise that the remark in the La Vallière fragment shows that Voltaire intended to present Eldorado as a foil to Paris and Parisian corruption. In much the same way critics have opined that Fielding's portrait of the gypsies in *Tom Jones* is a critical comment on the English and their government. Here again, Voltaire's debt to Fielding is strongly suggested by the La Place translation, which presents a jolly crew of *Égyptiens* or *Bohémiens* merry making at a wedding feast.[31] Following Fielding, La Place portrays the gypsies as a classless society, a utopia of rogues, adherents to a moral code prizing honor and abhorring disgrace—a society, moreover, governed by a benevolent but absolute despot known as "Sa Majesté Bohémienne." This pivotal figure, dressed exactly like his subjects, explains the history of the gypsy nation as well as its moral system.[32] To overcome the difficulty of having Candide speak familiarly with a king, Voltaire—always a stickler for protocol—found it convenient to create an intermediary character in Chapter 18 capable of explaining the history of Eldorado as well as its particular institutions. The "vieillard"—"le plus savant homme du

royaume" (*C* 187)—is yet another avatar of Voltaire himself, a fact revealed by his age as well as his reluctance to accompany Candide and Cacambo to court: "excusez-moi, leur dit-il, si mon âge me prive de l'honneur de vous accompagner" (*C* 189). Once at court, Candide and Cacambo are entertained by the king in a manner similar to that shown by "His Egyptian Majesty" to Tom and Partridge.[33] "Ce prince fit couvrir une table de quelques provisions choisies, où s'étant assis avec notre héros, il lui tint à peu près ce discours . . ." (*ET* II 323). The gypsy king's utterances also clearly point to what the Old Man says about Eldorado and its history in **Candide.**

Here again the *rapprochements d'expression* between the two novels are striking. Candide and Cacambo make the acquaintance of the Old Man through an innkeeper who tells them: "Je suis fort ignorant, et je m'en trouve bien" (*C* 187). The same idea is expressed by the gypsy king in his account of his nation's origins and history: "Il y a mille, ou deux mille ans plus ou moins (je ne puis vous en fixer le temps plus juste, *ne sachant ni lire, ni écrire*) il y fort longtemps, dis-je, qu'il arriva une *révolution* parmi les Égyptiens" (*ET* II 324). Once Candide and Cacambo meet the Old Man a few lines later, they learn about "les étonnantes *révolutions* du Pérou" (*C* 187) preceding the Spanish conquest of the New World. There follows a short history of the people of Eldorado and their contact with the Spanish in which the Old Man decries the "rapacité des nations de l'Europe" (*C* 188) and their "*inconcevable*" love of love of gold:

> Les Espagnols ont eu une connaissance confuse de ce pays, ils l'ont appelé Eldorado; et un Anglais, nommé le chevalier Raleigh, en a même approché il y a environ cent années; mais comme nous sommes entourés de rochers inabordables et de précipices, nous avons toujours été jusqu'à présent à l'abri de la rapacité des nations de l'Europe, qui ont une fureur inconcevable pour les cailloux et pour la fange de notre terre, et qui, pour en avoir, nous tueraient tous jusqu'au dernier.

(*C*: 188)

Similar themes of ambition, greed, war, and violence are prominent in the gypsy king's account of his people's distant past:

> Cette nation avait alors des seigneurs. Ces seigneurs, guidés par l'ambition, se firent la guerre les uns aux autres. Mais le roi les fit tous périr et établit une égalité parfaite parmi tous les sujets. Depuis ce temps nous sommes tous heureux.

(*ET* I 325)

Eldorado is not a classless society. Its citizens nevertheless all appear rich and content and enjoy a sort of communism similar to that of the gypsies. And as in gypsy society there are no law courts, lawyers, or prisons. Isolation has preserved its "innocence" and "félicité," and, finally, agreeable to Voltaire's anticlerical views, there are no priests. Or rather, everyone is a priest: "Le bon vieillard sourit. "Mes amis, dit-il, nous sommes tous prêtres"" (*C* 189). Critics have averred that the Eldorado chapters express Voltaire's deist convictions. Fielding's gypsy utopia, which is also a parable of government, makes no mention of religion.

Leaving Eldorado, and making his way back to Europe in Chapter 19, Candide encounters the pessimistic Philosopher Martin, counterweight to Pangloss. Martin becomes Candide's boon companion until the end of the tale where his voice dominates the novel's final chapters and conclusion. Another instance of the way in which *Candide* demonstrates the influence of *L'Enfant trouvé* is apparent in Chapter 21, where one of Martin's more trenchant utterances repeats almost verbatim La Place's characterization of the village busybody in *L'Enfant trouvé*. Deborah Wilkins is the servant whom Allworthy asked to find Tom's mother at the beginning of the novel (1.4). In the La Place translation the formidable Deborah is compared to a hawk (*épervier*), and in her zealous pursuit of the orphan's mother she terrorizes lesser mortals of the parish, called *petits oiseaux*:

> Ainsi qu'à l'aspect de l'épervier animal redoutable pour toute l'espèce emplumée, on voit les timides oiseaux fuyant en foule chercher leur sûreté dans le creux des arbres et des rochers, tandis que ce tyran enflé de sa puissance plane dans les airs en méditant de nouveaux forfaits [. . .]. Saisi par la beauté de cette comparaison, je prétends seulement faire entendre que s'il est dans la nature de l'épervier de faire main basse sur les petits oiseaux, il est également dans celle des Debora, mâles ainsi que femelles, d'insulter et de tyranniser le petit peuple.
>
> (*ET* I 16-17)

The same image, only slightly modified, turns up in *Candide* where, in line with Martin's pessimism, the analogy is drawn to its logical conclusion. Not only does the hawk terrorize "l'espèce emplumée," it is in its very nature to devour weak and defenseless "*pigeons*." Martin consequently invites us to conclude that men are by nature brutish, violent, and destructive:[34]

> —Croyez-vous, dit Martin; que les éperviers aient toujours mangé des pigeons quand ils en ont trouvé?— Oui, sans doute, dit Candide.—Eh bien! dit Martin, si les éperviers ont toujours eu le même caractère, pourquoi voulez-vous que les hommes aient changé le leur?
>
> (*C* 207)

As previously noted, Martin accompanies Candide to Paris and ultimately to Constantinople by way of Venice, a segment that others have suggested was inspired by Monbron's *Le Cosmopolite* (1750).[35] Recalling *Candide*'s sequacious construction, the final six books of *L'Enfant trouvé* are nevertheless revealing. Book 12

takes us to London where, in the course of *L'Enfant trouvé*'s lengthy *dénouement,* we discover two further narrative anecdotes that correspond to *Candide*'s final chapters.

The first is the Hamlet scene (Book 16:4) in which Tom, Partridge, and others go to the theatre. That segment corresponds to Candide's evening at the *comédie* in the company of the Perigourdine Abbé in Chapter 22 and, to a lesser degree, to the critique of tragedy delivered by "*un homme savant*" in the same chapter. Pomeau has written that the savant's indictment of one type of tragedy—"des rêves d'énergumène, en style barbare, des propos interrompus, de longues apostrophes aux dieux, parce qu'on ne sait point parler aux hommes, des maximes fausses, des lieux communs ampoulés" (*C* 216)—is an allusion to Crébillon père, one of Voltaire's rivals.[36] This may be. Voltaire must have nevertheless been aware that almost 25 years earlier, he used virtually the same language in his *Lettres philosophiques* to pass judgment on English tragedy in general and Shakespeare in particular. The propinquity of the two texts strongly suggesting that the savant's remark concerning "*des rêves d'énergumène*" alludes to Shakespeare rather than the comparatively mild Crébillon: "[. . .] leurs pièces presque toutes barbares, dépourvues de bienséances, d'ordre, de vraisemblance, ont des lueurs étonnantes au milieu de cette nuit. Le style est trop ampoulé, trop hors de la nature [. . .]."[37] Voltaire's complex relationship with Shakespeare, together with his jealousy of La Place's new-found role as the bard's "ambassador" in France, meant that he must have read the Hamlet scene with special interest. That scene is transferred to Paris in *Candide* where— not surprisingly—the famous *tragédienne* Mlle Clairon (with a concomitant allusion to Adrienne Lecouvreur) replaces the Shakespearian actor Garrick. Of special note is the influence of Partridge on Voltaire's portrait of the unsophisticated Candide. From the opening lines of *Hamlet,* Partridge is completely absorbed and, with a superb sense of ironic detachment, the novel recounts his responses to the play rather than the play itself: "Aussitôt la pièce commença, (c'était *Hamlet, Prince de Danemark*), Partridge fut tout yeux et tout oreilles" (*ET* III 42). Candide is likewise so enthralled at the theatre that in spite of the censure of his outspoken Parisian neighbors—"un des raisonneurs qui étaient à ses côtés lui dit dans un entr'acte: Vous avez grand tort de pleurer, cette actrice est fort mauvaise; l'acteur qui joue avec elle est plus mauvais" (*C* 210-11)—he is moved to tears: "Quel est, dit Candide, ce gros cochon qui me disait tant de mal de la pièce où j'ai tant pleuré, et des acteurs qui m'ont fait tant de plaisir?" (*C* 212). His enthusiasm fuels his desire to meet Mlle Clairon. Partridge, contrariwise, expresses total disdain for Garrick, and his dismissive comments about the celebrated actor oddly parallel the similarly dismissive comments about Mlle Clairon cited earlier: "En vérité, M. Partridge, dit

Madame Miller, vous n'êtes pas du goût de la ville entière dont tous les suffrages sont pour Hamlet qu'on regarde comme le meilleur comédien qui fût jamais. Lui? s'écria Partridge, avec un sourire méprisant, je jouerai, je vous assure, tout aussi bien que lui (*ET* III 49-50).

The second and final narrative segment common to both *Candide* and *L'Enfant trouvé* was inspired by the masked ball (13.7) to which Jones is invited by Lady Bellaston. This scene has its counterpart in Chapters 24, 25, and 26, where Candide travels to Venice at carnival time. Although we do not witness the carnival, it nonetheless permeates Voltaire's Venetian chapters and lends poignancy, as Jean Goldzink has argued, to the theme of disillusion and despair underscoring the entire segment.[38] The theatrical dimension of the city, linked metaphorically to the image of the carnival mask, is plainly suggested when Candide and Martin sup with the six deposed kings, each of whom states that he has come to Venice to attend the Carnival. At first glance Candide and Martin are incredulous since they take the assembly of kings to be a masquerade: "Candide et Martin ne doutèrent pas alors que ce ne fût une mascarade du carnival" (*C* 239). La Place also uses the word "*mascarade*" in reference to the masked ball.[39] One can hardly imagine the scene of masked revellers by candle light without picturing the Venetian Carnival, celebrated throughout the eighteenth century for its elegance and amorous intrigue. Voltaire was certainly aware that Tom's desperate attempts to find Sophia in a crowded room of disguised pleasure-seekers presents a situation reminiscent of the Carnival, where the potential for mistaken identity, unintended confessions, and seduction, is palpable:

Il [Jones] accosta indifféremment tout ce qu'il rencontrait de femmes qui, par la taille, l'air, ou la marche pouvaient ressembler à Sophie. Il essaya de leur dire à toutes quelque chose de fin et d'agaçant dans la vue de s'attirer une réponse qui pût déceler cette voix qu'il était bien sûr de ne pas méconnaître."

(*ET* II)

The protagonists' melancholy is common to both novels. Upon his arrival in Venice, Candide is distraught to learn that Cunégonde is not waiting for him and, discouraged by Martin, the usually cheerful Candide is downcast. In spite of his remaining fortune he refrains from celebrating in that city famous for pleasure: "Il tomba dans une mélancolie noire, et ne prit aucune part à l'opéra alla moda, ni aux autres divertissements du carnaval; pas une dame ne lui donna la moindre tentation" (*C* 225). Dressing for the masked ball, Jones is equally melancholy but, in his case, the mistaken thought that Sophia plans to meet him at the ball soon cheers him up:

Jones avait dans la tête que Sophie devait être au bal. Cette espérance lui donna plus d'esprit et de gaîté que

de lumières. La musique, et la nombreuse compagnie que bien des gens prétendent être d'excellents antidotes contre la tristesse."

(*ET* II 51)

Here again our two texts mirror each other in a curious way. That is both protagonists expect soon to be reunited with their beloved, and both are disappointed. As the philosophical Pangloss might have put it: "*mêmes causes, mêmes effets.*"

It is at this point—*Candide* Chapter 27—that the influence of *L'Enfant trouvé* breaks off. Why, we must ask, did Voltaire abandon Fielding's narrative before the conclusion of his own tale? In what way do the final chapters of *Candide* depart from *Tom Jones*?

Twenty-one of *Candide's* 30 chapters contain signs of the influence of *L'Enfant trouvé*. These intertextual echoes fall into a number of categories and are not of equal weight. Nor are they evenly distributed. The most telling verbal coincidences foreshadow *Candide's* characters, themes, and narrative and this is especially true of the dense multilayered borrowings in Chapters 1-3; 11, 12; 16-8; 21, 22; 24-7. Elsewhere, the echoes from La Place to Voltaire appear to hinge on a single word or phrase, which, taken alone provides only circumstantial evidence of a link between the two texts. The verbal clues identified here nevertheless add to the case built up by the other more extensive parallels that I have pointed out. Viewed as a whole, the striking similarities noted provide a glimpse of how Voltaire worked from a pre-existing text to concoct his own tale. What we have also seen is that, although he adapted the material borrowed—sometimes considerably—Voltaire nevertheless sought inspiration in *L'Enfant trouvé* well beyond *Candide's* first three chapters. Candide follows Tom Jones's lead in an almost step-by-step linear progression from one adventure to another, from his Somerset idyll to Upton and then finally to London where the novel ends. Critical segments of *Candide* rework almost word for word, line for line, similar anecdotes in La Place's *Enfant trouvé*, a novel that was more adaptation than translation *strictu sensu*.

In light of the accumulated verbal, thematic, and narrative analogies adduced here, even the most skeptical reader must surely admit that there is a strong case to see *L'Enfant trouvé* as *Candide's* elusive source. That source was not unique and in no wise precludes the absorption of personal anecdotes (there are many), nor as I have suggested, other written material. What *L'Enfant trouvé* does provide that other source material does not, however, is a both narrative and an ideological framework to which any number of anecdotes could be added (or from which subtracted). Judging by the degree to which *L'Enfant trouvé* anticipates *Candide*, it should now be plain that Voltaire not only read the novel carefully; he must also have made extensive notes of specific passages he wanted to incorporate into his work. Hence the significance of the La Vallière fragment recounting Candide's arrival in Paris which, as we have seen, provides a view of one (almost final) phase in what, we might assume, was a long chain of note-taking, writing, and revision. Part of this complex process of transformation involved compressing Fielding's sprawling thousand-page narrative into a work scarcely 100 pages long. At the same time, and conversely, *Candide* bursts the confines of Fielding's claustrophobic English novel, a novel in which a simple moonlit journey on foot takes on the heroic grandeur of *Don Quixote*. Tom and his cohorts embark on an expedition of staggering dimensions. Each encounter is more bizarre, more eccentric, more unsettling than the last: the result is Fielding's unique contribution to English literature— the comic epic. To be sure Voltaire's purpose in *Candide* was very different. *Candide* is a comic tale, but it not an epic tale. True, Voltaire's creations play out their adventures on four continents, submit to inhuman cruelty, are killed, and returned to life, and cross the ocean in the twinkling of an eye. They do not, however, exemplify *Tom Jones*'s moral earnestness. *Candide* is a satire, and an elaborate settling of accounts with Voltaire's innumerable enemies, real and imagined, individual and institutional. It is also a relentless attack on Optimism, dominated by its author in the guise of his omniscient narrator, but also by the tale's characters, several of whom give voice to Voltaire's own profound cynicism. *Candide*'s protagonists maintain a constant (one might say cold-blooded) ironic detachment. The novel's defining quality resides in their diabolical concert of voices rather than in any particular action. *Candide* is an internal (and infernal) debate in which Voltaire's private musings are atomized, personified, dramatized, projected, and magnified. It is a dispute where opposing views compete for the reader's attention, and where every action is the subject of a detached, tongue-in-cheek editorial comment.

Battistin has written "that the world of *Tom Jones,* like that of Pope's *Essay on Man* is characterized [. . .] by Order." And that that Order celebrates "the controlling hand of God."[40] Fielding's unwavering Optimism is manifest in the novel's symmetrical structure as well as in its irresistible progress towards the reunion of the archetypal couple and their harmonious re-insertion into the country paradise of their birth. The conclusion of *Candide* is poles apart; although it is not true to claim that Voltaire rejects *Tom Jones*'s famous happy ending. *Candide*'s paradise regained is founded on human intelligence, determination, and hard work. Re-uniting all the tales characters in Chapter 30, Providence nevertheless plays some role in helping reconstitute the best of all possible worlds. *L'Enfant trouvé* provided Voltaire with an ideological framework he could assimilate, interiorize, and ultimately bend to his own will. Still,

Candide is not quite an *anti-Tom Jones.* There can be little question, however that, writing *Candide,* Voltaire takes issue with the moral certainties Fielding, by his own admission inherited from Pope, and which Pope, in turn owed to Wolff and ultimately, to Leibniz.

Notes

1. This article is dedicated to mentor and friend, Professor René LeBlanc. Professor LeBlanc's encyclopedic knowledge of French literature coupled with his boundless enthusiasm inspired generations of undergraduates at Université Ste-Anne, Nova Scotia's only French language university.

2. Pomeau, R., *Voltaire en son Temps,* Fayard/ Voltaire Foundation (Paris/Oxford), vol. 1, pp. 176-9; See also Cottret, B., *Bolingbroke, exil et écriture au siècle des lumières* (Klincksieck, Paris 2000); Fletcher, D. J., "The Fortunes of Bolingbroke in France", *Studies,* 47 (1966): 209.

3. See Voltaire's Correspondence D135 (4 décembre 1722).

4. Voltaire would return to Bolingbroke and his ideas many times in his long career. In the last decade of his life of his life (1767) he published a deist manifesto under the title of *Examen de Milord Bolingbroke, ou le tombeau du fanatisme.* See Voltaire *Mélanges* (Galimard: Bibliothèque de la Pléiade, 1961), pp. 1019-117; see also R. Pomeau, *La Religion de Voltaire* (Nizet, édition revue et corrigée), pp. 175-6.

5. See Voltaire, *Lettres Philosophiques, Mélanges,* pp. 2-133.

6. In a letter dated 3 October 1759 (D8533), Voltaire upbraided Mme. du Deffand for indulging her taste in English novels: "Lire les romans anglais quand vous ne voulez pas lire l'ancien Testament. Dites-moi donc, s'il vous plait, où vous trouverez une histoire plus intéressante que celle de Joseph, devenu contrôleur général en Egypte, et reconnaissant ses frères. Comptez-vous pour rien Daniel qui confond si finement les deux vieillards? Quoi que Tobie ne soit pas si bon, cependant cela me parait meilleur que *Tom Jones,* dans lequel il n'y a rien de passable que le caractère d'un barbier."

7. Speaking of Richardson's *Clarissa* Voltaire wrote (12 April 1760, D8846): "pendant ma fièvre; cette lecture m'allumait le sang."

8. Langille, E. M., "La Place's *Histoire de Tom Jones, ou l'enfant trouvé* and *Candide,*" *Eighteenth Century Fiction,* 19/3 (Spring 2007): 267-89; Langille, E. M., "Indebted to Tom", *TLS* [*Times Literary Supplement*], 6 (April 2007): 15; Langille, E. M., "*L'Histoire de Tom Jones: ou l'enfant trouvé* (1750) et la genèse de *Candide,*" *RHLF* [*Revue d'histoire littéraire de la France*] (2008): 269-87.

9. *Les Avantures de Joseph Andrews et du Ministre Abraham Adams,* Londres par une Dame anglaise, (abbé Desfontaines), Londres 1743 (*JA* [*Joseph Andrews*]).

10. "La première chose qui se trouva sous sa main fut un chaudron rempli de sang de cochon: elle le saisit et le jeta à la tête du Ministre si adroitement qu'il n'en perdit pas une seule goute; de sorte que de son visage il coula, le long de sa barbe, sur ses habits; ce qui le rendit le plus effroyable objet qu'on puisse se figurer"; "Mais Joseph dans l'instant lui déchargea un pot de grès sur la tête avec tout ce qui était dedans [. . .] son sans mêlé de la liqueur dont le pot était rempli, distillait tout le long de son visage et de ses habits. Adams eut sa part du pot de chambre et pour achever, un des laquais lui avait frotté la barbe avec un linge qui trempait dans une cuve d'eau . . ." (*JA* 1: 200).

11. Langille, E. M., "Allusions to homosexuality in Voltaire's *Candide*: a reassessment", *SVEC* [*Studies in Voltaire and the Eighteenth Century*], 5 (2000): 53-63, 61.

12. "Pangloss était au désespoir de ne pas briller dans quelque université d'Allemagne" (*C* [*Candide*]: 255).

13. Ehrenpreis, I., *Fielding: Tom Jones* (London, 1964), p. 16.

14. "Pangloss, of course, represents philosophical optimism and Martin [. . .] philosophical pessimism. That is, Pangloss embodies the optimistic notion that ultimate reality can be known by reason, and Martin embodies the pessimistic notion that ultimate reality defies a rational accounting and can be known only through a manichaeistic mythology.[. . .] Juxtaposed with the other guides, Cacambo is a kind of neo-classical golden mean between the extremes. [. . .] He also represents the position of philosophical scepticism in the debate that propels th[e] book." Beck, Ervin, "Voltaire's *Candide*," *Explicator,* 57/4 (Summer 1999): 204.

15. Pomeau, R., "La Référence allemande dans *Candide*," in *Voltaire und Deutschland* (Stuttgart, 1979), pp. 167-74; Ferenczi, L., "Candide, est-il un roman allemand?," in *Voltaire und Deutschland* (Stuttgart 1979), pp. 175-81; Magnan, A., "Dossier de Voltaire en Prusse," *SVEC* (1986): 244.

16. Henry, P. "Travel in Candide; moving on but going nowhere," *Papers in Language and Literature* (Spring 1977); Stalloni, Y., "Lieux et personnages dans Candide," *Analyses et Réflexions sur Candide,* Ellipses (Paris, 1982), p. 83.

17. "Dans cette Partie Occidentale de l'Angleterre, vulgairement appelée Comté de Somerset, vivait dernièrement (& peut-être) vit encore un Gentil-homme nommé Alworthy, mortel si abondamment favorisé par la *Nature* et par la fortune, que l'une et l'autre semblaient s'être disputé la gloire de le combler de bienfaits. L'une l'avait doué d'une *figure agréable,* d'un bon tempérament, d'un *jugement sain & solide*; mais il devait à l'autre la possession du plus ample et du plus riche domaine de la Province" (*ET* I 1-2).

18. Deloffre, F., "Aux Origines de *Candide*: une économie de roman," *RHLF,* 1 (1998): 63-83; Deloffre, F., "Candide, roman de l'individu" dans *The King's Crown, Essays on XVIIIth Century Literature honoring Basil Guy,* sous la direction de Francis Assaf, Peeters, (Louvain, Paris, Dudley, MA, 2005), pp. 27-46; Deloffre, F., "Genèse de *Candide*: étude de la création des personnages et de l'élaboration du roman," *SVEC* (2006): 201-302.

19. "[. . .] Madame de Wortley-Montaigu, une des femmes d'Angleterre qui a le plus d'esprit et le plus de force dans l'esprit [. . .]" Voltaire, *Lettres Philosophiques* ("Sur l'insertion de la petite vérole"), *Mélanges,* 1961, p. 30-31; See also Pomeau, R., *Voltaire en son Temps,* vols I, 187, 191, 265.

20. "Et toi, compagne presque toujours du vrai génie, aimable humanité! fais passer dans mon cœur ce que tes sentiments ont de plus tendres. Si tes deux plus chers favoris, Allen et Lyttleton, sont seuls dépositaires de tes trésors" (*ET* III 5).

21. Candide, chassé du paradis terrestre, marcha longtemps sans savoir où, pleurant, levant les yeux au ciel, les tournant souvent vers le plus beau des châteaux, qui renfermait la plus belle des baronnettes; il se coucha sans souper au milieu des champs entre deux sillons; la neige tombait à gros flocons. Candide, tout transi, se traîna le lendemain vers la ville voisine, qui s'appelle Valdberghoff-trarbk-dikdorff, n'ayant point d'argent, mourant de faim et de lassitude. (*C* 122).

22. Pomeau, R., *Candide, ou l'Optimisme,* édition critique, Nizet, Paris, 1959, p. 30; Pomeau, R., *Voltaire en son Temps,* vol. 1, pp. 873-74.

23. "Je n'ai pas eu toujours les yeux éraillés et bordés d'écarlate; mon nez n'a pas toujours touché à mon menton, et je n'ai pas toujours été servante" (*C* 153).

24. Pomeau, R., "En marge des *Lettres philosophiques*: un essai de Voltaire sur le suicide", *Revue des Sciences Humaines* (1954): 285-94.

25. "engagez chaque passager à raconter son histoire, et s'il s'en trouve un seul qui n'ait souvent maudit sa vie, qui ne se soit souvent dit à lui-même qu'il était le plus malheureux des hommes, jetez-moi dans la mer la tête la première" (*C* 163).

26. Henry, Patrick, "The Metaphysical Puppets of
    Candide," *Romance Notes*, 17 (1976): 166-9; See
    also Vernier, France, "Les disfonctionnements des
    normes du conte dans *Candide*", *Littérature*, 1
    (1971): 17.

27. "Les Oreillons, habitants du pays, à qui les deux
    dames les avaient dénoncés, les avaient garrottés
    avec des cordes d'écorces d'arbre" (*C* 178).

28. Wade, Ira O., *Voltaire and 'Candide' a Study in
    the Fusion of History, Art and Philosophy, with
    the text of the La Vallière Manuscript of 'Candide'*
    (Princeton, NJ, London, 1959).

29. Reproduced facsimile and in Appendice 1 (pp.
    261-3), Pomeau in *Candide* (1980).

30. "Ils ne s'en aperçurent qu'après avoir marché
    l'espace d'environ six milles, lorsque, comptant
    entrer dans les faubourgs d'une grande ville, ils se
    trouvèrent dans un chemin très sale et très étroit"
    (*ET* II 316).

31. "On y remarquait même une sorte de décence et
    peut-être plus grande que dans certaines assem-
    blées bourgeoises, car ces gens-ci sont assujettis à
    un gouvernement et à des lois de leur façon et
    tous obéissent à une espèce de magistrat souverain
    qu'ils appellent leur roi" (*ET* II 322).

32. "Rien n'est si fatiguant que d'être sans cesse oc-
    cupé à rendre justice à ses égaux" (*ET* II 325).

33. "L'abondance était aussi de la fête et florissait
    dans cette grange. Il est vrai que la délicatesse et
    l'élégance n'en étaient pas mais le bon appétit des
    convives se passait fort bien d'elles. Beaucoup de
    lard, de volaille et de grosses viandes composaient
    le banquet, plus conforme à leur goût que tout ce
    que le plus fin et le plus couru des cuisiniers
    français eût pu leur présenter" (*ET* II 320).

    On servit quatre potages garnis chacun de deux
    perroquets, un contour bouilli qui pesait deux
    cents livres, deux signes rôtis d'un goût excellent,
    trois cents colibris dans un plat, et six cents
    oiseaux-mouches dans un autre; des ragoûts ex-
    quis, des pâtisseries délicieuses; le tout dans des
    plats d'une espèce de cristal de roche. Les garçons
    et les filles de l'hôtellerie versaient plusieurs li-
    queurs faites de cannes de sucre (*C* 185).

34. "Croyez-vous, dit Candide, que les hommes se
    soient toujours mutuellement massacrés comme ils
    font aujourd'hui? qu'ils aient toujours été ment-
    eurs, fourbes, perfides, ingrats, brigands, faibles,
    volages, lâches, envieux, gourmands, ivrognes,
    avares, ambitieux, sanguinaires, calomniateurs,
    débauchés, fanatiques, hypocrites et sots?" (*C* 206-
    7).

35. See Morize, A., "Le Candide de Voltaire", *Revue
    du XVIIIᵉ Siècle* (1913), 1; *Candide, Ou
    L'Optimisme,* edited by A. Morize, STMF (Paris

1913; reprinted 1957), p. xxv; Broome, J. H.,
"Voltaire and Fougeret de Monbron: a *Candide*
problem reconsidered", *MLR* [*Modern Language
Review*] 55/4 (Oct. 1960): 509-18.

36. See *Candide* (1980), p. 216, n. 19.

37. *Lettres Philosophiques*, p. 84.

38. *Candide, ou l'optimisme,* edited by Jean Goldzink,
    (Larousse 1990), p. 194.

39. "Ce n'est pas, dit cette bonne femme, que je
    conçoive le mal que certaines personnes trouvent
    dans ce qu'on appelle mascarades" (*ET* II 42).

40. Fielding's believed "that Providence guides the
    lives of men in the same way that his own omni-
    scient narrator conducts the actor worldings
    through complications of their own and others'
    making toward the final catastrophe when the cos-
    mic equivalent of poetic justice will be meted out
    to all," Battistin, M., and Battistin, R., *Henry
    Fielding, a Life* (New York, London, 1989), p.
    453.

Bibliography

Battistin, M., and Battistin, R., *Henry Fielding, a Life*
(New York and London: Routledge 1989).

———. "Tom Jones and 'His Egyptian Majesty'", *PMLA*
[*Proceedings of the Modern Language Association*], 82
(1967): 68-77.

Beck, Ervin, "Voltaire's *Candide*", *Explicator,* 57/4
(Summer 1999): 204.

Broome, J. H., "Voltaire and Fougeret de Monbron: a
Candide problem reconsidered," *MLR,* 55/4 (Oct. 1960):
509-18.

Charles, S., "Le *Tom Jones* de La Place ou la fabrique
d'un roman français", *RHLF,* 94/6 (1994): 931-58.

Cronk, N., "*Tom Jones* in Eighteenth Century France",
Drottningholms Slottsteatre, (1995): 94-6.

Cobb, L., *Pierre-Antoine de la Place: sa vie et son œuvre (1707-1793)* (Paris: De Boccard, 1928).

Cottret, B., *Bolingbroke, exil et écriture au siècle des
lumières* (Paris: Klincksieck, 2000).

Deloffre, F., "Aux Origines de *Candide*: une économie
de roman," *RHLF,* 98/1 (1998): 63-83.

———. "Candide, roman de l'individu" in *The King's
Crown, Essays on XVIIIᵗʰ Century Literature honoring
Basil Guy,* edited by Francis Assaf (Louvain, Paris and
Dudley, MA: Peeters, 2005), pp. 27-46.

———. "Genèse de *Candide*: étude de la création des
personnages et de l'élaboration du roman," *SVEC*
(2006): 201-302.

Ehrenpreis, I., *Fielding: Tom Jones* (London: Methuen, 1964).

Ferenczi, L., "Candide, est-il un roman allemand?" in *Voltaire und Deutschland* (Stuttgart: Mezlersche Verlagsbuch Handlung, 1979), pp. 175-181.

Fielding, H., *Histoire de Tom Jones, ou l'enfant trouvé,* traduction de l'anglais De M.Fielding par MDLP (P.-A. de La Place) (London: Nourse [Paris], 1750).

———. *Les Avantures de Joseph Andrews et du Ministre Abraham Adams,* Londres par une Dame anglaise, (abbé Desfontaines), (London, 1743).

Fletcher, D. J., "The Fortunes of Bolingbroke in France," *Studies,* 47 (1966): 209

Gunny, Ahmad, *Voltaire and English Literature, SVEC* (1979): 177.

Henry, P., "Travel in Candide: moving on but going nowhere," *Papers in Language and Literature,* 13 (Spring 1977): 193-7.

———. "The Metaphysical Puppets of *Candide,*" *Romance Notes,* 17 (1976): 166-9.

Langille, E. M., "Allusions to homosexuality in Voltaire's *Candide*: a reassessment," *SVEC* (2000): 53-63.

———. "La Place's *Histoire de Tom Jones, ou l'enfant trouvé* and *Candide*", *Eighteenth Century Fiction,* 19/3 (Spring 2007): 267-89.

———. "Indebted to Tom", *TLS,* (6 April 2007): 15.

———. "*L'Histoire de Tom Jones: ou l'enfant trouvé* (1750) et la genèse de *Candide*", *RHLF,* 2 (2008): 269-87.

Magnan, A., *Dossier de Voltaire en Prusse, SVEC* (1986): 244.

Mason, H., *Candide, optimism demolished* (New York: Twayne, 1992).

Mervaud, Ch., "Du carnaval au carnavalesque: l'épisode vénitien de *Candide*", in *Le Siècle de Voltaire: Hommage à René Pomeau,* ed. Sylvain Menant (Oxford: Voltaire Foundation 1987), pp. 651-62.

McMorran. W., *The Inn and the Traveller. Digressive Topographies in the Early Modern European Novel* (Oxford: European Humanities Research Centre, 2002), pp. 153-9.

Morize, A., "Le Candide de Voltaire", *Revue du XVIIIᵉ Siècle* (1913); reprinted as a monograph (Paris: Hachette, 1913).

Pavlovich, M., Catalogues des livres de la bibliothèque de Voltaire (BV) (Leningrad: Academy of Sciences, 1961).

Pomeau, R., *La Religion de Voltaire* (Paris: Nizet, 1960; reprinted 2000).

———. "En marge des *Lettres philosophiques*: un essai de Voltaire sur le suicide", *Revue des Sciences Humaines,* 75 (1954): 285-94.

———. "La Référence allemande dans *Candide*", in *Voltaire und Deutschland* (Stuttgart: Mezlersche Verlagsbuch Handlung, 1979), pp. 167-74.

———. *Voltaire en son Temps* (Paris and Oxford: Fayard and Voltaire Foundation, 1995).

Sandmann, M., "La Source anglaise de *Candide* (I et II)", *Zeitschrift fur Fransösiche Sprache und Literatur,* 83 (1973): 255-9.

Stalloni, Y., "Lieux et personnages dans Candide", *Analyses et Réflexions sur Candide* (Paris: Ellipses, 1982).

Vernier, France, "Les dysfonctionnements des normes du conte dans *Candide,*" *Littérature,* 1 (1971): 17-31.

Voltaire, *Candide, Ou L'Optimisme,* ed. A. Morize (STLF: Paris, 1913; reprinted 1957).

———. *Candide, ou l'Optimisme,* ed. René Pomeau (Paris: Nizet, 1959).

———. *Candide ou L'optimisme,* ed. René Pomeau, *Complete Works of Voltaire* (48 vols, Oxford: Voltaire Foundation, 1980).

———. *Candide, ou l'optimisme,* ed. Jean Goldzink (Paris: Larousse, 1990).

———. *Correspondence and Related Documents,* ed. T. Besterman, *Complete Works of Voltaire* (135 vols, Geneva, Banbury, Oxford: Institut et Musée Voltaire and Voltaire Foundation, 1968-77).

———. *Mélanges* (Paris: Galimard Bibliothèque de la Pléiade, 1961).

———. *Letters concerning the English Nation* (London, 1733).

———. *Letters concerning the English Nation,* ed. N. Cronk (Oxford World Classics, 1999).

Wade, Ira O., *Voltaire and 'Candide' a Study in the Fusion of History, Art and Philosophy, with the text of the La Vallière Manuscript of 'Candide'* (Princeton, NJ, London: University of Princeton Press, 1959).

Williams, David, "Voltaire's War with England 1760-1764." *SVEC,* 179 (1979): 79-100.

FURTHER READING

Criticism

Black, Moishe. "The Place of the Human Body in *Candide.*" *Studies on Voltaire & the Eighteenth Century* 278 (1990): 173-85.

Centers on body imagery in *Candide,* noting that while physicality is usually presented in a negative light in the novella, it contributes to Voltaire's concretization of the material world.

Braun, Theodore E. D. "Voltaire's *Zadig,* Chaos Theory, and the Problem of Determinism vs. Free Will." *Studies in Eighteenth Century Culture* 27 (1998): 195-207.

Explores the structure and themes of *Zadig* with reference to chaos theory, noting that doing so expands the possibilities of interpretation beyond the traditional, limited view of the *conte.*

Iotti, Gianni. "Voltaire as Story-Teller." In *The Cambridge Companion to Voltaire,* edited by Nicholas Cronk, pp. 109-23. Cambridge: Cambridge University Press, 2009.

Analyzes Voltaire's use of rhetoric, narration, and language in the *contes.*

Knapp, Bettina L. "Art and Inquiry in the Philosophical Tale." In *Voltaire Revisited,* pp. 144-200. New York: Twayne Publishers, 2000.

Detailed study of Voltaire's use of style to convey philosophic lessons in several *contes* and *Candide.*

Langille, E. M. "Allusions to Homosexuality in Voltaire's *Candide*: A Reassessment." *Studies on Voltaire & the Eighteenth Century* 5 (2000): 53-63.

Offers a detailed analysis of the theme of homosexuality in *Candide,* suggesting that Voltaire fashions it into a witty, "intricate joke" in the novella, whereas the same theme in his *Mémoires* is the object of biting satire.

———. "Cacombo and Candide: A New Look at Voltaire's 'Valet-Master' Duo." *Studies on Voltaire & the Eighteenth Century* 7 (2003): 3-17.

Argues that Candide's relationship with Cacombo reveals aspects of himself to himself, so that he can ultimately become the spokesman for Voltaire's ideas by the end of the novella.

Mason, Haydn. *Introduction to Voltaire*: Micromégas *and Other Short Fictions,* translated by Theo Cuffe, pp. vii-xxviii. London: Penguin Books, 2002.

Surveys Voltaire's short fiction, defines the main characteristics of the *contes,* and presents thematic summaries of individual tales.

Morrison, Ian R. "Leonardo Sciascia's *Candido* and Voltaire's *Candide.*" *The Modern Language Review* 97, Part I, (January 2002): 59-71.

Focuses on parallels between *Candide* and Sciascia's 1977 *Candido,* commenting on the two works' titles, similar passages, and use of subtitles.

Stewart, Philip. "*Candide.*" In *The Cambridge Companion to Voltaire,* edited by Nicholas Cronk, pp. 125-38. Cambridge: Cambridge University Press, 2009.

Discusses the presentation of idealism and experience in *Candide,* concluding that the final lesson of the novella is that "no one owns the truth."

Trapnell, William H. "Destiny in Voltaire's *Zadig* and *The Arabian Nights.*" *Studies on Voltaire & the Eighteenth Century* 278 (1990): 147-71.

Examines the influence of *The Arabian Nights* on Voltaire's *Zadig,* noting a similar view of fate in the two works, but stressing that Voltaire's commentary upon the workings of Providence extends further than that in the *Nights.*

Wood, Michael. "Notes on *Candide.*" *The New England Review* 20, 4 (2005): 192-202.

Examines the philosophical notion of optimism as presented in *Candide* and discusses the idea that "the fairy tale has turned sour, but the sourness has its reasons."

How to Use This Index

The main references

Calvino, Italo
  1923-1985 .... CLC **5, 8, 11, 22, 33, 39,
          73; SSC 3, 48**

list all author entries in the following Thomson Gale Literary Criticism series:

AAL = *Asian American Literature*
BG = *The Beat Generation: A Gale Critical Companion*
BLC = *Black Literature Criticism*
BLCS = *Black Literature Criticism Supplement*
CLC = *Contemporary Literary Criticism*
CLR = *Children's Literature Review*
CMLC = *Classical and Medieval Literature Criticism*
DC = *Drama Criticism*
FL = *Feminism in Literature: A Gale Critical Companion*
GL = *Gothic Literature: A Gale Critical Companion*
HLC = *Hispanic Literature Criticism*
HLCS = *Hispanic Literature Criticism Supplement*
HR = *Harlem Renaissance: A Gale Critical Companion*
LC = *Literature Criticism from 1400 to 1800*
NCLC = *Nineteenth-Century Literature Criticism*
NNAL = *Native North American Literature*
PC = *Poetry Criticism*
SSC = *Short Story Criticism*
TCLC = *Twentieth-Century Literary Criticism*
WLC = *World Literature Criticism, 1500 to the Present*
WLCS = *World Literature Criticism Supplement*

The cross-references

See also CA 85-88, 116; CANR 23, 61;
DAM NOV; DLB 196; EW 13; MTCW 1, 2;
RGSF 2; RGWL 2; SFW 4; SSFS 12

list all author entries in the following Thomson Gale biographical and literary sources:

AAYA = *Authors & Artists for Young Adults*
AFAW = *African American Writers*
AFW = *African Writers*
AITN = *Authors in the News*
AMW = *American Writers*
AMWR = *American Writers Retrospective Supplement*
AMWS = *American Writers Supplement*
ANW = *American Nature Writers*
AW = *Ancient Writers*
BEST = *Bestsellers*
BPFB = *Beacham's Encyclopedia of Popular Fiction: Biography and Resources*
BRW = *British Writers*
BRWS = *British Writers Supplement*
BW = *Black Writers*
BYA = *Beacham's Guide to Literature for Young Adults*
CA = *Contemporary Authors*
CAAS = *Contemporary Authors Autobiography Series*
CABS = *Contemporary Authors Bibliographical Series*
CAD = *Contemporary American Dramatists*
CANR = *Contemporary Authors New Revision Series*
CAP = *Contemporary Authors Permanent Series*
CBD = *Contemporary British Dramatists*
CCA = *Contemporary Canadian Authors*
CD = *Contemporary Dramatists*
CDALB = *Concise Dictionary of American Literary Biography*

CDALBS = *Concise Dictionary of American Literary Biography Supplement*
CDBLB = *Concise Dictionary of British Literary Biography*
CMW = *St. James Guide to Crime & Mystery Writers*
CN = *Contemporary Novelists*
CP = *Contemporary Poets*
CPW = *Contemporary Popular Writers*
CSW = *Contemporary Southern Writers*
CWD = *Contemporary Women Dramatists*
CWP = *Contemporary Women Poets*
CWRI = *St. James Guide to Children's Writers*
CWW = *Contemporary World Writers*
DA = *DISCovering Authors*
DA3 = *DISCovering Authors 3.0*
DAB = *DISCovering Authors: British Edition*
DAC = *DISCovering Authors: Canadian Edition*
DAM = *DISCovering Authors: Modules*
   DRAM: *Dramatists Module;* **MST:** *Most-studied Authors Module;*
   MULT: *Multicultural Authors Module;* **NOV:** *Novelists Module;*
   POET: *Poets Module;* **POP:** *Popular Fiction and Genre Authors Module*
DFS = *Drama for Students*
DLB = *Dictionary of Literary Biography*
DLBD = *Dictionary of Literary Biography Documentary Series*
DLBY = *Dictionary of Literary Biography Yearbook*
DNFS = *Literature of Developing Nations for Students*
EFS = *Epics for Students*
EXPN = *Exploring Novels*
EXPP = *Exploring Poetry*
EXPS = *Exploring Short Stories*
EW = *European Writers*
FANT = *St. James Guide to Fantasy Writers*
FW = *Feminist Writers*
GFL = *Guide to French Literature,* Beginnings to 1789, 1798 to the Present
GLL = *Gay and Lesbian Literature*
HGG = *St. James Guide to Horror, Ghost & Gothic Writers*
HW = *Hispanic Writers*
IDFW = *International Dictionary of Films and Filmmakers: Writers and Production Artists*
IDTP = *International Dictionary of Theatre: Playwrights*
LAIT = *Literature and Its Times*
LAW = *Latin American Writers*
JRDA = *Junior DISCovering Authors*
MAICYA = *Major Authors and Illustrators for Children and Young Adults*
MAICYAS = *Major Authors and Illustrators for Children and Young Adults Supplement*
MAWW = *Modern American Women Writers*
MJW = *Modern Japanese Writers*
MTCW = *Major 20th-Century Writers*
NCFS = *Nonfiction Classics for Students*
NFS = *Novels for Students*
PAB = *Poets: American and British*
PFS = *Poetry for Students*
RGAL = *Reference Guide to American Literature*
RGEL = *Reference Guide to English Literature*
RGSF = *Reference Guide to Short Fiction*
RGWL = *Reference Guide to World Literature*
RHW = *Twentieth-Century Romance and Historical Writers*
SAAS = *Something about the Author Autobiography Series*
SATA = *Something about the Author*
SFW = *St. James Guide to Science Fiction Writers*
SSFS = *Short Stories for Students*
TCWW = *Twentieth-Century Western Writers*
WLIT = *World Literature and Its Times*
WP = *World Poets*
YABC = *Yesterday's Authors of Books for Children*
YAW = *St. James Guide to Young Adult Writers*

Literary Criticism Series
Cumulative Author Index

Aldiss, Brian Wilson
See Aldiss, Brian W.
Aldrich, Ann
See Meaker, Marijane
Aldrich, Bess Streeter
1881-1954 .... **TCLC 125**
See also CLR 70; TCWW 2
Alegria, Claribel
See Alegria, Claribel
Alegria, Claribel 1924- .... **CLC 75; HLCS 1;
PC 26**
See also CA 131; CAAS 15; CANR 66, 94,
134; CWW 2; DAM MULT; DLB 145,
283; EWL 3; HW 1; MTCW 2; MTFW
2005; PFS 21
Alegria, Claribel Joy
See Alegria, Claribel
Alegria, Fernando 1918-2005 .... **CLC 57**
See also CA 9-12R; CANR 5, 32, 72; EWL
3; HW 1, 2
Aleixandre, Vicente 1898-1984 .... **HLCS 1;
TCLC 113**
See also CANR 81; DLB 108, 329; EWL 3;
HW 2; MTCW 1, 2; RGWL 2, 3
Alekseev, Konstantin Sergeivich
See Stanislavsky, Constantin
Alekseyer, Konstantin Sergeyevich
See Stanislavsky, Constantin
Aleman, Mateo 1547-1615(?) .... **LC 81**
Alencar, Jose de 1829-1877 .... **NCLC 157**
See also DLB 307; LAW; WLIT 1
Alencon, Marguerite d'
See de Navarre, Marguerite
Alepoudelis, Odysseus
See Elytis, Odysseus
Aleshkovsky, Joseph 1929- .... **CLC 44**
See also CA 121; 128; DLB 317
Aleshkovsky, Yuz
See Aleshkovsky, Joseph
Alexander, Barbara
See Ehrenreich, Barbara
Alexander, Lloyd 1924-2007 .... **CLC 35**
See also AAYA 1, 27; BPFB 1; BYA 5, 6,
7, 9, 10, 11; CA 1-4R; 260; CANR 1, 24,
38, 55, 113; CLR 1, 5, 48; CWRI 5; DLB
52; FANT; JRDA; MAICYA 1, 2; MAIC-
YAS 1; MTCW 1; SAAS 19; SATA 3, 49,
81, 129, 135; SATA-Obit 182; SUFW;
TUS; WYA; YAW
Alexander, Lloyd Chudley
See Alexander, Lloyd
Alexander, Meena 1951- .... **CLC 121**
See also CA 115; CANR 38, 70, 146; CP 5,
6, 7; CWP; DLB 323; FW
Alexander, Rae Pace
See Alexander, Raymond Pace
Alexander, Raymond Pace
1898-1974 .... **SSC 62**
See also CA 97-100; SATA 22; SSFS 4
Alexander, Samuel 1859-1938 .... **TCLC 77**
Alexander of Hales c.
1185-1245 .... **CMLC 128**
Alexeiev, Konstantin
See Stanislavsky, Constantin
Alexeyev, Constantin Sergeivich
See Stanislavsky, Constantin
Alexeyev, Konstantin Sergeyevich
See Stanislavsky, Constantin
Alexie, Sherman 1966- ..... **CLC 96, 154, 312;
NNAL; PC 53; SSC 107**
See also AAYA 28, 85; BYA 15; CA 138;
CANR 65, 95, 133, 174; CN 7; DA3;
DAM MULT; DLB 175, 206, 278; LATS
1:2; MTCW 2; MTFW 2005; NFS 17, 31,
38; PFS 39; SSFS 18
Alexie, Sherman Joseph, Jr.
See Alexie, Sherman

al-Farabi 870(?)-950 .... **CMLC 58**
See also DLB 115
Alfau, Felipe 1902-1999 .... **CLC 66**
See also CA 137
Alfieri, Vittorio 1749-1803 .... **NCLC 101**
See also EW 4; RGWL 2, 3; WLIT 7
Alfonso X 1221-1284 .... **CMLC 78**
Alfred, Jean Gaston
See Ponge, Francis
Alger, Horatio, Jr. 1832-1899 .... **NCLC 8, 83**
See also CLR 87, 170; DLB 42; LAIT 2;
RGAL 4; SATA 16; TUS
Al-Ghazali, Muhammad ibn Muhammad
1058-1111 .... **CMLC 50**
See also DLB 115
Algren, Nelson 1909-1981 ..... **CLC 4, 10, 33;
SSC 33**
See also AMWS 9; BPFB 1; CA 13-16R;
103; CANR 20, 61; CDALB 1941-1968;
CN 1, 2; DLB 9; DLBY 1981, 1982,
2000; EWL 3; MAL 5; MTCW 1, 2;
MTFW 2005; RGAL 4; RGSF 2
al-Hamadhani 967-1007 .... **CMLC 93**
See also WLIT 6
**al-Hariri, al-Qasim ibn 'Ali Abu
Muhammad al-Basri**
1054-1122 .... **CMLC 63**
See also RGWL 3
Ali, Ahmed 1908-1998 .... **CLC 69**
See also CA 25-28R; CANR 15, 34; CN 1,
2, 3, 4, 5; DLB 323; EWL 3
Ali, Monica 1967- .... **CLC 304**
See also AAYA 67; BRWS 13; CA 219;
CANR 158, 205; DLB 323
Ali, Tariq 1943- .... **CLC 173**
See also CA 25-28R; CANR 10, 99, 161,
196
Alighieri, Dante
See Dante
al-Kindi, Abu Yusuf Ya'qub ibn Ishaq c.
801-c. 873 .... **CMLC 80**
Allan, John B.
See Westlake, Donald E.
Allan, Sidney
See Hartmann, Sadakichi
Allan, Sydney
See Hartmann, Sadakichi
Allard, Janet CLC 59
Allen, Betsy
See Harrison, Elizabeth (Allen) Cavanna
Allen, Edward 1948- .... **CLC 59**
Allen, Fred 1894-1956 .... **TCLC 87**
Allen, Paula Gunn 1939-2008 . **CLC 84, 202,
280; NNAL**
See also AMWS 4; CA 112; 143; 272;
CANR 63, 130; CWP; DA3; DAM
MULT; DLB 175; FW; MTCW 2; MTFW
2005; RGAL 4; TCWW 2
Allen, Roland
See Ayckbourn, Alan
Allen, Sarah A.
See Hopkins, Pauline Elizabeth
Allen, Sidney H.
See Hartmann, Sadakichi
Allen, Woody 1935- ..... **CLC 16, 52, 195, 288**
See also AAYA 10, 51; AMWS 15; CA 33-
36R; CANR 27, 38, 63, 128, 172; DAM
POP; DLB 44; MTCW 1; SSFS 21
Allende, Isabel 1942- ... **CLC 39, 57, 97, 170,
264; HLC 1; SSC 65; WLCS**
See also AAYA 18, 70; CA 125; 130; CANR
51, 74, 129, 165, 208; CDWLB 3; CLR
99, 171; CWW 2; DA3; DAM MULT,
NOV; DLB 145; DNFS 1; EWL 3; FL 1:5;
FW; HW 1, 2; INT CA-130; LAIT 5;
LAWS 1; LMFS 2; MTCW 1, 2; MTFW
2005; NCFS 1; NFS 6, 18, 29; RGSF 2;
RGWL 3; SATA 163; SSFS 11, 16; WLIT
1

Alleyn, Ellen
See Rossetti, Christina
Alleyne, Carla D. CLC 65
Allingham, Margery (Louise)
1904-1966 .... **CLC 19**
See also CA 5-8R; 25-28R; CANR 4, 58;
CMW 4; DLB 77; MSW; MTCW 1, 2
Allingham, William 1824-1889 ...... **NCLC 25**
See also DLB 35; RGEL 2
Allison, Dorothy E. 1949- . **CLC 78, 153, 290**
See also AAYA 53; CA 140; CANR 66, 107;
CN 7; CSW; DA3; DLB 350; FW; MTCW
2; MTFW 2005; NFS 11; RGAL 4
Alloula, Malek CLC 65
Allston, Washington 1779-1843 .... **NCLC 2**
See also DLB 1, 235
Almedingen, E. M.
See Almedingen, Martha Edith von
Almedingen, Martha Edith von
1898-1971 .... **CLC 12**
See also CA 1-4R; CANR 1; SATA 3
Almodovar, Pedro 1949(?)- .... **CLC 114, 229;
HLCS 1**
See also CA 133; CANR 72, 151; HW 2
Almqvist, Carl Jonas Love
1793-1866 .... **NCLC 42**
**al-Mutanabbi, Ahmad ibn al-Husayn Abu
al-Tayyib al-Jufi al-Kindi**
915-965 .... **CMLC 66**
See also RGWL 3; WLIT 6
Alonso, Damaso 1898-1990 . **CLC 14; TCLC
245**
See also CA 110; 131; 130; CANR 72; DLB
108; EWL 3; HW 1, 2
Alov
See Gogol, Nikolai
al'Sadaawi, Nawal
See El Saadawi, Nawal
al-Shaykh, Hanan
See Shaykh, Hanan al-
Al Siddik
See Rolfe, Frederick (William Serafino Aus-
tin Lewis Mary)
Alta 1942- .... **CLC 19**
See also CA 57-60
Alter, Robert B. 1935- .... **CLC 34**
See also CA 49-52; CANR 1, 47, 100, 160,
201
Alter, Robert Bernard
See Alter, Robert B.
Alther, Lisa 1944- .... **CLC 7, 41**
See also BPFB 1; CA 65-68; CAAS 30;
CANR 12, 30, 51, 180; CN 4, 5, 6, 7;
CSW; GLL 2; MTCW 1
Althusser, L.
See Althusser, Louis
Althusser, Louis 1918-1990 .... **CLC 106**
See also CA 131; 132; CANR 102; DLB
242
Altman, Robert 1925-2006 .... **CLC 16, 116,
242**
See also CA 73-76; 254; CANR 43
Alurista
See Urista, Alberto
Alvarez, A. 1929- .... **CLC 5, 13**
See also CA 1-4R; CANR 3, 33, 63, 101,
134; CN 3, 4, 5, 6; CP 1, 2, 3, 4, 5, 6, 7;
DLB 14, 40; MTFW 2005
Alvarez, Alejandro Rodriguez
1903-1965 . **CLC 49; DC 32; TCLC 199**
See also CA 131; 93-96; EWL 3; HW 1
Alvarez, Julia 1950- .. **CLC 93, 274; HLCS 1**
See also AAYA 25, 85; AMWS 7; CA 147;
CANR 69, 101, 133, 166; DA3; DLB 282;
LATS 1:2; LLW; MTCW 2; MTFW 2005;
NFS 5, 9; PFS 39; SATA 129; SSFS 27,
31; WLIT 1
Alvaro, Corrado 1896-1956 .... **TCLC 60**
See also CA 163; DLB 264; EWL 3

Anthony, Florence
See Ai
Anthony, John
See Ciardi, John (Anthony)
Anthony, Peter
See Shaffer, Anthony; Shaffer, Peter
Anthony, Piers 1934- .... **CLC 35**
See also AAYA 11, 48; BYA 7; CA 200;
CAAE 200; CANR 28, 56, 73, 102, 133,
202; CLR 118; CPW; DAM POP; DLB 8;
FANT; MAICYA 2; MAICYAS 1; MTCW
1, 2; MTFW 2005; SAAS 22; SATA 84,
129; SATA-Essay 129; SFW 4; SUFW 1,
2; YAW
Anthony, Susan B(rownell)
1820-1906 .... **TCLC 84**
See also CA 211; FW
Antin, David 1932- .... **PC 124**
See also CA 73-76; CP 1, 3, 4, 5, 6, 7; DLB
169
Antin, Mary 1881-1949 .... **TCLC 247**
See also AMWS 20; CA 118; 181; DLB
221; DLBY 1984
Antiphon c. 480B.C.-c. 411B.C. .... **CMLC 55**
Antoine, Marc
See Proust, Marcel
Antoninus, Brother
See Everson, William
Antonioni, Michelangelo
1912-2007 .... **CLC 20, 144, 259**
See also CA 73-76; 262; CANR 45, 77
Antschel, Paul
See Celan, Paul
Anwar, Chairil 1922-1949 .... **TCLC 22**
See also CA 121; 219; EWL 3; RGWL 3
Anyidoho, Kofi 1947- .... **BLC 2:1**
See also BW 3; CA 178; CP 5, 6, 7; DLB
157; EWL 3
Anzaldua, Gloria (Evanjelina)
1942-2004 .... **CLC 200; HLCS 1**
See also CA 175; 227; CSW; CWP; DLB
122; FW; LLW; RGAL 4; SATA-Obit 154
Apess, William 1798-1839(?) .... **NCLC 73;
NNAL**
See also DAM MULT; DLB 175, 243
Apollinaire, Guillaume 1880-1918 .... **PC 7;
TCLC 3, 8, 51**
See also CA 104; 152; DAM POET; DLB
258, 321; EW 9; EWL 3; GFL 1789 to
the Present; MTCW 2; PFS 24; RGWL 2,
3; TWA; WP
Apollonius of Rhodes
See Apollonius Rhodius
Apollonius Rhodius c. 300B.C.-c.
220B.C. .... **CMLC 28**
See also AW 1; DLB 176; RGWL 2, 3
Appelfeld, Aharon 1932- ... **CLC 23, 47, 317;
SSC 42**
See also CA 112; 133; CANR 86, 160, 207;
CWW 2; DLB 299; EWL 3; RGHL;
RGSF 2; WLIT 6
Appelfeld, Aron
See Appelfeld, Aharon
Apple, Max 1941- .... **CLC 9, 33; SSC 50**
See also AMWS 17; CA 81-84; CANR 19,
54, 214; DLB 130
Apple, Max Isaac
See Apple, Max
Appleman, Philip (Dean) 1926- .... **CLC 51**
See also CA 13-16R; CAAS 18; CANR 6,
29, 56
Appleton, Lawrence
See Lovecraft, H. P.
Apteryx
See Eliot, T. S.
Apuleius, (Lucius Madaurensis) c. 125-c.
164 .... **CMLC 1, 84**
See also AW 2; CDWLB 1; DLB 211;
RGWL 2, 3; SUFW; WLIT 8

Aquin, Hubert 1929-1977 .... **CLC 15**
See also CA 105; DLB 53; EWL 3
Aquinas, Thomas 1224(?)-1274 .... **CMLC 33,
137**
See also DLB 115; EW 1; TWA
Aragon, Louis 1897-1982 .... **CLC 3, 22;
TCLC 123**
See also CA 69-72; 108; CANR 28, 71;
DAM NOV, POET; DLB 72, 258; EW 11;
EWL 3; GFL 1789 to the Present; GLL 2;
LMFS 2; MTCW 1, 2; RGWL 2, 3
Arany, Janos 1817-1882 .... **NCLC 34**
Aranyos, Kakay 1847-1910
See Mikszath, Kalman
Aratus of Soli c. 315B.C.-c.
240B.C. .... **CMLC 64, 114**
See also DLB 176
Arbuthnot, John 1667-1735 .... **LC 1**
See also BRWS 16; DLB 101
Archer, Herbert Winslow
See Mencken, H. L.
Archer, Jeffrey 1940- .... **CLC 28**
See also AAYA 16; BEST 89:3; BPFB 1;
CA 77-80; CANR 22, 52, 95, 136, 209;
CPW; DA3; DAM POP; INT CANR-22;
MTFW 2005
Archer, Jeffrey Howard
See Archer, Jeffrey
Archer, Jules 1915- .... **CLC 12**
See also CA 9-12R; CANR 6, 69; SAAS 5;
SATA 4, 85
Archer, Lee
See Ellison, Harlan
Archilochus c. 7th cent. B.C.- .... **CMLC 44**
See also DLB 176
Ard, William
See Jakes, John
Arden, John 1930- .... **CLC 6, 13, 15**
See also BRWS 2; CA 13-16R; CAAS 4;
CANR 31, 65, 67, 124; CBD; CD 5, 6;
DAM DRAM; DFS 9; DLB 13, 245;
EWL 3; MTCW 1
Arenas, Reinaldo 1943-1990 .. **CLC 41; HLC
1; TCLC 191**
See also CA 124; 128; 133; CANR 73, 106;
DAM MULT; DLB 145; EWL 3; GLL 2;
HW 1; LAW; LAWS 1; MTCW 2; MTFW
2005; RGSF 2; RGWL 3; WLIT 1
Arendt, Hannah 1906-1975 .... **CLC 66, 98;
TCLC 193**
See also CA 17-20R; 61-64; CANR 26, 60,
172; DLB 242; MTCW 1, 2
Aretino, Pietro 1492-1556 .... **LC 12, 165**
See also RGWL 2, 3
Arghezi, Tudor
See Theodorescu, Ion N.
Arguedas, Jose Maria 1911-1969 .... **CLC 10,
18; HLCS 1; TCLC 147**
See also CA 89-92; CANR 73; DLB 113;
EWL 3; HW 1; LAW; RGWL 2, 3; WLIT
1
Argueta, Manlio 1936- .... **CLC 31**
See also CA 131; CANR 73; CWW 2; DLB
145; EWL 3; HW 1; RGWL 3
Arias, Ron 1941- .... **HLC 1**
See also CA 131; CANR 81, 136; DAM
MULT; DLB 82; HW 1, 2; MTCW 2;
MTFW 2005
Ariosto, Lodovico
See Ariosto, Ludovico
Ariosto, Ludovico 1474-1533 ... **LC 6, 87; PC
42**
See also EW 2; RGWL 2, 3; WLIT 7
Aristides
See Epstein, Joseph

Aristides Quintilianus fl. c. 100-fl. c.
400 .... **CMLC 122**
Aristophanes 450B.C.-385B.C. . **CMLC 4, 51,
138; DC 2; WLCS**
See also AW 1; CDWLB 1; DA; DA3;
DAB; DAC; DAM DRAM, MST; DFS
10; DLB 176; LMFS 1; RGWL 2, 3;
TWA; WLIT 8
Aristotle 384B.C.-322B.C. .... **CMLC 31, 123;
WLCS**
See also AW 1; CDWLB 1; DA; DA3;
DAB; DAC; DAM MST; DLB 176;
RGWL 2, 3; TWA; WLIT 8
Arlt, Roberto 1900-1942 . **HLC 1; TCLC 29,
255**
See also CA 123; 131; CANR 67; DAM
MULT; DLB 305; EWL 3; HW 1, 2;
IDTP; LAW
Arlt, Roberto Godofredo Christophersen
See Arlt, Roberto
Armah, Ayi Kwei 1939- . **BLC 1:1, 2:1; CLC
5, 33, 136**
See also AFW; BRWS 10; BW 1; CA 61-
64; CANR 21, 64; CDWLB 3; CN 1, 2,
3, 4, 5, 6, 7; DAM MULT, POET; DLB
117; EWL 3; MTCW 1; WLIT 2
Armatrading, Joan 1950- .... **CLC 17**
See also CA 114; 186
Armin, Robert 1568(?)-1615(?) .... **LC 120**
Armitage, Frank
See Carpenter, John
Armstrong, Jeannette (C.) 1948- .... **NNAL**
See also CA 149; CCA 1; CN 6, 7; DAC;
DLB 334; SATA 102
Armytage, R.
See Watson, Rosamund Marriott
Arnauld, Antoine 1612-1694 .... **LC 169**
See also DLB 268
Arnette, Robert
See Silverberg, Robert
**Arnim, Achim von (Ludwig Joachim von
Arnim)** 1781-1831 .. **NCLC 5, 159; SSC
29**
See also DLB 90
Arnim, Bettina von 1785-1859 ...... **NCLC 38,
123**
See also DLB 90; RGWL 2, 3
Arnold, Matthew 1822-1888 ..... **NCLC 6, 29,
89, 126, 218; PC 5, 94; WLC 1**
See also BRW 5; CDBLB 1832-1890; DA;
DAB; DAC; DAM MST, POET; DLB 32,
57; EXPP; PAB; PFS 2; TEA; WP
Arnold, Thomas 1795-1842 .... **NCLC 18**
See also DLB 55
Arnow, Harriette (Louisa) Simpson
1908-1986 ...... **CLC 2, 7, 18; TCLC 196**
See also BPFB 1; CA 9-12R; 118; CANR
14; CN 2, 3, 4; DLB 6; FW; MTCW 1, 2;
RHW; SATA 42; SATA-Obit 47
Arouet, Francois-Marie
See Voltaire
Arp, Hans
See Arp, Jean
Arp, Jean 1887-1966 .... **CLC 5; TCLC 115**
See also CA 81-84; 25-28R; CANR 42, 77;
EW 10
Arrabal
See Arrabal, Fernando
Arrabal, Fernando 1932- .. **CLC 2, 9, 18, 58;
DC 35**
See also CA 9-12R; CANR 15; CWW 2;
DLB 321; EWL 3; LMFS 2
Arrabal Teran, Fernando
See Arrabal, Fernando
Arreola, Juan Jose 1918-2001 .... **CLC 147;
HLC 1; SSC 38**
See also CA 113; 131; 200; CANR 81;
CWW 2; DAM MULT; DLB 113; DNFS
2; EWL 3; HW 1, 2; LAW; RGSF 2

Ayckbourn, Alan 1939- ...... **CLC 5, 8, 18, 33, 74; DC 13**
See also BRWS 5; CA 21-24R; CANR 31, 59, 118; CBD; CD 5, 6; DAB; DAM DRAM; DFS 7; DLB 13, 245; EWL 3; MTCW 1, 2; MTFW 2005
Aydy, Catherine
See Tennant, Emma
Ayme, Marcel (Andre) 1902-1967 ... **CLC 11; SSC 41**
See also CA 89-92; CANR 67, 137; CLR 25; DLB 72; EW 12; EWL 3; GFL 1789 to the Present; RGSF 2; RGWL 2, 3; SATA 91
Ayrton, Michael 1921-1975 .... **CLC 7**
See also CA 5-8R; 61-64; CANR 9, 21
Aytmatov, Chingiz
See Aitmatov, Chingiz
Azorin
See Martinez Ruiz, Jose
Azuela, Mariano 1873-1952 .. **HLC 1; TCLC 3, 145, 217**
See also CA 104; 131; CANR 81; DAM MULT; EWL 3; HW 1, 2; LAW; MTCW 1, 2; MTFW 2005
Ba, Mariama 1929-1981 ...... **BLC 2:1; BLCS**
See also AFW; BW 2; CA 141; CANR 87; DLB 360; DNFS 2; WLIT 2
Baastad, Babbis Friis
See Friis-Baastad, Babbis Ellinor
Bab
See Gilbert, W(illiam) S(chwenck)
Babbis, Eleanor
See Friis-Baastad, Babbis Ellinor
Babel, Isaac
See Babel, Isaak (Emmanuilovich)
Babel, Isaak (Emmanuilovich) 1894-1941(?) .... **SSC 16, 78, 161; TCLC 2, 13, 171**
See also CA 104; 155; CANR 113; DLB 272; EW 11; EWL 3; MTCW 2; MTFW 2005; RGSF 2; RGWL 2, 3; SSFS 10; TWA
Babits, Mihaly 1883-1941 .... **TCLC 14**
See also CA 114; CDWLB 4; DLB 215; EWL 3
Babur 1483-1530 .... **LC 18**
Babylas
See Ghelderode, Michel de
Baca, Jimmy Santiago 1952- . **HLC 1; PC 41**
See also CA 131; CANR 81, 90, 146, 220; CP 6, 7; DAM MULT; DLB 122; HW 1, 2; LLW; MAL 5; PFS 40
Baca, Jose Santiago
See Baca, Jimmy Santiago
Bacchelli, Riccardo 1891-1985 .... **CLC 19**
See also CA 29-32R; 117; DLB 264; EWL 3
Bacchylides c. 520B.C.-c. 452B.C. .... **CMLC 119**
Bach, Richard 1936- .... **CLC 14**
See also AITN 1; BEST 89:2; BPFB 1; BYA 5; CA 9-12R; CANR 18, 93, 151; CPW; DAM NOV, POP; FANT; MTCW 1; SATA 13
Bach, Richard David
See Bach, Richard
Bache, Benjamin Franklin 1769-1798 .... **LC 74**
See also DLB 43
Bachelard, Gaston 1884-1962 ...... **TCLC 128**
See also CA 97-100; 89-92; DLB 296; GFL 1789 to the Present
Bachman, Richard
See King, Stephen
Bachmann, Ingeborg 1926-1973 ..... **CLC 69; TCLC 192**
See also CA 93-96; 45-48; CANR 69; DLB 85; EWL 3; RGHL; RGWL 2, 3

Bacigalupi, Paolo 1973- .... **CLC 309**
See also AAYA 86; CA 317; SATA 230
Bacon, Francis 1561-1626 ..... **LC 18, 32, 131**
See also BRW 1; CDBLB Before 1660; DLB 151, 236, 252; RGEL 2; TEA
Bacon, Roger 1214(?)-1294 ... **CMLC 14, 108**
See also DLB 115
Bacovia, G.
See Bacovia, George
Bacovia, George 1881-1957 .... **TCLC 24**
See Bacovia, George
See also CA 123; 189; CDWLB 4; DLB 220; EWL 3
Badanes, Jerome 1937-1995 .... **CLC 59**
See also CA 234
Bage, Robert 1728-1801 .... **NCLC 182**
See also DLB 39; RGEL 2
Bagehot, Walter 1826-1877 .... **NCLC 10**
See also DLB 55
Bagnold, Enid 1889-1981 .... **CLC 25**
See also AAYA 75; BYA 2; CA 5-8R; 103; CANR 5, 40; CBD; CN 2; CWD; CWRI 5; DAM DRAM; DLB 13, 160, 191, 245; FW; MAICYA 1, 2; RGEL 2; SATA 1, 25
Bagritsky, Eduard
See Dzyubin, Eduard Georgievich
Bagritsky, Edvard
See Dzyubin, Eduard Georgievich
Bagrjana, Elisaveta
See Belcheva, Elisaveta Lyubomirova
Bagryana, Elisaveta
See Belcheva, Elisaveta Lyubomirova
Bailey, Paul 1937- .... **CLC 45**
See also CA 21-24R; CANR 16, 62, 124; CN 1, 2, 3, 4, 5, 6, 7; DLB 14, 271; GLL 2
Baillie, Joanna 1762-1851 ...... **NCLC 71, 151**
See also DLB 93, 344; GL 2; RGEL 2
Bainbridge, Beryl 1934-2010 ..... **CLC 4, 5, 8, 10, 14, 18, 22, 62, 130, 292**
See also BRWS 6; CA 21-24R; CANR 24, 55, 75, 88, 128; CN 2, 3, 4, 5, 6, 7; DAM NOV; DLB 14, 231; EWL 3; MTCW 1, 2; MTFW 2005
Baker, Carlos (Heard) 1909-1987 .... **TCLC 119**
See also CA 5-8R; 122; CANR 3, 63; DLB 103
Baker, Elliott 1922-2007 .... **CLC 8**
See also CA 45-48; 257; CANR 2, 63; CN 1, 2, 3, 4, 5, 6, 7
Baker, Elliott Joseph
See Baker, Elliott
Baker, Jean H.
See Russell, George William
Baker, Nicholson 1957- .... **CLC 61, 165**
See also AMWS 13; CA 135; CANR 63, 120, 138, 190; CN 6; CPW; DA3; DAM POP; DLB 227; MTFW 2005
Baker, Ray Stannard 1870-1946 .... **TCLC 47**
See also CA 118; DLB 345
Baker, Russell 1925- .... **CLC 31**
See also BEST 89:4; CA 57-60; CANR 11, 41, 59, 137; MTCW 1, 2; MTFW 2005
Baker, Russell Wayne
See Baker, Russell
Bakhtin, M.
See Bakhtin, Mikhail Mikhailovich
Bakhtin, M. M.
See Bakhtin, Mikhail Mikhailovich
Bakhtin, Mikhail
See Bakhtin, Mikhail Mikhailovich
Bakhtin, Mikhail Mikhailovich 1895-1975 .... **CLC 83; TCLC 160**
See Bakhtin, Mikhail Mikhailovich
See also CA 128; 113; DLB 242; EWL 3
Bakshi, Ralph 1938(?)- .... **CLC 26**
See also CA 112; 138; IDFW 3

Bakunin, Mikhail (Alexandrovich) 1814-1876 .... **NCLC 25, 58**
See also DLB 277
Bal, Mieke 1946- .... **CLC 252**
See also CA 156; CANR 99
Bal, Mieke Maria Gertrudis
See Bal, Mieke
Baldwin, James 1924-1987 ...... **BLC 1:1, 2:1; CLC 1, 2, 3, 4, 5, 8, 13, 15, 17, 42, 50, 67, 90, 127; DC 1; SSC 10, 33, 98, 134; TCLC 229; WLC 1**
See also AAYA 4, 34; AFAW 1, 2; AMWR 2; AMWS 1; BPFB 1; BW 1; CA 1-4R; 124; CABS 1; CAD; CANR 3, 24; CDALB 1941-1968; CN 1, 2, 3, 4; CPW; DA; DA3; DAB; DAC; DAM MST, MULT, NOV, POP; DFS 11, 15; DLB 2, 7, 33, 249, 278; DLBY 1987; EWL 3; EXPS; LAIT 5; MAL 5; MTCW 1, 2; MTFW 2005; NCFS 4; NFS 4; RGAL 4; RGSF 2; SATA 9; SATA-Obit 54; SSFS 2, 18; TUS
Baldwin, William c. 1515-1563 .... **LC 113**
See also DLB 132
Bale, John 1495-1563 .... **LC 62**
See also DLB 132; RGEL 2; TEA
Ball, Hugo 1886-1927 .... **TCLC 104**
Ballard, James G.
See Ballard, J.G.
Ballard, James Graham
See Ballard, J.G.
Ballard, J.G. 1930-2009 ..... **CLC 3, 6, 14, 36, 137, 299; SSC 1, 53, 146**
See also AAYA 3, 52; BRWS 5; CA 5-8R; 285; CANR 15, 39, 65, 107, 133, 198; CN 1, 2, 3, 4, 5, 6, 7; DA3; DAM NOV, POP; DLB 14, 207, 261, 319; EWL 3; HGG; MTCW 1, 2; MTFW 2005; NFS 8; RGEL 2; RGSF 2; SATA 93; SATA-Obit 203; SCFW 1, 2; SFW 4
Ballard, Jim G.
See Ballard, J.G.
Balmont, Konstantin (Dmitriyevich) 1867-1943 .... **TCLC 11**
See also CA 109; 155; DLB 295; EWL 3
Baltausis, Vincas 1847-1910
See Mikszath, Kalman
Balzac, Guez de (?)-
See Balzac, Jean-Louis Guez de
Balzac, Honore de 1799-1850 ... **NCLC 5, 35, 53, 153; SSC 5, 59, 102, 153; WLC 1**
See also DA; DA3; DAB; DAC; DAM MST, NOV; DLB 119; EW 5; GFL 1789 to the Present; LMFS 1; NFS 33; RGSF 2; RGWL 2, 3; SSFS 10; SUFW; TWA
Balzac, Jean-Louis Guez de 1597-1654 .... **LC 162**
See also DLB 268; GFL Beginnings to 1789
Bambara, Toni Cade 1939-1995 ..... **BLC 1:1, 2:1; CLC 19, 88; SSC 35, 107; TCLC 116; WLCS**
See also AAYA 5, 49; AFAW 2; AMWS 11; BW 2, 3; BYA 12, 14; CA 29-32R; 150; CANR 24, 49, 81; CDALBS; DA; DA3; DAC; DAM MST, MULT; DLB 38, 218; EXPS; MAL 5; MTCW 1, 2; MTFW 2005; RGAL 4; RGSF 2; SATA 112; SSFS 4, 7, 12, 21
Bamdad, A.
See Shamlu, Ahmad
Bamdad, Alef
See Shamlu, Ahmad
Banat, D. R.
See Bradbury, Ray
Bancroft, Laura
See Baum, L. Frank
Bandello, Matteo 1485-1561 .... **SSC 143**
Banim, John 1798-1842 .... **NCLC 13**
See also DLB 116, 158, 159; RGEL 2

Banim, Michael 1796-1874 .... **NCLC 13**
See also DLB 158, 159

Banjo, The
See Paterson, A(ndrew) B(arton)

Banks, Iain 1954- .... **CLC 34**
See also BRWS 11; CA 123; 128; CANR
61, 106, 180; DLB 194, 261; EWL 3;
HGG; INT CA-128; MTFW 2005; SFW 4

Banks, Iain M.
See Banks, Iain

Banks, Iain Menzies
See Banks, Iain

Banks, Lynne Reid
See Reid Banks, Lynne

Banks, Russell 1940- . **CLC 37, 72, 187; SSC
42**
See also AAYA 45; AMWS 5; CA 65-68;
CAAS 15; CANR 19, 52, 73, 118, 195;
CN 4, 5, 6, 7; DLB 130, 278; EWL 3;
MAL 5; MTCW 2; MTFW 2005; NFS 13

Banks, Russell Earl
See Banks, Russell

Banville, John 1945- .. **CLC 46, 118, 224, 315**
See also CA 117; 128; CANR 104, 150,
176, 225; CN 4, 5, 6, 7; DLB 14, 271,
326; INT CA-128

Banville, Theodore (Faullain) de
1832-1891 .... **NCLC 9**
See also DLB 217; GFL 1789 to the Present

Baraka, Amiri 1934- .. **BLC 1:1, 2:1; CLC 1,
2, 3, 5, 10, 14, 33, 115, 213; DC 6; PC
4, 113; WLCS**
See also AAYA 63; AFAW 1, 2; AMWS 2;
BW 2, 3; CA 21-24R; CABS 3; CAD;
CANR 27, 38, 61, 133, 172; CD 3, 5, 6;
CDALB 1941-1968; CN 1, 2; CP 1, 2, 3,
4, 5, 6, 7; CPW; DA; DA3; DAC; DAM
MST, MULT, POET, POP; DFS 3, 11, 16;
DLB 5, 7, 16, 38; DLBD 8; EWL 3; MAL
5; MTCW 1, 2; MTFW 2005; PFS 9;
RGAL 4; TCLE 1:1; TUS; WP

Baratynsky, Evgenii Abramovich
1800-1844 .... **NCLC 103**
See also DLB 205

Barbauld, Anna Laetitia
1743-1825 .... **NCLC 50, 185**
See also CLR 160; DLB 107, 109, 142, 158,
336; RGEL 2

Barbellion, W. N. P.
See Cummings, Bruce F.

Barber, Benjamin R. 1939- .... **CLC 141**
See also CA 29-32R; CANR 12, 32, 64, 119

Barbera, Jack 1945- .... **CLC 44**
See also CA 110; CANR 45

Barbera, Jack Vincent
See Barbera, Jack

Barbey d'Aurevilly, Jules-Amedee
1808-1889 .... **NCLC 1, 213; SSC 17**
See also DLB 119; GFL 1789 to the Present

Barbour, John c. 1316-1395 .... **CMLC 33**
See also DLB 146

Barbusse, Henri 1873-1935 .... **TCLC 5**
See also CA 105; 154; DLB 65; EWL 3;
RGWL 2, 3

Barclay, Alexander c. 1475-1552 .... **LC 109**
See also DLB 132

Barclay, Bill
See Moorcock, Michael

Barclay, William Ewert
See Moorcock, Michael

Barclay, William Ewert
See Moorcock, Michael

Barea, Arturo 1897-1957 .... **TCLC 14**
See also CA 111; 201

Barfoot, Joan 1946- .... **CLC 18**
See also CA 105; CANR 141, 179

Barham, Richard Harris
1788-1845 .... **NCLC 77**
See also DLB 159

Baring, Maurice 1874-1945 .... **TCLC 8**
See also CA 105; 168; DLB 34; HGG

Baring-Gould, Sabine 1834-1924 ... **TCLC 88**
See also DLB 156, 190

Barker, Clive 1952- .... **CLC 52, 205; SSC 53**
See also AAYA 10, 54; BEST 90:3; BPFB
1; CA 121; 129; CANR 71, 111, 133, 187;
CPW; DA3; DAM POP; DLB 261; HGG;
INT CA-129; MTCW 1, 2; MTFW 2005;
SUFW 2

Barker, George Granville
1913-1991 .... **CLC 8, 48; PC 77**
See also CA 9-12R; 135; CANR 7, 38; CP
1, 2, 3, 4, 5; DAM POET; DLB 20; EWL
3; MTCW 1

Barker, Harley Granville
See Granville-Barker, Harley

Barker, Howard 1946- .... **CLC 37**
See also CA 102; CBD; CD 5, 6; DLB 13,
233

Barker, Jane 1652-1732 .... **LC 42, 82; PC 91**
See also DLB 39, 131

Barker, Pat 1943- .... **CLC 32, 94, 146**
See also BRWS 4; CA 117; 122; CANR 50,
101, 148, 195; CN 6, 7; DLB 271, 326;
INT CA-122

Barker, Patricia
See Barker, Pat

Barlach, Ernst (Heinrich)
1870-1938 .... **TCLC 84**
See also CA 178; DLB 56, 118; EWL 3

Barlow, Joel 1754-1812 .... **NCLC 23, 223**
See also AMWS 2; DLB 37; RGAL 4

Barnard, Mary (Ethel) 1909- .... **CLC 48**
See also CA 21-22; CAP 2; CP 1

Barnes, Djuna 1892-1982 .... **CLC 3, 4, 8, 11,
29, 127; SSC 3, 163; TCLC 212**
See also AMWS 3; CA 9-12R; 107; CAD;
CANR 16, 55; CN 1, 2, 3; CWD; DLB 4,
9, 45; EWL 3; GLL 1; MAL 5; MTCW 1,
2; MTFW 2005; RGAL 4; TCLE 1:1;
TUS

Barnes, Jim 1933- .... **NNAL**
See also CA 108, 175, 272; CAAE 175,
272; CAAS 28; DLB 175

Barnes, Julian 1946- .... **CLC 42, 141, 315**
See also BRWS 4; CA 102; CANR 19, 54,
115, 137, 195; CN 4, 5, 6, 7; DAB; DLB
194; DLBY 1993; EWL 3; MTCW 2;
MTFW 2005; SSFS 24

Barnes, Julian Patrick
See Barnes, Julian

Barnes, Peter 1931-2004 .... **CLC 5, 56**
See also CA 65-68; 230; CAAS 12; CANR
33, 34, 64, 113; CBD; CD 5, 6; DFS 6;
DLB 13, 233; MTCW 1

Barnes, William 1801-1886 .... **NCLC 75**
See also DLB 32

Barnfield, Richard 1574-1627 .... **LC 192**
See also DLB 172

Baroja, Pio 1872-1956 .... **HLC 1; SSC 112;
TCLC 8, 240**
See also CA 104; 247; EW 9

Baroja y Nessi, Pio
See Baroja, Pio

Baron, David
See Pinter, Harold

Baron Corvo
See Rolfe, Frederick (William Serafino Austin Lewis Mary)

Barondess, Sue K. 1926-1977 .... **CLC 3, 8**
See also CA 1-4R; 69-72; CANR 1

Barondess, Sue Kaufman
See Barondess, Sue K.

Baron de Teive
See Pessoa, Fernando

Baroness Von S.
See Zangwill, Israel

Barres, (Auguste-)Maurice
1862-1923 .... **TCLC 47**
See also CA 164; DLB 123; GFL 1789 to
the Present

Barreto, Afonso Henrique de Lima
See Lima Barreto, Afonso Henrique de

Barrett, Andrea 1954- .... **CLC 150**
See also CA 156; CANR 92, 186; CN 7;
DLB 335; SSFS 24

Barrett, Michele
See Barrett, Michele

Barrett, Michele 1949- .... **CLC 65**
See also CA 280

Barrett, Roger Syd
See Barrett, Syd

Barrett, Syd 1946-2006 .... **CLC 35**

Barrett, William (Christopher)
1913-1992 .... **CLC 27**
See also CA 13-16R; 139; CANR 11, 67;
INT CANR-11

Barrett Browning, Elizabeth
1806-1861 ...... **NCLC 1, 16, 61, 66, 170;
PC 6, 62; WLC 1**
See also AAYA 63; BRW 4; CDBLB 1832-
1890; DA; DA3; DAB; DAC; DAM MST,
POET; DLB 32, 199; EXPP; FL 1:2; PAB;
PFS 2, 16, 23; TEA; WLIT 4; WP

Barrie, Baronet
See Barrie, J. M.

Barrie, J. M. 1860-1937 .... **TCLC 2, 164**
See also BRWS 3; BYA 4, 5; CA 104; 136;
CANR 77; CDBLB 1890-1914; CLR 16,
124; CWRI 5; DA3; DAB; DAM DRAM;
DFS 7; DLB 10, 141, 156, 352; EWL 3;
FANT; MAICYA 1, 2; MTCW 2; MTFW
2005; SATA 100; SUFW; WCH; WLIT 4;
YABC 1

Barrie, James Matthew
See Barrie, J. M.

Barrington, Michael
See Moorcock, Michael

Barrol, Grady
See Bograd, Larry

Barry, Mike
See Malzberg, Barry N(athaniel)

Barry, Philip 1896-1949 .... **TCLC 11**
See also CA 109; 199; DFS 9; DLB 7, 228;
MAL 5; RGAL 4

Barry, Sebastian 1955- .... **CLC 282**
See also CA 117; CANR 122, 193; CD 5,
6; DLB 245

Bart, Andre Schwarz
See Schwarz-Bart, Andre

Barth, John 1930- ... **CLC 1, 2, 3, 5, 7, 9, 10,
14, 27, 51, 89, 214; SSC 10, 89**
See also AITN 1, 2; AMW; BPFB 1; CA
1-4R; CABS 1; CANR 5, 23, 49, 64, 113,
204; CN 1, 2, 3, 4, 5, 6, 7; DAM NOV;
DLB 2, 227; EWL 3; FANT; MAL 5;
MTCW 1; RGAL 4; RGSF 2; RHW;
SSFS 6; TUS

Barth, John Simmons
See Barth, John

Barthelme, Donald 1931-1989 ... **CLC 1, 2, 3,
5, 6, 8, 13, 23, 46, 59, 115; SSC 2, 55,
142**
See also AMWS 4; BPFB 1; CA 21-24R;
129; CANR 20, 58, 188; CN 1, 2, 3, 4;
DA3; DAM NOV; DLB 2, 234; DLBY
1980, 1989; EWL 3; FANT; LMFS 2;
MAL 5; MTCW 1, 2; MTFW 2005;
RGAL 4; RGSF 2; SATA 7; SATA-Obit
62; SSFS 17

Barthelme, Frederick 1943- ...... **CLC 36, 117**
See also AMWS 11; CA 114; 122; CANR
77, 209; CN 4, 5, 6, 7; CSW; DLB 244;
DLBY 1985; EWL 3; INT CA-122

Blume, Judy 1938- .... **CLC 12, 30**
See also AAYA 3, 26; BYA 1, 8, 12; CA 29-32R; CANR 13, 37, 66, 124, 186; CLR 2, 15, 69; CPW; DA3; DAM NOV, POP; DLB 52; JRDA; MAICYA 1, 2; MAIC-YAS 1; MTCW 1, 2; MTFW 2005; NFS 24; SATA 2, 31, 79, 142, 195; WYA; YAW

Blume, Judy Sussman
See Blume, Judy

Blunden, Edmund (Charles)
1896-1974 .... **CLC 2, 56; PC 66**
See also BRW 6; BRWS 11; CA 17-18; 45-48; CANR 54; CAP 2; CP 1, 2; DLB 20, 100, 155; MTCW 1; PAB

Bly, Robert 1926- ..... **CLC 1, 2, 5, 10, 15, 38, 128; PC 39**
See also AMWS 4; CA 5-8R; CANR 41, 73, 125; CP 1, 2, 3, 4, 5, 6, 7; DA3; DAM POET; DLB 5, 342; EWL 3; MAL 5; MTCW 1, 2; MTFW 2005; PFS 6, 17; RGAL 4

Bly, Robert Elwood
See Bly, Robert

Boas, Franz 1858-1942 .... **TCLC 56**
See also CA 115; 181

Bobette
See Simenon, Georges

Boccaccio, Giovanni 1313-1375 ... **CMLC 13, 57, 140; SSC 10, 87, 167**
See also EW 2; RGSF 2; RGWL 2, 3; SSFS 28; TWA; WLIT 7

Bochco, Steven 1943- .... **CLC 35**
See also AAYA 11, 71; CA 124; 138

Bock, Charles 1970- .... **CLC 299**
See also CA 274

Bode, Sigmund
See O'Doherty, Brian

Bodel, Jean 1167(?)-1210 .... **CMLC 28**

Bodenheim, Maxwell 1892-1954 .... **TCLC 44**
See also CA 110; 187; DLB 9, 45; MAL 5; RGAL 4

Bodenheimer, Maxwell
See Bodenheim, Maxwell

Bodker, Cecil
See Bodker, Cecil

Bodker, Cecil 1927- .... **CLC 21**
See also CA 73-76; CANR 13, 44, 111; CLR 23; MAICYA 1, 2; SATA 14, 133

Boell, Heinrich 1917-1985 ..... **CLC 2, 3, 6, 9, 11, 15, 27, 32, 72; SSC 23; TCLC 185; WLC 1**
See also BPFB 1; CA 21-24R; 116; CANR 24; CDWLB 2; DA; DA3; DAB; DAC; DAM MST, NOV; DLB 69, 329; DLBY 1985; EW 13; EWL 3; MTCW 1, 2; MTFW 2005; RGHL; RGSF 2; RGWL 2, 3; SSFS 20; TWA

Boell, Heinrich Theodor
See Boell, Heinrich

Boerne, Alfred
See Doeblin, Alfred

Boethius c. 480-c. 524 .... **CMLC 15, 136**
See also DLB 115; RGWL 2, 3; WLIT 8

Boff, Leonardo (Genezio Darci)
1938- .... **CLC 70; HLC 1**
See also CA 150; DAM MULT; HW 2

Bogan, Louise 1897-1970 .... **CLC 4, 39, 46, 93; PC 12**
See also AMWS 3; CA 73-76; 25-28R; CANR 33, 82; CP 1; DAM POET; DLB 45, 169; EWL 3; MAL 5; MBL; MTCW 1, 2; PFS 21, 39; RGAL 4

Bogarde, Dirk
See Van Den Bogarde, Derek Jules Gaspard Ulric Niven

Bogat, Shatan
See Kacew, Romain

Bogomolny, Robert L. 1938- .... **SSC 41; TCLC 11**
See also CA 121, 164; DLB 182; EWL 3; MJW; RGSF 2; RGWL 2, 3; TWA

Bogomolny, Robert Lee
See Bogomolny, Robert L.

Bogosian, Eric 1953- .... **CLC 45, 141**
See also CA 138; CAD; CANR 102, 148, 217; CD 5, 6; DLB 341

Bograd, Larry 1953- .... **CLC 35**
See also CA 93-96; CANR 57; SAAS 21; SATA 33, 89; WYA

Bohme, Jakob 1575-1624 .... **LC 178**
See also DLB 164

Boiardo, Matteo Maria 1441-1494 .... **LC 6, 168**

Boileau-Despreaux, Nicolas
1636-1711 .... **LC 3, 164**
See also DLB 268; EW 3; GFL Beginnings to 1789; RGWL 2, 3

Boissard, Maurice
See Leautaud, Paul

Bojer, Johan 1872-1959 .... **TCLC 64**
See also CA 189; EWL 3

Bok, Edward W(illiam)
1863-1930 .... **TCLC 101**
See also CA 217; DLB 91; DLBD 16

Boker, George Henry 1823-1890 . **NCLC 125**
See also RGAL 4

Boland, Eavan 1944- ... **CLC 40, 67, 113; PC 58**
See also BRWS 5; CA 143, 207; CAAE 207; CANR 61, 180; CP 1, 6, 7; CWP; DAM POET; DLB 40; FW; MTCW 2; MTFW 2005; PFS 12, 22, 31, 39

Boland, Eavan Aisling
See Boland, Eavan

Bolano, Roberto 1953-2003 .... **CLC 294**
See also CA 229; CANR 175

Bolingbroke, Viscount
See St. John, Henry

Boll, Heinrich
See Boell, Heinrich

Bolt, Lee
See Faust, Frederick

Bolt, Robert (Oxton) 1924-1995 ...... **CLC 14; TCLC 175**
See also CA 17-20R; 147; CANR 35, 67; CBD; DAM DRAM; DFS 2; DLB 13, 233; EWL 3; LAIT 1; MTCW 1

Bombal, Maria Luisa 1910-1980 .... **HLCS 1; SSC 37**
See also CA 127; CANR 72; EWL 3; HW 1; LAW; RGSF 2

Bombet, Louis-Alexandre-Cesar
See Stendhal

Bomkauf
See Kaufman, Bob (Garnell)

Bonaventura NCLC 35, 252
See also DLB 90

Bonaventure 1217(?)-1274 .... **CMLC 79**
See also DLB 115; LMFS 1

Bond, Edward 1934- .. **CLC 4, 6, 13, 23; DC 45**
See also AAYA 50; BRWS 1; CA 25-28R; CANR 38, 67, 106; CBD; CD 5, 6; DAM DRAM; DFS 3, 8; DLB 13, 310; EWL 3; MTCW 1

Bonham, Frank 1914-1989 .... **CLC 12**
See also AAYA 1, 70; BYA 1, 3; CA 9-12R; CANR 4, 36; JRDA; MAICYA 1, 2; SAAS 3; SATA 1, 49; SATA-Obit 62; TCWW 1, 2; YAW

Bonnefoy, Yves 1923- . **CLC 9, 15, 58; PC 58**
See also CA 85-88; CANR 33, 75, 97, 136; CWW 2; DAM MST, POET; DLB 258; EWL 3; GFL 1789 to the Present; MTCW 1, 2; MTFW 2005

Bonner, Marita
See Occomy, Marita (Odette) Bonner

Bonnin, Gertrude 1876-1938 .... **NNAL**
See also CA 150; DAM MULT; DLB 175

Bontemps, Arna 1902-1973 ... **BLC 1:1; CLC 1, 18; HR 1:2**
See also BW 1; CA 1-4R; 41-44R; CANR 4, 35; CLR 6; CP 1; CWRI 5; DA3; DAM MULT, NOV, POET; DLB 48, 51; JRDA; MAICYA 1, 2; MAL 5; MTCW 1, 2; PFS 32; SATA 2, 44; SATA-Obit 24; WCH; WP

Bontemps, Arnaud Wendell
See Bontemps, Arna

Boot, William
See Stoppard, Tom

Booth, Irwin
See Hoch, Edward D.

Booth, Martin 1944-2004 .... **CLC 13**
See also CA 93-96; 188; 223; CAAE 188; CAAS 2; CANR 92; CP 1, 2, 3, 4

Booth, Philip 1925-2007 .... **CLC 23**
See also CA 5-8R; 262; CANR 5, 88; CP 1, 2, 3, 4, 5, 6, 7; DLBY 1982

Booth, Philip Edmund
See Booth, Philip

Booth, Wayne C. 1921-2005 .... **CLC 24**
See also CA 1-4R; 244; CAAS 5; CANR 3, 43, 117; DLB 67

Booth, Wayne Clayson
See Booth, Wayne C.

Borchert, Wolfgang 1921-1947 .... **DC 42; TCLC 5**
See also CA 104; 188; DLB 69, 124; EWL 3

Borel, Petrus 1809-1859 .... **NCLC 41**
See also DLB 119; GFL 1789 to the Present

Borges, Jorge Luis 1899-1986 ... **CLC 1, 2, 3, 4, 6, 8, 9, 10, 13, 19, 44, 48, 83; HLC 1; PC 22, 32; SSC 4, 41, 100, 159; TCLC 109; WLC 1**
See also AAYA 26; BPFB 1; CA 21-24R; CANR 19, 33, 75, 105, 133; CDWLB 3; DA; DA3; DAB; DAC; DAM MST, MULT; DLB 113, 283; DLBY 1986; DNFS 1, 2; EWL 3; HW 1, 2; LAW; LMFS 2; MSW; MTCW 1, 2; MTFW 2005; PFS 27; RGHL; RGSF 2; RGWL 2, 3; SFW 4; SSFS 17; TWA; WLIT 1

Borne, Ludwig 1786-1837 .... **NCLC 193**
See also DLB 90

Borowski, Tadeusz 1922-1951 .... **SSC 48; TCLC 9**
See also CA 106; 154; CDWLB 4; DLB 215; EWL 3; RGHL; RGSF 2; RGWL 3; SSFS 13

Borrow, George (Henry)
1803-1881 .... **NCLC 9**
See also BRWS 12; DLB 21, 55, 166

Bosch (Gavino), Juan 1909-2001 ..... **HLCS 1**
See also CA 151; 204; DAM MST, MULT; DLB 145; HW 1, 2

Bosman, Herman Charles
1905-1951 .... **TCLC 49**
See also CA 160; DLB 225; RGSF 2

Bosschere, Jean de 1878(?)-1953 ... **TCLC 19**
See also CA 115; 186

Boswell, James 1740-1795 ...... **LC 4, 50, 182; WLC 1**
See also BRW 3; CDBLB 1660-1789; DA; DAB; DAC; DAM MST; DLB 104, 142; TEA; WLIT 3

Boto, Eza
See Beti, Mongo

Bottomley, Gordon 1874-1948 ..... **TCLC 107**
See also CA 120; 192; DLB 10

Bottoms, David 1949- .... **CLC 53**
See also CA 105; CANR 22; CSW; DLB 120; DLBY 1983

Branley, Franklyn M(ansfield)
    1915-2002 .... **CLC 21**
    See also CA 33-36R; 207; CANR 14, 39;
    CLR 13; MAICYA 1, 2; SAAS 16; SATA
    4, 68, 136
Brant, Beth (E.) 1941- .... **NNAL**
    See also CA 144; FW
Brant, Sebastian 1457-1521 .... **LC 112**
    See also DLB 179; RGWL 2, 3
Brathwaite, Edward Kamau
    1930- ... **BLC 2:1; BLCS; CLC 11, 305;
    PC 56**
    See also BRWS 12; BW 2, 3; CA 25-28R;
    CANR 11, 26, 47, 107; CDWLB 3; CP 1,
    2, 3, 4, 5, 6, 7; DAM POET; DLB 125;
    EWL 3
Brathwaite, Kamau
    See Brathwaite, Edward Kamau
Brautigan, Richard 1935-1984 .. **CLC 1, 3, 5,
    9, 12, 34, 42; PC 94; TCLC 133**
    See also BPFB 1; CA 53-56; 113; CANR
    34; CN 1, 2, 3; CP 1, 2, 3, 4; DA3; DAM
    NOV; DLB 2, 5, 206; DLBY 1980, 1984;
    FANT; MAL 5; MTCW 1; RGAL 4;
    SATA 56
Brautigan, Richard Gary
    See Brautigan, Richard
Brave Bird, Mary
    See Crow Dog, Mary
Braverman, Kate 1950- .... **CLC 67**
    See also CA 89-92; CANR 141; DLB 335
Brecht, Bertolt 1898-1956 .... **DC 3; TCLC 1,
    6, 13, 35, 169; WLC 1**
    See also CA 104; 133; CANR 62; CDWLB
    2; DA; DA3; DAB; DAC; DAM DRAM,
    MST; DFS 4, 5, 9; DLB 56, 124; EW 11;
    EWL 3; IDTP; MTCW 1, 2; MTFW 2005;
    RGHL; RGWL 2, 3; TWA
Brecht, Eugen Berthold Friedrich
    See Brecht, Bertolt
Brecht, Eugen Bertolt Friedrich
    See Brecht, Bertolt
Bremer, Fredrika 1801-1865 .... **NCLC 11**
    See also DLB 254
Brennan, Christopher John
    1870-1932 .... **TCLC 17**
    See also CA 117; 188; DLB 230; EWL 3
Brennan, Maeve 1917-1993 ... **CLC 5; TCLC
    124**
    See also CA 81-84; CANR 72, 100
Brenner, Jozef 1887-1919 .... **TCLC 13**
    See also CA 111; 240
Brent, Linda
    See Jacobs, Harriet A.
Brentano, Clemens (Maria)
    1778-1842 .... **NCLC 1, 191; SSC 115**
    See also DLB 90; RGWL 2, 3
Brent of Bin Bin
    See Franklin, (Stella Maria Sarah) Miles
    (Lampe)
Brenton, Howard 1942- .... **CLC 31**
    See also CA 69-72; CANR 33, 67; CBD;
    CD 5, 6; DLB 13; MTCW 1
Breslin, James
    See Breslin, Jimmy
Breslin, Jimmy 1930- .... **CLC 4, 43**
    See also CA 73-76; CANR 31, 75, 139, 187;
    DAM NOV; DLB 185; MTCW 2; MTFW
    2005
Bresson, Robert 1901(?)-1999 .... **CLC 16**
    See also CA 110; 187; CANR 49
Breton, Andre 1896-1966 .. **CLC 2, 9, 15, 54;
    PC 15; TCLC 247**
    See also CA 19-20; 25-28R; CANR 40, 60;
    CAP 2; DLB 65, 258; EW 11; EWL 3;
    GFL 1789 to the Present; LMFS 2;
    MTCW 1, 2; MTFW 2005; RGWL 2, 3;
    TWA; WP

Breton, Nicholas c. 1554-c. 1626 .... **LC 133**
    See also DLB 136
Breytenbach, Breyten 1939(?)- .. **CLC 23, 37,
    126**
    See also CA 113; 129; CANR 61, 122, 202;
    CWW 2; DAM POET; DLB 225; EWL 3
Bridgers, Sue Ellen 1942- .... **CLC 26**
    See also AAYA 8, 49; BYA 7, 8; CA 65-68;
    CANR 11, 36; CLR 18; DLB 52; JRDA;
    MAICYA 1, 2; SAAS 1; SATA 22, 90;
    SATA-Essay 109; WYA; YAW
Bridges, Robert (Seymour)
    1844-1930 .... **PC 28; TCLC 1**
    See also BRW 6; CA 104; 152; CDBLB
    1890-1914; DAM POET; DLB 19, 98
Bridie, James
    See Mavor, Osborne Henry
Brin, David 1950- .... **CLC 34**
    See also AAYA 21; CA 102; CANR 24, 70,
    125, 127; INT CANR-24; SATA 65;
    SCFW 2; SFW 4
Brink, Andre 1935- .... **CLC 18, 36, 106**
    See also AFW; BRWS 6; CA 104; CANR
    39, 62, 109, 133, 182; CN 4, 5, 6, 7; DLB
    225; EWL 3; INT CA-103; LATS 1:2;
    MTCW 1, 2; MTFW 2005; WLIT 2
Brink, Andre Philippus
    See Brink, Andre
Brinsmead, H. F.
    See Brinsmead, H(esba) F(ay)
Brinsmead, H. F(ay)
    See Brinsmead, H(esba) F(ay)
Brinsmead, H(esba) F(ay) 1922- ...... **CLC 21**
    See also CA 21-24R; CANR 10; CLR 47;
    CWRI 5; MAICYA 1, 2; SAAS 5; SATA
    18, 78
Brittain, Vera (Mary)
    1893(?)-1970 .... **CLC 23; TCLC 228**
    See also BRWS 10; CA 13-16; 25-28R;
    CANR 58; CAP 1; DLB 191; FW; MTCW
    1, 2
Broch, Hermann 1886-1951 ... **TCLC 20, 204**
    See also CA 117; 211; CDWLB 2; DLB 85,
    124; EW 10; EWL 3; RGWL 2, 3
Brock, Rose
    See Hansen, Joseph
Brod, Max 1884-1968 .... **TCLC 115**
    See also CA 5-8R; 25-28R; CANR 7; DLB
    81; EWL 3
Brodkey, Harold (Roy) 1930-1996 .. **CLC 56;
    TCLC 123**
    See also CA 111; 151; CANR 71; CN 4, 5,
    6; DLB 130
Brodskii, Iosif
    See Brodsky, Joseph
Brodskii, Iosif Alexandrovich
    See Brodsky, Joseph
Brodsky, Iosif Alexandrovich
    See Brodsky, Joseph
Brodsky, Joseph 1940-1996 ..... **CLC 4, 6, 13,
    36, 100; PC 9; TCLC 219**
    See also AAYA 71; AITN 1; AMWS 8; CA
    41-44R; 151; CANR 37, 106; CWW 2;
    DA3; DAM POET; DLB 285, 329; EWL
    3; MTCW 1, 2; MTFW 2005; PFS 35;
    RGWL 2, 3
Brodsky, Michael 1948- .... **CLC 19**
    See also CA 102; CANR 18, 41, 58, 147;
    DLB 244
Brodsky, Michael Mark
    See Brodsky, Michael
Brodzki, Bella **CLC 65**
Brome, Richard 1590(?)-1652 .... **LC 61**
    See also BRWS 10; DLB 58
Bromell, Henry 1947- .... **CLC 5**
    See also CA 53-56; CANR 9, 115, 116

Bromfield, Louis (Brucker)
    1896-1956 .... **TCLC 11**
    See also CA 107; 155; DLB 4, 9, 86; RGAL
    4; RHW
Broner, E. M. 1930-2011 .... **CLC 19**
    See also CA 17-20R; CANR 8, 25, 72, 216;
    CN 4, 5, 6; DLB 28
Broner, Esther Masserman
    See Broner, E. M.
Bronk, William 1918-1999 .... **CLC 10**
    See also AMWS 21; CA 89-92; 177; CANR
    23; CP 3, 4, 5, 6, 7; DLB 165
Bronstein, Lev Davidovich
    See Trotsky, Leon
Bronte, Anne 1820-1849 .... **NCLC 4, 71, 102,
    235**
    See also BRW 5; BRWR 1; DA3; DLB 21,
    199, 340; NFS 26; TEA
Bronte, (Patrick) Branwell
    1817-1848 .... **NCLC 109**
    See also DLB 340
Bronte, Charlotte 1816-1855 ...... **NCLC 3, 8,
    33, 58, 105, 155, 217, 229; SSC 167;
    WLC 1**
    See also AAYA 17; BRW 5; BRWC 2;
    BRWR 1; BYA 2; CDBLB 1832-1890;
    DA; DA3; DAB; DAC; DAM MST, NOV;
    DLB 21, 159, 199, 340; EXPN; FL 1:2;
    GL 2; LAIT 2; NFS 4, 36; TEA; WLIT 4
Bronte, Emily 1818-1848 .... **NCLC 16, 35,
    165, 244; PC 8; WLC 1**
    See also AAYA 17; BPFB 1; BRW 5;
    BRWC 1; BRWR 1; BYA 3; CDBLB
    1832-1890; DA; DA3; DAB; DAC; DAM
    MST, NOV, POET; DLB 21, 32, 199, 340;
    EXPN; FL 1:2; GL 2; LAIT 1; NFS 2;
    PFS 33; TEA; WLIT 3
Bronte, Emily Jane
    See Bronte, Emily
Brontes
    See Bronte, Anne; Bronte, (Patrick) Bran-
    well; Bronte, Charlotte; Bronte, Emily
Brooke, Frances 1724-1789 .... **LC 6, 48**
    See also DLB 39, 99
Brooke, Henry 1703(?)-1783 .... **LC 1**
    See also DLB 39
Brooke, Rupert 1887-1915 . **PC 24; TCLC 2,
    7; WLC 1**
    See also BRWS 3; CA 104; 132; CANR 61;
    CDBLB 1914-1945; DA; DAB; DAC;
    DAM MST, POET; DLB 19, 216; EXPP;
    GLL 2; MTCW 1, 2; MTFW 2005; PFS
    7; TEA
Brooke, Rupert Chawner
    See Brooke, Rupert
Brooke-Haven, P.
    See Wodehouse, P. G.
Brooke-Rose, Christine 1923(?)- ..... **CLC 40,
    184**
    See also BRWS 4; CA 13-16R; CANR 58,
    118, 183; CN 1, 2, 3, 4, 5, 6, 7; DLB 14,
    231; EWL 3; SFW 4
Brookner, Anita 1928- . **CLC 32, 34, 51, 136,
    237**
    See also BRWS 4; CA 114; 120; CANR 37,
    56, 87, 130, 212; CN 4, 5, 6, 7; CPW;
    DA3; DAB; DAM POP; DLB 194, 326;
    DLBY 1987; EWL 3; MTCW 1, 2; MTFW
    2005; NFS 23; TEA
Brooks, Cleanth 1906-1994 . **CLC 24, 86, 110**
    See also AMWS 14; CA 17-20R; 145;
    CANR 33, 35; CSW; DLB 63; DLBY
    1994; EWL 3; INT CANR-35; MAL 5;
    MTCW 1, 2; MTFW 2005
Brooks, George
    See Baum, L. Frank

DAM MST, NOV; DLB 9, 102, 329; EWL
3; LAIT 3; MAL 5; MTCW 1, 2; MTFW
2005; NFS 25; RGAL 4; RHW; SATA 1,
25; SSFS 33; TUS

Buck, Pearl Sydenstricker
See Buck, Pearl S.

Buckler, Ernest 1908-1984 .... **CLC 13**
See also CA 11-12; 114; CAP 1; CCA 1;
CN 1, 2, 3; DAC; DAM MST; DLB 68;
SATA 47

Buckley, Christopher 1952- .... **CLC 165**
See also CA 139; CANR 119, 180

Buckley, Christopher Taylor
See Buckley, Christopher

Buckley, Vincent (Thomas)
1925-1988 .... **CLC 57**
See also CA 101; CP 1, 2, 3, 4; DLB 289

Buckley, William F., Jr.
See Buckley, William F.

Buckley, William F. 1925-2008 .... **CLC 7, 18,
37**
See also AITN 1; BPFB 1; CA 1-4R; 269;
CANR 1, 24, 53, 93, 133, 185; CMW 4;
CPW; DA3; DAM POP; DLB 137; DLBY
1980; INT CANR-24; MTCW 1, 2;
MTFW 2005; TUS

Buckley, William Frank
See Buckley, William F.

Buckley, William Frank, Jr.
See Buckley, William F.

Buechner, Frederick 1926- ..... **CLC 2, 4, 6, 9**
See also AMWS 12; BPFB 1; CA 13-16R;
CANR 11, 39, 64, 114, 138, 213; CN 1,
2, 3, 4, 5, 6, 7; DAM NOV; DLBY 1980;
INT CANR-11; MAL 5; MTCW 1, 2;
MTFW 2005; TCLE 1:1

Buell, John (Edward) 1927- .... **CLC 10**
See also CA 1-4R; CANR 71; DLB 53

Buero Vallejo, Antonio 1916-2000 ... **CLC 15,
46, 139, 226; DC 18**
See also CA 106; 189; CANR 24, 49, 75;
CWW 2; DFS 11; EWL 3; HW 1; MTCW
1, 2

Bufalino, Gesualdo 1920-1996 .... **CLC 74**
See also CA 209; CWW 2; DLB 196

Buffon, Georges-Louis Leclerc
1707-1788 .... **LC 186**
See also DLB 313; GFL Beginnings to 1789

Bugayev, Boris Nikolayevich
1880-1934 .... **PC 11; TCLC 7**
See also CA 104; 165; DLB 295; EW 9;
EWL 3; MTCW 2; MTFW 2005; RGWL
2, 3

Bukowski, Charles 1920-1994 ... **CLC 2, 5, 9,
41, 82, 108; PC 18; SSC 45**
See also CA 17-20R; 144; CANR 40, 62,
105, 180; CN 4, 5; CP 1, 2, 3, 4, 5; CPW;
DA3; DAM NOV, POET; DLB 5, 130,
169; EWL 3; MAL 5; MTCW 1, 2;
MTFW 2005; PFS 28

Bulgakov, Mikhail 1891-1940 .... **SSC 18;
TCLC 2, 16, 159**
See also AAYA 74; BPFB 1; CA 105; 152;
DAM DRAM, NOV; DLB 272; EWL 3;
MTCW 2; MTFW 2005; NFS 8; RGSF 2;
RGWL 2, 3; SFW 4; TWA

Bulgakov, Mikhail Afanasevich
See Bulgakov, Mikhail

Bulgya, Alexander Alexandrovich
1901-1956 .... **TCLC 53**
See also CA 117; 181; DLB 272; EWL 3

Bullins, Ed 1935- ...... **BLC 1:1; CLC 1, 5, 7;
DC 6**
See also BW 2, 3; CA 49-52; CAAS 16;
CAD; CANR 24, 46, 73, 134; CD 5, 6;
DAM DRAM, MULT; DLB 7, 38, 249;
EWL 3; MAL 5; MTCW 1, 2; MTFW
2005; RGAL 4

Bulosan, Carlos 1911-1956 .... **AAL**
See also CA 216; DLB 312; RGAL 4

Bulwer-Lytton, Edward
1803-1873 .... **NCLC 1, 45, 238**
See also DLB 21; RGEL 2; SATA 23; SFW
4; SUFW 1; TEA

**Bulwer-Lytton, Edward George Earle
Lytton**
See Bulwer-Lytton, Edward

Bunin, Ivan
See Bunin, Ivan Alexeyevich

Bunin, Ivan Alekseevich
See Bunin, Ivan Alexeyevich

Bunin, Ivan Alexeyevich 1870-1953 ... **SSC 5;
TCLC 6, 253**
See also CA 104; DLB 317, 329; EWL 3;
RGSF 2; RGWL 2, 3; TWA

Bunting, Basil 1900-1985 ..... **CLC 10, 39, 47;
PC 120**
See also BRWS 7; CA 53-56; 115; CANR
7; CP 1, 2, 3, 4; DAM POET; DLB 20;
EWL 3; RGEL 2

Bunuel, Luis 1900-1983 ... **CLC 16, 80; HLC
1**
See also CA 101; 110; CANR 32, 77; DAM
MULT; HW 1

Bunyan, John 1628-1688 .... **LC 4, 69, 180;
WLC 1**
See also BRW 2; BYA 5; CDBLB 1660-
1789; CLR 124; DA; DAB; DAC; DAM
MST; DLB 39; NFS 32; RGEL 2; TEA;
WCH; WLIT 3

Buonarroti, Michelangelo
1568-1646 .... **PC 103**
See also DLB 339

Buravsky, Alexandr **CLC 59**

Burchill, Julie 1959- .... **CLC 238**
See also CA 135; CANR 115, 116, 207

Burckhardt, Jacob (Christoph)
1818-1897 .... **NCLC 49**
See also EW 6

Burford, Eleanor
See Hibbert, Eleanor Alice Burford

Burgess, Anthony 1917-1993 . **CLC 1, 2, 4, 5,
8, 10, 13, 15, 22, 40, 62, 81, 94**
See also AAYA 25; AITN 1; BRWS 1; CA
1-4R; 143; CANR 2, 46; CDBLB 1960 to
Present; CN 1, 2, 3, 4, 5; DA3; DAB;
DAC; DAM NOV; DLB 14, 194, 261;
DLBY 1998; EWL 3; MTCW 1, 2; MTFW
2005; NFS 15; RGEL 2; RHW; SFW 4;
TEA; YAW

Buridan, John c. 1295-c. 1358 ...... **CMLC 97**

Burke, Edmund 1729(?)-1797 .... **LC 7, 36,
146; WLC 1**
See also BRW 3; DA; DA3; DAB; DAC;
DAM MST; DLB 104, 252, 336; RGEL
2; TEA

Burke, James Lee 1936- .... **CLC 322**
See also AAYA 84; AMWS 14; CA 13-16R;
CAAS 19; CANR 7, 22, 41, 64, 106, 176,
219; CMW 4; CN 6, 7; CSW; DLB 226,
350

Burke, Kenneth (Duva) 1897-1993 ... **CLC 2,
24**
See also AMW; CA 5-8R; 143; CANR 39,
74, 136; CN 1, 2; CP 1, 2, 3, 4, 5; DLB
45, 63; EWL 3; MAL 5; MTCW 1, 2;
MTFW 2005; RGAL 4

Burke, Leda
See Garnett, David

Burke, Ralph
See Silverberg, Robert

Burke, Thomas 1886-1945 .. **SSC 158; TCLC
63**
See also CA 113; 155; CMW 4; DLB 197

Burke, Valenza Pauline
See Marshall, Paule

Burney, Fanny 1752-1840 .... **NCLC 12, 54,
107, 251**
See also BRWS 3; DLB 39; FL 1:2; NFS
16; RGEL 2; TEA

Burney, Frances
See Burney, Fanny

Burns, Robert 1759-1796 . **LC 3, 29, 40, 190;
PC 6, 114; WLC 1**
See also AAYA 51; BRW 3; CDBLB 1789-
1832; DA; DA3; DAB; DAC; DAM MST,
POET; DLB 109; EXPP; PAB; RGEL 2;
TEA; WP

Burns, Tex
See L'Amour, Louis

Burnshaw, Stanley 1906-2005 ..... **CLC 3, 13,
44**
See also CA 9-12R; 243; CP 1, 2, 3, 4, 5, 6,
7; DLB 48; DLBY 1997

Burr, Anne 1937- .... **CLC 6**
See also CA 25-28R

Burroughs, Augusten 1965- .... **CLC 277**
See also AAYA 73; CA 214; CANR 168,
218

Burroughs, Augusten Xon
See Burroughs, Augusten

Burroughs, Edgar Rice 1875-1950 . **TCLC 2,
32**
See also AAYA 11; BPFB 1; BYA 4, 9; CA
104; 132; CANR 131; CLR 157; DA3;
DAM NOV; DLB 8, 364; FANT; MTCW
1, 2; MTFW 2005; RGAL 4; SATA 41;
SCFW 1, 2; SFW 4; TCWW 1, 2; TUS;
YAW

Burroughs, William S. 1914-1997 . **CLC 1, 2,
5, 15, 22, 42, 75, 109; TCLC 121; WLC
1**
See also AAYA 60; AITN 2; AMWS 3; BG
1:2; BPFB 1; CA 9-12R; 160; CANR 20,
52, 104; CN 1, 2, 3, 4, 5, 6; CPW; DA;
DA3; DAB; DAC; DAM MST, NOV,
POP; DLB 2, 8, 16, 152, 237; DLBY
1981, 1997; EWL 3; GLL 1; HGG; LMFS
2; MAL 5; MTCW 1, 2; MTFW 2005;
RGAL 4; SFW 4

Burroughs, William Seward
See Burroughs, William S.

Burton, Sir Richard F(rancis)
1821-1890 .... **NCLC 42**
See also DLB 55, 166, 184, 366; SSFS 21

Burton, Robert 1577-1640 .... **LC 74, 195**
See also DLB 151; RGEL 2

Buruma, Ian 1951- .... **CLC 163**
See also CA 128; CANR 65, 141, 195

Bury, Stephen
See Stephenson, Neal

Busch, Frederick 1941-2006 .. **CLC 7, 10, 18,
47, 166**
See also CA 33-36R; 248; CAAS 1; CANR
45, 73, 92, 157; CN 1, 2, 3, 4, 5, 6, 7;
DLB 6, 218

Busch, Frederick Matthew
See Busch, Frederick

Bush, Barney (Furman) 1946- .... **NNAL**
See also CA 145

Bush, Ronald 1946- .... **CLC 34**
See also CA 136

Busia, Abena, P. A. 1953- .... **BLC 2:1**

Bustos, Francisco
See Borges, Jorge Luis

Bustos Domecq, Honorio
See Bioy Casares, Adolfo; Borges, Jorge
Luis

Butler, Octavia 1947-2006 . **BLC 2:1; BLCS;
CLC 38, 121, 230, 240**
See also AAYA 18, 48; AFAW 2; AMWS
13; BPFB 1; BW 2, 3; CA 73-76; 248;
CANR 12, 24, 38, 73, 145, 240; CLR 65;
CN 7; CPW; DA3; DAM MULT, POP;

DLB 33; LATS 1:2; MTCW 1, 2; MTFW
2005; NFS 8, 21, 34; SATA 84; SCFW 2;
SFW 4; SSFS 6; TCLE 1:1; YAW

Butler, Octavia E.
See Butler, Octavia

Butler, Octavia Estelle
See Butler, Octavia

Butler, Robert Olen, Jr.
See Butler, Robert Olen

Butler, Robert Olen 1945- .... **CLC 81, 162;
SSC 117**
See also AMWS 12; BPFB 1; CA 112;
CANR 66, 138, 194; CN 7; CSW; DAM
POP; DLB 173, 335; INT CA-112; MAL
5; MTCW 2; MTFW 2005; SSFS 11, 22

Butler, Samuel 1612-1680 .... **LC 16, 43, 173;
PC 94**
See also DLB 101, 126; RGEL 2

Butler, Samuel 1835-1902 .... **TCLC 1, 33;
WLC 1**
See also BRWS 2; CA 143; CDBLB 1890-
1914; DA; DA3; DAB; DAC; DAM MST,
NOV; DLB 18, 57, 174; RGEL 2; SFW 4;
TEA

Butler, Walter C.
See Faust, Frederick

Butor, Michel (Marie Francois)
1926- .... **CLC 1, 3, 8, 11, 15, 161**
See also CA 9-12R; CANR 33, 66; CWW
2; DLB 83; EW 13; EWL 3; GFL 1789 to
the Present; MTCW 1, 2; MTFW 2005

Butts, Mary 1890(?)-1937 ... **SSC 124; TCLC
77**
See also CA 148; DLB 240

Buxton, Ralph
See Silverstein, Alvin; Silverstein, Virginia
B.

Buzo, Alex
See Buzo, Alex

Buzo, Alex 1944- .... **CLC 61**
See also CA 97-100; CANR 17, 39, 69; CD
5, 6; DLB 289

Buzo, Alexander John
See Buzo, Alex

Buzzati, Dino 1906-1972 .... **CLC 36**
See also CA 160; 33-36R; DLB 177; RGWL
2, 3; SFW 4

Byars, Betsy 1928- .... **CLC 35**
See also AAYA 19; BYA 3; CA 33-36R,
183; CAAE 183; CANR 18, 36, 57, 102,
148; CLR 1, 16, 72; DLB 52; INT CANR-
18; JRDA; MAICYA 1, 2; MAICYAS 1;
MTCW 1; SAAS 1; SATA 4, 46, 80, 163,
223; SATA-Essay 108; WYA; YAW

Byars, Betsy Cromer
See Byars, Betsy

Byatt, A. S. 1936- .... **CLC 19, 65, 136, 223,
312; SSC 91**
See also BPFB 1; BRWC 2; BRWS 4; CA
13-16R; CANR 13, 33, 50, 75, 96, 133,
205; CN 1, 2, 3, 4, 5, 6; DA3; DAM NOV,
POP; DLB 14, 194, 319, 326; EWL 3;
MTCW 1, 2; MTFW 2005; RGSF 2;
RHW; SSFS 26; TEA

Byatt, Antonia Susan Drabble
See Byatt, A. S.

Byrd, William II 1674-1744 .... **LC 112**
See also DLB 24, 140; RGAL 4

Byrne, David 1952- .... **CLC 26**
See also CA 127; CANR 215

Byrne, John Joseph
See Leonard, Hugh

Byrne, John Keyes
See Leonard, Hugh

Byron, George Gordon
See Lord Byron

Byron, George Gordon Noel
See Lord Byron

Byron, Robert 1905-1941 .... **TCLC 67**
See also CA 160; DLB 195

C. 3. 3.
See Wilde, Oscar

Caballero, Fernan 1796-1877 .... **NCLC 10**

Cabell, Branch
See Cabell, James Branch

Cabell, James Branch 1879-1958 .... **TCLC 6**
See also CA 105; 152; DLB 9, 78; FANT;
MAL 5; MTCW 2; RGAL 4; SUFW 1

Cabeza de Vaca, Alvar Nunez
1490-1557(?) .... **LC 61**

Cable, George Washington
1844-1925 .... **SSC 4, 155; TCLC 4**
See also CA 104; 155; DLB 12, 74; DLBD
13; RGAL 4; TUS

Cabral de Melo Neto, Joao
1920-1999 .... **CLC 76**
See also CA 151; CWW 2; DAM MULT;
DLB 307; EWL 3; LAW; LAWS 1

Cabrera, Lydia 1900-1991 .... **TCLC 223**
See also CA 178; DLB 145; EWL 3; HW 1;
LAWS 1

Cabrera Infante, G. 1929-2005 ... **CLC 5, 25,
45, 120, 291; HLC 1; SSC 39**
See also CA 85-88; 236; CANR 29, 65, 110;
CDWLB 3; CWW 2; DA3; DAM MULT;
DLB 113; EWL 3; HW 1, 2; LAW; LAWS
1; MTCW 1, 2; MTFW 2005; RGSF 2;
WLIT 1

Cabrera Infante, Guillermo
See Cabrera Infante, G.

Cade, Toni
See Bambara, Toni Cade

Cadmus and Harmonia
See Buchan, John

Caedmon fl. 658-680 .... **CMLC 7, 133**
See also DLB 146

Caeiro, Alberto
See Pessoa, Fernando

Caesar, Julius
See Julius Caesar

Cage, John (Milton), (Jr.)
1912-1992 .... **CLC 41; PC 58**
See also CA 13-16R; 169; CANR 9, 78;
DLB 193; INT CANR-9; TCLE 1:1

Cahan, Abraham 1860-1951 .... **TCLC 71**
See also CA 108; 154; DLB 9, 25, 28; MAL
5; RGAL 4

Cain, Christopher
See Fleming, Thomas

Cain, G.
See Cabrera Infante, G.

Cain, Guillermo
See Cabrera Infante, G.

Cain, James M(allahan) 1892-1977 .. **CLC 3,
11, 28**
See also AITN 1; BPFB 1; CA 17-20R; 73-
76; CANR 8, 34, 61; CMW 4; CN 1, 2;
DLB 226; EWL 3; MAL 5; MSW; MTCW
1; RGAL 4

Caine, Hall 1853-1931 .... **TCLC 97**
See also RHW

Caine, Mark
See Raphael, Frederic

Calasso, Roberto 1941- .... **CLC 81**
See also CA 143; CANR 89, 223

Calderon de la Barca, Pedro
1600-1681 . **DC 3; HLCS 1; LC 23, 136**
See also DFS 23; EW 2; RGWL 2, 3; TWA

Caldwell, Erskine 1903-1987 ... **CLC 1, 8, 14,
50, 60; SSC 19, 147; TCLC 117**
See also AITN 1; AMW; BPFB 1; CA 1-4R;
121; CAAS 1; CANR 2, 33; CN 1, 2, 3,
4; DA3; DAM NOV; DLB 9, 86; EWL 3;
MAL 5; MTCW 1, 2; MTFW 2005;
RGAL 4; RGSF 2; TUS

Caldwell, Gail 1951- .... **CLC 309**
See also CA 313

Caldwell, (Janet Miriam) Taylor (Holland)
1900-1985 .... **CLC 2, 28, 39**
See also BPFB 1; CA 5-8R; 116; CANR 5;
DA3; DAM NOV, POP; DLBD 17;
MTCW 2; RHW

Calhoun, John Caldwell
1782-1850 .... **NCLC 15**
See also DLB 3, 248

Calisher, Hortense 1911-2009 .... **CLC 2, 4, 8,
38, 134; SSC 15**
See also CA 1-4R; 282; CANR 1, 22, 117;
CN 1, 2, 3, 4, 5, 6, 7; DA3; DAM NOV;
DLB 2, 218; INT CANR-22; MAL 5;
MTCW 1, 2; MTFW 2005; RGAL 4;
RGSF 2

Callaghan, Morley 1903-1990 ..... **CLC 3, 14,
41, 65; TCLC 145**
See also CA 9-12R; 132; CANR 33, 73;
CN 1, 2, 3, 4; DAC; DAM MST; DLB
68; EWL 3; MTCW 1, 2; MTFW 2005;
RGEL 2; RGSF 2; SSFS 19

Callaghan, Morley Edward
See Callaghan, Morley

Callimachus c. 305B.C.-c.
240B.C. .... **CMLC 18**
See also AW 1; DLB 176; RGWL 2, 3

Calvin, Jean
See Calvin, John

Calvin, John 1509-1564 .... **LC 37**
See also DLB 327; GFL Beginnings to 1789

Calvino, Italo 1923-1985 ... **CLC 5, 8, 11, 22,
33, 39, 73; SSC 3, 48; TCLC 183**
See also AAYA 58; CA 85-88; 116; CANR
23, 61, 132; DAM NOV; DLB 196; EW
13; EWL 3; MTCW 1, 2; MTFW 2005;
RGHL; RGSF 2; RGWL 2, 3; SFW 4;
SSFS 12, 31; WLIT 7

Camara Laye
See Laye, Camara

**Cambridge, A Gentleman of the University
of**
See Crowley, Edward Alexander

Camden, William 1551-1623 .... **LC 77**
See also DLB 172

Cameron, Carey 1952- .... **CLC 59**
See also CA 135

Cameron, Peter 1959- .... **CLC 44**
See also AMWS 12; CA 125; CANR 50,
117, 188; DLB 234; GLL 2

Camoens, Luis Vaz de 1524(?)-1580
See Camoes, Luis de

Camoes, Luis de 1524(?)-1580 . **HLCS 1; LC
62, 191; PC 31**
See also DLB 287; EW 2; RGWL 2, 3

Camp, Madeleine L'Engle
See L'Engle, Madeleine

Campana, Dino 1885-1932 .... **TCLC 20**
See also CA 117; 246; DLB 114; EWL 3

Campanella, Tommaso 1568-1639 .... **LC 32**
See also RGWL 2, 3

Campbell, Bebe Moore 1950-2006 . **BLC 2:1;
CLC 246**
See also AAYA 26; BW 2, 3; CA 139; 254;
CANR 81, 134; DLB 227; MTCW 2;
MTFW 2005

Campbell, John Ramsey
See Campbell, Ramsey

Campbell, John W. 1910-1971 .... **CLC 32**
See also CA 21-22; 29-32R; CANR 34;
CAP 2; DLB 8; MTCW 1; SCFW 1, 2;
SFW 4

Campbell, John Wood, Jr.
See Campbell, John W.

Campbell, Joseph 1904-1987 .... **CLC 69;
TCLC 140**
See also AAYA 3, 66; BEST 89:2; CA 1-4R;
124; CANR 3, 28, 61, 107; DA3; MTCW
1, 2

Carson, Rachel 1907-1964 .... **CLC 71**
See also AAYA 49; AMWS 9; ANW; CA 77-80; CANR 35; DA3; DAM POP; DLB 275; FW; LAIT 4; MAL 5; MTCW 1, 2; MTFW 2005; NCFS 1; SATA 23

Carson, Rachel Louise
See Carson, Rachel

Cartagena, Teresa de 1425(?)- .... **LC 155**
See also DLB 286

Carter, Angela 1940-1992 ...... **CLC 5, 41, 76; SSC 13, 85, 151; TCLC 139**
See also BRWS 3; CA 53-56; 136; CANR 12, 36, 61, 106; CN 3, 4, 5; DA3; DLB 14, 207, 261, 319; EXPS; FANT; FW; GL 2; MTCW 1, 2; MTFW 2005; RGSF 2; SATA 66; SATA-Obit 70; SFW 4; SSFS 4, 12; SUFW 2; WLIT 4

Carter, Angela Olive
See Carter, Angela

Carter, Martin (Wylde) 1927- .... **BLC 2:1**
See also BW 2; CA 102; CANR 42; CD-WLB 3; CP 1, 2, 3, 4, 5, 6; DLB 117; EWL 3

Carter, Nick
See Smith, Martin Cruz

Carter, Nick
See Smith, Martin Cruz

Carver, Raymond 1938-1988 ..... **CLC 22, 36, 53, 55, 126; PC 54; SSC 8, 51, 104**
See also AAYA 44; AMWS 3; BPFB 1; CA 33-36R; 126; CANR 17, 34, 61, 103; CN 4; CPW; DA3; DAM NOV; DLB 130; DLBY 1984, 1988; EWL 3; MAL 5; MTCW 1, 2; MTFW 2005; PFS 17; RGAL 4; RGSF 4; SSFS 3, 6, 12, 13, 23, 32; TCLE 1:1; TCWW 2; TUS

Cary, Elizabeth, Lady Falkland 1585-1639 .... **LC 30, 141**

Cary, (Arthur) Joyce (Lunel) 1888-1957 .... **TCLC 1, 29, 196**
See also BRW 7; CA 104; 164; CDBLB 1914-1945; DLB 15, 100; EWL 3; MTCW 2; RGEL 2; TEA

Casal, Julian del 1863-1893 .... **NCLC 131**
See also DLB 283; LAW

Casanova, Giacomo
See Casanova de Seingalt, Giovanni Jacopo

Casanova, Giovanni Giacomo
See Casanova de Seingalt, Giovanni Jacopo

Casanova de Seingalt, Giovanni Jacopo 1725-1798 .... **LC 13, 151**
See also WLIT 7

Casares, Adolfo Bioy
See Bioy Casares, Adolfo

Casas, Bartolome de las 1474-1566
See Las Casas, Bartolome de

Case, John
See Hougan, Carolyn

Casely-Hayford, J(oseph) E(phraim) 1866-1903 .... **BLC 1:1; TCLC 24**
See also BW 2; CA 123; 152; DAM MULT

Casey, John 1939- .... **CLC 59**
See also BEST 90:2; CA 69-72; CANR 23, 100, 225

Casey, John Dudley
See Casey, John

Casey, Michael 1947- .... **CLC 2**
See also CA 65-68; CANR 109; CP 2, 3; DLB 5

Casey, Patrick
See Thurman, Wallace (Henry)

Casey, Warren 1935-1988 .... **CLC 12**
See also CA 101; 127; INT CA-101

Casey, Warren Peter
See Casey, Warren

Casona, Alejandro
See Alvarez, Alejandro Rodriguez

Cassavetes, John 1929-1989 .... **CLC 20**
See also CA 85-88; 127; CANR 82

Cassian, Nina 1924- .... **PC 17**
See also CA 298; CWP; CWW 2

Cassill, R(onald) V(erlin) 1919-2002 .... **CLC 4, 23**
See also CA 9-12R; 208; CAAS 1; CANR 7, 45; CN 1, 2, 3, 4, 5, 6, 7; DLB 6, 218; DLBY 2002

Cassiodorus, Flavius Magnus Aurelius c. 490(?)-c. 583(?) .... **CMLC 43, 122**

Cassirer, Ernst 1874-1945 .... **TCLC 61**
See also CA 157

Cassity, (Allen) Turner 1929- .... **CLC 6, 42**
See also CA 17-20R; 223; CAAE 223; CAAS 8; CANR 11; CSW; DLB 105

Cassius Dio c. 155-c. 229 .... **CMLC 99**
See also DLB 176

Castaneda, Carlos (Cesar Aranha) 1931(?)-1998 .... **CLC 12, 119**
See also CA 25-28R; CANR 32, 66, 105; DNFS 1; HW 1; MTCW 1

Castedo, Elena 1937- .... **CLC 65**
See also CA 132

Castedo-Ellerman, Elena
See Castedo, Elena

Castellanos, Rosario 1925-1974 .... **CLC 66; HLC 1; SSC 39, 68**
See also CA 131; 53-56; CANR 58; CD-WLB 3; DAM MULT; DLB 113, 290; EWL 3; FW; HW 1; LAW; MTCW 2; MTFW 2005; RGSF 2; RGWL 2, 3

Castelvetro, Lodovico 1505-1571 .... **LC 12**

Castiglione, Baldassare 1478-1529 ..... **LC 12, 165**
See also EW 2; LMFS 1; RGWL 2, 3; WLIT 7

Castiglione, Baldesar
See Castiglione, Baldassare

Castillo, Ana 1953- .... **CLC 151, 279**
See also AAYA 42; CA 131; CANR 51, 86, 128, 172; CWP; DLB 122, 227; DNFS 2; FW; HW 1; LLW; PFS 21

Castillo, Ana Hernandez Del
See Castillo, Ana

Castle, Robert
See Hamilton, Edmond

Castro (Ruz), Fidel 1926(?)- .... **HLC 1**
See also CA 110; 129; CANR 81; DAM MULT; HW 2

Castro, Guillen de 1569-1631 .... **LC 19**

Castro, Rosalia de 1837-1885 ... **NCLC 3, 78; PC 41**
See also DAM MULT

Castro Alves, Antonio de 1847-1871 .... **NCLC 205**
See also DLB 307; LAW

Cather, Willa 1873-1947 .... **SSC 2, 50, 114; TCLC 1, 11, 31, 99, 132, 152, 264; WLC 1**
See also AAYA 24; AMW; AMWC 1; AMWR 1; BPFB 1; CA 104; 128; CDALB 1865-1917; CLR 98; DA; DA3; DAB; DAC; DAM MST, NOV; DLB 9, 54, 78, 256; DLBD 1; EWL 3; EXPN; EXPS; FL 1:5; LAIT 3; LATS 1:1; MAL 5; MBL; MTCW 1, 2; MTFW 2005; NFS 2, 19, 33; RGAL 4; RGSF 2; RHW; SATA 30; SSFS 2, 7, 16, 27; TCWW 1, 2; TUS

Cather, Willa Sibert
See Cather, Willa

Catherine II
See Catherine the Great

Catherine, Saint 1347-1380 ... **CMLC 27, 116**

Catherine the Great 1729-1796 .... **LC 69**
See also DLB 150

Cato, Marcus Porcius 234B.C.-149B.C. .... **CMLC 21**
See also DLB 211

Cato, Marcus Porcius, the Elder
See Cato, Marcus Porcius

Cato the Elder
See Cato, Marcus Porcius

Catton, (Charles) Bruce 1899-1978 . **CLC 35**
See also AITN 1; CA 5-8R; 81-84; CANR 7, 74; DLB 17; MTCW 2; MTFW 2005; SATA 2; SATA-Obit 24

Catullus c. 84B.C.-54B.C. ...... **CMLC 18, 141**
See also AW 2; CDWLB 1; DLB 211; RGWL 2, 3; WLIT 8

Cauldwell, Frank
See King, Francis

Caunitz, William J. 1933-1996 .... **CLC 34**
See also BEST 89:3; CA 125; 130; 152; CANR 73; INT CA-130

Causley, Charles (Stanley) 1917-2003 .... **CLC 7**
See also CA 9-12R; 223; CANR 5, 35, 94; CLR 30; CP 1, 2, 3, 4, 5; CWRI 5; DLB 27; MTCW 1; SATA 3, 66; SATA-Obit 149

Caute, (John) David 1936- .... **CLC 29**
See also CA 1-4R; CAAS 1, 33, 64, 120; CBD; CD 5, 6; CN 1, 2, 3, 4, 5, 6, 7; DAM NOV; DLB 14, 231

Cavafy, C. P.
See Cavafy, Constantine

Cavafy, Constantine 1863-1933 .... **PC 36; TCLC 2, 7**
See also CA 104; 148; DA3; DAM POET; EW 8; EWL 3; MTCW 2; PFS 19; RGWL 2, 3; WP

Cavafy, Constantine Peter
See Cavafy, Constantine

Cavalcanti, Guido c. 1250-c. 1300 .... **CMLC 54; PC 114**
See also RGWL 2, 3; WLIT 7

Cavallo, Evelyn
See Spark, Muriel

Cavanna, Betty
See Harrison, Elizabeth (Allen) Cavanna

Cavanna, Elizabeth
See Harrison, Elizabeth (Allen) Cavanna

Cavanna, Elizabeth Allen
See Harrison, Elizabeth (Allen) Cavanna

Cavendish, Margaret 1623-1673 . **LC 30, 132**
See also DLB 131, 252, 281; RGEL 2

Cavendish, Margaret Lucas
See Cavendish, Margaret

Caxton, William 1421(?)-1491(?) .... **LC 17**
See also DLB 170

Cayer, D. M.
See Duffy, Maureen

Cayrol, Jean 1911-2005 .... **CLC 11**
See also CA 89-92; 236; DLB 83; EWL 3

Cela, Camilo Jose
See Cela, Camilo Jose

Cela, Camilo Jose 1916-2002 .... **CLC 4, 13, 59, 122; HLC 1; SSC 71**
See also BEST 90:2; CA 21-24R; 206; CAAS 10; CANR 21, 32, 76, 139; CWW 2; DAM MULT; DLB 322; DLBY 1989; EW 13; EWL 3; HW 1; MTCW 1, 2; MTFW 2005; RGSF 2; RGWL 2, 3

Celan, Paul 1920-1970 ... **CLC 10, 19, 53, 82; PC 10**
See also CA 85-88; CANR 33, 61; CDWLB 2; DLB 69; EWL 3; MTCW 1; PFS 21; RGHL; RGWL 2, 3

Cela y Trulock, Camilo Jose
See Cela, Camilo Jose

Celine, Louis-Ferdinand 1894-1961 .. **CLC 1, 3, 4, 7, 47, 124**
See also CA 85-88; CANR 28; DLB 72; EW 11; EWL 3; GFL 1789 to the Present; MTCW 1; RGWL 2, 3

Cellini, Benvenuto 1500-1571 .... **LC 7**
See also WLIT 7

Cendrars, Blaise
See Sauser-Hall, Frederic

Coffin, Robert Peter Tristram
See Coffin, Robert P. Tristram
Cohan, George M. 1878-1942 .... **TCLC 60**
See also CA 157; DLB 249; RGAL 4
Cohan, George Michael
See Cohan, George M.
Cohen, Arthur A(llen) 1928-1986 ...... **CLC 7,**
31
See also CA 1-4R; 120; CANR 1, 17, 42;
DLB 28; RGHL
Cohen, Leonard 1934- .. **CLC 3, 38, 260; PC**
109
See also CA 21-24R; CANR 14, 69; CN 1,
2, 3, 4, 5, 6; CP 1, 2, 3, 4, 5, 6, 7; DAC;
DAM MST; DLB 53; EWL 3; MTCW 1
Cohen, Leonard Norman
See Cohen, Leonard
Cohen, Matt(hew) 1942-1999 .... **CLC 19**
See also CA 61-64; 187; CAAS 18; CANR
40; CN 1, 2, 3, 4, 5, 6; DAC; DLB 53
Cohen-Solal, Annie 1948- .... **CLC 50**
See also CA 239
Colegate, Isabel 1931- .... **CLC 36**
See also CA 17-20R; CANR 8, 22, 74; CN
4, 5, 6, 7; DLB 14, 231; INT CANR-22;
MTCW 1
Coleman, Emmett
See Reed, Ishmael
Coleridge, Hartley 1796-1849 .... **NCLC 90**
See also DLB 96
Coleridge, M. E.
See Coleridge, Mary E(lizabeth)
Coleridge, Mary E(lizabeth)
1861-1907 .... **TCLC 73**
See also CA 116; 166; DLB 19, 98
Coleridge, Samuel Taylor
1772-1834 ..... **NCLC 9, 54, 99, 111, 177,**
197, 231; PC 11, 39, 67, 100; WLC 2
See also AAYA 66; BRW 4; BRWR 2; BYA
4; CDBLB 1789-1832; DA; DA3; DAB;
DAC; DAM MST, POET; DLB 93, 107;
EXPP; LATS 1:1; LMFS 1; PAB; PFS 4,
5, 39; RGEL 2; TEA; WLIT 3; WP
Coleridge, Sara 1802-1852 .... **NCLC 31**
See also DLB 199
Coles, Don 1928- .... **CLC 46**
See also CA 115; CANR 38; CP 5, 6, 7
Coles, Robert 1929- .... **CLC 108**
See also CA 45-48; CANR 3, 32, 66, 70,
135, 225; INT CANR-32; SATA 23
Coles, Robert Martin
See Coles, Robert
Colette 1873-1954 ... **SSC 10, 93; TCLC 1, 5,**
16
See also CA 104; 131; DA3; DAM NOV;
DLB 65; EW 9; EWL 3; GFL 1789 to the
Present; GLL 1; MTCW 1, 2; MTFW
2005; RGWL 2, 3; TWA
Colette, Sidonie-Gabrielle
See Colette
Collett, (Jacobine) Camilla (Wergeland)
1813-1895 .... **NCLC 22**
See also DLB 354
Collier, Christopher 1930- .... **CLC 30**
See also AAYA 13; BYA 2; CA 33-36R;
CANR 13, 33, 102; CLR 126; JRDA;
MAICYA 1, 2; NFS 38; SATA 16, 70;
WYA; YAW 1
Collier, James Lincoln 1928- .... **CLC 30**
See also AAYA 13; BYA 2; CA 9-12R;
CANR 4, 33, 60, 102, 208; CLR 3, 126;
DAM POP; JRDA; MAICYA 1, 2; NFS
38; SAAS 21; SATA 8, 70, 166; WYA;
YAW 1
Collier, Jeremy 1650-1726 .... **LC 6, 157**
See also DLB 336
Collier, John 1901-1980 . **SSC 19; TCLC 127**
See also CA 65-68; 97-100; CANR 10; CN
1, 2; DLB 77, 255; FANT; SUFW 1

Collier, Mary 1690-1762 .... **LC 86**
See also DLB 95
Collingwood, R(obin) G(eorge)
1889(?)-1943 .... **TCLC 67**
See also CA 117; 155; DLB 262
Collins, Billy 1941- .... **PC 68**
See also AAYA 64; AMWS 21; CA 151;
CANR 92, 211; CP 7; MTFW 2005; PFS
18
Collins, Hunt
See Hunter, Evan
Collins, Linda 1931- .... **CLC 44**
See also CA 125
Collins, Merle 1950- .... **BLC 2:1**
See also BW 3; CA 175; DLB 157
Collins, Tom
See Furphy, Joseph
Collins, Wilkie 1824-1889 ... **NCLC 1, 18, 93,**
255; SSC 93
See also BRWS 6; CDBLB 1832-1890;
CMW 4; DFS 28; DLB 18, 70, 159; GL
2; MSW; NFS 39; RGEL 2; RGSF 2;
SUFW 1; WLIT 4
Collins, William 1721-1759 ...... **LC 4, 40; PC**
72
See also BRW 3; DAM POET; DLB 109;
RGEL 2
Collins, William Wilkie
See Collins, Wilkie
Collodi, Carlo 1826-1890 .... **NCLC 54**
See also CLR 5, 120; MAICYA 1,2; SATA
29, 100; WCH; WLIT 7
Colman, George
See Glassco, John
Colman, George, the Elder
1732-1794 .... **LC 98**
See also RGEL 2
Colonna, Vittoria 1492-1547 .... **LC 71**
See also RGWL 2, 3
Colt, Winchester Remington
See Hubbard, L. Ron
Colter, Cyrus J. 1910-2002 .... **CLC 58**
See also BW 1; CA 65-68; 205; CANR 10,
66; CN 2, 3, 4, 5, 6; DLB 33
Colton, James
See Hansen, Joseph
Colum, Padraic 1881-1972 .... **CLC 28**
See also BYA 4; CA 73-76; 33-36R; CANR
35; CLR 36; CP 1; CWRI 5; DLB 19;
MAICYA 1, 2; MTCW 1; RGEL 2; SATA
15; WCH
Colvin, James
See Moorcock, Michael
Colwin, Laurie (E.) 1944-1992 .... **CLC 5, 13,**
23, 84
See also CA 89-92; 139; CANR 20, 46;
DLB 218; DLBY 1980; MTCW 1
Comfort, Alex(ander) 1920-2000 .... **CLC 7**
See also CA 1-4R; 190; CANR 1, 45; CN
1, 2, 3, 4; CP 1, 2, 3, 4, 5, 6, 7; DAM
POP; MTCW 2
Comfort, Montgomery
See Campbell, Ramsey
Compton-Burnett, I. 1892(?)-1969 .... **CLC 1,**
3, 10, 15, 34; TCLC 180
See also BRW 7; CA 1-4R; 25-28R; CANR
4; DAM NOV; DLB 36; EWL 3; MTCW
1, 2; RGEL 2
Compton-Burnett, Ivy
See Compton-Burnett, I.
Comstock, Anthony 1844-1915 ...... **TCLC 13**
See also CA 110; 169
Comte, Auguste 1798-1857 .... **NCLC 54**
Conan Doyle, Arthur
See Doyle, Sir Arthur Conan
Conde (Abellan), Carmen
1901-1996 .... **HLCS 1**
See also CA 177; CWW 2; DLB 108; EWL
3; HW 2

Conde, Maryse 1937- .... **BLC 2:1; BLCS;**
CLC 52, 92, 247
See also BW 2, 3; CA 110, 190; CAAE 190;
CANR 30, 53, 76, 171; CWW 2; DAM
MULT; EWL 3; MTCW 2; MTFW 2005
Condillac, Etienne Bonnot de
1714-1780 .... **LC 26**
See also DLB 313
Condon, Richard 1915-1996 ...... **CLC 4, 6, 8,**
10, 45, 100
See also BEST 90:3; BPFB 1; CA 1-4R;
151; CAAS 1; CANR 2, 23, 164; CMW
4; CN 1, 2, 3, 4, 5, 6; DAM NOV; INT
CANR-23; MAL 5; MTCW 1, 2
Condon, Richard Thomas
See Condon, Richard
Condorcet
See Condorcet, marquis de Marie-Jean-
Antoine-Nicolas Caritat
Condorcet, marquis de
Marie-Jean-Antoine-Nicolas Caritat
1743-1794 .... **LC 104**
See also DLB 313; GFL Beginnings to 1789
Confucius 551B.C.-479B.C. .... **CMLC 19, 65;**
WLCS
See also DA; DA3; DAB; DAC; DAM
MST
Congreve, William 1670-1729 ... **DC 2; LC 5,**
21, 170; WLC 2
See also BRW 2; CDBLB 1660-1789; DA;
DAB; DAC; DAM DRAM, MST, POET;
DFS 15; DLB 39, 84; RGEL 2; WLIT 3
Conley, Robert J. 1940- .... **NNAL**
See also CA 41-44R, 295; CAAE 295;
CANR 15, 34, 45, 96, 186; DAM MULT;
TCWW 2
Connell, Evan S. 1924- .... **CLC 4, 6, 45**
See also AAYA 7; AMWS 14; CA 1-4R;
CAAS 2; CANR 2, 39, 76, 97, 140, 195;
CN 1, 2, 3, 4, 5, 6; DAM NOV; DLB 2,
335; DLBY 1981; MAL 5; MTCW 1, 2;
MTFW 2005
Connell, Evan Shelby, Jr.
See Connell, Evan S.
Connelly, Marc(us Cook) 1890-1980 . **CLC 7**
See also CA 85-88; 102; CAD; CANR 30;
DFS 12; DLB 7; DLBY 1980; MAL 5;
RGAL 4; SATA-Obit 25
Connelly, Michael 1956- .... **CLC 293**
See also AMWS 21; CA 158; CANR 91,
180; CMW 4; LNFS 2
Connolly, Paul
See Wicker, Tom
Connor, Ralph
See Gordon, Charles William
Conrad, Joseph 1857-1924 ..... **SSC 9, 67, 69,**
71, 153; TCLC 1, 6, 13, 25, 43, 57;
WLC 2
See also AAYA 26; BPFB 1; BRW 6;
BRWC 1; BRWR 2; BYA 2; CA 104; 131;
CANR 60; CDBLB 1890-1914; DA; DA3;
DAB; DAC; DAM MST, NOV; DLB 10,
34, 98, 156; EWL 3; EXPN; EXPS; LAIT
2; LATS 1:1; LMFS 1; MTCW 1, 2;
MTFW 2005; NFS 2, 16; RGEL 2; RGSF
2; SATA 27; SSFS 1, 12, 31; TEA; WLIT
4
Conrad, Robert Arnold
See Hart, Moss
Conroy, Donald Patrick
See Conroy, Pat
Conroy, Pat 1945- .... **CLC 30, 74**
See also AAYA 8, 52; AITN 1; BPFB 1;
CA 85-88; CANR 24, 53, 129, 233; CN
7; CPW; CSW; DA3; DAM NOV, POP;
DLB 6; LAIT 5; MAL 5; MTCW 1, 2;
MTFW 2005

Constant (de Rebecque), (Henri) Benjamin 1767-1830 .... NCLC **6, 182**
See also DLB 119; EW 4; GFL 1789 to the Present

Conway, Jill K. 1934- .... CLC **152**
See also CA 130; CANR 94

Conway, Jill Ker
See Conway, Jill K.

Conybeare, Charles Augustus
See Eliot, T. S.

Cook, Michael 1933-1994 .... CLC **58**
See also CA 93-96; CANR 68; DLB 53

Cook, Robin 1940- .... CLC **14**
See also AAYA 32; BEST 90:2; BPFB 1; CA 108; 111; CANR 41, 90, 109, 181, 219; CPW; DA3; DAM POP; HGG; INT CA-111

Cook, Roy
See Silverberg, Robert

Cooke, Elizabeth 1948- .... CLC **55**
See also CA 129

Cooke, John Esten 1830-1886 .... NCLC **5**
See also DLB 3, 248; RGAL 4

Cooke, John Estes
See Baum, L. Frank

Cooke, M. E.
See Creasey, John

Cooke, Margaret
See Creasey, John

Cooke, Rose Terry 1827-1892 ..... NCLC **110**; SSC **149**
See also DLB 12, 74

Cook-Lynn, Elizabeth 1930- .... CLC **93**; NNAL
See also CA 133; DAM MULT; DLB 175

Cooney, Ray CLC **62**
See also CBD

Cooper, Anthony Ashley 1671-1713 .. LC **107**
See also DLB 101, 336

Cooper, Dennis 1953- .... CLC **203**
See also CA 133; CANR 72, 86, 204; GLL 1; HGG

Cooper, Douglas 1960- .... CLC **86**

Cooper, Henry St. John
See Creasey, John

Cooper, J. California (?)- .... CLC **56**
See also AAYA 12; BW 1; CA 125; CANR 55, 207; DAM MULT; DLB 212

Cooper, James Fenimore
1789-1851 .... NCLC **1, 27, 54, 203**
See also AAYA 22; AMW; BPFB 1; CDALB 1640-1865; CLR 105; DA3; DLB 3, 183, 250, 254; LAIT 1; NFS 25; RGAL 4; SATA 19; TUS; WCH

Cooper, Joan California
See Cooper, J. California

Cooper, Susan Fenimore
1813-1894 .... NCLC **129**
See also ANW; DLB 239, 254

Coover, Robert 1932- .. CLC **3, 7, 15, 32, 46, 87, 161, 306**; SSC **15, 101**
See also AMWS 5; BPFB 1; CA 45-48; CANR 3, 37, 58, 115, 228; CN 1, 2, 3, 4, 5, 6, 7; DAM NOV; DLB 2, 227; DLBY 1981; EWL 3; MAL 5; MTCW 1, 2; MTFW 2005; RGAL 4; RGSF 2

Copeland, Stewart 1952- .... CLC **26**
See also CA 305

Copeland, Stewart Armstrong
See Copeland, Stewart

Copernicus, Nicolaus 1473-1543 .... LC **45**

Coppard, A(lfred) E(dgar)
1878-1957 .... SSC **21**; TCLC **5**
See also BRWS 8; CA 114; 167; DLB 162; EWL 3; HGG; RGEL 2; RGSF 2; SUFW 1; YABC 1

Coppee, Francois 1842-1908 .... TCLC **25**
See also CA 170; DLB 217

Coppola, Francis Ford 1939- ... CLC **16, 126**
See also AAYA 39; CA 77-80; CANR 40, 78; DLB 44

Copway, George 1818-1869 .... NNAL
See also DAM MULT; DLB 175, 183

Corbiere, Tristan 1845-1875 .... NCLC **43**
See also DLB 217; GFL 1789 to the Present

Corcoran, Barbara (Asenath)
1911-2003 .... CLC **17**
See also AAYA 14; CA 21-24R, 191; CAAE 191; CAAS 2; CANR 11, 28, 48; CLR 50; DLB 52; JRDA; MAICYA 2; MAIC-YAS 1; RHW; SAAS 20; SATA 3, 77; SATA-Essay 125

Cordelier, Maurice
See Giraudoux, Jean

Cordier, Gilbert
See Rohmer, Eric

Corelli, Marie
See Mackay, Mary

Corinna c. 225B.C.-c. 305B.C. ...... CMLC **72**

Corman, Cid 1924-2004 .... CLC **9**
See also CA 85-88; 225; CAAS 2; CANR 44; CP 1, 2, 3, 4, 5, 6, 7; DAM POET; DLB 5, 193

Corman, Sidney
See Corman, Cid

Cormier, Robert 1925-2000 .... CLC **12, 30**
See also AAYA 3, 19; BYA 1, 2, 6, 8, 9; CA 1-4R; CANR 5, 23, 76, 93; CDALB 1968-1988; CLR 12, 55, 167; DA; DAB; DAC; DAM MST, NOV; DLB 52; EXPN; INT CANR-23; JRDA; LAIT 5; MAICYA 1, 2; MTCW 1, 2; MTFW 2005; NFS 2, 18; SATA 10, 45, 83; SATA-Obit 122; WYA; YAW

Cormier, Robert Edmund
See Cormier, Robert

Corn, Alfred (DeWitt III) 1943- .... CLC **33**
See also CA 179; CAAE 179; CAAS 25; CANR 44; CP 3, 4, 5, 6, 7; CSW; DLB 120, 282; DLBY 1980

Corneille, Pierre 1606-1684 .. DC **21**; LC **28, 135**
See also DAB; DAM MST; DFS 21; DLB 268; EW 3; GFL Beginnings to 1789; RGWL 2, 3; TWA

Cornwell, David
See le Carre, John

Cornwell, David John Moore
See le Carre, John

Cornwell, Patricia 1956- .... CLC **155**
See also AAYA 16, 56; BPFB 1; CA 134; CANR 53, 131, 195; CMW 4; CPW; CSW; DAM POP; DLB 306; MSW; MTCW 2; MTFW 2005

Cornwell, Patricia Daniels
See Cornwell, Patricia

Cornwell, Smith
See Smith, David (Jeddie)

Corso, Gregory 1930-2001 .... CLC **1, 11**; PC **33, 108**
See also AMWS 12; BG 1:2; CA 5-8R; 193; CANR 41, 76, 132; CP 1, 2, 3, 4, 5, 6, 7; DA3; DLB 5, 16, 237; LMFS 2; MAL 5; MTCW 1, 2; MTFW 2005; WP

Cortazar, Julio 1914-1984 ... CLC **2, 3, 5, 10, 13, 15, 33, 34, 92**; HLC **1**; SSC **7, 76, 156**; TCLC **252**
See also AAYA 85; BPFB 1; CA 21-24R; CANR 12, 32, 81; CDWLB 3; DA3; DAM MULT, NOV; DLB 113; EWL 3; EXPS; HW 1, 2; LAW; MTCW 1, 2; MTFW 2005; RGSF 2; RGWL 2, 3; SSFS 3, 20, 28, 31, 34; TWA; WLIT 1

Cortes, Hernan 1485-1547 .... LC **31**

Cortez, Jayne 1936- .... BLC **2:1**
See also BW 2, 3; CA 73-76; CANR 13, 31, 68, 126; CWP; DLB 41; EWL 3

Corvinus, Jakob
See Raabe, Wilhelm (Karl)

Corwin, Cecil
See Kornbluth, C(yril) M.

Cosic, Dobrica 1921- .... CLC **14**
See also CA 122; 138; CDWLB 4; CWW 2; DLB 181; EWL 3

Costain, Thomas B(ertram)
1885-1965 .... CLC **30**
See also BYA 3; CA 5-8R; 25-28R; DLB 9; RHW

Costantini, Humberto 1924(?)-1987 . CLC **49**
See also CA 131; 122; EWL 3; HW 1

Costello, Elvis 1954(?)- .... CLC **21**
See also CA 204

Costenoble, Philostene
See Ghelderode, Michel de

Cotes, Cecil V.
See Duncan, Sara Jeannette

Cotter, Joseph Seamon Sr.
1861-1949 .... BLC **1:1**; TCLC **28**
See also BW 1; CA 124; DAM MULT; DLB 50

Cotton, John 1584-1652 .... LC **176**
See also DLB 24; TUS

Couch, Arthur Thomas Quiller
See Quiller-Couch, Sir Arthur (Thomas)

Coulton, James
See Hansen, Joseph

Couperus, Louis (Marie Anne)
1863-1923 .... TCLC **15**
See also CA 115; EWL 3; RGWL 2, 3

Coupland, Douglas 1961- .... CLC **85, 133**
See also AAYA 34; CA 142; CANR 57, 90, 130, 172, 213; CCA 1; CN 7; CPW; DAC; DAM POP; DLB 334

Coupland, Douglas Campbell
See Coupland, Douglas

Court, Wesli
See Turco, Lewis

Courtenay, Bryce 1933- .... CLC **59**
See also CA 138; CPW; NFS 32

Courtney, Robert
See Ellison, Harlan

Cousteau, Jacques 1910-1997 .... CLC **30**
See also CA 65-68; 159; CANR 15, 67, 201; MTCW 1; SATA 38, 98

Cousteau, Jacques-Yves
See Cousteau, Jacques

Coventry, Francis 1725-1754 .... LC **46**
See also DLB 39

Coverdale, Miles c. 1487-1569 .... LC **77**
See also DLB 167

Cowan, Peter (Walkinshaw)
1914-2002 .... SSC **28**
See also CA 21-24R; CANR 9, 25, 50, 83; CN 1, 2, 3, 4, 5, 6, 7; DLB 260; RGSF 2

Coward, Noel 1899-1973 ... CLC **1, 9, 29, 51**; DC **45**
See also AITN 1; BRWS 2; CA 17-18; 41-44R; CANR 35, 132, 190; CAP 2; CBD; CDBLB 1914-1945; DA3; DAM DRAM; DFS 3, 6; DLB 10, 245; EWL 3; IDFW 3, 4; MTCW 1, 2; MTFW 2005; RGEL 2; TEA

Coward, Noel Peirce
See Coward, Noel

Cowley, Abraham 1618-1667 .. LC **43**; PC **90**
See also BRW 2; DLB 131, 151; PAB; RGEL 2

Cowley, Malcolm 1898-1989 .... CLC **39**
See also AMWS 2; CA 5-8R; 128; CANR 3, 55; CP 1, 2, 3, 4; DLB 4, 48; DLBY 1981, 1989; EWL 3; MAL 5; MTCW 1, 2; MTFW 2005

Cowper, William 1731-1800 ..... NCLC **8, 94**; PC **40**
See also BRW 3; BRWR 3; DA3; DAM POET; DLB 104, 109; RGEL 2

Cox, William Trevor
See Trevor, William

Coyle, William
See Keneally, Thomas

Coyne, P. J.
See Masters, Hilary

Cozzens, James Gould 1903-1978 . **CLC 1, 4, 11, 92**
See also AMW; BPFB 1; CA 9-12R; 81-84; CANR 19; CDALB 1941-1968; CN 1, 2; DLB 9, 294; DLBD 2; DLBY 1984, 1997; EWL 3; MAL 5; MTCW 1, 2; MTFW 2005; RGAL 4

Crabbe, George 1754-1832 ... **NCLC 26, 121; PC 97**
See also BRW 3; DLB 93; RGEL 2

Crace, Jim 1946- .... **CLC 157; SSC 61**
See also BRWS 14; CA 128; 135; CANR 55, 70, 123, 180; CN 5, 6, 7; DLB 231; INT CA-135

Craddock, Charles Egbert
See Murfree, Mary Noailles

Craig, A. A.
See Anderson, Poul

Craik, Mrs.
See Craik, Dinah Maria (Mulock)

Craik, Dinah Maria (Mulock)
1826-1887 .... **NCLC 38**
See also DLB 35, 163; MAICYA 1, 2; RGEL 2; SATA 34

Cram, Ralph Adams 1863-1942 ..... **TCLC 45**
See also CA 160

Cranch, Christopher Pearse
1813-1892 .... **NCLC 115**
See also DLB 1, 42, 243

Crane, Harold Hart
See Crane, Hart

Crane, Hart 1899-1932 ... **PC 3, 99; TCLC 2, 5, 80; WLC 2**
See also AAYA 81; AMW; AMWR 2; CA 104; 127; CDALB 1917-1929; DA; DA3; DAB; DAC; DAM MST, POET; DLB 4, 48; EWL 3; MAL 5; MTCW 1, 2; MTFW 2005; RGAL 4; TUS

Crane, R(onald) S(almon)
1886-1967 .... **CLC 27**
See also CA 85-88; DLB 63

Crane, Stephen 1871-1900 ..... **PC 80; SSC 7, 56, 70, 129; TCLC 11, 17, 32, 216; WLC 2**
See also AAYA 21; AMW; AMWC 1; BPFB 1; BYA 3; CA 109; 140; CANR 84; CDALB 1865-1917; CLR 132; DA; DA3; DAB; DAC; DAM MST, NOV, POET; DLB 12, 54, 78, 357; EXPN; EXPS; LAIT 2; LMFS 2; MAL 5; NFS 4, 20; PFS 9; RGAL 4; RGSF 2; SSFS 4, 28, 34; TUS; WYA; YABC 2

Crane, Stephen Townley
See Crane, Stephen

Cranmer, Thomas 1489-1556 .... **LC 95**
See also DLB 132, 213

Cranshaw, Stanley
See Fisher, Dorothy (Frances) Canfield

Crase, Douglas 1944- .... **CLC 58**
See also CA 106; CANR 204

Crashaw, Richard 1612(?)-1649 .... **LC 24, 200; PC 84**
See also BRW 2; DLB 126; PAB; RGEL 2

Cratinus c. 519B.C.-c. 422B.C. ..... **CMLC 54**
See also LMFS 1

Craven, Margaret 1901-1980 .... **CLC 17**
See also BYA 2; CA 103; CCA 1; DAC; LAIT 5

Crawford, F(rancis) Marion
1854-1909 .... **TCLC 10**
See also CA 107; 168; DLB 71; HGG; RGAL 4; SUFW 1

Crawford, Isabella Valancy
1850-1887 .... **NCLC 12, 127**
See also DLB 92; RGEL 2

Crayon, Geoffrey
See Irving, Washington

Creasey, John 1908-1973 .... **CLC 11**
See also CA 5-8R; 41-44R; CANR 8, 59; CMW 4; DLB 77; MTCW 1

Crebillon, Claude Prosper Jolyot de (fils)
1707-1777 .... **LC 1, 28**
See also DLB 313; GFL Beginnings to 1789

Credo
See Creasey, John

Credo, Alvaro J. de
See Prado (Calvo), Pedro

Creeley, Robert 1926-2005 .... **CLC 1, 2, 4, 8, 11, 15, 36, 78, 266; PC 73**
See also AMWS 4; CA 1-4R; 237; CAAS 10; CANR 23, 43, 89, 137; CP 1, 2, 3, 4, 5, 6, 7; DA3; DAM POET; DLB 5, 16, 169; DLBD 17; EWL 3; MAL 5; MTCW 1, 2; MTFW 2005; PFS 21; RGAL 4; WP

Creeley, Robert White
See Creeley, Robert

Crenne, Helisenne de 1510-1560 .... **LC 113**
See also DLB 327

Crevecoeur, J. Hector St. John de
1735-1813 .... **NCLC 105**
See also AMWS 1; ANW; DLB 37

Crevecoeur, Michel Guillaume Jean de
See Crevecoeur, J. Hector St. John de

Crevel, Rene 1900-1935 .... **TCLC 112**
See also GLL 2

Crews, Harry 1935- .... **CLC 6, 23, 49, 277**
See also AITN 1; AMWS 11; BPFB 1; CA 25-28R; CANR 20, 57; CN 3, 4, 5, 6, 7; CSW; DA3; DLB 6, 143, 185; MTCW 1, 2; MTFW 2005; RGAL 4

Crichton, John Michael
See Crichton, Michael

Crichton, Michael 1942-2008 .. **CLC 2, 6, 54, 90, 242**
See also AAYA 10, 49; AITN 2; BPFB 1; CA 25-28R; 279; CANR 13, 40, 54, 76, 127, 179; CMW 4; CN 2, 3, 6, 7; CPW; DA3; DAM NOV, POP; DLB 292; DLBY 1981; INT CANR-13; JRDA; LNFS 1; MTCW 1, 2; MTFW 2005; NFS 34; SATA 9, 88; SATA-Obit 199; SFW 4; YAW

Crispin, Edmund
See Montgomery, Bruce

Cristina of Sweden 1626-1689 .... **LC 124**

Cristofer, Michael 1945(?)- .... **CLC 28**
See also CA 110; 152; CAD; CANR 150; CD 5, 6; DAM DRAM; DFS 15; DLB 7

Cristofer, Michael Ivan
See Cristofer, Michael

Criton
See Alain

Croce, Benedetto 1866-1952 .... **TCLC 37**
See also CA 120; 155; EW 8; EWL 3; WLIT 7

Crockett, David
See Crockett, Davy

Crockett, Davy 1786-1836 .... **NCLC 8**
See also DLB 3, 11, 183, 248

Crofts, Freeman Wills 1879-1957 .. **TCLC 55**
See also CA 115; 195; CMW 4; DLB 77; MSW

Croker, John Wilson 1780-1857 .... **NCLC 10**
See also DLB 110

Crommelynck, Fernand 1885-1970 .. **CLC 75**
See also CA 189; 89-92; EWL 3

Cromwell, Oliver 1599-1658 .... **LC 43**

Cronenberg, David 1943- .... **CLC 143**
See also CA 138; CCA 1

Cronin, A(rchibald) J(oseph)
1896-1981 .... **CLC 32**
See also BPFB 1; CA 1-4R; 102; CANR 5; CN 2; DLB 191; SATA 47; SATA-Obit 25

Cross, Amanda
See Heilbrun, Carolyn G.

Crothers, Rachel 1878-1958 .... **TCLC 19**
See also CA 113; 194; CAD; CWD; DLB 7, 266; RGAL 4

Croves, Hal
See Traven, B.

Crow Dog, Mary (?)- .... **CLC 93; NNAL**
See also CA 154

Crowfield, Christopher
See Stowe, Harriet Beecher

Crowley, Aleister
See Crowley, Edward Alexander

Crowley, Edward Alexander
1875-1947 .... **TCLC 7**
See also CA 104; GLL 1; HGG

Crowley, John 1942- .... **CLC 57**
See also AAYA 57; BPFB 1; CA 61-64; CANR 43, 98, 138, 177; DLBY 1982; FANT; MTFW 2005; SATA 65, 140; SFW 4; SUFW 2

Crowne, John 1641-1712 .... **LC 104**
See also DLB 80; RGEL 2

Crud
See Crumb, R.

Crumarums
See Crumb, R.

Crumb, R. 1943- .... **CLC 17**
See also CA 106; CANR 107, 150, 218

Crumb, Robert
See Crumb, R.

Crumbum
See Crumb, R.

Crumski
See Crumb, R.

Crum the Bum
See Crumb, R.

Crunk
See Crumb, R.

Crustt
See Crumb, R.

Crutchfield, Les
See Trumbo, Dalton

Cruz, Victor Hernandez 1949- ... **HLC 1; PC 37**
See also BW 2; CA 65-68; 271; CAAE 271; CAAS 17; CANR 14, 32, 74, 132; CP 1, 2, 3, 4, 5, 6, 7; DAM MULT, POET; DLB 41; DNFS 1; EXPP; HW 1, 2; LLW; MTCW 2; MTFW 2005; PFS 16; WP

Cryer, Gretchen (Kiger) 1935- .... **CLC 21**
See also CA 114; 123

Csath, Geza
See Brenner, Jozef

Cudlip, David R(ockwell) 1933- .... **CLC 34**
See also CA 177

Cuervo, Talia
See Vega, Ana Lydia

Cullen, Countee 1903-1946 ..... **BLC 1:1; HR 1:2; PC 20; TCLC 4, 37, 220; WLCS**
See also AAYA 78; AFAW 2; AMWS 4; BW 1; CA 108; 124; CDALB 1917-1929; DA; DA3; DAC; DAM MST, MULT, POET; DLB 4, 48, 51; EWL 3; EXPP; LMFS 2; MAL 5; MTCW 1, 2; MTFW 2005; PFS 3; RGAL 4; SATA 18; WP

Culleton, Beatrice 1949- .... **NNAL**
See also CA 120; CANR 83; DAC

Culver, Timothy J.
See Westlake, Donald E.

Cum, R.
See Crumb, R.

Davenport, Guy (Mattison, Jr.)
1927-2005 . **CLC 6, 14, 38, 241; SSC 16**
See also CA 33-36R; 235; CANR 23, 73;
CN 3, 4, 5, 6; CSW; DLB 130

David, Robert
See Nezval, Vitezslav

Davidson, Donald (Grady)
1893-1968 .... **CLC 2, 13, 19**
See also CA 5-8R; 25-28R; CANR 4, 84;
DLB 45

Davidson, Hugh
See Hamilton, Edmond

Davidson, John 1857-1909 .... **TCLC 24**
See also CA 118; 217; DLB 19; RGEL 2

Davidson, Sara 1943- .... **CLC 9**
See also CA 81-84; CANR 44, 68; DLB
185

Davie, Donald (Alfred) 1922-1995 .... **CLC 5,
8, 10, 31; PC 29**
See also BRWS 6; CA 1-4R; 149; CAAS 3;
CANR 1, 44; CP 1, 2, 3, 4, 5, 6; DLB 27;
MTCW 1; RGEL 2

Davie, Elspeth 1918-1995 .... **SSC 52**
See also CA 120; 126; 150; CANR 141;
DLB 139

Davies, Ray 1944- .... **CLC 21**
See also CA 116; 146; CANR 92

Davies, Raymond Douglas
See Davies, Ray

Davies, Rhys 1901-1978 .... **CLC 23**
See also CA 9-12R; 81-84; CANR 4; CN 1,
2; DLB 139, 191

Davies, Robertson 1913-1995 .. **CLC 2, 7, 13,
25, 42, 75, 91; WLC 2**
See also BEST 89:2; BPFB 1; CA 1, 33-
36R; 150; CANR 17, 42, 103; CN 1, 2, 3,
4, 5, 6; CPW; DA; DA3; DAB; DAC;
DAM MST, NOV, POP; DLB 68; EWL 3;
HGG; INT CANR-17; MTCW 1, 2;
MTFW 2005; RGEL 2; TWA

Davies, Sir John 1569-1626 .... **LC 85**
See also DLB 172

Davies, Walter C.
See Kornbluth, C(yril) M.

Davies, William Henry 1871-1940 ... **TCLC 5**
See also BRWS 11; CA 104; 179; DLB 19,
174; EWL 3; RGEL 2

Davies, William Robertson
See Davies, Robertson

Da Vinci, Leonardo 1452-1519 ..... **LC 12, 57,
60**
See also AAYA 40

Daviot, Gordon
See Mackintosh, Elizabeth

Davis, Angela Y. 1944- .... **CLC 77**
See also BW 2, 3; CA 57-60; CANR 10,
81; CSW; DA3; DAM MULT; FW

Davis, Angela Yvonne
See Davis, Angela Y.

Davis, B. Lynch
See Bioy Casares, Adolfo; Borges, Jorge
Luis

Davis, Frank Marshall 1905-1987 ... **BLC 1:1**
See also BW 2, 3; CA 125; 123; CANR 42,
80; DAM MULT; DLB 51

Davis, Gordon
See Hunt, E. Howard

Davis, H(arold) L(enoir) 1896-1960 . **CLC 49**
See also ANW; CA 178; 89-92; DLB 9,
206; SATA 114; TCWW 1, 2

Davis, Hart
See Poniatowska, Elena

Davis, Lydia 1947- .... **CLC 306**
See also CA 139; CANR 120, 171, 222;
DLB 130

Davis, Natalie Zemon 1928- .... **CLC 204**
See also CA 53-56; CANR 58, 100, 174

Davis, Rebecca Blaine Harding
See Davis, Rebecca Harding

Davis, Rebecca Harding 1831-1910 . **SSC 38,
109; TCLC 6, 267**
See also AMWS 16; CA 104; 179; DLB 74,
239; FW; NFS 14; RGAL 4; SSFS 26;
TUS

Davis, Richard Harding
1864-1916 .... **TCLC 24**
See also CA 114; 179; DLB 12, 23, 78, 79,
189; DLBD 13; RGAL 4

Davison, Frank Dalby 1893-1970 ..... **CLC 15**
See also CA 217; 116; DLB 260

Davison, Lawrence H.
See Lawrence, D. H.

Davison, Peter (Hubert) 1928-2004 . **CLC 28**
See also CA 9-12R; 234; CAAS 4; CANR
3, 43, 84; CP 1, 2, 3, 4, 5, 6, 7; DLB 5

Davys, Mary 1674-1732 .... **LC 1, 46**
See also DLB 39

Dawson, (Guy) Fielding (Lewis)
1930-2002 .... **CLC 6**
See also CA 85-88; 202; CANR 108; DLB
130; DLBY 2002

Day, Clarence (Shepard, Jr.)
1874-1935 .... **TCLC 25**
See also CA 108; 199; DLB 11

Day, John 1574(?)-1640(?) .... **LC 70**
See also DLB 62, 170; RGEL 2

Day, Thomas 1748-1789 .... **LC 1**
See also DLB 39; YABC 1

Day Lewis, C. 1904-1972 .. **CLC 1, 6, 10; PC
11; TCLC 261**
See also BRWS 3; CA 13-16; 33-36R;
CANR 34; CAP 1; CN 1; CP 1; CWRI 5;
DAM POET; DLB 77; EWL 3; MSW;
MTCW 1, 2; RGEL 2

Day Lewis, Cecil
See Day Lewis, C.

de Andrade, Carlos Drummond
See Drummond de Andrade, Carlos

de Andrade, Mario 1892(?)-1945 ... **TCLC 43**
See also CA 178; DLB 307; EWL 3; HW 2;
LAW; RGWL 2, 3

Deane, Norman
See Creasey, John

Deane, Seamus (Francis) 1940- ...... **CLC 122**
See also CA 118; CANR 42

de Athayde, Alvaro Coelho
See Pessoa, Fernando

de Beauvoir, Simone
See Beauvoir, Simone de

de Beer, P.
See Bosman, Herman Charles

De Botton, Alain 1969- .... **CLC 203**
See also CA 159; CANR 96, 201

de Brissac, Malcolm
See Dickinson, Peter

de Campos, Alvaro
See Pessoa, Fernando

de Chardin, Pierre Teilhard
See Teilhard de Chardin, (Marie Joseph)
Pierre

de Conte, Sieur Louis
See Twain, Mark

de Crenne, Helisenne c. 1510-c.
1560 .... **LC 113**

Dee, John 1527-1608 .... **LC 20**
See also DLB 136, 213

Deer, Sandra 1940- .... **CLC 45**
See also CA 186

De Ferrari, Gabriella 1941- .... **CLC 65**
See also CA 146

de Filippo, Eduardo 1900-1984 ... **TCLC 127**
See also CA 132; 114; EWL 3; MTCW 1;
RGWL 2, 3

Defoe, Daniel 1660(?)-1731 ..... **LC 1, 42, 108,
180; WLC 2**
See also AAYA 27; BRW 3; BRWR 1; BYA
4; CDBLB 1660-1789; CLR 61, 164; DA;
DA3; DAB; DAC; DAM MST, NOV;
DLB 39, 95, 101, 336; JRDA; LAIT 1;
LMFS 1; MAICYA 1, 2; NFS 9, 13, 30;
RGEL 2; SATA 22; TEA; WCH; WLIT 3

de Gouges, Olympe
See de Gouges, Olympe

de Gouges, Olympe 1748-1793 .... **LC 127**
See also DLB 313

de Gourmont, Remy(-Marie-Charles)
See Gourmont, Remy(-Marie-Charles) de

de Gournay, Marie le Jars
1566-1645 .... **LC 98**
See also DLB 327; FW

de Hartog, Jan 1914-2002 .... **CLC 19**
See also CA 1-4R; 210; CANR 1, 192; DFS
12

de Hostos, E. M.
See Hostos (y Bonilla), Eugenio Maria de

de Hostos, Eugenio M.
See Hostos (y Bonilla), Eugenio Maria de

Deighton, Len
See Deighton, Leonard Cyril

Deighton, Leonard Cyril 1929- ..... **CLC 4, 7,
22, 46**
See also AAYA 57, 6; BEST 89:2; BPFB 1;
CA 9-12R; CANR 19, 33, 68; CDBLB
1960- Present; CMW 4; CN 1, 2, 3, 4, 5,
6, 7; CPW; DA3; DAM NOV, POP; DLB
87; MTCW 1, 2; MTFW 2005

Dekker, Thomas 1572(?)-1632 ..... **DC 12; LC
22, 159**
See also CDBLB Before 1660; DAM
DRAM; DLB 62, 172; LMFS 1; RGEL 2

de Laclos, Pierre Ambroise Franois
See Laclos, Pierre-Ambroise Francois

Delacroix, (Ferdinand-Victor-)Eugene
1798-1863 .... **NCLC 133**
See also EW 5

Delafield, E. M.
See Dashwood, Edmee Elizabeth Monica
de la Pasture

de la Mare, Walter (John)
1873-1956 ..... **PC 77; SSC 14; TCLC 4,
53; WLC 2**
See also AAYA 81; CA 163; CDBLB 1914-
1945; CLR 23, 148; CWRI 5; DA3; DAB;
DAC; DAM MST, POET; DLB 19, 153,
162, 255, 284; EWL 3; EXPP; HGG;
MAICYA 1, 2; MTCW 2; MTFW 2005;
PFS 39; RGEL 2; RGSF 2; SATA 16;
SUFW 1; TEA; WCH

de Lamartine, Alphonse
See Lamartine, Alphonse de

Deland, Margaret(ta Wade Campbell)
1857-1945 .... **SSC 162**
See also CA 122; DLB 78; RGAL 4

Delaney, Franey
See O'Hara, John

Delaney, Shelagh 1939- .... **CLC 29; DC 45**
See also CA 17-20R; CANR 30, 67; CBD;
CD 5, 6; CDBLB 1960 to Present; CWD;
DAM DRAM; DFS 7; DLB 13; MTCW 1

Delany, Martin Robison
1812-1885 .... **NCLC 93**
See also DLB 50; RGAL 4

Delany, Mary (Granville Pendarves)
1700-1788 .... **LC 12**

Delany, Samuel R., Jr. 1942- .... **BLC 1:1;
CLC 8, 14, 38, 141, 313**
See also AAYA 24; AFAW 2; BPFB 1; BW
2, 3; CA 81-84; CANR 27, 43, 116, 172;
CN 2, 3, 4, 5, 6, 7; DAM MULT; DLB 8,
33; FANT; MAL 5; MTCW 1, 2; RGAL
4; SATA 92; SCFW 1, 2; SFW 4; SUFW
2

Delany, Samuel Ray
See Delany, Samuel R., Jr.

de la Parra, Ana Teresa Sonojo
See de la Parra, Teresa

de la Parra, Teresa 1890(?)-1936 .... **HLCS 2;
TCLC 185**
See also CA 178; HW 2; LAW

Delaporte, Theophile
See Green, Julien

De La Ramee, Marie Louise
1839-1908 .... **TCLC 43**
See also CA 204; DLB 18, 156; RGEL 2;
SATA 20

de la Roche, Mazo 1879-1961 .... **CLC 14**
See also CA 85-88; CANR 30; DLB 68;
RGEL 2; RHW; SATA 64

De La Salle, Innocent
See Hartmann, Sadakichi

de Laureamont, Comte
See Lautreamont

Delbanco, Nicholas 1942- ..... **CLC 6, 13, 167**
See also CA 17-20R, 189; CAAE 189;
CAAS 2; CANR 29, 55, 116, 150, 204;
CN 7; DLB 6, 234

Delbanco, Nicholas Franklin
See Delbanco, Nicholas

del Castillo, Michel 1933- .... **CLC 38**
See also CA 109; CANR 77

Deledda, Grazia (Cosima)
1875(?)-1936 .... **TCLC 23**
See also CA 123; 205; DLB 264, 329; EWL
3; RGWL 2, 3; WLIT 7

Deleuze, Gilles 1925-1995 .... **TCLC 116**
See also DLB 296

Delgado, Abelardo (Lalo) B(arrientos)
1930-2004 .... **HLC 1**
See also CA 131; 230; CAAS 15; CANR
90; DAM MST, MULT; DLB 82; HW 1,
2

Delibes, Miguel
See Delibes Setien, Miguel

Delibes Setien, Miguel 1920-2010 ...... **CLC 8,
18**
See also CA 45-48; CANR 1, 32; CWW 2;
DLB 322; EWL 3; HW 1; MTCW 1

DeLillo, Don 1936- ..... **CLC 8, 10, 13, 27, 39,
54, 76, 143, 210, 213**
See also AMWC 2; AMWS 6; BEST 89:1;
BPFB 1; CA 81-84; CANR 21, 76, 92,
133, 173; CN 3, 4, 5, 6, 7; CPW; DA3;
DAM NOV, POP; DLB 6, 173; EWL 3;
MAL 5; MTCW 1, 2; MTFW 2005; NFS
28; RGAL 4; TUS

de Lisser, H. G.
See De Lisser, H(erbert) G(eorge)

De Lisser, H(erbert) G(eorge)
1878-1944 .... **TCLC 12**
See also BW 2; CA 109; 152; DLB 117

Deloire, Pierre
See Peguy, Charles (Pierre)

Deloney, Thomas 1543(?)-1600 .... **LC 41; PC
79**
See also DLB 167; RGEL 2

Deloria, Ella (Cara) 1889-1971(?) ..... **NNAL**
See also CA 152; DAM MULT; DLB 175

Deloria, Vine, Jr. 1933-2005 .... **CLC 21, 122;
NNAL**
See also CA 53-56; 245; CANR 5, 20, 48,
98; DAM MULT; DLB 175; MTCW 1;
SATA 21; SATA-Obit 171

Deloria, Vine Victor, Jr.
See Deloria, Vine, Jr.

del Valle-Inclan, Ramon
See Valle-Inclan, Ramon del

Del Vecchio, John M(ichael) 1947- .. **CLC 29**
See also CA 110; DLBD 9

de Man, Paul (Adolph Michel)
1919-1983 .... **CLC 55**
See also CA 128; 111; CANR 61; DLB 67;
MTCW 1, 2

de Mandiargues, Andre Pieyre
See Pieyre de Mandiargues, Andre

DeMarinis, Rick 1934- .... **CLC 54**
See also CA 57-60, 184; CAAE 184; CAAS
24; CANR 9, 25, 50, 160; DLB 218;
TCWW 2

de Maupassant, Guy
See Maupassant, Guy de

Dembry, R. Emmet
See Murfree, Mary Noailles

Demby, William 1922- ...... **BLC 1:1; CLC 53**
See also BW 1, 3; CA 81-84; CANR 81;
DAM MULT; DLB 33

de Menton, Francisco
See Chin, Frank

Demetrius of Phalerum c.
307B.C.- .... **CMLC 34**

Demijohn, Thom
See Disch, Thomas M.

De Mille, James 1833-1880 .... **NCLC 123**
See also DLB 99, 251

Democritus c. 460B.C.-c.
370B.C. .... **CMLC 47, 136**

de Montaigne, Michel
See Montaigne, Michel de

de Montherlant, Henry
See Montherlant, Henry de

Demosthenes 384B.C.-322B.C. ...... **CMLC 13**
See also AW 1; DLB 176; RGWL 2, 3;
WLIT 8

de Musset, (Louis Charles) Alfred
See Musset, Alfred de

de Natale, Francine
See Malzberg, Barry N(athaniel)

de Navarre, Marguerite 1492-1549 .... **LC 61,
167; SSC 85**
See also DLB 327; GFL Beginnings to
1789; RGWL 2, 3

Denby, Edwin (Orr) 1903-1983 .... **CLC 48**
See also CA 138; 110; CP 1

de Nerval, Gerard
See Nerval, Gerard de

Denham, John 1615-1669 .... **LC 73**
See also DLB 58, 126; RGEL 2

Denis, Claire 1948- .... **CLC 286**
See also CA 249

Denis, Julio
See Cortazar, Julio

Denmark, Harrison
See Zelazny, Roger

Dennie, Joseph 1768-1812 .... **NCLC 249**
See also DLB 37, 43, 59, 73

Dennis, John 1658-1734 .... **LC 11, 154**
See also DLB 101; RGEL 2

Dennis, Nigel (Forbes) 1912-1989 ...... **CLC 8**
See also CA 25-28R; 129; CN 1, 2, 3, 4;
DLB 13, 15, 233; EWL 3; MTCW 1

Dent, Lester 1904-1959 .... **TCLC 72**
See also CA 112; 161; CMW 4; DLB 306;
SFW 4

Dentinger, Stephen
See Hoch, Edward D.

De Palma, Brian 1940- .... **CLC 20, 247**
See also CA 109

De Palma, Brian Russell
See De Palma, Brian

de Pizan, Christine
See Christine de Pizan

De Quincey, Thomas 1785-1859 ..... **NCLC 4,
87, 198**
See also BRW 4; CDBLB 1789-1832; DLB
110, 144; RGEL 2

De Ray, Jill
See Moore, Alan

Deren, Eleanora 1908(?)-1961 .. **CLC 16, 102**
See also CA 192; 111

Deren, Maya
See Deren, Eleanora

Derleth, August (William)
1909-1971 .... **CLC 31**
See also BPFB 1; BYA 9, 10; CA 1-4R; 29-
32R; CANR 4; CMW 4; CN 1; DLB 9;
DLBD 17; HGG; SATA 5; SUFW 1

Der Nister 1884-1950 .... **TCLC 56**
See also DLB 333; EWL 3

de Routisie, Albert
See Aragon, Louis

Derrida, Jacques 1930-2004 ...... **CLC 24, 87,
225**
See also CA 124; 127; 232; CANR 76, 98,
133; DLB 242; EWL 3; LMFS 2; MTCW
2; TWA

Derry Down Derry
See Lear, Edward

Dershowitz, Alan 1938- .... **CLC 298**
See also CA 25-28R; CANR 11, 44, 79,
159, 227

Dershowitz, Alan Morton
See Dershowitz, Alan

Dersonnes, Jacques
See Simenon, Georges

Der Stricker c. 1190-c. 1250 .... **CMLC 75**
See also DLB 138

Derzhavin, Gavriil Romanovich
1743-1816 .... **NCLC 215**
See also DLB 150

Desai, Anita 1937- . **CLC 19, 37, 97, 175, 271**
See also AAYA 85; BRWS 5; CA 81-84;
CANR 33, 53, 95, 133; CN 1, 2, 3, 4, 5,
6, 7; CWRI 5; DA3; DAB; DAM NOV;
DLB 271, 323; DNFS 2; EWL 3; FW;
MTCW 1, 2; MTFW 2005; SATA 63, 126;
SSFS 28, 31

Desai, Kiran 1971- .... **CLC 119**
See also BRWS 15; BYA 16; CA 171;
CANR 127; NFS 28

de Saint-Luc, Jean
See Glassco, John

de Saint Roman, Arnaud
See Aragon, Louis

Desbordes-Valmore, Marceline
1786-1859 .... **NCLC 97**
See also DLB 217

Descartes, Rene 1596-1650 ... **LC 20, 35, 150,
202**
See also DLB 268; EW 3; GFL Beginnings
to 1789

Deschamps, Eustache 1340(?)-1404 .. **LC 103**
See also DLB 208

De Sica, Vittorio 1901(?)-1974 .... **CLC 20**
See also CA 117

Desnos, Robert 1900-1945 ...... **TCLC 22, 241**
See also CA 121; 151; CANR 107; DLB
258; EWL 3; LMFS 2

Destouches, Louis-Ferdinand
See Celine, Louis-Ferdinand

De Teran, Lisa St. Aubin
See St. Aubin de Teran, Lisa

de Teran, Lisa St. Aubin
See St. Aubin de Teran, Lisa

de Tolignac, Gaston
See Griffith, D.W.

Deutsch, Babette 1895-1982 .... **CLC 18**
See also BYA 3; CA 1-4R; 108; CANR 4,
79; CP 1, 2, 3; DLB 45; SATA 1; SATA-
Obit 33

de Vere, Edward 1550-1604 .... **LC 193**
See also DLB 172

Devi, Mahasweta 1926- .. **CLC 290; SSC 165**

Deville, Rene
See Kacew, Romain

Drapier, M. B.
See Swift, Jonathan
Drayham, James
See Mencken, H. L.
Drayton, Michael 1563-1631 . **LC 8, 161; PC 98**
See also DAM POET; DLB 121; RGEL 2
Dreadstone, Carl
See Campbell, Ramsey
Dreiser, Theodore 1871-1945 .... **SSC 30, 114; TCLC 10, 18, 35, 83; WLC 2**
See also AMW; AMWC 2; AMWR 2; BYA 15, 16; CA 106; 132; CDALB 1865-1917; DA; DA3; DAC; DAM MST, NOV; DLB 9, 12, 102, 137, 361; DLBD 1; EWL 3; LAIT 2; LMFS 2; MAL 5; MTCW 1, 2; MTFW 2005; NFS 8, 17; RGAL 4; TUS
Dreiser, Theodore Herman Albert
See Dreiser, Theodore
Drexler, Rosalyn 1926- .... **CLC 2, 6**
See also CA 81-84; CAD; CANR 68, 124; CD 5, 6; CWD; MAL 5
Dreyer, Carl Theodor 1889-1968 ...... **CLC 16**
See also CA 116
Drieu la Rochelle, Pierre 1893-1945 .... **TCLC 21**
See also CA 117; 250; DLB 72; EWL 3; GFL 1789 to the Present
Drieu la Rochelle, Pierre-Eugene 1893-1945
See Drieu la Rochelle, Pierre
Drinkwater, John 1882-1937 .... **TCLC 57**
See also CA 109; 149; DLB 10, 19, 149; RGEL 2
Drop Shot
See Cable, George Washington
Droste-Hulshoff, Annette Freiin von 1797-1848 .... **NCLC 3, 133**
See also CDWLB 2; DLB 133; RGSF 2; RGWL 2, 3
Drummond, Walter
See Silverberg, Robert
Drummond, William Henry 1854-1907 .... **TCLC 25**
See also CA 160; DLB 92
Drummond de Andrade, Carlos 1902-1987 .... **CLC 18; TCLC 139**
See also CA 132; 123; DLB 307; EWL 3; LAW; RGWL 2, 3
Drummond of Hawthornden, William 1585-1649 .... **LC 83**
See also DLB 121, 213; RGEL 2
Drury, Allen (Stuart) 1918-1998 .... **CLC 37**
See also CA 57-60; 170; CANR 18, 52; CN 1, 2, 3, 4, 5, 6; INT CANR-18
Druse, Eleanor
See King, Stephen
Dryden, John 1631-1700 ..... **DC 3; LC 3, 21, 115, 188; PC 25; WLC 2**
See also BRW 2; BRWR 3; CDBLB 1660-1789; DA; DAB; DAC; DAM DRAM, MST, POET; DLB 80, 101, 131; EXPP; IDTP; LMFS 1; RGEL 2; TEA; WLIT 3
du Aime, Albert
See Wharton, William
du Aime, Albert William
See Wharton, William
du Bellay, Joachim 1524-1560 .... **LC 92**
See also DLB 327; GFL Beginnings to 1789; RGWL 2, 3
Duberman, Martin 1930- .... **CLC 8**
See also CA 1-4R; CAD; CANR 2, 63, 137, 174; CD 5, 6
Dubie, Norman (Evans) 1945- .... **CLC 36**
See also CA 69-72; CANR 12, 115; CP 3, 4, 5, 6, 7; DLB 120; PFS 12

Du Bois, W. E. B. 1868-1963 .... **BLC 1:1; CLC 1, 2, 13, 64, 96; HR 1:2; TCLC 169; WLC 2**
See also AAYA 40; AFAW 1, 2; AMWC 1; AMWS 2; BW 1, 3; CA 85-88; CANR 34, 82, 132; CDALB 1865-1917; DA; DA3; DAC; DAM MST, MULT, NOV; DLB 47, 50, 91, 246, 284; EWL 3; EXPP; LAIT 2; LMFS 2; MAL 5; MTCW 1, 2; MTFW 2005; NCFS 1; PFS 13; RGAL 4; SATA 42
Du Bois, William Edward Burghardt
See Du Bois, W. E. B.
Dubos, Jean-Baptiste 1670-1742 .... **LC 197**
Dubus, Andre 1936-1999 ..... **CLC 13, 36, 97; SSC 15, 118**
See also AMWS 7; CA 21-24R; 177; CANR 17; CN 5, 6; CSW; DLB 130; INT CANR-17; RGAL 4; SSFS 10; TCLE 1:1
Duca Minimo
See D'Annunzio, Gabriele
Ducharme, Rejean 1941- .... **CLC 74**
See also CA 165; DLB 60
du Chatelet, Emilie 1706-1749 .... **LC 96**
See also DLB 313
Duchen, Claire CLC 65
Duck, Stephen 1705(?)-1756 .... **PC 89**
See also DLB 95; RGEL 2
Duclos, Charles Pinot- 1704-1772 .... **LC 1**
See also GFL Beginnings to 1789
Ducornet, Erica 1943- .... **CLC 232**
See also CA 37-40R; CANR 14, 34, 54, 82; SATA 7
Ducornet, Rikki
See Ducornet, Erica
Dudek, Louis 1918-2001 .... **CLC 11, 19**
See also CA 45-48; 215; CAAS 14; CANR 1; CP 1, 2, 3, 4, 5, 6, 7; DLB 88
Duerrematt, Friedrich
See Durrenmatt, Friedrich
Duffy, Bruce 1953(?)- .... **CLC 50**
See also CA 172
Duffy, Maureen 1933- .... **CLC 37**
See also CA 25-28R; CANR 33, 68; CBD; CN 1, 2, 3, 4, 5, 6, 7; CP 5, 6, 7; CWD; CWP; DFS 15; DLB 14, 310; FW; MTCW 1
Duffy, Maureen Patricia
See Duffy, Maureen
Du Fu
See Tu Fu
Dugan, Alan 1923-2003 .... **CLC 2, 6**
See also CA 81-84; 220; CANR 119; CP 1, 2, 3, 4, 5, 6, 7; DLB 5; MAL 5; PFS 10
du Gard, Roger Martin
See Martin du Gard, Roger
du Guillet, Pernette 1520(?)-1545 ..... **LC 190**
See also DLB 327
Duhamel, Georges 1884-1966 .... **CLC 8**
See also CA 81-84; 25-28R; CANR 35; DLB 65; EWL 3; GFL 1789 to the Present; MTCW 1
du Hault, Jean
See Grindel, Eugene
Dujardin, Edouard (Emile Louis) 1861-1949 .... **TCLC 13**
See also CA 109; DLB 123
Duke, Raoul
See Thompson, Hunter S.
Dulles, John Foster 1888-1959 .... **TCLC 72**
See also CA 115; 149
Dumas, Alexandre (pere) 1802-1870 .... **NCLC 11, 71; WLC 2**
See also AAYA 22; BYA 3; CLR 134; DA; DA3; DAB; DAC; DAM MST, NOV; DLB 119, 192; EW 6; GFL 1789 to the Present; LAIT 1, 2; NFS 14, 19; RGWL 2, 3; SATA 18; TWA; WCH

Dumas, Alexandre (fils) 1824-1895 ...... **DC 1; NCLC 9**
See also DLB 192; GFL 1789 to the Present; RGWL 2, 3
Dumas, Claudine
See Malzberg, Barry N(athaniel)
Dumas, Henry L. 1934-1968 . **BLC 2:1; CLC 6, 62; SSC 107**
See also BW 1; CA 85-88; DLB 41; RGAL 4
du Maurier, Daphne 1907-1989 .. **CLC 6, 11, 59; SSC 18, 129; TCLC 209**
See also AAYA 37; BPFB 1; BRWS 3; CA 5-8R; 128; CANR 6, 55; CMW 4; CN 1, 2, 3, 4; CPW; DA3; DAB; DAC; DAM MST, POP; DLB 191; GL 2; HGG; LAIT 3; MSW; MTCW 1, 2; NFS 12; RGEL 2; RGSF 2; RHW; SATA 27; SATA-Obit 60; SSFS 14, 16; TEA
Du Maurier, George 1834-1896 ..... **NCLC 86**
See also DLB 153, 178; RGEL 2
Dunbar, Alice
See Nelson, Alice Ruth Moore Dunbar
Dunbar, Alice Moore
See Nelson, Alice Ruth Moore Dunbar
Dunbar, Paul Laurence 1872-1906 .... **BLC 1:1; PC 5; SSC 8; TCLC 2, 12; WLC 2**
See also AAYA 75; AFAW 1, 2; AMWS 2; BW 1, 3; CA 104; 124; CANR 79; CDALB 1865-1917; DA; DA3; DAC; DAM MST, MULT, POET; DLB 50, 54, 78; EXPP; MAL 5; PFS 33, 40; RGAL 4; SATA 34
Dunbar, William 1460(?)-1520(?) .... **LC 20; PC 67**
See also BRWS 8; DLB 132, 146; RGEL 2
Dunbar-Nelson, Alice
See Nelson, Alice Ruth Moore Dunbar
Dunbar-Nelson, Alice Moore
See Nelson, Alice Ruth Moore Dunbar
Duncan, Dora Angela
See Duncan, Isadora
Duncan, Isadora 1877(?)-1927 .... **TCLC 68**
See also CA 118; 149
Duncan, Lois 1934- .... **CLC 26**
See also AAYA 4, 34; BYA 6, 8; CA 1-4R; CANR 2, 23, 36, 111; CLR 29, 129; JRDA; MAICYA 1, 2; MAICYAS 1; MTFW 2005; SAAS 2; SATA 1, 36, 75, 133, 141, 219; SATA-Essay 141; WYA; YAW
Duncan, Robert 1919-1988 ... **CLC 1, 2, 4, 7, 15, 41, 55; PC 2, 75**
See also BG 1:2; CA 9-12R; 124; CANR 28, 62; CP 1, 2, 3, 4; DAM POET; DLB 5, 16, 193; EWL 3; MAL 5; MTCW 1, 2; MTFW 2005; PFS 13; RGAL 4; WP
Duncan, Sara Jeannette 1861-1922 .... **TCLC 60**
See also CA 157; DLB 92
Dunlap, William 1766-1839 ..... **NCLC 2, 244**
See also DLB 30, 37, 59; RGAL 4
Dunn, Douglas (Eaglesham) 1942- .... **CLC 6, 40**
See also BRWS 10; CA 45-48; CANR 2, 33, 126; CP 1, 2, 3, 4, 5, 6, 7; DLB 40; MTCW 1
Dunn, Katherine 1945- .... **CLC 71**
See also CA 33-36R; CANR 72; HGG; MTCW 2; MTFW 2005
Dunn, Stephen 1939- .... **CLC 36, 206**
See also AMWS 11; CA 33-36R; CANR 12, 48, 53, 105; CP 3, 4, 5, 6, 7; DLB 105; PFS 21
Dunn, Stephen Elliott
See Dunn, Stephen

Dunne, Finley Peter 1867-1936 ...... **TCLC 28**
See also CA 108; 178; DLB 11, 23; RGAL 4

Dunne, John Gregory 1932-2003 ..... **CLC 28**
See also CA 25-28R; 222; CANR 14, 50; CN 5, 6, 7; DLBY 1980

Dunsany, Lord
See Dunsany, Edward John Moreton Drax Plunkett

Dunsany, Edward John Moreton Drax Plunkett 1878-1957 .... **TCLC 2, 59**
See also CA 104; 148; DLB 10, 77, 153, 156, 255; FANT; MTCW 2; RGEL 2; SFW 4; SUFW 1

Duns Scotus, John
See Scotus, John Duns

Duong, Thu Huong 1947- .... **CLC 273**
See also CA 152; CANR 106, 166; DLB 348; NFS 23

Duong Thu Huong
See Duong, Thu Huong

du Perry, Jean
See Simenon, Georges

Durang, Christopher 1949- .... **CLC 27, 38**
See also CA 105; CAD; CANR 50, 76, 130; CD 5, 6; MTCW 2; MTFW 2005

Durang, Christopher Ferdinand
See Durang, Christopher

Duras, Claire de 1777-1832 .... **NCLC 154**

Duras, Marguerite 1914-1996 . **CLC 3, 6, 11, 20, 34, 40, 68, 100; SSC 40**
See also BPFB 1; CA 25-28R; 151; CANR 50; CWW 2; DFS 21; DLB 83, 321; EWL 3; FL 1:5; GFL 1789 to the Present; IDFW 4; MTCW 1, 2; RGWL 2, 3; TWA

Durban, (Rosa) Pam 1947- .... **CLC 39**
See also CA 123; CANR 98; CSW

Durcan, Paul 1944- .... **CLC 43, 70**
See also CA 134; CANR 123; CP 1, 5, 6, 7; DAM POET; EWL 3

d'Urfe, Honore
See Urfe, Honore d'

Durfey, Thomas 1653-1723 .... **LC 94**
See also DLB 80; RGEL 2

Durkheim, Emile 1858-1917 .... **TCLC 55**
See also CA 249

Durrell, Lawrence 1912-1990 .... **CLC 1, 4, 6, 8, 13, 27, 41**
See also BPFB 1; BRWR 3; BRWS 1; CA 9-12R; 132; CANR 40, 77; CDBLB 1945-1960; CN 1, 2, 3, 4; CP 1, 2, 3, 4, 5; DAM NOV; DLB 15, 27, 204; DLBY 1990; EWL 3; MTCW 1, 2; RGEL 2; SFW 4; TEA

Durrell, Lawrence George
See Durrell, Lawrence

Durrenmatt, Friedrich
See Durrenmatt, Friedrich

Durrenmatt, Friedrich 1921-1990 . **CLC 1, 4, 8, 11, 15, 43, 102**
See also CA 17-20R; CANR 33; CDWLB 2; CMW 4; DAM DRAM; DLB 69, 124; EW 13; EWL 3; MTCW 1, 2; RGHL; RGWL 2, 3

Dutt, Michael Madhusudan
1824-1873 .... **NCLC 118**

Dutt, Toru 1856-1877 .... **NCLC 29**
See also DLB 240

Dwight, Timothy 1752-1817 ... **NCLC 13, 245**
See also DLB 37; RGAL 4

Dworkin, Andrea 1946-2005 ..... **CLC 43, 123**
See also CA 77-80; 238; CAAS 21; CANR 16, 39, 76, 96; FL 1:5; FW; GLL 1; INT CANR-16; MTCW 1, 2; MTFW 2005

Dwyer, Deanna
See Koontz, Dean

Dwyer, K.R.
See Koontz, Dean

Dybek, Stuart 1942- .... **CLC 114; SSC 55**
See also CA 97-100; CANR 39; DLB 130; SSFS 23

Dye, Richard
See De Voto, Bernard (Augustine)

Dyer, Geoff 1958- .... **CLC 149**
See also CA 125; CANR 88, 209

Dyer, George 1755-1841 .... **NCLC 129**
See also DLB 93

Dylan, Bob 1941- ... **CLC 3, 4, 6, 12, 77, 308; PC 37**
See also AMWS 18; CA 41-44R; CANR 108; CP 1, 2, 3, 4, 5, 6, 7; DLB 16

Dyson, John 1943- .... **CLC 70**
See also CA 144

Dzyubin, Eduard Georgievich
1895-1934 .... **TCLC 60**
See also CA 170; DLB 359; EWL 3

E. V. L.
See Lucas, E(dward) V(errall)

Eagleton, Terence
See Eagleton, Terry

Eagleton, Terence Francis
See Eagleton, Terry

Eagleton, Terry 1943- .... **CLC 63, 132**
See also CA 57-60; CANR 7, 23, 68, 115, 198; DLB 242; LMFS 2; MTCW 1, 2; MTFW 2005

Earl of Orrey
See Boyle, Roger

Early, Jack
See Scoppettone, Sandra

Early, Tom
See Kelton, Elmer

East, Michael
See West, Morris L(anglo)

Eastaway, Edward
See Thomas, (Philip) Edward

Eastlake, William (Derry)
1917-1997 .... **CLC 8**
See also CA 5-8R; 158; CAAS 1; CANR 5, 63; CN 1, 2, 3, 4, 5, 6; DLB 6, 206; INT CANR-5; MAL 5; TCWW 1, 2

Eastland, Sam
See Watkins, Paul

Eastman, Charles A(lexander)
1858-1939 .... **NNAL; TCLC 55**
See also CA 179; CANR 91; DAM MULT; DLB 175; YABC 1

Eaton, Edith Maude 1865-1914 ... **AAL; SSC 157; TCLC 232**
See also CA 154; DLB 221, 312; FW

Eaton, (Lillie) Winnifred 1875-1954 .... **AAL**
See also CA 217; DLB 221, 312; RGAL 4

Eberhart, Richard 1904-2005 ...... **CLC 3, 11, 19, 56; PC 76**
See also AMW; CA 1-4R; 240; CANR 2, 125; CDALB 1941-1968; CP 1, 2, 3, 4, 5, 6, 7; DAM POET; DLB 48; MAL 5; MTCW 1; RGAL 4

Eberhart, Richard Ghormley
See Eberhart, Richard

Eberstadt, Fernanda 1960- .... **CLC 39**
See also CA 136; CANR 69, 128

Ebner, Margaret c. 1291-1351 ...... **CMLC 98**

Echegaray (y Eizaguirre), Jose (Maria Waldo) 1832-1916 .... **HLCS 1; TCLC 4**
See also CA 104; CANR 32; DLB 329; EWL 3; HW 1; MTCW 1

Echeverria, (Jose) Esteban (Antonino)
1805-1851 .... **NCLC 18**
See also LAW

Echo
See Proust, Marcel

Eckert, Allan W. 1931- .... **CLC 17**
See also AAYA 18; BYA 2; CA 13-16R; CANR 14, 45; INT CANR-14; MAICYA 2; MAICYAS 1; SAAS 21; SATA 29, 91; SATA-Brief 27

Eckhart, Meister 1260(?)-1327(?) .. **CMLC 9, 80, 131**
See also DLB 115; LMFS 1

Eckmar, F. R.
See de Hartog, Jan

Eco, Umberto 1932- .... **CLC 28, 60, 142, 248**
See also BEST 90:1; BPFB 1; CA 77-80; CANR 12, 33, 55, 110, 131, 195; CPW; CWW 2; DA3; DAM NOV, POP; DLB 196, 242; EWL 3; MSW; MTCW 1, 2; MTFW 2005; NFS 22; RGWL 3; WLIT 7

Eddison, E(ric) R(ucker)
1882-1945 .... **TCLC 15**
See also CA 109; 156; DLB 255; FANT; SFW 4; SUFW 1

Eddy, Mary (Ann Morse) Baker
1821-1910 .... **TCLC 71**
See also CA 113; 174

Edel, (Joseph) Leon 1907-1997 .. **CLC 29, 34**
See also CA 1-4R; 161; CANR 1, 22, 112; DLB 103; INT CANR-22

Eden, Emily 1797-1869 .... **NCLC 10**

Edgar, David 1948- .... **CLC 42; DC 44**
See also CA 57-60; CANR 12, 61, 112; CBD; CD 5, 6; DAM DRAM; DFS 15; DLB 13, 233; MTCW 1

Edgerton, Clyde 1944- .... **CLC 39**
See also AAYA 17; CA 118; 134; CANR 64, 125, 195; CN 7; CSW; DLB 278; INT CA-134; TCLE 1:1; YAW

Edgerton, Clyde Carlyle
See Edgerton, Clyde

Edgeworth, Maria 1768-1849 ... **NCLC 1, 51, 158; SSC 86**
See also BRWS 3; CLR 153; DLB 116, 159, 163; FL 1:3; FW; RGEL 2; SATA 21; TEA; WLIT 3

Edmonds, Paul
See Kuttner, Henry

Edmonds, Walter D(umaux)
1903-1998 .... **CLC 35**
See also BYA 2; CA 5-8R; CANR 2; CWRI 5; DLB 9; LAIT 1; MAICYA 1, 2; MAL 5; RHW; SAAS 4; SATA 1, 27; SATA-Obit 99

Edmondson, Wallace
See Ellison, Harlan

Edson, Margaret 1961- ...... **CLC 199; DC 24**
See also AMWS 18; CA 190; DFS 13; DLB 266

Edson, Russell 1935- .... **CLC 13**
See also CA 33-36R; CANR 115; CP 2, 3, 4, 5, 6, 7; DLB 244; WP

Edwards, Bronwen Elizabeth
See Rose, Wendy

Edwards, Eli
See McKay, Claude

Edwards, G(erald) B(asil)
1899-1976 .... **CLC 25**
See also CA 201; 110

Edwards, Gus 1939- .... **CLC 43**
See also CA 108; INT CA-108

Edwards, Jonathan 1703-1758 .... **LC 7, 54**
See also AMW; DA; DAC; DAM MST; DLB 24, 270; RGAL 4; TUS

Edwards, Marilyn
See French, Marilyn

Edwards, Sarah Pierpont 1710-1758 .. **LC 87**
See also DLB 200

Efron, Marina Ivanovna Tsvetaeva
See Tsvetaeva, Marina

Egeria fl. 4th cent. - .... **CMLC 70**

Eggers, Dave 1970- .... **CLC 241, 318**
See also AAYA 56; CA 198; CANR 138; MTFW 2005

Egoyan, Atom 1960- .... **CLC 151, 291**
See also AAYA 63; CA 157; CANR 151

Ehle, John (Marsden, Jr.) 1925- ...... **CLC 27**
See also CA 9-12R; CSW

Felsen, Henry Gregor 1916-1995 ..... **CLC 17**
See also CA 1-4R; 180; CANR 1; SAAS 2;
SATA 1

Felski, Rita CLC 65

Fenelon, Francois de Pons de Salignac de la
Mothe- 1651-1715 .... **LC 134**
See also DLB 268; EW 3; GFL Beginnings
to 1789

Fenno, Jack
See Calisher, Hortense

Fenollosa, Ernest (Francisco)
1853-1908 .... **TCLC 91**

Fenton, James 1949- .... **CLC 32, 209**
See also CA 102; CANR 108, 160; CP 2, 3,
4, 5, 6, 7; DLB 40; PFS 11

Fenton, James Martin
See Fenton, James

Ferber, Edna 1887-1968 .... **CLC 18, 93**
See also AITN 1; CA 5-8R; 25-28R; CANR
68, 105; DLB 9, 28, 86, 266; MAL 5;
MTCW 1, 2; MTFW 2005; RGAL 4;
RHW; SATA 7; TCWW 1, 2

Ferdousi
See Ferdowsi, Abu'l Qasem

Ferdovsi
See Ferdowsi, Abu'l Qasem

Ferdwsi
See Ferdowsi, Abu'l Qasem

Ferdowsi, Abolghasem Mansour
See Ferdowsi, Abu'l Qasem

Ferdowsi, Abolqasem
See Ferdowsi, Abu'l Qasem

Ferdowsi, Abol-Qasem
See Ferdowsi, Abu'l Qasem

Ferdowsi, Abu'l Qasem
940-1020(?) .... **CMLC 43**
See also CA 276; RGWL 2, 3; WLIT 6

Ferdowsi, A.M.
See Ferdowsi, Abu'l Qasem

Ferdowsi, Hakim Abolghasem
See Ferdowsi, Abu'l Qasem

Ferguson, Helen
See Kavan, Anna

Ferguson, Niall 1964- .... **CLC 134, 250**
See also CA 190; CANR 154, 200

Ferguson, Niall Campbell
See Ferguson, Niall

Ferguson, Samuel 1810-1886 .... **NCLC 33**
See also DLB 32; RGEL 2

Fergusson, Robert 1750-1774 .... **LC 29**
See also DLB 109; RGEL 2

Ferling, Lawrence
See Ferlinghetti, Lawrence

Ferlinghetti, Lawrence 1919(?)- .... **CLC 2, 6,**
10, 27, 111; PC 1
See also AAYA 74; BG 1:2; CA 5-8R; CAD;
CANR 3, 41, 73, 125, 172; CDALB 1941-
1968; CP 1, 2, 3, 4, 5, 6, 7; DA3; DAM
POET; DLB 5, 16; MAL 5; MTCW 1, 2;
MTFW 2005; PFS 28, 41; RGAL 4; WP

Ferlinghetti, Lawrence Monsanto
See Ferlinghetti, Lawrence

Fern, Fanny
See Parton, Sara Payson Willis

Fernandez, Vicente Garcia Huidobro
See Huidobro Fernandez, Vicente Garcia

Fernandez-Armesto, Felipe 1950- .... **CLC 70**
See also CA 142; CANR 93, 153, 189

Fernandez-Armesto, Felipe Fermin Ricardo
See Fernandez-Armesto, Felipe

Fernandez de Lizardi, Jose Joaquin
See Lizardi, Jose Joaquin Fernandez de

Ferre, Rosario 1938- ...... **CLC 139; HLCS 1;**
SSC 36, 106
See also CA 131; CANR 55, 81, 134; CWW
2; DLB 145; EWL 3; HW 1, 2; LAWS 1;
MTCW 2; MTFW 2005; WLIT 1

Ferrer, Gabriel (Francisco Victor) Miro
See Miro (Ferrer), Gabriel (Francisco
Victor)

Ferrier, Susan (Edmonstone)
1782-1854 .... **NCLC 8**
See also DLB 116; RGEL 2

Ferrigno, Robert 1947- .... **CLC 65**
See also CA 140; CANR 125, 161

Ferris, Joshua 1974- .... **CLC 280**
See also CA 262

Ferron, Jacques 1921-1985 .... **CLC 94**
See also CA 117; 129; CCA 1; DAC; DLB
60; EWL 3

Feuchtwanger, Lion 1884-1958 .... **TCLC 3**
See also CA 104; 187; DLB 66; EWL 3;
RGHL

Feuerbach, Ludwig 1804-1872 ..... **NCLC 139**
See also DLB 133

Feuillet, Octave 1821-1890 .... **NCLC 45**
See also DLB 192

Feydeau, Georges 1862-1921 .... **TCLC 22**
See also CA 113; 152; CANR 84; DAM
DRAM; DLB 192; EWL 3; GFL 1789 to
the Present; RGWL 2, 3

Feydeau, Georges Leon JulesMarie
See Feydeau, Georges

Fichte, Johann Gottlieb
1762-1814 .... **NCLC 62**
See also DLB 90

Ficino, Marsilio 1433-1499 .... **LC 12, 152**
See also LMFS 1

Fiedeler, Hans
See Doeblin, Alfred

Fiedler, Leslie A(aron) 1917-2003 ..... **CLC 4,**
13, 24
See also AMWS 13; CA 9-12R; 212; CANR
7, 63; CN 1, 2, 3, 4, 5, 6; DLB 28, 67;
EWL 3; MAL 5; MTCW 1, 2; RGAL 4;
TUS

Field, Andrew 1938- .... **CLC 44**
See also CA 97-100; CANR 25

Field, Eugene 1850-1895 .... **NCLC 3**
See also DLB 23, 42, 140; DLBD 13; MAI-
CYA 1, 2; RGAL 4; SATA 16

Field, Gans T.
See Wellman, Manly Wade

Field, Michael 1915-1971 .... **TCLC 43**
See also CA 29-32R

Fielding, Helen 1958- .... **CLC 146, 217**
See also AAYA 65; CA 172; CANR 127;
DLB 231; MTFW 2005

Fielding, Henry 1707-1754 .... **LC 1, 46, 85,**
151, 154; WLC 2
See also BRW 3; BRWR 1; CDBLB 1660-
1789; DA; DA3; DAB; DAC; DAM
DRAM, MST, NOV; DFS 28; DLB 39,
84, 101; NFS 18, 32; RGEL 2; TEA;
WLIT 3

Fielding, Sarah 1710-1768 .... **LC 1, 44**
See also DLB 39; RGEL 2; TEA

Fields, W. C. 1880-1946 .... **TCLC 80**
See also DLB 44

Fierstein, Harvey 1954- .... **CLC 33**
See also CA 123; 129; CAD; CD 5, 6;
CPW; DA3; DAM DRAM, POP; DFS 6;
DLB 266; GLL; MAL 5

Fierstein, Harvey Forbes
See Fierstein, Harvey

Figes, Eva 1932- .... **CLC 31**
See also CA 53-56; CANR 4, 44, 83, 207;
CN 2, 3, 4, 5, 6; DLB 14, 271; FW;
RGHL

Filippo, Eduardo de
See de Filippo, Eduardo

Finch, Anne 1661-1720 ..... **LC 3, 137; PC 21**
See also BRWS 9; DLB 95; PFS 30; RGEL
2

Finch, Robert (Duer Claydon)
1900-1995 .... **CLC 18**
See also CA 57-60; CANR 9, 24, 49; CP 1,
2, 3, 4, 5, 6; DLB 88

Findley, Timothy 1930-2002 .... **CLC 27, 102;**
SSC 145
See also AMWS 20; CA 25-28R; 206;
CANR 12, 42, 69, 109; CCA 1; CN 4, 5,
6, 7; DAC; DAM MST; DLB 53; FANT;
RHW

Fink, William
See Mencken, H. L.

Firbank, Louis 1942- .... **CLC 21**
See also CA 117

Firbank, (Arthur Annesley) Ronald
1886-1926 .... **TCLC 1**
See also BRWS 2; CA 104; 177; DLB 36;
EWL 3; RGEL 2

Firdaosi
See Ferdowsi, Abu'l Qasem

Firdausi
See Ferdowsi, Abu'l Qasem

Firdavsi, Abulqosimi
See Ferdowsi, Abu'l Qasem

Firdavsii, Abulqosim
See Ferdowsi, Abu'l Qasem

Firdawsi, Abu al-Qasim
See Ferdowsi, Abu'l Qasem

Firdosi
See Ferdowsi, Abu'l Qasem

Firdousi
See Ferdowsi, Abu'l Qasem

Firdousi, Abu'l-Qasim
See Ferdowsi, Abu'l Qasem

Firdovsi, A.
See Ferdowsi, Abu'l Qasem

Firdovsi, Abulgasim
See Ferdowsi, Abu'l Qasem

Firdusi
See Ferdowsi, Abu'l Qasem

Fish, Stanley 1938- .... **CLC 142**
See also CA 112; 132; CANR 90; DLB 67

Fish, Stanley E.
See Fish, Stanley

Fish, Stanley Eugene
See Fish, Stanley

Fisher, Dorothy (Frances) Canfield
1879-1958 .... **TCLC 87**
See also CA 114; 136; CANR 80; CLR 71;
CWRI 5; DLB 9, 102, 284; MAICYA 1,
2; MAL 5; YABC 1

Fisher, M(ary) F(rances) K(ennedy)
1908-1992 .... **CLC 76, 87**
See also AMWS 17; CA 77-80; 138; CANR
44; MTCW 2

Fisher, Roy 1930- .... **CLC 25; PC 121**
See also CA 81-84; CAAS 10; CANR 16;
CP 1, 2, 3, 4, 5, 6, 7; DLB 40

Fisher, Rudolph 1897-1934 ...... **BLC 1:2; HR**
1:2; SSC 25; TCLC 11, 255
See also BW 1, 3; CA 107; 124; CANR 80;
DAM MULT; DLB 51, 102

Fisher, Vardis (Alvero) 1895-1968 .... **CLC 7;**
TCLC 140
See also CA 5-8R; 25-28R; CANR 68; DLB
9, 206; MAL 5; RGAL 4; TCWW 1, 2

Fiske, Tarleton
See Bloch, Robert (Albert)

Fitch, Clarke
See Sinclair, Upton

Fitch, John IV
See Cormier, Robert

Fitzgerald, Captain Hugh
See Baum, L. Frank

FitzGerald, Edward 1809-1883 ...... **NCLC 9,**
153; PC 79
See also BRW 4; DLB 32; RGEL 2

Forsyth, Frederick 1938- .... **CLC 2, 5, 36**
See also BEST 89:4; CA 85-88; CANR 38, 62, 115, 137, 183; CMW 4; CN 3, 4, 5, 6, 7; CPW; DAM NOV, POP; DLB 87; MTCW 1, 2; MTFW 2005

Fort, Paul
See Stockton, Francis Richard

Forten, Charlotte
See Grimke, Charlotte L. Forten

Forten, Charlotte L. 1837-1914
See Grimke, Charlotte L. Forten

Fortinbras
See Grieg, (Johan) Nordahl (Brun)

Foscolo, Ugo 1778-1827 .... **NCLC 8, 97**
See also EW 5; WLIT 7

Fosse, Bob 1927-1987 .... **CLC 20**
See also AAYA 82; CA 110; 123

Fosse, Robert L.
See Fosse, Bob

Foster, Hannah Webster
1758-1840 .... **NCLC 99, 252**
See also DLB 37, 200; RGAL 4

Foster, Stephen Collins
1826-1864 .... **NCLC 26**
See also RGAL 4

Foucault, Michel 1926-1984 . **CLC 31, 34, 69**
See also CA 105; 113; CANR 34; DLB 242; EW 13; EWL 3; GFL 1789 to the Present; GLL 1; LMFS 2; MTCW 1, 2; TWA

Fouque, Friedrich (Heinrich Karl) de la Motte 1777-1843 .... **NCLC 2**
See also DLB 90; RGWL 2, 3; SUFW 1

Fourier, Charles 1772-1837 .... **NCLC 51**

Fournier, Henri-Alban 1886-1914 ... **TCLC 6**
See also CA 104; 179; DLB 65; EWL 3; GFL 1789 to the Present; RGWL 2, 3

Fournier, Pierre 1916-1997 .... **CLC 11**
See also CA 89-92; CANR 16, 40; EWL 3; RGHL

Fowles, John 1926-2005 .... **CLC 1, 2, 3, 4, 6, 9, 10, 15, 33, 87, 287; SSC 33, 128**
See also BPFB 1; BRWS 1; CA 5-8R; 245; CANR 25, 71, 103; CDBLB 1960 to Present; CN 1, 2, 3, 4, 5, 6, 7; DA3; DAB; DAC; DAM MST; DLB 14, 139, 207; EWL 3; HGG; MTCW 1, 2; MTFW 2005; NFS 21; RGEL 2; RHW; SATA 22; SATA-Obit 171; TEA; WLIT 4

Fowles, John Robert
See Fowles, John

Fox, Norma Diane
See Mazer, Norma Fox

Fox, Paula 1923- .... **CLC 2, 8, 121**
See also AAYA 3, 37; BYA 3, 8; CA 73-76; CANR 20, 36, 62, 105, 200; CLR 1, 44, 96; DLB 52; JRDA; MAICYA 1, 2; MTCW 1; NFS 12; SATA 17, 60, 120, 167; WYA; YAW

Fox, William Price, Jr.
See Fox, William Price

Fox, William Price 1926- .... **CLC 22**
See also CA 17-20R; CAAS 19; CANR 11, 142, 189; CSW; DLB 2; DLBY 1981

Foxe, John 1517(?)-1587 .... **LC 14, 166**
See also DLB 132

Frame, Janet 1924-2004 ...... **CLC 2, 3, 6, 22, 66, 96, 237; SSC 29, 127**
See also CA 1-4R; 224; CANR 2, 36, 76, 135, 216; CN 1, 2, 3, 4, 5, 6, 7; CP 2, 3, 4; CWP; EWL 3; MTCW 1,2; RGEL 2; RGSF 2; SATA 119; TWA

Frame, Janet Paterson
See Frame, Janet

France, Anatole 1844-1924 .... **TCLC 9**
See also CA 106; 127; DA3; DAM NOV; DLB 123, 330; EWL 3; GFL 1789 to the Present; MTCW 1, 2; RGWL 2, 3; SUFW 1; TWA

Francis, Claude **CLC 50**
See also CA 192

Francis, Dick 1920-2010 . **CLC 2, 22, 42, 102**
See also AAYA 5, 21; BEST 89:3; BPFB 1; CA 5-8R; CANR 9, 42, 68, 100, 141, 179; CDBLB 1960 to Present; CMW 4; CN 2, 3, 4, 5, 6; DA3; DAM POP; DLB 87; INT CANR-9; MSW; MTCW 1, 2; MTFW 2005

Francis, Paula Marie
See Allen, Paula Gunn

Francis, Richard Stanley
See Francis, Dick

Francis, Robert (Churchill)
1901-1987 .... **CLC 15; PC 34**
See also AMWS 9; CA 1-4R; 123; CANR 1; CP 1, 2, 3, 4; EXPP; PFS 12; TCLE 1:1

Francis, Lord Jeffrey
See Jeffrey, Francis

Franco, Veronica 1546-1591 .... **LC 171**
See also WLIT 7

Frank, Anne 1929-1945 ... **TCLC 17; WLC 2**
See also AAYA 12; BYA 1; CA 113; 133; CANR 68; CLR 101; DA; DA3; DAB; DAC; DAM MST; LAIT 4; MAICYA 2; MAICYAS 1; MTCW 1, 2; MTFW 2005; NCFS 2; RGHL; SATA 87; SATA-Brief 42; WYA; YAW

Frank, Annelies Marie
See Frank, Anne

Frank, Bruno 1887-1945 .... **TCLC 81**
See also CA 189; DLB 118; EWL 3

Frank, Elizabeth 1945- .... **CLC 39**
See also CA 121; 126; CANR 78, 150; INT CA-126

Frankl, Viktor E(mil) 1905-1997 ...... **CLC 93**
See also CA 65-68; 161; RGHL

Franklin, Benjamin
See Hasek, Jaroslav

Franklin, Benjamin 1706-1790 .. **LC 25, 134; WLCS**
See also AMW; CDALB 1640-1865; DA; DA3; DAB; DAC; DAM MST; DLB 24, 43, 73, 183; LAIT 1; RGAL 4; TUS

Franklin, Madeleine
See L'Engle, Madeleine

Franklin, Madeleine L'Engle
See L'Engle, Madeleine

Franklin, Madeleine L'Engle Camp
See L'Engle, Madeleine

Franklin, (Stella Maria Sarah) Miles (Lampe) 1879-1954 .... **TCLC 7**
See also CA 104; 164; DLB 230; FW; MTCW 2; RGEL 2; TWA

Franzen, Jonathan 1959- .... **CLC 202, 309**
See also AAYA 65; AMWS 20; CA 129; CANR 105, 166, 219; NFS 40

Fraser, Antonia 1932- .... **CLC 32, 107**
See also AAYA 57; CA 85-88; CANR 44, 65, 119, 164, 225; CMW; DLB 276; MTCW 1, 2; MTFW 2005; SATA-Brief 32

Fraser, George MacDonald
1925-2008 .... **CLC 7**
See also AAYA 48; CA 45-48, 180; 268; CAAE 180; CANR 2, 48, 74, 192; DLB 352; MTCW 2; RHW

Fraser, Sylvia 1935- .... **CLC 64**
See also CA 45-48; CANR 1, 16, 60; CCA 1

Frater Perdurabo
See Crowley, Edward Alexander

Frayn, Michael 1933- .... **CLC 3, 7, 31, 47, 176, 315; DC 27**
See also AAYA 69; BRWC 2; BRWS 7; CA 5-8R; CANR 30, 69, 114, 133, 166, 229; CBD; CD 5, 6; CN 1, 2, 3, 4, 5, 6, 7;

DAM DRAM, NOV; DFS 22, 28; DLB 13, 14, 194, 245; FANT; MTCW 1, 2; MTFW 2005; SFW 4

Fraze, Candida 1945- .... **CLC 50**
See also CA 126

Fraze, Candida Merrill
See Fraze, Candida

Frazer, Andrew
See Marlowe, Stephen

Frazer, J(ames) G(eorge)
1854-1941 .... **TCLC 32**
See also BRWS 3; CA 118; NCFS 5

Frazer, Robert Caine
See Creasey, John

Frazer, Sir James George
See Frazer, J(ames) G(eorge)

Frazier, Charles 1950- .... **CLC 109, 224**
See also AAYA 34; CA 161; CANR 126, 170; CSW; DLB 292; MTFW 2005; NFS 25

Frazier, Charles R.
See Frazier, Charles

Frazier, Charles Robinson
See Frazier, Charles

Frazier, Ian 1951- .... **CLC 46**
See also CA 130; CANR 54, 93, 193, 227

Frederic, Harold 1856-1898 ... **NCLC 10, 175**
See also AMW; DLB 12, 23; DLBD 13; MAL 5; NFS 22; RGAL 4

Frederick, John
See Faust, Frederick

Frederick the Great 1712-1786 .... **LC 14**

Fredro, Aleksander 1793-1876 .... **NCLC 8**

Freeling, Nicolas 1927-2003 .... **CLC 38**
See also CA 49-52; 218; CAAS 12; CANR 1, 17, 50, 84; CMW 4; CN 1, 2, 3, 4, 5, 6; DLB 87

Freeman, Douglas Southall
1886-1953 .... **TCLC 11**
See also CA 109; 195; DLB 17; DLBD 17

Freeman, Judith 1946- .... **CLC 55**
See also CA 148; CANR 120, 179; DLB 256

Freeman, Mary E(leanor) Wilkins
1852-1930 .... **SSC 1, 47, 113; TCLC 9**
See also CA 106; 177; DLB 12, 78, 221; EXPS; FW; HGG; MBL; RGAL 4; RGSF 2; SSFS 4, 8, 26; SUFW 1; TUS

Freeman, R(ichard) Austin
1862-1943 .... **TCLC 21**
See also CA 113; CANR 84; CMW 4; DLB 70

French, Albert 1943- .... **CLC 86**
See also BW 3; CA 167

French, Antonia
See Kureishi, Hanif

French, Marilyn 1929-2009 . **CLC 10, 18, 60, 177**
See also BPFB 1; CA 69-72; 286; CANR 3, 31, 134, 163, 220; CN 5, 6, 7; CPW; DAM DRAM, NOV, POP; FL 1:5; FW; INT CANR-31; MTCW 1, 2; MTFW 2005

French, Paul
See Asimov, Isaac

Freneau, Philip Morin 1752-1832 .. **NCLC 1, 111, 253**
See also AMWS 2; DLB 37, 43; RGAL 4

Freud, Sigmund 1856-1939 .... **TCLC 52**
See also CA 115; 133; CANR 69; DLB 296; EW 8; EWL 3; LATS 1:1; MTCW 1, 2; MTFW 2005; NCFS 3; TWA

Freytag, Gustav 1816-1895 .... **NCLC 109**
See also DLB 129

Friedan, Betty 1921-2006 .... **CLC 74**
See also CA 65-68; 248; CANR 18, 45, 74; DLB 246; FW; MTCW 1, 2; MTFW 2005; NCFS 5

Friedan, Betty Naomi
See Friedan, Betty

Friedlander, Saul
See Friedlander, Saul
Friedlander, Saul 1932- .... **CLC 90**
See also CA 117; 130; CANR 72, 214;
RGHL
Friedman, Bernard Harper
See Friedman, B.H.
Friedman, B.H. 1926-2011 .... **CLC 7**
See also CA 1-4R; CANR 3, 48
Friedman, Bruce Jay 1930- ...... **CLC 3, 5, 56**
See also CA 9-12R; CAD; CANR 25, 52,
101, 212; CD 5, 6; CN 1, 2, 3, 4, 5, 6, 7;
DLB 2, 28, 244; INT CANR-25; MAL 5;
SSFS 18
Friel, Brian 1929- .. **CLC 5, 42, 59, 115, 253;**
DC 8; SSC 76
See also BRWS 5; CA 21-24R; CANR 33,
69, 131; CBD; CD 5, 6; DFS 11; DLB
13, 319; EWL 3; MTCW 1; RGEL 2; TEA
Friis-Baastad, Babbis Ellinor
1921-1970 .... **CLC 12**
See also CA 17-20R; 134; SATA 7
Frisch, Max 1911-1991 ...... **CLC 3, 9, 14, 18,**
32, 44; TCLC 121
See also CA 85-88; 134; CANR 32, 74; CD-
WLB 2; DAM DRAM, NOV; DFS 25;
DLB 69, 124; EW 13; EWL 3; MTCW 1,
2; MTFW 2005; RGHL; RGWL 2, 3
Froehlich, Peter
See Gay, Peter
Fromentin, Eugene (Samuel Auguste)
1820-1876 .... **NCLC 10, 125**
See also DLB 123, 366; GFL 1789 to the
Present
Frost, Frederick
See Faust, Frederick
Frost, Robert 1874-1963 . **CLC 1, 3, 4, 9, 10,**
13, 15, 26, 34, 44; PC 1, 39, 71; TCLC
236; WLC 2
See also AAYA 21; AMW; AMWR 1; CA
89-92; CANR 33; CDALB 1917-1929;
CLR 67; DA; DA3; DAB; DAC; DAM
MST, POET; DLB 54, 284, 342; DLBD
7; EWL 3; EXPP; MAL 5; MTCW 1, 2;
MTFW 2005; PAB; PFS 1, 2, 3, 4, 5, 6,
7, 10, 13, 32, 35, 41; RGAL 4; SATA 14;
TUS; WP; WYA
Frost, Robert Lee
See Frost, Robert
Froude, James Anthony
1818-1894 .... **NCLC 43**
See also DLB 18, 57, 144
Froy, Herald
See Waterhouse, Keith
Fry, Christopher 1907-2005 .. **CLC 2, 10, 14;**
DC 36
See also BRWS 3; CA 17-20R; 240; CAAS
23; CANR 9, 30, 74, 132; CBD; CD 5, 6;
CP 1, 2, 3, 4, 5, 6, 7; DAM DRAM; DLB
13; EWL 3; MTCW 1, 2; MTFW 2005;
RGEL 2; SATA 66; TEA
Frye, (Herman) Northrop
1912-1991 .... **CLC 24, 70; TCLC 165**
See also CA 5-8R; 133; CANR 8, 37; DLB
67, 68, 246; EWL 3; MTCW 1, 2; MTFW
2005; RGAL 4; TWA
Fuchs, Daniel 1909-1993 .... **CLC 8, 22**
See also CA 81-84; CAAS 5; CANR
40; CN 1, 2, 3, 4, 5; DLB 9, 26, 28;
DLBY 1993; MAL 5
Fuchs, Daniel 1934- .... **CLC 34**
See also CA 37-40R; CANR 14, 48
Fuentes, Carlos 1928- .. **CLC 3, 8, 10, 13, 22,**
41, 60, 113, 288; HLC 1; SSC 24, 125;
WLC 2
See also AAYA 4, 45; AITN 2; BPFB 1;
CA 69-72; CANR 10, 32, 68, 104, 138,
197; CDWLB 3; CWW 2; DA; DA3;
DAB; DAC; DAM MST, MULT, NOV;
DLB 113; DNFS 2; EWL 3; HW 1, 2;

LAIT 3; LATS 1:2; LAW; LAWS 1;
LMFS 2; MTCW 1, 2; MTFW 2005; NFS
8; RGSF 2; RGWL 2, 3; TWA; WLIT 1
Fuentes, Gregorio Lopez y
See Lopez y Fuentes, Gregorio
Fuentes Macias, Carlos Manuel
See Fuentes, Carlos
Fuertes, Gloria 1918-1998 .... **PC 27**
See also CA 178, 180; DLB 108; HW 2;
SATA 115
Fugard, Athol 1932- .... **CLC 5, 9, 14, 25, 40,**
80, 211; DC 3
See also AAYA 17; AFW; BRWS 15; CA
85-88; CANR 32, 54, 118; CD 5, 6; DAM
DRAM; DFS 3, 6, 10, 24; DLB 225;
DNFS 1, 2; EWL 3; LATS 1:2; MTCW 1;
MTFW 2005; RGEL 2; WLIT 2
Fugard, Harold Athol
See Fugard, Athol
Fugard, Sheila 1932- .... **CLC 48**
See also CA 125
Fuguet, Alberto 1964- .... **CLC 308**
See also CA 170; CANR 144
Fujiwara no Teika 1162-1241 .... **CMLC 73**
See also DLB 203
Fukuyama, Francis 1952- .... **CLC 131, 320**
See also CA 140; CANR 72, 125, 170
Fuller, Charles (H.), (Jr.) 1939- ..... **BLC 1:2;**
CLC 25; DC 1
See also BW 2; CA 108; 112; CAD; CANR
87; CD 5, 6; DAM DRAM, MULT; DFS
8; DLB 38, 266; EWL 3; INT CA-112;
MAL 5; MTCW 1
Fuller, Henry Blake 1857-1929 .... **TCLC 103**
See also CA 108; 177; DLB 12; RGAL 4
Fuller, John (Leopold) 1937- .... **CLC 62**
See also CA 21-24R; CANR 9, 44; CP 1, 2,
3, 4, 5, 6, 7; DLB 40
Fuller, Margaret 1810-1850 ...... **NCLC 5, 50,**
211
See also AMWS 2; CDALB 1640-1865;
DLB 1, 59, 73, 183, 223, 239; FW; LMFS
1; SATA 25
Fuller, Roy (Broadbent) 1912-1991 ... **CLC 4,**
28
See also BRWS 7; CA 5-8R; 135; CAAS
10; CANR 53, 83; CN 1, 2, 3, 4, 5; CP 1,
2, 3, 4, 5; CWRI 5; DLB 15, 20; EWL 3;
RGEL 2; SATA 87
Fuller, Sarah Margaret
See Fuller, Margaret
Fuller, Thomas 1608-1661 .... **LC 111**
See also DLB 151
Fulton, Alice 1952- .... **CLC 52**
See also CA 116; CANR 57, 88, 200; CP 5,
6, 7; CWP; DLB 193; PFS 25
Fundi
See Baraka, Amiri
Furey, Michael
See Ward, Arthur Henry Sarsfield
Furphy, Joseph 1843-1912 .... **TCLC 25**
See also CA 163; DLB 230; EWL 3; RGEL
2
Furst, Alan 1941- .... **CLC 255**
See also CA 69-72; CANR 12, 34, 59, 102,
159, 193; DLB 350; DLBY 01
Fuson, Robert H(enderson) 1927- .... **CLC 70**
See also CA 89-92; CANR 103
Fussell, Paul 1924- .... **CLC 74**
See also BEST 90:1; CA 17-20R; CANR 8,
21, 35, 69, 135; INT CANR-21; MTCW
1, 2; MTFW 2005
Futabatei, Shimei 1864-1909 .... **TCLC 44**
See also CA 162; DLB 180; EWL 3; MJW
Futabatei Shimei
See Futabatei, Shimei
Futrelle, Jacques 1875-1912 .... **TCLC 19**
See also CA 113; 155; CMW 4

GAB
See Russell, George William
Gaberman, Judie Angell
See Angell, Judie
Gaboriau, Emile 1835-1873 .... **NCLC 14**
See also CMW 4; MSW
Gadda, Carlo Emilio 1893-1973 ...... **CLC 11;**
TCLC 144
See also CA 89-92; DLB 177; EWL 3;
WLIT 7
Gaddis, William 1922-1998 ... **CLC 1, 3, 6, 8,**
10, 19, 43, 86
See also AMWS 4; BPFB 1; CA 17-20R;
172; CANR 21, 48, 148; CN 1, 2, 3, 4, 5,
6; DLB 2, 278; EWL 3; MAL 5; MTCW
1, 2; MTFW 2005; RGAL 4
Gage, Walter
See Inge, William (Motter)
Gaiman, Neil 1960- .... **CLC 319**
See also AAYA 19, 42, 82; CA 133; CANR
81, 129, 188; CLR 109; DLB 261; HGG;
MTFW 2005; SATA 85, 146, 197, 228;
SFW 4; SUFW 2
Gaiman, Neil Richard
See Gaiman, Neil
Gaines, Ernest J. 1933- ..... **BLC 1:2; CLC 3,**
11, 18, 86, 181, 300; SSC 68, 137
See also AAYA 18; AFAW 1, 2; AITN 1;
BPFB 2; BW 2, 3; BYA 6; CA 9-12R;
CANR 6, 24, 42, 75, 126; CDALB 1968-
1988; CLR 62; CN 1, 2, 3, 4, 5, 6, 7;
CSW; DA3; DAM MULT; DLB 2, 33,
152; DLBY 1980; EWL 3; EXPN; LAIT
5; LATS 1:2; MAL 5; MTCW 1, 2;
MTFW 2005; NFS 5, 7, 16; RGAL 4;
RGSF 2; RHW; SATA 86; SSFS 5; YAW
Gaines, Ernest James
See Gaines, Ernest J.
Gaitskill, Mary 1954- .... **CLC 69, 300**
See also CA 128; CANR 61, 152, 208; DLB
244; TCLE 1:1
Gaitskill, Mary Lawrence
See Gaitskill, Mary
Gaius Suetonius Tranquillus
See Suetonius
Galdos, Benito Perez
See Perez Galdos, Benito
Gale, Zona 1874-1938 .... **DC 30; SSC 159;**
TCLC 7
See also CA 105; 153; CANR 84; DAM
DRAM; DFS 17; DLB 9, 78, 228; RGAL
4
Galeano, Eduardo 1940- ... **CLC 72; HLCS 1**
See also CA 29-32R; CANR 13, 32, 100,
163, 211; HW 1
Galeano, Eduardo Hughes
See Galeano, Eduardo
Galiano, Juan Valera y Alcala
See Valera y Alcala-Galiano, Juan
Galilei, Galileo 1564-1642 .... **LC 45, 188**
Gallagher, Tess 1943- .... **CLC 18, 63; PC 9**
See also CA 106; CP 3, 4, 5, 6, 7; CWP;
DAM POET; DLB 120, 212, 244; PFS 16
Gallant, Mavis 1922- ..... **CLC 7, 18, 38, 172,**
288; SSC 5, 78
See also CA 69-72; CANR 29, 69, 117;
CCA 1; CN 1, 2, 3, 4, 5, 6, 7; DAC; DAM
MST; DLB 53; EWL 3; MTCW 1, 2;
MTFW 2005; RGEL 2; RGSF 2
Gallant, Roy A(rthur) 1924- .... **CLC 17**
See also CA 5-8R; CANR 4, 29, 54, 117;
CLR 30; MAICYA 1, 2; SATA 4, 68, 110
Gallico, Paul 1897-1976 .... **CLC 2**
See also AITN 1; CA 5-8R; 69-72; CANR
23; CN 1, 2; DLB 9, 171; FANT; MAI-
CYA 1, 2; SATA 13
Gallico, Paul William
See Gallico, Paul

Gallo, Max Louis 1932- .... **CLC 95**
   See also CA 85-88

Gallois, Lucien
   See Desnos, Robert

Gallup, Ralph
   See Whitemore, Hugh (John)

Galsworthy, John 1867-1933 .... **SSC 22;**
   TCLC 1, 45; WLC 2
   See also BRW 6; CA 104; 141; CANR 75;
   CDBLB 1890-1914; DA; DA3; DAB;
   DAC; DAM DRAM, MST, NOV; DLB
   10, 34, 98, 162, 330; DLBD 16; EWL 3;
   MTCW 2; RGEL 2; SSFS 3; TEA

Galt, John 1779-1839 .... **NCLC 1, 110**
   See also DLB 99, 116, 159; RGEL 2; RGSF
   2

Galvin, James 1951- .... **CLC 38**
   See also CA 108; CANR 26

Gamboa, Federico 1864-1939 .... **TCLC 36**
   See also CA 167; HW 2; LAW

Gandhi, M. K.
   See Gandhi, Mohandas Karamchand

Gandhi, Mahatma
   See Gandhi, Mohandas Karamchand

Gandhi, Mohandas Karamchand
   1869-1948 .... **TCLC 59**
   See also CA 121; 132; DA3; DAM MULT;
   DLB 323; MTCW 1, 2

Gann, Ernest Kellogg 1910-1991 ..... **CLC 23**
   See also AITN 1; BPFB 2; CA 1-4R; 136;
   CANR 1, 83; RHW

Gao Xingjian
   See Xingjian, Gao

Garber, Eric
   See Holleran, Andrew

Garber, Esther
   See Lee, Tanith

Garcia, Cristina 1958- .... **CLC 76**
   See also AMWS 11; CA 141; CANR 73,
   130, 172; CN 7; DLB 292; DNFS 1; EWL
   3; HW 2; LLW; MTFW 2005; NFS 38;
   SATA 208

Garcia Lorca, Federico 1898-1936 ...... **DC 2;**
   HLC 2; PC 3; TCLC 1, 7, 49, 181,
   197; WLC 2
   See also AAYA 46; CA 104; 131; CANR
   81; DA; DA3; DAB; DAC; DAM DRAM,
   MST, MULT, POET; DFS 4; DLB 108;
   EW 11; EWL 3; HW 1, 2; LATS 1:2;
   MTCW 1, 2; MTFW 2005; PFS 20, 31,
   38; RGWL 2, 3; TWA; WP

Garcia Marquez, Gabriel 1928- .... **CLC 2, 3,**
   8, 10, 15, 27, 47, 55, 68, 170, 254; HLC
   1; SSC 8, 83, 162; WLC 3
   See also AAYA 3, 33; BEST 89:1, 90:4;
   BPFB 2; BYA 12, 16; CA 33-36R; CANR
   10, 28, 50, 75, 82, 128, 204; CDWLB 3;
   CPW; CWW 2; DA; DA3; DAB; DAC;
   DAM MST, MULT, NOV, POP; DLB 113,
   330; DNFS 1, 2; EWL 3; EXPN; EXPS;
   HW 1, 2; LAIT 2; LATS 1:2; LAW;
   LAWS 1; LMFS 2; MTCW 1, 2; MTFW
   2005; NCFS 3; NFS 1, 5, 10; RGSF 2;
   RGWL 2, 3; SSFS 1, 6, 16, 21; TWA;
   WLIT 1

Garcia Marquez, Gabriel Jose
   See Garcia Marquez, Gabriel

Garcia Marquez, Gabriel Jose
   See Garcia Marquez, Gabriel

Garcilaso de la Vega, El Inca
   1539-1616 .... **HLCS 1; LC 127**
   See also DLB 318; LAW

Gard, Janice
   See Latham, Jean Lee

Gard, Roger Martin du
   See Martin du Gard, Roger

Gardam, Jane 1928- .... **CLC 43**
   See also CA 49-52; CANR 2, 18, 33, 54,
   106, 167, 206; CLR 12; DLB 14, 161,
   231; MAICYA 1, 2; MTCW 1; SAAS 9;
   SATA 39, 76, 130; SATA-Brief 28; YAW

Gardam, Jane Mary
   See Gardam, Jane

Gardens, S. S.
   See Snodgrass, W. D.

Gardner, Herb(ert George)
   1934-2003 .... **CLC 44**
   See also CA 149; 220; CAD; CANR 119;
   CD 5, 6; DFS 18, 20

Gardner, John, Jr. 1933-1982 ... **CLC 2, 3, 5,**
   7, 8, 10, 18, 28, 34; SSC 7; TCLC 195
   See also AAYA 45; AITN 1; AMWS 6;
   BPFB 2; CA 65-68; 107; CANR 33, 73;
   CDALBS; CN 2, 3; CPW; DA3; DAM
   NOV, POP; DLB 2; DLBY 1982; EWL 3;
   FANT; LATS 1:2; MAL 5; MTCW 1, 2;
   MTFW 2005; NFS 3; RGAL 4; RGSF 2;
   SATA 40; SATA-Obit 31; SSFS 8

Gardner, John 1926-2007 .... **CLC 30**
   See also CA 103; 263; CANR 15, 69, 127,
   183; CMW 4; CPW; DAM POP; MTCW
   1

Gardner, John Champlin, Jr.
   See Gardner, John, Jr.

Gardner, John Edmund
   See Gardner, John

Gardner, Miriam
   See Bradley, Marion Zimmer

Gardner, Noel
   See Kuttner, Henry

Gardons, S.S.
   See Snodgrass, W. D.

Garfield, Leon 1921-1996 .... **CLC 12**
   See also AAYA 8, 69; BYA 1, 3; CA 17-
   20R; 152; CANR 38, 41, 78; CLR 21,
   166; DLB 161; JRDA; MAICYA 1, 2;
   MAICYAS 1; SATA 1, 32, 76; SATA-Obit
   90; TEA; WYA; YAW

Garland, (Hannibal) Hamlin
   1860-1940 ... **SSC 18, 117; TCLC 3, 256**
   See also CA 104; DLB 12, 71, 78, 186;
   MAL 5; RGAL 4; RGSF 2; TCWW 1, 2

Garneau, (Hector de) Saint-Denys
   1912-1943 .... **TCLC 13**
   See also CA 111; DLB 88

Garner, Alan 1934- .... **CLC 17**
   See also AAYA 18; BYA 3, 5; CA 73-76,
   178; CAAE 178; CANR 15, 64, 134; CLR
   20, 130; CPW; DAB; DAM POP; DLB
   161, 261; FANT; MAICYA 1, 2; MTCW
   1, 2; MTFW 2005; SATA 18, 69; SATA-
   Essay 108; SUFW 1, 2; YAW

Garner, Helen 1942- .... **SSC 135**
   See also CA 124; 127; CANR 71, 206; CN
   4, 5, 6, 7; DLB 325; GLL 2; RGSF 2

Garner, Hugh 1913-1979 .... **CLC 13**
   See also CA 69-72; CANR 31; CCA 1; CN
   1, 2; DLB 68

Garnett, David 1892-1981 .... **CLC 3**
   See also CA 5-8R; 103; CANR 17, 79; CN
   1, 2; DLB 34; FANT; MTCW 2; RGEL 2;
   SFW 4; SUFW 1

Garnier, Robert c. 1545-1590 .... **LC 119**
   See also DLB 327; GFL Beginnings to 1789

Garrett, George 1929-2008 ... **CLC 3, 11, 51;**
   SSC 30
   See also AMWS 7; BPFB 2; CA 1-4R, 202;
   272; CAAE 202; CAAS 5; CANR 1, 42,
   67, 109, 199; CN 1, 2, 3, 4, 5, 6, 7; CP 1,
   2, 3, 4, 5, 6, 7; CSW; DLB 2, 5, 130, 152;
   DLBY 1983

Garrett, George P.
   See Garrett, George

Garrett, George Palmer
   See Garrett, George

Garrett, George Palmer, Jr.
   See Garrett, George

Garrick, David 1717-1779 .... **LC 15, 156**
   See also DAM DRAM; DLB 84, 213;
   RGEL 2

Garrigue, Jean 1914-1972 .... **CLC 2, 8**
   See also CA 5-8R; 37-40R; CANR 20; CP
   1; MAL 5

Garrison, Frederick
   See Sinclair, Upton

Garrison, William Lloyd
   1805-1879 .... **NCLC 149**
   See also CDALB 1640-1865; DLB 1, 43,
   235

Garro, Elena 1920(?)-1998 .. **HLCS 1; TCLC**
   153
   See also CA 131; 169; CWW 2; DLB 145;
   EWL 3; HW 1; LAWS 1; WLIT 1

Garshin, Vsevolod Mikhailovich
   1855-1888 .... **NCLC 257**
   See also DLB 277

Garth, Will
   See Hamilton, Edmond; Kuttner, Henry

Garvey, Marcus (Moziah, Jr.)
   1887-1940 ..... **BLC 1:2; HR 1:2; TCLC**
   41
   See also BW 1; CA 120; 124; CANR 79;
   DAM MULT; DLB 345

Gary, Romain
   See Kacew, Romain

Gascar, Pierre
   See Fournier, Pierre

Gascoigne, George 1539-1577 .... **LC 108**
   See also DLB 136; RGEL 2

Gascoyne, David (Emery)
   1916-2001 .... **CLC 45**
   See also CA 65-68; 200; CANR 10, 28, 54;
   CP 1, 2, 3, 4, 5, 6, 7; DLB 20; MTCW 1;
   RGEL 2

Gaskell, Elizabeth 1810-1865 ... **NCLC 5, 70,**
   97, 137, 214; SSC 25, 97
   See also AAYA 80; BRW 5; BRWR 3; CD-
   BLB 1832-1890; DAB; DAM MST; DLB
   21, 144, 159; RGEL 2; RGSF 2; TEA

Gass, William H. 1924- . **CLC 1, 2, 8, 11, 15,**
   39, 132; SSC 12
   See also AMWS 6; CA 17-20R; CANR 30,
   71, 100; CN 1, 2, 3, 4, 5, 6, 7; DLB 2,
   227; EWL 3; MAL 5; MTCW 1, 2;
   MTFW 2005; RGAL 4

Gassendi, Pierre 1592-1655 .... **LC 54**
   See also GFL Beginnings to 1789

Gasset, Jose Ortega y
   See Ortega y Gasset, Jose

Gates, Henry Louis, Jr. 1950- ... **BLCS; CLC**
   65
   See also AMWS 20; BW 2, 3; CA 109;
   CANR 25, 53, 75, 125, 203; CSW; DA3;
   DAM MULT; DLB 67; EWL 3; MAL 5;
   MTCW 2; MTFW 2005; RGAL 4

Gatos, Stephanie
   See Katz, Steve

Gautier, Theophile 1811-1872 ... **NCLC 1, 59,**
   243; PC 18; SSC 20
   See also DAM POET; DLB 119, 366; EW
   6; GFL 1789 to the Present; RGWL 2, 3;
   SUFW; TWA

Gautreaux, Tim 1947- .... **CLC 270; SSC 125**
   See also CA 187; CANR 207; CSW; DLB
   292

Gautreaux, Tim Martin
   See Gautreaux, Tim

Gay, John 1685-1732 ...... **DC 39; LC 49, 176**
   See also BRW 3; DAM DRAM; DLB 84,
   95; RGEL 2; WLIT 3

Gay, Oliver
   See Gogarty, Oliver St. John

Goldman, William W.
See Goldman, William

Goldmann, Lucien 1913-1970 .... **CLC 24**
See also CA 25-28; CAP 2

Goldoni, Carlo 1707-1793 .... **LC 4, 152**
See also DAM DRAM; DFS 27; EW 4;
RGWL 2, 3; WLIT 7

Goldsberry, Steven 1949- .... **CLC 34**
See also CA 131

Goldsmith, Oliver 1730(?)-1774 .... **DC 8; LC 2, 48, 122; PC 77; WLC 3**
See also BRW 3; CDBLB 1660-1789; DA;
DAB; DAC; DAM DRAM, MST, NOV,
POET; DFS 1; DLB 39, 89, 104, 109, 142,
336; IDTP; RGEL 2; SATA 26; TEA;
WLIT 3

Goldsmith, Peter
See Priestley, J(ohn) B(oynton)

Goldstein, Rebecca 1950- .... **CLC 239**
See also CA 144; CANR 99, 165, 214;
TCLE 1:1

Goldstein, Rebecca Newberger
See Goldstein, Rebecca

Gombrowicz, Witold 1904-1969 .... **CLC 4, 7, 11, 49; TCLC 247**
See also CA 19-20; 25-28R; CANR 105;
CAP 2; CDWLB 4; DAM DRAM; DLB
215; EW 12; EWL 3; RGWL 2, 3; TWA

Gomez de Avellaneda, Gertrudis
1814-1873 .... **NCLC 111**
See also LAW

Gomez de la Serna, Ramon
1888-1963 .... **CLC 9**
See also CA 153; 116; CANR 79; EWL 3;
HW 1, 2

Gomez-Pena, Guillermo 1955- .... **CLC 310**
See also CA 147; CANR 117

Goncharov, Ivan Alexandrovich
1812-1891 .... **NCLC 1, 63**
See also DLB 238; EW 6; RGWL 2, 3

Goncourt, Edmond de 1822-1896 ... **NCLC 7**
See also DLB 123; EW 7; GFL 1789 to the
Present; RGWL 2, 3

Goncourt, Edmond Louis Antoine Huot de
See Goncourt, Edmond de

Goncourt, Jules Alfred Huot de
See Goncourt, Jules de

Goncourt, Jules de 1830-1870 .... **NCLC 7**
See Goncourt, Jules de
See also DLB 123; EW 7; GFL 1789 to the
Present; RGWL 2, 3

Gongora (y Argote), Luis de
1561-1627 .... **LC 72**
See also RGWL 2, 3

Gontier, Fernande 19(?)- .... **CLC 50**

Gonzalez Martinez, Enrique
See Gonzalez Martinez, Enrique

Gonzalez Martinez, Enrique
1871-1952 .... **TCLC 72**
See also CA 166; CANR 81; DLB 290;
EWL 3; HW 1, 2

Goodison, Lorna 1947- .... **BLC 2:2; PC 36**
See also CA 142; CANR 88, 189; CP 5, 6,
7; CWP; DLB 157; EWL 3; PFS 25

Goodman, Allegra 1967- .... **CLC 241**
See also CA 204; CANR 162, 204; DLB
244, 350

Goodman, Paul 1911-1972 ..... **CLC 1, 2, 4, 7**
See also CA 19-20; 37-40R; CAD; CANR
34; CAP 2; CN 1; DLB 130, 246; MAL
5; MTCW 1; RGAL 4

Goodweather, Hartley
See King, Thomas

GoodWeather, Hartley
See King, Thomas

Googe, Barnabe 1540-1594 .... **LC 94**
See also DLB 132; RGEL 2

Gordimer, Nadine 1923- ...... **CLC 3, 5, 7, 10, 18, 33, 51, 70, 123, 160, 161, 263; SSC 17, 80, 154; WLCS**
See also AAYA 39; AFW; BRWS 2; CA
5-8R; CANR 3, 28, 56, 88, 131, 195, 219;
CN 1, 2, 3, 4, 5, 6, 7; DA; DA3; DAB;
DAC; DAM MST, NOV; DLB 225, 326,
330; EWL 3; EXPS; INT CANR-28;
LATS 1:2; MTCW 1, 2; MTFW 2005;
NFS 4; RGEL 2; RGSF 2; SSFS 2, 14,
19, 28, 31; TWA; WLIT 2; YAW

Gordon, Adam Lindsay
1833-1870 .... **NCLC 21**
See also DLB 230

Gordon, Caroline 1895-1981 . **CLC 6, 13, 29, 83; SSC 15; TCLC 241**
See also AMW; CA 11-12; 103; CANR 36;
CAP 1; CN 1, 2; DLB 4, 9, 102; DLBD
17; DLBY 1981; EWL 3; MAL 5; MTCW
1, 2; MTFW 2005; RGAL 4; RGSF 2

Gordon, Charles William
1860-1937 .... **TCLC 31**
See also CA 109; DLB 92; TCWW 1, 2

Gordon, Mary 1949- .. **CLC 13, 22, 128, 216; SSC 59**
See also AMWS 4; BPFB 2; CA 102;
CANR 44, 92, 154, 179, 222; CN 4, 5, 6,
7; DLB 6; DLBY 1981; FW; INT CA-
102; MAL 5; MTCW 1

Gordon, Mary Catherine
See Gordon, Mary

Gordon, N. J.
See Bosman, Herman Charles

Gordon, Sol 1923- .... **CLC 26**
See also CA 53-56; CANR 4; SATA 11

Gordone, Charles 1925-1995 .... **BLC 2:2; CLC 1, 4; DC 8**
See also BW 1, 3; CA 93-96; 180; 150;
CAAE 180; CAD; CANR 55; DAM
DRAM; DLB 7; INT CA-93-96; MTCW
1

Gore, Catherine 1800-1861 .... **NCLC 65**
See also DLB 116, 344; RGEL 2

Gorenko, Anna Andreevna
See Akhmatova, Anna

Gor'kii, Maksim
See Gorky, Maxim

Gorky, Maxim 1868-1936 ..... **SSC 28; TCLC 8; WLC 3**
See also CA 105; 141; CANR 83; DA;
DAB; DAC; DAM DRAM, MST, NOV;
DFS 9; DLB 295; EW 8; EWL 3; MTCW
2; MTFW 2005; RGSF 2; RGWL 2, 3;
TWA

Goryan, Sirak
See Saroyan, William

Gosse, Edmund (William)
1849-1928 .... **TCLC 28**
See also CA 117; DLB 57, 144, 184; RGEL
2

Gotlieb, Phyllis 1926-2009 .... **CLC 18**
See also CA 13-16R; CANR 7, 135; CN 7;
CP 1, 2, 3, 4; DLB 88, 251; SFW 4

Gotlieb, Phyllis Fay Bloom
See Gotlieb, Phyllis

Gottesman, S. D.
See Kornbluth, C(yril) M.; Pohl, Frederik

Gottfried von Strassburg fl. c.
1170-1215 .... **CMLC 10, 96, 132**
See also CDWLB 2; DLB 138; EW 1;
RGWL 2, 3

Gotthelf, Jeremias 1797-1854 .... **NCLC 117**
See also DLB 133; RGWL 2, 3

Gottschalk c. 804-c. 866 .... **CMLC 130**
See also DLB 148

Gottschalk, Laura Riding
See Jackson, Laura

Gould, Lois 1932(?)-2002 .... **CLC 4, 10**
See also CA 77-80; 208; CANR 29; MTCW
1

Gould, Stephen Jay 1941-2002 .... **CLC 163**
See also AAYA 26; BEST 90:2; CA 77-80;
205; CANR 10, 27, 56, 75, 125; CPW;
INT CANR-27; MTCW 1, 2; MTFW 2005

Gourmont, Remy(-Marie-Charles) de
1858-1915 .... **TCLC 17**
See also CA 109; 150; GFL 1789 to the
Present; MTCW 2

Gournay, Marie le Jars de
See de Gournay, Marie le Jars

Govier, Katherine 1948- .... **CLC 51**
See also CA 101; CANR 18, 40, 128; CCA
1

Gower, John c. 1330-1408 .... **LC 76; PC 59**
See also BRW 1; DLB 146; RGEL 2

Goyen, (Charles) William
1915-1983 .... **CLC 5, 8, 14, 40**
See also AITN 2; CA 5-8R; 110; CANR 6,
71; CN 1, 2, 3; DLB 2, 218; DLBY 1983;
EWL 3; INT CANR-6; MAL 5

Goytisolo, Juan 1931- .... **CLC 5, 10, 23, 133; HLC 1**
See also CA 85-88; CANR 32, 61, 131, 182;
CWW 2; DAM MULT; DLB 322; EWL
3; GLL 2; HW 1, 2; MTCW 1, 2; MTFW
2005

Gozzano, Guido 1883-1916 .... **PC 10**
See also CA 154; DLB 114; EWL 3

Gozzi, (Conte) Carlo 1720-1806 .... **NCLC 23**

Grabbe, Christian Dietrich
1801-1836 .... **NCLC 2**
See also DLB 133; RGWL 2, 3

Grace, Patricia 1937- .... **CLC 56**
See also CA 176; CANR 118; CN 4, 5, 6,
7; EWL 3; RGSF 2; SSFS 33

Grace, Patricia Frances
See Grace, Patricia

Gracian, Baltasar 1601-1658 .... **LC 15, 160**

Gracian y Morales, Baltasar
See Gracian, Baltasar

Gracq, Julien 1910-2007 ..... **CLC 11, 48, 259**
See also CA 122; 126; 267; CANR 141;
CWW 2; DLB 83; GFL 1789 to the
present

Grade, Chaim 1910-1982 .... **CLC 10**
See also CA 93-96; 107; DLB 333; EWL 3;
RGHL

Grade, Khayim
See Grade, Chaim

Graduate of Oxford, A
See Ruskin, John

Grafton, Garth
See Duncan, Sara Jeannette

Grafton, Sue 1940- .... **CLC 163, 299**
See also AAYA 11, 49; BEST 90:3; CA 108;
CANR 31, 55, 111, 134, 195; CMW 4;
CPW; CSW; DA3; DAM POP; DLB 226;
FW; MSW; MTFW 2005

Graham, John
See Phillips, David Graham

Graham, Jorie 1950- .... **CLC 48, 118; PC 59**
See also AAYA 67; CA 111; CANR 63, 118,
205; CP 4, 5, 6, 7; CWP; DLB 120; EWL
3; MTFW 2005; PFS 10, 17; TCLE 1:1

Graham, R. B. Cunninghame
See Cunninghame Graham, Robert Bontine

Graham, Robert
See Haldeman, Joe

Graham, Robert Bontine Cunninghame
See Cunninghame Graham, Robert Bontine

Graham, Tom
See Lewis, Sinclair

Graham, W(illiam) S(ydney)
1918-1986 .... **CLC 29; PC 127**
See also BRWS 7; CA 73-76; 118; CP 1, 2,
3, 4; DLB 20; RGEL 2

Gurganus, Allan 1947- .... **CLC 70**
See also BEST 90:1; CA 135; CANR 114;
CN 6, 7; CPW; CSW; DAM POP; DLB
350; GLL 1

Gurney, A. R.
See Gurney, A(lbert) R(amsdell), Jr.

Gurney, A(lbert) R(amsdell), Jr.
1930- .... **CLC 32, 50, 54**
See also AMWS 5; CA 77-80; CAD; CANR
32, 64, 121; CD 5, 6; DAM DRAM; DLB
266; EWL 3

Gurney, Ivor (Bertie) 1890-1937 ... **TCLC 33**
See also BRW 6; CA 167; DLBY 2002;
PAB; RGEL 2

Gurney, Peter
See Gurney, A(lbert) R(amsdell), Jr.

Guro, Elena (Genrikhovna)
1877-1913 .... **TCLC 56**
See also DLB 295

Gustafson, James M(oody) 1925- ... **CLC 100**
See also CA 25-28R; CANR 37

Gustafson, Ralph (Barker)
1909-1995 .... **CLC 36**
See also CA 21-24R; CANR 8, 45, 84; CP
1, 2, 3, 4, 5, 6; DLB 88; RGEL 2

Gut, Gom
See Simenon, Georges

Guterson, David 1956- .... **CLC 91**
See also CA 132; CANR 73, 126, 194; CN
7; DLB 292; MTCW 2; MTFW 2005;
NFS 13

Guthrie, A(lfred) B(ertram), Jr.
1901-1991 .... **CLC 23**
See also CA 57-60; 134; CANR 24; CN 1,
2, 3; DLB 6, 212; MAL 5; SATA 62;
SATA-Obit 67; TCWW 1, 2

Guthrie, Isobel
See Grieve, C. M.

Gutierrez Najera, Manuel
1859-1895 .... **HLCS 2; NCLC 133**
See also DLB 290; LAW

Guy, Rosa 1925- .... **CLC 26**
See also AAYA 4, 37; BW 2; CA 17-20R;
CANR 14, 34, 83; CLR 13, 137; DLB 33;
DNFS 1; JRDA; MAICYA 1, 2; SATA 14,
62, 122; YAW

Guy, Rosa Cuthbert
See Guy, Rosa

Gwendolyn
See Bennett, (Enoch) Arnold

H. D.
See Doolittle, Hilda

H. de V.
See Buchan, John

Haavikko, Paavo Juhani 1931- .. **CLC 18, 34**
See also CA 106; CWW 2; EWL 3

Habbema, Koos
See Heijermans, Herman

Habermas, Juergen 1929- .... **CLC 104**
See also CA 109; CANR 85, 162; DLB 242

Habermas, Jurgen
See Habermas, Juergen

Hacker, Marilyn 1942- ...... **CLC 5, 9, 23, 72,
91; PC 47**
See also CA 77-80; CANR 68, 129; CP 3,
4, 5, 6, 7; CWP; DAM POET; DLB 120,
282; FW; GLL 2; MAL 5; PFS 19

Hadewijch of Antwerp fl. 1250- ... **CMLC 61**
See also RGWL 3

Hadrian 76-138 .... **CMLC 52**

Haeckel, Ernst Heinrich (Philipp August)
1834-1919 .... **TCLC 83**
See also CA 157

Hafiz c. 1326-1389(?) .... **CMLC 34; PC 116**
See also RGWL 2, 3; WLIT 6

Hagedorn, Jessica T. 1949- .... **CLC 185**
See also CA 139; CANR 69, 231; CWP;
DLB 312; RGAL 4

Hagedorn, Jessica Tarahata
See Hagedorn, Jessica T.

Haggard, H(enry) Rider
1856-1925 .... **TCLC 11**
See also AAYA 81; BRWS 3; BYA 4, 5;
CA 108; 148; CANR 112; DLB 70, 156,
174, 178; FANT; LMFS 1; MTCW 2; NFS
40; RGEL 2; RHW; SATA 16; SCFW 1,
2; SFW 4; SUFW 1; WLIT 4

Hagiosy, L.
See Larbaud, Valery (Nicolas)

Hagiwara, Sakutaro 1886-1942 .... **PC 18;
TCLC 60**
See also CA 154; EWL 3; RGWL 3

Hagiwara Sakutaro
See Hagiwara, Sakutaro

Haig, Fenil
See Ford, Ford Madox

Haig-Brown, Roderick (Langmere)
1908-1976 .... **CLC 21**
See also CA 5-8R; 69-72; CANR 4, 38, 83;
CLR 31; CWRI 5; DLB 88; MAICYA 1,
2; SATA 12; TCWW 2

Haight, Rip
See Carpenter, John

Haij, Vera
See Jansson, Tove (Marika)

Hailey, Arthur 1920-2004 .... **CLC 5**
See also AITN 2; BEST 90:3; BPFB 2; CA
1-4R; 233; CANR 2, 36, 75; CCA 1; CN
1, 2, 3, 4, 5, 6, 7; CPW; DAM NOV, POP;
DLB 88; DLBY 1982; MTCW 1, 2;
MTFW 2005

Hailey, Elizabeth Forsythe 1938- ..... **CLC 40**
See also CA 93-96; 188; CAAE 188; CAAS
1; CANR 15, 48; INT CANR-15

Haines, John 1924-2011 .... **CLC 58**
See also AMWS 12; CA 17-20R; CANR
13, 34; CP 1, 2, 3, 4, 5; CSW; DLB 5,
212; TCLE 1:1

Haines, John Meade
See Haines, John

Hakluyt, Richard 1552-1616 .... **LC 31**
See also DLB 136; RGEL 2

Haldeman, Joe 1943- .... **CLC 61**
See also AAYA 38; CA 53-56, 179; CAAE
179; CAAS 25; CANR 6, 70, 72, 130,
171, 224; DLB 8; INT CANR-6; SCFW
2; SFW 4

Haldeman, Joe William
See Haldeman, Joe

Hale, Janet Campbell 1947- .... **NNAL**
See also CA 49-52; CANR 45, 75; DAM
MULT; DLB 175; MTCW 2; MTFW 2005

Hale, Sarah Josepha (Buell)
1788-1879 .... **NCLC 75**
See also DLB 1, 42, 73, 243

Halevy, Elie 1870-1937 .... **TCLC 104**

Haley, Alex 1921-1992 . **BLC 1:2; CLC 8, 12,
76; TCLC 147**
See also AAYA 26; BPFB 2; BW 2, 3; CA
77-80; 136; CANR 61; CDALBS; CPW;
CSW; DA; DA3; DAB; DAC; DAM MST,
MULT, POP; DLB 38; LAIT 5; MTCW
1, 2; NFS 9

Haley, Alexander Murray Palmer
See Haley, Alex

Haliburton, Thomas Chandler
1796-1865 .... **NCLC 15, 149**
See also DLB 11, 99; RGEL 2; RGSF 2

Hall, Donald 1928- ... **CLC 1, 13, 37, 59, 151,
240; PC 70**
See also AAYA 63; CA 5-8R; CAAS 7;
CANR 2, 44, 64, 106, 133, 196; CP 1, 2,
3, 4, 5, 6, 7; DAM POET; DLB 5, 342;
MAL 5; MTCW 2; MTFW 2005; RGAL
4; SATA 23, 97

Hall, Donald Andrew, Jr.
See Hall, Donald

Hall, Frederic Sauser
See Sauser-Hall, Frederic

Hall, James
See Kuttner, Henry

Hall, James Norman 1887-1951 ..... **TCLC 23**
See also CA 123; 173; LAIT 1; RHW 1;
SATA 21

Hall, Joseph 1574-1656 .... **LC 91**
See also DLB 121, 151; RGEL 2

Hall, Marguerite Radclyffe
See Hall, Radclyffe

Hall, Radclyffe 1880-1943 ...... **TCLC 12, 215**
See also BRWS 6; CA 110; 150; CANR 83;
DLB 191; MTCW 2; MTFW 2005; RGEL
2; RHW

Hall, Rodney 1935- .... **CLC 51**
See also CA 109; CANR 69; CN 6, 7; CP
1, 2, 3, 4, 5, 6, 7; DLB 289

Hallam, Arthur Henry
1811-1833 .... **NCLC 110**
See also DLB 32

Halldor Laxness
See Gudjonsson, Halldor Kiljan

Halleck, Fitz-Greene 1790-1867 .... **NCLC 47**
See also DLB 3, 250; RGAL 4

Halliday, Michael
See Creasey, John

Halpern, Daniel 1945- .... **CLC 14**
See also CA 33-36R; CANR 93, 174; CP 3,
4, 5, 6, 7

Hamann, Johann Georg 1730-1788 .. **LC 198**
See also DLB 97

Hamburger, Michael 1924-2007 ... **CLC 5, 14**
See also CA 5-8R, 196; 261; CAAE 196;
CAAS 4; CANR 2, 47; CP 1, 2, 3, 4, 5, 6,
7; DLB 27

Hamburger, Michael Peter Leopold
See Hamburger, Michael

Hamill, Pete 1935- .... **CLC 10, 261**
See also CA 25-28R; CANR 18, 71, 127,
180

Hamill, William Peter
See Hamill, Pete

Hamilton, Alexander 1712-1756 .... **LC 150**
See also DLB 31

Hamilton, Alexander
1755(?)-1804 .... **NCLC 49**
See also DLB 37

Hamilton, Clive
See Lewis, C. S.

Hamilton, Edmond 1904-1977 .... **CLC 1**
See also CA 1-4R; CANR 3, 84; DLB 8;
SATA 118; SFW 4

Hamilton, Elizabeth 1758-1816 ... **NCLC 153**
See also DLB 116, 158

Hamilton, Eugene (Jacob) Lee
See Lee-Hamilton, Eugene (Jacob)

Hamilton, Franklin
See Silverberg, Robert

Hamilton, Gail
See Corcoran, Barbara (Asenath)

Hamilton, (Robert) Ian 1938-2001 . **CLC 191**
See also CA 106; 203; CANR 41, 67; CP 1,
2, 3, 4, 5, 6, 7; DLB 40, 155

Hamilton, Jane 1957- .... **CLC 179**
See also CA 147; CANR 85, 128, 214; CN
7; DLB 350; MTFW 2005

Hamilton, Mollie
See Kaye, M.M.

Hamilton, Patrick 1904-1962 .... **CLC 51**
See also BRWS 16; CA 176; 113; DLB 10,
191

Hamilton, Virginia 1936-2002 .... **CLC 26**
See also AAYA 2, 21; BW 2, 3; BYA 1, 2,
8; CA 25-28R; 206; CANR 20, 37, 73,
126; CLR 1, 11, 40, 127; DAM MULT;
DLB 33, 52; DLBY 2001; INT CANR-

Hebbel, Friedrich 1813-1863 . **DC 21; NCLC 43**
See also CDWLB 2; DAM DRAM; DLB 129; EW 6; RGWL 2, 3

Hebert, Anne 1916-2000 .... **CLC 4, 13, 29, 246; PC 126**
See also CA 85-88; 187; CANR 69, 126; CCA 1; CWP; CWW 2; DA3; DAC; DAM MST, POET; DLB 68; EWL 3; GFL 1789 to the Present; MTCW 1, 2; MTFW 2005; PFS 20

Hebreo, Leon c. 1460-1520 .... **LC 193**
See also DLB 318

Hecht, Anthony (Evan) 1923-2004 .... **CLC 8, 13, 19; PC 70**
See also AMWS 10; CA 9-12R; 232; CANR 6, 108; CP 1, 2, 3, 4, 5, 6, 7; DAM POET; DLB 5, 169; EWL 3; PFS 6; WP

Hecht, Ben 1894-1964 ..... **CLC 8; TCLC 101**
See also CA 85-88; DFS 9; DLB 7, 9, 25, 26, 28, 86; FANT; IDFW 3, 4; RGAL 4

Hedayat, Sadeq 1903-1951 . **SSC 131; TCLC 21**
See also CA 120; EWL 3; RGSF 2

Hegel, Georg Wilhelm Friedrich 1770-1831 .... **NCLC 46, 151**
See also DLB 90, 366; TWA

Heidegger, Martin 1889-1976 .... **CLC 24**
See also CA 81-84; 65-68; CANR 34; DLB 296; MTCW 1, 2; MTFW 2005

Heidenstam, (Carl Gustaf) Verner von 1859-1940 .... **TCLC 5**
See also CA 104; DLB 330

Heidi Louise
See Erdrich, Louise

Heifner, Jack 1946- .... **CLC 11**
See also CA 105; CANR 47

Heijermans, Herman 1864-1924 .... **TCLC 24**
See also CA 123; EWL 3

Heilbrun, Carolyn G. 1926-2003 ..... **CLC 25, 173, 303**
See also BPFB 1; CA 45-48; 220; CANR 1, 28, 58, 94; CMW; CPW; DLB 306; FW; MSW

Heilbrun, Carolyn Gold
See Heilbrun, Carolyn G.

Hein, Christoph 1944- .... **CLC 154**
See also CA 158; CDWLB 2; CWW 2; DLB 124

Heine, Heinrich 1797-1856 .... **NCLC 4, 54, 147, 249; PC 25**
See also CDWLB 2; DLB 90; EW 5; PFS 37; RGWL 2, 3; TWA

Heinemann, Larry 1944- .... **CLC 50**
See also CA 110; CAAS 21; CANR 31, 81, 156; DLBD 9; INT CANR-31

Heinemann, Larry Curtiss
See Heinemann, Larry

Heiney, Donald (William) 1921-1993 . **CLC 9**
See also CA 1-4R; 142; CANR 3, 58; FANT

Heinlein, Robert A. 1907-1988 .. **CLC 1, 3, 8, 14, 26, 55; SSC 55**
See also AAYA 17; BPFB 2; BYA 4, 13; CA 1-4R; 125; CANR 1, 20, 53; CLR 75; CN 1, 2, 3, 4; CPW; DA3; DAM POP; DLB 8; EXPS; JRDA; LAIT 5; LMFS 2; MAICYA 1, 2; MTCW 1, 2; MTFW 2005; NFS 40; RGAL 4; SATA 9, 69; SATA-Obit 56; SCFW 1, 2; SFW 4; SSFS 7; YAW

Heinrich von dem Tuerlin fl. c. 1230- .... **CMLC 133**
See also DLB 138

Hejinian, Lyn 1941- .... **PC 108**
See also CA 153; CANR 85, 214; CP 4, 5, 6, 7; CWP; DLB 165; PFS 27; RGAL 4

Held, Peter
See Vance, Jack

Heldris of Cornwall fl. 13th cent.
- .... **CMLC 97**

Helforth, John
See Doolittle, Hilda

Heliodorus fl. 3rd cent. - .... **CMLC 52**
See also WLIT 8

Hellenhofferu, Vojtech Kapristian z
See Hasek, Jaroslav

Heller, Joseph 1923-1999 . **CLC 1, 3, 5, 8, 11, 36, 63; TCLC 131, 151; WLC 3**
See also AAYA 24; AITN 1; AMWS 4; BPFB 2; BYA 1; CA 5-8R; 187; CABS 1; CANR 8, 42, 66, 126; CN 1, 2, 3, 4, 5, 6; CPW; DA; DA3; DAB; DAC; DAM MST, NOV, POP; DLB 2, 28, 227; DLBY 1980, 2002; EWL 3; EXPN; INT CANR-8; LAIT 4; MAL 5; MTCW 1, 2; MTFW 2005; NFS 1; RGAL 4; TUS; YAW

Hellman, Lillian 1905-1984 . **CLC 2, 4, 8, 14, 18, 34, 44, 52; DC 1; TCLC 119**
See also AAYA 47; AITN 1, 2; AMWS 1; CA 13-16R; 112; CAD; CANR 33; CWD; DA3; DAM DRAM; DFS 1, 3, 14; DLB 7, 228; DLBY 1984; EWL 3; FL 1:6; FW; LAIT 3; MAL 5; MBL; MTCW 1, 2; MTFW 2005; RGAL 4; TUS

Hellman, Lillian Florence
See Hellman, Lillian

Heloise c. 1095-c. 1164 .... **CMLC 122**

Helprin, Mark 1947- .... **CLC 7, 10, 22, 32**
See also CA 81-84; CANR 47, 64, 124, 222; CDALBS; CN 7; CPW; DA3; DAM NOV, POP; DLB 335; DLBY 1985; FANT; MAL 5; MTCW 1, 2; MTFW 2005; SSFS 25; SUFW 2

Helvetius, Claude-Adrien 1715-1771 .. **LC 26**
See also DLB 313

Helyar, Jane Penelope Josephine 1933- .... **CLC 17**
See also CA 21-24R; CANR 10, 26; CWRI 5; SAAS 2; SATA 5; SATA-Essay 138

Hemans, Felicia 1793-1835 ...... **NCLC 29, 71**
See also DLB 96; RGEL 2

Hemingway, Ernest 1899-1961 .. **CLC 1, 3, 6, 8, 10, 13, 19, 30, 34, 39, 41, 44, 50, 61, 80; SSC 1, 25, 36, 40, 63, 117, 137; TCLC 115, 203; WLC 3**
See also AAYA 19; AMW; AMWC 1; AMWR 1; BPFB 2; BYA 2, 3, 13, 15; CA 77-80; CANR 34; CDALB 1917-1929; CLR 168; DA; DA3; DAB; DAC; DAM MST, NOV; DLB 4, 9, 102, 210, 308, 316, 330; DLBD 1, 15, 16; DLBY 1981, 1987, 1996, 1998; EWL 3; EXPN; EXPS; LAIT 3, 4; LATS 1:1; MAL 5; MTCW 1, 2; MTFW 2005; NFS 1, 5, 6, 14; RGAL 4; RGSF 2; SSFS 17; TUS; WYA

Hemingway, Ernest Miller
See Hemingway, Ernest

Hempel, Amy 1951- .... **CLC 39**
See also AMWS 21; CA 118; 137; CANR 70, 166; DA3; DLB 218; EXPS; MTCW 2; MTFW 2005; SSFS 2

Henderson, F. C.
See Mencken, H. L.

Henderson, Mary
See Mavor, Osborne Henry

Henderson, Sylvia
See Ashton-Warner, Sylvia (Constance)

Henderson, Zenna (Chlarson) 1917-1983 .... **SSC 29**
See also CA 1-4R; 133; CANR 1, 84; DLB 8; SATA 5; SFW 4

Henkin, Joshua 1964- .... **CLC 119**
See also CA 161; CANR 186; DLB 350

Henley, Beth 1952- ... **CLC 23, 255; DC 6, 14**
See also AAYA 70; CA 107; CABS 3; CAD; CANR 32, 73, 140; CD 5, 6; CSW; CWD; DA3; DAM DRAM, MST; DFS 2, 21, 26; DLBY 1986; FW; MTCW 1, 2; MTFW 2005

Henley, Elizabeth Becker
See Henley, Beth

Henley, William Ernest 1849-1903 .. **PC 127; TCLC 8**
See also CA 105; 234; DLB 19; RGEL 2

Hennissart, Martha 1929- .... **CLC 2**
See also BPFB 2; CA 85-88; CANR 64; CMW 4; DLB 306

Henry VIII 1491-1547 .... **LC 10**
See also DLB 132

Henry, O. 1862-1910 . **SSC 5, 49, 117; TCLC 1, 19; WLC 3**
See also AAYA 41; AMWS 2; CA 104; 131; CDALB 1865-1917; DA; DA3; DAB; DAC; DAM MST; DLB 12, 78, 79; EXPS; MAL 5; MTCW 1, 2; MTFW 2005; RGAL 4; RGSF 2; SSFS 2, 18, 27, 31; TCWW 1, 2; TUS; YABC 2

Henry, Oliver
See Henry, O.

Henry, Patrick 1736-1799 .... **LC 25**
See also LAIT 1

Henryson, Robert 1430(?)-1506(?) ..... **LC 20, 110; PC 65**
See also BRWS 7; DLB 146; RGEL 2

Henschke, Alfred
See Klabund

Henson, Lance 1944- .... **NNAL**
See also CA 146; DLB 175

Hentoff, Nat(han Irving) 1925- .... **CLC 26**
See also AAYA 4, 42; BYA 6; CA 1-4R; CAAS 6; CANR 5, 25, 77, 114; CLR 1, 52; DLB 345; INT CANR-25; JRDA; MAICYA 1, 2; SATA 42, 69, 133; SATA-Brief 27; WYA; YAW

Heppenstall, (John) Rayner 1911-1981 .... **CLC 10**
See also CA 1-4R; 103; CANR 29; CN 1, 2; CP 1, 2, 3; EWL 3

Heraclitus c. 540B.C.-c. 450B.C. ... **CMLC 22**
See also DLB 176

Herbert, Edward 1583-1648 .... **LC 177**
See also DLB 121, 151, 252; RGEL 2

Herbert, Frank 1920-1986 ... **CLC 12, 23, 35, 44, 85**
See also AAYA 21; BPFB 2; BYA 4, 14; CA 53-56; 118; CANR 5, 43; CDALBS; CPW; DAM POP; DLB 8; INT CANR-5; LAIT 5; MTCW 1, 2; MTFW 2005; NFS 17, 31; SATA 9, 37; SATA-Obit 47; SCFW 1, 2; SFW 4; YAW

Herbert, George 1593-1633 . **LC 24, 121; PC 4**
See also BRW 2; BRWR 2; CDBLB Before 1660; DAB; DAM POET; DLB 126; EXPP; PFS 25; RGEL 2; TEA; WP

Herbert, Zbigniew 1924-1998 ..... **CLC 9, 43; PC 50; TCLC 168**
See also CA 89-92; 169; CANR 36, 74, 177; CDWLB 4; CWW 2; DAM POET; DLB 232; EWL 3; MTCW 1; PFS 22

Herbert of Cherbury, Lord
See Herbert, Edward

Herbst, Josephine (Frey) 1897-1969 .... **CLC 34; TCLC 243**
See also CA 5-8R; 25-28R; DLB 9

Herder, Johann Gottfried von 1744-1803 .... **NCLC 8, 186**
See also DLB 97; EW 4; TWA

Heredia, Jose Maria 1803-1839 ...... **HLCS 2; NCLC 209**
See also LAW

Hergesheimer, Joseph 1880-1954 ... **TCLC 11**
See also CA 109; 194; DLB 102, 9; RGAL 4

Herlihy, James Leo 1927-1993 .... **CLC 6**
See also CA 1-4R; 143; CAD; CANR 2; CN 1, 2, 3, 4, 5

Herman, William
See Bierce, Ambrose

Hermogenes fl. c. 175- .... **CMLC 6**

Hernandez, Felisberto 1902-1964 .... **SSC 152**
See also CA 213; EWL 3; LAWS 1

Hernandez, Jose 1834-1886 .... **NCLC 17**
See also LAW; RGWL 2, 3; WLIT 1

Herodotus c. 484B.C.-c. 420B.C. .. **CMLC 17**
See also AW 1; CDWLB 1; DLB 176;
RGWL 2, 3; TWA; WLIT 8

Herr, Michael 1940(?)- .... **CLC 231**
See also CA 89-92; CANR 68, 142; DLB
185; MTCW 1

Herrick, Robert 1591-1674 .. **LC 13, 145; PC 9**
See also BRW 2; BRWC 2; DA; DAB;
DAC; DAM MST, POP; DLB 126; EXPP;
PFS 13, 29, 39; RGAL 4; RGEL 2; TEA;
WP

Herring, Guilles
See Somerville, Edith Oenone

Herriot, James 1916-1995 .... **CLC 12**
See also AAYA 1, 54; BPFB 2; CA 77-80;
148; CANR 40; CLR 80; CPW; DAM
POP; LAIT 3; MAICYA 2; MAICYAS 1;
MTCW 2; SATA 86, 135; SATA-Brief 44;
TEA; YAW

Herris, Violet
See Hunt, Violet

Herrmann, Dorothy 1941- .... **CLC 44**
See also CA 107

Herrmann, Taffy
See Herrmann, Dorothy

Hersey, John 1914-1993 .. **CLC 1, 2, 7, 9, 40, 81, 97**
See also AAYA 29; BPFB 2; CA 17-20R;
140; CANR 33; CDALBS; CN 1, 2, 3, 4,
5; CPW; DAM POP; DLB 6, 185, 278,
299, 364; MAL 5; MTCW 1, 2; MTFW
2005; RGHL; SATA 25; SATA-Obit 76;
TUS

Hersey, John Richard
See Hersey, John

Hervent, Maurice
See Grindel, Eugene

Herzen, Aleksandr Ivanovich
1812-1870 .... **NCLC 10, 61**
See also DLB 277

Herzen, Alexander
See Herzen, Aleksandr Ivanovich

Herzl, Theodor 1860-1904 .... **TCLC 36**
See also CA 168

Herzog, Werner 1942- .... **CLC 16, 236**
See also AAYA 85; CA 89-92; CANR 215

Hesiod fl. 8th cent. B.C.- .... **CMLC 5, 102**
See also AW 1; DLB 176; RGWL 2, 3;
WLIT 8

Hesse, Hermann 1877-1962 ... **CLC 1, 2, 3, 6, 11, 17, 25, 69; SSC 9, 49; TCLC 148, 196; WLC 3**
See also AAYA 43; BPFB 2; CA 17-18;
CAP 2; CDWLB 2; DA; DA3; DAB;
DAC; DAM MST, NOV; DLB 66, 330;
EW 9; EWL 3; EXPN; LAIT 1; MTCW
1, 2; MTFW 2005; NFS 6, 15, 24; RGWL
2, 3; SATA 50; TWA

Hewes, Cady
See De Voto, Bernard (Augustine)

Heyen, William 1940- .... **CLC 13, 18**
See also CA 33-36R; 220; CAAE 220;
CAAS 7; CANR 98, 188; CP 3, 4, 5, 6, 7;
DLB 5; RGHL

Heyerdahl, Thor 1914-2002 .... **CLC 26**
See also CA 5-8R; 207; CANR 5, 22, 66,
73; LAIT 4; MTCW 1, 2; MTFW 2005;
SATA 2, 52

Heym, Georg (Theodor Franz Arthur)
1887-1912 .... **TCLC 9**
See also CA 106; 181

Heym, Stefan 1913-2001 .... **CLC 41**
See also CA 9-12R; 203; CANR 4; CWW
2; DLB 69; EWL 3

Heyse, Paul (Johann Ludwig von)
1830-1914 .... **TCLC 8**
See also CA 104; 209; DLB 129, 330

Heyward, (Edwin) DuBose
1885-1940 .... **HR 1:2; TCLC 59**
See also CA 108; 157; DLB 7, 9, 45, 249;
MAL 5; SATA 21

Heywood, John 1497(?)-1580(?) .... **LC 65**
See also DLB 136; RGEL 2

Heywood, Thomas 1573(?)-1641 . **DC 29; LC 111**
See also DAM DRAM; DLB 62; LMFS 1;
RGEL 2; TEA

Hiaasen, Carl 1953- .... **CLC 238**
See also CA 105; CANR 22, 45, 65, 113,
133, 168; CMW 4; CPW; CSW; DA3;
DLB 292; LNFS 2, 3; MTCW 2; MTFW
2005; SATA 208

Hibbert, Eleanor Alice Burford
1906-1993 .... **CLC 7**
See also BEST 90:4; BPFB 2; CA 17-20R;
140; CANR 9, 28, 59; CMW 4; CPW;
DAM POP; MTCW 2; MTFW 2005;
RHW; SATA 2; SATA-Obit 74

Hichens, Robert (Smythe)
1864-1950 .... **TCLC 64**
See also CA 162; DLB 153; HGG; RHW;
SUFW

Higgins, Aidan 1927- .... **SSC 68**
See also CA 9-12R; CANR 70, 115, 148;
CN 1, 2, 3, 4, 5, 6, 7; DLB 14

Higgins, George V(incent)
1939-1999 .... **CLC 4, 7, 10, 18**
See also BPFB 2; CA 77-80; 186; CAAS 5;
CANR 17, 51, 89, 96; CMW 4; CN 2, 3,
4, 5, 6; DLB 2; DLBY 1981, 1998; INT
CANR-17; MSW; MTCW 1

Higginson, Thomas Wentworth
1823-1911 .... **TCLC 36**
See also CA 162; DLB 1, 64, 243

Higgonet, Margaret CLC 65

Highet, Helen
See MacInnes, Helen (Clark)

Highsmith, Mary Patricia
See Highsmith, Patricia

Highsmith, Patricia 1921-1995 ...... **CLC 2, 4, 14, 42, 102**
See also AAYA 48; BRWS 5; CA 1-4R; 147;
CANR 1, 20, 48, 62, 108; CMW 4; CN 1,
2, 3, 4, 5; CPW; DA3; DAM NOV, POP;
DLB 306; GLL 1; MSW; MTCW 1, 2;
MTFW 2005; NFS 27; SSFS 25

Highwater, Jamake (Mamake)
1942(?)-2001 .... **CLC 12**
See also AAYA 7, 69; BPFB 2; BYA 4; CA
65-68; 199; CAAS 7; CANR 10, 34, 84;
CLR 17; CWRI 5; DLB 52; DLBY 1985;
JRDA; MAICYA 1, 2; SATA 32, 69;
SATA-Brief 30

Highway, Tomson 1951- ..... **CLC 92; DC 33; NNAL**
See also CA 151; CANR 75; CCA 1; CD 5,
6; CN 7; DAC; DAM MULT; DFS 2;
DLB 334; MTCW 2

Hijuelos, Oscar 1951- .... **CLC 65; HLC 1**
See also AAYA 25; AMWS 8; BEST 90:1;
CA 123; CANR 50, 75, 125, 205; CPW;
DA3; DAM MULT, POP; DLB 145; HW
1, 2; LLW; MAL 5; MTCW 2; MTFW
2005; NFS 17; RGAL 4; WLIT 1

Hikmet, Nazim 1902-1963 .... **CLC 40**
See also CA 141; 93-96; EWL 3; PFS 38,
41; WLIT 6

Hildegard von Bingen
1098-1179 .... **CMLC 20, 118**
See also DLB 148

Hildesheimer, Wolfgang 1916-1991 .. **CLC 49**
See also CA 101; 135; DLB 69, 124; EWL
3; RGHL

Hill, Aaron 1685-1750 .... **LC 148**
See also DLB 84; RGEL 2

Hill, Geoffrey 1932- ... **CLC 5, 8, 18, 45, 251; PC 125**
See also BRWR 3; BRWS 5; CA 81-84;
CANR 21, 89; CDBLB 1960 to Present;
CP 1, 2, 3, 4, 5, 6, 7; DAM POET; DLB
40; EWL 3; MTCW 1; RGEL 2; RGHL

Hill, George Roy 1921-2002 .... **CLC 26**
See also CA 110; 122; 213

Hill, John
See Koontz, Dean

Hill, Susan 1942- .... **CLC 4, 113**
See also BRWS 14; CA 33-36R; CANR 29,
69, 129, 172, 201; CN 2, 3, 4, 5, 6, 7;
DAB; DAM MST, NOV; DLB 14, 139;
HGG; MTCW 1; RHW; SATA 183

Hill, Susan Elizabeth
See Hill, Susan

Hillard, Asa G. III CLC 70

Hillerman, Anthony Grove
See Hillerman, Tony

Hillerman, Tony 1925-2008 ...... **CLC 62, 170**
See also AAYA 40; BEST 89:1; BPFB 2;
CA 29-32R; 278; CANR 21, 42, 65, 97,
134; CMW 4; CPW; DA3; DAM POP;
DLB 206, 306; MAL 5; MSW; MTCW 2;
MTFW 2005; RGAL 4; SATA 6; SATA-
Obit 198; TCWW 2; YAW

Hillesum, Etty 1914-1943 .... **TCLC 49**
See also CA 137; RGHL

Hilliard, Noel (Harvey) 1929-1996 ... **CLC 15**
See also CA 9-12R; CANR 7, 69; CN 1, 2,
3, 4, 5, 6

Hillis, Rick 1956- .... **CLC 66**
See also CA 134

Hilton, James 1900-1954 .... **TCLC 21**
See also AAYA 76; CA 108; 169; DLB 34,
77; FANT; SATA 34

Hilton, Walter 1343-1396(?) .. **CMLC 58, 141**
See also DLB 146; RGEL 2

Himes, Chester (Bomar)
1909-1984 .... **BLC 1:2; CLC 2, 4, 7, 18, 58, 108; TCLC 139**
See also AFAW 2; AMWS 16; BPFB 2; BW
2; CA 25-28R; 114; CANR 22, 89; CMW
4; CN 1, 2, 3; DAM MULT; DLB 2, 76,
143, 226; EWL 3; MAL 5; MSW; MTCW
1, 2; MTFW 2005; RGAL 4

Himmelfarb, Gertrude 1922- .... **CLC 202**
See also CA 49-52; CANR 28, 66, 102, 166

Hinde, Thomas 1926- .... **CLC 6, 11**
See also CA 5-8R; CN 1, 2, 3, 4, 5, 6; EWL
3

Hine, (William) Daryl 1936- .... **CLC 15**
See also CA 1-4R; CAAS 15; CANR 1, 20;
CP 1, 2, 3, 4, 5, 6, 7; DLB 60

Hinkson, Katharine Tynan
See Tynan, Katharine

Hinojosa, Rolando 1929- .... **HLC 1**
See also CA 131; CAAS 16; CANR 62;
DAM MULT; DLB 82; EWL 3; HW 1, 2;
LLW; MTCW 2; MTFW 2005; RGAL 4

Hinton, S. E. 1950- .... **CLC 30, 111**
See also AAYA 2, 33; BPFB 2; BYA 2, 3;
CA 81-84; CANR 32, 62, 92, 133;
CDALBS; CLR 3, 23; CPW; DA; DA3;
DAB; DAC; DAM MST, NOV; JRDA;
LAIT 5; MAICYA 1, 2; MTCW 1, 2;
MTFW 2005; NFS 5, 9, 15, 16, 35; SATA
19, 58, 115, 160; WYA; YAW

Hinton, Susan Eloise
See Hinton, S. E.

Hippius, Zinaida
See Gippius, Zinaida

Hooker, (Peter) Jeremy 1941- .... **CLC 43**
See also CA 77-80; CANR 22; CP 2, 3, 4, 5, 6, 7; DLB 40

Hooker, Richard 1554-1600 .... **LC 95**
See also BRW 1; DLB 132; RGEL 2

Hooker, Thomas 1586-1647 .... **LC 137**
See also DLB 24

hooks, bell 1952(?)- .... **BLCS; CLC 94**
See also BW 2; CA 143; CANR 87, 126, 211; DLB 246; MTCW 2; MTFW 2005; SATA 115, 170

Hooper, Johnson Jones
1815-1862 .... **NCLC 177**
See also DLB 3, 11, 248; RGAL 4

Hope, A(lec) D(erwent) 1907-2000 .... **CLC 3, 51; PC 56**
See also BRWS 7; CA 21-24R; 188; CANR 33, 74; CP 1, 2, 3, 4, 5; DLB 289; EWL 3; MTCW 1, 2; MTFW 2005; PFS 8; RGEL 2

Hope, Anthony 1863-1933 .... **TCLC 83**
See also CA 157; DLB 153, 156; RGEL 2; RHW

Hope, Brian
See Creasey, John

Hope, Christopher 1944- .... **CLC 52**
See also AFW; CA 106; CANR 47, 101, 177; CN 4, 5, 6, 7; DLB 225; SATA 62

Hope, Christopher David Tully
See Hope, Christopher

Hopkins, Gerard Manley
1844-1889 .... **NCLC 17, 189; PC 15; WLC 3**
See also BRW 5; BRWR 2; CDBLB 1890-1914; DA; DA3; DAB; DAC; DAM MST, POET; DLB 35, 57; EXPP; PAB; PFS 26, 40; RGEL 2; TEA; WP

Hopkins, John (Richard) 1931-1998 .. **CLC 4**
See also CA 85-88; 169; CBD; CD 5, 6

Hopkins, Pauline Elizabeth
1859-1930 .... **BLC 1:2; TCLC 28, 251**
See also AFAW 2; BW 2, 3; CA 141; CANR 82; DAM MULT; DLB 50

Hopkinson, Francis 1737-1791 .... **LC 25**
See also DLB 31; RGAL 4

Hopkinson, Nalo 1960- .... **CLC 316**
See also AAYA 40; CA 196, 219; CAAE 219; CANR 173; DLB 251

Hopley, George
See Hopley-Woolrich, Cornell George

Hopley-Woolrich, Cornell George
1903-1968 .... **CLC 77**
See also CA 13-14; CANR 58, 156; CAP 1; CMW 4; DLB 226; MSW; MTCW 2

Horace 65B.C.-8B.C. .. **CMLC 39, 125; PC 46**
See also AW 2; CDWLB 1; DLB 211; RGWL 2, 3; WLIT 8

Horatio
See Proust, Marcel

Horgan, Paul (George Vincent O'Shaughnessy) 1903-1995 .. **CLC 9, 53**
See also BPFB 2; CA 13-16R; 147; CANR 9, 35; CN 1, 2, 3, 4, 5; DAM NOV; DLB 102, 212; DLBY 1985; INT CANR-9; MTCW 1, 2; MTFW 2005; SATA 13; SATA-Obit 84; TCWW 1, 2

Horkheimer, Max 1895-1973 .... **TCLC 132**
See also CA 216; 41-44R; DLB 296

Horn, Peter
See Kuttner, Henry

Hornby, Nicholas Peter John
See Hornby, Nick

Hornby, Nick 1957(?)- .... **CLC 243**
See also AAYA 74; BRWS 15; CA 151; CANR 104, 151, 191; CN 7; DLB 207, 352

Horne, Frank 1899-1974 .... **HR 1:2**
See also BW 1; CA 125; 53-56; DLB 51; WP

Horne, Richard Henry Hengist
1802(?)-1884 .... **NCLC 127**
See also DLB 32; SATA 29

Hornem, Horace Esq.
See Lord Byron

Horne Tooke, John 1736-1812 ..... **NCLC 195**

Horney, Karen (Clementine Theodore Danielsen) 1885-1952 .... **TCLC 71**
See also CA 114; 165; DLB 246; FW

Hornung, E(rnest) W(illiam)
1866-1921 .... **TCLC 59**
See also CA 108; 160; CMW 4; DLB 70

Horovitz, Israel 1939- .... **CLC 56**
See also CA 33-36R; CAD; CANR 46, 59; CD 5, 6; DAM DRAM; DLB 7, 341; MAL 5

Horton, George Moses
1797(?)-1883(?) .... **NCLC 87**
See also DLB 50

Horvath, odon von 1901-1938
See von Horvath, Odon
See also EWL 3

Horvath, Oedoen von -1938
See von Horvath, Odon

Horwitz, Julius 1920-1986 .... **CLC 14**
See also CA 9-12R; 119; CANR 12

Horwitz, Ronald
See Harwood, Ronald

Hospital, Janette Turner 1942- .... **CLC 42, 145, 321**
See also CA 108; CANR 48, 166, 200; CN 5, 6, 7; DLB 325; DLBY 2002; RGSF 2

Hosseini, Khaled 1965- .... **CLC 254**
See also CA 225; LNFS 1, 3; SATA 156

Hostos, E. M. de
See Hostos (y Bonilla), Eugenio Maria de

Hostos, Eugenio M. de
See Hostos (y Bonilla), Eugenio Maria de

Hostos, Eugenio Maria
See Hostos (y Bonilla), Eugenio Maria de

Hostos (y Bonilla), Eugenio Maria de
1839-1903 .... **TCLC 24**
See also CA 123; 131; HW 1

Houdini
See Lovecraft, H. P.

Houellebecq, Michel 1958- ...... **CLC 179, 311**
See also CA 185; CANR 140, 231; MTFW 2005

Hougan, Carolyn 1943-2007 .... **CLC 34**
See also CA 139; 257

Household, Geoffrey 1900-1988 .... **CLC 11**
See also BRWS 17; CA 77-80; 126; CANR 58; CMW 4; CN 1, 2, 3, 4; DLB 87; SATA 14; SATA-Obit 59

Housman, A. E. 1859-1936 . **PC 2, 43; TCLC 1, 10; WLCS**
See also AAYA 66; BRW 6; CA 104; 125; DA; DA3; DAB; DAC; DAM MST, POET; DLB 19, 284; EWL 3; EXPP; MTCW 1, 2; MTFW 2005; PAB; PFS 4, 7, 40; RGEL 2; TEA; WP

Housman, Alfred Edward
See Housman, A. E.

Housman, Laurence 1865-1959 .... **TCLC 7**
See also CA 106; 155; DLB 10; FANT; RGEL 2; SATA 25

Houston, Jeanne Wakatsuki 1934- .... **AAL**
See also AAYA 49; CA 103, 232; CAAE 232; CAAS 16; CANR 29, 123, 167; LAIT 4; SATA 78, 168; SATA-Essay 168

Hove, Chenjerai 1956- .... **BLC 2:2**
See also CP 7; DLB 360

Howard, E. J.
See Howard, Elizabeth Jane

Howard, Elizabeth Jane 1923- ..... **CLC 7, 29**
See also BRWS 11; CA 5-8R; CANR 8, 62, 146, 210; CN 1, 2, 3, 4, 5, 6, 7

Howard, Maureen 1930- .... **CLC 5, 14, 46, 151**
See also CA 53-56; CANR 31, 75, 140, 221; CN 4, 5, 6, 7; DLBY 1983; INT CANR-31; MTCW 1, 2; MTFW 2005

Howard, Richard 1929- .... **CLC 7, 10, 47**
See also AITN 1; CA 85-88; CANR 25, 80, 154, 217; CP 1, 2, 3, 4, 5, 6, 7; DLB 5; INT CANR-25; MAL 5

Howard, Robert E 1906-1936 .... **TCLC 8**
See also AAYA 80; BPFB 2; BYA 5; CA 105; 157; CANR 155; FANT; SUFW 1; TCWW 1, 2

Howard, Robert Ervin
See Howard, Robert E

Howard, Sidney (Coe) 1891-1939 .... **DC 42**
See also CA 198; DFS 29; DLB 7, 26, 249; IDFW 3, 4; MAL 5; RGAL 4

Howard, Warren F.
See Pohl, Frederik

Howe, Fanny 1940- .... **CLC 47**
See also CA 117; 187; CAAE 187; CAAS 27; CANR 70, 116, 184; CP 6, 7; CWP; SATA-Brief 52

Howe, Fanny Quincy
See Howe, Fanny

Howe, Irving 1920-1993 .... **CLC 85**
See also AMWS 6; CA 9-12R; 141; CANR 21, 50; DLB 67; EWL 3; MAL 5; MTCW 1, 2; MTFW 2005

Howe, Julia Ward 1819-1910 . **PC 81; TCLC 21**
See also CA 117; 191; DLB 1, 189, 235; FW

Howe, Susan 1937- .... **CLC 72, 152; PC 54**
See also AMWS 4; CA 160; CANR 209; CP 5, 6, 7; CWP; DLB 120; FW; RGAL 4

Howe, Tina 1937- .... **CLC 48; DC 43**
See also CA 109; CAD; CANR 125; CD 5, 6; CWD; DLB 341

Howell, James 1594(?)-1666 .... **LC 13**
See also DLB 151

Howells, W. D.
See Howells, William Dean

Howells, William D.
See Howells, William Dean

Howells, William Dean 1837-1920 ... **SSC 36; TCLC 7, 17, 41**
See also AMW; CA 104; 134; CDALB 1865-1917; DLB 12, 64, 74, 79, 189; LMFS 1; MAL 5; MTCW 2; RGAL 4; TUS

Howes, Barbara 1914-1996 .... **CLC 15**
See also CA 9-12R; 151; CAAS 3; CANR 53; CP 1, 2, 3, 4, 5, 6; SATA 5; TCLE 1:1

Hrabal, Bohumil 1914-1997 ...... **CLC 13, 67; TCLC 155**
See also CA 106; 156; CAAS 12; CANR 57; CWW 2; DLB 232; EWL 3; RGSF 2

Hrabanus Maurus 776(?)-856 .... **CMLC 78**
See also DLB 148

Hroswitha of Gandersheim
See Hrotsvit of Gandersheim

Hrotsvit of Gandersheim c. 935-c. 1000 .... **CMLC 29, 123**
See also DLB 148

Hsi, Chu 1130-1200 .... **CMLC 42**

Hsun, Lu
See Shu-Jen, Chou

Hubbard, L. Ron 1911-1986 .... **CLC 43**
See also AAYA 64; CA 77-80; 118; CANR 52; CPW; DA3; DAM POP; FANT; MTCW 2; MTFW 2005; SFW 4

Hubbard, Lafayette Ronald
See Hubbard, L. Ron

Huch, Ricarda (Octavia)
1864-1947 .... **TCLC 13**
See also CA 111; 189; DLB 66; EWL 3

L. S.
  See Stephen, Sir Leslie
Labe, Louise 1521-1566 .... **LC 120**
  See also DLB 327
Labrunie, Gerard
  See Nerval, Gerard de
La Bruyere, Jean de 1645-1696 .. **LC 17, 168**
  See also DLB 268; EW 3; GFL Beginnings
  to 1789
LaBute, Neil 1963- .... **CLC 225**
  See also CA 240
Lacan, Jacques (Marie Emile)
  1901-1981 .... **CLC 75**
  See also CA 121; 104; DLB 296; EWL 3;
  TWA
Laclos, Pierre-Ambroise Francois
  1741-1803 .... **NCLC 4, 87, 239**
  See also DLB 313; EW 4; GFL Beginnings
  to 1789; RGWL 2, 3
La Colere, Francois
  See Aragon, Louis
Lacolere, Francois
  See Aragon, Louis
Lactantius c. 250-c. 325 .... **CMLC 118**
La Deshabilleuse
  See Simenon, Georges
Lady Gregory
  See Gregory, Lady Isabella Augusta (Persse)
Lady of Quality, A
  See Bagnold, Enid
La Fayette, Marie-(Madelaine Pioche de la
  Vergne) 1634-1693 .... **LC 2, 144**
  See also DLB 268; GFL Beginnings to
  1789; RGWL 2, 3
Lafayette, Marie-Madeleine
  See La Fayette, Marie-(Madelaine Pioche
  de la Vergne)
Lafayette, Rene
  See Hubbard, L. Ron
La Flesche, Francis 1857(?)-1932 ...... **NNAL**
  See also CA 144; CANR 83; DLB 175
La Fontaine, Jean de 1621-1695 . **LC 50, 184**
  See also DLB 268; EW 3; GFL Beginnings
  to 1789; MAICYA 1, 2; RGWL 2, 3;
  SATA 18
LaForet, Carmen 1921-2004 .... **CLC 219**
  See also CA 246; CWW 2; DLB 322; EWL
  3
LaForet Diaz, Carmen
  See LaForet, Carmen
Laforgue, Jules 1860-1887 .... **NCLC 5, 53,**
  221; PC 14; SSC 20
  See also DLB 217; EW 7; GFL 1789 to the
  Present; RGWL 2, 3
Lagerkvist, Paer 1891-1974 ... **CLC 7, 10, 13,**
  54; SSC 12; TCLC 144
  See also CA 85-88; 49-52; DA3; DAM
  DRAM, NOV; DLB 259, 331; EW 10;
  EWL 3; MTCW 1, 2; MTFW 2005; RGSF
  2; RGWL 2, 3; SSFS 33; TWA
Lagerkvist, Paer Fabian
  See Lagerkvist, Paer
Lagerkvist, Par
  See Lagerkvist, Paer
Lagerloef, Selma
  See Lagerlof, Selma
Lagerloef, Selma Ottiliana Lovisa
  See Lagerlof, Selma
Lagerlof, Selma 1858-1940 .... **TCLC 4, 36**
  See also CA 108; 188; CLR 7; DLB 259,
  331; MTCW 2; RGWL 2, 3; SATA 15;
  SSFS 18, 35
Lagerlof, Selma Ottiliana Lovisa
  See Lagerlof, Selma

La Guma, Alex 1925-1985 .. **BLCS; CLC 19;**
  TCLC 140
  See also AFW; BW 1, 3; CA 49-52; 118;
  CANR 25, 81; CDWLB 3; CN 1, 2, 3;
  CP 1; DAM NOV; DLB 117, 225; EWL
  3; MTCW 1, 2; MTFW 2005; WLIT 2;
  WWE 1
La Guma, Justin Alexander
  See La Guma, Alex
Lahiri, Jhumpa 1967- .... **CLC 282; SSC 96**
  See also AAYA 56; AMWS 21; CA 193;
  CANR 134, 184; DLB 323; MTFW 2005;
  NFS 31; SSFS 19, 27
Laidlaw, A. K.
  See Grieve, C. M.
Lainez, Manuel Mujica
  See Mujica Lainez, Manuel
Laing, R(onald) D(avid) 1927-1989 . **CLC 95**
  See also CA 107; 129; CANR 34; MTCW 1
Laishley, Alex
  See Booth, Martin
Lamartine, Alphonse de
  1790-1869 .... **NCLC 11, 190; PC 16**
  See also DAM POET; DLB 217; GFL 1789
  to the Present; RGWL 2, 3
Lamartine, Alphonse Marie Louis Prat de
  See Lamartine, Alphonse de
Lamb, Charles 1775-1834 ..... **NCLC 10, 113;**
  SSC 112; WLC 3
  See also BRW 4; CDBLB 1789-1832; DA;
  DAB; DAC; DAM MST; DLB 93, 107,
  163; RGEL 2; SATA 17; TEA
Lamb, Lady Caroline 1785-1828 ... **NCLC 38**
  See also DLB 116
Lamb, Mary Ann 1764-1847 ...... **NCLC 125;**
  SSC 112
  See also DLB 163; SATA 17
Lame Deer 1903(?)-1976 .... **NNAL**
  See also CA 69-72
La Mettrie, Julien Offroy de
  1709-1751 .... **LC 202**
  See also DLB 313
Lamming, George 1927- .... **BLC 1:2, 2:2;**
  CLC 2, 4, 66, 144
  See also BW 2, 3; CA 85-88; CANR 26,
  76; CDWLB 3; CN 1, 2, 3, 4, 5, 6, 7; CP
  1; DAM MULT; DLB 125; EWL 3;
  MTCW 1, 2; MTFW 2005; NFS 15;
  RGEL 2
Lamming, George William
  See Lamming, George
L'Amour, Louis 1908-1988 .... **CLC 25, 55**
  See also AAYA 16; AITN 2; BEST 89:2;
  BPFB 2; CA 1-4R; 125; CANR 3, 25, 40;
  CPW; DA3; DAM NOV, POP; DLB 206;
  DLBY 1980; MTCW 1, 2; MTFW 2005;
  RGAL 4; TCWW 1, 2
Lampedusa, Giuseppe di
  1896-1957 .... **TCLC 13**
  See also CA 111; 164; DLB 177; EW 11;
  EWL 3; MTCW 2; MTFW 2005; RGWL
  2, 3; WLIT 7
Lampman, Archibald 1861-1899 .. **NCLC 25,**
  194
  See also DLB 92; RGEL 2; TWA
Lancaster, Bruce 1896-1963 .... **CLC 36**
  See also CA 9-10; CANR 70; CAP 1; SATA
  9
Lanchester, John 1962- .... **CLC 99, 280**
  See also CA 194; DLB 267
Landau, Mark Alexandrovich
  See Aldanov, Mark (Alexandrovich)
Landau-Aldanov, Mark Alexandrovich
  See Aldanov, Mark (Alexandrovich)
Landis, Jerry
  See Simon, Paul
Landis, John 1950- .... **CLC 26**
  See also CA 112; 122; CANR 128

Landolfi, Tommaso 1908-1979 .... **CLC 11, 49**
  See also CA 127; 117; DLB 177; EWL 3
Landon, Letitia Elizabeth
  1802-1838 .... **NCLC 15**
  See also DLB 96
Landor, Walter Savage
  1775-1864 .... **NCLC 14**
  See also BRW 4; DLB 93, 107; RGEL 2
Landwirth, Heinz
  See Lind, Jakov
Lane, Patrick 1939- .... **CLC 25**
  See also CA 97-100; CANR 54; CP 3, 4, 5,
  6, 7; DAM POET; DLB 53; INT CA-97-
  100
Lane, Rose Wilder 1887-1968 ...... **TCLC 177**
  See also CA 102; CANR 63; SATA 29;
  SATA-Brief 28; TCWW 2
Lang, Andrew 1844-1912 .... **TCLC 16**
  See also CA 114; 137; CANR 85; CLR 101;
  DLB 98, 141, 184; FANT; MAICYA 1, 2;
  RGEL 2; SATA 16; WCH
Lang, Fritz 1890-1976 .... **CLC 20, 103**
  See also AAYA 65; CA 77-80; 69-72;
  CANR 30
Lange, John
  See Crichton, Michael
Langer, Elinor 1939- .... **CLC 34**
  See also CA 121
Langland, William 1332(?)-1400(?) .... **LC 19,**
  120
  See also BRW 1; DA; DAB; DAC; DAM
  MST, POET; DLB 146; RGEL 2; TEA;
  WLIT 3
Langstaff, Launcelot
  See Irving, Washington
Langton, Stephen c. 1165-1228 ... **CMLC 125**
Lanier, Sidney 1842-1881 . **NCLC 6, 118; PC**
  50
  See also AMWS 1; DAM POET; DLB 64;
  DLBD 13; EXPP; MAICYA 1; PFS 14;
  RGAL 4; SATA 18
Lanyer, Aemilia 1569-1645 .... **LC 10, 30, 83;**
  PC 60
  See also DLB 121
Lao Tzu c. 6th cent. B.C.-3rd cent.
  B.C. .... **CMLC 7, 125**
Lao-Tzu
  See Lao Tzu
Lapine, James (Elliot) 1949- .... **CLC 39**
  See also CA 123; 130; CANR 54, 128; DFS
  25; DLB 341; INT CA-130
La Ramee, Pierre de 1515(?)-1572 .... **LC 174**
  See also DLB 327
Larbaud, Valery (Nicolas)
  1881-1957 .... **TCLC 9**
  See also CA 106; 152; EWL 3; GFL 1789
  to the Present
Larcom, Lucy 1824-1893 .... **NCLC 179**
  See also AMWS 13; DLB 221, 243
Lardner, Ring 1885-1933 .... **SSC 32, 118;**
  TCLC 2, 14
  See also AMW; BPFB 2; CA 104; 131;
  CDALB 1917-1929; DLB 11, 25, 86, 171;
  DLBD 16; MAL 5; MTCW 1, 2; MTFW
  2005; RGAL 4; RGSF 2; TUS
Lardner, Ring W., Jr.
  See Lardner, Ring
Lardner, Ringold Wilmer
  See Lardner, Ring
Laredo, Betty
  See Codrescu, Andrei
Larkin, Maia
  See Wojciechowska, Maia (Teresa)
Larkin, Philip 1922-1985 ...... **CLC 3, 5, 8, 9,**
  13, 18, 33, 39, 64; PC 21
  See also BRWR 3; BRWS 1; CA 5-8R; 117;
  CANR 24, 62; CDBLB 1960 to Present;
  CP 1, 2, 3, 4; DA3; DAB; DAM MST,
  POET; DLB 27; EWL 3; MTCW 1, 2;
  MTFW 2005; PFS 3, 4, 12; RGEL 2

Author Index

Li Ho 791-817 .... **PC 13**

Li Ju-chen c. 1763-c. 1830 .... **NCLC 137**

Liking, Werewere 1950- .... **BLC 2:2**
See also CA 293; DLB 360; EWL 3

Lilar, Francoise
See Mallet-Joris, Francoise

Liliencron, Detlev
See Liliencron, Detlev von

Liliencron, Detlev von 1844-1909 .. **TCLC 18**
See also CA 117

Liliencron, Friedrich Adolf Axel Detlev von
See Liliencron, Detlev von

Liliencron, Friedrich Detlev von
See Liliencron, Detlev von

Lille, Alain de
See Alain de Lille

Lillo, George 1691-1739 .... **LC 131**
See also DLB 84; RGEL 2

Lilly, William 1602-1681 .... **LC 27**

Lima, Jose Lezama
See Lezama Lima, Jose

Lima Barreto, Afonso Henrique de
1881-1922 .... **TCLC 23**
See also CA 117; 181; DLB 307; LAW

Lima Barreto, Afonso Henriques de
See Lima Barreto, Afonso Henrique de

Limonov, Eduard
See Limonov, Edward

Limonov, Edward 1944- .... **CLC 67**
See also CA 137; DLB 317

Lin, Frank
See Atherton, Gertrude (Franklin Horn)

Lin, Yutang 1895-1976 .... **TCLC 149**
See also CA 45-48; 65-68; CANR 2; RGAL
4

Lincoln, Abraham 1809-1865 .... **NCLC 18,
201**
See also LAIT 2

Lincoln, Geoffrey
See Mortimer, John

Lind, Jakov 1927-2007 ... **CLC 1, 2, 4, 27, 82**
See also CA 9-12R; 257; CAAS 4; CANR
7; DLB 299; EWL 3; RGHL

Lindbergh, Anne Morrow
1906-2001 .... **CLC 82**
See also BPFB 2; CA 17-20R; 193; CANR
16, 73; DAM NOV; MTCW 1, 2; MTFW
2005; SATA 33; SATA-Obit 125; TUS

Lindbergh, Anne Spencer Morrow
See Lindbergh, Anne Morrow

Lindholm, Anna Margaret
See Haycraft, Anna

Lindsay, David 1878(?)-1945 .... **TCLC 15**
See also CA 113; 187; DLB 255; FANT;
SFW 4; SUFW 1

Lindsay, Nicholas Vachel
See Lindsay, Vachel

Lindsay, Vachel 1879-1931 ..... **PC 23; TCLC
17; WLC 4**
See also AMWS 1; CA 114; 135; CANR
79; CDALB 1865-1917; DA; DA3; DAC;
DAM MST, POET; DLB 54; EWL 3;
EXPP; MAL 5; RGAL 4; SATA 40; WP

Linke-Poot
See Doeblin, Alfred

Linney, Romulus 1930-2011 .... **CLC 51**
See also CA 1-4R; CAD; CANR 40, 44,
79; CD 5, 6; CSW; RGAL 4

Linton, Eliza Lynn 1822-1898 .... **NCLC 41**
See also DLB 18

Li Po 701-763 .... **CMLC 2, 86; PC 29**
See also PFS 20, 40; WP

Lippard, George 1822-1854 .... **NCLC 198**
See also DLB 202

Lipsius, Justus 1547-1606 .... **LC 16**

Lipsyte, Robert 1938- .... **CLC 21**
See also AAYA 7, 45; CA 17-20R; CANR
8, 57, 146, 189; CLR 23, 76; DA; DAC;
DAM MST, NOV; JRDA; LAIT 5; MAI-
CYA 1, 2; NFS 35; SATA 5, 68, 113, 161,
198; WYA; YAW

Lipsyte, Robert Michael
See Lipsyte, Robert

Lish, Gordon 1934- .... **CLC 45; SSC 18**
See also CA 113; 117; CANR 79, 151; DLB
130; INT CA-117

Lish, Gordon Jay
See Lish, Gordon

Lispector, Clarice 1925(?)-1977 .... **CLC 43;
HLCS 2; SSC 34, 96**
See also CA 139; 116; CANR 71; CDWLB
3; DLB 113, 307; DNFS 1; EWL 3; FW;
HW 2; LAW; RGSF 2; RGWL 2, 3; WLIT
1

Liszt, Franz 1811-1886 .... **NCLC 199**

Littell, Robert 1935(?)- .... **CLC 42**
See also CA 109; 112; CANR 64, 115, 162,
217; CMW 4

Little, Malcolm
See Malcolm X

Littlewit, Humphrey Gent.
See Lovecraft, H. P.

Litwos
See Sienkiewicz, Henryk (Adam Alexander
Pius)

Liu, E. 1857-1909 .... **TCLC 15**
See also CA 115; 190; DLB 328

Lively, Penelope 1933- .... **CLC 32, 50, 306**
See also BPFB 2; CA 41-44R; CANR 29,
67, 79, 131, 172, 222; CLR 7, 159; CN 5,
6, 7; CWRI 5; DAM NOV; DLB 14, 161,
207, 326; FANT; JRDA; MAICYA 1, 2;
MTCW 1, 2; MTFW 2005; SATA 7, 60,
101, 164; TEA

Lively, Penelope Margaret
See Lively, Penelope

Livesay, Dorothy (Kathleen)
1909-1996 .... **CLC 4, 15, 79**
See also AITN 2; CA 25-28R; CAAS 8;
CANR 36, 67; CP 1, 2, 3, 4, 5; DAC;
DAM MST, POET; DLB 68; FW; MTCW
1; RGEL 2; TWA

Livius Andronicus c. 284B.C.-c.
204B.C. .... **CMLC 102**

Livy c. 59B.C.-c. 12 .... **CMLC 11**
See also AW 2; CDWLB 1; DLB 211;
RGWL 2, 3; WLIT 8

Li Yaotang
See Jin, Ba

Li-Young, Lee
See Lee, Li-Young

Lizardi, Jose Joaquin Fernandez de
1776-1827 .... **NCLC 30**
See also LAW

Llewellyn, Richard
See Llewellyn Lloyd, Richard Dafydd Vivian

Llewellyn Lloyd, Richard Dafydd Vivian
1906-1983 .... **CLC 7, 80**
See also CA 53-56; 111; CANR 7, 71; DLB
15; NFS 30; SATA 11; SATA-Obit 37

Llosa, Jorge Mario Pedro Vargas
See Vargas Llosa, Mario

Llosa, Mario Vargas
See Vargas Llosa, Mario

Lloyd, Manda
See Mander, (Mary) Jane

Lloyd Webber, Andrew 1948- .... **CLC 21**
See also AAYA 1, 38; CA 116; 149; DAM
DRAM; DFS 7; SATA 56

Llull, Ramon c. 1235-c. 1316 .... **CMLC 12,
114**

Lobb, Ebenezer
See Upward, Allen

Lochhead, Liz 1947- .... **CLC 286**
See also BRWS 17; CA 81-84; CANR 79;
CBD; CD 5, 6; CP 2, 3, 4, 5, 6, 7; CWD;
CWP; DLB 310

Locke, Alain Leroy 1885-1954 .... **BLCS; HR
1:3; TCLC 43**
See also AMWS 14; BW 1, 3; CA 106; 124;
CANR 79; DLB 51; LMFS 2; MAL 5;
RGAL 4

Locke, John 1632-1704 .... **LC 7, 35, 135**
See also DLB 31, 101, 213, 252; RGEL 2;
WLIT 3

Locke-Elliott, Sumner
See Elliott, Sumner Locke

Lockhart, John Gibson 1794-1854 .. **NCLC 6**
See also DLB 110, 116, 144

Lockridge, Ross (Franklin), Jr.
1914-1948 .... **TCLC 111**
See also CA 108; 145; CANR 79; DLB 143;
DLBY 1980; MAL 5; RGAL 4; RHW

Lockwood, Robert
See Johnson, Robert

Lodge, David 1935- .... **CLC 36, 141, 293**
See also BEST 90:1; BRWS 4; CA 17-20R;
CANR 19, 53, 92, 139, 197; CN 1, 2, 3,
4, 5, 6, 7; CPW; DAM POP; DLB 14,
194; EWL 3; INT CANR-19; MTCW 1,
2; MTFW 2005

Lodge, David John
See Lodge, David

Lodge, Thomas 1558-1625 .... **LC 41**
See also DLB 172; RGEL 2

Loewinsohn, Ron(ald William)
1937- .... **CLC 52**
See also CA 25-28R; CANR 71; CP 1, 2, 3,
4

Logan, Jake
See Smith, Martin Cruz

Logan, John (Burton) 1923-1987 .... **CLC 5**
See also CA 77-80; 124; CANR 45; CP 1,
2, 3, 4; DLB 5

Lo-Johansson, (Karl) Ivar
1901-1990 .... **TCLC 216**
See also CA 102; 131; CANR 20, 79, 137;
DLB 259; EWL 3; RGWL 2, 3

Lo Kuan-chung 1330(?)-1400(?) .... **LC 12**

Lomax, Pearl
See Cleage, Pearl

Lomax, Pearl Cleage
See Cleage, Pearl

Lombard, Nap
See Johnson, Pamela Hansford

Lombard, Peter 1100(?)-1160(?) ... **CMLC 72**

Lombino, Salvatore
See Hunter, Evan

London, Jack 1876-1916 .... **SSC 4, 49, 133;
TCLC 9, 15, 39; WLC 4**
See also AAYA 13, 75; AITN 2; AMW;
BPFB 2; BYA 4, 13; CA 110; 119; CANR
73; CDALB 1865-1917; CLR 108; DA;
DA3; DAB; DAC; DAM MST, NOV;
DLB 8, 12, 78, 212; EWL 3; EXPS;
JRDA; LAIT 3; MAICYA 1, 2,; MAL 5;
MTCW 1, 2; MTFW 2005; NFS 8, 19,
35; RGAL 4; RGSF 2; SATA 18; SFW 4;
SSFS 7, 35; TCWW 1, 2; TUS; WYA;
YAW

London, John Griffith
See London, Jack

Long, Emmett
See Leonard, Elmore

Longbaugh, Harry
See Goldman, William

Luxemburg, Rosa 1870(?)-1919 ..... **TCLC 63**
　　See also CA 118
Lu Xun 1881-1936 .... **SSC 158**
　　See also CA 243; DLB 328; RGSF 2;
　　RGWL 2, 3
Luzi, Mario (Egidio Vincenzo)
　　1914-2005 .... **CLC 13**
　　See also CA 61-64; 236; CANR 9, 70;
　　CWW 2; DLB 128; EWL 3
L'vov, Arkady CLC 59
Lydgate, John c. 1370-1450(?) ..... **LC 81, 175**
　　See also BRW 1; DLB 146; RGEL 2
Lyly, John 1554(?)-1606 .... **DC 7; LC 41, 187**
　　See also BRW 1; DAM DRAM; DLB 62,
　　167; RGEL 2
L'Ymagier
　　See Gourmont, Remy(-Marie-Charles) de
Lynch, B. Suarez
　　See Borges, Jorge Luis
Lynch, David 1946- .... **CLC 66, 162**
　　See also AAYA 55; CA 124; 129; CANR
　　111
Lynch, David Keith
　　See Lynch, David
Lynch, James
　　See Andreyev, Leonid
Lyndsay, Sir David 1485-1555 .... **LC 20**
　　See also RGEL 2
Lynn, Kenneth S(chuyler)
　　1923-2001 .... **CLC 50**
　　See also CA 1-4R; 196; CANR 3, 27, 65
Lynx
　　See West, Rebecca
Lyons, Marcus
　　See Blish, James
Lyotard, Jean-Francois
　　1924-1998 .... **TCLC 103**
　　See also DLB 242; EWL 3
Lyre, Pinchbeck
　　See Sassoon, Siegfried
Lytle, Andrew (Nelson) 1902-1995 ... **CLC 22**
　　See also CA 9-12R; 150; CANR 70; CN 1,
　　2, 3, 4, 5, 6; CSW; DLB 6; DLBY 1995;
　　RGAL 4; RHW
Lyttelton, George 1709-1773 .... **LC 10**
　　See also RGEL 2
Lytton, Edward G.E.L. Bulwer-Lytton
　　Baron
　　See Bulwer-Lytton, Edward
Lytton of Knebworth, Baron
　　See Bulwer-Lytton, Edward
Maalouf, Amin 1949- .... **CLC 248**
　　See also CA 212; CANR 194; DLB 346
Maas, Peter 1929-2001 .... **CLC 29**
　　See also CA 93-96; 201; INT CA-93-96;
　　MTCW 2; MTFW 2005
Mac A'Ghobhainn, Iain
　　See Smith, Iain Crichton
Macaulay, Catharine 1731-1791 .... **LC 64**
　　See also BRWS 17; DLB 104, 336
Macaulay, (Emilie) Rose
　　1881(?)-1958 .... **TCLC 7, 44**
　　See also CA 104; DLB 36; EWL 3; RGEL
　　2; RHW
Macaulay, Thomas Babington
　　1800-1859 .... **NCLC 42, 231**
　　See also BRW 4; CDBLB 1832-1890; DLB
　　32, 55; RGEL 2
MacBeth, George (Mann)
　　1932-1992 .... **CLC 2, 5, 9**
　　See also CA 25-28R; 136; CANR 61, 66;
　　CP 1, 2, 3, 4, 5; DLB 40; MTCW 1; PFS
　　8; SATA 4; SATA-Obit 70
MacCaig, Norman (Alexander)
　　1910-1996 .... **CLC 36**
　　See also BRWS 6; CA 9-12R; CANR 3, 34;
　　CP 1, 2, 3, 4, 5, 6; DAB; DAM POET;
　　DLB 27; EWL 3; RGEL 2

MacCarthy, Sir (Charles Otto) Desmond
　　1877-1952 .... **TCLC 36**
　　See also CA 167
MacDiarmid, Hugh
　　See Grieve, C. M.
MacDonald, Anson
　　See Heinlein, Robert A.
Macdonald, Cynthia 1928- .... **CLC 13, 19**
　　See also CA 49-52; CANR 4, 44, 146; DLB
　　105
MacDonald, George 1824-1905 .... **TCLC 9,
　　113, 207**
　　See also AAYA 57; BYA 5; CA 106; 137;
　　CANR 80; CLR 67; DLB 18, 163, 178;
　　FANT; MAICYA 1, 2; RGEL 2; SATA 33,
　　100; SFW 4; SUFW; WCH
Macdonald, John
　　See Millar, Kenneth
MacDonald, John D. 1916-1986 .. **CLC 3, 27,
　　44**
　　See also BPFB 2; CA 1-4R; 121; CANR 1,
　　19, 60; CMW 4; CPW; DAM NOV, POP;
　　DLB 8, 306; DLBY 1986; MSW; MTCW
　　1, 2; MTFW 2005; SFW 4
Macdonald, John Ross
　　See Millar, Kenneth
Macdonald, Ross
　　See Millar, Kenneth
MacDonald Fraser, George
　　See Fraser, George MacDonald
MacDougal, John
　　See Blish, James
MacDowell, John
　　See Parks, Tim
MacEwen, Gwendolyn (Margaret)
　　1941-1987 .... **CLC 13, 55**
　　See also CA 9-12R; 124; CANR 7, 22; CP
　　1, 2, 3, 4; DLB 53, 251; SATA 50; SATA-
　　Obit 55
MacGreevy, Thomas 1893-1967 .... **PC 82**
　　See also CA 262
Macha, Karel Hynek 1810-1846 .... **NCLC 46**
Machado (y Ruiz), Antonio
　　1875-1939 .... **TCLC 3**
　　See also CA 104; 174; DLB 108; EW 9;
　　EWL 3; HW 2; PFS 23; RGWL 2, 3
Machado de Assis, Joaquim Maria
　　1839-1908 . **BLC 1:2; HLCS 2; SSC 24,
　　118; TCLC 10**
　　See also CA 107; 153; CANR 91; DLB 307;
　　LAW; RGSF 2; RGWL 2, 3; TWA; WLIT
　　1
Machaut, Guillaume de c.
　　1300-1377 .... **CMLC 64**
　　See also DLB 208
Machen, Arthur
　　See Jones, Arthur Llewellyn
Machen, Arthur Llewelyn Jones
　　See Jones, Arthur Llewellyn
Machiavelli, Niccolo 1469-1527 ... **DC 16; LC
　　8, 36, 140; WLCS**
　　See also AAYA 58; DA; DAB; DAC; DAM
　　MST; EW 2; LAIT 1; LMFS 1; NFS 9;
　　RGWL 2, 3; TWA; WLIT 7
MacInnes, Colin 1914-1976 .... **CLC 4, 23**
　　See also CA 69-72; 65-68; CANR 21; CN
　　1, 2; DLB 14; MTCW 1, 2; RGEL 2;
　　RHW
MacInnes, Helen (Clark)
　　1907-1985 .... **CLC 27, 39**
　　See also BPFB 2; CA 1-4R; 117; CANR 1,
　　28, 58; CMW 4; CN 1, 2; CPW; DAM
　　POP; DLB 87; MSW; MTCW 1, 2;
　　MTFW 2005; SATA 22; SATA-Obit 44
Mackay, Mary 1855-1924 .... **TCLC 51**
　　See also CA 118; 177; DLB 34, 156; FANT;
　　RGEL 2; RHW; SUFW 1

Mackay, Shena 1944- .... **CLC 195**
　　See also CA 104; CANR 88, 139, 207; DLB
　　231, 319; MTFW 2005
Mackenzie, Compton (Edward Montague)
　　1883-1972 .... **CLC 18; TCLC 116**
　　See also CA 21-22; 37-40R; CAP 2; CN 1;
　　DLB 34, 100; RGEL 2
Mackenzie, Henry 1745-1831 .... **NCLC 41**
　　See also DLB 39; RGEL 2
Mackey, Nathaniel 1947- .... **BLC 2:3; PC 49**
　　See also CA 153; CANR 114; CP 6, 7; DLB
　　169
Mackey, Nathaniel Ernest
　　See Mackey, Nathaniel
MacKinnon, Catharine
　　See MacKinnon, Catharine A.
MacKinnon, Catharine A. 1946- .... **CLC 181**
　　See also CA 128; 132; CANR 73, 140, 189;
　　FW; MTCW 2; MTFW 2005
Mackintosh, Elizabeth
　　1896(?)-1952 .... **TCLC 14**
　　See also CA 110; CMW 4; DLB 10, 77;
　　MSW
Macklin, Charles 1699-1797 .... **LC 132**
　　See also DLB 89; RGEL 2
MacLaren, James
　　See Grieve, C. M.
MacLaverty, Bernard 1942- ..... **CLC 31, 243**
　　See also CA 116; 118; CANR 43, 88, 168;
　　CN 5, 6, 7; DLB 267; INT CA-118; RGSF
　　2
MacLean, Alistair 1922(?)-1987 .. **CLC 3, 13,
　　50, 63**
　　See also CA 57-60; 121; CANR 28, 61;
　　CMW 4; CP 2, 3, 4, 5, 6, 7; CPW; DAM
　　POP; DLB 276; MTCW 1; SATA 23;
　　SATA-Obit 50; TCWW 2
MacLean, Alistair Stuart
　　See MacLean, Alistair
Maclean, Norman (Fitzroy)
　　1902-1990 .... **CLC 78; SSC 13, 136**
　　See also AMWS 14; CA 102; 132; CANR
　　49; CPW; DAM POP; DLB 206; TCWW
　　2
MacLeish, Archibald 1892-1982 ... **CLC 3, 8,
　　14, 68; DC 43; PC 47**
　　See also AMW; CA 9-12R; 106; CAD;
　　CANR 33, 63; CDALBS; CP 1, 2; DAM
　　POET; DFS 15; DLB 4, 7, 45; DLBY
　　1982; EWL 3; EXPP; MAL 5; MTCW 1,
　　2; MTFW 2005; PAB; PFS 5; RGAL 4;
　　TUS
MacLennan, (John) Hugh
　　1907-1990 .... **CLC 2, 14, 92**
　　See also CA 5-8R; 142; CANR 33; CN 1,
　　2, 3, 4; DAC; DAM MST; DLB 68; EWL
　　3; MTCW 1, 2; MTFW 2005; RGEL 2;
　　TWA
MacLeod, Alistair 1936- .. **CLC 56, 165; SSC
　　90**
　　See also CA 123; CCA 1; DAC; DAM
　　MST; DLB 60; MTCW 2; MTFW 2005;
　　RGSF 2; TCLE 1:2
Macleod, Fiona
　　See Sharp, William
MacNeice, (Frederick) Louis
　　1907-1963 .... **CLC 1, 4, 10, 53; PC 61**
　　See also BRW 7; CA 85-88; CANR 61;
　　DAB; DAM POET; DLB 10, 20; EWL 3;
　　MTCW 1, 2; MTFW 2005; RGEL 2
MacNeill, Dand
　　See Fraser, George MacDonald
Macpherson, James 1736-1796 .... **CMLC 28;
　　LC 29, 196; PC 97**
　　See also BRWS 8; DLB 109, 336; RGEL 2
Macpherson, (Jean) Jay 1931- .... **CLC 14**
　　See also CA 5-8R; CANR 90; CP 1, 2, 3, 4,
　　6, 7; CWP; DLB 53

Mankiewicz, Herman (Jacob)
1897-1953 .... **TCLC 85**
See also CA 120; 169; DLB 26; IDFW 3, 4
Manley, (Mary) Delariviere
1672(?)-1724 .... **LC 1, 42**
See also DLB 39, 80; RGEL 2
Mann, Abel
See Creasey, John
Mann, Emily 1952- .... **DC 7**
See also CA 130; CAD; CANR 55; CD 5,
6; CWD; DFS 28; DLB 266
Mann, Erica
See Jong, Erica
Mann, (Luiz) Heinrich 1871-1950 ... **TCLC 9**
See also CA 106; 164, 181; DLB 66, 118;
EW 8; EWL 3; RGWL 2, 3
Mann, Paul Thomas
See Mann, Thomas
Mann, Thomas 1875-1955 ...... **SSC 5, 80, 82;**
TCLC 2, 8, 14, 21, 35, 44, 60, 168, 236;
WLC 4
See also BPFB 2; CA 104; 128; CANR 133;
CDWLB 2; DA; DA3; DAB; DAC; DAM
MST, NOV; DLB 66, 331; EW 9; EWL 3;
GLL 1; LATS 1:1; LMFS 1; MTCW 1, 2;
MTFW 2005; NFS 17; RGSF 2; RGWL
2, 3; SSFS 4, 9; TWA
Mannheim, Karl 1893-1947 .... **TCLC 65**
See also CA 204
Manning, David
See Faust, Frederick
Manning, Frederic 1882-1935 .... **TCLC 25**
See also CA 124; 216; DLB 260
Manning, Olivia 1915-1980 .... **CLC 5, 19**
See also CA 5-8R; 101; CANR 29; CN 1,
2; EWL 3; FW; MTCW 1; RGEL 2
Mannyng, Robert c. 1264-c.
1340 .... **CMLC 83**
See also DLB 146
Mano, D. Keith 1942- .... **CLC 2, 10**
See also CA 25-28R; CAAS 6; CANR 26,
57; DLB 6
Mansfield, Katherine 1888-1923 .. **SSC 9, 23,**
38, 81; TCLC 2, 8, 39, 164; WLC 4
See also BPFB 2; BRW 7; CA 104; 134;
DA; DA3; DAB; DAC; DAM MST; DLB
162; EWL 3; EXPS; FW; GLL 1; MTCW
2; RGEL 2; RGSF 2; SSFS 2, 8, 10, 11,
29; TEA; WWE 1
Mansfield, Kathleen
See Mansfield, Katherine
Manso, Peter 1940- .... **CLC 39**
See also CA 29-32R; CANR 44, 156
Mantecon, Juan Jimenez
See Jimenez, Juan Ramon
Mantel, Hilary 1952- .... **CLC 144, 309**
See also CA 125; CANR 54, 101, 161, 207;
CN 5, 6, 7; DLB 271; RHW
Mantel, Hilary Mary
See Mantel, Hilary
Manton, Peter
See Creasey, John
Man Without a Spleen, A
See Chekhov, Anton
Manzano, Juan Franciso
1797(?)-1854 .... **NCLC 155**
Manzoni, Alessandro 1785-1873 ... **NCLC 29,**
98
See also EW 5; RGWL 2, 3; TWA; WLIT 7
Map, Walter 1140-1209 .... **CMLC 32**
Mapu, Abraham (ben Jekutiel)
1808-1867 .... **NCLC 18**
Mara, Sally
See Queneau, Raymond
Maracle, Lee 1950- .... **NNAL**
See also CA 149

Marat, Jean Paul 1743-1793 .... **LC 10**
Marcel, Gabriel Honore 1889-1973 . **CLC 15**
See also CA 102; 45-48; EWL 3; MTCW 1,
2
March, William 1893-1954 .... **TCLC 96**
See also CA 108; 216; DLB 9, 86, 316;
MAL 5
Marchbanks, Samuel
See Davies, Robertson
Marchi, Giacomo
See Bassani, Giorgio
Marcus Aurelius
See Aurelius, Marcus
Marcuse, Herbert 1898-1979 .... **TCLC 207**
See also CA 188; 89-92; DLB 242
Marguerite
See de Navarre, Marguerite
Marguerite d'Angouleme
See de Navarre, Marguerite
Marguerite de Navarre
See de Navarre, Marguerite
Margulies, Donald 1954- .... **CLC 76**
See also AAYA 57; CA 200; CD 6; DFS 13;
DLB 228
Marias, Javier 1951- .... **CLC 239**
See also CA 167; CANR 109, 139, 232;
DLB 322; HW 2; MTFW 2005
Marie de France c. 12th cent. - ...... **CMLC 8,**
111; PC 22
See also DLB 208; FW; RGWL 2, 3
Marie de l'Incarnation 1599-1672 ..... **LC 10,**
168
Marier, Captain Victor
See Griffith, D.W.
Mariner, Scott
See Pohl, Frederik
Marinetti, Filippo Tommaso
1876-1944 .... **TCLC 10**
See also CA 107; DLB 114, 264; EW 9;
EWL 3; WLIT 7
Marino, Giambattista 1569-1625 ...... **LC 181**
See also DLB 339; WLIT 7
Marivaux, Pierre Carlet de Chamblain de
1688-1763 .... **DC 7; LC 4, 123**
See also DLB 314; GFL Beginnings to
1789; RGWL 2, 3; TWA
Markandaya, Kamala 1924-2004 ...... **CLC 8,**
38, 290
See also BYA 13; CA 77-80; 227; CN 1, 2,
3, 4, 5, 6, 7; DLB 323; EWL 3; MTFW
2005; NFS 13
Markfield, Wallace (Arthur)
1926-2002 .... **CLC 8**
See also CA 69-72; 208; CAAS 3; CN 1, 2,
3, 4, 5, 6, 7; DLB 2, 28; DLBY 2002
Markham, Edwin 1852-1940 .... **TCLC 47**
See also CA 160; DLB 54, 186; MAL 5;
RGAL 4
Markham, Robert
See Amis, Kingsley
Marks, J.
See Highwater, Jamake (Mamake)
Marks-Highwater, J.
See Highwater, Jamake (Mamake)
Markson, David M. 1927-2010 .... **CLC 67**
See also AMWS 17; CA 49-52; CANR 1,
91, 158; CN 5, 6
Markson, David Merrill
See Markson, David M.
Marlatt, Daphne (Buckle) 1942- .... **CLC 168**
See also CA 25-28R; CANR 17, 39; CN 6,
7; CP 4, 5, 6, 7; CWP; DLB 60; FW
Marley, Bob
See Marley, Robert Nesta
Marley, Robert Nesta 1945-1981 ...... **CLC 17**
See also CA 107; 103

Marlowe, Christopher 1564-1593 . **DC 1; LC**
22, 47, 117, 201; PC 57; WLC 4
See also BRW 1; BRWR 1; CDBLB Before
1660; DA; DA3; DAB; DAC; DAM
DRAM, MST; DFS 1, 5, 13, 21; DLB 62;
EXPP; LMFS 1; PFS 22; RGEL 2; TEA;
WLIT 3
Marlowe, Stephen 1928-2008 .... **CLC 70**
See also CA 13-16R; 269; CANR 6, 55;
CMW 4; SFW 4
Marmion, Shakerley 1603-1639 .... **LC 89**
See also DLB 58; RGEL 2
Marmontel, Jean-Francois 1723-1799 .. **LC 2**
See also DLB 314
Maron, Monika 1941- .... **CLC 165**
See also CA 201
Marot, Clement c. 1496-1544 .... **LC 133**
See also DLB 327; GFL Beginnings to 1789
Marquand, John P(hillips)
1893-1960 .... **CLC 2, 10**
See also AMW; BPFB 2; CA 85-88; CANR
73; CMW 4; DLB 9, 102; EWL 3; MAL
5; MTCW 2; RGAL 4
Marques, Rene 1919-1979 .. **CLC 96; HLC 2**
See also CA 97-100; 85-88; CANR 78;
DAM MULT; DLB 305; EWL 3; HW 1,
2; LAW; RGSF 2
Marquez, Gabriel Garcia
See Garcia Marquez, Gabriel
Marquez, Gabriel Garcia
See Garcia Marquez, Gabriel
Marquis, Don(ald Robert Perry)
1878-1937 .... **TCLC 7**
See also CA 104; 166; DLB 11, 25; MAL
5; RGAL 4
Marquis de Sade
See Sade, Donatien Alphonse Francois
Marric, J. J.
See Creasey, John
Marryat, Frederick 1792-1848 .... **NCLC 3**
See also DLB 21, 163; RGEL 2; WCH
Marsden, James
See Creasey, John
Marse, Juan 1933- .... **CLC 302**
See also CA 254; DLB 322
Marsh, Edith Ngaio
See Marsh, Ngaio
Marsh, Edward 1872-1953 .... **TCLC 99**
Marsh, Ngaio 1895-1982 .... **CLC 7, 53**
See also CA 9-12R; CANR 6, 58; CMW 4;
CN 1, 2, 3; CPW; DAM POP; DLB 77;
MSW; MTCW 1, 2; RGEL 2; TEA
Marshall, Alan
See Westlake, Donald E.
Marshall, Allen
See Westlake, Donald E.
Marshall, Garry 1934- .... **CLC 17**
See also AAYA 3; CA 111; SATA 60
Marshall, Paule 1929- .... **BLC 1:3, 2:3; CLC**
27, 72, 253; SSC 3
See also AFAW 1, 2; AMWS 11; BPFB 2;
BW 2, 3; CA 77-80; CANR 25, 73, 129,
209; CN 1, 2, 3, 4, 5, 6, 7; DA3; DAM
MULT; DLB 33, 157, 227; EWL 3; LATS
1:2; MAL 5; MTCW 1, 2; MTFW 2005;
NFS 36; RGAL 4; SSFS 15
Marshallik
See Zangwill, Israel
Marsilius of Inghen c.
1340-1396 .... **CMLC 106**
Marsten, Richard
See Hunter, Evan
Marston, John 1576-1634 ...... **DC 37; LC 33,**
172
See also BRW 2; DAM DRAM; DLB 58,
172; RGEL 2

Martel, Yann 1963- .... **CLC 192, 315**
    See also AAYA 67; CA 146; CANR 114,
    226; DLB 326, 334; LNFS 2; MTFW
    2005; NFS 27

Martens, Adolphe-Adhemar
    See Ghelderode, Michel de

Martha, Henry
    See Harris, Mark

Marti, Jose 1853-1895 ..... **HLC 2; NCLC 63;**
    PC 76
    See also DAM MULT; DLB 290; HW 2;
    LAW; RGWL 2, 3; WLIT 1

Martial c. 40-c. 104 .... **CMLC 35; PC 10**
    See also AW 2; CDWLB 1; DLB 211;
    RGWL 2, 3

Martin, Ken
    See Hubbard, L. Ron

Martin, Richard
    See Creasey, John

Martin, Steve 1945- .... **CLC 30, 217**
    See also AAYA 53; CA 97-100; CANR 30,
    100, 140, 195, 227; DFS 19; MTCW 1;
    MTFW 2005

Martin, Valerie 1948- .... **CLC 89**
    See also BEST 90:2; CA 85-88; CANR 49,
    89, 165, 200

Martin, Violet Florence 1862-1915 .. **SSC 56;**
    TCLC 51

Martin, Webber
    See Silverberg, Robert

Martindale, Patrick Victor
    See White, Patrick

Martin du Gard, Roger
    1881-1958 .... **TCLC 24**
    See also CA 118; CANR 94; DLB 65, 331;
    EWL 3; GFL 1789 to the Present; RGWL
    2, 3

Martineau, Harriet 1802-1876 ...... **NCLC 26,**
    137
    See also BRWS 15; DLB 21, 55, 159, 163,
    166, 190; FW; RGEL 2; YABC 2

Martines, Julia
    See O'Faolain, Julia

Martinez, Enrique Gonzalez
    See Gonzalez Martinez, Enrique

Martinez, Jacinto Benavente y
    See Benavente, Jacinto

Martinez de la Rosa, Francisco de Paula
    1787-1862 .... **NCLC 102**
    See also TWA

Martinez Ruiz, Jose 1873-1967 .... **CLC 11**
    See also CA 93-96; DLB 322; EW 3; EWL
    3; HW 1

Martinez Sierra, Gregorio
    See Martinez Sierra, Maria

Martinez Sierra, Gregorio
    1881-1947 .... **TCLC 6**
    See also CA 115; EWL 3

Martinez Sierra, Maria 1874-1974 .. **TCLC 6**
    See also CA 250; 115; EWL 3

Martinez Sierra, Maria de la O'LeJarraga
    See Martinez Sierra, Maria

Martinsen, Martin
    See Follett, Ken

Martinson, Harry (Edmund)
    1904-1978 .... **CLC 14**
    See also CA 77-80; CANR 34, 130; DLB
    259, 331; EWL 3

Marti y Perez, Jose Julian
    See Marti, Jose

Martyn, Edward 1859-1923 .... **TCLC 131**
    See also CA 179; DLB 10; RGEL 2

Marut, Ret
    See Traven, B.

Marut, Robert
    See Traven, B.

Marvell, Andrew 1621-1678 ... **LC 4, 43, 179;**
    PC 10, 86; WLC 4
    See also BRW 2; BRWR 2; CDBLB 1660-
    1789; DA; DAB; DAC; DAM MST,
    POET; DLB 131; EXPP; PFS 5; RGEL 2;
    TEA; WP

Marx, Karl 1818-1883 .... **NCLC 17, 114**
    See also DLB 129; LATS 1:1; TWA

Marx, Karl Heinrich
    See Marx, Karl

Masaoka, Shiki -1902
    See Masaoka, Tsunenori

Masaoka, Tsunenori 1867-1902 ..... **TCLC 18**
    See also CA 117; 191; EWL 3; RGWL 3;
    TWA

Masaoka Shiki
    See Masaoka, Tsunenori)

Masefield, John (Edward)
    1878-1967 .... **CLC 11, 47; PC 78**
    See also CA 19-20; 25-28R; CANR 33;
    CAP 2; CDBLB 1890-1914; CLR 164;
    DAM POET; DLB 10, 19, 153, 160; EWL
    3; EXPP; FANT; MTCW 1, 2; PFS 5;
    RGEL 2; SATA 19

Maso, Carole 1955(?)- .... **CLC 44**
    See also CA 170; CANR 148; CN 7; GLL
    2; RGAL 4

Mason, Bobbie Ann 1940- ... **CLC 28, 43, 82,**
    154, 303; SSC 4, 101
    See also AAYA 5, 42; AMWS 8; BPFB 2;
    CA 53-56; CANR 11, 31, 58, 83, 125,
    169; CDALBS; CN 5, 6, 7; CSW; DA3;
    DLB 173; DLBY 1987; EWL 3; EXPS;
    INT CANR-31; MAL 5; MTCW 1, 2;
    MTFW 2005; NFS 4; RGAL 4; RGSF 2;
    SSFS 3, 8, 20; TCLE 1:2; YAW

Mason, Ernst
    See Pohl, Frederik

Mason, Hunni B.
    See Sternheim, (William Adolf) Carl

Mason, Lee W.
    See Malzberg, Barry N(athaniel)

Mason, Nick 1945- .... **CLC 35**

Mason, Tally
    See Derleth, August (William)

Mass, Anna CLC 59

Mass, William
    See Gibson, William

Massinger, Philip 1583-1640 .. **DC 39; LC 70**
    See also BRWS 11; DLB 58; RGEL 2

Master Lao
    See Lao Tzu

Masters, Edgar Lee 1868-1950 ...... **PC 1, 36;**
    TCLC 2, 25; WLCS
    See also AMWS 1; CA 104; 133; CDALB
    1865-1917; DA; DAC; DAM MST,
    POET; DLB 54; EWL 3; EXPP; MAL 5;
    MTCW 1, 2; MTFW 2005; PFS 37;
    RGAL 4; TUS; WP

Masters, Hilary 1928- .... **CLC 48**
    See also CA 25-28R; 217; CAAE 217;
    CANR 13, 47, 97, 171, 221; CN 6, 7;
    DLB 244

Masters, Hilary Thomas
    See Masters, Hilary

Mastrosimone, William 1947- .... **CLC 36**
    See also CA 186; CAD; CD 5, 6

Mathe, Albert
    See Camus, Albert

Mather, Cotton 1663-1728 .... **LC 38**
    See also AMWS 2; CDALB 1640-1865;
    DLB 24, 30, 140; RGAL 4; TUS

Mather, Increase 1639-1723 .... **LC 38, 161**
    See also DLB 24

Mathers, Marshall
    See Eminem

Mathers, Marshall Bruce
    See Eminem

Matheson, Richard 1926- .... **CLC 37, 267**
    See also AAYA 31; CA 97-100; CANR 88,
    99; DLB 8, 44; HGG; INT CA-97-100;
    SCFW 1, 2; SFW 4; SUFW 2

Matheson, Richard Burton
    See Matheson, Richard

Mathews, Harry 1930- .... **CLC 6, 52**
    See also CA 21-24R; CAAS 6; CANR 18,
    40, 98, 160; CN 5, 6, 7

Mathews, John Joseph 1894-1979 .. **CLC 84;**
    NNAL
    See also CA 19-20; 142; CANR 45; CAP 2;
    DAM MULT; DLB 175; TCWW 1, 2

Mathias, Roland 1915-2007 .... **CLC 45**
    See also CA 97-100; 263; CANR 19, 41;
    CP 1, 2, 3, 4, 5, 6, 7; DLB 27

Mathias, Roland Glyn
    See Mathias, Roland

Matsuo Basho 1644(?)-1694 ..... **LC 62; PC 3,**
    125
    See also DAM POET; PFS 2, 7, 18; RGWL
    2, 3; WP

Mattheson, Rodney
    See Creasey, John

Matthew, James
    See Barrie, J. M.

Matthew of Vendome c. 1130-c.
    1200 .... **CMLC 99**
    See also DLB 208

Matthews, (James) Brander
    1852-1929 .... **TCLC 95**
    See also CA 181; DLB 71, 78; DLBD 13

Matthews, Greg 1949- .... **CLC 45**
    See also CA 135

Matthews, William (Procter III)
    1942-1997 .... **CLC 40**
    See also AMWS 9; CA 29-32R; 162; CAAS
    18; CANR 12, 57; CP 2, 3, 4, 5, 6; DLB
    5

Matthias, John (Edward) 1941- .... **CLC 9**
    See also CA 33-36R; CANR 56; CP 4, 5, 6,
    7

Matthiessen, F(rancis) O(tto)
    1902-1950 .... **TCLC 100**
    See also CA 185; DLB 63; MAL 5

Matthiessen, Francis Otto
    See Matthiessen, F(rancis) O(tto)

Matthiessen, Peter 1927- ... **CLC 5, 7, 11, 32,**
    64, 245
    See also AAYA 6, 40; AMWS 5; ANW;
    BEST 90:4; BPFB 2; CA 9-12R; CANR
    21, 50, 73, 100, 138; CN 1, 2, 3, 4, 5, 6,
    7; DA3; DAM NOV; DLB 6, 173, 275;
    MAL 5; MTCW 1, 2; MTFW 2005; SATA
    27

Maturin, Charles Robert
    1780(?)-1824 .... **NCLC 6, 169**
    See also BRWS 8; DLB 178; GL 3; HGG;
    LMFS 1; RGEL 2; SUFW

Matute (Ausejo), Ana Maria 1925- .. **CLC 11**
    See also CA 89-92; CANR 129; CWW 2;
    DLB 322; EWL 3; MTCW 1; RGSF 2

Maugham, W. S.
    See Maugham, W. Somerset

Maugham, W. Somerset 1874-1965 ... **CLC 1,**
    11, 15, 67, 93; SSC 8, 94, 164; TCLC
    208; WLC 4
    See also AAYA 55; BPFB 2; BRW 6; CA
    5-8R; 25-28R; CANR 40, 127; CDBLB
    1914-1945; CMW 4; DA; DA3; DAB;
    DAC; DAM DRAM, MST, NOV; DFS
    22; DLB 10, 36, 77, 100, 162, 195; EWL
    3; LAIT 3; MTCW 1, 2; MTFW 2005;
    NFS 23, 35; RGEL 2; RGSF 2; SATA 54;
    SSFS 17

Maugham, William S.
    See Maugham, W. Somerset

Maugham, William Somerset
    See Maugham, W. Somerset

Maupassant, Guy de 1850-1893 ..... **NCLC 1, 42, 83, 234; SSC 1, 64, 132; WLC 4**
See also BYA 14; DA; DA3; DAB; DAC; DAM MST; DLB 123; EW 7; EXPS; GFL 1789 to the Present; LAIT 2; LMFS 1; RGSF 2; RGWL 2, 3; SSFS 4, 21, 28, 31; SUFW; TWA

Maupassant, Henri Rene Albert Guy de
See Maupassant, Guy de

Maupin, Armistead 1944- .... **CLC 95**
See also CA 125; 130; CANR 58, 101, 183; CPW; DA3; DAM POP; DLB 278; GLL 1; INT CA-130; MTCW 2; MTFW 2005

Maupin, Armistead Jones, Jr.
See Maupin, Armistead

Maurhut, Richard
See Traven, B.

Mauriac, Claude 1914-1996 .... **CLC 9**
See also CA 89-92; 152; CWW 2; DLB 83; EWL 3; GFL 1789 to the Present

Mauriac, Francois (Charles)
1885-1970 .... **CLC 4, 9, 56; SSC 24**
See also CA 25-28; CAP 2; DLB 65, 331; EW 10; EWL 3; GFL 1789 to the Present; MTCW 1, 2; MTFW 2005; RGWL 2, 3; TWA

Mavor, Osborne Henry 1888-1951 .. **TCLC 3**
See also CA 104; DLB 10; EWL 3

Maxwell, Glyn 1962- .... **CLC 238**
See also CA 154; CANR 88, 183; CP 6, 7; PFS 23

Maxwell, William (Keepers, Jr.)
1908-2000 .... **CLC 19**
See also AMWS 8; CA 93-96; 189; CANR 54, 95; CN 1, 2, 3, 4, 5, 6, 7; DLB 218, 278; DLBY 1980; INT CA-93-96; MAL 5; SATA-Obit 128

May, Elaine 1932- .... **CLC 16**
See also CA 124; 142; CAD; CWD; DLB 44

Mayakovski, Vladimir 1893-1930 ... **TCLC 4, 18**
See also CA 104; 158; EW 11; EWL 3; IDTP; MTCW 2; MTFW 2005; RGWL 2, 3; SFW 4; TWA; WP

Mayakovski, Vladimir Vladimirovich
See Mayakovski, Vladimir

Mayakovsky, Vladimir
See Mayakovski, Vladimir

Mayhew, Henry 1812-1887 .... **NCLC 31**
See also BRWS 16; DLB 18, 55, 190

Mayle, Peter 1939(?)- .... **CLC 89**
See also CA 139; CANR 64, 109, 168, 218

Maynard, Joyce 1953- .... **CLC 23**
See also CA 111; 129; CANR 64, 169, 220

Mayne, William 1928-2010 .... **CLC 12**
See also AAYA 20; CA 9-12R; CANR 37, 80, 100; CLR 25, 123; FANT; JRDA; MAICYA 1, 2; MAICYAS 1; SAAS 11; SATA 6, 68, 122; SUFW 2; YAW

Mayne, William James Carter
See Mayne, William

Mayo, Jim
See L'Amour, Louis

Maysles, Albert 1926- .... **CLC 16**
See also CA 29-32R

Maysles, David 1932-1987 .... **CLC 16**
See also CA 191

Mazer, Norma Fox 1931-2009 .... **CLC 26**
See also AAYA 5, 36; BYA 1, 8; CA 69-72; 292; CANR 12, 32, 66, 129, 189; CLR 23; JRDA; MAICYA 1, 2; SAAS 1; SATA 24, 67, 105, 168, 198; WYA; YAW

Mazzini, Guiseppe 1805-1872 .... **NCLC 34**

McAlmon, Robert (Menzies)
1895-1956 .... **TCLC 97**
See also CA 107; 168; DLB 4, 45; DLBD 15; GLL 1

McAuley, James Phillip 1917-1976 .. **CLC 45**
See also CA 97-100; CP 1, 2; DLB 260; RGEL 2

McBain, Ed
See Hunter, Evan

McBrien, William 1930- .... **CLC 44**
See also CA 107; CANR 90

McBrien, William Augustine
See McBrien, William

McCabe, Pat
See McCabe, Patrick

McCabe, Patrick 1955- .... **CLC 133**
See also BRWS 9; CA 130; CANR 50, 90, 168, 202; CN 6, 7; DLB 194

McCaffrey, Anne 1926- .... **CLC 17**
See also AAYA 6, 34; AITN 2; BEST 89:2; BPFB 2; BYA 5; CA 25-28R, 227; CAAE 227; CANR 15, 35, 55, 96, 169; CLR 49, 130; CPW; DA3; DAM NOV, POP; DLB 8; JRDA; MAICYA 1, 2; MTCW 1, 2; MTFW 2005; SAAS 11; SATA 8, 70, 116, 152; SATA-Essay 152; SFW 4; SUFW 2; WYA; YAW

McCaffrey, Anne Inez
See McCaffrey, Anne

McCall, Nathan 1955(?)- .... **CLC 86**
See also AAYA 59; BW 3; CA 146; CANR 88, 186

McCall Smith, Alexander
See Smith, Alexander McCall

McCann, Arthur
See Campbell, John W.

McCann, Colum 1965- .... **CLC 299**
See also CA 152; CANR 99, 149; DLB 267

McCann, Edson
See Pohl, Frederik

McCarthy, Charles
See McCarthy, Cormac

McCarthy, Charles, Jr.
See McCarthy, Cormac

McCarthy, Cormac 1933- .... **CLC 4, 57, 101, 204, 295, 310**
See also AAYA 41; AMWS 8; BPFB 2; CA 13-16R; CANR 10, 42, 69, 101, 161, 171; CN 6, 7; CPW; CSW; DA3; DAM POP; DLB 6, 143, 256; EWL 3; LATS 1:2; LNFS 3; MAL 5; MTCW 2; MTFW 2005; NFS 36, 40; TCLE 1:2; TCWW 2

McCarthy, Mary 1912-1989 ...... **CLC 1, 3, 5, 14, 24, 39, 59; SSC 24**
See also AMW; BPFB 2; CA 5-8R; 129; CANR 16, 50, 64; CN 1, 2, 3, 4; DA3; DLB 2; DLBY 1981; EWL 3; FW; INT CANR-16; MAL 5; MBL; MTCW 1, 2; MTFW 2005; RGAL 4; TUS

McCarthy, Mary Therese
See McCarthy, Mary

McCartney, James Paul
See McCartney, Paul

McCartney, Paul 1942- .... **CLC 12, 35**
See also CA 146; CANR 111

McCauley, Stephen 1955- .... **CLC 50**
See also CA 141

McClaren, Peter .... **CLC 70**

McClure, Michael 1932- .... **CLC 6, 10**
See also BG 1:3; CA 21-24R; CAD; CANR 17, 46, 77, 131, 231; CD 5, 6; CP 1, 2, 3, 4, 5, 6, 7; DLB 16; WP

McClure, Michael Thomas
See McClure, Michael

McCorkle, Jill 1958- .... **CLC 51**
See also CA 121; CANR 113, 218; CSW; DLB 234; DLBY 1987; SSFS 24

McCorkle, Jill Collins
See McCorkle, Jill

McCourt, Francis
See McCourt, Frank

McCourt, Frank 1930-2009 .... **CLC 109, 299**
See also AAYA 61; AMWS 12; CA 157; 288; CANR 97, 138; MTFW 2005; NCFS 1

McCourt, James 1941- .... **CLC 5**
See also CA 57-60; CANR 98, 152, 186

McCourt, Malachy 1931- .... **CLC 119**
See also SATA 126

McCoy, Edmund
See Gardner, John

McCoy, Horace (Stanley)
1897-1955 .... **TCLC 28**
See also AMWS 13; CA 108; 155; CMW 4; DLB 9

McCrae, John 1872-1918 .... **TCLC 12**
See also CA 109; DLB 92; PFS 5

McCreigh, James
See Pohl, Frederik

McCullers, Carson 1917-1967 . **CLC 1, 4, 10, 12, 48, 100; DC 35; SSC 9, 24, 99; TCLC 155; WLC 4**
See also AAYA 21; AMW; AMWC 2; BPFB 2; CA 5-8R; 25-28R; CABS 1, 3; CANR 18, 132; CDALB 1941-1968; DA; DA3; DAB; DAC; DAM MST, NOV; DFS 5, 18; DLB 2, 7, 173, 228; EWL 3; EXPS; FW; GLL 1; LAIT 3, 4; MAL 5; MBL; MTCW 1, 2; MTFW 2005; NFS 6, 13; RGAL 4; RGSF 2; SATA 27; SSFS 5, 32; TUS; YAW

McCullers, Lula Carson Smith
See McCullers, Carson

McCulloch, John Tyler
See Burroughs, Edgar Rice

McCullough, Colleen 1937- ...... **CLC 27, 107**
See also AAYA 36; BPFB 2; CA 81-84; CANR 17, 46, 67, 98, 139, 203; CPW; DA3; DAM NOV, POP; MTCW 1, 2; MTFW 2005; RHW

McCunn, Ruthanne Lum 1946- .... **AAL**
See also CA 119; CANR 43, 96; DLB 312; LAIT 2; SATA 63

McDermott, Alice 1953- .... **CLC 90**
See also AMWS 18; CA 109; CANR 40, 90, 126, 181; CN 7; DLB 292; MTFW 2005; NFS 23

McDonagh, Martin 1970(?)- .... **CLC 304**
See also AAYA 71; BRWS 12; CA 171; CANR 141; CD 6

McElroy, Joseph 1930- .... **CLC 5, 47**
See also CA 17-20R; CANR 149; CN 3, 4, 5, 6, 7

McElroy, Joseph Prince
See McElroy, Joseph

McElroy, Lee
See Kelton, Elmer

McEwan, Ian 1948- ... **CLC 13, 66, 169, 269; SSC 106**
See also AAYA 84; BEST 90:4; BRWS 4; CA 61-64; CANR 14, 41, 69, 87, 132, 179, 232; CN 3, 4, 5, 6, 7; DAM NOV; DLB 14, 194, 319, 326; HGG; MTCW 1, 2; MTFW 2005; NFS 32; RGSF 2; SUFW 2; TEA

McEwan, Ian Russell
See McEwan, Ian

McFadden, David 1940- .... **CLC 48**
See also CA 104; CP 1, 2, 3, 4, 5, 6, 7; DLB 60; INT CA-104

McFarland, Dennis 1950- .... **CLC 65**
See also CA 165; CANR 110, 179

McGahern, John 1934-2006 .... **CLC 5, 9, 48, 156; SSC 17**
See also CA 17-20R; 249; CANR 29, 68, 113, 204; CN 1, 2, 3, 4, 5, 6, 7; DLB 14, 231, 319; MTCW 1

McGinley, Patrick (Anthony) 1937- . **CLC 41**
See also CA 120; 127; CANR 56; INT CA-127

266; EWL 3; LAIT 1, 4; LATS 1:2; MAL
5; MTCW 1, 2; MTFW 2005; RGAL 4;
RGHL; TUS; WYAS 1

Miller, Frank 1957- .... **CLC 278**
See also AAYA 45; CA 224

Miller, Henry (Valentine)
1891-1980 .... **CLC 1, 2, 4, 9, 14, 43, 84;**
TCLC 213; WLC 4
See also AMW; BPFB 2; CA 9-12R; 97-
100; CANR 33, 64; CDALB 1929-1941;
CN 1, 2; DA; DA3; DAB; DAC; DAM
MST, NOV; DLB 4, 9; DLBY 1980; EWL
3; MAL 5; MTCW 1, 2; MTFW 2005;
RGAL 4; TUS

Miller, Hugh 1802-1856 .... **NCLC 143**
See also DLB 190

Miller, Jason 1939(?)-2001 .... **CLC 2**
See also AITN 1; CA 73-76; 197; CAD;
CANR 130; DFS 12; DLB 7

Miller, Sue 1943- .... **CLC 44**
See also AMWS 12; BEST 90:3; CA 139;
CANR 59, 91, 128, 194, 231; DA3; DAM
POP; DLB 143

Miller, Walter M(ichael, Jr.)
1923-1996 .... **CLC 4, 30**
See also BPFB 2; CA 85-88; CANR 108;
DLB 8; SCFW 1, 2; SFW 4

Millett, Kate 1934- .... **CLC 67**
See also AITN 1; CA 73-76; CANR 32, 53,
76, 110; DA3; DLB 246; FW; GLL 1;
MTCW 1, 2; MTFW 2005

Millhauser, Steven 1943- ... **CLC 21, 54, 109,**
300; SSC 57
See also AAYA 76; CA 110; 111; CANR
63, 114, 133, 189; CN 6, 7; DA3; DLB 2,
350; FANT; INT CA-111; MAL 5; MTCW
2; MTFW 2005

Millhauser, Steven Lewis
See Millhauser, Steven

Millin, Sarah Gertrude 1889-1968 ... **CLC 49**
See also CA 102; 93-96; DLB 225; EWL 3

Milne, A. A. 1882-1956 .... **TCLC 6, 88**
See also BRWS 5; CA 104; 133; CLR 1,
26, 108; CMW 4; CWRI 5; DA3; DAB;
DAC; DAM MST; DLB 10, 77, 100, 160,
352; FANT; MAICYA 1, 2; MTCW 1, 2;
MTFW 2005; RGEL 2; SATA 100; WCH;
YABC 1

Milne, Alan Alexander
See Milne, A. A.

Milner, Ron(ald) 1938-2004 .. **BLC 1:3; CLC**
56
See also AITN 1; BW 1; CA 73-76; 230;
CAD; CANR 24, 81; CD 5, 6; DAM
MULT; DLB 38; MAL 5; MTCW 1

Milnes, Richard Monckton
1809-1885 .... **NCLC 61**
See also DLB 32, 184

Milosz, Czeslaw 1911-2004 .... **CLC 5, 11, 22,**
31, 56, 82, 253; PC 8; WLCS
See also CA 81-84; 230; CANR
23, 51, 91, 126; CDWLB 4; CWW 2;
DA3; DAM MST, POET; DLB 215, 331;
EW 13; EWL 3; MTCW 1, 2; MTFW
2005; PFS 16, 29, 35; RGHL; RGWL 2,
3

Milton, John 1608-1674 ... **LC 9, 43, 92, 205;**
PC 19, 29; WLC 4
See also AAYA 65; BRW 2; BRWR 2; CD-
BLB 1660-1789; DA; DA3; DAB; DAC;
DAM MST, POET; DLB 131, 151, 281;
EFS 1:1, 2:2; EXPP; LAIT 1; PAB; PFS
3, 17, 37; RGEL 2; TEA; WLIT 3; WP

Min, Anchee 1957- .... **CLC 86, 291**
See also CA 146; CANR 94, 137, 222;
MTFW 2005

Minehaha, Cornelius
See Wedekind, Frank

Miner, Valerie 1947- .... **CLC 40**
See also CA 97-100; CANR 59, 177; FW;
GLL 2

Minimo, Duca
See D'Annunzio, Gabriele

Minot, Susan (Anderson) 1956- ...... **CLC 44,**
159
See also AMWS 6; CA 134; CANR 118;
CN 6, 7

Minus, Ed 1938- .... **CLC 39**
See also CA 185

Mirabai 1498(?)-1550(?) .... **LC 143; PC 48**
See also PFS 24

Miranda, Javier
See Bioy Casares, Adolfo

Mirbeau, Octave 1848-1917 .... **TCLC 55**
See also CA 216; DLB 123, 192; GFL 1789
to the Present

Mirikitani, Janice 1942- .... **AAL**
See also CA 211; DLB 312; RGAL 4

Mirk, John (?)-c. 1414 .... **LC 105**
See also DLB 146

Miro (Ferrer), Gabriel (Francisco Victor)
1879-1930 .... **TCLC 5**
See also CA 104; 185; DLB 322; EWL 3

Misharin, Alexandr **CLC 59**

Mishima, Yukio
See Hiraoka, Kimitake

Mishima Yukio
See Hiraoka, Kimitake

Miss C. L. F.
See Grimke, Charlotte L. Forten

Mister X
See Hoch, Edward D.

Mistral, Frederic 1830-1914 .... **TCLC 51**
See also CA 122; 213; DLB 331; GFL 1789
to the Present

Mistral, Gabriela 1899-1957 .... **HLC 2; PC**
32; TCLC 2
See also BW 2; CA 104; 131; CANR 81;
DAM MULT; DLB 283, 331; DNFS;
EWL 3; HW 1, 2; LAW; MTCW 1, 2;
MTFW 2005; PFS 37; RGWL 2, 3; WP

Mistry, Rohinton 1952- ... **CLC 71, 196, 281;**
SSC 73
See also BRWS 10; CA 141; CANR 86,
114; CCA 1; CN 6, 7; DAC; DLB 334;
SSFS 6

Mitchell, Clyde
See Ellison, Harlan; Silverberg, Robert

Mitchell, David 1969- .... **CLC 311**
See also BRWS 14; CA 210; CANR 159,
224

Mitchell, Emerson Blackhorse Barney
1945- .... **NNAL**
See also CA 45-48

Mitchell, James Leslie 1901-1935 .... **TCLC 4**
See also BRWS 14; CA 104; 188; DLB 15;
RGEL 2

Mitchell, Joni 1943- .... **CLC 12**
See also CA 112; CCA 1

Mitchell, Joseph (Quincy)
1908-1996 .... **CLC 98**
See also CA 77-80; 152; CANR 69; CN 1,
2, 3, 4, 5, 6; CSW; DLB 185; DLBY 1996

Mitchell, Margaret 1900-1949 .... **TCLC 11,**
170
See also AAYA 23; BPFB 2; BYA 1; CA
109; 125; CANR 55, 94; CDALBS; DA3;
DAM NOV, POP; DLB 9; LAIT 2; MAL
5; MTCW 1, 2; MTFW 2005; NFS 9, 38;
RGAL 4; RHW; TUS; WYAS 1; YAW

Mitchell, Margaret Munnerlyn
See Mitchell, Margaret

Mitchell, Peggy
See Mitchell, Margaret

Mitchell, S(ilas) Weir 1829-1914 .... **TCLC 36**
See also CA 165; DLB 202; RGAL 4

Mitchell, W(illiam) O(rmond)
1914-1998 .... **CLC 25**
See also CA 77-80; 165; CANR 15, 43; CN
1, 2, 3, 4, 5, 6; DAC; DAM MST; DLB
88; TCLE 1:2

Mitchell, William (Lendrum)
1879-1936 .... **TCLC 81**
See also CA 213

Mitford, Mary Russell 1787-1855 ... **NCLC 4**
See also DLB 110, 116; RGEL 2

Mitford, Nancy 1904-1973 .... **CLC 44**
See also BRWS 10; CA 9-12R; CN 1; DLB
191; RGEL 2

Miyamoto, (Chujo) Yuriko
1899-1951 .... **TCLC 37**
See also CA 170, 174; DLB 180

Miyamoto Yuriko
See Miyamoto, (Chujo) Yuriko

Miyazawa, Kenji 1896-1933 .... **TCLC 76**
See also CA 157; EWL 3; RGWL 3

Miyazawa Kenji
See Miyazawa, Kenji

Mizoguchi, Kenji 1898-1956 .... **TCLC 72**
See also CA 167

Mo, Timothy (Peter) 1950- .... **CLC 46, 134**
See also CA 117; CANR 128; CN 5, 6, 7;
DLB 194; MTCW 1; WLIT 4; WWE 1

Mo, Yan
See Yan, Mo

Moberg, Carl Arthur
See Moberg, Vilhelm

Moberg, Vilhelm 1898-1973 .... **TCLC 224**
See also CA 97-100; 45-48; CANR 135;
DLB 259; EW 11; EWL 3

Modarressi, Taghi (M.) 1931-1997 ... **CLC 44**
See also CA 121; 134; INT CA-134

Modiano, Patrick (Jean) 1945- .... **CLC 18,**
218
See also CA 85-88; CANR 17, 40, 115;
CWW 2; DLB 83, 299; EWL 3; RGHL

Mofolo, Thomas 1875(?)-1948 .... **BLC 1:3;**
TCLC 22
See also AFW; CA 121; 153; CANR 83;
DAM MULT; DLB 225; EWL 3; MTCW
2; MTFW 2005; WLIT 2

Mofolo, Thomas Mokopu
See Mofolo, Thomas

Mohr, Nicholasa 1938- .... **CLC 12; HLC 2**
See also AAYA 8, 46; CA 49-52; CANR 1,
32, 64; CLR 22; DAM MULT; DLB 145;
HW 1, 2; JRDA; LAIT 5; LLW; MAICYA
2; MAICYAS 1; RGAL 4; SAAS 8; SATA
8, 97; SATA-Essay 113; WYA; YAW

Moi, Toril 1953- .... **CLC 172**
See also CA 154; CANR 102; FW

Mojtabai, A(nn) G(race) 1938- ..... **CLC 5, 9,**
15, 29
See also CA 85-88; CANR 88

Moliere 1622-1673 ..... **DC 13; LC 10, 28, 64,**
125, 127, 200; WLC 4
See also DA; DA3; DAB; DAC; DAM
DRAM, MST; DFS 13, 18, 20; DLB 268;
EW 3; GFL Beginnings to 1789; LATS
1:1; RGWL 2, 3; TWA

Molin, Charles
See Mayne, William

Molina, Antonio Munoz 1956- .... **CLC 289**
See also DLB 322

Molnar, Ferenc 1878-1952 .... **TCLC 20**
See also CA 109; 153; CANR 83; CDWLB
4; DAM DRAM; DLB 215; EWL 3;
RGWL 2, 3

Momaday, N. Scott 1934- ...... **CLC 2, 19, 85,**
95, 160; NNAL; PC 25; WLCS
See also AAYA 11, 64; AMWS 4; ANW;
BPFB 2; BYA 12; CA 25-28R; CANR 14,
34, 68, 134; CDALBS; CN 2, 3, 4, 5, 6,
7; CPW; DA; DA3; DAB; DAC; DAM
MST, MULT, NOV, POP; DLB 143, 175,

256; EWL 3; EXPP; INT CANR-14; LAIT 4; LATS 1:2; MAL 5; MTCW 1, 2; MTFW 2005; NFS 10; PFS 2, 11, 37, 41; RGAL 4; SATA 48; SATA-Brief 30; TCWW 1, 2; WP; YAW

Momaday, Navarre Scott
See Momaday, N. Scott

Momala, Ville i
See Moberg, Vilhelm

Monette, Paul 1945-1995 .... **CLC 82**
See also AMWS 10; CA 139; 147; CN 6; DLB 350; GLL 1

Monroe, Harriet 1860-1936 .... **TCLC 12**
See also CA 109; 204; DLB 54, 91

Monroe, Lyle
See Heinlein, Robert A.

Montagu, Elizabeth 1720-1800 .... **NCLC 7, 117**
See also DLB 356; FW

Montagu, Lady Mary Wortley 1689-1762 .... **LC 9, 57, 204; PC 16**
See also DLB 95, 101, 366; FL 1:1; RGEL 2

Montagu, W. H.
See Coleridge, Samuel Taylor

Montague, John (Patrick) 1929- ..... **CLC 13, 46; PC 106**
See also BRWS 15; CA 9-12R; CANR 9, 69, 121; CP 1, 2, 3, 4, 5, 6, 7; DLB 40; EWL 3; MTCW 1; PFS 12; RGEL 2; TCLE 1:2

Montaigne, Michel de 1533-1592 . **LC 8, 105, 194; WLC 4**
See also DA; DAB; DAC; DAM MST; DLB 327; EW 2; GFL Beginnings to 1789; LMFS 1; RGWL 2, 3; TWA

Montaigne, Michel Eyquem de
See Montaigne, Michel de

Montale, Eugenio 1896-1981 ... **CLC 7, 9, 18; PC 13**
See also CA 17-20R; 104; CANR 30; DLB 114, 331; EW 11; EWL 3; MTCW 1; PFS 22; RGWL 2, 3; TWA; WLIT 7

Montemayor, Jorge de 1521(?)-1561(?) .... **LC 185**
See also DLB 318

Montesquieu, Charles-Louis de Secondat 1689-1755 .... **LC 7, 69, 189**
See also DLB 314; EW 3; GFL Beginnings to 1789; TWA

Montessori, Maria 1870-1952 ...... **TCLC 103**
See also CA 115; 147

Montgomery, Bruce 1921(?)-1978 .... **CLC 22**
See also CA 179; 104; CMW 4; DLB 87; MSW

Montgomery, L. M. 1874-1942 ..... **TCLC 51, 140**
See also AAYA 12; BYA 1; CA 108; 137; CLR 8, 91, 145; DA3; DAC; DAM MST; DLB 92, 362; JRDA; DLBD 14; MAICYA 1, 2; MTCW 2; MTFW 2005; RGEL 2; SATA 100; TWA; WCH; WYA; YABC 1

Montgomery, Lucy Maud
See Montgomery, L. M.

Montgomery, Marion, Jr. 1925- .... **CLC 7**
See also AITN 1; CA 1-4R; CANR 3, 48, 162; CSW; DLB 6

Montgomery, Marion H. 1925-
See Montgomery, Marion, Jr.

Montgomery, Max
See Davenport, Guy (Mattison, Jr.)

Montgomery, Robert Bruce
See Montgomery, Bruce

Montherlant, Henry de 1896-1972 .... **CLC 8, 19**
See also CA 85-88; 37-40R; DAM DRAM; DLB 72, 321; EW 11; EWL 3; GFL 1789 to the Present; MTCW 1

Montherlant, Henry Milon de
See Montherlant, Henry de

Monty Python
See Chapman, Graham; Cleese, John (Marwood); Gilliam, Terry; Idle, Eric; Jones, Terence Graham Parry; Palin, Michael

Moodie, Susanna (Strickland) 1803-1885 .... **NCLC 14, 113**
See also DLB 99

Moody, Hiram
See Moody, Rick

Moody, Hiram F. III
See Moody, Rick

Moody, Minerva
See Alcott, Louisa May

Moody, Rick 1961- .... **CLC 147**
See also CA 138; CANR 64, 112, 179; MTFW 2005

Moody, William Vaughan 1869-1910 .... **TCLC 105**
See also CA 110; 178; DLB 7, 54; MAL 5; RGAL 4

Mooney, Edward
See Mooney, Ted

Mooney, Ted 1951- .... **CLC 25**
See also CA 130; CANR 229

Moorcock, Michael 1939- ...... **CLC 5, 27, 58, 236**
See also AAYA 26; CA 45-48; CAAS 5; CANR 2, 17, 38, 64, 122, 203; CN 5, 6, 7; DLB 14, 231, 261, 319; FANT; MTCW 1, 2; MTFW 2005; SATA 93, 166; SCFW 1, 2; SFW 4; SUFW 1, 2

Moorcock, Michael John
See Moorcock, Michael

Moorcock, Michael John
See Moorcock, Michael

Moore, Al
See Moore, Alan

Moore, Alan 1953- .... **CLC 230**
See also AAYA 51; CA 204; CANR 138, 184; DLB 261; MTFW 2005; SFW 4

Moore, Alice Ruth
See Nelson, Alice Ruth Moore Dunbar

Moore, Brian 1921-1999 ... **CLC 1, 3, 5, 7, 8, 19, 32, 90**
See also BRWS 9; CA 1-4R; 174; CANR 1, 25, 42, 63; CCA 1; CN 1, 2, 3, 4, 5, 6; DAB; DAC; DAM MST; DLB 251; EWL 3; FANT; MTCW 1, 2; MTFW 2005; RGEL 2

Moore, Edward
See Muir, Edwin

Moore, G. E. 1873-1958 .... **TCLC 89**
See also DLB 262

Moore, George Augustus 1852-1933 ... **SSC 19, 134; TCLC 7, 265**
See also BRW 6; CA 104; 177; DLB 10, 18, 57, 135; EWL 3; RGEL 2; RGSF 2

Moore, Lorrie 1957- .... **CLC 39, 45, 68, 165, 315; SSC 147**
See also AMWS 10; CA 116; CANR 39, 83, 139, 221; CN 5, 6, 7; DLB 234; MTFW 2005; SSFS 19

Moore, Marianne 1887-1972 . **CLC 1, 2, 4, 8, 10, 13, 19, 47; PC 4, 49; WLCS**
See also AMW; CA 1-4R; 33-36R; CANR 3, 61; CDALB 1929-1941; CP 1; DA; DA3; DAB; DAC; DAM MST, POET; DLB 45; DLBD 7; EWL 3; EXPP; FL 1:6; MAL 5; MBL; MTCW 1, 2; MTFW 2005; PAB; PFS 14, 17, 38; RGAL 4; SATA 20; TUS; WP

Moore, Marianne Craig
See Moore, Marianne

Moore, Marie Lorena
See Moore, Lorrie

Moore, Michael 1954- .... **CLC 218**
See also AAYA 53; CA 166; CANR 150

Moore, Thomas 1779-1852 .... **NCLC 6, 110**
See also BRWS 17; DLB 96, 144; RGEL 2

Moorhouse, Frank 1938- .... **SSC 40**
See also CA 118; CANR 92; CN 3, 4, 5, 6, 7; DLB 289; RGSF 2

Mootoo, Shani 1958(?)- .... **CLC 294**
See also CA 174; CANR 156

Mora, Pat 1942- .... **HLC 2**
See also AMWS 13; CA 129; CANR 57, 81, 112, 171; CLR 58; DAM MULT; DLB 209; HW 1, 2; LLW; MAICYA 2; MTFW 2005; PFS 33, 35, 40; SATA 92, 134, 186, 232

Moraga, Cherríe 1952- ... **CLC 126, 250; DC 22**
See also CA 131; CANR 66, 154; DAM MULT; DLB 82, 249; FW; GLL 1; HW 1, 2; LLW

Moran, J.L.
See Whitaker, Rod

Morand, Paul 1888-1976 .... **CLC 41; SSC 22**
See also CA 184; 69-72; DLB 65; EWL 3

Morante, Elsa 1918-1985 .... **CLC 8, 47**
See also CA 85-88; 117; CANR 35; DLB 177; EWL 3; MTCW 1, 2; MTFW 2005; RGHL; RGWL 2, 3; WLIT 7

Moravia, Alberto
See Pincherle, Alberto

Morck, Paul
See Rolvaag, O.E.

More, Hannah 1745-1833 ...... **NCLC 27, 141**
See also DLB 107, 109, 116, 158; RGEL 2

More, Henry 1614-1687 .... **LC 9**
See also DLB 126, 252

More, Sir Thomas 1478(?)-1535 ... **LC 10, 32, 140**
See also BRWC 1; BRWS 7; DLB 136, 281; LMFS 1; NFS 29; RGEL 2; TEA

Moreas, Jean
See Papadiamantopoulos, Johannes

Moreton, Andrew Esq.
See Defoe, Daniel

Moreton, Lee
See Boucicault, Dion

Morgan, Berry 1919-2002 .... **CLC 6**
See also CA 49-52; 208; DLB 6

Morgan, Claire
See Highsmith, Patricia

Morgan, Edwin 1920-2010 .... **CLC 31**
See also BRWS 9; CA 5-8R; CANR 3, 43, 90; CP 1, 2, 3, 4, 5, 6, 7; DLB 27

Morgan, Edwin George
See Morgan, Edwin

Morgan, (George) Frederick 1922-2004 .... **CLC 23**
See also CA 17-20R; 224; CANR 21, 144; CP 2, 3, 4, 5, 6, 7

Morgan, Harriet
See Mencken, H. L.

Morgan, Jane
See Cooper, James Fenimore

Morgan, Janet 1945- .... **CLC 39**
See also CA 65-68

Morgan, Lady 1776(?)-1859 .... **NCLC 29**
See also DLB 116, 158; RGEL 2

Morgan, Robin (Evonne) 1941- .... **CLC 2**
See also CA 69-72; CANR 29, 68; FW; GLL 2; MTCW 1; SATA 80

Morgan, Scott
See Kuttner, Henry

Morgan, Seth 1949(?)-1990 .... **CLC 65**
See also CA 185; 132

Morgenstern, Christian (Otto Josef Wolfgang) 1871-1914 .... **TCLC 8**
See also CA 105; 191; EWL 3

Mulock, Dinah Maria
   See Craik, Dinah Maria (Mulock)
Multatuli 1820-1881 .... **NCLC 165**
   See also RGWL 2, 3
Munday, Anthony 1560-1633 .... **LC 87**
   See also DLB 62, 172; RGEL 2
Munford, Robert 1737(?)-1783 .... **LC 5**
   See also DLB 31
Mungo, Raymond 1946- .... **CLC 72**
   See also CA 49-52; CANR 2
Munnings, Clare
   See Conway, Jill K.
Munro, Alice 1931- .... **CLC 6, 10, 19, 50, 95,**
      222; SSC 3, 95; WLCS
   See also AAYA 82; AITN 2; BPFB 2; CA
      33-36R; CANR 33, 53, 75, 114, 177; CCA
      1; CN 1, 2, 3, 4, 5, 6, 7; DA3; DAC;
      DAM MST, NOV; DLB 53; EWL 3;
      LNFS 3; MTCW 1, 2; MTFW 2005; NFS
      27; RGEL 2; RGSF 2; SATA 29; SSFS 5,
      13, 19, 28; TCLE 1:2; WWE 1
Munro, Alice Anne
   See Munro, Alice
Munro, H. H.
   See Saki
Munro, Hector H.
   See Saki
Munro, Hector Hugh
   See Saki
Murakami, Haruki 1949- .... **CLC 150, 274**
   See also CA 165; CANR 102, 146, 212;
      CWW 2; DLB 182; EWL 3; LNFS 2;
      MJW; RGWL 3; SFW 4; SSFS 23
Murakami Haruki
   See Murakami, Haruki
Murasaki, Lady
   See Murasaki Shikibu
Murasaki Shikibu 978(?)-1026(?) .. **CMLC 1,**
      79
   See also EFS 1:2, 2:2; LATS 1:1; RGWL 2,
      3
Murdoch, Iris 1919-1999 .. **CLC 1, 2, 3, 4, 6,**
      8, 11, 15, 22, 31, 51; TCLC 171
   See also BRWS 1; CA 13-16R; 179; CANR
      8, 43, 68, 103, 142; CBD; CDBLB 1960
      to Present; CN 1, 2, 3, 4, 5, 6; CWD;
      DA3; DAB; DAC; DAM MST, NOV;
      DLB 14, 194, 233, 326; EWL 3; INT
      CANR-8; MTCW 1, 2; MTFW 2005; NFS
      18; RGEL 2; TCLE 1:2; TEA; WLIT 4
Murdoch, Jean Iris
   See Murdoch, Iris
Murfree, Mary Noailles 1850-1922 .. **SSC 22;**
      TCLC 135
   See also CA 122; 176; DLB 12, 74; RGAL
      4
Murglie
   See Murnau, F.W.
Murnau, Friedrich Wilhelm
   See Murnau, F.W.
Murnau, F.W. 1888-1931 .... **TCLC 53**
   See also CA 112
Murphy, Arthur 1727-1805 .... **NCLC 229**
   See also DLB 89, 142; RGEL 2
Murphy, Richard 1927- .... **CLC 41**
   See also BRWS 5; CA 29-32R; CP 1, 2, 3,
      4, 5, 6, 7; DLB 40; EWL 3
Murphy, Sylvia 1937- .... **CLC 34**
   See also CA 121
Murphy, Thomas 1935- .... **CLC 51**
   See also CA 101; DLB 310
Murphy, Thomas Bernard
   See Murphy, Thomas
Murphy, Tom
   See Murphy, Thomas
Murray, Albert 1916- .... **BLC 2:3; CLC 73**
   See also BW 2; CA 49-52; CANR 26, 52,
      78, 160; CN 7; CSW; DLB 38; MTFW
      2005

Murray, Albert L.
   See Murray, Albert
Murray, Diane Lain Johnson
   See Johnson, Diane
Murray, James Augustus Henry
      1837-1915 .... **TCLC 117**
Murray, Judith Sargent
      1751-1820 .... **NCLC 63, 243**
   See also DLB 37, 200
Murray, Les 1938- .... **CLC 40**
   See also BRWS 7; CA 21-24R; CANR 11,
      27, 56, 103, 199; CP 1, 2, 3, 4, 5, 6, 7;
      DAM POET; DLB 289; DLBY 2001;
      EWL 3; RGEL 2
Murray, Leslie Allan
   See Murray, Les
Murry, J. Middleton
   See Murry, John Middleton
Murry, John Middleton
      1889-1957 .... **TCLC 16**
   See also CA 118; 217; DLB 149
Musgrave, Susan 1951- .... **CLC 13, 54**
   See also CA 69-72; CANR 45, 84, 181;
      CCA 1; CP 2, 3, 4, 5, 6, 7; CWP
Musil, Robert (Edler von)
      1880-1942 ... **SSC 18; TCLC 12, 68, 213**
   See also CA 109; CANR 55, 84; CDWLB
      2; DLB 81, 124; EW 9; EWL 3; MTCW
      2; RGSF 2; RGWL 2, 3
Muske, Carol
   See Muske-Dukes, Carol
Muske, Carol Anne
   See Muske-Dukes, Carol
Muske-Dukes, Carol 1945- .... **CLC 90**
   See also CA 65-68, 203; CAAE 203; CANR
      32, 70, 181; CWP; PFS 24
Muske-Dukes, Carol Ann
   See Muske-Dukes, Carol
Muske-Dukes, Carol Anne
   See Muske-Dukes, Carol
Musset, Alfred de 1810-1857 . **DC 27; NCLC**
      7, 150
   See also DLB 192, 217; EW 6; GFL 1789
      to the Present; RGWL 2, 3; TWA
Musset, Louis Charles Alfred de
   See Musset, Alfred de
Mussolini, Benito (Amilcare Andrea)
      1883-1945 .... **TCLC 96**
   See also CA 116
Mutanabbi, Al-
   See al-Mutanabbi, Ahmad ibn al-Husayn
      Abu al-Tayyib al-Jufi al-Kindi
Mutis, Alvaro 1923- .... **CLC 283**
   See also CA 149; CANR 118; DLB 283;
      EWL 3; HW 1; LAWS 1
My Brother's Brother
   See Chekhov, Anton
Myers, L(eopold) H(amilton)
      1881-1944 .... **TCLC 59**
   See also CA 157; DLB 15; EWL 3; RGEL
      2
Myers, Walter Dean 1937- ...... **BLC 1:3, 2:3;**
      CLC 35
   See also AAYA 4, 23; BW 2; BYA 6, 8, 11;
      CA 33-36R; CANR 20, 42, 67, 108, 184;
      CLR 4, 16, 35, 110; DAM MULT, NOV;
      DLB 33; INT CANR-20; JRDA; LAIT 5;
      LNFS 1; MAICYA 1, 2; MAICYAS 1;
      MTCW 2; MTFW 2005; NFS 30, 33, 40;
      SAAS 2; SATA 41, 71, 109, 157, 193,
      229; SATA-Brief 27; SSFS 31; WYA;
      YAW
Myers, Walter M.
   See Myers, Walter Dean
Myles, Symon
   See Follett, Ken

Nabokov, Vladimir 1899-1977 ... **CLC 1, 2, 3,**
      6, 8, 11, 15, 23, 44, 46, 64; SSC 11, 86,
      163; TCLC 108, 189; WLC 4
   See also AAYA 45; AMW; AMWC 1;
      AMWR 1; BPFB 2; CA 5-8R; 69-72;
      CANR 20, 102; CDALB 1941-1968; CN
      1, 2; CP 2; DA; DA3; DAB; DAC; DAM
      MST, NOV; DLB 2, 244, 278, 317; DLBD
      3; DLBY 1980, 1991; EWL 3; EXPS;
      LATS 1:2; MAL 5; MTCW 1, 2; MTFW
      2005; NCFS 4; NFS 9; RGAL 4; RGSF
      2; SSFS 6, 15; TUS
Nabokov, Vladimir Vladimirovich
   See Nabokov, Vladimir
Naevius c. 265B.C.-201B.C. .... **CMLC 37**
   See also DLB 211
Nafisi, Azar 1955- .... **CLC 313**
   See also CA 222; CANR 203; DLB 366;
      LNFS 2
Nagai, Kafu 1879-1959 .... **TCLC 51**
   See also CA 117; 276; DLB 180; EWL 3;
      MJW
Nagai, Sokichi
   See Nagai, Kafu
Nagai Kafu
   See Nagai, Kafu
na gCopaleen, Myles
   See O Nuallain, Brian
na Gopaleen, Myles
   See O Nuallain, Brian
Nagy, Laszlo 1925-1978 .... **CLC 7**
   See also CA 129; 112
Naidu, Sarojini 1879-1949 .... **TCLC 80**
   See also EWL 3; RGEL 2
Naipaul, Shiva 1945-1985 .... **CLC 32, 39;**
      TCLC 153
   See also CA 110; 112; 116; CANR 33; CN
      2, 3; DA3; DAM NOV; DLB 157; DLBY
      1985; EWL 3; MTCW 1, 2; MTFW 2005
Naipaul, Shivadhar Srinivasa
   See Naipaul, Shiva
Naipaul, Vidiahar Surajprasad
   See Naipaul, V.S.
Naipaul, V.S. 1932- .. **CLC 4, 7, 9, 13, 18, 37,**
      105, 199; SSC 38, 121
   See also BPFB 2; BRWS 1; CA 1-4R;
      CANR 1, 33, 51, 91, 126, 191, 225; CD-
      BLB 1960 to Present; CDWLB 3; CN 1,
      2, 3, 4, 5, 6, 7; DA3; DAB; DAC; DAM
      MST, NOV; DLB 125, 204, 207, 326, 331;
      DLBY 1985, 2001; EWL 3; LATS 1:2;
      MTCW 1, 2; MTFW 2005; NFS 37, 39;
      RGEL 2; RGSF 2; SSFS 29; TWA; WLIT
      4; WWE 1
Nair, Kamala
   See Das, Kamala
Nakos, Lilika 1903-1989 .... **CLC 29**
   See also CA 217
Nalapat, Kamala
   See Das, Kamala
Napoleon
   See Yamamoto, Hisaye
Narayan, R. K. 1906-2001 ..... **CLC 7, 28, 47,**
      121, 211; SSC 25, 154
   See also BPFB 2; CA 81-84; 196; CANR
      33, 61, 112; CN 1, 2, 3, 4, 5, 6, 7; DA3;
      DAM NOV; DLB 323; DNFS 1; EWL 3;
      MTCW 1, 2; MTFW 2005; RGEL 2;
      RGSF 2; SATA 62; SSFS 5, 29; WWE 1
Narayan, Rasipuram Krishnaswami
   See Narayan, R. K.
Nash, Fredric Ogden
   See Nash, Ogden
Nash, Ogden 1902-1971 ...... **CLC 23; PC 21;**
      TCLC 109
   See also CA 13-14; 29-32R; CANR 34, 61,
      185; CAP 1; CP 1; DAM POET; DLB 11;
      MAICYA 1, 2; MAL 5; MTCW 1, 2; PFS
      31; RGAL 4; SATA 2, 46; WP

Niven, Larry 1938- .... **CLC 8**
 See also AAYA 27; BPFB 2; BYA 10; CA
 21-24R, 207; CAAE 207; CAAS 12;
 CANR 14, 44, 66, 113, 155, 206; CPW;
 DAM POP; DLB 8; MTCW 1, 2; SATA
 95, 171; SCFW 1, 2; SFW 4
Niven, Laurence Van Cott
 See Niven, Larry
Niven, Laurence VanCott
 See Niven, Larry
Nixon, Agnes Eckhardt 1927- .... **CLC 21**
 See also CA 110
Nizan, Paul 1905-1940 .... **TCLC 40**
 See also CA 161; DLB 72; EWL 3; GFL
 1789 to the Present
Nkosi, Lewis 1936-2010 ... **BLC 1:3; CLC 45**
 See also BW 1, 3; CA 65-68; CANR 27,
 81; CBD; CD 5, 6; DAM MULT; DLB
 157, 225; WWE 1
Nodier, (Jean) Charles (Emmanuel)
 1780-1844 .... **NCLC 19**
 See also DLB 119; GFL 1789 to the Present
Noguchi, Yone 1875-1947 .... **TCLC 80**
Nolan, Brian
 See O Nuallain, Brian
Nolan, Christopher 1965-2009 .... **CLC 58**
 See also CA 111; 283; CANR 88
Nolan, Christopher John
 See Nolan, Christopher
Noon, Jeff 1957- .... **CLC 91**
 See also CA 148; CANR 83; DLB 267;
 SFW 4
Nordan, Lewis (Alonzo) 1939- .... **CLC 304**
 See also CA 117; CANR 40, 72, 121; CSW;
 DLB 234, 350
Norden, Charles
 See Durrell, Lawrence
Nordhoff, Charles Bernard
 1887-1947 .... **TCLC 23**
 See also CA 108; 211; DLB 9; LAIT 1;
 RHW 1; SATA 23
Norfolk, Lawrence 1963- .... **CLC 76**
 See also CA 144; CANR 85; CN 6, 7; DLB
 267
Norman, Marsha (Williams) 1947- . **CLC 28,
 186; DC 8**
 See also CA 105; CABS 3; CAD; CANR
 41, 131; CD 5, 6; CSW; CWD; DAM
 DRAM; DFS 2; DLB 266; DLBY 1984;
 FW; MAL 5
Normyx
 See Douglas, (George) Norman
Norris, Benjamin Franklin, Jr.
 See Norris, Frank
Norris, Frank 1870-1902 ...... **SSC 28; TCLC
 24, 155, 211**
 See also AAYA 57; AMW; AMWC 2; BPFB
 2; CA 110; 160; CDALB 1865-1917; DLB
 12, 71, 186; LMFS 2; MAL 5; NFS 12;
 RGAL 4; TCWW 1, 2; TUS
Norris, Kathleen 1947- .... **CLC 248**
 See also CA 160; CANR 113, 199
Norris, Leslie 1921-2006 .... **CLC 14**
 See also CA 11-12; 251; CANR 14, 117;
 CAP 1; CP 1, 2, 3, 4, 5, 6, 7; DLB 27,
 256
North, Andrew
 See Norton, Andre
North, Anthony
 See Koontz, Dean
North, Captain George
 See Stevenson, Robert Louis
North, Captain George
 See Stevenson, Robert Louis
North, Milou
 See Erdrich, Louise
Northrup, B. A.
 See Hubbard, L. Ron

North Staffs
 See Hulme, T(homas) E(rnest)
Northup, Solomon 1808-1863 ...... **NCLC 105**
Norton, Alice Mary
 See Norton, Andre
Norton, Andre 1912-2005 .... **CLC 12**
 See also AAYA 83; BPFB 2; BYA 4, 10,
 12; CA 1-4R; 237; CANR 2, 31, 68, 108,
 149; CLR 50; DLB 8, 52; JRDA; MAI-
 CYA 1, 2; MTCW 1; SATA 1, 43, 91;
 SUFW 1, 2; YAW
Norton, Caroline 1808-1877 .. **NCLC 47, 205**
 See also DLB 21, 159, 199
Norway, Nevil Shute
 See Shute, Nevil
Norwid, Cyprian Kamil
 1821-1883 .... **NCLC 17**
 See also RGWL 3
Nosille, Nabrah
 See Ellison, Harlan
Nossack, Hans Erich 1901-1977 .... **CLC 6**
 See also CA 93-96; 85-88; CANR 156;
 DLB 69; EWL 3
Nostradamus 1503-1566 .... **LC 27**
Nosu, Chuji
 See Ozu, Yasujiro
Notenburg, Eleanora (Genrikhovna) von
 See Guro, Elena (Genrikhovna)
Nova, Craig 1945- .... **CLC 7, 31**
 See also CA 45-48; CANR 2, 53, 127, 223
Novak, Joseph
 See Kosinski, Jerzy
Novalis 1772-1801 .... **NCLC 13, 178; PC 120**
 See also CDWLB 2; DLB 90; EW 5; RGWL
 2, 3
Novick, Peter 1934- .... **CLC 164**
 See also CA 188
Novis, Emile
 See Weil, Simone
Nowlan, Alden (Albert) 1933-1983 ... **CLC 15**
 See also CA 9-12R; CANR 5; CP 1, 2, 3;
 DAC; DAM MST; DLB 53; PFS 12
Noyes, Alfred 1880-1958 ...... **PC 27; TCLC 7**
 See also CA 104; 188; DLB 20; EXPP;
 FANT; PFS 4; RGEL 2
Nugent, Richard Bruce
 1906(?)-1987 .... **HR 1:3**
 See also BW 1; CA 125; CANR 198; DLB
 51; GLL 2
Nunez, Elizabeth 1944- .... **BLC 2:3**
 See also CA 223; CANR 220
Nunn, Kem CLC 34
 See also CA 159; CANR 204
Nussbaum, Martha Craven 1947- .. **CLC 203**
 See also CA 134; CANR 102, 176, 213
Nwapa, Flora (Nwanzuruaha)
 1931-1993 .... **BLCS; CLC 133**
 See also BW 2; CA 143; CANR 83; CD-
 WLB 3; CLR 162; CWRI 5; DLB 125;
 EWL 3; WLIT 2
Nye, Robert 1939- .... **CLC 13, 42**
 See also BRWS 10; CA 33-36R; CANR 29,
 67, 107; CN 1, 2, 3, 4, 5, 6, 7; CP 1, 2, 3,
 4, 5, 6, 7; CWRI 5; DAM NOV; DLB 14,
 271; FANT; HGG; MTCW 1; RHW;
 SATA 6
Nyro, Laura 1947-1997 .... **CLC 17**
 See also CA 194
O. Henry
 See Henry, O.
Oates, Joyce Carol 1938- .. **CLC 1, 2, 3, 6, 9,
 11, 15, 19, 33, 52, 108, 134, 228; SSC 6,
 70, 121; WLC 4**
 See also AAYA 15, 52; AITN 1; AMWS 2;
 BEST 89:2; BPFB 2; BYA 11; CA 5-8R;
 CANR 25, 45, 74, 113, 129, 165; CDALB
 1968-1988; CN 1, 2, 3, 4, 5, 6, 7; CP 5,
 6, 7; CPW; CWP; DA; DA3; DAB; DAC;
 DAM MST, NOV, POP; DLB 2, 5, 130;

DLBY 1981; EWL 3; EXPS; FL 1:6; FW;
 GL 3; HGG; INT CANR-25; LAIT 4;
 MAL 5; MBL; MTCW 1, 2; MTFW 2005;
 NFS 8, 24; RGAL 4; RGSF 2; SATA 159;
 SSFS 1, 8, 17, 32; SUFW 2; TUS
Obradovic, Dositej 1740(?)-1811 . **NCLC 254**
 See also DLB 147
O'Brian, E.G.
 See Clarke, Arthur C.
O'Brian, Patrick 1914-2000 .... **CLC 152**
 See also AAYA 55; BRWS 12; CA 144; 187;
 CANR 74, 201; CPW; MTCW 2; MTFW
 2005; RHW
O'Brien, Darcy 1939-1998 .... **CLC 11**
 See also CA 21-24R; 167; CANR 8, 59
O'Brien, Edna 1932- ..... **CLC 3, 5, 8, 13, 36,
 65, 116, 237; SSC 10, 77**
 See also BRWS 5; CA 1-4R; CANR 6, 41,
 65, 102, 169, 213; CDBLB 1960 to
 Present; CN 1, 2, 3, 4, 5, 6, 7; DA3; DAM
 NOV; DLB 14, 231, 319; EWL 3; FW;
 MTCW 1, 2; MTFW 2005; RGSF 2;
 WLIT 4
O'Brien, E.G.
 See Clarke, Arthur C.
O'Brien, Fitz-James 1828-1862 ..... **NCLC 21**
 See also DLB 74; RGAL 4; SUFW
O'Brien, Flann
 See O Nuallain, Brian
O'Brien, Richard 1942- .... **CLC 17**
 See also CA 124
O'Brien, Tim 1946- .... **CLC 7, 19, 40, 103,
 211, 305; SSC 74, 123**
 See also AAYA 16; AMWS 5; CA 85-88;
 CANR 40, 58, 133; CDALBS; CN 5, 6,
 7; CPW; DA3; DAM POP; DLB 152;
 DLBD 9; DLBY 1980; LATS 1:2; MAL
 5; MTCW 2; MTFW 2005; NFS 37;
 RGAL 4; SSFS 5, 15, 29, 32; TCLE 1:2
O'Brien, William Timothy
 See O'Brien, Tim
Obstfelder, Sigbjorn 1866-1900 ..... **TCLC 23**
 See also CA 123; DLB 354
O'Casey, Brenda
 See Haycraft, Anna
O'Casey, Sean 1880-1964 .... **CLC 1, 5, 9, 11,
 15, 88; DC 12; WLCS**
 See also BRW 7; CA 89-92; CANR 62;
 CBD; CDBLB 1914-1945; DA3; DAB;
 DAC; DAM DRAM, MST; DFS 19; DLB
 10; EWL 3; MTCW 1, 2; MTFW 2005;
 RGEL 2; TEA; WLIT 4
O'Cathasaigh, Sean
 See O'Casey, Sean
Occom, Samson 1723-1792 .... **LC 60; NNAL**
 See also DLB 175
Occomy, Marita (Odette) Bonner
 1899(?)-1971 ..... **HR 1:2; PC 72; TCLC
 179**
 See also BW 2; CA 142; DFS 13; DLB 51,
 228
Ochs, Phil(ip David) 1940-1976 .... **CLC 17**
 See also CA 185; 65-68
O'Connor, Edwin (Greene)
 1918-1968 .... **CLC 14**
 See also CA 93-96; 25-28R; MAL 5
O'Connor, Flannery 1925-1964 ..... **CLC 1, 2,
 3, 6, 10, 13, 15, 21, 66, 104; SSC 1, 23,
 61, 82, 111; TCLC 132; WLC 4**
 See also AAYA 7; AMW; AMWR 2; BPFB
 3; BYA 16; CA 1-4R; CANR 3, 41;
 CDALB 1941-1968; DA; DA3; DAB;
 DAC; DAM MST, NOV; DLB 2, 152;
 DLBD 12; DLBY 1980; EWL 3; EXPS;
 LAIT 5; MAL 5; MBL; MTCW 1, 2;
 MTFW 2005; NFS 3, 21; RGAL 4; RGSF
 2; SSFS 2, 7, 10, 19, 34; TUS
O'Connor, Frank 1903-1966
 See O'Donovan, Michael Francis

O'Connor, Mary Flannery
See O'Connor, Flannery
O'Dell, Scott 1898-1989 .... **CLC 30**
See also AAYA 3, 44; BPFB 3; BYA 1, 2, 3, 5; CA 61-64; 129; CANR 12, 30, 112; CLR 1, 16, 126; DLB 52; JRDA; MAICYA 1, 2; SATA 12, 60, 134; WYA; YAW
Odets, Clifford 1906-1963 ..... **CLC 2, 28, 98; DC 6; TCLC 244**
See also AMWS 2; CA 85-88; CAD; CANR 62; DAM DRAM; DFS 3, 17, 20; DLB 7, 26, 341; EWL 3; MAL 5; MTCW 1, 2; MTFW 2005; RGAL 4; TUS
O'Doherty, Brian 1928- .... **CLC 76**
See also CA 105; CANR 108
O'Donnell, K. M.
See Malzberg, Barry N(athaniel)
O'Donnell, Lawrence
See Kuttner, Henry
O'Donovan, Michael Francis
1903-1966 .... **CLC 14, 23; SSC 5, 109**
See also BRWS 14; CA 93-96; CANR 84; DLB 162; EWL 3; RGSF 2; SSFS 5, 34
Oe, Kenzaburo 1935- ... **CLC 10, 36, 86, 187, 303; SSC 20**
See also CA 97-100; CANR 36, 50, 74, 126; CWW 2; DA3; DAM NOV; DLB 182, 331; DLBY 1994; EWL 3; LATS 1:2; MJW; MTCW 1, 2; MTFW 2005; RGSF 2; RGWL 2, 3
Oe Kenzaburo
See Oe, Kenzaburo
O'Faolain, Julia 1932- .... **CLC 6, 19, 47, 108**
See also CA 81-84; CAAS 2; CANR 12, 61; CN 2, 3, 4, 5, 6, 7; DLB 14, 231, 319; FW; MTCW 1; RHW
O'Faolain, Sean 1900-1991 ...... **CLC 1, 7, 14, 32, 70; SSC 13; TCLC 143**
See also CA 61-64; 134; CANR 12, 66; CN 1, 2, 3, 4; DLB 15, 162; MTCW 1, 2; MTFW 2005; RGEL 2; RGSF 2
O'Flaherty, Liam 1896-1984 .... **CLC 5, 34; SSC 6, 116**
See also CA 101; 113; CANR 35; CN 1, 2, 3; DLB 36, 162; DLBY 1984; MTCW 1, 2; MTFW 2005; RGEL 2; RGSF 2; SSFS 5, 20
Ogai
See Mori Ogai
Ogilvy, Gavin
See Barrie, J. M.
O'Grady, Standish (James)
1846-1928 .... **TCLC 5**
See also CA 104; 157
O'Grady, Timothy 1951- .... **CLC 59**
See also CA 138
O'Hara, Frank 1926-1966 .... **CLC 2, 5, 13, 78; PC 45**
See also CA 9-12R; 25-28R; CANR 33; DA3; DAM POET; DLB 5, 16, 193; EWL 3; MAL 5; MTCW 1, 2; MTFW 2005; PFS 8, 12, 34, 38; RGAL 4; WP
O'Hara, John 1905-1970 . **CLC 1, 2, 3, 6, 11, 42; SSC 15**
See also AMW; BPFB 3; CA 5-8R; 25-28R; CANR 31, 60; CDALB 1929-1941; DAM NOV; DLB 9, 86, 324; DLBD 2; EWL 3; MAL 5; MTCW 1, 2; MTFW 2005; NFS 11; RGAL 4; RGSF 2
O'Hara, John Henry
See O'Hara, John
O'Hehir, Diana 1929- .... **CLC 41**
See also CA 245; CANR 177
O'Hehir, Diana F.
See O'Hehir, Diana
Ohiyesa
See Eastman, Charles A(lexander)

Okada, John 1923-1971 .... **AAL**
See also BYA 14; CA 212; DLB 312; NFS 25
O'Kelly, Seamus 1881(?)-1918 .... **SSC 136**
Okigbo, Christopher 1930-1967 ..... **BLC 1:3; CLC 25, 84; PC 7, 128; TCLC 171**
See also AFW; BW 1, 3; CA 77-80; CANR 74; CDWLB 3; DAM MULT, POET; DLB 125; EWL 3; MTCW 1, 2; MTFW 2005; RGEL 2
Okigbo, Christopher Ifenayichukwu
See Okigbo, Christopher
Okri, Ben 1959- .... **BLC 2:3; CLC 87, 223; SSC 127**
See also AFW; BRWS 5; BW 2, 3; CA 130; 138; CANR 65, 128; CN 5, 6, 7; DLB 157, 231, 319, 326; EWL 3; INT CA-138; MTCW 2; MTFW 2005; RGSF 2; SSFS 20; WLIT 2; WWE 1
Old Boy
See Hughes, Thomas
Olds, Sharon 1942- .. **CLC 32, 39, 85; PC 22**
See also AMWS 10; CA 101; CANR 18, 41, 66, 98, 135, 211; CP 5, 6, 7; CPW; CWP; DAM POET; DLB 120; MAL 5; MTCW 2; MTFW 2005; PFS 17
Oldstyle, Jonathan
See Irving, Washington
Olesha, Iurii
See Olesha, Yuri (Karlovich)
Olesha, Iurii Karlovich
See Olesha, Yuri (Karlovich)
Olesha, Yuri (Karlovich) 1899-1960 . **CLC 8; SSC 69; TCLC 136**
See also CA 85-88; DLB 272; EW 11; EWL 3; RGWL 2, 3
Olesha, Yury Karlovich
See Olesha, Yuri (Karlovich)
Oliphant, Mrs.
See Oliphant, Margaret (Oliphant Wilson)
Oliphant, Laurence 1829(?)-1888 .. **NCLC 47**
See also DLB 18, 166
Oliphant, Margaret (Oliphant Wilson)
1828-1897 ... **NCLC 11, 61, 221; SSC 25**
See also BRWS 10; DLB 18, 159, 190; HGG; RGEL 2; RGSF 2; SUFW
Oliver, Mary 1935- ... **CLC 19, 34, 98; PC 75**
See also AMWS 7; CA 21-24R; CANR 9, 43, 84, 92, 138, 217; CP 4, 5, 6, 7; CWP; DLB 5, 193, 342; EWL 3; MTFW 2005; PFS 15, 31, 40
Olivi, Peter 1248-1298 .... **CMLC 114**
Olivier, Laurence (Kerr) 1907-1989 . **CLC 20**
See also CA 111; 150; 129
O.L.S.
See Russell, George William
Olsen, Tillie 1912-2007 .... **CLC 4, 13, 114; SSC 11, 103**
See also AAYA 51; AMWS 13; BYA 11; CA 1-4R; 256; CANR 1, 43, 74, 132; CDALBS; CN 2, 3, 4, 5, 6, 7; DA; DA3; DAB; DAC; DAM MST; DLB 28, 206; DLBY 1980; EWL 3; EXPS; FW; MAL 5; MTCW 1, 2; MTFW 2005; RGAL 4; RGSF 2; SSFS 1, 32; TCLE 1:2; TCWW 2; TUS
Olson, Charles 1910-1970 . **CLC 1, 2, 5, 6, 9, 11, 29; PC 19**
See also AMWS 2; CA 13-16; 25-28R; CABS 2; CANR 35, 61; CAP 1; CP 1; DAM POET; DLB 5, 16, 193; EWL 3; MAL 5; MTCW 1, 2; RGAL 4; WP
Olson, Charles John
See Olson, Charles
Olson, Merle Theodore
See Olson, Toby
Olson, Toby 1937- .... **CLC 28**
See also CA 65-68; CAAS 11; CANR 9, 31, 84, 175; CP 3, 4, 5, 6, 7

Olyesha, Yuri
See Olesha, Yuri (Karlovich)
Olympiodorus of Thebes c. 375-c. 430 .... **CMLC 59**
Omar Khayyam
See Khayyam, Omar
Ondaatje, Michael 1943- ..... **CLC 14, 29, 51, 76, 180, 258, 322; PC 28**
See also AAYA 66; CA 77-80; CANR 42, 74, 109, 133, 172; CN 5, 6, 7; CP 1, 2, 3, 4, 5, 6, 7; DA3; DAB; DAC; DAM MST; DLB 60, 323, 326; EWL 3; LATS 1:2; LMFS 2; MTCW 2; MTFW 2005; NFS 23; PFS 8, 19; TCLE 1:2; TWA; WWE 1
Ondaatje, Philip Michael
See Ondaatje, Michael
Oneal, Elizabeth 1934- .... **CLC 30**
See also AAYA 5, 41; BYA 13; CA 106; CANR 28, 84; CLR 13, 169; JRDA; MAICYA 1, 2; SATA 30, 82; WYA; YAW
Oneal, Zibby
See Oneal, Elizabeth
O'Neill, Eugene 1888-1953 ..... **DC 20; TCLC 1, 6, 27, 49, 225; WLC 4**
See also AAYA 54; AITN 1; AMW; AMWC 1; CA 110; 132; CAD; CANR 131; CDALB 1929-1941; DA; DA3; DAB; DAC; DAM DRAM, MST; DFS 2, 4, 5, 6, 9, 11, 12, 16, 20, 26, 27; DLB 7, 331; EWL 3; LAIT 3; LMFS 2; MAL 5; MTCW 1, 2; MTFW 2005; RGAL 4; TUS
O'Neill, Eugene Gladstone
See O'Neill, Eugene
Onetti, Juan Carlos 1909-1994 ... **CLC 7, 10; HLCS 2; SSC 23; TCLC 131**
See also CA 85-88; 145; CANR 32, 63; CDWLB 3; CWW 2; DAM MULT, NOV; DLB 113; EWL 3; HW 1, 2; LAW; MTCW 1, 2; MTFW 2005; RGSF 2
O'Nolan, Brian
See O Nuallain, Brian
Ono no Komachi fl. c. 850- .... **CMLC 134**
O Nuallain, Brian 1911-1966 .... **CLC 1, 4, 5, 7, 10, 47**
See also BRWS 2; CA 21-22; 25-28R; CAP 2; DLB 231; EWL 3; FANT; RGEL 2; TEA
Ophuls, Max
See Ophuls, Max
Ophuls, Max 1902-1957 .... **TCLC 79**
See also CA 113
Opie, Amelia 1769-1853 .... **NCLC 65**
See also DLB 116, 159; RGEL 2
Oppen, George 1908-1984 ..... **CLC 7, 13, 34; PC 35; TCLC 107**
See also CA 13-16R; 113; CANR 8, 82; CP 1, 2, 3; DLB 5, 165
Oppenheim, E(dward) Phillips
1866-1946 .... **TCLC 45**
See also CA 111; 202; CMW 4; DLB 70
Oppenheimer, Max
See Ophuls, Max
Opuls, Max
See Ophuls, Max
Orage, A(lfred) R(ichard)
1873-1934 .... **TCLC 157**
See also CA 122
Origen c. 185-c. 254 .... **CMLC 19**
Orlovitz, Gil 1918-1973 .... **CLC 22**
See also CA 77-80; 45-48; CN 1; CP 1, 2; DLB 2, 5
Orosius c. 385-c. 420 .... **CMLC 100**
O'Rourke, P. J. 1947- .... **CLC 209**
See also CA 77-80; CANR 13, 41, 67, 111, 155, 217; CPW; DAM POP; DLB 185
O'Rourke, Patrick Jake
See O'Rourke, P. J.
Orrery
See Boyle, Roger

Orris
See Ingelow, Jean

Ortega y Gasset, Jose 1883-1955 ...... **HLC 2; TCLC 9**
See also CA 106; 130; DAM MULT; EW 9; EWL 3; HW 1, 2; MTCW 1, 2; MTFW 2005

Ortese, Anna Maria 1914-1998 .... **CLC 89**
See also DLB 177; EWL 3

Ortiz, Simon
See Ortiz, Simon J.

Ortiz, Simon J. 1941- . **CLC 45, 208; NNAL; PC 17**
See also AMWS 4; CA 134; CANR 69, 118, 164; CP 3, 4, 5, 6, 7; DAM MULT, POET; DLB 120, 175, 256, 342; EXPP; MAL 5; PFS 4, 16; RGAL 4; SSFS 22; TCWW 2

Ortiz, Simon Joseph
See Ortiz, Simon J.

Orton, Joe
See Orton, John Kingsley

Orton, John Kingsley 1933-1967 ...... **CLC 4, 13, 43; DC 3; TCLC 157**
See also BRWS 5; CA 85-88; CANR 35, 66; CBD; CDBLB 1960 to Present; DAM DRAM; DFS 3, 6; DLB 13, 310; GLL 1; MTCW 1, 2; MTFW 2005; RGEL 2; TEA; WLIT 4

Orwell, George 1903-1950 .... **SSC 68; TCLC 2, 6, 15, 31, 51, 123, 128, 129; WLC 4**
See also BPFB 3; BRW 7; BYA 5; CA 104; 132; CDBLB 1945-1960; CLR 68, 171; DA; DA3; DAB; DAC; DAM MST, NOV; DLB 15, 98, 195, 255; EWL 3; EXPN; LAIT 4, 5; LATS 1:1; MTCW 1, 2; MTFW 2005; NFS 3, 7; RGEL 2; SATA 29; SCFW 1, 2; SFW 4; SSFS 4; TEA; WLIT 4; YAW X

Osborne, David
See Silverberg, Robert

Osborne, Dorothy 1627-1695 .... **LC 141**

Osborne, George
See Silverberg, Robert

Osborne, John 1929-1994 .... **CLC 1, 2, 5, 11, 45; DC 38; TCLC 153; WLC 4**
See also BRWS 1; CA 13-16R; 147; CANR 21, 56; CBD; CDBLB 1945-1960; DA; DAB; DAC; DAM DRAM, MST; DFS 4, 19, 24; DLB 13; EWL 3; MTCW 1, 2; MTFW 2005; RGEL 2

Osborne, Lawrence 1958- .... **CLC 50**
See also CA 189; CANR 152

Osbourne, Lloyd 1868-1947 .... **TCLC 93**

Osceola
See Blixen, Karen

Osgood, Frances Sargent
1811-1850 .... **NCLC 141**
See also DLB 250

Oshima, Nagisa 1932- .... **CLC 20**
See also CA 116; 121; CANR 78

Oskison, John Milton
1874-1947 .... **NNAL; TCLC 35**
See also CA 144; CANR 84; DAM MULT; DLB 175

Osofisan, Femi 1946- .... **CLC 307**
See also AFW; BW 2; CA 142; CANR 84; CD 5, 6; CDWLB 3; DLB 125; EWL 3

Ossian c. 3rd cent. -
See Macpherson, James

Ossoli, Sarah Margaret
See Fuller, Margaret

Ossoli, Sarah Margaret Fuller
See Fuller, Margaret

Ostriker, Alicia 1937- .... **CLC 132**
See also CA 25-28R; CAAS 24; CANR 10, 30, 62, 99, 167; CWP; DLB 120; EXPP; PFS 19, 26

Ostriker, Alicia Suskin
See Ostriker, Alicia

Ostrovsky, Aleksandr Nikolaevich
See Ostrovsky, Alexander

Ostrovsky, Alexander 1823-1886 .. **NCLC 30, 57**
See also DLB 277

Osundare, Niyi 1947- .... **BLC 2:3**
See also AFW; BW 3; CA 176; CDWLB 3; CP 7; DLB 157

Otero, Blas de 1916-1979 .... **CLC 11**
See also CA 89-92; DLB 134; EWL 3

O'Trigger, Sir Lucius
See Horne, Richard Henry Hengist

Otto, Rudolf 1869-1937 .... **TCLC 85**

Otto, Whitney 1955- .... **CLC 70**
See also CA 140; CANR 120

Otway, Thomas 1652-1685 .. **DC 24; LC 106, 170**
See also DAM DRAM; DLB 80; RGEL 2

Ouida
See De La Ramee, Marie Louise

Ouologuem, Yambo 1940- .... **CLC 146, 293**
See also CA 111; 176

Ousmane, Sembene 1923-2007 .... **BLC 1:3, 2:3; CLC 66**
See also AFW; BW 1, 3; CA 117; 125; 261; CANR 81; CWW 2; DLB 360; EWL 3; MTCW 1; WLIT 2

Ovid 43B.C.-17 .... **CMLC 7, 108; PC 2**
See also AW 2; CDWLB 1; DA3; DAM POET; DLB 211; PFS 22; RGWL 2, 3; WLIT 8; WP

Owen, Hugh
See Faust, Frederick

Owen, Wilfred (Edward Salter)
1893-1918 ..... **PC 19, 102; TCLC 5, 27; WLC 4**
See also BRW 6; CA 104; 141; CDBLB 1914-1945; DA; DAB; DAC; DAM MST, POET; DLB 20; EWL 3; EXPP; MTCW 2; MTFW 2005; PFS 10, 37; RGEL 2; WLIT 4

Owens, Louis (Dean) 1948-2002 ... **CLC 321; NNAL**
See also CA 137, 179; 207; CAAE 179; CAAS 24; CANR 71

Owens, Rochelle 1936- .... **CLC 8**
See also CA 17-20R; CAAS 2; CAD; CANR 39; CD 5, 6; CP 1, 2, 3, 4, 5, 6, 7; CWD; CWP

Oz, Amos 1939- ...... **CLC 5, 8, 11, 27, 33, 54; SSC 66**
See also AAYA 84; CA 53-56; CANR 27, 47, 65, 113, 138, 175, 219; CWW 2; DAM NOV; EWL 3; MTCW 1, 2; MTFW 2005; RGHL; RGSF 2; RGWL 3; WLIT 6

Ozeki, Ruth L. 1956- .... **CLC 307**
See also CA 181

Ozick, Cynthia 1928- . **CLC 3, 7, 28, 62, 155, 262; SSC 15, 60, 123**
See also AMWS 5; BEST 90:1; CA 17-20R; CANR 23, 58, 116, 160, 187; CN 3, 4, 5, 6, 7; CPW; DA3; DAM NOV, POP; DLB 28, 152, 299; DLBY 1982; EWL 3; EXPS; INT CANR-23; MAL 5; MTCW 1, 2; MTFW 2005; RGAL 4; RGHL; RGSF 2; SSFS 3, 12, 22

Ozu, Yasujiro 1903-1963 .... **CLC 16**
See also CA 112

Pabst, G. W. 1885-1967 .... **TCLC 127**

Pacheco, C.
See Pessoa, Fernando

Pacheco, Jose Emilio 1939- .... **HLC 2**
See also CA 111; 131; CANR 65; CWW 2; DAM MULT; DLB 290; EWL 3; HW 1, 2; RGSF 2

Pa Chin
See Jin, Ba

Pack, Robert 1929- .... **CLC 13**
See also CA 1-4R; CANR 3, 44, 82; CP 1, 2, 3, 4, 5, 6, 7; DLB 5; SATA 118

Packer, Vin
See Meaker, Marijane

Padgett, Lewis
See Kuttner, Henry

Padilla (Lorenzo), Heberto
1932-2000 .... **CLC 38**
See also AITN 1; CA 123; 131; 189; CWW 2; EWL 3; HW 1

Paerdurabo, Frater
See Crowley, Edward Alexander

Page, James Patrick 1944- .... **CLC 12**
See also CA 204

Page, Jimmy 1944-
See Page, James Patrick

Page, Louise 1955- .... **CLC 40**
See also CA 140; CANR 76; CBD; CD 5, 6; CWD; DLB 233

Page, Patricia Kathleen
See Page, P.K.

Page, P.K. 1916-2010 .... **CLC 7, 18; PC 12**
See also CA 53-56; CANR 4, 22, 65; CCA 1; CP 1, 2, 3, 4, 5, 6, 7; DAC; DAM MST; DLB 68; MTCW 1; RGEL 2

Page, Stanton
See Fuller, Henry Blake

Page, Thomas Nelson 1853-1922 .... **SSC 23**
See also CA 118; 177; DLB 12, 78; DLBD 13; RGAL 4

Pagels, Elaine
See Pagels, Elaine Hiesey

Pagels, Elaine Hiesey 1943- .... **CLC 104**
See also CA 45-48; CANR 2, 24, 51, 151; FW; NCFS 4

Paget, Violet 1856-1935 .. **SSC 33, 98; TCLC 5**
See also CA 104; 166; DLB 57, 153, 156, 174, 178; GLL 1; HGG; SUFW 1

Paget-Lowe, Henry
See Lovecraft, H. P.

Paglia, Camille 1947- .... **CLC 68**
See also CA 140; CANR 72, 139; CPW; FW; GLL 2; MTCW 2; MTFW 2005

Pagnol, Marcel (Paul)
1895-1974 .... **TCLC 208**
See also CA 128; 49-52; DLB 321; EWL 3; GFL 1789 to the Present; MTCW 1; RGWL 2, 3

Paige, Richard
See Koontz, Dean

Paine, Thomas 1737-1809 ...... **NCLC 62, 248**
See also AMWS 1; CDALB 1640-1865; DLB 31, 43, 73, 158; LAIT 1; RGAL 4; RGEL 2; TUS

Pakenham, Antonia
See Fraser, Antonia

Palamas, Costis
See Palamas, Kostes

Palamas, Kostes 1859-1943 .... **TCLC 5**
See also CA 105; 190; EWL 3; RGWL 2, 3

Palamas, Kostis
See Palamas, Kostes

Palazzeschi, Aldo 1885-1974 .... **CLC 11**
See also CA 89-92; 53-56; DLB 114, 264; EWL 3

Pales Matos, Luis 1898-1959 .... **HLCS 2**
See Pales Matos, Luis
See also DLB 290; HW 1; LAW

Paley, Grace 1922-2007 ... **CLC 4, 6, 37, 140, 272; SSC 8, 165**
See also AMWS 6; CA 25-28R; 263; CANR 13, 46, 74, 118; CN 2, 3, 4, 5, 6, 7; CPW; DA3; DAM POP; DLB 28, 218; EWL 3; EXPS; FW; INT CANR-13; MAL 5; MBL; MTCW 1, 2; MTFW 2005; RGAL 4; RGSF 2; SSFS 3, 20, 27

Pausanias c. 1st cent. - .... **CMLC 36**
Paustovsky, Konstantin (Georgievich)
    1892-1968 .... **CLC 40**
    See also CA 93-96; 25-28R; DLB 272;
    EWL 3
Pavese, Cesare 1908-1950 .... **PC 13; SSC 19;**
    TCLC 3, 240
    See also CA 104; 169; DLB 128, 177; EW
    12; EWL 3; PFS 20; RGSF 2; RGWL 2,
    3; TWA; WLIT 7
Pavic, Milorad 1929-2009 .... **CLC 60**
    See also CA 136; CDWLB 4; CWW 2; DLB
    181; EWL 3; RGWL 3
Pavlov, Ivan Petrovich 1849-1936 . **TCLC 91**
    See also CA 118; 180
Pavlova, Karolina Karlovna
    1807-1893 .... **NCLC 138**
    See also DLB 205
Payne, Alan
    See Jakes, John
Payne, John Howard 1791-1852 .. **NCLC 241**
    See also DLB 37; RGAL 4
Payne, Rachel Ann
    See Jakes, John
Paz, Gil
    See Lugones, Leopoldo
Paz, Octavio 1914-1998 . **CLC 3, 4, 6, 10, 19,**
    51, 65, 119; HLC 2; PC 1, 48; TCLC
    211; WLC 4
    See also AAYA 50; CA 73-76; 165; CANR
    32, 65, 104; CWW 2; DA; DA3; DAB;
    DAC; DAM MST, MULT, POET; DLB
    290, 331; DLBY 1990, 1998; DNFS 1;
    EWL 3; HW 1, 2; LAW; LAWS 1; MTCW
    1, 2; MTFW 2005; PFS 18, 30, 38; RGWL
    2, 3; SSFS 13; TWA; WLIT 1
p'Bitek, Okot 1931-1982 . **BLC 1:3; CLC 96;**
    TCLC 149
    See also AFW; BW 2, 3; CA 124; 107;
    CANR 82; CP 1, 2, 3; DAM MULT; DLB
    125; EWL 3; MTCW 1, 2; MTFW 2005;
    RGEL 2; WLIT 2
Peabody, Elizabeth Palmer
    1804-1894 .... **NCLC 169**
    See also DLB 1, 223
Peacham, Henry 1578-1644(?) .... **LC 119**
    See also DLB 151
Peacock, Molly 1947- .... **CLC 60**
    See also CA 103, 262; CAAE 262; CAAS
    21; CANR 52, 84; CP 5, 6, 7; CWP; DLB
    120, 282
Peacock, Thomas Love
    1785-1866 .... **NCLC 22; PC 87**
    See also BRW 4; DLB 96, 116; RGEL 2;
    RGSF 2
Peake, Mervyn 1911-1968 .... **CLC 7, 54**
    See also CA 5-8R; 25-28R; CANR 3; DLB
    15, 160, 255; FANT; MTCW 1; RGEL 2;
    SATA 23; SFW 4
Pearce, Ann Philippa
    See Pearce, Philippa
Pearce, Philippa 1920-2006 .... **CLC 21**
    See also BYA 5; CA 5-8R; 255; CANR 4,
    109; CLR 9; CWRI 5; DLB 161; FANT;
    MAICYA 1; SATA 1, 67, 129; SATA-Obit
    179
Pearl, Eric
    See Elman, Richard (Martin)
Pearson, Jean Mary
    See Gardam, Jane
Pearson, Thomas Reid
    See Pearson, T.R.
Pearson, T.R. 1956- .... **CLC 39**
    See also CA 120; 130; CANR 97, 147, 185;
    CSW; INT CA-130
Peck, Dale 1967- .... **CLC 81**
    See also CA 146; CANR 72, 127, 180; GLL
    2

Peck, John (Frederick) 1941- .... **CLC 3**
    See also CA 49-52; CANR 3, 100; CP 4, 5,
    6, 7
Peck, Richard 1934- .... **CLC 21**
    See also AAYA 1, 24; BYA 1, 6, 8, 11; CA
    85-88; CANR 19, 38, 129, 178; CLR 15,
    142; INT CANR-19; JRDA; MAICYA 1,
    2; SAAS 2; SATA 18, 55, 97, 110, 158,
    190, 228; SATA-Essay 110; WYA; YAW
Peck, Richard Wayne
    See Peck, Richard
Peck, Robert Newton 1928- .... **CLC 17**
    See also AAYA 3, 43; BYA 1, 6; CA 81-84,
    182; CAAE 182; CANR 31, 63, 127; CLR
    45, 163; DA; DAC; DAM MST; JRDA;
    LAIT 3; MAICYA 1, 2; NFS 29; SAAS
    1; SATA 21, 62, 111, 156; SATA-Essay
    108; WYA; YAW
Peckinpah, David Samuel
    See Peckinpah, Sam
Peckinpah, Sam 1925-1984 .... **CLC 20**
    See also CA 109; 114; CANR 82
Pedersen, Knut 1859-1952 .. **TCLC 2, 14, 49,**
    151, 203
    See also AAYA 79; CA 104; 119; CANR
    63; DLB 297, 330; EW 8; EWL 8; MTCW
    1, 2; RGWL 2, 3
Peele, George 1556-1596 .... **DC 27; LC 115**
    See also BRW 1; DLB 62, 167; RGEL 2
Peeslake, Gaffer
    See Durrell, Lawrence
Peguy, Charles (Pierre)
    1873-1914 .... **TCLC 10**
    See also CA 107; 193; DLB 258; EWL 3;
    GFL 1789 to the Present
Peirce, Charles Sanders
    1839-1914 .... **TCLC 81**
    See also CA 194; DLB 270
Pelagius c. 350-c. 418 .... **CMLC 118**
Pelecanos, George P. 1957- .... **CLC 236**
    See also CA 138; CANR 122, 165, 194;
    DLB 306
Pelevin, Victor 1962- .... **CLC 238**
    See also CA 154; CANR 88, 159, 197; DLB
    285
Pelevin, Viktor Olegovich
    See Pelevin, Victor
Pellicer, Carlos 1897(?)-1977 .... **HLCS 2**
    See also CA 153; 69-72; DLB 290; EWL 3;
    HW 1
Pena, Ramon del Valle y
    See Valle-Inclan, Ramon del
Pendennis, Arthur Esquir
    See Thackeray, William Makepeace
Penn, Arthur
    See Matthews, (James) Brander
Penn, William 1644-1718 .... **LC 25**
    See also DLB 24
Penny, Carolyn
    See Chute, Carolyn
PEPECE
    See Prado (Calvo), Pedro
Pepys, Samuel 1633-1703 ... **LC 11, 58; WLC**
    4
    See also BRW 2; CDBLB 1660-1789; DA;
    DA3; DAB; DAC; DAM MST; DLB 101,
    213; NCFS 4; RGEL 2; TEA; WLIT 3
Percy, Thomas 1729-1811 .... **NCLC 95**
    See also DLB 104
Percy, Walker 1916-1990 .... **CLC 2, 3, 6, 8,**
    14, 18, 47, 65
    See also AMWS 3; BPFB 3; CA 1-4R; 131;
    CANR 1, 23, 64; CN 1, 2, 3, 4; CPW;
    CSW; DA3; DAM NOV, POP; DLB 2;
    DLBY 1980, 1990; EWL 3; MAL 5;
    MTCW 1, 2; MTFW 2005; RGAL 4; TUS
Percy, William Alexander
    1885-1942 .... **TCLC 84**
    See also CA 163; MTCW 2

Perdurabo, Frater
    See Crowley, Edward Alexander
Perec, Georges 1936-1982 .... **CLC 56, 116**
    See also CA 141; DLB 83, 299; EWL 3;
    GFL 1789 to the Present; RGHL; RGWL
    3
Pereda (y Sanchez de Porrua), Jose Maria
    de 1833-1906 .... **TCLC 16**
    See also CA 117
Pereda y Porrua, Jose Maria de
    See Pereda (y Sanchez de Porrua), Jose
    Maria de
Peregoy, George Weems
    See Mencken, H. L.
Perelman, S(idney) J(oseph)
    1904-1979 .. **CLC 3, 5, 9, 15, 23, 44, 49;**
    SSC 32
    See also AAYA 79; AITN 1, 2; BPFB 3;
    CA 73-76; 89-92; CANR 18; DAM
    DRAM; DLB 11, 44; MTCW 1, 2; MTFW
    2005; RGAL 4
Peret, Benjamin 1899-1959 .... **PC 33; TCLC**
    20
    See also CA 117; 186; GFL 1789 to the
    Present
Perets, Yitskhok Leybush
    See Peretz, Isaac Loeb
Peretz, Isaac Leib (?)-
    See Peretz, Isaac Loeb
Peretz, Isaac Loeb 1851-1915 .... **SSC 26;**
    TCLC 16
    See Peretz, Isaac Leib
    See also CA 109; 201; DLB 333
Peretz, Yitzhok Leibush
    See Peretz, Isaac Loeb
Perez Galdos, Benito 1843-1920 ..... **HLCS 2;**
    TCLC 27
    See also CA 125; 153; EW 7; EWL 3; HW
    1; RGWL 2, 3
Peri Rossi, Cristina 1941- .. **CLC 156; HLCS**
    2
    See also CA 131; CANR 59, 81; CWW 2;
    DLB 145, 290; EWL 3; HW 1, 2
Perlata
    See Peret, Benjamin
Perloff, Marjorie G(abrielle)
    1931- .... **CLC 137**
    See also CA 57-60; CANR 7, 22, 49, 104
Perrault, Charles 1628-1703 .. **LC 2, 56; SSC**
    144
    See also BYA 4; CLR 79, 134; DLB 268;
    GFL Beginnings to 1789; MAICYA 1, 2;
    RGWL 2, 3; SATA 25; WCH
Perrotta, Tom 1961- .... **CLC 266**
    See also CA 162; CANR 99, 155, 197
Perry, Anne 1938- .... **CLC 126**
    See also CA 101; CANR 22, 50, 84, 150,
    177; CMW 4; CN 6, 7; CPW; DLB 276
Perry, Brighton
    See Sherwood, Robert E(mmet)
Perse, St.-John
    See Leger, Alexis Saint-Leger
Perse, Saint-John
    See Leger, Alexis Saint-Leger
Persius 34-62 .... **CMLC 74**
    See also AW 2; DLB 211; RGWL 2, 3
Perutz, Leo(pold) 1882-1957 .... **TCLC 60**
    See also CA 147; DLB 81
Peseenz, Tulio F.
    See Lopez y Fuentes, Gregorio
Pesetsky, Bette 1932- .... **CLC 28**
    See also CA 133; DLB 130
Peshkov, Alexei Maximovich
    See Gorky, Maxim
Pessoa, Fernando 1888-1935 .... **HLC 2; PC**
    20; TCLC 27, 257
    See also CA 125; 183; CANR 182; DAM
    MULT; DLB 287; EW 10; EWL 3; RGWL
    2, 3; WP

Pessoa, Fernando Antonio Nogueira
See Pessoa, Fernando

Peterkin, Julia Mood 1880-1961 ...... **CLC 31**
See also CA 102; DLB 9

Peter of Blois c. 1135-c. 1212 ...... **CMLC 127**

Peters, Joan K(aren) 1945- .... **CLC 39**
See also CA 158; CANR 109

Peters, Robert L(ouis) 1924- .... **CLC 7**
See also CA 13-16R; CAAS 8; CP 1, 5, 6, 7; DLB 105

Peters, S. H.
See Henry, O.

Petofi, Sandor 1823-1849 .... **NCLC 21**
See also RGWL 2, 3

Petrakis, Harry Mark 1923- .... **CLC 3**
See also CA 9-12R; CANR 4, 30, 85, 155; CN 1, 2, 3, 4, 5, 6, 7

Petrarch 1304-1374 .... **CMLC 20; PC 8**
See also DA3; DAM POET; EW 2; LMFS 1; RGWL 2, 3; WLIT 7

Petrarch, Francesco
See Petrarch

Petronius c. 20-66 .... **CMLC 34**
See also AW 2; CDWLB 1; DLB 211; RGWL 2, 3; WLIT 8

Petrov, Eugene
See Kataev, Evgeny Petrovich

Petrov, Evgenii
See Kataev, Evgeny Petrovich

Petrov, Evgeny
See Kataev, Evgeny Petrovich

Petrovsky, Boris
See Mansfield, Katherine

Petry, Ann 1908-1997 ...... **CLC 1, 7, 18; SSC 161; TCLC 112**
See also AFAW 1, 2; BPFB 3; BW 1, 3; BYA 2; CA 5-8R; 157; CAAS 6; CANR 4, 46; CLR 12; CN 1, 2, 3, 4, 5, 6; DLB 76; EWL 3; JRDA; LAIT 1; MAICYA 1, 2; MAICYAS 1; MTCW 1; NFS 33; RGAL 4; SATA 5; SATA-Obit 94; TUS

Petry, Ann Lane
See Petry, Ann

Petursson, Halligrimur 1614-1674 .... **LC 8**

Peychinovich
See Vazov, Ivan (Minchov)

Phaedrus c. 15B.C.-c. 50 .... **CMLC 25**
See also DLB 211

Phelge, Nanker
See Richards, Keith

Phelps (Ward), Elizabeth Stuart
See Phelps, Elizabeth Stuart

Phelps, Elizabeth Stuart
1844-1911 .... **TCLC 113**
See also CA 242; DLB 74; FW

Pheradausi
See Ferdowsi, Abu'l Qasem

Philip, M(arlene) Nourbese 1947- .. **CLC 307**
See also BW 3; CA 163; CWP; DLB 157, 334

Philippe de Remi c. 1247-1296 ... **CMLC 102**

Philips, Katherine 1632-1664 ..... **LC 30, 145; PC 40**
See also DLB 131; RGEL 2

Philipson, Ilene J. 1950- .... **CLC 65**
See also CA 219

Philipson, Morris H. 1926- .... **CLC 53**
See also CA 1-4R; CANR 4

Phillips, Caryl 1958- ..... **BLCS; CLC 96, 224**
See also BRWS 5; BW 2; CA 141; CANR 63, 104, 140, 195; CBD; CD 5, 6; CN 5, 6, 7; DA3; DAM MULT; DLB 157; EWL 3; MTCW 2; MTFW 2005; WLIT 4; WWE 1

Phillips, David Graham
1867-1911 .... **TCLC 44**
See also CA 108; 176; DLB 9, 12, 303; RGAL 4

Phillips, Jack
See Sandburg, Carl

Phillips, Jayne Anne 1952- .... **CLC 15, 33, 139, 296; SSC 16**
See also AAYA 57; BPFB 3; CA 101; CANR 24, 50, 96, 200; CN 4, 5, 6, 7; CSW; DLBY 1980; INT CANR-24; MTCW 1, 2; MTFW 2005; RGAL 4; RGSF 2; SSFS 4

Phillips, Richard
See Dick, Philip K.

Phillips, Robert (Schaeffer) 1938- .... **CLC 28**
See also CA 17-20R; CAAS 13; CANR 8; DLB 105

Phillips, Ward
See Lovecraft, H. P.

Philo c. 20B.C.-c. 50 .... **CMLC 100**
See also DLB 176

Philostratus, Flavius c. 179-c.
244 .... **CMLC 62**

Phiradausi
See Ferdowsi, Abu'l Qasem

Piccolo, Lucio 1901-1969 .... **CLC 13**
See also CA 97-100; DLB 114; EWL 3

Pickthall, Marjorie L(owry) C(hristie)
1883-1922 .... **TCLC 21**
See also CA 107; DLB 92

Pico della Mirandola, Giovanni
1463-1494 .... **LC 15**
See also LMFS 1

Piercy, Marge 1936- .... **CLC 3, 6, 14, 18, 27, 62, 128; PC 29**
See also BPFB 3; CA 21-24R, 187; CAAE 187; CAAS 1; CANR 13, 43, 66, 111; CN 3, 4, 5, 6, 7; CP 1, 2, 3, 4, 5, 6, 7; CWP; DLB 120, 227; EXPP; FW; MAL 5; MTCW 1, 2; MTFW 2005; PFS 9, 22, 32, 40; SFW 4

Piers, Robert
See Anthony, Piers

Pieyre de Mandiargues, Andre
1909-1991 .... **CLC 41**
See also CA 103; 136; CANR 22, 82; DLB 83; EWL 3; GFL 1789 to the Present

Pil'niak, Boris
See Vogau, Boris Andreyevich

Pil'niak, Boris Andreevich
See Vogau, Boris Andreyevich

Pilnyak, Boris 1894-1938
See Vogau, Boris Andreyevich

Pinchback, Eugene
See Toomer, Jean

Pincherle, Alberto 1907-1990 .. **CLC 2, 7, 11, 27, 46; SSC 26**
See also CA 25-28R; 132; CANR 33, 63, 142; DAM NOV; DLB 127; EW 12; EWL 3; MTCW 2; MTFW 2005; RGSF 2; RGWL 2, 3; WLIT 7

Pinckney, Darryl 1953- .... **CLC 76**
See also BW 2, 3; CA 143; CANR 79

Pindar 518(?)B.C.-438(?)B.C. .... **CMLC 12, 130; PC 19**
See also AW 1; CDWLB 1; DLB 176; RGWL 2

Pineda, Cecile 1942- .... **CLC 39**
See also CA 118; DLB 209

Pinero, Arthur Wing 1855-1934 .... **TCLC 32**
See also CA 110; 153; DAM DRAM; DLB 10, 344; RGEL 2

Pinero, Miguel (Antonio Gomez)
1946-1988 .... **CLC 4, 55**
See also CA 61-64; 125; CAD; CANR 29, 90; DLB 266; HW 1; LLW

Pinget, Robert 1919-1997 .... **CLC 7, 13, 37**
See also CA 85-88; 160; CWW 2; DLB 83; EWL 3; GFL 1789 to the Present

Pink Floyd
See Barrett, Syd; Gilmour, David; Mason, Nick; Waters, Roger; Wright, Rick

Pinkney, Edward 1802-1828 .... **NCLC 31**
See also DLB 248

Pinkwater, D. Manus
See Pinkwater, Daniel

Pinkwater, Daniel 1941- .... **CLC 35**
See also AAYA 1, 46; BYA 9; CA 29-32R; CANR 12, 38, 89, 143; CLR 4; CSW; FANT; JRDA; MAICYA 1, 2; SAAS 3; SATA 8, 46, 76, 114, 158, 210; SFW 4; YAW

Pinkwater, Daniel M.
See Pinkwater, Daniel

Pinkwater, Daniel Manus
See Pinkwater, Daniel

Pinkwater, Manus
See Pinkwater, Daniel

Pinsky, Robert 1940- .... **CLC 9, 19, 38, 94, 121, 216; PC 27**
See also AMWS 6; CA 29-32R; CAAS 4; CANR 58, 97, 138, 177; CP 3, 4, 5, 6, 7; DA3; DAM POET; DLBY 1982, 1998; MAL 5; MTCW 2; MTFW 2005; PFS 18; RGAL 4; TCLE 1:2

Pinta, Harold
See Pinter, Harold

Pinter, Harold 1930-2008 ...... **CLC 1, 3, 6, 9, 11, 15, 27, 58, 73, 199; DC 15; WLC 4**
See also BRWR 1; BRWS 1; CA 5-8R; 280; CANR 33, 65, 112, 145; CBD; CD 5, 6; CDBLB 1960 to Present; CP 1; DA; DA3; DAB; DAC; DAM DRAM, MST; DFS 5, 7, 14, 25; DLB 13, 310, 331; EWL 3; IDFW 3, 4; LMFS 2; MTCW 1, 2; MTFW 2005; RGEL 2; RGHL; TEA

Piozzi, Hester Lynch (Thrale)
1741-1821 .... **NCLC 57**
See also DLB 104, 142

Pirandello, Luigi 1867-1936 .. **DC 5; SSC 22, 148; TCLC 4, 29, 172; WLC 4**
See also CA 104; 153; CANR 103; DA; DA3; DAB; DAC; DAM DRAM, MST; DFS 4, 9; DLB 264, 331; EW 8; EWL 3; MTCW 2; MTFW 2005; RGSF 2; RGWL 2, 3; SSFS 30, 33; WLIT 7

Pirdousi
See Ferdowsi, Abu'l Qasem

Pirdousi, Abu-l-Qasim
See Ferdowsi, Abu'l Qasem

Pirsig, Robert M(aynard) 1928- ... **CLC 4, 6, 73**
See also CA 53-56; CANR 42, 74; CPW 1; DA3; DAM POP; MTCW 1, 2; MTFW 2005; NFS 31; SATA 39

Pisan, Christine de
See Christine de Pizan

Pisarev, Dmitrii Ivanovich
See Pisarev, Dmitry Ivanovich

Pisarev, Dmitry Ivanovich
1840-1868 .... **NCLC 25**
See also DLB 277

Pix, Mary (Griffith) 1666-1709 ..... **LC 8, 149**
See also DLB 80

Pixerecourt, (Rene Charles) Guilbert de
1773-1844 .... **NCLC 39**
See also DLB 192; GFL 1789 to the Present

Plaatje, Sol(omon) T(shekisho)
1878-1932 .... **BLCS; TCLC 73**
See also BW 2, 3; CA 141; CANR 79; DLB 125, 225

Plaidy, Jean
See Hibbert, Eleanor Alice Burford

Planche, James Robinson
1796-1880 .... **NCLC 42**
See also RGEL 2

Plant, Robert 1948- .... **CLC 12**

Plante, David 1940- .... **CLC 7, 23, 38**
See also CA 37-40R; CANR 12, 36, 58, 82, 152, 191, 230; CN 2, 3, 4, 5, 6, 7; DAM NOV; DLBY 1983; INT CANR-12; MTCW 1

Pteleon
See Grieve, C. M.

Puckett, Lute
See Masters, Edgar Lee

Puig, Manuel 1932-1990 .... **CLC 3, 5, 10, 28, 65, 133; HLC 2; TCLC 227**
See also BPFB 3; CA 45-48; CANR 2, 32, 63; CDWLB 3; DA3; DAM MULT; DLB 113; DNFS 1; EWL 3; GLL 1; HW 1, 2; LAW; MTCW 1, 2; MTFW 2005; RGWL 2, 3; TWA; WLIT 1

Pulitzer, Joseph 1847-1911 .... **TCLC 76**
See also CA 114; DLB 23

Pullman, Philip 1946- .... **CLC 245**
See also AAYA 15, 41; BRWS 13; BYA 8, 13; CA 127; CANR 50, 77, 105, 134, 190; CLR 20, 62, 84; JRDA; MAICYA 1, 2; MAICYAS 1; MTFW 2005; SAAS 17; SATA 65, 103, 150, 198; SUFW 2; WYAS 1; YAW

Purchas, Samuel 1577(?)-1626 .... **LC 70**
See also DLB 151

Purdy, A(lfred) W(ellington)
1918-2000 .... **CLC 3, 6, 14, 50**
See also CA 81-84; 189; CAAS 17; CANR 42, 66; CP 1, 2, 3, 4, 5, 6, 7; DAC; DAM MST, POET; DLB 88; PFS 5; RGEL 2

Purdy, James 1914-2009 .... **CLC 2, 4, 10, 28, 52, 286**
See also AMWS 7; CA 33-36R; 284; CAAS 1; CANR 19, 51, 132; CN 1, 2, 3, 4, 5, 6, 7; DLB 2, 218; EWL 3; INT CANR-19; MAL 5; MTCW 1; RGAL 4

Purdy, James Amos
See Purdy, James

Purdy, James Otis
See Purdy, James

Pure, Simon
See Swinnerton, Frank Arthur

Pushkin, Aleksandr Sergeevich
See Pushkin, Alexander

Pushkin, Alexander 1799-1837 . **NCLC 3, 27, 83; PC 10; SSC 27, 55, 99; WLC 5**
See also DA; DA3; DAB; DAC; DAM DRAM, MST, POET; DLB 205; EW 5; EXPS; PFS 28, 34; RGSF 2; RGWL 2, 3; SATA 61; SSFS 9; TWA

Pushkin, Alexander Sergeyevich
See Pushkin, Alexander

P'u Sung-ling 1640-1715 .... **LC 49; SSC 31**

Putnam, Arthur Lee
See Alger, Horatio, Jr.

Puttenham, George 1529(?)-1590 ...... **LC 116**
See also DLB 281

Puzo, Mario 1920-1999 .... **CLC 1, 2, 6, 36, 107**
See also BPFB 3; CA 65-68; 185; CANR 4, 42, 65, 99, 131; CN 1, 2, 3, 4, 5, 6; CPW; DA3; DAM NOV, POP; DLB 6; MTCW 1, 2; MTFW 2005; NFS 16; RGAL 4

Pygge, Edward
See Barnes, Julian

Pyle, Ernest Taylor
See Pyle, Ernie

Pyle, Ernie 1900-1945 .... **TCLC 75**
See also CA 115; 160; DLB 29, 364; MTCW 2

Pyle, Howard 1853-1911 .... **TCLC 81**
See also AAYA 57; BYA 2, 4; CA 109; 137; CLR 22, 117; DLB 42, 188; DLBD 13; LAIT 1; MAICYA 1, 2; SATA 16, 100; WCH; YAW

Pym, Barbara (Mary Crampton)
1913-1980 .... **CLC 13, 19, 37, 111**
See also BPFB 3; BRWS 2; CA 13-14; 97-100; CANR 13, 34; CAP 1; DLB 14, 207; DLBY 1987; EWL 3; MTCW 1, 2; MTFW 2005; RGEL 2; TEA

Pynchon, Thomas 1937- .. **CLC 2, 3, 6, 9, 11, 18, 33, 62, 72, 123, 192, 213; SSC 14, 84; WLC 5**
See also AMWS 2; BEST 90:2; BPFB 3; CA 17-20R; CANR 22, 46, 73, 142, 198; CN 1, 2, 3, 4, 5, 6, 7; CPW 1; DA; DA3; DAB; DAC; DAM MST, NOV, POP; DLB 2, 173; EWL 3; MAL 5; MTCW 1, 2; MTFW 2005; NFS 23, 36; RGAL 4; SFW 4; TCLE 1:2; TUS

Pynchon, Thomas Ruggels, Jr.
See Pynchon, Thomas

Pynchon, Thomas Ruggles
See Pynchon, Thomas

Pythagoras c. 582B.C.-c. 507B.C. . **CMLC 22**
See also DLB 176

Q
See Quiller-Couch, Sir Arthur (Thomas)

Qian, Chongzhu
See Qian, Zhongshu

Qian, Sima 145B.C.-c. 89B.C. .... **CMLC 72**
See also DLB 358

Qian, Zhongshu 1910-1998 .... **CLC 22**
See also CA 130; CANR 73, 216; CWW 2; DLB 328; MTCW 1, 2

Qroll
See Dagerman, Stig (Halvard)

Quarles, Francis 1592-1644 .... **LC 117**
See also DLB 126; RGEL 2

Quarrington, Paul 1953-2010 .... **CLC 65**
See also CA 129; CANR 62, 95, 228

Quarrington, Paul Lewis
See Quarrington, Paul

Quasimodo, Salvatore 1901-1968 .... **CLC 10; PC 47**
See also CA 13-16; 25-28R; CAP 1; DLB 114, 332; EW 12; EWL 3; MTCW 1; RGWL 2, 3

Quatermass, Martin
See Carpenter, John

Quay, Stephen 1947- .... **CLC 95**
See also CA 189

Quay, Timothy 1947- .... **CLC 95**
See also CA 189

Queen, Ellery
See Dannay, Frederic; Hoch, Edward D.; Lee, Manfred B.; Marlowe, Stephen; Sturgeon, Theodore (Hamilton); Vance, Jack

Queneau, Raymond 1903-1976 ..... **CLC 2, 5, 10, 42; TCLC 233**
See also CA 77-80; 69-72; CANR 32; DLB 72, 258; EW 12; EWL 3; GFL 1789 to the Present; MTCW 1, 2; RGWL 2, 3

Quevedo, Francisco de 1580-1645 ...... **LC 23, 160**

Quiller-Couch, Sir Arthur (Thomas)
1863-1944 .... **TCLC 53**
See also CA 118; 166; DLB 135, 153, 190; HGG; RGEL 2; SUFW 1

Quin, Ann 1936-1973 .... **CLC 6**
See also CA 9-12R; 45-48; CANR 148; CN 1; DLB 14, 231

Quin, Ann Marie
See Quin, Ann

Quincey, Thomas de
See De Quincey, Thomas

Quindlen, Anna 1953- .... **CLC 191**
See also AAYA 35; AMWS 17; CA 138; CANR 73, 126; DA3; DLB 292; MTCW 2; MTFW 2005

Quinn, Martin
See Smith, Martin Cruz

Quinn, Peter 1947- .... **CLC 91**
See also CA 197; CANR 147

Quinn, Peter A.
See Quinn, Peter

Quinn, Simon
See Smith, Martin Cruz

Quintana, Leroy V. 1944- ...... **HLC 2; PC 36**
See also CA 131; CANR 65, 139; DAM MULT; DLB 82; HW 1, 2

Quintilian c. 40-c. 100 .... **CMLC 77**
See also AW 2; DLB 211; RGWL 2, 3

Quiroga, Horacio (Sylvestre)
1878-1937 ... **HLC 2; SSC 89; TCLC 20**
See also CA 117; 131; DAM MULT; EWL 3; HW 1; LAW; MTCW 1; RGSF 2; WLIT 1

Quoirez, Francoise
See Sagan, Francoise

Raabe, Wilhelm (Karl) 1831-1910 . **TCLC 45**
See also CA 167; DLB 129

Rabe, David 1940- .... **CLC 4, 8, 33, 200; DC 16**
See also CA 85-88; CABS 3; CAD; CANR 59, 129, 218; CD 5, 6; DAM DRAM; DFS 3, 8, 13; DLB 7, 228; EWL 3; MAL 5

Rabe, David William
See Rabe, David

Rabelais, Francois 1494-1553 .... **LC 5, 60, 186; WLC 5**
See also DA; DAB; DAC; DAM MST; DLB 327; EW 2; GFL Beginnings to 1789; LMFS 1; RGWL 2, 3; TWA

Rabi'a al-'Adawiyya c. 717-c. 801 .... **CMLC 83**
See also DLB 311

Rabinovitch, Sholem 1859-1916 .... **SSC 33, 125; TCLC 1, 35**
See also CA 104; DLB 333; TWA

Rabinovitsh, Sholem Yankev
See Rabinovitch, Sholem

Rabinowitz, Sholem Yakov
See Rabinovitch, Sholem

Rabinowitz, Solomon
See Rabinovitch, Sholem

Rabinyan, Dorit 1972- .... **CLC 119**
See also CA 170; CANR 147

Rachilde
See Vallette, Marguerite Eymery; Vallette, Marguerite Eymery

Racine, Jean 1639-1699 .. **DC 32; LC 28, 113**
See also DA3; DAB; DAM MST; DFS 28; DLB 268; EW 3; GFL Beginnings to 1789; LMFS 1; RGWL 2, 3; TWA

Radcliffe, Ann 1764-1823 .. **NCLC 6, 55, 106, 223**
See also BRWR 3; DLB 39, 178; GL 3; HGG; LMFS 1; RGEL 2; SUFW; WLIT 3

Radclyffe-Hall, Marguerite
See Hall, Radclyffe

Radiguet, Raymond 1903-1923 ...... **TCLC 29**
See also CA 162; DLB 65; EWL 3; GFL 1789 to the Present; RGWL 2, 3

Radishchev, Aleksandr Nikolaevich
1749-1802 .... **NCLC 190**
See also DLB 150

Radishchev, Alexander
See Radishchev, Aleksandr Nikolaevich

Radnoti, Miklos 1909-1944 .... **TCLC 16**
See also CA 118; 212; CDWLB 4; DLB 215; EWL 3; RGHL; RGWL 2, 3

Rado, James 1939- .... **CLC 17**
See also CA 105

Radvanyi, Netty 1900-1983 .... **CLC 7**
See also CA 85-88; 110; CANR 82; CDWLB 2; DLB 69; EWL 3

Rae, Ben
See Griffiths, Trevor

Raeburn, John (Hay) 1941- .... **CLC 34**
See also CA 57-60

Ragni, Gerome 1942-1991 .... **CLC 17**
See also CA 105; 134

Rahv, Philip
See Greenberg, Ivan

Remark, Erich Paul
See Remarque, Erich Maria
Remarque, Erich Maria 1898-1970 . **CLC 21**
See also AAYA 27; BPFB 3; CA 77-80; 29-
32R; CDWLB 2; CLR 159; DA; DA3;
DAB; DAC; DAM MST, NOV; DLB 56;
EWL 3; EXPN; LAIT 3; MTCW 1, 2;
MTFW 2005; NFS 4, 36; RGHL; RGWL
2, 3
Remington, Frederic S(ackrider)
1861-1909 .... **TCLC 89**
See also CA 108; 169; DLB 12, 186, 188;
SATA 41; TCWW 2
Remizov, A.
See Remizov, Aleksei (Mikhailovich)
Remizov, A. M.
See Remizov, Aleksei (Mikhailovich)
Remizov, Aleksei (Mikhailovich)
1877-1957 .... **TCLC 27**
See also CA 125; 133; DLB 295; EWL 3
Remizov, Alexey Mikhaylovich
See Remizov, Aleksei (Mikhailovich)
Renan, Joseph Ernest 1823-1892 . **NCLC 26,
145**
See also GFL 1789 to the Present
Renard, Jules(-Pierre) 1864-1910 .. **TCLC 17**
See also CA 117; 202; GFL 1789 to the
Present
Renart, Jean fl. 13th cent. - .... **CMLC 83**
Renault, Mary 1905-1983 .... **CLC 3, 11, 17**
See also BPFB 3; BYA 2; CA 81-84; 111;
CANR 74; CN 1, 2, 3; DA3; DLBY 1983;
EWL 3; GLL 1; LAIT 1; MTCW 2;
MTFW 2005; RGEL 2; RHW; SATA 23;
SATA-Obit 36; TEA
Rendell, Ruth
See Rendell, Ruth
Rendell, Ruth 1930- ...... **CLC 28, 48, 50, 295**
See also BEST 90:4; BPFB 3; BRWS 9;
CA 109; CANR 32, 52, 74, 127, 162, 190,
227; CN 5, 6, 7; CPW; DAM POP; DLB
87, 276; INT CANR-32; MSW; MTCW
1, 2; MTFW 2005
Rendell, Ruth Barbara
See Rendell, Ruth
Renoir, Jean 1894-1979 .... **CLC 20**
See also CA 129; 85-88
Rensie, Willis
See Eisner, Will
Resnais, Alain 1922- .... **CLC 16**
Restif de la Bretonne, Nicolas-Anne-Edme
1734-1806 .... **NCLC 257**
See also DLB 314; GFL Beginnings to 1789
Revard, Carter 1931- .... **NNAL**
See also CA 144; CANR 81, 153; PFS 5
Reverdy, Pierre 1889-1960 .... **CLC 53**
See also CA 97-100; 89-92; DLB 258; EWL
3; GFL 1789 to the Present
Reverend Mandju
See Su, Chien
Rexroth, Kenneth 1905-1982 .... **CLC 1, 2, 6,
11, 22, 49, 112; PC 20, 95**
See also BG 1:3; CA 5-8R; 107; CANR 14,
34, 63; CDALB 1941-1968; CP 1, 2, 3;
DAM POET; DLB 16, 48, 165, 212;
DLBY 1982; EWL 3; INT CANR-14;
MAL 5; MTCW 1, 2; MTFW 2005;
RGAL 4
Reyes, Alfonso 1889-1959 .... **HLCS 2; TCLC
33**
See also CA 131; EWL 3; HW 1; LAW
Reyes y Basoalto, Ricardo Eliecer Neftali
See Neruda, Pablo
Reymont, Wladyslaw (Stanislaw)
1868(?)-1925 .... **TCLC 5**
See also CA 104; DLB 332; EWL 3
Reynolds, John Hamilton
1794-1852 .... **NCLC 146**
See also DLB 96

Reynolds, Jonathan 1942- .... **CLC 6, 38**
See also CA 65-68; CANR 28, 176
Reynolds, Joshua 1723-1792 .... **LC 15**
See also DLB 104
Reynolds, Michael S(hane)
1937-2000 .... **CLC 44**
See also CA 65-68; 189; CANR 9, 89, 97
Reza, Yasmina 1959- .... **CLC 299; DC 34**
See also AAYA 69; CA 171; CANR 145;
DFS 19; DLB 321
Reznikoff, Charles 1894-1976 ..... **CLC 9; PC
124**
See also AMWS 14; CA 33-36; 61-64; CAP
2; CP 1, 2; DLB 28, 45; RGHL; WP
Rezzori, Gregor von
See Rezzori d'Arezzo, Gregor von
Rezzori d'Arezzo, Gregor von
1914-1998 .... **CLC 25**
See also CA 122; 136; 167
Rhine, Richard
See Silverstein, Alvin; Silverstein, Virginia
B.
Rhodes, Eugene Manlove
1869-1934 .... **TCLC 53**
See also CA 198; DLB 256; TCWW 1, 2
R'hoone, Lord
See Balzac, Honore de
Rhys, Jean 1890-1979 .... **CLC 2, 4, 6, 14, 19,
51, 124; SSC 21, 76**
See also BRWS 2; CA 25-28R; 85-88;
CANR 35, 62; CDBLB 1945-1960; CD-
WLB 3; CN 1, 2; DA3; DAB; DAM NOV; DLB
36, 117, 162; DNFS 2; EWL 3; LATS 1:1;
MTCW 1, 2; MTFW 2005; NFS 19;
RGEL 2; RGSF 2; RHW; TEA; WWE 1
Ribeiro, Darcy 1922-1997 .... **CLC 34**
See also CA 33-36R; 156; EWL 3
Ribeiro, Joao Ubaldo (Osorio Pimentel)
1941- .... **CLC 10, 67**
See also CA 81-84; CWW 2; EWL 3
Ribman, Ronald (Burt) 1932- .... **CLC 7**
See also CA 21-24R; CAD; CANR 46, 80;
CD 5, 6
Ricci, Nino 1959- .... **CLC 70**
See also CA 137; CANR 130; CCA 1
Ricci, Nino Pio
See Ricci, Nino
Rice, Anne 1941- .... **CLC 41, 128**
See also AAYA 9, 53; AMWS 7; BEST
89:2; BPFB 3; CA 65-68; CANR 12, 36,
53, 74, 100, 133, 190; CN 6, 7; CPW;
CSW; DA3; DAM POP; DLB 292; GL 3;
GLL 2; HGG; MTCW 2; MTFW 2005;
SUFW 2; YAW
Rice, Elmer (Leopold) 1892-1967 ...... **CLC 7,
49; DC 44; TCLC 221**
See also CA 21-22; 25-28R; CAP 2; DAM
DRAM; DFS 12; DLB 4, 7; EWL 3;
IDTP; MAL 5; MTCW 1, 2; RGAL 4
Rice, Tim 1944- .... **CLC 21**
See also CA 103; CANR 46; DFS 7
Rice, Timothy Miles Bindon
See Rice, Tim
Rich, Adrienne 1929- ..... **CLC 3, 6, 7, 11, 18,
36, 73, 76, 125; PC 5, 129**
See also AAYA 69; AMWR 2; AMWS 1;
CA 9-12R; CANR 20, 53, 74, 128, 199;
CDALBS; CP 1, 2, 3, 4, 5, 6, 7; CSW;
CWP; DA3; DAM POET; DLB 5, 67;
EWL 3; EXPP; FL 1:6; FW; MAL 5;
MBL; MTCW 1, 2; MTFW 2005; PAB;
PFS 15, 29, 39; RGAL 4; RGHL; WP
Rich, Adrienne Cecile
See Rich, Adrienne
Rich, Barbara
See Graves, Robert
Rich, Robert
See Trumbo, Dalton

Richard, Keith
See Richards, Keith
Richards, David Adams 1950- .... **CLC 59**
See also CA 93-96; CANR 60, 110, 156;
CN 7; DAC; DLB 53; TCLE 1:2
Richards, I(vor) A(rmstrong)
1893-1979 .... **CLC 14, 24**
See also BRWS 2; CA 41-44R; 89-92;
CANR 34, 74; CP 1, 2; DLB 27; EWL 3;
MTCW 2; RGEL 2
Richards, Keith 1943- .... **CLC 17**
See also CA 107; CANR 77
Richardson, Anne
See Roiphe, Anne
Richardson, Dorothy Miller
1873-1957 .... **TCLC 3, 203**
See also BRWS 13; CA 104; 192; DLB 36;
EWL 3; FW; RGEL 2
Richardson, Ethel Florence Lindesay
1870-1946 .... **TCLC 4**
See also CA 105; 190; DLB 197, 230; EWL
3; RGEL 2; RGSF 2; RHW
Richardson, Henrietta
See Richardson, Ethel Florence Lindesay
Richardson, Henry Handel
See Richardson, Ethel Florence Lindesay
Richardson, John 1796-1852 .... **NCLC 55**
See also CCA 1; DAC; DLB 99
Richardson, Samuel 1689-1761 ...... **LC 1, 44,
138, 204; WLC 5**
See also BRW 3; CDBLB 1660-1789; DA;
DAB; DAC; DAM MST, NOV; DLB 154;
RGEL 2; TEA; WLIT 3
Richardson, Willis 1889-1977 .... **HR 1:3**
See also BW 1; CA 124; DLB 51; SATA 60
**Richardson Robertson, Ethel Florence
Lindesay**
See Richardson, Ethel Florence Lindesay
Richler, Mordecai 1931-2001 .... **CLC 3, 5, 9,
13, 18, 46, 70, 185, 271**
See also AITN 1; CA 65-68; 201; CANR
31, 62, 111; CCA 1; CLR 17; CN 1, 2, 3,
4, 5, 7; CWRI 5; DAC; DAM MST, NOV;
DLB 53; EWL 3; MAICYA 1, 2; MTCW
1, 2; MTFW 2005; RGEL 2; RGHL;
SATA 44, 98; SATA-Brief 27; TWA
Richter, Conrad (Michael)
1890-1968 .... **CLC 30**
See also AAYA 21; AMWS 18; BYA 2; CA
5-8R; 25-28R; CANR 23; DLB 9, 212;
LAIT 1; MAL 5; MTCW 1, 2; MTFW
2005; RGAL 4; SATA 3; TCWW 1, 2;
TUS; YAW
Ricostranza, Tom
See Ellis, Trey
Riddell, Charlotte 1832-1906 .... **TCLC 40**
See also CA 165; DLB 156; HGG; SUFW
Riddell, Mrs. J. H.
See Riddell, Charlotte
Ridge, John Rollin 1827-1867 ...... **NCLC 82;
NNAL**
See also CA 144; DAM MULT; DLB 175
Ridgeway, Jason
See Marlowe, Stephen
Ridgway, Keith 1965- .... **CLC 119**
See also CA 172; CANR 144
Riding, Laura
See Jackson, Laura
Riefenstahl, Berta Helene Amalia
1902-2003 .... **CLC 16, 190**
See also CA 108; 220
Riefenstahl, Leni
See Riefenstahl, Berta Helene Amalia
Riffe, Ernest
See Bergman, Ingmar
Riffe, Ernest Ingmar
See Bergman, Ingmar

Roiphe, Anne 1935- .... **CLC 3, 9**
  See also CA 89-92; CANR 45, 73, 138, 170,
  230; DLBY 1980; INT CA-89-92
Roiphe, Anne Richardson
  See Roiphe, Anne
Rojas, Fernando de 1475-1541 ... **HLCS 1, 2;**
  LC 23, 169
  See also DLB 286; RGWL 2, 3
Rojas, Gonzalo 1917-2011 .... **HLCS 2**
  See also CA 178; HW 2; LAWS 1
Rojas Zorrilla, Francisco de
  1607-1648 .... **LC 204**
Rolaag, Ole Edvart
  See Rolvaag, O.E.
Roland (de la Platiere), Marie-Jeanne
  1754-1793 .... **LC 98**
  See also DLB 314
Rolfe, Frederick (William Serafino Austin
  Lewis Mary) 1860-1913 .... **TCLC 12**
  See also CA 107; 210; DLB 34, 156; GLL
  1; RGEL 2
Rolland, Romain 1866-1944 .... **TCLC 23**
  See also CA 118; 197; DLB 65, 284, 332;
  EWL 3; GFL 1789 to the Present; RGWL
  2, 3
Rolle, Richard c. 1300-c. 1349 ...... **CMLC 21**
  See also DLB 146; LMFS 1; RGEL 2
Rolvaag, O.E.
  See Rolvaag, O.E.
Rolvaag, O.E.
  See Rolvaag, O.E.
Rolvaag, O.E. 1876-1931 .... **TCLC 17, 207**
  See also AAYA 75; CA 117; 171; DLB 9,
  212; MAL 5; NFS 5; RGAL 4; TCWW 1,
  2
Romain Arnaud, Saint
  See Aragon, Louis
Romains, Jules 1885-1972 .... **CLC 7**
  See also CA 85-88; CANR 34; DLB 65,
  321; EWL 3; GFL 1789 to the Present;
  MTCW 1
Romero, Jose Ruben 1890-1952 .... **TCLC 14**
  See also CA 114; 131; EWL 3; HW 1; LAW
Ronsard, Pierre de 1524-1585 . **LC 6, 54; PC**
  11, 105
  See also DLB 327; EW 2; GFL Beginnings
  to 1789; RGWL 2, 3; TWA
Rooke, Leon 1934- .... **CLC 25, 34**
  See also CA 25-28R; CANR 23, 53; CCA
  1; CPW; DAM POP
Roosevelt, Franklin Delano
  1882-1945 .... **TCLC 93**
  See also CA 116; 173; LAIT 3
Roosevelt, Theodore 1858-1919 ..... **TCLC 69**
  See also CA 115; 170; DLB 47, 186, 275
Roper, Margaret c. 1505-1544 .... **LC 147**
Roper, William 1498-1578 .... **LC 10**
Roquelaure, A. N.
  See Rice, Anne
Rosa, Joao Guimaraes
  See Guimaraes Rosa, Joao
Rose, Wendy 1948- . **CLC 85; NNAL; PC 13**
  See also CA 53-56; CANR 5, 51; CWP;
  DAM MULT; DLB 175; PFS 13; RGAL
  4; SATA 12
Rosen, R.D. 1949- .... **CLC 39**
  See also CA 77-80; CANR 62, 120, 175;
  CMW 4; INT CANR-30
Rosen, Richard
  See Rosen, R.D.
Rosen, Richard Dean
  See Rosen, R.D.
Rosenberg, Isaac 1890-1918 .... **TCLC 12**
  See also BRW 6; CA 107; 188; DLB 20,
  216; EWL 3; PAB; RGEL 2
Rosenblatt, Joe
  See Rosenblatt, Joseph

Rosenblatt, Joseph 1933- .... **CLC 15**
  See also CA 89-92; CP 3, 4, 5, 6, 7; INT
  CA-89-92
Rosenfeld, Samuel
  See Tzara, Tristan
Rosenstock, Sami
  See Tzara, Tristan
Rosenstock, Samuel
  See Tzara, Tristan
Rosenthal, M(acha) L(ouis)
  1917-1996 .... **CLC 28**
  See also CA 1-4R; 152; CAAS 6; CANR 4,
  51; CP 1, 2, 3, 4, 5, 6; DLB 5; SATA 59
Ross, Barnaby
  See Dannay, Frederic; Lee, Manfred B.
Ross, Bernard L.
  See Follett, Ken
Ross, J. H.
  See Lawrence, T. E.
Ross, John Hume
  See Lawrence, T. E.
Ross, Martin 1862-1915
  See Martin, Violet Florence
  See also DLB 135; GLL 2; RGEL 2; RGSF
  2
Ross, (James) Sinclair 1908-1996 ... **CLC 13;**
  SSC 24
  See also CA 73-76; CANR 81; CN 1, 2, 3,
  4, 5, 6; DAC; DAM MST; DLB 88;
  RGEL 2; RGSF 2; TCWW 1, 2
Rossetti, Christina 1830-1894 ... **NCLC 2, 50,**
  66, 186; PC 7, 119; WLC 5
  See also AAYA 51; BRW 5; BRWR 3; BYA
  4; CLR 115; DA; DA3; DAB; DAC;
  DAM MST, POET; DLB 35, 163, 240;
  EXPP; FL 1:3; LATS 1:1; MAICYA 1, 2;
  PFS 10, 14, 27, 34; RGEL 2; SATA 20;
  TEA; WCH
Rossetti, Christina Georgina
  See Rossetti, Christina
Rossetti, Dante Gabriel 1828-1882 . **NCLC 4,**
  77; PC 44; WLC 5
  See also AAYA 51; BRW 5; CDBLB 1832-
  1890; DA; DAB; DAC; DAM MST,
  POET; DLB 35; EXPP; RGEL 2; TEA
Rossi, Cristina Peri
  See Peri Rossi, Cristina
Rossi, Jean-Baptiste 1931-2003 .... **CLC 90**
  See also CA 201; 215; CMW 4; NFS 18
Rossner, Judith 1935-2005 .... **CLC 6, 9, 29**
  See also AITN 2; BEST 90:3; BPFB 3; CA
  17-20R; 242; CANR 18, 51, 73; CN 4, 5,
  6, 7; DLB 6; INT CANR-18; MAL 5;
  MTCW 1, 2; MTFW 2005
Rossner, Judith Perelman
  See Rossner, Judith
Rostand, Edmond 1868-1918 . **DC 10; TCLC**
  6, 37
  See also CA 104; 126; DA; DA3; DAB;
  DAC; DAM DRAM, MST; DFS 1; DLB
  192; LAIT 1; MTCW 1; RGWL 2, 3;
  TWA
Rostand, Edmond Eugene Alexis
  See Rostand, Edmond
Roth, Henry 1906-1995 ... **CLC 2, 6, 11, 104;**
  SSC 134
  See also AMWS 9; CA 11-12; 149; CANR
  38, 63; CAP 1; CN 1, 2, 3, 4, 5, 6; DA3;
  DLB 28; EWL 3; MAL 5; MTCW 1, 2;
  MTFW 2005; RGAL 4
Roth, (Moses) Joseph 1894-1939 ... **TCLC 33**
  See also CA 160; DLB 85; EWL 3; RGWL
  2, 3
Roth, Philip 1933- ... **CLC 1, 2, 3, 4, 6, 9, 15,**
  22, 31, 47, 66, 86, 119, 201; SSC 26,
  102; WLC 5
  See also AAYA 67; AMWR 2; AMWS 3;
  BEST 90:3; BPFB 3; CA 1-4R; CANR 1,
  22, 36, 55, 89, 132, 170; CDALB 1968-

1988; CN 3, 4, 5, 6, 7; CPW 1; DA; DA3;
  DAB; DAC; DAM MST, NOV, POP;
  DLB 2, 28, 173; DLBY 1982; EWL 3;
  MAL 5; MTCW 1, 2; MTFW 2005; NFS
  25; RGAL 4; RGHL; RGSF 2; SSFS 12,
  18; TUS
Roth, Philip Milton
  See Roth, Philip
Rothenberg, Jerome 1931- .... **CLC 6, 57; PC**
  129
  See also CA 45-48; CANR 1, 106; CP 1, 2,
  3, 4, 5, 6, 7; DLB 5, 193
Rotter, Pat CLC 65
Roumain, Jacques 1907-1944 .... **BLC 1:3;**
  TCLC 19
  See also BW 1; CA 117; 125; DAM MULT;
  EWL 3
Roumain, Jacques Jean Baptiste
  See Roumain, Jacques
Rourke, Constance Mayfield
  1885-1941 .... **TCLC 12**
  See also CA 107; 200; MAL 5; YABC 1
Rousseau, Jean-Baptiste 1671-1741 ...... **LC 9**
Rousseau, Jean-Jacques 1712-1778 .... **LC 14,**
  36, 122, 198; WLC 5
  See also DA; DA3; DAB; DAC; DAM
  MST; DLB 314; EW 4; GFL Beginnings
  to 1789; LMFS 1; RGWL 2, 3; TWA
Roussel, Raymond 1877-1933 .... **TCLC 20**
  See also CA 117; 201; EWL 3; GFL 1789
  to the Present
Rovit, Earl (Herbert) 1927- .... **CLC 7**
  See also CA 5-8R; CANR 12
Rowe, Elizabeth Singer 1674-1737 ..... **LC 44**
  See also DLB 39, 95
Rowe, Nicholas 1674-1718 .... **LC 8**
  See also DLB 84; RGEL 2
Rowlandson, Mary 1637(?)-1678 .... **LC 66**
  See also DLB 24, 200; RGAL 4
Rowley, Ames Dorrance
  See Lovecraft, H. P.
Rowley, William 1585(?)-1626 ..... **DC 43; LC**
  100, 123
  See also DFS 22; DLB 58; RGEL 2
Rowling, J.K. 1965- .... **CLC 137, 217**
  See also AAYA 34, 82; BRWS 16; BYA 11,
  13, 14; CA 173; CANR 128, 157; CLR
  66, 80, 112; LNFS 1, 2, 3; MAICYA 2;
  MTFW 2005; SATA 109, 174; SUFW 2
Rowling, Joanne Kathleen
  See Rowling, J.K.
Rowson, Susanna Haswell
  1762(?)-1824 .... **NCLC 5, 69, 182**
  See also AMWS 15; DLB 37, 200; RGAL 4
Roy, Arundhati 1961- .... **CLC 109, 210**
  See also CA 163; CANR 90, 126, 217; CN
  7; DLB 323, 326; DLBY 1997; EWL 3;
  LATS 1:2; MTFW 2005; NFS 22; WWE
  1
Roy, Gabrielle 1909-1983 .... **CLC 10, 14;**
  TCLC 256
  See also CA 53-56; 110; CANR 5, 61; CCA
  1; DAB; DAC; DAM MST; DLB 68;
  EWL 3; MTCW 1; RGWL 2, 3; SATA
  104; TCLE 1:2
Roy, Suzanna Arundhati
  See Roy, Arundhati
Royko, Mike 1932-1997 .... **CLC 109**
  See also CA 89-92; 157; CANR 26, 111;
  CPW
Rozanov, Vasilii Vasil'evich
  See Rozanov, Vassili
Rozanov, Vasily Vasilyevich
  See Rozanov, Vassili
Rozanov, Vassili 1856-1919 .... **TCLC 104**
  See also DLB 295; EWL 3

Rozewicz, Tadeusz 1921- ...... **CLC 9, 23, 139**
See also CA 108; CANR 36, 66; CWW 2;
DA3; DAM POET; DLB 232; EWL 3;
MTCW 1, 2; MTFW 2005; RGHL;
RGWL 3

Ruark, Gibbons 1941- .... **CLC 3**
See also CA 33-36R; CAAS 23; CANR 14,
31, 57; DLB 120

Rubens, Bernice (Ruth) 1923-2004 . **CLC 19,
31**
See also CA 25-28R; 232; CANR 33, 65,
128; CN 1, 2, 3, 4, 5, 6, 7; DLB 14, 207,
326; MTCW 1

Rubin, Harold
See Robbins, Harold

Rudkin, (James) David 1936- .... **CLC 14**
See also CA 89-92; CBD; CD 5, 6; DLB 13

Rudnik, Raphael 1933- .... **CLC 7**
See also CA 29-32R

Ruffian, M.
See Hasek, Jaroslav

Rufinus c. 345-410 .... **CMLC 111**

Ruiz, Jose Martinez
See Martinez Ruiz, Jose

Ruiz, Juan c. 1283-c. 1350 .... **CMLC 66**

Rukeyser, Muriel 1913-1980 . **CLC 6, 10, 15,
27; PC 12**
See also AMWS 6; CA 5-8R; 93-96; CANR
26, 60; CP 1, 2, 3; DA3; DAM POET;
DLB 48; EWL 3; FW; GLL 2; MAL 5;
MTCW 1, 2; PFS 10, 29; RGAL 4; SATA-
Obit 22

Rule, Jane 1931-2007 .... **CLC 27, 265**
See also CA 25-28R; 266; CAAS 18; CANR
12, 87; CN 4, 5, 6, 7; DLB 60; FW

Rule, Jane Vance
See Rule, Jane

Rulfo, Juan 1918-1986 .. **CLC 8, 80; HLC 2;
SSC 25**
See also CA 85-88; 118; CANR 26; CD-
WLB 3; DAM MULT; DLB 113; EWL 3;
HW 1, 2; LAW; MTCW 1, 2; RGSF 2;
RGWL 2, 3; WLIT 1

Rumi
See Rumi, Jalal al-Din

Rumi, Jalal al-Din 1207-1273 ...... **CMLC 20;
PC 45, 123**
See also AAYA 64; RGWL 2, 3; WLIT 6;
WP

Runeberg, Johan 1804-1877 .... **NCLC 41**

Runyon, (Alfred) Damon
1884(?)-1946 .... **TCLC 10**
See also CA 107; 165; DLB 11, 86, 171;
MAL 5; MTCW 2; RGAL 4

Rush, Benjamin 1746-1813 .... **NCLC 251**
See also DLB 37

Rush, Norman 1933- .... **CLC 44, 306**
See also CA 121; 126; CANR 130; INT CA-
126

Rushdie, Ahmed Salman
See Rushdie, Salman

Rushdie, Salman 1947- .... **CLC 23, 31, 55,
100, 191, 272; SSC 83; WLCS**
See also AAYA 65; BEST 89:3; BPFB 3;
BRWS 4; CA 108; 111; CANR 33, 56,
108, 133, 192; CLR 125; CN 4, 5, 6, 7;
CPW 1; DA3; DAB; DAC; DAM MST,
NOV, POP; DLB 194, 323, 326; EWL 3;
FANT; INT CA-111; LATS 1:2; LMFS 2;
MTCW 1, 2; MTFW 2005; NFS 22, 23;
RGEL 2; RGSF 2; TEA; WLIT 4

Rushforth, Peter 1945-2005 .... **CLC 19**
See also CA 101; 243

Rushforth, Peter Scott
See Rushforth, Peter

Ruskin, John 1819-1900 .... **TCLC 63**
See also BRW 5; BYA 5; CA 114; 129; CD-
BLB 1832-1890; DLB 55, 163, 190;
RGEL 2; SATA 24; TEA; WCH

Russ, Joanna 1937-2011 .... **CLC 15**
See also BPFB 3; CA 25-28; CANR 11, 31,
65; CN 4, 5, 6, 7; DLB 8; FW; GLL 1;
MTCW 1; SCFW 1, 2; SFW 4

Russ, Richard Patrick
See O'Brian, Patrick

Russell, George William
1867-1935 .... **TCLC 3, 10**
See also BRWS 8; CA 104; 153; CDBLB
1890-1914; DAM POET; DLB 19; EWL
3; RGEL 2

Russell, Jeffrey Burton 1934- .... **CLC 70**
See also CA 25-28R; CANR 11, 28, 52, 179

Russell, (Henry) Ken(neth Alfred)
1927- .... **CLC 16**
See also CA 105

Russell, William Martin 1947- .... **CLC 60**
See also CA 164; CANR 107; CBD; CD 5,
6; DLB 233

Russell, Willy
See Russell, William Martin

Russo, Richard 1949- .... **CLC 181**
See also AMWS 12; CA 127; 133; CANR
87, 114, 194; NFS 25

Rutebeuf fl. c. 1249-1277 .... **CMLC 104**
See also DLB 208

Rutherford, Mark
See White, William Hale

Ruysbroeck, Jan van 1293-1381 ... **CMLC 85**

Ruyslinck, Ward
See Belser, Reimond Karel Maria de

Ryan, Cornelius (John) 1920-1974 ..... **CLC 7**
See also CA 69-72; 53-56; CANR 38

Ryan, Michael 1946- .... **CLC 65**
See also CA 49-52; CANR 109, 203; DLBY
1982

Ryan, Tim
See Dent, Lester

Rybakov, Anatoli (Naumovich)
1911-1998 .... **CLC 23, 53**
See also CA 126; 135; 172; DLB 302;
RGHL; SATA 79; SATA-Obit 108

Rybakov, Anatolii (Naumovich)
See Rybakov, Anatoli (Naumovich)

Ryder, Jonathan
See Ludlum, Robert

Ryga, George 1932-1987 .... **CLC 14**
See also CA 101; 124; CANR 43, 90; CCA
1; DAC; DAM MST; DLB 60

Rymer, Thomas 1643(?)-1713 .... **LC 132**
See also DLB 101, 336

S. H.
See Hartmann, Sadakichi

S. L. C.
See Twain, Mark

S. S.
See Sassoon, Siegfried

Sa'adawi, al- Nawal
See El Saadawi, Nawal

Saadawi, Nawal El
See El Saadawi, Nawal

Saadiah Gaon 882-942 .... **CMLC 97**

Saba, Umberto 1883-1957 .... **TCLC 33**
See also CA 144; CANR 79; DLB 114;
EWL 3; RGWL 2, 3

Sabatini, Rafael 1875-1950 .... **TCLC 47**
See also BPFB 3; CA 162; RHW

Sabato, Ernesto 1911-2011 .... **CLC 10, 23;
HLC 2**
See also CA 97-100; CANR 32, 65; CD-
WLB 3; CWW 2; DAM MULT; DLB 145;
EWL 3; HW 1, 2; LAW; MTCW 1, 2;
MTFW 2005

Sa-Carneiro, Mario de 1890-1916 . **TCLC 83**
See also DLB 287; EWL 3

Sacastru, Martin
See Bioy Casares, Adolfo

Sacher-Masoch, Leopold von
1836(?)-1895 .... **NCLC 31**

Sachs, Hans 1494-1576 .... **LC 95**
See also CDWLB 2; DLB 179; RGWL 2, 3

Sachs, Marilyn 1927- .... **CLC 35**
See also AAYA 2; BYA 6; CA 17-20R;
CANR 13, 47, 150; CLR 2; JRDA; MAI-
CYA 1, 2; SAAS 2; SATA 3, 68, 164;
SATA-Essay 110; WYA; YAW

Sachs, Marilyn Stickle
See Sachs, Marilyn

Sachs, Nelly 1891-1970 .. **CLC 14, 98; PC 78**
See also CA 17-18; 25-28R; CANR 87;
CAP 2; DLB 332; EWL 3; MTCW 1;
MTFW 2005; PFS 20; RGHL; RGWL 2,
3

Sackler, Howard (Oliver)
1929-1982 .... **CLC 14**
See also CA 61-64; 108; CAD; CANR 30;
DFS 15; DLB 7

Sacks, Oliver 1933- .... **CLC 67, 202**
See also CA 53-56; CANR 28, 50, 76, 146,
187, 230; CPW; DA3; INT CANR-28;
MTCW 1, 2; MTFW 2005

Sacks, Oliver Wolf
See Sacks, Oliver

Sackville, Thomas 1536-1608 .... **LC 98**
See also DAM DRAM; DLB 62, 132;
RGEL 2

Sadakichi
See Hartmann, Sadakichi

Sa'dawi, Nawal al-
See El Saadawi, Nawal

Sade, Donatien Alphonse Francois
1740-1814 .... **NCLC 3, 47**
See also DLB 314; EW 4; GFL Beginnings
to 1789; RGWL 2, 3

Sade, Marquis de
See Sade, Donatien Alphonse Francois

Sadoff, Ira 1945- .... **CLC 9**
See also CA 53-56; CANR 5, 21, 109; DLB
120

Saetone
See Camus, Albert

Safire, William 1929-2009 .... **CLC 10**
See also CA 17-20R; 290; CANR 31, 54,
91, 148

Safire, William L.
See Safire, William

Safire, William Lewis
See Safire, William

Sagan, Carl 1934-1996 .... **CLC 30, 112**
See also AAYA 2, 62; CA 25-28R; 155;
CANR 11, 36, 74; CPW; DA3; MTCW 1,
2; MTFW 2005; SATA 58; SATA-Obit 94

Sagan, Francoise 1935-2004 ...... **CLC 3, 6, 9,
17, 36**
See also CA 49-52; 231; CANR 6, 39, 73,
216; CWW 2; DLB 83; EWL 3; GFL
1789 to the Present; MTCW 1, 2; MTFW
2005; TWA

Sahgal, Nayantara (Pandit) 1927- .... **CLC 41**
See also CA 9-12R; CANR 11, 88; CN 1,
2, 3, 4, 5, 6, 7; DLB 323

Said, Edward W. 1935-2003 .... **CLC 123**
See also CA 21-24R; 220; CANR 45, 74,
107, 131; DLB 67, 346; MTCW 2; MTFW
2005

Saikaku, Ihara 1642-1693 .... **LC 141**
See also RGWL 3

Saikaku Ihara
See Saikaku, Ihara

Saint, H(arry) F. 1941- .... **CLC 50**
See also CA 127

St. Aubin de Teran, Lisa 1953- .... **CLC 36**
See also CA 118; 126; CANR 215; CN 6,
7; INT CA-126

DFS 17; DLB 7, 9, 86; DLBY 1981; EWL 3; LAIT 4; MAL 5; MTCW 1, 2; MTFW 2005; NFS 39; RGAL 4; RGSF 2; SATA 23; SATA-Obit 24; SSFS 14; TUS

Sarraute, Nathalie 1900-1999 .... **CLC 1, 2, 4, 8, 10, 31, 80; TCLC 145**
See also BPFB 3; CA 9-12R; 187; CANR 23, 66, 134; CWW 2; DLB 83, 321; EW 12; EWL 3; GFL 1789 to the Present; MTCW 1, 2; MTFW 2005; RGWL 2, 3

Sarton, May 1912-1995 ... **CLC 4, 14, 49, 91; PC 39; TCLC 120**
See also AMWS 8; CA 1-4R; 149; CANR 1, 34, 55, 116; CN 1, 2, 3, 4, 5, 6; CP 1, 2, 3, 4, 5, 6; DAM POET; DLB 48; DLBY 1981; EWL 3; FW; INT CANR-34; MAL 5; MTCW 1, 2; MTFW 2005; RGAL 4; SATA 36; SATA-Obit 86; TUS

Sartre, Jean-Paul 1905-1980 . **CLC 1, 4, 7, 9, 13, 18, 24, 44, 50, 52; DC 3; SSC 32; WLC 5**
See also AAYA 62; CA 9-12R; 97-100; CANR 21; DA; DA3; DAB; DAC; DAM DRAM, MST, NOV; DFS 5, 26; DLB 72, 296, 321, 332; EW 12; EWL 3; GFL 1789 to the Present; LMFS 2; MTCW 1, 2; MTFW 2005; NFS 21; RGHL; RGSF 2; RGWL 2, 3; SSFS 9; TWA

Sassoon, Siegfried 1886-1967 .. **CLC 36, 130; PC 12**
See also BRW 6; CA 104; 25-28R; CANR 36; DAB; DAM MST, NOV, POET; DLB 20, 191; DLBD 18; EWL 3; MTCW 1, 2; MTFW 2005; PAB; PFS 28; RGEL 2; TEA

Sassoon, Siegfried Lorraine
See Sassoon, Siegfried

Satterfield, Charles
See Pohl, Frederik

Satyremont
See Peret, Benjamin

Saul, John 1942- .... **CLC 46**
See also AAYA 10, 62; BEST 90:4; CA 81-84; CANR 16, 40, 81, 176, 221; CPW; DAM NOV, POP; HGG; SATA 98

Saul, John W.
See Saul, John

Saul, John Woodruff III
See Saul, John

Saunders, Caleb
See Heinlein, Robert A.

Saura (Atares), Carlos 1932-1998 .... **CLC 20**
See also CA 114; 131; CANR 79; HW 1

Sauser, Frederic Louis
See Sauser-Hall, Frederic

Sauser-Hall, Frederic 1887-1961 ..... **CLC 18, 106**
See also CA 102; 93-96; CANR 36, 62; DLB 258; EWL 3; GFL 1789 to the Present; MTCW 1; WP

Saussure, Ferdinand de
1857-1913 .... **TCLC 49**
See also DLB 242

Savage, Catharine
See Brosman, Catharine Savage

Savage, Richard 1697(?)-1743 .... **LC 96**
See also DLB 95; RGEL 2

Savage, Thomas 1915-2003 .... **CLC 40**
See also CA 126; 132; 218; CAAS 15; CN 6, 7; INT CA-132; SATA-Obit 147; TCWW 2

Savan, Glenn 1953-2003 .... **CLC 50**
See also CA 225

Savonarola, Girolamo 1452-1498 ...... **LC 152**
See also LMFS 1

Sax, Robert
See Johnson, Robert

Saxo Grammaticus c. 1150-c.
1222 .... **CMLC 58, 141**

Saxton, Robert
See Johnson, Robert

Sayers, Dorothy L(eigh) 1893-1957 . **SSC 71; TCLC 2, 15, 237**
See also BPFB 3; BRWS 3; CA 104; 119; CANR 60; CDBLB 1914-1945; CMW 4; DAM POP; DLB 10, 36, 77, 100; MSW; MTCW 1, 2; MTFW 2005; RGEL 2; SSFS 12; TEA

Sayers, Valerie 1952- .... **CLC 50, 122**
See also CA 134; CANR 61; CSW

Sayles, John 1950- .... **CLC 7, 10, 14, 198**
See also CA 57-60; CANR 41, 84; DLB 44

Sayles, John Thomas
See Sayles, John

Scalapino, Leslie 1947-2010 .... **PC 114**
See also CA 123; CANR 67, 103; CP 5, 6, 7; CWP; DLB 193

Scamander, Newt
See Rowling, J.K.

Scammell, Michael 1935- .... **CLC 34**
See also CA 156; CANR 222

Scannel, John Vernon
See Scannell, Vernon

Scannell, Vernon 1922-2007 .... **CLC 49**
See also CA 5-8R; 266; CANR 8, 24, 57, 143; CN 1, 2; CP 1, 2, 3, 4, 5, 6, 7; CWRI 5; DLB 27; SATA 59; SATA-Obit 188

Scarlett, Susan
See Streatfeild, Noel

Scarron 1847-1910
See Mikszath, Kalman

Scarron, Paul 1610-1660 .... **LC 116**
See also GFL Beginnings to 1789; RGWL 2, 3

Sceve, Maurice c. 1500-c. 1564 . **LC 180; PC 111**
See also DLB 327; GFL Beginnings to 1789

Schaeffer, Susan Fromberg
1940-2011 .... **CLC 6, 11, 22**
See also CA 49-52; CANR 18, 65, 160; CN 4, 5, 6, 7; DLB 28, 299; MTCW 1, 2; MTFW 2005; SATA 22

Schama, Simon 1945- .... **CLC 150**
See also BEST 89:4; CA 105; CANR 39, 91, 168, 207

Schama, Simon Michael
See Schama, Simon

Schary, Jill
See Robinson, Jill

Schell, Jonathan 1943- .... **CLC 35**
See also CA 73-76; CANR 12, 117, 187

Schelling, Friedrich Wilhelm Joseph von
1775-1854 .... **NCLC 30**
See also DLB 90

Scherer, Jean-Marie Maurice
See Rohmer, Eric

Schevill, James (Erwin) 1920- .... **CLC 7**
See also CA 5-8R; CAAS 12; CAD; CD 5, 6; CP 1, 2, 3, 4, 5

Schiller, Friedrich von 1759-1805 ...... **DC 12; NCLC 39, 69, 166**
See also CDWLB 2; DAM DRAM; DLB 94; EW 5; RGWL 2, 3; TWA

Schisgal, Murray (Joseph) 1926- .... **CLC 6**
See also CA 21-24R; CAD; CANR 48, 86; CD 5, 6; MAL 5

Schlee, Ann 1934- .... **CLC 35**
See also CA 101; CANR 29, 88; SATA 44; SATA-Brief 36

Schlegel, August Wilhelm von
1767-1845 .... **NCLC 15, 142**
See also DLB 94; RGWL 2, 3

Schlegel, Friedrich 1772-1829 .... **NCLC 45, 226**
See also DLB 90, 366; EW 5; RGWL 2, 3; TWA

Schlegel, Johann Elias (von)
1719(?)-1749 .... **LC 5**

Schleiermacher, Friedrich
1768-1834 .... **NCLC 107**
See also DLB 90

Schlesinger, Arthur M., Jr.
1917-2007 .... **CLC 84**
See Schlesinger, Arthur Meier
See also AITN 1; CA 1-4R; 257; CANR 1, 28, 58, 105, 187; DLB 17; INT CANR-28; MTCW 1, 2; SATA 61; SATA-Obit 181

Schlink, Bernhard 1944- .... **CLC 174**
See also CA 163; CANR 116, 175, 217; RGHL

Schmidt, Arno (Otto) 1914-1979 ...... **CLC 56**
See also CA 128; 109; DLB 69; EWL 3

Schmitz, Aron Hector 1861-1928 ..... **SSC 25; TCLC 2, 35, 244**
See also CA 104; 122; DLB 264; EW 8; EWL 3; MTCW 1; RGWL 2, 3; WLIT 7

Schnackenberg, Gjertrud 1953- ...... **CLC 40; PC 45**
See also AMWS 15; CA 116; CANR 100; CP 5, 6, 7; CWP; DLB 120, 282; PFS 13, 25

Schnackenberg, Gjertrud Cecelia
See Schnackenberg, Gjertrud

Schneider, Leonard Alfred
1925-1966 .... **CLC 21**
See also CA 89-92

Schnitzler, Arthur 1862-1931 ..... **DC 17; SSC 15, 61; TCLC 4**
See also CA 104; CDWLB 2; DLB 81, 118; EW 8; EWL 3; RGSF 2; RGWL 2, 3

Schoenberg, Arnold Franz Walter
1874-1951 .... **TCLC 75**
See also CA 109; 188

Schonberg, Arnold
See Schoenberg, Arnold Franz Walter

Schopenhauer, Arthur 1788-1860 . **NCLC 51, 157**
See also DLB 90; EW 5

Schor, Sandra (M.) 1932(?)-1990 ..... **CLC 65**
See also CA 132

Schorer, Mark 1908-1977 .... **CLC 9**
See also CA 5-8R; 73-76; CANR 7; CN 1, 2; DLB 103

Schrader, Paul (Joseph) 1946- . **CLC 26, 212**
See also CA 37-40R; CANR 41; DLB 44

Schreber, Daniel 1842-1911 .... **TCLC 123**

Schreiner, Olive 1855-1920 .... **TCLC 9, 235**
See also AFW; BRWS 2; CA 105; 154; DLB 18, 156, 190, 225; EWL 3; FW; RGEL 2; TWA; WLIT 2; WWE 1

Schreiner, Olive Emilie Albertina
See Schreiner, Olive

Schulberg, Budd 1914-2009 .... **CLC 7, 48**
See also AMWS 18; BPFB 3; CA 25-28R; 289; CANR 19, 87, 178; CN 1, 2, 3, 4, 5, 6, 7; DLB 6, 26, 28; DLBY 1981, 2001; MAL 5

Schulberg, Budd Wilson
See Schulberg, Budd

Schulberg, Seymour Wilson
See Schulberg, Budd

Schulman, Arnold
See Trumbo, Dalton

Schulz, Bruno 1892-1942 .. **SSC 13; TCLC 5, 51**
See also CA 115; 123; CANR 86; CDWLB 4; DLB 215; EWL 3; MTCW 2; MTFW 2005; RGSF 2; RGWL 2, 3

Schulz, Charles M. 1922-2000 .... **CLC 12**
See also AAYA 39; CA 9-12R; 187; CANR 6, 132; INT CANR-6; MTFW 2005; SATA 10; SATA-Obit 118

Schulz, Charles Monroe
See Schulz, Charles M.

116, 159, 178; EXPN; FL 1:3; GL 3; HGG; LAIT 1; LMFS 1, 2; NFS 1, 37; RGEL 2; SATA 29; SCFW 1, 2; SFW 4; TEA; WLIT 3

Shelley, Percy Bysshe 1792-1822 .. **NCLC 18, 93, 143, 175; PC 14, 67; WLC 5**
See also AAYA 61; BRW 4; BRWR 1; CD-BLB 1789-1832; DA; DA3; DAB; DAC; DAM MST, POET; DLB 96, 110, 158; EXPP; LMFS 1; PAB; PFS 2, 27, 32, 36; RGEL 2; TEA; WLIT 3; WP

Shepard, James R.
See Shepard, Jim

Shepard, Jim 1956- .... **CLC 36**
See also AAYA 73; CA 137; CANR 59, 104, 160, 199, 231; SATA 90, 164

Shepard, Lucius 1947- .... **CLC 34**
See also CA 128; 141; CANR 81, 124, 178; HGG; SCFW 2; SFW 4; SUFW 2

Shepard, Sam 1943- .... **CLC 4, 6, 17, 34, 41, 44, 169; DC 5**
See also AAYA 1, 58; AMWS 3; CA 69-72; CABS 3; CAD; CANR 22, 120, 140, 223; CD 5, 6; DA3; DAM DRAM; DFS 3, 6, 7, 14; DLB 7, 212, 341; EWL 3; IDFW 3, 4; MAL 5; MTCW 1, 2; MTFW 2005; RGAL 4

Shepherd, Jean (Parker)
1921-1999 .... **TCLC 177**
See also AAYA 69; AITN 2; CA 77-80; 187

Shepherd, Michael
See Ludlum, Robert

Sherburne, Zoa (Lillian Morin)
1912-1995 .... **CLC 30**
See also AAYA 13; CA 1-4R; 176; CANR 3, 37; MAICYA 1, 2; SAAS 18; SATA 3; YAW

Sheridan, Frances 1724-1766 .... **LC 7**
See also DLB 39, 84

Sheridan, Richard Brinsley
1751-1816 . **DC 1; NCLC 5, 91; WLC 5**
See also BRW 3; CDBLB 1660-1789; DA; DAB; DAC; DAM DRAM, MST; DFS 15; DLB 89; WLIT 3

Sherman, Jonathan Marc 1968- .... **CLC 55**
See also CA 230

Sherman, Martin 1941(?)- .... **CLC 19**
See also CA 116; 123; CAD; CANR 86; CD 5, 6; DFS 20; DLB 228; GLL 1; IDTP; RGHL

Sherwin, Judith Johnson
See Johnson, Judith

Sherwood, Frances 1940- .... **CLC 81**
See also CA 146, 220; CAAE 220; CANR 158

Sherwood, Robert E(mmet)
1896-1955 .... **DC 36; TCLC 3**
See also CA 104; 153; CANR 86; DAM DRAM; DFS 11, 15, 17; DLB 7, 26, 249; IDFW 3, 4; MAL 5; RGAL 4

Shestov, Lev 1866-1938 .... **TCLC 56**

Shevchenko, Taras 1814-1861 .... **NCLC 54**

Shiel, M. P. 1865-1947 .... **TCLC 8**
See also CA 106; 160; DLB 153; HGG; MTCW 2; MTFW 2005; SCFW 1, 2; SFW 4; SUFW

Shiel, Matthew Phipps
See Shiel, M. P.

Shields, Carol 1935-2003 . **CLC 91, 113, 193, 298; SSC 126**
See also AMWS 7; CA 81-84; 218; CANR 51, 74, 98, 133; CCA 1; CN 6, 7; CPW; DA3; DAC; DLB 334, 350; MTCW 2; MTFW 2005; NFS 23

Shields, David 1956- .... **CLC 97**
See also CA 124; CANR 48, 99, 112, 157

Shields, David Jonathan
See Shields, David

Shiga, Naoya 1883-1971 .... **CLC 33; SSC 23; TCLC 172**
See also CA 101; 33-36R; DLB 180; EWL 3; MJW; RGWL 3

Shiga Naoya
See Shiga, Naoya

Shilts, Randy 1951-1994 .... **CLC 85**
See also AAYA 19; CA 115; 127; 144; CANR 45; DA3; GLL 1; INT CA-127; MTCW 2; MTFW 2005

Shimazaki, Haruki 1872-1943 .... **TCLC 5**
See also CA 105; 134; CANR 84; DLB 180; EWL 3; MJW; RGWL 3

Shimazaki Toson
See Shimazaki, Haruki

Shirley, James 1596-1666 .... **DC 25; LC 96**
See also DLB 58; RGEL 2

Sholem Aleykhem
See Rabinovitch, Sholem

Sholokhov, Mikhail 1905-1984 ..... **CLC 7, 15**
See also CA 101; 112; DLB 272, 332; EWL 3; MTCW 1, 2; MTFW 2005; RGWL 2, 3; SATA-Obit 36

Sholokhov, Mikhail Aleksandrovich
See Sholokhov, Mikhail

Sholom Aleichem 1859-1916 ....
See Rabinovitch, Sholem

Shone, Patric
See Hanley, James

Showalter, Elaine 1941- .... **CLC 169**
See also CA 57-60; CANR 58, 106, 208; DLB 67; FW; GLL 2

Shreve, Susan
See Shreve, Susan Richards

Shreve, Susan Richards 1939- .... **CLC 23**
See also CA 49-52; CAAS 5; CANR 5, 38, 69, 100, 159, 199; MAICYA 1, 2; SATA 46, 95, 152; SATA-Brief 41

Shteyngart, Gary 1972- .... **CLC 319**
See also AAYA 68; CA 217; CANR 175

Shteyngart, Igor
See Shteyngart, Gary

Shue, Larry 1946-1985 .... **CLC 52**
See also CA 145; 117; DAM DRAM; DFS 7

Shu-Jen, Chou 1881-1936 . **SSC 20; TCLC 3**
See also CA 104; EWL 3

Shulman, Alix Kates 1932- .... **CLC 2, 10**
See also CA 29-32R; CANR 43, 199; FW; SATA 7

Shuster, Joe 1914-1992 .... **CLC 21**
See also AAYA 50

Shute, Nevil 1899-1960 .... **CLC 30**
See also BPFB 3; CA 102; 93-96; CANR 85; DLB 255; MTCW 2; NFS 9, 38; RHW 4; SFW 4

Shuttle, Penelope (Diane) 1947- .... **CLC 7**
See also CA 93-96; CANR 39, 84, 92, 108; CP 3, 4, 5, 6, 7; CWP; DLB 14, 40

Shvarts, Elena 1948-2010 .... **PC 50**
See also CA 147

Sidhwa, Bapsi 1939-
See Sidhwa, Bapsy (N.)

Sidhwa, Bapsy (N.) 1938- .... **CLC 168**
See also CA 108; CANR 25, 57; CN 6, 7; DLB 323; FW

Sidney, Mary 1561-1621 .... **LC 19, 39, 182**
See also DLB 167

Sidney, Sir Philip 1554-1586 .... **LC 19, 39, 131, 197; PC 32**
See also BRW 1; BRWR 2; CDBLB Before 1660; DA; DA3; DAB; DAC; DAM MST, POET; DLB 167; EXPP; PAB; PFS 30; RGEL 2; TEA; WP

Sidney Herbert, Mary
See Sidney, Mary

Siegel, Jerome 1914-1996 .... **CLC 21**
See also AAYA 50; CA 116; 169; 151

Siegel, Jerry
See Siegel, Jerome

Sienkiewicz, Henryk (Adam Alexander Pius)
1846-1916 .... **TCLC 3**
See also CA 104; 134; CANR 84; DLB 332; EWL 3; RGSF 2; RGWL 2, 3

Sierra, Gregorio Martinez
See Martinez Sierra, Gregorio

Sierra, Maria de la O'LeJarraga Martinez
See Martinez Sierra, Maria

Sigal, Clancy 1926- .... **CLC 7**
See also CA 1-4R; CANR 85, 184; CN 1, 2, 3, 4, 5, 6, 7

Siger of Brabant 1240(?)-1284(?) . **CMLC 69**
See also DLB 115

Sigourney, Lydia H.
See Sigourney, Lydia Howard

Sigourney, Lydia Howard
1791-1865 .... **NCLC 21, 87**
See also DLB 1, 42, 73, 183, 239, 243

Sigourney, Lydia Howard Huntley
See Sigourney, Lydia Howard

Sigourney, Lydia Huntley
See Sigourney, Lydia Howard

Siguenza y Gongora, Carlos de
1645-1700 .... **HLCS 2; LC 8**
See also LAW

Sigurjonsson, Johann
See Sigurjonsson, Johann

Sigurjonsson, Johann 1880-1919 ... **TCLC 27**
See also CA 170; DLB 293; EWL 3

Sikelianos, Angelos 1884-1951 .... **PC 29; TCLC 39**
See also EWL 3; RGWL 2, 3

Silkin, Jon 1930-1997 .... **CLC 2, 6, 43**
See also CA 5-8R; CAAS 5; CANR 89; CP 1, 2, 3, 4, 5, 6; DLB 27

Silko, Leslie 1948- .... **CLC 23, 74, 114, 211, 302; NNAL; SSC 37, 66, 151; WLCS**
See also AAYA 14; AMWS 4; ANW; BYA 12; CA 115; 122; CANR 45, 65, 118, 226; CN 4, 5, 6, 7; CP 4, 5, 6, 7; CPW 1; CWP; DA; DA3; DAC; DAM MST, MULT, POP; DLB 143, 175, 256, 275; EWL 3; EXPP; EXPS; LAIT 4; MAL 5; MTCW 2; MTFW 2005; NFS 4; PFS 9, 16; RGAL 4; RGSF 2; SSFS 4, 8, 10, 11; TCWW 1, 2

Silko, Leslie Marmon
See Silko, Leslie

Sillanpaa, Frans Eemil 1888-1964 ... **CLC 19**
See also CA 129; 93-96; DLB 332; EWL 3; MTCW 1

Sillitoe, Alan 1928-2010 . **CLC 1, 3, 6, 10, 19, 57, 148, 318**
See also AITN 1; BRWS 5; CA 9-12R, 191; CAAE 191; CAAS 2; CANR 8, 26, 55, 139, 213; CDBLB 1960 to Present; CN 1, 2, 3, 4, 5, 6; CP 1, 2, 3, 4, 5; DLB 14, 139; EWL 3; MTCW 1, 2; MTFW 2005; RGEL 2; RGSF 2; SATA 61

Silone, Ignazio 1900-1978 .... **CLC 4**
See also CA 25-28; 81-84; CANR 34; CAP 2; DLB 264; EW 12; EWL 3; MTCW 1; RGSF 2; RGWL 2, 3

Silone, Ignazione
See Silone, Ignazio

Siluriensis, Leolinus
See Jones, Arthur Llewellyn

Silver, Joan Micklin 1935- .... **CLC 20**
See also CA 114; 121; INT CA-121

Silver, Nicholas
See Faust, Frederick

Silverberg, Robert 1935- .... **CLC 7, 140**
See also AAYA 24; BPFB 3; BYA 7, 9; CA 1-4R; CAAE 186; CAAS 186; CANR 1, 20, 36, 85, 140, 175; CLR 59; CN 6, 7; CPW; DAM POP; DLB 8; INT CANR-

20; MAICYA 1, 2; MTCW 1, 2; MTFW 2005; SATA 13, 91; SATA-Essay 104; SCFW 1, 2; SFW 4; SUFW 2

Silverstein, Alvin 1933- .... **CLC 17**
See also CA 49-52; CANR 2; CLR 25; JRDA; MAICYA 1, 2; SATA 8, 69, 124

Silverstein, Shel 1932-1999 .... **PC 49**
See also AAYA 40; BW 3; CA 107; 179; CANR 47, 74, 81; CLR 5, 96; CWRI 5; JRDA; MAICYA 1, 2; MTCW 2; MTFW 2005; SATA 33, 92; SATA-Brief 27; SATA-Obit 116

Silverstein, Sheldon Allan
See Silverstein, Shel

Silverstein, Virginia B. 1937- .... **CLC 17**
See also CA 49-52; CANR 2; CLR 25; JRDA; MAICYA 1, 2; SATA 8, 69, 124

Silverstein, Virginia Barbara Opshelor
See Silverstein, Virginia B.

Sim, Georges
See Simenon, Georges

Simak, Clifford D(onald) 1904-1988 . **CLC 1, 55**
See also CA 1-4R; 125; CANR 1, 35; DLB 8; MTCW 1; SATA-Obit 56; SCFW 1, 2; SFW 4

Simenon, Georges 1903-1989 .... **CLC 1, 2, 3, 8, 18, 47**
See also BPFB 3; CA 85-88; 129; CANR 35; CMW 4; DA3; DAM POP; DLB 72; DLBY 1989; EW 12; EWL 3; GFL 1789 to the Present; MSW; MTCW 1, 2; MTFW 2005; RGWL 2, 3

Simenon, Georges Jacques Christian
See Simenon, Georges

Simic, Charles 1938- .... **CLC 6, 9, 22, 49, 68, 130, 256; PC 69**
See also AAYA 78; AMWS 8; CA 29-32R; CAAS 4; CANR 12, 33, 52, 61, 96, 140, 210; CP 2, 3, 4, 5, 6, 7; DA3; DAM POET; DLB 105; MAL 5; MTCW 2; MTFW 2005; PFS 7, 33, 36; RGAL 4; WP

Simmel, Georg 1858-1918 .... **TCLC 64**
See also CA 157; DLB 296

Simmons, Charles (Paul) 1924- .... **CLC 57**
See also CA 89-92; INT CA-89-92

Simmons, Dan 1948- .... **CLC 44**
See also AAYA 16, 54; CA 138; CANR 53, 81, 126, 174, 204; CPW; DAM POP; HGG; SUFW 2

Simmons, James (Stewart Alexander) 1933- .... **CLC 43**
See also CA 105; CAAS 21; CP 1, 2, 3, 4, 5, 6, 7; DLB 40

Simmons, Richard
See Simmons, Dan

Simms, William Gilmore 1806-1870 .... **NCLC 3, 241**
See also DLB 3, 30, 59, 73, 248, 254; RGAL 4

Simon, Carly 1945- .... **CLC 26**
See also CA 105

Simon, Claude 1913-2005 ... **CLC 4, 9, 15, 39**
See also CA 89-92; 241; CANR 33, 117; CWW 2; DAM NOV; DLB 83, 332; EW 13; EWL 3; GFL 1789 to the Present; MTCW 1

Simon, Claude Eugene Henri
See Simon, Claude

Simon, Claude Henri Eugene
See Simon, Claude

Simon, Marvin Neil
See Simon, Neil

Simon, Myles
See Follett, Ken

Simon, Neil 1927- .... **CLC 6, 11, 31, 39, 70, 233; DC 14**
See also AAYA 32; AITN 1; AMWS 4; CA 21-24R; CAD; CANR 26, 54, 87, 126; CD 5, 6; DA3; DAM DRAM; DFS 2, 6, 12, 18, 24, 27; DLB 7, 266; LAIT 4; MAL 5; MTCW 1, 2; MTFW 2005; RGAL 4; TUS

Simon, Paul 1941(?)- .... **CLC 17**
See also CA 116; 153; CANR 152

Simon, Paul Frederick
See Simon, Paul

Simonon, Paul 1956(?)- .... **CLC 30**

Simonson, Helen 1963- .... **CLC 318**
See also CA 307

Simonson, Rick CLC 70

Simpson, Harriette
See Arnow, Harriette (Louisa) Simpson

Simpson, Louis 1923- ... **CLC 4, 7, 9, 32, 149**
See also AMWS 9; CA 1-4R; CAAS 4; CANR 1, 61, 140; CP 1, 2, 3, 4, 5, 6, 7; DAM POET; DLB 5; MAL 5; MTCW 1, 2; MTFW 2005; PFS 7, 11, 14; RGAL 4

Simpson, Mona 1957- .... **CLC 44, 146**
See also CA 122; 135; CANR 68, 103, 227; CN 6, 7; EWL 3

Simpson, Mona Elizabeth
See Simpson, Mona

Simpson, N.F. 1919-2011 .... **CLC 29**
See also CA 13-16R; CBD; DLB 13; RGEL 2

Simpson, Norman Frederick
See Simpson, N.F.

Sinclair, Andrew (Annandale) 1935- . **CLC 2, 14**
See also CA 9-12R; CAAS 5; CANR 14, 38, 91; CN 1, 2, 3, 4, 5, 6, 7; DLB 14; FANT; MTCW 1

Sinclair, Emil
See Hesse, Hermann

Sinclair, Iain 1943- .... **CLC 76**
See also BRWS 14; CA 132; CANR 81, 157; CP 5, 6, 7; HGG

Sinclair, Iain MacGregor
See Sinclair, Iain

Sinclair, Irene
See Griffith, D.W.

Sinclair, Julian
See Sinclair, May

Sinclair, Mary Amelia St. Clair (?)-
See Sinclair, May

Sinclair, May 1865-1946 .... **TCLC 3, 11**
See also CA 104; 166; DLB 36, 135; EWL 3; HGG; RGEL 2; RHW; SUFW

Sinclair, Roy
See Griffith, D.W.

Sinclair, Upton 1878-1968 ...... **CLC 1, 11, 15, 63; TCLC 160; WLC 5**
See also AAYA 63; AMWS 5; BPFB 3; BYA 2; CA 5-8R; 25-28R; CANR 7; CDALB 1929-1941; DA; DA3; DAB; DAC; DAM MST, NOV; DLB 9; EWL 3; INT CANR-7; LAIT 3; MAL 5; MTCW 1, 2; MTFW 2005; NFS 6; RGAL 4; SATA 9; TUS; YAW

Sinclair, Upton Beall
See Sinclair, Upton

Singe, (Edmund) J(ohn) M(illington) 1871-1909 .... **WLC**

Singer, Isaac
See Singer, Isaac Bashevis

Singer, Isaac Bashevis 1904-1991 .. **CLC 1, 3, 6, 9, 11, 15, 23, 38, 69, 111; SSC 3, 53, 80, 154; WLC 5**
See also AAYA 32; AITN 1, 2; AMW; AMWR 2; BPFB 3; BYA 1, 4; CA 1-4R; 134; CANR 1, 39, 106; CDALB 1941-1968; CLR 1; CN 1, 2, 3, 4; CWRI 5; DA; DA3; DAB; DAC; DAM MST, NOV;

DLB 6, 28, 52, 278, 332, 333; DLBY 1991; EWL 3; EXPS; HGG; JRDA; LAIT 3; MAICYA 1, 2; MTCW 1, 2; MTFW 2005; RGAL 4; RGHL; RGSF 2; SATA 3, 27; SATA-Obit 68; SSFS 2, 12, 16, 27, 30; TUS; TWA

Singer, Israel Joshua 1893-1944 .... **TCLC 33**
See also CA 169; DLB 333; EWL 3

Singh, Khushwant 1915- .... **CLC 11**
See also CA 9-12R; CAAS 9; CANR 6, 84; CN 1, 2, 3, 4, 5, 6, 7; DLB 323; EWL 3; RGEL 2

Singleton, Ann
See Benedict, Ruth

Singleton, John 1968(?)- .... **CLC 156**
See also AAYA 50; BW 2, 3; CA 138; CANR 67, 82; DAM MULT

Siniavskii, Andrei
See Sinyavsky, Andrei (Donatevich)

Sinibaldi, Fosco
See Kacew, Romain

Sinjohn, John
See Galsworthy, John

Sinyavsky, Andrei (Donatevich) 1925-1997 .... **CLC 8**
See also CA 85-88; 159; CWW 2; EWL 3; RGSF 2

Sinyavsky, Andrey Donatovich
See Sinyavsky, Andrei (Donatevich)

Sirin, V.
See Nabokov, Vladimir

Sissman, L(ouis) E(dward) 1928-1976 .... **CLC 9, 18**
See also CA 21-24R; 65-68; CANR 13; CP 2; DLB 5

Sisson, C(harles) H(ubert) 1914-2003 .... **CLC 8**
See also BRWS 11; CA 1-4R; 220; CAAS 3; CANR 3, 48, 84; CP 1, 2, 3, 4, 5, 6, 7; DLB 27

Sitting Bull 1831(?)-1890 .... **NNAL**
See also DA3; DAM MULT

Sitwell, Dame Edith 1887-1964 ..... **CLC 2, 9, 67; PC 3**
See also BRW 7; CA 9-12R; CANR 35; CDBLB 1945-1960; DAM POET; DLB 20; EWL 3; MTCW 1, 2; MTFW 2005; RGEL 2; TEA

Siwaarmill, H. P.
See Sharp, William

Sjoewall, Maj 1935- .... **CLC 7**
See also BPFB 3; CA 65-68; CANR 73; CMW 4; MSW

Sjowall, Maj
See Sjoewall, Maj

Skelton, John 1460(?)-1529 ..... **LC 71; PC 25**
See also BRW 1; DLB 136; RGEL 2

Skelton, Robin 1925-1997 .... **CLC 13**
See also AITN 2; CA 5-8R; 160; CAAS 5; CANR 28, 89; CCA 1; CP 1, 2, 3, 4, 5, 6; DLB 27, 53

Skolimowski, Jerzy 1938- .... **CLC 20**
See also CA 128

Skram, Amalie (Bertha) 1846-1905 .... **TCLC 25**
See also CA 165; DLB 354

Skvorecky, Josef 1924- . **CLC 15, 39, 69, 152**
See also CA 61-64; CAAS 1; CANR 10, 34, 63, 108; CDWLB 4; CWW 2; DA3; DAC; DAM NOV; DLB 232; EWL 3; MTCW 1, 2; MTFW 2005

Skvorecky, Josef Vaclav
See Skvorecky, Josef

Slade, Bernard 1930-
See Newbound, Bernard Slade

Slaughter, Carolyn 1946- .... **CLC 56**
See also CA 85-88; CANR 85, 169; CN 5, 6, 7

Slaughter, Frank G(ill) 1908-2001 ... **CLC 29**
See also AITN 2; CA 5-8R; 197; CANR 5, 85; INT CANR-5; RHW

Slavitt, David R. 1935- .... **CLC 5, 14**
See also CA 21-24R; CAAS 3; CANR 41, 83, 166, 219; CN 1, 2; CP 1, 2, 3, 4, 5, 6, 7; DLB 5, 6

Slavitt, David Rytman
See Slavitt, David R.

Slesinger, Tess 1905-1945 .... **TCLC 10**
See also CA 107; 199; DLB 102

Slessor, Kenneth 1901-1971 .... **CLC 14**
See also CA 102; 89-92; DLB 260; RGEL 2

Slowacki, Juliusz 1809-1849 .... **NCLC 15**
See also RGWL 3

Small, David 1945- .... **CLC 299**
See also CLR 53; MAICYA 2; SATA 50, 95, 126, 183, 216; SATA-Brief 46

Smart, Christopher 1722-1771 .... **LC 3, 134; PC 13**
See also DAM POET; DLB 109; RGEL 2

Smart, Elizabeth 1913-1986 .... **CLC 54; TCLC 231**
See also CA 81-84; 118; CN 4; DLB 88

Smiley, Jane 1949- ...... **CLC 53, 76, 144, 236**
See also AAYA 66; AMWS 6; BPFB 3; CA 104; CANR 30, 50, 74, 96, 158, 196, 231; CN 6, 7; CPW 1; DA3; DAM POP; DLB 227, 234; EWL 3; INT CANR-30; MAL 5; MTFW 2005; NFS 32; SSFS 19

Smiley, Jane Graves
See Smiley, Jane

Smith, A(rthur) J(ames) M(arshall) 1902-1980 .... **CLC 15**
See also CA 1-4R; 102; CANR 4; CP 1, 2, 3; DAC; DLB 88; RGEL 2

Smith, Adam 1723(?)-1790 .... **LC 36**
See also DLB 104, 252, 336; RGEL 2

Smith, Alexander 1829-1867 .... **NCLC 59**
See also DLB 32, 55

Smith, Alexander McCall 1948- ..... **CLC 268**
See also CA 215; CANR 154, 196; SATA 73, 179

Smith, Anna Deavere 1950- ...... **CLC 86, 241**
See also CA 133; CANR 103; CD 5, 6; DFS 2, 22; DLB 341

Smith, Betty (Wehner) 1904-1972 .... **CLC 19**
See also AAYA 72; BPFB 3; BYA 3; CA 5-8R; 33-36R; DLBY 1982; LAIT 3; NFS 31; RGAL 4; SATA 6

Smith, Charlotte (Turner) 1749-1806 .... **NCLC 23, 115; PC 104**
See also DLB 39, 109; RGEL 2; TEA

Smith, Clark Ashton 1893-1961 .... **CLC 43**
See also AAYA 76; CA 143; CANR 81; FANT; HGG; MTCW 2; SCFW 1, 2; SFW 4; SUFW

Smith, Dave
See Smith, David (Jeddie)

Smith, David (Jeddie) 1942- .... **CLC 22, 42**
See also CA 49-52; CAAS 7; CANR 1, 59, 120; CP 3, 4, 5, 6, 7; CSW; DAM POET; DLB 5

Smith, Iain Crichton 1928-1998 .... **CLC 64**
See also BRWS 9; CA 21-24R; 171; CN 1, 2, 3, 4, 5, 6; CP 1, 2, 3, 4, 5, 6; DLB 40, 139, 319, 352; RGSF 2

Smith, John 1580(?)-1631 .... **LC 9**
See also DLB 24, 30; TUS

Smith, Johnston
See Crane, Stephen

Smith, Joseph, Jr. 1805-1844 .... **NCLC 53**

Smith, Kevin 1970- .... **CLC 223**
See also AAYA 37; CA 166; CANR 131, 201

Smith, Lee 1944- .... **CLC 25, 73, 258; SSC 142**
See also CA 114; 119; CANR 46, 118, 173, 225; CN 7; CSW; DLB 143; DLBY 1983; EWL 3; INT CA-119; RGAL 4

Smith, Martin
See Smith, Martin Cruz

Smith, Martin Cruz 1942- .. **CLC 25; NNAL**
See Smith, Martin Cruz
See also BEST 89:4; BPFB 3; CA 85-88; CANR 6, 23, 43, 65, 119, 184; CMW 4; CPW; DAM MULT, POP; HGG; INT CANR-23; MTCW 2; MTFW 2005; RGAL 4

Smith, Patti 1946- .... **CLC 12, 318**
See also CA 93-96; CANR 63, 168, 232

Smith, Pauline (Urmson) 1882-1959 .... **TCLC 25**
See also DLB 225; EWL 3

Smith, R. Alexander McCall
See Smith, Alexander McCall

Smith, Rosamond
See Oates, Joyce Carol

Smith, Seba 1792-1868 .... **NCLC 187**
See also DLB 1, 11, 243

Smith, Sheila Kaye
See Kaye-Smith, Sheila

Smith, Stevie 1902-1971 .... **CLC 3, 8, 25, 44; PC 12**
See also BRWR 3; BRWS 2; CA 17-18; 29-32R; CANR 35; CAP 2; CP 1; DAM POET; DLB 20; EWL 3; MTCW 1, 2; PAB; PFS 3; RGEL 2; TEA

Smith, Wilbur 1933- .... **CLC 33**
See also CA 13-16R; CANR 7, 46, 66, 134, 180; CPW; MTCW 1, 2; MTFW 2005

Smith, Wilbur Addison
See Smith, Wilbur

Smith, William Jay 1918- .... **CLC 6**
See also AMWS 13; CA 5-8R; CANR 44, 106, 211; CP 1, 2, 3, 4, 5, 6, 7; CSW; CWRI 5; DLB 5; MAICYA 1, 2; SAAS 22; SATA 2, 68, 154; SATA-Essay 154; TCLE 1:2

Smith, Woodrow Wilson
See Kuttner, Henry

Smith, Zadie 1975- .... **CLC 158, 306**
See also AAYA 50; CA 193; CANR 204; DLB 347; MTFW 2005; NFS 40

Smolenskin, Peretz 1842-1885 .... **NCLC 30**

Smollett, Tobias (George) 1721-1771 ... **LC 2, 46, 188**
See also BRW 3; CDBLB 1660-1789; DLB 39, 104; RGEL 2; TEA

Snodgrass, Quentin Curtius
See Twain, Mark

Snodgrass, Thomas Jefferson
See Twain, Mark

Snodgrass, W. D. 1926-2009 .... **CLC 2, 6, 10, 18, 68; PC 74**
See also AMWS 6; CA 1-4R; 282; CANR 6, 36, 65, 85, 185; CP 1, 2, 3, 4, 5, 6, 7; DAM POET; DLB 5; MAL 5; MTCW 1, 2; MTFW 2005; PFS 29; RGAL 4; TCLE 1:2

Snodgrass, W. de Witt
See Snodgrass, W. D.

Snodgrass, William de Witt
See Snodgrass, W. D.

Snodgrass, William De Witt
See Snodgrass, W. D.

Snorri Sturluson 1179-1241 .. **CMLC 56, 134**
See also RGWL 2, 3

Snow, C(harles) P(ercy) 1905-1980 ... **CLC 1, 4, 6, 9, 13, 19**
See also BRW 7; CA 5-8R; 101; CANR 28; CDBLB 1945-1960; CN 1, 2; DAM NOV; DLB 15, 77; DLBD 17; EWL 3; MTCW 1, 2; MTFW 2005; RGEL 2; TEA

Snow, Frances Compton
See Adams, Henry

Snyder, Gary 1930- . **CLC 1, 2, 5, 9, 32, 120; PC 21**
See also AAYA 72; AMWS 8; ANW; BG 1:3; CA 17-20R; CANR 30, 60, 125; CP 1, 2, 3, 4, 5, 6, 7; DA3; DAM POET; DLB 5, 16, 165, 212, 237, 275, 342; EWL 3; MAL 5; MTCW 2; MTFW 2005; PFS 9, 19; RGAL 4; WP

Snyder, Gary Sherman
See Snyder, Gary

Snyder, Zilpha Keatley 1927- .... **CLC 17**
See also AAYA 15; BYA 1; CA 9-12R, 252; CAAE 252; CANR 38, 202; CLR 31, 121; JRDA; MAICYA 1, 2; SAAS 2; SATA 1, 28, 75, 110, 163, 226; SATA-Essay 112, 163; YAW

Soares, Bernardo
See Pessoa, Fernando

Sobh, A.
See Shamlu, Ahmad

Sobh, Alef
See Shamlu, Ahmad

Sobol, Joshua 1939- .... **CLC 60**
See also CA 200; CWW 2; RGHL

Sobol, Yehoshua 1939-
See Sobol, Joshua

Socrates 470B.C.-399B.C. .... **CMLC 27**

Soderberg, Hjalmar 1869-1941 ...... **TCLC 39**
See also DLB 259; EWL 3; RGSF 2

Soderbergh, Steven 1963- .... **CLC 154**
See also AAYA 43; CA 243

Soderbergh, Steven Andrew
See Soderbergh, Steven

Sodergran, Edith 1892-1923 .... **TCLC 31**
See also CA 202; DLB 259; EW 11; EWL 3; RGWL 2, 3

Soedergran, Edith Irene
See Sodergran, Edith

Softly, Edgar
See Lovecraft, H. P.

Softly, Edward
See Lovecraft, H. P.

Sokolov, Alexander V. 1943- .... **CLC 59**
See also CA 73-76; CWW 2; DLB 285; EWL 3; RGWL 2, 3

Sokolov, Alexander Vsevolodovich
See Sokolov, Alexander V.

Sokolov, Raymond 1941- .... **CLC 7**
See also CA 85-88

Sokolov, Sasha
See Sokolov, Alexander V.

Soli, Tatjana CLC 318
See also CA 307

Solo, Jay
See Ellison, Harlan

Sologub, Fedor
See Teternikov, Fyodor Kuzmich

Sologub, Feodor
See Teternikov, Fyodor Kuzmich

Sologub, Fyodor
See Teternikov, Fyodor Kuzmich

Solomons, Ikey Esquir
See Thackeray, William Makepeace

Solomos, Dionysios 1798-1857 .... **NCLC 15**

Solwoska, Mara
See French, Marilyn

Solzhenitsyn, Aleksandr 1918-2008 ... **CLC 1, 2, 4, 7, 9, 10, 18, 26, 34, 78, 134, 235; SSC 32, 105; WLC 5**
See also AAYA 49; AITN 1; BPFB 3; CA 69-72; CANR 40, 65, 116; CWW 2; DA; DA3; DAB; DAC; DAM MST, NOV; DLB 302, 332; EW 13; EWL 3; EXPS; LAIT 4; MTCW 1, 2; MTFW 2005; NFS 6; PFS 38; RGSF 2; RGWL 2, 3; SSFS 9; TWA

Styron, William 1925-2006 .. **CLC 1, 3, 5, 11, 15, 60, 232, 244; SSC 25**
See also AMW; AMWC 2; BEST 90:4; BPFB 3; CA 5-8R; 255; CANR 6, 33, 74, 126, 191; CDALB 1968-1988; CN 1, 2, 3, 4, 5, 6, 7; CPW; CSW; DA3; DAM NOV, POP; DLB 2, 143, 299; DLBY 1980; EWL 3; INT CANR-6; LAIT 2; MAL 5; MTCW 1, 2; MTFW 2005; NCFS 1; NFS 22; RGAL 4; RGHL; RHW; TUS

Styron, William C.
See Styron, William

Styron, William Clark
See Styron, William

Su, Chien 1884-1918 .... **TCLC 24**
See also CA 123; EWL 3

Suarez Lynch, B.
See Bioy Casares, Adolfo; Borges, Jorge Luis

Suassuna, Ariano Vilar 1927- .... **HLCS 1**
See also CA 178; DLB 307; HW 2; LAW

Suckert, Kurt Erich
See Malaparte, Curzio

Suckling, Sir John 1609-1642 . **LC 75; PC 30**
See also BRW 2; DAM POET; DLB 58, 126; EXPP; PAB; RGEL 2

Suckow, Ruth 1892-1960 ...... **SSC 18; TCLC 257**
See also CA 193; 113; DLB 9, 102; RGAL 4; TCWW 2

Sudermann, Hermann 1857-1928 .. **TCLC 15**
See also CA 107; 201; DLB 118

Sue, Eugene 1804-1857 .... **NCLC 1**
See also DLB 119

Sueskind, Patrick
See Suskind, Patrick

Suetonius c. 70-c. 130 .... **CMLC 60**
See also AW 2; DLB 211; RGWL 2, 3; WLIT 8

Su Hsuan-ying
See Su, Chien

Su Hsuean-ying
See Su, Chien

Sui Sin Far
See Eaton, Edith Maude

Sukenick, Ronald 1932-2004 ..... **CLC 3, 4, 6, 48**
See also CA 25-28R, 209; 229; CAAE 209; CAAS 8; CANR 32, 89; CN 3, 4, 5, 6, 7; DLB 173; DLBY 1981

Suknaski, Andrew 1942- .... **CLC 19**
See also CA 101; CP 3, 4, 5, 6, 7; DLB 53

Sullivan, Vernon
See Vian, Boris

Sully Prudhomme, Rene-Francois-Armand 1839-1907 .... **TCLC 31**
See also CA 170; DLB 332; GFL 1789 to the Present

Sulpicius Severus c. 363-c. 425 ... **CMLC 120**

Su Man-shu
See Su, Chien

Sumarokov, Aleksandr Petrovich 1717-1777 .... **LC 104**
See also DLB 150

Summerforest, Ivy B.
See Kirkup, James

Summers, Andrew James
See Summers, Andy

Summers, Andy 1942- .... **CLC 26**
See also CA 255

Summers, Hollis (Spurgeon, Jr.) 1916- .... **CLC 10**
See also CA 5-8R; CANR 3; CN 1, 2, 3; CP 1, 2, 3, 4; DLB 6; TCLE 1:2

Summers, (Alphonsus Joseph-Mary Augustus) Montague 1880-1948 .... **TCLC 16**
See also CA 118; 163

Sumner, Gordon Matthew
See Sting

Sun Tzu c. 400B.C.-c. 320B.C. ...... **CMLC 56**

Surayya, Kamala
See Das, Kamala

Surayya Kamala
See Das, Kamala

Surdas c. 1478-c. 1583 .... **LC 163**
See also RGWL 2, 3

Surrey, Henry Howard 1517-1574 ... **LC 121; PC 59**
See also BRW 1; RGEL 2

Surtees, Robert Smith 1805-1864 .. **NCLC 14**
See also DLB 21; RGEL 2

Susann, Jacqueline 1921-1974 .... **CLC 3**
See also AITN 1; BPFB 3; CA 65-68; 53-56; MTCW 1, 2

Su Shi
See Su Shih

Su Shih 1037-1101 .... **CMLC 15, 139**
See also RGWL 2, 3

Suskind, Patrick 1949- .... **CLC 44, 182**
See also BPFB 3; CA 145; CWW 2

Suso, Heinrich c. 1295-1366 .... **CMLC 87**

Sutcliff, Rosemary 1920-1992 .... **CLC 26**
See also AAYA 10; BRWS 16; BYA 1, 4; CA 5-8R; 139; CANR 37; CLR 1, 37, 138; CPW; DAB; DAC; DAM MST, POP; JRDA; LATS 1:1; MAICYA 1, 2; MAIC-YAS 1; RHW; SATA 6, 44, 78; SATA-Obit 73; WYA; YAW

Sutherland, Efua (Theodora Morgue) 1924-1996 .... **BLC 2:3**
See also AFW; BW 1; CA 105; CWD; DLB 117; EWL 3; IDTP; SATA 25

Sutro, Alfred 1863-1933 .... **TCLC 6**
See also CA 105; 185; DLB 10; RGEL 2

Sutton, Henry
See Slavitt, David R.

Su Yuan-ying
See Su, Chien

Su Yuean-ying
See Su, Chien

Suzuki, D. T.
See Suzuki, Daisetz Teitaro

Suzuki, Daisetz T.
See Suzuki, Daisetz Teitaro

Suzuki, Daisetz Teitaro 1870-1966 .... **TCLC 109**
See also CA 121; 111; MTCW 1, 2; MTFW 2005

Suzuki, Teitaro
See Suzuki, Daisetz Teitaro

Svareff, Count Vladimir
See Crowley, Edward Alexander

Svevo, Italo
See Schmitz, Aron Hector

Swados, Elizabeth 1951- .... **CLC 12**
See also CA 97-100; CANR 49, 163; INT CA-97-100

Swados, Elizabeth A.
See Swados, Elizabeth

Swados, Harvey 1920-1972 .... **CLC 5**
See also CA 5-8R; 37-40R; CANR 6; CN 1; DLB 2, 335; MAL 5

Swados, Liz
See Swados, Elizabeth

Swan, Gladys 1934- .... **CLC 69**
See also CA 101; CANR 17, 39; TCLE 1:2

Swanson, Logan
See Matheson, Richard

Swarthout, Glendon (Fred) 1918-1992 .... **CLC 35**
See also AAYA 55; CA 1-4R; 139; CANR 1, 47; CN 1, 2, 3, 4, 5; LAIT 5; NFS 29; SATA 26; TCWW 1, 2; YAW

Swedenborg, Emanuel 1688-1772 ..... **LC 105**

Sweet, Sarah C.
See Jewett, Sarah Orne

Swenson, May 1919-1989 ...... **CLC 4, 14, 61, 106; PC 14**
See also AMWS 4; CA 5-8R; 130; CANR 36, 61, 131; CP 1, 2, 3, 4; DA; DAB; DAC; DAM MST, POET; DLB 5; EXPP; GLL 2; MAL 5; MTCW 1, 2; MTFW 2005; PFS 16, 30, 38; SATA 15; WP

Swift, Augustus
See Lovecraft, H. P.

Swift, Graham 1949- .... **CLC 41, 88, 233**
See also BRWC 2; BRWS 5; CA 117; 122; CANR 46, 71, 128, 181, 218; CN 4, 5, 6, 7; DLB 194, 326; MTCW 2; MTFW 2005; NFS 18; RGSF 2

Swift, Jonathan 1667-1745 ..... **LC 1, 42, 101, 201; PC 9; WLC 6**
See also AAYA 41; BRW 3; BRWC 1; BRWR 1; BYA 5, 14; CDBLB 1660-1789; CLR 53, 161; DA; DA3; DAB; DAC; DAM MST, NOV, POET; DLB 39, 95, 101; EXPN; LAIT 1; NFS 6; PFS 27, 37; RGEL 2; SATA 19; TEA; WCH; WLIT 3

Swinburne, Algernon Charles 1837-1909 ... **PC 24; TCLC 8, 36; WLC 6**
See also BRW 5; CA 105; 140; CDBLB 1832-1890; DA; DA3; DAB; DAC; DAM MST, POET; DLB 35, 57; PAB; RGEL 2; TEA

Swinfen, Ann CLC 34
See also CA 202

Swinnerton, Frank (Arthur) 1884-1982 .... **CLC 31**
See also CA 202; 108; CN 1, 2, 3; DLB 34

Swinnerton, Frank Arthur 1884-1982 .... **CLC 31**
See also CA 108; DLB 34

Swithen, John
See King, Stephen

Syjuco, Miguel 1976- .... **CLC 318**
See also CA 305

Sylvia
See Ashton-Warner, Sylvia (Constance)

Symmes, Robert Edward
See Duncan, Robert

Symonds, John Addington 1840-1893 .... **NCLC 34**
See also BRWS 14; DLB 57, 144

Symons, Arthur 1865-1945 ... **PC 119; TCLC 11, 243**
See also BRWS 14; CA 107; 189; DLB 19, 57, 149; RGEL 2

Symons, Julian (Gustave) 1912-1994 .... **CLC 2, 14, 32**
See also CA 49-52; 147; CAAS 3; CANR 3, 33, 59; CMW 4; CN 1, 2, 3, 4, 5; CP 1, 3, 4; DLB 87, 155; DLBY 1992; MSW; MTCW 1

Synge, Edmund John Millington
See Synge, John Millington

Synge, J. M.
See Synge, John Millington

Synge, John Millington 1871-1909 ...... **DC 2; TCLC 6, 37, 257**
See also BRW 6; BRWR 1; CA 104; 141; CDBLB 1890-1914; DAM DRAM; DFS 18; DLB 10, 19; EWL 3; RGEL 2; TEA; WLIT 4

Syruc, J.
See Milosz, Czeslaw

Szirtes, George 1948- .... **CLC 46; PC 51**
See also CA 109; CANR 27, 61, 117; CP 4, 5, 6, 7

Szymborska, Wislawa 1923- ... **CLC 99, 190; PC 44**
See also AAYA 76; CA 154; CANR 91, 133, 181; CDWLB 4; CWP; CWW 2; DA3; DLB 232, 332; DLBY 1996; EWL 3; MTCW 2; MTFW 2005; PFS 15, 27, 31, 34, 41; RGHL; RGWL 3

T. O., Nik
See Annensky, Innokenty (Fyodorovich)

Tabori, George 1914-2007 .... **CLC 19**
See also CA 49-52; 262; CANR 4, 69; CBD; CD 5, 6; DLB 245; RGHL

Tacitus c. 55-c. 117 .... **CMLC 56, 131**
See also AW 2; CDWLB 1; DLB 211; RGWL 2, 3; WLIT 8

Tadjo, Veronique 1955- .... **BLC 2:3**
See also DLB 360; EWL 3

Tagore, Rabindranath 1861-1941 .... **PC 8; SSC 48; TCLC 3, 53**
See also CA 104; 120; DA3; DAM DRAM, POET; DFS 26; DLB 323, 332; EWL 3; MTCW 1, 2; MTFW 2005; PFS 18; RGEL 2; RGSF 2; RGWL 2, 3; TWA

Taine, Hippolyte Adolphe
1828-1893 .... **NCLC 15**
See also EW 7; GFL 1789 to the Present

Talayesva, Don C. 1890-(?) .... **NNAL**

Talese, Gay 1932- .... **CLC 37, 232**
See also AITN 1; AMWS 17; CA 1-4R; CANR 9, 58, 137, 177; DLB 185; INT CANR-9; MTCW 1, 2; MTFW 2005

Tallent, Elizabeth 1954- .... **CLC 45**
See also CA 117; CANR 72; DLB 130

Tallmountain, Mary 1918-1997 .... **NNAL**
See also CA 146; 161; DLB 193

Tally, Ted 1952- .... **CLC 42**
See also CA 120; 124; CAD; CANR 125; CD 5, 6; INT CA-124

Talvik, Heiti 1904-1947 .... **TCLC 87**
See also EWL 3

Tamayo y Baus, Manuel
1829-1898 .... **NCLC 1**

Tammsaare, A(nton) H(ansen)
1878-1940 .... **TCLC 27**
See also CA 164; CDWLB 4; DLB 220; EWL 3

Tam'si, Tchicaya U
See Tchicaya, Gerald Felix

Tan, Amy 1952- ..... **AAL; CLC 59, 120, 151, 257**
See also AAYA 9, 48; AMWS 10; BEST 89:3; BPFB 3; CA 136; CANR 54, 105, 132; CDALBS; CN 6, 7; CPW 1; DA3; DAM MULT, NOV, POP; DLB 173, 312; EXPN; FL 1:6; FW; LAIT 3, 5; MAL 5; MTCW 2; MTFW 2005; NFS 1, 13, 16, 31, 35; RGAL 4; SATA 75; SSFS 9; YAW

Tan, Amy Ruth
See Tan, Amy

Tandem, Carl Felix
See Spitteler, Carl

Tandem, Felix
See Spitteler, Carl

Tania B.
See Blixen, Karen

Tanizaki, Jun'ichiro 1886-1965 ... **CLC 8, 14, 28; SSC 21**
See also CA 93-96; 25-28R; DLB 180; EWL 3; MJW; MTCW 2; MTFW 2005; RGSF 2; RGWL 2

Tanizaki Jun'ichiro
See Tanizaki, Jun'ichiro

Tannen, Deborah 1945- .... **CLC 206**
See also CA 118; CANR 95

Tannen, Deborah Frances
See Tannen, Deborah

Tanner, William
See Amis, Kingsley

Tante, Dilly
See Kunitz, Stanley

Tao Lao
See Storni, Alfonsina

Tapahonso, Luci 1953- .... **NNAL; PC 65**
See also CA 145; CANR 72, 127, 214; DLB 175

Tarantino, Quentin 1963- .... **CLC 125, 230**
See also AAYA 58; CA 171; CANR 125

Tarantino, Quentin Jerome
See Tarantino, Quentin

Tarassoff, Lev
See Troyat, Henri

Tarbell, Ida 1857-1944 .... **TCLC 40**
See also CA 122; 181; DLB 47

Tarbell, Ida Minerva
See Tarbell, Ida

Tarchetti, Ugo 1839(?)-1869 .... **SSC 119**

Tardieu d'Esclavelles,
Louise-Florence-Petronille
See Epinay, Louise d'

Tarkington, (Newton) Booth
1869-1946 .... **TCLC 9**
See also BPFB 3; BYA 3; CA 110; 143; CWRI 5; DLB 9, 102; MAL 5; MTCW 2; NFS 34; RGAL 4; SATA 17

Tarkovskii, Andrei Arsen'evich
See Tarkovsky, Andrei (Arsenyevich)

Tarkovsky, Andrei (Arsenyevich)
1932-1986 .... **CLC 75**
See also CA 127

Tartt, Donna 1964(?)- .... **CLC 76**
See also AAYA 56; CA 142; CANR 135; LNFS 2; MTFW 2005

Tasso, Torquato 1544-1595 .... **LC 5, 94**
See also EFS 1:2, 2:1; EW 2; RGWL 2, 3; WLIT 7

Tate, (John Orley) Allen 1899-1979 .. **CLC 2, 4, 6, 9, 11, 14, 24; PC 50**
See also AMW; CA 5-8R; 85-88; CANR 32, 108; CN 1, 2; CP 1, 2; DLB 4, 45, 63; DLBD 17; EWL 3; MAL 5; MTCW 1, 2; MTFW 2005; RGAL 4; RHW

Tate, Ellalice
See Hibbert, Eleanor Alice Burford

Tate, James 1943- .... **CLC 2, 6, 25**
See also CA 21-24R; CANR 29, 57, 114, 224; CP 1, 2, 3, 4, 5, 6, 7; DLB 5, 169; EWL 3; PFS 10, 15; RGAL 4; WP

Tate, James Vincent
See Tate, James

Tate, Nahum 1652(?)-1715 .... **LC 109**
See also DLB 80; RGEL 2

Tauler, Johannes c. 1300-1361 ...... **CMLC 37**
See also DLB 179; LMFS 1

Tavel, Ronald 1936-2009 .... **CLC 6**
See also CA 21-24R; 284; CAD; CANR 33; CD 5, 6

Taviani, Paolo 1931- .... **CLC 70**
See also CA 153

Tawada, Yoko 1960- .... **CLC 310**
See also CA 296

Taylor, Bayard 1825-1878 .... **NCLC 89**
See also DLB 3, 189, 250, 254, 366; RGAL 4

Taylor, C(ecil) P(hilip) 1929-1981 .... **CLC 27**
See also CA 25-28R; 105; CANR 47; CBD

Taylor, Charles 1931- .... **CLC 317**
See also CA 13-16R; CANR 11, 27, 164, 200

Taylor, Charles Margrave
See Taylor, Charles

Taylor, Edward 1642(?)-1729 ..... **LC 11, 163; PC 63**
See also AMW; DA; DAB; DAC; DAM MST, POET; DLB 24; EXPP; PFS 31; RGAL 4; TUS

Taylor, Eleanor Ross 1920- .... **CLC 5**
See also CA 81-84; CANR 70

Taylor, Elizabeth 1912-1975 .... **CLC 2, 4, 29; SSC 100**
See also CA 13-16R; CANR 9, 70; CN 1, 2; DLB 139; MTCW 1; RGEL 2; SATA 13

Taylor, Frederick Winslow
1856-1915 .... **TCLC 76**
See also CA 188

Taylor, Henry 1942- .... **CLC 44**
See also CA 33-36R; CAAS 7; CANR 31, 178; CP 6, 7; DLB 5; PFS 10

Taylor, Henry Splawn
See Taylor, Henry

Taylor, Kamala
See Markandaya, Kamala

Taylor, Mildred D. 1943- .... **CLC 21**
See also AAYA 10, 47; BW 1; BYA 3, 8; CA 85-88; CANR 25, 115, 136; CLR 9, 59, 90, 144; CSW; DLB 52; JRDA; LAIT 3; MAICYA 1, 2; MTFW 2005; SAAS 5; SATA 135; WYA; YAW

Taylor, Peter (Hillsman) 1917-1994 .. **CLC 1, 4, 18, 37, 44, 50, 71; SSC 10, 84**
See also AMWS 5; BPFB 3; CA 13-16R; 147; CANR 9, 50; CN 1, 2, 3, 4, 5; CSW; DLB 218, 278; DLBY 1981, 1994; EWL 3; EXPS; INT CANR-9; MAL 5; MTCW 1, 2; MTFW 2005; RGSF 2; SSFS 9; TUS

Taylor, Robert Lewis 1912-1998 .... **CLC 14**
See also CA 1-4R; 170; CANR 3, 64; CN 1, 2; SATA 10; TCWW 1, 2

Tchekhov, Anton
See Chekhov, Anton

Tchicaya, Gerald Felix 1931-1988 .. **CLC 101**
See also CA 129; 125; CANR 81; EWL 3

Tchicaya U Tam'si
See Tchicaya, Gerald Felix

Teasdale, Sara 1884-1933 .... **PC 31; TCLC 4**
See also CA 104; 163; DLB 45; GLL 1; PFS 14; RGAL 4; SATA 32; TUS

Tecumseh 1768-1813 .... **NNAL**
See also DAM MULT

Tegner, Esaias 1782-1846 .... **NCLC 2**

Teilhard de Chardin, (Marie Joseph) Pierre
1881-1955 .... **TCLC 9**
See also CA 105; 210; GFL 1789 to the Present

Temple, Ann
See Mortimer, Penelope (Ruth)

Tennant, Emma 1937- .... **CLC 13, 52**
See also BRWS 9; CA 65-68; CAAS 9; CANR 10, 38, 59, 88, 177; CN 3, 4, 5, 6, 7; DLB 14; EWL 3; SFW 4

Tenneshaw, S.M.
See Silverberg, Robert

Tenney, Tabitha Gilman
1762-1837 .... **NCLC 122, 248**
See also DLB 37, 200

Tennyson, Alfred 1809-1892 ... **NCLC 30, 65, 115, 202; PC 6, 101; WLC 6**
See also AAYA 50; BRW 4; BRWR 3; CD-BLB 1832-1890; DA; DA3; DAB; DAC; DAM MST, POET; DLB 32; EXPP; PAB; PFS 1, 2, 4, 11, 15, 19; RGEL 2; TEA; WLIT 4; WP

Teran, Lisa St. Aubin de
See St. Aubin de Teran, Lisa

Terence c. 184B.C.-c. 159B.C. ...... **CMLC 14, 132; DC 7**
See also AW 1; CDWLB 1; DLB 211; RGWL 2, 3; TWA; WLIT 8

Teresa de Jesus, St. 1515-1582 .... **LC 18, 149**

Teresa of Avila, St.
See Teresa de Jesus, St.

Terkel, Louis
See Terkel, Studs

Terkel, Studs 1912-2008 .... **CLC 38**
See also AAYA 32; AITN 1; CA 57-60; 278; CANR 18, 45, 67, 132, 195; DA3; MTCW 1, 2; MTFW 2005; TUS

Terkel, Studs Louis
See Terkel, Studs

Terry, C. V.
See Slaughter, Frank G(ill)

Terry, Megan 1932- .... **CLC 19; DC 13**
See also CA 77-80; CABS 3; CAD; CANR 43; CD 5, 6; CWD; DFS 18; DLB 7, 249; GLL 2

Tertullian c. 155-c. 245 .... **CMLC 29**

Tertz, Abram
See Sinyavsky, Andrei (Donatevich)

Tesich, Steve 1943(?)-1996 .... **CLC 40, 69**
See also CA 105; 152; CAD; DLBY 1983

Tesla, Nikola 1856-1943 .... **TCLC 88**
See also CA 157

Teternikov, Fyodor Kuzmich
1863-1927 .... **TCLC 9, 259**
See also CA 104; DLB 295; EWL 3

Tevis, Walter 1928-1984 .... **CLC 42**
See also CA 113; SFW 4

Tey, Josephine
See Mackintosh, Elizabeth

Thackeray, William Makepeace
1811-1863 ...... **NCLC 5, 14, 22, 43, 169, 213; WLC 6**
See also BRW 5; BRWC 2; CDBLB 1832-1890; DA; DA3; DAB; DAC; DAM MST, NOV; DLB 21, 55, 159, 163; NFS 13; RGEL 2; SATA 23; TEA; WLIT 3

Thakura, Ravindranatha
See Tagore, Rabindranath

Thames, C. H.
See Marlowe, Stephen

Tharoor, Shashi 1956- .... **CLC 70**
See also CA 141; CANR 91, 201; CN 6, 7

Thelwall, John 1764-1834 .... **NCLC 162**
See also DLB 93, 158

Thelwell, Michael Miles 1939- .... **CLC 22**
See also BW 2; CA 101

Theo, Ion
See Theodorescu, Ion N.

Theobald, Lewis, Jr.
See Lovecraft, H. P.

Theocritus c. 310B.C.- .... **CMLC 45**
See also AW 1; DLB 176; RGWL 2, 3

Theodorescu, Ion N. 1880-1967 .... **CLC 80**
See also CA 167; 116; CDWLB 4; DLB 220; EWL 3

Theriault, Yves 1915-1983 .... **CLC 79**
See also CA 102; CANR 150; CCA 1; DAC; DAM MST; DLB 88; EWL 3

Therion, Master
See Crowley, Edward Alexander

Theroux, Alexander 1939- .... **CLC 2, 25**
See also CA 85-88; CANR 20, 63, 190; CN 4, 5, 6, 7

Theroux, Alexander Louis
See Theroux, Alexander

Theroux, Paul 1941- .... **CLC 5, 8, 11, 15, 28, 46, 159, 303**
See also AAYA 28; AMWS 8; BEST 89:4; BPFB 3; CA 33-36R; CANR 20, 45, 74, 133, 179; CDALBS; CN 1, 2, 3, 4, 5, 6, 7; CP 1; CPW 1; DA3; DAM POP; DLB 2, 218; EWL 3; HGG; MAL 5; MTCW 1, 2; MTFW 2005; RGAL 4; SATA 44, 109; TUS

Theroux, Paul Edward
See Theroux, Paul

Thesen, Sharon 1946- .... **CLC 56**
See also CA 163; CANR 125; CP 5, 6, 7; CWP

Thespis fl. 6th cent. B.C.- .... **CMLC 51**
See also LMFS 1

Thevenin, Denis
See Duhamel, Georges

Thibault, Jacques Anatole Francois
See France, Anatole

Thiele, Colin 1920-2006 .... **CLC 17**
See also CA 29-32R; CANR 12, 28, 53, 105; CLR 27; CP 1, 2; DLB 289; MAICYA 1, 2; SAAS 2; SATA 14, 72, 125; YAW

Thiong'o, Ngugi Wa
See Ngugi wa Thiong'o

Thistlethwaite, Bel
See Wetherald, Agnes Ethelwyn

Thomas, Audrey (Callahan) 1935- .... **CLC 7, 13, 37, 107, 289; SSC 20**
See also AITN 2; CA 21-24R; 237; CAAE 237; CAAS 19; CANR 36, 58; CN 2, 3, 4, 5, 6, 7; DLB 60; MTCW 1; RGSF 2

Thomas, Augustus 1857-1934 .... **TCLC 97**
See also MAL 5

Thomas, D.M. 1935- ..... **CLC 13, 22, 31, 132**
See also BPFB 3; BRWS 4; CA 61-64, 303; CAAE 303; CAAS 11; CANR 17, 45, 75; CDBLB 1960 to Present; CN 4, 5, 6, 7; CP 1, 2, 3, 4, 5, 6, 7; DA3; DLB 40, 207, 299; HGG; INT CANR-17; MTCW 1, 2; MTFW 2005; RGHL; SFW 4

Thomas, Donald Michael
See Thomas, D.M.

Thomas, Dylan 1914-1953 . **PC 2, 52; SSC 3, 44; TCLC 1, 8, 45, 105; WLC 6**
See also AAYA 45; BRWR 3; BRWS 1; CA 104; 120; CANR 65; CDBLB 1945-1960; DA; DA3; DAB; DAC; DAM DRAM, MST, POET; DLB 13, 20, 139; EWL 3; EXPP; LAIT 3; MTCW 1, 2; MTFW 2005; PAB; PFS 1, 3, 8; RGEL 2; RGSF 2; SATA 60; TEA; WLIT 4; WP

Thomas, Dylan Marlais
See Thomas, Dylan

Thomas, (Philip) Edward 1878-1917 . **PC 53; TCLC 10**
See also BRW 6; BRWS 3; CA 106; 153; DAM POET; DLB 19, 98, 156, 216; EWL 3; PAB; RGEL 2

Thomas, J. F.
See Fleming, Thomas

Thomas, Joyce Carol 1938- .... **CLC 35**
See also AAYA 12, 54; BW 2, 3; CA 113; 116; CANR 48, 114, 135, 206; CLR 19; DLB 33; INT CA-116; JRDA; MAICYA 1, 2; MTCW 1, 2; MTFW 2005; SAAS 7; SATA 40, 78, 123, 137, 210; SATA-Essay 137; WYA; YAW

Thomas, Lewis 1913-1993 .... **CLC 35**
See also ANW; CA 85-88; 143; CANR 38, 60; DLB 275; MTCW 1, 2

Thomas, M. Carey 1857-1935 .... **TCLC 89**
See also FW

Thomas, Paul
See Mann, Thomas

Thomas, Piri 1928-2011 .... **CLC 17; HLCS 2**
See also CA 73-76; HW 1; LLW; SSFS 28

Thomas, R(onald) S(tuart)
1913-2000 .... **CLC 6, 13, 48; PC 99**
See also BRWS 12; CA 89-92; 189; CAAS 4; CANR 30; CDBLB 1960 to Present; CP 1, 2, 3, 4, 5, 6, 7; DAB; DAM POET; DLB 27; EWL 3; MTCW 1; RGEL 2

Thomas, Ross (Elmore) 1926-1995 .. **CLC 39**
See also CA 33-36R; 150; CANR 22, 63; CMW 4

Thompson, Francis (Joseph)
1859-1907 .... **TCLC 4**
See also BRW 5; CA 104; 189; CDBLB 1890-1914; DLB 19; RGEL 2; TEA

Thompson, Francis Clegg
See Mencken, H. L.

Thompson, Hunter S. 1937(?)-2005 .. **CLC 9, 17, 40, 104, 229**
See also AAYA 45; BEST 89:1; BPFB 3; CA 17-20R; 236; CANR 23, 46, 74, 77, 111, 133; CPW; CSW; DA3; DAM POP; DLB 185; MTCW 1, 2; MTFW 2005; TUS

Thompson, Hunter Stockton
See Thompson, Hunter S.

Thompson, James Myers
See Thompson, Jim

Thompson, Jim 1906-1977 .... **CLC 69**
See also BPFB 3; CA 140; CMW 4; CPW; DLB 226; MSW

Thompson, Judith (Clare Francesca)
1954- .... **CLC 39**
See also CA 143; CD 5, 6; CWD; DFS 22; DLB 334

Thomson, James 1700-1748 .... **LC 16, 29, 40**
See also BRWS 3; DAM POET; DLB 95; RGEL 2

Thomson, James 1834-1882 .... **NCLC 18**
See also DAM POET; DLB 35; RGEL 2

Thoreau, Henry David 1817-1862 .. **NCLC 7, 21, 61, 138, 207; PC 30; WLC 6**
See also AAYA 42; AMW; ANW; BYA 3; CDALB 1640-1865; DA; DA3; DAB; DAC; DAM MST; DLB 1, 183, 223, 270, 298, 366; LAIT 2; LMFS 1; NCFS 3; RGAL 4; TUS

Thorndike, E. L.
See Thorndike, Edward L(ee)

Thorndike, Edward L(ee)
1874-1949 .... **TCLC 107**
See also CA 121

Thornton, Hall
See Silverberg, Robert

Thorpe, Adam 1956- .... **CLC 176**
See also CA 129; CANR 92, 160; DLB 231

Thorpe, Thomas Bangs
1815-1878 .... **NCLC 183**
See also DLB 3, 11, 248; RGAL 4

Thubron, Colin 1939- .... **CLC 163**
See also CA 25-28R; CANR 12, 29, 59, 95, 171, 232; CN 5, 6, 7; DLB 204, 231

Thubron, Colin Gerald Dryden
See Thubron, Colin

Thucydides c. 455B.C.-c.
399B.C.- .... **CMLC 17, 117**
See also AW 1; DLB 176; RGWL 2, 3; WLIT 8

Thumboo, Edwin Nadason 1933- .... **PC 30**
See also CA 194; CP 1

Thurber, James 1894-1961 .... **CLC 5, 11, 25, 125; SSC 1, 47, 137**
See also AAYA 56; AMWS 1; BPFB 3; BYA 5; CA 73-76; CANR 17, 39; CDALB 1929-1941; CWRI 5; DA; DA3; DAB; DAC; DAM DRAM, MST, NOV; DLB 4, 11, 22, 102; EWL 3; EXPS; FANT; LAIT 3; MAICYA 1, 2; MAL 5; MTCW 1, 2; MTFW 2005; RGAL 4; RGSF 2; SATA 13; SSFS 1, 10, 19; SUFW; TUS

Thurber, James Grover
See Thurber, James

Thurman, Wallace (Henry)
1902-1934 .. **BLC 1:3; HR 1:3; TCLC 6**
See also BW 1, 3; CA 104; 124; CANR 81; DAM MULT; DLB 51

Tibullus c. 54B.C.-c. 18B.C. .... **CMLC 36**
See also AW 2; DLB 211; RGWL 2, 3; WLIT 8

Ticheburn, Cheviot
See Ainsworth, William Harrison

Ticknor, George 1791-1871 .... **NCLC 255**
See also DLB 1, 59, 140, 235

van Ostaijen, Paul 1896-1928 .... **TCLC 33**
  See also CA 163
Van Peebles, Melvin 1932- .... **CLC 2, 20**
  See also BW 2, 3; CA 85-88; CANR 27,
  67, 82; DAM MULT
van Schendel, Arthur(-Francois-Emile)
  1874-1946 .... **TCLC 56**
  See also EWL 3
van Schurman, Anna Maria
  1607-1678 .... **LC 199**
Van See, John
  See Vance, Jack
Vansittart, Peter 1920-2008 .... **CLC 42**
  See also CA 1-4R; 278; CANR 3, 49, 90;
  CN 4, 5, 6, 7; RHW
Van Vechten, Carl 1880-1964 ... **CLC 33; HR**
  1:3
  See also AMWS 2; CA 183; 89-92; DLB 4,
  9, 51; RGAL 4
van Vogt, A(lfred) E(lton) 1912-2000 . **CLC 1**
  See also BPFB 3; BYA 13, 14; CA 21-24R;
  190; CANR 28; DLB 8, 251; SATA 14;
  SATA-Obit 124; SCFW 1, 2; SFW 4
Vara, Madeleine
  See Jackson, Laura
Varda, Agnes 1928- .... **CLC 16**
  See also CA 116; 122
Vargas Llosa, Jorge Mario Pedro
  See Vargas Llosa, Mario
Vargas Llosa, Mario 1936- .. **CLC 3, 6, 9, 10,**
  15, 31, 42, 85, 181, 318; HLC 2
  See also BPFB 3; CA 73-76; CANR 18, 32,
  42, 67, 116, 140, 173, 213; CDWLB 3;
  CWW 2; DA; DA3; DAB; DAC; DAM
  MST, MULT, NOV; DLB 145; DNFS 2;
  EWL 3; HW 1, 2; LAIT 5; LATS 1:2;
  LAW; LAWS 1; MTCW 1, 2; MTFW
  2005; RGWL 2, 3; SSFS 14; TWA; WLIT
  1
Varnhagen von Ense, Rahel
  1771-1833 .... **NCLC 130**
  See also DLB 90
Vasari, Giorgio 1511-1574 .... **LC 114**
Vasilikos, Vasiles
  See Vassilikos, Vassilis
Vasiliu, Gheorghe
  See Bacovia, George
Vassa, Gustavus
  See Equiano, Olaudah
Vassilikos, Vassilis 1933- .... **CLC 4, 8**
  See also CA 81-84; CANR 75, 149; EWL 3
Vaughan, Henry 1621-1695 ... **LC 27; PC 81**
  See also BRW 2; DLB 131; PAB; RGEL 2
Vaughn, Stephanie CLC 62
Vazov, Ivan (Minchov) 1850-1921 . **TCLC 25**
  See also CA 121; 167; CDWLB 4; DLB
  147
Veblen, Thorstein B(unde)
  1857-1929 .... **TCLC 31**
  See also AMWS 1; CA 115; 165; DLB 246;
  MAL 5
Vega, Ana Lydia 1946- .... **SSC 150**
  See also CA 193; CWW 2; EWL 3
Vega, Lope de 1562-1635 ... **DC 44; HLCS 2;**
  LC 23, 119
  See also EW 2; RGWL 2, 3
Veldeke, Heinrich von c. 1145-c.
  1190 .... **CMLC 85**
Vendler, Helen 1933- .... **CLC 138**
  See also CA 41-44R; CANR 25, 72, 136,
  190; MTCW 1, 2; MTFW 2005
Vendler, Helen Hennessy
  See Vendler, Helen
Venison, Alfred
  See Pound, Ezra
Ventsel, Elena Sergeevna
  1907-2002 .... **CLC 59**
  See also CA 154; CWW 2; DLB 302

Venttsel', Elena Sergeevna
  See Ventsel, Elena Sergeevna
Verdi, Marie de
  See Mencken, H. L.
Verdu, Matilde
  See Cela, Camilo Jose
Verga, Giovanni (Carmelo)
  1840-1922 ..... **SSC 21, 87; TCLC 3, 227**
  See also CA 104; 123; CANR 101; EW 7;
  EWL 3; RGSF 2; RGWL 2, 3; WLIT 7
Vergil 70B.C.-19B.C. .. **CMLC 9, 40, 101; PC**
  12; WLCS
  See also AW 2; CDWLB 1; DA; DA3;
  DAB; DAC; DAM MST, POET; DLB
  211; EFS 1:1, 2:1; LAIT 1; LMFS 1;
  RGWL 2, 3; WLIT 8; WP
Vergil, Polydore c. 1470-1555 .... **LC 108**
  See also DLB 132
Verhaeren, Emile (Adolphe Gustave)
  1855-1916 .... **TCLC 12**
  See also CA 109; EWL 3; GFL 1789 to the
  Present
Verlaine, Paul 1844-1896 .. **NCLC 2, 51, 230;**
  PC 2, 32
  See also DAM POET; DLB 217; EW 7;
  GFL 1789 to the Present; LMFS 2; RGWL
  2, 3; TWA
Verlaine, Paul Marie
  See Verlaine, Paul
Verne, Jules 1828-1905 .... **TCLC 6, 52, 245**
  See also AAYA 16; BYA 4; CA 110; 131;
  CLR 88; DA3; DLB 123; GFL 1789 to
  the Present; JRDA; LAIT 2; LMFS 2;
  MAICYA 1, 2; MTFW 2005; NFS 30, 34;
  RGWL 2, 3; SATA 21; SCFW 1, 2; SFW
  4; TWA; WCH
Verne, Jules Gabriel
  See Verne, Jules
Verus, Marcus Annius
  See Aurelius, Marcus
Very, Jones 1813-1880 .... **NCLC 9; PC 86**
  See also DLB 1, 243; RGAL 4
Very, Rev. C.
  See Crowley, Edward Alexander
Vesaas, Tarjei 1897-1970 .... **CLC 48**
  See also CA 190; 29-32R; DLB 297; EW
  11; EWL 3; RGWL 3
Vialis, Gaston
  See Simenon, Georges
Vian, Boris 1920-1959(?) .... **TCLC 9**
  See also CA 106; 164; CANR 111; DLB
  72, 321; EWL 3; GFL 1789 to the Present;
  MTCW 2; RGWL 2, 3
Viator, Vacuus
  See Hughes, Thomas
Viaud, Julien 1850-1923 .... **TCLC 11, 239**
  See also CA 107; DLB 123; GFL 1789 to
  the Present
Viaud, Louis Marie Julien
  See Viaud, Julien
Vicar, Henry
  See Felsen, Henry Gregor
Vicente, Gil 1465-c. 1536 .... **LC 99**
  See also DLB 318; IDTP; RGWL 2, 3
Vicker, Angus
  See Felsen, Henry Gregor
Vico, Giambattista
  See Vico, Giovanni Battista
Vico, Giovanni Battista 1668-1744 .... **LC 138**
  See also EW 3; WLIT 7
Vidal, Eugene Luther Gore
  See Vidal, Gore
Vidal, Gore 1925- ...... **CLC 2, 4, 6, 8, 10, 22,**
  33, 72, 142, 289
  See also AAYA 64; AITN 1; AMWS 4;
  BEST 90:2; BPFB 3; CA 5-8R; CAD;
  CANR 13, 45, 65, 100, 132, 167; CD 5,
  6; CDALBS; CN 1, 2, 3, 4, 5, 6, 7; CPW;
  DA3; DAM NOV, POP; DFS 2; DLB 6,

152; EWL 3; GLL 1; INT CANR-13;
  MAL 5; MTCW 1, 2; MTFW 2005;
  RGAL 4; RHW; TUS
Viereck, Peter 1916-2006 .... **CLC 4; PC 27**
  See also CA 1-4R; 250; CANR 1, 47; CP 1,
  2, 3, 4, 5, 6, 7; DLB 5; MAL 5; PFS 9,
  14
Viereck, Peter Robert Edwin
  See Viereck, Peter
Vigny, Alfred de 1797-1863 .... **NCLC 7, 102;**
  PC 26
  See also DAM POET; DLB 119, 192, 217;
  EW 5; GFL 1789 to the Present; RGWL
  2, 3
Vigny, Alfred Victor de
  See Vigny, Alfred de
Vilakazi, Benedict Wallet
  1906-1947 .... **TCLC 37**
  See also CA 168
Vile, Curt
  See Moore, Alan
Villa, Jose Garcia 1914-1997 ... **AAL; PC 22;**
  TCLC 176
  See also CA 25-28R; CANR 12, 118; CP 1,
  2, 3, 4; DLB 312; EWL 3; EXPP
Villard, Oswald Garrison
  1872-1949 .... **TCLC 160**
  See also CA 113; 162; DLB 25, 91
Villarreal, Jose Antonio 1924- .... **HLC 2**
  See also CA 133; CANR 93; DAM MULT;
  DLB 82; HW 1; LAIT 4; RGAL 4
Villaurrutia, Xavier 1903-1950 ...... **TCLC 80**
  See also CA 192; EWL 3; HW 1; LAW
Villaverde, Cirilo 1812-1894 .... **NCLC 121**
  See also LAW
Villehardouin, Geoffroi de
  1150(?)-1218(?) .... **CMLC 38**
Villiers, George 1628-1687 .... **LC 107**
  See also DLB 80; RGEL 2
Villiers de l'Isle Adam, Jean Marie Mathias
  Philippe Auguste 1838-1889 ... **NCLC 3,**
  237; SSC 14
  See also DLB 123, 192; GFL 1789 to the
  Present; RGSF 2
Villon, Francois 1431-1463(?) .... **LC 62, 166;**
  PC 13
  See also DLB 208; EW 2; RGWL 2, 3;
  TWA
Vine, Barbara
  See Rendell, Ruth
Vinge, Joan (Carol) D(ennison)
  1948- .... **CLC 30; SSC 24**
  See also AAYA 32; BPFB 3; CA 93-96;
  CANR 72; SATA 36, 113; SFW 4; YAW
Viola, Herman J(oseph) 1938- .... **CLC 70**
  See also CA 61-64; CANR 8, 23, 48, 91;
  SATA 126
Violis, G.
  See Simenon, Georges
Viramontes, Helena Maria 1954- ... **HLCS 2;**
  SSC 149
  See also CA 159; CANR 182; CLR 285;
  DLB 122, 350; HW 2; LLW
Virgil
  See Vergil
Visconti, Luchino 1906-1976 .... **CLC 16**
  See also CA 81-84; 65-68; CANR 39
Vitry, Jacques de
  See Jacques de Vitry
Vittorini, Elio 1908-1966 .... **CLC 6, 9, 14**
  See also CA 133; 25-28R; DLB 264; EW
  12; EWL 3; RGWL 2, 3
Vivekananda, Swami 1863-1902 .... **TCLC 88**
Vives, Juan Luis 1493-1540 .... **LC 170**
  See also DLB 318

Walker, Ted
See Walker, Edward Joseph
Wallace, David Foster 1962-2008 .... **CLC 50, 114, 271, 281; SSC 68**
See also AAYA 50; AMWS 10; CA 132; 277; CANR 59, 133, 190; CN 7; DA3; DLB 350; MTCW 2; MTFW 2005
Wallace, Dexter
See Masters, Edgar Lee
Wallace, (Richard Horatio) Edgar 1875-1932 .... **TCLC 57**
See also CA 115; 218; CMW 4; DLB 70; MSW; RGEL 2
Wallace, Irving 1916-1990 .... **CLC 7, 13**
See also AITN 1; BPFB 3; CA 1-4R; 132; CAAS 1; CANR 1, 27; CPW; DAM NOV, POP; INT CANR-27; MTCW 1, 2
Wallant, Edward Lewis 1926-1962 ... **CLC 5, 10**
See also CA 1-4R; CANR 22; DLB 2, 28, 143, 299; EWL 3; MAL 5; MTCW 1, 2; RGAL 4; RGHL
Wallas, Graham 1858-1932 .... **TCLC 91**
Waller, Edmund 1606-1687 .... **LC 86; PC 72**
See also BRW 2; DAM POET; DLB 126; PAB; RGEL 2
Walley, Byron
See Card, Orson Scott
Walls, Jeannette 1960(?)- .... **CLC 299**
See also CA 242; CANR 220
Walpole, Horace 1717-1797 ..... **LC 2, 49, 152**
See also BRW 3; DLB 39, 104, 213; GL 3; HGG; LMFS 1; RGEL 2; SUFW 1; TEA
Walpole, Hugh 1884-1941 .... **TCLC 5**
See also CA 104; 165; DLB 34; HGG; MTCW 2; RGEL 2; RHW
Walpole, Hugh Seymour
See Walpole, Hugh
Walrond, Eric (Derwent) 1898-1966 . **HR 1:3**
See also BW 1; CA 125; DLB 51
Walser, Martin 1927- .... **CLC 27, 183**
See also CA 57-60; CANR 8, 46, 145; CWW 2; DLB 75, 124; EWL 3
Walser, Robert 1878-1956 ..... **SSC 20; TCLC 18, 267**
See also CA 118; 165; CANR 100, 194; DLB 66; EWL 3
Walsh, Gillian Paton
See Paton Walsh, Jill
Walsh, Jill Paton
See Paton Walsh, Jill
Walter, Villiam Christian
See Andersen, Hans Christian
Walter of Chatillon c. 1135-c. 1202 .... **CMLC 111**
Walters, Anna L(ee) 1946- .... **NNAL**
See also CA 73-76
Walther von der Vogelweide c. 1170-1228 .... **CMLC 56**
Walton, Izaak 1593-1683 .... **LC 72**
See also BRW 2; CDBLB Before 1660; DLB 151, 213; RGEL 2
Walzer, Michael 1935- .... **CLC 238**
See also CA 37-40R; CANR 15, 48, 127, 190
Walzer, Michael Laban
See Walzer, Michael
Wambaugh, Joseph, Jr. 1937- ...... **CLC 3, 18**
See also AITN 1; BEST 89:3; BPFB 3; CA 33-36R; CANR 42, 65, 115, 167, 217; CMW 4; CPW 1; DA3; DAM NOV, POP; DLB 6; DLBY 1983; MSW; MTCW 1, 2
Wambaugh, Joseph Aloysius
See Wambaugh, Joseph, Jr.
Wang Wei 699(?)-761(?) . **CMLC 100; PC 18**
See also TWA
Warburton, William 1698-1779 .... **LC 97**
See also DLB 104

Ward, Arthur Henry Sarsfield 1883-1959 .... **TCLC 28**
See also CA 108; 173; CMW 4; DLB 70; HGG; MSW; SUFW
Ward, Douglas Turner 1930- .... **CLC 19**
See also BW 1; CA 81-84; CAD; CANR 27; CD 5, 6; DLB 7, 38
Ward, E. D.
See Lucas, E(dward) V(errall)
Ward, Mrs. Humphry 1851-1920
See Ward, Mary Augusta
See also RGEL 2
Ward, Mary Augusta 1851-1920 ... **TCLC 55**
See Ward, Mrs. Humphry
See also DLB 18
Ward, Nathaniel 1578(?)-1652 .... **LC 114**
See also DLB 24
Ward, Peter
See Faust, Frederick
Warhol, Andy 1928(?)-1987 .... **CLC 20**
See also AAYA 12; BEST 89:4; CA 89-92; 121; CANR 34
Warner, Francis (Robert Le Plastrier) 1937- .... **CLC 14**
See also CA 53-56; CANR 11; CP 1, 2, 3, 4
Warner, Marina 1946- .... **CLC 59, 231**
See also CA 65-68; CANR 21, 55, 118; CN 5, 6, 7; DLB 194; MTFW 2005
Warner, Rex (Ernest) 1905-1986 ...... **CLC 45**
See also CA 89-92; 119; CN 1, 2, 3, 4; CP 1, 2, 3, 4; DLB 15; RGEL 2; RHW
Warner, Susan (Bogert) 1819-1885 .... **NCLC 31, 146**
See also AMWS 18; DLB 3, 42, 239, 250, 254
Warner, Sylvia (Constance) Ashton
See Ashton-Warner, Sylvia (Constance)
Warner, Sylvia Townsend 1893-1978 .. **CLC 7, 19; SSC 23; TCLC 131**
See also BRWS 7; CA 61-64; 77-80; CANR 16, 60, 104; CN 1, 2; DLB 34, 139; EWL 3; FANT; FW; MTCW 1, 2; RGEL 2; RGSF 2; RHW
Warren, Mercy Otis 1728-1814 .... **NCLC 13, 226**
See also DLB 31, 200; RGAL 4; TUS
Warren, Robert Penn 1905-1989 .. **CLC 1, 4, 6, 8, 10, 13, 18, 39, 53, 59; PC 37; SSC 4, 58, 126; WLC 6**
See also AITN 1; AMW; AMWC 2; BPFB 3; BYA 1; CA 13-16R; 129; CANR 10, 47; CDALB 1968-1988; CN 1, 2, 3, 4; CP 1, 2, 3, 4; DA; DA3; DAB; DAC; DAM MST, NOV, POET; DLB 2, 48, 152, 320; DLBY 1980, 1989; EWL 3; INT CANR-10; MAL 5; MTCW 1, 2; MTFW 2005; NFS 13; RGAL 4; RGSF 2; RHW; SATA 46; SATA-Obit 63; SSFS 8; TUS
Warrigal, Jack
See Furphy, Joseph
Warshofsky, Isaac
See Singer, Isaac Bashevis
Warton, Joseph 1722-1800 ... **LC 128; NCLC 118**
See also DLB 104, 109; RGEL 2
Warton, Thomas 1728-1790 .... **LC 15, 82**
See also DAM POET; DLB 104, 109, 336; RGEL 2
Waruk, Kona
See Harris, (Theodore) Wilson
Warung, Price
See Astley, William
Warwick, Jarvis
See Garner, Hugh
Washington, Alex
See Harris, Mark

Washington, Booker T. 1856-1915 . **BLC 1:3; TCLC 10**
See also BW 1; CA 114; 125; DA3; DAM MULT; DLB 345; LAIT 2; RGAL 4; SATA 28
Washington, Booker Taliaferro
See Washington, Booker T.
Washington, George 1732-1799 .... **LC 25**
See also DLB 31
Wassermann, (Karl) Jakob 1873-1934 .... **TCLC 6**
See also CA 104; 163; DLB 66; EWL 3
Wasserstein, Wendy 1950-2006 . **CLC 32, 59, 90, 183; DC 4**
See also AAYA 73; AMWS 15; CA 121; 129; 247; CABS 3; CAD; CANR 53, 75, 128; CD 5, 6; CWD; DA3; DAM DRAM; DFS 5, 17, 29; DLB 228; EWL 3; FW; INT CA-129; MAL 5; MTCW 2; MTFW 2005; SATA 94; SATA-Obit 174
Waterhouse, Keith 1929-2009 .... **CLC 47**
See also BRWS 13; CA 5-8R; 290; CANR 38, 67, 109; CBD; CD 6; CN 1, 2, 3, 4, 5, 6, 7; DLB 13, 15; MTCW 1, 2; MTFW 2005
Waterhouse, Keith Spencer
See Waterhouse, Keith
Waters, Frank (Joseph) 1902-1995 .. **CLC 88**
See also CA 5-8R; 149; CAAS 13; CANR 3, 18, 63, 121; DLB 212; DLBY 1986; RGAL 4; TCWW 1, 2
Waters, Mary C. **CLC 70**
Waters, Roger 1944- .... **CLC 35**
Watkins, Frances Ellen
See Harper, Frances Ellen Watkins
Watkins, Gerrold
See Malzberg, Barry N(athaniel)
Watkins, Gloria Jean
See hooks, bell
Watkins, Paul 1964- .... **CLC 55**
See also CA 132; CANR 62, 98, 231
Watkins, Vernon Phillips 1906-1967 .... **CLC 43**
See also CA 9-10; 25-28R; CAP 1; DLB 20; EWL 3; RGEL 2
Watson, Irving S.
See Mencken, H. L.
Watson, John H.
See Farmer, Philip Jose
Watson, Richard F.
See Silverberg, Robert
Watson, Rosamund Marriott 1860-1911 .... **PC 117**
See also CA 207; DLB 240
Watson, Sheila 1909-1998 .... **SSC 128**
See also AITN 2; CA 155; CCA 1; DAC; DLB 60
Watts, Ephraim
See Horne, Richard Henry Hengist
Watts, Isaac 1674-1748 .... **LC 98**
See also DLB 95; RGEL 2; SATA 52
Waugh, Auberon (Alexander) 1939-2001 .... **CLC 7**
See also CA 45-48; 192; CANR 6, 22, 92; CN 1, 2, 3; DLB 14, 194
Waugh, Evelyn 1903-1966 ... **CLC 1, 3, 8, 13, 19, 27, 44, 107; SSC 41; TCLC 229; WLC 6**
See also AAYA 78; BPFB 3; BRW 7; CA 85-88; 25-28R; CANR 22; CDBLB 1914-1945; DA; DA3; DAB; DAC; DAM MST, NOV, POP; DLB 15, 162, 195, 352; EWL 3; MTCW 1, 2; MTFW 2005; NFS 13, 17, 34; RGEL 2; RGSF 2; TEA; WLIT 4
Waugh, Evelyn Arthur St. John
See Waugh, Evelyn
Waugh, Harriet 1944- .... **CLC 6**
See also CA 85-88; CANR 22

Literary Criticism Series
Cumulative Topic Index

This index lists all topic entries in Gale's *Children's Literature Review* (CLR), *Classical and Medieval Literature Criticism* (CMLC), *Contemporary Literary Criticism* (CLC), *Drama Criticism* (DC), *Literature Criticism from 1400 to 1800* (LC), *Nineteenth-Century Literature Criticism* (NCLC), *Short Story Criticism* (SSC), and *Twentieth-Century Literary Criticism* (TCLC). The index also lists topic entries in the Gale Critical Companion Collection, which includes the following publications: *The Beat Generation* (BG), *Feminism in Literature* (FL), *Gothic Literature* (GL), and *Harlem Renaissance* (HR).

Topic Index

Topic Index

Topic Index

SSC Cumulative Nationality Index

Nationality Index

SSC-167 Title Index

Title Index